PUBLIC PAPERS OF THE PRESIDENTS
OF THE
UNITED STATES

PUBLIC PAPERS OF THE PRESIDENTS
OF THE
UNITED STATES

William J. Clinton

1997
(IN TWO BOOKS)

BOOK I—JANUARY 1 TO JUNE 30, 1997

UNITED STATES GOVERNMENT PRINTING OFFICE
WASHINGTON : 1998

Published by the
Office of the Federal Register
National Archives and Records Administration

For sale by the
Superintendent of Documents
U.S. Government Printing Office
Washington, DC 20402

Foreword

On the morning of May 2, 1997, on the banks of the Tidal Basin, I participated in the dedication ceremony for the Franklin Delano Roosevelt Memorial, honoring this great leader of the "American Century." Later that afternoon, in Baltimore, Maryland, I announced an historic agreement to balance the Federal budget. These two events—one, a reflection on our past, the other, a promise for our future—embodied the new American consensus on the role of Government that I have worked hard to forge since my first days as President.

We have quelled the contentious debate between those who view Government as the problem and those who view it as the solution. It is neither—as I stated in my Second Inaugural Address, which I had the great privilege to deliver. The challenges of a new age require not time-worn slogans but action. They require a limited, flexible Government characterized by fiscal discipline, enlightened innovation, and a commitment to creating opportunity for all Americans. The Government's role—and its responsibility—is to affirm these cherished values in changing times.

Committed to these principles, America entered 1997 peaceful and secure, prosperous and stable, and determined to meet the challenges of the 21st Century. We discarded outdated dogmas and forged new relationships. In our own hemisphere, we celebrated the close friendship between the United States and Mexico, redefining our partnership in the face of new priorities—from combating drugs to preserving the environment. Across the Atlantic, where the barricades of the Cold War once stood, we built new alliances for global security and commerce. We completed new agreements: from the ratification of the landmark Chemical Weapons Convention, to the Founding Act that joins NATO and the Russian Federation in practical cooperation. In Helsinki, President Yeltsin and I agreed to pursue even deeper cuts in our nuclear arsenals. And in Denver, where I hosted the annual summit of the world's industrialized democracies, we worked to combat new security threats, prepared our countries to succeed in the global economy, and opened a new chapter in the history of Europe.

Here at home, too, we set new and higher goals, refusing to grow complacent in our success. America's economy was the strongest in a generation. Inflation remained low while employment surged, defying conventional wisdom, and both crime rates and welfare rolls were down dramatically. And to ensure that all Americans will share in the promise of the new century, I launched a national campaign to lift our standards of education. In my State of the Union Address I called not for a Federal mandate, but for a national commitment to tough, smart standards in education basics.

In June, at the University of California at San Diego, I opened a national dialogue on another challenge: race. When we finally lift the burden of race, it will not be because a law made it happen. It will be because the American people confronted and dispelled the myths that divide us. Americans of all backgrounds have responded to this challenge, leaving me more confident than ever that we will not come apart but come together; that we will enter the 21st Century not as separate, distinct groups, but as one America—at once diverse, and as the Founders declared, indivisible.

Preface

This book contains the papers and speeches of the 42d President of the United States that were issued by the Office of the Press Secretary during the period January 1–June 30, 1997. The material has been compiled and published by the Office of the Federal Register, National Archives and Records Administration.

The material is presented in chronological order, and the dates shown in the headings are the dates of the documents or events. In instances when the release date differs from the date of the document itself, that fact is shown in the textnote. Every effort has been made to ensure accuracy: Remarks are checked against a tape recording, and signed documents are checked against the original. Textnotes and cross references have been provided by the editors for purposes of identification or clarity. Speeches were delivered in Washington, DC, unless indicated. The times noted are local times. All materials that are printed full-text in the book have been indexed in the subject and name indexes, and listed in the document categories list.

The Public Papers of the Presidents series was begun in 1957 in response to a recommendation of the National Historical Publications Commission. An extensive compilation of messages and papers of the Presidents covering the period 1789 to 1897 was assembled by James D. Richardson and published under congressional authority between 1896 and 1899. Since then, various private compilations have been issued, but there was no uniform publication comparable to the Congressional Record or the United States Supreme Court Reports. Many Presidential papers could be found only in the form of mimeographed White House releases or as reported in the press. The Commission therefore recommended the establishment of an official series in which Presidential writings, addresses, and remarks of a public nature could be made available.

The Commission's recommendation was incorporated in regulations of the Administrative Committee of the Federal Register, issued under section 6 of the Federal Register Act (44 U.S.C. 1506), which may be found in title 1, part 10, of the Code of Federal Regulations.

A companion publication to the Public Papers series, the Weekly Compilation of Presidential Documents, was begun in 1965 to provide a broader range of Presidential materials on a more timely basis to meet the needs of the contemporary reader. Beginning with the administration of Jimmy Carter, the Public Papers series expanded its coverage to include additional material as printed in the Weekly Compilation. That coverage provides a listing of the President's daily schedule and meetings, when announced, and other items of general interest issued by the Office of the Press Secretary. Also included are lists of the President's nominations submitted to the Senate, materials released by the Office of the Press Secretary that are not printed full-text in the book, and proclamations, Executive orders, and other Presidential documents released by the Office of the Press Secretary and published in the *Federal Register*. This information appears in the appendixes at the end of the book.

Volumes covering the administrations of Presidents Hoover, Truman, Eisenhower, Kennedy, Johnson, Nixon, Ford, Carter, Reagan, and Bush are also included in the Public Papers series.

The Public Papers of the Presidents publication program is under the direction of Frances D. McDonald, Director of the Presidential Documents and Legislative Division. The series is produced by the Presidential Documents Unit, Gwen H. Estep, Chief. The Chief Editor of this book was Karen Howard Ashlin, assisted by Scott Andreae, Brad Brooks, Anna Glover, Margaret A. Hemmig, Carolyn W. Hill, Maxine Hill, Michael Hoover, Alfred Jones, and Michael J. Sullivan.

The frontispiece and photographs used in the portfolio were supplied by the White House Photo Office. The typography and design of the book were developed by the Government Printing Office under the direction of Michael F. DiMario, Public Printer.

Raymond A. Mosley
Director of the Federal Register

John W. Carlin
Archivist of the United States

Contents

Cabinet

Secretary of State .... Madeleine K. Albright

Secretary of the Treasury .... Robert E. Rubin

Secretary of Defense .... William S. Cohen

Attorney General .... Janet Reno

Secretary of the Interior .... Bruce Babbitt

Secretary of Agriculture .... Dan Glickman

Secretary of Commerce .... William M. Daley

Secretary of Labor .... Alexis M. Herman

Secretary of Health and Human Services .... Donna E. Shalala

Secretary of Housing and Urban
Development .... Andrew M. Cuomo

Secretary of Transportation .... Rodney E. Slater

Secretary of Energy .... Federico Peña

Secretary of Education .... Richard W. Riley

Secretary of Veterans Affairs .... Jesse Brown

United States Representative to the
United Nations .... Bill Richardson

Administrator of the Environmental
Protection Agency .... Carol M. Browner

United States Trade Representative .... Charlene Barshefsky

Director of the Office of Management
and Budget .... Franklin D. Raines

Chief of Staff to the President .... Erskine B. Bowles

Counselor to the President .... Thomas F. McLarty III

Chair of the Council of Economic Advisers ..... Janet Yellen

Director of National Drug Control Policy .... Barry R. McCaffrey

Administrator of the Small Business
Administration .... Aida Alvarez

Director of the Federal Emergency
Management Agency .... James Lee Witt

Administration of William J. Clinton

1997

Letter to Congressional Leaders on Continuation of the National Emergency With Respect to Libya
January 2, 1997

Dear Mr. Speaker: (Dear Mr. President:)

Section 202(d) of the National Emergencies Act (50 U.S.C. 1622(d)) provides for the automatic termination of a national emergency unless, prior to the anniversary date of its declaration, the President publishes in the *Federal Register* and transmits to the Congress a notice stating that the emergency is to continue in effect beyond the anniversary date. In accordance with this provision, I have sent the enclosed notice, stating that the Libyan emergency is to continue in effect beyond January 7, 1997, to the *Federal Register* for publication. Similar notices have been sent annually to the Congress and the *Federal Register* since December 23, 1986. The most recent notice appeared in the *Federal Register* on January 3, 1996.

The crisis between the United States and Libya that led to the declaration of a national emergency on January 7, 1986, has not been resolved. The Government of Libya has continued its actions and policies in support of terror-

ism, despite the calls by the United Nations Security Council, in Resolutions 731 (1992), 748 (1992), and 883 (1993), that it demonstrate by concrete actions its renunciation of such terrorism. Such Libyan actions and policies pose a continuing unusual and extraordinary threat to the national security and vital foreign policy interests of the United States. For these reasons, I have determined that it is necessary to maintain in force the broad authorities necessary to apply economic pressure to the Government of Libya to reduce its ability to support international terrorism.

Sincerely,

WILLIAM J. CLINTON

NOTE: Identical letters were sent to Newt Gingrich, Speaker of the House of Representatives, and Albert Gore, Jr., President of the Senate. The notice is listed in Appendix D at the end of this volume.

Statement on Review of Title III of the Cuban Liberty and Democratic Solidarity (LIBERTAD) Act of 1996
January 3, 1997

Last July, I allowed title III of the Cuban Liberty and Democratic Solidarity Act (LIBERTAD Act) to come into force but suspended for 6 months the right it grants to American nationals to bring suit against foreign firms trafficking in confiscated properties in Cuba. I took this step so that we could have time to develop a more common approach with our allies and trading partners to promote democracy, human rights, and fundamental freedoms in Cuba. We and our allies agree on the vital need for a transition to democracy on the island, but differences over how to achieve that aim have

often overshadowed the goal itself. That is why I decided to make maximum use of title III to increase pressure on the Castro regime by working with our allies—not against them—to accelerate change in Cuba.

Over the past 6 months, our efforts have yielded real progress. Thanks to the tireless efforts of Under Secretary of Commerce Stuart Eizenstat, who serves as my Special Representative for the Promotion of Democracy in Cuba, the international community is more united behind the cause of freedom in Cuba than ever

1

before in the 38-year history of Castro's oppressive regime.

Today, in order to consolidate and build on the momentum we have generated for democratic change in Cuba, I have decided to extend for another 6 months the suspension of the right to file suit under title III of the Cuban Liberty and Democratic Solidarity Act.

A number of developments show the strengthened international consensus for change in Cuba. The European Union, acting consistent with its traditional democratic values, in December adopted an historic "Common Position" binding all 15 member nations to promote democracy and reform in Cuba. The EU's action explicitly makes any improvement in political or economic relations with Cuba contingent on concrete advances in human rights and political freedoms on the island. At the Ibero-American Summit in Santiago in November, heads of state from Latin America, Spain, and Portugal called for democracy and full respect for human rights, thus emphasizing Cuba's isolation as the hemisphere's only nondemocratic nation.

Governments and nongovernmental organizations are increasing their backing for dissidents on the island and keeping international attention focused on repression in Cuba. A new European Platform for Human Rights and Democracy in Cuba is being created to help coordinate NGO activity to strengthen independent groups in Cuba. European business leaders and organizations are supporting a set of best business practices so, if they invest in Cuba, it will benefit Cuban workers and not the government. Eu-

rope's major labor organization, the International Confederation of Free Trade Unions, has strongly condemned Castro's labor practices and called for free trade unions.

These and other steps have sent a clarion message of hope to the Cuban people. They underscore that it is Castro who is isolated, not those who welcome the democratic tide of history. They demonstrate the international community's resolve to end the dictatorship so the people of Cuba can enjoy the freedom and prosperity they deserve.

The international momentum we have built to promote democracy in Cuba must be preserved and strengthened. During the coming 6 months and thereafter, we will continue working with our allies to develop the most comprehensive, effective measures to promote democracy in Cuba that we can. We also will continue to enforce title IV of the LIBERTAD Act.

The law requires that I review title III every 6 months. I would expect to continue suspending the right to file suit so long as America's friends and allies continue their stepped-up efforts to promote a transition to democracy in Cuba. I hope, furthermore, that the momentum created by the EU's actions will lead to similar Cuba democracy efforts by others, including governments in our own hemisphere.

The Cuban people have lived under tyranny for too long. We must sustain our efforts to hasten the arrival of democracy in Cuba. As a result of increasing international pressure, we have never been closer to that day. We will not be satisfied until that day arrives.

Letter to Congressional Leaders on Review of Title III of the Cuban Liberty and Democratic Solidarity (LIBERTAD) Act of 1996
January 3, 1997

Dear _____:

Pursuant to subsection 306(c)(2) of the Cuban Liberty and Democratic Solidarity (LIBERTAD) Act of 1996 (Public Law 104–114), (the "Act"), I hereby determine and report to the Congress that suspension for 6 months beyond February 1, 1997, of the right to bring an action under Title III of the Act is necessary to the national interests of the United States and will expedite a transition to democracy in Cuba.

Sincerely,

WILLIAM J. CLINTON

NOTE: Identical letters were sent to Jesse Helms, chairman, and Claiborne Pell, ranking member, Senate Committee on Foreign Relations; Mark O. Hatfield, chairman, and Robert C. Byrd, ranking member, Senate Committee on Appropriations;

Benjamin A. Gilman, chairman, and Lee H. Hamilton, ranking member, House Committee on International Relations; and Robert L. Livingston, chairman, and David R. Obey, ranking member, House Committee on Appropriations.

The President's Radio Address
January 4, 1997

Good morning, and Happy New Year. I look forward to 1997 with great optimism. As we enter this new year, I'm preparing to enter my second term as your President, committed to continuing our mission of preparing our people for the 21st century, meeting our new challenges, and strengthening our oldest values. We will work to give our people the tools they need to make the most of their own lives, to build strong families and strong communities. And as we work to expand opportunity, we will also seek responsibility from every American.

This approach is working. In just 4 years we have replaced trickle-down economics with invest-and-grow economics, responsibility, and opportunity. We've cut the deficit by 60 percent, increased our trade to record levels. We have over 11 million new jobs.

In just 4 years, working with citizens and communities all over America to solve our social problems, we have replaced political rhetoric with a strategy of giving people the tools to solve their problems and demanding responsibility from all of our citizens. It's working, too. Crime has dropped for the last 4 years as we work to put 100,000 police on our streets and take gangs and guns away from our children. The welfare rolls have dropped by 2.1 million—that's a record reduction—as we work to help people find work but to require them to pursue work and education and to be responsible parents.

But there's still a lot more to do if we're going to make sure the American dream is a reality for all of our citizens in the 21st century. And we still have some pretty big problems in our society. None stands in our way of achieving our goals for America more than the epidemic of teen pregnancy. Today I want to talk to you about the progress we've made in preventing it and to tell you about the new steps we're taking to see to it that our progress carries into the new year and beyond.

We know many of our social problems have their roots in the breakdown of our families. We know children who are born to teen parents are more likely to drop out of school, get involved in crime and drugs, and end up in poverty; more likely to suffer ill health, even to die as infants. And teen parents often find their own lives are changed forever. Too many don't finish school, not ever, and therefore they never learn the skills they need to succeed as workers and parents in our new economy.

That's why our administration has worked so hard to reduce teen pregnancies, to increase responsibility among teen parents, and to prepare young people to be good parents at the right time. Last year I took executive action to require young mothers to stay in school or lose their welfare payments. We challenged members of the private sector to take action, and they did, with a national campaign to prevent teen pregnancy and community initiatives all over our Nation.

We're mounting an unprecedented crackdown on child support enforcement. Now child support collections are up over 50 percent compared to 4 years ago. And we've worked with community-based groups in the character education movement in our schools to help parents teach young people right from wrong.

Today we have new evidence that this approach is starting to work. Last year we learned that the teen birth rate has dropped for the 4th year in a row and that out-of-wedlock birth rates dropped for the first time in 19 years. According to a new report by the Department of Health and Human Services, the teen birth rates dropped more than 10 percent over 3 years in Wisconsin, Washington, and 8 other States. And altogether, from 1991 to 1995, the teen birth rate in America has dropped by 8 percent.

The progress we're making on teen pregnancy shows that we can overcome even our most stubborn and serious problems. Because of the energy and the effort of the American people, as I said, the crime rate is dropping, the welfare rolls have dropped dramatically, and poverty is down. We can meet our challenges if we'll meet them together, in our homes, our communities, and as a nation. But let me be clear: The teen pregnancy rate is still intolerably high in America. Too many children are still having children. So we must do more. As I enter my second term, I want to tell you the new and comprehensive steps my administration will take to further reduce the number of out-of-wedlock births.

First, we'll step up support for programs at the local level that work, providing $7½ million for pioneering programs like the one at Emory University in Atlanta, where young people teach their peers about abstinence and responsibility.

Second, we'll spread the word about these programs so that what works in one community can be tried quickly in more communities.

Third, we'll forge even stronger partnerships with businesses, clergy, and community groups who are committed to dealing with this issue.

And fourth, we'll see to it that we use the most up-to-date research methods to track teen pregnancy trends. We have to make sure our efforts are actually paying off.

Finally, we'll carry out the strong provisions of the welfare reform law I signed last year, which requires teen mothers who receive welfare not only to stay in school but to live at home or in an adult-supervised setting. It sets up second-chance homes where young mothers who can't go home still have a safe place to raise a child and turn their lives around. And it institutes the toughest ever child support measures.

We've made some significant progress in the effort against teen pregnancy in the last few years. With the new steps I'm announcing today, we'll continue our fight against children having children. All of you need to help us send the strongest possible message: It's wrong to be pregnant or father a child unless you are married and ready to take on the responsibilities of parenthood.

What we're doing to prevent teen pregnancy as a nation is an example of how we can master many of the challenges of our time. The National Government cannot solve all our problems, but it can help by giving individuals, families, and communities the tools they need to take responsibility and solve those problems for themselves.

As President, I'm committed to marshaling all the forces in our society to mobilizing our citizens, our communities, our businesses, our schools to meet our challenges. That is the way we will keep the promise of America alive for all our citizens as we move into the 21st century.

Thanks for listening, and Happy New Year.

NOTE: The President spoke at 10:06 a.m. from the Mahogany Run Golf Course in St. Thomas, U.S. Virgin Islands.

Statement on the Decline in Serious Crime
January 5, 1997

These new FBI statistics show that for the fifth year in a row, serious crime in this country has declined. This is the longest period of decline in over 25 years.

At the beginning of my administration, we set out to change this country's approach to crime by putting more officers on our streets through community policing and taking guns out of the hands of criminals. We are making a difference. Today, our neighborhoods are safer, and we are restoring the American people's confidence that crime can be reduced.

But our work is not done. We must continue to move in the right direction by adding more police officers, cracking down on gangs, and reducing gun and drug violence. That is why I have placed curbing juvenile violence at the top of my anticrime agenda for the new year.

NOTE: This statement was embargoed for release until 6 p.m.

Remarks at the Ecumenical Prayer Breakfast
January 6, 1997

Thank you very much, Mr. Vice President and Tipper and ladies and gentlemen. Hillary and I are delighted to welcome you to the White House. We look forward to these breakfasts. As Al said, we have been doing them on a regular basis now, normally around—just after Labor Day as we sort of rededicate ourselves to the labor of the new year. But this year, we are doing it now for two reasons: One is, obviously, this is on the brink of the Inauguration and a new 4-year term for the President and for our country; the other is, we were otherwise occupied last Labor Day. [*Laughter*]

This is a wonderful day to be here. We asked Father Stephanopoulos to pray today because, as all of you know, this is the celebration of Epiphany in the Christian faith, a time of recognizing Christmas in the Orthodox tradition. I also wanted you to pray so that I could say that we were all very impressed with the size of the book contract that—[*laughter*]—that your son got, and we know we can depend upon you to make sure the church gets its 10 percent of that contract. We are very proud of him and very grateful to have him here.

This is the day in the Christian tradition when the wise men came bearing gifts for the baby Jesus. And we have much to be thankful for and much to pray for, but I think what I would say today is that I asked you to come here to share with me your thoughts and to share with you some of ours in the hope that we might all become wiser.

I am very grateful for the progress that our country has made in the last 4 years, grateful that we have been given a chance to play a role in that progress, and mindful that whatever has been done which is good has been done by us together.

One of my college roommates, who I think is a really smart guy, said to me the other day when we were together and joking about our lost youth, he said, "Oh, and one other thing," as he was leaving. He said, "Don't ever forget that great Presidents do not do great things. Great Presidents get a lot of other people to do great things. And there is over 250 million of us now, so that's a lot of greatness if you can get us all to do the right thing," which

I thought was an interesting way of saying in part what the magic and genius of democracy is all about.

So we're thinking a lot now about how we're going to build our bridge to the 21st century, what we're going to do in this next term. I've listened to all of these experts talk about how hard it is for Presidents to be effective in the second term because, after all, they just got reelected because things went well in their first term, not because they had actually thought through what they were going to do in their second term. But we've tried to overcome that disability.

There are a lot of particulars that we could discuss today, but what I'd like for you to think about a little bit, from your perspective and what you can do—two things: What are we going to do; and secondly, and more importantly I think, how are we going to do it? In what spirit shall we proceed?

In any great democracy there are always differences about what are we going to do. There always have been, there always will be, and these are altogether healthy. It would be—America wouldn't last very long, I think, if 100 percent of the people agreed 100 percent of the time on 100 percent of the issues. What keeps us going—we all know that none of us has perfect and infinite understanding of these complex matters facing our country and facing the world. But we have devised a system—we have nurtured and maintained it now for over 200 years—in which people can reconcile their differences and come to a consensus and an agreement which will push the country forward. So we are enlarged when we come to agreement after honest debate in the right way; we are diminished if, in the way we treat each other, we preclude the possibility of resolution and going forward. And at times like this, when things are changing so much, we need the right spirit more because we have more to decide, more to deal with. And yet, at times like this, we are in some ways put at risk by the absence of that spirit of reconciliation and respect.

There are several specific things I hope we can talk about later that I think we could reach broad agreement on. For example, some of you think I made a mistake when I signed the welfare reform bill, and I don't. But one thing that we all ought to be able to agree on is, the bill will not succeed—the bill does nothing, it just changes the rules. It doesn't put anybody to work. In 4 years we have reduced by 2.1 million the number of people on welfare, the biggest reduction in history, by doing the kinds of things that now this bill requires every State to do. We just went out and worked with the States and came up with innovative ways to get around old rules and regulations and do them anyway. Now every State has got to try to do that for every person.

My objective here is, once and for all, to take the politics out of poverty and to treat all able-bodied people the same at the community level. What I long for is a system of community-based support for people who are out of work through no fault of their own but a system of community-based norms that require people who can work to work when there is work. Now, if you say that everybody who is able-bodied can only stay on welfare 2 years continuously unless the State decides to continue to support them for some other reason—and we did give a fund so that hardship cases could be treated in that way—then every community has to have a system for putting those people to work.

Now, let me pause at this; you can all think about this. This new law gives every State the right to give the welfare check to any employer, including a church, as an employment and training subsidy, who will hire someone from welfare. If every church in America just hired one family, the welfare problem would go way down. If every church in America challenged every member of that church who had 25 or more employees to hire another family, the problem would go away, and we would really have a system in which in times of recession we'd have more people unemployed at the community level. In good times we'd have fewer people, but we would always have a community-based commitment that crossed party lines and religious lines and every other line to give able-bodied people the dignity of work and support them in the most important work they do, which is raising their children.

The second thing I wanted to talk about a little bit is this whole business of immigration. The things I don't like about the welfare law have nothing to do with welfare and everything to do with the way we tried to save money, I thought unfairly, on legal immigrants. Our administration has done a lot to cut down on illegal immigration, but we believe that legal immigration has served our country well. It has, however, made us more diverse. And so immigration is really the touchstone where we deal with not only what are we going to do but how are we going to do it.

I believe that we have learned a lot in 220 years—really more than 300 years—about how hard it is for people of different races to get along. We know that that is difficult in all societies and all times, and it's something you just have to keep working at. But now America is not a white and black America. America is a country with scores, hundreds of different racial, ethnic, and religious groups. Our biggest county, Los Angeles County, now has over 160 different racial and ethnic groups within one county. But it's all over America. Wayne County, where Detroit, Michigan, is, has now over 140 different racial and ethnic groups. Detroit was a place where we used to think of where you basically had white ethnics who immigrated from Central and Eastern Europe and African-Americans and white Southerners who immigrated out of the South because they couldn't make a living in places like my home State in the Depression and later—now, 140 different racial and ethnic groups.

How are we going to deal with that? Against the background of what you see in Bosnia, Rwanda, Northern Ireland, the Middle East, all of these things, these destructive impulses people have, how can we prove in America that we can all get along, not without giving up our basic beliefs but in finding a ground of mutual respect? It seems to me that that may be the single most significant decision facing the United States. We have a lot of other things we have to deal with in the next 4 years, the whole question of the entitlements burden when the baby boomers retire and education initiatives that I intend to push and finishing the work of balancing the budget and all that. That's fine, but if we can all find a way to hold up to the world not only the example of our freedom but the example of our freedom in the 21st century global interdependent world in which anybody from anywhere can live here, and if you show up for work or you show up for school and you do what you're supposed to do and you're a good citizen, you can be part of our country, and we'll respect your faith, we'll respect your differences, and we'll find a way to work together, then I believe the preeminence of the United States will be assured throughout the next century. And I think you have to think about it in long terms like that.

What causes a society to rise and fall? We clearly are proving that we're getting back to our basic values. The crime rate is going down. You saw the—has gone down now for several years in a row for the first time in 25 years. We have inequality among working people going down—and I'm very proud of that—for the first time in 20 years. We have a lot of our other social problems being ameliorated, the teen pregnancy rate dropping substantially for the first time in a good while. Drugs, alcohol, tobacco are still a problem for very young people. Drug use is going down in society as a whole but still going up among young people.

So we're on the cusp here, maybe, of turning a lot of our social problems around. We know what we ought to do. Can we do it in the right way, in a spirit of reconciliation? And can we recognize that in this exciting new world there's no way in the world for us to know the answer to all these questions that are out there before us?

And that's the last point I'd like to make. If we do things in the right way, we'll get enough of the right answers to keep moving our country forward and to keep doing the right thing for the rest of the world. And we won't be right all the time, but that's just because we're human. So that's the last thought I would like to leave with you.

The beginning of wisdom, I think, is humility and respect for what you may not know. Now, we were talking around the table here about the last speech Cardinal Bernardin gave in which he said that the precious gift of time should not be wasted on acrimony and division. And he said that knowing he just had a little bit of time left. The truth is, all of us just have a little bit of time left. He just knew it, and we don't. And 3 weeks or 30 years, it's a little bit of time in the life of a country, the life of the world.

So I say to you—I ask for your guidance, for your prayers for our country, for the efforts that all of us are making. I ask for your specific involvement, particularly in the two issues I've mentioned, on the welfare and immigration issues. But most important of all, I ask for your help in creating a sense of reconciliation, the right sort of spirit in which we can deal with these issues. As people of faith on this Epiphany, I think we should all ask that that be made evident to us.

Thank you, and God bless you.

NOTE: The President spoke at 9:59 a.m. in the State Dining Room at the White House. In his remarks, he referred to Rev. Robert G. Stephanopoulos, Holy Trinity Cathedral, New York, NY, who gave the invocation, and the late Joseph Cardinal Bernardin, former Archbishop of Chicago.

Remarks on Receiving the Report of the Presidential Advisory Committee on Gulf War Veterans' Illnesses and an Exchange With Reporters
January 7, 1997

The President. Thank you very much to Dr. Lashof and the members of the Presidential Advisory Committee on Gulf War Illnesses; Secretary White; Secretary Brown; Secretary Shalala; Deputy Director Tenet. I'd like to say a special word of thanks to Dr. Jack Gibbons for the work that he did on this. I thank Senator Rockefeller, Senator Specter, Congressman Lane Evans for their interest and their pursuit of this issue, and all the representatives of the military and veterans organizations who are here.

I am pleased to accept this report. I thank Dr. Lashof and the committee for their extremely thorough and dedicated work over 18 months now. I pledge to you and to all the veterans of this country, we will now match your efforts with our action.

Six years ago hundreds of thousands of Americans defended our vital interest in the Persian Gulf. They faced a dangerous enemy, harsh conditions, lengthy isolation from their families. And they went to victory for our country with lightning speed. When they came home, for reasons that we still don't fully understand, thousands of them became ill. They served their country with courage and skill and strength, and they must now know that they can rely upon us. And we must not, and will not, let them down.

Three years ago I asked the Secretaries of Defense, Health and Human Services, and Veterans Affairs to form the Persian Gulf Veterans Coordinating Board to strengthen our efforts to care for our veterans and find the causes of their illnesses. I signed landmark legislation that pays disability benefits to Gulf war veterans with undiagnosed illnesses. DOD and VA established toll-free lines and medical evaluation programs.

I am especially grateful to the First Lady who took this matter to heart and first brought it to my attention quite a long while ago now. I thank her for reaching out to the veterans and for making sure that their voices would be heard.

To date, we have provided Gulf war veterans with more than 80,000 free medical exams. We've approved more than 26,000 disability claims. HHS, DOD, and the Veterans Department have sponsored more than 70 research projects to identify the possible causes of the illnesses.

But early on, it became clear that answers were not emerging fast enough. Hillary and I shared the frustration and concerns of many veterans and their families. We realized the issues were so complex they demanded a more comprehensive effort. That is why, in May of 1995, I asked some of our Nation's best doctors and scientists, as well as Gulf war veterans themselves, to form a Presidential advisory committee that could provide an open and thorough and independent review of the Government's response to veterans' health concerns and the causes of their ailments.

Since that time, we have made some real progress. The Department of Defense, with the CIA, launched a review of more than 5 million pages of Gulf war documents, declassifying some 23,000 pages of materials and putting them on the Internet. Through this effort, we discovered important information concerning the possible exposure of our troops to chemical agents in the wake of our destruction of an arms depot in southern Iraq.

The committee made clear and the Defense Department agrees that this new information demands a new approach, focusing on what happened not only during but after the war and what it could mean for our troops. Based on the committee's guidance, the Department of Defense has restructured and intensified its efforts, increasing tenfold its investigating team, tracking down and talking to veterans who may have been exposed to chemical agents, and devoting millions of dollars to research on the possible effects of low-level chemical exposure.

I'm determined that this investigation will be comprehensive and credible. We haven't ended the suffering. We don't have all the answers, and I won't be satisfied until we have done everything humanly possible to find them. That's why I welcome this committee's report and its suggestions on how to make our commitment even stronger. I also take seriously the concern regarding DOD's investigation of possible chemical exposure. I'm determined to act swiftly on these findings not only to help the veterans who are sick but to apply the lessons of this experience to the future.

I've asked the Secretaries of Defense, Health and Human Services, and Veterans Affairs to report to me in 60 days with concrete, specific action plans for implementing these recommendations. And I am directing Secretary-designate Cohen, when confirmed by the Senate, to make this a top priority of the Defense Department. I'm also announcing two other immediate initiatives.

First, I've asked this committee to stay in business for 9 more months to provide independent, expert oversight of DOD's efforts to investigate chemical exposure, and also to monitor the Governmentwide response to the broader recommendations. The committee's persistent public effort has helped to bring much new information to light, and I have instructed them to fulfill their oversight role with the same intensity, resolve, and vigor they have brought to their work so far. Dr. Lashof has agreed to continue, and I trust the other committee members will as well.

Second, I'm accepting Secretary Brown's proposal to reconsider the regulation that Gulf war veterans with undiagnosed illnesses must prove their disabilities emerged within 2 years of their return in order to be eligible for benefits. Experience has shown that many disabled veterans have their claims denied because they fall outside the 2-year timeframe. I've asked Secretary

Brown to report back to me in 60 days with a view toward extending that limit.

And we will do whatever we can and whatever it takes to research Gulf war illnesses as thoroughly as possible. Every credible possibility must be fully explored, including low-level chemical exposure and combat stress.

I know that Congress shares our deep concern, and let me again thank Senator Specter, Senator Rockefeller, and Congressman Evans for being here. Caring for our veterans is not a partisan issue. It is a national obligation, and I thank them for the approach that they have taken.

As we continue to investigate Gulf war illnesses, let me again take this opportunity to urge the Congress to ratify the Chemical Weapons Convention which would make it harder for rogue states to acquire chemical weapons in the future and protect the soldiers of the United States and our allies in the future.

This report is not the end of the road, any more than it is the beginning. We have a lot of hard work that's been done, and we have made some progress, but the task is far from over. The committee's assessment gives me confidence that we are on the right track, but we have much yet to learn and much to do.

As we do make progress, we will make our findings public. We will be open in how we view Gulf war illnesses and all their possible causes, open to the veterans whose care is in our hands, open to the public looking to us for answers. I pledge to our veterans and to every American, we will not stop until we have done all we can to care for our Gulf war veterans, to find out why they are sick, and to help to make them healthy again.

Thank you very much.

Q. Mr. President, this has been studied to death. Do you believe that there is a Gulf war illness?

The President. I believe that there are a lot of veterans who got sick as a result of their service in the Gulf. And I leave it to the experts to determine whether there is one or a proliferation of them and exactly what the causal connection were. That has been apparent for some time. That's why the Congress agreed to support our efforts that for the first time gave disability payments for people with undiagnosed conditions.

But let me say that I think that this committee has done a good job. I think—I want to compliment the work that has been done in the last few months by John White in the Defense Department in facing up to the things which were not done before. No one has ever suggested that anybody intentionally imposed—exposed American soldiers to these dangers, and there is nothing—there is no reason that anyone in this Government should ever do anything but just try to get to the truth and get it out and do what is right by the veterans.

And there are also—I think we need to be a little humble about this. There are a lot of things that we still don't know. That's what Dr. Lashof said. And that's why these research projects are so very important.

And the final thing I'd like to say is we don't know all the answer here. You heard that—Dr. Lashof said that sometimes, when people are exposed to substances that can cause cancer, it may not be manifest for 10 years, which is why I want to thank Secretary Brown for urging that we scrap the 2-year rule. We have to be vigilant about this. And my successor will be working on this. We will be monitoring this for a long time to come.

But we've got a process now the American people and the veterans and their families can have confidence in. We've got the appropriate commitment of personnel and money. And more important, we've got the appropriate commitment of the heart and the mind. And I'm convinced now that we will do justice to this issue and to the people that have been affected by it.

NOTE: The President spoke at 10:55 a.m. in the Roosevelt Room at the White House. In his remarks, he referred to Joyce Lashof, Chair, Presidential Advisory Committee on Gulf War Veterans' Illnesses.

Message to the Congress Transmitting the Report of the Department of Housing and Urban Development
January 7, 1997

To the Congress of the United States:

Pursuant to the requirements of 42 U.S.C. 3536, I transmit herewith the 31st Annual Report of the Department of Housing and Urban Development, which covers calendar year 1995.

WILLIAM J. CLINTON

The White House,

January 7, 1997.

NOTE: This message was released by the Office of the Press Secretary on January 8.

Message to the Congress Transmitting the Report of the Department of Energy
January 7, 1997

To the Congress of the United States:

In accordance with the requirements of section 657 of the Department of Energy Organization Act (Public Law 95–91; 42 U.S.C. 7267), I transmit herewith the Annual Report of the Department of Energy, which covers the years 1994 and 1995.

WILLIAM J. CLINTON

The White House,

January 7, 1997.

NOTE: This message was released by the Office of the Press Secretary on January 8.

Message to the Congress Transmitting a Report on Hazardous Materials Transportation
January 7, 1997

To the Congress of the United States:

In accordance with Public Law 103–272, as amended (49 U.S.C. 5121(e)), I transmit herewith the Biennial Report on Hazardous Materials Transportation for Calendar Years 1994–1995 of the Department of Transportation.

WILLIAM J. CLINTON

The White House,

January 7, 1997.

NOTE: This message was released by the Office of the Press Secretary on January 8.

Message to the Senate Transmitting Conventional Weapons Convention Protocols on Mines, Incendiary Weapons, and Blinding Lasers With Documentation
January 7, 1997

To the Senate of the United States:

I transmit herewith, for the advice and consent of the Senate to ratification, the following Protocols to the 1980 Convention on Prohibitions or Restrictions on the Use of Certain Conventional Weapons Which May Be Deemed to Be Excessively Injurious or to Have Indiscriminate Effects: the amended Protocol on Prohibitions or Restrictions on the Use of Mines, Booby-Traps and Other Devices (Protocol II or the amended Mines Protocol); the Protocol on Prohibitions or Restrictions on the Use of Incendiary Weapons (Protocol III or the Incendiary Weapons Protocol); and the Protocol on Blinding Laser Weapons (Protocol IV). Also transmitted for the information of the Senate is the report of the Department of State with respect to these Protocols, together with article-by-article analyses.

The most important of these Protocols is the amended Mines Protocol. It is an essential step forward in dealing with the problem of anti-personnel landmines (APL) and in minimizing the very severe casualties to civilians that have resulted from their use. It is an important precursor to the total prohibition of these weapons that the United States seeks.

Among other things, the amended Mines Protocol will do the following: (1) expand the scope of the original Protocol to include internal armed conflicts, where most civilian mine casualties have occurred; (2) require that all remotely delivered anti-personnel mines be equipped with self-destruct devices and backup self-deactivation features to ensure that they do not pose a long-term threat to civilians; (3) require that all nonremotely delivered anti-personnel mines that are not equipped with such devices be used only within controlled, marked, and monitored minefields to protect the civilian population in the area; (4) require that all anti-personnel mines be detectable using commonly available technology to make the task of mine clearance easier and safer; (5) require that the party laying mines assume responsibility for them to ensure against their irresponsible and indiscriminate use; and (6) provide more effec-

tive means for dealing with compliance problems to ensure that these restrictions are actually observed. These objectives were all endorsed by the Senate in its Resolution of Ratification of the Convention in March 1995.

The amended Mines Protocol was not as strong as we would have preferred. In particular, its provisions on verification and compliance are not as rigorous as we had proposed, and the transition periods allowed for the conversion or elimination of certain noncompliant mines are longer than we thought necessary. We shall pursue these issues in the regular meetings that the amended Protocol provides for review of its operation.

Nonetheless, I am convinced that this amended Protocol will, if generally adhered to, save many lives and prevent many tragic injuries. It will, as well, help to prepare the ground for the total prohibition of anti-personnel landmines to which the United States is committed. In this regard, I cannot overemphasize how seriously the United States takes the goal of eliminating APL entirely. The carnage and devastation caused by anti-personnel landmines—the hidden killers that murder and maim more than 25,000 people every year—must end.

On May 16, 1996, I launched an international effort to this end. This initiative sets out a concrete path to a global ban on anti-personnel landmines and is one of my top arms control priorities. At the same time, the policy recognizes that the United States has international commitments and responsibilities that must be taken into account in any negotiations on a total ban. As our work on this initiative progresses, we will continue to consult with the Congress.

The second of these Protocols—the Protocol on Incendiary Weapons—is a part of the original Convention but was not sent to the Senate for advice and consent with the other 1980 Protocols in 1994 because of concerns about the acceptability of the Protocol from a military point of view. Incendiary weapons have significant potential military value, particularly with respect to flammable military targets that cannot so

11

readily be destroyed with conventional explosives.

At the same time, these weapons can be misused in a manner that could cause heavy civilian casualties. In particular, the Protocol prohibits the use of air-delivered incendiary weapons against targets located in a city, town, village, or other concentration of civilians, a practice that caused very heavy civilian casualties in past conflicts.

The executive branch has given very careful study to the Incendiaries Protocol and has developed a reservation that would, in our view, make it acceptable from a broader national security perspective. This proposed reservation, the text of which appears in the report of the Department of State, would reserve the right to use incendiaries against military objectives located in concentrations of civilians where it is judged that such use would cause fewer casualties and less collateral damage than alternative weapons.

The third of these three Protocols—the new Protocol on Blinding Lasers—prohibits the use or transfer of laser weapons specifically designed to cause permanent blindness to unenhanced vision (that is, to the naked eye or to the eye with corrective devices). The Protocol also requires Parties to take all feasible precautions in the employment of other laser systems to avoid the incidence of such blindness.

These blinding lasers are not needed by our military forces. They are potential weapons of the future, and the United States is committed to preventing their emergence and use. The United States supports the adoption of this new Protocol.

I recommend that the Senate give its early and favorable consideration to these Protocols and give its advice and consent to ratification, subject to the conditions described in the accompanying report of the Department of State. The prompt ratification of the amended Mines Protocol is particularly important, so that the United States can continue its position of leadership in the effort to deal with the humanitarian catastrophe of irresponsible landmine use.

WILLIAM J. CLINTON

The White House,
January 7, 1997.

NOTE: This message was released by the Office of the Press Secretary on January 8.

Letter to Congressional Leaders Reporting on Iraq's Compliance With United Nations Security Council Resolutions
January 7, 1997

Dear Mr. Speaker: (Dear Mr. President:)

Consistent with the Authorization for Use of Military Force Against Iraq Resolution (Public Law 102–1) and as part of my effort to keep the Congress fully informed, I am reporting on the status of efforts to obtain Iraq's compliance with the resolutions adopted by the U.N. Security Council (UNSC). This report covers the period from November 4 to the present.

Saddam Hussein remains a threat to his people and the region. The United States successfully responded to the increased threat resulting from Saddam's attack on Irbil in late August, but he continues to try to manipulate local rivalries in northern Iraq to his advantage. The United States and our coalition partners continue to enforce the no-fly zone over southern Iraq. Enforcement of the northern no-fly zone

also continues uninterrupted, despite a restructuring of operations. Because of changes in its mission as a result of the closing last fall of the Military Command Center (MCC) in the city of Zakho, Iraq and the shift of humanitarian assistance in the north under UNSCR 986 to international organizations, the designation "Provide Comfort" will no longer be used to describe the operation. The United Kingdom will continue to take part in this mission; however, France has chosen not to continue to participate in this endeavor. None of these changes affect our firm commitment to ensuring that the northern no-fly zone is fully enforced.

Besides our air operations, we will continue to maintain a strong U.S. presence in the region in order to deter Saddam. U.S. force levels have returned to approximate pre-Operation Desert

Strike levels, with land and carrier based aircraft, surface warships, a Marine amphibious task force, a Patriot missile battalion, and a mechanized battalion task force deployed in support of USCINCCENT operations. As an additional deterrent against Iraqi aggression, F–117 aircraft remain deployed to Kuwait. Since submission of my last report, USCINCCENT has completed the initial phases of Operation Desert Focus, with the relocation and consolidation of all combatant forces in Saudi Arabia into more secure facilities throughout Saudi Arabia. To enhance force protection throughout the region, additional military security personnel have been deployed for continuous rotation. USCINCCENT continues to closely monitor the security situation in the region to ensure adequate force protection is provided for all deployed forces.

United Nations Security Council Resolution (UNSCR) 949, adopted in October 1994, demands that Iraq not threaten its neighbors or U.N. operations in Iraq and that it not redeploy or enhance its military capacity in southern Iraq. In view of Saddam's reinforced record of unreliability, it is prudent to retain a significant U.S. force presence in the region in order to maintain the capability to respond rapidly to possible Iraqi aggression or threats against its neighbors.

In northern Iraq, we have made some limited progress in strengthening the October 23 cease-fire and encouraging political reconciliation between the two main Iraqi Kurd groups, the Kurdistan Democratic Party (KDP) and the Patriotic Union of Kurdistan (PUK). Assistant Secretary of State for Near Eastern Affairs Robert Pelletreau co-chaired talks between the KDP and the PUK in Turkey on October 30 and November 15, alongside representatives of the Turkish and British governments. During these talks, we obtained agreement from the two parties that the neutral, indigenous Peace Monitoring Force (PMF) would demarcate and observe the cease-fire line. To support the PMF, I have directed, under the authorities of sections 552(c) and 614 of the Foreign Assistance Act of 1961, as amended, the drawdown of up to $4 million in Department of Defense commodities and services, and the Secretary of State has made a determination under which we will provide up to $3 million for uniforms, tents, generators and other non-lethal supplies. Issues related to PMF operations are discussed regularly by a

Supervisory Peace Monitoring Group that meets in Ankara and is composed of U.S., U.K. and Turkish representatives, as well as members of the indigenous relevant parties. In these and other high level meetings, this Administration has consistently warned all concerned that internecine warfare in the north can only work to the advantage of Saddam Hussein and Iran, which we believe has no role to play in the area. In this connection, we remain concerned about the KDP's links to Baghdad and the PUK's ties to Iran.

Despite the cease-fire and other efforts, many residents of northern Iraq continued to face threats from Baghdad due to their association with U.S.-affiliated nongovernmental organizations, who had undertaken relief work in northern Iraq over the past few years. In response, this Administration, with the assistance of Turkey, conducted a third humanitarian evacuations operation of approximately 3,780 residents of northern Iraq whose lives were directly threatened by the Iraqi regime. All of the evacuees are being processed on Guam under the U.S. refugee resettlement program, while most of the 2,700 evacuated under two previous operations are now resettled in the United States.

The United States, working through the United Nations and humanitarian relief organizations, continues to provide humanitarian assistance to the people of northern Iraq. We have contributed more than $15 million this fiscal year to programs in the north administered by the U.N. International Children's Emergency Fund (UNICEF) and the World Food Program (WFP). Security conditions in northern Iraq remain tenuous at best, with Iranian and PKK (Kurdistan Workers Party) activity adding to the ever-present threat from Baghdad.

On December 9, the U.N. Secretary General submitted his formal report to the UNSC stating that all necessary conditions for implementation of UNSCR 986 had been met. Following this action, the resolution went into effect 12:01 a.m. on December 10. UNSCR 986 authorizes Iraq to sell up to $2 billion of oil during an initial 180-day period, with the possibility of UNSC renewal of subsequent 180-day periods. Resolution 986 provides that the proceeds of this limited oil sale, all of which must be deposited in a U.N. escrow account, will be used to purchase food, medicine, and other materials and supplies for essential civilian needs for all Iraqi

13

citizens, and to fund vital U.N. activities regarding Iraq. Critical to the success of UNSCR 986 is Iraq's willingness to follow through on its commitments under 986 to allow the U.N. to monitor the distribution of food and medical supplies to the Iraqi people.

We have already seen good evidence that the safeguards systems is working: when Saddam Hussein pushed a button in Kirkuk on December 10 to turn on the flow of oil before any oil contracts had been approved by the U.N., the U.N. made him turn it off. The oil flow began again, under proper U.N. supervision, a short time later.

The Government of Iraq has, since my last report, continued to flout its obligations under a number of Security Council resolutions in other ways. Under the terms of relevant UNSC resolutions, Iraq must grant the United Nations Special Commission on Iraq (UNSCOM) inspectors immediate, unconditional, and unrestricted access to any location in Iraq they wish to examine, and access to any Iraqi official whom they wish to interview, so that UNSCOM may fully discharge its mandate. Iraq continues, as it has for the past 5 years, to fail to live up either to the letter or the spirit of this commitment.

In his October 11 semiannual written report to the Security Council, UNSCOM Executive Chairman Rolf Ekeus outlined in comprehensive detail Iraq's past and ongoing efforts to conceal evidence of its weapons of mass destruction (WMD) programs. In his December 18 briefing to the Security Council, Ekeus urged it to take action to reverse Iraq's current blocking of UNSCOM removal of 130 SCUD motors from Iraq for analysis. As reported to the press by Security Council President Fulci that day, Ekeus informed the Council that he thought significant numbers of SCUD missiles still exist in Iraq. As long as Saddam refuses to cooperate fully with U.N. weapons inspectors, UNSCOM will be impeded in its efforts to fulfill its mandate to ensure that Iraq's WMD program has been eliminated. We will continue to fully support the mandate and the efforts of the Special Commission to obtain Iraqi compliance with all relevant U.N. resolutions.

The implementation of the export/import monitoring mechanism approved by the Security Council in Resolution 1051 began on October 1. Resolution 1051 approved a mechanism to monitor Iraq's undertaking to reacquire proscribed weapons capabilities by requiring that Iraq inform the U.N. in advance of any imports of dual-use items and that countries provide timely notification of the export to Iraq of dual-use items.

Iraq also continues to stall and obfuscate rather than work in good faith toward accounting for the hundreds of Kuwaitis and third-country nationals who disappeared at the hands of Iraqi authorities during the occupation. It has also failed to return all of the stolen Kuwaiti military equipment and the priceless Kuwaiti cultural and historical artifacts, which were looted during the occupation.

Iraq's repression of its Shi'a population continues with policies aimed at destroying the Marsh Arabs' way of life in Southern Iraq, as well as the ecology of the southern marshes. The human rights situation throughout Iraq remains unchanged. Saddam Hussein shows no signs of complying with UNSCR 688, which demands that Iraq cease the repression of its own people.

The Multinational Interception Force (MIF) remains on station in the Arabian Gulf. Our commitment to the enforcement of the sanctions regime is clearly demonstrated by the significant investment we have made with our naval forces in this area. Since my last report, 10 vessels have been intercepted and diverted for sanctions violations. Most of the vessels diverted have been engaged in illegal oil smuggling, but in recent weeks, we have begun to intercept smaller boats attempting to smuggle Iraqi dates as well. Traditionally, our naval forces encounter an increase in date smugglers as Ramadan approaches.

We continue to note suspected smugglers using the territorial waters of Iran to avoid interception by the MIF. Due to the geography of the Gulf, it is possible to transit from Iraqi ports to the UAE and the Indian Ocean without entering international waters. We believe, and have confirmed in some instances, that smugglers utilize these routes to export Iraqi petroleum products in violation of UNSCR 661. We believe that there are elements within the Iranian government who profit from charging "protection fees" for the safe passage through Iranian waters. We have presented evidence of this to the United Nations Sanctions Committee, and I am pleased to report that the Committee has decided to admonish Iran for failing to halt sanctions violators in its waters.

The recent implementation of UNSCR 986 will increase the workload of our naval forces participating in the MIF. We are prepared to meet the increased monitoring effort in the coming months. The surge in maritime traffic expected to occur with the implementation of UNSCR 986 will necessitate extreme vigilance to ensure that those who would profit from illegal trade with Iraq are not given the opportunity to succeed.

The United Nations Compensation Commission (UNCC), established pursuant to UNSCR 687, continues to resolve claims against Iraq arising from Iraq's unlawful invasion and occupation of Kuwait. The UNCC has issued over 1 million awards worth approximately $5.2 billion. At its most recent meeting, the UNCC Governing Council approved an award of $610 million on the claim by the Kuwait national oil company for the costs of extinguishing the oil well fires ignited by Iraq at the end of the Gulf War. The UNCC has authorized to date only limited payments for fixed awards for serious personal injury or death because additional funds to pay awards have been unavailable due to Iraq's refusal to comply with all relevant sanctions. With the advent of oil sales under UNSCR 986, however, 30 percent of the proceeds (which is anticipated to be as much as $100 million per month) will be allocated to the Compensation Fund. These proceeds will be used to make installment payments on awards already made and to finance the operations of the UNCC.

To conclude, Iraq remains a serious threat to regional peace and stability. I remain determined to see Iraq comply fully with all of its obligations under U.N. Security Council resolutions. My Administration will continue to oppose any relaxation of sanctions until Iraq demonstrates its peaceful intentions through such compliance.

I appreciate the support of the Congress for our efforts and shall continue to keep the Congress informed about this important issue.

Sincerely,

WILLIAM J. CLINTON

NOTE: Identical letters were sent to Newt Gingrich, Speaker of the House of Representatives, and Strom Thurmond, President pro tempore of the Senate. This letter was released by the Office of the Press Secretary on January 8.

Message to the Congress Transmitting Legislation on the Appointment of the United States Trade Representative
January 8, 1997

To the Congress of the United States:

I am pleased to transmit herewith for your immediate consideration and enactment legislation to provide a waiver from certain provisions relating to the appointment of the United States Trade Representative.

This draft bill would authorize the President, acting by and with the advice and consent of the Senate, to appoint Charlene Barshefsky as the United States Trade Representative, notwithstanding any limitations imposed by certain provisions of law. The Lobbying Disclosure Act of 1995 amended the provisions of the Trade Act of 1974 regarding the appointment of the United States Trade Representative and the Deputy United States Trade Representatives by imposing certain limitations on their appointment. These limitations only became effective with respect to the appointment of the United States Trade Representative and Deputy United States Trade Representatives on January 1, 1996, and do not apply to individuals who were serving in one of those positions on that date and continue to serve in them. Because Charlene Barshefsky was appointed Deputy United States Trade Representative on May 28, 1993, and has continued to serve in that position since then, the limitations in the Lobbying Disclosure Act, which became effective on January 1, 1996, do not apply to her in her capacity as Deputy United States Trade Representative and it is appropriate that they not apply to her if she is appointed to be the United States Trade Representative.

I have today nominated Charlene Barshefsky to be the next United States Trade Representative. She has done an outstanding job as Deputy United States Trade Representative since 1993 and as Acting United States Trade Representative for the last 9 months. I am confident she will make an excellent United States Trade Rep-

resentative. I urge the Congress to take prompt and favorable action on this legislation.

WILLIAM J. CLINTON

The White House,
January 8, 1997.

Remarks on Receiving a Report on Student Loan Default Rates and an Exchange With Reporters
January 9, 1997

The President. Thank you very much, Fiona. And I want to thank all the young people for coming here and for representing the best in our country and the best of our future. I also want to thank Secretary Riley for this report and for the work that he and the good people at the Department of Education have done every day for the last 4 years.

When I ran for this office in 1992, at every stop along the way, I always said one of the most important things for me to do in the next 4 years was to open the doors of college education wider by passing a loan program that would allow people to pay their college loans back as a percentage of their income, to have more options to pay their college loans back so no young person need ever fear going to college because of the crushing burden of debt on them in the early years after they got out, but that at the same time, we had to have more responsibility by dramatically lowering the student default rate.

I went to law school and college on scholarships and loans and jobs, and I felt very strongly that it ought to be easier for people to go but that it ought to be harder to evade your obligation to repay the debt. And we have worked very, very hard to achieve those objectives. And that's why we've worked hard to expand college loans and lower their costs through the direct loan program. I'm glad that Fiona is a direct-loan student. We've seen the results of that throughout the country, and we believe that when those loans start to be repaid, they will lower the default rate even more.

We expanded Pell grants and work-study programs in the last session of Congress to their highest level in history. We had the biggest in-

crease in Pell grants in 20 years, and we added 200,000 more work-study slots. AmeriCorps was created, and it lets young people, obviously, earn money for a college education by serving in their communities.

And in addition to that, as this report points out, we have strengthened the basic bargain. There has been more opportunity, but there is more responsibility. The default rate on student loans that is being announced today is the lowest in the history of America. It has dropped 40 percent since I took office. It is now below 11 percent. We want it to go lower still, but we can be proud of the fact that more young people who go to college are showing that, along with everything else, they have learned the important lesson of their responsibility to pay the loan back. And that means savings of hundreds of millions of dollars to our taxpayers, savings which will make it easier for us to balance the budget and easier for us to invest more in education.

We have done our part by placing tough sanctions on schools that didn't do their part to prevent defaults, and in some cases, we actually took away eligibility for Federal loan programs. When necessary, we have tracked down defaulters and made them pay. Frankly, a stronger economy has also helped to produce today's good news. More young people who get out of college can get good jobs and repay their loans more easily, and that's very, very important.

But the bottomline is that this report shows that our strategy of opportunity and responsibility is working. It's working because of the steps that have been taken to improve student loans and strengthen the economy. It's working because of the changes that were made in the loan program by Congress a few years ago. And it's working because more and more young people are taking advantage of a college education and then taking the opportunity to be responsible in paying their loans back.

Now, as we begin this second term, I just want to reiterate my commitment to ensuring that every person in this country has the tools that he or she needs to make the most of their own lives, that we open the doors of college education to everyone. The core of my second term efforts to build a bridge to the 21st century will be dramatic advancements in education. The fact is that some people who want to go to college still can't get there, so our first step should be to provide more opportunity. We can do that through the HOPE Scholarships tax cuts that I have proposed. They would allow Americans to deduct from their tax bill, dollar for dollar, the cost of the typical community college tuition for up to 2 years, to make the first 2 years of college as universal as a high school diploma is today. They would allow the typical family to deduct up to $10,000 a year from their taxes for the cost of any college tuition. They would allow a family—I mean more families, many more families to save through IRA's and then to withdraw from those IRA's penalty-free if the money is being used to finance a college education.

Especially now that more and more students are taking responsibility for their own education, we simply have to do more to open the doors wider. The HOPE Scholarship tax cuts would make college affordable for every person in this country willing to work for it, especially when you couple that with the availability of the loans and the work-studies. America needs these tax cuts to help America pay for college, and I hope Congress will help us to pass them into law.

Let me also point out one of our other proposals that I've had on the table in Congress for 4 years now, which I am determined to get passed in this next Congress, is the "GI bill" for America's workers. A lot of people in the work force need to go back to school. There are now scores of different training programs that we propose to consolidate and send a skills grant to people who lose their jobs or people who are dramatically unemployed and let them

make the decision to use this skills grant in the same way, to finance a college education.

And let me finally say that while we can make sure that everyone can go to college, it's also important that everyone be prepared to go. We have to set the highest standards for public education in this country so that highly trained teachers demand peak performance from students. We should require that students pass tests that actually test whether they learn what the standards say they're supposed to know before they go on from grade to grade. We should reward teachers who do well and make it possible for local schools to remove those who do not. We should expand public school choice and improve and expand on charter schools run by teachers and parents that survive only if they produce results. We should make sure every child can read independently by the third grade, and I hope that we'll have another 100,000 young people helping in that million-person brigade of volunteers we're going to need to teach our young people to read. And we should finish the job of connecting every classroom to the Internet by the year 2000.

If every 8-year-old can read, every 12-year-old can log on to the Internet, and every 18-year-old can go to college, America will enter the 21st century with every person able to have the skills that he or she needs to succeed in building a good life.

So let me say that these young people here—they're a shining example of opportunity and responsibility—give me the hope that we will succeed. And I thank you, Fiona, and I thank all the others and all of them like you all across America today who will be watching this and who will be building our future.

Thank you, and thank you, Mr. Secretary.

Legislative Agenda

Q. What do you think is the chance of getting these through Congress?

The President. Well, I think they'll be very good. You know, we've worked very hard on our budget, and our OMB Director, Frank Raines, has begun conversations with Members of Congress already. I have spoken, obviously, on many occasions with Senator Lott and Senator Daschle, Speaker Gingrich and Leader Gephardt. And if the atmosphere—I can now only add to what I've already said—if the atmosphere of this Congress reflects what happened in the last 2 months of the last Congress, I think the American people will get their balanced budget; they will get these education tax cuts; they will get the next step of welfare reform to create jobs for people who are going to be moving from welfare to work; and it will be a very, very good time. The atmosphere so far feels good to me, and if we just keep working on it, I think we can get there.

Q. Mr. President, have you made all of your final budget decisions? And is there any possibility of your reopening any of those decisions, specifically on Medicare?

The President. Well, let me answer you this way. I have completed sometime ago the work on the budget. We still have to work around the edges from time to time. It is a good budget; it is a credible budget. I also am pleased that the OMB and the Congressional Budget Office have been working together to try to narrow the gaps between them in all these assumptions they have for the budget. And I'm confident that we can produce one that will bring balance under either set of assumptions, and I intend to do that. And the budget will reflect the priorities I laid before the American people in the campaign and will be consistent

with what I have said over the last 4 or 5 years about this.

Now, I also expect there to be a negotiating process with the Congress, and I will work with them in good faith, as I have said all along. But I think this budget will show that I am making a clear effort to reach out to them, to meet them halfway, and to get this job done.

Q. In what year will the budget you present in February actually reach a balanced budget?

The President. In 2002, the same year we——

Q. The same year.

The President. ——all along.

Q. Does that mean that on Medicare you are going to go for raising the premiums and so forth? And you spoke in generalities, but is there anything you can——

The President. Well, it means I don't want to remove all the suspense from my budget presentation. [*Laughter*]

Thank you very much.

NOTE: The President spoke at 10:31 a.m. in the Oval Office at the White House. In his remarks, he referred to Fiona Rose, University of Michigan student who introduced the President.

Remarks on Presenting the Arts and Humanities Awards
January 9, 1997

Thank you very much. When Hillary said that, I was so hoping that there wouldn't be even one loud stage whisper saying, "I wish he had made that choice." [*Laughter*]

I am so delighted to be here to honor the 1996 recipients of the National Medal of the Arts and the Charles Frankel Prize. They are men and women whose accomplishments speak to the breadth and depth of our creative and intellectual genius.

I want to begin by thanking Jane Alexander, Sheldon Hackney, Diane Frankel, and John Brademas for their energetic and wise leadership in promoting the arts and humanities across our country. I thank them for what they have done. This cold day is a rather apt metaphor for a lot of what they have labored through the last couple of years, and we are all in their debt for standing firm.

I thank the United States Marine Band for being here. I'm always so proud of them and the work they do for our country. I thank the magnificent Harlem Boys Choir for their wonderful music and for being here. All of you who are supporters of the arts who are here, I thank you for being here, supporters of the humanities. I see Secretary and Mrs. Riley and Congressman Dicks and Congressman Rangel. There may be other Members here; I apologize for not introducing you, but for those of you in other positions of public responsibility, in particular, I thank you for standing up for the arts and humanities.

Each year this ceremony gives us an opportunity to celebrate the extraordinary contributions of individual American artists, writers, and thinkers, to reflect on the role of the arts and humanities in our own lives and in the life of our great democracy. We are a nation whose strength and greatness are derived from the rich heritage and diversity of our people, from the richness of our artistic and intellectual traditions. For more than 200 years, our freedom has depended not only upon our system of government and the resolve of our people but upon the ferment of ideas that shape our public discourse and on the flow of creative expression that unites us as a people.

Today we are on the eve of a new century. The arts and humanities are more essential than ever to the endurance of our democratic values of tolerance, pluralism, and freedom and to our understanding of where we are and where we need to go. At a momentous time in our history like this, when so much is happening to change the way we work and live, the way we relate to one another, and the way we relate to the rest of the world, we cannot fully understand the past nor envision the future we need to pursue without the arts and humanities.

It is, after all, through the arts and humanities that we unleash our individual and collective imaginations. And imagination is, in the end, the animating force of a democracy committed to constant renewal, the force that allows us to conceive of a brighter future and a better world, that allows us to overcome new challenges and grave difficulties. By imagining a better America and acting to achieve it, we make our greatest progress.

That is why we must sustain our Nation's commitment for the arts and humanities to build that bridge to the 21st century I am so committed to. We must have our theaters, our orchestras, our dance troupes, our exhibits, our lectures, our scholarship. We must have them all to strengthen and preserve our culture and instill in our children the democratic ideals we claim to cherish. And we must have them so that our young people can imagine what their lives might be like if they were better. For all the speeches I might give, the children struggling to overcome difficult circumstances, simply seeing the powerful example of the Harlem Boys Choir is probably more persuasive than any words I could ever utter.

Today the average American spends about 80 cents to support Federal funding of the arts and humanities, about as much as it costs to buy a can of soda pop in a vending machine. In some places it costs more than that. [*Laughter*] This tiny investment means that from Providence to Portland, from Minneapolis to Miami,

from Dallas to Des Moines, Americans of all walks of life can share in the great artistic and intellectual life of our Nation.

In America, we should all be able to enjoy art, ideas, and culture, no matter what our station in life. And our children should be able to be exposed to them, no matter what their station in life. For children, Federal support of the arts and humanities is particularly critical. Think of how often we hear stories about children who, unable to find safe outlets for their ideas, their emotions, their enormous physical energy, travel instead down the wrong road to destruction and despair. But across our Nation, Federal support to the arts and humanities has enabled tens of thousands of those children to see their first play, their first ballet, their first Monet. What a transforming experience it can be when a young person discovers his or her own gifts for music, for dance, for painting, for drama, for poetry, photography, or writing.

One man who knows firsthand about the power of art to change young people's lives is the artist who designed the medal that some of our honorees will receive today. Bob Graham is one of our Nation's finest sculptors. After the Los Angeles riots, he decided to hire inner-city gang members as assistants and apprentices in his studio in southern California. These young men have recharted their futures and found that instead of feeling alienated by society, they are now valued for the contributions they are making to society.

The earlier we start developing these creative impulses for artistic and intellectual potential, the better off our children and we will be. As Hillary wrote in her book, we know a great deal more today about the importance of providing such stimulation for children in the very first years of life. We know how important it is for children to hear words, listen to stories, develop their imaginations. That's one reason I'm challenging all of our people to work with us toward a goal of making sure every boy and girl in our country can read a book independently by the third grade.

Perhaps no one has done as much to show the power of the written word on children, not to mention on their parents, as Maurice Sendak, one of our honorees today. I'm delighted that he will join Hillary tomorrow at the Georgetown University Medical Center to read to children who are getting their checkups there. And I thank them both to help to kick off a national effort to educate Americans about reading even to our very youngest children.

For the better part of this century, the world has looked to the United States not simply for military and economic and political leadership but for cultural leadership as well. So as we embark upon this new century, let us make sure that our Nation remains the cultural oasis it is today. I am optimistic about our prospects because of the commitment and the dedication of those of you who are gathered here and because our Nation is honored and blessed by the artists and thinkers we recognize today.

In an age when words and images and ideas are too often diluted, devalued, and distorted, when what we see and hear is routinely reduced to catch phrases and instant images, the men and women on this stage represent instead the profound, lasting, and transcendent qualities of American cultural life.

Now it gives me great pleasure to present the 1996 National Medal of Arts awards and the Charles Frankel Prize. First, the men and women being awarded the National Medal of Arts.

Last month we paid tribute to our first honoree at the Kennedy Center, and I'm proud to honor him again. For some 40 years, playwright Edward Albee has been a dominate and inspirational figure in American theater. His plays offer raw and provocative portrayals of the human experience. He has challenged actors, audiences, and fellow writers to explore the complexities of our emotions, attitudes, and relationships. A native of Washington, DC, he won the Pulitzer Prize three times for "A Delicate Balance," "Seascape," and most recently for "Three Tall Women." I ask you to join me in congratulating Edward Albee. [*Applause*]

[*At this point, the President and the First Lady congratulated Mr. Albee and presented the medal.*]

Audiences from Russia to the Philippines to our own shores have experienced firsthand conductor Sarah Caldwell's passion for music and her commitment to bring some of our world's most difficult yet beautiful operas to the stage. Sarah Caldwell has dedicated her life to promoting and introducing opera to new audiences here and around the world. She conducted her first opera at Tanglewood in 1947, founded the Boston Opera 10 years later, and went on to become the first woman ever to conduct the New York Metropolitan Opera. She is truly opera's First Lady. And if you will forgive me a small amount of parochialism, she has come a long way from our native State of Arkansas— [*laughter*]—and I am very proud of her.

[*The President and the First Lady congratulated Ms. Caldwell and presented the medal.*]

A photographer whose work has inspired both peers and casual viewers and a teacher whose ideas and methods have influenced university curricula, Harry Callahan is a national treasure. More than 50 years ago, he discovered the camera's power to capture the sublime and seemingly everyday subjects: nature, the city, and people. His subtle, contemplative pictures convey an intensely personal vision of the world. They have graced photography exhibitions in some of the finest museums around the world. A native of Detroit, his work reminds us that there is always much more than meets the eye.

[*The President and the First Lady congratulated Mr. Callahan and presented the medal.*]

I'm delighted to honor a woman who has spent some four decades creating and nurturing one of the leading artistic institutions in our Nation's Capital. The Arena Stage is a living legacy of the vision, the talent, and the creative energies of Zelda Fichandler. The Arena is one of our country's leading regional theaters and under her leadership has brought plays such as "Inherit the Wind," "After the Fall," and "The Crucible" to audiences in Russia, Hong Kong, and Israel. In 1976 she and the Arena became the first company based outside New York to win a Tony.

[*The President and the First Lady congratulated Ms. Fichandler and presented the medal.*]

Thank you very much for all you have done.

Musician, composer, and bandleader Eduardo (Lalo) Guerrero has spent a creative life celebrating and exploring his Mexican-American heritage in music from mariachis to orchestra pieces. An Arizona native, he began his career while still in his teens, composing what later became the unofficial anthem of Mexico. In the 60 years since, he has been prolific and inspired, composing songs that have topped the charts on both sides of the border. In 1980 the Smithsonian Institution named him a national folk treasure. And we are honored to honor him today.

[*The President and the First Lady congratulated Mr. Guerrero and presented the medal.*]

He still has his salsa, you see. [*Laughter*]

First, let me say that we are glad to see Lionel Hampton here safe and sound. A legendary bandleader, singer, and the first musician to make a vibraphone sing and swing, he has been delighting jazz audiences for over half a century. Anyone who has ever heard his music knows that he is much more than a performer; he is a pioneer. When Louis Armstrong invited him to play the vibraphones at a recording session in 1936, he realized he had found his calling. He mastered the vibes quickly and performed the first jazz vibraphone solo ever recorded. In 1936 he joined the Benny Goodman Trio, but soon he formed his own band and over the years has nurtured the talents of many jazz leaders, including Quincy Jones and Dinah Washington. He is a lion of American music, and he still makes the vibraphone sing.

[*The President and the First Lady congratulated Mr. Hampton and presented the medal.*]

Dancer, choreographer, and teacher Bella Lewitzky first began creating dances in her hometown of Redlands, California, when she was just 7 years old. With Lester Horton, she founded the Dance Theater of Los Angeles in 1946. Twenty years later, she formed the Lewitzky Dance Company, a troupe that has performed to critical acclaim around the world. Now in her 80th year, when it would be just as easy to rest upon her well-deserved laurels, she is eagerly looking to start new projects, and I hope all of you have inspired her here today.

[*The President and the First Lady congratulated Ms. Lewitzky and presented the medal.*]

Vera List has touched generations of students, teachers, artists, performers, audiences, and artistic institutions across America. For more than half a century, she has lent her vision, energy, and resources to philanthropic efforts to promote the arts at universities, museums, and through artistic endowments. The charitable foundation that she and her husband, Albert, created in 1945 helped to underwrite the construction of the Metropolitan Opera House at Lincoln Center more than three decades ago. She has sponsored an opera performance for under-privileged children, PBS broadcasts highlighting the American artist, and many other varied and worthy arts projects. She has done what private citizens must do if we are going to bring the arts to all the American people, and we thank her for it.

[*The President and the First Lady congratulated Ms. List and presented the medal.*]

We would be hard-pressed to find any American who doesn't recognize Robert Redford as one of our Nation's most acclaimed actors, directors, and producers. He won an Academy Award for Best Director for "Ordinary People." He's won numerous other awards and made wonderful movies. The most important thing to me about Robert Redford is that he could have been well satisfied to be a movie superstar but instead chose an entirely different life, because for years and years and years, he has supported and encouraged many young and emerging screenwriters and directors through the Sundance Institute in Utah. He's helped to promote nontraditional cinema. He's opened the doors for many new artists and their films. I can say also, in an area not covered by today's awards, he has been a passionate advocate of preserving our natural heritage and protecting our environment. And the Vice President and I were honored to have him with us at the Grand Canyon a few months ago when we set aside 1.7 million acres, the Grand Staircase-Escalante National Monument in southern Utah, a cause that he pressed for for years and years and years. It is very important when a person with immense talent, resources, and fame tries to give the gift of creativity back to people who would otherwise never have a chance to fulfill their own God-given abilities. We honor him for that today and thank him.

[*The President and the First Lady congratulated Mr. Redford and presented the medal.*]

Throughout a lifetime as an author and illustrator, Maurice Sendak has singlehandedly revolutionized children's literature. In works such as "Where the Wild Things Are," he has created heroes and adventures that have captured the imagination of generations of young readers. His books have helped children to explore and resolve their feelings of anger, boredom, fear, frustration, and jealousy. Hillary and I read "Where the Wild Things Are" alone to our daughter scores and scores of times. And I can tell you, he helped me to explore my feelings of anger, boredom, fear, frustration, and jealousy. [*Laughter*] His books have become staples of children's libraries and family bookshelves. They will always be a beloved part of our national culture, and they have done a great deal to help our children find their own imaginations.

[*The President and the First Lady congratulated Mr. Sendak and presented the medal.*]

We were having a picture—Mr. Sendak said that, "This is my first grown-up award." [*Laughter*]

I feel that I should sing about our next honoree—but I won't; relax. [*Laughter*] Stephen Sondheim is one of our Nation's finest composers and lyricists. Not only are his words and melodies timeless, appealing to all generations, they mirror the history and experiences we share as Americans. His work is indelibly etched on our national cultural landscape. Who among us can't rattle off some words from "West Side Story," "A Funny Thing Happened on the Way to the Forum," "Gypsy," "A Little Night Music," or "Sweeney Todd"? Decade after decade, Stephen Sondheim continues to delight audiences here and around the world with his treasured lyrics. He has won five Tony Awards, was awarded the Pulitzer Prize in 1993, received the Kennedy Center Honor for Lifetime Achievement in 1993. But he has given us more than we could ever give to him.

Stephen Sondheim.

[*The President and the First Lady congratulated Mr. Sondheim and presented the medal.*]

In less than 30 years, the Boys Choir of Harlem has become one of the world's finest singing ensembles. The choir gives 100 concerts every year and has performed at the White House, the United Nations, and all around the world. These accomplishments would be enough to merit a medal, but the Boys Choir of Harlem has also changed and saved lives. Over the years it has recognized and nurtured the God-given potential of thousands of young people whose talents might otherwise have gone unnoticed. The 550 boys and girls who attend the Choir Academy of Harlem learn much more than how to sing on key and in harmony. They learn that through discipline, hard work, and cooperation, anything is possible and dreams do come true. I again say they are a powerful, shining symbol to all the young people of this country about

what they can become if the rest of us will just do our part to give them the chance.

[*The President and the First Lady congratulated choir director Walter Turnbull and presented the medal.*]

I now have the honor of introducing the recipients of the Charles Frankel Prize.

Poet, professor of poems, and activist for poetry Rita Dove helps us to find the extraordinary in the ordinary moments of our lives. She has used her gift for language, her penetrating insight, and her sensitivity to the world around her to mine the richness of the African-American experience as well as the experience of everyday living. Winner of the Pulitzer Prize in 1987 and recently Poet Laureate of the United States, she is considered one of our finest poets, and she truly is a life force of poetry.

[*The President and the First Lady congratulated Ms. Dove and presented the prize.*]

Best-selling author, historian, and political commentator Doris Kearns Goodwin has enriched our understanding and appreciation of the people and institutions that have shaped American government, American history, and American politics. Her great gift is to tell the story of America through rigorous scholarship, engaging prose, and anecdotes and details that bring alive major events and political figures. She has worked in the White House, taught at Harvard, written books about President Johnson, the Kennedys, and the Roosevelts. Her latest work, "No Ordinary Time," won the Pulitzer Prize in 1994. And I can tell you it made the details of the White House come alive. I actually had the book, walking from room to room, imagining what it all looked like all those long years ago. In that book alone, she did a great service to the United States in helping us to understand our history, our leaders, and what this country is really all about.

[*The President and the First Lady congratulated Ms. Goodwin and presented the prize.*]

Political philosopher, public servant, builder of civil society Daniel Kemmis has dedicated his life to reawakening America's sense of community, of citizenship, of working together for the common good. In his books and lectures and during his tenure in politics, he has spread the gospel of community involvement and explored the roots and true meaning of our democracy. He is a welcome and convincing voice against cynicism and social divisiveness. As we look to the next century, with ours the strongest, most vibrant democracy in the world but increasingly more diverse, the question of whether we will learn to identify ourselves in terms of our obligations and our opportunities in the larger community, to learn to work together across the lines that divide us with mutual respect for the common good is perhaps the greatest question facing the American people. Daniel Kemmis has helped to make sure we give the right answer.

[*The President and the First Lady congratulated Mr. Kemmis and presented the prize.*]

Arturo Madrid is pioneering the field of Latino studies in the United States. He's been an advocate for expanding educational opportunities for Hispanic students all across America. As professor of modern Spanish and Latin American literature and founder of the Tomas Rivera Center, the Nation's leading think-tank on Latino issues, he has helped Americans discern and appreciate the impact of Hispanic life on American culture and literature. An entire generation of Latino academics at the Nation's top universities owe some part of their success to Arturo Madrid's work. And now as we see Americans of Hispanic heritage the fastest growing group of our fellow citizens, the full impact of his work is bound to be felt in the future. So we thank him for what he has done and for what he has done that will be felt in generations yet to come.

[*The President and the First Lady congratulated Mr. Madrid and presented the prize.*]

Bill Moyers has received about every award there is in his field, quite simply because he has proved himself a giant in broadcast journal-ism. For more than 25 years, he has used the power of television to tackle some of the most difficult and complex issues facing our Nation, to explore the world of ideas, and to help millions of viewers better understand each other and the society in which we live. At a time in which the media often is used to truncate, oversimplify, and distort ideas in a way that divides rather than enlighten, the work of Bill Moyers' life is truly and profoundly important and encouraging. Though he is known to most Americans now as a broadcaster, his career has been as wide-ranging as his documentaries. He has been a newspaper reporter and a publisher, a campaign aide, a Deputy Director for the Peace Corps, and when he was still just a child, Presidential Press Secretary to President Johnson. Most important to me, he is a living rebuke to everybody's preconceptions about Baptist preachers. [*Laughter*] He is truly a 20th century renaissance man.

[*The President and the First Lady congratulated Mr. Moyers and presented the prize.*]

When I gave him the award, he said, "Now they'll make us pay for that one." [*Laughter*]

Ladies and gentlemen, I ask you to join me in giving one more hand to every one of these outstanding Americans. They are terrific. [*Applause*] And now, appropriately, our program will close with the Boys Choir of Harlem's rendition of "Amazing Grace."

NOTE: The President spoke at 1 p.m. in the Mellon Auditorium at the Department of Commerce. In his remarks, he referred to Jane Alexander, Chairman, National Endowment for the Arts; Sheldon Hackney, Chairman, National Endowment for the Humanities; Diane B. Frankel, Director, Institute of Museum Services; and John Brademas, Chairman, President's Committee on the Arts and Humanities.

Remarks at the Arts and Humanities Awards Dinner
January 9, 1997

Good evening, ladies and gentlemen. Welcome to the White House. Hillary and I are delighted to have all of your here tonight. This afternoon we had the honor to award 16 men and women and the Harlem Boys Choir our country's highest recognition for achievement in the arts and humanities.

Tonight we come together to salute the honorees again for their profound contributions to our cultural life. At a time when so many forces seem determined to divide us, not simply here but all around the world, the arts and humanities unite us as a people in all of our rich diversity. They give voice to our collective experience and deepen our understandings of ourselves and one another.

At the dawn of a new century in a rapidly changing world, we need our artists, our writers, our thinkers more than ever to help us find that common thread that is woven through all of our lives, to help give our children the imagination they need to visualize the future they must make, and to reach across the lines that divide us. The people we have honored today have dedicated their lives to this purpose, and I join all Americans in thanking them for their life's work.

I ask all of you now to please join me in a toast to our honorees and to the United States of America.

Hear! Hear!

[*At this point, the President toasted the honorees.*]

Thank you very much.

NOTE: The President spoke at 8:30 p.m. in the State Dining Room at the White House.

Remarks Prior to a Meeting With Business Leaders and an Exchange With Reporters
January 10, 1997

The President. Good morning, everybody. We are here in the Cabinet Room to meet with business leaders and members of the Cabinet to discuss what we all have to do together to provide jobs and training for people who will be making the transition from welfare to work as mandated by the new welfare reform law.

But before we talk more about this, I want to report some good economic news. The Department of Labor reported this morning—on Secretary Reich's last day on the payroll—where is he? [*Laughter*] He's ending with a bang. The report says that 11.2 million new jobs have now been created in the past 4 years. This is the first time in the history of our economy that over 11 million jobs have been created during one 4-year administration. It is a great tribute to the private sector in America. It is further evidence that our economy is strong, and finally, that our economic strategy to bring down the deficit, expand trade, and invest in our people is working.

I want to thank Secretary Reich for all he has done. I also want to acknowledge—there are two other outgoing members of the administration that had a great role in this economic recovery, Secretary Kantor, both as trade ambassador and as Commerce Secretary, and of course, Mr. Panetta, who was OMB Director at the time we adopted our economic plan.

The meeting we are convening here this morning builds on the exceptional efforts that have been made over the last 4 years to allow States and local communities the freedom to test their own welfare reform strategies. Last year I signed into law an approach that revolutionized welfare and made it a national mandate to move people who are able-bodied from welfare to work within 2 years. But as I have said repeatedly since that time, that was not the end of welfare reform; it was only the next step.

Now we have to launch a national effort in every State and every community to make sure that the jobs are there for people who have to make the transition from welfare to work. As a first step in that effort, every State has to tailor a welfare reform plan that requires and rewards work, imposes time limits, increases child care payments, and demands personal responsibility. We've already given the green light to 26 of our States to carry out the welfare reform plans they have designated. Today I am pleased to announce that three more States, Louisiana, Maryland, and North Carolina, have been given approval to implement their plans.

The steps we've taken over the last 4 years, working with individual States and communities, have helped to reduce the welfare rolls by 2.1 million people. Those efforts and the stronger economy have led to the biggest reduction in welfare rolls in the history of this country. But welfare reform now must go on to the next step, and it cannot succeed by Government action alone. There cannot be in our efforts to balance the budget enough money to have some big public works program here to put everyone to work who is required to move into the work force within 2 years. So welfare reform, if it's going to work, will have to have the leadership of the private sector in turning welfare checks into paychecks.

Now, our balanced budget plan has provisions in it to support the business community in helping to create a million more jobs. But today we are going to meet with these business leaders to talk about what specifically they and others can do to help to move people from welfare to work and also to talk about what they can do to help make sure that the States and the communities in this country have actually designed plans that will be attractive to the private sector in helping businesses of all sizes, not just larger businesses, to move from welfare to work and, I might also add, nonprofit organizations who are also eligible to participate in these initiatives. Just a few days ago we had our annual prayer breakfast here, and I challenged the religious organizations, as employers, to participate in this program.

So a number of these companies represented around this table have already been very active in this. We're going to have a good meeting, and I look forward to success. But I do want to make it clear to the American people, that welfare reform law did not put anybody to work. Unless we can create new jobs in the private sector within the 2-year timeline, the welfare reform effort will not succeed. And we're depending on the leaders around this table, people like them throughout America, to help us to achieve that goal.

Conspiracy To Manipulate the Media

Q. Mr. President, do you think there is a right-wing cabal in the press against you?

The President. No.

Presidential Immunity From Civil Charges

Q. Mr. President, are you concerned that the purely legal question that goes to the Supreme Court on Monday in your civil case will become a pretext for hauling out the whole story again and causing you more difficulty?

The President. I don't have any control over what anyone else does. I can only control what I do. It's not going to cause me any difficulty because I'm going to do my job here.

National Economy

Q. Mr. President, you referred to the jobs figures that came out earlier today as good news. As you're aware, not only was the December report pretty strong but both the October and November reports were revised upwards. Are you concerned at all that this strength may signal a building up of inflationary pressures in the economy?

The President. No. Based on the conversation I had with Chairman Greenspan last week, that's one of the things—or I guess earlier this week—one of the things that he noted—Secretary Rubin and I were there—was that the normal inflation pressures, at least if you go back till the end of World War II, that you would see with this kind of job growth and by modern standards a low unemployment rate just have not materialized. And he speculated on a number of the reasons why that might be so.

But I basically believe, as long as we're competitive, as long as our markets are open, as long as we're reaching out to new markets around the world, as long as we're seeing American workers continue to upgrade their skills and American businesses employ technology and better production techniques to improve their productivity, that we can keep this going without undue inflation. At least now there's no evidence of it. The only place we've had any spike in inflation is in energy prices, which was unrelated to the general growth in jobs. So I'm very hopeful right now.

Federal Reserve Board Nominations

Q. When do you expect to nominate replacements for the two Fed Governors who are leaving? Do you have any people in mind?

The President. I don't know. One of them just materialized. But I'll turn my attention to it, and I'll do it in a timely fashion.

Political Consultant Dick Morris

Q. Did Dick Morris violate his confidence by writing a book and taking credit for everything good that happened to you in the last several months?

The President. I thought the last sentence of the introduction of his book said that he was not responsible for my getting reelected, I was. [*Laughter*] So I would think that you would have to say that was a rather selective reading of the book, if that's the way you read it. [*Laughter*]

NOTE: The President spoke at 10:15 a.m. in the Cabinet Room at the White House.

Remarks to the 1996 National Hockey League Champion Colorado Avalanche
January 10, 1997

I'd like to welcome all of you to the White House, especially Representative Diana DeGette; and Charlie Lyons, the president of Ascent Entertainment; and of course the 1996 Stanley Cup winners, the Colorado Avalanche.

I'm pleased that all of you could join us today to congratulate the team, especially the people who have come all the way from Colorado. Ice hockey is one of the fastest, most exciting games going, and there was an article in one of the papers yesterday detailing all the cities in America that now want a hockey franchise. I think it's because Colorado won the championship so quickly. [*Laughter*]

When you watch an amazing team like the Avalanche take the ice, you understand why children all over our country for the first time are trying on skates and crowding the rinks. This was a very awe-inspiring performance that this team turned in this year.

No one could have anticipated the kind of season you've had when you moved to Denver just 18 months ago, rolling over the NHL like the avalanche you are so well named for. You swept the final series against the Florida Panthers, a great team who deserve a lot of credit for being the youngest expansion team to make it to the Stanley Cup final after only 3 years in the league. And as the Avalanche played out the final minutes of the triple overtime game that brought you to victory, you also showed what teamwork is all about. I may show those final minutes to the Cabinet repeatedly over the next 2 years. [*Laughter*]

In one short season, you captured the heart of your new home city and gave Colorado its first major sports championship ever. Your coach, Marc Crawford, is the third youngest coach in history to lead a team to a Stanley Cup victory. That's a remarkable achievement, something I can identify with. I used to be the youngest person doing things—[*laughter*]—a long time ago. At 27, Joe Sakic brings incredible talent and maturity to the team, and I see him here recovering from his recent injury. I hope you'll be back on your skates soon. Your outstanding goalie, Patrick Roy, must be used to this by now. Of course, this is his third Stanley Cup victory. I understand he's an avid golfer as well, and the difference is, of course, in golf you're not allowed to block the other person's shots. [*Laughter*] I must say, there have been a lot of times when I wished there had been someone there to block mine.

This victory belongs to every player on the team. By bringing home to Denver and to Colorado their first ever professional sports championship, you have justified the loyalty and pride of some ferociously loyal and proud fans. And I think it highly likely that you'll keep them happy again this year too. After your win against the Senators last night, I know you're number one in the NHL again.

Now I'd like to introduce the commissioner of the National Hockey League, Gary Bettman, to continue the program.

NOTE: The President spoke at 3:34 p.m. in the East Room at the White House. In his remarks, he referred to Charlie Lyons, chairman, and Joe Sakic, center, Colorado Avalanche.

Letter to Congressional Leaders Reporting on Economic Sanctions Against Libya
January 10, 1997

Dear Mr. Speaker: *(Dear Mr. President:)*

I hereby report to the Congress on the developments since my last report of July 22, 1996, concerning the national emergency with respect to Libya that was declared in Executive Order 12543 of January 7, 1986. This report is submitted pursuant to section 401(c) of the National Emergencies Act, 50 U.S.C. 1641(c); section 204(c) of the International Emergency Economic Powers Act (IEEPA), 50 U.S.C. 1703(c); and section 505(c) of the International Security and Development Cooperation Act of 1985, 22 U.S.C. 2349aa–9(c).

1. On January 2, 1997, I renewed for another year the national emergency with respect to Libya pursuant to IEEPA. This renewal extended the current comprehensive financial and trade embargo against Libya in effect since 1986. Under these sanctions, all trade with Libya is prohibited, and all assets owned or controlled by the Libyan government in the United States or in the possession or control of U.S. persons are blocked.

2. There have been two amendments to the Libyan Sanctions Regulations, 31 C.F.R. Part 550 (the "Regulations"), administered by the Office of Foreign Assets Control (OFAC) of the Department of the Treasury, since my last report on July 22, 1996. The Libyan Sanctions Regulations were amended on August 22, 1996, to add the Antiterrorism and Effective Death Penalty Act of 1996 (Public Law 104–132; 110 Stat. 1214–1319 (the "Antiterrorism Act") as an authority for the Regulations. (61 *Fed. Reg.* 43460, August 23, 1996). On April 24, 1996, I signed into law the Antiterrorism Act. Section 321 of the Antiterrorism Act (18 U.S.C. 2332d) makes it a criminal offense for United States persons, except as provided in regulations issued by the Secretary of the Treasury in consultation with the Secretary of State, to engage in financial transactions with the governments of countries designated under section 6(j) of the Export Administration Act (50 U.S.C. App. 2405) as supporting international terrorism. United States persons who engage in such transactions are subject to criminal fines under title 18, United States Code, imprisonment for up to 10 years, or both. Because the Regulations already prohibited such transactions, with minor exceptions for transactions found to be in the public interest, no substantive change to the prohibitions of the Regulations was necessary. A copy of the amendment is attached.

The Regulations were amended on October 21, 1996 (61 *Fed. Reg.* 54936, October 23, 1996), to implement section 4 of the Federal Civil Penalties Inflation Adjustment Act of 1990, as amended by the Debt Collection Improvement Act of 1996, by adjusting for inflation the amount of the civil monetary penalties that may be assessed under the Regulations. The Regulations, as amended, increase the maximum civil monetary penalty provided by law from $10,000 to $11,000 per violation.

The amended Regulations also reflect an amendment to 18 U.S.C. 1001 contained in section 330016(1)(L) of Public Law 103–322; 108 Stat. 2147. The amendment strikes the $10,000 maximum on fines imposed for fraudulent dealing with Federal agencies. Finally, the amendment notes the availability of higher criminal fines pursuant to the formulas set forth in 18 U.S.C. 3571. A copy of the amendment is attached.

3. During the current 6-month period, OFAC reviewed numerous applications for licenses to authorize transactions under the Regulations. Consistent with OFAC's ongoing scrutiny of banking transactions, the largest category of license approvals (49) concerned requests by non-Libyan persons or entities to unblock transfers interdicted because of what appeared to be Government of Libya interests. Several previously issued licenses were amended to authorize the provision of legal services to the Government of Libya in connection with actions in U.S. courts in which the Government of Libya was named as defendant.

Minister Louis Farrakhan and the Nation of Islam applied for a license to receive a gift of up to $1 billion from the Government of Libya as well as for Minister Farrakhan to collect $250,000 in prize money that accompanied the Ghadafi Prize for Human Rights awarded to

Minister Farrakhan in Tripoli. The application was denied on Foreign policy grounds.

4. During the current 6-month period, OFAC continued to emphasize to the international banking community in the United States the importance of identifying and blocking payments made by or on behalf of Libya. The office worked closely with the banks to assure the effectiveness of interdiction software systems used to identify such payments. During the reporting period, more than 100 transactions potentially involving Libya were interdicted.

5. Since my last report, OFAC collected 14 civil monetary penalties totaling more than $165,000 for violations of the U.S. sanctions against Libya. Twelve of the violations involved the failure of banks to block funds transfers to Libyan-owned or -controlled financial institutions. Two U.S. corporations paid OFAC penalties totaling $105,000 for export violations as part of global plea agreements with the Department of Justice. Sixty-one other cases are in active penalty processing.

On August 7, 1996, a major U.S. exporter entered a guilty plea and was sentenced in the U.S. District Court for the Western District of Kentucky for Libyan sanctions violations. The company and four co-conspirators were charged with aiding and abetting the exportation and attempted exportation of oil well drilling equipment to Libya through Italy in 1995 and 1996. The company paid $3 million in criminal fines and aggregate criminal penalties paid by individuals totaled $211,000. In addition, a major U.S. manufacturer in Milwaukee, Wisconsin agreed to pay $2 million in criminal fines, in addition to the civil penalty noted above, for violation of the Libyan sanctions involving a commercial project in Libya. Numerous investigations carried over from prior reporting periods are continuing and new reports of violations are being pursued.

6. The expenses incurred by the Federal Government in the 6-month period from July 6, 1996, through January 5, 1997, that are directly attributable to the exercise of powers and authorities conferred by the declaration of the Libyan national emergency are estimated at approximately $670,000. Personnel costs were largely centered in the Department of the Treasury (particularly in the Office of Foreign Assets Control, the Office of the General Counsel, and the U.S. Customs Service), the Department of State, and the Department of Commerce.

7. The policies and actions of the Government of Libya continue to pose an unusual and extraordinary threat to the national security and foreign policy of the United States. In adopting UNSCR 883 in November 1993, the Security Council determined that the continued failure of the Government of Libya to demonstrate by concrete actions its renunciation of terrorism, and in particular its continued failure to respond fully and effectively to the requests and decisions of the Security Council in Resolutions 731 and 748, concerning the bombing of the Pan Am 103 and UTA 772 flights, constituted a threat to international peace and security. The United States will continue to coordinate its comprehensive sanctions enforcement efforts with those of other U.N. member states. We remain determined to ensure that the perpetrators of the terrorist acts against Pan Am 103 and UTA 772 are brought to justice. The families of the victims in the murderous Lockerbie bombing and others acts of Libyan terrorism deserve nothing less. I shall continue to exercise the powers at my disposal to apply economic sanctions against Libya fully and effectively, so long as those measures are appropriate, and will continue to report periodically to the Congress on significant developments as required by law.

Sincerely,

WILLIAM J. CLINTON

NOTE: Identical letters were sent to Newt Gingrich, Speaker of the House of Representatives, and Albert Gore, Jr., President of the Senate.

Message on the Observance of Ramadan
January 10, 1997

Warm greetings to all those celebrating the sacred month of Ramadan.

Each year during Ramadan, Muslims across America and around the world commemorate God's revelation of the Koran to Muhammad with a month of rigorous fasting and devout prayer. This period of discipline for body, mind, and spirit draws the Muslim community closer not only to God, but also to their fellow human beings.

By experiencing hunger during Ramadan, the followers of Muhammad learn true compassion for the poor of the world who go hungry every day. By reflecting on God's teachings in the Koran, they learn humility and the beauty of forgiveness. And, by their example of devotion and self-discipline during Ramadan, Muslims remind us all that our true strength is derived, not from food and drink, but from closeness to God.

As the crescent moon marks the beginning of Ramadan again this year, Hillary and I extend our best wishes for a holy and memorable observance.

BILL CLINTON

NOTE: This message was released by the Office of the Press Secretary on January 11.

The President's Radio Address
January 11, 1997

Good morning. Today I want to talk about how to build upon the progress we've made together in working against crime and violence, and especially how we can fight against youth crime.

Four years ago it seemed to many Americans as if the forces of crime and violence had gained an intractable hold over our country, and law-abiding Americans were afraid that from now on they would just have to put up with the insecurity and loss that goes with rampant crime. I was determined to turn that around, to give people the tools they need to take back their streets and schools and neighborhoods, to reestablish a sense of security and true freedom in our country, and to restore our people's faith in the power of law and order.

We had a comprehensive plan to fight crime, to put 100,000 new community police officers on the street and tough new penalties on the books, to keep guns away from criminals by passing the Brady bill and banning assault weapons, to steer young people away from crime, gangs, and drugs in the first place. This approach is working.

This week the FBI reported that serious crime dropped another 3 percent last year, dropping for the 5th year in a row, the longest decline in more than 25 years. This is great news, not because it gives us a chance to sit back and rest on our laurels but because it does show all of us that if we work together we can make a difference.

Now that we've finally turned the crime on the run, we have to redouble our efforts. We have to drive the forces of violence further and further into retreat. And as we move forward, we have to remember that we're not just fighting against crime; we're fighting for the kind of nation we want to build together for the 21st century, for an America where people feel safe when they walk around the block at night and untroubled when they kiss their children goodbye in the morning, an America where nobody's grandmother lives across the street from a crack house and nobody's child walks to school through a neighborhood overrun by gangs. We're fighting for our children and for their future.

As I begin my second term as President, the next stage in our fight must center on keeping our children safe and attacking the scourge of juvenile crime and gangs. I want every police officer, prosecutor, and citizen in America working together to keep our young people safe and young criminals off the streets. This should be

America's top priority in the fight for law and order over the next 4 years. I pledge it will be mine.

We must help parents protect their children and bring order and discipline to their lives. That's why I support school uniforms and community-based curfews. That's why we made zero tolerance for guns in schools the law of the land and passed Megan's Law to demand that States tell a community whenever a dangerous sexual predator enters its midst. Now we must do more to give young people something to say yes to, after school, on weekends, and in the summer. And we must finish the job of putting 100,000 police on our streets.

At the same time, young people must understand that if they break the law, they will be punished, and if they commit violent crimes, they will be punished severely. I am determined to break the backs of criminal gangs that have ruined too many lives and stolen too many futures by bringing the full force of the law against them.

One of the most difficult problems facing law enforcement in this fight is the power of gang members to thwart the criminal justice system by threatening and intimidating the witnesses against them. Too many people in too many communities will not testify about gang crimes because they are afraid of violent reprisal. We must not allow the voice of justice to be frightened into silence by the violent threats of gangs.

Today the Justice Department is releasing a report called "Preventing Gang and Drug-Related Witness Intimidation." This report is a handbook for police officers, prosecutors, and judges to help them overcome the dangerous obstacle witness intimidation poses to the steady march of justice. It details the problems they face and helps to provide a blueprint for them to follow that will significantly help State and local gang investigation and prosecution. Starting today, the Justice Department will distribute this report to thousands of police departments, prosecutors, and judges across America.

In the coming weeks, I will submit to Congress comprehensive legislation to combat youth violence and drug abuse. Together with all our other efforts against youth violence, this will be the top crime fighting priority of my second term. I've asked the Attorney General to closely examine the growing threat of witness intimidation by gangs and to recommend strong measures to stop it that can be included in this legislation. We must not allow the very gangs we're fighting to grind the wheels of justice to a halt.

Over the past 4 years we've shown that we can roll back crime and violence. Now is no time to let up. There is still too much of it. But if we continue to work together, to stand up for what is right, to work with our community police officers, to take responsibility for ourselves and our families and the other children in our communities who need a guiding hand and an encouraging word, if we'll do all these things, we can keep the crime rate coming down and we can build the future our children deserve.

Thanks for listening.

NOTE: The address was recorded at 4:55 p.m. on January 10 in the Roosevelt Room at the White House for broadcast at 10:06 a.m. on January 11.

Remarks on Presenting the Congressional Medal of Honor to African-American Heroes of World War II
January 13, 1997

The President. Secretary Perry, Secretary Brown, other members of the administration, General Shalikashvili and the members of the Joint Chiefs, General Powell, Senator Craig, Senator Kempthorne, Congressman Miller, the members of the families and friends of the medal recipients, and Mr. Vernon Baker. I'd like to begin by thanking Shaw University; its president, Talbert Shaw; and all the authors of the Shaw study on the nomination of outstanding African-American soldiers for the Medal of Honor in the United States Army during World War II.

I also want to commend the Department of the Army officials, former and present, who commissioned this study and saw it through. Together, your support and painstaking research made this day possible. Without it, we would not be able to meet our obligation as a people to an extraordinary group of soldiers to whom we owe the greatest debt. Because of the hard work you have done, history has been made whole today and our Nation is bestowing honor on those who have long deserved it.

Fifty-two years ago on an August day, Harry Truman stood where I stand now and awarded 28 Medals of Honor to veterans of World War II in the largest such ceremony ever held. President Truman described those medal recipients as a great cross-section of the United States. "These men love peace but are able to adjust themselves to the necessity of war," he said.

I believe Harry Truman was one of our greatest Presidents. He had not a shred of discrimination in his bones. He integrated the Armed Forces. But that day, something was missing from his cross-section of America. No African-American who deserved the Medal of Honor for his service in World War II received it. Today we fill the gap in that picture and give a group of heroes, who also love peace but adapted themselves to war, the tribute that has always been their due. Now and forever, the truth will be known about these African-Americans who gave so much that the rest of us might be free.

Today we recognize seven men as being among the bravest of the brave. Each of them distinguished himself with extraordinary valor in the famous words, "at the risk of his life, above and beyond the call of duty." In the greatest struggle in human history, they helped to lead the forces of freedom to victory. Their deeds remind us anew of the indomitable power of the human spirit. And they always will be remembered by men and women who cherish liberty.

As recipients of the Medal of Honor, their names join the roles of America's heroes, along with Sergeant York, Eddie Rickenbacker, Jimmy Doolittle, Audie Murphy, General Robert Foley and Senator Bob Kerrey, and only some 3,400 Americans in the entire history of the United States.

For these men, heroism was a habit. Ruben Rivers of Oklahoma was awarded a Silver Star while fighting in France in late 1944. A week later he was terribly wounded when his tank hit a mine. Refusing an order to withdraw, Ser-geant Rivers took command of another tank. He radioed in, "I see him. We'll fight him." And he kept on fighting until his second tank was hit and he was killed.

Edward Carter, the son of missionaries, was crossing an open field in Germany when he was wounded five times. But Staff Sergeant Carter continued to advance, and when eight of the enemy tried to capture him, he killed six, took two prisoner, and brought them back for interrogation.

In the face of overwhelming danger, they never wavered. As he led a task force in France, Lieutenant Charles Thomas was wounded by intense fire. While helping others to find cover, he was wounded again and again and again. But he refused evacuation until he had made sure that his forces could return fire effectively.

While scouting a forward position, Private First Class Willy James was pinned down for an hour. But he made his way back to his platoon, planned a counterattack, and volunteered to lead the assault and then was killed going to the aid of his wounded platoon leader.

They were selfless. When Private George Watson's ship was attacked by enemy bombers, over and over and over again he helped others to make it to liferafts so that they might live, until he himself was so exhausted, he was pulled down by the tow of the sinking ship.

When the enemy surged into a town in Italy and drove out our forces, Lieutenant John Fox volunteered to remain behind in an observation force post. He directed defensive artillery fire, and eventually he insisted that that artillery fire be aimed at his own position. He said, "There are more of them than there are of us." The barrage he so bravely ordered killed him. And when our forces recovered the position, they found his riddled body among that of 100 German soldiers.

One of these heroes is here today. In an assault on a mountain stronghold in Italy, Lieutenant Vernon Baker wiped out three enemy machine gun nests, an observer post, and a dugout. I must say that Mr. Baker has not quite abandoned doing the impossible. I learned before this ceremony that he is now 77 years young, but last year he got the better of a mountain lion that was stalking him. [*Laughter*] I was also very moved, as I'm sure many of you were, by the comments quoted in today's Washington Post—or last weekend—about Mr. Baker's creed in life. He was asked how he bore up under the lack of respect and dignity and honor after all these years. And he said, "Give respect before you expect it, treat people the way you want to be treated, remember the mission, set the example, keep going." Those are words for all of us.

When Vernon Baker's commanding officer first wrote his award recommendation, he observed that Lieutenant Baker "desperately wanted the men of his company to hold their ground and was willing to sacrifice his own life in an effort to win our battle." That passage was never forwarded. When Ruben Rivers died, no award recommendation was made for the deeds we remember today. It was felt that the Silver Star he had already been—he had been given already was reward enough for a black man.

But when victory was complete in World War II, our Government made a pledge to correct cases in which Medals of Honor were deserved but not awarded. Today America honors that pledge. On behalf of the United States Congress, I award the Medal of Honor, our Nation's highest military award, to Vernon Baker; Edward Carter, Jr.; John Fox; Willy F. James, Jr.; Ruben Rivers; Charles Thomas; and George Watson.

A soldier who receives the Medal of Honor usually needs no further description. But we must remember something else here today. These heroes distinguish themselves in another almost unique way. In the tradition of African-Americans who have fought for our Nation as far back as Bunker Hill, they were prepared to sacrifice everything for freedom even though freedom's fullness was denied to them.

We remember Edward Carter, who unsuccessfully requested combat duty for 3 years, because until 1944 African-Americans were not allowed into action. When his request was finally granted, it was at the cost of his sergeant's stripes, because an African-American was not allowed to command white troops. Now those injustices are past.

Our military is among the most integrated institutions in America, a beacon to society, and among the most successful, for America is stronger than ever. In the service of General Colin Powell, General Benjamin Davis, General

Chappie James, and countless other outstanding African-Americans, we see the enormous strength that America's diversity has given us. The men we honor here today help to make their historic progress possible. They were denied their Nation's highest honor, but their deeds could not be denied, and they cleared the way to a better world.

Today, America is profoundly thankful for the patriotism and the nobility of these men and for the example they set, which helped us to find the way to become a more just, more free nation. They helped America to become more worthy of them and more true to its ideals.

To the families of the recipients who are gone, may you take comfort in the honor that has finally been done to your loved ones. And may God embrace their souls. And God bless you, Vernon Baker, and God bless America.

Commander, post the orders.

[*At this point, Comdr. John Richardson, USN, read the citations, and Lt. Col. Michael G. Mudd, USA, assisted the President in presenting the medals.*]

The President. I think it might be an appropriate way to close to say that when I gave Mr. Watson's medal to the Sergeant Major of the Army, he looked at it and smiled and he said, "This is indicative of the type of soldiers we have today, a group of people in our military, men and women, that really do reflect the vast and rich texture of our Nation."

As we adjourn, I would like to pay special respect to the other African-Americans who are here who are now or have been in uniform, to the other Medal of Honor winners who are here, and to all of you who have worked so that this day might become a reality. And to all of you again I say, your Nation thanks you, and God bless you.

Thank you.

NOTE: The President spoke at 11:12 a.m. in the East Room at the White House. In his remarks, he referred to Gen. Colin L. Powell, USA (ret.), former chairman of the Joint Chiefs of Staff, and Sergeant Major of the Army Gene C. McKinney.

Statement on Multiparty Talks on the Future of Northern Ireland
January 13, 1997

I welcome the resumption of the multiparty talks on the future of Northern Ireland in Belfast today. As the new year begins, I urge the British and Irish Governments and the leaders of Northern Ireland's political parties to press forward with their efforts to achieve a lasting settlement that will ensure peace, justice, prosperity, and opportunity for the people they represent. I am proud of the contribution that Senator George Mitchell and his two cochairmen are making to these important negotiations.

I am deeply outraged by the end of the IRA cease-fire, which threatens to plunge Northern Ireland into a senseless spiral of violence. As we start a new year, I call again on the IRA to restore its cease-fire immediately. I have always believed that the Belfast talks will have a better chance of success if all the elected parties, including Sinn Fein, are at the table, but that can only happen if the IRA declares and implements a cease-fire in both words and deeds. I remain convinced that if such an action

is taken, substantive and inclusive talks would soon follow.

As I saw during my visit to Northern Ireland just over a year ago, the overwhelming majority of the people yearn for a just and lasting settlement and an end to the conflict that has divided them for so long. I am committed to supporting the courageous people of both traditions who are working toward that goal. And I urge the loyalists to maintain their cease-fire and refrain from descending into a cycle of escalating violence.

Sadly, sectarian clashes during the summer revealed again the depth of suspicion and animosity between the two communities of Northern Ireland. When we look back in another year's time, I pray that we will call to mind images of hope and promise, reconciliation and peace in Northern Ireland. My administration remains committed to supporting the British and Irish Governments, the political leaders, and the people of Northern Ireland as they work to reach a just and lasting settlement.

Letter to Congressional Leaders Transmitting a Report on the Intelligence Community Budget
January 13, 1997

Dear Mr. Chairman:

As required by section 501 of the Intelligence Authorization Act for Fiscal Year 1997, I transmit herewith the Report on Executive Branch Oversight of the Intelligence Community Budget. This report describes actions taken to ensure adequate oversight by the executive branch of the budget of the National Reconnaissance Office and the budgets of other elements of the intelligence community within the Department of Defense.

Sincerely,

WILLIAM J. CLINTON

NOTE: Identical letters were sent to Larry Combest, chairman, House Permanent Select Committee on Intelligence; Floyd Spence, chairman, House Committee on National Security; Arlen Specter, chairman, Senate Select Committee on Intelligence; and Strom Thurmond, chairman, Senate Committee on Armed Services. This letter was released by the Office of the Press Secretary on January 14.

Remarks on Presenting the Presidential Medal of Freedom to Secretary of Defense William J. Perry at Fort Myer, Virginia
January 14, 1997

Thank you very much. General Shalikashvili, Mrs. Shalikashvili, distinguished leaders of the United States Armed Forces, Members of Congress, service members in our Armed Forces assembled here today, friends of Secretary and Mrs. Perry, and to Bill and Lee and your children and your grandchildren, your other family members who are here today. Let me say that for Hillary and me this is a bittersweet day, a great privilege for us to be here to honor Bill and Lee, a great regret that our Nation will be losing—as all nations must and we, too, must from time to time—one of the ablest people who ever served the United States in any position. We come to honor Bill Perry, the leader, the statesman, and the friend of America's Armed Forces.

Once he was asked if he had ever aspired to a career in Government service, and he replied, "No. I was a math major." Fortunately for the rest of us, he set aside his love of mathematics and engineering to serve in demanding levels of Government where the clarity and precision of his training and insight and ability were highly valued and sorely needed. He did so with remarkable distinction, accomplishment, and integrity. And I agree with Shali: When the history of our time is written, Bill Perry may well be recorded as the most productive, effective Secretary of Defense the United States ever had.

His association with our military dates to his service as an enlisted man at the end of World War II, then as an Army Reserve officer. At Stanford he helped to educate and sharpen some of our Nation's great young minds. As a businessman, he created jobs and prosperity for his home State of California. As Under Secretary of Defense in the late 1970's, it was his vision and drive and leadership that brought from the drawing board to deployment in record time many of the advanced technologies that were vital to our Nation's victory in Operation Desert Storm. Bill Perry was one of the great and, indeed, unsung heroes of the Gulf war.

But we gather today, first and foremost, to honor and thank Bill and Lee for their last 3 years leading the Defense Department. This was a difficult job but the perfect one for Bill Perry.

He completed the post-cold-war drawdown of our Armed Forces while increasing their readiness capabilities and technological edge, something no one thought could be done. The simple fact is that this is one of the great managerial achievements in our country's history. Today our troops are the best trained, the best equipped, the best prepared fighting force in the world. And they have proven that again and again on Bill Perry's watch, from Haiti to Bosnia to the Persian Gulf.

Bill Perry downsized without downgrading morale. He always valued and honored the service of people who do the hard work of ensuring our security. And as the Vice President well knows, he brought reinventing Government right into the E wing of the Pentagon with commonsense acquisition and financial reform. He never let the crisis of the moment deter him from meeting the long-term challenges and seizing the long-term opportunities to build a more secure future for the United States.

He led our successful effort to dismantle and de-target thousands of Russian nuclear warheads once aimed at American cities and to eliminate nuclear warheads from Kazakstan, Ukraine, and Belarus. The cooperative threat reduction program he managed has helped keep nuclear materials from falling into the hands of rogue states and terrorists. He helped to build a new security architecture in Europe through NATO's Partnership For Peace program. He reinvigorated our security ties with Japan and established new security relationships with Russia, China, and our neighbors in Latin America.

The Department of Defense is the largest and most complex organization in our Nation's Government. He ran it hands-on. This method would be demanding enough at any Federal agency, but when your headquarters is the Pentagon and your staff numbers 3 million, what Bill calls "management by walking around" is all the more remarkable. But as has been said today by others who know well, it is his affinity for and his commitment to our Nation's troops, the men and women who serve at home, abroad, and at sea and who are sent into harm's way at a moment's notice, which I most admire.

In many of our private meetings together over the last 3 years, Bill Perry would always—always—bring up the welfare, the morale, the interests, and the future of our men and women in uniform who are enlisted personnel and their families. Secretary Perry's many trips abroad—and as the most traveled Defense Secretary in the history of the United States, there were many trips—were as much about checking in with our troops and their families and checking on their quality of life as they were about meeting with defense ministers and military leaders in other lands.

As a former private, his heart never left the members of the enlisted corps. As a former lieutenant, he understood the leadership demands we place upon our junior officers. But above all, he understood that whether enlisted or officer, military service is the ultimate expression of patriotism by those who choose to wear our uniform.

I will miss Bill Perry for many things, for his thoughtful temperament and manner, for speaking with the mathematician's unadorned clarity, a rarity in Washington. Teddy Roosevelt said that those of us in positions of authority should speak softly and carry a big stick. Bill Perry spoke softly and carried the biggest stick in the world with great care and a great effect. His quiet confidence was always an incredible comfort to me. There were qualities which our allies relied upon, and as long as he was Secretary of Defense, I never went to bed a single night worried about the security of the United States or the welfare of our men and women in uniform. His practice of bipartisanship earned Bill Perry the trust and respect of the Congress and the American people as well as credibility abroad as an American who could speak for the entire country.

Many of you know that Secretary Perry's personal hero is his predecessor General George Marshall. During the crisis days of World War II, Marshall lived right here at Fort Myer and then went on to become a great Secretary of State and the third Secretary of Defense. While Bill Perry is one of just 16 to follow him in that difficult job, I believe he is the successor George Marshall would be most proud of.

The measure of a great Defense Secretary is whether he leaves our military stronger and our Nation safer than on the day he took office. It is, and we are.

And so it is my great privilege as President, as Commander in Chief, and as a grateful American citizen, to present William J. Perry with the Presidential Medal of Freedom, the Nation's highest civilian award.

Commander, publish the order.

NOTE: The President spoke at 10:40 a.m. in Conmy Hall. In his remarks, he referred to General Shalikashvili's wife, Joan, and Secretary Perry's wife, Leonilla. Following the President's remarks, Spec. John Christ, USA, 3d U.S. Infantry (the Old Guard), read the citation.

Statement on the National Economy
January 14, 1997

Today's Consumer Price Index report makes clear that 1996 was an exceptional year for the economy in terms of low inflation and low unemployment. Indeed, the report confirms that the combined rate of unemployment and inflation, the so-called misery index, was lower in 1996 than in any year since 1968. We also learned that in the last 3 years we have had stronger real average hourly wage growth than during any 3-year period in nearly two decades (1976–1978). Moreover, the core inflation rate in 1996 was as low as any year since 1965.

This is good news for the American people and more evidence that our economic strategy is working. Now is the time to work together in a bipartisan fashion and build on our success. That's why we will continue our efforts to reduce the deficit to zero, expand trade, and increase educational opportunities.

Statement on 1997 Appropriations for the Immigration and Naturalization Service
January 14, 1997

For many years, the Immigration and Naturalization Service did not receive sufficient resources to carry out some of its vital functions. As a result, control of our borders suffered and illegal immigration flourished.

Four years ago, we began an effort to revitalize the INS by providing the resources and commitment to fulfill our responsibilities. During this period, INS funding has grown 105 percent. Our borders have been greatly strengthened with more personnel and better technology, workplace enforcement has gotten tougher, and a record number of criminal aliens have been deported.

Today's announcement represents continuing wise management of the additional resources requested by me and provided by the Congress. And it represents my administration's continuing commitment to an immigration policy that recognizes the value of legal immigration while strengthening our efforts to restrict illegal immigration.

Remarks on the Israeli-Palestinian Agreement on Hebron and an Exchange With Reporters
January 14, 1997

The President. A few minutes ago, Prime Minister Netanyahu and Chairman Arafat called me to tell me that they have reached agreement on the Israeli redeployment in Hebron. This achievement brings to a successful conclusion the talks that were launched in Washington last September, and it brings us another step closer to a lasting, secure Middle East peace.

Once again, the Israelis and the Palestinians have shown they can resolve their differences and help to build a brighter future for their children by finding ways to address each other's concerns. And once again, the forces of peace have prevailed over a history of division.

Israel will promptly redeploy its troops. The parties will establish practical security arrangements to strengthen stability and improve cooperation. There will also be an agreed roadmap for further redeployment by Israel. The Palestinians have reaffirmed their commitments, including their commitment to fight terrorism.

I thank Prime Minister Netanyahu and Chairman Arafat for their leadership. King Hussein also deserves special recognition and gratitude for his work for peace. I also want to express my appreciation to President Mubarak for his support. Finally, let me thank Secretary Christopher, who worked on this all weekend long, and our United States team. And especially let me thank our Special Middle East Coordinator, Dennis Ross, who has worked so hard and so long to help conclude this agreement.

Today's agreement is not an end in itself. Bringing its words to life will require active and continuous cooperation between Israeli and Palestinian officials. It will demand every effort to stop those who would choose confrontation over cooperation. In short, this is not a time to relax. It is a time to reinforce our commitment to peace.

That's why it is so important that the Israelis and the Palestinians have agreed to continue to work on the remaining issues contained in their agreements. As they do, the United States will do all it can to help. We will do everything we can to build a just and durable peace, a peace that will mean a better life for Israelis, for Palestinians, for all the people of the Middle East.

And now I'd like to ask Mr. Berger to come up here and give you the details from our perspective of what's happened over the last couple weeks.

Q. Sir, if it took so long for this agreement to be worked out, sir, on a relatively minor point of redeploying troops in Hebron, what does—is it a bad omen for the other unresolved issues that they now face?

The President. No. I think it's a good omen, because—keep in mind this agreement was not just about the Hebron redeployment. It was about a timetable for further redeployment. It was about other arrangements that would shape their future working relationship. So this is—there's much more in this agreement now. And Mr. Berger can answer more questions about it.

NOTE: The President spoke at 8:27 p.m. in the Briefing Room at the White House. In his remarks, he referred to Prime Minister Binyamin Netanyahu of Israel; Chairman Yasser Arafat of the Palestinian Authority; King Hussein I of Jordan; and President Hosni Mubarak of Egypt.

Remarks on Mexico's Repayment of Loans From the United States and an Exchange With Reporters
January 15, 1997

The President. Good morning, and welcome. Ambassador Silva Herzog, Chairman Greenspan, Secretary Rubin, Deputy Secretary Summers and other members of the administration, Mr. McLarty, Mr. Berger, Congressman Richardson, Congressman Matsui, Congressman Frank, ladies and gentlemen. Just a few moments ago, President Ernesto Zedillo of Mexico called me to tell me that Mexico had issued instructions to repay the remaining $3.5 billion of the $13½ billion the United States loaned to Mexico 2 years ago in the wake of the peso's collapse.

In 1995, when my administration put together this emergency support package, Mexico was in crisis. Today the United States is being repaid more than 3 years ahead of schedule. We have earned more than half a billion dollars on our loan. Our exports to Mexico are at an all-time high, and the Mexican economy is back on track.

Two years ago, helping our friend and neighbor in a time of need was quite controversial. Some said that we should not get involved, that the money would never be repaid, that Mexico should fend for itself. They were wrong. Today the American people can be proud that we did the right thing by Mexico and the right thing for the United States and the right thing to protect global prosperity.

The financial crisis in Mexico was also America's problem. We had to act to prevent the crisis from destabilizing our third largest trading partner, spreading to other emerging markets from Latin America to Asia, and threatening the sales of goods and services that generate jobs for American workers. By taking action, we protected a strong and growing market for American products that supports 700,000 jobs here. We helped Mexico to sustain its program of democratic reform and economic growth. And we helped to give the Mexican people renewed hope for a more secure future.

I want to thank Secretary Rubin and his team at Treasury, Deputy Secretary Summers and Under Secretary Shafer, for the remarkable job they have done. I want to thank Chairman Greenspan for his support of this course of action and for the close cooperation that he offered the Treasury Department in working through this. Together they put together an emergency $20 billion loan support package that allowed Mexico to work itself out of the crisis while working itself back to financial and economic health. We also led an international effort to make available up to $50 billion in emergency support from international financial institutions.

For its part, Mexico put in place a tough adjustment program to get its economic house in order. Today, in thanking President Zedillo for the good news we have received, I also want to applaud him and his team for the skill and courage they have demonstrated in sticking to their program of reform and reviving Mexico's economy. The Mexican economy grew by over 4 percent in 1996. The exchange rate has stabilized. Inflation has been cut nearly in half. Close to one million new jobs have been restored to Mexico since the crisis bottomed out. And Mexico has regained the confidence of international investors. This is a remarkable turnaround. Following its 1982 financial crisis, it took 7 years—7 years—for Mexico to return to the private financial markets. This time it took 7 months.

After the 1982 crisis, Mexico imposed prohibitive tariffs, and U.S. exports fell 50 percent, not recovering for 7 years. This time Mexico continued to fulfill its NAFTA commitments, and our exports are already 11 percent above pre-crisis levels.

Mexico's immediate financial crisis was our first order of business, but our work didn't stop there. With our G–7 allies in the international financial institutions, we agreed at the Halifax summit in 1995 to long-term safeguards to prevent similar crises from occurring in the future and to deal with them effectively if they do. Mexico will face new challenges as it moves forward on economic and political reform, as it works to strengthen the social safety net and raise living standards for the poor and fights the scourge of drug trafficking. The United States will continue to support and encourage these efforts. And I want to underscore that our administration and this President are committed to strengthening our engagement throughout Latin America in the months and years ahead, just as we are committed to the need for American leadership because there are times when only America can get the job done.

It now gives me great pleasure to invite Ambassador Silva Herzog and Secretary Rubin to sign a protocol that officially terminates the special loan agreement between the United States and Mexico and brings our emergency support program to a very successful conclusion.

[*At this point, Treasury Secretary Robert Rubin and Mexican Ambassador to the United States Jesus Silva Herzog Flores signed the protocol.*]

Possible Visit to Mexico

Q. Mr. President, do you plan to visit Mexico to celebrate this?

The President. The answer to your question is I do plan to visit Mexico and soon. We have not fixed a date yet, but I told President Zedillo that I would be there as soon as I could. And I think it will be actually quite soon.

Mexican Economy

Q. Mr. President, it seems just a few months ago the peso was in trouble once again. I'm wondering if you feel in your mind, do your advisers feel that that the Mexican economy is on very certain footing right now?

The President. Do you want to answer that? [*Laughter*]

Secretary Rubin. If the President is going to learn to do these things, then I'll answer your question. [*Laughter*]

The President. I thought since you make so much more money than I do. [*Laughter*]

Secretary Rubin. There is a point to that. [*Laughter*] The answer is that I think the accomplishments—or we think the accomplishments of Mexico have been enormous. President Zedillo, Minister Ortiz, and the others have really had enormous political courage in following the track they've been on.

Having said that, while a great deal has been accomplished, there is also a great deal to do going forward, and we look forward to being helpful to, and working with, the Mexican Government.

Speaker Newt Gingrich

Q. Mr. President, what do you think about the political warfare that's sprung up around the ethics case of Speaker Newt Gingrich?

The President. I want it to be over. I want it to be over. You know, the American people have given us larger responsibilities. I think in general, at least in my experience in my brief time here the last 4 years, way too much time and energy and effort is spent on all these things, leaving too little time and emotional energy for the work of the people. So that's what I think. I want it to be over, whatever—the Speaker should do whatever is appropriate, and we should get on with it, put it behind us, and go on with the business of the country.

Thank you.

NOTE: The President spoke at 11:22 a.m. in the Roosevelt Room at the White House. During the exchange, Secretary Rubin referred to Foreign Minister Guillermo Ortiz Martinez of Mexico.

Statement on the Bombing of a Women's Health Clinic in Atlanta, Georgia
January 16, 1997

Our thoughts and prayers are with the law enforcement officers and other citizens injured this morning and with their families.

The double bombing at a women's health clinic in Atlanta this morning was a vile and malevolent crime. Make no mistake: Anyone who brings violence against a woman trying to exercise her constitutional rights is committing an act of terror. It is always wrong. And it should be punished severely.

Nobody has a right to use violence in America to advance their own convictions over the rights of others. It is precisely because we take the constitutional rights and individual liberties of all our people so seriously that I fought for and signed new legislation in 1994 to make it a Federal crime to interfere with a woman exercising her constitutional right to visit a women's health center.

Federal investigators from the FBI, ATF, the Marshals, and the U.S. Attorney are on the ground in Atlanta and working closely with local law enforcement. We will pursue this investigation aggressively and methodically. We will get to the bottom of this, and we will punish those responsible to the fullest extent the law provides.

Remarks on the World War II Memorial and on Presenting the Presidential Medal of Freedom to Former Senator Bob Dole
January 17, 1997

Thank you very much, General Woerner, for your kind words and for your fine work. I thank you on behalf of all Americans for all the American Battle Monuments Commission does all around the world to ensure that our fallen heroes receive the honor they deserve.

Mr. Vice President, to the members of the Cabinet, Senator and Mrs. Dole and Robin, Majority Leader Lott and many Members of Congress who are here today, to the representatives of the veterans service organizations, the members of the American Battle Monuments Commission, my fellow Americans. Let me begin by thanking Congresswoman Marcy Kaptur, Governor Hugh Carey, Commissioner Wheeler, Dr. Williams, my good friend Jess Hay, and all the members of the American Battle Monuments Commission and the World War II Memorial Advisory Board for their efforts to create the first national memorial to all who served in World War II. I want to congratulate also Professor St. Florian and his team on their design. I have reviewed it, and it is very impressive.

The World War II Memorial will commemorate one of the great defining passages in our Nation's history. Fittingly, it will be flanked by the Washington Monument and the Lincoln Memorial. For if the Revolutionary War marks the birth of our Republic and the Civil War its greatest trial, then surely America's triumph in World War II will forever signal our coming of age. Roused by the threat of tyranny and fascism, provoked by an infamous attack, millions of Americans fought under freedom's flag, carrying it to far-off places whose names still stir our souls.

At home, our Nation turned as one to the task of building a mighty arsenal for our democratic warriors. Out of the crucible of global conflict and total war, the greatest struggle humankind has ever known, America emerged as the world's most powerful force for peace and freedom and prosperity. With this memorial we pay lasting homage to the 16 million men and women who took up arms in that battle.

Some of the bravest among them were those who fought for freedom themselves were denied. Earlier this week, I had the chance to recognize the extraordinary courage of seven African-American soldiers with the Nation's highest military honor, an award that was richly deserved as long as it was overdue. But I say today that we owe them and all the veterans of World War II a debt that can never be fully repaid. As I said, and had the honor to say in Normandy: When they were young, they saved the world.

This memorial also quite rightly remembers the heroics and hardships of those on the homefront. Many of the families who started the war with a star in the window ended it with sorrow in their hearts, their loved ones lost forever. But our Americans scrimped and saved, making do with 3 gallons of gas a week and two pairs of shoes a year. With the American Red Cross they worked to tend the wounded and send millions of care packages overseas. They ran the factories, manned in many cases by women, that churned out the planes, the tanks, the ships that enabled the allies to control the land, the air, and the sea.

In war, this generation of heroes summoned the collective resolve to defend our most cherished values, to defeat the most fearsome enemies. In peace, they came home and drew on that strength and unity to meet the challenges of a new era. Their leaders did not seek to withdraw from the world but to build alliances and institutions, to promote our prosperity, and to secure our victory in the long cold war. This memorial will stand as a lasting tribute to what Americans can achieve when they work together.

It is especially appropriate at this time that we also honor the remarkable service of one of our Nation's most distinguished World War II veterans who has spent the last 50 years of his life building America and a better world, Senator Bob Dole.

Fifty-one years ago, during a fierce fight in Italy's Po Valley, Second Lieutenant Bob Dole was going to the aid of a fallen comrade when a shell struck him down. He would bear the burden of that terrible injury from that day forward. His recuperation was long and uncertain. Yet Senator Dole turned adversity to advantage and pain to public service, embodying the motto of the State that he loved and went on to serve so well: *Ad astra per aspera*, to the stars through difficulties.

Son of the soil, citizen, soldier, and legislator, Bob Dole understands the American people, their struggles, their triumphs, and their dreams.

Through five decades of public service that took him from county attorney to Senate majority leader and the longest serving leader of his party in history, he never forgot his roots in Russell, Kansas. He has stood up for what he believed, championing the interests of his State's hardworking farmers, helping the disabled through leading the way to the Americans with Disabilities Act, extending the Voting Rights Act, playing a key role in the National Commission on Social Security Reform, and always, always supporting the leadership of our country: first, throughout that long twilight struggle of the cold war and, now in this new era, reasserting America's indispensable role for peace and freedom, security and prosperity.

In times of conflict and crisis, he has worked to keep America united and strong. In this city often known for taking itself too seriously, we are all better for his fine sense of humor. But our country is better for his courage, his determination, and his willingness to go the long course to lead America.

I am pleased to be able to recognize Bob Dole's record of achievement with the highest honor our Nation can bestow on a citizen, the Presidential Medal of Freedom. Through it, we honor not just his individual achievement but his clear embodiment of the common values and beliefs that join us as a people, values and beliefs that he has spent his life advancing.

Senator Dole, a grateful nation presents this award with respect for the example you have set for Americans today and for Americans in generations yet to come.

I now ask the military aide to read the citation. Major, post the orders.

NOTE: The President spoke at 10:33 a.m. in the East Room at the White House. In his remarks, he referred to Gen. Fred F. Woerner, USA (ret.), Chairman, and Hugh Carey and F. Haydn Williams, Commissioners, American Battle Monuments Commission; Senator Dole's daughter, Robin; Pete Wheeler and Jess Hay, members, World War II Memorial Advisory Board; and architect Friedrich St. Florian, winner of the World War II Memorial design competition. Following the President's remarks, Maj. Charles Raderstorf, USMC, read the medal citation.

The President's Radio Address
January 18, 1997

Good morning. Today I want to talk with you about the progress we have made in response to last year's disturbing rash of arsons and other destructive acts directed at houses of worship throughout our country. But before I do, I want to condemn another act of violent terror, the recent bombing of the women's health center in Atlanta. That, too, is wrong, and we also must stop it.

Now, in the aftermath of these terrible crimes against the houses of worship, many of us ask ourselves, why? Were these fires fueled by a sudden upsurge in racial and religious hostility? Were they set for personal gain or revenge? Or were they merely random acts of violence? Whatever the causes of the crimes, they offended every citizen who cherishes America's proud heritage of religious and ethnic diversity, every citizen who remembers that religious freedom, justice, and equality are the founding principles of our great democracy. As one who was raised in the church and who continues to be guided by the enduring lessons I learned there, I joined with all Americans of conscience in demanding swift action to combat these crimes, to help the churches rebuild, and to prevent any more fires.

Seven months ago, I established the National Church Arson Task Force to coordinate the efforts of more than 200 FBI and ATF agents deployed to work with local and State law enforcement agencies, churches, and citizens to catch and prosecute those responsible for these crimes. This week, the task force released its first interim report. The report shows that we have been remarkably successful in solving the crimes. Since January 1995, 143 suspects have been arrested in connection with 107 fires at churches and other houses of worship. This rate of arrest is double the general rate of arrest for arsons, and three-quarters of these arrests occurred during the 7 months following the formation of the task force. So far, 48 defendants have been convicted on Federal and State charges in connection with 43 fires.

This work has been supported by $3 million in Justice Department grants to help local communities intensify their enforcement and surveillance efforts. In addition, Congress authorized the Department of Housing to administer a $10 million loan guarantee to assist with the rebuilding of churches. And the Federal Emergency Management Agency continues to work with communities to increase awareness and help build local arson prevention coalitions. This Federal effort must continue until all those responsible are brought to justice and no more fires burn.

But even more impressive than our Government effort has been the tremendous outpouring of assistance that has flowed from every corner of our country in response to these crimes. People have crossed lines of faith and race and region to link arms in a united effort to rebuild and protect our houses of worship. And by doing so, they have shown us that America is still a country that cares about its neighbors, a country that comes together in the face of common threats to defend the common ground of our values. I am reminded of what Joseph said in Genesis when he met up with the brothers who sold him into slavery: "You meant evil against me, but God meant it for good."

I saw this up close this past August when Hillary and I, along with the Vice President and Tipper Gore, picked up paintbrushes and hammers to help rebuild Salem Baptist Church in Fruitland, Tennessee. One of the earliest supporters of the rebuilding of this tiny black church was the congregation of a white church 3 miles down the road that also had suffered a suspicious fire.

On a national level, we saw groups like the National Council of Churches, the Anti-Defamation League, the Southern Christian Leadership Council, the National Association of Evangelicals, and the NAACP come together as one to tackle this problem. And we received strong bipartisan support from Congress for our work. The insurance industry, at the urging of the Vice President, also became a partner in the rebuilding effort.

These groups, and others of good will all over America, stepped forward to live out the lesson of the man whose birthday celebration this year coincides with my second Inauguration on Monday. Thirty-four years ago in his famous speech on The Mall in Washington, Dr. Martin Luther

King recognized the need for biracial cooperation. In talking of his fellow Americans who stood with him in the civil rights struggle, he said, "Their destiny is tied up with our destiny, and they have come to realize that their freedom is inextricably bound to our freedom. We cannot walk alone."

My fellow citizens, we must not walk alone into the 21st century. This next week as we focus on the Inauguration and the future of our great country, my greatest hope is that we as Americans will continue to find strength in our diversity, that the world will always look to us as a champion of racial and religious liberty, that we will have the wisdom to heal our divisions and walk together into a bright new day.

Thanks for listening.

NOTE: The address was recorded at 12:03 p.m. on January 17 in the Oval Office at the White House for broadcast at 10:06 a.m. on January 18.

Statement on the Death of Paul Tsongas
January 18, 1997

Paul Tsongas was a great American. He cared deeply about his beloved State of Massachusetts and about our country and its future. In a life devoted to public service, he set an unparalleled example of integrity, candor, and commitment. On behalf of the entire Nation, Hillary and I extend to his family our deepest sympathy and our profound gratitude for his life and work.

Remarks at a Democratic National Committee Brunch
January 19, 1997

Thank you very much. Thank you. When I see all of you here with your enthusiasm—this is actually the first event I have attended—and I see the pictures of all the thousands and thousands of people in the shivering cold who were out on The Mall yesterday, all the children taking in the exhibits, and I sense the freedom and the feeling and the enthusiasm on the streets as I—maybe this will be better the second time around. It's pretty good. I like this.

I want to thank my friend Alan Solomont for taking on this immense responsibility. And obviously, I'm indebted to my longtime friend Governor Roy Romer and to Steve Grossman and to Carol Pensky. I'll have more to say about all that the day after tomorrow. I thank Don Fowler and Chris Dodd and Marvin and Scott and everybody else that helped us so much in the last 4 years. And I ask you only to think about this—I have to be very careful because I've been thinking about nothing but my Inaugural Address; if I'm not careful I'll give you half of it right here. [*Laughter*] How can I say this differently?

I actually, in the darkest days of 1994 and '95, always believed that we would be doing this on this day. But it didn't have so much to do with me or even our wonderful Vice President, but what I think about the American people, what makes us tick, where we are in history, and where we have to go. And I ask you to think about that, because we've come a long way here in building a party that is true to the internal principles of the Democratic Party but geared to the challenges of the present and the future.

And I've run my last race, but we haven't done all the work we need to do for our country for the 21st century. And we have to maintain both the commitment to progress and a commitment to community. That's what's unique about us; we believe that we'll all do better if we all do better. That's what's unique about the Democratic Party.

And so, with a heart full of gratitude for all that has been done for me, I ask you to redouble your efforts and to renew your commitment and not to grow exhausted from doing so in the next few years, because we've only begun to scratch the surface of what can be done to mobilize younger people, what can be done to mobilize people who have never been active in political affairs before to participate, financially and as citizens, in our common endeavors. And we have to do that. We have to leave here with a system, with a structure for ordinary citizens to participate more in the affairs and the life of this party in order to have really been successful.

In that regard, I would like to mention just two other people. First of all, I would like to thank Reverend Jackson, who is over here to my left, appropriately enough, who has never flagged in his belief in our country and his determination to get more people involved in it, to get people to register to vote, to vote, to participate. We all need to do more of what he has been doing.

The second thing I'd like to ask all of you to do on this Sunday, each in your own way, is to say a prayer of gratitude for the life of Senator Paul Tsongas. You know, we had an interesting campaign in 1992. I had read both the books that he had written by that time. We went all over New Hampshire, in that wonderful atmosphere that only New Hampshire has, where you're supposed to meet every voter 3 times before they take you seriously. [*Laughter*] And we had—he and I had these crazy ideas that people might actually not object to policy wonks running for President. It might be a good thing if the President actually knew something about the problems of the country. [*Laughter*] And it was really quite an interesting

phenomenon, the town meetings that the two of us had and the crowds that would show up just to hear people talk about the issues.

And my admiration for him and for his sense of commitment to our future, to the integrity of the political process, and to the ultimate ability of America always to renew itself, only grew with all of our contacts. Our country is deeply indebted to him for having had the courage to stay active in public life and to battle through his own illness and his own pain and his own disappointment to continue to fight for America's well-being. That is citizenship in the best sense. So I ask you to say a prayer of gratitude for the life and the soul and the family of Paul Tsongas.

Finally, let me encourage you to have a wonderful time. This is supposed to be fun in the best sense. I hope you enjoy it. And I hope every day for the next 4 years you will always be immensely proud of what you did to make this day come about.

Thank you, and God bless you.

NOTE: The President spoke at 12:44 p.m. at the Mayflower Hotel. In his remarks, he referred to the following Democratic National Committee officials: Alan Solomont, incoming national finance chair; Gov. Roy Romer of Colorado, incoming general chair; Steve Grossman, incoming national chair; Carol Pensky, incoming treasurer; Donald L. Fowler, outgoing national chair; Senator Christopher J. Dodd, outgoing general chair; Marvin Rosen, outgoing finance chair; and Scott Pastrick, outgoing treasurer; and civil rights leader Jesse Jackson.

Inaugural Address
January 20, 1997

My fellow citizens, at this last Presidential Inauguration of the 20th century, let us lift our eyes toward the challenges that await us in the next century. It is our great good fortune that time and chance have put us not only at the edge of a new century, in a new millennium, but on the edge of a bright new prospect in human affairs, a moment that will define our course and our character for decades to comes. We must keep our old democracy forever young.

Guided by the ancient vision of a promised land, let us set our sights upon a land of new promise.

The promise of America was born in the 18th century out of the bold conviction that we are all created equal. It was extended and preserved in the 19th century, when our Nation spread across the continent, saved the Union, and abolished the awful scourge of slavery.

Then, in turmoil and triumph, that promise exploded onto the world stage to make this the

American Century. And what a century it has been. America became the world's mightiest industrial power, saved the world from tyranny in two World Wars and a long cold war, and time and again reached out across the globe to millions who, like us, longed for the blessings of liberty.

Along the way, Americans produced a great middle class and security in old age, built unrivaled centers of learning and opened public schools to all, split the atom and explored the heavens, invented the computer and the microchip, and deepened the wellspring of justice by making a revolution in civil rights for African-Americans and all minorities and extending the circle of citizenship, opportunity, and dignity to women.

Now, for the third time, a new century is upon us and another time to choose. We began the 19th century with a choice: to spread our Nation from coast to coast. We began the 20th century with a choice: to harness the industrial revolution to our values of free enterprise, conservation, and human decency. Those choices made all the difference. At the dawn of the 21st century, a free people must now choose to shape the forces of the information age and the global society, to unleash the limitless potential of all our people, and yes, to form a more perfect Union.

When last we gathered, our march to this new future seemed less certain than it does today. We vowed then to set a clear course to renew our Nation. In these 4 years, we have been touched by tragedy, exhilarated by challenge, strengthened by achievement. America stands alone as the world's indispensable nation. Once again, our economy is the strongest on Earth. Once again, we are building stronger families, thriving communities, better educational opportunities, a cleaner environment. Problems that once seemed destined to deepen, now bend to our efforts. Our streets are safer, and record numbers of our fellow citizens have moved from welfare to work. And once again, we have resolved for our time a great debate over the role of Government. Today we can declare: Government is not the problem, and Government is not the solution. We—the American people—we are the solution. Our Founders understood that well and gave us a democracy strong enough to endure for centuries, flexible enough to face our common challenges and advance our common dreams in each new day.

As times change, so Government must change. We need a new Government for a new century, humble enough not to try to solve all our problems for us but strong enough to give us the tools to solve our problems for ourselves, a Government that is smaller, lives within its means, and does more with less. Yet where it can stand up for our values and interests around the world, and where it can give Americans the power to make a real difference in their everyday lives, Government should do more, not less. The preeminent mission of our new Government is to give all Americans an opportunity, not a guarantee but a real opportunity, to build better lives.

Beyond that, my fellow citizens, the future is up to us. Our Founders taught us that the preservation of our liberty and our Union depends upon responsible citizenship. And we need a new sense of responsibility for a new century. There is work to do, work that Government alone cannot do: teaching children to read, hiring people off welfare rolls, coming out from behind locked doors and shuttered windows to help reclaim our streets from drugs and gangs and crime, taking time out of our own lives to serve others.

Each and every one of us, in our own way, must assume personal responsibility not only for ourselves and our families but for our neighbors and our Nation. Our greatest responsibility is to embrace a new spirit of community for a new century. For any one of us to succeed, we must succeed as one America. The challenge of our past remains the challenge of our future: Will we be one Nation, one people, with one common destiny, or not? Will we all come together, or come apart?

The divide of race has been America's constant curse. And each new wave of immigrants gives new targets to old prejudices. Prejudice and contempt cloaked in the pretense of religious or political conviction are no different. These forces have nearly destroyed our Nation in the past. They plague us still. They fuel the fanaticism of terror. And they torment the lives of millions in fractured nations all around the world.

These obsessions cripple both those who hate and of course those who are hated, robbing both of what they might become. We cannot, we will not, succumb to the dark impulses that lurk in the far regions of the soul everywhere. We shall overcome them. And we shall replace them with the generous spirit of a people who feel at home with one another. Our rich texture of racial, religious, and political diversity will be a godsend in the 21st century. Great rewards will come to those who can live together, learn together, work together, forge new ties that bind together.

As this new era approaches, we can already see its broad outlines. Ten years ago, the Internet was the mystical province of physicists; today, it is a commonplace encyclopedia for millions of schoolchildren. Scientists now are decoding the blueprint of human life. Cures for our most feared illnesses seem close at hand. The world is no longer divided into two hostile camps. Instead, now we are building bonds with nations that once were our adversaries. Growing connections of commerce and culture give us a chance to lift the fortunes and spirits of people the world over. And for the very first time in all of history, more people on this planet live under democracy than dictatorship.

My fellow Americans, as we look back at this remarkable century, we may ask, can we hope not just to follow but even to surpass the achievements of the 20th century in America and to avoid the awful bloodshed that stained its legacy? To that question, every American here and every American in our land today must answer a resounding, "Yes!" This is the heart of our task. With a new vision of Government, a new sense of responsibility, a new spirit of community, we will sustain America's journey.

The promise we sought in a new land, we will find again in a land of new promise. In this new land, education will be every citizen's most prized possession. Our schools will have the highest standards in the world, igniting the spark of possibility in the eyes of every girl and every boy. And the doors of higher education will be open to all. The knowledge and power of the information age will be within reach not just of the few but of every classroom, every library, every child. Parents and children will have time not only to work but to read and play together. And the plans they make at their kitchen table will be those of a better home, a better job, the certain chance to go to college.

Our streets will echo again with the laughter of our children, because no one will try to shoot them or sell them drugs anymore. Everyone who can work, will work, with today's permanent under class part of tomorrow's growing middle class. New miracles of medicine at last will reach not only those who can claim care now but the children and hard-working families too long denied.

We will stand mighty for peace and freedom and maintain a strong defense against terror and destruction. Our children will sleep free from the threat of nuclear, chemical, or biological weapons. Ports and airports, farms and factories will thrive with trade and innovation and ideas. And the world's greatest democracy will lead a whole world of democracies.

Our land of new promise will be a nation that meets its obligations, a nation that balances its budget but never loses the balance of its values, a nation where our grandparents have secure retirement and health care and their grandchildren know we have made the reforms necessary to sustain those benefits for their time, a nation that fortifies the world's most productive economy even as it protects the great natural bounty of our water, air, and majestic land. And in this land of new promise, we will have reformed our politics so that the voice of the people will always speak louder than the din of narrow interests, regaining the participation and deserving the trust of all Americans.

Fellow citizens, let us build that America, a nation ever moving forward toward realizing the full potential of all its citizens. Prosperity and power, yes, they are important, and we must maintain them. But let us never forget, the greatest progress we have made and the greatest progress we have yet to make is in the human heart. In the end, all the world's wealth and a thousand armies are no match for the strength and decency of the human spirit.

Thirty-four years ago, the man whose life we celebrate today spoke to us down there, at the other end of this Mall, in words that moved the conscience of a nation. Like a prophet of old, he told of his dream that one day America would rise up and treat all its citizens as equals before the law and in the heart. Martin Luther King's dream was the American dream. His quest is our quest: the ceaseless striving to live out our true creed. Our history has been built on such dreams and labors. And by our dreams and labors, we will redeem the promise of America in the 21st century.

To that effort I pledge all my strength and every power of my office. I ask the Members of Congress here to join in that pledge. The American people returned to office a President of one party and a Congress of another. Surely they did not do this to advance the politics of petty bickering and extreme partisanship they plainly deplore. No, they call on us instead to be repairers of the breach and to move on with America's mission. America demands and deserves big things from us, and nothing big ever came from being small. Let us remember the timeless wisdom of Cardinal Bernardin, when facing the end of his own life. He said, "It is wrong to waste the precious gift of time on acrimony and division."

Fellow citizens, we must not waste the precious gift of this time. For all of us are on that same journey of our lives, and our journey, too, will come to an end. But the journey of our America must go on.

And so, my fellow Americans, we must be strong, for there is much to dare. The demands of our time are great, and they are different. Let us meet them with faith and courage, with patience and a grateful, happy heart. Let us shape the hope of this day into the noblest chapter in our history. Yes, let us build our bridge, a bridge wide enough and strong enough for every American to cross over to a blessed land of new promise.

May those generations whose faces we cannot yet see, whose names we may never know, say of us here that we led our beloved land into a new century with the American dream alive for all her children, with the American promise of a more perfect Union a reality for all her people, with America's bright flame of freedom spreading throughout all the world.

From the height of this place and the summit of this century, let us go forth. May God strengthen our hands for the good work ahead, and always, always bless our America.

NOTE: The President spoke at 12:05 p.m. at the West Front of the Capitol. Prior to the address, Chief Justice William H. Rehnquist administered the oath of office.

Remarks at the Inaugural Luncheon
January 20, 1997

Thank you very much. First let me thank Senator Warner and Senator Ford, Speaker Gingrich, Leader Gephardt, Senator Lott, Senator Daschle, the Inaugural committee for the wonderful job they did with the morning ceremony. I thank all the participants. My good friend Jessye Norman, thank you. You were magnificent. And I thank Santita Jackson and all the choirs who sang today. They were wonderful. And I thank my friend of nearly 25 years Miller Williams for that wonderful poem. I will take it as an admonition and keep it close to my heart. Thank you.

Hillary and Chelsea and I have had a wonderful day. We got up early and went to a church service, and it ran a little late; Reverend Jackson was speaking. [*Laughter*] It wasn't his fault; we all were carried away. And it put us all in the right frame of mind for this happy moment.

I feel a great deal of gratitude for many things, but Senator, when I heard you telling that fascinating story of the fight between President Roosevelt and Harry Byrd, Sr., I felt an enormous amount of gratitude that at least so far you have not released the letter you made me write you to make sure we could hold this ceremony today. [*Laughter*] And I thank you for that.

We've been doing this a long time, our country has, and I just want to say to all of you that I worked for a long time on what exactly I would say today, and I believe it very much. I believe we're at a unique moment in history. I believe that the only problems we've never solved in America are the problems of the heart, particularly relating to race. We get better at them, but we've never quite gotten over it.

I believe that it is more possible to imagine our future and shape it now than at any time in the history of the country, with the exception of our entry into the industrial age, when we also had peace and prosperity, and our entry into the 19th century, when Thomas Jefferson decided to buy Louisiana, a decision that Senator Lott and I especially appreciate—[*laughter*]—and a lot of others.

So this is a unique moment. And because it is, to some extent, without precedent and because it is different, we have to imagine the future before we can create it. And when you do something like that, it requires you to make alliances and get outside of barriers that normally govern your lives. So I meant very much what I said about the bipartisan nature of our common task. And tomorrow we will start to work on it.

For today, I think we should all, as the previous speakers have said, enjoy being Americans, enjoy the parade, enjoy the balls, but most of all, enjoy the great gift of our citizenship.

Thank you, and God bless you all.

NOTE: The President spoke at 2:25 p.m. in Statuary Hall at the Capitol. In his remarks, he referred to vocalists Jessye Norman and Santita Jackson; and poet Miller Williams of Arkansas. Prior to the President's remarks, Senator John Warner, chairman, Joint Congressional Committee on Inaugural Ceremonies, introduced the President, and Senator Wendell H. Ford, committee vice-chairman, presented him with an engraved crystal bowl.

Proclamation 6968—National Day of Hope and Renewal, 1997
January 20, 1997

By the President of the United States of America

A Proclamation

Today as we celebrate the last Presidential Inauguration of the 20th century and raise our sights with hope and humility toward the challenges of a new age, let us together ask God's guidance and blessing.

This day marks not a personal or political victory but the triumph of a free people who have freely chosen the course our country will take as we prepare for the 21st century.

During the past 4 years, we have grown together as a people and as a Nation. Touched by tragedy, strengthened by achievement, exhilarated by the challenges and opportunities ahead, we have come a long way on our journey to change America's course for the better. We have always been a people of hope—hope that we can make tomorrow brighter than today, hope that we can fulfill our Nation's enduring promise of freedom and opportunity. And we have always known that, by the grace of God and our mutual labor, we can make our hopes reality.

Today, we live in an age of possibility—a moment of rich opportunity that brings with it a deep responsibility for the future and the generations to come. We must seize this special moment with a commitment to do right by those who will follow us in this blessed land.

Dr. Martin Luther King, Jr., whose life and vision we honor today, recognized that the destiny of each American is bound to the destiny

of all Americans; that if we are to go forward, we must go forward together. So, let us pledge today to continue our national journey together. Let us reaffirm our commitment to our shared values of family and faith, work and opportunity. And let us resolve to work together, one Nation under God, to build a bridge of hope and renewal to a new American century.

Now, Therefore, I, William J. Clinton, President of the United States of America, by the authority vested in me by the Constitution and laws of the United States, do hereby proclaim January 20, 1997, a National Day of Hope and Renewal, and I call upon the citizens of this great Nation to observe this day by reflecting on their obligations to one another and to our beloved country and by facing the future with a spirit of hope and renewal.

In Witness Whereof, I have hereunto set my hand this twentieth day of January, in the year of our Lord nineteen hundred and ninety-seven, and of the Independence of the United States of America the two hundred and twenty-first.

WILLIAM J. CLINTON

[Filed with the Office of the Federal Register, 8:45 a.m., January 22, 1997]

NOTE: This proclamation was published in the *Federal Register* on January 23. It is included here as an example of the proclamations which are listed in Appendix D at the end of this volume and compiled annually in title 3 of the *Code of Federal Regulations.*

Remarks Prior to a Meeting With the Economic Team and an Exchange With Reporters
January 21, 1997

Budget Proposal

The President. Are we all here? Are we all awake? [*Laughter*] Are we all cogent?

Q. How about you?

The President. Yes, I'm fine. I got a good night's sleep last night.

Yesterday was a great day of celebration for us, but it's time to get down to work. I told everyone at all the balls yesterday that I felt better at the second Inauguration than the first because the country was better but that I wanted us to see it not as a reward for the first 4 years but a mandate for the next 4. And that's what I want to be working on today.

I wanted to begin this second term by meeting first with our economic team to discuss finishing the job of balancing the budget. I said yesterday that we need a new Government for the new century ahead, and that means a Government that lives within its means, that our parties must work together, and that we have to be repairers of the breach that has developed in our partisan system over the last 4 years and too often among our people.

To that end, on February 6th I will submit a balanced budget. As I said yesterday, we have to do—what I will do—maintain our commitment to a balanced budget and the balance of our values. That's why we will also expand education, research, and technology, protect the environment, and preserve health care for our parents and our children.

The only way we can actually balance the budget is if we seize this moment to work together. And I'm going to do my best to reach out to the Republicans. So today I want to announce that our balanced budget will contain Medicare reforms that will make the program work better and will meet my goal of securing the Medicare Trust Fund for 10 years. It will save $138 billion over 6 years. And it should bring us much closer to bipartisan agreement, because based on the scoring of the Congressional Budget Office last year, this means that we're meeting the Republicans halfway. I want to meet them halfway on this and on many other issues. And I hope they'll meet me halfway.

I'm determined that if we'll do that, we can resolve our remaining differences and reach agreement to balance the budget and do a lot of other good things for the American people as well. I'm looking forward to it, and I hope this first gesture is one that will be treated in good faith and responded to in kind.

Reprimand of Speaker Gingrich

Q. Mr. President, what effect do you think today's House vote on Mr. Gingrich will have on your stated effort yesterday and today to repair the breach?

The President. Well, of course, it depends on how everyone reacts to it. But I believe I said what I needed to say in the Inaugural. I think the House should do its business, and then we should get back to the people's business.

Budget Negotiations

Q. Mr. President, on the $138 billion, what does that come to over 5 years, since you're going to be submitting a 5-year balanced budget proposal, not a 6-year balanced budget proposal?

The President. It's about a hundred. But the point is that the Republicans will be, too. In other words, the ratio will be about the same.

Q. And do you expect them to simply accept that or to see that as an opening bargaining position, going forward in the negotiations to try to find some sort of common ground, given the history of the so-called Mediscare tactics that were used against them during the campaign?

The President. Well, first of all, as you know, I dispute that. I vetoed a budget that had $270 billion in Medicare cuts. Throughout the campaign and in the debates, I pointed out that the Republicans and I had moved closer together at the end, but that if we adopted a 15 percent across-the-board tax cut it would push the Medicare number back to a number I vetoed. I don't think that's Mediscare. So I just dispute that.

But the main thing is we've got to get up today and do the work of the country. There are lots of elements to this budget. Medicare is not the only one, but it's a very important one. And I do believe, obviously, if we adopt a balanced budget plan in a bipartisan way, then we all have to take responsibility for the decisions, and we all have to take responsibility, therefore, for complimenting those in the other party who take the same decision we do. And so I'm just trying to create the conditions in which we can do that, and I think meeting them halfway on this and perhaps a number of other issues is the way to go.

Q. Mr. President—[*inaudible*]—will the cuts come from providers or beneficiaries?

The President. You'll be briefed on all that, I think, as soon as this is over. But we believe there are substantial savings to be made in the Medicare program, and we're going to offer our ways of doing it.

Campaign Finance Practices

Q. Mr. President, the Democratic National Committee has decided to stop taking even legal—what are now legal contributions from foreigners. Can we ask you—I assume you've had a lot to do with that, and is it a sign that perhaps there were problems in the past?

The President. We're going over there in a few minutes, and I'll be addressing all that then.

White House Access

Q. Mr. President, you're making announcements on new, tighter restrictions on access to the White House later today as well?

The President. Well, I'm going over there in a few minutes, so I'll have more to say about it.

Balanced Budget Amendment

Q. You heard Alan Greenspan—[*inaudible*]—constitutional amendment? [*Laughter*] He says he has reservations about that.

The President. Good for him.

Q. Is that a result of the meeting you had with him the other day?

The President. No, I think Mr. Greenspan makes his own conclusions.

Q. What about——

The Vice President. Everyone but Wolf [Wolf Blitzer, CNN] leaves. [*Laughter*]

The President. [*Inaudible*]—makes his own—[*inaudible*]—but I was very pleased to hear him say that.

Press Secretary Mike McCurry. Wolf, Greenspan is still on the access list. [*Laughter*]

The President. We've got new rules on access to the press. You guys are staying here. [*Laughter*]

NOTE: The President spoke at 2:24 p.m. in the Cabinet Room at the White House. In his remarks, he referred to Alan Greenspan, Chairman, Federal Reserve Board. A portion of these remarks could not be verified because the tape was incomplete.

Remarks to a Democratic National Committee Meeting
January 21, 1997

Thank you. Please be seated. Thank you. You know, maybe the Vice President should stay up all night more often. [*Laughter*] He's on a roll today.

I received on Saturday, a day early, very courteously from the New York Times, a copy of the New York Times Sunday Magazine, just preceding the day of the Inauguration, and it had a lot of nice things in it—an article about whether I believed in anything. [*Laughter*] The conclusion was accurate: that I believed in civil rights and that I believed that Government can do good things for people that they can't do on their own.

But far more important, the Sunday crossword puzzle had as its theme "Inauguration," with several very clever clues like "Movie about Presidential aspirations"—"Hope Dreams," instead of "Hoop Dreams." You get it? But the most important clue in the whole thing was "Mathematical rules governing the Vice President's macarena." And the answer was "Al-Gore-rhythms." [*Laughter*] And it struck me that a major part of the history of this time will be the "Al-Gore-rhythms" that have reverberated across America.

Ladies and gentlemen, I come here more than anything else to thank you, to thank our outgoing leaders and our incoming leaders, to thank the members of the Democratic National Committee and all those whom you represent who are active in our party, who were there in that vast crowd yesterday along the parade route and even more of them who were back home just watching and cheering on television.

I was asked many times yesterday how it felt the second time around. And I always said, "Better. It feels better." Better because America is better than it was 4 years ago. And you should feel a great deal of pride in that.

Just before I left to come over here, one of my staff members told me that Newsweek is about to issue the book it puts out every 4 years on the Presidential election, and the title this year is "Back From the Dead." [*Laughter*] Well, I have some mixed feelings about that, because I always felt the pulse. [*Laughter*] But for your role in bringing us back from whatever it was we were in right after 1994's election, I thank you, and I hope you'll always be very proud of it.

I want to say a special word of thanks, as the Vice President did, to Senator Chris Dodd for going all across this country and for being a powerful and eloquent voice and for proving that politics can be noble and can be fun and that we need not be ashamed of being Democrats or being involved in the American political system. I want to thank Don Fowler, who has toiled in our vineyards for decades, for being willing to leave his comfortable and encouraging surroundings and come up here and live in what is not always the most hospitable climate for 2 years to fight this battle.

Their efforts resulted not only in the first Democrat to be reelected in 60 years but to gains in the House and to gains in the statehouses across the country. We celebrate the election of the first Asian-American Governor in the history of America and the first woman Governor of New Hampshire in the history of America; one million small donors now, one million ordinary citizens sending in their money to support the Democratic Party; and a real revival of State parties throughout the country, a revival, which, I might add, we must continue and strengthen and build upon.

I want to thank the Democrats who helped in our Inaugural: Terry McAuliffe, Ann Jordan, Craig Smith, and Deb Willhite. And a special word of thanks to the man who oversaw it all, whom you honored earlier here today, Harold Ickes, for this Inauguration, for two brilliant na-

tional conventions, for the beginning of an organization in New York, which after 5 years of effort produced 1.6 million votes in plurality for the Clinton/Gore ticket in 1996.

I would like to say a special word of thanks, and I can't enumerate them all, but I would be remiss if I did not say a special word of thanks to the American labor movement for the support it has given to our efforts and to our progress. And a special word of thanks for their role in one of the still untold stories of the last 4 years—the teachers of this country for the advances we continue to make in investment and opportunity for education in the last 4 years.

I want to thank Roy Romer and Steve Grossman for their willingness to come into this great party and to build it and to go forward. Roy Romer and I have been friends for a very long time now. I think it would be no offense to any of our colleagues if I would say that, at least when I left the governorship in 1992— I think it was true then; I think it is true now— there is no Governor in America more respected or who has accomplished more than Roy Romer, not a single one in either party. Today, he is recognized as being the person who knows the most about education and our national drive toward having high standards. He has proved in Colorado that you can be for restoring the environment and growing the economy. He has proved that you can care about families and children and do things that will help them along their way in life. He is an unreconstructed, clear reformer and a brilliant consensus builder and a great, strong voice, and I thank him for his willingness to do this.

I want to thank my friend Steve Grossman who has labored in our vineyard. He's been a State party chair and active in our finance operations. He's been a success in business and a success in running AIPAC. I told him if he could get everybody in AIPAC to get along, he could certainly get everybody in the Democratic Committee to get along. [*Laughter*] He took the reins of the Massachusetts party in 1991 and '92 after the '90 elections when they were at a low ebb and began the process of rebuilding, which led in 1996 to the first all-Democratic delegation for Congress in Massachusetts since 1872 and, just as an aside, a 62 percent vote for the Clinton/Gore ticket in the election.

Yesterday I said that I wanted us to build a land of new promise in America in the next century, with a new kind of Government, a new sense of responsibility, and a new spirit of community at home, in the world, and in our dealings with each other. I called for a spirit of reconciliation, and I think, to me, as much as anything else it means we have to give each other the benefit of the doubt.

I thank Reverend Jackson for his moving comments on the legacy of Martin Luther King in our church service yesterday. One person told me this morning that the spirit of reconciliation may have been represented more vividly yesterday than anything else by the fact that we had Christians and Jews and Muslims in the same house of worship, and we had white Pentecostals and African-Americans singing the same song and finding the same soul yesterday.

What I'd like to take a few minutes to do, because there is always some question about this, before we look forward to the future, I want you to be proud of the legacy you have made, and I want you to understand very clearly what it is in the last 4 years. Over the last 30 years, until the last two elections, our friends in the Republican Party were moving toward a dominance of the Presidency in the national political debate, and there were positive elements in their message. They stood for a strong defense. They stood for a strong economy rooted in free enterprise. They said that they would stand for the basic values of our country. But they also divided us in certain ways that at least we Democrats do not agree with. Beginning nearly 30 years ago, they began to subtly use, and then sometimes not so subtly use, rhetoric to divide our people one from another, first on race, and then later there were divisions based on religion and politics, which made it much more difficult for us to come together.

Then, starting in 1981, they advanced two other elements. One was supply-side economics; we Democrats called it trickle-down. And the argument was that there really is a Santa Claus, that the deficits don't matter, and that they'll go away anyway with supply-side economics if we just cut taxes, particularly for people in upper incomes. And in addition to that there was the clear, explicit, expressed argument that Government is the problem with America.

Now, I would argue to you that in the last 4 years, part of the historic legacy of our administration and our Democrats in Congress and in America is that we ended the illusion of supply-side economics, not until it had quadrupled

our national debt, tripled our annual deficit, but early enough to stop it from causing permanent disaster. And we ended the notion that Government is the problem. It was very powerful rhetorically, but the American people never knew what it meant until the other party won the Congress in 1995 and had the Government shut down twice over the battle of the budget. But make no mistake, our view prevailed, and you should be proud of it.

And we have not ended but we have at least eased this notion that we can advance our country by becoming divided one against the other. People know that as they become ever more multiracial, multiethnic, multireligious, that is a recipe for destruction. In fairness, I think the awful tragedy of Oklahoma City had a lot to do with our coming of age. We realized that we could not love our country and hate our Government, that the people who work for our Government were our neighbors and friends, they had children, too, in their child care centers while their mothers and fathers went to work every day.

But I think the fact that the Democratic Party was a clear and constant voice for reconciliation and for not permitting our racial or our religious or our political differences to consume us has made this country a better place and has dramatically changed the political debate forever as we look toward the future. That is a part of your legacy, and you should be proud of it.

I also want to tell you that there are at least six things that are a part of our positive legacy that I think we should go forward with. They must be the basis of our mobilizing our State parties, of recruiting good, new candidates, of getting people to show up when you have these meetings back home, and of making people proud to be Democrats and of making people believe that they ought to send a small check to the Democratic Party on a regular basis. If they don't want big money and organized money to dominate the process, they have to give the little money. And they must do that for positive reasons.

Let's be candid. One of the most interesting things that happened in the last year was we had a huge upsurge of giving among ordinary Democrats when we were standing against the budget and reversing supply-side economics and reversing the idea that Government was the problem. And after the battles had been won against the negative forces, there weren't so many people that thought they needed to send the small checks again. They said, "Well, President Clinton and Vice President Gore are going to get reelected." But the question is, what are we going to do? So you need to know what the positive legacy of the last 4 years is so you will be ennobled and emboldened about what we can accomplish in the next 4.

One, we replaced supply-side economics with invest-and-grow economics, reducing the deficit, investing more in education and science and technology, standing for free and fair trade around the world. And that's what produced the largest number of jobs in any 4-year term in history, record small businesses, and declining inequality among working people for the first time in 20 years. That's a part of your legacy, and you should be proud of it.

Number two, we reversed the expansion of social problems which people thought were inevitable. The crime rate has dropped now in all 4 years. The crime bill is working. The welfare rolls have had their biggest reduction in history as people have moved from welfare to work. People are dying to go to work if the jobs are out there for them, if the training is out there for them, and if there is a system there to move people through. And that indicates what we have to do in the years ahead. Child support collection is up 50 percent. You should be proud of these things.

Just 4 years ago, most people thought the crime rate was going to go on forever. Now we can visualize a time when our children can walk safely from home to school, to play in the park across the street and not fear that somebody will come up to them and try to shoot them or sell them dope. We can do that now because that is what we have done in the last 4 years. We've turned these things around. That is a huge surpassing achievement, part of your legacy, and you should be proud of it.

We Democrats have restored the primacy of family and community to our social policies. That's what the Family and Medical Leave Act was all about. That's what the earned-income tax credit, which is now giving tax reductions to people with incomes up to $30,000 a year who have children in their home, was all about. That's what our reforms in retirement—we secured the retirement of 40 million people, made it easier for people in small business to get retirement. That's what it was all about, putting

family and community in the center of our social concern. That's what the Vice President and Henry Cisneros were doing with the empowerment zone initiative, trying to let people and communities all across America seize control of their situation and make it better. That's what we were doing with the V-chip. That's what we were doing in trying to protect our children against tobacco advertisements. That's what we were doing with the zero tolerance for guns and drugs in schools, putting family and community back at the center of our concern, so that now no one thinks of family values as being the Government is the problem, the Government is the enemy.

Now, the question is, what can we do together to build strong families and strong communities. That's part of our legacy, and you ought to be proud of it.

The fourth thing we did, again I say, was not only to stand against the forces of division but to say that community is a good thing, that we'll be better off in the future in the global society if we can all work together and learn together and build new ties that bind us together. We'll be better off. You can see it in what we did with affirmative action. Mend it, yes, but don't end it until it's not needed anymore. You can see it with what we did with immigration. Protect the borders, yes. People are in the criminal justice system, send them home. Be tough on the workplace. Don't let people go in and take jobs away from American workers because their employers want to bring in people to work for slave wages. But don't denigrate the immigrants who have made this country a great land. Except for the Native Americans, we're all from somewhere else.

You can see it in our response to the church burnings. You can see it in response to what we did with the Religious Freedom Restoration Act, trying to liberate people from the notion that there was never a time when they could express their religious convictions in a public forum. You can see it in what was done here after Oklahoma City or in response to the militias. We are affirmatively building an American community. It is part of the legacy of this administration and this party, and you should be proud of it. You can see it in the way we've reasserted the role of America's leadership around the world, and yes, you can see it in the way we have resolved the fight over Government.

I was curious to see how people commented about that. Government is not the problem. Government is not the solution. We have to be the solution. Government is the instrument by which we give each other the tools to make the most of our own lives, which means that we have downsized the Government with the Vice President's reinventing Government initiative. But there are times when the Government should do more, more on family leave, more on helping people succeed at home and at work, more in opening the doors of college education to everyone, more in investing in early childhood education. And we can't rest until the people who are still shut out of the health care system, especially the children of poor working people, have access to it.

Now, you have to make this legacy apparent to the folks back home. And in order to do it, we have got to end the divisions in thinking in our mind. We all talk about how the so-called bipolar world is over—freedom versus communism—but the bipolar mind is still holding us back. We think you can balance the budget and invest in the future. We think we cannot only protect but improve the environment and grow the economy. We think we can be strong at home, and in order to do it we have to be strong abroad and vice versa. We don't believe that every issue has to go into a Democrat or a Republican or a liberal or a conservative box.

I think you can make a compelling case that balancing the budget in a proper way is a very liberal thing to do because otherwise we'll never have the political support in this country or the money to invest in the future of the people that are otherwise left out.

I think you can make a case that educating—investing in the education of our children and providing families decent health care when the kids are young is a very conservative thing to do, because otherwise you cannot conserve the basic strength and security and values of the country over the long run.

We're in a period of change. We've got to stop this. Who ever said the Republicans should own crime? I never met a Democrat who was happy to have his child mugged. Who ever said the Republicans own welfare reform? Those of us who've known people on welfare know how bad they want to get off. You have to help change the way people think about these things.

And to do that, you have to help build a positive future.

Now, in the State of the Union message, I will be talking more about the specific things that I want to do in the future. But I want to talk today about this whole issue of campaign finance reform for two reasons. One is campaign finance reform—elections are too expensive, and they take too much money, and it takes too much time to raise the money, and it always raises questions.

But there's a bigger problem, which is the more that elections become the province of very expensive ad wars, the less people are likely to participate. I think the Democrats ought to be on record not only for campaign finance reform, but we need to find ways, Mr. Chairman, Mr. Vice Chairs, all the new officers here—we've got to find ways to encourage affirmatively the increase of participation of people at the polls.

Reverend Jackson's spent his whole life going around and registering people to vote. If young voters had voted in 1996 in the same percentages they did in 1992, the election would have been even more dramatic in the outcome and the congressional results would have been different. We have to lift the participation of people. And we need to see campaign finance reform not only as restoring the trust of citizens in their Government but as one step of increasing the participation of people in our common affairs. You cannot have a national community if half the community doesn't show up. Everybody's got to be there.

But we, the Democrats, have to continue to be and intensify our efforts for campaign finance reform, and it has to be a bipartisan solution. Today Senator John McCain and Senator Russ Feingold and Representative Chris Shays and Marty Meehan, in the House and the Senate, a Democrat, a Republican, are introducing their bipartisan campaign finance reform legislation. It is tough. It is balanced. It is credible. It should become the law of the land. We know from experience—I went through this for 4 years—that all you have to do to kill campaign finance reform is just not do it. Nobody ever wants a vote up on the tote board, "I killed this bill", so they just keep letting it die in the Senate with the filibuster.

Delay will mean the death of reform one more time if it happens. So I ask Members of Congress in both parties to act now. While the public is watching, while the momentum is building, act now; don't delay. You've got a good bill. You've got a good forum. Resolve the differences and go forward.

I also ask that we not wait. Today, let us resume our call to our friends in the Republican Party. Together, let's stop accepting soft money, even before the reform becomes law. If you will do it, we will do it. We have offered our hand, time and again. Why not just say yes?

Today, as a first step, the Democratic Party has announced several changes unilaterally in the way we raise money. I thank the DNC for agreeing with the position that we took in the campaign not to accept contributions from noncitizens and foreign-owned businesses and for taking other steps to limit contributions that may otherwise raise questions about the integrity of the process. These are sound and necessary first steps in the reforms we need. We should go forward from there and take the next step.

Now, let me say again, let's be realistic about this. There have been problems with this all along the way. But there's a great deal of interest in this in the press, and in the spirit of reconciliation let me say that we need to be candid about this. On the other side, our friends may not think that they have any interest in campaign finance reform. Why should they? They raise more money. They raise more foreign money. They raise more money in big contributions, and we take all the heat. It's a free ride.

Secondly, let's be candid. Once you're in office, whether you're a Democrat or a Republican, if you've done a good job and you've got friends out there and they can relate to you,

you at least know that maybe even if it's bad for your party or bad for your country, maybe you can protect yourself if some wave of hysteria comes along that threatens to wash you away, and at least if you can raise the money, you can have your own case heard. I say that to make this point: We hear a lot in America about the cynicism that exists between the public and the politicians or how cynical the press are about politicians. The problem with cynicism is that it always eventually becomes a two-way street. You cannot end cynicism unless all parties involved are willing to give each other the benefit of the doubt.

And so I ask now for an honest, open effort to pass this bill. And I ask for an honest, open understanding that the Supreme Court decision allowing all of these third-party expenditures will complicate our task. But we can make it better if we will suspend our cynicism and instead put our energies into getting something done for America. Will you help us do that? Will all of you help us do that? Stand up if you believe in it. Stand up if you'll fight for it. We can do this, and I want you to help.

Thank you, and God bless you.

NOTE: The President spoke at 4:14 p.m. at the Washington Hilton Hotel. In his remarks, he referred to Terence McAuliffe and Ann Dibble Jordan, cochairs, and Craig Smith and Debbie Willhite, co-executive directors, Presidential Inaugural Committee. A portion of these remarks could not be verified because the tape was incomplete.

Message to the Congress on Continuation of the Emergency With Respect to Terrorists Who Threaten To Disrupt the Middle East Peace Process
January 21, 1997

To the Congress of the United States:

Section 202(d) of the National Emergencies Act (50 U.S.C. 1622(d)) provides for the automatic termination of a national emergency unless, prior to the anniversary date of its declaration, the President publishes in the *Federal Register* and transmits to the Congress a notice stating that the emergency is to continue in effect beyond the anniversary date. In accordance with

this provision, I have sent the enclosed notice to the *Federal Register* for publication, stating that the emergency declared with respect to grave acts of violence committed by foreign terrorists that disrupt the Middle East peace process, is to continue in effect beyond January 23, 1997. The first notice continuing this emergency was published in the *Federal Register* last year on January 22, 1996.

The crisis with respect to the grave acts of violence committed by foreign terrorists that threaten to disrupt the Middle East peace process that led to the declaration of a national emergency, on January 23, 1995, has not been resolved. Terrorist groups continue to engage in activities with the purpose or effect of threatening the Middle East peace process, and which are hostile to U.S. interests in the region. Such actions threaten vital interests of the national security, foreign policy, and economy of the United States. For these reasons, I have determined that it is necessary to maintain in force the broad authorities necessary to deny any financial support from the United States for foreign terrorists that threaten to disrupt the Middle East peace process.

WILLIAM J. CLINTON

The White House,
January 21, 1997.

NOTE: The notice of January 21 is listed in Appendix D at the end of this volume.

Exchange With Reporters
January 22, 1997

16th Street Explosion

Q. [Inaudible]—the explosion near the abortion clinic this morning—any thoughts on that?

The President. Let me say that we do not yet have all the facts involving the incidents this morning. But Federal officials are working with the local law enforcement officials to get to the bottom of this. I want to emphasize again, as I had to do just a few days ago, that acts of violence against people who are trying to exercise their constitutional rights are acts of terror. They are illegal. They are wrong. And we will do our very best to investigate them, to catch who is doing it, and to make sure they're punished. But as to the incidents this morning, we are still investigating them. The facts are unfolding. Whatever happened, there is never an excuse for an act of violence against someone exercising a constitutional right.

Q. [Inaudible]—at the Mayflower, Mr. President?

The President. We're on top of the situation, I believe. We're doing our very best. And obviously I'm concerned about the safety of anybody involved that might be subject to that sort of thing. But the investigators are there, and we're working hard on it.

NOTE: The exchange began at 9:14 a.m. on the South Lawn at the White House, prior to the President's departure for Chicago, IL.

Remarks at Stanley Field Middle School in Northbrook, Illinois
January 22, 1997

The President. I was just thinking, if I had had a class like this when I was their age, I might have gotten into a different line of work. *[Laughter]* This is fascinating. Thank you very much, guys. I'm glad you learned about Newton's laws doing this, and I'm glad you learned how to do this.

I just thought of something—you should know too, one of you made the point about conservation of materials. Interestingly enough, in many manufacturing enterprises today, that's one of the major sources of adding productivity and profitability to the enterprise. Being environmentally responsible is just learning how to continue to get more and more and more output out of fewer and fewer raw materials. And that applies not only to stable materials like that but also to energy input. So a big part of what technology and learning is doing to all kinds of production is allowing people to produce more output of products and services with fewer material input. Very interesting, so I'm glad you did it.

[*At this point, Secretary of Education Richard Riley commented on standards in education, and then the students continued their demonstration.*]

The President. The one thing I would say to you—we have to go, but you are going to live in the most exciting period of time in human history, in terms of what people can do with their minds and their imaginations and what people can do on their own. It's going to be a very, very exciting time. But it will only be an exciting time for people who can access it. That's why the learning is so important.

Someday you may be building—one of you may be building trains that go 500 miles an hour, that people get in, and therefore, then, they don't pollute the air. And they all travel together, so they can read while they're studying during their commute times. You may be doing

things you can't even imagine now because of what you're learning.

And that's the thing I would emphasize. You can't imagine what someday you might be doing with what you're just now learning here. And I envy you in that way. I think that the 21st century will be a time of enormous possibility for young people like you, and all you really need to tap it is a great education. And I'm glad you're getting it.

Thank you.

Teacher. I know they can do it. Well, thank you so much. We're very pleased to have you come.

The President. I'm glad to see you. Thank you.

Teacher. Thank you for coming.

The President. I wish I could see all the cars driving. What you should do, you should make a movie of this. You should have everybody— inspire classes all over America.

NOTE: The President spoke at 11:05 a.m. in the eighth grade science classroom.

Remarks to the First in the World Consortium in Northbrook
January 22, 1997

Thank you very much. First of all, let me thank Mary Hamblet for her introduction and for that fine statement about the thrill of teaching and the changes of teaching. Would all the teachers in the audience please stand? Thank you very much. [*Applause*] I thank you all very, very much.

Thank you, Dr. Kimmelman, for your leadership in the First in the World Consortium. I thank all the other superintendents and administrators who are here. Thank you, Congressman Porter, for your leadership for education and, I might add, for your leadership for safe streets in the United States, in the Congress. I appreciate that very much.

Thank you, Secretary Riley. Everything Dr. Kimmelman said about you was true, even if you did have to write his speech for him. [*Laughter*] I like it that the Secretary of Education is prouder of being a grandfather than anything else in his life. I think that's a good signal for America's future.

We're glad to be joined today also by Mayor Daley and Congressman Blagojevich. Welcome. Cook County Assessor Tom Hines; your State senator, Cathy Parker. Welcome. Thank you for being here. Village presidents Nancy Firfer and Mark Damisch, thank you also for coming. I thank the Glenbrook Concert Orchestra for the music. Thank you all.

I am honored to be here with all of you, humbled and encouraged by your passionate commitment to education. I came today to talk about your remarkable success, hoping it will reverberate all across America and people will want to know what has been done here and how, and to talk about why and how this must be done all across America.

As we come to the end of this century and set about the business of preparing America for the next century, as I said in my Inaugural Address, it is especially important that we be able to say we have kept the American dream of opportunity alive for all of our children. I think all of us know in our heart of hearts that that will be a slogan and a dream only, unless we give to all of our children and expect from all of our children world-class educational opportunities and world-class learning.

What I want to do in the next 2 weeks leading up to my State of the Union Address to the Congress and to the American people, is to lay out some concrete things we can do in Washington to help to achieve those objectives. We do live in a time of enormous possibility. I was just—you know, it's—the last couple of days is the first free time I've had in a while—[*laughter*]—and I was trying to create some more space in our living quarters in the White House, and I was moving some reference books around that our daughter sometimes uses and her father and mother sometime use. But I was—there was one on the Age of Reason and one on the Age of Enlightenment. And I really do think there's a good chance that the 21st century will be called something like the Age of Possibility or the Age of Promise, when people write about it 100 years from now, because it really will be possible for more people across the world to live out their dreams and live up to their God-given abilities than ever before in human history. It will be possible. But "possible" or an "Age of Promise," those are operative words. There are no guarantees here.

And in order to realize that promise, we've got to make sure our people are prepared for it. There is a veritable revolution in the way we work and live because of science and technology. The world which was once divided by the cold war is now united by not only free markets and open trade but by common security challenges that threaten all open societies. Young people are continually entering jobs that weren't invented a couple of years ago. The young people in this great hall today will be doing jobs, many of them that have not been imagined by any of us here. And it's very important to understand that.

I spent a day at the National Institute of Health not very long ago going through in some detail the status of the human genome project. And it is clear to me that before very long, when young parents like Secretary Riley's son and daughter-in-law come home with a baby from the hospital, there really will be a map of the baby's genetic code available to the parents. Some of it, of course, will occasionally be troubling and profoundly worrying. But by and large what it will do is to give us a way of maximizing the health and potential of all people from medical care to diet to exercise to understanding how they can best live their lives from the beginning. No one would ever have imagined this.

Just in the last couple of years, we've seen the first successful treatment for stroke. It now seems possible that we might actually be able to repair some of the damage done by strokes. We have uncovered two genes that seem to be at the basis of either the cause of, or dramatic propensity to, breast cancer. We have seen nerve transplants to the spines of laboratory animals which has given movement to the lower limbs of laboratory animals that had their spines severed.

The Internet was literally, as I said in the Inaugural Address, the mystical province of physicists 10 years ago. Today, it's an encyclopedia that 8- and 9-year-old kids teach their parents how to use. [*Laughter*]

When I became President, 3 million Americans—thanks in large measure to technology—were working in their homes full time. At the end of my first term, 12 million Americans were. At the end of my second term, it is estimated that 30 million Americans will be. Not all good—it will also pose some new challenges: How can we continue to maintain our community? How can people work together in teams productively if they either need to or have to do some of their work at home?

But change is out there. At a time like this, it is critical that we not only know certain things but that we be able to learn for a lifetime. And we know that requires an enormous grounding, not only in the subjects we master but in the way we learn, which is why I was so glad in the introduction to hear Mary talk about different ways of teaching. Because the way teachers are teaching now engage the children in a learning process that they can then apply to any other subject that they have to face throughout their lives, so that they can become lifetime learners.

Now, this is really not all that new. Education has been at the heart of America's progress for over 200 years. First of all, our Founding Fathers were highly literate people. Where would we be if Thomas Jefferson had known nothing about the great philosophers who went before him?

Right after the Civil War, as the country was spreading westward and occupying the whole continent, the Congress provided for the establishment of land-grant institutions, like the great State universities in Illinois, in my home State, all across the country. Abraham Lincoln really oversaw it during the Civil War, the idea, but the institutions themselves were actually created after the Civil War. It dramatically changed America, the idea that we could actually give people a college degree who lived in a place as far west as Illinois, which was on the edge of the frontier when Mr. Lincoln was elected President.

Then, at the beginning of this century, we finally made public schools like this available to all of our children. People moved from farm to factory, from the country to the city, and it became essential that everyone at least have some basic education. After World War II, out of a sense of national obligation, we gave all of the veterans a chance to go to college, and it was one of the central elements in exploding the great middle class and creating the kind of middle class communities we have here in this consortium. It was a phenomenal thing.

Now, the Government did not do that for anyone. All it said was, you served your country; here's a college degree if you can get it—if you can get it. And that's the beauty of education; you can't really give it to anyone. You can put it out there, and you can help people, but the students themselves have to seize it.

Now, this has been an obsession of mine for a long time. I grew up in a State—when I was born in my home State, our per capita income was only a little over half the national average right after World War II. And I know that everything good that's happened there in an economic way has been in no small measure the result of our elevating the levels of education. In a much more personal sense, I am absolutely certain that I would not be standing here as President today if it had not been for my teachers. It is clear, and I'm certain.

When I became Governor almost 20 years ago now, we began to do things to try to help advance the cause of education. My daughter just had one of her best friends up here to the Inauguration who is a student at a school of mathematics and science that I established as one of my last acts as Governor. Dr. Kimmelman mentioned the National Education Goals, which were promulgated by the Gov-

ernors and President Bush in 1989. I had the honor of being the Democratic Governor whose job it was to draft the goals.

So I know a lot about those goals. And I thought they were very good then; I think they're better now, because the wealth of our country now no longer primarily depends upon our oil, our gold, our land, or our factories. It is now and will increasingly be measured in the minds and creativity of our people and our achievements in science and technology and also in the humanities, because we have to learn how to manage all this new power we're giving to ourselves.

We have to, in short, commit ourselves for the first time now to have the best education in the world, not just for the few but for the many. We have the best higher education system in the world; there's no question about it. But we do not have the best system of education in the world from start to finish for all of our children, and we cannot be satisfied until that is exactly what we have in the United States of America. Now, the Congressman said this; the Secretary said this; Dr. Kimmelman said this. In America, we have a unique heritage. Our educational system is a local system governed by local school boards and the people they appoint; governed by laws enacted at the State level, not the national level. And the Federal Government's role in education basically is a fairly recent vintage. It goes back about 30 years or so.

But essentially what the Federal Government has tried to do over time is to equalize opportunity in education by opening the doors of college to more people, by recognizing that some districts don't have the resources and some States don't have the resources to meet the needs of people, by dealing with the problems of populations who have needs that may be more expensive. And I think one of the great advances in education in my lifetime has been the provision of educational services through the school systems to students with disabilities, enabling them to achieve enormous things.

And then, increasingly, over the last 10 to 12 years, the Education Department has tried to do more in research and in spurring reform. And since I have been in this office, we have moved in all those areas. We've dramatically increased the number of people in Head Start. We've improved and expanded college scholarships, college loans, and work-study, adding

200,000 more places there at the end of the last Congress—thank you, Congressman Porter—and the biggest increase in Pell grants in 20 years. We've done that. We've helped 70,000 young people work their way through college by serving their community in the AmeriCorps program.

And we did pass two things that I thought were very important for grassroots reform. One was the so-called school to work program, which helps deal with young people who aren't going to 4-year colleges but do need further education. We know now that unless you have at least 2 years of education after high school, young people this day and age are almost certain to be put in jobs where their incomes go down, not up.

The other was the Goals 2000 program, which had a simple idea. We should have a system by which school districts and States can establish very high national standards but have more flexibility school by school, district by district, to decide how to meet those standards. That's what Goals 2000 was about. So it just simply says, we at the national level will give the States some money and then the States can give it to school districts. If they will figure out—if they will, A, set high standards for themselves and then, B, figure out how they want to meet those standards and be held accountable for them.

And that's what this First in the World Consortium did. There is no better model for what we were trying to do in the entire United States of America than what you have done here. And you should be very proud of yourselves.

Now, as we look to the next 4 years, there are some things that I'd like to do in that first category, that basket of things I mentioned. I do think there are more things we need to do in the area of equal opportunity and helping deal with resource problems.

The most important thing we can do is to open the doors of college to all and to make sure that the first 2 years of college become as universal by the year 2000 as a high school diploma is today, and I think—that's clear that we know how to do that. We have proposed a $1,500 tax credit for people for the first 2 years of college, which is the cost of a typical community college tuition in America; a $10,000 a year tax deduction for the cost of any college tuition—I can see you adding it up now— [*laughter*]—and making it easier for more people to take out IRA's and then withdraw from

them, tax-free, if the money is used to pay for a college education. I think all of those things will help.

We've proposed to collapse all these Federal programs, about 70 of them that pay for various kinds of job training, and get rid of all of them, put the money in a fund, and send every unemployed or underemployed person who would be eligible for any of them a simple voucher, a skills grant that they could then take to the nearest community college or other educational institution to decide on their own what kind of training they need, which I think is a very important idea.

We have funds in there to complete our work of connecting all of our schools to the information superhighway by the year 2000, which will make it possible for the first time in history for students in the poorest or in the most remote school districts to have access to the same information other children have in the same way at the same time. It can literally revolutionize educational opportunity in a way that I believe is very important.

And finally, it's not a problem here, but I've spent a lot of time in our schools, and it's very hard to lift children up in schools that are falling down. The educational infrastructure of the country has deteriorated dramatically, number one. Number two, we have for the first time a group of young people coming in that are going to be bigger than the baby boom cohort. We have now the largest number of young people in our schools in history. I'm glad for that; it takes a big burden off us baby boomers that— [*laughter*]—the kids are taking over again. It also means great things for how we're going to pay for all of our retirement several years down the road. [*Laughter*] But in the near term, I have championed a proposal that has been spearheaded by Senator Carol Moseley-Braun that will spark a 20 percent increase in school construction and renovation that I think is very important, by having the Federal Government use limited monies to leverage down the interest rates when school districts make an extra effort to do things that have to be done in their schools. That is also important.

And finally, for the districts that need it, I also have been a great champion of the charter school program, and that is all in our budget. The mayor and I are going down to Chicago in a few moments to talk to the school board about that.

Now, all of these things will help, but how are we going to get the standards? There are two things that we're going to do in the next 4 years, I hope, that I believe will make all of the difference. Number one is we are going to hire 30,000 reading specialists to mobilize a million volunteers to teach every 8-year-old in the country to read independently by the third grade. Now, we can talk all about the standards in the world, but if the children literally cannot read—an astonishing percentage of our young people are not proficient in reading when they have to learn these things—then we can't achieve very much later on.

It is true that our student population is the most diverse in history in terms of race, ethnicity, religion, national origin. But that can be a great asset for the United States. There is no other large democracy as diverse as ours. And in a global society, in a global economy, that's a huge, huge asset. But we have to have the language of common parlance in order to enable us all to function together. And we simply have to provide the resources and the people, and we're going to need a lot of volunteers to do this, but it will literally revolutionize education in America if we have universal literacy by the third grade. And that is the goal of this, and I hope all of you will support that.

But the most important thing we can do is something that the Federal Government should not do directly, but something I'm convinced will not happen unless we get out here and beat the drum for it and work for it, and that is to have recognized high standards for math and science and other basic subjects that are national in scope, measured by national and international standards, adopted locally, implemented locally, but nationally recognized and nationally tested throughout the United States. Until we do that, we will never know whether we have achieved our goal of international excellence in education for every student in the United States. And I ask your support for that.

This has never happened. People have talked about this. When we wrote the national education goals, we anticipated that we would have to develop a set of national standards, not Federal Government standards, national standards. The councils of mathematics teachers and science teachers have done a lot of work on this. A lot of work has been done on this.

But nobody has yet been willing to say, or at least we haven't had enough people willing

to say, whether they were Governors or State superintendents of education or local school boards, "We're all going to accept these, and we want to have some tests we can give to our students which will measure not how smart they are, not what they might have happened to learn but whether they know the things that we say are essential for every student to know in math and in science in order to succeed and win in the world they're going to live in." That is what we must do as a nation, and we have delayed too long. We shouldn't delay anymore. By the time we start the new century, we ought to have these standards adopted, embraced, and evaluated in every school district in the United States, and I want you to lead the way, just as you are here.

I have heard all the arguments in the world against this. But no one has yet made a compelling case to me for how calculus is different in Chicago from Little Rock, Arkansas, or Cody, Wyoming, or for that matter, Germany or Singapore or any other place in the world. That is what is the genius behind what you've done here with this First in the World education consortium.

We already know we're not doing well enough as a nation. What our students in general learned in math in the eighth grade is learned in Japan in the seventh grade. Even more troubling to me, what each year students in Germany and Japan learn 10 to 20 math subjects in depth, our students are asked to cover 35 math subjects and therefore don't learn any of them in depth.

Last year, educators around the world gave a half a million students, including 40,000 in the United States, the same test at the same time to give us a clear picture—our first clear picture—of what world-class education really means and how close we are to meeting it. We learned that our eighth graders are above the international average in science but below it in math. We know that every child in America, however—we can see that from the tests—we know that every child in America can meet these high standards if we have the courage and the vision simply to recognize the standards, to set them as the bar we're trying to jump over, to teach them, and to test whether children have learned them.

I do not understand why we are so afraid to do this. Don't we believe in our children more than this? And I do not believe there is a rule that says if you happen to be poor, you can't learn these things. I don't believe that either. When we were writing these goals—I remember it was about 2:30 in the morning—we got to this thing, "What are we going to say about math and science?" And somebody said, "We're going to be first in the world in math and science in the 21st century." And another person said, "Well, that will never happen. Now, how can we set a goal we know we can't meet?" So they looked at me and said, "What do you think, Bill?" And I said, "Well, okay, suppose we just say our goal is to be third in the world." [*Laughter*] There was no more discussion. We wrote the goal. Our goal was to be first in the world.

And this is not political rhetoric. Every single examination of the capacity of the human brain has shown that over 90 percent of the people in our country can learn way over 90 percent of what they need to know to do very, very well in the world we're going to live in. Sure, it will be harder for some than others. Some subjects are harder for some people than others. Not everybody will know everything on every exam, but we can do this. And we can no longer hide behind our love of local control of the schools and use that as an excuse not to hold ourselves to high standards. It has nothing to do with local control. There's no school board in America that controls the content of algebra.

I just left a junior high school where I saw these young people making their own automobiles out of paper and rubber bands and paper clips. Stand up there. Where are the students in that class? Here they are. All of the students in the class I just visited, stand up. [*Applause*] So they built these light little cars with their paper wheels, and they wound up this propeller with a rubber band that was tied across the whole length of the car, and then it went ahead. And they said, "This demonstrates one of Newton's laws of motion, which is that every action generates an equal and opposite reaction." And they also talked about how the wheels had to be round instead of flat, but they couldn't be too slick, because there would have been no friction, and then no motion would be possible.

Now, that is—the rule for that is not different in California. [*Laughter*] It is still the same. And I told these young people when I saw them with their cars, I said, "If I would have had a class like this when I was 13, I might be

in a different line of work today." [*Laughter*] It was so exciting. But to pretend that somehow holding ourselves to these standards and agreeing that there has to be some uniform way of measuring them is giving up local control, is just an excuse to avoid being held accountable because we're afraid we can't make it. And it's selling our kids down the drain, and it's wrong. It is not right.

So what happened when you did it? What does that report say? It says, in effect, that the eighth graders from the First in the World Consortium tied for first in the world in science and tied for second in the world in math. I think that's pretty good for their first time out.

That happened because—look around this room. Can you imagine a school district or a set of school districts with more genuine local control than this one, with—more than these— more parental involvement, more committed teachers, more—you know, you've got local control. But you didn't use it as an excuse not to throw your hat in the ring. I think it's great that it came out this way. But if you had finished eighth and ninth, I would still be here to pat you on the back because you had the guts to do it.

That's the important thing. That's the important thing. When we were coming out here on the airplane, the Congressman and Mayor Daley and Secretary Riley and Kevin O'Keefe of our staff, we were talking about, you know, what men talk about on airplanes, we were talking about basketball—[*laughter*]—and how Michael Jordan scored 51 points last night. And Kevin O'Keefe reminded me that there was somewhere a basketball coach who had removed Michael Jordan from the high school basketball team. Now, what's the point of that? [*Laughter*]

You know, we laugh about it. The coach might have made the right decision, and the decision he made may have spurred him on to what he later did. But the point is, it's okay if you're not winning when you start. It's okay. I know more about—but Scottie Pippen, who is from my home State, was essentially the manager of a college basketball team when he was a freshman in a very small school—couldn't even make the team. By the time he was a senior in college, he was the best player in that division in the United States, and he was only beginning. When you play a game like that, you know how to measure people. I mean, there is a way you keep score there.

Again, we're not talking about young people's human worth. You don't diminish somebody's human worth, you enhance their human worth when you help them to develop their capacities. So I cannot say again, I am elated that you scored so well. I almost wish you hadn't done quite this well, so I would—because everybody else is going to say, "Well, we wouldn't do that well." That's not the point. That is not the point. The point is to know the truth so you can do better. That is the point.

Finally, let me say that there are things that we can do in the Department of Education. We can validate this testing mechanism. One of the problems I had—there are lots of standardized tests in America today, you know. Most kids are tested until the tests are coming out their ears. But what are the relevant tests? These tests shouldn't be IQ tests. These should be effort tests and effort directed in the right direction. The thing that's good about this test is, this test measures whether these young people know what it is important to know in mathematics and science at this point in their life, if they're going to be very successful at a later point in their lives and if their nations are going to be successful. That's the important thing.

So we can help. We can help with the Goals 2000 program. We can help with the charter schools. We can help schools to join in this movement toward setting strong national standards and then to know that if they give the students examinations, that the tests are relevant to what it is they're saying the children should know in the standards. We can do that.

The schools can push ahead. We could have every superintendent in the country prepared to give the speech that we heard this superintendent give today. We can do that. But what really will have to happen is that business leaders and parents and community leaders, religious leaders, people that are at the grassroots level are going to have to demand that this be done and are going to have to say, "Do not be afraid. And if it doesn't come out okay the first time, don't worry." We're going to use that not as a stick to beat somebody to death with but as a spur to lift people up with. That's what we have to say.

And so again I say: The young people in this room today are going to live in the greatest age of possibility, the greatest age of promise ever known. Our obligation as Americans is to give all of them the chance to make the most of their God-given abilities, to give all of them the chance to live out their dreams, to take whatever they have and make the most of it. And we will never get this job done unless we do what this First in the World Consortium has done. And if we do it, sure as the world, America will be number one.

Thank you, and God bless you.

NOTE: The President spoke at 12:08 p.m. in the gymnasium at the Glenbrook North High School. In his remarks, he referred to Mary Hamblet, teacher, Wood Oaks Junior High School; Paul Kimmelman, consortium coordinator; Mayor Richard M. Daley of Chicago; Nancy Firfer, village president, Glenview; Mark Damisch, village president, Northbrook; and Chicago Bulls basketball players Michael Jordan and Scottie Pippen. A portion of these remarks could not be verified because the tape was incomplete.

Interview With Al Hunt of WBIS in Chicago, Illinois
January 22, 1997

Part I

Mr. Hunt. Mr. President, I want to thank you for being one of our first guests on S-Plus on our second day of broadcast.

The President. Thank you.

National Economy

Mr. Hunt. All right. Let me start off with a question about the economy. You oversaw a very good economy during your first administration, average growth of about 2½ percent a year, and yet there's still not enough money to do some of the things you want to do, and there's still income and wage disparities. Do you think it's reasonable in a second Clinton administration to look for slightly faster growth, say 3 to 4 percent a year?

The President. Well, of course, the conventional wisdom is that it should slow down, but I don't believe that. Let me say what I want to do is to keep a sustained period of growth going. If we could ratchet it up a little bit, it would be even better, but if we could average 4½—let's say 2½ percent for 8 years in a row, that would have quite a compound effect, actually, in our economy.

Keep in mind, when we started, we thought our plan would reduce the deficit by 50 percent; it did by 63 percent. And over the long run, we are opening up investment dollars to help educate people, to help move people from welfare to work, to help invest in science and technology, to help do the things we need to be doing here, and to make some of the tax changes that will reduce inequality, as well.

Mr. Hunt. But you can do that at 2½ percent the next 4 years?

The President. Well, you can do some of it. For example, in the last 4 years when we had to really do a lot of the hardest work on the deficit reduction, we were able to—because growth took care of part of our deficit problem, we were able to cut spending overall but still increase spending in education and in science and technology, primarily, and then deal with the problems of health care costs.

I think if we can keep growth between 2½ and 3 percent, and if we can avert a huge increase in health care inflation—you know, there have been a lot of disturbing articles in the press in the last couple of days, well, health care inflation is coming back now. If we can avoid that—and we're going to try hard to do that—then I believe we'll have some money for the kinds of investments we need.

I also would point out that in—we won't know until later this year, but in 1996 we saw that in 1995 inequality among working people began to go down for the first time in 20 years, for a number of reasons. Most of the new jobs are coming in high-wage areas, and the impact of the tax changes of '93 on workers with incomes of $30,000 a year or less was very positive. So I think we may be able to see declining inequality now for several years if we can continue with good new jobs and education.

Mr. Hunt. In that context, the other day Chairman Greenspan of the Federal Reserve worried that wages may be rising so fast that it could threaten a renewed inflation, which would cause higher interest rates. Do you share that concern?

The President. Well, so far—I don't yet, but there are two reasons why I don't. Number one, so far, workers have gotten, finally, some real raises, and they should. But you haven't seen a lot of demands for wage increases all out of line with profitability growth in given enterprises. You haven't seen any kind of demands that people would say are outrageous, even in tight labor markets.

And I think that workers are very sophisticated now, and they're very sensitive to—they want a fair deal, so if their business is doing very well they'd like to participate in that, but they also understand that they can't kill the goose that laid the golden egg. And I think there's a lot more sophistication among working people, both members of labor unions and people who are not members of labor unions but are working in enterprises where they have to make those judgments.

Now, in addition to that, I think productivity increases are continuing to be brisk, and there's now, finally, a lot of scholarship coming out indicating that we may have underestimated productivity in the last several years, especially in the service industries. And I think if that happens, if we can keep the productivity going, and we can keep our markets open—we can keep competing, keep expanding our horizons in competition overseas in trade—that we can have some appropriate wage growth without having inflation. That's the goal, anyway.

Budget Negotiations

Mr. Hunt. You mentioned earlier the deficit reduction. What do you think of the odds right now that you can reach an agreement with Congress on a balanced budget by the year 2002?

The President. I think they're quite high.

Mr. Hunt. You do?

The President. I do.

Mr. Hunt. Better than 50 percent?

The President. I do.

Mr. Hunt. In that context, I know that you favor a very specific targeted reduction in the capital gains tax rate, just for specific endeavors. But could you envision accepting what the Republicans are advocating, namely a broad-based unconditional reduction in capital gains taxes?

The President. Well, let me say I can envision being more flexible on capital gains. I think it's a mistake to do a very expensive retroactivity provision. It's unnecessary. It doesn't contribute to economic growth. And it will cause a lot of, you know, problems in other decisions we have to make.

But I've always made it clear that I'm flexible on capital gains. I've never been philosophically opposed, as some of my fellow Democrats are. But I think a lot of us are open to that. What I want to do is to make sure that whatever we do we pay for and that we take care of first things first. And I hope that my education proposals will receive a favorable ear, and I hope that the Congress will be flexible about that. And I've decided to keep all options open.

Yesterday, when I offered Medicare savings that literally were halfway between where I was and where the Republicans were when we broke off negotiations in 1996, I met them halfway. I want to do that as much as I can in every way. So I think we've got very good odds.

Mr. Hunt. Meet them halfway on taxes also?

The President. Well, I want to meet them halfway insofar as I can. On the other hand, we have to ask, you know, how much of a tax cut do they want and how is it going to be paid for and what are we going to do without. So we just have to get to that.

But I'm not in stone on any of these things. I have proposed what I think is best for the country. I want them to propose, and then we'll have to work it out.

Medicare and Social Security Reform

Mr. Hunt. Your Medicare proposal the other day was quite well received by just about everyone on Capitol Hill. But let me ask you, why not go a little bit further, as even Bob Rubin at one point endorsed, and have wealthier senior citizens pay a little bit more for Medicare than middle income and poorer——

The President. Well, as you know, I proposed that back in 1993 as part of our health care reform plan. And I'm not necessarily opposed to that. But I think that we ought to look at that in terms of a long-term fix for Medicare. But if we do it, people are entitled to know that it's not the Tweedledee, Tweedledum; that is, it's not a tax cut here and a premium rise there.

And what I'd like to do—what I was trying to demonstrate, what I'm trying to demonstrate in my budget here is that through the right kind of disciplined management of Medicare we can achieve a 10-year life on the trust fund

and a balanced budget. If we want to do more in that area to lengthen the life of the Medicare Trust Fund, then that's something Congress and I need to discuss in the context of Medicare and Social Security reform. But I also believe we have an excellent chance to make some decisions which will be helpful to the country over the long run with regard to what happens to the entitlements, not in the next 10 years but in the next 15 to 30 years, when the baby boomers like me all come into the system.

Mr. Hunt. Do you think, then, there is a good chance for a major reform of Social Security in your second administration? Let me ask you just one specific on that. As you know, the Social Security advisory commission the other day—they were divided on a number of things, but one thing that they were unanimous on, on Social Security, was that the retirement eligibility age ought to be gradually increased. Do you support that?

The President. Well, let me say—here's what I think they believe. Right now we're increasing the retirement eligibility age to 67. So when you say "increase," there are two ways you can do it. You can bump it up to 68 or 69, but it's happening over a period of very many years. Or you can accelerate, you can move it up instead of 1 month a year, you can move it up 2 months a year or 3 months a year, something like that, and accelerate that coming on.

I think what we need to do is get together in some sort of bipartisan fashion—either a bipartisan representation of Congress with the affected groups or a commission, but a commission that would have a very short timespan. Because last year, you know, Senator Kerrey and Senator Danforth looked at a number of these things, explored a number of these options, so we have their work.

Mr. Hunt. You're talking about an entitlement commission, not just a Medicare commission?

The President. Yes, correct. And now we've got the work that the Social Security commission has done, although they couldn't agree, which shows you how difficult it is. And a lot of people even on Wall Street have reservations about whether this idea of putting more of the present Social Security savings into the stock market is a good one or not.

Mr. Hunt. Let me just close this. You said there were two ways to go. Does either way seem effective to you now on increasing retirement age?

The President. Well, I think—we discussed a couple of years ago whether it would be an appropriate thing to kind of, to accelerate the timetable from a month a year, 2 months a year, whatever, what would that look like.

I would have to see more evidence on raising the years, simply because I don't know—you know, I could work until I'm 68. And one of the reasons I went to law school is so no one could ever force me to retire, so I'd be able to work until I drop, because I'm a workaholic and I enjoy it and I think it is a good thing. But I don't know how many people out there work in jobs that are physically or emotionally so stressful that we would really be putting them under a lot of difficulty should we do that.

And so I just need—that's why I've said over and over again, I'm prepared to make these decisions with the Congress, I'm prepared to take responsibility for them, but we need to agree upon a process that is bipartisan and fairly quick. I think that from beginning to end, whatever we do, we need to be finished by the middle of next year.

Bipartisanship

Mr. Hunt. Mr. President, the chief Republican in any bipartisan negotiations this year, almost everyone on Capitol Hill says, will be Senate Majority Leader Trent Lott. What are your relations like with Senator Lott? How do you two southerners deal with one another?

The President. Well, I think we understand each other. And I like him. I like dealing with him. As of this date, he has always been very straightforward with me. If he couldn't do something, he would tell me, "I can't do that." If he disagreed with me, he would say, "I disagree." If he thought we could work something out, he would say, "Let me see," and he'd always get back to me and say yes or no. And I have tried to treat him in the same way.

I think we have some similarities in our upbringing and, obviously, in the culture in which we grew up. I feel very comfortable relating to him, and I do like him personally. And I think that he's a man who—he has his strong political convictions, but I believe he loves our country, and I believe that it really—he measures himself in no small measure by what he achieves and whether he actually gets something done for the country.

So, if we can keep the kind of atmospherics that existed in the last month or two of the last Congress in this Congress, I think we're going to do just fine.

Mr. Hunt. It sounds like different chemistry than you had in the beginning of the last Congress with Republican leaders. Is that fair?

The President. Yes, although I developed—all I had to do to have a good chemistry with Senator Dole was just spend some more time with him. In the first 2 years of my Presidency before he became majority leader, when he was minority leader, I think he had an understandable reluctance to be at the White House very much and to spend a lot of time with me or with our people, because he knew he was going to run for President and because he thought it didn't matter so much because he was a minority leader. Once he became majority leader he understood that we had to meet and work together, and we fairly quickly established a pretty good rapport.

Part II
Professional and College Basketball

Mr. Hunt. Let me turn to a couple of sports questions. We are in Chicago right now.

The President. Home of the Bulls.

Mr. Hunt. Not only the home of the Bulls, but there's one Chicago Bull from a little town called Hamburg, Arkansas.

The President. Hamburg, Arkansas. Scottie Pippen.

Mr. Hunt. Tell us what you know about that Chicago Bull.

The President. He's a remarkable man. I really admire him very much. And you know, we don't know each other well, but in Arkansas everybody knows everybody else. [*Laughter*] You know, it's a small State. But he came out of a small town. He went to a fairly small school in Arkansas.

Mr. Hunt. The Razorbacks didn't even recruit him?

The President. No, he went to a division II school, and he didn't make that team as a freshman. And then I watched him go from a sophomore, sort of making the team. And then by the time he was a senior he was the best player in his division in the United States. I mean, just—and then of course he was drafted in the pros. And then every year he just got better and better and better, you know, for 5 or 6 years he was just exploding in his capacity every year.

So I think of all the people playing for basketball today you would have to say that he was a little bit of a late bloomer, but he exploded when he got going. I mean, for a man who—he literally started sort of from his sophomore year in college, and he just kept—whatever the bar was he always reached it and went over it. And he's still doing that.

Mr. Hunt. Did you see him play in college?

The President. One time. And he was good. He was really good. And, you know, now it's not even the same. I mean, he's like on another planet now.

Mr. Hunt. I know your favorite team is the Arkansas Razorbacks. But you and Patrick Ewing also share an alma mater together.

The President. Yes, Georgetown.

Mr. Hunt. Do you follow your former Georgetown Hoyas?

The President. I do. I always root for the Razorbacks and the Hoyas. I keep up. Georgetown is having a little bit of a tough season this year, but over the long run it's hard to think of a program that's done more than John Thompson's has to produce both good basketball teams and college graduates. And I think that's—I wish more people would model the Georgetown program.

Mr. Hunt. Let me ask you about that. You talked in your Inaugural speech about personal responsibility, you talked about the need for a more civil discourse, and you mentioned role models. What effect do you think it has on kids when famous athletes like Dennis Rodman engage in those well-publicized antics? Does it worry you?

The President. It does. It worries me more now than it used to, than it would have 20 years ago, because, first of all, all of us know the pervasiveness of the media in our culture. It means that we all know everything like that when it happens, instantaneously.

And secondly, there are an awful lot of young people out there, particularly young boys and young men, who don't have immediate, positive male role models who can contradict a lapse by an athlete. And I say this—I'm a big Dennis Rodman fan. I mean, I think he's an extraordinary athlete, and he's a very interesting man. And I don't mind at all some of the more unusual manifestations of his personality. But I think when he does a destructive thing like that, it's a bad thing. I'm sure in his heart of hearts he really regrets it.

You know, we all would hate to be judged on what we did in the darkest hour of the dark-

est day of our lives. And, unfortunately, when athletes are under all this pressure, they're also being watched all the time, when they're under the most stress and most likely to do or say something they wish they hadn't. And I'm sure in his heart of hearts he regrets doing that. But I would hope that at some point, in addition to paying this enormous fine and also trying to pay the gentleman that he kicked—which I think is a good thing—that he'll find a way to say, "I shouldn't have done it, and I really regret it."

Because I think it will only make him bigger, it will only make his fans think more of him. And it will send who knows what signal to some young person out there who, like Dennis Rodman, has enormous abilities and a terrific imagination and is a little bit different from the run of the mill person and therefore really identifies with Dennis Rodman. There's lots of kids out there like that, real smart, real able, a little bit different. And they've got to be fascinated by him. So I hope he'll find a way to say that—and I say that as I'm a real admirer of his basketball talent, and I find him a fascinating man. But he might be able to help some young people if he just says, "That's something I shouldn't have done, and I'm not going to do that anymore."

Mr. Hunt. You are a genuine basketball aficionado. Who is the greatest basketball player you've ever seen?

The President. Oh, Jordan.

Mr. Hunt. Is he?

The President. Oh, yes.

Mr. Hunt. In a league by himself?

The President. I wouldn't say that. I've seen some great players. I saw Michael Jordan play when he was a senior in college and North Carolina came to play Arkansas, and they were ranked first and we were, I don't know, fifth or sixth or something. And we beat them by one point. But it was a fascinating game. And he just is—you know, he's a wonderful player. But basketball, I suppose next to golf, is my favorite sport, although you can tell by the way I'm built and move around I have to be a spectator more than a player. [*Laughter*]

I have never been much of a player, but I love it. And the thing that I find exciting about pro ball is that it's played at such a high level that it seems to me that year-in, year-out on the whole, the group of players is getting better. I believe that is accurate. And so I think some day, you know, Michael may have the kinds of things that we—you know, he scored 51 points last night. His team has a bad night, and it happens to be on the night he's having a good night—you know, he can do something like that. Someday we may take it for granted, that level of achievement. Some day there may be 20, 30 players in this league who can do that, just because of the level of competition they're bringing out of one another—you know, the way they're growing and going. But——

Mr. Hunt. I'll never have time for anything else if that happens, Mr. President. I'm just going to go to those games.

The President. No, it's just fascinating to watch. But I think, for me, he's the—because he has both offensive and defensive skills and a level of physical mobility and control, the combination of those things that I've never seen it before.

Super Bowl XXXI

Mr. Hunt. Let me ask you one final question. You will never run again for national office. You're going to retire undefeated from that. So you don't have to worry about Wisconsin's 11 electoral votes or Massachusetts' 12. Who's going to win the Super Bowl on Sunday, Packers or Patriots?

The President. I still have feelings for those places. [*Laughter*] I'll give you an analysis. I won't call it.

Mr. Hunt. All right.

The President. I think, first of all, there's an enormous psychological energy coming out of Green Bay. They've waited a long time to get back to the Super Bowl. They had this proud heritage. And it really is a home team. They don't have the kind of—they never worry about the team moving. They don't have to worry about the franchise leaving if you don't build a new stadium. They don't have to worry about building a skybox for wealthy people—you know, keep the money coming in. And it's always going to be sold out, because it belongs to the community and the leaders of the community.

And I think that, plus the fact that they played a very tough NFC schedule and ranked first in offense and third in defense and they've got great wideouts and great tight ends and a good running program. You know, that's a very rare thing to see that. I think that gives them a lot going.

Now, the flip side is the New England team has come alive defensively in the last five games in a way that's highly unusual. You rarely—if something funny—something fundamentally different has happened to them. And it's the one thing that makes me believe that—you know, the last several Super Bowls, the NFC team has won fairly handily. But if you look at the fact that the Patriots have a very skilled quarterback, a fabulous coach who is very savvy in circumstances like this——

Mr. Hunt. And has been there before.

The President. ——and been there before. And something happened, it was almost like a transformation of their defense in the last half dozen games of this year. I think you have to say that this could be the most interesting Super Bowl we've had in a long time.

Mr. Hunt. You're not going to predict the winner. Will you predict a close game?

The President. Yes, I will. I think that this is likely to be a—I think it is likely to be a closer game than the last four or five we've seen. The problem has been, you know, that the NFC basically has been beefier. So when a team—when the Cowboys or the 49ers come out of it as they have tended to come out the last several years, not only do they have this great reservoir of talent, but this great reservoir of talent was tested in a steady way during the year. So that when the best team came out of the AFC, they even—not only have they had—very often they weren't as strong pound for pound, particularly in physical strength. That was the thing that the Cowboys had, you know, on both sides of the line. In the end they would win at the end on their just brute strength as much as anything else. But the AFC teams hadn't been subject to that level of competition on a sustained basis.

I think this may be a little different. And as I said, you've got to ask yourself what happened to this team that turned it into a, literally, a brilliant defensive team in the last third of this year. There's something there. And I think it's—we've got a chance to see an exciting game.

Mr. Hunt. We'll watch on Sunday. And on that note, Mr. President, I want to thank you very much again for being one of our first guests on S-Plus.

The President. Thank you.

NOTE: The interview began at 5:06 p.m. at the Chicago Cultural Center. This interview was released by the Office of the Press Secretary in two parts: Part I was released on January 22, and part II was released on January 24. In his remarks, the President referred to former Senator John C. Danforth; John Thompson, Georgetown University men's basketball coach; and Dennis Rodman, Chicago Bulls basketball player.

Statement on Senate Confirmation of Madeleine K. Albright as Secretary of State and William S. Cohen as Secretary of Defense
January 22, 1997

I applaud the Senate for acting so swiftly on the nominations of Madeleine Albright and William Cohen. In confirming both Ambassador Albright as Secretary of State and Senator Cohen as Secretary of Defense by unanimous votes, the Senate has recognized the extraordinary capabilities of these two outstanding individuals.

Equally important, the Senate has sent a strong signal to the world of its determination to work in a constructive and bipartisan spirit with the administration on our Nation's foreign policy and national defense. I welcome that resolve. Nothing is more important for maintaining America's leadership in the world than preserving the bipartisan consensus on national security policy that was so vital to our success in World War II and the cold war. I look forward to a continuation of that spirit of bipartisan cooperation as the Senate takes up the nominations of Congressman Bill Richardson to be Ambassador to the United Nations and Anthony Lake to be Director of Central Intelligence.

Remarks at the Swearing-In of Madeleine K. Albright as Secretary of State and an Exchange With Reporters
January 23, 1997

The President. Welcome. Mr. Vice President, Secretary-designate Albright, members of your family, Senator Helms, Senator Mikulski. Is Congressman Hamilton here? Under Secretary Tarnoff. I'm very pleased to preside at Madeleine Albright's swearing-in today. I thank the Senate for its swift and unanimous approval of her nomination. That reflects the confidence that all of us have in this remarkable American. It also sends a strong signal of the Senate's willingness to work with us to fashion a constructive and bipartisan foreign policy to advance the national interest of America.

This is a time of great hope and opportunity. If we are going to realize its promise, we must recognize that our global leadership is essential. In the next century, no less than this one, America must continue to be the world's greatest force for peace and freedom and prosperity. Madeleine Albright has the strength and wisdom to help ensure that America remains the indispensable nation.

Arriving on our shores as a refugee from tyranny and oppression, she worked her way up with determination and character to attain our Nation's highest diplomatic office. She knows from her life's experience that freedom has its price and democracy its rewards. Her story is the best of America's story, told with courage, compassion, and conviction.

As our U.N. Ambassador these last 4 years, she has stood unflinchingly for America's interest and values. Now as our Secretary of State, she will help lead the effort to build a world where America makes the most of its partnerships with friends and allies around the world, where America leads the fight for a world that is safer from weapons of terror and mass destruction, where America leads the fight for a world that is safer from organized crime, drug trafficking, and all terrorist activity, and where expanded trade brings growth and opportunity, where peace and freedom know no frontiers.

Just as I have benefited time and again from her counsel and her judgment, the American people will benefit from her leadership and her ability to speak to them about the importance of our being strong abroad in order to have a strong, good life here at home.

On their behalf, I ask now that the Vice President swear Madeleine Albright into her new office.

[*At this point, Vice President Gore administered the oath of office, and Secretary Albright made brief remarks.*]

Q. Madam Secretary, what is your first order of business?

Secretary Albright. To go over to the State Department and tell them all that we have a very important job to do with the hard work of our foreign service and civil service who works in the State Department. And then I will plan the next steps. But my first goal is really to go and work with the excellent people that have provided the backbone of America's diplomatic service.

Q. Madam Secretary, now that you've made history, how else do you intend to differ from your predecessor?

Secretary Albright. I'm basically interested in serving the President of the United States and the people of the United States as best I can. I'm very proud to be an American. And I hope very much that the American people will be proud of me as I perform this service for the United States.

Thank you.

Q. Are you going to be tough on the new Secretary-General, as you were on his predecessor? [*Laughter*]

Secretary Albright. I think we are going to meet with the new Secretary-General. I'm very pleased, actually, that his—the first official trip that—the first visit here that the President is going to have after his Inauguration is with the United Nations Secretary-General. My first official act will be to meet with the President and the new Secretary-General in a little while. And I think that is a very good sign of the support that the United States is going to give to the United Nations. And as the Vice President said last night, we are committed to the United Nations.

Thank you.

The President. Thank you.

NOTE: The President spoke at 12:18 p.m. in the Oval Office at the White House.

Remarks Following Discussions With United Nations Secretary-General Kofi Annan and an Exchange With Reporters
January 23, 1997

The President. Good afternoon. Secretary-General and your distinguished staff, Mr. Vice President, Madam Secretary.

The President of the United States must exercise the leadership of our country for peace and freedom, for security and prosperity in the world. When we must, we will act alone. But when we can, we must work with others to spread the cost and the risks of engagement and to make our own leadership more effective.

The United Nations is critical in advancing the progress and peace of the world. It vaccinates children against disease, helps refugees to stay safe and go home, teaches farmers how to grow good crops, guards against the spread of nuclear weapons. And from Angola to the Middle East, U.N. peacekeepers are giving diplomacy a chance to work and peace a chance to take hold.

That is the kind of burden-sharing we need to seize the promise and meet the perils of a world growing ever closer together. That's why last year I believed so strongly that the United Nations needed new leadership, a Secretary-General who could rebuild the institution to take on the challenges of the future. I am very pleased that the U.N. chose Kofi Annan for the job. He is a man who shares that vision and is clearly prepared to act, an experienced diplomat, a proven reformer, a man committed to a revitalized United Nations, one that upholds its timeless mission but that adapts to new times.

We had a good discussion. We talked about the need to put the U.N. back on sound financial footing. That will demand far-reaching reform, the elimination of waste, streamlining staff, wiping out overlap and abuse. The Secretary-General and I agree that the U.N. must pursue this course of reform. It's clear to me that he is prepared and determined to get the job done.

As the U.N. moves to reform, it must know also that the United States is prepared to pay its way. In the weeks ahead, I will be working with Congress to reach an agreement through which America can pay our arrears to the U.N., meet our obligations, and continue to spur real progress. We cannot expect to lead through the United Nations unless we are prepared to pay our own way and to pay what we owe as they do what they should along the path of reform. As long as the United States does its part—as long as the United Nations does its part, we simply have to be prepared to pay our debts and to pay our dues.

Today we are proud as Americans to stand as the indispensable nation, the world's leading force for peace and freedom and security and prosperity. But we cannot sustain our leadership or, more importantly, our goals for a better world, alone. And we cannot sustain it by words alone. Our well-being at home depends upon our engagement around the world. We have to have the resources to meet that challenge and to assume the responsibilities of leadership. Meeting our commitment to the United Nations is a crucial part of that task, and I might say also, on Secretary Albright's first day in office, adequately funding our foreign policy operations through the State Department and our other diplomatic missions is also a critical part of that task.

I'm very encouraged that the Secretary-General will be meeting with congressional leaders during his visit here to Washington. I look forward to working with the Congress and with the Secretary-General to renew the United Nations for the century ahead, and I'm very glad that he is the first leader that I have met with after my Inauguration.

Mr. Secretary-General, would you like to say a few words? Welcome to Washington.

[*At this point, Secretary-General Annan made brief remarks.*]

The President. Thank you very much.

U.S. Debt to the United Nations

Q. Mr. President, why did you wait so long to want to pay back your debts? And is it conditional on reforms?

The President. First of all, I wanted to pay it back all along. Our budget will actually have a plan to pay it back and to pay it back in a prompt fashion. As a practical matter, I know from consulting with the Members of Congress that we won't be able to secure support in the Congress for paying the arrears unless they're convinced that reform is going forward.

But you know, the United States has been, I think, very fortunate to have hosted the United Nations since its creation, to have supported it and worked with it in ways large and small. And we have been immensely benefited by the burden-sharing and humanitarian work that the United Nations has done. So I am determined to see that we pay our way. And I think it's a part of—I'll say again, it's a part of having the proper attitude toward our foreign policy operations in general.

I'm gratified that Secretary Albright and Secretary Cohen were confirmed yesterday. I hope that Bill Richardson and Tony Lake will be promptly confirmed so we can put our whole foreign policy team on the field and go to work. But we have to recognize that our diplomacy and our leadership cannot be through the defense budget alone. We also have to have an adequate diplomatic budget to do the work that has to be done. And that is—a part of that is paying our U.N. way.

Q. Mr. President, what do you think about——

Q. Mr. President, if you put the U.N. on a scale of 1 to 10, where would you place it?

The President. Rising rapidly. [*Laughter*]

Canada-Cuba Trade Agreement

Q. What do you think about Canada's trade deal with Cuba?

The President. Excuse me?

Q. Canada's trade deal with Cuba?

The President. What about it?

Q. What is your reaction to it? Do you have any?

The President. Well, my reaction is I'm gratified that the Canadians, along with the Europeans, are now talking more to the Cubans about human rights and democratic reforms. I'm skeptical, frankly, that it will—that the recent discussions between the Canadians and the Cubans will lead to advances. I believe that our policy is the proper one, but I'm glad that the Canadians are trying to make something good happen in Cuba.

U.S. Debt to the United Nations

Q. Gentlemen, would the two of you like to have a common strategy about how to get a reluctant Congress to give up this money?

The President. Well, I think we have common interests there. I've already told you that I'm utterly convinced that the Secretary-General has a chance to genuinely reform the United Nations for the 21st century because he is committed to do it and because he and his team have the capacity to do it. And I think all that remains is for him to establish an appropriate relationship with our Congress. And I think he'll do it and do quite well with it. And we don't need to coordinate a strategy for that. No secret here, we've told you everything we've just said in there.

Thank you very much.

NOTE: The President spoke at 1:21 p.m. in the Roosevelt Room at the White House.

Memorandum on Increasing Seatbelt Use
January 23, 1997

Memorandum for the Secretary of Transportation

Subject: Increasing Seatbelt Use Nationwide

We have made steady progress in improving highway safety over the years. However, there are still far too many tragic and unnecessary deaths and injuries on the Nation's roads. As a first line of defense, we must all wear seatbelts. Seatbelts protect passengers not only in frontal crashes, but also in side, rear, and rollover crashes, saving about 10,000 lives a year. I understand that about 70 percent of the population use seatbelts. Increasing seatbelt use will clearly save more lives and reduce injuries.

I hereby direct you, working with the Congress, the States, and other concerned Americans, including the automobile and insurance industries, and safety and consumer groups, to report back to me in 45 days with a plan to increase the use of seatbelts nationwide. The plan shall address, among other things, the State laws that require the use of seatbelts, assistance from the Department of Transportation to improve those State laws, and a comprehensive education campaign on behalf of the public and private sector to help the public understand the need to wear seatbelts.

You are authorized and directed to publish this memorandum in the *Federal Register*.

WILLIAM J. CLINTON

NOTE: This memorandum was not received for publication in the *Federal Register*.

Remarks at the Swearing-In of William S. Cohen as Secretary of Defense and an Exchange With Reporters
January 24, 1997

The President. Good morning. Mr. Vice President, Secretary-about-to-be Cohen, Janet, Secretary Perry, Deputy Secretary White, General Shalikashvili, General Ralston, Senator Inouye, Senator Levin, Senator McCain, Senator Stevens, Senator Thurmond, Senator Collins, Senator Snowe. I'm delighted today to be here along with all of you for Senator Cohen's swearing-in.

I want to congratulate him on the swift confirmation of his nomination. It says a great deal about this extraordinary man that his Senate colleagues paid him the tribute of a unanimous vote of approval. In so doing, the Senate sent a strong signal of its intention to work in a constructive and bipartisan spirit to preserve and enhance our national security.

Bill Cohen is the embodiment of that spirit. Throughout his years as a Senator and a Congressman, he's reached across the divisions of party to strengthen our defenses, shaping the START I arms control treaty, helping reorganize the Department of Defense, guiding the most important deliberations about our Armed Forces. He has never forgotten, as he said so eloquently in his testimony on Wednesday, that at the end of every debate stand our soldiers, sailors, airmen, and marines, who look to us for leadership, not political strife.

As we move forward to face the challenges of the next century, America's leadership in the world will depend upon that understanding, just as it did in World War II and the cold war. We know that to seize all the possibilities of this moment and to keep the United States the greatest force for peace and freedom, for security and prosperity, we must continue to have the best-trained, best-equipped, best-prepared troops on Earth, because at the heart of America's power is our military strength and will.

Whether they are deterring a dangerous tyrant in the Persian Gulf, helping the people of Bosnia build peace in their shattered land, defending democracy in the cold war's last frontier on the Korean Peninsula, or standing watch for liberty here at home, our Armed Forces maintain America's status as the indispensable nation.

In Bill Cohen, our military will have a Secretary of Defense with the vision, judgment, and dedication that our era demands. He has served the people of Maine with tremendous distinction. And now I'm pleased that all Americans will benefit from his leadership and his wisdom.

On their behalf, I now ask the Vice President to swear William Cohen into his new office.

[*At this point, Vice President Gore administered the oath of office, and Secretary Cohen made brief remarks.*]

Pentagon Priorities

Q. What will be your top priority at the Pentagon? Are you going to hit the deck running? [*Laughter*]

Secretary Cohen. I intend to hit it running. My first—I have a full day starting immediately after this ceremony. I'm going to be paying a final visit with Secretary Perry. I'm going to be meeting with General Shalikashvili and Deputy Secretary White to discuss matters this afternoon. I'm sending messages to all of our troops today, along with the commanders of the regional commands. I'll be meeting later this afternoon with all of the service chiefs and secretaries, and then beginning some budget deliberations and briefings, starting at 5:30 this afternoon with John Hamre. So I have a fairly full schedule today.

And we'll look forward to starting this process of trying to retain and attract the best qualified people in our military, to make sure that we provide them with the best equipment, training, and that we seek to modernize our forces for the future. So all of that is very high on my agenda.

Q. Are you going to ask for more money? [*Laughter*]

Secretary Cohen. I'm going to do my best to see to it that we have the best military that the world has ever seen.

The President. Everybody else does. [*Laughter*]

Secretary Cohen. I see Senator Stevens over to my right, and I'm sure that I'll be calling upon him for assistance as we go through the budgetary process.

Q. What is the budget for defense—a secret?

The President. We're releasing it in a few days.

Thank you all very much.

NOTE: The President spoke at 10:10 a.m. in the Oval Office at the White House. In his remarks, he referred to Secretary Cohen's wife, Janet Langhart.

Remarks Announcing the Presidents' Summit for America's Future
January 24, 1997

The President. I thank the Vice President and the First Lady for their remarks. Obviously, I am delighted to have President Bush, General Powell, and Secretary Cisneros back. Henry's only been off the payroll a day or two. [*Laughter*] I didn't really know if he'd come. [*Laughter*]

I thank so many people here who have advocated national service and citizen service of various kinds for a long time. Especially I'd like to acknowledge, in addition to Harris Wofford and Bob Goodwin, Eli Segal and Ray Chambers; Al From with the Democratic Leadership Council; Charles Moskos, the national scholar of citizen service, who was for all this years before the rest of us knew it was an issue. Thank you, sir, for all your lifetime of work devoted to the proposition that the American people can forge their own destiny and solve their own problems. We thank you.

This is an extraordinary collection of Americans who have gathered here, not only on the stage but out here in the room, to advance the cause of citizen service. Much of the work of America cannot be done by government. Much other work cannot be done by government alone. The solution must be the American people through voluntary service to others. The challenges we face today, especially those that face our children, require something of all of us, parents, religious and community groups, business, labor organizations, schools, teachers, our great national civic and service organizations, every citizen.

One of my proudest moments as President was signing the bill creating the Corporation for National Service and AmeriCorps. During the last 3 years, about 50,000 Americans have earned aid for college by serving in their communities, doing real work to address critical problems, cleaning up rivers, working with the police to make the streets safe, helping children learn to read, and doing many, many more things in every State in the country.

These AmeriCorps members and even larger numbers of Senior Service Corps and student volunteers have really helped to revive the spirit of service in America. I noticed just a few days before the Inauguration the publication of a national poll—I can mention that now and you think I have no self-interest, you see—[*laughter*]—the publication of a national poll that said that young people are serving in their communities in far higher percentages than just a few years ago.

I think this is a culmination of years and years of effort. When President Bush held this office, he understood that so much of what is good in America has to be done and is being done by people who are outside Washington and outside the Federal Government. And we share his hope that by holding up examples of ordinary Americans engaged in extraordinary service, by holding up those thousand points of light, they will grow by the power of their example into millions of points of light. And we thank you for that.

Citizen service belongs to no party, no ideology. It is an American idea which every American should embrace. Today I am pleased to announce that we are taking an important step to give more Americans the opportunity to fulfill that promise. On April 27th in Philadelphia, with the support and leadership of the Corporation for National Service, the Points of Light Foundation, General Colin Powell, and Secretary Henry Cisneros, President Bush and I will convene the first Presidents' summit on citizen service. Our goal is to mobilize America's citizen power in a united effort to solve our common problems, especially those that threaten our young people.

Leaders from a broad spectrum will come with commitments in hand, concrete pledges of support, and volunteers to solve their local problems. In preparation for the summit some of our most prominent corporations and service organizations have already stepped forward. Big Brothers-Big Sisters has pledged to double their mentoring relations, matching 200,000 deserving young people with caring adults through the year 2000. And they have pledged to compound their efforts by having these adult volunteers actually do other citizen service projects with the young people they mentor. They not only will be serving the young but calling on the young to serve. Lens Crafters will provide one million needy Americans, especially children, with free vision care by the year 2003. Columbia HCA, a leading health care company, has committed to immunize one million children through their health care facilities by the year 2000. And that is just the beginning.

I am delighted that General Colin Powell, who has served our country in so very many ways, has agreed to serve once again, this time as general chair of the summit. General, we're grateful that you're joining us. And I remember well when you had your retirement ceremony, you said that you were going to devote more of your life to helping young people to have better lives and better futures. There is nothing—nothing—you could do that would have a bigger impact on that goal than this. And we are very grateful to you, sir.

All of you know that I believe Henry Cisneros is the finest HUD Secretary who ever served our country. He had a special way of getting people to take responsibility for their own lives and of generating real interpersonal human contacts in places where they had been too long absent. He just has a great new leadership job at Univision, and I am very grateful that he was willing to take substantial time out of an already very busy schedule in a new and fulfilling, in some ways more rewarding life—[*laughter*]—to do what I know he loves best, which is to help people realize their own promise. Thank you, Henry, for doing this.

Finally, let me say I am deeply honored to be embarking on this joint venture with President Bush. As far as I know, there's not much of a precedent for this sort of thing, at least in recent history, but there should be. It must be true that the things which unite us as citizens are bigger than any one person, one party, one election, or one ideology. They can only be solved if we come together in partnership to lift each other up, a person at a time, a family at a time, a neighborhood at a time, a school at a time.

The organizers of this effort have wisely chosen Philadelphia as the site of the summit, for the reasons that the Vice President said. I'm reminded at the close of the Constitutional Convention, Benjamin Franklin made an observation about a design of the Sun that was hanging low on the horizon in the chair that General Washington sat in to preside over the Convention. And after the Constitutional Convention was over, he said there had been a lot of speculation about whether it was a rising or a setting Sun; having seen the Constitution he could say that it was definitely a rising Sun. I believe we can look at this assemblage today, look forward to Independence Hall in Philadelphia, and say this is a rising Sun.

I thank all of you. I thank especially those who are here on this platform. And I'd like to ask all of you to join me as we hear from our speakers. First, President Bush, to be followed by General Powell and Henry Cisneros.

Mr. President, welcome back.

[*At this point, former President George Bush, former Chairman of the Joint Chiefs of Staff Gen. Colin L. Powell, USA (ret.), and former Secretary of Housing and Urban Development Henry G. Cisneros made brief remarks.*]

The President. Well, let me again thank President Bush and General Powell and Secretary Cisneros and all the rest of you for being here; especially the Members of Congress, members of the administration, the mayors, and others who are here.

We are going to adjourn now and have a reception. But as we leave I'd like to just ask that we keep in mind the last point that Secretary Cisneros made. I imagine that Ray Chambers was a happy and successful man before he decided to give his whole life over to other people's welfare. But I can't imagine that he emanated the glow that he does today that we all see and that you see in the lives of other people who give.

And I guess—you know, our wealth and power are very important in America, and they must be maintained. But the pursuit of happiness involves more. And it really is true that in giving, we receive. So if we give a lot, we'll get a lot, and our country will enter this new century in wonderful, wonderful shape.

Thank you all, and God bless you. We're adjourned.

NOTE: The President spoke at 2:52 p.m. in the East Room at the White House. In his remarks, he referred to Harris Wofford, Chief Executive Officer, and Eli Segal, board member, Corporation for National and Community Service; Robert F. Goodwin, president, Points of Light Foundation; Raymond G. Chambers, president, Amerlior Foundation; Al From, president, Democratic Leadership Council; and Charles C. Moskos, professor of sociology, Northwestern University.

The President's Radio Address
January 25, 1997

Good morning. Today I'm pleased to announce a major new step toward protecting the health and safety of all Americans, especially our children.

Almost a week ago, in my Inaugural Address, I told the American people that we must lead our country into the 21st century with the American dream alive for all our children, with the American promise of a more perfect Union a reality for all our people, with the light of our freedom illuminating all the world.

I believe we will make this vision real by doing what we've always done in moments of great change—holding fast to our enduring values. Central among these is the belief that we work tirelessly to make our families stronger and our children safer. Nothing is more important to meeting this goal than seeing to it that Americans live in a world with clean air, safe food, pure water. Hard-working American parents deserve the peace of mind that comes from knowing that the meal they set before their children is safe.

That's why I was so concerned by what happened in Washington State and in two other Western States this fall. Apple juice contaminated with a deadly strain of *E. coli* bacteria reached supermarket shelves. More than a dozen children, some as young as 2, were hospitalized, and one child died.

I'm sure just about every parent in America remembers what *E. coli* can do. Four years ago this month, tragedy struck hundreds of families in the Western United States when they took their children to fast-food restaurants that served them hamburgers tainted by the *E. coli* bacteria. Five hundred people became ill, some of them severely, and four children lost their lives.

Our administration has made it a top priority to protect the health and safety of all Americans. I signed into law legislation to keep harmful pesticides off our fruits and vegetables and legislation that keeps our drinking water safe and pure. We put in place strong new protections to ensure that seafood is safe. And last summer we announced steps to modernize our meat and poultry food safety system for the first time in 90 years. These new safety rules will begin to take effect next week. From now on, all meat and poultry plants will be required to test for *E. coli*.

We have built a solid foundation for the health of America's families. But clearly we must do more. No parent should have to think twice about the juice that they pour their children at breakfast or a hamburger ordered during dinner out. That's why today I'm announcing new steps to use cutting-edge technology to keep our food safe and to protect our children from deadly bacteria. We must continue to modernize the food safety system put in place at the dawn of the 20th century so that it can meet the demands of the 21st century.

First, we will put in place a nationwide early warning system for food-borne illness. Right now the Centers for Disease Control, the Food and Drug Administration, and the Agriculture Department sponsor five centers across the country whose mission is to post a lookout for food-borne diseases like *E. coli* bacteria and salmonella. Working with State and local governments, these sentinel sites in California, Oregon, Minnesota, Georgia, and Connecticut actively track outbreaks of illnesses caused by contaminated food. Today I'm announcing we'll increase the number of these sites from five to eight and link them to other State health agencies. This expanded early warning system will enable us to catch outbreaks sooner and give us the data we need to help us prevent outbreaks from happening in the first place.

Second, we will see to it that the early warning system uses state-of-the-art technology to keep our food safe. We'll increase the number of expert disease detectives to investigate and control food-borne disease outbreaks. We will give these experts the technology to use sophisticated new DNA fingerprinting methods to trace dangerous bacteria to their source. We will create a permanent DNA fingerprint library so we can immediately recognize an illness if it reappears. And we will use advance communication networks to speed outbreak information to hospitals and public health agencies all around America.

Third, I'm directing Secretary of Agriculture Dan Glickman, Secretary of Health and Human Services Donna Shalala, and the Administrator of the Environmental Protection Agency, Carol Browner, to work with communities, farmers, businesses, consumer protection groups, and all levels of Government to come up with additional measures to improve food safety. I want them to pay special attention to research and public education efforts. I want them to focus on what sort of partnerships the Government can form with the private sector to meet our goals. And I want them to report back to me with their findings within 90 days.

Finally, let me add that these new public health investments are paid for, line by line, dime by dime, in the balanced budget I will officially send to Congress next month. With this new early warning system to track food-borne illness, we are saying loud and clear that we will use the world's best science to make the world's most bountiful food supply safer than ever before for our families and for our children. Together we will see to it that our people and our Nation are prepared for the 21st century.

Thanks for listening.

NOTE: The address was recorded at 1:26 p.m. on January 24 in the Roosevelt Room at the White House for broadcast at 10:06 a.m. on January 25.

Memorandum on Improving the Safety of the Nation's Food Supply
January 25, 1997

Memorandum for the Secretary of Agriculture, Secretary of Health and Human Services, Administrator of the Environmental Protection Agency

Subject: Improving the Safety of the Nation's Food Supply

Americans rightly expect to have the world's safest food supply. Although our food is unmatched in quantity and quality, we can do better in our efforts to eliminate disease caused by microorganisms and other contaminants. Americans still suffer thousands of food-related deaths and millions of food-related illnesses.

The 21st century will present new and greater challenges in this area. Novel pathogens are emerging. Long-understood pathogens are growing resistant to treatment. Americans eat more foods prepared outside the home, and we consume record levels of imported food—some of which moves across the globe overnight. These changing circumstances require greatly strengthened systems of coordination, surveillance, prevention, research, and education.

My Administration has already taken a number of steps to improve food safety. We modernized the meat, poultry, and seafood safety systems. I signed into law new legislation to keep harmful pesticides off our fruits and vegetables—and legislation that keeps our drinking water safe and pure. Today, I announced a new national early warning system for food-borne illness. The system will allow us to respond more quickly to disease outbreaks and to better prevent them in the future.

But we need to do more. Government, consumers, and industry must work together to further reduce food-borne disease and to ensure our food supply is the safest in the world.

I hereby direct that you work with consumers, producers, industry, States, universities, and the public to identify additional ways to improve the safety of our food supply through government and private sector action, including public-private partnerships. Your recommendations should identify steps to further improve surveillance, inspections, research, risk assessment, education, and coordination among local, State, and Federal health authorities. You should report back to me within 90 days with your recommendations.

WILLIAM J. CLINTON

The President's News Conference
January 28, 1997

The President. Good afternoon. Please be seated. Before I take your questions, I would like to make a brief statement about the balanced budget that I will send to Congress next week.

This budget shows that we can meet two of our most crucial national priorities at the same time. It proves we can protect our children from a future burdened by reckless debt even as we give them the educational opportunities they need to make the most of the 21st century.

The budget finally moves us beyond the false choices that have held us back for too long and shows that we can cut our debt and invest in our children. The budget will help to renew our public schools. It will expand Head Start, help rebuild crumbling classrooms. It will double funding for public charter schools, giving parents more choice in how they educate their children. It will increase funding for Goals 2000 by 26 percent. And it will help our students to reach high standards and master the basics of reading, writing, math, and science.

It will also enable us to connect our schools and our libraries to the information superhighway. The budget more than doubles our investment in technology to hook our children up to computers and the Internet, and it increases by a third our investment in partnerships with teachers and industries to develop quality educational programming and technology. In short, the budget will connect our children to the best educational technology in the world.

It will also open the doors of college education wider than ever before. I'd like to take a minute now simply to outline our unprecedented commitment to higher education. With this budget, national support for college education in the year 2002 will be more than double what it was on the day I first took office, going from $24 billion to $58 billion per year. The budget will fully pay for a $1,500-a-year tuition tax credit, a HOPE scholarship for the first 2 years of college, to make the typical community college affordable for every American and to achieve our goal of making 2 years of college education as universal as a high school diploma is today.

It will also allow a working family to deduct up to $10,000 a year for taxes for the cost of any college tuition or job training. And with our special IRA for education, most parents will be able to save for college tuition without ever paying a penny in taxes.

In addition, my balanced budget takes further steps to widen the circle of educational opportunity. It provides a 25 percent increase in funding for Pell grants, the largest increase in the maximum scholarship in 20 years, so that over 4 million students will get up to $3,000 a year. We'll make 130,000 more students eligible for these scholarships, and we will open the scholarships to 218,000 older, low income Americans who want to go to college.

Second, under the balanced budget we will present, we will continue to reform our student loan programs to make college loans easier for students to get and easier to pay back. We will cut interest rates on loans to students while they're in school. We will cut loan fees for 4 million low and middle income students in half. Fees on 2½ million more will be cut by 25 percent. Taken together, these two steps will save American families $2.6 billion over 5 years.

Third, we will increase funding again for work-study positions for students. That will take us, over about a 3-year period, from 700,000 work-study positions to 1 million work-study positions per year. And it will help us to meet our goal of getting 100,000 of those work-study students to participate as tutors in our initiative to make sure that all of our 8-year-olds can read independently.

To encourage community service, we will also provide tax incentives to encourage loan forgiveness for students who, after college, choose professions that give something back, people who use their education to work as teachers, in homeless shelters, as doctors in remote rural areas.

All together, these proposals will move us much closer to our clear national goal: an America where every 8-year-old can read, where every 12-year-old can log on to the Internet, where every 18-year-old can go to college, where all Americans will have the knowledge they need to meet the challenges of the 21st century. I am very proud of this budget.

Finally, let me say a word about campaign finance reform. We all know we need to find a new way to finance our campaigns and to bring the aggregate spending levels under control. Anyone who is involved in politics must accept responsibility for this problem and take responsibility to repair it. That is true for me and true for others as well.

Last week, I met with Senators John McCain and Russ Feingold, and Representatives Chris Shays and Marty Meehan. They have introduced tough, balanced, credible, bipartisan campaign finance reform legislation. I pledged my support to them. I pledge it again today. I pledge to do all I can to help them pass this legislation. Any legislation we pass should be bipartisan, should limit spending, and should leave the playing field level between parties and between incumbents and challengers.

This is our best chance in a generation to give the American people campaigns that are worthy of the world's oldest continuous democracy. I call on the members of both parties to work with us to get the job done.

Helen [Helen Thomas, United Press International].

Campaign Finance Reform

Q. Mr. President, my question ties into that. What should the American people think of a Presidential campaign in which a day at the White House is sold for $250,000 a couple and the Republican Party sells a season ticket of access to Capitol Hill for $250,000?

The President. Well, first, let me say I dispute a little bit the characterization there. I can't speak for the Republicans; they'll have to speak for themselves. But the people who were there on the day in question were not charged a fee. Some of them were our contributors—had contributed in the past—they had raised money for me in the past. Some of them had not. And so I don't think it's quite an accurate characterization.

But I will say this: If you look at the money that was raised and spent not only by the parties and their respective campaign committees in the Senate and House but also by all these independent—apparently independent third-party committees and you look at the exponential cost of the campaigns related to communications,

surely we can use this opportunity to make something positive come out of this.

I mean, I think that all of us—as I said, again—every one of us who has participated in this system, even if we did it because we thought we had to do it to survive or to just keep up, has to take some responsibility for its excess, and I take mine. But we have got to do something about it. And the only way we can do anything about it is to pass the legislation, the McCain-Feingold bill or some acceptable variation thereof.

Terry [Terence Hunt, Associated Press].

Q. Mr. President, with all the focus on the Democrat fundraising right now, why are you attending a million-dollar fundraiser tonight? What kind of an image do you think this leaves? And why do these donors make these big-money contributions? What do they get in return?

The President. Well, first of all, under all conceivable campaign finance reform scenarios, it will still be necessary for the parties to raise some money. And neither party has the capacity to raise all their money from direct mail campaigns and contributions of $100 or less. The Business Council, the group that is having this fundraiser tonight, is one that would be quite consistent with the McCain-Feingold bill, were it to pass. And I, frankly, am very appreciative of the fact that these folks have been willing to come and help us and that we have increased the ranks of particularly younger, more entrepreneurial people in the Democratic Party supporting us. So I think it's an important thing to do. I don't think there's anything wrong with raising money for the political process. The problem is, it is the volume of money, the amount of money, the time it takes to raise, the inevitable questions that are raised.

Now, I can tell you what they get from me. I don't know—you have to ask them what they expect. What they get from me, I think, is a respectful hearing if they have some concern about issues. I think it's a good thing when contributors care about the country and have some particular area of expertise they want to contribute. But nobody buys a guaranteed result, nor should they ever. They should get a respectful hearing, and the President should do what's right for the country.

Wolf [Wolf Blitzer, CNN].

Taxes

Q. Mr. President, in your new budget that you'll submit next week to Congress there will be tax cut proposals, including some of the education tax cut proposals you outlined today. But there also, presumably, will be some tax increases in the form of what you would describe as corporate welfare, getting rid of some of the tax breaks that big business have now. Some Republicans are already suggesting that netwise, your budget proposal will have a net increase in taxes as opposed to a net decrease. Is that a fair assessment of your budget?

The President. No. I believe that's incorrect. And let me say, I also believe—and again, I'm speaking from memory now; I have not discussed this with Mr. Raines in the last several weeks. But I believe that—number one, I believe it's incorrect, that we do have a net tax cut. Number two——

Q. Tax increase.

The President. No, we have a net tax cut. Number two, I believe that virtually all of the corporate loophole closings that we have in this budget are ones that we had discussed with and reached at least general agreement on with the congressional leadership back during the budget negotiations, when we were having them last year. I believe that to be the case. And if it's not, I'll stand corrected, but that's accurate.

Yes, Gene [Gene Gibbons, Reuters].

President Boris Yeltsin of Russia

Q. Mr. President, Boris Yeltsin has been out of work for more than 6 months now because of his health problems. How has that affected your ability to do business with the Russian Government? And a related question: How will Yeltsin's health problems affect the timing and location of the next U.S.-Soviet summit, which had been set for March?

The President. Well, first, let me make the most important statement I think I can make to your question, which is, I have no private information that is inconsistent with the public statements of the Russian Government on President Yeltsin's health. I have no reason to believe, based on any information I have, that his condition is any different from what the Russian Government has said it is—first thing.

Secondly, I had been very impressed by the extent to which President Yeltsin made appropriate delegations to Mr. Chernomyrdin during the period of his convalescence leading up to the surgery and then in this period after the surgery when he developed his illness. And the Vice President and Mr. Chernomyrdin are going to meet pretty soon, and their ongoing relationship—we have a huge, full agenda. And we have been given no impression by the Russians that we aren't still going to have the Yeltsin-Clinton meeting in the March timeframe.

I think it's very important—you know, we have to work through the NATO-Russia relationship in connection with expansion and other issues. We have a lot of other security issues. We have to deal with the START II issues, with where we go after START II. We have a lot of economic issues that are still to be resolved. And so I think we'll go right on, and I expect to have that meeting in March. And I expect it to be an important one and, I hope, a successful one.

Mr. Donvan [John Donvan, ABC News].

Bipartisanship

Q. Mr. President, in your Inaugural Address 8 days ago, you outlined some quite lofty goals, for example, the education proposals you were speaking about today. But in the days since, many questions in the press and in Congress have focused on issues like campaign fundraising. My question is whether you are worried that the well is being poisoned even now for the realization of these goals before you can even get out of the gate, particularly on the issue of bipartisanship?

The President. No. But all I can do is speak for myself. I have tried to conduct the Presidency and to guard my words in a way that would make it clear that I intend to follow through on my commitment to try to establish a working partnership and a dynamic center, not a stable, stale one but a dynamic one, with people in both parties. I think we will have to continue to work on that.

As these—you know, just a few days ago, there were—when someone asked me if I thought that in the House the issue over the Speaker would poison the well, and I didn't, and I don't. I don't think it has. I just think that when matters come up that have to be dealt with, they need to be dealt with and disposed of. But the American people expect us to focus on how we can lift their lives and improve our conditions and move our people together and deal with the things that are before us. And I think if we do that and do it in a good-faith way, we'll be able to go forward.

Now, I'm very encouraged—let me just say this—the most encouraging thing has been, to me, the way that my budget proposals have been received. Even in criticism they have not been rejected outright. You know, 4 years ago when I came here, nobody in Congress took a President's budget seriously. They said, "Oh, his budget scenario is always rosy. The numbers are always cooked." And we now have 4 years in a row when I have presented conservative budget figures, when we've brought the deficit down by over 60 percent, and when, now, both sides are keeping their powder dry enough to create the possibility we can reach a balanced budget agreement. So, on balance, I'm still quite hopeful.

Peter [Peter Maer, NBC Mutual Radio].

Terrorist Attack in Dhahran, Saudi Arabia

Q. Mr. President, both your Attorney General and the FBI Director recently expressed concerns about the level of cooperation from Saudi Arabia into the investigation into the bombing that killed 19 American soldiers last year. What's your assessment of their level of cooperation, and do you have confidence in the security of the U.S. men who are still on duty there?

The President. Let me answer the second question first. We have worked very hard, as you know, since the Khobar incident, to enhance the security of our Armed Forces personnel in Saudi Arabia. In that endeavor, we have received the cooperation of the Saudi Government. We have relocated a large number of people. We have done a lot of work. We've invested a lot of money; so have they. And we believe that there is no such thing as a risk-free world, but we believe that our Armed Forces are more secure today. And we feel good about that.

On the investigation, clearly, for our point of view, in our Government, the FBI is in charge of that. They have sought the answers to some more questions. The Saudi Government has assured us from the very highest levels that they would get answers for those questions, and so I expect that to happen. And that's all I can tell you at this time. The process is ongoing. The investigation is ongoing. The relationship is ongoing.

As you can imagine, this creates—an investigation of this kind raises all kinds of complex questions about cooperation against sovereignty, about what other interests of that nation might be in play. But I'm confident that in the end they will do what I have been assured personally by the highest levels of the Saudi Government they should do.

Q. So you're satisfied with the level to this date?

The President. Well, it's still in process. We have to see if it comes out all right. But we still have—there are further requests for information that are ongoing. We'll see how it comes out.

Yes, Mr. Neikirk [Bill Neikirk, Chicago Tribune].

Hong Kong

Q. Mr. President, the Chinese have been making a lot of noises about clamping down on civil liberties in Hong Kong. How concerned are you about this, and will this upset our relationship in any way?

The President. Well, it wouldn't help anything. I'm concerned about it, and I think the—we don't know yet what's going to happen. But the Chinese have basically said that it would be a part of China, but its system would be left intact. And I think there may be some ambivalence about what it means to leave their system intact. And I think maybe some would assume that you could impose political uniformity on Hong Kong and leave its economic vibrancy intact. It really is, in some ways, almost a perfect open market, you know. And I don't know if that's true or not. It's a complex society.

I think anyone who has ever been to Hong Kong more than once—and I've been there on several occasions in my life—probably leaves with the feeling I have, that you could go there a thousand times and you might not ever understand it all. It's a complicated society. And I'm not so sure that it can exist, with all of its potential to help China modernize its own economy and open opportunities for its own people, if the civil liberties of the people are crushed.

So I think it would be wrong on its own merits, but I think it might wind up being less useful to China. So I would hope very much that they would look for ways to maximize the continuation not only of the economic system but of the personal freedoms that the people of Hong Kong have enjoyed in making it such an economic engine.

Yes.

Webster Hubbell and the Lippo Group

Q. Mr. President, the Lippo Group hired your friend Webb Hubbell after he resigned in a scandal from the Justice Department and just a few months before he went to jail for embezzlement. So far, no one has been able to determine what kind of work he was doing or why he was paid a sum reportedly in excess of $200,000. Does anything about this arrangement strike you as unusual or suspicious? And given that there have been public suggestions this money was offered to encourage his silence before the Whitewater investigator, have you taken any steps yourself to assure yourself that this is not the case?

The President. First of all, I didn't know about it. To the best of my recollection, I didn't know anything about his having that job until I read about it in the press. And I can't imagine who could have ever arranged to do something improper like that and no one around here to know about it. It was just not—we did not know anything about it, and I can tell you categorically that that did not happen. I knew nothing about it, none of us did, before it happened. And I didn't personally know anything about it until I read about it in the press.

So I don't think—I think when somebody makes a charge like that, there ought to be some burden on them to come forward with some evidence to substantiate their charge instead of saying, "We'll make a charge; see if you can disprove it." That's not the way things work, and that's a pretty irresponsible charge to make without knowing—having some evidence of it. And I'm just telling you it's not so.

Yes, Rita [Rita Braver, CBS News].

Campaign Finance and White House Access

Q. Back on this issue of fundraising. You've talked about it maybe in general terms, but specifically last week the White House put out a list of coffees. It showed that at one coffee that included the Comptroller of the Currency, the Secretary of the Treasury, there were people who—bankers who had contributed something like $325,000. You attended that coffee. There was another coffee with another regulator of the Consumer Product Safety Commission;

something like $500,000 was contributed by people who were at that coffee. And I wondered if, in retrospect, you had any feelings about, number one, regulators being at political coffees, and also your own participation. Obviously, you're not going to be doing this again for your own reelection, but is this something that you have decided you will continue doing, and what have you come to in your own mind on this issue?

The President. I have a different opinion about my participation and the regulators' participation. First, let me tell you about—I can only comment on the first instance you mentioned, the bankers meeting. I think it is an appropriate thing and can be a good thing for the President and for the Secretary of Treasury to meet with a group of bankers and listen to them and listen to their concerns and, if they have certain issues, to explore those issues.

I can tell you categorically that no decision ever came out of any of those coffees where I or anyone else said, "This person is a contributor of ours; do what they asked us to do." But I think those meetings are good. I think the President should keep in touch with people. I think he should listen to people. I never learn very much when I'm talking, and I normally learn something when I'm listening. So I think that they're good.

In retrospect, since the DNC sponsored it, I do not think the Comptroller of the Currency should have been there. I agree with Mr. Ludwig, and he should have been told who was sponsoring it, and it would have been better had he not come. I agree with that. But I think there is a distinction to be made between the President meeting with people, listening to them, and then, at least if they raise some serious issues, having them looked into. But I never made a decision for anybody because they were contributors of mine. I don't—but I do think it's important to listen to people.

But you're right—or he was right, it would have been better if he had not been there. Regulators should not come to meetings that are sponsored—have any kind of political sponsorship, I don't think.

Q. So you intend to keep going with these coffees, sir? Do you intend to keep going with these coffees?

The President. I don't know. But I can tell you—well, I intend to keep going with coffees. I don't know whether they'll be sponsored by the DNC or whether we'll just bring them in through our own regular offices. But I also had lots and lots and lots of coffees over the last 4 years that had nothing to do with the DNC, where a lot of people came were not contributors or even active supporters of mine, but they were from different walks of life around the country. And I found them very helpful, where I would just sit down and talk for 4 or 5 minutes and then listen for an hour or so and maybe ask questions based on whatever people had to say to me.

I think it's an effective way for the President to hear firsthand how the operations of the Government or developments in the country are affecting people. So I think that the coffees themselves are a very good device. But I do believe, particularly if sponsored by a political party, it's not appropriate for the regulator to be there.

Social Security and the Budget

Q. Thank you, Mr. President. A number of Democrats in Congress oppose a balanced budget amendment to the Constitution unless the Government promises to stop spending surplus Social Security funds, borrowing and spending them. Would you—though you oppose an amendment, you will propose a balanced budget; will you stop using surplus Social Security funds?

The President. Well, the using—the funds that are collected on Social Security are going to be invested in some way. When you say "using," what they do, they cover the deficit by basically being sold for Government securities. Social Security is not, therefore, in effect separated from the Government. But those securities will come back with interest to the Government later on. And by then, what will have to happen is, when we start running short of money 20 years or so from now, the Government will have to have been on a balanced budget for some years by then, so that when the bonds are repaid, they can be used to pay Social Security.

We couldn't right now, neither the Republicans nor I and the Congress, could produce a balanced budget tomorrow that could pass, if you said the Social Security funds cannot be counted, if you will, as part of the budget.

But let me say—you raise an interesting question, however, which is why I don't favor this amendment—I've given the Congress a plan to balance the budget. I've made it clear that we

will work with them to meet the Congressional Budget Office budgetary projections. And we're going to do this. And now they know that I have credibility because we've worked on it for 4 years and we've done almost two-thirds of the work.

When you amend the Constitution, you do it forever. No one can foresee the circumstances that will come a generation from now or 50 years from now or even 10 years from now. And the way I read the amendment, it would almost certainly require after a budget is passed, if the economic estimates turn out to be wrong, the executive branch, the President, the Treasury Department, to impound Social Security checks or to turn it over to courts to decide what to be done. And it would put us in a position, in my view, of doing things that are counterproductive.

The Congress—[*inaudible*]—is about to vote on this—the House is—against a background of 4 years of stable growth and 4 years of declining deficits. But we don't know what external factors in the world might be brought to bear on our country in the next 10 or 15 years that might have terribly counterproductive impulses if we were cutting aid to children and raising taxes in the teeth of a big recession or we were impounding Social Security checks or something of that kind. I just think that the Congress has an obligation to think of what could happen here in the future and ask themselves whether they really want to straitjacket the United States.

What we ought to do is follow prudent policies, balance the budget, and go forward. But we shouldn't compromise what might happen 10, 15 years from now with an amendment to the Constitution. I think it's bad economic policy and bad policy. And I think we're going to wind up with some decisions in the courts and some decisions on Social Security and aid to kids and other things that future generations won't be very grateful to us for just because it seemed so popular now because we haven't balanced the budget since 1969.

Q. If I may, Mr. President, could I just follow up? Mr. President, could I just follow up on one thing? There are a number of reform plans around that would give people part of their taxes back to put into private accounts. If it was only part of their taxes and some sort of safety net was preserved, would you favor some private accounts out of Social Security tax money?

The President. Well, first of all, I would favor nothing that would compromise the integrity of the system. Secondly, even the Social Security Advisory Commission couldn't agree on that, so I can't make a decision on that, to support something like that, without knowing more about it.

There are two different options that were recommended—or three different ones—and I just—I think that what we need to do, as I've said before, we need to make some changes in Social Security to lengthen its life a little bit. We don't want to start getting in trouble in 2019; it ought to have a longer lifespan than that. And we ought to do it through a bipartisan process that is either like the one that was done in 1983 or that at least consults all the people who will be affected by it. And I think that if we start now, we can make modest changes that won't be too burdensome to anybody, that will secure Social Security for another 50 years. And I think that's what we ought to be doing.

District of Columbia

Q. Mr. President, I wonder if we could just shift the focus briefly to something you've become much more interested in lately, the troubled Capital City here. The District of Columbia Congresswoman has reintroduced her wide-ranging tax cut plan today, which offers relief on the Federal level for everybody, and the working poor would indeed be eliminated, as you know. She is also saying today that she wants your help on this and she thinks that her tax plan should be included in your new DC recovery plan, that the one cannot work without the other, and that time is fast slipping out for the Capital City, that action needs to be taken soon or we're going to go down the tubes.

The President. Well, let me say, I believe that we should have a three-point plan. One is the thing that Congresswoman Norton and I agree on, that we should have the Federal Government assume those things that are now burdening the District of Columbia that in every other place in the country those costs are borne by State governments, not local governments. You can't expect any city to function and be successful if they have to pay the State's cost as well as the city's cost, raise taxes when people can go right across the Potomac River or right up the road into Maryland and have the same cost

borne in a different way. So I think that responsibility shift is important.

Secondly, I think the Federal Government needs a more disciplined effort to see what else we can do within the resources we now have to help DC in law enforcement, in education, in transportation, right across—and housing and homelessness.

Thirdly, I think there needs to be an economic incentive in the form of tax relief. Now, I haven't seen what Congresswoman Norton introduced today. The last time this came up, the folks at Treasury and OMB thought that the proposal was more costly than we could afford. But I intend to make one, and I think it will be a significant incentive for people to invest in DC and to help to grow the economy here. I think that's a very important component. So I agree with her on the general point. I just have to see the specifics before I can make a commitment.

Yes, Mara [Mara Liasson, National Public Radio].

Q. I wonder if I could just follow up?

China and Human Rights

Q. Your annual human rights report is about to come out this week. It's reported that it will say there are no active dissidents in China. They're either all exiled, or they're in jail. Does this mean that your policy of constructive engagement has failed to get the kind of results you wanted to get on China's human rights behavior?

The President. It means that we have not made the progress in human rights that I think—that I had hoped to make, yes. But it does not mean that if we had followed a policy of isolating ourselves from China, when no one else in the world was prepared to do that, that we would have gotten better results. And I think—I still believe, over the long run, being engaged with China, working with them where we can agree—which helps us on a whole range of security issues that directly bear on the welfare of the American people, like the problems on the Korean Peninsula—and continuing to be honest and forthright and insistent where we disagree has the greatest likelihood of having a positive impact on China.

Keep in mind, the time horizon here for how we judge them has to be broadened a little bit. They tend to look at things in a long-time horizon. They're going through some significant changes themselves within their country, economic and political changes. And I believe that the impulses of the society and the nature of the economic change will work together, along with the availability of information from the outside world, to increase the sphere of liberty over time. I don't think there is any way that anyone who disagrees with that in China can hold back that, just as eventually the Berlin Wall fell. I just think it's inevitable. And I regret that we haven't had more progress there more quickly, but I still believe that the policy we're following is the correct one.

Jim [Jim Miklaszewski, NBC News].

Campaign Finance Reform

Q. Mr. President, some lawmakers on Capitol Hill still think it would be a good idea to appoint an independent counsel to investigate some of the campaign fundraising that occurred last year. And at the same time—what's your latest thinking on that? And at the same time, if I may, you often decry what you call a cynicism that you believe is pervasive in Washington, but given the amounts of money that were raised last year, the way they were raised, and some of the explanations for the way they were raised, isn't the public entitled to a little bit of healthy skepticism, if not cynicism, about the entire process?

The President. Well, to answer your first question, I'm going to take Bob Dole's advice because that's a decision for the Attorney General to make. And to answer your second question, yes, healthy skepticism is warranted. But keep in mind, I would say to the skeptics, the vast majority—indeed, a huge percentage, way, way over 90 percent—I don't know what it would be—the vast majority of the money that was raised by both the Democrats and the Republicans was raised in a perfectly lawful fashion, completely consistent with the requirements of the law. The vast majority of the people who gave money to both the Democrats and the Republicans were people who believed passionately in the course that those two parties were pursuing and the candidates and what they were trying to do—and to their House committees and the Senate committees.

The problem is that the margins create great problems because of the sheer volume of money that is being raised today. As I said before, it's too much money, takes too much time to raise, raises too many questions. And the cyni-

cism is well—and the skepticism is well-founded. If it becomes cynicism, then it removes the incentive on the part of the Congress to pass campaign finance reform because cynics will say it won't make any difference anyway.

If you look at the present campaign laws, I think you can make a compelling case. I have not heard this point made, but I believe it to be true. I believe when these reforms arose out of the Watergate thing back in the mid-seventies, I think they worked pretty well for several years. I believe they elevated the reputation of politics, and I think the reforms worked pretty well. What happened is, no system in a world changing like ours can be maintained indefinitely, because the economy changes and particularly—look at how your work has changed. When you travel with me, you carry these little computers around, and you run these pictures up on computers, and you send them from the plane somewhere else. I mean, just think of all the things that have changed. This system has not been fixed in over 20 years. During that 20 years, there has been an explosion in ways of communicating with people and an exponential increase in the cost of communicating. And a system which I would argue to you really worked pretty well, after it was passed in '74 and going forward, has been overtaken by events.

So, cynical, no; healthy skepticism, you bet. We should always be skeptical. But we need to change the system. It's got to be—it's just outdated.

Ellen [Ellen Ratner, Talk Radio News Service].

Welfare Reform

Q. Mr. President, what specific mechanisms do you plan on working with the private sector in terms of creating more welfare jobs for people who are on welfare?

The President. Primarily two. One, I will offer a special tax incentive—there was a story about it today, I think, in the New York Times—a special tax incentive that'll be a 50 percent credit for up to $10,000 a year in pay for people who are clearly, provably hired from welfare and put into new jobs.

Secondly, we have given the States—and there was a story, I think, in the Post today talking about how a lot of the States are trying to push this down to the community level. That's good. That's not bad, that's good, as long as they give the communities the means they need.

The second thing is that every community should know that the employers in that community, if they hire people from welfare to work, can get what used to be the welfare check for at least a year to use as an employment and training subsidy. Why? The welfare rolls have gone down 2.1 million in the last 4 years; it's the biggest drop in history. I think a fair reading of it would say about half of this decline came from an improved economy and about half of it came from intensified efforts to move people from welfare to work. Now, I don't have any scientific division, but anyway, there's some division there.

The rest of the people that are on welfare now, by and large, are people who will be more difficult to move from welfare to work and have stay there. So I think we're going to have to give some incentives. But if it works and if every community in the country would set up an employment council and turn this into a family and an employment program like Kansas City has and all employers have those two incentives, I think we'll be able to meet the requirements of this welfare reform bill in a way that will be good for the people on welfare and good for their kids.

Kathy [Kathy Lewis, Dallas Morning News].

Legal Immigrants and the Budget

Q. Mr. President, the chairman of the House Ways and Means Committee over the weekend laid down some markers for what he thinks would create chances for your budget to be alive on arrival on the Hill. On welfare, one of the things he mentioned was increased spending for legal immigrants, and he said he hoped you wouldn't insist on it. How do you deal with that in your budget, and will you continue to insist on it?

The President. Well, let me say, I like Mr. Archer very much, and we've had a good relationship, and I appreciate what he said about me meeting him halfway on Medicare. But there have been reports in the last couple of days about Republican Governors with high immigrant populations coming back to their Republican congressional leaders and saying, "Please reconsider this."

My budget will contain funds and propose changes consistent with the promises I made when I signed the welfare reform bill and when

I campaigned to the American people on this issue. I believe that the bill is counterproductive in the way it treats legal immigrants who through no fault of their own wind up in desperate circumstances and in other ways that I think are not good for families and children.

So I will propose some changes. And I hope that when we get all through here—again, I hope this will be treated just like the budget issue—I would ask our friends on the Republican side and the Democrats who care as passionately about this as I do to keep our powder dry. Let us make our case on the merits. Let them hear from the Republican Governors of places like Texas and New York that have these huge immigrant populations of good people that are making great contributions to this country, that are working like crazy and making this a better place, and listen to the practical impact of the law that's now there on the immigrant population. And I'm not sure we can't get some changes. I'm very hopeful that we can, and I'm going to give it my very best effort.

Q. Mr. President——

The President. Wait a minute, I'll take a couple of more. Just a minute.

Deborah [Deborah Mathis, Gannett News Service]. No, no, Sarah's [Sarah McClendon, McClendon News Service] next. Let Deborah talk.

Go ahead.

Campaign Finance Reform

Q. To follow up on Jim Miklaszewski's question, the people are not just skeptical or cynical about politics or about campaign finance. They are more specifically cynical and skeptical and suspicious of this White House, of this administration, partly because of the way information has trickled out, the way memories have been stubborn and sometimes revised at the last moment—at an opportune moment, it would seem. And I'm wondering what's new about the White House now and the way you handle delicate information, and what you want to tell the people about it?

The President. First of all, I want to tell the people, when you get asked hundreds of questions, it's not possible to remember the answer to every one. I think some of these people make honest mistakes. I read things in your reports all the time that aren't quite factually accurate, but I don't think you deliberately did it. It's impossible to do—we're living in a society that is deluged in information. So I think that what we've all got to be candid enough to say is, no one is blameless here; it costs so much money to pay for these campaigns, that mistakes were made here by people who either did it deliberately or inadvertently. Now, it's up to others to decide whether those mistakes were made deliberately or inadvertently. It's up to me to do what I can to clean up the system.

Now, what should they believe about us? Well, first of all, I got the Democratic Party to make some unilateral changes in its fundraising policies and asked our friends in the Republican Party to do the same and offered to completely get rid of the so-called soft money, the larger contributions, if they would. Secondly, we're out here working hard as a party, as a White House, and me personally as President, to pass the McCain-Feingold bill which would put an end to these problems and modernize this system. So I think that's quite important.

Now, I do not believe you will ever get the politics out of politics. That is—and that's not bad. I think people who fight for candidates and who help them and who help parties will be people that the people who represent them want to hear from and want to maintain access to. I don't think there is anything wrong with that. That's the way the system works. And I don't think anyone should imply that your first obligation once you get elected is to stop talking to the people that helped you get there.

But I think that we've got to improve the system. And I understand why the cynicism is there. But again I will say, I'd ask you to look— way, way over 90 percent of all the people who gave money and way over 90 percent of all the people who gave—of all the money that was raised is clearly consistent with the law in both parties, as far as I know. I mean, I can't really speak for the Republicans, but I'd be astonished if that were not so. I would be astonished if it were not so.

So there is no pattern and practice here of trying to push our system over the brink into corruption. What happens is, there is a race to get as much money as you can to keep from being buried by the other people and to make sure you can get your own message out and, at the edges, errors are made. And when they're made, they need to be confessed, and we need to assume responsibility for them. And that's what I'm trying to do up here today. But I can't say, Deborah, in response to your question,

that I know that any of these people who gave insufficient answers to you did it in a deliberate or deceptive way, because a lot of times people just ask questions, and they don't have all the answers. And they're trying to cooperate and don't do such a good job.

Sarah, go ahead. I promised you a question.

Health Care

Q. Sir, the National Coalition on Health Care has issued a wonderful report. It's the largest consumer organization on the subject. They say that at 58 million people, 60 percent of those people were against the present health care system as being totally inadequate, and they don't have faith in it. Now, we heard last year a lot of stuff about how people were satisfied with the most wonderful health care system in the world. Well, apparently, that's baloney, according to this report. And there's a lot of talk being done about preserving Medicare, but Medicare won't do it. It won't go all the way to take care of the people of this country. And this report shows that they simply cannot meet the big bills of hospitals and doctors. Aren't you going to try again this year with Hillary to devise a good national health care program for this country?

The President. Well, I read that report, and I found it very interesting. But I think what that report was saying—and again, I don't want to read between the lines, all I did was read a news column on it—but I can tell you what I got out of it, and then let me respond to your question. What I got out of it was people said, "Well, I may feel good about my doctor or my local hospital, but I'm worried about the security of this system. I'm worried about whether, if managed care controls everything, whether I'll lose any control over important decisions affecting my life. I'm worried about whether if I lose insurance here, whether I can take it there."

And what I think we have to do is to recognize that our society—and I think we've played a role in it here, but I think the whole system deserves credit for it—we've done a much better job in holding down inflation in medical care and bringing it closer to the general rate of inflation. There's some indication it's going up again, but I hope we can keep it down. And we have done a better job of some other things, like ending the 48-hour delivery rule and all that. But we have not—or the 24-hour delivery.

But we have not done enough to increase access to affordable care for people who don't have coverage, to deal with the problem that there are still a lot of children in working families that are poor who aren't covered and to deal with the fact that there are people who are unemployed who, even though we just made it legal for them to carry their insurance with them when the Kennedy-Kassebaum bill passed last year, they can't afford to do that.

So in my budget, we will have, in effect, an unemployment health insurance plan to help people, families who have insurance keep it when they're employed. And I intend over the next 4 years to work very hard to try to find other ways, as I said, in a step-by-step way to allow people affordable access to this system. It will never be completely stable for anyone until everyone at least has affordable access to it.

Yes, one foreign person over here.

Middle East Peace Process

Q. Mr. President—Mr. President, both Israel and Syria seem willing and ready to come to the negotiating table, and they both want American diplomacy as an honest broker. Prime Minister Netanyahu will come to Washington next month. How will you act together to energize this track and reach comprehensive peace in the Middle East, which is clearly a top priority of your administration?

The President. Well, Prime Minister Netanyahu, Chairman Arafat, King Hussein, and President Mubarak are all coming here in the next couple of months. And I must say again how much I appreciate the agreement reached on Hebron and the other understandings reached between Prime Minister Netanyahu and Chairman Arafat and the fact that so far things seem to be being implemented in an appropriate way and going all right.

There will never be a comprehensive peace in the Middle East until we resolve this matter with Syria—between Syria and Israel. And that requires the willingness of the parties. What our experience has been, mine, the Secretary of State, Secretary Christopher, and now Secretary Albright, Mr. Ross, and our whole team—has been that when both parties want to make peace, no matter how far apart they seem, we've found a way to get there. If they're not sure it's time to make peace, no matter how close it seems to an outsider, we don't seem to be

able to bridge the gap. So you can be sure that that will be a major focus of our discussion, whether we can find a way to work together.

Yes.

Medicare

Q. Mr. President, your Medicare reform plan was criticized for relying too heavily on savings squeezed from health care providers. Why shouldn't Americans who can afford to pay higher Medicare premiums pay them?

The President. Let me respond to the criticism. First of all, in my health care reform proposal I supported higher income—increases in Medicare premiums on higher income Americans, but it was part of a comprehensive health care reform. What I was attempting to do, after meeting at some length with Secretary Shalala who worked through these issues with me, the specifics of the Medicare reform, was to demonstrate that we could balance the budget, meet the Republicans halfway, and put 10 years on the life of the Trust Fund without a premium increase. If we're going to have a longer term Medicare reform—I have never said that I would rule that out, but I didn't want to rule it in. I presented a budget that was consistent with my priorities. And I'm prepared to meet with Senator Lott and discuss that and other issues. But I presented a budget that I though was the best budget to achieve our objectives.

You've been trying to stand up all this time. Go ahead.

Campaign Fundraising Investigation

Q. Thank you, sir. When you are finished here, Mr. President, Senator Thompson is expected to go to the Senate floor to discuss his committee's investigation into these fundraising issues. I'm wondering if you would like to say something to him regarding White House cooperation and the possibility of looking into Republican fundraising as well.

The President. I have instructed everybody here to fully cooperate with him. My new Counsel, Mr. Ruff, is going to meet with Senator Thompson and the appropriate people, and we will be fully cooperative. I think that's very important.

And on the question of the Republicans, I just want him to be fair. I think that it's very important to be fair and even-handed, because I'm confident that any investigations will reveal what I said, that the vast majority of people who give do so well within the law and with the best of motives; they really believe in what they're doing—on both sides. And what we need to do is find out whether there are any systematic flaws here that need to be addressed and address them. But in the end, I'm telling you, no matter what this hearing uncovers, in the end, if you want to get rid of—if you want to turn cynicism back into skepticism, you have to pass McCain-Feingold or some other acceptable campaign finance reform.

Mr. Cannon [Carl Cannon, Baltimore Sun]. I'll take one more question.

Capital Gains Taxes

Q. Mr. President, in Chicago the day you gave your acceptance speech at the convention, you unveiled a plan in which homeowners would not have to pay virtually any capital gains taxes. We haven't heard much about it since then. And my question is, is that going to be in your budget, that proposal, and will you go a little further if the Republicans want to do a little more on capital gains?

The President. The answer is, yes, my homeowners exemption, capital gains exemption is in the budget. Everything I talked about at Chicago is in the budget. And the capital gains issue has never been a particularly high priority with me because I've never seen it demonstrated as a big engine of economic growth overall and because I thought the previous— as you know, this is nothing new—the proposal that the Republicans made in their budget I thought was entirely excessive and would really almost squander money by having it be retroactive.

But what I've—I have tried to practice what I preach here. I want to keep our powder dry; I want them to keep their powder dry. I will present a budget. I know what my priorities are. I know what theirs are on the taxes. And then what we need to do is to meet each other in good faith. This and all other issues can best be resolved by an early attempt to work through to a balanced budget agreement.

Thank you very much.

NOTE: The President's 134th news conference began at 2:30 p.m. in the East Room at the White House. In his remarks, he referred to former Senator Bob Dole, 1996 Republican nominee for President; Prime Minister Binyamin Netanyahu of Israel; Chairman Yasser Arafat of the Palestinian Authority; King Hussein I of Jordan; and President Hosni Mubarak of Egypt.

Preface to the Report Entitled "Support for a Democratic Transition in Cuba"
January 28, 1997

The promotion of democracy abroad is one of the primary foreign policy objectives of my Administration. These efforts reflect our ideals and reinforce our interests—preserving America's security and enhancing our prosperity. Democracies are less likely to go to war with one another or to abuse the rights of their peoples. They make for better trading partners. And each one is a potential ally in the struggle against the forces of hatred and intolerance, whether rogue nations, those who foment ethnic and religious hatred, or terrorists who traffic in weapons of mass destruction.

Today, freedom's reach is broader than ever. For the first time in history, two thirds of all nations have governments elected by their own people. As newly democratic nations have left the dark years of authoritarian government behind, millions of their citizens around the world have begun to experience the political and economic freedoms that they were so long and so wrongfully denied.

Creating open societies and democratic institutions and building free markets are major tasks that call for courage and commitment. To face these challenges, many democratizing and newly democratic governments have turned to developed democratic nations and international institutions for assistance and support. The United States has been at the forefront of these efforts, lending help in numerous areas in which we have long experience—for example, building democratic institutions and the institutions of a market economy, and protecting human rights through an effective and impartial justice system.

Cubans, like the other peoples of this hemisphere, of Eastern Europe, and of the former Soviet Union, desire to be free. The United States is committed to help the Cuban people in a transition to democracy. We will continue working with others in the international community who share our desire to welcome Cuba into the ranks of prosperous democratic nations, where it will proudly join the other thirty-four countries in this hemisphere.

This document outlines the assistance that a democratizing Cuba is likely to seek during its transition, and the ways in which the United States and the international community will try to help. It draws from the experiences of other countries that have embarked upon similar transitions and highlights some of the lessons learned from those processes. It is my sincere hope that it will contribute to a better understanding of the international community's potential role in a transition to democracy and underscore the strong commitment of the American people to support the Cuban people when they embark upon that process of change.

WILLIAM J. CLINTON

NOTE: An original was not available for verification of the content of this preface.

Letter to Congressional Leaders Transmitting the Report Entitled "Support for a Democratic Transition in Cuba"
January 28, 1997

Dear Mr. Chairman:

Pursuant to section 202(g) of the Cuban Liberty and Democratic Solidarity (LIBERTAD) Act of 1996 (Public Law 104–114), I hereby transmit to you a report concerning assistance to a free and independent Cuba, entitled "Support for a Democratic Transition in Cuba."

The report includes an addendum of indicative roles for various agencies of the United States Government. This is for internal United States Government use and is not intended for publication. The remainder of the report will be translated into Spanish to be communicated to the Cuban people pursuant to section 202(f) of the Act.

Sincerely,

WILLIAM J. CLINTON

NOTE: Identical letters were sent to Jesse Helms, chairman, Senate Committee on Foreign Relations; Ted Stevens, chairman, Senate Committee on Appropriations; Benjamin A. Gilman, chairman, House Committee on International Relations; and Robert L. Livingston, chairman, House Committee on Appropriations.

Message to the Senate Transmitting the Thailand-United States Taxation Convention With Documentation
January 28, 1997

To the Senate of the United States:

I transmit herewith for Senate advice and consent to ratification the Convention Between the Government of the United States of America and the Government of the Kingdom of Thailand for the Avoidance of Double Taxation and the Prevention of Fiscal Evasion with Respect to Taxes on Income, signed at Bangkok, November 26, 1996. An enclosed exchange of notes, transmitted for the information of the Senate, provides clarification with respect to the application of the Convention in specified cases. Also transmitted is the report of the Department of State concerning the Convention.

This Convention, which is similar to other tax treaties between the United States and developing nations, provides maximum rates of tax to be applied to various types of income and protection from double taxation of income. The Convention also provides for the exchange of information to prevent fiscal evasion and sets forth standard rules to limit the benefits of the Convention to persons that are not engaged in treaty shopping.

I recommend that the Senate give early and favorable consideration to this Convention and give its advice and consent to ratification.

WILLIAM J. CLINTON

The White House,
January 28, 1997.

Remarks at a Democratic Business Council Dinner
January 28, 1997

Thank you very much. Well, thank you, Carol. Thank you, Steve. Roy, I won't ever make you stay in that bed again. [*Laughter*] I was simply trying to get even for all the nights he's bent my ear. [*Laughter*]

I want to thank all the officers of the Democratic Party who are here, all the distinguished elected officials, and all the members of our administration who are here. And I want to thank you.

Some of you may have noticed that I had a press conference today where there was one or two questions about campaign finance. [*Laughter*] And they said, "Well, does it set a good example that you're going to this fundraiser tonight?" And I said, "Yes, I think it does, because there is no system which has been offered which is completely publicly funded from start to finish and funds the political parties. So we have to depend upon people to help us."

And this group, as Alan Solomont said earlier, has been responsible for dramatically increasing the number of business people and entrepreneurs all across America that have been a part of our party, broadening our base, giving us a chance to go forward. I thank you, Tom, for being willing to take over the leadership of it. I think it's a good thing if people like Tom or Steve, who had a very successful career in business and worked at the grassroots level, want to come in and be part of the Democratic Party.

I also think it's terribly important that the President see as many people as possible, from as many walks of life as possible, from as many places in this country as possible, who actually know something about what's going on in the country and how people are living and what the challenges are.

And as I said today, I never had anyone in 4 years who asked me to make a decision as President based on being a financial contributor, and I have never made such a decision. But I think we should listen to each other. I mean, you all have to listen to me all the time, and every now and then for me to take a little time to listen to you I think is pretty good because even Presidents need to learn. And almost no one learns when they're talking, and almost no one fails to learn when they're listening.

So I think this is a good thing, and I welcome you here, and I hope you're glad to be here. And let me also say that—[*applause*]—thank you. Having said that, I do want to compliment the new leadership of the party and the old leadership of the party for taking some unilateral initiatives to push the campaign finance reform system along by coming out against things that are legal that we're not going to do anymore because we want to try to push the system along, saying that if you can't vote, you shouldn't contribute, that companies that are primarily foreign-owned should not contribute, and that we would limit our large contributions. I think that's a good thing.

But I also would urge you to help us pass a campaign finance reform bill that is fair, that is bipartisan, that does not give undue advantage to either party, and that gives challengers as well as incumbents a fair chance at the ears, the minds, and the hearts of the voters. I think that's a very important thing to do.

We were talking around the table here at dinner—my impression is—and I ran for Congress in 1974 and got beat, by the way, but I did all right—but that was the first election under the old campaign finance reform, which was then the new campaign finance reform law. And my impression is that it did work to give people a greater degree of confidence that there were reasonable rules, regulations, and balance in the funding system.

What's happened now is, the explosion of technology and the escalation of cost and the multiplication of the way people communicate with one another and the proliferation of various groups who are doing it and two Supreme Court decisions have basically swamped the old system.

Now, there are very few of you who run enterprises who, even if you've been in business 20 years, could possibly be using the same communication system with the same budget in the same way that you were 20 years ago. So it is unreasonable to expect that our Nation could have the right balance drawn between having a system that is largely privately financed but has adequate rules of disclosure, rules of conduct, and limitations, with a system that was written over 20 years ago, during which time we've had the biggest explosion in differences in the way people communicate and relate to each other politically than in any 20-year period certainly in the 20th century. So I hope you will help us get that done.

The other point I'd like to make to you tonight is that you ought to be proud of what you have done. You know that the—sort of the superficial results. In '96 we had our first successful reelection for a President in 60 years. And someone, just to make sure I understood that, sent me the January 4, 1937 copy of Life Magazine, which I had framed and hung up in the White House so I don't forget that.

We elected a Democrat the first Asian-American Governor in the United States, something I'm very proud of. That's another thing I want to say. We welcome first-generation immigrant Americans into the Democratic Party; we want them here. And it has been my personal experience—one of the richest aspects of being President and running for President twice has been getting to know in a personal way very large numbers of people who are first-generation Americans, who still come to our shores seeking opportunity and making opportunity. And virtually without exception, they give this country many times over what they ever ask from it. And I think that is a very good thing.

We had the first woman Governor ever in the State of New Hampshire. And we carried New Hampshire for the second time, and that's only happened three times in the history of the State, that a Democrat's won there twice. And I'm very grateful to them.

We had 100 new Democratic legislators. We picked up some seats in the House.

So we're—those things were good. But what I want you to do is just take a minute tonight to look behind that, to understand what I believe 20, 30 years from now when people look back on this time, what they will say about it. For almost 30 years, the other party has dominated Presidential politics, and the salient issues dividing the voters, I would argue, have been the power of appeals to people's differences based on race and religion and extreme political views, as opposed to appeal to community.

In the last 16 years, the argument of what we Democrats called trickle-down economics and what the other fellows called supply-side economics—that is, that if you cut taxes enough you would generate so much revenue the budget would be balanced, and if it wasn't it didn't really matter, and we quadrupled our debt in 12 years following that theory—and the argument that the Government is the problem and so if we just chocked Washington full of people who hated their Government, things would be wonderful out in the country—if you go all the way back to '68 and watch the Presidential elections unfold, any analysis would say that those things were very powerful components of that.

What has happened in just the last 4 years? Number one, we haven't abolished the divisive feelings Americans have about each other, but we've come a long way toward subordinating them to the idea that we are one community, and we're better off if we relate to each other across the lines that divide us, and it's a big part of our meal ticket to the 21st century. That is a huge, significant step forward.

And even in places where people didn't agree with me about specific issues—for example, when I stood up for the proposition that affirmative action should be reformed but not abolished at this point in time—in California the voters disagreed in the vote on the initiative, but they voted for the Clinton/Gore ticket for reelection. Why? Because I think people know deep down inside, we've got to go forward together. That's a big thing. It's a significant change.

Number two, the theory of trickle-down economics was tested and abolished in 1993 with our budget, our much maligned budget passed only by members of our party. Four years later, we know who was right and who was wrong. We have had—[applause]—the deficit went down by almost two-thirds. Inequality decreased among working families for the first time in 20 years. We increased our investment in education and technology. And the economy produced 11 million jobs plus for the first time in a 4-year term in history. So we replaced trickle-down economics with invest-and-grow economics—and trade and reach out to the rest of the world. It's working. That is a significant thing.

And the third thing we did, I talked about in the Inaugural. We said Government is not the problem—that's wrong—but Government is not the solution. We have to be the solution. Democratic Government is simply the gift our Founders gave us to meet our challenges and to pursue our dreams that must be met and pursued in common. And the primary function of Government today is to give people the tools they need to make the most of their own lives, to build strong careers, strong families, and strong communities, and then to keep us the world's strongest force for peace and freedom and democracy. And we have done that. And you should be very proud of that. That is what you helped to create.

There are other things. Social problems used to be rhetorical instruments of political campaigns which no one really expected to change very much. So whether you were tough on crime or not was largely a function of who could talk tougher in campaigns. We went out and wrote a crime bill based on what the police officers, the community patrol people, the community leaders in this country said would work to bring the crime rate down and to contribute to what people were doing in some communities already in America to bring the crime rate down. And we know that community policing, we know that tougher punishment for repeat offenders, and we know that giving young kids something to say yes to as well as something to say no to all work. And we've had now 4 years of declining crime. That is a very significant thing. Nobody has to believe that crime is inevitable anymore.

We had—long before this welfare bill passed, we were out there giving States and communities permission to try new things that would move people from welfare to work, and 2.1 million people now have moved in only 4 years from welfare to work, the biggest decline in American history.

And let me just say—I want to say some more about that in a minute, but my decision to sign the welfare reform bill was based in large measure on my unshakable conviction that we can go the rest of the way and that we have to build a community-based system where able-bodied people are not segregated, the unemployed, from those on welfare. We need a family- and work-oriented, community-based system of full employment for people who are capable of working.

And of course, when the economy is down, there will be more people out of work. And when the economy is working, there will be more people in work. But you have to play a role in that, and I'll say something about that in a minute.

This was a huge deal. Nobody believes that the welfare rolls have to grow forever now— 2.1 million fewer people on welfare. So social problems are something more than the rhetoric of campaigns now, they're about how people live.

We've also put what I think of as the right kind of family values back at the center of our policymaking. What is it we can do to help families cope with the challenges of family and work and family and culture? That's what the Family and Medical Leave Act was all about. That's what the V-chip and the television rating systems were all about. That's what all that was about. How are people going to juggle all these balls and still do the most important thing in life, which is to do a good job raising their children? It's the number one job any person ever has. How can we do that?

Well, we're moving in the right direction on that. All these changes have been made in just the last 4 years. It's a good basis from which we have to go forward. And I'm going to give the State of the Union Address in a few days, and I will focus on what I hope we can do together, working with the Republicans to balance the budget, to put education front and center on our national agenda so we have national standards and we open the doors of college to all, to build on this families first agenda, and to keep the crime rate coming down, and to expand health care coverage, and to reform the systems of Social Security and Medicare so they're there for the next generation and they don't bankrupt the budget, and to continue to reach out to the rest of the world.

And this is the last thing I'd like to say. Because I believe we should talk, and I should also listen as well as talk, I always tell people who contribute to our efforts that you have even more opportunities and responsibilities to make your voice heard. And I would like to just say two things. There are many things I will ask for your help on, but I want to serve notice there are two things that I will ask for your help on.

Number one relates to what Mr. Grossman used to do before he came to the party. I said if Steve Grossman could run AIPAC and keeps those folks together, he ought to be able to unify the Democrats. And all the members of AIPAC thought that was funny.

But one of the things that we have to recognize is, there is no such thing in the 21st century as being strong at home and therefore saying you don't care what happens abroad. We cannot be strong at home unless we are also strong abroad. And that is about more than the defense budget. That means they're going—that means, among other things, now that they're reforming the United Nations, we have new leadership, we've got to pay the money we owe them. We can't any longer be the biggest debtor at the U.N. We've got to show up and pay our way. We can't expect to lead the world if we won't even do the minimal required of a responsible country.

And number two, we have to invest some measure of our money. We spend less of our budget than any great country in the world on foreign affairs, but we have to spend enough to enable our country to lead the way for peace and freedom. And I hope you will help us convince the Congress of that, and our fellow citizens.

Second, and closer to home, I know that this welfare reform bill can be made to work. I think we have to change some of the provisions relating to immigrants and some other things, but the substance of the bill simply says, if you're able-bodied, within 2 years you have to move from welfare to work. And if you do, as Governor Romer said, we'll give you more child care; we'll support you in other ways; we'll

keep the health care guarantee for your kids; we'll help you with transportation. But you have to do it.

Now, you might say that is inherently impossible because last year in a boom economy there were six applicants for every entry-level job opening in Chicago and nine for every entry-level job opening in St. Louis. So how can you do that? The answer is, I can't, but you can. And now every State in the country has the power today to take the welfare check and give it to an employer as a wage and training supplement for a year or more and, if it's a small-business employer, to keep covering the children with health care. Every one.

I've asked the Congress to adopt a special tax credit that would give every employer who hires someone certified from welfare, up to $10,000 a year in salary, a 50 percent tax credit. Those two things together are more than enough incentive for people to marginally add to the work force if they've got a healthy business and they want to do something for their country.

And you think about it. If small business, medium-sized and large, and for-profit and private institutions like churches and community groups, if we said—businesses saying, "For every 25 employees I've got, if I have these incentives at the grassroots level, I'll hire somebody off welfare," this problem would go away tomorrow. Oh, yeah, there would be people who would have a hard time making it, and they'd fall on and off the rolls, and we'd have to work with education and training and preparing people. But the problem, as a big problem, would go away. And we would have what I have always wanted, which is a community-based system that treats all people who are out of work with dignity—dignity by giving them the support they need for their children and dignity by giving them the expectation that if they're able-bodied, they will work when they can. A good thing to do.

But I just would say to you, we have to set an example here. And we are going to have to go out and find the people to do this. And all of you are going to have to help me do this. And I'll have an organized way of doing that which I will explain to you over the next several days and give you a better chance to participate in it.

But that's what being a Democrat means. We can be pro-business and have a social conscience. We can be for very high standards in school and still be compassionate for people that need a hand up. We need to do things that prove that you don't have to make false choices—you can grow the economy, protect the environment; you can balance the budget and invest in education; you can be strong at home and be strong abroad. And we can build a unifying vision that will bring this country together and move it forward.

That's what I want you to be a part of. I want you to be excited. I want you to be happy. I want you to be proud to be a part of what we're trying to do. And I want you to be a part of what we're trying to do. You are very welcome.

Thank you, and God bless you all.

NOTE: The President spoke at 8:12 p.m. at the Sheraton Carlton Hotel. In his remarks, he referred to Carol Pensky, treasurer, Steve Grossman, national chair, Gov. Roy Romer of Colorado, general chair, and Alan Solomont, national finance chair, Democratic National Committee; C. Thomas Hendrickson, chair, Democratic Business Council; Gov. Gary Locke of Washington; and Gov. Jeanne Shaheen of New Hampshire.

Letter to Congressional Leaders Reporting on Terrorists Who Threaten To Disrupt the Middle East Peace Process
January 28, 1997

Dear Mr. Speaker: (Dear Mr. President:)

I hereby report to the Congress on the developments concerning the national emergency with respect to terrorists who threaten to disrupt the Middle East peace process that was declared in Executive Order 12947 of January 23, 1995. This report is submitted pursuant to section 401(c) of the National Emergencies Act, 50 U.S.C. 1641(c), and section 204(c) of the International Emergency Economic Powers Act (IEEPA), 50 U.S.C. 1703(c). Since the crisis with respect to the grave acts of violence committed by foreign terrorists that threaten the Middle East peace process has not been resolved, on January 21, 1997, I renewed this national emergency in accordance with section 202(d) of the National Emergencies Act (50 U.S.C. 1622(d)).

1. On January 23, 1995, I signed Executive Order 12947, "Prohibiting Transactions with Terrorists Who Threaten To Disrupt the Middle East Peace Process" (the "Order") (60 *Fed. Reg.* 5079, January 25, 1995). The order blocks all property subject to U.S. jurisdiction in which there is any interest of 12 terrorist organizations that threaten the Middle East peace process as identified in an Annex to the order. The order also blocks the property and interests in property subject to U.S. jurisdiction of persons designated by the Secretary of State, in coordination with the Secretary of the Treasury and the Attorney General, who are found (1) to have committed, or to pose a significant risk of committing, acts of violence that have the purpose or effect of disrupting the Middle East peace process, or (2) to assist in, sponsor, or provide financial, material, or technological support for, or services in support of, such acts of violence. In addition, the order blocks all property and interests in property subject to U.S. jurisdiction in which there is any interest of persons determined by the Secretary of the Treasury, in coordination with the Secretary of State and the Attorney General, to be owned or controlled by, or to act for or on behalf of, any other person designated pursuant to the order (collectively "Specially Designated Terrorists" or "SDTs").

The order further prohibits any transaction or dealing by a United States person or within the United States in property or interests in property of SDTs, including the making or receiving of any contribution of funds, goods, or services to or for the benefit of such persons. This prohibition includes donations that are intended to relieve human suffering. Designations of persons blocked pursuant to the order are effective upon the date of determination by the Secretary of State or his delegate, or the Director of the Office of Foreign Assets Control (OFAC) acting under authority delegated by the Secretary of the Treasury. Public notice of blocking is effective upon the date of filing with the *Federal Register* or upon prior actual notice.

2. On January 25, 1995, the Department of the Treasury issued a notice listing persons blocked pursuant to Executive Order 12947 who have been designated by the President as terrorist organizations threatening the Middle East peace process or who have been found to be owned or controlled by, or to be acting for or on behalf of, these terrorist organizations (60 *Fed. Reg.* 5084, January 25, 1995). The notice identified 31 entities that act for or on behalf of the 12 Middle East terrorist organizations listed in the Annex to Executive Order 12947, as well as 18 individuals who are leaders or representatives of these groups. In addition the notice provides 9 name variations or pseudonyms used by the 18 individuals identified. The list identifies blocked persons who have been found to have committed, or to pose a risk of committing, acts of violence that have the purpose of disrupting the Middle East peace process or to have assisted in, sponsored, or provided financial, material, or technological support for, or service in support of, such acts of violence, or are owned or controlled by, or to act for or on behalf of other blocked persons. The Department of the Treasury issued three additional notices adding the names of three individuals, as well as their pseudonyms, to the List of SDTs (60 *Fed. Reg.* 41152, August 11, 1995; 60 *Fed. Reg.* 44932, August 29, 1995; and 60 *Fed. Reg.* 58435, November 27, 1995). The OFAC, in coordination with the Secretary of State and the Attorney General, is continuing to expand the list of Specially Designated Terrorists, including both organizations and individuals, as additional information is developed.

3. On February 2, 1996, the OFAC issued the Terrorism Sanctions Regulations (the "TSRs") (61 *Fed. Reg.* 3805, February 2, 1996). The TSRs implement the President's declaration of a national emergency and imposition of sanctions against certain persons whose acts of violence have the purpose or effect of disrupting the Middle East peace process.

4. The expenses incurred by the Federal Government in the 6-month period from July 23, 1996, through January 22, 1997, that are directly attributable to the exercise of powers and authorities conferred by the declaration of the national emergency with respect to organizations that disrupt the Middle East peace process are estimated at approximately $285,000.

5. Executive Order 12947 provides this Administration with a new tool for combating fundraising in this country on behalf of organizations that use terror to undermine the Middle East peace process. The order makes it harder for such groups to finance these criminal activities by cutting off their access to sources of support in the United States and to U.S. financial facilities. It is also intended to reach charitable contributions to designated organizations and individuals to preclude diversion of such donations to terrorist activities.

In addition, comprehensive counterterrorism legislation was enacted on April 24, 1996, that would strengthen our ability to prevent terrorist acts, identify those who carry them out, and bring them to justice. The combination of Executive Order 12947 and the Antiterrorism and Effective Death Penalty Act of 1996 demonstrate the United States determination to confront and combat those who would seek to destroy the Middle East peace process, and our commitment to the global fight against terrorism.

I shall continue to exercise the powers at my disposal to apply economic sanctions against extremists seeking to destroy the hopes of peaceful coexistence between Arabs and Israelis as long as these measures are appropriate, and will continue to report periodically to the Congress on significant developments pursuant to 50 U.S.C. 1703(c).

Sincerely,

WILLIAM J. CLINTON

NOTE: Identical letters were sent to Newt Gingrich, Speaker of the House of Representatives, and Albert Gore, Jr., President of the Senate. This letter was released by the Office of the Press Secretary on January 29.

Remarks Prior to a Meeting With Military Leaders and an Exchange With Reporters in Arlington, Virginia
January 29, 1997

The President. Let me say, first of all, I'm delighted to have a chance to be back at the Pentagon to meet with our commanders-in-chief. This is the first meeting for Secretary Cohen and our new national security team. We're all looking forward to it.

America is very proud of our men and women in uniform, and they have maintained an extraordinary tempo of operations for the last several years, being deployed in many different places for long periods of time. And the leadership and planning that has gone into these operations are a tribute to the people around this table and to others in our Armed Forces. And I'm looking forward to discussing what we're going to do in the next year and having this meeting.

War Crimes in Bosnia

Q. Mr. President, do you think that U.S. troops could play a role in trying to arrest some of the accused war criminals that are out and about in Bosnia at the moment?

The President. I think that the agreement that was struck at Dayton and signed in the Paris Peace Treaty says what our military believes is responsible, that if we're going to go there and do the UNPROFOR mission, it would be impossible to do that and spend your time taking affirmative action over—as a police force, in effect, international police force—but that if they come in contact with people who are wanted and where there is, in effect, a warrant out for them, they ought to apprehend them. But I think it would be very difficult for them to do the mission, particularly with a smaller number of people, and in effect spend full-time doing that.

It's always—I think at Dayton—everyone knew from Dayton on that this was one of the most difficult things, that they couldn't walk away from this evidence of war crimes and that

there needed to be some way of proceeding, but that there was no way that you could effectively do the job of UNPROFOR, which was the most important thing to try to stabilize the country and the borders, and in effect make that the primary mission.

Maybe I ought to let General Joulwan answer that question, but I think that's the right answer.

Gen. George A. Joulwan. Yes, Mr. President. [*Laughter*]

Q. Do you oppose the international group that's been proposed?

The President. Well, what I want to look—I have asked—at the University of Connecticut, when I spoke at the—Senator Dodd not very long ago—I said I thought we ought to consider whether there should be a permanent international war crimes tribunal, which of course would require some sort of way of carrying out its mandate. But that—if we do that, we need to look at it not just in terms of Bosnia but over the long run.

We need to recognize that we can't expect people who are sent into a very volatile situation and ask us to stabilize borders, to ensure the security of cross-border crossings, and all the other things that UNPROFOR has had to do, you can't expect those same people to do this other work unless they literally come in contact with those who should be arrested and returned. So there would have to be a completely different way of dealing with it if we're going to have a permanent war crimes tribunal, which I think has a lot of merit.

NOTE: The President spoke at 10:25 a.m. in the Army Conference Room at the Pentagon. In his remarks, the President referred to Gen. George A. Joulwan, USA, Supreme Allied Commander, Europe. A tape was not available for verification of the content of these remarks.

Remarks on Presenting the Presidential Awards for Excellence in Microenterprise Development
January 30, 1997

Thank you. Welcome to the White House. I would like to begin with a word of thanks to, first, Secretary Rubin, who became Treasury Secretary and, before that, head of the National Economic Council, with a passion rare for someone in his previous line of work—*[laughter]*—rare, to bring the benefits of enterprise to people who had been too long denied them, and an absolute conviction, too rare all across our country, that just because people were poor and in distress did not mean they could not do better, did not mean that we could not spread the benefits of enterprise to the cities and to the isolated rural areas where they had been too long absent.

I'd also like to thank the First Lady for beginning this obsession, almost, that we have with microenterprise with me. I guess—I asked her before I came up here, and we were laughing—you know, one of the great burdens of growing older is that you can't remember when something happened even if you remember exactly what happened. *[Laughter]* And I said, "Now, when was it that I came home and told you, 'I hope I live long enough to see Muhammad Yunus win a Nobel Prize'?"—*[laughter]*—because it was my first exposure, through our friends in Chicago who brought me in touch with him, to the whole idea that microenterprise might be exploded across a nation. And she said, "I think it was '85, but it might have been '86." So to be literally accurate, more than 10 years ago—*[laughter]*—we started the long road which we could not have predicted would bring us all to this day.

These awards for excellence in microenterprise development simply recognize that our country has been and will be built on the enterprise of our people, on their ideas, their energies, their willingness to take risks, their willingness to pursue their dreams. That is the story of all the new businesses in this country. And with the right opportunity, those kinds of dreams can become real for countless numbers of people to support their families and strengthen their communities and build our country into the kind of nation we want in a new century.

Indeed, it is now a commonplace observance that often the greatest contributions, economic contributions, in our communities come from the smallest businesses in the aggregate. They literally can transform communities, offering a path to success for Americans who would otherwise not have had it.

If we can spread the opportunity for microenterprise, for making that first beginning across this country, we can offer a new path to success for Americans who today are left out of the economic mainstream. In rural America it may be a person who once worked on a family farm. In urban areas it may be a parent who can't juggle an office or a plant job with a family or who's been left out of the work force for childrearing or who is struggling to move from welfare to work. It might be older Americans who are retired from their previous jobs. It might be people with disabilities who aren't mobile but who have a skill, an idea, a capacity to contribute. It might be laid off workers looking for a second chance.

There are huge numbers of people in our country, as all of you know, who are literally brimming with initiative and desire, who are willing to be responsible and work hard. Microenterprise helps to put such people on their feet and gives people with courage and genius a chance to reach for the stars. To do that, they must have opportunity. There are people often who need these opportunities who are completely unable to get proper business training or loans or even a hearing from a lender under the established systems. But when the opportunity is not there for them, make no mistake about it, their loss is also our loss. For every person whose potential goes unfulfilled, there is a problem or the absence of an opportunity that affects the entire Nation.

And when they have an opportunity, we move closer together in our common goals for our society, for after all, all of us want every American to be able to be responsible and to work and to find fulfillment. We want to raise the incomes of people who can be fully participating in our society. We want to promote the growth of business. We want to ensure that everybody has a stake in the success of our communities, because we know there are no unsuccessful communities where everybody has a stake in its success.

As the First Lady has said with a lot of her compelling examples today, we have seen the value of microenterprise demonstrated in much poorer countries, bringing new dignity and better lives for women and children, especially. But we know it has also worked in America. One of the things that we worked to do in our home State was to create a community development bank and a good-faith fund microenterprise program.

Since I became President, we have tried to go national with this micro idea in a very macro way. And again, I say it would not have been possible if it hadn't been for the support of Secretary Rubin and his considerable persuasive powers in convincing other people who had never thought about it that this was in fact a good idea. We want microenterprise to take root everywhere. We recognize, however, that our efforts alone are not enough. We have to have a partnership between the public and private sectors if we're going to have adequate support of microenterprise development all across the United States.

I also want to emphasize that microenterprise must be part of a larger strategy to help every American make the most of his or her own life. There are many pieces to the strategy, and we must all play a role to have the whole strategy succeed. We also reformed the Community Reinvestment Act, to revive communities in distress and ensure that private sector capital flows to all—all—credit-worthy borrowers without prejudice. That is unleashing billions of dollars in private investment in those communities, and I am committed to maintaining that effort.

In 1992, I called for a nationwide network of community development banks, while asking the Nation's banks and thrifts to make sound investments to expand opportunity, enterprise, and homeownership in distressed communities. Last year, Treasury's Community Development Financial Institutions Fund made its first round of awards to 32 CDFI's around the Nation. This is an initiative with enormous potential to help people who have been left out come in and be lifted up by their own endeavors.

Before recognizing the awardees, I want to make two further announcements today in support of these common efforts. First, we are committed to increase the Community Development Financial Institutions Fund by a billion dollars over the next 5 years. That is almost triple its current funding. [*Applause*] Thank you. And all of you know that properly run, these funds can create more jobs with $100,000 than some traditional efforts can with a million. So I ask for your support and your continued demonstration that this is a good investment for all Americans.

Second, I want to announce a bold new effort to help Americans in hard-hit communities go to work. We have finalized a new $10-million welfare-to-work partnership between Chase Manhattan Bank, the Rockefeller Foundation, and the Department of Housing and Urban Development. This three-way partnership will fund two private sector welfare-to-work projects designed to raise employment rates by as much as 20 to 30 percent in high poverty urban neighborhoods. More than 15 sites will be funded in both projects; three of them, Brooklyn and Central Harlem in New York City and Sandtown-Winchester in Baltimore, have already been selected for one project. Los Angeles, Cleveland, San Antonio, Seattle, and Louisville are among the finalists for the other.

I'd like to ask Peter Goldmark, the president of the Rockefeller Foundation; William Harrison, the vice president of the Chase Manhattan Corporation and Chase Bank; and Michael Stegman, Assistant Secretary at HUD, to stand so we can all thank you for your work in putting together this very amazing and very hopeful project. Gentlemen, would you please stand? [*Applause*]

Microenterprise, by giving people the tools they need to help themselves, will reinforce efforts like this. And that's what our award recipients do every day. Today we recognize them for their successful efforts. They are the engineers and the pioneers of potential. We need more of them in America. I'd like to ask each of them to stand as I announce their endeavors and their award.

First, the Women's Self-Employment Project is a leader in advocating for low income women in Chicago and assisting them to pursue self-employment to lift themselves from poverty and welfare dependency. It trains the women in entrepreneurship, marketing, and in getting loans. It has served more than 3,000 women in the past 10 years. Most of the clients have household incomes of $15,000. And listen to this, their business survival rate is 79 percent. Accepting for the Women's Self-Employment Project the award for excellence in program delivery, poverty alleviation, is Connie Evans. Thank you, Connie.

ACCION U.S. Network has made an impact in New York, Chicago, San Diego, Albuquerque, San Antonio, and El Paso. Its name—"action" in Spanish—translates into opportunity for people it serves through specialized, streamlined loans. Most of its several thousand borrowers are Hispanic or low income entrepreneurs of homebased businesses. It also lends to others who lack access to credit. One of its best success stories is that of Safaraaz Saalim who went from being homeless to running a successful one-man salad restaurant in downtown San Diego. I'll go there next time I'm there. [*Laughter*] ACCION has shown itself to be a model of disciplined management.

The Cascadia Revolving Fund operates in rural and urban communities of the Pacific Northwest—no, no, we're going to do them together; I know what I'm doing—[*laughter*]—providing intensive services to new and young businesses and helping them to stay in business. That's a big accomplishment because Cascadia specializes in high risk businesses. It is focused on helping low income people, women-owned firms, and businesses that locate in economically distressed communities.

For their work, ACCION and Cascadia Revolving Fund are receiving awards for excellence in program delivery, access to credit, and the recipients are Bill Burrus for ACCION and Patricia Grossman for the Cascadia Revolving Fund. Let's give them a hand. [*Applause*]

The North Carolina Rural Economic Development Center established a microenterprise loan program several years ago to combat the problem of lack of capital to start up businesses in rural areas. Its solution: a highly effective model for statewide delivery of microenterprise services. It makes both individual and group loans and provides business training through local community-based partners. These partners identify potential borrowers and underwrite their loans. This is community action at its best, growing the economy at the grassroots. And we have another winner in this category as well. [*Laughter*]

From its base in Cambridge, Massachusetts, Working Capital also provides small loans to groups of business owners who form peer groups. To further help the cause, Working Cap-

ital created the microenterprise toolkit, a step-by-step guide to starting a microenterprise program. This innovation will help spawn a whole new wave of entrepreneurs, something all of us can cheer.

For their leaps in creativity, the awards for excellence in program innovation go to Billy Ray Hall of the North Carolina Rural Economic Development Center and Jeffrey Ashe of Working Capital. Let's give them a hand. [*Applause*]

The Nebraska Microenterprise Partnership Fund is a model of public-private partnership. It is an intermediary, raising money from public and private sources to build a statewide grassroots network of microfunds. In just a short time, the Partnership Fund has sown the seeds of a strong network of microenterprise, demonstrating that Federal, State, and local government can in fact work with community-based organizations to support the smallest businesses.

The Self-Employment Learning Project of Washington, DC, is the preeminent effort to research and evaluate the development of microenterprise and the people it serves in the United States. It has been instrumental in setting down the foundation for the growth of microenterprise and promoting its potential as a road to economic opportunity. Before the Learning Project was established in 1991, there was little information on microenterprise, and well, here we' are today celebrating them and more information. It has been a real engine in our progress, and I hope today that we are helping the Self-Employment Learning Project to get more information out about this around the country.

For their fine work, they receive awards for excellence in public or private support of microenterprise development: Gene Severens of the Nebraska Microenterprise Partnership Fund and Peggy Clark of the Self-Employment Learning Project.

Again, let me thank all of you for being here. Again, I thank Secretary Rubin. I also want to thank Brian Atwood of AID and Phil Lader, the Small Business Administrator, for their intense support of our microenterprise efforts.

And let me say, as all of you know, we have only scratched the surface. And I hope by our being together here today, you will go home reenergized. And I hope that because of the publicity this event generates, you will all get hundreds of calls asking you—[*laughter*]—how more communities and more neighborhoods can become involved in this great endeavor. And

I hope that we can depend upon Senator Kennedy and Congressman Davis to have yet another good project to become evangelical about. [*Laughter*]

Thank you all very much, and good day. Thank you.

NOTE: The President spoke at 2:53 p.m. in the East Room at the White House. In his remarks, he referred to development economist Muhammad Yunus, managing director, Grameen Bank, Bangladesh.

Executive Order 13034—Extension of Presidential Advisory Committee on Gulf War Veterans' Illnesses
January 30, 1997

By the authority vested in me as President by the Constitution and the laws of the United States of America, it is hereby ordered as follows:

Section 1. Extension. The Presidential Advisory Committee on Gulf War Veterans' Illnesses (the "Committee"), established pursuant to Executive Order 12961 of May 26, 1995, is hereby extended for the purposes set forth herein. All provisions of that order relating to membership and administration shall remain in effect. All Committee appointments, as well as the President's designation of a Chairperson, shall remain in effect. The limitations set forth in section 2(c)–(e) and section 4(a) of Executive Order 12961 shall also remain in effect. The Committee shall remain subject to the Federal Advisory Committee Act, as amended, 5 U.S.C. App. 2.

Sec. 2. Functions. (a) The Committee shall report to the President through the Secretary of Defense, the Secretary of Veterans Affairs, and the Secretary of Health and Human Services.

(b) The Committee shall have two principal roles:

(1) Oversight of the ongoing investigation being conducted by the Department of Defense with the assistance, as appropriate, of other executive departments and agencies into possible chemical or biological warfare agent exposures during the Gulf War; and

(2) Evaluation of the Federal Government's plan for and progress towards the implementation of the Committee's recommendations contained in its Final Report submitted on December 31, 1996.

(c) The Committee shall provide advice and recommendations related to its oversight and evaluation responsibilities.

(d) The Committee may also provide additional advice and recommendations prompted by any new developments related to its original functions as set forth in section 2(b) of Executive Order 12961.

(e) The Committee shall submit by letter a status report by April 30, 1997, and a final supplemental report by October 31, 1997, unless otherwise directed by the President.

Sec. 3. General Provisions. (a) The Committee shall terminate 30 days after submitting its final supplemental report.

(b) This order is intended only to improve the internal management of the executive branch and it is not intended to create any right, benefit or trust responsibility, substantive or procedural, enforceable at law or equity by a party against the United States, its agencies, its officers, or any person.

WILLIAM J. CLINTON

The White House,
January 30, 1997.

[Filed with the Office of the Federal Register, 10:55 a.m., January 31, 1997]

NOTE: This Executive order was published in the *Federal Register* on February 3. It is included here as an example of the numbered Executive orders which are listed in Appendix D at the end of this volume and compiled annually in title 3 of the *Code of Federal Regulations*.

Statement on the Death of Representative Frank Tejeda
January 31, 1997

Hillary and I were saddened to learn today of the death of Congressman Frank Tejeda. Congressman Tejeda spent the last years of his life not only fighting for the citizens of San Antonio but also courageously battling cancer. Frank was a friend who dedicated himself to serving his country and community. He will long be remembered for his perseverance in the face of adversity. He endeared himself to all who knew him, always looking out for the best interests of his constituents, members of the military, and the Hispanic and veterans' communities in particular. We will miss him greatly. Our thoughts and prayers are with his children, Marissa, Sonya, and Frank, his mother, Lillie, his extended family members, and his many friends at this difficult time.

Statement on Funding for International Family Planning
January 31, 1997

In the next few weeks, Congress will face an important vote about the United States' support for voluntary family planning in developing countries.

The funds to continue our support have already been approved, as part of our Fiscal Year '97 budget. At issue is whether the money will be released on March 1, or whether it will be further delayed by 4 months, until July.

It is my determination that a delay will cause serious, irreversible, and avoidable harm. In the balance are the lives and well-being of many thousands of women and children and American credibility as the leader in family planning programs around the world.

Opponents of this funding have tried to mischaracterize this upcoming vote and the work of United States Agency for International Development in family planning. So, let me be clear: The United States provides family planning support where it is wanted and needed. We are prohibited by law from ever funding abortion—and we abide faithfully by that law. Indeed, the work we have funded in developing countries has been supportive of families, helping them to flourish. It has improved women's health and women's station in life. It has allowed generations of children to grow and be educated in safer and healthier environments. It has been instrumental in helping to prevent the spread of disease, including AIDS. And, make no mistake: It has prevented untold numbers of abortions and maternal deaths. This much is clear: In preventing abortions, maternal and child deaths, family planning has been proven effective.

If we delay support for family planning by even 4 months, denying safe and effective contraception to couples who depend on these programs, we will see a rise in unintended pregnancies and maternal deaths and a tragic recourse to unsafe and unsanitary methods to terminate those pregnancies.

I want to emphasize this vote should have nothing to do with partisan politics. In fact, right now, a bipartisan group of legislators in the House and the Senate are hard at work to pass this bill for the timely release of funds. And for a generation, through administrations led by both parties, the United States has led the world in family planning programs. Studies show that our efforts, as part of an international strategy, have prevented more than 500 million unintended pregnancies.

Rapid population growth undermines economic and social development in poor countries. With our support for family planning, the scarce resources in developing countries—from infrastructure and environment to nutrition and education—can be better used to allow progress for their people.

Maintaining and building on this progress depends on our being consistent in our actions and adhering to our values.

Cooperative international efforts to address rapid population growth serve American foreign policy interests in protecting the Earth's environment, promoting human rights, and improving basic standards of health. It enhances the social, economic, and political status of women. It ensures global economic progress and strong markets for United States exports. It encourages international stability and it reduces pressures that lead to refugee flows and migration.

I appeal to the Members of Congress to examine the consequences of a delay, to weigh those against the benefits of fulfilling an urgent and continuing American commitment, and to vote for the March 1, 1997, unconditional release of these voluntary international family planning funds.

If Congress fails to take this simple action, we risk a cost to humanity that we will bear well into the next century.

Surely, we agree that we must do all we can to prevent unintended pregnancies and abortions. With passage of this bill, we can do that. The decision is now in the hands of the Congress.

Letter to Congressional Leaders on Funding for International Family Planning
January 31, 1997

Dear _____:

Pursuant to the authority vested in me by section 518A(d) of the Foreign Operations, Export Financing, and Related Programs Appropriations Act, 1997 (Public Law 104–208) (the "Act"), I hereby find that the July 1, 1997, limitation on obligations imposed by subsection (a) of section 518A is having a negative impact on the proper functioning of the population planning program. Subject to a joint resolution of approval by the Congress to be adopted no later than February 28, 1997, as specified in section 518A(d) of the Act, funds for these activities may be made available beginning March 1, 1997.

Sincerely,

WILLIAM J. CLINTON

NOTE: Identical letters were sent to Newt Gingrich, Speaker of the House of Representatives; Albert Gore, Jr., President of the Senate; Ted Stevens, chairman, and Robert C. Byrd, ranking member, Senate Committee on Appropriations; and Robert L. Livingston, chairman, and David R. Obey, ranking member, House Committee on Appropriations.

The President's Radio Address
February 1, 1997

Good morning. As a parent, I know how important it is to take responsibility for our children when they need us most; when they're sick, when they need to go to the doctor, or when there's a parent-teacher conference at school. Fortunately, Hillary and I have never had to risk our jobs to be there for our daughter. We've never had to make the choice between being good parents and good workers.

Today I want to talk with you about what we have done and what more we must do as a people to give that same assurance to every American family. One of the things I wanted most to do when I became President was to help parents succeed both at home and at work. That's why I was so proud to make the Family and Medical Leave Act the very first bill I signed as President, exactly 4 years ago this Wednesday. Family and medical leave allows people in companies with 50 or more employees to take up to 12 weeks of unpaid leave to care for a newborn or a newly adopted child or to be with a family member who is seriously ill without fear of losing their job.

Today, over half of all American workers share this important benefit, people like Christy Sens, a first-grade teacher from Fairfax, Virginia, who is here with me today. Christy was among the first Americans to make use of the new family leave law in 1993 when she and her husband were expecting their first child. She thought she would be forced to choose between the 6 weeks her school allowed her for new mothers or taking a whole year off without pay. Because of our new law, she was able to spend 12 full weeks at home recovering from her pregnancy and spending precious time with her new daughter. Christy used the benefit again in 1995 for the birth of her second child.

Family leave is not only family-friendly, it's employer-friendly as well. Also with me today is Stan Sorrell, president and CEO of the Calvert Group, an investment firm in Bethesda, Maryland, and two of his employees who have also used family leave. The Calvert Group started a family and medical leave program 3 years before it became the law of the land. Like almost 90 percent of the businesses covered by the law, they found that family leave is easy to administer and costs them little or nothing. So we know it's working for both families and businesses. After all, in these past 4 years, American business has created over 11 million new jobs, more than any other 4-year term in our history.

Now we must make it even easier for parents to live up to their responsibilities to their children and to their employers. Today I call upon Congress to expand the family leave law to give parents an additional 24 hours of unpaid leave each year to take a child or an elderly relative to a regular doctor's appointment or to attend parent-teacher conferences at school. In so doing, we'll make our families stronger and our workers more productive, building the kind of country and economy we all want for our children.

We also must address the fact that too many workers still do not know about the family leave law. That's why I'm pleased to announce that we're launching a multimedia public education campaign to spread the word about family leave to make sure employers and employees have the facts and to make sure everyone knows how to make this law work for them. It's simply not enough to help people have the tools to succeed; we also have to make sure they know what those tools are.

The centerpiece of this campaign is a new 800 number that any American can call to learn about family and medical leave. It's 1–800–959–FMLA. That's 1–800–959–FMLA. You can also get information through our Labor Department's website on the Internet: www.dol.gov. That's www.dol.gov.

By expanding family leave to cover children's doctor visits and parent-teacher conferences and by helping more Americans to learn about the opportunity of family leave, we can enable millions of more of our fellow citizens to meet their responsibilities both at home and at work. That's how we must prepare our people for a new century full of new promise and possibility.

As parents, teachers, and business people, as members of the work force and members of our communities, we all share a stake in the strength of our families. Our society can never be stronger than the children we raise or the families in which we raise them. That's why family leave is more than just a single issue or accomplishment. It is at the heart of our approach to preparing America for the 21st century by ensuring that we can all meet our obligations and make the most of our God-given gifts.

Thanks for listening.

NOTE: The President spoke at 10:06 a.m. from the Oval Office at the White House.

Statement on the Death of Herb Caen
February 1, 1997

Hillary and I were saddened to learn of the passing of Herb Caen, the San Francisco Chronicle's legendary columnist, and we extend our condolences to his family, friends, and most of all, the city he loved. Maybe it's not right to call an "institution" someone who deflated many overstuffed institutions with a brisk three dots, but surely no one knew better the vibrancy and eccentricities of the city, his city, San Francisco, than did Herb Caen. If we listen carefully on those cool mornings when the fog has boiled through the Golden Gate, out beyond the clat-tering of cables underfoot and the low moan of the horn at Alcatraz, maybe we will still hear Herb Caen's wonderful, witty, irrepressible voice. Herb Caen . . . he will be missed . . . a lot.

Remarks at the National Governors' Association Dinner
February 2, 1997

Ladies and gentlemen, Governor and Mrs. Miller, Governor and Mrs. Voinovich, all the Governors and spouses and children and friends who are here, the leaders of the National Governors' Association, welcome back to the White House.

As all of you know, this is a very special dinner for Hillary and for me. I had to pinch myself this afternoon when I was preparing these notes—very elaborate—*[laughter]*—when I realized that this is the fifth time I have had the honor of hosting this dinner, which I also attended 12 times as a Governor.

Four years ago when you came here, I told you that I would do my best to chart a new course for our country, to give you a strong economy, a smaller and less obtrusive Federal Government, still one that could be very effective and innovative in dealing with the challenges before us and in forging a new partnership with the Governors to devolve more decisionmaking to the State level. Four years later, we can look back and see that that strategy has worked, thanks to your efforts and what all of us here have been able to do, working together.

Our economy is the strongest it's been in 30 years. Our Government is the smallest it's been since President Kennedy was here. Today one of our major newspapers carried a story chronicling the record decline in the welfare rolls over the last 4 years—2¼ million people—and at last giving the Governors and the States committed to welfare reform a share of the credit, along with the rising economy, for moving people from welfare to work. So this is a good time. Crime rates have dropped now for 5 years in a row, and we know now what to do to keep them coming down.

The main thing I want to say tonight is that we all, together, have an incredible opportunity, standing as we do on the edge of a new century, a new millennium, but also a profoundly different time in human affairs and standing at this point not only as the world's only superpower but one that is free of external threat and internal economic crisis, which means we have an opportunity almost unique in our history to think about not only what we need to do for our people today and tomorrow but what America needs 20 years from now, 50 years from now.

That is the sort of thing that people who were here before us thought about at the end of World War II, and the decisions they made gave us 50 pretty good years as Americans. Tuesday night, when I speak in the State of the Union Address, I'm going to ask the Congress to cross party lines with each other and with me and to think about how we can build the next 50 years for America, how we can bring about true excellence and complete opportunity in education, how we can finish the job of welfare reform so that everyone we are now requiring to work genuinely has the chance to work, how we can meet the other challenges that are before us. Many of them involve the leadership, the initiative, the strength and steadiness of our Nation's Governors.

And so I pledge to you to continue the partnership we've had, to try to deepen it, to try to enrich it, and beginning tomorrow, to try to continue to listen to you and to your concerns and to hear your advice. This has been a good 4 years for America. I look forward to the next 4. And I look forward to our continued partnership.

The National Governors' Association has been a unique and immensely valuable institution for the United States because it gives the Governors a chance, without regard to their regional and political differences, to reach common positions for the people of their States and to bring those positions not only to life in their States but also to bring them to Washington, where it's too often easy to forget about the real lives of real people out in the country. I know you will be doing that here, and I hope together we will be advancing those lives for 4 more years.

I now ask you to join me in a toast to our partnership, to the Governors, and especially to Governor and Mrs. Miller and to Governor and Mrs. Voinovich.

NOTE: The President spoke at 8:50 p.m. in the State Dining Room at the White House. In his remarks, he referred to Gov. Bob Miller of Nevada, National Governors' Association chairman, and his wife, Sandy; and Gov. George V. Voinovich of Ohio, NGA vice chairman, and his wife, Janet.

Remarks at the National Governors' Association Meeting
February 3, 1997

Good morning, Governor Miller, Governor Voinovich; good morning to all the Governors who are here. It was wonderful to see all of you last night, and I'm glad to welcome you back to the White House.

This is an unusual opportunity for our country and for every State. The Nation is strong; we are at peace; we have extraordinary prosperity. But we know we're living through a time of great change in the way we work, in the way we live, the way we relate to each other, that there are significant challenges which if not faced will have destructive consequences for our Nation in the years ahead. So as we stand on the edge of this new century and this profoundly new era, we have a unique opportunity and a common responsibility, which is to take action together to try to prepare this country not just for the next 4 years but for the next 50 years.

In the State of the Union Address tomorrow night, I'm going to lay out the challenges that I see not only for the President and the Congress but also for the States and local communities and private citizens. Because there will be a great deal in that speech about the States

and the issues of education and welfare reform and other issues of common concern, I want to invite any of you who can stay, to stay tomorrow night and to come into the Chamber of the Capitol and sit as a group, as many as would like to stay, and be there at the State of the Union Address.

I know that many of you have concerns about welfare reform or Medicaid spending or education, the environment, transportation. I'm looking forward to addressing those concerns, beginning today at this meeting but also every day for the next 4 years. I want every one of you to feel that you can always call this White House and that you will have someone, even if we don't always agree, who understands your concerns and will do his best to address them. And I thank you.

Mr. Chairman.

NOTE: The President spoke at 9:50 a.m. in the East Room at the White House. In his remarks, he referred to Gov. Bob Miller of Nevada and Gov. George V. Voinovich of Ohio, chairman and vice chairman of the association.

Remarks at the Democratic Governors Association Dinner
February 3, 1997

Thank you. Thank you, Governor Dean, for that wonderful introduction. And I thank the

orchestra for playing me in. [*Laughter*] Thank you, Governor Rossello, for your leadership here in the DGA. And to our DNC general chair, Governor Roy Romer, thank you for agreeing to do that. I hope it made the Democratic Governors feel better; it sure made me feel better when you did it. Our Democratic national chairman, Steve Grossman, thank you for being here tonight. And thank you, Santita, for singing again. You got me in a good humor before I had to come out and speak.

You all know that the Vice President is coming over later. I'm just the warmup act. [*Laughter*] But that's probably as it should be. At least that's what he asked me to say right before I left the White House. [*Laughter*]

I thank you for understanding why I can't be here all evening. As you know, the State of the Union is tomorrow night, and I hope that the Governors who are here will be staying for it. We have a place for all of you.

It's a very different city than it was a year ago. A year ago, we had a cold wave and a cold wave in politics so bad that it shut the Government down. And the American people had something to say about it in the months ahead after that and then definitively in November. And it's a lot warmer outside this year than it was last year. And I like it.

All of you know that I have been deeply indebted to my own experience as a Governor and to the Democratic Governors for many of the ideas that we have brought to bear over the last 4 years. Our country has produced 11.2 million jobs for the first time in history in a 4-year Presidential administration. We have—crime has come down in every year. The welfare rolls have dropped by 2¼ million, the largest amount in history. Inequality among working people has started back down again, after a 20-year increase, with particular drops for single parents working to support their children; the elderly; and African-Americans.

In the last 4 years, thanks to the work that we have done together, we have, first of all, reversed our country's addiction to supply-side economics and substituted for it an economics based on investing in people, expanding trade, reducing the deficit, and ultimately balancing the budget in the right way.

We have restored the family and community as the centerpiece of our social agenda with initiatives like the family and medical leave law, which we celebrated the fourth anniversary of just this week and which I hope to expand in this coming session of the Congress, and I hope you will help me do that.

When it comes to crime and welfare, we replaced rhetoric with action, and that's why results have flowed. We have redefined the role of the Government. No longer do the American people believe, and no longer are they being told, that Government is the enemy. They know that the role of Government is to be our partner to give us the tools to solve our problems and to create the conditions in which Americans can flourish.

And finally, we have reaffirmed the importance of our national community. No longer is it commonplace in our national politics to see victory come from dividing Americans by race, by gender, or in any other way. And I'm proud of that, perhaps proudest of all that we have rebuked the people who want to divide us as a nation. That's what the Democratic Party is all about.

In the next 4 years—well, you have to wait until tomorrow night to hear about that. [*Laughter*] But let me say that in the next 4 years, I will still depend upon the Democratic Governors for your ideas; two of them you know I have embraced with particular vigor: the HOPE scholarship, pioneered by Governor Zell Miller in Georgia, and the idea of providing national certification to the most excellent teachers in America, pioneered by Governor Jim Hunt in North Carolina. I thank you both for that.

What I want to leave you with is that I think in the last 4 years we've basically unlocked the potential of our country by fixing a lot of things that were wrong and by redefining what the stakes are. In the next 4 years, we have to take initiatives to shape America for the next 50 years. And what I want you to think about when you go back home is this: It's not very often that a country has a period of such enormous peace and prosperity and yet is still confronted by such great challenges. And what has brought us to this moment in history is the incredible rate and scope of change of the time in which we live.

We're not just moving into a new century and a new millennium; we're moving into a whole new way of doing things. It's changing the way family life works. It's changing the way work life works. It's changing the way people relate to each other in society and across national borders. It poses particular challenges for our educators but also challenges for all the rest of us.

We're also learning a lot of things that impose new responsibilities on us. I know that the Democratic Governors heard from my friend Rob Reiner, who is sitting out here at this table, who is passionately concerned about what happens to children from the time they're born until they're 2 or 3 years old. We now know things about those years that we never knew before. And that imposes upon us responsibilities we' never had before because we now know we can prevent problems from occurring we didn't think we could, and we can unleash potential we didn't know was there and that requires us to behave in a different way.

So tomorrow night, I'm going to try to talk about the next steps I think we have to take. But I want you to think in big terms about this. Every time a Governor is elected who has real vision and real understanding and a real willingness to take prudent risks to tap the potential of this moment, we have advanced the cause of freedom and democracy, and we've given more people a chance to light up their own lives. That's really what all this is about.

Democracies normally don't do very well in times of peace and prosperity. They sort of get complacent and kind of go to the golf course twice a week. [*Laughter*] Sounds like a good idea to me. [*Laughter*] Unfortunately, we don't have that luxury now, not if we're going to do what we ought to do.

So that's what this is about tonight. In the next 2 years, we'll be seeing 38 Governors' races come up for a vote of the people, affecting 80 percent of the people who live in this country. And the decisions that will be made by those Governors will chart the course for the next century. This is a very, very important time to be making these judgments. And I can tell you, having now been President for 4 years and having been a Governor for 12 years—I could tell you a lot of things about that—[*laughter*]—but the point I want to make is there are a lot of things that a President can do and a lot of things a President can't. There are some things that can and will only be done by the Governors of this country, working with people throughout the States. It matters a great deal. You know that. That's why you're here tonight.

But as you think about this tonight and tomorrow night at the State of the Union and the work that I'm going to help you do in the next 2 years to try to make sure we elect more people from our party to the statehouses to move this country forward, just remember, usually democracies get lazy in times of peace and prosperity. The changes and the challenges of this time do not permit us to do this. If we do it, we will regret it for a very long time. If we don't, you ain't seen nothing yet.

Thank you, and God bless you.

NOTE: The President spoke at 6:40 p.m. in the Regency Ballroom at the Omni Shoreham Hotel. In his remarks, he referred to Gov. Howard Dean of Vermont, chair, Democratic Governors Association; Gov. Pedro Rossello of Puerto Rico; Gov. Roy Romer of Colorado; singer Santita Jackson; and Rob Reiner, founder, I Am Your Child campaign.

Letter to Congressional Leaders and the Chairman of the Federal Communications Commission Reporting on Radio Frequency Spectrum Reallocation
February 4, 1997

Dear _____:

Title VI of the Omnibus Budget Reconciliation Act of 1993 directs the Secretary of Commerce to prepare a report identifying at least 200 megahertz (MHz) of the radio frequency spectrum for reallocation, over a period of 15 years, from Federal Government use to non-federal Government use. This title also directs the President to notify the Federal Communications Commission and both Houses of Congress as actions are taken under this title. Including the reallocation of the 25 MHz reported in this notice, actions have now been completed to reallocate 120 MHz of spectrum for use by non-federal Government entities.

Under delegated authority, the National Telecommunications and Information Administration (NTIA) is responsible for managing the Federal Government's use of the radio frequency spectrum. On March 22, 1995, former Secretary of Commerce Ronald Brown submitted to you NTIA's Spectrum Reallocation Final Report; this report presented a schedule for reallocating specified frequency bands over the period extending to January 1999. The NTIA report identified the frequency band 4635–4660 MHz for reallocation in January 1997.

I am pleased to inform you that the Federal Government frequency assignments in the 4635–4660 MHz frequency band have been withdrawn by NTIA in compliance with section 114 of the Act. In addition, appropriate modifications have been made to the United States Table of Frequency Allocations for Federal Government stations to reflect the completed spectrum reallocation actions.

Sincerely,

WILLIAM J. CLINTON

NOTE: Identical letters were sent to Newt Gingrich, Speaker of the House of Representatives; Albert Gore, Jr., President of the Senate; and Reed E. Hundt, Chairman of the Federal Communications Commission.

Message to the Congress Transmitting the Estonia-United States Fisheries Agreement
February 4, 1997

To the Congress of the United States:

In accordance with the Magnuson Fishery Conservation and Management Act of 1976 (16 U.S.C. 1801 *et seq.*), I transmit herewith an Agreement between the Government of the United States of America and the Government of the Republic of Estonia Extending the Agreement of June 1, 1992, Concerning Fisheries Off the Coasts of the United States, with annex, as extended ("the 1992 Agreement"). The Agreement, which was effected by an exchange of notes at Tallinn on June 3 and 28, 1996, extends the 1992 Agreement to June 30, 1998.

In light of the importance of our fisheries relationship with the Republic of Estonia, I urge that the Congress give favorable consideration to this Agreement at an early date.

WILLIAM J. CLINTON

The White House,
February 4, 1997.

Message to the Congress Transmitting the Lithuania-United States Fisheries Agreement
February 4, 1997

To the Congress of the United States:

In accordance with the Magnuson Fishery Conservation and Management Act of 1976 (16 U.S.C. 1801 *et seq.*), I transmit herewith an Agreement between the Government of the United States of America and the Government of the Republic of Lithuania Extending the Agreement of November 12, 1992, Concerning Fisheries Off the Coasts of the United States, with annex, as extended ("the 1992 Agreement"). The Agreement, which was effected by an exchange of notes at Vilnius on June 5 and October 15, 1996, extends the 1992 Agreement to December 31, 1998.

In light of the importance of our fisheries relationship with the Republic of Lithuania, I urge that the Congress give favorable consideration to this Agreement at an early date.

WILLIAM J. CLINTON

The White House,

February 4, 1997.

Address Before a Joint Session of the Congress on the State of the Union
February 4, 1997

Mr. Speaker, Mr. Vice President, Members of the 105th Congress, distinguished guests, and my fellow Americans: I think I should start by saying thanks for inviting me back. I come before you tonight with a challenge as great as any in our peacetime history and a plan of action to meet that challenge, to prepare our people for the bold new world of the 21st century.

We have much to be thankful for. With 4 years of growth, we have won back the basic strength of our economy. With crime and welfare rolls declining, we are winning back our optimism, the enduring faith that we can master any difficulty. With the cold war receding and global commerce at record levels, we are helping to win an unrivaled peace and prosperity all across the world.

My fellow Americans, the state of our Union is strong. But now we must rise to the decisive moment, to make a nation and a world better than any we have ever known. The new promise of the global economy, the information age, unimagined new work, life-enhancing technology, all these are ours to seize. That is our honor and our challenge. We must be shapers of events, not observers, for if we do not act, the moment will pass, and we will lose the best possibilities of our future.

We face no imminent threat, but we do have an enemy. The enemy of our time is inaction. So tonight I issue a call to action: action by this Congress, action by our States, by our people, to prepare America for the 21st century; action to keep our economy and our democracy strong and working for all our people; action to strengthen education and harness the forces of technology and science; action to build stronger families and stronger communities and a safer environment; action to keep America the world's strongest force for peace, freedom, and prosperity; and above all, action to build a more perfect Union here at home.

The spirit we bring to our work will make all the difference. We must be committed to the pursuit of opportunity for all Americans, responsibility from all Americans, in a community of all Americans. And we must be committed to a new kind of Government, not to solve all our problems for us but to give our people, all our people, the tools they need to make the most of their own lives.

And we must work together. The people of this Nation elected us all. They want us to be partners, not partisans. They put us all right here in the same boat, they gave us all oars, and they told us to row. Now, here is the direction I believe we should take.

First, we must move quickly to complete the unfinished business of our country, to balance the budget, renew our democracy, and finish the job of welfare reform.

Over the last 4 years, we have brought new economic growth by investing in our people, expanding our exports, cutting our deficits, creating over 11 million new jobs, a 4-year record. Now we must keep our economy the strongest in the world. We here tonight have an historic opportunity. Let this Congress be the Congress that finally balances the budget. [*Applause*] Thank you.

In 2 days I will propose a detailed plan to balance the budget by 2002. This plan will balance the budget and invest in our people while protecting Medicare, Medicaid, education, and the environment. It will balance the budget and build on the Vice President's efforts to make our Government work better, even as it costs less. It will balance the budget and provide middle class tax relief to pay for education and health care, to help to raise a child, to buy and sell a home.

Balancing the budget requires only your vote and my signature. It does not require us to rewrite our Constitution. I believe it is both unnecessary and unwise to adopt a balanced budget amendment that could cripple our country in time of economic crisis and force unwanted results, such as judges halting Social Security checks or increasing taxes. Let us at least agree, we should not pass any measure—no measure should be passed that threatens Social Security. Whatever your view on that, we all must concede: We don't need a constitutional amendment; we need action.

Whatever our differences, we should balance the budget now. And then, for the long-term health of our society, we must agree to a bipartisan process to preserve Social Security and reform Medicare for the long run, so that these fundamental programs will be as strong for our children as they are for our parents.

And let me say something that's not in my script tonight. I know this is not going to be easy. But I really believe one of the reasons the American people gave me a second term was to take the tough decisions in the next 4 years that will carry our country through the next 50 years. I know it is easier for me than for you to say or do. But another reason I was elected is to support all of you, without regard to party, to give you what is necessary to join in these decisions. We owe it to our country and to our future.

Our second piece of unfinished business requires us to commit ourselves tonight, before the eyes of America, to finally enacting bipartisan campaign finance reform. Now, Senators McCain and Feingold, Representatives Shays and Meehan have reached across party lines here to craft tough and fair reform. Their proposal would curb spending, reduce the role of special interests, create a level playing field between challengers and incumbents, and ban contributions from noncitizens, all corporate sources, and the other large soft money contributions that both parties receive.

You know and I know that this can be delayed. And you know and I know the delay will mean the death of reform. So let's set our own deadline. Let's work together to write bipartisan campaign finance reform into law and pass McCain-Feingold by the day we celebrate the birth of our democracy, July the fourth.

There is a third piece of unfinished business. Over the last 4 years, we moved a record 2¼ million people off the welfare rolls. Then last year, Congress enacted landmark welfare reform legislation, demanding that all able-bodied recipients assume the responsibility of moving from welfare to work. Now each and every one of us has to fulfill our responsibility, indeed, our moral obligation, to make sure that people who now must work, can work.

Now we must act to meet a new goal: 2 million more people off the welfare rolls by the year 2000. Here is my plan: Tax credits and other incentives for businesses that hire people off welfare; incentives for job placement firms and States to create more jobs for welfare recipients; training, transportation, and child care to help people go to work.

Now I challenge every State: Turn those welfare checks into private sector paychecks. I challenge every religious congregation, every community nonprofit, every business to hire someone off welfare. And I'd like to say especially to every employer in our country who ever criticized the old welfare system, you can't blame that old system anymore. We have torn it down. Now do your part. Give someone on welfare the chance to go to work.

Tonight I am pleased to announce that five major corporations, Sprint, Monsanto, UPS, Burger King, and United Airlines, will be the first to join in a new national effort to marshal America's businesses, large and small, to create jobs so that people can move from welfare to work.

We passed welfare reform. All of you know I believe we were right to do it. But no one can walk out of this Chamber with a clear conscience unless you are prepared to finish the job.

And we must join together to do something else, too, something both Republican and Democratic Governors have asked us to do, to restore basic health and disability benefits when misfortune strikes immigrants who came to this country legally, who work hard, pay taxes, and obey the law. To do otherwise is simply unworthy of a great nation of immigrants.

Now, looking ahead, the greatest step of all, the high threshold of the future we must now cross, and my number one priority for the next 4 years is to ensure that all Americans have the best education in the world.

Let's work together to meet these three goals: Every 8-year-old must be able to read; every 12-year-old must be able to log on to the Internet; every 18-year-old must be able to go to college; and every adult American must be able to keep on learning for a lifetime.

My balanced budget makes an unprecedented commitment to these goals, $51 billion next year. But far more than money is required. I have a plan, a call to action for American education, based on these 10 principles:

First, a national crusade for education standards, not Federal Government standards but national standards, representing what all our students must know to succeed in the knowledge economy of the 21st century. Every State and school must shape the curriculum to reflect these standards and train teachers to lift students up to them. To help schools meet the standards and measure their progress, we will lead an effort over the next 2 years to develop national tests of student achievement in reading and math. Tonight I issue a challenge to the Nation: Every State should adopt high national standards, and by 1999, every State should test every fourth grader in reading and every eighth grader in math to make sure these standards are met.

Raising standards will not be easy, and some of our children will not be able to meet them at first. The point is not to put our children down but to lift them up. Good tests will show us who needs help, what changes in teaching to make, and which schools need to improve. They can help us end social promotions, for no child should move from grade school to junior high or junior high to high school until he or she is ready.

Last month our Secretary of Education, Dick Riley, and I visited northern Illinois, where eighth-grade students from 20 school districts, in a project aptly called First in the World, took the Third International Math and Science Study. That's a test that reflects the world-class standards our children must meet for the new era. And those students in Illinois tied for first in the world in science and came in second in math. Two of them, Kristen Tanner and Chris Getsler, are here tonight, along with their teacher, Sue Winski. They're up there with the First Lady. And they prove that when we aim high and challenge our students, they will be the best in the world. Let's give them a hand. Stand up, please. [*Applause*]

Second, to have the best schools, we must have the best teachers. Most of us in this Chamber would not be here tonight without the help of those teachers; I know that I wouldn't be here. For years, many of our educators, led by North Carolina's Governor Jim Hunt and the National Board for Professional Teaching Standards, have worked very hard to establish nationally accepted credentials for excellence in teaching. Just 500 of these teachers have been certified since 1995. My budget will enable 100,000 more to seek national certification as master teachers. We should reward and recognize our best teachers, and as we reward them, we should quickly and fairly remove those few who don't measure up. And we should challenge more of our finest young people to consider teaching as a career.

Third, we must do more to help all our children read. Forty percent—40 percent—of our 8-year-olds cannot read on their own. That's why we have just launched the America Reads initiative, to build a citizen army of one million volunteer tutors to make sure every child can read independently by the end of the third grade. We will use thousands of AmeriCorps volunteers to mobilize this citizen army. We want at least 100,000 college students to help, and tonight I am pleased that 60 college presidents have answered my call, pledging that thousands of their work-study students will serve for one year as reading tutors. This is also a challenge to every teacher and every principal: You must use these tutors to help students read. And it is especially a challenge to our parents: You must read with your children every night.

This leads to the fourth principle: Learning begins in the first days of life. Scientists are now discovering how young children develop emotionally and intellectually from their very first days and how important it is for parents to begin immediately talking, singing, even reading to their infants. The First Lady has spent years writing about this issue, studying it. And she and I are going to convene a White House conference on early learning and the brain this spring, to explore how parents and educators can best use these startling new findings.

We already know we should start teaching children before they start school. That's why this balanced budget expands Head Start to one million children by 2002. And that is why the Vice President and Mrs. Gore will host their annual family conference this June on what we can do to make sure that parents are an active part of their children's learning all the way through school. They've done a great deal to highlight the importance of family in our life, and now they're turning their attention to getting more parents involved in their children's learning all the way through school. And I thank you, Mr. Vice President, and I thank you especially, Tipper, for what you do.

Fifth, every State should give parents the power to choose the right public school for their children. Their right to choose will foster competition and innovation that can make public schools better. We should also make it possible for more parents and teachers to start charter schools, schools that set and meet the highest standards and exist only as long as they do. Our plan will help America to create 3,000 of these charter schools by the next century, nearly 7 times as there are in the country today, so that parents will have even more choices in sending their children to the best schools.

Sixth, character education must be taught in our schools. We must teach our children to be good citizens. And we must continue to promote order and discipline, supporting communities that introduce school uniforms, impose curfews, enforce truancy laws, remove disruptive students from the classroom, and have zero tolerance for guns and drugs in school.

Seventh, we cannot expect our children to raise themselves up in schools that are literally falling down. With the student population at an all-time high and record numbers of school buildings falling into disrepair, this has now become a serious national concern. Therefore, my budget includes a new initiative, $5 billion to help communities finance $20 billion in school construction over the next 4 years.

Eighth, we must make the 13th and 14th years of education, at least 2 years of college, just as universal in America by the 21st century as a high school education is today, and we must open the doors of college to all Americans. To do that, I propose America's HOPE scholarship, based on Georgia's pioneering program: 2 years of a $1,500 tax credit for college tuition, enough to pay for the typical community college. I also propose a tax deduction of up to $10,000 a year for all tuition after high school, an expanded IRA you can withdraw from tax-free for education, and the largest increase in Pell grant scholarships in 20 years. Now, this plan will give most families the ability to pay no taxes on money they save for college tuition. I ask you to pass it and give every American who works hard the chance to go to college.

Ninth, in the 21st century, we must expand the frontiers of learning across a lifetime. All our people, of whatever age, must have the chance to learn new skills. Most Americans live near a community college. The roads that take them there can be paths to a better future. My "GI bill" for America's workers will transform the confusing tangle of Federal training programs into a simple skill grant to go directly into eligible workers' hands. For too long, this bill has been sitting on that desk there without action. I ask you to pass it now. Let's give more of our workers the ability to learn and to earn for a lifetime.

Tenth, we must bring the power of the information age into all our schools. Last year, I challenged America to connect every classroom and library to the Internet by the year 2000, so that, for the first time in our history, children in the most isolated rural towns, the most comfortable suburbs, the poorest inner-city schools, will have the same access to the same universe of knowledge.

That is my plan, a call to action for American education. Some may say that it is unusual for a President to pay this kind of attention to education. Some may say it is simply because the President and his wonderful wife have been obsessed with this subject for more years than they can recall. That is not what is driving these proposals.

We must understand the significance of this endeavor. One of the greatest sources of our strength throughout the cold war was a bipartisan foreign policy. Because our future was at stake, politics stopped at the water's edge. Now I ask you and I ask all our Nation's Governors, I ask parents, teachers, and citizens all across America for a new nonpartisan commitment to education, because education is a critical national security issue for our future, and politics must stop at the schoolhouse door.

To prepare America for the 21st century, we must harness the powerful forces of science and technology to benefit all Americans. This is the first State of the Union carried live in video over the Internet. But we've only begun to spread the benefits of a technology revolution that should become the modern birthright of every citizen.

Our effort to connect every classroom is just the beginning. Now we should connect every hospital to the Internet, so that doctors can instantly share data about their patients with the best specialists in the field. And I challenge the private sector tonight to start by connecting every children's hospital as soon as possible, so that a child in bed can stay in touch with school, family, and friends. A sick child need no longer be a child alone.

We must build the second generation of the Internet so that our leading universities and national laboratories can communicate in speeds 1,000 times faster than today, to develop new medical treatments, new sources of energy, new ways of working together.

But we cannot stop there. As the Internet becomes our new town square, a computer in every home, a teacher of all subjects, a connection to all cultures, this will no longer be a dream but a necessity. And over the next decade, that must be our goal.

We must continue to explore the heavens, pressing on with the Mars probes and the international space station, both of which will have practical applications for our everyday living.

We must speed the remarkable advances in medical science. The human genome project is now decoding the genetic mysteries of life. American scientists have discovered genes linked to breast cancer and ovarian cancer and medication that stops a stroke in progress and begins to reverse its effects and treatments that dramatically lengthen the lives of people with HIV and AIDS.

Since I took office, funding for AIDS research at the National Institutes of Health has increased dramatically to $1.5 billion. With new resources, NIH will now become the most powerful discovery engine for an AIDS vaccine, working with other scientists to finally end the threat of AIDS. Remember that every year— every year—we move up the discovery of an AIDS vaccine will save millions of lives around the world. We must reinforce our commitment to medical science.

To prepare America for the 21st century, we must build stronger families. Over the past 4 years, the family and medical leave law has helped millions of Americans to take time off to be with their families. With new pressures on people in the way they work and live, I believe we must expand family leave so that workers can take time off for teacher conferences and a child's medical checkup. We should pass flextime, so workers can choose to be paid for overtime in income or trade it in for time off to be with their families.

We must continue, step by step, to give more families access to affordable, quality health care. Forty million Americans still lack health insurance. Ten million children still lack health insurance; 80 percent of them have working parents who pay taxes. That is wrong. My balanced budget will extend health coverage to up to 5 million of those children. Since nearly half of all children who lose their insurance do so because their parents lose or change a job, my budget will also ensure that people who temporarily lose their jobs can still afford to keep their health insurance. No child should be without a doctor just because a parent is without a job.

My Medicare plan modernizes Medicare, increases the life of the Trust Fund to 10 years, provides support for respite care for the many families with loved ones afflicted with Alzheimer's, and for the first time, it would fully pay for annual mammograms.

Just as we ended drive-through deliveries of babies last year, we must now end the dangerous and demeaning practice of forcing women home from the hospital only hours after a mastectomy. I ask your support for bipartisan legislation to guarantee that a woman can stay in the hospital for 48 hours after a mastectomy. With us tonight is Dr. Kristen Zarfos, a Connecticut surgeon whose outrage at this practice spurred a national movement and inspired this legislation. I'd like her to stand so we can thank her for her efforts. Dr. Zarfos, thank you. [*Applause*]

In the last 4 years, we have increased child support collections by 50 percent. Now we should go further and do better by making it a felony for any parent to cross a State line in an attempt to flee from this, his or her most sacred obligation.

Finally, we must also protect our children by standing firm in our determination to ban the advertising and marketing of cigarettes that endanger their lives.

To prepare America for the 21st century, we must build stronger communities. We should start with safe streets. Serious crime has dropped 5 years in a row. The key has been community policing. We must finish the job of putting 100,000 community police on the streets of the United States. We should pass the victims' rights amendment to the Constitution. And I ask you to mount a full-scale assault on juvenile crime with legislation that declares war on gangs with new prosecutors and tougher penalties; extends the Brady bill so violent teen criminals will not be able to buy handguns; requires child safety locks on handguns to prevent unauthorized use; and helps to keep our schools open after hours, on weekends, and in the summer, so our young people will have someplace to go and something to say yes to.

This balanced budget includes the largest antidrug effort ever, to stop drugs at their source, punish those who push them, and teach our young people that drugs are wrong, drugs are illegal, and drugs will kill them. I hope you will support it.

Our growing economy has helped to revive poor urban and rural neighborhoods. But we must do more to empower them to create the conditions in which all families can flourish and to create jobs through investment by business and loans by banks. We should double the number of empowerment zones. They've already brought so much hope to communities like Detroit, where the unemployment rate has been cut in half in 4 years. We should restore contaminated urban land and buildings to productive use. We should expand the network of community development banks. And together we must pledge tonight that we will use this empowerment approach, including private-sector tax incentives, to renew our Capital City, so that Washington is a great place to work and live and once again the proud face America shows the world.

We must protect our environment in every community. In the last 4 years, we cleaned up 250 toxic waste sites, as many as in the previous 12. Now we should clean up 500 more, so that our children grow up next to parks, not poison. I urge you to pass my proposal to make big polluters live by a simple rule: If you pollute our environment, you should pay to clean it up.

In the last 4 years, we strengthened our Nation's safe food and clean drinking water laws. We protected some of America's rarest, most beautiful land in Utah's Red Rocks region, created three new national parks in the California desert, and began to restore the Florida Everglades. Now we must be as vigilant with our rivers as we are with our lands. Tonight I announce that this year I will designate 10 American Heritage Rivers, to help communities alongside them revitalize their waterfronts and clean up pollution in the rivers, proving once again that we can grow the economy as we protect the environment.

We must also protect our global environment, working to ban the worst toxic chemicals and to reduce the greenhouse gases that challenge our health even as they change our climate.

Now, we all know that in all of our communities, some of our children simply don't have what they need to grow and learn in their own homes or schools or neighborhoods. And that means the rest of us must do more, for they are our children, too. That's why President Bush, General Colin Powell, former Housing Secretary Henry Cisneros will join the Vice President and me to lead the Presidents' Summit of Service in Philadelphia in April.

Our national service program, AmeriCorps, has already helped 70,000 young people to work their way through college as they serve America. Now we intend to mobilize millions of Americans to serve in thousands of ways. Citizen service is an American responsibility which all Americans should embrace, and I ask your support for that endeavor.

I'd like to make just one last point about our national community. Our economy is measured in numbers and statistics, and it's very important. But the enduring worth of our Nation lies in our shared values and our soaring spirit. So instead of cutting back on our modest efforts to support the arts and humanities, I believe we should stand by them and challenge our artists, musicians, and writers, challenge our museums, libraries, and theaters. We should challenge all Americans in the arts and humanities to join with our fellow citizens to make the year 2000 a national celebration of the American spirit in every community, a celebration of our common culture in the century that has passed and in the new one to come in the new millennium, so that we can remain the world's beacon not only of liberty but of creativity long after the fireworks have faded.

To prepare America for the 21st century, we must master the forces of change in the world and keep American leadership strong and sure for an uncharted time. Fifty years ago, a farsighted America led in creating the institutions that secured victory in the cold war and built a growing world economy. As a result, today more people than ever embrace our ideals and share our interests. Already we have dismantled many of the blocs and barriers that divided our parents' world. For the first time, more people live under democracy than dictatorship, including every nation in our own hemisphere but one, and its day, too, will come.

Now we stand at another moment of change and choice and another time to be farsighted, to bring America 50 more years of security and prosperity. In this endeavor, our first task is to help to build, for the very first time, an undivided, democratic Europe. When Europe is stable, prosperous, and at peace, America is more secure. To that end, we must expand NATO by 1999, so that countries that were once our adversaries can become our allies. At the special NATO summit this summer, that is what we will begin to do. We must strengthen NATO's Partnership For Peace with non-member allies. And we must build a stable partnership between NATO and a democratic Russia. An expanded NATO is good for America, and a Europe in which all democracies define their future not in terms of what they can do to each other but in terms of what they can do together for the good of all—that kind of Europe is good for America.

Second, America must look to the East no less than to the West. Our security demands it. Americans fought three wars in Asia in this century. Our prosperity requires it. More than 2 million American jobs depend upon trade with Asia. There, too, we are helping to shape an Asia-Pacific community of cooperation, not conflict. Let our progress there not mask the peril that remains. Together with South Korea, we must advance peace talks with North Korea and bridge the cold war's last divide. And I call on Congress to fund our share of the agreement under which North Korea must continue to freeze and then dismantle its nuclear weapons program.

We must pursue a deeper dialog with China for the sake of our interests and our ideals. An isolated China is not good for America; a China playing its proper role in the world is. I will go to China, and I have invited China's President to come here, not because we agree on everything but because engaging China is the best way to work on our common challenges like ending nuclear testing and to deal frankly with our fundamental differences like human rights.

The American people must prosper in the global economy. We've worked hard to tear down trade barriers abroad so that we can create good jobs at home. I am proud to say that today America is once again the most competitive nation and the number one exporter in the world.

Now we must act to expand our exports, especially to Asia and Latin America, two of the fastest growing regions on Earth, or be left behind as these emerging economies forge new ties with other nations. That is why we need the authority now to conclude new trade agreements that open markets to our goods and services even as we preserve our values.

We need not shrink from the challenge of the global economy. After all, we have the best workers and the best products. In a truly open market, we can out-compete anyone, anywhere on Earth.

But this is about more than economics. By expanding trade, we can advance the cause of freedom and democracy around the world. There is no better example of this truth than Latin America, where democracy and open markets are on the march together. That is why I will visit there in the spring to reinforce our important tie.

We should all be proud that America led the effort to rescue our neighbor Mexico from its economic crisis. And we should all be proud that last month Mexico repaid the United States 3 full years ahead of schedule, with half a billion dollar profit to us.

America must continue to be an unrelenting force for peace from the Middle East to Haiti, from Northern Ireland to Africa. Taking reasonable risks for peace keeps us from being drawn into far more costly conflicts later.

With American leadership, the killing has stopped in Bosnia. Now the habits of peace must take hold. The new NATO force will allow reconstruction and reconciliation to accelerate. Tonight I ask Congress to continue its strong support of our troops. They are doing a remarkable job there for America, and America must do right by them.

Fifth, we must move strongly against new threats to our security. In the past 4 years, we agreed to ban—we led the way to a worldwide agreement to ban nuclear testing. With Russia, we dramatically cut nuclear arsenals, and we stopped targeting each other's citizens. We are acting to prevent nuclear materials from falling into the wrong hands and to rid the world of landmines. We are working with other nations with renewed intensity to fight drug traffickers and to stop terrorists before they act and hold them fully accountable if they do.

Now we must rise to a new test of leadership, ratifying the Chemical Weapons Convention. Make no mistake about it. It will make our troops safer from chemical attack. It will help us to fight terrorism. We have no more important obligations, especially in the wake of what we now know about the Gulf war. This treaty has been bipartisan from the beginning, supported by Republican and Democratic administrations and Republican and Democratic Members of Congress and already approved by 68 nations. But if we do not act by April 29th, when this convention goes into force with or without us, we will lose the chance to have Americans leading and enforcing this effort. Together we must make the Chemical Weapons Convention law, so that at last we can begin to outlaw poison gas from the Earth.

Finally, we must have the tools to meet all these challenges. We must maintain a strong and ready military. We must increase funding for weapons modernization by the year 2000, and we must take good care of our men and women in uniform. They are the world's finest.

We must also renew our commitment to America's diplomacy and pay our debts and dues to international financial institutions like the World Bank and to a reforming United Nations. Every dollar we devote to preventing conflicts, to promoting democracy, to stopping the spread of disease and starvation, brings a sure return in security and savings. Yet international affairs spending today is just one percent of the Federal budget, a small fraction of what America invested in diplomacy to choose leadership over escapism at the start of the cold war. If America is to continue to lead the world, we here who lead America simply must find the will to pay our way.

A farsighted America moved the world to a better place over these last 50 years. And so it can be for another 50 years. But a shortsighted America will soon find its words falling on deaf ears all around the world.

Almost exactly 50 years ago, in the first winter of the cold war, President Truman stood before a Republican Congress and called upon our country to meet its responsibilities of leadership. This was his warning; he said, "If we falter, we may endanger the peace of the world, and we shall surely endanger the welfare of this Nation." That Congress, led by Republicans like

Senator Arthur Vandenberg, answered President Truman's call. Together, they made the commitments that strengthened our country for 50 years. Now let us do the same. Let us do what it takes to remain the indispensable nation, to keep America strong, secure, and prosperous for another 50 years.

In the end, more than anything else, our world leadership grows out of the power of our example here at home, out of our ability to remain strong as one America. All over the world, people are being torn asunder by racial, ethnic, and religious conflicts that fuel fanaticism and terror. We are the world's most diverse democracy, and the world looks to us to show that it is possible to live and advance together across those kinds of differences.

America has always been a nation of immigrants. From the start, a steady stream of people in search of freedom and opportunity have left their own lands to make this land their home. We started as an experiment in democracy fueled by Europeans. We have grown into an experiment in democratic diversity fueled by openness and promise.

My fellow Americans, we must never, ever believe that our diversity is a weakness. It is our greatest strength. Americans speak every language, know every country. People on every continent can look to us and see the reflection of their own great potential, and they always will, as long as we strive to give all of our citizens, whatever their background, an opportunity to achieve their own greatness.

We're not there yet. We still see evidence of abiding bigotry and intolerance in ugly words and awful violence, in burned churches and bombed buildings. We must fight against this, in our country and in our hearts.

Just a few days before my second Inauguration, one of our country's best known pastors, Reverend Robert Schuller, suggested that I read Isaiah 58:12. Here's what it says: "Thou shalt raise up the foundations of many generations, and thou shalt be called the repairer of the breach, the restorer of paths to dwell in." I placed my hand on that verse when I took the oath of office, on behalf of all Americans, for no matter what our differences in our faiths, our backgrounds, our politics, we must all be repairers of the breach.

I want to say a word about two other Americans who show us how. Congressman Frank Tejeda was buried yesterday, a proud American whose family came from Mexico. He was only 51 years old. He was awarded the Silver Star, the Bronze Star, and the Purple Heart fighting for his country in Vietnam. And he went on to serve Texas and America fighting for our future here in this Chamber. We are grateful for his service and honored that his mother, Lillie Tejeda, and his sister, Mary Alice, have come from Texas to be with us here tonight. And we welcome you.

Gary Locke, the newly elected Governor of Washington State, is the first Chinese-American Governor in the history of our country. He's the proud son of two of the millions of Asian-American immigrants who have strengthened America with their hard work, family values, and good citizenship. He represents the future we can all achieve. Thank you, Governor, for being here. Please stand up. [*Applause*]

Reverend Schuller, Congressman Tejeda, Governor Locke, along with Kristen Tanner and Chris Getsler, Sue Winski and Dr. Kristen Zarfos, they're all Americans from different roots whose lives reflect the best of what we can become when we are one America. We may not share a common past, but we surely do share a common future. Building one America is our most important mission, the foundation for many generations of every other strength

we must build for this new century. Money cannot buy it. Power cannot compel it. Technology cannot create it. It can only come from the human spirit.

America is far more than a place. It is an idea, the most powerful idea in the history of nations. And all of us in this Chamber, we are now the bearers of that idea, leading a great people into a new world. A child born tonight will have almost no memory of the 20th century. Everything that child will know about America will be because of what we do now to build a new century.

We don't have a moment to waste. Tomorrow there will be just over 1,000 days until the year 2000; 1,000 days to prepare our people; 1,000 days to work together; 1,000 days to build a bridge to a land of new promise. My fellow Americans, we have work to do. Let us seize those days and the century.

Thank you, God bless you, and God bless America.

NOTE: The President spoke at 9:15 p.m. in the House Chamber of the Capitol. The Executive order of September 11, 1997, establishing the American Heritage Rivers initiative was published in the *Federal Register* at 62 FR 48445.

Remarks on the Death of Ambassador Pamela Harriman
February 5, 1997

Hillary and I were very sad to learn that our good friend and America's outstanding Ambassador to France, Pamela Harriman, passed away just a few moments ago in Paris.

She was an extraordinary United States Ambassador, representing our country as well as our Government to the people of France and to the Government, earning the trust of the leaders and the admiration of people. She was one of the most unusual and gifted people I ever met, with an extraordinary life, from her years growing up in Great Britain to being a part of what the British went through in World War II as the Prime Minister's daughter-in-law and then her remarkable life in America with Averell Harriman, with all the work she did as a force for political activism for the Demo-

cratic Party, and with the friends she had in both parties, in business, in labor, and in politics.

Our country will miss her. We are deeply indebted to the work she did in France in maintaining our relationships with one of our oldest and closest allies. She was a source of judgment, an inspiration to me, a source of constant good humor and charm and real friendship, and we will miss her very, very much.

I had a good talk this morning with her son, Winston Churchill, and our prayers are with him and the rest of her family and her legion of friends. She will be brought home to America later this week, and we'll have more announcements about her funeral later.

America has lost a great public servant and another immigrant who became a great American.

Thank you.

NOTE: The President spoke at 10:28 a.m. on the South Lawn at the White House, prior to his departure for Augusta, GA.

Remarks Prior to a Roundtable Discussion on Education in Augusta, Georgia
February 5, 1997

The President. First of all, I want to thank all of you for agreeing to be part of this, and I'll be very brief because I want to hear from you.

I very much appreciate the fact that Senator Coverdell and Senator Cleland and Congressman Norwood came down with me today, along with Governor and Mrs. Miller. And I wanted to, after the State of the Union last night—which I believe was the most extensive treatment a President has ever given to the question of education in the State of the Union—I wanted to come here because I know a lot about what you've done here and what you're trying to do, and I think it's very important that the American people respond to the challenge that I laid out last night to make American education the best in the world, to understand that it won't be done overnight, and not to be afraid of trying to reach higher standards.

I went over—and I won't belabor it now, but this is a little booklet that I had done that Secretary of Education Riley, who is here with us today, put together for us, incorporating the 10 points that I made in the State of the Union last night. But in virtually every one of these areas, the State of Georgia is trying to move forward, and that's the important thing, whether it's opening the doors of college education with a HOPE scholarship or the pre-kindergarten program or the remarkable thing you're trying to do on the Internet, which will have a huge impact around the country if you do it, because then a lot of other States will get in here and help us. The Vice President and I have been trying to get all the schools hooked up by the year 2000, but we might get there ahead of time if every State would take the kind of action that you're taking here.

Then the thing that I really want to focus on is how we can achieve the objectives that were set out way back in 1989 by the Governors and then-President Bush. How can we achieve those national education goals? The only way we can ever do it is if we maintain the right blend of local control of our schools, State leadership, but adherence to high national standards so everybody understands what the bar is we're trying to reach.

And what we're going to try to do is to get the States and the school districts of the country and all the teachers organizations, the other educators, and the parents especially to accept the notion that there ought to be high standards and we ought to measure to see how our kids are doing, not to put them down but to lift them up and to support the whole educational process and make a specific effort to mobilize a lot of people to make sure our children are literate and that they can read independently at the appropriate level, at least by the time they get out of the third grade. So that's what we're going to do. And I think—what I hope will come out of this today is that by our being here people will see what you're trying to do in Georgia. They'll be interested in it, it will spark similar activities around the country, and we'll see a kind of a cascading effect.

You know, when the American people make up their mind to do something, they can get out ahead of the leaders in a hurry, and that's a good thing. When we started this hooking up the Internet, for example, we went to California, which is our biggest State, and had a NetDay and hooked up 20 percent of the schools in California. And we had this organized effort to get everybody else to do it. And within no time, the amount of activity outstripped the organization; people just went on and did it, just like you're doing. And that's what you want to happen.

So I'm very hopeful, I'm very excited, and I hope that now we can just hear from you. And Mr. Swearingen, I think you're going to run this show, so——

Carl Swearingen. We'll try, sir.

The President. ——the floor is yours.

NOTE: The President spoke at 1:17 p.m. in the Physical Education Athletic Complex at Augusta State University. In his remarks, he referred to Gov. Zell Miller of Georgia and Carl Swearingen, chairman, Georgia's Partnership for Excellence in Education. A portion of these remarks could not be verified because the tape was incomplete.

Remarks at Augusta State University in Augusta
February 5, 1997

Thank you so much, Tanya. She did a great job, didn't she? Let's give her a hand. I thought she was terrific. [*Applause*]

Dr. Bloodworth, thank you for making me feel so welcome here at Augusta State today. I must say, when I came in, Dr. Bloodworth had his whole family there, and you can't say that he's not trying to practice what he preaches. His son, Paul, has a Georgia HOPE scholarship, and his daughter, Nicole, was an AmeriCorps volunteer last year. If we could get everybody to follow that lead, we'd have no problems at all in America within no time. That's great.

I thank Mayor Sconyers for coming to meet me at the airport and for being here. He made a politician's promise. He promised that I would get some good barbecue before I left town, and I'm going to see if he keeps it.

I thank the many members of the Georgia Legislature who are here, and I know they have a pivotal role in education. My good friend Commissioner Tommy Irvin, I thank him for being here. I thank Secretary Riley for being willing to serve as Education Secretary. He has established a remarkable record already, and we just got started. And I thank him.

I thank Senator Coverdell and Congressman Norwood for coming down here with me on Air Force One today, along with Senator Cleland. I have to tell you this. I've known Max Cleland for a long time; I admire him for many things. When we go back home on Air Force One today, he will be landing at Andrews Air Force Base for the first time since he landed there as a terribly wounded veteran from the Vietnam war. He has come a long way, and we are proud of him.

I'd like to thank the other students who are here from the Augusta Technical Institute and its president, Terry Elam; Dr. Francis Tedesco and the students of the Medical College of Georgia; Dr. Shirley Lewis and the students of Payne College; and of course, the students and faculty of Augusta State. Thank you for being here.

When I arrived today, to read the local paper, I was wondering if any of you would come, because the local paper had a history of Presidents coming to Augusta, and there were so many and they came so often, I thought this might just be another day at the office. [*Laughter*] I read that my very first predecessor, George Washington, visited a precursor of your school, the Richmond School, in 1791—Richmond Academy. And he, George Washington, apparently did not give a speech; instead, he sat through oral exams. [*Laughter*] I'm glad you're letting me talk today. [*Laughter*] After the State of the Union last night, I'm so tired I couldn't pass any exam, written or oral. But it's certainly good to be at a place where no one I hear speaking has an accent. [*Laughter*]

In my State of the Union Address last night, I sought to challenge all of you to rise to the moment of preparing America for the 21st century. What I want all of you to understand is two things.

Number one, we really are moving into a time where more people from more walks of life will have a chance to rise higher and to live out more of their dreams than at any time in history. You must believe that. That is true— not a guarantee but a chance.

Number two, we all tend to think that the times we live in are normal. If you look at the whole sweep of human history, if you look at the whole sweep of American history, this is a highly unusual time. Why? Because we now

119

enjoy both prosperity and peace, but we're living in a time of such change we can't afford to just sit back and enjoy it, because the speed at which we're changing the way we work and live and relate to each other and the rest of the world is so great and its scope is so profound that we have lots of work to do.

But this is a blessing, not a curse. Very rarely have our people in this country ever had the freedom just to come together and totally shape our own future, unforced by a war, unforced by domestic turmoil, unforced by depression. We can sit here and construct a future for the children of America that is better than any time in all of human history, and we had better get at the work of doing it.

I came here today for some good reasons. Senator Cleland mentioned that President Roosevelt used to come to Georgia a lot, to Warm Springs. When Roosevelt came here and saw the plight of so many Georgians living in abject poverty, he got the inspiration to electrify rural America. For us it's hard to imagine today. Most families are wondering whether they can afford a computer in their home. When Roosevelt came to Georgia, a lot of families couldn't turn on a light. And he had this inspiration that electricity ought to be given to something besides people who lived in the cities. And the rural electrification effort was born, out of the inspiration he saw in Georgia.

And now, as we prepare for the new century, we have to give people another way to turn the lights on. We have to give everybody the tools to make the most of their own lives. And the most important thing we can do is to give people a good education, not just in terms of what they know but to put all of our people in a position that they can keep on learning for a lifetime. And that's why I came to Georgia, because Governor Miller, with the HOPE scholarship, with the pre-kindergarten program, with the commitment to hook up all your schools to the Internet, with all the other initiatives, has turned the lights on, and America is seeing the light.

It is no secret that I am a great admirer of your Governor. He spoke for me in New York in 1992 and talked about the house his mother built with her own hands. And with his thick Georgia accent, he pierced the deafest ears of people who never heard anybody talk like that before. [*Laughter*] And no one who heard that speech will ever forget the vivid image of

his mother crossing the creek with the rocks in her hand.

Governor Miller is the son of a teacher. He became a teacher himself. He's given his life to bringing education to every child here. But he has something else that's very important and embodied in that Marine Corps pin he wears on his lapel every day. Whatever he decides to do, he does with the same conviction and intensity and doggedness that he showed when he was a member of the United States Marines. And I'm glad he's fighting for you and your future, and I'm grateful that he's fought for me.

I also want to say to you something else. In the world in which we are living, we can do things together that will create the opportunities for people to make a great deal of their lives. But you will have to work harder to make more of it than the people did when rural electrification came in. We could come together and set up an authority and run those powerlines out and then all people had to do was flip a switch and the lights came on. Now we can come together and create the greatest structure of education in the world, but you can't just flip a switch. You have to go to work. You have to make the most of those opportunities.

No one can force-feed an education. People have to want it badly, deeply, in a way that makes learning not only important but fun. But it is work, and it is work that every American citizen must be prepared to do for himself or herself and with all of our children, every single one of them.

Last year I had the opportunity to speak at Princeton University in New Jersey. It was a great honor for me because they only ask the President to speak every 50 years, when they celebrate a 50th anniversary, and I just sort of fell into it. But I talked to them about how important it was for people not to believe that America's future rested solely on the young people who would graduate from our most elite institutions of higher education, that America's future rested on our ability to give everybody a higher education.

And I asked Governor Miller to go up there with me, and there we were, two southern boys sort of ogling the Ivy League. And I asked the people of Princeton to support taking Georgia's HOPE scholarship national, to give hope to all of America with a HOPE scholarship in every State, in every community. That's what I asked the Congress to approve last night: $1,500 tax credit to make a typical community college or other 2-year program available to virtually everyone in the United States and a $10,000 tax deduction for the cost of any tuition after high school at any program, undergraduate or graduate, and an expanded IRA you can withdraw from tax-free for education, and the biggest increase in Pell grants in 20 years. We can educate America with that program.

But I ask you to remember, too, that last night I said there were 10 principles to this program. Secretary Riley, in no time at all given the miracles of modern technology, has got them written up for us here. We'll be glad to send you a copy if you want one. But there are 10 things we have to do. Even though we're balancing the budget and cutting spending, I recommended $51 billion for education, by far the biggest amount of money the National Government has ever committed to education.

But it is not enough. And briefly, let me say to you that there are other things we must do, the most important of which is to make up our minds that we are finally going to achieve international excellence in education and that we do believe that all our children can learn. A lot of people don't believe that. I believe people perform according to their expectations, their support, and how we treat them and what we offer them.

We should begin with the proposition that every 8-year-old should be able to read, every 12-year-old should be able to get on to the Internet, every 18-year-old should be able to go on to college, every adult should keep on learning for a lifetime. We must start with the elemental principle that there should be national standards of excellence in education—not Federal Government standards, not something that takes away local control, not something that undermines the State's role in leading the way in education—but algebra is the same in Georgia as it is in Utah. We have to set up national standards for what every student must learn.

Teachers should be trained to help students meet these standards. There should be national tests reflecting the standards. All the teachers will understand this when I say it: There are lots of standardized tests; what we need are tests that reflect standards. And they're two very different things. Every State by 1999 should agree not only to have high standards but to have all their fourth graders take a national test, the same one, in reading, and all their eighth graders take a national test, the same one, in mathematics.

If you saw last night, if you watched the State of the Union, you know that there were 20 school districts that did something a lot of school districts wouldn't dare do, in northern Illinois. They agreed to go together to try to achieve international excellence in math and science for their eighth graders, and they agreed to take, with students from all over the world, the Third International Math and Science Survey. It is truly an international test reflecting what students should know worldwide at that point in their careers.

And the kids from those 20 school districts who took the test—a representative sample of them—of all their students—they tied for first in science and tied for second in math. But what I told them after the speech was over is I'd have been proud of them if they had finished dead last, because they had the courage to say, "We want to know how we stand against what we have to know." And I want you to support everybody in America doing that.

A lot of this intellectual work is like every other kind of work. We have to set the standards high and then train to meet the standards. People who work out can't do 100 pushups the first time they try. Not every student, not every school district, not every State will do all that well on these examinations the first time they're given. That is not the point. The point is to find out what we know and what we need to learn. We're not trying to put anybody down. We've got a whole country to lift up to a new century where learning will determine our future.

The second thing we have to do is to value our teachers more, to train them better and support them more. Many of our finest educators have worked hard to establish a system of national credentials for excellence in teaching. Five hundred master teachers have been certified by the national board since 1995. I offered a budget to the Congress last night that would permit 100,000 more teachers to be certified, so we could have at least one teacher in every school in America who had been through a rigorous training program that that teacher could then share with every other teacher in the school, to support the teachers who are going to determine the quality of education of our children.

The third thing I want to do is to do more to help our children read. There was a story in the press a couple of days ago which pointed out that we now have four school districts in America where the children in the school districts speak as their native tongue over 100 different languages. You want me to say that again? That's unbelievable, isn't it? Four. Atlanta—I don't know how many tongues there are, but Atlanta is the headquarters to more international companies than any other city in the country. They must have 50 or 60 there.

Now, one consequence of this, along with increasing poverty over the last 20 years of young children, is that 40 percent of our 8-year-olds can't read at grade level. And that simply means they can't read a third-grade book by themselves, 4 out of 10. How many are capable of doing it with the brain they've got up there? Nearly all of them. You must believe this; otherwise we're just up here talking to ourselves. Nearly all of them are capable of doing this.

So we have a lot of work to do, and our schools cannot do it all alone. We need more help from the parents, but we also need more help from the rest of us. I am committed to mobilizing a citizen army of a million people to be trained as tutors and to be willing to tutor children in every community in this country so that by the year 2000 every 8-year-old can pick up a book and say, "I can read this book all by myself." And I want you to help us do it.

We're going to use a lot of our AmeriCorps volunteers to mobilize the system, but we need a million people. I have asked that at least 100,000 of the 200,000 new work-study slots that we created in last year's budget be devoted to college students who are willing to work as tutors. And last night I said 60 presidents have already pledged thousands of their work-study students to do that. I hope some of you in this room today will say, "I'd be honored to try to teach a child to read so that child can have the same opportunity I have today to be a student in a university." I hope you will do that. Your country needs you to do that.

The fourth point I want to make is that we have to start teaching children very early. Georgia has what I believe is the most extensive pre-kindergarten program in the United States. Good for you. Good for you. We have extended Head Start coverage to 3-year-olds in the last couple of years. And that's a very good thing.

But we have to begin even earlier. We now know that children's brains develop more than half of their capacity—not what they know but their capacity to learn—within the first 4 years. We now know that a child with parents who have confidence that they can help that child and understand what they're supposed to do will get as many as 700,000 positive contacts from the parents in the first 4 years of life. A child with a parent who feels ill-equipped for the job, who has no idea what to do, who desperately loves her child but just doesn't know, may have given that child as few as 150,000 positive contacts in the first 4 years. You tell me which child is going to be better when they're 18, given what we know now from these scientists.

So we have got to support, all of us, everything we can do to help get out there and convince parents, even if they don't have a good education, they can do something very important for their children from the day they are born. That is my wife's strong commitment and mine. We're going to bring together scientists and educators from all over America this spring at a conference on early childhood development and the brain. And we're going to try to take all these new discoveries, so that when our children do get to school, the teachers will be able to do what they want to do with them, because they have been given the opportunity to develop in a wholesome, positive way in the first 3 or 4 years of their lives. And I hope you will support everything that is being done here to that end.

Next we want to support more innovation in our public schools. And I want to compliment Georgia for its magnet schools and for the charter school program you've just started. It's unfamiliar to most Americans, but basically charter schools are public schools that are free from some of the rules and regulations that other schools have to follow, created by teachers, parents, and others with a certain mission. But they can exist only as long as they fulfill the mission. If they don't produce educational excellence, they don't keep their charter. And Georgia is leading the way there, too.

Last night I asked the Congress to give me enough funds to support 3,000 of those schools. That's 7 times as many as there are in the United States today. But that, again, is an important part of innovation. Eventually, we need to get to the point where every school is just like these charter schools—every school is just like these magnet schools. They all have their own personality; they only have their own culture; they have their own standards; and they work. But the best way to do it is to create models in every school district of the United States, and that's what the charter school movement will do. And that's another reason I'm very proud of the State of Georgia for trying to lead the way.

The next point I want to make is—somebody has got a sign up there to say they have a middle school and they wear school uniforms. Hold that sign up there. "Mr. President, Glen Hills Middle School Wears Uniforms." Thank you very much. Stand up without the sign. Stand up. There you go, good for you. [*Applause*] Thank you. Now, I promise we did not organize this. I didn't even know they were going to be there. [*Laughter*]

Last night I said our schools need to teach character education. We need to teach young people to be good citizens. And we need to support these schools when they try to find their own way to do that. Schools that require school uniforms, that's one way to do that. I've been in school districts where the crime rate dropped, the violence in the school dropped, the dropout rate dropped, and the wealthier kids as well as the poorer kids liked it better when they adopted their own uniform of their own choosing in a way that helped them preserve order in the schools. That's one way of creating school identity. It normally works in grade school and junior high better than high school, for obvious reasons, but it can have a positive impact.

The point is that we need to recognize that our schools are molding the character of our young people, and we should not discourage them. One of the best things Secretary Riley has done, of all the wonderful things he's done, is to get out here and push the teaching of character education and to try to make it clear that we do not have to have a value-free environment in schools. That is cancerous. We should have a valued environment in the schools. And I thank him for that, and I know you believe that.

The seventh thing we're trying to do is help the school districts that are absolutely overwhelmed with growth, with a lot of buildings that are falling down, get out of the hole they're in. The National Government's never done this before, and I wouldn't be doing it now, but

we have 52 million public school students, the largest number in history, with more buildings falling down than any time in history. I've been in school districts where half the kids were going to class in trailers outside the regular building.

And we need to do what we can to support local efforts. So if people at the local level are willing to put up their funds to try to build the buildings and repair the buildings that the schools need, we want to be in a position to support what they're doing. And we think with a modest expenditure we can help to spark $20 billion more in school construction and repair over the next 4 years. And that's what we intend to do, and I hope you'll support that.

Just two other points very quickly. Learning has got to become a lifetime endeavor. Ask someone who works in a bank whether it's different being a bank teller today than it was 10 years ago. Go into any working environment and see how different it is now from the way it was just a few years ago. I spent a lot of time working with law enforcement. Do you want to know one reason that the crime rate's dropped in America for 5 years in a row for the first time in years and years and years— is that our law enforcement officers in a lot of our bigger cities where the crime rate's very high have become basically high-tech managers of criminal justice resources to support local neighborhoods. In New York, they had a precipitous drop in the crime rate when they realized that they could have computer reports every single day of every offense in that vast city, put it up on a map, study the patterns of crime, and put the police into the neighborhood working with the people—changing it on a daily basis.

Every kind of work is different. That's why I have asked the Congress to pass what I call a "GI bill"—you heard Max Cleland talking about the GI bill—what I call a "GI bill" for America's workers.

We've got 70 different training programs the Federal Government has put up for people who are unemployed or underemployed over time. Every one of them had a good justification. Today, we don't need that anymore. Nearly every American is within driving distance of a community college or another community-based educational institution like this one—nearly every American. So I say get rid of that, put the money in a pot, send a skill grant to every adult who's eligible for it, and let that man or woman figure out where to get the best education. They'll figure it out in no time, and it will be a place like Augusta State. That's what will happen. And I hope you will ask your Members of Congress to support that.

Last thing I want to say is this. We have got to do what Governor Miller plans to do here; we have got to harness the full force of technology to every school in the United States. Now, I have this argument all the time with people my age who aren't very good on a computer—that includes me; I'm not saying they aren't and I am—but a lot of people come up to me and they say, "Now, Mr. President, I like your education program, but I think you're overdoing this Internet deal. I mean, you know, what good is the Internet if people can't read and write?" The point is that a lot of these kids will be more interested in learning to read and write if they have access to technology. And if we hook up all of our schools to the Internet, it will mean that for the very first time in the entire history of the United States of America, the kids in the poorest schools, the kids in the most isolated rural schools, and the kids in the wealthiest schools will all have access to the same universe of knowledge in the same way at the same time. That's never happened in the history of the country before. It will revolutionize what it means to be a student. And it will also say to all these kids that now feel like nobody cares about them, "You're just as important as anybody else. You matter. You can learn whatever you want. You can be whatever you want to be."

This is not about technology. This is about unleashing the power of the human mind that resides in every single one of our young people. So I say, what Zell Miller is doing here in Georgia will put you ahead of the pack, but the most important thing is, it may make everyone in America want to do this even faster than I thought we could do it. Every class, every school—eventually every home will have a connection to every school through a computer.

And let me just give you one example. I visited a school district in New Jersey that was doing so poorly the State was literally going to shut it down and take it over. Most of the students were lower income. Many of them were from first-generation immigrant families whose parents did not speak English. And I saw the Bell Atlantic phone company, along with some other companies, go in there, put computers in all the classrooms, give them to all the kids and to a lot of the children who were having trouble, actually put personal computers in the homes and teach the parents, the immigrant parents, how to E-mail the teachers and the principals.

And you say, "Why are they doing all that? These people need to learn to read, write, count, speak basic English." All I know is, 3 years later this school district that was going to be shut down had a lower dropout rate, a higher graduation rate, and higher test scores than the average in the State of New Jersey, which has the second highest per capita income in the United States of America. Don't tell me all of our kids can't learn. They can learn if we do it right and we help them and we support them.

But again I say, we have a limited amount of time. You don't know how long America can go in a state of prosperity and peace where everything looks rosy to the country. You don't know how long we can go still tolerating in a passive way the loss of as many kids as we're losing to crime, to drugs, to all the problems we have. We don't have a lot of time. There really are just a few days over 1,000 days until the year 2000. But very few societies in all human history have had the opportunity we have to have peace, prosperity, opportunity, and the chance to forge our own future.

This is a call to action. I am committed to doing my part. You must do yours.

Thank you, and God bless you. And God bless America.

NOTE: The President spoke at 3 p.m. in the Physical Education Athletic Complex. In his remarks, he referred to Tanya Davis, chair, student senate, who introduced the President, and William Bloodworth, Jr., president, Augusta State University; Mayor Larry Sconyers of Augusta; Tommy Irvin, Georgia commissioner of agriculture; Terry Elam, president, Augusta Technical Institute; Francis J. Tedesco, president, Medical College of Georgia; and Shirley Lewis, president, Payne College. A portion of these remarks could not be verified because the tape was incomplete.

Remarks at the National Prayer Breakfast
February 6, 1997

Thank you very much, Congressman Barrett. I want to thank you for making it possible for me to follow Dr. Carson. [*Laughter*] And that business about worrying about whether the Secret Service would take you away if you talked too long, if that were true I wouldn't be here today. I'd be long gone. [*Laughter*] That biochemical description of—I got a real problem; I can't remember my home phone number anymore. [*Laughter*]

Senator Akaka, Mr. Speaker, Congressman Gephardt, to all the Members of Congress and the Governors who are here and our leaders and visitors from other lands and ministers and citizens from the United States. I've had a wonderful day today. I would like not to pour cold water on the day, but just as you go through the day I would like to ask all of you to remember the heartbreaking loss that our friends in Israel have sustained in the last couple of days with 73 of their finest young soldiers dying in that horrible accident in the air.

I would like to also say that, like all of you, I was very elevated by this experience, as I always am. I thought Dr. Carson was wonderful. I thought the Scriptures were well chosen. I appreciate Doug Coe and all the people who work on the prayer breakfast so much.

I would like to just say a couple of things very briefly. In my Inaugural Address and again in my State of the Union, I quoted Isaiah 58:12, which Reverend Robert Schuller sent to me a few days before I started my second term, to remind us that we should all be repairers of the breach. And it's a very moving thing. And basically the political press here read it in the proper way; they said Clinton wants the Republicans and Democrats to make nice to each other and do constructive things.

But then I got to thinking about who is it that's in the breach. Who has fallen between the cracks? If we repaired the breach, who would we be lifting out of the hole? And very briefly, I'd like to just mention three things and to ask you not only to pray for these three groups of people but also to do something about it. I don't know about you, but whenever I hear somebody like Dr. Carson speak, I can clap better than anybody in the audience. Then the next day, when I get up and try to live by what he said I was supposed to do, it turned out to be harder than it was to clap. So I would like to ask you to think about who is in the breach, if we're supposed to be repairers of the breach.

The first group of people that are in the breach are the poor in America, and they're different then they used to be. When I was a boy, most poor people were old. In 1995, we learned last year, we had the lowest rate of poverty among older Americans in the history of the country. We have succeeded in taking them out of poverty, virtually all of them. We should be proud of that and grateful. Today, almost all the poor are young, very young people without much education, a lot of mothers like Dr. Carson's mother, struggling, doing the best they can to raise their kids.

We just passed this welfare reform bill which I signed and voted for because I believed it. And we did it because we believed that the welfare system had gone from being a system that helped the poor to help themselves to move off welfare, to a system that trapped people because the family unit has changed and there are so many single parents out there having children, and there isn't the stigma on it there used to be. And a lot of people now seem to be stuck on that system from generation to generation. So we changed it—we didn't change it; we tore it down. We threw it away. We said, "There's no longer a national guarantee that you can always get a check from the Government just because you're poor and you've got little babies in your home. Now the kids can have health care and we'll give them food, but you don't get an income check every month. And you've got to go to work if you're able to."

So the people that are in the breach are the people that we say have to go to work, who want to go to work, who can't go to work. And you have to help us repair the breach. Two and a quarter million people moved off the welfare rolls in the last 4 years. A million of them, more or less, were adults who went to work; the others were their children—a million out of 11 million new jobs created.

In the next 4 years, there's about, more or less, 10 million more people left on welfare, about 3½ million adults, maybe 4, most of them able-bodied. And all of them are supposed to lose their benefits if they're able-bodied after 2 years unless they go to work. Where are they going to get the jobs? You're going to have to give them—private employers, churches, community nonprofits. I see the Governor of Michigan, the Governor of North Dakota here. They can actually take the welfare check and give it to you now as an employment or a training subsidy or to help you deal with transportation or child care or whatever.

But you better hire them. And if you don't, this whole thing will be a fraud, and we will not have repaired the breach. And all that we dreamed of doing, which is to create more Dr. Carsons out of those children of welfare recipients, will go down the drain because we come to places like this and clap for people like him and then we get up tomorrow morning and we don't repair the breach and do what we're supposed to do. And I need you to help.

The second people who have fallen between the cracks are people around the world who are in trouble that we could help without troubling ourselves very much. I'm proud of what our country has done in Bosnia and the Balkans—you should be too—in the Middle East, in Haiti, to help our neighbors in Mexico. Impulses—the American people are generous. I want to thank the Speaker for supporting me when only 15 percent of the American people thought we were right when we tried to help our friends in Mexico. Thank goodness they proved us right, Mr. Speaker, otherwise we might be out in the south 40 somewhere today.

But still our country has this idea that somehow it demeans us to pay our dues to the United Nations or to participate in the World Bank or—there's lots of things more important than that—or just to give Secretary Albright, who's here, the basic tools of diplomacy. This is an interdependent world. We can get a long way with having the finest defense in the world, but we also have to help people become what they can be.

So I ask you to think about that. We're not talking about spending a lot of money here. It's only one percent of our budget. But we can't walk away from our obligations to the rest of the world. We can be a model for the rest of the world, but we also know that we have

to model the behavior we advocate, which is to give a helping hand when we can.

The third people who are in the breach and are in a deep hole and need to be lifted up are the politicians. And we need your help. We need your help. And some members of the press, they're in that breach with us, too, and they need your help. [*Laughter*]

This is funny, but I'm serious now. And tomorrow, I want you to wake—I want you to laugh today and wake up and be serious tomorrow. This town is gripped with people who are self-righteous, sanctimonious, and hypocritical; all of us are that way sometimes. I plead guilty, from time to time. We also tend to get—we spend an enormous amount of time here in Washington trying to get even. And it doesn't matter who started it.

I remember when I came here one time, I got so mad at our friends in the Congress and the Republican Party because they were real mean to me over something. I went back to the White House, and I asked somebody who had been there a while in Washington, and I said, "Now, why in the world did they do that?" They said, "It's payback time." I said, "What do you mean?" They said, "Well, they think the Democrats in Congress did this to Republican Presidents." I said, "I didn't even live here then. Why are they paying me back?" They said, "Oh, you don't understand. You've just got to pay back."

So then, pretty soon I was behaving that way. I'd wake up in the morning, and my heart was getting a little harder. "Now, who can I get even with?" You think—this happens to you, doesn't it? "Who can I get even with?" And sometimes you can't get even with the person that really did it to you, so you just go find somebody else, because you've got to get even with somebody. Pretty soon, everybody's involved in this great act.

You know how cynical the press is about the politicians, you know. They think we're all whatever they think. What you should know is that the politicians have now become just as cynical about the press, because cynicism breeds cynicism.

We're in a world of hurt. We need help. We are in the breach. We are in the hole here. This country has the most astonishing opportunity we have ever had. We happen to be faced with this time of great change and challenge. We're going into this enormous new world. And instead of going into it hobbled with economic distress or foreign pressures, we are free of any threat to our existence and our economy is booming. And it's like somebody said, "Here's this brave new world, and I'm going to let you prepare for it and walk into it in the best shape you've ever been in." And instead of doing that, half of us want to sit down, and the other half of us want to get in a fight with each other. We are in the breach. And we need you to help us get out of it.

The United States is better than that. We owe more than that to our people, to our future, and to the world. We owe more than that to our heritage, to everybody from George Washington on, that made us what we are today. And cynicism and all this negative stuff is just sort of a cheap excuse for not doing your best with your life. And it's not a very pleasant way to live, frankly—not even any fun.

I try to tell everybody around the White House all the time, I have concluded a few things in my life, and one of them is that you don't ever get even. The harder you try, the more frustrated you're going to be, because nobody ever gets even. And when you do, you're not really happy. You don't feel fulfilled.

So I ask you to pray for us. I went to church last Sunday where Hillary and I always go, at the Foundry Methodist Church, and the pastor gave a sermon on Romans 12:16 through 21 and a few other verses. But I'm going to quote the relevant chapters. "Do not be wise in your own estimation." It's hard to find anybody here that can fit that. "Never pay back evil for evil to anyone." "If possible, so far as it depends upon you, be at peace with all men." "Never take your own vengeance." "If your enemy is hungry, feed him. If he is thirsty, give him a drink." "Do not be overcome by evil, but overcome evil with good."

Pray for the people in public office that we can rid ourselves of this toxic atmosphere of cynicism and embrace with joy and gratitude this phenomenal opportunity and responsibility before us. Do not forget people in the rest of the world who depend upon the United States for more than exhortation. And most of all, remember that in every Scripture of every faith, there are hundreds and hundreds and hundreds of admonitions not to forget those among us who are poor. They are no longer entitled to a handout, but they surely deserve, and we are ordered to give them, a hand up.

Thank you, and God bless you all.

NOTE: The President spoke at 9:28 a.m. at the Washington Hilton Hotel. In his remarks, he referred to Representative Bill Barrett, chairman, 1997 National Prayer Breakfast; Dr. Ben Carson, director of pediatric neurosurgery, Johns Hopkins Hospital; Doug Coe, who helped organize the event; and Governors John Engler of Michigan and Edward T. Schafer of North Dakota.

Remarks on the 1998 Budget
February 6, 1997

Good morning. In my State of the Union Address, I issued a call to action to prepare our people for the 21st century. I said that to do that we first had to finish the unfinished business of America, beginning with balancing the budget.

Today I am submitting to Congress my plan to balance the budget by 2002. It will spur economic growth, promote education and our other priorities, and eliminate the Federal deficit for the very first time in three decades. I am proud of this budget, and I want to thank the people here on the economic team who worked with me on it. Thank you.

For too many years, it seemed as if our deficit would grow forever, that there was nothing we could do about it. As a result, our economy and our people suffered. Four years ago I took office with a plan to reduce the deficit in half in 4 years, as we invested in our people. In fact, the deficit has been cut by nearly two-thirds, from $290 billion in 1992 to $107 billion in 1996. That makes it, as a proportion of our economy, the smallest of any major nation in the world.

Our economy, therefore, has gotten stronger. It's the strongest it's been in a generation. The American people have produced over 11 million jobs—that's the most ever in a single Presidential term—along with record numbers of new businesses and rising incomes.

Finishing this job of balancing the budget will not be easy, but it is vital for the continued health of our economy. Balancing the budget will free up billions of dollars in private investment. It will keep interest rates low, allowing our people to start new businesses, buy a home or a new car. It will prove that when we set our minds to it, we can make our Government live within its means.

My plan balances the budget while maintaining the balance of our values.

First, it eliminates the deficit by 2002 through detailed, difficult cuts in hundreds of Government programs.

Second, it increases investment in education and training to $51 billion in 1998, a 20 percent increase. It provides tax cuts to help families pay for college, increases Pell grant scholarships for deserving students, advances the America Reads initiative to help every 8-year-old read independently, commits to helping connect every classroom to the Internet by the year 2000. As I said in the State of the Union, education is a key national security issue, and politics should stop at the schoolhouse door.

Third, it provides targeted tax relief for the middle class, to pay for education, health care, to buy and sell a home. It provides a $500-per-child tax credit to help families raise their children.

Fourth, it takes critical steps to extend health care to more Americans. It secures the Medicare Trust Fund for 10 years, making necessary reforms to help the program meet these budget targets and also to maintain its fundamental purpose. It will cover as many as 5 million presently uninsured children and help working people who are temporarily between jobs keep their health insurance. For the first time, it would fully cover annual mammograms for older women and provide some respite care support for the many families who are caring for a family member with Alzheimer's.

Fifth, it advances our interests as the world's indispensable nation, reversing the downward spiral in international affairs spending, strengthening our ability to promote peace, and fighting global problems like drug trafficking, terrorism, and nuclear proliferation. And this budget meets our responsibilities to the community of nations by the concrete plan to promote reform, pay

our bills, and put the United Nations back on sound financial footing.

I support a balanced budget. I am proposing a balanced budget. I do not support a constitutional amendment to balance the budget for reasons I have already outlined. I think it is neither necessary or wise, and it could have numerous unwanted consequences. It could throw our budget into the courts. It could force judges to make decisions they would normally never make and that they know they should not be making. And all that it takes to balance the budget is discipline and action.

I'd also like to say this. We believe our balanced budget plan will keep the budget more or less in balance. And I say that because it's impossible to predict everything that will happen. But based on the projections we now have, we believe we can maintain a balanced budget for more than two decades. So this is not going to be a one-time thing. And Director Raines will talk more about this when he goes through the details. But one of the things I think Americans have been afraid of is that even if we balance the budget, it will be a one-year blip, and then we'll go right back to the same problems we've had in the past, particularly as the baby boomers age and move into the retirement years. We do not believe that is going to happen with this budget. And Secretary Rubin and Mr. Raines can explain why, and I know you'll want to question them on that, but that is one of the most important findings of the work that we have been doing. We believe we can keep this budget in balance for a good long time.

Finally, let me say this. It is obvious—and most of you have reported on this—that there are still differences between the parties about how we should do this, but I am convinced those differences can be bridged. I have reviewed them in general, at least. I have been very impressed by the cooperative attitude which has been expressed by the leaders of the Republican Party in Congress. Some of the differences we have are truly principle differences, and we'll have to work hard to have an honorable compromise. But I believe that we can do it as long as the Republicans and the Democrats agree that we have to achieve this goal.

We've got the best chance in a generation to do it. The lion's share of the savings that we needed to make from the nightmarish projections we had 4 years ago have been put in place already, and it remains for us to take the last steps. I am confident we will, and I intend to do everything I can—everything I can over the next few months to see that we achieve this goal.

Now, I'd like to ask the Vice President to say a few words, and then we'll follow with

Secretary Rubin, Mr. Raines, and however else they want to elucidate the budget.

Mr. Vice President.

NOTE: The President spoke at 11:58 a.m. in Room 450 of the Old Executive Office Building.

Message to Federal Workers
February 6, 1997

As I begin my second term as President, I want all of you to know how proud I am of your hard work and accomplishments during the past four years. I came to Washington with a high regard for civil servants, and you have only confirmed that opinion.

And I'm not the only one who has been impressed. Four years ago, public confidence in the federal government was at an all-time low. But you have begun to change that attitude. Even in a time of leaner budgets and smaller staffs, you have improved service to the public, forged effective partnerships with communities and private businesses, and discarded old-fashioned management systems. Now, for the first time in decades, public opinion of federal agencies is markedly on the rise. Congratulations—

the credit for this stunning turnaround goes to you.

Vice President Gore and I are excited and optimistic about the prospects for America in the next four years. We are on the right track to the twenty-first century and are picking up speed as we continue to work with you to reinvent government. I believe that our nation will enter that new century stronger, more confident, and more capable than ever before. And I believe that a large part of that success will be achieved because of the energy and talent of each of you—the men and women of the federal government.

Thank you for all you do on behalf of your fellow Americans.

BILL CLINTON

Remarks Prior to Discussions With Prime Minister Viktor Chernomyrdin of Russia and an Exchange With Reporters
February 7, 1997

President Clinton. I want to welcome Prime Minister Chernomyrdin to the White House and thank him for the work that he and the Vice President have done over the last couple of days dealing with the issues involving the relationships of Russia and the United States and NATO and Russia and a number of other issues. And I want to thank them for the work they've done to prepare the way for my meeting with President Yeltsin in Helsinki on March 20th and 21st.

And I also want to thank President Ahtisaari of Finland for hosting us at that meeting. I'm looking forward to it. It will be very important,

and I feel quite optimistic about it because of the good relationships I've always had with President Yeltsin and because of the work that the Prime Minister and the Vice President have done.

Helsinki Summit and NATO Expansion

Q. Two questions, Mr. President. Number one, was Helsinki chosen to accommodate the health of President Yeltsin? And two, how do you convince the President and Mr. Chernomyrdin that NATO expansion is not the threat that they seem to think it is?

President Clinton. Well, first of all, Helsinki was decided upon for a number of reasons, but it worked well for both of us, and I feel good about it. I'm looking forward to going back there.

Q. Was health one of the reasons?

President Clinton. Secondly, we just have started our meeting here, but I think you have to see this issue in the context of our—all American-Russian relations and the fact that Russia has emerged as a great democratic nation with such strong sense of partnership with the European countries. The best evidence of that is what we're all doing together in Bosnia today— for our partnership there.

Juvenile Crime

Q. Mr. President, one of the global issues on the forefront today is also the CDC report on suicide and homicide among juveniles. How do you react to the fact that the United States is leading the richest nations among homicides and suicides among 15-year-olds and under?

President Clinton. I'm very concerned about it, and we're working on it. That's one of the reasons that I made such a big issue of juvenile crime and violence in the State of the Union. There is some indication that it is going down now after years and years and years of exploding. The last figures we have for 1995 were somewhat encouraging.

It's an unacceptable condition. And we have too many children out there raising themselves on our streets, too many children who have not been embraced by their communities, who can't get what they need in their own families. The rest of us have to do better. And a big part of what I hope we can work together on with the Congress is the whole juvenile justice package, which I think will be passed and then fully implemented, along with the community efforts that are going on in places like Boston, which is a good model, where there hasn't been a single juvenile homicide in 18 months, I think, in a long time.

If we can learn from what's working out there, we can turn this around. But we ought to be sensitive about it, not only because we don't rank well compared to all of the nations but because it means we're losing too many of our children.

Q. Were you shocked by it?

President Clinton. No. I'm shocked by—I was shocked but not surprised, because I knew that we would have the worst record on this.

1998 Budget

Q. Senator Lott says he is greatly depressed by your budget proposal. What did you think about that?

President Clinton. Well, I had a good visit with him today; I'm trying to put him in a better frame of mind about it. We know that from the last 2 years that they have different priorities than I do in balancing the budget. But the American people should remember this administration has a record now; we've cut the deficit by 63 percent. We're serious about balancing the budget, but we think we have to do it in a way that protects our values and invests in our future.

If the charge is that I have invested more in education and in the health and welfare of poor children in this country, then that's a charge I'm guilty of. I presented a budget that invested a lot more in education and in the health and welfare of poor children, and I'm guilty of that. But I think that's good for America, to make it stronger, and we'll still balance the budget.

Q. Did you talk to Senator Lott——

President Clinton. Let me just make one more comment on that. We are just beginning this process, and I took no offense about what he said today. I'm very encouraged by the remarks that have been made by the House leaders and the Senate leaders in the budget process. I think he thinks that maybe there's a bigger difference between us, and we'll have to work harder, but we always knew we were going to have to work hard to reconcile the differences between us. We can do this.

But if you look at the differences between us and you look at how close we are to a balanced budget, we can do it, and I'm convinced we will do it. And I think what I want to do is make sure we do it in a way that's best for the American people and deals with this enormous problem we have, especially of our young people—giving them the right kind of education, keeping them out of trouble, giving them decent health care and—because I don't want to have to keep reading years from now the kind of rankings that were just quoted to me from the CDC.

[*At this point, one group of reporters left the room, and another group entered.*]

Prime Minister Chernomyrdin's Visit

President Clinton. First, let me say that we are honored to welcome Prime Minister Chernomyrdin back to Washington. And I very much appreciate the work that he and the Vice President have done and will do after this meeting on issues between our two countries. And I'm especially grateful that they worked out a time for President Yeltsin and me to meet in Helsinki on March 20th and 21st. I thank President Ahtisaari for agreeing to host us, and I'm delighted to be going back to Helsinki and very, very anxious to have my meeting with President Yeltsin.

Russia and NATO

Q. Mr. President, would you agree to sign a legal binding agreement with Russia on European security guarantees?

President Clinton. Well, I believe that we ought to work out an agreement between NATO and Russia—the United States—which ensures that Russia will have a leading role in European security affairs. There are all kinds of—the question you asked me and the way you ask it leaves a lot of landmines open there. I believe that we can work out an agreement that will be sufficiently satisfactory to both parties, that we can get that.

But I don't want to say yes to the question you ask because that would imply things which might make any agreement we could reach meaningless. We want a meaningful agreement that is signed and public and that the parties feel bound to but that actually means something.

Five Nation Summit

Q. Mr. President, would you like to go to Paris to that summit of five nations? Looks like Russia supports that, the French, the Germans.

President Clinton. First of all, I want to have my meeting with President Yeltsin. I think that's the most important thing. We have to meet first. Chancellor Kohl has been to see President Yeltsin. President Chirac's seen him. And I haven't seen him in several months, and I'm anxious to see him. We've talked on the phone, but I want to have a meeting first. And before we all get together we need to be very clear on what it is we'll be discussing and what we expect the results to be. So I want to defer a decision on that until I have a chance to have my visit with President Yeltsin.

Helsinki Summit and NATO Expansion

Q. Mr. President, can the summit in Helsinki influence in any way the timetable of the NATO expansion?

President Clinton. Well, we intend to have our meeting in the summertime and make the decisions that we have agreed already to make on that. That's a decision that's already been made by NATO. But what I think that the summit in Helsinki can do is to make it clear that no one has any intention of providing any increased threat to the security of Russia.

I have worked very hard for 4 years to elevate the role of Russia in the international forums, in the economic forums like the G–7, in security partnerships like the remarkable partnership we have in Bosnia. I'm convinced that the operation in Bosnia would not have the credibility it does today if you didn't have Russia and the United States and the European parties in there.

My whole vision of the future is a partnership of all of Europe's democracies, obviously including Russia, as I said in my State of the Union Address. So I think we'll be able to talk about that and make some real progress.

Vice President Gore. And we're going to have a discussion in here in just a minute, so you need to give them a chance. [*Laughter*]

President Clinton. They're going to do a press conference——

[*A question was asked in Russian, and a translation was not provided.*]

Prime Minister Chernomyrdin. It's a step forward—[*inaudible*]—express the importance for the meeting with the President and the President of Russia. It will be one of the critical stages in terms of—[*inaudible*]—in Europe. The upcoming summit, and the questions—[*inaudible*]—a wide range, and the decisions will be extremely important for the relationship between our two countries and for European security as well, as well as for the arms control, for economic questions.

NOTE: The President spoke at 1:40 p.m. in the Oval Office at the White House. In his remarks, he referred to President Boris Yeltsin of Russia; President Martti Ahtisaari of Finland; Chancellor Helmut Kohl of Germany; and President Jacques Chirac of France. A tape was not available for verification of the content of these remarks.

Statement on the National Economy
February 7, 1997

Today we learned that during the full 4 years of my first term, the economy added 11.5 million new jobs—the first time any administration has ever created more than 11 million jobs and well above the 8 million new jobs I had set as our goal. The combined rate of unemployment and inflation was lower than during any other administration since Lyndon Johnson was President. And the deficit fell by 63 percent, from $290 billion in 1992 to $107 billion in 1996. Now we must continue our work of balancing the budget while investing in people. The budget I released yesterday will balance the budget by 2002, contributing to continued strong growth with low inflation. I look forward to working with congressional leaders to pass a balanced budget that maintains our crucial investments in education and training.

Letter to Congressional Leaders on Cyprus
February 7, 1997

Dear Mr. Speaker: (Dear Mr. Chairman:)

In accordance with Public Law 95–384 (22 U.S.C. 2373(c)), I submit to you this report on progress toward a negotiated settlement of the Cyprus question. The previous submission covered progress through September 30, 1996. The current submission covers the period October 1 through November 30, 1996.

The tragic violence on Cyprus in August and September was detailed in my last report. Sadly, included in this report is an account of an additional killing on October 13.

Nonetheless, these senseless acts need not be repeated. The United Nations has been working very hard to obtain agreement on a series of practical measures to reduce the prospects for further violence along the Island's cease-fire lines. My Administration fully supports the U.N. package. A U.S. interagency team that visited the region put the issue on its agenda and urged the parties to implement all the steps in the U.N. package.

Given the events of the past summer and fall, we are disappointed that the United Nations attempts to obtain this agreement have not yet succeeded. We will continue to press the issue with the parties. Cooperation on these steps, although modest, could have a beneficial effect on larger settlement efforts.

Although it is properly the subject of my next report, I should also note my concern about the recent decision of the Government of Cyprus to purchase SA–10 anti-aircraft missile systems and the resulting threats of a military strike from Ankara. We have forcefully made our concern known to both governments. At the same time, we remain committed to pursuing a comprehensive settlement on Cyprus. As Secretary Albright stated during her confirmation hearings: "We are prepared to play a heightened role in promoting a resolution in Cyprus, but, for any initiative to bear fruit, the parties must agree to steps that will reduce tensions and make direct negotiations possible."

Sincerely,

WILLIAM J. CLINTON

NOTE: Identical letters were sent to Newt Gingrich, Speaker of the House of Representatives, and Jesse Helms, chairman, Senate Committee on Foreign Relations.

Message on the Observance of Id al-Fítr
February 7, 1997

On behalf of all Americans, I want to extend greetings to all Muslims in the United States and around the world as you celebrate Id al-Fítr.

This celebration, which marks the end of a month of fasting and sacrifice, is an occasion for rejoicing. It is an opportunity for Muslims to gather in joy, as well as in remembrance of those less fortunate.

It is also an opportunity for all of us to rededicate ourselves, not only to achieving spiritual growth, but also to the cause of peace between all peoples of the earth. It is our common challenge and our shared responsibility to create a better world for ourselves and our children.

To all who practice the faith of Islam, in the United States and abroad, Hillary and I extend our very best wishes. May peace be with you and your families, and may God grant you health and prosperity now and in the year ahead.

BILL CLINTON

The President's Radio Address
February 8, 1997

The President. Good morning. This morning the Vice President and I are going to talk about the progress we've made to bring 21st century technology to our students and our schools.

In my State of the Union Address Tuesday night, I issued a call to action to all Americans to prepare our people for the 21st century. The very heart of this mission and my number one priority these next 4 years is to give our children the best education in the world.

Education is about opportunity, about giving our children the tools to make the most of their God-given potential. This is a goal every American must share for every other American. That's why I'm calling for a new, nonpartisan commitment to education. During the cold war, America had a bipartisan commitment to foreign policy and politics stopped at the water's edge. Today, education is a critical national security issue for our future, and our politics must stop at the schoolhouse door.

My plan calls for world-class standards for students, teachers, and schools. It calls for expanding Head Start, rebuilding crumbling schools, opening the doors of college wider than ever before, and ensuring that workers can learn and earn for a lifetime.

To give our children the best education, we must help them to harness the powerful forces of technology. That's why we've challenged America to connect every classroom and library to the Internet by the year 2000. For the first time in history, children in the most isolated rural towns, the most comfortable suburbs, and the poorest inner-city schools will have the same access to the same universe of knowledge.

We've come a long way toward meeting that goal, and we owe much of that progress to the leadership of the Vice President who will now say a few words about our efforts.

[At this point, the Vice President made brief remarks.]

The President. Thank you, Mr. Vice President. We are making a lot of progress. Today we're issuing a report prepared by Secretary Riley and the Department of Education that shows that 65 percent of our schools are now connected to the Internet, almost double the number of schools connected in 1994. But it's not enough to connect every school; we must connect every classroom and every library as well. Since 1994, we have more than quadrupled the number of classrooms with a direct link to the Internet, but the vast majority still do not have access. That's why we're now launching an aggressive, three-part plan to finish the job.

First, my balanced budget plan makes an unprecedented commitment to education technology, doubling the technology literacy initiative the Vice President just mentioned and providing a total of $500 million for computers, teacher training, and educational software for our schools.

Second, we're working to ensure that every school and library can afford the Internet. Under the Telecommunications Act, the Federal Communications Commission is now developing a plan to give schools and libraries access to the Internet at a dramatically discounted rate. Fees for most schools will be cut in half. Fees for our poorest schools will be almost free. I urge the FCC to act quickly. And I call upon the telecommunications industry to support this effort.

Third, this April 19th, parents, teachers, business people, and volunteers from all walks of life will answer our call and hold NetDays in all 50 States, connecting tens of thousands of schools, classrooms, and libraries to the Internet.

By doubling our investment in education technology, by dramatically lowering the Internet rates for schools and libraries by mobilizing Americans all across the country to help wire our schools, we will meet our goal of connecting every classroom and library to the information superhighway by the year 2000. That's how we must prepare our children for the 21st century, with the full promise of the information age at their fingertips. And it's an important way to give our children the world's best education and the chance to make the most of their own lives.

Thanks for listening.

NOTE: The address was recorded at 12:38 p.m. on February 7 in the Roosevelt Room at the White House for broadcast at 10:06 a.m. on February 8.

Remarks to the Maryland General Assembly in Annapolis, Maryland
February 10, 1997

Thank you all for that wonderful reception. Thank you, Mr. Speaker, for what you said. Thank you, Senator Miller, for that 10-year walk down memory lane. [*Laughter*] It is true that when I met his mother I fell in love with her, even before I found out she had 10 kids. [*Laughter*] It's not often you meet a person who can elect you if her family votes for you. [*Laughter*]

Thank you, Governor Glendening, for your leadership here on so many issues. Lieutenant Governor Kathleen Kennedy Townsend, Attorney General Curran, Treasurer Dixon, my old friend Comptroller Louie Goldstein. I was in the first grade when he became comptroller. [*Laughter*] The walking argument against term limits, you know. It's amazing. [*Laughter*]

I'd like to thank so many Members of your very distinguished congressional delegation for joining me today: Senator Sarbanes and Senator Mikulski; Representative Wayne Gilchrest, your Congressman; Representative Connie Morella; Representative Ben Cardin; Representative Al Wynn; and Representative Elijah Cummings.

Now, I know that Ben was formerly the speaker here and that Al and Elijah and Connie and Senator Sarbanes were all members of this body. It kind of makes you wonder how Senator Mikulski and Congressman Gilchrest got elected to Congress. [*Laughter*] It's obviously a good training program here. [*Laughter*]

I'd like to thank the president of the Maryland State Board of Education, Christopher Cross, for being here. When he worked for President Bush, he and I stayed up all night one night writing the national education goals, which began the process which bring us to this point today. Thank you, sir, for being here. And I'd like to thank your State superintendent of education, Nancy Grasmick, for being here.

Then there are two people who are not here, who are here with us in spirit, and I would like to ask that we all remember them today, our good friend Congressman Steny Hoyer and his late wife, Judy, who was one of the finest educators this State ever had. And I know we miss them today. Steny and his family are in our prayers, and we are grateful for the dedication of Judy Hoyer's life to the children and the people of Maryland.

I would also like to say I'm very glad to be here with two members of my Cabinet, Secretary of Education Dick Riley and the Secretary of Health and Human Services, Donna Shalala. They have served our administration and, more importantly, the American people exceptionally well, and I thank them for their presence here today. And when I finish talking, if you want anything else, call them. [*Laughter*]

I should also say, since Senator Miller mentioned it, that my college roommate, who lived on the Eastern Shore, Tom Kaplan, is here. And he's still my friend after all these years, which is either a great tribute to his patience or to the roots and values of the people of Maryland. So I'm glad he's here.

I wanted to come here today to talk in greater detail about the issues I discussed in the State of the Union that require us to prepare America for the 21st century. It is important that we gather here at this turning point in our history. It was, after all, in this statehouse that George Washington resigned his commission as general of the Continental Army. In fact, it was right down the hall in the Lieutenant Governor's office that Thomas Jefferson wrote George Washington's words of resignation. It was here that the Treaty of Paris was prepared and ratified, ending the Revolutionary War and beginning the greatest experiment in democracy and opportunity the world has ever known.

Just think what began here in this building. What an experiment it has been, all the turmoil we have survived, the Civil War, the two World Wars, the cold war, the social upheaval, all the triumphs of our country in civil rights and women's rights, the environmental movement, workers' rights, bringing in all the immigrants, the explosion in science and technology, the political, the economic, the social achievements of this country. What an incredible experiment it has been since the events of so long ago when the treaty ending the Revolutionary War was signed and ratified here.

At each step along the way, how did we keep growing, how did we overcome, how did we work through, how did we reach higher? We always had responsible citizens. We were always able to come together as one country. And we were always driven by a clear vision.

I would argue to you that we are at another turning point today, and we need responsible citizens, a united country, and a clear vision. We face a moment of peace and prosperity, and it gives us an extraordinary opportunity to actually decide what kind of future we want for America in the 21st century and then go to work to build it. It is very important that we understand that such moments are extremely rare in our history.

We have perhaps had only one before. After World War II, we dominated the world economically. We were the most powerful country in the world militarily. We had some ability to decide our future, and thank goodness we did the right thing with the Marshall plan and rebuilding Europe and Japan, our former friends and our former foes. But we were constrained by the cold war.

At the beginning of this century probably is the time most like this one when we entered the industrial era as a powerful and wealthy country at peace. But never have we been quite like this, as the world's only superpower, just completing 4 years where we produced more new jobs than at any other 4-year period in our history, looking toward a world that is full of troubles, to be sure, but so full of explosive opportunities.

We have an incredible responsibility—we in America and you in Maryland. Thanks to the leadership of your Governor and the work that all of you have done, unemployment's at a 6-year low. Things are going well for you here. Your family incomes have risen to fourth in the Nation. Your welfare rolls have dropped almost 25 percent since 1995. Student achievement has risen, and more schools are meeting the high standards you have set. We are well positioned.

But it is a moment of choice. We cannot afford to squander this moment in complacency or division. That's normally what happens to people when they sort of get happy and satisfied. They get complacent, or they fall out over little things. And this is not a time for us to squander in petty bickering or small ambitions. This is a time for us to build a new century.

We have to meet all the challenges we still have. There are still too many poor children in this country and too many lives of children being lost on the streets of America every day. There are still too many of our areas in our cities and isolated rural areas that have not felt the uplift of the economic recovery. We still have not balanced the budget. We still have not finished all the unfinished business of the cold war. Not everybody who works hard is feeling the opportunities that are available in America. We have unfinished business.

Then we have new challenges that we have to face. We have to prepare for the aging of the baby boomers. I know I'm the oldest one; that's a self-interest plea here, I think. [*Laughter*] We have to prepare for the aging of the baby boomers. We have to make sure that we're ready for this new worldwide competition. We have to meet the new security threats of the 21st century, in terrorism and ethnic and religious and racial conflicts. We have to meet the new environmental challenges of the 21st century, most of which will be global in nature.

So there are challenges out there. But the most important thing is, there are staggering opportunities. More people will have more chances to live out their dreams than any people who ever lived in the history of the Earth, if we do the right things—if we do the right things.

We have worked for the last 4 years essentially to try to make sure America works again, that we are functioning at a reasonable level of proficiency so that we can have the freedom to do that, to shape our future. And we have changed the economic course of this country away from supply-side economics to investment economics, to move toward a balanced budget, to reduce the deficits, the interest rates, to expand our trade around the world and to invest in our people. And the results have been good.

We've tried to move the debate over social policy in Washington away from rhetoric to reality, centered on families and communities. You've got now 5 years of declining crime. You've got the biggest drop in welfare rolls in history. You've got real efforts being made through the family leave law and other things to help people succeed in raising their children and in the workplace. We're in a position now to know what works and to know that we can have confidence that if we work together, we can make a difference in assaulting our most profound challenges here at home.

We've tried to define the role of Government away from the old fight that's dominated America almost ever since World War II, to say Government is not the problem; Government is not the solution. Government's job is to create the conditions and give people the tools to solve their problems and make the most of their own lives.

So now we have this chance. And it's hard when you're not threatened by a foreign enemy to whip people up to a fever pitch of common, intense, sustained, disciplined endeavor. But that is what we must do, my fellow Americans. That is what we must do.

We are strong enough to shape a future that will take advantage of all this life-enhancing technology, of these new economic opportunities, of the new opportunities we have to build a structure of peace around the world, of the new opportunities we have to put the information age at the fingertips of the poorest as well as the wealthiest children in our country. And we had better do this. Our children and our grandchildren will never forgive us if we blow this chance to make their future the best future in the history of this country.

It is obvious that to prepare our people for the 21st century we will need a new, more far-reaching, deeper partnership in America. The era of big Government is over, both because we can't go on running national deficits till the end of time and because the nature of our problems requires a different approach. But the era of big national challenges is far from over. It will never be over. And the ones we face are very big indeed.

National leadership can point the way. It can move barriers out of the way that have prevented our States, our cities, and our people from solving their own problems. But the real responsibilities of building this future are ones we all must bear together. I will do my part. I will do what I can to see that the National Government does its part. But in turn, you must work with me and with others to make sure that we seize this opportunity while we stand strong enough to do so.

Today I want to talk about two critical areas, giving our children the best education and finishing the job of welfare reform, breaking the cycle of dependency, moving millions of more people from welfare to work. Taken together, these issues really are at the core of our national mission to prepare America for the 21st century.

Everyone must have the tools to succeed in the knowledge economy. That means education and training. Everyone willing to work hard with those tools must have a chance to do so. That means finishing the job of welfare reform. Education and welfare reform are about bringing all Americans to the starting line of the economy, then making sure all of them are ready to run the race. Our number one priority must be to ensure that America has the best education in the world.

I cannot add much to the statement we made so long ago in the national education goals, 7 years ago now—almost 8 years ago—but my shorthand statement is: Every 8-year-old has to be able to read, every 12-year-old should be able to log on to the Internet, every 18-year-old should be able to go to college, and every adult American should be able to keep on learning for an entire lifetime. That should be our goal.

Because our future was at stake in the cold war, we had a bipartisan foreign policy. Politics stopped at the water's edge. Well, now our future is at stake, in large measure depending upon whether we can give all of our people world-class education. Therefore, we must have a nonpartisan commitment to education, and politics should stop at the schoolhouse door in the 21st century.

It is not enough for Members of Congress and members of the State legislatures and elected executives to embrace this commitment. Our businesses, our educators, our parents, all our citizens must make the same commitment. I'm gratified that you have a number of Maryland parents and teachers and business people committed to education here today. I thank them for being here, and I thank you for inviting them.

In my State of the Union Address, I laid out a 10-point call to action for American education, which is embodied in this booklet. And I want to say just a few words about a number of issues today and then focus on one in particular. And I want to thank the State of Maryland for taking the lead in doing so many of the right things. A lot of you have worked with me, going back long years in the past when I was a Governor, on these educational issues, and I thank you for what you've done.

First, every child has to be able to read independently by the third grade. I'm pleased that the University of Maryland at College Park has already pledged more than 2,300 of its students to work as reading tutors over the next 5 years. That is a great thing. We're going to use 35,000 of our AmeriCorps volunteers to help to try to mobilize a million of these students. We think we can get at least 100,000 out of the new

work-study students approved by Congress in the last budget. Then all the schools have to make use of volunteers once they are trained. But we have to do this.

You just think about it. If 40 percent of our children can't read at grade level, how in the wide world do we expect them to learn algebra, trigonometry, calculus, physics, biology, chemistry? It is very important. Unless we get this done, the rest cannot happen. And it is going to take a national effort of monumental proportions to do it. But we can do it, because the children can do it. The children can do it. They just need for us to do our job, and they then will do the rest. So I want you to help us to finish that job.

We must expand public school choice. And Baltimore City has done that through its charter schools. We must rebuild crumbling schools. And you heard the Governor say that's a priority for him as well. We must make it possible for all of our children to have access—the same access, in the same time, to the same knowledge. That's what hooking up all these classrooms to the Internet is all about. And I thank Maryland for its commitment to that objective.

In the last 4 years, we have opened the doors of college wider than ever before through the direct college loan program and expanded Pell grants, 200,000 more work-study positions, and the AmeriCorps program. But we have to do more. And I am very pleased, Governor, that you have proposed these State HOPE scholarships to open the doors of college.

I just came back from Georgia—Secretary Riley and I went to Augusta—230,000 people in the State of Georgia who maintained a B average have had their tuition and their schoolbooks paid for by the State HOPE scholarship program. In a representative crowd there, I had person after person after person of all ages telling me, "I was a HOPE scholar; I had a chance to go to college; I never could have done it otherwise; I wouldn't have made it otherwise."

There is no better expenditure of our money. It will raise the per capita income of this State more quickly. It will get over inequalities in income groups more quickly, and it will bring people together for a stronger future more quickly than anything else.

So I applaud the proposal you have put before the legislature here, and I also tell you I will do my best to pass our national version of the HOPE scholarship to give a tax credit of $1,500 for 2 years—that's the typical cost of community college tuition—and a tax deduction of up to $10,000 a year for the cost of tuition for any education after high school. This will make a difference.

We also propose making the IRA available to more savers and then let people withdraw from their IRA tax-free if the money is used to pay for education—and the biggest increase in Pell grant scholarships for needy students in 20 years. And our "GI bill" for America's workers would take the 70 different Federal programs for job training, put them in one big block, and send a skill grant to an unemployed or an underemployed worker and say, "Here, you take it to the nearest institution of education and get the training you need." Nearly every American lives within driving distance of a community college or another community-based university or educational institution that can provide the training today that all people know they need to have a better future. So we need to do these things together, and they will make a big difference.

I also believe we have to teach our children to be good citizens as well as good students. And I'd like to thank the Lieutenant Governor for supporting the statewide program of character education you have here, to have a statewide code of discipline, to remove disruptive students from the classroom, to promote community curfews. And again, I thank you for being the only State in America to require community service to graduate from high school. You have the first class of seniors graduating today. That's a good thing. That's a good thing.

To give you some idea how long it takes for some of these things to catch on, 10 years ago, in 1987, the then-Republican Governor of New Jersey and now the president of Drew University, Tom Kean, and I cochaired a Carnegie commission study on middle school, and one of our recommendations was that national service should be a requirement for public school students. People should learn that they are connected to others in their community and make it a positive, good, wholesome thing. Only Maryland has done it so far. But I certainly hope—perhaps my presence here will help—I hope other States will follow your lead. This is an important part of building a common future for America.

Let me say the most important thing we can do in education is to hold our students to high standards. Children will grow according to the expectations we have of them. They cannot be expected to know what it is they should know or even how high they can soar until we give them the right set of expectations. When 40 percent of our third graders are not reading as well as they should or, to put it in plain language, when 40 percent of 8-year-olds cannot read a book on their own that they ought to be able to read, we have a lot to do. When students in Germany or Singapore learn 15 to 20 math subjects in depth each year, while our students typically race through 30 to 35 without learning any in depth in a given year, we aren't doing what we should be doing to prepare them for a knowledge economy that demands that they be able to think and reason and analyze, in short, demands that they be able to learn for a lifetime of working in ways that have not yet been invented, perhaps not yet even imagined. This is impossible without a good foundation in the basics.

Maryland is making a good start. You've developed clear standards for what children should learn by the third, fifth, and eighth grades, in particular, in reading and math, and clear tests to measure them school district by school district and school by school. You're holding schools accountable for making the grade, rewarding excellence, intervening in schools that aren't performing. Because you have set high standards, you have seen 5 years of steady, sustained progress toward meeting those standards.

But Maryland and all other States must do more. To compete and win in the 21st century, we must have a high standard of excellence that all States agree on. That is why I called, in my State of the Union Address, for national standards of excellence in the basics, not Federal Government standards but national standards representing what all our students must know to succeed in a new century. I called upon every State to test every fourth grader in reading and every eighth grader in math by 1999, according to the national standards, to make sure they're being met.

We already have widely accepted rigorous national standards in both reading and math and widely used tests based on those standards. In reading, Maryland and more than 40 other States have participated in a test called the National Assessment of Education Progress or, as all of us educational junkies call it, the NAEP test. It measures a State's overall performance against a high national standard of excellence. It's a good test. In math, tens of thousands of students across our Nation have already taken the Third International Math and Science Survey, called the TIMSS test, a test that reflects the world-class standards our children must meet for the new era. As I said in my State of the Union, last month Secretary Riley and I visited northern Illinois, where eighth grade students from 20 districts took the test and tied for first in the world for science and second in math. We know it is the world standard, and we know the world standard is the right standard to which we should all hold ourselves.

Unfortunately, these current tests, both the Assessment of Education Progress for the fourth grade reading test and the Third International Survey in Math and Science for the eighth graders, do not provide individual scores; they only measure how an entire State is doing. What we need are tests that will measure the performance of each and every student, each and every school, each and every district, so that parents and teachers will know how every child is doing compared to other students in other schools, other States, and other countries, not just compared to them but, more importantly, compared against what they need to know.

It is a false thing to compare all kids against one another unless all children are first held to a high standard. That's what we want to know. That's the only thing that really matters. That is why I'm presenting a plan to help all students in all States meet these standards and to measure them.

Over the next 2 years, our Department of Education will support the development for new tests for fourth grade reading based on the National Assessment of Education Progress and eighth grade math based on the International Math and Science Survey, to show how every student measures up to existing, widely accepted standards. These tests will be developed by independent test experts in consultation with leading math and reading teachers. The Federal Government will not require them, but they will be available to every State and every school district that chooses to administer them. I believe every State must participate and that every parent has a right to honest, accurate information about how his or her child is doing based on real, meaningful national standards.

Now, already in the last week I have heard some people saying, "Sounds like a Federal power grab to me." That's nonsense. We will not attempt to require them. They are not Federal Government standards. They are national standards. But we have been hiding behind a very small fig leaf for very long, and the results are not satisfactory. Anybody who says that a country as big and diverse as ours can't possibly have national standards in the basics, I say from Maryland to Michigan to Montana, reading is reading and math is math. No school board is in charge of algebra, and no State legislature can enact the laws of physics. And it is time we started acting the way we know we should.

There's another thing that will be said now and that you will have to confront, because I know how much—I've been through a zillion State legislative sessions; everybody's got a new idea and everybody wants more money and there's never enough to go around. And you will be told—and it is true—that we have lots of standardized tests. That's true, there are lots of standardized tests, but there is no national test testing the standards. That's a very different thing. There is no national exam given to all of our children that says, here's what a good fourth grader ought to learn.

Keep in mind, we don't want Johnny to make a better score than Mary on this test. We want 100 percent of our kids to pass this test. And then when a lot of them don't, we don't want to give them an F. We want to give them a hand up. We want to say, "We haven't done what we should, and we're going to do this."

It is amazing, you know, we take it for granted we have the best military in the world. Think how silly it would be if everyplace in America where we do basic training, they said, "Well, you know, Louisiana is a long way from Georgia. We couldn't have possibly have uniform standards for basic training in the military. Just sort of come up with whatever you think will be good, and we'll hope it works the next time we're in the Persian Gulf." [*Laughter*] You're laughing. That's what we do. And even if you do the very best you can, we don't know the truth. It's wrong for these children not to know the truth. This is not a put-down, now, this is a lift-up.

We've got the most diverse democracy in the world. We have 4 school districts now where the children's first languages comprise over 100 different languages, in 4 school districts in America. Who are we kidding that we're going to create the kind of country we want, where everybody's got a chance to make it, when we haven't even taken the first elemental step to say, here's how everyone should read by the fourth grade; here's the math everybody ought to know by the eighth grade?

There is more to do after that, but let's start with something that really matters. We've never done it. This has nothing to do with local control of education. Secretary Riley has done more to get rid of Federal rules and regulations, to give States and local school districts more control without the rules and more flexibility than anybody has in a long time. But no matter how much flexibility you have, sooner or later your children are going to have to face the fact that they either can read or they can't, they either can do the math or they can't, they know algebra or they don't. And if we play around with all these games and hide-and-seek excuses, in the end the only people that are going to be hurt are those kids, and the rest of the country will pay the price from now on. And we've got to stop it. [*Applause*] Thank you.

I want to give you two pieces of good news, one of which you can be especially proud of. You all know that the business community has been calling for this for a long time. Governor Glendening was recently with the other Governors last year at an education summit in New York with the business community, and they were saying we have to have standards. Today I'm proud to say that the national Business Roundtable is endorsing our call for national tests for fourth grade reading and eighth grade math. They will join our crusade to make American education the best in the world. And I want to thank especially Norm Augustine, who is the CEO of Lockheed Martin and the head of the Business Roundtable's education task force and who has done a lot to help you in Maryland with your schools. Just before the speech today, your State board of education chairman, Chris Cross, told me that the State board of education intends to incorporate these news tests of national standards into your State's program. And I thank you, sir, for that, and I thank you for that.

Let me say that throughout my public career, I have been very interested in this whole issue of education. There are lots of other things I'd like to talk to you about today. I hope you will support the work that we are doing with the National Board of Certification for Master Teachers, to certify teachers in educational ex-

cellence. Governor Hunt from North Carolina has been working on that for years, and we certified the last teachers—the first teachers in 1995 but only 500 since 1995. We believe we need at least one master teacher in every school district, hopefully in every school in America, someone who has been through the special, rigorous program of training and evaluation here so that then that teacher can share what he or she has learned with all the other teachers in the school. Our budget contains enough funds—and it's a relatively low-cost program— to provide for another 100,000 master teachers in the next 4 years. So I hope you will support that as well.

But let me say—I guess you can tell I feel strongly about this, but I have spent a lot of time in our schools, a lot of time listening to teachers, a lot of time listening to parents. I've worked harder on this issue over the course of my public life than anything else because it has a unique role in our history and an even more powerful role in our future. It is, of course, the key to individual opportunity. It is also the key to responsible citizenship. I am convinced it is the key to giving us the understanding we need to live together as one nation in the midst of all of our diversity. It is also the key to maintaining our world leadership for peace and freedom and prosperity. Only if every American has the full use of his or her mind can our country move forward together.

So I hope that all of you will keep this in mind. I hope that you will push this, and I hope you will lead the way. I want to be able to take this crusade across the country and tell people, if they don't believe we can do it, call Maryland. You've had the courage to do it. Stand up. [*Applause*]

Now, let me just say a couple of words about welfare reform, because that's very important. For years and years and years, all the Governors—I was one of them—said we want more control over the State's welfare system; we want to do that. We could reform the welfare system. We could make it work. We could end the culture of poverty and dependency. Well, you got it. [*Laughter*] And this has got to be a focus of your efforts now, because this is very, very important.

We ended the old welfare system basically in two steps. First of all, in the last 4 years, Secretary Shalala and I worked with 43 of the 50 States to launch welfare reform experiments which, along with a growing economy and a 50 percent increase in child support collection—something I'm very proud of—helped to reduce the welfare rolls by 2¼ million. That's the biggest drop in welfare rolls in the history of the country, an 18 percent drop. You can be proud of that and proud of what you did. Here in Maryland you did better than the national average. You used your waiver to move 51,000 people off the welfare rolls, and you had about a 25 percent drop. And you can be proud of that.

You also answered my call to revoke the driver's licenses of people who deliberately—who can and don't pay their child support. And I think that's a good thing. We're going to do more to collect child support. We can move 800,000 more people off welfare tomorrow if people just paid the child support they owe and that they are capable of paying. So I thank you for that.

Now we come to the hard part. The new law, supported by the Governors and all State associations, says that every able-bodied person on welfare must move to work within 2 years, that the States can have a little cushion fund to support those who can't move into the work force either because they're disabled or because the economy is not so hot.

But now, think of this challenge. In the last 4 years, 2¼ million people moved from welfare to work in an economy that produced 11.5 million jobs. That's a record for any 4-year administration. We have to do at least that well in the next 4 years. That reduced the welfare rolls by about 20 percent, 18 to 20 percent.

So you've got about 10 million people left and about—maybe a little more than 10 million—and about 4½ million of them are adults and about 4 million, anyway, are going to be able-bodied and able enough to physically work. And then there will be some moving in and out of the work force as there always is, as people retire and all. But through deliberate efforts we're going to have to create at least 2 million jobs. And if we don't do it, what will happen?

Keep in mind, this welfare reform bill has this ringing declaration: Everybody who can work, everybody who's able to work has to take responsibility for their own lives, no more permanent dependency full of moral precepts. Well, the morality shoe is now on the other foot. Those of us who supported that, we now have

a moral obligation to say, everybody we told, "You have to go to work" actually is able to work. Because if we are not able to do that, then the law's consequence will not be to liberate people from dependency but to make people who are dying to go to work even worse off just because they couldn't find a job.

This is a serious, stiff challenge. And the challenge is primarily on you and the employer community, which is the way you said you wanted it. But it's there now. You know that great old country music star Chet Atkins used to say, "You got to be careful what you ask for in this life; you might get it." So here it is. What are we going to do? Is there a way out? Yes, there is. Can we do this? You bet we can. You bet we can. We can to it, but we have to do it together. And we have to do it with discipline. And we need a plan. And it needs to go down to every community. And we're going to have to ask people to help. And you need to really closely follow your numbers and make sure you're doing what it takes to be done.

How are we going to do it? First, we have to pass the Federal program that I recommended, which will give tax credits to private employers of up to 50 percent of a salary up to $10,000 to hire people, only if they hire people from welfare to work. And then we have to support the provisions of the welfare reform law which continue the health care, continue the nutrition, and provide much more money for child care than the previous law. That's the good news.

This legislation also gives you the authority for the first time to take money that had been used on welfare checks and give it to private employers as a wage or training supplement. Now, this can be very important in convincing nonprofit employers who don't pay taxes anyway to hire people off welfare and make an extra effort. All the community nonprofits, every church or other religious organization in the State of Maryland of any size, without regard to their faith, they're all under an admonition to care for the poor. Now you can say, "We'll give you a little money to help, if you will do the rest."

Missouri had a program like this in Kansas City, where they gave the welfare check to private employers for more than a year—they could keep it for a couple years—as a wage and training premium if they would hire people off welfare. I met a man who had a data-processing storage company with 25 employees, and 5 of his employees he'd hired from the welfare rolls, and he loved it. And they loved it.

And if we can do it, it is better to hire people in small groups or one-on-one, because you're trying to lift people out of a culture of dependency into a mainstream culture of work. But this man was willing to do that. And they have to pay about $1.75 above the minimum wage to get the wage subsidy there and to give people a living income. But still it costs them less than the minimum wage to do it.

Florida has just decided to follow suit. And I hope other States will follow that lead. You've got to—believe me—to meet these job targets, your employer community is going to need every last option you can give them. And somebody's got to have a plan—I mean a game plan, that challenges every sector and every community to do what has to be done. So I urge you to use the flexibility you have been given to do that.

Secondly, I urge you to make sure that the money you have saved from welfare reform will be used to move even more people to work. I know Maryland has taken its considerable savings from welfare reform efforts and put them into a special rainy-day fund to create jobs and to move people from welfare to work. And that's something other States ought to copy, because if welfare reform is going to succeed in the beginning, all States are going to have to use those savings on efforts like child care, wage subsidies, employment incentives, or other ways to create private sector jobs.

Let me just say one other thing. I hope as you do this you will not forget a sort of a parallel population not on welfare, and those are young, single men who are unemployed who are eligible for food stamps but not welfare. Keep in mind, their loss to the work force is an enormous loss to our society. It leads to higher crime. It leads to fewer two-parent families. It leads to robbing them of the potential of what they might become. And a lot of places now are beginning to try to—instead of talking just about the welfare population—[*inaudible*]—the young, unemployed population so that these young, single men can be treated in the right way, too.

And in Missouri, what they did, we gave them a waiver, and they actually took the food stamp payments for the young, single men and gave them to employers with the same sort of incentive as the welfare payments for young women going from welfare to work. So I urge you to think about that.

Finally, let me say, what is our vision? I can tell you what my vision—why do we do all this? Here's my vision. Here's where I hope we'll be in a few years. I hope all over America in a few years, we will have a community-based, employment-family support system for people who are out of work and people will come into this system whether they come off the welfare rolls or off the employment rolls through the unemployment rolls and we won't make a distinction. It will just be good people with kids or without kids, depending, who are out of work who need to get back into the work force. And we'll have a system for moving them back in, and we'll have a system of subsidies for people at the margins so that employers will be encouraged to make that extra effort to restore people to the dignity of work. And meanwhile, we'll always be helping people support their children in fulfilling their first and most important job.

Now, that's my vision. That's what I hope we would get out of this welfare reform effort. But the next 2 years are going to be critical, because about 2 years from now, people are going to start running out of their 2-year time limit, and then the spotlight will shift from all of them to all of us. And we will be asked, what did we do when the welfare reform bill passed? What did we do to make sure that those we told, "You have to go to work," had the chance to go to work? So I urge you to think about this.

This is exciting, but it's bracing, because our society has never done anything like this before in ordinary times. And I do not believe that when the bill passed, people had really focused on the dimensions of the challenge. I had, and I was willing to make it. I'm willing to try to—to jump off this cliff, to hold up this high standard. I think we can do this. I think we can develop a work-based society that does not have people trapped in permanent dependence. But it's going to take everybody thinking about it, working on it, and doing things they had not done in the past. And so I ask you to do that.

I just want to make one final point the Governor's already mentioned. I know Maryland is considering using its own money to continue providing some basic benefits for legal immigrants who have lost Federal aid now that the Federal bans have taken effect. That's the right thing to do, but you shouldn't have to do it all by yourself. That's why every State and every Governor, Republican or Democrat, I hope will join with us to try to persuade the Congress to restore just the basic health and disability benefits that used to be available until this new law passed when misfortune strikes them.

The argument made by the majority when they passed this was, when an immigrant comes to America, you've got to sign a piece of paper that says you're not going to take public benefits. Now, that's an understandable policy. We shouldn't be inviting people to come here just to get on welfare or to get on Medicaid or Medicare. But we can solve that, and did, by simply saying that every immigrant has a sponsor and the sponsor's income will be deemed the immigrant's income until the immigrant becomes a citizen. That's the way to solve that.

But if you have all these immigrants coming here, and even before they can become citizens—suppose an Indian from New Delhi comes to Maryland to develop computer software programs for one of your growing businesses, and stays here 3 years, and has a 1-year-old child and a 3-year-old child. What does that person do if he or his spouse gets hit by a car or is the victim of a crime or one of the children is born with cerebral palsy and they don't have regular health care that will take care of all these things?

What do we say? "Tough luck. You had misfortune. Yes, you've worked hard; yes, you've paid your taxes; yes, you've been perfectly legal; yes, you've complied with every provision of the law; yes, you didn't try to sneak in our country, you waited your turn just like everybody else, but I'm sorry. Yes, we took the benefit of your brain; you made us a richer, stronger country; we wanted you in here; you had skills we needed, but I'm sorry"? This is wrong, folks. This is unworthy of a great nation of immigrants, and we ought to fix it.

When you get right down to it, all this business about education reform and welfare reform and what do we have to do to prepare our country for the 21st century and will we have the discipline, strength, and courage to take advantage of this unique moment in history—it really comes down to two questions: What does America mean, and what does it mean to be an American?

America must always be a nation becoming. We're never there. We're always becoming: becoming a more perfect union, full of new promise for our own people and new hopes for the world. And what does it mean to be an American? We're the ones who have to make that happen.

Thank you, and God bless you.

NOTE: The President spoke at 11:20 a.m. at the Maryland State House. In his remarks, he referred to Casper R. Taylor, Jr., speaker, Maryland House of Delegates, and Thomas V. Miller, Jr., president, Maryland State Senate; Gov. Parris N. Glendening of Maryland; State Attorney General J. Joseph Curran, Jr.; State Treasurer Thomas N. Dixon; and State Comptroller Louis L. Goldstein.

Message to the Congress on Canadian Whaling Activities
February 10, 1997

To the Congress of the United States:

On December 12, 1996, Secretary of Commerce Michael Kantor certified under section 8 of the Fishermen's Protective Act of 1967, as amended (the "Pelly Amendment") (22 U.S.C. 1978), that Canada has conducted whaling activities that diminish the effectiveness of a conservation program of the International Whaling Commission (IWC). The certification was based on the issuance of whaling licenses by the Government of Canada in 1996 and the subsequent killing of two bowhead whales under those licenses. This message constitutes my report to the Congress pursuant to subsection (b) of the Pelly Amendment.

In 1991, Canadian natives took a bowhead whale from the western Arctic stock, under a Canadian permit. In 1994, Canadian natives took another bowhead whale from one of the eastern Arctic stocks, without a permit.

In 1996, under Canadian permits, one bowhead whale was taken in the western Canadian Arctic on July 24 and one bowhead whale was taken in the eastern Canadian Arctic on August 17. The whale in the eastern Arctic was taken from a highly endangered stock. The IWC has expressed particular concern about whaling on this stock, which is not known to be recovering.

None of the Canadian whale hunts described above was authorized by the IWC. Canada withdrew from the IWC in 1982. In those instances where Canada issued whaling licenses, it did so without consulting the IWC. In fact, Canada's 1996 actions were directly contrary to IWC advice. At the 1996 Annual Meeting, the IWC passed a resolution encouraging Canada to refrain from issuing whaling licenses and to rejoin the IWC. However, Canada has recently advised the United States that it has no plans to rejoin the IWC and that it intends to continue granting licenses for the taking of endangered bowhead whales.

Canada's unilateral decision to authorize whaling outside of the IWC is unacceptable. Canada's conduct jeopardizes the international effort that has allowed whale stocks to begin to recover from the devastating effects of historic whaling.

I understand the importance of maintaining traditional native cultures, and I support aboriginal whaling that is managed through the IWC. The Canadian hunt, however, is problematic for two reasons.

First, the whaling took place outside the IWC. International law, as reflected in the 1982 United Nations Convention on the Law of the Sea, obligates countries to work through the appropriate international organization for the conservation and management of whales. Second, whaling in the eastern Canadian Arctic poses a particular conservation risk, and the decision to take this risk should not have been made unilaterally.

I believe that Canadian whaling on endangered whales warrants action at this time.

Accordingly, I have instructed the Department of State to oppose Canadian efforts to address takings of marine mammals within the newly formed Arctic Council. I have further instructed the Department of State to oppose Canadian efforts to address trade in marine mammal products within the Arctic Council. These actions grow from our concern about Canada's efforts to move whaling issues to fora other than the IWC and, more generally, about the taking of marine mammals in ways that are inconsistent with sound conservation practices.

Second, I have instructed the Department of Commerce, in implementing the Marine Mammal Protection Act, to withhold consideration of any Canadian requests for waivers to the existing moratorium on the importation of seals and/or seal products into the United States.

Finally, the United States will continue to urge Canada to reconsider its unilateral decision to authorize whaling on endangered stocks and to authorize whaling outside the IWC.

I believe the foregoing measures are more appropriate in addressing the problem of Canadian whaling than the imposition of import prohibitions at this time.

I have asked the Departments of Commerce and State to keep this situation under close review.

WILLIAM J. CLINTON

The White House,
February 10, 1997.

NOTE: This message was released by the Office of the Press Secretary on February 11.

Message to the Congress Reporting Budget Rescissions and Deferrals
February 10, 1997

To the Congress of the United States:

In accordance with the Congressional Budget and Impoundment Control Act of 1974, I herewith report nine proposed rescissions of budgetary resources, totaling $397 million, and one revised deferral, totaling $7 million.

The proposed rescissions affect the Departments of Agriculture, Defense-Military, Energy, Housing and Urban Development, and Justice, and the General Services Administration. The deferral affects the Social Security Administration.

WILLIAM J. CLINTON

The White House,

February 10, 1997.

NOTE: This message was released by the Office of the Press Secretary on February 11. The report detailing the proposed rescissions and deferral was published in the *Federal Register* on February 21.

Remarks on Campaign Finance Reform Legislation and an Exchange With Reporters
February 11, 1997

The President. In the State of the Union Address I asked the Congress to pass bipartisan campaign finance reform by July the Fourth, and I pointed out that delay would mean the death of reform, as it has in the last several years. I am very pleased to welcome to the White House today this bipartisan group of House Members who are now all cosponsors of the Shays-Meehan legislation. They are coming together in a bipartisan way to limit the influence of money in our campaigns for Congress and in financing the political parties and to level the playing field.

And I feel very, very strongly that they have done a good thing for our country. I am supporting their efforts very strongly, and I want to do whatever I can to work with them to help this legislation pass.

As soon as I leave here I'm going up to the Hill to a meeting of the bipartisan leadership of Congress, to which the Speaker and Senator Lott invited me after the State of the Union. And this is one of the issues I intend to raise there. I'm very encouraged by what I've heard here today, and we're determined to go forward.

Mr. Vice President.

[*At this point, the Vice President, Representative Christopher Shays, and Representative Martin T. Meehan made brief remarks.*]

The President. Thank you all.

Q. Isn't this blocking the barn after the horse has gone?

The President. No. How can you say that? There will be a whole set of new elections up. There are elections in '98; there are elections in 2000; there are elections in 2002. I hope there will be elections 200 years from now.

Q. Is this all a product of lessons learned from the last campaign?

The President. No. Most of these people have wanted to do this for many years. Keep in mind, we had—in each of the last 4 years we had a serious campaign finance reform effort that died because of the parliamentary procedures in the Senate which permit 40 plus 1 to block a vote and because we didn't have more of this. I think this is the most important thing. The House is staking out a position—these Members are—that they're going to try to reach not only across party lines but across philosophical lines. I mean, just look around this table here and you'll see people who differ on a lot of substantive issues but want to change the rules by which they work in the public interest. That's really, to me, the most encouraging thing.

If you look around this table you see not only party difference, you see people from every region in our country, you see people who are in various different positions on the substance of most of the major issues facing us. But they are united in wanting to change the rules. And I think that there can be an engine of bipartisan and grassroots reform here that we have not seen before. People have wanted to do this for a long time, but I think they've got a chance to break through the last dam and get the job done. And I'm going to support them every way I can.

O.J. Simpson Civil Trial

Q. Mr. President, how disturbing is it to you that black and white jurors and black and white Americans in general viewed the same evidence in the O.J. Simpson trial but came generally to drastically different conclusions?

The President. Well, first of all, as to the jury verdict, I have nothing to add to what I said after the last jury verdict. We have a system here in this country which I think we should all respect. The only people who heard all the evidence were the people who were sitting in the jury box, in both cases. And civil trials and criminal trials are very different in different ways. So I have nothing to add to that. I respect the jury verdict.

And in terms of the way Americans see the world differently, generally based on their race, that troubles me, and I spoke about it at some length at the University of Texas last year when we had the Million Man March here in Washington, and I was down there. I think the only answer to that is for us to spend more time listening to each other and try to put ourselves in each other's shoes and understand why we see the world in different ways and keep trying to overcome that.

I would say that even though it's disturbing, we have succeeded so far in managing the world's most multiethnic, diverse democracy better than a lot of countries that are smaller than we are with fewer differences within them. And we just—this is a work that's never done—that our different attitudes, our different viewpoints in some ways are the great strength of America, but if they're too—if we're too estranged, if the divide is too great, then we can't hold the country together. And we just have to keep working on it. And I intend to—I've worked on it hard for 4 years; we're talking about what else we might do.

But in terms of the jury verdict, that's the system we have in America. It's over as far as I'm concerned. We need to get on with other things. But we always need to be working to try to bridge these divides between us.

Budget Negotiations

Q. Mr. President, what are you hoping to achieve in the budget talks today? What are you hoping to achieve in budget talks this morning?

The President. The next step of what we talked about—what I talked about at the State of the Union. I think we have got an enormous opportunity here to do great things together, because I think there is a consensus all across the country and among both parties that we have a lot of great challenges, some significant, indeed, unparalleled opportunities. And the whole system is kind of tending toward movement instead of paralysis again. And that's a good thing for America. And I'm going to do what I can to keep it going this morning.

NOTE: The President spoke at 10 a.m. in the Cabinet Room at the White House prior to a meeting with bipartisan congressional cosponsors of the "Campaign Reform Act of 1997."

Remarks Prior to a Meeting With Congressional Leaders
February 11, 1997

First, I want to thank Senator Lott for hosting this. I thank the Speaker and Senator Lott and the leadership for inviting us to come down here and meet with the bipartisan leadership today. I think it's a very important first step after the State of the Union Address. It indicates we want to work together.

We'll discuss a lot of issues, I'm sure. I just want to emphasize, too, I think it's imperative that we pass a bipartisan balanced budget this year. And I think it's imperative that we find a way to work together on education reform, and we'll be talking about how we can do that.

There are many other things, but I want to emphasize those two above all.

The reception that I received in Maryland yesterday was a reception for the importance of education standards and educational opportunity in America as we move into this new century. And so I'm optimistic, I'm hopeful, and I'm gratified to be invited to be here.

NOTE: The President spoke at 11:10 a.m. in the President's Bill Signing Room at the Capitol. A tape was not available for verification of the content of these remarks.

Remarks Following a Screening of Excerpts From the Film "Thomas Jefferson"
February 11, 1997

Thank you. First of all, I know I speak for all of us when I thank Ken Burns and all of those who made this magnificent film possible. Thank you, especially, Jack Smith, for your work in making it possible and sponsoring it.

If you think about what Ken Burns has given to America with "The Civil War," "The West," "Baseball," and "Thomas Jefferson," I think Mr. Jefferson would be very proud of you, Mr. Burns. And I know we all are, and we thank you so much.

I think every American President has been inspired by Jefferson's ideals, affected by his decisions, fascinated by his character. Two of my most prized personal possessions are an original printing of the "Notes on Virginia" and a printing of Daniel Webster's marvelous eulogy to John Adams and Thomas Jefferson delivered in Faneuil Hall in August of 1826. And from time to time when I feel some sense of despair, just for the heck of it, I take them down and open the pages and start reading.

I always thought that the fact that both of them died on the 50th anniversary of the Declaration of Independence was the best evidence the modern world has on the question of whether God is. It is impossible to believe this happened by accident.

And so, I ask all of you to leave here tonight with a sense of gratitude to Thomas Jefferson but also with the firm conviction that the thing he was most right about was in leaving us a system that would always be in the act of becoming, that his unshakable belief that the future could be better than the present extended even to himself and to his contemporaries, to their failures and to their successes. And that is what we must always believe. You make a better present if you think about the future being brighter and if you really believe in the potential of every single human spirit. Thomas Jefferson did, and so should we.

I hope you'll now join us in the State Dining Room, and you'll all be able to talk about what you liked most about the movie. But let me say again, we're gratified to have you all here. Hillary and I have looked forward to this evening for a long time, and we are especially grateful for all of you who had any part in this magnificent gift to the people of the United States.

Thank you.

NOTE: The President spoke at 8:45 p.m. in the East Room at the White House. In his remarks, he referred to Ken Burns, producer of the film, and Jack Smith, president, General Motors Corp.

Remarks on Receiving the Final Report of the White House Commission on Aviation Safety and Security and an Exchange With Reporters
February 12, 1997

The President. Thank you very much, Mr. Vice President. Secretary Peña, Secretary-designate Slater; Senator Lautenberg, thank you for your support and involvement. And a special thanks to all the members of this very distinguished Commission for the work that they did.

This report lays out a clear plan of action to ensure that America's airways and airplanes will remain the safest and that our passengers the most secure in the world well into the next century.

Our aviation infrastructure is just as important to us today as the great railroads were in the 1800's or the interstate highway system became in the second half of the 20th century. Just as they made us competitive in the economies of the 19th and 20th century, a modernized national airspace system will determine our ability to compete in the 21st century.

147

It is fitting that the Vice President is leading this effort. One of the great legacies of Al Gore, Sr.'s service in the United States Senate was his leadership in building our interstate highway system. The mission to modernize and improve our airspace system for the challenges of the next century is every bit as important and historic, and I thank him for the work he has done.

I also want to commend the members of this Commission for first taking on the task and especially the family members of the victims of airline disasters, those serving on the Commission, those who wrote to us, those who testified before us about how to improve our interaction with families in the aftermath of disasters. Out of their personal tragedy they have made a valuable contribution to all of us.

The recommendations in this report are strong, and we will put them into action. We will use all the tools of modern science to make flying as safe as possible. We will bring our air traffic control system into the 21st century, and we will do it by converting to space age satellite technology. We will also change the way we inspect older aircraft, to include an examination of wiring and hydraulic systems, all to ensure that every plane carrying passengers, regardless of its age, is as safe as it can be.

We are doing all these things so that we can cut the fatal accident rate by 80 percent in 5 years—in 10 years—and so that by the year 2005 our air traffic control system will be the finest in the world. We are also taking steps to improve security for all American travelers.

I want to say a word about two of the report's most important recommendations on accident reduction and security. First, it's important to note that air travel is still our safest mode of transportation and America has the lowest accident rate in the world. We have to keep it the lowest and keep working to improve. The FAA and the airline industry have been partners in this effort for years. Today I am pleased to announce that NASA will join them. NASA has agreed to dedicate up to a half a billion dollars in research and development budget over the next 5 years to help make sure we do achieve our accident reduction goal.

Second, aviation security is one of the major fronts of our three-part counterterrorism strategy. On September 9th, I accepted the Commission's 20 initial policy recommendations on security. We acted quickly to implement these rec-

ommendations. We have begun installing 54 bomb detection machines in America's airports. We are training and deploying over 100 bomb-sniffing dog teams. The FAA is hiring 300 new special agents to test airport security. And the FBI is adding 644 agents and 620 support personnel in 1997 to counterterrorism efforts.

We are taking action to make our people more secure. But we cannot afford to rest. The balanced budget I submitted to Congress last week contains $100 million for future aviation security improvements, as the Commission recommends. I urge the Congress to provide this critical funding. This unprecedented Federal commitment reflects our resolve to do everything we can to protect our people and to prevent terrorism.

Again, let me thank the Vice President and the Commission for this remarkable report. Your work should give the American people confidence that air travel in the 21st century will be better and safer than ever before.

Thank you very much.

The Vice President. Mr. President, I think we're going to have a chance to visit with each of them. I want to just note that every single member of the Commission signed the final recommendations. And it was unanimous on every section, with the exception of one dissent in one part of the report from one Commissioner. Every member of the Commission has signed it.

American Airlines Labor Dispute

Q. Mr. President, on aviation, if American Airlines and its pilots can't come to an agreement by Friday, are you inclined to use your power to declare a national emergency and therefore avoid the disruption of a strike? [*Laughter*]

The President. You're going to have another shot at me tomorrow, you know. [*Laughter*] First of all, today I want to say this and just this. This issue has huge implications for our country and, in particular, for specific parts of our country. I have been following it very closely. Today I want to say that the time has not expired, and I want to encourage the parties to make maximum use of the mediation board process. That's what ought to be done today, and that's all I have to say about it today.

Thank you.

NOTE: The President spoke at 1:47 p.m. in the Roosevelt Room at the White House.

Statement on Campaign Finance Reform Legislation
February 12, 1997

In my State of the Union Address, I said that delay would mean the death of campaign finance reform, and I called on the Congress to act by July 4, 1997. Passage of effective finance reform must be a priority for this Congress, but we will succeed only if citizens all across the country make clear to elected officials that change is urgent and that public support is broad and deep. Project Independence can help break the logjam that has blocked reform for so long. By building support for the McCain-Feingold and Shays-Meehan campaign finance reform bills, Project Independence will give citizens a voice as we work to reform our politics and renew our democracy.

Remarks at the Funeral of Ambassador Pamela Harriman
February 13, 1997

We gather in tribute to Pamela Harriman, patriot and public servant, American Ambassador and citizen of the world, mother, grandmother, great-grandmother, and sister, and for so many of us here, a cherished friend. She adopted our country with extraordinary devotion. Today her country bids her farewell with profound gratitude.

Hillary and I have often talked about what made Pamela so remarkable. It was more than her elegance, as unforgettable as that was. It was more than the lilt of her voice and her laughter, more even, than the luminous presence that could light up a room, a convention hall, or even the City of Lights itself. It was more than her vibrant sense of history and the wisdom that came to her from the great events she had lived and those she had helped to shape, from the Battle of Britain to the peace accord in Bosnia. I think it was most of all that she was truly indomitable.

One day the train she was on to London was bombed twice, during the Blitz. She simply brushed off the shards of glass, picked herself up, and went to the office to do her work at the Ministry of Supply. She was 21 years old.

More than 40 years later, all of us who knew her saw the same resolve and strength again and again, most tenderly, in the way she gave not only love but dignity and pride to Averell who, as long as he was with her, was at the summit, even to his last days.

In 1991, she put her indomitability to a new test in American politics, forming an organization with a name that made the pundits chuckle because it did seem a laughable oxymoron in those days: Democrats for the Eighties. For members of our party at that low ebb, she became organizer, inspirer, sustainer, a captain of our cause in a long march back to victory. She lifted our spirits and our vision.

I will never forget how she was there for Hillary and for me in 1992: wise counsel, friend, a leader in our ranks who never doubted the outcome, or if she did, covered it so well with her well-known bravado that no one could have suspected. Today I am here in no small measure because she was there.

She was one of the easiest choices I made for any appointment when I became President. As she left to become our Ambassador to France, she told us all with a smile, "Now my home in Paris will be your home. Please come and visit, but not all at once." [*Laughter*] It seemed she had been having us at her home all at once for too many years. So a lot of us took her up on her invitation to come to Paris. After Hillary and I had been there the first time, I must say I wondered which one of us got the better job. [*Laughter*]

In many ways her whole life was a preparation for these last 4 years of singular service and achievement. She represented America with wisdom, grace, and dignity, earning the confidence of France's leaders, the respect of its people, the devotion of her staff.

Born a European, an American by choice, as she liked to say, Pamela worked hard to build the very strongest ties between our two countries and continents. She understood that to make yourself heard you had to know how to listen. And with the special appreciation of one not native born, she felt to her bones America's special leadership role in the world.

Today, we see her legacy in the growing promise of a Europe undivided, secure, and free, a legacy that moved President Chirac last week to confer upon Pamela the Grand Cross of the Legion of Honor, France's highest award. He said then that seldom since Benjamin Franklin and Thomas Jefferson had America been so well served in France.

There is one image of Pamela Harriman I will always treasure. I can see her now, standing on the windswept beaches of Normandy on the 50th anniversary of D-Day. She had told many of us of the long, tense night in England half a century before, as they waited for news about the transports plowing toward the shore, filled with young soldiers, American, British, and Free French. Now, 50 years later, history had come full circle, and she was there as an active life force in the greatest continuing alliance for freedom the world has ever known.

I was so glad that Randolph read a few moments ago from the book of Sir Winston Churchill's essays that Pamela loved so well and gave to so many of us who were her friends. The passage he read not only describes her own life, it is her valediction to us, her final instruction about how we should live our lives. And I think she would like this service to be not only grand, as it is, but to be a final instruction from her to us about what we should now do.

Let me quote just a portion of what was said a few moments ago. "Let us reconcile ourselves to the mysterious rhythm of our destinies such as they must be in this time—in this world of time and space. Let us treasure our joys but not bewail our sorrows. The glory of light cannot exist without the shadows. Life is a whole, and the journey has been well worth making."

Throughout her glorious journey, Pamela Harriman lightened the shadows of our lives. Now she is gone. In the mysterious rhythm of her destiny, she left us at the pinnacle of her public service, with the promise of her beloved America burning brighter because of how she lived in her space and time. What a journey it was and well worth making.

May God comfort her family and countless friends, and may He keep her soul indomitable forever.

NOTE: The President spoke at 10:26 a.m. at Washington National Cathedral. In his remarks, he referred to Pamela Harriman's late husband, W. Averell Harriman; her grandson, Randolph Churchill; and President Jacques Chirac of France.

Remarks Prior to Discussions With Prime Minister Binyamin Netanyahu of Israel and an Exchange With Reporters
February 13, 1997

President Clinton. Let me say two things. First of all, I'm delighted to have the Prime Minister back in Washington, and I applaud the terrific effort that he and Chairman Arafat made to resolve the issues relating to Hebron. And I'm looking forward to the next steps.

The second thing I'd like to say is, we are going to have a press conference after this is over, and because we have a lot of things to discuss and a limited amount of time to discuss them, I would prefer if we would defer all questions until the press conference. I will give you an extended opportunity to ask questions related to this, and I know you have some other questions on other things, but I'd rather answer them at the press conference.

Q. And I'll obey you for a change. [*Laughter*]

Q. Sir, I like your tie.

President Clinton. Thank you. Pamela Harriman gave me that the last time I was in Paris. That's why I wore it today. Her last gift to me was this tie. That's why I wore it today.

[*At this point, one group of reporters left the room, and another group entered.*]

President Clinton. Let me make a brief statement, if I might. First of all, I am very, very pleased that the Prime Minister is back in Washington. I'm looking forward to our meeting. I want, once again, to congratulate him for the agreement that was made with Chairman Arafat over Hebron. It was a brave and wise thing to do. Obviously, the United States wants to make whatever contribution we can to the continuation of a peace process.

The second thing I would like to say is that we have a lot of things to discuss here, as you might imagine, and a limited time in which to discuss them. I will be happy to take your questions, but I would like to defer it until our press conference. And at least I and I think the Prime Minister will be willing to stay for a reasonable period of time to get virtually all the questions out. But we need to get on with our meeting now.

Q. Mr. President, are you willing to take— [*inaudible*]—the Hamas member, to Israel——

President Clinton. I'll answer the questions at the press conference.

Prime Minister Netanyahu. This is the Israeli press, Mr. President.

President Clinton. No, it's okay.

Q. What's wrong with the Israeli press?

Prime Minister Netanyahu. A very good press.

President Clinton. Nothing. [*Laughter*] Wait, wait, wait. The Prime Minister wants to make a statement.

Prime Minister Netanyahu. It's a very brief statement, but I think it says a lot. I'm very, very happy to be here with President Clinton again. We have seen him personally and his staff make a tremendous contribution for peace. I think their contribution for the Hebron agreement was decisive, and it reflects and reaffirms the leadership for peace that President Clinton has shown throughout his term of office.

I think we've taken bold steps for peace. It's time that we see such steps from our partners as well. And if we have this mutuality, we will have, I think, a great future, a different future and hope for our children and our grandchildren.

Q. Mr. President, can you take one question?

President Clinton. At the press conference. I will answer at the press conference. And I promise, if he doesn't call on you, I will.

NOTE: The President spoke at 1:12 p.m. in the Oval Office at the White House. In his remarks, he referred to Chairman Yasser Arafat of the Palestinian Authority. A tape was not available for verification of the content of these remarks.

The President's News Conference With Prime Minister Binyamin Netanyahu of Israel
February 13, 1997

President Clinton. Good afternoon. Please be seated. I'm pleased to welcome Prime Minister Netanyahu back to the White House for his fourth visit since taking office. He comes at a time of great sadness in Israel, following the terrible helicopter accident of 9 days ago. We know that in Israel every death is in the family. And on behalf of the American people, Mr. Prime Minister, once again I would like to extend our deepest sympathies to the loved ones of the victims and to all the people of Israel.

Since our meeting in October, we have traveled a very long way. Then we met in a time of crisis; now there is a renewed sense of promise in the Middle East. I want to congratulate the Prime Minister for concluding the Hebron agreement last month with Chairman Arafat. They have reached a milestone on the way to a secure and lasting peace. The agreement solved the immediate issue of redeployment and laid out a roadmap for the next steps that must be taken to fulfill existing agreements and to move ahead to the pivotal questions of the future.

Beyond the specific commitments made, the Hebron accord is important because it renewed the partnership between Israelis and Palestinians, a partnership that is essential to the success of the peace process. The United States is proud to have helped in this effort.

Today the Prime Minister and I discussed what Israelis and Palestinians need to do next to strengthen this relationship that is so central to all our hopes for the Middle East. We have an opportunity to build on the new momentum coming out of last month's agreement. It must not be wasted.

The release of Palestinian prisoners earlier this week was an important sign of Israel's respect for past agreements and its willingness to take into account Palestinian needs. Both sides must show the same kind of determination as they seek to resolve on the basis of reciprocity the issues that remain. The challenges will be great, but the Prime Minister and Chairman Arafat have shown that the will is there. Just as America has been by Israel's side each step of the way, in the journey that lies ahead we will help Israel and its partners move forward.

The achievement of Hebron is a call to action, and it must be heeded. The United States and Israel share a goal of a comprehensive settlement and a powerful belief that peace and security are indivisible.

The Prime Minister and I exchanged ideas on how to revive negotiations between Syria and Israel. I believe both nations want to conclude a peace agreement, and the United States will work with them to achieve that goal. We also believe it is important that Israel and Lebanon achieve an agreement to complete the circle of peace.

We agreed on the need for increased contact and better ties between Arab States and Israel. This will be a priority in my meetings with other Middle East leaders over the next month. It's time to reinvigorate talks that bring together Israelis, Arabs, and the international community to address regional issues such as water resources and environmental protection and to clear the way to more trade between Israel and Arab nations.

To make peace meaningful, reconciliation must deepen. And Arabs and Israelis must both harvest more of the fruits of peace. The pursuit of peace and the practice of terror are incompat-

ible. For negotiations to succeed, there must be a climate of stability and tranquility. For peace to endure, Arabs and Israelis must know the calm of a normal life.

Prime Minister Netanyahu and I reviewed our shared efforts to combat terror, including the 2-year, $100 million program I announced last year. Those funds have allowed Israel to invest in research and development for new technologies, to procure state-of-the-art security equipment, to streamline the passage of goods and people from the West Bank and Gaza. That way Israel has more security, and Palestinians have more economic opportunity.

Finally, I reaffirmed to the Prime Minister America's unshakable determination to continue helping Israel to meet its security needs. The delivery of F–15–I fighters beginning this year will strengthen Israel's air defenses against any attack. And our cooperation on theater missile defenses through early warning systems and defensive programs like the Arrow is reducing the chance that Israelis again will fear missile attacks from distant enemies.

When Binyamin Netanyahu first visited the White House as Prime Minister, I pledged that we would preserve and strengthen the bonds between our two nations. With this meeting we have taken another step to fulfill that promise, to deepen the partnership that has made it possible for so many extraordinary changes to occur in the Middle East since 1993, through the agreements last month and through other things that will now be done to sustain us as we move forward toward our common dream of a comprehensive peace.

Thank you, Mr. Prime Minister. The floor is yours.

Prime Minister Netanyahu. Thank you. Mr. President, I want to thank you first for the very moving words that you expressed, your sharing of our grief, the sharing of the American people of the great sorrow of the people of Israel in our recent tragedy. I think you've shown yourself to be a great champion of peace and an exceptional friend of Israel. And I must say that both of these attitudes were in evidence today in our discussions, discussions between friends who wish to achieve peace and security.

We discussed the progress and the various tracks of peace, both with the Palestinians and as we hope with the Syrians. And I found, as always in my discussions with you, Mr. President, your unshakable commitment to Israel's security and understanding of how security is intertwined with peace and a desire to assist us with our Arab partners to walk on that road of peace and security.

I think that the strength of the American-Israel relationship is a fundamental factor in the pursuit of peace, of a secure peace in the Middle East. And I come out of these meetings with renewed confidence in our ability to progress on that road.

Thank you, Mr. President.

President Clinton. Now, we'll start with Terry [Terence Hunt, Associated Press], and we'll alternate between American and Israeli journalists. And the Prime Minister will call on the journalists from Israel.

Syria

Q. Mr. President, you mentioned Syria. What are the prospects for restarting peace talks with Syria? And the Prime Minister was said to be bringing a territorial compromise on the Golan Heights. Did you discuss that, and what can you tell us about it? Do you think it might work?

President Clinton. I would very much like to see the talks resume. And I think it's an important part of continuing the process, keeping it alive, keeping the momentum going. We had an extensive discussion about the whole issue of every aspect of the peace process. But I think the only way the United States has been able to be a constructive force in this process for the last several years is not to say anything which will undermine the prospects of its success. So if I—I'm going to follow the rule I've followed since I first came to this job: Until we have something to say publicly, anything I comment on will only undermine the chances of peace.

I do feel encouraged by the discussions we've had, that there are things worth working on, working through. I'm hopeful that we can get the Syrian track going again. But I have nothing specific to say at this time.

Middle East Peace Process

Q. Mr. President, I believe that you had a very lengthy private talk with Prime Minister Netanyahu. In your private conversation today, did he outline to you how does he see the future Middle East or the permanent settlements—peace settlements in the Middle East between Israel and Syria, between Israel and the Palestinians or the Palestinian Authority? Privately, did he say anything to you about it?

President Clinton. You mean you want me to make the private talk not private anymore? [*Laughter*] No, the answer—yes, the answer is, I believe he has thought through a way consistent with the security of the people of Israel that a comprehensive peace might be achieved. We all know that there are a lot of things out there that still have to be resolved. But I was impressed that it's obvious that he has been thinking very hard about this and thinking about it from a security point of view and from a point of view of peace and long-term harmony and prosperity of peoples in the region. I was encouraged by that.

Helen [Helen Thomas, United Press International].

Lebanon

Q. Mr. President, assuming that Ambassador Indyk was correctly quoted on our policy in Lebanon and assuming that we still have a tradition of supporting territorial integrity, why are you against the withdrawal of Israeli troops from Lebanon at this time?

President Clinton. I believe it is imperative that Israel maintain the security of its northern border, and therefore, I have believed that the United States should be somewhat deferential under these circumstances, which are quite unusual, as we've seen repeatedly over the last few years, in the decisions that Israel would make. So it's up to the Prime Minister to announce the policy of his country, not me, on this issue.

Q. Even to the point of occupying someone else's country?

President Clinton. Do you want to make a comment about it?

Prime Minister Netanyahu. Thanks. [*Laughter*]

President Clinton. Get me off the hot seat. [*Laughter*]

Prime Minister Netanyahu. Well, we have no desire, Helen, to be in Lebanon. We're there simply because there's a desire of some people in Lebanon to be in Israel, specifically, to launch attacks against Israel. They've been doing that over the years. I'm talking about Hezbollah at this stage. And we have said that we would withdraw from Lebanon if we could secure our northern border. Our concern is that if we simply walked away to the border, the Hezbollah and other terrorists would just come to the fence and attack our towns and villages and our citizens from that improved position.

My view is that we can achieve an ultimate withdrawal from Lebanon if we could have somebody dismantle the Hezbollah military capacity in the south of the country and take up the slack—preferably it should be the Lebanese army. That is something that we're prepared to negotiate with the Government of Lebanon, and it's no secret with Syria, that has more than a minor influence in Lebanon. That is our position. It hasn't changed.

Iran and Saudi Arabia

Q. Mr. President, Mr. Prime Minister, Iran is developing long-range missiles with Russian know-how. Is that a clear and present danger to Israel? On another—friends of the United States, the Saudis, will get the latest technology from United States. Will that be a danger to Israel's qualitative edge? Thank you.

President Clinton. Let me answer the second question first, and then I'll answer them both. First of all, with regard to Saudi Arabia, we have had a long and very important defense partnership which persists to this day and which has contributed, I believe, to the security of Israel. We have not been asked by the Saudi Government for F–16's, which I take it is the import of your question, so I will get to the specifics. Obviously, any request they would make of us we would have to seriously consider. But any decision that I make about that has to be made in a way that is consistent with our first commitment which is to do nothing that will undermine the qualitative edge of Israeli security forces in the Middle East.

Now, with regard to the second question, we are obviously concerned about Iran from many perspectives, not only from the build-up of its conventional military forces but also from the continued determination of the government to support terrorists in the region and beyond. And we are doing what we can to stem the tide of terrorism. And I will say again, we will do what we can to make sure that no development in any other country that is beyond our control or influence will be permitted to erode Israel's qualitative security edge. That is our responsibility, and we'll do our best to fulfill it.

Bill [Bill Plante, CBS News].

China and Campaign Financing

Q. Mr. President, your Press Secretary said earlier today that you were surprised and concerned by reports that there may have been plans made in the Chinese Embassy to funnel foreign contributions to the Democratic National Committee this year. Does this give you concern that there could be industrial or economic espionage as a target of this? And do you think this tips the scales in favor of having an independent counsel on the campaign finance question?

President Clinton. Well, first of all, the—let me answer—the second question has and should be answered entirely by the Justice Department. The statute about that depends not on the gravity of the subject but on what the targets are. And it's fairly well covered. The Justice Department has spoken to that and will continue to speak to that and will make the decisions. I don't want to have any comment about it.

On the first, let me say that, first of all, this is a serious set of questions raised here. And the first I knew about any of it was last evening. They obviously have to be thoroughly investigated. And I do not want to speculate or accuse anyone of anything. I do not—I know nothing about it other than what I heard last night, which is reflected entirely in the article this morning in the Post. But obviously, it would be a very serious matter for the United States if any country were to attempt to funnel funds to one of our political parties for any reason whatever.

So I think we just have to let the investigation proceed, and we should all support it in every way we can. It has to be vigorous, and it has to be thorough.

Lebanon and Syria

Q. Mr. President, is it the American view that it's possible to reach a settlement in Lebanon without first reaching an overall settlement with Syria? And if so, will the American Government do something to seek such a solution?

President Clinton. Well, let me say I would support any reasonable efforts to reach a comprehensive settlement with Lebanon that the Government of Israel thought was feasible and was willing to undertake. I think that we all know what the facts are there, and we all understand. You just heard the Prime Minister talk about the problems along the border. I think we all understand it would be at least certainly a lot easier to do if there were also an agreement with Syria.

You know, we have a special feeling in this country for Lebanon, and we have a lot of the sons and daughters of Lebanon who are American citizens now. And it is a particularly grievous thing for us to see the relationships between Israel and Lebanon in the position they're in. But we have to look at this over the long run. I think that—we have talked about this frankly; we've had several conversations about this. We have to do what we think is possible, and Israel has to do what we think is possible. If it became possible to have a real and meaningful agreement, would I be for that? You bet I would. Is it now? I'm not sure.

And you may want to——

Prime Minister Netanyahu. I think you said it very well.

American Airlines Labor Dispute

Q. Mr. President?

President Clinton. Yes, John [John Palmer, NBC News]?

Q. Mr. President, I wondered if you could give us your assessment of the impact of a possible American Airlines strike at midnight tomorrow night? Have you received the Department of Transportation report on that impact and how serious would it be? And would you plan to invoke any special powers and keep them on the job through an emergency decree?

President Clinton. Today I want to say no more than I did yesterday, except to reemphasize that it should be obvious to everyone looking at this that it cannot be a good thing for American Airlines, but more importantly, it cannot be a good thing for the people of the United States, and indeed people coming to the United States from other parts of the world, for a significant interruption to occur in the operations of this airline.

We've had so many problems with our airlines for several years. And now they've been doing quite well for the last couple of years. Our administration has worked very hard on that. This is an important part of America being seen as a vibrant, reliable, successful nation. And it would be quite disruptive if it occurs.

So I want to say today, I want to reiterate my call to the parties to use the mediator and think about how they can reach out to one another in the best interest of the Nation as well

of American and its employees, all of its employees.

Israel-Syria Peace Talks

Q. Mr. President, do you really think that Israel and Syria can resume the peace talks in an atmosphere like we have today, where Hezbollah keeps its terror activity and the Syrian and Iranian support? And what are you going to do about it, if anything—if you are going to do anything about it?

President Clinton. Well, actually, we spend quite a lot of time trying to do something about terrorists everywhere. We invest a lot of our resources and our efforts in working with our friends in Israel and throughout the world trying to prevent terrorists from conducting successful operations and trying to track them down and punish them and extradite them and do what needs to be done when they do.

So I think our—I think the United States has a clearer, more unambiguous position on terrorism, whether it affects our people directly or not, than virtually any other large industrial country in the world. And I will continue to do that.

However, it has been obvious for some time to the overwhelming majority of people in Israel—which is why the Prime Minister has done what he's done and why his predecessors did what they did—that in the long run, there had to be a comprehensive peace in the region to end all the violence. And I applaud him for doing that.

When we seek to make peace, we obviously are dealing with people with whom we have been angry, angry enough to take up arms, people with whom we have not had a relationship of trust. And that is what makes every step along the way so difficult. But I think to renounce the possibility of peace is not the right course. To stand up to terrorism in every way we can is the right course.

National Economy

Q. In your economic report of the President, which was released this week, you said that the economy's health was the strongest it had been in decades. Today the stock market closed at about 7,000 for the first time. Are you concerned about the speed of that rise? Do you think it may well be justified, given what you see as a pretty strong fundamental economy?

President Clinton. I think it was 3,200 when I took office. [*Laughter*] And I got a call from a little town in the mountains of north Arkansas, from a friend of mine who was talking to his Republican stockbroker, who said, "If it ever hits 4,000, even I will vote for him." [*Laughter*]

Let me say, my own view is that anything we say about this is likely to either have no effect or an adverse one. The market has produced a remarkable growth, but the economy is growing. Obviously, the concern is, you know, are the returns to stocks, returns to investment greater than can be justified based on the productivity and profit prospects of the companies that are being traded? But if you look at the stability and the growth that we've enjoyed and the prospects we have for stable growth with no inflation, it's hard to say that it's completely out of the question.

More and more—keep in mind, one of the reasons this market has gone up is that just a few years ago only about a third of the American people owned stocks, either directly or indirectly through their retirement investments and mutual funds; today over 40 percent of the American people do.

So, on balance, this has been a positive thing. Obviously, you know—some people say, "Well, gosh, we don't want another 1987 here." But even after 1987, we had a rather rapid rebound. So I think what I need to do is to try to work on keeping the economy healthy. Let's go on and balance the budget. Let's invest in our future, and let's try to create a better worldwide trading system. Let's follow our strategy, and then let the market take care of itself, as long as there is no destructive element in it. That's what I think we should do.

Want to take one more?

Alleged Hamas Terrorist Abu Marzook

Q. Mr. President and Mr. Prime Minister, are you considering once again the question of bringing Mr. Abu Marzook to trial in Israel?

President Clinton. The answer to that question is, we did not discuss it because it's a matter within the American courts. And there is nothing I can do about, nothing the Prime Minister can do about it. It's in our courts, and we can't discuss it until it's resolved in the courts.

Prime Minister Netanyahu. I can only reaffirm that. But I can also tell you that, Mr. President, like you, I have a habit of not dealing—not

commenting on our stock market, which has been going up. [*Laughter*] But I will say that when the Israeli stock market reaches 7,000 I will comment on it. [*Laughter*]

Second Term Cabinet Nominees

President Clinton. Before I go I have to—since I didn't get a question on it, I have—there is one thing I want to say something about, just because I've heard it suggested that maybe I don't have a great interest in this. I've just literally not been asked about it.

I have been very well-pleased with the treatment that my nominees for the Cabinet have received who have gotten their hearings and been taken to a vote. There are still some who have not gotten a hearing yet, and let me mention in particular Tony Lake. We've now answered all the questions that we've been asked. We've sent it up to the committee. And I think he ought to be given a hearing and a vote.

And I'd like to remind everybody involved in this that it was Tony Lake who came up with the strategy that we implemented to end the bloodiest war in Europe since World War II. He was a terrific success as the National Security Adviser to the President. He has worked in these fields for 30 years. He fully understands the intelligence operations. He is superbly qualified. If someone has some reason to oppose him, let them oppose him in a hearing and then in a vote on the floor. But in view of his service, not to me but to this country, and the positive consequences of that service, whether it's Bosnia, Haiti, the agreements with Russia, you name it, he deserves—his service to this country deserved a hearing and a vote on the floor of the Senate. And I hope he will get it.

Thank you very much.

Q. [*Inaudible*]

President Clinton. Well, I obviously feel that way about that, but you know, you've got this on the record about that. I think she'll sail through if we ever get her to a vote. The same thing about Secretary Peña. But I wanted to—I'm on the record, I think, with Alexis. I just wanted to be on the record with Tony.

NOTE: The President's 135th news conference began at 4:34 p.m. in the East Room at the White House. In his remarks, he referred to U.S. Ambassador to Israel Martin S. Indyk and Secretary of Labor-designate Alexis Herman.

Statement on the Killing of a British Soldier in Northern Ireland
February 13, 1997

I am grieved and outraged by the callous killing of a British soldier in Northern Ireland yesterday. The First Lady and I extend our deepest sympathy to the soldier's family and to the British Government and people on the loss of this young man. We wish the authorities success in bringing the murderers swiftly to justice.

All those who care about the future of Northern Ireland must join me in condemning this cowardly crime. I remain convinced that the people of both of Northern Ireland's traditions want to take the path of peace and reconciliation, not hatred and violence.

The Belfast talks chaired by Senator Mitchell continue to have my full support. I urge all those taking part, who share a commitment to democratic values, to move as rapidly as possible into substantive negotiation about the future of Northern Ireland.

The loyalists and their leaders have shown great courage and restraint in not allowing themselves to be drawn into an escalating spiral of violence. I urge them to remain steadfast.

Remarks on Receiving the "Adoption 2002" Report and an Exchange With Reporters
February 14, 1997

The President. Thank you very much, Olivia. Ladies and gentlemen and boys and girls, thank you all for being here. I also want to say a special word of thanks to some Members of Congress who are not here today but who have done an enormous amount of work on this issue, including Senators Rockefeller, Chafee, and DeWine, and Congresswoman Kennelly and Congressman Camp.

Let me begin by also saying Happy Valentine's Day. All the kids look wonderful. The rest of us look all right, too—[*laughter*]—but the kids look especially wonderful.

I want to thank you, Olivia, for the work you've done. And I want to thank the First Lady for the work she has done on this issue over more than 20 years now. I'll never forget the first conversation we had, shortly after we were married, about a case that she had involving a child in foster care who wanted to become an adopted child. I didn't know very much about it before then, and ever since then this issue has been of consuming interest to me because of what I learned through her. And I thank her for that.

We know that our children's fundamental well-being depends upon safety and stability, that without these, children have a very hard time in this complicated, challenging world of ours. We know that far too many of our own children are indeed now in danger in the homes in which they live. The public child welfare system was created to provide a temporary haven for those children but not to let them languish forever in foster care.

As you heard Olivia say, we have nearly half a million of our children in foster care today. Nearly 100,000 will never return to their original homes. Many of those children still will never know what it's like to live in a real home until they grow up and start their own families. But it does not have to be that way. We can find adoptive and other permanent families for waiting children like these fine children who have joined us today and the children whose valentines you see hanging behind me and here in front.

In December I asked the Department of Health and Human Services to come up with an aggressive legislative and administrative strategy to double the number of children we move from foster care to permanent homes annually by the year 2002 and to move them there much more quickly. I'm proud to say that the Department went to work to produce this blueprint for achieving our goal.

Now we have to move quickly to put this plan into action, so that no child is deprived of a safe and permanent home for even one day longer than necessary. Every agency of every State, every family court, every case worker in the country must understand that children's health and safety are the paramount concerns of the child welfare system, especially when determining whether to remove a child from his or her home or return them there. We'll work with Congress to make sure the law explicitly reflects this priority. We'll issue guidelines to the States so there will be no question as to the law's meaning.

Second, to meet the goal of moving 54,000 children into permanent homes in 2002, we'll work with States and set yearly targets. We'll give them, as my balanced budget does, $10 million a year for the next 3 years to give them the assistance they need, to State agencies, courts, and communities, to devise such a system. We'll also have $10 million to establish competitive grants for States to develop model strategies for moving children from foster care to permanent families.

Third, we'll propose legislation that gives States bonuses, as Olivia said, for every child that is adopted over the prior year's total, with even larger bonuses when the child has special needs. The balanced budget will start paying for these bonuses, but we know they'll pay for themselves, since foster care costs far more than adoption. This isn't just cost effective; of course, it's the right thing to do.

Fourth, to achieve our goal of moving children more quickly, we'll work with Congress to shorten from 18 to 12 months the time a child waits for the first hearing. And we're going to call it a permanency planning hearing, so that there's no mistake as to its purpose.

Fifth, to give credit for model strategies that are working, we'll give national awards for excellence every year in November, National Adoption Month.

Finally, we'll redouble our efforts to make sure no child of one race is deprived of a loving home when a family of another race is prepared to give it. That is illegal and wrong and often hurts our very neediest children. The Department of Health and Human Services will continue to ensure that States are meeting their obligations under this law.

Putting this plan into action today will mean that we are ensuring that no child will languish in foster care when loving families are out there

ready, willing, and able to open their hearts and their homes. This is just one part of our strategy to guarantee the well-being of our most vulnerable children. By giving States the flexibility to develop their own strategies, we're moving closer to achieving that goal.

I'm proud to announce that we have approved Ohio's request for a waiver in dealing with their child welfare system. This is the fifth of its kind, and there will be more to come. It gives Ohio the authority to design and to test a managed care approach to improve child welfare services and move children out of foster care more quickly.

By working together across party lines at every level of government, in businesses, religious groups, communities, and in our homes, we can make sure that every child in America grows up in a safe and nurturing home. That is a goal every American should be proud to support. That is a gift of love we can make to all of our children. And if you look at the children here today, it's hard to think of anything more important we could be doing to say, Happy Valentine's Day.

Thank you.

[At this point, the President and the First Lady greeted the children, and then the President took questions from reporters.]

American Airlines Labor Dispute

Q. Mr. President, both sides of the American Airlines dispute seem to keep putting the ball into your court. How do you feel about being put into that position? Both sides of the dispute seem to keep putting the ball into your court.

The President. They need to go back to work. They've got a few more hours of work to do.

Q. Let me put it this way: What's the upside and the downside of your acting one way or the other?

The President. I'm going to have a meeting on this later this afternoon to get an update, and then I think I should make myself available for questions after I see where we are in a couple hours.

NOTE: The President spoke at 12:51 p.m. in the Oval Office at the White House. In his remarks, he referred to Olivia A. Golden, Acting Assistant Secretary of Health and Human Services, Administration for Children and Families.

Message on the Observance of Presidents' Day
February 14, 1997

I am pleased to join all Americans in celebrating Presidents' Day, 1997.

Each year at this time, we reflect with pride and gratitude on the achievements of our former Presidents; and we pay special tribute to George Washington and Abraham Lincoln, two extraordinary leaders whose clarity of vision and strength of character did so much to shape our country's destiny.

Presidents Washington and Lincoln led America at pivotal moments in our history, moments that profoundly affected our nation's character and course for decades to follow. George Washington helped to win our liberty and give us a democracy strong enough to endure through the centuries and flexible enough to survive the fresh challenges that face each generation of Americans. During the dark days of the Civil War, Abraham Lincoln held together the frayed fabric of our Union and reaffirmed our founders' commitment to the self-evident truths of liberty and equality.

Today we stand at another defining moment in our national journey. We must chart a course for America into a new century and a new millennium. Inspired by the wisdom of Washington and strengthened by the determination of Lincoln, we will build a new American community, based on responsible citizenship and a resolve to realize the full potential of all our citizens. In this way, we can best keep faith with the remarkable leaders whose memory we honor today.

Best wishes for a wonderful observance.

BILL CLINTON

Statement on the Establishment of an Emergency Board in the Dispute Between American Airlines and the Allied Pilots Association
February 14, 1997

As you know, I have been closely following the labor negotiations between American Airlines and its pilots represented by the Allied Pilots Association. I want to compliment the parties, the National Mediation Board, its chairman Kenneth Hipp, and mediator Harry Bickford for their hard work to date. Progress has been made over the last several days and especially in the last few hours. Despite these good-faith efforts, however, the parties have been unable to reach a tentative agreement by the 12:01 a.m. strike deadline.

To facilitate an agreement, and because I believe that a strike would have an immediate and adverse impact on the traveling public, I am creating a Presidential emergency board to work with the parties and to make recommendations regarding a resolution. No strike will occur while the Presidential emergency board is in place.

A strike would cause a severe disruption to both domestic and international air transportation. American Airlines is the Nation's second largest airline; it carries over 220,000 passengers every day. It would be extremely difficult for other carriers to fill the void. The Department of Transportation has estimated that approximately 43,000 passengers per day would not be accommodated by other airlines. The disruption would be particularly felt in Dallas, Miami, Chicago, New York, and Puerto Rico where American provides a large percentage of existing flights. It would also affect the nations of the Caribbean, many of whom rely heavily on American Airlines for air service to and from their shores.

In the event of a strike, most of the 90,000 American and American Eagle employees would be placed on leave. The majority of these employees are based in Texas, Illinois, New York, California, Florida, and Oklahoma. Many of the elected officials from the States led by Senators Graham and Hutchison and Representative Martin Frost and Governor Chiles have made clear to my administration that a strike would severely affect their economies.

American transports almost 10 percent of the Nation's air cargo. A strike could increase and cause delays for shippers and the U.S. Postal Service.

I was also particularly concerned that a strike would be especially disruptive over a holiday weekend, when hundreds of thousands of citizens rely on our air transit system.

This dispute needs to be resolved as soon as possible. I urge the parties to continue to use the National Mediation Board and the Presidential emergency board to redouble their efforts to reach an agreement. They owe that to each other and to the traveling public.

NOTE: The Executive order of February 15 establishing the emergency board is listed in Appendix D at the end of this volume.

The President's Radio Address
February 15, 1997

Good morning. Today I'm pleased to announce a major new step in our efforts to protect America's children: a universal system for attaching child safety seats in cars. This system, developed by a blue ribbon commission of industry and consumer groups, will make safety seats easier to install and more secure on the road. It will save young lives.

In my State of the Union Address, I issued a call to action to all Americans to prepare our people for the 21st century. Building strong families is central to that mission. That's why we must do all that we can to help parents do all they can to live up to one of the greatest responsibilities anyone can have, to care for a child.

Parents are always on the lookout to make sure their children are safe. That's especially true when you get in the car. Thousands of children are killed in car accidents every year; tens of thousands more are injured.

Even though America's cars and roads are the safest in the world, we must make them safer. That's why today, the final day of National Child Passenger Safety Week, I'd like to talk with you about the steps we're taking to save more lives on the road.

First, we will continue to stress the fundamental rules of safety: seatbelts, safety seats for small children, children 12 and under buckled up and in the back seat. Last month, I instructed the outgoing Transportation Secretary, Federico Peña, to develop a plan to get more Americans to wear seatbelts. I'm delighted to be joined today by our new Transportation Secretary, Rodney Slater, who came to us from the Federal Highway Administration. He knows a lot about this issue, and he will present that plan to me in March. When he does, I will be ready to review it and act on it.

We must also continue to support law enforcement in its effort to increase compliance with safety laws.

Second, we have taken action to make it clear that on America's roads there is no room for alcohol or drugs. We fought to make it illegal for all young people under 21 to drive with any alcohol in their blood, and 34 States now have these zero-tolerance laws. We're also developing a plan to make teens pass a drug test as a condition of getting a driver's license.

Third, we've worked to make air bags, one of our most important safety tools, safer for children. All cars and safety seats now come with warning labels to remind drivers to keep children in the back seat. Plans are underway to permit manufacturers to install less powerful air bags and to phase in a new generation of "smart" air bags. Air bags have saved a lot of lives. With these improvements, they'll save even more.

And today we're taking a fourth step: We will make child safety seats safer. These seats are the most effective safety device to protect very young children. In car crashes, they reduce the risk of death or serious injury to infants by 70 percent. They cut the fatality and injury rate for children aged 1 to 4 in half. But while all 50 States have car seat laws, studies show that 40 percent of the time young children do not even ride in safety seats, and even when they are placed in child safety seats, 80 percent of the time children are either not fully secured or the car seats are not properly attached.

The fact is, despite parents' best efforts, car seats are hard to install. Not all 100 models of car seats fit in all 900 models of passenger cars. And even when they do, it's no simple task to put them in place. Seat belts are not designed primarily to hold child safety seats. Anyone who's wrestled with a car seat knows what I'm talking about. Thousands of frustrated parents have called our Transportation Department hotline with questions about how to use car seats properly.

Parents are not alone in their concerns. Automobile and car seat makers, consumer organizations, the medical community all have felt there was too much confusion surrounding child seat safety. In response to this problem, my administration convened a blue ribbon panel, with representatives from all these groups, to find ways to make it easier for parents to protect their children with safe, secure car seats.

Today I am pleased that we are acting on the panel's number one proposal, a universal system for attaching car safety seats. Under a Transportation Department plan, every car safety seat would have two standard buckles at its base. Every car would be equipped with stand-ard latches in the back seat designed specifically to fasten to these buckles. There would also be universal attachments to secure the top of the safety seat to the car's interior, so car seats would be locked in from top to bottom. This plan will go out for public comment next week. If approved, the new safety system could be on the market by 1999.

A car seat can protect a child from the violence of the worst crashes. So today we are acting to solve a problem that's been around for too long. We're taking steps to make sure that your child's car seat will stay put in your car every time. With this plan, we're moving closer to the day when safe, well-attached car seats will be the rule of the road.

Together, these efforts represent a new spirit of cooperation in America, with industry and Government working with the American people to support our families as they seek to make life safer and better for our children.

Thanks for listening.

NOTE: The address was recorded at 2:09 p.m. on February 14 in the Oval Office at the White House for broadcast at 10:06 a.m. on February 15.

Statement on the Telecommunications Services Agreement
February 15, 1997

I am pleased to announce that American-led negotiations in Geneva have resulted today in a landmark agreement that will liberalize world trade in telecommunications services. Telecommunications services trade—including telephone, data, satellite, and cellular services—is already a $600 billion industry. It is expected to grow to more than $1 trillion over the next 10 years. U.S. telecommunications firms are the most competitive in the world. This agreement will open markets in nations that account for over 90 percent of the world's telecommunications trade and allow U.S. companies to compete on an equal basis. Today's agreement will bring clear benefits to American workers, businesses, and consumers alike—new jobs, new markets, and lower prices—and will spread the benefits of a technology revolution to citizens around the world.

Just 2 months ago the United States led efforts to complete the information technology agreement, which zeroes out tariffs on a broad range of information technology goods, such as computers, telephone equipment, and semiconductors. Today's agreement opens markets for the services for which many of those information technology products are used—basic telecommunications. These are critical steps toward realization of the American vision of a global information infrastucture.

I want to thank the Vice President for his important role in launching these negotiations nearly 3 years ago. I also want to congratulate America's Trade Representative-designate, Ambassador Charlene Barshefsky, for her skilled and determined efforts. This important agreement advances our interests and opens new opportunities for growth, prosperity, and progress. I also want to thank FCC Chairman Reed Hundt and Deputy U.S. Trade Representative Jeff Lang who helped bring these negotiations to their successful conclusion.

Remarks in a Roundtable Discussion on Welfare Reform in New York City
February 18, 1997

The President. I now know that I came here because after a long holiday weekend, I needed a little good preaching to wake up for the rest of the week. [*Laughter*]

Let me thank you, Dr. Forbes, for welcoming me here, and Dr. Washington, for giving me the chance, just before we began, to walk through the beautiful sanctuary upstairs which I have heard about and known about for many years. The legendary story of Harry Emerson Fosdick and John D. Rockefeller even made its way to me many years ago.

I want to thank Senator Moynihan and Congressman Rangel for being here, as well as Congresswoman Nydia Velázquez and Congresswoman Carol Maloney; thank you for being here. The members of the panel, thank you all. I want to especially say a word of thanks to Secretary of Health and Human Services Donna Shalala, who literally just got off an airplane this morning from South Africa, where she went with the Vice President, and got off one airplane and got on mine and came here. So if she nods out during the ceremony—[*laughter*]—we will forgive her.

Let me get right to business. I came here because I wanted to know a little about what this church is doing and because I wanted to say to the people of New York City and New York what is required of us to do together under this welfare reform law.

By way of background, in the last 4 years and before the law was passed—before the law was changed, the welfare rolls in America were reduced by almost 2.3 million. I received just yesterday an analysis by the Council of Economic Advisers—and that's a record, by the way; the welfare rolls had never gone down by that much in a 4-year period before—the Council of Economic Advisers saying to me that they thought about half of the welfare rolls reduction had come because the economy had improved.

We, after all, had 11½ million new jobs in the last 4 years, and no 4-year period had produced that many before. But about 30 percent of these jobs had materialized—or this movement had materialized because of the welfare reform efforts already going on in 43 States, people in the States making an extra effort to move people from welfare to work. And about 20 percent happened for reasons that cannot be identified. But among other things, we had a 50 percent increase in child support collections over the last 4 years, and anything of that magnitude always enables some people to move out of the welfare rolls and out of the ranks of poverty.

Now, that's what happened in the last 4 years. In the next 4 years—I won't go through all the details of it, but Secretary Shalala and my staff have provided me with an analysis which says that, in essence, the welfare roll law now says that after a certain amount of time, everybody who's able to work should be in the work force, and therefore welfare can't be for a lifetime. And then there are all kinds of rules and regulations and requirements. But the bottom line is we have to move about a million people from the welfare rolls to the work rolls in the next 4 years. That's about the same number of people we moved in the last 4 years, because the average welfare family actually has about 2½, 2.7 people in it.

Now, the problem is, in the last 4 years we had 11½ million jobs. If we can produce 11½ million jobs in the next 4 years, we'll be doing fine. But we have to do it without knowing that for sure. And how are we going to do this? That's what I want to talk about today. And more importantly, how can we not just move people for 1 month or 2 or 3 or 4 or 5 or 6 months into a job but how can we help people who have been trapped in a culture of dependence and poverty to move to a culture of independence, family, and work?

I think it is fair to assume that whenever you reduce the welfare rolls, the people who are most employable move off first. Therefore, the people who are left may be more difficult to employ than the ones who have already moved.

I want to talk about just three or four things that we intend to continue to do. Number one, we believe that child support collections will continue to increase because we've made significant changes in the law to help us do that.

Number two, we have asked the Congress to pass a bill which would give employers who hire people from welfare to work or who hire single men off food stamps, who have no income and get food stamps, into the work force would get a 50 percent tax credit for a salary of up to $10,000. So a maximum tax credit—actual reduction of the tax bill of $5,000, which is quite a significant incentive.

Thirdly, we recommend funds to States and to cities sufficient to create about 380,000 jobs in the public sector over the next 4 years.

Fourthly, I would remind you that the existing law provides for now more funds for child care than before, $4 billion, and continuing support for health care for people who have public assistance and who move into the work force.

Now, in addition to that, if you look at this pattern, I also want to point out that the State has some flexibility right now. The State of New York, for example, right now, can offer all or part of a monthly welfare check to an employer as a wage and training subsidy if the employer will hire someone off welfare. For a single man on food stamps but with no welfare check, the State of New York can cash out the food stamps and give it to the employer as a wage and training subsidy under the new law.

Secretary Shalala and I will work together to give some States the flexibility under the old law, and the results, the preliminary results are quite encouraging. The State of Florida has just announced a program to try this.

How are we going to get all these people jobs? Let me give you some numbers. This country has 826,000 private sector business employers with 20 or more employees. A lot of them have a lot more than 20 employees. We have 1.1 million nonprofit organizations; many of them are large enough to hire someone else. We have 135,000 religious—churches, synagogues, mosques, and others—with 200 or more members. Obviously, if half that many—50 percent of them—hired one person, we could get there. And a lot of the big companies can hire more than one.

The point I want to make is that this is a manageable problem—if you look at the tax credits, if you look at the cash incentives that the States can offer, it's a manageable problem. But it will not work unless out of this we create what Dr. Forbes talked about at the beginning, in this partnership of hope here.

We have got to create a community-based system, supporting work and family, to make welfare a transitional program that is a program of support and movement to independence. The way the law is written, we have several years to phase in what has to be done, but we've worked out the numbers. We think we have to move another million people from the welfare rolls into the job market, which would reduce the overall rolls by about almost 3 million if we did that, with the children. So that's the background. Those are the incentives we can bring to the table. But we have to have your help to set up this network.

Let me just say one other thing that has particular impact in New York and five or six other States. I think it is imperative that in this budget we are about to pass, that Congress include the provisions that I have recommended to restore benefits to legal immigrants who have been damaged and have health and other problems through no fault of their own. And I assure you I intend to fight hard for that, and I know that your delegation will, but we need your support. The Congress needs to understand that there are an awful lot of people who came here legally who are not on welfare, who are out working, who are paying taxes, and who wound up getting hurt and needing disability or health benefits through no fault of their own. And I think it's a mistake to cut them off. And so we're working on that, and I'd ask for your help on that.

I'd like to turn the program back over to Dr. Forbes, but let me just say again, we've moved about a million people into the work force in the last 4 years and reduced the welfare rolls by 2.3 million. To meet the requirements of the law, it is a calculation of the Department of Health and Human Services, we have to meet another million in the next 4 years. We may or may not create 11½ million new jobs in the next 4 years. If we did it twice in a row, it would be something for sure. Whether or not we do, we're going to have to do that. We can only do it if churches, nonprofits, and private employers make maximum use of tax credits, if the cities and States get the funds that I recommended to hire people in the public sector, and if the States provide the kind of flexibility to private employers everywhere in America that some have done in some places.

You should know that Indiana and Wisconsin reduced their welfare rolls by 40 percent in the last 4 years—40 percent—by aggressive efforts and without particularly ungenerous programs either, just aggressive efforts. This can be done, and I need your help to do it. And I do think it's part of all of our mission in life, Doctor, to do this, anyway.

Thank you.

[At this point, the discussion began.]

The President. Let me say, with all respect, I don't think it's that simple. I don't think it's accurate to say that this bill destroys the safety net for poor people. It maintains a Federal guarantee for poor women and children for nutrition, a Federal guarantee for health care, spends $4 billion more on child care, and says, simply, that if you are able bodied, you cannot stay on welfare forever without going into the work force. And the way the work participation requirements were put on States, by the year 2000 about 40 percent of all the able-bodied people in the welfare—able-bodied adults have to be in—have had some work experience within a given 2-year period. That's what it says.

Now, I hardly—and when you consider the fact that the welfare population, Earl, is different than it used to be and that there are some people who are on it perpetually, I think it is a good thing, not a bad thing, that we did that.

Number two, I do not think it is so simple to say that at any given moment in time there are a fixed number of people who have to be hired by all the employers in America, and if they hire a few more, they're all going down the tubes and lose money. This bill that I have proposed will give a 50 percent tax credit, up to $5,000 a year, for people who hire people. That means you can hire somebody for $10,000 a year and, in effect, the out-of-pocket cost to you is less than the minimum wage.

I met a man with only 25 employees in Kansas City, and 5 of his employees were former welfare recipients. And they were happy at work, and he was happy with them. And he only hired them because he figured that the marginal cost of hiring them, since he got the welfare check as a wage subsidy for a couple of years, lowered his risk of adding to the work force. And sure enough, when he added to the work force, he generated some more work and it turned out to be a profitable decision for him.

I talked to a former Governor last week who's back in private business, who's got a small business, who told me once I explained the proposal to him that he would now go hire three or four people from the welfare rolls because it lowered the marginal cost of adding employees to him. And there is no reason to believe, if we all work on this, that we can't create another million jobs over 4 years without bankrupting businesses and that it wouldn't be better for people who otherwise are going to be permanently dependent on welfare.

And it is not true that we have withdrawn all supports. We are spending more on child care. I want to also spend $3 billion on public service related jobs to create over a third of a million there. And the health care and the nutrition guarantees are still there. So I think it will be a good thing if we make this work, but there is no automatic system for doing it, and that's why we need your help.

[The discussion continued.]

The President. Let me say this, first of all, I agree with what you said about people being in college—people who are going to college who are full-time students. We are looking at whether—if there's some way to get—to deal with that because I don't think people should be pulled out of college. I agree with that.

Secondly, for one thing, you just—from the point of view of the State of New York, this is a—we're trying to work this out because the States basically have control of this. The State of New York would be much better with you as a college graduate, which is the point you tried to make. So I believe that.

Now, the other problem is these training programs essentially are all run by the States and the cities. But I will do some—you've given me some things that we need to obviously do some work on. We need to make sure that there is an adequate training and preparation. That's one of the things I know that you've talked about—what you can do here because an awful lot of people who move from welfare, who are just thrown into these jobs, don't last because they were never prepared for them in the first place, and they're traumatized as a result of it. And oftentimes, just basic preparation of a few months can make a—a few weeks even— can make all the difference in the world. So we'll go back and do—we will pay some more attention to that.

But on the college education thing, I think you're right, and I think we ought to find some way to accommodate that, and we're working on that.

[The discussion continued.]

The President. If I could just make one point on that. Next to education and child care, the thing we hear most all around the country from people who seek to move from welfare to work or very often even to go to college is whether they have adequate transportation. And this ISTEA act that Lew just mentioned, which is— it took me a long time to remember what all those little letters were for. But the bottom line is, I asked the new Secretary of Transportation, Rodney Slater, to look at that to see that we were allocating enough money in here not only for mass transit but also for the appropriate subsidies to make sure that poor people could have access to this. Otherwise they won't be able to get to work.

And this is an interesting opportunity for New York to make an alliance with smaller cities. For example, there was just a study on Atlanta, which said that in—something like 80 percent of the entry-level jobs in the city of Atlanta were filled by people who lived in low-income neighborhoods in Atlanta. In the suburban towns outside, just that touch Atlanta, only 55 percent were. And it was clearly the result of the inadequate ability of low-income people to access transportation to get there.

So this is a huge issue, Lou. It's a huge issue for welfare reform and basically for the integrity of poor families to be able to sort of aspire and move and do things.

Senator, were you going to say something about this?

Senator Daniel Patrick Moynihan. Yes. We very much appreciate your endorsing the existing formula, Mr. President. *[Laughter]*

The President. Is that what I did?

Senator Moynihan. Wyoming, Montana——

The President. I thought we could do a little better on mass transit.

Senator Moynihan. The newspapers out there, did you hear that? *[Laughter]*

The President. Never misses a lick. *[Laughter]*

[The discussion continued.]

The President. Let me say, as I'm sure you know, all the Members of Congress who are present here supported the efforts we made last year to raise the minimum wage. And that, plus doubling the earned-income tax credit, the refundable earned-income tax credit for lower income working people, led in 1995, before the minimum wage even went into—we had the biggest drop in poverty, in the poverty rate among single women with children in 20 years. And so I couldn't agree with you more.

We have still 20 percent of our kids living in poverty. And it's not very complicated. I mean, it's the reverse of why we have lowered the poverty rate among our seniors to 11 percent, and it's the lowest it's ever been in history because we met a national, common commitment to investing in retirement and health care for seniors. And one of the things that I earnestly hope we can do is to—in the next 2 years is to do something really significant to deal with the fact there's still 10 million children in our country without health care. And they're not primarily people who are presently on public assistance because they're eligible for Medicaid.

But education, health care, and safety are the three big priorities that we have for our children. And I think they're all very important, and we're nowhere near where we ought to be there.

[The discussion continued.]

The President. Let me just say very briefly, I think you're right on both counts. We have five American corporations, including UPS and Sprint, Monsanto, Burger King, and somebody I've left out—United Airlines—who have agreed to head a national effort to get major corporations to hire and train people in good jobs.

The second point you made, though, is absolutely right, we have to have—this will not work unless we also have a floor plan for publicly financed jobs for people in training programs in the beginning and also just continuing support for higher education. I'll give you an example. We've been working very hard for months now to try to get a new agreement among the world's nations on telecommunications services, giving American companies the right to compete in other countries for telecommunications services. We finally got an agreement that was far better than I ever dreamed we could get. It is estimated it will bring a million new jobs to America—this one agreement—a million new jobs over the next 10 years, but not one of those new jobs will be a low-skilled job. Every one of those jobs will require a level of skills and education that the folks that want to go to work but don't have those skills desperately need.

[The discussion continued.]

The President. One of the best things we did in the last session of Congress, in the last days, was to add 200,000 more work-study slots. There was another 100,000 in my new budget. If they pass, we will go to a million people on work-study in this country in the next 2 years.

If we can do that, surely—if you think about the numbers you're talking about, you're talking about maybe 100,000 nationwide of the million people that must be in the work force—surely we can get some consideration for permitting a certain number of hours worked on the campus in connection with the legislation. I want to say that I think the one thing that I know that is not working, the way this thing is being applied now, is rules that in effect force people out of college. You know, we're cutting off our nose to spite our face. These are not people who do not want to work. So I will work on that for you.

[A participant presented the President with a gift.]

The President. Thank you.

NOTE: The President spoke at 11:07 a.m. at Riverside Church. In his remarks, he referred to Rev. Dr. James Forbes, senior minister, Riverside Church; Rev. James Washington, chair, Riverside Church Council; Earl G. Graves, chief executive officer, Black Enterprise magazine; and Lewis Rudin, chairman, Association for a Better New York.

Remarks at the Business Enterprise Awards Luncheon in New York City
February 18, 1997

Thank you very much, Jim and Norman, and to all of you who are involved in the Business Enterprise Trust; our host, the New York Public Library, thank you for this magnificent room; and to—especially to our awardees.

I'm glad Bill Moyers told that story about Calvin Coolidge and Alice Roosevelt Longworth because I was looking at these—I had a great time today. I sort of hate it that I have to speak; I was having such a good time looking at the films and looking at the people. But I was thinking to myself, why am I here, because this is such an interesting program; what do they need me here for? And then I thought, well, Norman Lear has been trying to get me to come here for 4 years. *[Laughter]* He's hard to say no to. Every person's friendship carries a certain burden; you know that. That's it. *[Laughter]* And as Calvin Coolidge said, "A man's got to eat." *[Laughter]* So, Norman, I want to thank you for that stick of bread and the cookie at lunch. It was great. *[Laughter]*

Ladies and gentlemen, Norman Lear told that old story about his grandfather; in 1981, I had the distinction of entering my name for the first time in Ripley's when I became the youngest former Governor in the history of the American Republic. *[Laughter]* With dim career prospects—and in my entire State only one person offered me a job—Norman Lear called me and asked me if I would consider coming to work in another one of his endeavors. And I never forgot it, mostly because no one else wanted me to come to work at anything. *[Laughter]* And we've been friends ever since. He doesn't have to do this. He does it because he believes in it and he loves it and he believes that all of us have a higher purpose in our endeavors.

I have known Jim Burke for a long time. In his former life, he headed a great company with two plants in my State that were the embodiment of a lot of what you recognize here every year. And since then, he has headed the Partnership for a Drug-Free America. I don't think any American citizen could wish to have a person in charge of the endeavor to make our country drug-free who is deeper, more committed, more passionate, more whole-hearted than Jim Burke. America owes him an enormous debt of gratitude for his efforts there.

I was thinking about what all this meant today in terms of what I actually need to talk to you about as President. What does Marriott's efforts to provide real services to many of their employees, including a lot of them whose first language is not English and who weren't born here—what does that mean for what I have to say? What does Motorola's commitment to lifetime education and training for its employees—something we do in the military, I might add, but something which Motorola does at an investment of 3 times the industry average—what does that mean? What does the incredible story of Olmec Toys mean? If I ever need anything sold, I'm calling you. [*Laughter*] I've now run all my elections; where were you when I needed you? [*Laughter*] What does it mean for children to be able to see in their toys their dreams, and imagine that there is a connection between their small lives and their big dreams?

I don't know how many of you read Max DePree's books, but I have, and when I read "Leadership Is An Art" I was overwhelmed. I said to myself, why in the living daylights didn't I know that already? Why haven't I been doing that? Why would anybody ever try to do it any other way? What does all this mean?

What I think it means is not only that it's possible to be a good business person and a good citizen, that it's possible to do things like grow the economy and preserve the environment, that you can make a profit and still be decent to your employees, that you can be efficient and still recognize the dignity and the importance of the larger society of which you're a part—that's all true—but I think what it really means is that the most fulfilled people in life are those whose lives are most whole and most in harmony with others with whom they live and come in contact and work, and that in a funny way we're all trying, in different ways, to end the isolation of our endeavors and find some real integrity, some wholeness to them, to connect ourselves to each other in a way that enables us to flourish as individuals and to find personal success by making the whole stronger and better.

And that brings me to what I actually need to talk to you about today, which is how we're going to do that for those among us who are the poorest Americans, who are on welfare and who are now the object of the welfare reform law which I signed last year, because they, too, deserve that. And in some ways, those who have become permanently dependent on public assistance have been isolated from the rest of us by people whose political views span the entire spectrum.

I hear people who think of themselves as conservative, demeaning people on welfare sometimes by saying, "Well, none of them want to go to work," and you know, "The only answer to that is just to walk away. They won't do anything unless they're faced with starvation." And then I hear people who are more liberal, demeaning them in a way that can be equally deadening by saying, "Well, the poor things, they can't work, and so we have to just take care of them. Of course, we'll take care of them at a substandard level, so that every month, from now to the rest of their lives, they'll always be acutely conscious of what they cannot do and cannot be and cannot become."

I believe that we never intended to create a class of permanently dependent people in our society. I believe it only happened because the welfare system we set up for people who had genuine misfortune—the typical welfare recipient 60 years ago was a West Virginia miner's widow with no education and no expectation of being in the work force and children running around the house that had to be cared for and a society that did not require high levels of education for success.

Today, basically, there are two groups of people on welfare. Half the people in this system or any other system would work just fine for it because they run into a little trouble and then they need a little help. But they get themselves out of it, and they go right on about their business and don't get back on welfare again. And they do just fine. And this system—it's not very good, but it's about as good as anything else because they made it work and they go on with their lives.

Then there are the rest of the people on welfare, slightly more than half, who essentially have become part of a group of people in America known in a kind of pejorative sense often as a permanent underclass, mostly younger women and their young children with little or no education, little or no job experience, little or no ability to move into the work force on a sustained basis.

There are another group of people, by the way, that have not been part of this public debate at all, who are at least as big a social concern to me, and those are the single men who are ineligible to get welfare payments in almost every State because they're single men, they don't have children they're supporting, and they live on food stamps and whatever else they can scrounge up. But they're hardly ever in the work force, and we have paid for that as well. The isolation of these people from the rest of us has cost them in ways that are obvious, but we have paid as well—all the families that haven't been formed, all the jobs and all the economic activity that hasn't been there.

So for 4 years, we've been working on this because I believe we could do better. And in 4 years, we've had the biggest reduction in welfare rolls in history, 2¼ million. But it happened for several reasons. It happened about half because we had 11½ million jobs in the last 4 years, and that had never happened before. It happened about 30 percent because over 40 States were already working on welfare reform, moving people from welfare to work. And we don't really know why the other 20 percent got off welfare, partly because we had a 50 percent increase in child support collections.

But now we have a law that says every State must design a system to move able-bodied people who are adults from welfare to work in 2 years. That's what the law says. And I won't bore you with all the details, but let me give you the bottom line. The bottom line is that in the next 4 years, with a smaller welfare population and people who are therefore harder to place, we have to move as many people into the work force as we did in the last 4 years when we had 11½ million jobs and a 50 percent increase in child support enforcement and 43 States already out there working on welfare reform.

And you have to help. And you have to find a way to make it good business. And I believe you can. And that's what I came here to say. We cannot be the country we ought to be if 20 percent of our children are living in poverty. We cannot be the country we ought to be if we say there are all these folks out here that literally we're prepared to have physically separate from us. And if any of you have ever really

spent any time with folks on welfare, you know that most of them are actually dying to go to work. And a painful number literally don't know the first thing about how. And we have a lot of work to do.

But what I want to say to you is this is not an insurmountable problem. Let me just give you a couple of numbers. Keep in mind I said in order to meet the requirements of the law, which I have carefully reviewed now, we'll have to move about a million people more into the work force. That will reduce the welfare rolls by about 2.7 million because of the size of welfare families.

Now, how in the wide world are we going to do this? Well, the first thing you need to know is that there are about 826,000 businesses in America with more than 20 employees. There are 1.1 million nonprofit organizations in America—I don't have the employment breakdown on them. There are 135,000 houses of worship in America with 200 or more members, and over 200,000 with 100 or more members.

Under the new law, every State in the country can take what used to be the welfare check and actually just go give it to an employer to train—properly train, not have some momentary, fly-by-night, meaningless education program but to actually properly train the employee—and to pay a wage subsidy to help train people on literally the habits of work. There is no excuse not to do that. If the law passes that I have proposed, we'll also have a 50 percent tax credit of up to $10,000 for doing it.

Every State can—for single men who don't get welfare checks—can give food stamp funds to the employer for the same purpose. The tax credits are no good to the houses of worship and the community nonprofits who don't pay taxes, but the cash subsidies would be. There are all kinds of things that can be done. But if you just look at the sheer numbers of employers out there, we could do this million people in a snap and help to break the back of the isolated underclass in America and make poverty what it used to be, at least in our imagination, which is a way-station on the way to the middle class for people who would work and learn.

Over the weekend, Charlene Barshefsky, our Trade Ambassador, concluded an agreement on telecommunications that industry leaders estimate will bring one million new jobs to America—that one agreement—in the next 10 years. But none of them will go to people who are illiterate. None of them will go to people who can't find their way on a bus or a subway to work. None of them will go to people who literally don't have the self-confidence to be able to look people dead in the eye and talk to them and relate to them.

This country will never be what it ought to be if there are people who are literally beyond the message of Max DePree or Motorola or Olmec Toys or all these other things. We have got to realize, especially because so many of them are children, that they are our responsibility, too.

And so I ask you today, whether you belong in the category of folks who've criticized the welfare system without really knowing anybody on welfare, or whether you belong in a category of folks who patronize people on welfare and therefore undersold what they could become, or whether, like most of us, you've probably done a little bit of both in your life, they are our people. They are a big part of our future.

The law now says that those who can work have to work. And now that we, as a nation, have put that requirement on them, we have to make sure that those who have to work can work. It is our highest responsibility. But we should do it not with any spirit other than a desire to further what we saw in every one of these films today and to make sure every American can be a part of the whole. And if that happens, they will be better, but so will we.

Thank you, and God bless you.

NOTE: The President spoke at 1:42 p.m. at the New York Public Library. In his remarks, he referred to Jim Burke, chairman, and Norman Lear, founder, Business Enterprise Trust; and journalist Bill Moyers.

Letter to Congressional Leaders Transmitting the Second Africa Trade and Development Report
February 18, 1997

Dear _____:

I am pleased to submit the second of five annual reports on the Administration's Comprehensive Trade and Development Policy for Africa as required by section 134 of the Uruguay Round Agreements Act. Our policy seeks to accelerate the pace of sustainable economic development for the countries of Africa.

This Second Africa Trade and Development Report reflects our conviction that economic development in Sub-Saharan Africa will benefit both Africans and Americans. Stronger economies will better enable African nations to address a variety of complex problems that transcend regional boundaries. In an increasingly competitive global economy, the United States cannot afford to neglect a vast region that contains almost 10 percent of the world's population. Our efforts to help Africa develop will also create more export opportunities for U.S. goods and services and more jobs at home. These efforts to strengthen African economies will also reduce the cost in later years for large-scale U.S. humanitarian aid and enhance local and regional capacity to address transnational problems that threaten regional stability.

Many African countries have made significant progress in the struggle for development in recent years. With assistance from the World Bank and the International Monetary Fund, more than 30 Sub-Saharan African nations have instituted economic reform programs, and, since 1990, nearly as many have held elections.

Nevertheless, there is much more to be done. The United States and other developed nations must do our part to promote economic growth and development in the region. Additionally, African governments must recognize that the failure of many to open their markets to increased international trade has inhibited regional economic growth.

This second report summarizes the status of ongoing programs discussed in last year's African trade and development report and introduces several initiatives designed to spur investment, development, and trade over the near to medium term. These programs and initiatives seek to achieve five basic objectives set forth in the first report: trade liberalization and promotion, investment liberalization and promotion, development of the private sector, infrastructure enhancement, and economic and democratic reforms implemented by many Sub-Saharan African governments in recent years.

Working with the Congress, the U.S. private sector, the countries of Africa, and our other trading partners, the Administration looks forward to developing additional initiatives to promote trade, investment, and development in Africa.

Sincerely,

WILLIAM J. CLINTON

NOTE: Identical letters were sent to Jesse Helms, chairman, and Joseph R. Biden, Jr., ranking member, Senate Committee on Foreign Relations; William V. Roth, Jr., chairman, and Daniel Patrick Moynihan, ranking member, Senate Committee on Finance; Benjamin A. Gilman, chairman, and Lee H. Hamilton, ranking member, House Committee on International Relations; and Bill Archer, chairman, and Charles B. Rangel, ranking member, House Committee on Ways and Means.

Remarks at a Democratic Senatorial Campaign Committee Dinner in New York City
February 18, 1997

Thank you very much. First, let me thank Shelby and Katherine for taking us in tonight. I don't want to be adopted, but this makes the White House look like public housing. [*Laughter*] It is wonderful public housing. [*Laughter*] I really do appreciate their taking us in, and I thank all of you for coming.

And I thank Senator Leahy, Senator Biden, as well as Senators Kerrey and Torricelli. I thank you, Congressman Rangel, for being here. And I don't think—Senator Moynihan is not here anymore; he was here earlier.

I thank the people who are here from New York and New Jersey for the enormous victory you gave to Al Gore and to me on election day. It's the first time I've had a chance to say formally, thank you, here in this part of the world. I am very grateful. I also want to thank Bob Kerrey for agreeing to take on this job again and for what he said.

This has been an eventful time for our country. We just celebrated an Inauguration. We just had a very good State of the Union and response to it. We are working with Members of Congress in both parties on the right kind of balanced budget agreement. I'm working on the Middle East again and have some hope there. We just had the American Airlines strike deferred. And just a couple of days ago, our Trade Ambassador, Charlene Barshefsky, concluded a trade agreement that we believe will create a million new high-wage American jobs in the next

decade. It is a good time for the country, and we are moving in the right direction.

As I said at the State of the Union and I'd like to say again, what we're doing in a larger sense is preparing our country for a new century and a new millennium, and our goal ought to be to give more people than ever before the chance to live out their own dreams and to live in harmony with their brothers and sisters across racial and religious and ethnic lines and to make this country once again the greatest hope for freedom and peace and prosperity throughout the next century. That's the best thing, I think, not only for us but for the rest of the world.

And in order to do that, we need to understand very clearly why we're here today and what happened. The economy is better because we changed the economic policy of the country. We don't have trickle-down economics anymore; we've got investment economics. We brought the deficit down, expanded trade, invested in our people and our technology, and we have 11½ million jobs to show for it. We ought to be glad of that and proud of it.

We went beyond rhetoric and tough talk in crime and welfare reform. We had the biggest drop in welfare rolls in history and 5 years of dropping in crime. And people are actually beginning to conceive that their streets might be safe again. We put family and community not at the center of our talk but at the center of our social policy with things like the Family and Medical Leave Act and the V-chip and the television ratings and the initiative against teen smoking.

And these things are making a difference in people's lives. And that's what happened in the election. We steadfastly stood against those who sought to use race or religion to divide the American people and took some pretty unpopular positions clear across the country in California on affirmative action and immigration initiatives. But the people of California stayed with us because they knew we were trying to bring out the best in the American people and we all have to go forward together.

And let me just say, finally, we rejected, I think conclusively, the dominant political theory of the last 16 years, which is that Government is the problem. It is not the problem. That is not true. Neither is it the salvation. But the market will not solve all the problems in the world, and the market will not solve all the problems of America. And that is one of the things that makes me a Democrat. Senator Kerrey and I talked for nearly an hour on the phone several weeks ago about it. And we believe the job of Government is to provide the conditions and the tools for people to solve their own problems, seize their own opportunities, and make the most of their own lives.

We have reduced the size of the Government more than our counterparts in the other party, reduced the size of regulation. We have led the way toward a lot of changes, through the Vice President's efforts, that needed to be made. But we do not believe that that which we do together through our Government is the enemy of America and its future. We believe we have to work together to make the most of the future. That's why we're here tonight.

And when we look ahead—I want to say something about what Bob said. I appreciate the fact that you came here knowing you might be targeted for the exercise of your constitutional right to stand up and support the people you believe in. And I thank you for being here. I thank you for being here.

You need to know, as people who invest in this, exactly what happened in the last election to the best of our ability to know it. I want you to know two things. Number one, for reasons I cannot explain or defend, our party did not check all the contributions that were given. Therefore, less than 2 percent of the total had

been returned either because they were not lawful or because they raised questions even though they were clearly lawful. They were not all illegal, but we just decided we didn't even want any questions raised about ours. All it did was get more questions raised, but we did it in good faith. And 99.9 percent of all the people who contributed to us—one million, I might add, in the last cycle—one million for the first time have not had their contributions questioned. Indeed, more than 99.9 percent.

So everything you have had to endure, including some of the calls you have received, have come because of what was done by less than one-tenth of one percent of the total number of contributors we had, involving less than 2 percent of the money we raised. But it was wrong not to check those contributions. And if your party had been doing its job, you wouldn't be hearing about all that today. That is everybody's responsibility, from me down, who didn't know about it and should have. But it will never happen again. You can rest assured.

And so we now have to ask ourselves, never mind about this, what is the right thing for the country? Here's why I believe we ought to pass campaign finance reform. I don't agree, as some people do, that a large contribution is automatically suspect and automatically compromises a public official. I don't agree with that. But I do agree that if it costs too much money for a party to do its business and for candidates to do theirs, that you have to raise so much money and it takes so much time to raise it, that it undermines the quality and erodes the independence of the political system. And I think all of you would agree with that.

And so what I want to ask you to do is to support a bipartisan solution to this. The McCain-Feingold bill, I think, is a good bill. It restricts the overall spending. It restricts the size of contributions. It leaves an even playing field between the parties and between challengers and incumbents. And it gives people a discount—candidates—for the cost of communicating over the airwaves, which is so terrifically expensive.

If we did that, we could all still come here, we could all still gather, we could all still give, we could all still do it, but we could do it knowing that our fellow citizens who cannot afford to come here tonight would think they were more equally represented in the political arena. And we could do so knowing that these people that we support when they run and work hard—and keep in mind, my campaigns are over now, so I'm doing this on behalf of them—that we know that they can spend an appropriate amount of time going out and raising funds and listening to people and hearing out the concerns of people in their districts, their States, and their nations, but that it won't take all their time and it won't take all your time. Besides that, it won't cost you as much money. [*Laughter*] But the main thing is, it will be better for our country.

So if there's one group of people I would like to see in the forefront of advocating a reasonable bipartisan campaign finance reform, it is the contributors of the Democratic Party, the Democratic Committee, the Democratic Senatorial Committee, the Democratic House Committee, the people that helped me become President. So I ask you, please help me do that and give our own Members the courage they need to demand that our friends on the other side join us and do this. We need to just put this behind us.

The system was created in '74. It worked fine for us for a while. It's been overtaken by events. You understand it better than anybody else. You're on the receiving end of it. Help me pass campaign finance reform this year. I need your help, and I want you to do it.

The other thing I want to tell you is this: We have a chance this year to pass a balanced budget, to do some things in welfare reform that will really prove that we're not just being tough and talking and saying, people who can work, must work, but to actually give people a chance to work and to get an education. We have a chance to expand our trade networks, particularly in Latin America and Asia, in ways we never have before. The First Lady and our daughter are about to go to Africa on a sweeping trip there.

We have a chance to pass significant improvements in health care for children. We have a chance to do a number of things in foreign affairs to make the world safer. We have a chance to deal with the entitlements problem for the next generation. All of this can be done this year.

It can only be done if I can maintain an atmosphere of both openness to members of the Republican Party who want to work with us and if the Democrats know that we are proceeding with conviction to prepare this country for the next century consistent with what we pledged to do in the election.

And what I want to ask you to do is to continue to give me your support in a constructive way. When we deal with these issues, if you have some suggestion, let me know. If you can mobilize support, do it. But just remember, every day is a day we're moving closer to a new century and a new millennium, and if we do our job, we will open the greatest period in American history. If we fail to do our job, our children and grandchildren should never forgive us. And if something happens that we don't do it in Washington, we ought to make sure it is not the responsibility of our Democrats in the Senate or the House or the White House.

Every day we get up and go to work there to try to make this country a better place. Ultimately, when you get right down to the bottom line, that is what you have supported and what I promise you you will continue to support. And I want you always to be proud of it and always to believe in it.

Thank you, and God bless you all.

NOTE: The President spoke at 9 p.m. at the residence of Shelby and Katherine Bryan.

Remarks in a Roundtable Discussion on Juvenile Crime in Boston, Massachusetts
February 19, 1997

The President. Thank you very much, Mr. Mayor, and let me thank all the panelists who are here and all of those who are in the audience, people who represent law enforcement groups around America, people who represent the families who have suffered loss.

We are here today for a simple reason: Boston proves that we can take the streets back of our country from juvenile violence and crime, from murder, from lost lives; that we can give our children back their childhood and we can give our streets and our neighborhoods back to the families who live on them.

And what we are trying to do in Washington, what I am determined to do in this legislative session, is to take the lessons learned and the triumphs achieved here in Boston and the progress made and embody it in a legislative proposal that the Attorney General has worked very hard with me on to try to give other communities the chance to do what you have done here. It's not a very complicated strategy, but it's the most sensible one we can follow.

Between 1990 and 1995, juvenile homicides dropped by 80 percent in the city of Boston. Since July of 1995, not a single child under 16 has been killed by a gun in this city. Our anti-gang and youth violence strategy essentially rests on four elements, all of which can be found in what has been done here: first, targeting violent gangs and juveniles with more prosecutors and tougher laws; second, working to make our children gun-free and drug-free; third, streamlining and reforming our juvenile justice system; and fourth, giving our young people something to say yes to, not just looking for ways to punish those who have done wrong but to give kids a chance to make some positive steps and actually have a little constructive fun in their lives. I've seen that here in Boston, too.

I have a lot to be grateful to the mayor for, but one of the things that I'm especially grateful for is that he gave me a chance early on in his term to sit and meet with his youth council, the young people that have advised him and worked with him, along with Sister Jean, who has been to Washington to help us out a couple of times.

And I have seen the remarkable balance of your program; I'm excited about it. I also know that for this to succeed nationwide everyone has a part to play. We can pass laws in Washington, we can be supportive at the Federal level, but we have to have the support of grassroots citizens, of business leaders, religious leaders, as well as those in law enforcement and parents and obviously the political leaders here.

So, Mr. Mayor, I'm glad to be here. Governor, Senator, Congressmen, thank you all for having us here, and I think I'd like to let you go on with the program now and listen.

[*At this point, the discussion began.*]

The President. If I could just say very briefly, in support of not only what the Justice Department has done, but also we have Ray Kelly here who's our Under Secretary of the Treasury for Enforcement: We do recognize that one of our important roles nationally—and I want to thank all the Members of the Senate and the House that are here for their support—is to do what we can to at least disarm people who should not have guns.

And I think the Brady bill has helped, the assault weapons bill has helped, the work the Treasury has done to try to be more disciplined in who can be federally licensed to sell guns has helped. There are fewer than half the number of people licensed to sell guns today than there were 4 years ago, fewer than half. And I thank you for that, for your efforts there.

And in this bill we have two other things: We extend the provisions of the Brady bill to violent juvenile offenders, and we require some sort of trigger or gun lock mechanism to be on guns that are in the reach of children. I think that's very important. I thank you for what you're doing.

[*The discussion continued.*]

The President. Thank you very much, Mayor. I don't think we can possibly minimize the role that you have played in all this, the impetus you gave to everybody else. You are someone who is as gifted as anyone I've ever known at bringing people together and making people feel comfortable, when they're from different walks of life, in the same room together working on the same thing. I think the enormous trust the people of this city have in you is one of the reasons this has happened. And I thank you for that.

Let me also say just briefly, in closing, two points. Number one, when I asked Janet Reno to become Attorney General, I knew that I was—that we were together taking a chance, because I had been a State attorney general and a Governor, dealing with crime problems— Governor of a small State dealing with crime problems on a community basis. And she had been a prosecuting attorney in a very large and a very complicated county, with enormous and very challenging problems. But neither one of us had ever dealt with the Federal system except on the other end of it.

I did it because we believed together that the only way we would ever get the crime rate going back down and start saving children's lives and giving people the confidence they need to deal with all the other challenges—the economic, the educational, the other challenges we face—is if the lessons that were being manifested at the community level in America could somehow sweep the country and be reflected in national policy.

When I became President and I discovered that Senator Biden, then the Chairman of the Senate committee that had control of this legislation, believed the same thing, we fated a lot of heat and became vulnerable to a lot of very—what was in the short run quite effective political rhetoric, you know, we were trying to take everybody's guns away and throwing money at these problems and all that. But you see, now, 4 years later, we know the truth, that what we have tried to do is simply give more people like Mayor Menino and Probation Officer Brooks and Commissioner Evans and Captain Dunford and all the others a chance to succeed all over America. That's what we've tried to do.

It is a very simple strategy, but it will work. It will work. And today the juvenile program I'm going to announce is basically an attempt to take what you have proved works here and give those tools to every community in the Nation to follow. Let me just say, no disrespect to anybody else, but you know the people I listened most closely to today were Terry and Lanita because they're going to be around here long after I'm gone.

And what we have to do, the rest of us, is to construct a system that works for them and that works for parents like the Cherys, who lost a child because of the failures of America and who have spent their lives now trying to make sure it doesn't happen to anybody else. So this is a huge deal.

There was a report—I will just close with this—there was a report that was issued a few weeks ago by the Centers for Disease Control in Atlanta, saying that 75 percent of all the teenagers who lose their lives, who are murdered, in the entire industrial world are murdered in America—75 percent. Now, that hasn't happened in Boston in over a year and a half. If it doesn't happen in Boston, it doesn't have to happen anyplace else. We can turn this around.

America now knows we can bring the crime rate down. Now America has to learn that we can save our children and that we do not have to put up with this and that the only way to solve it is the way you have solved it, but that we have a job in Washington to create the conditions and give you the tools which will make it possible for you to solve it. That's what we're trying to do. But let's not forget what the stakes are.

You know, I've spent a lot of time—we had a big telecommunications trade agreement that we finished last weekend which will create a million new jobs in America over the next 12 years. I want every child in Boston to be alive to have a chance to get one of those jobs.

Let's do first things first. Let's get this done, and let's remember that what we're really trying to do is make what you've done here possible for children in communities all across America.

Thank you very much.

NOTE: The President spoke at 10:19 a.m. in the McCormack Building. In his remarks, he referred to Mayor Thomas Menino of Boston; Sister Jean Gribaudo, the mayor's youth adviser; Gov. William Weld of Massachussetts; Tanya Brooks, Suffolk County Superior Court probation officer; Paul Evans, Boston police commissioner; Robert P. Dunford, Boston area C–11 police district captain; Terry Thompson and Lanita Tolentino, members of the Mayor's Youth Council; and Joseph and Tina Chery, whose son was a victim of gang crossfire in 1993. The release also included remarks by Attorney General Janet Reno.

Remarks at the University of Massachusetts in Boston
February 19, 1997

Thank you. Mr. Mayor; Commissioner Evans; Probation Officer Tanya Brooks; President Bulger; Chancellor Sherry Penney; Governor Weld; Senator Kerry; Congressman Moakley;

Congressman Kennedy—I understand you're also an alumni of this university; Attorney General Harshbarger, the president of the National Association of Attorneys General; thank you all for welcoming me here.

And I'm delighted to be here with two of my great partners in this endeavor, our wonderful Attorney General, Janet Reno, and the Under Secretary of the Treasury for Enforcement, Ray Kelly. Thank you for being here. We're all glad to be here.

I want to thank all the police officers for being here, especially the Voices in Blue for singing the national anthem. They were great. Great job, gentlemen. And I'd like to thank the students at the University of Massachusetts at Boston. I know that 80 percent of the students—I've been told at least that 80 percent of the students here are working virtually full-time while pursuing their degrees. That's a great tribute to you. And if our budget passes, we'll have the direct loan program, the AmeriCorps program, tax cuts for tuition, and a huge increase in Pell grants and work-study. I hope it will help you all.

Oh, there's one more thing before I begin my prepared remarks. This is my first trip to Boston and to Massachusetts in 1997, and if you will forgive me a purely personal remark, I want to thank the people of Massachusetts for giving me the biggest margin of victory of any State in the country. Thank you very much. [*Applause*] Thank you.

Let me begin, if I might, by trying to put today's event into some context. You heard the mayor talking about declining crime generally in Boston. Let me just ask you to go back to 4 or 5 years ago. When I assumed this office, I wanted to do basically two big things. One is, I wanted to kind of get America fixed up; I wanted things to work again. And then I wanted to get all of us together to focus on what we need to do to prepare our people for a new century; to preserve the American dream for everyone who is willing to work for it without regard to their background or where they start out in life; to preserve a sense of community that embraces every American who is willing to be a responsible citizen; and to create a sense that our families, our neighborhoods, our workplaces, our schools, all of our organizations were working again; and to maintain our leadership in a rapidly changing world. But first we had to make sure things would work.

And the first thing we worked through in Washington was an economic program that was designed to change the whole economic direction of the last several years, to get away from spending ourselves into immediate prosperity through constant deficits to a longer-term strategy to bring the deficit down, get interest rates down, invest in our people, and prove we could trade and compete with the rest of the world.

Now, I just got a report this morning on the last inflationary numbers of that 4-year period, which says that the core rate of inflation—that is the basic things people buy—the inflation rate dropped from 3½ percent to 2½ percent in the previous 4 years; and that the combined rates of unemployment and inflation on average through 4 years, together were 8.7 percent. That's the lowest since Lyndon Johnson was the President of the United States, and that's a good sign. That's a good sign.

But what I want to ask you to focus on today is that in some ways the whole question of having safe streets, safe neighborhoods, safe schools, and safe children has to be prior to economic opportunity, because if people are living in constant fear, if their lives are always disoriented, if they are completely unpredictable, then it is very hard to say to them, "You should stay in school. You should learn all you can. You should look forward to a better future. The 21st century will give you more chances to live out your dreams than ever before." And if the answer you get back is, "What do you mean, man, I'm trying to stay alive until lunch time," then it is very difficult to make this country work.

So we have spent a lot of time, as you heard the previous speakers discuss, working on this. I asked the Attorney General to assume her office because she was a prosecutor in a big urban county in America with a world of problems and because she had learned that only by empowering the people who lived there that she worked with could she not only catch criminals but, more importantly, prevent crime and save children for a better future. And we have been working with the attorney generals, with the prosecutors, with community leaders, with others all across the country for 4 years to try to create the conditions that would make it possible for normal life to prevail in our cities and in other places which had been victimized by crime.

When we passed the crime bill in 1994 with the help of all the Members of Congress here on this platform—and I thank them for it—we made a commitment to put 100,000 new police on our streets so we could go back to community policing. Why? Because violent crime had tripled in 30 years, and the police forces had increased by 10 percent—300 percent against 10 percent. What happened? As a result, people felt overwhelmed and more and more police officers had to ride together in cars instead of walking on streets in neighborhoods and working with their neighbors, so that in a bizarre way, we actually reduced the coverage of the police just so they could be safe.

And now this whole concept of neighborhood or community policing, which Boston has done so brilliantly, is sweeping the country. That, plus the Brady bill, plus the ban on the assault weapons, plus the new efforts to steer young people away from crime, plus tougher penalties for serious offenders, all those things now taking hold all across America have given us 5 years of declining crime for the first time in decades. And that is very, very good news.

But we have to now look at step two because until last year's statistics, we had this heartbreaking, heartbreaking evidence that the crime rate in America was going down, but the crime rate among juveniles under 18 was going up. Violence among adults was going down, even young adults; violence among juveniles going up. Drug use among adults, people over 18, going down dramatically; drug use among people under 18 going up.

Last year, we began to see some hope that it might be dropping off, but we haven't even had 2 years in a row. But we know that in Boston there have been big changes. And we know that we just started the largest class of children in our schools in history. There are now about 52 million young Americans in our schools, the largest school-age population ever, even bigger than the biggest baby boom year, now in our schools.

And so we know we've got about 6 years to turn this juvenile crime thing around, or our country is going to be living with chaos. And my successors will not be giving speeches about the wonderful opportunities of the global economy, they'll be trying to keep body and soul together for people on the streets of these cities if we don't do everywhere in America what you have begun to do in Boston and save our children.

So the crime bill in '94, the 100,000 police, the neighborhood policing, the Brady bill, the assault weapons ban, all those things were step one. Step two has got to be a very sharp and disciplined focus on the problems of juvenile violence, juvenile crime, juvenile gangs. Ninety-five percent of our largest cities and 88 percent of our smaller cities report that they are plagued by gang crime. Experts predict the number of people arrested for violent crimes will double by the year 2010 unless we do something about it. Fighting, therefore, juvenile crime has got to become our top law enforcement priority.

When Boston launched Operation Night Light, when police and probation officers together can make nightly visits to the homes of young people on probation to make sure they're not in violation; when you had your Operation Cease-Fire vigorously enforcing graffiti, truancy, noise statutes to reclaim neighborhoods and the conditions of ordinary life; when you launched the Boston gun project to shut down illegal gun dealers who sell to young people, by tracing serial numbers and severely punishing those who break the law—these things will work.

Seventy percent of your young people on probation are now sticking to it. That's a huge percentage if you compare it to other places around the country. Youth murders have dropped 80 percent in 5 years, and as you have heard twice already, you haven't had a single child killed with a gun in a year and a half in this city. How I would pray that could happen in every city in America.

I want to compliment the mayor on his youth council and meeting with young people who are representative of the city every 6 weeks. And I'd like to thank the young woman from the council who appeared today, Lanita, on the program. I'd like to thank the young people who have been on probation who are making something of their lives. Young Terry Thompson was on our program today. I thank him for being a model of that.

What I want to say to you is that we cannot permit this to be only an achievement in Boston, because if it is only an achievement in Boston, it will be harder for Boston to continue to achieve. Sooner or later, what we have to do is to create the notion that it is normal for kids not to get shot, and so nobody claps when you say no kid has been killed.

Do you realize when I was the age of the young people who were on our program today—one is 19, I think the other is 17—if I had stood up as a young person there, wanting to be noticed, wanting to give a nice speech, wanting to give accounting of myself, and I had said, "We haven't had a young person killed in our town for the last year and a half," do you know what everybody would have said? "So what? What's that fool talking about?" [*Laughter*] Today everybody claps. We have to keep working until the answer is, "So what?" That ought to be the answer, shouldn't it? Isn't that what you want? [*Applause*]

The truth is that all across our country children are still killing children for shoes, for jackets, for turf. And we can stop it. The truth is that Boston and just a few other cities have removed any fig leaf of excuse that we can't do anything about it. You have now proved that it can be stopped, and therefore there is no excuse for not stopping it. And the United States of America, through the Congress, this year, should pass a law to give every community the tools that you have used to make your city safe again, so that we can do it everywhere in America.

I have four parts to the legislation that I am presenting Congress today. First, we have to break the backs of the gangs and punish juveniles who commit violent crimes with real severity. We have to finish putting 100,000 police on the street. And we have to make sure communities have the resources to prosecute people who violate the law. This bill will help communities to hire new prosecutors to directly deal with violent juveniles; to launch antigang units; to pursue, prosecute, and punish members who really hurt people. It will give judges more power to crack down on gang members who intimidate witnesses, and it will give Federal prosecutors for the first time the authority in appropriate circumstances to prosecute serious violent juveniles as adults.

The second thing we have to do is to keep drugs and guns away from our children. The Brady bill—listen to this—has already blocked more than 60,000 felons, fugitives, and stalkers from buying a handgun. That's an old small number. We'll have some new ones in the next few days. But it doesn't permit someone who commits a violent crime as a juvenile from buying a handgun once he or she turns 18. I think we should close that loophole and extend the

Brady bill so that anyone who commits a violent crime should not be given the right to buy a handgun.

Our plan would also require child safety locks on handguns to prevent unauthorized use and tragic accident. We ought to do that. We have begun an effort actually modeled on the Boston gun project in 17 other cities to crack down on those who illegally sell guns to young people.

And I said this in the former meeting—I want to say it again because I think most Americans don't know it. The Treasury Department that license people who sell guns—they have to have a Federal license—has cracked down on that whole process in the last 3 years, and there are now fewer than half the licensed Federal gun dealers there were just 3 years ago. We are trying to get control of this process.

Our plan has the largest antidrug effort ever to stop drugs at their source, punish those who push them, and most importantly, to keep working to steer young people away from them. General McCaffrey, our Nation's drug czar, has recommended that I had asked for funding to launch a massive national advertising campaign to deal with something that I had thought—wrongly—was basic, and that is how dangerous drugs are. It is clear that the main reason that drug use among teenagers is going up, while it is going down among people between the ages of 18 and 35, is that too many teenagers no longer believe that drugs are not only wrong and illegal but they can kill them. That—it is clear.

And it is clear that a lot of young adults who used to be a big part of the drug problem now do understand that they can die from this as well as be punished for it. And somehow we have got to bring the attitudes of the teenagers in line with the attitudes of the young adults so that we can deal with that. And we'll be working with that.

I think every State should now begin to require drug tests of people for essential services like driver's licenses. That would send a strong message out and be unpopular with a lot of young people who otherwise think their President is a pretty good fellow. [*Laughter*] But I think it's the right thing to do.

The third thing we have to do is to reform the juvenile justice system so that it can handle today's juvenile offenders. Most systems were designed to deal with truants and other minor problems, not violent problems. And we need more people like this fine probation officer that introduced me today and more of those folks working with the police.

The story you have created here is the story we want to recreate in every community in the country. I want to hear more stories. I want it to be normal when I go some place and say, we go together, and we got into people's homes, and we visit with them at night, and they're glad to see us, and they understand that we're all on the same side and we're trying to save these kids' lives and give them a future. That's the story we want to hear everywhere.

We have to have more special court proceedings for young people, with greater flexibility to handle juveniles and tougher penalties to punish those who are really gone and then more flexibility and other opportunities to save those that ought to be saved. The real answer to this has got to be prevention. We have got to prevent these things from happening in the first place. That's what all the law enforcement people know.

Finally, we have to help our young people to stay on the right track. Our strategy will help to fund 1,000 new after-school initiatives in communities across the country to help keep schools open after school, on the weekends, in the summer. Listen to this: More than 50 percent of the juvenile crime in America occurs in the 3 hours after school is closed and before the parents are home. That's a stunning statistic. You take 3 or 4 hours out of the day, and you've cut the problem in half. Now, we don't want our young people left alone on street corners when they can be in school or at home. And we have to have ways that help our educators, our parents, our religious and community leaders to try to save these kids.

This anti-gang and youth violence strategy is based on what we know works. It is really a national framework to give other communities the chance to get the resources to do what you're trying to do in Boston. That is all it is. Tough when you should be tough; smart when you should be smart; compassionate when you should be compassionate; using everybody, building partnerships, letting everybody play a role; requiring communities to take responsibility for their own streets and their own kids and then giving you the outside support you need—that is all this bill does.

It is the critical next step in our fight to have a safe America and to give our children a safe childhood. And I ask you here in Massachusetts to send a clear message. We know if this can be done in Boston, it can be done in every community, in every neighborhood of every size in the United States, and we ask the United States Congress to do what you've done here in Massachusetts: cross all party lines, throw politics away, throw the speeches in the trashcan, join hands. Let's do what works and make America the safe place it has to be.

Let me just make one other point to you. The citizens of this country have got to do their part—every citizen. And one of the things that I want to announce today that I'm very proud of is—that I think will help make all of you be better citizens and to support community policing, which is clearly the single most decisive element in bringing the crime rate, the neighborhood policing system.

Not very long ago I was made aware of a problem that—like a lot of problems ordinary people have that Presidents don't know about because our lives are so isolated—I learned that a lot of the 911 numbers were breaking down because 911 was being clogged up not only by genuine emergencies but by other legitimate calls that weren't really emergencies. And so I asked the Federal Communications Commission to set up a national community policing number for non-emergencies so that 911 calls would always go through when there was a matter of life and death, but all the other calls could be handled as well. This morning, the FCC announced that they are designating and setting aside the numbers 311 as a national non-emergency community policing number. And I believe it will help you.

So to all of you out here who are just citizens, I say: Use both numbers, and talk to your neighbors about using them in the right way. Be a part of a neighborhood watch. Support these community police officers, these probation officers, and do what you can to play your part. We'll do our part. You have to do your part.

If this country is going to be the country it ought to be in the 21st century, we can't have any more reports like the one that came out of the Center for Disease Control a few days ago saying that 75 percent of all the kids murdered in the industrial world are killed in the United States. What we've got to do is to create the record of the last year and a half in Boston for the United States. If you give our kids back their lives and their future, they will make America the world's greatest country in the 21st century.

Thank you very much.

NOTE: The President spoke at 12:22 p.m. at the Clark Athletic Center. In his remarks, he referred to Mayor Thomas Menino of Boston; Paul Evans, Boston police commissioner; William Bulger, president, and Sherry H. Penney, chancellor, University of Massachusetts; Gov. William Weld and Attorney General L. Scott Harshbarger of Massachusetts; and Lanita Tolentino and Terry Thompson, members of the Mayor's Youth Council. A portion of these remarks could not be verified because the tape was incomplete.

Statement on the Death of Deng Xiaoping
February 19, 1997

I was saddened today to learn of the death of Deng Xiaoping, China's senior statesman. Over the past two decades, Mr. Deng was an extraordinary figure on the world stage and the driving force behind China's decision to normalize relations with the United States. His historic visit to our country in 1979 laid the foundation for the rapid expansion of relations and cooperation between China and the United States.

Mr. Deng's long life spanned a century of turmoil, tribulation, and remarkable change in China. He spurred China's historic economic reform program, which greatly improved living standards in China and modernized much of the nation.

China today plays an important role in world affairs in no small part because of Mr. Deng's decision to open his country to the outside world. The continued emergence of China as a great power that is stable politically and open economically, that respects human rights and the rule of law, and that becomes a full partner in building a secure international order, is profoundly in America's interest and in the world's interest.

I want to convey my personal condolences to China's President Jiang Zemin, to Mr. Deng's widow, Zhuo Lin, and to the Chinese people.

Remarks on Medicaid Patient Protection and an Exchange With Reporters
February 20, 1997

The President. Thank you. I was just sitting here thinking that, in the spirit of full disclosure, the Vice President and Secretary Shalala may have a particular vested interest in health care issues—that they both just got back from South Africa, and when they got back he got on a plane and went to Los Angeles to speak to the AFL–CIO convention; he got back at 4 o'clock this morning. And she got on a plane and went to New York with me to a welfare reform event. And I don't see how either one of them are still standing up. [*Laughter*] But they probably have a strong interest in what happened here today.

Let me thank, if I might, first of all, all the Members of Congress who are here from both parties for their leadership on this issue; and Bruce Vladeck and Bruce Fried for what they have done; and the representatives of the groups over here to my right for being here and for supporting our endeavors.

Today I'm pleased to announce that we're taking steps to see that Medicaid beneficiaries continue to get access to the fullest quality health care. In recent years, the medical community and the insurance industry have joined to reform and improve American health care, working with us, and much of this progress has come through managed care, which emphasizes prevention, provides better care, and controls costs at the same time, when the plans are the best and the right kind of managed care plans.

On the whole, the growth of managed care has been a good thing for our country. But we also know—we've seen enough to know that we have to make absolutely sure that this rapid transformation does not lead to a decline in the quality of health care.

That's why I've been concerned about these so-called gag rules that some HMO's and other health care plans have, rules that restrict the ability of health care professionals to administer proper medical care, that prevent doctors and nurses from telling patients about alternate and sometimes more expensive care that are not covered by the plans that they're in. This is unacceptable. Patients in HMO's and other health plans should know that their doctors will give them the very best information, the very most complete information, the widest possible range of information when it comes to their treatment. And there shouldn't be a shadow of doubt about this.

In December, as Secretary Shalala just said, we took action to give Medicare beneficiaries the right to know about their treatment options. Today we take the next step, acting to protect 13 million Medicaid beneficiaries, children, the disabled, elderly Americans. I'm directing Secretary Shalala to inform all State Medicaid directors that it's illegal for health care plans to prohibit doctors from discussing any treatment options with their patients. Families facing illness simply should not have to worry that the doctor they trust does not have the freedom to tell them what they need to know. Patients have the fundamental right to know they are getting the best medical treatment, not simply the cheapest.

And this must be only the beginning. We can act today to protect Medicare and Medicaid beneficiaries because they are Federal programs and because Government is the largest purchaser of managed care in our Nation. But to protect 130 million Americans enrolled in managed care throughout the private sector, the Congress must act.

That's why I'm so pleased that Members of Congress from both parties, led by those who are here with us today in the House, have come together with the support of doctors, nurses, health care professionals, and consumers to craft legislation that will ban all gag rules for all Americans in all HMO's and other health care plans. I urge the Congress to send me this legis-lation, and when they do, I will promptly sign it into law.

The bipartisan legislation shows how we can work together as we continue, step by step, to give more families access to quality, affordable health care. I hope we can build on this record of accomplishment and that Congress will join me to pass a balanced budget that extends health care coverage to children; helps people who temporarily lose their jobs to keep their health insurance; covers, through Medicare, assistance for families with Alzheimer's victims and provides for annual mammograms; and that reforms Medicaid for the next decade. Today we built a strong foundation for the health of American families, and we can now make sure that it lasts for a long time.

Let me close again by thanking these Members of Congress who are here and saying that while we have done the right thing for Medicare and Medicaid, we need their legislation to do the right thing for the majority of our fellow citizens who are now covered by private managed care plans.

Q. Where lies the fault; is it the insurance industry?

The President. Well, I think—what I think is we're going to have a continuing tension between the need for controlling costs and competition and managing health care, and the need to make sure that you don't shortcut the quality of care, which has been the hallmark of our medical care in America for those who had access to it.

And what we are trying to do, and I think what these Members of Congress are trying to do, is to strike the right balance, to permit managed care to go forward and even to flourish but to try to set the conditions in which it will operate so that we guarantee that quality of care is not sacrificed.

Mexico

Q. Mr. President, how serious of a blow is it that Mexico's drug czar has been arrested, given the fact that so much of the illegal drugs coming into the United States comes through or originates in Mexico?

The President. Well, I would—I think that the American people should have two reactions: first of all, that this is a very serious revelation and deeply troubling; secondly, the fact—we should be encouraged by President Zedillo's determination because the Government has taken this action, the President has personally taken this action, and they've made it public. And they're obviously saying to the world and to the people of Mexico, we will not tolerate corruption if we can find it and root it out, even if it's at the highest level.

So I'm troubled by it, but I'm also encouraged by the strong action President Zedillo has taken. And you may be sure that this will continue to be at the top of our agenda, and when we meet in the not-too-distant future, we will talk more about it. But we've worked very hard with Mexico. And you know, the more success we had in South America in shutting down routes, particularly airplane routes and, to some extent, overland—routes over water, the more these operations have moved into Mexico, which is a big country with a lot of opportunities, to find places that are sparsely populated to set up these transit operations and, to some extent, processing operations. So we have to have Mexico's cooperation.

And this is a serious thing. I regret it, but, on the other hand, I'm very encouraged that President Zedillo has moved promptly and aggressively to deal with the situation.

Q. Have you made a decision on certification?

The President. Excuse me?

Q. Have you made a decision on certification?

The President. I have not, and I have not made—I don't believe I've been given a recommendation yet by the Secretary of State on it.

Q. Mike McCurry said today, following on that last question, that this incident would be a factor in the decision whether or not to certify. Why will it be a factor, and how so?

The President. Well, first of all, let me reiterate, there is a process for doing this that has not been completed, and I have to get the recommendation first. But as I say, as a factor in the certification decision, I would imagine it is a mixed factor. On the one hand, it's troubling because we knew and it's been widely reported that local police organizations at various places in Mexico are highly vulnerable to all the money that was being thrown at them from the drug lords. And the military had been thought to be an antidote to that, a counterweight. So it's troubling.

But on the other hand, I'll say again that they have not fooled around with this. When the President discovered it, he's taken strong action. It's been very public. It's been non-apol-

ogetic. And so I'm encouraged by that. So I would think that this would cut both ways on the certification question.

China and Cabinet Nominees

Q. Mr. President, do you see any change in policy with China now that Deng is dead?

The President. We expect basic continuity here. The Chinese, perhaps mindful of some of the problems they've had in their long history in transitions—Deng Xiaoping set in motion a process which has been well underway for more than 2 years now. And I think that that is something that we can all appreciate, that there has been a basic continuity there.

So I think that our policy is the right policy. We will continue to engage strongly with China. I look forward to all the meetings which are going to occur, including Secretary Albright's trip and then the Vice President's trip later and then the exchange of visits by the two Presidents. The policy we are following of engaging with China, to work where we agree and to honestly air our disagreements and work through them, is the right policy for the people of the United States and, indeed, for the world in the 21st century. If you imagine what the world will look like 30 years from now, 40 years from now, we can do nothing other than what we are doing. It is the right thing to do.

Let me just make one other comment here, because this came up at the last press briefing I had, about the status of our nominations for the Cabinet in the Senate. I have been gratified by the treatment that the Cabinet members who have been confirmed have received by both parties and the prompt dealing with their nominations. I said something about Mr. Lake when I last was with the press.

The only other comment I want to make today is there has still not been a hearing scheduled for Alexis Herman. I think that is a big mistake. She enjoys wide support among labor—the labor unions endorsed her yesterday strongly—and she has wide support among business. I don't know that there's ever been a person nominated for Secretary of Labor that had as much broad support in the business and the labor communities. She's clearly well-qualified. If anybody wants to vote against her for whatever reason, they're plainly free to do that, but she deserves a hearing, and if she gets a hearing, she's going to be confirmed. And I think Senator Jeffords is a good man and a fair man, and

I believe he will give her a hearing. But it's imperative that it be done. It's now midway through February, and I think it's time to get on with this.

Thank you.

NOTE: The President spoke at 11:05 a.m. in the Oval Office at the White House. In his remarks, he referred to Bruce Vladeck, Administrator, Health Care Financing Administration; Bruce Fried, Director, HCFA Office of Managed Care; Gen. Jesus Gutierrez Rebollo, Director of Mexico's National Institute to Combat Drugs, dismissed for allegedly protecting a Mexican drug trafficker; President Ernesto Zedillo of Mexico; Deng Xiaoping, former President of China; and Anthony Lake, nominee for Director of Central Intelligence.

Remarks Announcing the District of Columbia College Reading Tutor Initiative
February 21, 1997

Thank you very much. Thank you, General Becton, for the introduction. Thank you, Principal Andrea Robinson, for making the First Lady and me feel so very welcome here in Garrison today. Delegate Norton, Mr. Mayor, all the college presidents who are here, some out in the audience, but especially those here behind me who are part of our announcement today: Dr. Ladner of American University, Brother Patrick Ellis of Catholic, Dr. I. King Jordan of Gallaudet, Father Leo O'Donovan of Georgetown, Stephen Trachtenberg of George Washington, Pat McGuire of Trinity, Patrick Swygert of Howard.

To the Council members who are here today, Hilda Mason and Harry Thomas, Judge Hamilton. To the School Board members who are here and others who are here who are part of our endeavor. I would like to especially acknowledge the Librarian of Congress, Dr. Jim Billington; the Secretary of Education, Secretary Dick Riley; Carol Rasco, the National Director of our America Reads program; Frank Raines, the Director of the Office of Management and Budget; and Harris Wofford, who heads our national service program.

I'd also like to thank Dr. Robert Corrigan from San Francisco State University, who is here. He and Father O'Donovan are two of the 21 steering committee members for our national effort to get volunteers in colleges all over America involved in helping our children to read. So I'm delighted to be here with this distinguished assemblage.

Two weeks ago in my State of the Union Address I spoke of the importance of renewing our great Capital City to make it the finest place to learn, to work, to live, to make it once again the proud face America shows to the world. This is a city of truly remarkable strengths. I saw that when I lived here as a student so very many years ago now. I see it now, having come back as President. We see the majesty of the monuments, the beauty of the parks, the commitment of community and business leaders. But most importantly, we see it in the eyes of our children.

I was just in Stephanie Abney's first grade class, where Hillary and I read "The Tortoise and the Hare" to the students, and they could have been reading it back to us. And I thought about those wonderful children and all the others who are here. They deserve the best future we can give them, and we can give them a better future. And that is what this is all about.

As the First Lady said, this endeavor will require us to be more like the tortoise than the hare. We will have to move slowly but deliberately, and we will not be able to sit down and rest. But if we do that, like the tortoise, we will win the race. This is our city. All of us who live here, all of us who work here, all of us who want America's Capital to be a world capital, second to none; all of us have an obligation to work with the mayor, with General Becton, with the control board, with Delegate Norton, with all the leaders of the city to help to renew and to revitalize Washington, DC. I pledge to you today that we, my personal family and my official family, will be with you as you make those efforts, every step of the way.

I'd like to say a special word of appreciation to three people who have been particularly important to me in this endeavor: First, to the First Lady, who has been telling me for a long time that we had to do more, we owed it to Washington to do more, and that we could do more. Second, to Frank Raines, the Director of the Office of Management and Budget, who came up with the proposal we have made to relieve the District of Columbia of some of its unfair and unnecessary financial burdens and reallocate responsibility among the State and Federal Government. And third—I didn't know if she was here with us today, but I finally spotted her in the audience—to Carol Thompson-Cole, thank you very much for all that you have done to help us to get this effort off the ground.

So we've made this proposal to the Congress to relieve the District government of some of its financial burdens. As I have said many times, one of the major problems of the District of Columbia is that it has too often been a "not quite" place. It's not quite a State, but it's not quite a city. So it has been loaded up with responsibilities that normally are only borne by States. I think that is wrong, and I think we should do better about that.

To strengthen the city's economic base, we also must provide some financial incentives for people to move businesses and to move themselves back into the city. We must expand the empowerment approach that has worked so well across the country. In Detroit, one of our empowerment zone cities, the unemployment rate was cut in half in 4 years—in half—and investment was flooding back, business was coming back, people were coming back to live in the city. We can do this in every city in America, and we must.

To help home rule succeed, we have to change the relationship between the District and our Nation's Government. Sometimes the District gets the worst of all worlds. It's not quite independent, but the dependencies it has carry burdens that cannot be borne by any community. So we need to work that out.

But let's not kid ourselves, there are some things that have to be done here that must be done by the people of the District of Columbia. And the two that are most important in my view are making the schools work for these children and making the streets safe for them to walk and live on.

What I want to say to you today is that I know you can do this. I have been not only here at Garrison, but I have been in the Kramer Junior High School in Anacostia, which has been adopted by my Secret Service detail—it's one of the presents they gave me for a birthday once—best present I could ever be given by my Secret Service detail. And they go to Kramer—they're in there all the time—and I get regular reports about the progress they're making. I have been to Thomas Jefferson Junior High School, which is near the Capitol, probably 5 times in the last 10 years. I've been to Eastern High School and to a number of other schools in the District. You can do this. This school system can be great for all of its children, and what we want to do is to help.

I'd also like to say that you can do the other things you have to do, too. Public safety can succeed here. I started the week in Boston, where no child has been murdered in a year and a half, not a single child in a year and a half, not one. And no manna dropped from Heaven, no outside force lifted them up. They did some things together in a disciplined, organized, determined way that changed the future of children. And now it can be done everywhere. So I am hopeful.

But let's begin with education. All of you know that the world we are moving toward will put a higher premium on education than ever before. It has always been important. A certain amount of it has always been essential for people to get along in life. It is now more critical than ever before, not only for the individual futures of every one of these little kids here but for how the rest of us do as well. For the skeptics who are about my age, I could only say that we ought to be working hard to give these children a good education so they will support us in our old age—*[laughter]*—in a style that we'll be comfortable with.

We can only be a strong, united community if we can educate all our people. If you look around—just look at these children today. America is building the most genuinely diverse democracy in all of human history. No one has ever tried to do this before, and we did it almost without thinking, just by being a nation of successive waves of immigrants. We became more and more and more diverse. And by continuing to advance the cause of civil rights and civil liberties, we've made different people more and more and more at home in our country. And then all of a sudden we wake up on the edge of the 21st century with 4 school districts in our country where children's native tongues number more than 100—in 4 different school districts.

This is a great challenge because all children, even of the same race and the same religious background, as every teacher could tell you, are different. All children are different anyway. And when you think of this diversity we have to manage, it's even a greater challenge. But it's also the greatest opportunity that has ever been served up to any people in human history. And if we seize that opportunity, if we prove that all of our children can learn and they can all be given opportunities and they can all make a contribution, we will be richly rewarded.

We know that there are some remarkable success stories in the District of Columbia, and we know the District's schools have to do better. That's why I am so grateful that, after a lifetime of service to his nation, General Becton has taken on yet another important challenge and a true act of patriotism. We are committed to supporting him.

We know that we have to mobilize people from all walks of life, and I was glad to hear all the different volunteer groups recognized, particularly the seniors and the VISTA volunteers and, of course, a great personal pride of mine, the AmeriCorps volunteers. And I thank some of them who are here today, and I thank them for being here.

We need to start with simple, clear goals that we know are important, number one, and, number two, that we can determine whether we have met. One of the real problems that I find in all human endeavors is that sometimes we don't clarify our goals and make sure we're going after the important ones. And then sometimes, even if we've got a good goal, we set it up so we never can tell whether we've met it or not.

One of our goals has to be to make sure every 8-year-old in this country can read a book on his or her own, and every 8-year-old in this school and every 8-year-old in this city can do the same in the next 4 years. That is a very important thing, and we can find out whether that is being done.

The Secretary of Education and I intend to make it possible for States and the District, by the year 1999, to give an examination to every fourth grader in reading and every eighth grader in math to see whether they know what they're supposed to know, based on national basic standards. And so we will know whether every 8-year-old can read in 1999. And we are being given a few years to get the job done. We also know that these children can do the job if they're given the support, the discipline, the love that they need.

But today, in America as a whole, 40 percent—4 of every 10—8-year-olds cannot read as well as they should read. Now, part of that is because so many of them's first language is not English. But a lot of it is because—indeed, the lion's share of it is because they simply are not learning as they should. Many times the teachers have more than they can do. Many times the teachers don't have the support they need for all the different challenges that the children bring into the classroom in their early lives. Many times, as General Becton indicated, we need more help from the parents at home. Many times the parents themselves need help to learn to read well enough to read to their children.

So we know that this is a complicated problem. That does not, however, relieve us of the burden of solving it. In fact, what it does is impose upon more of us the responsibility to help to solve it. I'm glad to see my friend Bill Milliken here, and I was glad to hear General Becton recognize the Cities and Communities in Schools program because they have for years, in small rural cities in my home State and in big urban places like Washington, tried to remind the community that our children are everyone's responsibility and there must be a community approach to dealing with this.

And that's what we're here to talk about today with regard to a simple but profoundly important goal, that every 8-year-old must be able to read independently. We intend to use thousands of AmeriCorps volunteers to mobilize and train a citizen army of one million reading tutors. We want at least 100,000 college students to help, to build our army of reading tutors on college campuses all across America. That's what the America Reads program Secretary Riley and Carol Rasco are spearheading is all about.

Last fall, I worked with the Congress to create over 200,000 new work-study jobs on America's college campuses, the program that enables young people to work their way through college. My present budget calls for another 100,000 work-study positions to be made available to our college campuses. I want a portion of those new positions to be devoted to community service—to letting people work not just on the campus but, more importantly, in the community and especially teaching our children to read.

College presidents nationwide have answered the call. Many of them are here today, the local college presidents behind me, others in the audience. They have pledged thousands of their work-study students and thousands who do not receive work-study assistance to serve for one year as reading tutors.

The District of Columbia is rising to meet that challenge. Today, thanks to the support of General Becton and the willing leadership of the university presidents behind me, over the next 5 years, thousands of college students, AmeriCorps participants, volunteers, parents, and teachers will work together to help DC's children learn to read so that they can meet that national goal.

The presidents of seven DC area colleges and universities—American, Catholic, Gallaudet, Georgetown, George Washington, Howard, and Trinity—have pledged nearly 700 students next year and thousands of students over the next 5 years to serve as reading tutors in DC's public schools. And we should all thank them for it. And we should note, too, that there are several hundred students from these seven schools who are already working in our city as tutors and as other public servants.

These new tutors, the vast majority of whom will be work-study students, will begin in the 18 District schools General Becton has identified as most in need of this kind of partnership, including Garrison. But we hope the effort will expand to many more of DC's schools. In each of the 18 schools we will place two AmeriCorps participants who will work full time to coordinate the effort and recruit more volunteers.

I might say that one of the things I have learned in visiting schools all across America, in all different kinds of settings, is that it requires an organized effort by the schools to effectively use the volunteers, and sometimes volunteers aren't in the schools simply because the school either hasn't taken the time or doesn't have the resources to organize bringing them in and using them effectively. So that's one of the things that we hope we can accomplish with our AmeriCorps volunteers.

Finally, with the help of AmeriCorps and DC businesses, General Becton will open a family resource center in each school so that parents have the support and assistance they need to read to their own children, so that they can be the first and best teachers for our students.

After Hillary and I read the book to the 6-year-olds today—out of the mouths of babes—the children came up to see us. The first question they asked was, "Now, did you read to your daughter when she was a little girl?" [*Laughter*] "Every night," I said. And the second question was, "Now, did your parents read to you when you were a little boy?" The first two questions they asked. So we do have to make it possible for these parents to do their jobs.

That's another thing I've noticed over the years: Almost every parent, no matter how young they might be, no matter how uneducated they might be, desperately wants to do a good job. And we have to give them the resources to do it and the strength and self-confidence to do it.

Now, as I said, we're plotting out a race here for a tortoise, not a hare. This is not going to be done overnight. Children are not built in a day. But it is a very important start. To truly renew our Capital City, we clearly have to start with our children. With the creation of this new DC Reads partnership, thousands of college students and volunteers will help our public school children learn to read. In so doing, they'll be taking more responsibility for their city that has given them an opportunity to get an education. They'll be creating more opportunity for the children who live here. They'll be building a stronger and a better-prepared community for the 21st century. I believe they will inspire this entire community to pitch in and work together to lift up the children of the District of Columbia and make this Capital worthy of its great heritage and the bright future of our Nation.

We want to do more to improve education throughout the District. We'll offer more support to the Department of Education, to the District schools, sharing our expertise in a broad range of areas. Our Cabinet agencies will build on the many partnerships they've established over the past years. We'll continue to adopt schools, to donate computers and educational software and supplies, to become engaged ourselves as tutors and volunteers throughout the public schools. AmeriCorps will build on the work that it has done, not just in tutoring but also in repairing crumbling schools and correcting fire code violations so schools can open on time and recruiting even more volunteers.

But the most important work will be done by parents and teachers, by students and volunteers, by government and business working together. The spirit of common cause is how we must meet this challenge and, indeed, all the challenges of the District of Columbia in education, in building safe streets, in economic development, in restoring the health of the city's finances, and the proper balance of responsibilities between the city and the National Government. We are committed to this task.

Hillary and I are honored to be here with you today, and we thank every one of you for what you're doing to give our children the future they deserve.

Thank you, and God bless you.

NOTE: The President spoke at 11:25 a.m. in the auditorium at Garrison Elementary School. In his remarks, he referred to Gen. Julius Becton, USA (ret.), superintendent, District of Columbia public schools; Andrea Robinson, principal, Garrison Elementary School; Delegate Eleanor Holmes Norton and Mayor Marion Barry, Jr., of the District of Columbia; Benjamin Ladner, president, American University; Hilda Mason and Harry L. Thomas, Sr., members of the District of Columbia City Council; Eugene N. Hamilton, Chief Judge of the Superior Court of the District of Columbia; Robert A. Corrigan, president, San Francisco State University; Carol Thompson-Cole, adviser to the President for the District of Columbia; and William E. Milliken, president, Communities In Schools, Inc.

The President's Radio Address
February 22, 1997

Good morning. Today I want to talk with you about our economy, what we can do to keep it growing, offering opportunities to all Americans who work for them.

When I took office 4 years ago, my most important job was to renew our economy. We put in place an economic plan that cut the deficit even as we increased investments in our people and expanded exports to record levels. We cut the deficit by 63 percent, from $290 billion a year in 1992 to $107 billion last year. Proportionally, it is now the smallest of any major economy. This has created the conditions for American businesses and workers to thrive, and they have.

Over the last several weeks, we've received the full data on our country's economic progress for the last 4 years. The economy created 11½ million new jobs for the first time ever in a single term. That includes a million construction jobs and millions of other good paying jobs. Entrepreneurs have started a record number of new businesses, hundreds of thousands of them owned by women and minorities. We've had the largest increase in homeownership ever, a big drop in the poverty rate, and a big increase in family income. And just this week, we learned that the combined rate of unemployment and inflation over the last 4 years is the lowest for a Presidential term since the 1960's.

Now we must continue our progress. We cut the deficit by two-thirds; it's time to finish the job. We must balance the budget to keep interest rates down and investment up and jobs coming in. But we must do it the right way. Today our economy is growing steady and strong. If we want to keep it growing, producing jobs and opportunity for our people as we enter a new century, then we simply must finish the job of balancing the budget, and we must do it this year. That is the only way to keep interest rates low, to keep confidence high, to give businesses the ability to innovate for tomorrow. We must pass a balanced budget plan this year or face the consequences in years to come.

This month I submitted my plan to balance the budget by 2002. Our plan makes the hard decisions necessary to lock in the savings achieved and to ensure that the budget remains in balance in the future. It saves $350 billion over the next 5 years, enough not only to balance the budget but also to cut taxes. It makes tough and specific cuts in spending and ensures that those cuts will be carried out by imposing strict limits on the amounts Congress can spend each year. It ends hundreds of wasteful Government programs and projects, eliminates $34 billion in corporate subsidies businesses don't need, and makes reforms in entitlement programs so they'll cost less in the future, extending the life of the Medicare Trust Fund for a decade while preserving quality health care for elderly Americans.

Even as the plan balances the budget, it also maintains the balance of our values. To prepare our people for the 21st century, I have challenged our Nation to build the world's best educational system. My plan increases investment in education and training to $51 billion in 1998, a 20 percent increase. It provides tax cuts to help families pay for college, increases Pell grant scholarships for deserving students, advances the America Reads initiative to help every 8-year-old read on his or her own, and advances our goal of connecting every single classroom and library to the Internet by the year 2000. It invests in our people in other ways as well, giving them tax cuts to help them raise their children or buy a home, extending health care coverage to 5 million more children, protecting the environment.

That is the right way to balance the budget. And balancing the budget only requires Congress' vote and my signature; it does not require us to rewrite our Constitution. We must balance the budget, but a balanced budget amendment could cause more harm than good. It would prevent us from responding to foreign challenges abroad or economic trouble at home, if to do so resulted in even a minor budget deficit. And because it would write a specific economic policy into our Constitution, it could force the Secretary of the Treasury to cut Social Security, or drive the budget into courts of law when a deficit occurred when Congress was not working on the budget. In a court of law, judges could be forced to halt Social Security checks or to raise taxes just to meet the demands of the constitutional amendment.

These are results no one wants to see happen, but a balanced budget amendment could surely produce them. Instead, we should simply act this year and act together, for Democrats and Republicans have an historic opportunity to reach across party lines to enact the first balanced budget in a generation. Soon we will begin discussions with bipartisan leaders in Congress to craft a final plan. By coming to an agreement this year, we can take a giant step to prepare our country for the 21st century and give our children the future they deserve.

Thanks for listening.

NOTE: The address was recorded at 5:17 p.m. on February 21 in the Roosevelt Room at the White House for broadcast at 10:06 a.m. on February 22.

Statement on the Death of Albert Shanker
February 22, 1997

Hillary and I were deeply saddened today to learn of the passing of Albert Shanker. Al spent his life in pursuit of one of the noblest of causes, the improvement of our public schools. Since 1964, he led educational organizations, first as the president of the United Federation of Teachers in New York and for 22 years as the president of the American Federation of Teachers. He challenged the country's teachers and schools to provide our children with the very best education possible and made a crusade out of the need for educational standards. He believed, as I do, that children should not go through school without learning the basics of reading, writing, and arithmetic. Our thoughts and prayers are with his wife, Eadie, and his family tonight.

Remarks to the National Association for Equal Opportunity in Higher Education
February 24, 1997

Thank you very much. Good morning. Welcome to the White House. Dr. Ponder, Dr. Wilson, Dr. Shaw. Where's Bill Gray? Is he here? You're hiding your light under a bushel back there. [*Laughter*] I wanted to say again to all of you how grateful I am to Bill Gray for the historic role that he assumed in restoring democracy to Haiti. We've got another year behind us now, Bill, and we're still going. Thank you. Dr. Payne and Dr. Hackley, Mr. Secretary. I'd also like to thank Catherine LeBlanc for her work on the White House Initiative on Historically Black Colleges and Universities.

Welcome to the White House. I'm especially glad you could join us during Black History Month as we pay tribute to the contributions of African-Americans to American life. None of those has been more important than our Nation's historically black colleges and universities. When the doors of college were closed to all but white students and black people's aspirations were scorned, historically black colleges and universities gave young African-Americans the high quality education they deserved, the pride they needed to rise above cruelty and bigotry, as the graduates and teachers of HBCU's haven't just taken care of themselves, they fought for freedom and equal opportunity for all other Americans as well. This has been important throughout our history, and in the future it will be more important than ever before, because education will be more important than ever before. To prepare our people for the new century, every young American must have the world's best education.

You know better than anyone how much a difference an education can make. To name just a few of the young Americans who were educated at HBCU's, you'd have to look at Justice Marshall, Congresswoman Barbara Jordan, Reverend Jesse Jackson, NAACP President Kweisi Mfume, Nobel Prize winner Toni Morrison, and of course Dr. King. Eighty-five percent of our Nation's black physicians, 80 percent of our African-American Federal judges, 75 percent of our black Ph.D.'s, 50 percent of our black business executives and elected officials all were educated at HBCU's.

Historically black colleges and universities have served with distinction, of course, in terms of their contributions to our administration: our former Secretary of Energy, Hazel O'Leary; former Surgeon General, Dr. Joycelyn Elders; the Director of Presidential Personnel, Bob Nash; and, of course, as the Vice President said, Alexis Herman, who is here with us today and who did a superb job for us as Director of Public Liaison and, with your help, will be a great Secretary of Labor, and I want your help. [*Applause*] Thank you.

Over the last 4 years, we have put in place a comprehensive college opportunity strategy to make college available to every American citizen. I directed the Department of Education and the White House initiative on historical colleges to work to increase funding to HBCU's. We've made student loans less expensive and much easier to obtain under the direct student loan program. AmeriCorps, our national service program, has given tens of thousands of young people the chance to earn college tuition while serving in their communities. We have created already in the last budget 200,000 more work-study positions to help students work their way through college, and in the new budget there is another 100,000, which will mean we will go from 700,000 to one million work-study slots in only 4 years.

We know that financial aid is critically important. But some of your colleges, as many as 90 percent of the students receive financial aid. Last year we increased the Pell grant program by 20 percent, taking the maximum grant up to $2,700 from about, wherever it was, $2,460. That was the biggest increase in 20 years.

This year's budget is bigger still. It increases Pell grants by another 25 percent, the largest increase again in well over 20 years, and increases the maximum Pell grant award to $3,000 per year. It expands the program to include older students who are starting college late or returning to school. It raises the maximum family income level to include hundreds of thousands of families who did not qualify for Pell grants before. In total, these changes will help almost 350,000 more families send a family member to college. The balanced budget also includes a $10,000 tax deduction to help families pay for college and a $1,500 HOPE scholarship tax credit, which is enough to pay for the tuition at the typical community college in America for 2 years.

This college opportunity agenda will open the doors of college wider than ever before. Now we need to work to make sure that the Congress, without regard to party, will enact these changes into law.

Before I answer questions now, I'd like to ask for your help with one more thing. We all know that literacy is the basic tool of learning. But 40 percent of our children cannot read independently by the time they're 8 years old. We can and must do better. My budget includes more than $2 billion to help us with the literacy challenge, but that is not enough.

I launched our America Reads initiative to mobilize an army of reading tutors all across America. And I asked college and university presidents to help me achieve that. I sent a senior member of the White House staff, Carol Rasco, to the Department of Education to work with Secretary Riley to make sure the America Reads initiative does that. We have dedicated several thousand AmeriCorps volunteers to becoming trained so they can, in turn, train reading tutors to work with schools, with parents, and with children to help make sure our children can read.

But now we need a lot of volunteers—as many as a million—and a lot of them will have to come from students. I am pleased to say that over 80 college presidents have already committed thousands of their work-study students to participate as reading tutors. I hope you will join them and commit a percentage of your own work-study students to help our children learn to read, because without literacy, the job manuals and the history books are both closed, and so are the doors of college. We need your help to open them wider.

I'm looking forward to working with you in the months and the years ahead but especially this year to make sure that we pass this education agenda in Congress, number one, and number two, that we enlist the idealism, the ability, and the energy of our young college students in helping us to teach our children to read.

Thank you very much.

NOTE: The President spoke at 10:50 a.m. in the State Dining Room at the White House. In his remarks, he referred to Henry Ponder, president, and Harrison Wilson, board of directors chairman, National Association for Equal Opportunity in Higher Education; Talbert O. Shaw, president, Shaw University; William H. Gray III, president, United Negro College Fund; Joyce Payne, director, Office for the Advancement of Public Black Colleges; and Vic Hackley, chair, President's Advisory Board on Historically Black Colleges and Universities.

Remarks to the American Council on Education
February 24, 1997

Thank you very much. Mr. Secretary, that was a good speech—[*laughter*]—and fully illustrated Clinton's third law of politics, which is, whenever possible, be introduced by someone you have appointed to high position. [*Laughter*] Their objectivity is stunning. [*Laughter*]

I thank Secretary Riley and all the people at the Department of Education for the work that they do. Stan Ikenberry, I'm glad to be here today with all of you. President Knapp, thank you for your moving remarks about the HOPE scholarship. You all laughed when Barry

said he was making a great sacrifice by going to the Aspen Institute, but in Georgia, that's what they think. [*Laughter*]

President-elect Myers, and to my friend Barry Munitz—you know, we're all in a lather up here in Washington these days about campaign contributions. Everybody hates them, but nobody wants to go to public funding. So we seem destined to some period of handwringing. And since we're in a spirit of full disclosure, I have to tell you that in addition to my coming here today, I received a gratuity, which I intend to disclose before the whole world. I complimented Barry on his watch, and he gave it to me. [*Laughter*] And cravenly, as we politicians are, I took it without blinking. [*Laughter*] He swears it cost $18. [*Laughter*]

But I'll tell you why I bragged on it—and all of you more or less of my age group can identify with this—look how big the numbers are. I can—[*laughter*]—it's the first watch I've ever seen that I don't need glasses for. The more expensive they are, the smaller the numbers get. [*Laughter*] So, thank you, Barry.

I would like to begin today, if I might, with a very personal and serious word. This is the first opportunity I have had, really, to say something publicly about the death of Al Shanker yesterday, one of the greatest educators of the 20th century in this country. He was my friend for many years. I considered him my colleague. He believed that all children could learn with high expectations and high standards, high-quality teaching, and high accountability. He literally lived a life that was nothing less than a crusade, with intense passion and power. And I know that all of you will join me in wishing his wife and his family and the members of the American Federation of Teachers the best, and giving them our sadness and our thanks for a remarkable American who did his job very, very well.

I also want to come here to thank you. Secretary Riley said, in his inimitable way, that this is a big day for us—and this is a big day for us—starting with the community colleges and their trustees and then going to this organization which represents, I thought at last count, almost 1,700 2- and 4-year colleges and universities. Your views matter, your voice is heard, and your endorsement of our college opportunity agenda, including the HOPE scholarships, the tax deduction for tuition, and the large increase in Pell grants, will help to bring that opportunity into reality and to fulfill my dream of opening the doors of college to every single American who wants to go. Thank you very, very much. I'm grateful to you.

This is a remarkable time in the history of our democracy. At the end of the cold war we find ourselves as the world's remaining superpower, with a special responsibility to try to shape the future in a way that will advance the cause of peace and prosperity. We find our own economy strong and growing, producing more jobs in the last 4 years than in any comparable term in our history, with record numbers of new businesses being formed each and every year.

We know that this is a time of enormous change, but the impulse to satisfaction, I'm sure, is great. Normally, when democracies have times this good, one of two things happens, sometimes both at the same time: People get very self-satisfied and begin to relax and therefore miss the underlying currents of what is really going on for the future, or they become too easily preoccupied with small matters and begin to divide among themselves over things that bring them down instead of lift them up. We must give in to neither impulse.

Because the growth of the global economy and the absolute explosion in scientific and technical information associated with the information age give us an opportunity but not a guarantee, an opportunity for undreamed of new jobs and careers, for greater knowledge and understanding, not just for greater material wealth but for enhancements in the quality of lives for families and communities, it is literally true that in the era toward which we are moving more people than ever before in all of human history will have a chance to live out their dreams. But it is also true that the chance cannot be realized unless we give them the power to make the most of their own lives. So this is no time to rest.

Four years ago we knew we couldn't rest, and we set about laying the foundation for progress by changing the economic policy of the country to focus on investing in our people, getting our fiscal house in order, emphasizing science and technology, and opening the doors of trade with the rest of the world. We changed our social policy, centering it clearly on family and community and focusing on action instead of rhetoric. The result is that we've had marked drops in crime, the biggest drop in welfare rolls in the history of the country, the family and medical leave law, action to stop teenagers from being exposed illegally to the sales and marketing of cigarettes, and a number of other initiatives.

Our foreign policy has begun to articulate the world that we want to make, working in an interdependent way with allies and friends of like mind throughout the world not only to advance the cause of peace and freedom and prosperity but to stand up against the new threats to our security.

Along the way, we have fought—and I hope largely resolved—the battle that has dominated America for nearly 20 years now over what the proper role of our Nation's Government should be. You hardly hear anyone saying anymore that Government is the enemy.

It was interesting—in the last couple of days Hillary and I went to see—or brought in the movie—we have a theater at the White House; it's the best perk of the job, I think—[*laughter*]—but we had about all the seriousness we could stand, and we watched that movie "Dante's Peak," about the volcano exploding. And I couldn't help thinking, you know, the hero works for the U.S. Geological Service, and his life is saved in the end by a contraption developed not here at home for uses on the ground but by NASA for use in space. And I thought, the Government is not the enemy. The role of the Government is to create the conditions and to give people the tools to build strong lives and families and communities and a strong nation, and to give people the chance to live out their dreams.

Now that that foundation has been laid, and now that I believe we have also moved away from the very dangerous rhetoric of the last several years that seeks to divide us against one another based on our racial or ethnic or religious or other differences, toward an understanding that it is actually a great godsend for us to be the world's most multiethnic, multiracial, multireligious democracy, we now can actually seize the opportunities that are before us. But the first and most important thing we have to do is to recognize that, beginning at the beginning, our education system will not provide us the opportunity to do that unless we change it.

For the beginning years, we have to raise standards. For our colleges and universities, which are plainly the finest in the world, we simply have to make sure that the access is there for everyone who should go to have a chance to go.

The main point I want to make is that we actually are in a position now to mold our future untroubled by war abroad or disruption at home in a way that is very, very rare in human history. We have no idea how long this moment of tranquility will last. We have no idea how long we will be fully free to wake up and say, "what am I going to do today," without being impinged

upon by some external force that will shape us.

I was interested when the Secretary talked about Abraham Lincoln and the land grant. I used to teach at a land grant school, so I like that. But it's interesting that President Lincoln signed that land grant bill during the Civil War. And Lincoln once said during the Civil War—he gave a statement today that I would be ridiculed nationwide if I said—he said, "My policy is to have no policy. I am controlled by events." Well, of course, he did have a policy. He had the most important one of all: "I'm going to hold this Union together if we all have to die to do it, including me." That was his policy. But he also told an important truth. When the wheel runs off and things fall apart, you are to some extent controlled by events.

Today, in a rare moment, America is not especially controlled by events, but we cannot be unmindful of the larger historical trends which will shape our future. And it is the moral obligation of every person in a position of responsibility in the United States to take this opportunity not to lay down on the job and not to fall into mindless debates but to lift our sights and our visions to take advantage of this rare moment and make the most of it. And we could do no better than to give our people the finest set of educational opportunities in the world and to make sure very single one of them has those opportunities.

I was encouraged by the report I got out back, very brief, about the words that Senator Lott said earlier here today. During the cold war we had a bipartisan foreign policy, because—literally because the future of the country was at stake. Everybody agreed: We'd like to fight with you, and we'd like to kick you out if you're not in our party, but politics should stop at the water's edge.

Today, in the information age, politics should stop at the schoolhouse door, because our security depends upon our ability to give all our people the finest education in the world. My shorthand expression for what we're trying to do, and you will all recognize there are many other things at stake, is that we have to create an America in which every 8-year-old can read, every 12-year-old can log on to the Internet, every 18-year-old can go on to college, and every adult can keep on learning for a lifetime. My balanced budget makes an unprecedented commitment to these goals: $51 billion next year. But far more than money is required.

Three weeks ago at the State of the Union, I issued a call to action for American education based on 10 principles necessary to prepare our people for the 21st century:

First, we have to set world-class standards for our schools and develop a system of accountability, beginning for the first time with national standards-based reading tests in the fourth grade and math tests in the eighth grade.

Second, we have to make sure we have the best teachers in the world.

Third, we must make sure that every child can read on his or her own by the third grade. I see my friend the president of the Miami-Dade Community College out here, the largest community college in our country and one of the most diverse student bodies. Forty percent of the 8-year-olds in this country cannot read a book on their own, 40 percent. And we have to do better than that if we want all of our children to be in 2- and 4-year colleges when their time comes.

Fourth, we have to make sure parents are more deeply involved in a constructive way in their child's learning from birth. The First Lady and I are going to host a conference on early childhood learning and brain development in the spring here.

Fifth, we have to give parents more power to choose the right public schools for their children and encourage school reforms like charter schools that set and meet high standards.

Sixth, we should encourage the teaching of character education in our schools—and Secretary Riley has done a marvelous job of that—and promote order and discipline at the same time by supporting local school initiatives like school uniforms or truancy enforcements or curfews and demanding zero tolerance for guns and drugs. I have seen in the most difficult neighborhoods in this country that children do not have to put up with violent, disruptive, and destructive school environments. There are schools that are succeeding against all the odds. And if some can, all can. And until they all do, none of us should be satisfied.

Seventh, we should support school construction at the national level. I believe, for the very first time—because we have record numbers of school populations now—for the first time we've got a group bigger than the baby boomers coming through, and the schools are growing at

record rates while their facilities are deteriorating at record rates.

Eighth, we should make sure that learning is available for a lifetime by transforming what can only be described as a tangle of Federal training programs into a simple skill grant that goes directly to workers. People who need and are eligible for Federal training help, nearly all of them, live within driving distance of a community-based educational institution that can give them what they need. And we do not need a lot of Federal programs to get between them and those institutions. I have been trying for 4 years to pass this program. I hope you will help me get this done in this session of Congress, to create a new "GI bill" for America's workers that simply gives people a skills grant and lets them take it to the institution of education nearest them most able to meet their needs.

Ninth, we are determined to connect every classroom and library in this country to the Internet by the year 2000, and we're making good progress on that.

But finally, and the thing that you have endorsed today, is our effort to meet the last goal, to throw open the doors of college to all people who are willing to work for the opportunity.

As the Secretary said, we have always expanded education. He began with Abraham Lincoln, and we might have begun with Thomas Jefferson, who advocated, even as he advocated buying Louisiana—for which I'm very grateful; otherwise I wouldn't be President—*[laughter]*—and America becoming a continental nation, that we should educate all of our children. Thomas Jefferson even advocated the education of every single child, boy or girl, of slave families in America. And we know from the beginning that it was the education of our leaders that gave them the vision to chart the course which has brought us to this day.

I do believe, based on the sheer economic realities and the need for greater understanding of our interdependence in the world in which we're living, that we have to make the first 2 years of college as universal as a high school education is today. Fifteen years ago, the typical worker with a college degree earned 38 percent more than a high school graduate; today, it is 69 percent. Two years of college alone means a 20 percent increase in learning and a quarter of a million dollars more in earnings over a lifetime.

Now, over the past 4 years we have put in place an unprecedented college opportunity strategy: student loans provided directly to people who need them and that enable people to repay those loans as a percentage of their income; AmeriCorps, which has already helped 70,000 young people earn their way through college by serving their communities and their country; 200,000 more students in work-study as a result of last year's budget; and a very large increase in Pell grants last year, taking the maximum grant to $2,700 and expanding the number of people eligible.

The plan I have put before the Congress in my balanced budget would expand work-study again so that one million students will be able to work their way through college by the year 2000. We want 100,000 of these new work-study students to join our America Reads efforts to help make sure all our 8-year-olds can read independently by the year 2000.

I know that more than 80 college presidents have already committed thousands of their work-study students to work as reading tutors. I thank those of you who are here leading this effort, many of you on the front row here, and I'd like to ask all the rest of you to join us. Go back home, look at how many people you've got in work-study, see how many you could allocate to this effort.

We're going to have about 35,000 AmeriCorps students trained especially to train tutors. We're going to challenge the parents and the schools to open up to make sure we can get these volunteers in there to teach these kids to read. We cannot expect the schools to operate efficiently if children have to leave the third grade not even being able to read. They will never learn what they need to know. And college students will relate well to these young kids and have a chance to literally revolutionize future learning in America.

A lot of these children are not just poor kids, they simply—many of them come out of cultures where their first language is not English, and they did not learn to read properly. We should not let them go past the third grade without knowing we have all done everything we humanly can to make sure that they can read independently. So I thank those of you from the bottom of my heart who have volunteered already, and I ask the rest of you to join in that crusade. We need you, and it will make all the difference.

Finally, let me say we have got to do more in other areas. For 3 years in a row now we've expanded Pell grants for deserving students. But our budget this year—our balanced budget contains the largest increase in Pell grant scholarships in 20 years. We are adding $1.7 billion in grants, a 25 percent increase, which will make 348,000 more students eligible, many of them older students, and will increase the maximum grant to $3,000. And for 4 million low and middle income students, the budget will cut student loan fees in half.

But if we're truly going to set a new standard, a 14-year standard, we've got to do more. That's why I have proposed America's HOPE scholarship based on the Georgia pioneering program: 2 years of a tax credit of $1,500 for college tuition, enough to pay for the typical community college. We know it will work because of the testimonial you have already heard from President Knapp.

Second, I propose a tax deduction of up to $10,000 a year for all tuition after high school to help families send children or parents to college or to graduate or medical school or any other education after high school.

Third, I propose an expanded IRA, expanded in terms of eligibility, in terms of who can save, and in terms of purpose, so that families can save tax-free to pay for education. Together these proposals mean that a family could save money for college tuition and never pay a penny of taxes on it. For example, families could put up to $2,000 of income into the IRA each year without paying taxes, then withdraw up to $10,000 a year for tuition and deduct that from income so that there will not be any taxes when they're paid out.

Cutting taxes to help people pay directly for college has never been done before on a national level. But we have cut taxes for years to help people buy a home or invest in a business because that's the way we thought we could encourage people to invest in their future and build the American dream. And it has worked. In the last 4 years we have seen homeownership rise to a 15-year high, and if the rate of increase continues, by the year 2000 more than two-thirds of Americans will live in their own home, an all-time record. In the last 4 years we have seen in each successive year a record number of new businesses formed in America. Today we ought to have that same kind of encouragement to invest in education, an even more important investment for the future. And I think that it is highly appropriate to adopt this device to achieve that goal.

Let me assure you, the Treasury Department is committed to working with the Department of Education and all of you to make this tax plan work. The IRS will not interfere with the affairs of educational institutions. We are committed to making this simple and straightforward for the academic community and especially for the students of every age. The plan will give families the power to choose the right education for themselves and the flexibility to decide the best way in which to pay for that education.

Now, just think about what this could mean. A young person who can't afford tuition or whose family can't afford it can now go down to a local community college right away and sign up if they meet the standards, because the HOPE scholarship will pay for it. Someone with a new family who is worried about college costs down the road can multiply his or her savings power by putting tuition money in an IRA tax-free every year while the children are growing up. Then, when they're 40 and worried they might need more education to move ahead but can't spare time off from work, not only can they withdraw from the IRA for the kids but the parents can go part time or at night. But all can go to college without tax consequences.

My plan is simple: $1,500-a-year tax cut for individuals to pay for college for 2 years; a $10,000-a-year tax deduction for families for any year of tuition after high school; an expanded IRA to help families save tax-free for education; plus the more and larger Pell grant scholarships for deserving students, 300,000 more work-study positions, AmeriCorps, the direct loan program.

This plan will throw open the doors of college and give every American the great chance to make the most of the world that we are moving into. College is opportunity for tomorrow. And creating that opportunity is our responsibility today.

I thank you again for your support of this plan. As we work in the weeks and months ahead to craft a bipartisan balanced budget, your endorsement today will be an historic element in making sure that this will be part of the ultimate budget plan. We need a balanced budget, but it has to reflect our values, and it has to pave the way to a better future.

Today we have committed to expanding educational opportunities by enacting the HOPE scholarship tax cut, the college tax deduction, the Pell grant increases, the work-study increases. I thank you for standing with us. You are standing for opportunity for generations to come in a way that will change America forever for the better.

Thank you, and God bless you.

NOTE: The President spoke at 2:14 p.m. at the Grand Hyatt Hotel. In his remarks, he referred to Stanley O. Ikenberry, president, Michelle Tolela Myers, incoming chair, and Barry Munitz, outgoing chair, American Council on Education; Charles Knapp, incoming president, Aspen Institute, Washington, DC; and Eduardo Padron, president, Miami-Dade Community College.

Statement on the Death of Martin Slate
February 24, 1997

Hillary and I were deeply saddened to learn of the death of Marty Slate. Marty has been a dear friend since our years at Yale Law School and was the quintessential public servant.

From his days as a Freedom Rider in Mississippi to his years as a senior civil servant at the Equal Employment Opportunity Commission and the Internal Revenue Service, Marty spent his entire life working to make sure our laws were fair and applied justly.

Four years ago, I was delighted when Marty answered my call to return to public service. As Executive Director of the Pension Benefit Guaranty Corporation, he brought a new standard of excellence to that agency. He improved the PBGC's level of customer service and its financial management, winning an Innovation in American Government Award from the John F. Kennedy School and several Vice Presidential Hammer Awards for Excellence in Government.

Marty fought successfully for important new legislation that brought renewed financial stability to the Corporation, expanded pension coverage, and ensured that millions of Americans' pensions were more secure.

Hillary and I will miss him greatly. Our thoughts and prayers are with Cookie and his family on this sad day.

Statement on the First Anniversary of the Downing of American Civilian Aircraft by Cuba
February 24, 1997

One year ago, four innocent civilians were killed when their aircraft were brutally shot down by the Cuban regime. Without warning, Cuban MiG's fired air-to-air missiles at two small unarmed planes in international airspace. Three U.S. citizens and one permanent resident were the victims: Carlos Costa, Armando Alejandre, Mario de la Peña, and Pablo Morales.

Today we join the families in honoring the memory of these men as we carry forward our efforts to seek justice for their deaths. An investigation by the International Civil Aviation Organization last June confirmed that the shootdown was unlawful and without any justification. The U.N. Security Council last February and again in June strongly deplored Cuba's illegal use of violence against the aircraft. The Castro regime, however, has consistently rejected the judgment of the international community. As we did one

year ago, we call on Cuba to take full responsibility for its actions and provide assurances that an outrage like this will never happen again.

The shootdown and the Cuban Government's continuing repression of human rights activists and independent journalists underscore the need to continue working for a peaceful transition to democracy in Cuba. The United States continues to lead the international effort to achieve that goal, and over the past year, more of our friends and allies than ever before have joined with us to help bring democracy to Cuba.

On this anniversary, with the memory of the four victims in our prayers, the United States reaffirms its commitment to help bring democracy, respect for human rights, and prosperity to the people of Cuba, who have too long been denied these essentials of a decent life.

Letter to Congressional Leaders Transmitting a Report on the Enlargement of the North Atlantic Treaty Organization
February 24, 1997

Dear Mr. Chairman:

Pursuant to section 1048 of the National Defense Authorization Act for Fiscal Year 1997, I transmit herewith a report on the enlargement of the North Atlantic Treaty Organization.

For over 50 years, successive Presidents and Congresses have maintained a firm, bipartisan consensus that the security of Europe is vital to the national security of the United States. It remains so. NATO, even as it evolves and adapts to a changing world, remains the core of the transatlantic alliance that has served American interests for two generations.

Inclusion of new members into NATO's ranks is an indispensable element of a broader American strategy to create an undivided, democratic Europe for the 21st century. By extending the underpinnings of security beyond the arbitrary line of the Cold War, NATO can strengthen democratic and free market reforms for all of Europe, just as it has done for Western Europe in the decades since 1949. By admitting new states to the alliance, NATO will limit and help eliminate a potentially destabilizing vacuum in Europe, widening the circle of like-minded nations sharing common values and willing to shoulder common responsibilities and burdens. Already, the prospect of NATO enlargement has strengthened stability and democracy, and promoted regional cooperation among the states of Central and Eastern Europe.

The enlargement of NATO is not directed against any state; NATO does not see any nation as its enemy. By extending security and stability throughout Europe, NATO enlargement will serve the interests of all of Europe's democracies—whether they are current members, new members, or nonmembers. The United States looks forward to the building of a strong, dynamic relationship and unprecedented partnership between NATO and Russia.

NATO enlargement is moving ahead. NATO has agreed to hold a Summit on July 8–9 in Madrid at which one or more nations will be invited to begin negotiations on accession to the Washington Treaty; I have called for NATO to welcome new members by 1999, and NATO has accepted this goal. Continued close and bipartisan cooperation between the Congress and the executive branch are, and will remain, the

keys to achieving this objective. Addition of new members to the North Atlantic alliance must be submitted to the Senate for its advice and consent, and both houses of the Congress will have to approve the resources necessary to make enlargement a reality.

I thank the Congress for the constructive role it has played in recent years to advance the enlargement of NATO. I look forward to working with the Congress to achieve our common objective of a wider circle of security, prosperity, and common values embracing an integrated Europe and the United States.

Sincerely,

WILLIAM J. CLINTON

NOTE: Identical letters were sent to Jesse Helms, chairman, Senate Committee on Foreign Relations; Benjamin A. Gilman, chairman, House Committee on International Relations; Strom Thurmond, chairman, Senate Committee on Armed Services; and Floyd Spence, chairman, House Committee on National Security.

Letter to National Bioethics Advisory Commission Chair Harold Shapiro on Cloning Technology Issues
February 24, 1997

Dear Dr. Shapiro:

As you know, it was reported today that researchers have developed techniques to clone sheep. This represents a remarkable scientific discovery, but one that raises important questions. While this technological advance could offer potential benefits in such areas as medical research and agriculture, it also raises serious ethical questions, particularly with respect to the

possible use of this technology to clone human embryos.

Therefore, I request that the National Bioethics Advisory Commission undertake a thorough review of the legal and ethical issues associated with the use of this technology, and report back to me within ninety days with recommendations on possible federal actions to prevent its abuse.

Sincerely,

BILL CLINTON

Remarks to the Democratic Business Council
February 24, 1997

Thank you very much, Tom and Carol. Chairman Grossman and Alan Solomont and Paul

DeNino, thank you for taking on this important work.

Let me begin by thanking all of you for being here tonight and for your support, for the things that you said earlier, and your high hopes for our country. And let me remind you that we are involved in an extraordinary endeavor with a great opportunity. In the last 4 years we changed the economic policy of this country, and we now are committed to investing in our people, expanding our trade, and balancing our budget, and the consequences have been truly extraordinary.

In the last 4 years, for the first time ever in one Presidential administration, we had 11½ million more jobs and record numbers of new businesses in every single year. The so-called misery index is the combined rates of unemployment and inflation. It's the lowest it has been in America since the 1960's. And every one of you who supported our efforts, who fought for our policies, who stood up for what we are trying to do played a role in that, and you should be proud of that.

We changed the direction of social policy in this country, putting family and community at the center of our concerns and substituting action for rhetoric. And that's one of the reasons, thanks to the crime bill, that we've had years of declining crime now and people actually can believe that their streets can be made safe for their children; one of the reasons we've had the largest decline in welfare rolls in the history of the United States.

We now have—I was telling the folks at the table tonight, from 1972 to 1989, it was an average of 4.8 percent of the American people on public assistance. When I took office there were almost 5½ percent of the people on welfare. Today, it's 4.6, lower than the average since 1972 and going down.

And the only thing I would ask you is, any one of you—my friend Stan Chesley has already hired two people off the welfare rolls. We have to set an example. We can't just exhort people. We now have to hire one million people from welfare to work in the next 4 years to meet the targets of the welfare reform law. Meeting the target of the welfare reform law means requiring people who can work to work but not cutting anybody off public assistance who is honestly committed to supporting her children and cannot find a job. So we changed the law. Now we have to do our part.

And I want to invite all of you to be part of what is a great and, I might add, a bipartisan

effort to hire one million more people off the welfare rolls. And I ask for your support to pass the legislation in Congress to give special tax credits of up to 50 percent of a salary, capping out at $10,000 a year, for anyone who hires anyone from welfare into the work force. We can do this.

And I know we can do it; I've added up all the numbers of all the employers of all sizes, of all kinds in America. This is a snap if we will just make a commitment as a country to do it. We owe it to the children in those families who deserve a chance to see their parents and themselves move into the middle class and have a shot at what we're all trying to build for our children in the new century.

Let me say that today we had some very, very good news on the education front. You know from the State of the Union that I believe this should be the primary focus of our new endeavors in the next 4 years. And today meeting in Washington, the National Convention of Community Colleges and all their trustees, and the American Council on Education, which includes 1,700 leaders of 2- and 4-year colleges and universities in America, both endorsed the education plan I put before the American people and the Congress in the State of the Union Address. So this is a good day.

And we are going to be able to create a country in the next 4 years where every 8-year-old can read independently, where every 12-year-old and every classroom and library in America is hooked up to the Internet, where every 18-year-old has a chance to go on to college, and where our adults can continue to learn for a lifetime. These things are good things, and we are moving in the right direction.

I can also tell you that I am confident that we will continue to reach out in a positive way to the rest of the world. The Secretary of State has had a great first trip on her first trip as Secretary of State around the world. I've been very proud of her, and I hope you have. And we have to continue to do that.

Let me just make one last point here. In the last 4 years if you were to ask me, "What did you do that was most significant," well, those of us who count votes might say, "Well, you passed that economic plan in '93 by one vote, and it brought the country back and that's what happened in '96." Those of us who worry about the safety of our streets might say, "If it hadn't been for the crime bill passing and the Brady bill and the assault weapons ban, well, we wouldn't have the crime rate coming down." Others might say the family and medical leave law and the other things we did surrounding family. Others might say the fact that we defeated the other party's attempt to drastically change the course of America by beating back the '95 budget, and we killed, I think, once and for all the dominant rhetoric of the last 20 years, which is that Government is the enemy.

Government is not the enemy. Neither is Government the solution. But we now know that every modern society that seeks to fulfill the potential of its people needs, through its Government, leadership in creating conditions and giving people the tools to make the most of their own lives.

I told somebody today that Hillary and I over the weekend needed a little break from all this seriousness, and we watched "Dante's Peak" at the White House movie theater—best perk about being President, the theater. [*Laughter*] And it's a movie about volcanoes, and I think it's a rather interesting movie because I'm interested in volcanoes. But I thought it was interesting that it was this movie, and the hero of the movie was an employee of the U.S. Geological Service. And the hero was nearly killed by the volcano, and in the end his life is saved by a technical contraption developed not for volcanoes but for space by NASA. Government is not the enemy. [*Laughter*] They would have had no movie but for the Government. [*Laughter*]

And I think we've earned the right to say that, that this Government is now smaller by 285,000 people than the day I took the oath of office the first time—285,000, the smallest since President Kennedy was in office; hundreds of programs gone; thousands of pages of regulation gone; the reinventing Government effort led by the Vice President still gathering steam, not about to just sit around and do no more.

But we have got to say these are things we have to do as a country, as partners. But apart from all that, I think maybe the thing that I would highlight is that in the last 4 years I hope we have created the conditions for seeing this country fulfill all of its potential because we have rejected the politics of division, whether it was based on race or religion or anything else.

I think I made the right decision in saying we should mend affirmative action and not end

it. I think I made the right decision in saying that I did not think that we should turn our backs on legal immigrants in this country; this is a nation of immigrants. I think we did the right thing to support the Religious Freedom Restoration Act and protect the religious liberties even of people whose politics are very different from mine and who believe they have a religious duty to try to remove me from office the last election. [*Laughter*]

That's what made this country great. The first amendment guaranteed freedom of speech, freedom of assembly, freedom of association, and freedom of religious faith. I think we did the right thing to try to combat in a very aggressive way these church burnings. And I might say, the recent bombing of the gay nightclub in Atlanta reminds us that this work is not over. That was wrong, and we have to stand against those things. We have got to go forward together. We don't have anybody to waste.

And we surely have figured out finally that it is a great advantage to the United States to be the largest, most multiethnic, multireligious, diverse democracy in the world. We're still learning how to deal with it. But we still have to reach out to the rest of the world. We have to compete and win. And we have to educate our people to live and to be a humanizing, democratizing, freedom- and peace-promoting influence in the rest of the world. We can't do any of that unless we do it as one America. And I think that is a lasting legacy which you can all be proud of. And we have more work to do on that, and we will be doing more work.

Let me finally say that I appreciate your being here for our party because this is not something a President can do alone. I'm glad to see Secretary of Transportation Rodney Slater here tonight, who's going to acquit himself so well in that job, and my friend and sort of family member, Senator Barbara Boxer, here, who needs your help to get reelected in 2 years, and I hope you'll help her. She deserves it.

And we're trying to do this together, and we're trying to do it together with the Republicans in Congress insofar as we and they—to be fair to them, because we have honest differences—insofar as we and they can in good conscience do that. The atmosphere is different here. And we have to keep it positive, constructive, building, trying to get something done to make this country great.

And the last thing I want to leave you with is this. I said this in the State of the Union, but I want all of you to think about it because it applies to our personal lives and our business lives as well as the life of this Nation. It is rare when things are going well on almost all fronts. You have to go back a good while to find a time when the economy was as strong as it is, when it was working for small businesses as well as big businesses, when the welfare rolls were going down, the poverty rate was dropping, the inequality among classes of working people was dropping, when all these things are happening at the same time, and when we're not threatened from without. And the tendency when things are going that well is either to relax and just sort of lay back and let things happen and have a good time, or to, frankly, find small things to fight about and fall out about and to be divided about. It sounds counterintuitive, but it's true. If you think about it in your own life, you see that. And we must not do either one of those things.

This is a unique moment in the history of a country. When Abraham Lincoln was President, in the middle of the Civil War, someone asked him what his policy was, and he gave an answer that if I were to give it I would be nationally ridiculed. He said, "My policy is to have no policy. I am controlled by events." Think how you would feel if I said that. [*Laughter*]

Now, the truth is, he did have a policy. His policy was "I'm going to hold the Union together if I have to—if everybody in the country has to die, including me." That was his policy, and he adhered to it. But it was also true that on a day-to-day basis he could have no policy, he was controlled by events. We are not controlled by events. We get to shape events. It is rare when this happens to a country.

And we cannot blow this opportunity, either by being complacent or by falling out over small things. This is a time to be big and visionary and active and aggressive and a time to do it together. That is what I want you to be invested in. That is what I want you to feel that you are participating in.

And whenever we announce a new initiative you agree with, or results of something you support, I want you to understand that it is all part of a bigger effort to create a country in which, really for the first time in our history, every person actually does have a chance to live out his or her dreams, a country which really can help to shape a world where there is more peace, more freedom, more prosperity, and in which we are organized in a different way to meet the different challenges to our security and to our values around the world.

This is a very good time, but it imposes a special responsibility on us because nobody is beating us on the back with a lash, making us do the right thing. Our existence is not hanging by a thread so that we pray for the largeness of spirit that people seek when they know that. We just have to do it because we understand that this is a unique opportunity, and we are not going to pass it by.

Thank you, and God bless you.

NOTE: The President spoke at 8:10 p.m. at the Sheraton Carlton Hotel. In his remarks, he referred to C. Thomas Hendrickson, chair, Democratic Business Council; Carol Pensky, treasurer, Steve Grossman, national chair, Alan D. Solomont, national finance chair, and Paul DeNino, finance director, Democratic National Committee; and attorney Stanley M. Chesley.

Remarks Announcing the 1997 National Drug Control Strategy and an Exchange With Reporters
February 25, 1997

The President. Thank you very much. First of all, thank you, Nathan, for your introduction and your commitment, and I thank all the young people who are here from the Boys and Girls Club, from the D.A.R.E. programs. I want to thank the members of the President's Drug Policy Council who are standing here behind me and those out in the audience who have been introduced by the Vice President and by General McCaffrey. And I thank the Members of

Congress for being here and their support, and all the rest of you who are involved in this battle.

Let me say a special word of appreciation to General McCaffrey. He has literally been tireless in developing a national strategy to reduce illegal drug use and, more importantly, to implement it in a way that makes a difference in the lives of all Americans. I knew that he was well-suited for the job. I had had a lot of exposure to General McCaffrey before I asked him to do this job. But even so, I have been surprised by the increased intensity of his tenacity and focus, and for that I am grateful. I think it gives us a chance to turn this situation among our young people around, with all of your help.

Let me say at the outset, one of the things that I have tried to do and one of the reasons I like this drug policy so much is that it is focused on children and therefore it is a part of what I think ought to be our overall mission, which is to give our children a safe, wholesome, constructive upbringing that begins with a drug-free life, appropriate health care, safe streets, and a decent education.

I want to thank the Attorney General—today the Justice Department has announced something else that I think is important. I'd just like to begin, because I think we need to look at this in terms of the safety of our children. Today the Justice Department announced that in the first 28 months since the Brady bill went into effect—another law directed to the safety of our children—more than 186,000 felons, fugitives, and stalkers were blocked from buying guns over the counter, more than 186,000, from March of 1994 to the end of June of 1996. And more than 70 percent were rejected because the applicant was an indicted or convicted felon. Now, it seems to me that, for all those who are still out there campaigning against the Brady bill, those of us who support it can now rest our case. It's the right thing to do for America. It's making us safer. It's giving these children a chance to grow up drug-free. And I ask all of you in law enforcement to redouble your efforts to support it and to do what we can to defend it.

Our five-part drug strategy is another part of making America safer for our children. In 10 years, a young person, a young man or woman Nathan's age, will be in his or her early twenties, a time when a person should be well on the road to becoming a contributing member of society, an adult with responsible duties. Those 10 years, they're a pivotal 10 years. We're learning all the time about how formative the young years are in a person's life when intelligence is formed, but we also need to concentrate on the formative years when not only intelligence but good judgment is formed and decisions are made about whether people will be good citizens, good workers, good parents, and among other things, drug-free. What happens to people in those 10 years should be an integral part of every drug strategy. This is an urgent issue.

You know, there is hardly a day that passes when we don't read in the newspaper about yet another child becoming a victim of violence. Every American should be angry that a 9-year-old cannot make her way safely to her grandmother's door in a Chicago housing project—angry that she was brutally attacked and left for dead. That child will suffer with great physical and emotional pain for the rest of her life. A portion of her childhood was taken from her. And whenever an attack like that happens, a portion of our humanity is taken from all of us.

Last week in Chicago, Hillary asked that anyone who has information about that attack contact the local law enforcement officials. I want to extend that call today and ask that all of us do more to keep watch over our children. We have to become angry whenever any child, one single child, becomes prey for drugs or violence or abuse, and we should use our anger to take action.

Last week I unveiled our youth violence strategy to keep gangs, guns, and drugs off our street and called for new protections for our children, including safety locks on guns and extending the Brady bill to violent youthful offenders. But fundamentally this course will only change if all of us can teach our children right from wrong and if all of us can help them to steer away to a more productive, positive life.

That is what we have to focus on in this drug strategy. We know what works. We know what works. There are people here who have been working in this vineyard for years and years and years. We know that bipartisan cooperation works. We know persistence and community action works. All were factors in reducing illegal drug use by half in the last 15 years. But we also know that during this time, drug use by adolescents, almost unbelievably, went up. And I might add, until last year so was the crime rate by young people going up while the overall crime rate was dropping. And the two things were clearly related.

This is not a problem confined only to the poor or to those in inner cities. It cuts across from rich to middle class to poor, from urban to suburban to rural. In each of these places there are children who are getting in trouble when they ought to be choosing a better life. Among eighth graders in the last few years, drug use is up 150 percent. An eighth grader, typically, is 13 or 14 years old. That's why prevention is important at that age and indeed even considerably younger. If we teach our children well, more of them will live well away from harm's way.

Our drug strategy must be more than a year-to-year approach but a guide to action for the next decade for those critical 10 years of these young people's lives, to reduce drug use and its consequences, and to keep our young people out of the kind of harm that the invasion of drugs into their bodies will cause. We should first begin by giving our children the straight facts. We know that the more children are aware of the dangers of drugs and believe the facts, the more likely they are to avoid them. We propose to add up to $175 million to seed a far-reaching media campaign to get out the facts and shape the attitudes of these young people. We'll be seeking matching funds from the private sector for a total of $350 million because this must be a shared responsibility. If a child does watch television—and what child doesn't—he or she should not be able to escape these messages.

And again, let me say I want to thank General McCaffrey for bringing this idea to me and pointing out how much we had permitted public advertising aimed at young people about the dangers of drugs to decline over the last few years. That is one of the seminal contributions that he has made to my understanding of this issue, and I appreciate it, and I ask the Congress to help us to get this job done.

Second, we must reduce drug-related crime and violence. Drug trafficking supports gangs and sets off gang warfare. A million Americans are arrested every year for violating the drug laws. Let me say that again: A million Americans are arrested every year for violating drug laws. Three-quarters of the growth in the number of Federal prison inmates is due to drug offenses.

We will enforce the law vigorously, but we have to do more than make more jail space. I saw yesterday that two of our largest States, Florida and California, now have prison budgets bigger than their higher education budgets, that prison construction is growing all over America much faster than constructions in our colleges and universities, even though enrollment is going up and older people are trying to go back to college.

We have to do more to prevent these things from occurring in the first place, more to take the guns out of hands of criminals and juveniles, more to use the criminal justice system to reduce drug demand and break the cycle of drugs and violence. Drug courts and mandatory drug testing and treatment are effective. I'm pleased to announce that the Justice Department is providing $16 million in grants to more than 125 communities across our Nation for planning, implementing, or improving drug courts. I have seen them work; I know they will make a difference.

Third, we have to work to eliminate the social consequences of illegal drug use. A third of all AIDS and HIV cases are drug-related—a third. More than 3.6 million Americans, as the General said, are addicted to drugs. Drugs kill 14,000 of our fellow citizens every year. Often, people who use illegal drugs are people who go to class or hold jobs or have families. They drain our productivity. We can begin to reduce these circumstances if we can further decrease the number of casual drug users and if we can help chronic users to overcome their dependency. It is important that we try to do both.

Fourth, we have to do more to shield our frontiers against drug trafficking. We all know that this is a very difficult task. Hundreds of millions of people enter our Nation every year. Hundreds of millions of tons of cargo are shipped here every year. Just one millionth of all that cargo is illegal drugs. One millionth of all that cargo is illegal drugs. But that is still far too much and an awful lot of cargo. Our job is to stop it without hurting the legal commerce and movement that makes us the trade leader of the world. Along our border to the south with Mexico, crime and violence linked to drugs must be brought under control. Our 1998 budget will bring considerable reinforcement to that border.

Fifth, we have to reduce drug cultivation, production, and trafficking abroad and at home.

We've made a start by supporting alternatives to drug crops. In Peru, coca cultivation dropped by 18 percent. In the next decade, we want to completely eliminate the cultivation of coca for illicit consumption. If we help with alternative crops, that is a viable, viable policy in many cases.

We've also had some successes against trafficking. The Coast Guard's Operation Frontier Shield in the eastern Caribbean between October 1st and December 1st of last year seized 14,000 pounds of illicit drugs, compared to 5,400 pounds for the entire previous year. It seized seven smuggling vessels and achieved an 80 percent interdiction rate, versus 20 percent in the previous year. We can do better with interdiction, and we're learning to do it.

Throughout the Caribbean and in South America, we've captured more than 100 tons of cocaine a year. With the cooperation of other nations and with regional organizations, we're committed to building on our record of success. And when Secretary Albright returns from her trip this afternoon, we'll be looking at certification on counternarcotics operations. We are committed to cooperating with our friends in Latin America. That's one of the reasons why I asked Mack McLarty to be my special envoy to the Americas. We want to cooperate with them, but we want them to cooperate with us as well. We want to reduce our demand for drugs, but we are determined to reduce the supply as well.

Finally, let me say we have to do more to work together here at home. On May 21st I will host the first White House mayors conference on drug control, to bring together not only mayors but police officers and prosecutors, too, to make sure that in every community we are doing the very best job we can. I want parents, teachers, law enforcement, and other community leaders to help us. I want our young people to help us, most of all. We did not create this problem overnight, and it will not be solved overnight, but over that critical decade of these young people's lives who are here, we can lift a whole generation away from the grip of a terrible menace.

Thanks to the efforts of many people, we now have a rational, coherent, and long-term strategy. Its ultimate success will depend upon the support it receives from every American. And ultimately, it will depend upon the willingness of our young people to listen, to learn, to be strong, and to find support. The rest of us have to be that support. There is no more urgent priority.

Thank you very much.

1996 Campaign Financing

Q. Mr. President, in a short time we in the media will have access to documents which reportedly contain your feelings that overnight stays at the White House could be used as a motivation to get——

The President. This is not a national priority.

Q. ——could be used as a motivation for getting people to contribute more to the Democratic National Committee.

The President. That's not what they contain.

Q. Well, I'm—we have not seen these documents yet.

The President. Well, I'll tell you what. I'll be glad to answer the questions, but you should see it first. What the document says—there's a document in there that points out that in early 1995, a lot of the people that helped me get elected President in '92 thought that they had gotten estranged, in effect, from me, that we had not kept in touch with them. And Terry McAuliffe sent me a memo suggesting things we ought to do to reestablish contact, which I thought was a good memo. And I told him to proceed. And I told Nancy Hernreich, in addition to that, that I wanted to ask some of my friends who had helped me when I got elected President that I hadn't been in touch with to come to the White House and spend the night with me. That is a reference to that.

And later, by the way, today, sometime, we're going to release the people—the number of people who stayed at the White House in the last 4 years, and you will see that the people that worked for me and helped to raise funds for me were a small percentage of the total number of people who stayed at the White House. But they were my friends, and I was proud to have them here. And I do not believe people who lawfully raise money for people running for office are bad people. I think they're good people. They make the system work that we have now. I'm proud that they helped me, and I was proud to have them here. I did not have any strangers here. The Lincoln Bedroom was never sold. That was one more false story we have had to endure. And the facts will show what the truth is.

Thank you very much.

NOTE: The President spoke at 11:37 a.m. in Room 450 of the Old Executive Office Building. In his remarks, he referred to Boys and Girls Club member Nathan Habel, who introduced the President; Terence McAuliffe, finance chair, Clinton/Gore '96; and Nancy Hernreich, Deputy Assistant to the President and Director of Oval Office Operations.

Message to the Congress Transmitting the 1997 National Drug Control Strategy
February 25, 1997

To the Congress of the United States:

I am pleased to transmit the *1997 National Drug Control Strategy* to the Congress. This strategy renews our bipartisan commitment to reducing drug abuse and its destructive consequences. It reflects the combined and coordinated Federal effort that is directed by National Drug Control Policy Director Barry McCaffrey and includes every department and over 50 agencies. It enlists all State and local leaders from across the country who must share in the responsibility to protect our children and all citizens from the scourge of illegal drugs.

In the *1996 National Drug Control Strategy,* we set forth the basis of a coherent, rational, long-term national effort to reduce illicit drug use and its consequences. Building upon that framework, the *1997 National Drug Control Strategy* adopts a 10-year national drug-control strategy that includes quantifiable measures of effectiveness. The use of a long-term strategy, with annual reports to the Congress and consistent outreach to the American people on our progress, will allow us to execute a dynamic, comprehensive plan for the Nation and will help us to achieve our goals.

We know from the past decade of Federal drug control efforts that progress in achieving our goals will not occur overnight. But our success in reducing casual drug use over the last decade demonstrates that drug abuse is not an incurable social ill. Thanks to the bipartisan efforts of the Congress and the past three administrations, combined with broad-based efforts of citizens and communities throughout the United States, we have made tremendous progress since the 1970's in reducing drug use.

Nonetheless, we are deeply concerned about the rising trend of drug use by young Americans. While overall use of drugs in the United States has fallen dramatically—by half in 15 years—adolescent drug abuse continues to rise. That is why the number one goal of our strategy is to motivate America's youth to reject illegal drugs and substance abuse.

Our strategy contains programs that will help youth to recognize the terrible risks associated with the use of illegal substances. The cornerstone of this effort will be our national media campaign that will target our youth with a consistent anti-drug message. But government cannot do this job alone. We challenge the national media and entertainment industry to join us—by renouncing the glamorization of drug abuse and realistically portraying its consequences.

All Americans must accept responsibility to teach young people that drugs are wrong, drugs are illegal, and drugs are deadly. We must renew our commitment to the drug prevention strategies that deter first-time drug use and halt the progression from alcohol and tobacco use to illicit drugs.

While we continue to teach our children the dangers of drugs, we must also increase the safety of our citizens by substantially reducing drug-related crime and violence. At the beginning of my Administration, we set out to change this country's approach to crime by putting more police officers on our streets, taking guns out of the hands of criminals and juveniles, and breaking the back of violent street gangs. We are making a difference. For the fifth year in a row serious crime in this country has declined. This is the longest period of decline in over 25 years. But our work is far from done and we must continue to move in the right direction.

More than half of all individuals brought into the Nation's criminal justice systems have substance abuse problems. Unless we also break the cycle of drugs and violence, criminal addicts will end up back on the street, committing more crimes, and back in the criminal justice system, still hooked on drugs. The criminal justice system should reduce drug demand—not prolong or tolerate it. Our strategy implements testing and sanctions through coerced abstinence as a way to reduce the level of drug use in the population of offenders under criminal justice supervision, and thereby reduce the level of other criminal behavior.

Our strategy supports the expansion of drug-free workplaces, which have proven so successful and we will continue to seek more effective, efficient, and accessible drug treatment to ensure that we are responsive to emerging drug-abuse trends.

We must continue to shield America's air, land, and sea frontiers from the drug threat. By devoting more resources to protecting the Southwest border than ever before, we are increasing drug seizures, stopping drug smugglers, and disrupting major drug trafficking operations. We must continue our interdiction efforts, which have greatly disrupted the trafficking patterns of cocaine smugglers and have blocked the free flow of cocaine through the western Caribbean into Florida and the Southeast.

Our comprehensive effort to reduce the drug flow cannot be limited to seizing drugs as they enter the United States. We must persist in our efforts to break foreign and domestic sources of supply. We know that by working with source and transit nations, we can greatly reduce foreign supply. International criminal narcotics organizations are a threat to our national security. But if we target these networks, we can dismantle them—as we did the Cali Cartel.

We will continue to oppose all calls for the legalization of illicit drugs. Our vigilance is needed now more than ever. We will continue to ensure that all Americans have access to safe and effective medicine. However, the current drug legalization movement sends the wrong message to our children. It undermines the concerted efforts of parents, educators, businesses, elected leaders, community groups, and others to achieve a healthy, drug-free society.

I am confident that the national challenge of drug abuse can be met by extending our strategic vision into the future, educating citizens, treating addiction, and seizing the initiative in dealing with criminals who traffic not only in illegal drugs but in human misery and lost lives.

Every year drug abuse kills 14,000 Americans and costs taxpayers nearly $70 billion. Drug abuse fuels spouse and child abuse, property and violent crime, the incarceration of young men and women, the spread of AIDS, workplace and motor vehicle accidents, and absenteeism in the work force.

For our children's sake and the sake of this Nation, this menace must be confronted through a rational, coherent, cooperative, and long-range strategy. I ask the Congress to join me in a partnership to carry out this national , strategy to reduce illegal drug use and its devastating impact on America.

WILLIAM J. CLINTON

The White House,
February 25, 1997.

Message to the Congress Transmitting the United Kingdom-United States Supplementary Social Security Agreement
February 25, 1997

To the Congress of the United States:

Pursuant to section 233(e)(1) of the Social Security Act, as amended by the Social Security Amendments of 1977 (Public Law 95–216, 42 U.S.C. 433(e)(1)), I transmit herewith the Supplementary Agreement Amending the Agreement Between the Government of the United States of America and the Government of the United Kingdom of Great Britain and Northern Ireland on Social Security (the Supplementary Agreement), which consists of two separate instruments: a principal agreement and an administrative arrangement. The Supplementary Agreement, signed at London on June 6, 1996, is intended to modify certain provisions of the original United States-United Kingdom Social Security Agreement signed at London February 13, 1984.

The United States-United Kingdom Social Security Agreement is similar in objective to the social security agreements with Austria, Belgium, Canada, Finland, France, Germany, Greece, Ireland, Italy, Luxembourg, The Netherlands, Norway, Portugal, Spain, Sweden, and Switzerland. Such bilateral agreements provide for limited coordination between the U.S. and foreign social security systems to eliminate dual social security coverage and taxation, and to help prevent the loss of benefit protection that can occur when workers divide their careers between two countries.

The Supplementary Agreement, which would amend the 1984 Agreement to update and clarify several of its provisions, is necessitated by changes that have occurred in U.S. and English law in recent years. Among other things, the Supplementary Agreement removes certain restrictions in the original agreement concerning payment of UK disability benefits to residents of the United States. The Supplementary Agreement will also make a number of minor revisions in the Agreement to take account of other changes in U.S. and English law that have occurred in recent years.

The United States-United Kingdom Social Security Agreement, as amended, would continue to contain all provisions mandated by section 233 and other provisions that I deem appropriate to carry out the provisions of section 233, pursuant to section 233(c)(4) of the Act.

I also transmit for the information of the Congress a report prepared by the Social Security Administration explaining the key points of the Supplementary Agreement, along with a paragraph-by-paragraph explanation of the effect of the amendments on the principal agreement and the related administrative arrangement. Annexed to this report is the report required by section 233(e)(1) of the Act on the effect of the Agreement, as amended, on income and expenditures of the U.S. Social Security program and the number of individuals affected by the amended Agreement. The Department of State and the Social Security Administration have recommended the Supplementary Agreement and related documents to me.

I commend the United States-United Kingdom Supplementary Social Security Agreement and related documents.

WILLIAM J. CLINTON

The White House,
February 25, 1997.

Memorandum on Federal Policies Targeted to Children in Their Earliest Years
February 24, 1997

Memorandum for the Heads of Executive Departments and Agencies

Subject: Federal Policies Targeted to Children in Their Earliest Years

Over the past few years, scientific research has demonstrated that the earliest years of life—before children reach school-age—are critical to cognitive, emotional, and physical development. We know that emotional nourishment, intellectual stimulation, parental and community support, good nutrition, proper health care, quality child care, and safe housing during the first years of life form the foundation for a child's ability to learn, thrive in school, work productively, and contribute fully to society.

Across the Federal Government, we are making great strides to enhance development during the earliest years of life by investing in research, educating parents and care-givers, and supporting programs that provide early intervention to disadvantaged families. I am committed to accelerating our efforts to target the earliest years of life. We all have a stake in ensuring that every child is given the opportunity to fulfill his or her God-given potential.

Today, I am directing the heads of executive departments and agencies to report to me within 30 days with:

1. a comprehensive list and assessment of existing projects and programs funded by your agency that target the earliest years of life—including any existing qualitative

205

or quantitative evidence of success, as well as current funding levels and number of clients served—and a description of any proposed improvements to such projects and programs.

2. a comprehensive list and assessment of any planned projects and programs of your agency that target the earliest years of life, including projected funding levels and number of clients to be served; and

3. specific proposals for additional projects and programs this year that could be undertaken to improve the earliest years of life that do not require new spending or

that fall within the proposals in the FY 1998 Budget, or that could be developed for consideration in the FY 1999 Budget, within the limits of my Balanced Budget Plan.

I am also directing the establishment of a senior level interagency working group to share, examine, and develop these assessments and proposals.

WILLIAM J. CLINTON

NOTE: This memorandum was released by the Office of the Press Secretary on February 26.

Remarks Welcoming President Eduardo Frei of Chile
February 26, 1997

President Frei, Mrs. Frei, members of the Chilean delegation, distinguished guests. On behalf of the American people, I am delighted to welcome President Frei back to the United States and to return the warm hospitality the people of Chile showed to the First Lady when she visited there 2 years ago.

Today the countries of our hemisphere stand together facing a new era. Never have the Americas been more free or more prosperous. Never have we had a better opportunity to create a community of nations united by shared values and common purpose. Now, by acting together to deepen our democracy, to spur economic growth, to strengthen our partnership, the United States and Chile can bring concrete benefits to our own people, to all the Americas, and to the world and fulfill the promise of our times.

Chile's return to democracy, a heroic and courageous struggle, has helped to fuel freedom's march all across our hemisphere. Its economic reforms have set the standard for success throughout our region with impressive growth, unmatched financial stability, and high rates of job creation and the reduction of poverty.

During the last 3 years, Mr. President, your determination to expand opportunity at home and forge new links abroad has displayed the power of open societies and open markets to lift the lives of our people. The friendship we celebrate today has its roots in the fight for freedom that gave birth to both our countries. Almost two centuries ago, in 1811, that shared heritage was reflected in Chile's decision to hold its first national congress on July 4th, the anniversary of our own independence.

Now our ties are bearing fruit in a growing partnership that advances our ideals and our interests. Just as we joined hands to help peace take hold in El Salvador, we are working side by side to keep peace on the border between Peru and Ecuador and to help them reach a lasting settlement. Together we are striving to follow the roadmap set by our hemisphere's 34 democracies in the Miami Summit of the Americas in 1994. We are working to make trade in the Americas more free and fair, the key to jobs and growth and opportunity for all our people in the next century. And by advancing human rights, fighting drugs, and protecting the air and the water we share, we are proving that democracies deliver.

And now our sights are set on the second summit, which Chile will host in March of 1998. We must consolidate the historic advance of the Americas from dictatorship, war, and command economies to democracy, cooperation, and open markets.

Mr. President, almost 30 years ago your father, President Eduardo Frei Montalva, said, "Great perspectives will open before us if we are united." Today the United States and Chile are united, and we can see great new horizons of hope all across our hemisphere.

We must take advantage of this historic opportunity to advance into the future together, making the success of our efforts to promote peace and freedom and prosperity in the Americas a model for all the world.

NOTE: The President spoke at 10:16 a.m. on the South Lawn at the White House, where President Frei was accorded a formal welcome with full military honors. In his remarks, he referred to President Frei's wife, Marta.

Remarks Prior to Discussions With President Eduardo Frei of Chile and an Exchange With Reporters
February 26, 1997

President Clinton. Let me say very briefly that President Frei and I are going to have a press conference after this meeting of ours, and we'll answer your questions then. But I want to welcome him to the United States and once again to point out the truly astonishing record that Chile has established in the last several years in growing a powerful democracy and having remarkable economic growth and reducing poverty. And we are especially glad that Chile has agreed to host the next Summit of the Americas meetings in Santiago in 1994, following up on the one that we had, of course, in Miami—in 1998, they'll be in 1998—the one we had in Miami in 1994.

And Mr. President, we're glad to have you here and we thank you very much for everything you've done. And we look forward to a unique partnership.

President Frei. I would like to specially thank the invitation and especially now at this point when the relations between Chile and the United States are so especially outstanding and promising.

Thank you for this being an invitation, the first one in your second term. And I'm sure we'll have the opportunity to discuss major issues on restrengthening our democracy, growth—sustained economic growth, alleviation of poverty, and the advantages we have experienced as being an open economy.

We begin this visit with tremendous confidence, optimism, and as true partners. And we will be expecting you in March of next year at the second Summit of the Americas.

President Clinton. I'll be there.

Q. Mr. President, during the ceremony, Chairman Greenspan was on the Hill expressing

some deep concerns about the direction of the market. Do you share that concern?

President Clinton. I'll answer questions at the press conference. Thank you.

Q. Are you going to call Senator Torricelli? Are you going to call Senator Torricelli about——

Vice President Gore. Gracias. Vamos.

Q. ——amendment?

President Clinton. That's a good question. [*Laughter*]

[*At this point, one group of reporters left the room, and another group entered.*]

President Clinton. Let me begin by saying again how deeply honored I am that President Frei is here and that he has favored the United States with our first state visit of my second term as President. We believe we have established a genuine partnership with Chile that will only deepen in the years ahead.

The American people are terribly impressed by the remarkable transformation of Chile in the last several years, the growth of the deep democracy, the powerful economic advances, the reduction in poverty, the assumption of leadership by Chile in the region and in the world. And I'm looking forward to building on that partnership. And again let me say I'm very pleased that President Frei is here at my first state visit in my second term.

President Frei. I would like to thank you once again, Mr. President, for this invitation to this state visit, the first one of your second term. We've come here with great optimism at a time where the relations between the United States and Chile are at its utmost.

We are partners not only in this hemisphere, but globally we have been working as partners. We want to keep on working together in furtherance of democracy and to defeat poverty in the end. Chile has a rich experience in foreign trade, and we plan to share that as well.

Thank you for the warm welcome and for your kind words about my father, Mr. President. Thank you, and we will continue to consolidate together democracy. And we expect you in March of next year when you come to the Summit of the Americas.

Q. President Clinton, will you——

Vice President Gore. We're going to wait for the press conference.

President Clinton. We'll do questions, and they'll be equally divided at the press conference.

NOTE: The President spoke at 10:28 a.m. in the Oval Office at the White House. A tape was not available for verification of the content of these remarks.

The President's News Conference With President Eduardo Frei of Chile
February 26, 1997

President Clinton. Good afternoon. Please be seated. First, let me say it's been a great pleasure to welcome President Frei to the White House. We meet in an historic moment for our hemisphere, when the foundation of democracy and free markets is firmly in place. Now we must lead in building on that foundation to forge a future of peace and prosperity.

Chile is the window through which we see the Americas of tomorrow, a multiparty democracy, a firm commitment to human rights, proven economic reform. President Frei is working hard to make sure that all Chileans benefit from Chile's economic growth, lifting people from poverty and raising their aspirations. Chile is also an active global citizen, promoting peace from El Salvador to Iraq, sending civilian police to Bosnia, ratifying the Chemical Weapons Convention.

At the crossroads of trade among the world's most dynamic economies, Chile can be a cornerstone of the vibrant free trade area we are working to build in our hemisphere. Together, the United States and Chile are showing the promise of partnership in the Americas. Today President Frei and I reaffirmed our commitment to build on that partnership at the Summit of the Americas that Chile will host in March of 1998.

At the summit in Miami in 1994, we charted a roadmap for collective action. Now we must set further milestones for progress that will benefit our people: deepening democracy, advancing trade, expanding opportunity, fighting drugs, and protecting the environment. I look forward to attending the Santiago summit and to working closely with President Frei to build on Miami's success.

We also discussed the importance of open trade, both in boosting prosperity and in bolstering freedom and democracy. I repeated to the President what I told the Congress: I believe we must have fast-track authority to conclude new trade agreements that open markets to America's products and that advance our values. The United States simply cannot afford to sit on the sidelines while others share in the fruits of Latin America's remarkable growth.

Chile's strong record of reform, good government, and sound fiscal policies make it an excellent candidate for the first use of such authority. Our administration remains committed to concluding a comprehensive free trade agreement with Chile. In that regard, I'm pleased to announce that I've asked the Secretary of Agriculture, Dan Glickman, to travel to Chile to inaugurate a new consultative process to promote our agricultural trade. Our countries have also agreed to launch negotiations on an open skies agreement.

And finally, I want to mention something near to my heart, our Fulbright exchange program, the oldest in Latin America. Today Chile's decision to share this program's cost will help our people to build even stronger ties as we enter the 21st century.

Over the next several months, as I visit Latin America and the Caribbean, I'll continue to advance the important agenda we focused on today, consolidating the historic journey of the Americas toward democracy, open markets, mutual respect, and cooperation. We are weaving a fabric of an integrated hemisphere, a community where people live, work, and learn together as friends on behalf of peace and progress.

Before I ask President Frei to speak, I'd like to say just a few words, if I might, to the American people and the American press about our continued determination and our ongoing efforts to get to the bottom of the question of Gulf war illnesses. This week, as a result of the ongoing review we instituted several months ago, new documents have come to light further suggesting that our troops could have been exposed to chemical agents during the Gulf war. As soon as we get any new information, we share it with our veterans and the American people, and we will act appropriately on any information we uncover.

I want to caution everyone that it is important not to prejudge the actions or the developments that occurred in the previous administration. We simply have to get to the bottom of it. Today I've written to Dr. Joyce Lashof, the Chair of our action committee on Gulf war illnesses, and asked the PAC to focus on the documents that have come to light this week. It is essential that we get all the help we can from the PAC in understanding the full significance of the documents and any other new information that might come to light. We cannot stop until we get all the answers about Gulf war illnesses.

And now I'd like to ask President Frei to make an opening statement. And we'll take your questions.

Mr. President.

President Frei. Thank you, Mr. President. I would like in the first place to reiterate our thanks for this invitation. Chile is a country that in the recent years has consolidated its democracy. It has had sustained growth in the last 14 years, with average development and growth rates of 7 percent a year. And that has strengthened and consolidated our economy.

We have given a front battle against poverty, bringing down to half the level of poverty we had during the eighties. And at the same time, we've done it within the framework of a tremendous opening to foreign trade—international trade. Chile has today economic complementation agreements with more than 30 countries. We are members of MERCOSUR starting October of last year. We are members

of APEC, as the only South American country. And we are negotiating an agreement with the European Union.

For all these reasons, at this working meeting we have discussed all the items—hemispheric ideas, the Summit of the Americas to be held in March of '98 in Chile, what are the main items and subjects and what we will focus on during the year: consolidation of democracy, free trade, struggle against poverty, and also very preeminent subjects that we have agreed to include in that Summit of the Americas, and that is education, science, technology, and training as the essential and foremost tool to leave under development.

We have talked also about our participation in the United Nations and in all those issues of world peace. We have representatives of our armed forces in Iraq, and we will take part with members of our police forces in Bosnia. And we are very active seeking in Latin America the peaceful settlement of disputes. And this has been proven by our participation in several conflicts we've had in Latin America and very recently in those difficulties between Peru and Ecuador, whereby we have actively participated to consolidate peace in the region.

Also, we have reviewed our bilateral relation. In the last years of my government, the increase of bilateral trade between Chile and the U.S. has had an explosive increase; it has increased more than 50 percent in the last 2 or 3 years. Only in 1996 we've had investments of American firms equivalent to all of the American investment we had in Chile in the previous 15 years. And so with an exchange of more than $6.2 billion—of course, there are sensitive issues, especially in agricultural sectors. And we have expressed our way of thinking and our ideas as to trade, the points of interest to Chile, to the United States. And as the President has stated, our Secretaries of Agriculture will meet so as to jointly look for a solution to these problems that we believe always can emerge in such a vast, broad, and diversified trade relation as the one we have.

Also, we have spoken of politics. We are interested in the 1998 summit to speak of politics as we did in the Iberia-American summit of Santiago. Usually we used to discuss environment, free trade, and education. This time we raised the subject of democratic governance, good government, how to make our democracies effective in Latin America, how to solve the very specific and concrete problems of the people.

And that item, that subject, we want to include it in the summit of next year. We know that democracy has to be built every single day with great effort and sacrifice, and that is why this conversation has been very open, candid. We are a small country. We are no power neither as to population nor are we an economic power. But with certain dignity we do have the capability of raising before the United States a very wealthy bilateral relation of great development and to work together in the hemisphere and in global policies.

I believe that Chile, and this I say here solemnly, Chile is no example, nor model. What we've done is to build an experience based on our history. And of course, drawing upon the lessons and work of many, many generations, we have been able to consolidate this development model, this development process. And we have a historic opportunity. Never before has the country been in a position to view upon the future in a different manner.

If we act in this way, I think that in the next years we can leave underdevelopment behind. That is what we want in Chile. That is what we want to build. And we feel partners with the United States in this major endeavor, that as a Latin American country I will be able to leave behind poverty, margination, and build a better future for our children. That is our task, the major project.

And I feel today that, upon arrival to the United States, being received by the President and highest authorities, and when speaking tomorrow before the joint session of Congress—first time a Chilean President will have this honor—it's not an honor for the President, it's an honor to the country, for what we've been, for what we are, and what we are building.

Thank you, Mr. President.

1996 Campaign Financing

Q. Sir, the documents yesterday show you raised a great deal of money from people you entertained at the White House. Did you pay for their food and such? And can you really say the White House was not used as a fundraising tool?

President Clinton. Absolutely. Look at the list of the people. We put it out there. A vast majority, I think almost seven-eighths of them, were people that I had relationships with that were

independent of my campaign for President in '92. But some people did come and stay with me who helped me, and I think that's entirely appropriate. I don't think people who support you and help you through tough times and who believe in what you're doing should be disqualified from being the President's guests at the White House. But any Presidential guest at the White House, whether they're family members or dignitaries or whatever, their costs are not borne by the taxpayers.

Mr. President, would you like to call on someone?

Free Trade and Fast-Track Authority

Q. A question for President Clinton. In Chile, your political will with regard to Chile's accession to NAFTA is well-known. However, at this point, with all the time that's gone by, we're asking for more concrete steps. Among those steps you are about to take, are you going to ask for fast-track authority from Congress?

President Clinton. Yes. I am going to ask for fast-track authority from Congress. In my State of the Union Address I said that I would. And I want to reiterate today that I believe the first use of that authority should be to conclude a comprehensive trade agreement with Chile, and I would hope that the Congress would support that endeavor. I believe the President's speech to the Congress tomorrow will be very helpful in that regard. And I'm delighted that he came here; I'm delighted that this is my first state visit since I was reelected President.

And I wish it had been done before, but it was simply not possible to pass through Congress. I do believe we'll get the fast-track authority, and I believe we'll conclude an agreement. But we have a lot of work to do. And as I said, the fact that the President is going to speak to Congress tomorrow to a joint session is a historic thing not only for Chile, but it's very important for the United States and for the future of this whole region.

Terry [Terence Hunt, Associated Press].

1996 Campaign Financing

Q. Mr. President, in the documents that were released yesterday, two high-ranking White House officials, Harold Ickes and Evelyn Lieberman, refer to DNC coffees at the White House as fundraisers. That, of course, would be illegal. How do you explain their choice of words, and do you think that any of the fund-raising activities came close to skirting the line, going across the line into illegality?

President Clinton. No. We got strict advice about—legal advice about what the rules were, and everyone involved knew what the rules were. Did we hope that the people that came there would support me, particularly after we got into a political season, when we were doing this? Of course we did. But there was no solicitation during the events. And the guidelines, which I believe were made available to you also yesterday in the documents, made it clear that there was to be no price tag on the events. Did the people hope that the folks that came to the events would subsequently support me? Yes, they did. And I think that was clear to everyone involved at the time. But there was no solicitation at the White House, and the guidelines made clear that there was to be no price tag on the events.

Q. But the language in those memos?

President Clinton. I think my own view is—and I haven't talked to the people, but that's how much they hoped would come out of their endeavors after the coffees were over. And I think, if you will ask them, you'll find that sometimes they did, and sometimes they didn't.

Chile and NAFTA

Q. President Clinton, Chile is a country with a small economy and a small population. Why do you think it deserves to be part of NAFTA?

President Clinton. I think that Chile deserves to be part of NAFTA because it is the most successful democratic free market economy in Latin America, with high rates of growth, a deeply entrenched democracy, having overcome very well-documented, extreme difficulties in building that democracy over the last few decades. And really I think Chile is looked to as a leader in our hemisphere on political and economic matters. And I can't imagine how we could have a set of free trade agreements with our neighbors in Latin America that Chile was not a part of.

And what I'm hoping is that others in our hemisphere who have now embraced democracy will see what Chile has done economically, not simply in having high rates of growth but also in reducing poverty, spreading the benefits of economic growth to more people. The commitments that the President has articulated in education, for example, that the First Lady saw

so clearly when she was down there 2 years ago—I'm hoping that that will spread across our hemisphere and that when we come to Santiago next year there will be a deep feeling among all the other nations there represented that we should press on to create a free trade area of the Americas and that it should help more countries to bring the benefits to their people that the Chilean people are beginning to realize.

So the symbolic significance of Chile is far beyond the size of the economy, although I wouldn't minimize the size of the economy and its potential for growth.

Claire [Claire Shipman, CNN].

1996 Campaign Financing

Q. Mr. President, given all the public attention at this point on the fundraising issue, and the calls now from Capitol Hill from Democrats and Republicans for an independent counsel, don't you think it might make sense at this point to have an independent counsel to take some of the pressure off?

President Clinton. Well, I think what I always think about that. There is a statute, and that is a decision for the Attorney General to make. It should not be a political decision. It's a legal decision; the Attorney General has to make it.

Q. Would you be opposed to an independent counsel?

President Clinton. I'm not going to comment. I never have. It is a decision that should be made strictly on the law, based—by the Attorney General, not based on any politics. But the evidence that we made clear yesterday, I think is—I've answered the questions about that, and I don't think there is a legal issue there.

Trade and Domestic Politics in Chile

Q. President Frei, have you been told by President Clinton the strategy he will use in the months ahead to propose fast-track on Congress? And also, a domestic question—have you decided—are you close to a decision to who will be president of the Christian Democrats in Chile?

President Clinton. I'm glad you asked him a domestic question. Thank you. [*Laughter*]

President Frei. What we think as to free trade is to show exactly what our experience has been, more than taking part as to—or referring to the decisions that the U.S. Government or Congress have to make. We are interested; of course we are. Why? Because as I said before, we have economic complementation agreements with more than 30 countries. Our foreign trade is highly diversified in Asia, Europe, and America. Our trade with Latin America is very similar to the one we have with the United States. That is why we have aggressively sought these agreements, allowing a small nation to consolidate those markets. Today if we had foreign trade—I mean, imports, exports, and related services—they account for practically 55 percent of our GDP. And so today at least 6 or 7 out of 10 jobs in Chile depend on international trade.

And that is why we believe that this has been beneficial for the country. And also, Chilean firms have gone abroad and invested more than $15 billion in the southern cone of America— unprecedented fact—practically 20 percent of our GDP. And this has meant the creation of an area not only of free trade but of integration. We are working in physical integration, energy integration, and we are contributing to improve our quality of life in the continent and particularly in our country.

That is why we've grown in recent years at rates—permanent rates about 6 or 7 percent, I would say. The last 14 years, we have a savings and investment rate that reaches unprecedented figures. Last year we had a saving investment rate of 28 percent, 28.5 of our GDP. And domestic savings, there the state contributes with 5 percent to domestic savings. And for 5 years we've had fiscal surplus.

Our accounts are in order, and thus we are firmly convinced that free trade not only is a pillar and foundation for Chile's development but an essential condition to consolidate our political, social, and economic project. And that is why, of course, we are interested, and we are certainly interested in the agreement with the United States. We signed with Canada in November an agreement following the guidelines of NAFTA, and that includes labor and environmental clauses that we are also ready and willing to accept.

So this is our vision of the country, how is our country going to be in the 21st century, and we are working toward that. And that is why we expect and the U.S. Government and Congress to define this, which is a road for Chile, of course, but it is also a road to be followed by the Americas.

And as to the Christian Democrat Party in Chile, the President of the Republic is President of all Chileans and does not take part in active politics. There in Chile, I am head of state and head of government, and the decisions of the parties are independent decisions. And the Christian Democratic Party, of which I've been a member for more than 35 years, elects its authorities democratically, universal suffrage process which is underway, and at the end of March they will hold that election. All the members will vote, and they will democratically elect their authorities.

Consumer Price Index

Q. Mr. President, are you ready to endorse Senator Lott's call for a commission of economists to once and for all settle this issue of whether the CPI overstates inflation?

President Clinton. Let me say, first of all, I support a cost of living increase that is appropriate. I think it's important that it be accurate. There have been questions raised and opinions offered about that. And I think it's important that we agree to a procedure that will have credibility not only among both parties and their leaders in Congress but even more importantly out there among the American people. This is not a question for the budget; this is a question about the long-term viability of our systems and whether the CPI is an accurate reflection of how much the cost of living of Americans goes up every year.

I appreciate Senator Lott's suggestion and I have—it is one of the things that I have considered, and I think we'll have some sort of an announcement on that in the not too distant future. But I think it's important for me to make sure that whatever we do has not only the confidence of Senator Lott, Senator Daschle, Speaker Gingrich, and Leader Gephardt and the members of their caucuses but also of the people out there in the country that will be living with whatever decision is made on this.

So I think he made a good, constructive suggestion. I think we ought to take that under advisement. And we need to see what other options there are out there, and then we need to go forward, and I expect to do that.

Free Trade and Fast-Track Authority

Q. President Clinton, since the Miami summit, not much progress has been done with regard to the free trade areas of the Americas. Do you think that the various regional processes in Latin America have been making much more headway, and do you think that the next summit is going to concentrate more on that than the FTAA?

President Clinton. Well, I think the answer to your question is it depends in large measure on what we do here. Since the United States did not renew fast-track authority, there was not much more we could do. But a lot of progress has been made within South America, for example. Chile reached an agreement with the MERCOSUR countries, and a lot of other things have been going on there. And then we've been working on some specific issues with a lot of nations in our hemisphere.

But I believe that our ability to get a free trade area of the Americas—Chile also, I think, made separate agreements with both Canada and Mexico. So our ability to get a free trade area of the Americas and to build what I think is potentially the most powerful economic unit in the early part of the next century now rests

with the willingness of Congress to approve the fast-track authority and our ability to get back on track and try to be a constructive, cooperative part of this process. And I intend to do whatever I can to achieve that.

And as I said, I'm delighted that the President is going to address Congress tomorrow. There's an enormous amount of admiration for Chile in the United States Congress, across party lines, for all kinds of reasons. And I think his words will be heard, and I think they will be exceedingly helpful.

Thank you very much.

NOTE: The President's 136th news conference began at 1:16 p.m. in Room 450 of the Old Executive Office Building. In his remarks, he referred to the President's Advisory Committee on Gulf War Veterans' Illnesses (PAC). President Frei spoke in Spanish, and his remarks were translated by an interpreter.

Memorandum on Gulf War Documents
February 26, 1997

Memorandum for the Chairperson of the Presidential Advisory Committee on Gulf War Veterans' Illnesses

Subject: Gulf War Documents

I've made it very clear from the early days of my Administration that the welfare of Gulf War veterans is a national priority. My strong and continuing commitment, reflected in the establishment and recent extension of the Presidential Advisory Committee on Gulf War Veterans' Illnesses, is to leave no stone unturned on behalf of those who served in the Persian Gulf theater. This commitment entails ensuring both that sick Gulf War veterans receive the medical care they require and that all relevant information that may help us understand the risks they faced is brought to light.

As you are aware, the Central Intelligence Agency, working in cooperation with the Department of Defense, has recently declassified several documents relating to the ongoing investigation of possible chemical warfare agent exposure of U.S. forces during demolition operations at Khamisiyah after the Gulf War. These docu-

ments indicate that: (1) U.S. Army units were warned of the possibility that there were chemical munitions at the Khamisiyah ammunition depot prior to seizing that objective during the ground war in February 1991; and (2) in November 1991, the Central Intelligence Agency prepared a classified message documenting the possibility that U.S. forces conducting demolition operations at the Khamisiyah facility were exposed to chemical warfare agents.

While the many issues related to Gulf War illnesses are complex and entail consideration of massive quantities of information, there must be no question of this Nation's commitment to protecting its soldiers on the battlefield and then ensuring that they receive the care they require upon returning home. This is a joint bipartisan responsibility that my Administration and the Congress take very seriously.

Accordingly, in conducting your oversight of the ongoing investigation being undertaken by the Department of Defense, with the assistance of other executive departments and agencies, into possible chemical or biological agent exposures during the Gulf War, I am directing your attention to the recently declassified documents. You have a vital role in assisting me, the Congress, and the American public in understanding their full significance.

These documents have been provided to the Inspectors General of the United States Army and the Central Intelligence Agency, both of whom are conducting investigations relating to Khamisiyah. There are two important questions raised by these recently declassified documents that must be resolved by these investigations: (1) When did we have sufficient evidence to conclude that chemical munitions were present at Khamisiyah and that U.S. forces conducting demolition activities may have been exposed to chemical warfare agents; and (2) Once we had that information, what actions were taken by whom to investigate this alarming possibility and were those actions sufficient.

Your oversight efforts should take full account of the evidence disclosed by these ongoing investigations, as well as the information being developed by the Office of the Special Assistant for Gulf War Illnesses at the Department of Defense. Your preliminary assessment relating to the adequacy of the investigations concerning these issues should be provided as soon as possible within the next 60 days, and no later than April 30, 1997, the date specified in Executive Order 13034 for your interim status report.

Thank you for your continuing efforts and those of your fellow members and supporting staff. Your Committee's dedicated efforts are truly indispensable to ensuring that no stone is left unturned on behalf of Gulf War veterans.

WILLIAM J. CLINTON

Statement on Senate Action on the Balanced Budget Amendment
February 26, 1997

I have made clear my concerns about the balanced budget amendment, and I am pleased that Senator Torricelli has made the difficult decision to oppose that measure.

Now it's time to get down to the hard work of balancing the budget. I look forward to work-

ing with both Republicans and Democrats in Congress to enact a plan that balances the budget in 5 years while protecting education and other critical investments in America's future.

Message to the Congress Transmitting a Report on Weapons of Mass Destruction
February 26, 1997

To the Congress of the United States:

The National Defense Authorization Act for Fiscal Year 1997 (Public Law 104–201), title XIV, section 1411 requires the President to transmit a report to the Congress that assesses the capabilities of the Federal Government to prevent and respond to terrorist incidents involving weapons of mass destruction and to support

State and local prevention and response efforts. In accordance with this provision, I transmit the attached report on the subject issue.

WILLIAM J. CLINTON

The White House,
February 26, 1997.

Remarks at the State Dinner Honoring President Eduardo Frei of Chile
February 26, 1997

Ladies and gentlemen, Mr. President, Mrs. Frei, members of the Chilean delegation, distinguished guests, welcome to the White House. Mr. President, I enjoyed our meeting today, especially your perspective as a trained engineer committed to building bridges. [*Laughter*] You have more experience and credibility at that than I have, but I am glad to be your partner in building those bridges.

The United States respects the extraordinary accomplishments of the Chilean people, the brave struggle to reclaim democracy which has cast the light of liberty over your land and over the entire hemisphere. The United States respects the extraordinary economic achievements of Chile, which have shined the light of hope over your land and the entire hemisphere.

Beyond democracy, you have advanced equality before the law and good government. Beyond economic growth, you have advanced fuller participation in Chile's prosperity, reducing poverty and increasing education so that all may have their chance. Under your leadership, Chile is a crossroads for global commerce, a force of freedom and peace, a valued partner of the United States in building a better world for the 21st century.

Three decades ago, Mr. President, during the time of the Alliance for Progress launched by President Kennedy, your father made plans for a state visit to our country. That visit never came to pass. And in the years that followed, the bright hopes that our nations had for cooperation in our hemisphere went unrealized. Now we stand at a moment of unprecedented promise for the Americas. Just as you donned your father's ceremonial sash when you took office, you have completed the journey to the United States that he once set out to make.

Now we must make our bold journey into tomorrow together. Mr. President, I gave a book of poems by your great Chilean poet Pablo Neruda to my wife for our 20th wedding anniversary. In his "Ode to the Sea," Neruda wrote these words that speak to us tonight across the years: "We'll put the affairs of mankind in order, big things first, then all the rest. We will make you see an Earth, we will make you perform miracles, because inside us, inside our struggle is our daily bread, our fish, and our miracle."

Mr. President, you have put big things first: democracy, justice, freedom, the future. In so doing, you have given the Chilean people the chance to reach deep within themselves to perform miracles.

Tonight it's my great honor to ask all those here present to join me in toasting you, Mrs. Frei, people of Chile, and the bright promise of our partnership.

NOTE: The President spoke at 8:57 p.m. in the State Dining Room at the White House. In his remarks, he referred to President Frei's wife, Marta.

Remarks to the Business Council
February 27, 1997

Thank you, and good morning. Thank you, Larry. Thank you, Mr. Vice President. I want to thank the other officers and all of you who are here today for inviting me to come by. There are a lot of members of my administration here. I know Secretary Rubin spoke earlier, and Chief of Staff Erskine Bowles is here; Gene Sperling, the Director of the National Economic Council; and Maria Echaveste, who is my new Assistant for Public Liaison and Alexis Herman's successor—some of you may not know her. Maria, where are you? Stand up there. I wanted you to know because she'll be relating to you. I want to thank you for the support that so many of you have given to Alexis Herman in the job that she held and in the job that I'm confident she will hold as the Secretary of Labor.

Over the last 4 years, I have worked with many of you in this group to grapple with a lot of great issues facing our Nation, from reducing the deficit to expanding trade, to investing in new opportunities for a new century. The Vice President talked about the record that our people together have amassed in the last 4 years, and it is an impressive one and one we can all be proud of.

I understand you had a panel earlier this morning speculating on what has now become the conversation that we all have, which is, can it be possible that we have repealed the business cycle? Or if it hasn't been repealed, has at least it been shaved a little? And I think there is some argument for that if you look at the better inventory control, the changing nature of the economy, the more service jobs, the nature of global competition and technology, and the greater sophistication at the Fed. I mean, there are a lot of reasons for it, but I think there are some indications that we have had some real ability to manage this. But I think the most important thing to remember is that the underlying fundamentals have been good because of the productivity of the American people and our willingness to compete. And I think that if we want this to continue, which is the real question, we have to continue to do the things that will make it likely that success will prevail for another 4 years and into the next century.

It is relatively rare for a country to have both peace and prosperity and the opportunity to shape its own destiny at a time when there are so many fundamental changes in the way we work and live and relate to each other and the rest of the world. You go back to the history of the country; that is a relatively rare opportunity. And when it comes along, it's easy to miss because when things are going generally quite well, people are either complacent or they tend to—one of the unfortunate aspects of human nature—they tend to either be complacent or to be all heated up over small things, not big things, to fall out over petty divisions, not larger ones.

And so I think it is quite important that the business leadership of our Nation keep our country focused on the big questions: What will it take to ensure the long-term prosperity of America? What will it take to assure that America continues to be the world's leading force for peace and freedom and security in the new world of the 21st century? What will it take to guarantee a whole new generation of Americans, not a certainty but at least a fair opportunity, to be a part of this enormous, new, exciting age? What kinds of things do we have to do?

It seems to me clear that we have to finish the job of balancing the budget, to keep the interest rates down and the investment up, and to keep the economy growing. And it seems clear that we have to do a lot more than we have done to dramatically improve education at every level.

I'd like to talk about those two things and then mention one or two others today. I realize that whenever I talk about the skill levels of the work force to this group, I am preaching to the saved, but I think it is worth pointing out that between 1992 and 2000, 89 percent of the new jobs created in this economy will require post-high school levels of literacy and math skills. And virtually 100 percent of those jobs will pay what is now an above average wage. But only half the people entering the work force are even nominally prepared for these jobs. Our education system is still turning out millions of young people who simply are not equipped for the new world of work.

We know that we lag behind the rest of the world in math and science and that this poses a severe and growing competitive disadvantage for our country. We know that our young people have to do a better job of learning basic things and of developing the capacity to learn for a lifetime. That's why in the State of the Union Address I challenged our Nation to establish national standards in every school, in every community, in every classroom in the country and to be willing to measure whether every child has met those standards in learning, beginning at the beginning with a test of every fourth grader in reading and a test of every eighth grader in math by 1999.

Now, this may seem strange; for all of us who have had children come up through schools, we know that there are a lot of standardized tests out there. But what many people don't understand is that there are not tests to national standards. That's very different from a standardized test. If you have the right—if you have standards that every child should know in a subject and every child is tested, then that's a test everybody could pass. There's no curve grading. You either know what you're supposed to know or you don't. And how you rank in an average is utterly irrelevant unless you know what you are supposed to know.

And it is appalling that we have hidden behind a good idea, local control of our schools, to advance a very bad proposition that algebra is somehow different in Alaska than it is in south Florida, that geography is different in the northern part of Maine than it is in San Diego. This is not true. And no other country which seeks to do well in the modern economy would permit its children to keep coming up through an educational system that could not tell you whether our children know what they are supposed to know.

This is especially important now that so many of our young people come from other countries. Just across the river here in Fairfax County, there is one of the four school districts in America where the schoolchildren's native tongues number more than 100. And if—there are 40 percent of our kids in the third grade today who cannot read a book on their own. And we will never change this until we, first of all, say what the standards are and then, second, find a way to measure everyone.

Now, today, we've made some progress in this in the last 10 or 12 years. And some of you have helped me to work on it when I was a Governor. Today, through the National Assessment of Education Progress, for example, we can measure how States are doing or how school districts are doing, but still no parent can learn if a son or a daughter is actually meeting tough national standards. Our goal should be not to drive these children down but to lift them up.

Today the Department of Education is releasing the annual assessment of math performance through the National Assessment of Education Progress. It is based on a sample in the States that participate, and most States do participate now. Across the country and in almost every State, our math performance has improved in the 4th, 8th, and 12th grades. Secretary Riley will release the full results today. The scores are getting better, but they also show you why every child should be tested based on these standards, for about 30 to 35 percent of the children tested still have not mastered basic math skills, those which must be known in order to continue to learn for a lifetime.

So what I'd like to do is to just remind you of how you couldn't function if you couldn't measure and how things that you take for granted in the day-to-day operations of your business have literally been avoided in education under the guise of preserving local control. This has

nothing to do with local control. Dick Riley, since he's been the Secretary of Education, has done more in 4 years, I believe, than any of his predecessors to try to relax unnecessary Federal rules and regulations that hamstring how local school districts spend Federal money. This is not what this is about. This is about whether you really believe if a child reads "The Little Engine That Could," it's the same in New Orleans as it is in Minneapolis. No election to a school board or no State legislative action can change the fundamental elements on a chemistry table. And yet we have never been willing to subject ourselves to this sort of rigorous examination in an appropriate way.

We should begin at the beginning with fourth grade reading tests and the eighth grade math tests and then build it up. I think it is highly unlikely that we can do this unless we have strong support from the business community. I know that the Business Roundtable last month endorsed the concept of tests. I am grateful for that. I am profoundly grateful for it. But what I want you to understand is, we're going to go and make sure that they're developed. The standards-based tests that are out there now, which are basically the Third International Math and Science Survey and the National Assessment of Education Progress, are very good. We just have to find a way to either take them or a variant of them and then fix it so all the— so a State could get them and give them to school districts and all the students could take them and they could be properly scored.

But what I need you to know is that we still need your support. Right now there's a lot of enthusiasm for this. The Vice President and First Lady and I, we're going to go make a lot of State legislative trips. We're going to try to advocate this around the country. But we still do not have the power to require States to do this. This must be a voluntary thing. But the business community can create the conditions in which every State will have to embrace this challenge and no one can run away.

And again I say, we have to create the mentality that failing is not bad. What is bad is hiding the truth. What is bad is not taking the available tools to find out what the truth is, because we know that way over 90 percent of the kids in this country can learn what they need to know, but you have to start with where you are. And we know that if we have high expectations and then we measure them, we will eventually see people rise to them.

So I thank you for the endorsement, but you've got to stay with us, and you've got to help us. And when we need business leadership to help convince this State or that State or the other State to do this, we've got to have you there, because it won't work unless all 50 States do it and everybody recognizes that this has nothing to do with local control and everything to do with international competitiveness and giving our children, every single one of them, a chance to live the life that they ought to have the chance to live. And we need you very much.

Let me also say, with regard to the balanced budget—we don't have to have a long conversation about this today, but it now seems clear that the balanced budget amendment will not pass. I think that is a good thing, for the reasons that I have said elsewhere. But I think it must also be clear to the American people that we must make sure that a balanced budget does pass, passes this year, and passes as soon as we can reasonably pass it. We have to now go beyond the constitutional debate to get to the specifics. I am convinced that if we pass a balanced budget plan this year, it will moderate interest rates, spur more investment, and keep growth going. I believe that.

All the indicators we see that have been shown to me by Frank Raines and the Office of Management and Budget, supported by Secretary Rubin, indicate that if we can pass a balanced budget this year, dealing with the fundamentals that we're talking about—trying to better manage the Medicare program, the Medicaid program, looking at the long-term health of all the other programs—that we could keep it more or less in balance for two decades, based on what we now know. Obviously, there will be differences from year to year, depending on the performance of the economy. But you can look at the fundamentals and the demographics of things over two decades and pretty well know where you are. So it is very important that we do this.

Now, I believe that we've shown, this administration, that we care about this and that we're willing to work with the Congress. Before I took office the administration's budget projections had usually been an illusion to avoid the difficult decisions that administrations didn't want to make so that Congress would have to make them. Of course very often Congress didn't

make them, either, and each side took what the other wanted. So if one wanted tax cuts and the other wanted spending programs and, oh, by the way, they wanted to control spending, the tax cuts and the spending programs took preference over the controlling of the spending, and we wound up with a $290 billion a year deficit and a quadruple Federal debt in 12 years. Last year the deficit was $107 billion, proportionately the smallest of any major economy in the world, 63 percent lower than it had been in 1992.

So this is working. We have been working together first with the Democratic Congress, then with the Republican Congress, always driving it down. What has made it possible are conservative, realistic budget projections that every year have been more conservative for the deficit than what actually occurred. In other words, the deficit was even lower than we projected it to be in every year with our economic assessments.

And sometimes when you read in the press, there's a difference between the Congressional Budget Office and the Office of Management and Budget and it looks big in one year, the truth is that we have narrowed these differences dramatically now. They're not breathtaking differences, and it's enabled us to get together and work together to have budgets that make sense.

The other thing I think is important is, you hear a lot of criticism saying, "Well, whenever they have one of these plans, all the savings are in the out years." That's not quite true. But if you look at the way Medicare or Medicaid works, particularly in the Medicare program, if you look at the way some of these other programs work, the savings, by definition, compound themselves in a way that will always make the savings look bigger in the out years. The trick is to pass a plan that legally locks in tomorrow's savings today and that places strict limits on the amounts of money Congress can spend each year. If you do that, then the framework will be created which will permit us to get to balance in 2002. And it will have great credibility in the market.

I know that's true because of things we've tried to do with entitlements, including placing a cap, a per capita cap on Medicaid, and extending the life of the Medicare Trust Fund for a decade by having very rigorous spending controls that will facilitate the movement to managed care, have elicited so much criticism. And I know that, therefore, they're likely to work. I mean, it's just—it's not easy to do this. You all face these kind of decisions all the time.

But I do want to say, you will see a lot of our differences aired publicly—the executive, the Congress, the parties within the Congress. But this budget is well within reach. This is well within reach. And it's well within reach in a way that also would permit us to create a bipartisan process to deal with the long-term challenges of the entitlements in Medicare and Social Security as well.

So you should feel positive about that. But my advice would be here and my appeal to you is to tell every one of us, every time you get a chance to say it, that you cannot celebrate Thanksgiving this year without a balanced budget. Get the job done this year. We need it done this year. If you don't, it will have a destructive impact on the markets. If you do, it will have a positive one.

But you should know, when you hear all the debates, it is in the nature of the things for the differences to be amplified. The fact is that we are well within range of being able to get this done if we'll all just hunker down and kind of turn down the rhetoric and treat each other with good faith. We can get this job done in a way that I think is very good for the economy.

Let me just mention two other things I'd like to ask for your help on. The first is to help in getting a budget out and in supporting a policy in both parties that fulfills our responsibilities in the world today as the world's indispensable nation.

We had a bipartisan foreign policy during most of the cold war because we knew our neck was on the line, and politics stopped at the water's edge. Now it is more difficult to build a bipartisan foreign policy because the elements of it are more diverse. For example, economic policy and trade has a lot more to do with it than previously, or at least we're aware that it does—I think it was always a big part of our foreign policy—and because no one perceives that our neck is on the line. But the truth is that the whole world is looking to see whether America will fulfill its responsibilities to lead in an increasingly interdependent world, not only economically interdependent but environmentally interdependent and politically interdependent.

Increasingly, the security threats we face are those that cross borders, like terrorism and narcotrafficking. And this is a very complex time. We are in the process of building new structures, new understandings, new ways of working together. And it is important that America lead. That begins with trade.

We had great victories in 1993 with NAFTA and with the GATT, and in the last 4 years we've had 200 separate trade agreements. We had a great victory the other day for the cause of global trade and for the American economy. When Ambassador Barshefsky concluded the telecommunications agreement, it was a great thing. But we have been now 2 years without fast-track authority for the President.

Latin America is looking at us. President Frei in Chile—they just had—three Asian heads of government paid visits to Chile in the last 3 or 4 months. And the whole world in Latin America is looking to see what we're going to do. The same thing in Asia. So we really need to pass the fast-track authority. We need to do it this year, and we need to do it as soon as possible. And I hope that all of you will help us do this.

I think most Members of Congress understand—let me just give you two examples—how China defines its greatness over the next 20 years will shape the next 50 years of life in America and the world. I think most Members of Congress understand that how we work through this business of trying to create a united, democratic Europe and a relationship between NATO and Russia, that that will have a lot to do with the way we live in the next 50 years.

But we must understand that our neighbors to the south of us are still our greatest opportunity for the future. All but one of them are democracies. They are committed to free market economics. Other people around the world are looking to them, and we cannot pass up the chance to build closer trade ties with them. This will benefit America and will help us to deal, as I said, not just with economic matters but with political matters, with environmental matters, with a whole host of other issues. So I implore you to do what you can to help us get this done this year.

Beyond that, we have to pass a balanced budget plan that still has a diplomatic budget for the United States. We have continued to lower our spending on diplomacy dramatically, in a way that I think has been very counterproductive for our interests. Our request is simply to give us one penny of every Federal dollar to promote peace, to fight problems like drug trafficking and terrorism, nuclear proliferation, and to meet our obligations to the international community through the World Bank, the IMF, the other international financial institutions.

My budget does reverse a downward spiral in foreign affairs spending that's been going on a long time. But you know, our Embassies around the world are working around the clock. We've had to close a lot of our consulates. We've had to weaken the efforts that we were making to help American firms win contracts and protect intellectual property rights and fight unfair business practices. We live in an interdependent world. We cannot afford to say that we just simply will see the United States Government quit the field. And I feel very strongly about this. I know that many of you do. But I ask you to help us do that. It's not a big deal in the budget, but it's a part that always, always gets cut, and it's not in our interest to cut it.

The last thing I would like to do is to ask you, as I have before, to help us finish the job of welfare reform. Over the last 4 years, with 11½ million new jobs in the economy, about 2¼ million people moved off welfare. That's the largest reduction in the welfare rolls in history. There are now 4.6 percent of the population, about 10 million people, on public assistance. That is below the historic average since 1972. From 1972 to 1990 the historic average was 4.8 percent of the population on public assistance. In 1994 we got up to 5.4 percent. So in a booming economy, we got down to 4.6 percent, and of that, 2.25 million people who have moved off welfare, approximately a million of them moved into jobs. Depending on whose study you read, the average welfare family has between 2.3 and 2.8 people. There are very few families where there's a single mother with a zillion kids. It's mostly one child or two children in the families.

Now, in the new law, the new law says that the States can let people who are able-bodied stay on welfare for 5 years and no longer; that they're not supposed to stay on welfare more than 2 years at a pop without being in the work force; that the States can establish sort

of a contingency fund of about 20 percent to take care of people who are not physically or mentally able to work or who live in areas of very high unemployment.

It is obvious to me that if you look at all the studies—and the Council of Economic Advisers gave me a report on this, by the way, estimating that of the 2¼ million people that moved off the welfare rolls, about half of them moved off because of the good economy, about 30 percent of them moved off because 43 States were making extra efforts to move people from welfare to work, and about 20 percent of them moved off for—we don't know why—maybe because there was a 50 percent increase in child support payments, collections. And that will always lift some people off welfare. Maybe there are other reasons.

But the point I'm trying to make is that to meet the requirements of this new law, which is graduated in the standards that it applies to these timetables I just mentioned, we have to move another million people into the work force from the welfare rolls in the next 4 years. And there is a law that requires it, so we have to do it whether or not the private economy produces 11½ million jobs.

Now, five companies, including members of this organization, Monsanto, Sprint—who else— Federal Express, United Airlines, and Burger King, I think, agreed to head up a national coalition to get other companies to hire people from welfare to work. If you look at what's been done in Kansas City, you see that every State has the option to offer companies the welfare check as a cash subsidy for people who will pay well above the minimum wage as an employment and training subsidy. We're trying to get more small businesses into this. We are also trying to pass through Congress a 50 percent tax credit for salaries of up to $10,000 a year, tied much more tightly than any of these jobs tax credits have in the past to just people who move from public assistance—that is, from welfare to work, or single men who can't get welfare who move from food stamps to work.

There are a lot of things which can be done which lower the marginal cost to companies of hiring new people. But in the end this must be assumed as a mission by business people. You know, we've all complained for years that the welfare system leaves people on it that are permanently dependent, and they get used to receiving a check and don't go to work. Well, the truth is, that was never true for half the people. For half the people, the welfare system worked just fine. They got in a tough spot; they needed a little help; they got the help; and they got off welfare and they went on with their lives. But it is true that about half the people were more or less permanently dependent on it. Those are the ones that will be harder to place. So we've got to get another million people, and they're going to be harder to place. And we have got to have your help.

So that's the last thing I will say. I want you to help us balance the budget. I want you to support the education standards movement, not just in the Congress but asking the States that you operate in to embrace these tests, not letting anybody run away. I want you to help us continue to lead the world with fast-track and a decent diplomatic budget. And I want every one of you to ask yourselves personally, what can we do in our company to end the cycle of welfare dependency? If we do this we will have done a thing of historic significance for the American people, because it will end the culture of poverty. There will always be people who are out of work, but no one will be looked at as a permanent dependent of the State if they're able-bodied, if you do your part and we do ours.

Thank you very much.

NOTE: The President spoke at 10:32 a.m. in the ballroom at the Park Hyatt Hotel. In his remarks, he referred to Larry Bossidy, Business Council chairman, and President Eduardo Frei of Chile.

Statement on the Domestic Reduction in Deaths From AIDS
February 27, 1997

I was greatly encouraged by today's report from the Centers for Disease Control and Prevention on the historic reduction in the number of Americans dying of AIDS, further evidence that this terrible epidemic is beginning to yield to our sustained national public health investment in AIDS research, prevention, and care.

In these last 4 years, we have steadily increased our national commitment to fighting HIV and AIDS. We have increased funding for the programs by more than 50 percent, developed the first-ever national AIDS strategy, accelerated approval of successful new AIDS drugs by the Food and Drug Administration, strengthened and focused the Office of AIDS Research at the National Institutes of Health, and created a White House Office of National AIDS Policy.

We have made good progress, but it is also clear that the AIDS epidemic is not over. We must continue to press ahead if we are to meet our ultimate goal—the end to this epidemic, a cure for those who are living with HIV, and a vaccine to protect everyone from this virus.

That is why I am so pleased that the Department of Health and Human Services is today releasing another $202 million in funds under the Ryan White Comprehensive AIDS Resources Emergency Act to provide high-quality treatment to people living in 49 U.S. cities. Funds for the CARE act have increased 158 percent over the last 4 years and the number of cities receiving this assistance has grown from 26 to 49. While we will continue to care for those who are already sick, we must also sustain our commitment to prevention. The only way that we can assure that a person will not die of AIDS is to make sure they don't become infected with HIV in the first place.

Today's report is very good news, but we must not relax our efforts. In the months and years ahead, we must continue to work together as a nation to further our progress against this deadly epidemic, and while we do so, we must remember that every person who is living with HIV or AIDS is someone's son or daughter, brother or sister, parent or grandparent. They deserve our respect and they need our love.

Message to the Congress on Continuation of the National Emergency With Respect to Cuba
February 27, 1997

To the Congress of the United States:

Section 202(d) of the National Emergencies Act (50 U.S.C. 1622(d)) provides for the automatic termination of a national emergency unless, prior to the anniversary date of its declaration, the President publishes in the *Federal Register* and transmits to the Congress a notice stating that the emergency is to continue in effect beyond the anniversary date. In accordance with this provision, I have sent the enclosed notice, stating that the emergency declared with respect to the Government of Cuba's destruction of two unarmed U.S.-registered civilian aircraft in international airspace north of Cuba on February 24, 1996, is to continue in effect beyond March 1, 1997, to the *Federal Register* for publication.

WILLIAM J. CLINTON

The White House,
February 27, 1997.

NOTE: The notice is listed in Appendix D at the end of this volume.

Remarks on the Initiative To Protect Youth From Tobacco
February 28, 1997

Thank you, Anna Santiago, for the power of your example and for that very fine introduction. I want to thank all the young people who are here, the advocates who are here, the Members of Congress who are here who have championed this battle for so long. Especially, I thank the Vice President, Secretary Shalala for what they have done.

And of course, I want to have a special word of thanks to David Kessler. I think he's had a bigger impact on the lives and health and the future of the American people than any person who ever held the job of FDA Commissioner before him, and I thank him very much. Because of David Kessler, we have been able to undertake this initiative to protect our young people from tobacco. Because of your actions over the last 6 years, more AIDS and cancer patients are getting better drugs faster, as well; more people are getting better information on their food labels; every American can go to bed knowing that the food on their tables, the medicines in their cabinets are safe. You've left us a great legacy. All Americans should be grateful to you, and we'll do our best to replace you. The Vice President and I would like to be invited to Yale from time to time to give a speech. [*Laughter*]

Let me say that the reason we're all here today is to ensure that Anna and all the young people behind me, and the young people all across America for whom they stand today, have a chance to live out their dreams. They can only do that if they choose positive and healthy lifestyles and if we give them the support they need to make those choices. That's why the number one goal of the drug strategy we announced earlier this week is to motivate our children to reject illegal drugs.

Most of us have an instinctive urge to protect our young people from danger. We teach them to look both ways before crossing the street. We tell them not to touch a hot stove. We make sure they bundle up before going out in the cold. We should wrap that same protective arm around them when it comes to resisting smoking and the advertising and marketing of cigarettes.

More Americans die every year from smoking-related diseases than from AIDS, car accidents, murders, suicides, and fires combined. Today it's estimated that 4½ million of our children and adolescents smoke. Another 1 million use smokeless tobacco. The problem is getting worse. Smoking rates among eighth graders have risen 50 percent in the last 6 years. One out of every three young people who picks up this deadly habit will have their lives shortened from the terrible diseases caused by smoking. As parents, as leaders, as citizens, all of us have a moral obligation to do what we can to protect them. That's why last August the FDA took bold action to protect our children from the dangers of tobacco. We knew it would be a tough battle, but the health and well-being of our children are worth that. We set a goal of reducing tobacco use by children and adolescents by 50 percent over 7 years. To do that, we initiated the Nation's first-ever comprehensive effort to restrict access and limit the appeal of tobacco to children.

Today is the first day that some of these rules take effect, quite appropriately on David Kessler's last day on the Federal payroll. First, we're making the law of the land what is already the law in every State: no sale of tobacco products to anyone under age 18. Second, we're now requiring age verification by photo ID for anyone under the age of 27 for the purchase of tobacco products. From now on, in every store in America, our children will be told, "No ID, no sale." By requiring ID checks for people under 27, store clerks and managers will no longer have to guess the age of those seeking to buy cigarettes.

Studies show that minors succeed in buying cigarettes over the counter nearly 70 percent of the time. That simply must stop. With these new requirements, we'll help to keep cigarettes out of reach of our young people while giving store clerks and managers a tool they need to make sure they're not inadvertently violating the law by selling to minors.

Before we came out here, Secretary Shalala asked Anna if all of her efforts and all of these efforts were having any impact in reducing the tendency of her peers to smoke. And she said, "Yeah, a lot of them are quitting because it's too much hassle now." [*Laughter*] That's the idea. [*Laughter*] That's good.

Over the last 3 weeks, we've conducted massive education campaigns to let retailers know how they can comply with these new rules. We've even prepared this new guide, "A Retailer's Guide to the New Federal Regulations"— appealing advertising, multi-color. [*Laughter*] This has been made available to 500,000 retailers around the country. I want every retailer and every community across our Nation to join with us in this important effort.

Parents must continue to be the first line of defense, but all the rest of us have to make these rules work, and the retailers can play a major role. I honestly believe the overwhelming majority of them want to do so, and most of them are parents too. They have children too. We have a common interest in doing this job together. And we hope this guide will help them to achieve that goal.

Cigarettes are still legal for adults. If they want to smoke, they can do so. But we have now clearly as a nation drawn a line where our children are concerned. We have done it together. We are committed together. And now we must make it real together.

Thank you very much.

NOTE: The President spoke at 10:47 a.m. in the Roosevelt Room at the White House. In his remarks, he referred to Anna Santiago, Campaign for Tobacco Free Kids 1996 Advocate of the Year.

Statement on the Death of Peggy Browning
February 28, 1997

Hillary and I were saddened to learn of the death of Peggy Browning. Through her devotion to the law and determination in encouraging fair labor practices, Peggy contributed greatly to constructive and harmonious labor relations in this country. Her distinguished career was marked by compassion, good judgment, and, especially in recent months, courage. Her dedicated service will be sorely missed. Our prayers and sympathies are with her family at this time.

Statement on the Third Anniversary of the Brady Act
February 28, 1997

Today marks the third anniversary of the implementation of the Brady act—one of the most effective public safety measures ever.

The facts speak for themselves. Earlier this week, I announced that during its first 28 months, the Brady act prevented more than 186,000 felons, fugitives, and stalkers from buying a handgun. Every month the Brady act blocks an average of 6,600 illegal over-the-counter gun sales, with indicted or convicted felons constituting more than 70 percent of the rejections.

These statistics should end any remaining doubt that might exist. The Brady act is working.

This important public safety measure is the result of the tireless efforts of two courageous Americans, Jim and Sarah Brady. The Bradys have waged a moral and political battle to save lives and to keep handguns out of the hands of criminals. Their dedication to ending gun violence and making our streets safer is an inspiration to law enforcement and all Americans. Last year, I was deeply honored to bestow upon Jim the Presidential Medal of Freedom, the highest honor our Nation can bestow on a citizen.

I look forward to working with the Bradys to pass my anti-gang and youth violence legislation, which will require child safety locks for all handguns and apply the Brady act to anyone who has committed a violent juvenile offense.

NOTE: Public Law 103–159, "To provide for a waiting period before the purchase of a handgun, and for the establishment of a national instant criminal background check system to be contacted by firearms dealers before the transfer of any firearm," approved November 30, 1993, took effect on February 28, 1994.

Statement on Signing International Population Assistance Program Legislation
February 28, 1997

Today I am pleased to sign into law H.J. Res. 36, which approves a Presidential finding related to international population programs. Approval of this joint resolution permits the release on March 1 of funds previously appropriated for international population assistance programs administered by the U.S. Agency for International Development (USAID). In making these funds available without further delay we are assuring that these programs will continue to serve the many millions of women and men whose health and well-being—and ability to plan their own futures—depend on family planning services supported by USAID. Moreover, we are underscoring the indisputable fact that family planning reduces abortion—as best evidenced by significant declines in abortion rates as family planning services are becoming available in Russia and Central and Eastern Europe.

The passage of this joint resolution at the opening of the 105th Congress is particularly gratifying as it signifies what we can accomplish by working together—Democrats and Republicans. By agreeing to secure the timely release of these funds, we are assuring that the United States will continue to lead the world in providing voluntary family planning assistance. More importantly, we are helping the women of the world to prevent millions of unintended pregnancies, permit the healthy spacing of births, prevent the spread of sexually transmitted diseases, including HIV/AIDS, reduce recourse to abortion, and avert deaths from childbirth that often leave infants and their siblings motherless.

It is clear to me—and I am delighted that a strong bipartisan group of legislators in the House and Senate has joined in affirming the view—that family planning is a key element of our comprehensive strategy to improve women's health and station in life, and to increase child survival rates. By their votes, Members of Congress have shown their concern for the well-being of the poorest families around the globe.

WILLIAM J. CLINTON

The White House,
February 28, 1997.

NOTE: H.J. Res. 36, approved February 28, was assigned Public Law No. 105–3.

Memorandum on Delegation of Responsibility for Defense Acquisition Management
February 28, 1997

Memorandum for the Director of the Office of Management and Budget

Subject: Delegation of Responsibility for Submitting a Legislative Proposal Pursuant to Section 809(e) of the National Defense Authorization Act for Fiscal Year 1997

By the authority vested in me as President by the Constitution and laws of the United States of America, including the National Defense Authorization Act for Fiscal Year 1997

(Public Law 104–201) ("Act") and section 301 of title 3 of the United States Code, I hereby delegate to you the responsibility for submitting a legislative proposal to the Congress as required under section 809(e) of the Act.

You are authorized and directed to publish this memorandum in the *Federal Register*.

WILLIAM J. CLINTON

NOTE: This memorandum was not received for publication in the *Federal Register*.

The President's Radio Address
March 1, 1997

Good morning. Today I want to talk about what we must do to strengthen our effort to keep drugs away from our neighborhoods and out of our children's lives.

First, we must fight drugs before they reach our borders and keep them out of America. This is a battle we must fight together with other nations. Every year the President is legally required to certify whether other nations are doing their part. Yesterday I accepted Secretary of State Madeleine Albright's recommendation to certify Mexico, to certify that Mexico is cooperating with us in this fight.

Mexican President Zedillo is fighting a tough, uphill battle against the drug cartels which corrupt Mexico's law enforcement agencies. But President Zedillo has taken brave action, firing more than 1,200 tainted officials, extraditing criminals for the first time, passing tough laws, arresting his own drug czar for corruption. In the past year, their seizures of marijuana, co-

caine, and heroin are up, drug-related arrests have increased, and eradication efforts have reached record levels.

Make no mistake about it; Mexico has a serious drug problem. But Mexico's leaders recognize that problem, and they have the will to fight it. We must do whatever we can to give them the means to succeed. Stamping out the drug trade is a long-term battle. It won't be won overnight. We will continue to press our Mexican partners to take tough action that will protect all our people from drugs.

Stopping drugs at their source is a critical part of the antidrug strategy I announced earlier this week. My balanced budget pays for the largest antidrug effort ever. Under the leadership of our national drug czar, General Barry McCaffrey, who's here with me at the radio address this morning, this plan will crack down on drug dealers and help parents teach their children just how dangerous drugs are. We must give our children the straight facts. They need to hear a constant drumbeat from all of us: Drugs are wrong; drugs are illegal; drugs can kill you. The more children know about how dangerous drugs are, the less likely they are to use them. Our drug strategy includes an unprecedented national advertising campaign to get out the facts and shape the attitudes of young people about drugs.

And we must do more to sever the dangerous connection between illegal drugs and violent crime. Illegal drugs are involved with the vast majority of violent crimes in America: drug dealers carrying guns, violent criminals on drugs, and out-of-control gang wars over drug-trafficking turf. One million Americans are arrested every year for breaking the drug laws. Two-thirds of all the men in State prisons have abused drugs regularly.

Unfortunately, most of the people who enter jail as drug addicts leave jail still addicted or about to become addicts again. When criminals on parole or ex-convicts out of jail go back on drugs, the chances are enormously high they will commit new crimes. According to some experts, 60 percent of all the heroin and cocaine sold in America is sold to people on bail, parole, or probation. Two-thirds of prisoners with a history of heroin or cocaine use who are released without treatment are back on drugs within just 3 months. We must break this cycle of crime and drugs once and for all.

Last fall Congress passed my proposal to require drug testing and treatment for prison inmates and convicts on parole. Our prisons must not be illegal drug markets, and anyone given a chance to go straight and live a better life must be absolutely drug-free. The bill I signed said to the States, we want to continue helping you build prisons, but if you want the money to do that, you must start drug testing prisoners and parolees.

In December I announced Justice Department guidelines to help States meet this requirement. The guidelines are straightforward.

By March 1, 1998, one year from today, every State must submit to the Attorney General a clearly defined, comprehensive plan to test prisoners and parolees, to treat those who need it and punish those who go back on drugs.

Today I'm announcing that I am sending all 50 Governors a letter to make it clear that General McCaffrey and Attorney General Reno are prepared to help every State get this job done. We'll provide guidance and resources, experts, technical assistance, access to new technology. We'll give that to every State that needs help in developing its plans. At the same time, this, too, should be perfectly clear: Any State without a prisoner and parolee drug testing plan one year from today will lose Federal prison assistance until a plan is submitted. We want to help States build the prison space they need, but we will not help to build prisons that tolerate drugs by turning a blind eye.

The Federal Government and State governments must work together as partners to get this done. It's time to say to inmates, if you stay on drugs, you'll stay in jail; if you want out of jail, you have to get off drugs. It's time to say to parolees, if you go back on drugs, you'll go back to jail; if you want to stay out of jail, stay off drugs.

We must fight drugs on every front, on our streets and in our schools, at our borders and in our homes. Every American must accept this responsibility. There is no more insidious threat to a good future than illegal drugs. I'm counting on all of you to help us win the fight against them.

Thanks for listening.

NOTE: The address was recorded at 4:28 p.m. on February 28 in the Roosevelt Room at the White House for broadcast at 10:06 a.m. on March 1. The Presidential determination of February 28 on certification for major narcotics producing and transit countries is listed in Appendix D at the end of this volume.

Remarks Prior to Discussions With Chairman Yasser Arafat of the Palestinian Authority and an Exchange With Reporters
March 3, 1997

President Clinton. Good morning. I'm glad to welcome Chairman Arafat here. This is our sixth meeting, and I'm hopeful that it will be as productive as our previous ones have. You will remember the last time he was here, last fall, we were facing a very difficult situation with regard to Hebron, and because of the efforts that he made in working with the Israelis, an agreement was reached, a timetable was established, and we're moving forward. And I'm hopeful that we can keep doing that. This is also a difficult moment, but I think we can work through it and go forward, and I appreciate his coming to see me.

Middle East Peace Process

Q. Mr. Chairman, are the new settlements designed by the Israelis to make the annexation a fait accompli of East Jerusalem?

Chairman Arafat. Not only for Jerusalem but also for Bethlehem, because their target is to squeeze and to isolate Jerusalem but, at the same time, to build the settlements at the entrance of Bethlehem, to replace Har Homa, our capital—in the city of Bethlehem during the 2,000 years of our celebration for our Jesus Christ.

Q. What are you going to do about it?

Chairman Arafat. I am sure that His Excellency will push for—to prevent it.

Q. Mr. President, what do you think about the settlement?

President Clinton. Well, what I think about the settlement is what I think about all these issues. You know, the important thing is for these people on both sides to be building confidence and working together. And so I would prefer the decision not have been made, because I don't think it builds confidence, I think it builds mistrust. And I wish that it had not been made.

Q. Mr. President, the Jerusalem Embassy Act declares that the United States should recognize Jerusalem as Israel's capital. Is Jerusalem Israel's capital, and does Israel have the right to build within the municipal boundaries of Jerusalem?

President Clinton. Well, you know, I've been asked that question a lot, and I'm going to give you the same answer I always give. I do not believe, now that the parties have reached the agreement they reached in 1993 and they have made this the final status issue, that the United States can serve any useful purpose by saying, or especially by doing, anything which seems to prejudge what should be a final status issue between the parties. I think that would be a big mistake.

1996 Campaign Financing

Q. Vice President Gore, did you solicit money in the White House, Mr. Gore, during the campaign?

Vice President Gore. I'll talk with you all later, not during this.

President Clinton. Nice tie, Ron [Ron Fournier, Associated Press].

Q. Thank you. Got that in Arkansas.

Storms in Arkansas

Q. Do you want to say anything about the storms?

Q. Are you going to Arkansas?

President Clinton. I'm going down tomorrow. I'm very concerned about it. I talked over the weekend to—I talked to the Governor twice and the mayor of Little Rock and Representative Malone in Arkadelphia. You know, it's a bad situation. More people were killed in 18 hours than in the 12 years I was Governor, I believe, combined, in the tornadoes.

Q. Did you know anybody that was hurt or killed?

President Clinton. Not to my knowledge, although I did recognize a couple of people on television last night who had lost their homes. One man said—did you see that—where he had given away a couch to the Goodwill Industries, and whoever got the couch had their home destroyed and the couch was blown back into his house. [*Laughter*]

Q. You're going down——

President Clinton. I recognized three or four people on television. But I'm going down there. I'll see tomorrow.

Chelsea Clinton's Birthday

Q. You had a good birthday celebration?

President Clinton. Wonderful. Chelsea had a good birthday. New York was good.

NOTE: The President spoke at 10:12 a.m. in the Oval Office at the White House. In his remarks, he referred to Gov. Mike Huckabee of Arkansas; Mayor Jim Dailey of Little Rock, AR; and State Representative Percy Malone. A tape was not available for verification of the content of these remarks.

Remarks at the Unveiling Ceremony for the Coalition for America's Children Public Service Announcement
March 3, 1997

I want to thank all those who have been a part of this. Alex Kroll, thank you for what you said and for reminding us that we're about the business of helping parents, not disrespecting the difficulties they face. Christine Benero, thank you. Eva Kasten, the executive vice president of the Advertising Council, thank you. I thank the Benton Foundation, the AT&T Foundation, the Packard Foundation. I'd like to thank the people in our administration probably most directly involved in helping our children who are here today, Secretary Riley, Secretary Shalala, and Harris Wofford, the head of the Corporation for National Service.

But most of all, I want to thank Bradley Pine and Lonzo Warren for coming here to share their story. Their relationship is a powerful example of what could be done all over America if we move from vague rhetoric to specific action directed at helping and supporting all of our children. Just think of what would happen in this country if every single child who needed a mentor had one. Think of what would happen if every person out there who is willing to volunteer to help knew where to go and how to do it. The public service message we just saw, that Hillary and I were honored to participate in, is simply designed to remind every American that there are children out there who need our support and to tell every American who wants to serve that there is a way to serve and we will help you do it.

We know that being a parent is the most difficult and important job in the world, and we know that everyone has to help. Hillary has been working on these children's issues since before I met her, a long time ago now, and I think that the book that she wrote did capture the image of the village raising our children. But it should not be allowed to obscure the fact that what that really means is that each and every one of us has a personal responsibility to do our part. And also, thanks to this effort, it will be easier for people to understand how to exercise that responsibility.

I'm especially fond of the work that we have done in this regard. We've done all we could to encourage citizen service. We now have more than 50,000 young people working in AmeriCorps, earning money to go to college. Many, many of them are helping our children in supportive ways.

Last summer, we launched our America Reads program to try to mobilize one million volunteer tutors in America to make sure that by the year 2000 every single 8-year-old in this country can read independently and will have a chance to make the most of his or her education. Today I am pleased to announce that Scholastic Books is donating one million books to help us reach that goal. We need more companies like Scholastic Books to give more Americans the opportunity to serve.

In January I was proud to stand right here with President Bush and General Colin Powell and former Secretary of Housing and Urban Development Henry Cisneros to announce that we are convening the first-ever Presidents' Summit of Service in April in Philadelphia to bring together business, religious, community leaders committed to support citizen service with resources and volunteers. With their help, I hope we can make the plea we make in this public service announcement a reality for tens of thousands of more people in the United States.

This public service announcement is just what it seems to be. It seeks to help in mobilizing a volunteer force of Americans. It reflects the wisdom that no impersonal bureaucracy can ever replace the magic that we saw here between

Bradley and Lonzo or the feeling that Lonzo expressed for his own family who are here with him today. What we can do is to make it possible for more things like that to happen and to give our children the basic supports they need to make it happen. But in the end, we must make this vast, big complicated society of ours more of a society in which we all feel that we should volunteer, and, like Bradley, we know we're going to be better off for doing it. We'll get more out of it than we give. We have to create the networks to facilitate that kind of voluntarism.

The public service announcement, as you saw, gives people a number to call, a website to visit, to learn about organizations in their very own communities where they can volunteer their time, to become a reading tutor or a math coach or a mentor to a child in need. Beginning today, anyone visiting the White House home page on the Internet will be able to connect to the coalition's website with just a click of the mouse and find out what they can do to help.

The more people this message reaches, the more children will be helped. So far, some of our biggest television, cable, and radio networks have committed to air this message during times when it will have the best chance of inspiring the largest number of people. Newsweek, the New York Times, and People magazine will also run the message in their pages, and movie-goers will see it in theaters all over the country, thanks to promotion slide and cinema advertisers. This is a very good start, but let me encourage other media organizations around the country to help to make sure this message is heard by as many people as possible, to help to work with us to encourage the spirit of service in America, to strengthen our families, to improve the lives of our children one at a time.

Whenever you think about what else we can do, just think of Bradley and Lonzo and multiply it by millions and imagine the America we can make together.

Thank you. God bless you.

NOTE: The President spoke at 12:17 p.m. in the East Room at the White House. In his remarks, he referred to Alex Kroll, chairman, Advertising Council; Christine Benero, chair, Coalition for America's Children; Lonzo Warren, a 15-year-old high school student from Hyattsville, MD, and his mentor, Bradley R. Pine; and Gen. Colin L. Powell, USA (ret.), former Chairman, Joint Chiefs of Staff.

Message to the Congress Transmitting the Second Supplementary Canada-United States Social Security Agreement
March 3, 1997

To the Congress of the United States:

Pursuant to section 233(e)(1) of the Social Security Act (the "Act"), as amended by the Social Security Amendments of 1977 (Public Law 95–216, 42 U.S.C. 433(e)(1)), I transmit herewith the Second Supplementary Agreement Amending the Agreement Between the Government of the United States of America and the Government of Canada with Respect to Social Security (the Second Supplementary Agreement). The Second Supplementary Agreement, signed at Ottawa on May 28, 1996, is intended to modify certain provisions of the original United States-Canada Social Security Agreement signed at Ottawa March 11, 1981, which was amended once before by the Supplementary Agreement of May 10, 1983.

The United States-Canada Social Security Agreement is similar in objective to the social security agreements with Austria, Belgium, Finland, France, Germany, Greece, Ireland, Italy, Luxembourg, The Netherlands, Norway, Portugal, Spain, Sweden, Switzerland, and the United Kingdom. Such bilateral agreements provide for limited coordination between the U.S. and foreign social security systems to eliminate dual social security coverage and taxation, and to help prevent the loss of benefit protection that can occur when workers divide their careers between two countries.

The Second Supplementary Agreement provides Canada with a specific basis to enter into a mutual assistance arrangement with the United States. This enables each Governments' Social

Security agency to assist the other in enhancing the administration of their respective foreign benefits programs. The Social Security Administration has benefited from a similar mutual assistance arrangement with the United Kingdom. The Second Supplementary Agreement will also make a number of minor revisions in the Agreement to take into account other changes in U.S. and Canadian law that have occurred in recent years.

The United States-Canada Social Security Agreement, as amended, would continue to contain all provisions mandated by section 233 and other provisions that I deem appropriate to carry out the provisions of section 233, pursuant to section 233(c)(4) of the Act.

I also transmit for the information of the Congress a report prepared by the Social Security Administration explaining the key points of the Second Supplementary Agreement, along with a paragraph-by-paragraph explanation of the effect of the amendments on the Agreement. Annexed to this report is the report required by section 233(e)(1) of the Act on the effect of the Agreement, as amended, on income and expenditures of the U.S. Social Security program and the number of individuals affected by the amended Agreement. The Department of State and the Social Security Administration have recommended the Second Supplementary Agreement and related documents to me.

I commend the United States-Canada Second Supplementary Social Security Agreement and related documents.

WILLIAM J. CLINTON

The White House,
March 3, 1997.

Remarks Announcing the Prohibition on Federal Funding for Cloning of Human Beings and an Exchange With Reporters
March 4, 1997

The President. Good morning. I'm glad to be joined this morning by the Vice President; Secretary Shalala; Dr. Harold Varmus, the head of NIH; Dr. Harold Shapiro, the president of Princeton and the Chairman of our Bioethics Advisory Commission; and Dr. Jack Gibbons, the President's adviser on science and technology, all of whom know a lot about and care a lot about this issue we are discussing today.

The recent breakthrough in animal cloning is one that could yield enormous benefits, enabling us to reproduce the most productive strains of crop and livestock, holding out the promise of revolutionary new medical treatments and cures, helping to unlock the greatest secrets of the genetic code. But like the splitting of the atom, this is a discovery that carries burdens as well as benefits.

Science often moves faster than our ability to understand its implications. That is why we have a responsibility to move with caution and care to harness the powerful forces of science and technology so that we can reap the benefit while minimizing the potential danger.

This new discovery raises the troubling prospect that it might someday be possible to clone human beings from our own genetic material. There is much about cloning that we still do not know. But this much we do know: Any discovery that touches upon human creation is not simply a matter of scientific inquiry, it is a matter of morality and spirituality as well.

My own view is that human cloning would have to raise deep concerns, given our most cherished concepts of faith and humanity. Each human life is unique, born of a miracle that reaches beyond laboratory science. I believe we must respect this profound gift and resist the temptation to replicate ourselves. At the very least, however, we should all agree that we need a better understanding of the scope and implications of this most recent breakthrough. Last week I asked our National Bioethics Advisory Commission, headed by President Harold Shapiro of Princeton, to conduct a thorough review of the legal and the ethical issues raised by this new cloning discovery and to recommend possible actions to prevent its abuse, reporting back to me by the end of May.

In the meantime, I am taking further steps to prevent human cloning. The Federal Government currently restricts the use of Federal funds for research involving human embryos. After reviewing these restrictions, our administration believes that there are loopholes that could allow the cloning of human beings if the technology were developed. Therefore, today I am issuing a directive that bans the use of any Federal funds for any cloning of human beings. Effective immediately, no Federal agency may support, fund, or undertake such activity.

Of course, a great deal of research and activity in this area is supported by private funds. That is why I am urging the entire scientific and medical community, every foundation, every university, every industry that supports work in this area, to heed the Federal Government's example. I'm asking for a voluntary moratorium on the cloning of human beings until our Bioethics Advisory Commission and our entire Nation have had a real chance to understand and debate the profound ethical implications of the latest advances.

As we gain a fuller understanding of this technology, we must proceed not just with caution but also with a conscience. By insisting that not a single taxpayer dollar supports human cloning and by urging a moratorium on all private research in this area, we can ensure that as we move forward on this issue, we weigh the concerns of faith and family and philosophy and values, not merely of science alone.

Thank you very much.

1996 Campaign Financing

Q. Mr. President, how do you think the Vice President did in his rebuttal yesterday, and do you agree with him that you two are in a separate category in terms of fundraising from Federal property?

The President. Well, I agree with—number one, I thought he did very well, and I agree with the statement he made, and I agree that what he did was legal. But I also agree with the decision that he made.

I would remind you that we knew we had a very stiff challenge. We were fighting a battle not simply for our reelection but over the entire direction of the country for years to come and the most historic philosophical battle we've had in America in quite a long time over the direction of the budget, over our commitment to education, over whether we would dismantle large chunks of our environmental regulations and our public health regulations. It was a significant thing for America, and we knew that

we were going to be outspent and outraised, but we knew we had to do everything we could to at least be competitive enough to get our message out. In fact, that is what happened. We were outspent and outraised by more than $200 million, but thanks to the Vice President's efforts and those of thousands of others and a million small donors, we were able to get our message out.

Q. But did you overdo it in a sense that now you're regretting, obviously—you must be—all the things that have happened since then?

The President. The only thing I regret—and I regret this very much, as I have said—is that a decision was made, which I did not approve of or know about, to stop the rigorous review of checks coming in to the Democratic Committee so that some funds were accepted which should not have been accepted. I regret that very much. And I have said that I feel—as the titular head of the Democratic Party, I feel responsible for that. I think all of us in the line of command are. And I was very proud of Governor Romer and Mr. Grossman and the entire Democratic Committee. When they made a full accounting, they went over all the checks, they did something as far as I know no party has done in modern history, and they gave back money that was not only clearly illegal but that was questionable, and they're going on. I regret that very much, because that never should have happened in the first place.

For the rest, I think the Vice President said he thought that some changes were in order, but I don't regret the fact that we worked like crazy to raise enough money to keep from being rolled over by the biggest juggernaut this country had seen in a very long time. And I think it would have been a very bad thing for the American people if that budget had passed, if their plans to dramatically dismantle the environmental protections and the public health protections the country had passed, and I am glad we stood up to it. I'm glad we fought the battles of '95 and '96, and I'm glad it came out the way it did. And we had to be aggressive and strong within the law, and I'm very proud of what the Vice President did.

Q. Don't you think it puts the Vice President in a vulnerable——

Human Cloning

Q. Mr. President, what is the extent of your order today? How much funds—do you know how much funds were being spent toward this human cloning, if any?

The President. We attempted previously to have a ban on this, going back to '94, I believe. The nature of the new discovery raised the prospect that the technology was not covered specifically by the nature of the ban. So as far as I know, nothing is going on in Government-funded research. I just want to make sure that we keep it that way, because our research dollars are spread all across the country in different institutions.

With regard to the private sector, let me say that our staff here in the White House has been in touch with a number of people in the biotech industry, and they seem to be glad that we called and anxious to participate in a moratorium until we think through the implications of this.

I mean, I imagine a lot of you, not as journalists but in your own private homes, have sat around talking about this discovery in the last few days. I know we have in our home. And I just think that we need the best minds that we can bring to bear and the distinguished people on the bioethics advisory committee to think through this, tell us about what we may be missing about—if there's anything positive that could come from this, and also think through the other implications, how can we get the benefits of our deep desire to find any possible cure for any malady that's out there without raising the kind of ethical implications that, in effect, we're in the business where people are trying to play God or to replicate themselves.

1996 Campaign Financing

Q. Mr. President, Democrats and Republicans are bogged down in Congress over whether to conduct hearings on the fundraising issue. Do you want to see that happen, and would you so tell your Democrats, your fellow Democrats up on the Hill?

The President. My understanding is that the Democrats have no objection whatever to the hearings. They just believe that they ought not to go on forever and that they don't need to—they're disputing whether $6½ million needs to be spent. That's something that they need to work out among themselves.

I certainly have no objection to hearings. I've always assumed that they would occur, but I think that the American people are entitled to know that some prudence will be exercised in how much money is spent, because there's a lot of other things out there to be done, and we have the public's business to get on with as well, a lot of other issues that need to be dealt with. And what I'm hoping that we can do is to just reconcile how this is going to be dealt with and maybe spend some of that money to properly fund the Federal Election Commission so they can do the kind of audits they're supposed to do and do the job that they actually have the power to do on the books right now and get on with the big business, get on with balancing the budget, get on with passing the education program, get on with doing the other things that are out there for us to do. And so I'm going to do everything I can to facilitate that.

But it is a decision for the Senate and for the House—in the House—to decide how these hearings will proceed and how they will be funded. But I don't think anybody objects to having hearings. We want them to be fair. We want them to be bipartisan. We want them to be balanced. And as I understand it, the big fight in the Senate is, will there be a date certain for ending, and will there be a limit to how much is spent?

And let me say this: Whatever the hearings produce, in the end, the only real question is, will they produce campaign finance reform? Whatever they produce, will they produce campaign finance reform? I still believe that the only way for the Congress to really deal with this and any questions from the past is to change the system. And we have the McCain-Feingold bill out there. It's a good vehicle. I have endorsed it. I would happily sign it the way it is, but they may want to debate that in some way or another. But the main thing that I want to say again is that there is no excuse for not voting on and passing a good bipartisan campaign finance reform bill this year. There is no excuse. That is the main issue.

Thank you.

NOTE: The President spoke at 9:25 a.m. in the Oval Office at the White House. In his remarks, he referred to Gov. Roy Romer of Colorado, general chair, and Steve Grossman, national chair, Democratic National Committee.

Memorandum on the Prohibition on Federal Funding for Cloning of Human Beings
March 4, 1997

Memorandum for the Heads of Executive Departments and Agencies

Subject: Prohibition on Federal Funding for Cloning of Human Beings

Recent accounts of advances in cloning technology, including the first successful cloning of an adult sheep, raise important questions. They potentially represent enormous scientific breakthroughs that could offer benefits in such areas as medicine and agriculture. But the new technology also raises profound ethical issues, particularly with respect to its possible use to clone humans. That is why last week I asked our National Bioethics Advisory Commission to thoroughly review the legal and ethical issues associated with the use of this technology and report back to me in 90 days.

Federal funds should not be used for cloning of human beings. The current restrictions on the use of Federal funds for research involving human embryos do not fully assure this result. In December 1994, I directed the National Institutes of Health not to fund the creation of human embryos for research purposes. The Congress extended this prohibition in FY 1996 and FY 1997 appropriations bills, barring the Department of Health and Human Services from supporting certain human embryo research. However, these restrictions do not explicitly cover human embryos created for implantation and do not cover all Federal agencies. I want to make it absolutely clear that no Federal funds will be used for human cloning. Therefore, I hereby direct that no Federal funds shall be allocated for cloning of human beings.

WILLIAM J. CLINTON

Remarks on Surveying Tornado Damage and an Exchange With Reporters in Arkadelphia, Arkansas
March 4, 1997

The President. Ladies and gentlemen, first let me say that I very much appreciate the work that has been done here. I know this has been a very difficult thing, but I have been so impressed by the local officials, the volunteers, the police and fire personnel, the Army Reserve, the other military people. You've got a lot to be proud of.

I want to thank Governor Huckabee—and I see Mrs. Huckabee over there in a Red Cross jacket—for what they have done, and Congressman Jay Dickey, who came down with me today. I want to thank all the Arkansans who are part of our operation. In addition to James Lee Witt, I know that Mack McLarty and Bruce Lindsey and Craig Smith came down with me today. And we have a lot of people here representing our various agencies. Rodney Slater has been here since Sunday, and as I was walking up and down the streets, I heard several people

say, "Well, I don't want you to fix my building, but I would like a new road in some place or another in Clark County." [*Laughter*] So we'll do our best to behave on that.

I also have the new director of the Small Business Administration here, Aida Alvarez, who served in the Housing and Urban Development Department with me. And we're going to be working with Judge Runyan and Mayor Kolb and Senator Ross and Representative Malone and all the other local leaders here to try to help you get back on track.

You know, James Lee said this, but when I became President, one of the things that I wanted to do—and I never thought my native State would need it, but I wanted to make sure that when disaster strikes anywhere in America, the United States Government would do its part and would be there promptly and would stay for the long haul and would be concerned and be able to deal with problems that may look small in Washington but are as big as anything in life to people who face them when a disaster strikes. And I can't say enough about the work he's done. But I have to tell you, you know—he mentioned this—we've seen five 100-year floods in the Middle West like nothing I'd ever seen. We've seen flooding in the Southeast. We've worked on the aftermath of a hurricane in Florida. We saw the Pacific Northwest washed out. We've seen fires and floods and earthquakes in California. But nothing has quite affected me the way this has today, and I think it's because I've been coming to Arkadelphia for more than 40 years.

We flew over College Station in Saline County coming down here, and I spent an enormous amount of time in those places when I was Governor. And I look into the eyes of so many people here today, and I wish there were more I could say and do. But I can tell you this—I'll make you a little prediction. Within 2 years, what we're looking at today will look better than it did before the storm hit because of all of you, and we're going to do what we can to help you.

Let me just go over some details here. I've got a few notes—everybody makes fun—when I was Governor I never used notes, but now my memory is failing me, so I need notes. [*Laughter*] The disaster declaration I signed on Sunday provides for emergency aid, temporary housing, grants, and low interest loans. FEMA has set up an 800 number, and the people that are eligible for financial help will be getting it beginning just in the next couple of days. I think that since James Lee's been there, we've turned these checks around pretty quick. So I think there shouldn't be people in too much of a tight, within a matter of just a few days.

The Department of Defense is already helping, as all of you know, in clearing debris. The SBA can provide long-term, low-interest loans. I know for a lot of small-business people that seems like a losing proposition now, but I think if you look at the terms you will find them very helpful. I also know that the local banks here have gone out of their way to try to be helpful already and have sent very positive signals out in this community.

Let me just mention two other things, mostly for other parts of the State. Today we're making farmers also eligible in the affected counties for emergency low-interest loans. And as I told the

Governor coming down, the Labor Department will be providing some funds to the State which will enable people who have lost their jobs temporarily or—I hope not, but if it should happen—permanently because of this tornado, to be hired to help and be part of the cleanup so their families won't be without an income and so we can speed up the cleanup. And I hope that will be helpful.

The third thing I'd like to say is that we're looking here at a long-term process. I am, I must say, terrifically impressed with all the folks I've seen out here cleaning up, all the people from the utilities and the contractors and the football teams. I was walking down the street, I said, "I believe there's more brawn per square inch in this town today than any other place in America." We've got more physical strength here, and I've been very impressed.

But you look around at this destruction. It's going to be a long-term rebuilding process, not only for the individuals who lost their businesses but for this community. And a lot of thought has to go into this. Each and every person who lost a business will have to decide, "Well, what am I going to do? Am I going to rebuild here or not? Or, if I'm going to rebuild, am I going to do it somewhere else?" And the county has to decide what to do about the courthouse site. A lot of decisions have to be made.

And we have decided that what we should do is to put together a task force representing all the different departments in the Federal Government that could be of any help, that will be able to work with you over the long run. I don't want you to think that the Federal Government comes down here, there's an emergency, sends out a few checks, and then we walk away. So we're going to set up a long-term task force. We will be with you all the way. And again I will say, I predict that within a couple of years, Arkadelphia will be back stronger than ever and you will like what you see here. You will have to plan your own future. You will have to execute it. But we want to stay with you.

Let me also tell you that these storm centers—and you already know this, but I have to say this to people in other States who've been afflicted—if you've been looking at the television you have seen people literally buried in avalanches of water in Ohio, in Kentucky, and in West Virginia. Today I'm declaring a major disaster in Kentucky and Ohio because of the floods that are there, and we will begin to immediately help them. The Vice President and Mr. Witt are going to go to those two States tomorrow to view the damage and to report back to me.

The final thing I'd like to say is that when I heard about this, the first thing that struck me was not only the physical devastation but that the number of people who died here in the space of about 18 hours are equal—almost equal to the number of people who died from tornadoes in the entire 12 years that I had the honor of being Governor of Arkansas. And so Hillary and I said a prayer for those people and their families, and I would just like to ask that all the rest of us who were unscathed by this keep those folks in mind, as well as those who were injured and those who lost everything they had. They're all going to need our help.

There are people here who have come from other States already to help. And if we keep the right spirit and all of you keep the light in your eyes that I saw today when person after person after person said, "Well, we'll get over this. This is Arkansas. We know how to behave. We know what to do." You do know what to do, and I'll be honored to help you every step of the way. And I thank you for giving me the chance to share this with you today. As difficult as it is, I very much wanted to be here, and I'm glad I came.

Thank you.

1996 Campaign Financing

Q. Mr. President, a couple of questions on other topics. One question, apparently there is some effort on the Hill to get the legislation—Trent Lott and others have called for an independent counsel. Is that appropriate at this time?

The President. It's a legal question.

Q. OK, one other question——

The President. I have nothing else to say.

Q. Did the White House ever get a heads up from DOJ or from the FBI on the Chinese——

The President. I want to refer—ask them. Ask the White House. They're the appropriate person you're supposed to ask.

Q. Did you?

The President. No.

NOTE: The President spoke at 2:35 p.m. at the corner of Seventh and Clinton Streets. In his remarks, he referred to Gov. Mike Huckabee of Arkansas and his wife, Janet; Clark County Judge Grady Runyan; Mayor Mike Kolb of Arkadelphia; State Senator Mike Ross; and State Representative Percy Malone.

Statement on Senate Action on the Balanced Budget Amendment
March 4, 1997

I am pleased that the Senate has heeded the warnings of eminent economists and constitutional experts from across the political spectrum, and defeated the balanced budget constitutional amendment.

At the same time, let me be clear: While I oppose a constitutional amendment, I am committed to achieving the bipartisan goal of balancing the budget by 2002. Last year, I sent Congress a plan to balance the budget, and I submitted a balanced budget plan again a few weeks ago.

The constitutional amendment could have caused or worsened recessions, permitted a minority of legislators to hold the Nation's credit-worthiness hostage, involved unelected judges in spending and tax policy, and threatened Social Security and other vital benefits.

Now that the amendment vote has taken place, I call on Congress to join me in passing a plan to balance the budget by 2002 while protecting our values, strengthening education, and providing targeted tax relief to working families.

At the end of Congress' last session, we saw several instances of productive bipartisan cooperation. I hope that we can continue this spirit of bipartisanship and make progress for the American people by reaching agreement on a balanced budget plan this year. All it takes is their votes and my signature.

It's time to do the real work of balancing the budget.

Message to the Senate Transmitting the Hong Kong-United States Extradition Agreement With Documentation
March 3, 1997

To the Senate of the United States:

With a view to receiving the advice and consent of the Senate to ratification as a treaty, I transmit herewith the Agreement Between the Government of the United States of America and the Government of Hong Kong for the Surrender of Fugitive Offenders signed at Hong Kong on December 20, 1996 (hereinafter referred to as "the Agreement"). In addition, I transmit for the information of the Senate, the report of the Department of State with respect to the Agreement. As a treaty, this Agreement will not require implementing legislation.

This Agreement will, upon entry into force, enhance cooperation between the law enforcement communities of the United States and Hong Kong, and will provide a framework and basic protections for extraditions after the reversion of Hong Kong to the sovereignty of the People's Republic of China on July 1, 1997. Given the absence of an extradition treaty with the People's Republic of China, this Treaty would provide the means to continue an extradition relationship with Hong Kong after reversion and avoid a gap in law enforcement. It will thereby make a significant contribution to international law enforcement efforts.

The provisions in this Agreement follow generally the form and content of extradition treaties recently concluded by the United States. In addition, the Agreement contains several provisions specially designed in light of the particular status of Hong Kong. The Agreement's basic protections for fugitives are also made expressly applicable to fugitives surrendered by the two parties before the new treaty enters into force.

I recommend that the Senate give early and favorable consideration to the Agreement and give its advice and consent to its ratification as a treaty.

WILLIAM J. CLINTON

The White House,
March 3, 1997.

NOTE: This message was released by the Office of the Press Secretary on March 5.

Remarks on Signing the Memorandum on Child Safety Lock Devices for Handguns and an Exchange With Reporters
March 5, 1997

The President. Good morning. I'd like to welcome here Senators Biden and Boxer, Durbin and Feinstein, Kohl; Congressmen Conyers, Schumer, and Congresswoman Carolyn McCarthy; along with Deputy Attorney General Jamie Gorelick; Treasury's Under Secretary for Enforcement, Ray Kelly; our friends Jim and Sarah Brady; and members of the law enforcement community. Did I leave anyone from Congress out? Senators? Did I get everybody? Good.

Four years ago we made a commitment to take our streets back from crime and violence with a comprehensive plan: first, to put 100,000 community police officers on our streets, to put new, tough penalties on the books, to steer young people away from crime and gangs and drugs, to keep guns out of the hands of criminals with the assault weapons ban and the Brady bill. Last week I announced that the Brady bill has already stopped 186,000 felons, fugitives, and stalkers from purchasing handguns.

Repeatedly I have said that fighting the scourge of juvenile crime and violence will be my top law enforcement priority in the next 4 years. Two weeks ago I submitted to Congress my antigang and youth violence strategy. One of this bill's key provisions will require gun dealers to provide safety locks with every handgun they sell, to prevent unauthorized use by teenage criminals and to protect children too young to know what they're doing.

Today I announce a series of new steps we must take immediately to protect our children, our neighbors, and our police officers from tragedies caused by firearms in the wrong hands. First, we must keep guns out of the hands of children.

The Centers for Disease Control report that nearly 1.2 million children return from school to a home with no adult supervision but with a loaded and unlocked firearm. Easy access means deadly consequences. Children and teenagers cause over 10,000 unintentional shootings every year. Guns cause one in every four deaths of teenagers age 15 to 19. Last month the Centers for Disease Control reported that the rate of children from birth to age 14 who are killed by firearms in America is nearly 12 times higher than in 25 other industrialized countries combined.

America cannot tolerate this. Until Congress makes child safety locks the law of the land, we must do everything we can to prevent unauthorized firearms use.

I want to make sure the Federal Government is doing its part. Each year the Federal Government issues thousands of handguns to law enforcement agents. Unfortunately, we know all too well that even firearms issued to law enforcement are sometimes tragically misused. Today I am directing that every Federal agency shall require child safety locking devices with every handgun issued. The directive I'm about to sign requires every department and every agency to develop a plan to accomplish this commonsense safety measure and to implement it as soon as possible. And Congress should pass my proposal to require these locks with every handgun in the very near future. If it's good enough for law enforcement, it's good enough for all our citizens.

The second step we're taking today will make it harder for people to come to America, purchase weapons, and commit crimes against Americans. We were all shocked to learn of the foreign gunman who shot seven people on top of the Empire State Building, killing one of them, and then killing himself. He apparently bought this gun after living in a Florida motel for just 3 weeks. Federal law requires legal aliens to live at least 90 days in a State before they are allowed to purchase a handgun. But the application to buy a gun does not even ask how long an applicant has lived at his or her current address.

As a first step to reduce illegal handgun purchases by foreigners, today I'm announcing that the Bureau of Alcohol, Tobacco and Firearms will immediately require applicants to certify that they have been residents for at least 90 days in the State where they are trying to buy a gun. But this is not enough. I call on Congress to pass the bill sponsored by Senators Kennedy and Durbin and Congressman Schumer that will prohibit all foreign visitors from buying or carrying guns in the United States.

Finally, as we work to make all our people safer, we must never forget our special obligation to police officers, like those who are with me today, who risk their lives to protect us all. It is long past time for Congress to listen to America's law enforcement officers and ban cop-killer bullets once and for all.

I have sent this legislation to Congress twice before, and they failed to act. They should not delay this effort again. We don't need to study this issue any more to determine what specific materials can be used to make armor-piercing bullets. We need a simple test and a straightforward ban. If a bullet can tear through a bulletproof vest like a hot knife through butter, it should be against the law, and that is the bottom line. These bullets are designed for one purpose only, to kill police officers. They have no place on our streets.

Three simple steps to make our children, our streets, and our law enforcement officers safer: child safety locks on handguns, new rules to prevent foreign criminals from buying guns in the United States, a straightforward ban on cop-killer bullets. I will do my part. I thank the Members of Congress who are here especially for their leadership, and I ask the Congress to act on this important legislation.

Now, let me sign this order here, and then I'll answer any questions you have.

[At this point, the President signed the memorandum.]

Thank you.

Assault Weapons Ban

Q. The police were outgunned in Los Angeles. Do you think there's also a problem with police departments not having enough firepower?

The President. There could be, but I think the real problem is—the way we sought to deal with that is by dealing with the assault weapons ban. I think most police departments will be adequately armed if we can get the assault weapons out of the hands of the criminals and if we have tougher enforcement of the Brady bill. It's—186,000 blocked sales is no small number, even in a big country like ours—186,000. That's pretty impressive.

1996 Campaign Financing

Q. What do you think of the Republicans suggesting they'll vote tomorrow in the Senate on insisting there be an independent counsel on campaign financial fundraising?

The President. Well, I think, you know, there is a law on that. It's a legal question. It shouldn't be a political one.

Gun Control Legislation

Q. Mr. President, why would you think now that things in the Congress would be any different this time around for cop-killer bullets or for some of these other measures than before?

The President. Because of the clear demonstration of public support. Keep in mind that this Congress, which had originally come into office with a commitment to repeal the—I mean, the last Congress, the Congress of '95–'96, which came to Congress with a commitment to repeal the assault weapons ban and weaken or repeal the Brady bill actually agreed with me to strengthen the Brady bill at the end of the last session of Congress in late 1996. So I think there has been a sea change in the shift of attitude in the Congress as the American people have crystallized their opinions on these issues and made it known.

Furthermore, I think there will be broad support—even broader support for the child safety locks. I would be surprised if you don't have a lot of the gunowners groups—if they didn't support this, it would surprise me. I mean, this is consistent with a lot of the things that they have said in the past, so I think we would have a good chance on that.

And on the cop-killer bullets, I think that—you asked my hope. My hope is based on the action that this Congress took at the last session where they voted with us to extend the impact of the Brady bill.

1996 Campaign Financing

Q. Mr. President, with the new subpoenas coming out on the Lippo connection to the White House, are you satisfied that there's been no undue influence by outside influence on—by outside countries on either your White House or on your former—your very good friend Web Hubbell?

The President. I have no reason to believe that there has been. But I think that everybody should comply with the information, and we have. And you know, Mr. Burton asked us yesterday, I think, for some information relating to the allegation of an attempt by the Chinese to influence the American election. And when we have made that—when—we said in our letter to the Justice Department that we assumed anything that we got would be given to the House and Senate Intelligence Committees because we didn't want to raise any questions, we just want to get to the bottom of that. And so, they have it, and whatever is appropriate for them to share with Mr. Burton, they can. I just think we—

Q. Is Burton grandstanding?

The President. I don't want to get into that. But I believe that the House and Senate committees—Intelligence Committees—have anything that we had. And so they can share it with them as is appropriate.

Q. Do you have any reason to believe there was influence——

The President. No.

Q. ——attempted influence?

The President. I do not, but I think we have to get—you know, there's an investigation. As I said, the charge is serious; we need to get to the bottom of it. But I have no reasons to believe—I have no personal evidence, but that's not the issue. The issue is this charge has been made, it's—anytime you allege that another government attempted to influence an American election, that's a serious thing and has to be looked into. But I have no personal evidence, but I want the investigation to proceed, and I want the Justice Department to get to the bottom of it. And I expect that they will.

NOTE: The President spoke at 10:33 a.m. in the Oval Office at the White House. In his remarks, he referred to former White House Press Secretary James S. Brady, who was wounded in the 1981 assassination attempt on President Ronald Reagan; Mr. Brady's wife, Sarah, head of Hand Gun Control, Inc.; and Representative Dan Burton, chairman, House Committee on Government Reform and Oversight.

Memorandum on Child Safety Lock Devices for Handguns
March 5, 1997

Memorandum for the Heads of Executive Departments and Agencies

Subject: Child Safety Lock Devices for Handguns

Every day, firearms claim the lives of too many children. Firearms cause 12 percent of fatalities among American children and teens, and one of every four deaths of teenagers ages 15 to 19. These numbers represent not only violent crimes, but also tragic gun accidents. Firearms are now the fourth leading cause of accidental deaths among children ages 5 to 14. Moreover, firearms have become the primary method by which young people commit suicide.

According to a Centers for Disease Control study released earlier this month, the rate of firearm deaths among children up to 14 years old is nearly 12 times higher in the United States than in 25 other industrialized countries combined. The Center also estimates that nearly 1.2 million unsupervised children return from school to a home that has a loaded or unlocked firearm.

Recently, my Administration sent to the Congress our "Anti-Gang and Youth Violence Act of 1997," draft legislation that includes a provision requiring all Federal Firearms Licensed dealers to provide a safety lock device with every firearm sold. Safety lock devices will help to reduce the unauthorized use of handguns by a child at play or a teen who wants to commit a crime. Just as important, safety lock devices can also help deter gun theft.

I have urged the Congress to move this legislation quickly. In the meantime, the Federal Government can serve as an example of gun safety for the Nation by taking an important step to reduce handgun accidents and protect our children from injury and death.

Every year, the Federal Government issues thousands of handguns to our law enforcement agents. While some agencies have already adopted a policy of distributing safety locks for these handguns, this policy should be universally adopted across the Federal Government. That is why I direct you to develop and implement a policy requiring that a safety lock device— as defined in our draft legislation—be provided with any and every handgun issued by your agency to law enforcement officers. You should ensure that all Federal law enforcement officers are informed of this policy and that all issued safety lock devices are accompanied by instructions for their proper use.

All Americans have a responsibility to ensure that guns do not fall into the hands of our children. Your response to this directive will help ensure that this does not happen. Taking this simple step can have a dramatic impact on saving the lives of our children. You should proceed as quickly as possible to carry out this directive.

WILLIAM J. CLINTON

Statement on the Recess of Belfast Talks
March 5, 1997

As the Belfast talks on the future of Northern Ireland recess today for the British and local election campaigns, I want to emphasize the strong support of the United States for these historic negotiations. They offer an unparalleled opportunity for the Northern Ireland political parties and the British and Irish Governments to achieve a just and lasting settlement to the conflict that has haunted the people of Northern Ireland for too long. Violence can have no place in this democratic process. For the talks to be inclusive, as they are intended to be, the IRA must declare and implement an unequivocal cease-fire.

Under the skilled chairmanship of Senator George Mitchell and his colleagues, the talks have made useful progress. When the talks reconvene in June, it is important that they move quickly into substantive negotiations. I hope the participants will return to Stormont on June 3 determined to work creatively to make real progress. If they do, they will have my full support for the negotiations and their eventual outcome.

NOTE: The statement referred to George J. Mitchell, Special Assistant to the President for Northern Ireland.

Message to the Congress on Continuation of the National Emergency With Respect to Development of Iranian Petroleum Resources
March 5, 1997

To the Congress of the United States:

Section 202(d) of the National Emergencies Act (50 U.S.C. 1622(d)) provides for the automatic termination of a national emergency unless, prior to the anniversary date of its declaration, the President publishes in the *Federal Register* and transmits to the Congress a notice stating that the emergency is to continue in effect beyond the anniversary date. In accordance with this provision, I have sent the enclosed notice, stating that the Iran emergency declared on March 15, 1995, pursuant to the International Emergency Economic Powers Act (50 U.S.C. 1701–1706) is to continue in effect beyond March 15, 1997, to the *Federal Register* for publication. This emergency is separate from that declared on November 14, 1979, in connection with the Iranian hostage crisis and therefore requires separate renewal of emergency authorities.

The factors that led me to declare a national emergency with respect to Iran on March 15, 1995, have not been resolved. The actions and policies of the Government of Iran, including its support for international terrorism, efforts to undermine the Middle East peace process, and its acquisition of weapons of mass destruction and the means to deliver them, continue to threaten the national security, foreign policy, and economy of the United States. Accordingly, I have determined that it is necessary to maintain in force the broad authorities that are in place by virtue of the March 15, 1995, declaration of emergency.

WILLIAM J. CLINTON

The White House,
March 5, 1997.

NOTE: The notice is listed in Appendix D at the end of this volume.

Remarks to a Joint Session of the Michigan State Legislature in Lansing
March 6, 1997

Thank you. Thank you very much, Mr. Speaker, Governor. Thank you all for that wonderful welcome in this magnificent capitol. I'm delighted to be here today with so many of your State officials—Lieutenant Governor Binsfeld; your State board of education president, Kathleen Strauss. I don't know if Frank Kelley met Theodore Roosevelt, but he did meet me when I became attorney general. [*Laughter*] And some days I feel about that old. I want to thank the mayor of Lansing, Mayor Hollister, for meeting me at the airport, and all the other State officials and dignitaries who are here—Representative Sikkema, thank you, sir; and Senator Cherry and Senator Posthumus.

I want to thank the Members of Congress and others who flew down here with me today—your former Governor, Jim Blanchard and his wife, Janet; Congressman Dingell; your Congresswoman from here, Congressman Debbie Stabenow; Representative Levin; Representative Kilpatrick; Representative Conyers; Representative Stupak; Representative Camp; and Representative Hoekstra and Representative Barcia. Did I get them all? [*Laughter*] Nine, we only had nine here. I could only muster nine, but that's a quorum—[*laughter*]—even in the State legislature—of the Michigan delegation. I thank them for coming down.

Thank you, Wendell Anthony, for your invocation, and thank you for making me feel so welcome.

When I came in, the Speaker and I were looking up at this magnificent ceiling, and I noticed that the seal of the State of Michigan was right next to the seal of my home State of Arkansas. And maybe one reason for that is that the Congress approved us coming into the Union at the same time.

I was reading also the account of Theodore Roosevelt coming here 90 years ago. I know you have partisan differences today. You might be interested to know that 90 years ago there were 32 Republicans and no Democrats in the Senate. [*Laughter*] If you clap too much, I've got a great closing line—Governor, you'll get mad at it. [*Laughter*] There were 95 Republicans and 5 Democrats in the House. And it was the aftermath of the Civil War.

I say this because our two States have been entwined in an interesting way over the course of time. We were allowed together into the Union because Michigan was a free State and Arkansas was a Southern slave State, and Michigan became the party—adhering to the party of Abraham Lincoln, of freedom, and the party of Theodore Roosevelt, which the Governor explained. And most of us Democrats are pretty proud of those folks, too. They represent the best in America.

Then, after the Great Depression, Michigan basically became the home of tens of thousands of people from my State who simply could not make a living anymore on the farm, and the

factories of Michigan gave people from Arkansas, black and white together, the chance to come up here and build a decent, middle class life and educate their children and be a part of what was then America's future. So anybody from my roots must be exceedingly grateful to the people of Michigan and the history and the heritage of Michigan.

When Theodore Roosevelt was here, he was going to Michigan State to address the graduates there, just as I did a couple of years ago. And I might say the president of Michigan State is here, and I told him today that he gave me a picture of Theodore Roosevelt's address to the graduates at Michigan State, and it now hangs on my office wall at the White House at the entrance to my little private office off the Oval Office, and I look up there and see Teddy Roosevelt speaking every day that I go to work.

Before that, he came here, and when he spoke here I suppose the place looked about like it does now, thanks to your magnificent renovation, and I applaud you for doing this. People all over America should remember it's worth investing a little money to protect your roots and your heritage and the beauty and meaning of what we were as well as what we hope to be.

In 1907 when Teddy Roosevelt came here, we were at the dawn of the industrial era. This building had been wired for electricity only 2 years before he showed up. And when President Roosevelt left here to go to the college campus, he got in a newfangled contraption called a Reo automobile. I read the newspaper article from your local paper from 1907 this morning, and it said that it was something of a risk for him to get into the car, but it was probably the wave of the future; who knew what would turn out. [*Laughter*] Then, like a good politician, I read that when he was at Michigan State, at the campus, he learned that there were, in fact, two different car manufacturers competing with one another in Lansing, so he took the other one back. [*Laughter*] He took a Reo out and an Olds back.

That was a rare moment. Just think what happened from that moment to this one. Think about the century that that moment and this one spans—all but 10 years of this century—and why it became the American Century, what a big part of it Michigan was, building a great middle class; offering a haven to people from all over America and to immigrants who would come here from other lands to work, to make their way; building an industrial power that could prevail in two World Wars and overcome a Great Depression; building an ethical power that could live up to the meaning of its Constitution in the civil rights revolution and expanding opportunities to young people to vote and to women to fully participate in the life of America. Just think what has happened in the 20th century.

When Roosevelt was here in 1907, it was a rare moment. We were moving onto the stage as a world power. Everyone recognized it. We had by then been a nation for more than 100 years, and everybody knew there was something unique about America, a free democracy where people could vote and decide and make their judgments. And it was growing and being nourished. We were exceedingly prosperous by the standards of the time.

And Roosevelt knew that you had to make the most of peace and prosperity and leadership, and he did. And so did his successor, Woodrow Wilson. And because of them together and the work they did with like-minded members of both parties, we built an era that set the framework for America's leadership, growth, and prosperity, and the explosion of people into the middle class, which became the hallmark of Michigan's greatness.

When I was a kid in Arkansas, our per capita income was barely half the national average. We all knew if you could find your way up here and got a job, you could still make a good living. That all began at the beginning of this century. It is a very rare thing for a country to have peace and prosperity and the possibility of shaping its own future. Abraham Lincoln said in the Civil War, "My policy is to have no policy. I'm controlled by events." If I said that, I would be ridiculed, rightly so. But he was controlled by events. He did have a policy; it was to keep the Union together and then to liberate us from the scourge of slavery. But he was controlled by events.

When the Depression came on and President Roosevelt called for an era of bold experimentation, he was controlled by events to some extent. He couldn't say the major issue in America is the climate or even education or anything else. He was controlled by events, and the war did that. And to some extent, the cold war did that for us. When Sputnik went up and we

got into the space race and wound up winning it, we were almost forced into it. Now we have peace and prosperity on the edge of an era of unimaginable possibility.

We just finished 4 years where our country, for the first time during one administration, has produced 11½ million jobs. Michigan—the unemployment rate has dropped, and the Governor said your welfare rolls are down 30 percent. You see this kind of progress, this energy, this movement, this possibility in America—dramatic new advances in science and technology occurring. This is a rare time.

What happens to people, usually, when they are prosperous and unthreatened? Well, they usually get complacent, and then they normally find some reason to fall out with one another, usually over something incredibly petty, just in the nature of human events. And I come here to say to you today, we here in America and you here especially in Michigan who have done so much for so long, we cannot afford to do that. We owe something better to our children. We have been given this unique opportunity, the same sort of opportunity we had when your predecessors were listening to Theodore Roosevelt here 90 years ago, except one on an even grander scale, and we have to make the most of it. We have to build America in the new century. And we also have to know that we have to do it as one America.

I am gratified that Governor Engler said what he did about the education program today. I am gratified that this bipartisan State legislature has given me such a warm welcome, for we have to forge a new partnership for a new time.

While the era of big Government is truly over—the Federal Government now has 285,000 fewer people working for it than it did on the day I took the oath of office—the era of big challenges for our Nation is not over. And now, we know that national leadership can and must point the way, but the real responsibility is one we all share.

Especially, there are two areas I want to discuss today—educational excellence, high standards for all students; and welfare reform, breaking the cycle of dependency for everyone capable of independence in America—for these issues are at the core of what it means to prepare America for the 21st century, giving all Americans not only the opportunity but the tools they need to make the most of their own lives in this new global knowledge economy.

The Governor referred to this in his remarks. When I gave the State of the Union Address, I said that during the cold war, because our national security was threatened by communism, politics stopped at the water's edge. Today, our national security depends upon our ability to develop the capacities of all of our people, so politics should stop at the schoolhouse door.

Between 1992 and 2000—think of this—89 percent of the new jobs created in this economy will require more than high school levels of literacy and math skills, but only half the people entering the work force are prepared for these high-paying jobs, even though about 80 percent of them are high school graduates. Our schools are still turning out millions of young people who simply are not equipped for the new world of work. That is why our number one priority must be to make our system of public education the best in the world, and you must believe we can do this.

A few years ago, almost 8 years ago now, I had the honor of joining the other Governors then serving with President Bush at the University of Virginia to write the national education goals. I still think they're pretty good goals. If you ask me what the consequences would be if they were implemented, we could say bluntly that it would mean that every 8-year-old would be able to read independently, every 12-year-old could now log on to the Internet, every 18-year-old could go to college, and every adult American could keep on learning for a lifetime. That is what I want to be the reality in this country.

In the State of the Union Address, I laid out a 10-point plan, a call to action for American education that describes the steps I believe we must all take, beginning with the youngest children, expanding and improving early childhood learning. The First Lady and I will be having a conference on early childhood learning and the brain to try to deal with these enormously significant new findings over the last couple of years, what we know about not only when children learn but how they learn and what happens if we don't do for them what they should do.

An enormous percentage of the capacity of the brain to absorb information to operate is developed in the first 4 years. I'll just give you one statistic: The average child that grows up in a family with two parents caring for that child, even if they both work, that have reasonably good educations and deal with the basic developmental tasks, will give that child 700,000 positive interactions in the first 4 years. The average child being raised by a single parent with low self-esteem and low self-confidence and no training in parenting will get 150,000 positive interactions and spend roughly 7 times as much time before a television doing nothing, in the first 4 years. This has enormous consequences for the way we become. So we're going to talk about that.

We have to open the doors of college wider than ever. If 90 percent of the jobs require more than a high school education, and the 1990 census shows that the only group of younger workers whose incomes went up instead of down after you adjust for inflation were those that had at least 2 years of some kind of training after high school, we ought to make the 13th and 14th years of education just as universal by the year 2000 as a high school education is today.

I know that for years Michigan has been in the forefront of that, helping people to save for college. I have a proposal to provide tax credits for the cost of a typical community college for 2 years, and tax deductions up to $10,000 a year for the tuition cost in any post-high school education, and an expanded IRA that can be used for the same purpose. We have to do this.

We also have to give more of our workers the ability to keep on learning for a lifetime. For 4 years, through a Democratic Congress and a Republican Congress, I have been given equal opportunity to fail to pass the "GI bill" for American workers. But it seems to me to be a simple idea. I just want to take the 70-odd programs that were developed with the best of intentions over the years, for this training program, that training program, and the other one, put them in a big fund, and when a worker becomes eligible for help through unemployment or underemployment, send them a skills grant and let them take it to the local community college or the nearest education institution. They can find out for themselves what they need to do to improve their education. We don't need all that stuff in the middle of them, between them and the money. Send them the money, let them get the education. I hope you will help me pass that in the Congress. I think it is a good thing.

I want to help for the very first time through an innovative program to use Federal funds to lower the interest rates on local bond issues to help schools with enormous building problems to repair their broken infrastructure or build new facilities when they are doing their part. This is a very important thing. We have the largest number of schoolchildren—as Secretary Riley never lets me forget—we have the largest number of schoolchildren in history in our schools this year, the first time we've ever had a bigger group than the baby boom generation. I have been to schools where the buildings were falling down. My wife was in a school this week where some of the floors were closed, and the kids were going to school on some floors and couldn't go into other floors or other rooms because they didn't comply with the building codes. I have been into other schools with beautiful old school buildings surrounded by temporary facilities to hold the children.

So I think it's an appropriate thing for us to do, not to try to take over this function and not to try to substitute for people assuming responsibility, but when there's a terrible problem and people are doing their own work, if we can, by a prudent and limited investment, lower the cost of that so that more people can afford to do more construction and repair, I think we should.

I'm also strongly committed—the Vice President and I have been working on this very hard—to getting every classroom and every library in the country hooked up to the Internet by the year 2000. And I want to thank your Congresswoman, Debbie Stabenow, for the work that she's done in supporting that.

Secretary Riley has awarded Michigan a grant of $8.6 million for the technology literacy challenge to help your classrooms move into the 21st century, and I ask all of you to support that. There is enormous willingness in the private sector to help us get this done, and it can revolutionize—just think of it—if we can hook up every classroom and every library to the Internet by the year 2000, for the first time in the history of the country ever—ever—children in the poorest district, the richest districts, the middle class districts, all of them will have access to the same learning in the same way in the same time.

And those of you who have children or know children who are already proficient in using the Internet, it's a stunning thing. The other day, my daughter picked a topic to do a research paper on, and she said, "Dad, can you get me a couple of books on this out of the library?" I came home with four books, and she had eight citations she had gotten off the Internet—eight articles and things. So my labors were one-third of her research project.

This is an incredible thing. If we make this available to all children, it will change in a breathtaking way what people can become, what our children can imagine themselves becoming. And I ask you to help us do that.

I thank you, Governor, for what you said about our support for greater discipline and safety and character education in the schools. I have proposed funding 1,000 new community school programs across the country to help our schools stay open after school, on the weekends, in the summertime, to try to give those children who need some positive place to go, some support, some help to stay out of trouble, a place to do that.

I have studied very carefully this problem of rising juvenile crime when overall crime has been going down dramatically in America. And the communities that are reversing that trend, that had juvenile crime going down are the places that make sure that all those kids have something positive to say yes to, even as they're being told to say no to the wrong things. So I want the schools to be able to do that in every community where it's needed in the United States.

We have to make sure that we do everything we can to help our classroom teachers be the best they can be. For years, educators worked to establish nationally accepted credentials for excellence in teaching through the National Board for Professional Teaching Standards, which is headquartered here in Detroit, Michigan.

Now, Michigan has the third highest number of board-certified master teachers in the country, and that's a good thing. But there are still only a few hundred who have been board certified. My new budget will enable 100,000 teachers all across America to seek certification as master teachers. And our goal should be to have one certified master teacher in every single school in America. That will make more master teachers we need for those schools, and I hope we can do it.

As has already been said today, I do believe that we need a strong system of public education that gives parents and communities more freedom and flexibility. I think we should work together to give parents more choices for what public schools their children attend all across America. I think we should help teachers, parents, museums, and others to create new public charter schools.

I have proposed to double the budget of the program so that we can increase by tenfold the number of charter schools we have by the year 2000, to create—[*applause*]—and I think it's important to emphasize what we want. We want high standards, schools that are open to all children regardless of their backgrounds. We want an example of accountability which will then spread to all other public schools. But we want to say to them, you can stay open only as long as you do a good job. That's what the charter means; that's what a charter is.

Ultimately, what we want to do is to prove that we have a model here that can be used everywhere else. It is simply not true that if you have a few public schools that all the rest of them can't be good, if some of them are good that they all can't be good. That is not true. It is not true that because it's a public institution we can't achieve excellence everywhere. If that were true, we'd have some good Army units and some bad Army units, and we'd be afraid to go to war, and you wouldn't sleep well at night. Isn't that right?

So you do not have to accept the feeling that you know this wonderful principal, and if only everybody else could be that way. That is simply not true. Leadership can be taught, leadership can be trained, and 90 percent of the children in this country plus—99 percent of them—can learn what they need to know to succeed and triumph in the modern world. They can do it, and we have to do it. [*Applause*]

Now that you've clapped, I will say they are capable of it, but they don't know it today. Let's face the facts. The truth is that 40 percent of the fourth graders in this country still cannot read a book on their own. In Germany or Singapore, students learn 15 to 20 math subjects in depth every year. Typically in the United States, we run over 30 or 35 every year in a superficial way. Then we have these comparative tests. They normally win, especially since they stay in school longer than we do, day-in and day-out, year-in and year-out.

But without these skills, children will not be able to develop the capacity to think and to reason and to analyze complex problems. All these skills will be essential to succeeding in

the world of the 21st century in jobs that have not been invented or even imagined yet.

Now, what do we have to have? We have got to have high standards, high expectations, and high levels of accountability. That is why I have challenged our Nation to meet these national standards in the basics, not Federal Government standards but national standards, representing what every child, wherever he or she lives, however poor, rich, or middle class he or she is, must know to do well in the world of the 21st century. And I think we should begin by having every State test every fourth grader in reading and every eighth grader in math by 1999 to make sure these basic standards are met.

We already have widely accepted rigorous standards in both reading and math and widely used tests that are based on these standards. They're just not given to everyone or designed to be given to everyone. Michigan and more than 40 other States have participated in a test called the National Assessment of Education Progress. The education committee members in the audience call it the NAEP test. It measures a State's overall performance against a high national standard of excellence. Just last week we released the annual assessment of math performance and it shows, across the country, that our 4th, 8th, and 12th graders are doing better. And as the Governor said, Michigan's score is among the most improved in the Nation.

Tens of thousands of students across the country have also taken the Third International Math and Science Survey, a test that reflects world-class standards our children must meet in math and science. The headquarters for that test is just down the road at Michigan State. And I want to thank Dr. William Schmidt at Michigan State for his leadership of this important study. I think he's here with us today. Where are you, Dr. Schmidt? He's here somewhere. Thank you very much, sir.

If you saw the State of the Union Address, you know there are a group of children in northern Illinois that took this test in 20 school districts north of Chicago, and they finished tied for first in science and tied for second in math, I think—very impressive.

Unfortunately, these tests also don't provide scores for individuals; they simply measure how an entire area or group of people are doing. What we need are exams that will literally measure the performance of each and every student in each and every school. That way, parents and teachers will know how every child is doing compared to other students in other schools, other States, and other countries. And most important of all, they will know how the child is doing compared to what you need to know to go forward.

And I want to make it clear what the difference is. It doesn't matter if your child makes the highest grade in the class if nobody gets over the standards bar. Conversely, in this sense it doesn't matter if your child makes the lowest grade in the class if everybody gets over the standards bar. That's the difference. We have a lot of these standardized tests. We need tests that test to the standards, that say whether you have crossed the threshold of what you must know to do well in the world of tomorrow.

That's why I'm presenting a plan to help the States meet and measure these standards. Over the next 2 years, the Department of Education will support the development of new tests for the fourth grade reading and the eighth grade math, to show how every student measures up to high and widely accepted standards. They'll be developed by independent experts in consultation with leading math and reading teachers. The Federal Government will not require them, but these tests will be made available to every State that chooses to administer them. That is the significance of the announcement that the Governor made. I want to create a climate in which no one can say no, in which it's voluntary but you are ashamed if you don't give your kids the chance to do this.

Together we are saying this. This is not a partisan issue. There is no Democratic or Republican way to teach. There is no Maryland or Michigan way to learn. Reading is reading; math is math. No school board or State legislature can rewrite the rules of algebra in Alaska to make them different than they are in Arkansas. It cannot be done. Every State must put politics aside, work in a bipartisan fashion, test our children in the same rigorous way. Politics should stop at the schoolhouse door.

This will not be easy. Some of our children won't do very well at first. We don't need to make them feel like failures; we need to make them understand we're doing this so we can know how to measure their success. If they don't do very well at first, it's probably more our fault than theirs. And a lot of it, I will say again, is because when we see people in

difficult circumstances, sometimes out of the goodness of our heart, we exercise our compassion by expecting less of them. And we are selling their future right down the drain every time we do it.

I can tell you, over the last several years—you know, I was a Governor a long time. I served with Governor Engler; I served with Governor Blanchard; I served with Governor Milliken. I have been all over this country to schools. I have seen schools in areas with high murder rates, where it was unsafe to get in the school, where there were no guns, no knives, no dope, no dropout, and test scores were above the State average. I could go through example after example after example. And every time I see one, I get more hopeful and more angry, because if you can have one good school where the kids are learning against all the odds and all the obstacles, then you know when you leave that school there is no excuse for that not happening everywhere. This will help that happen everywhere. This will help that happen everywhere.

Let me make a comment now about one other part of this education program that I think is very important, and that's our America Reads program. We announced it here in Michigan last August in Wyandotte, when I was there on my train trip. And I did it with the help of two elementary school students, Justin Whitney and Elizabeth Schweyen. We announced the America Reads challenge. We set a goal mobilizing a million volunteer tutors to help every 8-year-old learn to read independently. We're going to use 11,000 of our AmeriCorps volunteers to mobilize and train the army. We're going to get at least 100,000 college students to help. And I might say in the last budget we added 200,000 more work-study slots, and there's another 100,000 in this budget, so we'll go to a million kids on work-study, and I want 100,000 of that extra 300,000 to help teach our children to read. And I'm pleased that 16 Michigan college presidents have already pledged to provide their fair share of those students.

I don't know if you remember what we did that hot August day, but Elizabeth and Justin read "The Little Engine That Could" to me, and I said I want every child to be able to do this and say, "Here's this book, and I can read this all by myself." Today Elizabeth and Justin are here with us, and I would like to ask them to stand up. Where are they? They're out there. There they are. [*Applause*] Thank you.

I will do what I can to help your young people be ready to be tested. I am asking the Department of Education and the National Science Foundation to identify and coordinate resources throughout the Federal Government and through the nonprofit sector that can be used to help students to meet the math standards. I want to help young people learn more science as well and to make the Government a resource. The Federal Government has some of the world's most esteemed laboratories and research institutions. We ought to make sure every high school math and science teacher has easy access to the work of these laboratories and the experts there through the Internet, and we're going to do our best to set up that kind of system and make it available to all of your teachers so they can in turn make it available to your students. We can do this. We can do this.

We can also meet the challenge of welfare reform, and I can't leave here without talking to you about it for a couple of minutes, because I want to make it clear where we are now, and this is something else we've got to do together. In the last 4 years, the welfare rolls went down by 2½ million people, the largest drop in the history of the country. Now, how did that happen? And Michigan had a reduction of 30 percent, above the national average. How did that happen?

We know that about half the drop was the result of the economy producing 11½ million jobs. We know about 30 percent to a third of it was the result of the fact that 43 of our States had vigorous welfare reform experiments, and the ones that were statewide, like yours, had better results. We know that there was some result from the fact that we increased child support collections, working together to get really tough within the States and across State lines. Child support collections went up by 50 percent in the last 4 years, and we know that helped some people to get off welfare.

Now we have a new law, and the new law says there should be time limits for how long a person could be on welfare; there should be time limits for how long a person could be on welfare consecutively—2 years before getting a job. There are tough work requirements. We leave the medical aid and food aid to poor children and their families in place. We increased the aid going in child care at the Federal level,

and then we give the States the flexibility to decide how to design the program to move people from welfare to work and support them at an appropriate level in the meantime.

Now, that's what it does. I signed the bill, and I thought it was the right thing to do. But I also want you to know that we have to do now something else; we have to make it work. That law was not the end of welfare reform; it was the beginning. It gave this problem to you. You remember what that old country musician Chet Atkins said: "You got to be careful what you ask for in this old life; you might get it." And so now you have it.

Now, we have been telling poor people they have to be more responsible: "If you can work, you have to work. You've got to succeed at home as parents and in the work force." Now we have a responsibility. You're telling people they've got to go to work; we've got to make sure there's a job there for them if they go to work.

Let me say precisely what this means, because I want to be precise. I think it's very important that since the States have responsibility here, every State needs to know exactly how many jobs have we got to create in Michigan only for people to move from welfare to work, how many jobs in Arkansas, how many jobs in Arizona, how many jobs, and how many jobs would that mean we'd have to do by county, and how are we going to do this.

Basically, if you look at the law's requirements and the fact that it's phased in, the requirement for States to put a certain number of people at work, you will have to—as a nation, we will have to create about another million, a little bit less, maybe 900,000 jobs for welfare recipients only, and move approximately another 2½ million people off welfare in the next 4 years to meet the requirements of the law.

Now, in the last 4 years, we did it with 43 of the 50 States having welfare reform experiments, but only some of them were statewide. But we also had 11½ million jobs. We never had that many before. Maybe we'll do it again. I'd like that a lot, and I'll work on it hard. But no one can predict with any certainty what will happen.

So you must imagine, how will we make it more attractive—and we don't have the money to have big public service employment. I do have some money in my budget to give to the urban areas especially and to isolated rural areas with high impact unemployment to help them do work that needs to be done anyway in their cities. But that won't get the job done. Most of this will have to be done by private employers.

Our plan will give tax credits of up to 50 percent of the salary up to $10,000 a year for people that hire people right off the welfare roll and do not replace someone else; they hire them for a real new job. It will give other incentives for businesses to hire people off welfare and incentives for job placement firms and for States to create more jobs for welfare recipients. You'll get more money if you create more jobs for them. And if your past is any indication, you'll be one of those that will be claiming the incentives, and that's a good thing. And it does provide more money for training and for child care, and in our budget for the new transportation bill, more money for transportation, because that's a big issue in a lot of places for moving people from welfare to work.

But you are going to have to get help. And the private employer community and the community nonprofits community and the religious community, they're all going to have to help. You also have the option to do something else: You can, totally at your own discretion, let people take some or all of the welfare check and you can give it to the employer as an employment and training subsidy. And some States are going to have to do that because their training dollars are inadequate, so they're going to have to depend on on-the-job training. Missouri is doing this now in the Kansas City area; Florida has adopted a version of it; a number of other States have. I urge you to look at that. I think it's a legitimate thing to give a private employer, for a limited period of time, a subsidy for training and for hiring people who are otherwise very hard to hire.

That's another point I want to make. Keep in mind, about half the welfare caseload gets off on their own. It's the other half that we have to liberate from permanent dependency, and it's harder for them to get into the work force and harder for them to stay and harder for them to learn the basic things. And so we're going to have to go out to our employers and say, "Hey, we want to help you." Or in the case of the churches and the nonprofits, the tax credit is not worth anything to them because they don't pay taxes anyway, but the wage subsidy would be worth something to them to get them to enlist.

So, you know, I have really collected—how many employers are there in America with more than 100 employees? How many nonprofits are there? How many religious institutions are there with more than 100 members in the congregation or more than 200 members? Every State needs this information. Every community needs this information. And those folks need to be hit up to do their part, especially if you ever heard anybody in your local neighborhood cussing the welfare system who works people. Go back and say, "Okay, we got rid of it. Now what are you going to do? What are you going to do? We need your help."

The last thing I wanted to say is—and this may be a moderate problem in Michigan, will be a huge problem in some States—I signed the welfare reform bill, but I said when I signed it I thought we made a mistake to eliminate all aid to legal immigrants. Now, when an immigrant comes to America, they say—they have to promise that they won't try to get on welfare and they won't take any public money. That is true. But it's also true it takes 5 years to become a citizen; meanwhile you work and you pay taxes. And in a country like ours that lets in a significant number of immigrants—in your largest county now, you have people from over 140 different racial and ethnic groups—bad things are going to happen to good people just when they show up every day. There will be car wrecks; there will be serious illnesses; there will be crime victims; and I personally think it's wrong to either dump that problem on the door of the State legislature or, in the alternative, just tell them to do without. And this is a great nation of immigrants. I think this is unworthy of us, and I'm going to try to change it, and I hope that you will support that. It would be good for you if you do.

Thank you for making me feel so welcome today. Let me say again, you ought to go back and get the local paper and read the article about Teddy Roosevelt. You ought to think about what happened in the intervening 90 years. You ought to realize that we have an even greater opportunity now, and with it a greater responsibility to forge a new partnership to deal with the new possibilities of this bright new era. And if we seize this responsibility of ours, there is no telling what can happen—good and wonderful and positive for America.

So it is our duty, but it is our good fortune. You ought to go home tonight and thank God that you got a chance to serve the public at this moment in time. It is a rare time. And you ought to wake up tomorrow determined to do it with greater energy and enthusiasm and dedication than ever before.

Thank you, and God bless you.

NOTE: The President spoke at 11:36 a.m. in the House of Representatives Chamber at the State Capitol. In his remarks, he referred to Speaker of the House Curtis Hertel, House Majority Leader Ken Sikkema, Senate Minority Leader John Cherry, and Senate Majority Leader Dick Posthumus, Michigan State Legislature; Gov. John Engler, Lt. Gov. Connie Binsfeld, and Attorney General Frank J. Kelley of Michigan; Mayor Dick Hollister of Lansing; Rev. Wendell Anthony, Fellowship Chapel, Detroit, MI, who gave the invocation; William Schmidt, professor, Michigan State University; and James J. Blanchard and William Milliken, former Governors of Michigan.

Memorandum on Educational Excellence in Math and Science
March 6, 1997

Memorandum for the Secretary of Education, the Director of the National Science Foundation

Subject: Preparing Students to Meet National Standards of Excellence in Eighth Grade Math and Improving Math and Science Education

Since the early 1980s, U.S. elementary and secondary school students have begun taking tougher courses, and we are starting to see the results. National Assessment of Educational Progress scores have improved in math and science, with gains in mathematics equal to at least one grade level. On the Scholastic Aptitude Test (SAT), average math scores are at their highest in 25 years, even as the number and diversity of test-takers have increased. However, the eighth-grade results of the 41-Nation Third International Math and Science Study (TIMSS), released last fall, show that the United States is below average in math and just above average in science. That isn't acceptable; in this technology-rich information era, our students need to perform much better in both subjects, but especially in math, if they are to excel at higher-level math and science courses that are critical to college admission and success and to citizenship, productive employment, and lifelong learning.

The first step in raising achievement is lifting expectations and setting high standards for what students should know and be able to do. Our National Assessment of Educational Progress, TIMSS, and the standards developed by the National Council of Teachers of Mathematics give us a solid framework to build on. Last month, to help parents and teachers learn who needs help, what changes in teaching to make, and which schools need to improve, I asked the Secretary of Education to develop a voluntary national test for individual eighth-grade students based on widely accepted, challenging national standards in mathematics. The national test will be available to States and local school districts to give to their students in the spring of 1999, and will measure whether students have reached a high level of mathematics proficiency.

The primary responsibility for achieving high standards rests with students, teachers, parents, and schools in local communities across America. However, it is imperative that we work to ensure that Federal resources support student success as well. We must ensure that Federal programs, research, and human resources are used as effectively as possible to help improve teaching and learning.

Therefore, I direct the Secretary of Education and the Director of the National Science Foundation to form an interagency working group and to develop an action strategy for using Federal resources to assist States and local school systems to prepare students to meet challenging math standards in eighth grade, and for involving the mathematics, scientific, and technical communities in support of these efforts.

The action strategy should include recommendations for the use of Federal resources to help States, local school districts, and schools to improve teaching, upgrade curriculum, and integrate technology and high-quality instructional materials into the classroom, as well as motivate students and help them understand how math concepts are applied in the real world. The strategy should identify significant Federal programs, activities, and partnerships available to improve teaching and learning, ensure that these resources are appropriately focused on helping students reach challenging math standards, and determine how these resources can best support State and local reforms. In developing this strategy, the interagency group should review the current status of improvements in math education and identify and address critical areas of need, drawing on research and input from educators and professional organizations.

Because teaching and learning in math and science are so integrally related, and because success in both subjects is vitally important in this information era, the working group should also review how Federal resources and partnerships with other organizations can help improve student achievement in science.

The working group should make its recommendations and submit its action strategy to me within 90 days.

WILLIAM J. CLINTON

Statement on the Death of President Cheddi Jagan of Guyana
March 6, 1997

It was with deep regret that I learned of the death early today of President Cheddi Jagan of the Co-operative Republic of Guyana. President Jagan was a respected statesman in our hemisphere of democracies. He was one of the founders of the People's Progressive Party and for over 45 years played an active role in his country's political life. I remember warmly our meeting at the Miami Summit of the Americas in December 1994. President Jagan was a champion of the poor who devoted himself to alleviating poverty in his country and throughout the Caribbean.

On behalf of the American people, I extend my deepest sympathies to the Jagan family and the people of Guyana.

Letter to Congressional Leaders Transmitting a Report on International Agreements
March 6, 1997

Dear Mr. Speaker: (*Dear Mr. Chairman:*)
Pursuant to subsection (b) of the Case-Zablocki Act (1 U.S.C. 112b(b)), I hereby transmit a report prepared by the Department of State concerning international agreements.
Sincerely,

WILLIAM J. CLINTON

NOTE: Identical letters were sent to Newt Gingrich, Speaker of the House of Representatives, and Jesse Helms, chairman, Senate Committee on Foreign Relations.

Message to the Congress Transmitting a Report on the Trade Agreements Program
March 6, 1997

To the Congress of the United States:

As required by section 163 of the Trade Act of 1974, as amended (19 U.S.C. 2213), I transmit herewith the 1997 Trade Policy Agenda and 1996 Annual Report on the Trade Agreements Program.

WILLIAM J. CLINTON

The White House,
March 6, 1997.

The President's News Conference
March 7, 1997

The President. Good afternoon, ladies and gentlemen. Today we learned some very good news about the American economy. Our Nation has created almost 600,000 new jobs in the first 2 months of 1997, almost 12 million since January of 1992. At the same time, the deficit has been reduced by 63 percent; investment in our people has increased; inflation remains low. Our economy is on the right track. But to stay on that right track, we have to balance the budget while we go forward with the work that leads to continued growth and low inflation. That's what our balanced budget will do, eliminating the deficit in 5 years and strengthening critical investments for the future of all of our people.

Last week the Congressional Budget Office certified that even under its assumptions, because of the protections we built into the budget, it would be balanced by 2002. So I am hopeful, and I want to say again that the talks we have been continually having with congressional leaders in both parties will produce a balanced budget agreement this year and in the not too distant future.

I also want to talk a moment about our commitments to our Gulf war veterans. And I thank Secretary Brown and the other veterans leaders who are here, including Elaine Larson from the Presidential Advisory Committee on Gulf War Illnesses, the leadership of the Veterans of Foreign Wars and other veterans organizations, and the Persian Gulf veterans who join with us here today.

Two months ago, when I accepted the final report of the Presidential Advisory Committee on Gulf War Illnesses, I pledged to the Committee and to all America's veterans that we would match their efforts with action. Today I am announcing three important steps to meet that pledge and our debt to our veterans.

First, I have approved Secretary Brown's recommendation for the new regulations to extend the eligibility period for compensation for Persian Gulf veterans with undiagnosed illnesses. We aim to raise significantly the window for Gulf veterans to claim the compensation they have earned. Under current regulations, veterans with undiagnosed illnesses must prove their disabilities emerged within 2 years of their return from the Gulf in order to be eligible for benefits. Experience has shown that many disabled veterans have had their claims denied because they fall outside that 2-year timeframe. The proposed new regulations would extend the timeframe through the year 2001. That is 10 years after the cessation of hostilities in the Gulf war. Gulf war veterans who became ill as a result of their service should receive the compensation they deserve even if science cannot yet pinpoint the cause of their illnesses.

Second, I have accepted from the Secretaries of Defense, Health and Human Services, and Veterans Affairs a comprehensive action plan to implement the recommendations of the Presidential Advisory Committee's final report. I asked for this plan within 60 days, and they delivered. The plan addresses outreach, medical and clinical issues, research, coordination, investigations, and chemical and biological weapons. It will help us to do an even better job of caring for Gulf war veterans and finding out why they're sick.

Third and finally, as the Committee recommended, I have initiated a Presidential review directive process to make sure that in any future troop deployments, we act on lessons learned in the Gulf to better protect the health of our service men and women and their families. We need to focus on better communication, better data, and better service.

The Committee's work and a massive, intensive, ongoing review of millions of pages of documents by the Department of Defense and the CIA continues to bring new information to light, including recently released documents about possible exposure of our troops to chemical agents. The scope of the efforts is substantial, and if there is additional information, it will be found and released. We will be asking two very important questions about any such new information. First, should it change the research or health care programs we have in place to care for our veterans? And second, how will it help us to make the policy changes we need to better protect our forces in future deployments?

What is most important is that we remain relentless in our search for the facts and that as we do get new information, we share it with our veterans, with Congress, and with the American people, and that we act on any information we uncover. That is what we have done and what we must continue to do. I will not stop until we've done everything we can to provide the care and to find the answers for Gulf war veterans that they need and deserve.

And again let me say, I thank all of you for your work and for being with us here today.

Now I'll be glad to take your questions, and I think, Terry [Terence Hunt, Associated Press], you're the first.

1996 Campaign Financing

Q. Yes, sir, Mr. President. We learned this week that the Vice President solicited campaign contributions in the White House and that the First Lady's Chief of Staff accepted a $50,000 campaign contribution in the White House. This comes on the heels of news about White House sleepovers and White House coffees for big-money donors. You, sir, promised to have the most ethical administration in history. How does all of this square with that?

The President. Well, first of all, let's take them one by one. I don't believe that they undermine the case. But let me begin by saying there were problems in the fundraising in 1996 which have been well-identified. And the Democratic Party commissioned its own audit, did a review, made the results public, and took appropriate action. I think that is very important, and I'm proud of that.

The second thing I want to say is, I thought the Vice President did a good job of explaining what he did and why, and explaining exactly what he intended to do in the future.

With regard to Maggie Williams, I'd like to make a comment about that. She is an honorable person. She was put in a rather unusual circumstance, and as a courtesy, she agreed to do what the relevant regulation plainly provides for, which is to forward the check on to the Democratic National Committee. Now, in retrospect, with all of the publicity that's attended the whole contribution issue, would it have been better if Maggie Williams had said, "Look, I can do this under the regulations, but I decided I shouldn't do it. And I want you to go mail it in yourself or take it over there yourself"— that would have been a better thing to do. And in the future, I expect that the White House will follow that course should such an occasion ever arise again.

But finally, I want to make the point I have been trying to make to the American people. We had to work hard within the law to raise a lot of money, to be competitive. We did work hard, and I'm glad we did, because the stakes were high and the divisions between us in Washington at that time were very great. We still fell over $200 million short of the money raised by the committees of the Republican Party.

The real problem and the reason you have some of the questions you have, I think—unless you just believe that all transactions between contributors and politicians are inherently suspect, which I don't believe and I think is wrong for either party—the real problem is these campaigns cost too much money, they take too much time, and they will continue to do so until we pass campaign finance reform. If we pass campaign finance reform, as I've asked, by July 4th, then the situation will get better. If we don't, we will still be raising too much money, and it will take too much time and effort on the part of everyone involved. So I'm hopeful that we can.

But I believe that both the Vice President and Maggie Williams are highly ethical people, and I do not believe that either one would knowingly do anything wrong.

This business of raising money takes a lot of time, and if you have to do too much of it, it will take too much time and raise too many questions. But I do not agree with the inherent premise that some have advanced that there is somehow something intrinsically wrong with a person that wants to give money to a person running for office and that if you accept it, that something bad has happened. I don't agree with that. I don't think there is something intrinsically bad. But the system is out of whack, and I think we all know it and we all know it's not going to get better until and unless we pass a reasonable campaign finance reform law.

Helen [Helen Thomas, United Press International].

Q. Mr. President, Governor Romer said that Maggie Williams was wrong to accept the check, and you obviously seem to agree in retrospect. But——

The President. No, no, I'm not going to say Maggie Williams did anything wrong. And I don't want to be—you all will have to deal with this as best you can, but I want to be clear. She is an honorable person. There is a regulation that deals with this which explicitly says that when something—if you receive a contribution and all you do is just pass it on and you've been involved in no way in any solicitation on public property and you're just passing it through, that that is what the regulation provides for. It is explicit and clear.

What I said was, I think that she would say in retrospect and I would say, given the extreme sensitivity now everyone has to all these contribution issues, that she should have said to the gentleman in question, "Look, I can do this legally, but I don't want to do it because I think we should remove all question, all doubt. I think you ought to go mail it yourself. Go take it down there yourself." And that's what I think the White House should do in the future if someone physically is present in the White House and attempts to do that.

Q. Mr. President, in your zeal for funds during the last campaign, didn't you put the Vice President and Maggie and all the others in your administration topside in a very vulnerable position?

The President. I disagree with that. How are we vulnerable, because—only vulnerable if you think it is inherently bad to raise funds and you believe that these transactions are between people who are almost craven. I mean, that's how—I don't agree with that. Maggie Williams, in this case, was completely passive. She didn't ask someone to come in and give her a check. And she had no reason to believe there was anything wrong with it, with the check involved. She just simply did what the regulation explicitly provides for, which is to pass it on.

Now, in the case of the Vice President, he can speak for himself, but I have to tell you, we knew what we were facing. We knew no matter what happened, we would be badly outspent. We believed in what we stood for. From time to time, we were surprised we had as many folks who were willing to stick with us as there were. But we are proud of the fact that, within the limits of the law, we worked hard to raise money so that we could get our message out there and we would not be buried, literally buried, by the amount of money that the other side had at their disposal.

There were the problems that we identified, which we've been very forthright about. We got an external auditor to come into the Democratic Party. They have taken the steps to correct them. But it was—we had never faced anything like that before in American politics, and we did the very best we could with it. And I don't think we were compromised by fighting for what we believed in within the limits of the law.

I do believe that this system is not good now. It is so expensive. It requires too much time, too much energy. And the more effort you put into it, the more opportunity you have for some sort of—something going wrong. So what I think has to be done is we have to reform the law. But until we get some energy behind an effort to reform the law, you know, if it's just me and Senator McCain and Senator Feingold and a few others who support us for it, we can't pass it, and you will be left with the same system next time and the time after that and the time after that. And because of the exponential rise in the cost of buying air time and other means of communication, we'll have all these questions all over again, time and time and time again.

Go ahead—Rita [Rita Braver, CBS News] first, and then Wolf [Wolf Blitzer, Cable News Network]. I'll just do it that way.

White House Access

Q. I'm going to ask your forbearance, because this question is a little bit long. But this is about Johnny Chung, the person who gave the check to Maggie Williams. In April of '95, about a month after he gave that check, he came in here to the White House; he brought in five Chinese officials. Someone on your staff sent a memo to the National Security Council saying that you were not certain you'd want photos of you with these people floating around. I wanted to ask you why you were worried about that, and also why, after a highly knowledgeable NSC official wrote back that he was a hustler who will continue to make efforts to bring in his friends into contact with the President and First Lady and whose clients might not always be in favor of business ventures the President would support—why did he keep getting back in here? What was your relationship to him? And he now says that it was at least implicit, if not explicit, that he would get this access for the money he gave.

The President. Well, first of all, you asked me two questions really.

Q. Four. [*Laughter*]

The President. Why did I—well, I'll answer the two I can remember, then if I don't suit you, you can ask again. [*Laughter*]

I just had—as I have said before on this question of White House access, we did not have an adequate system here. I assumed, wrongly as it turned out, that there were kind of established procedures which were sort of handed on from administration to administration that had nothing to do with whoever happened to be here about—that controlled and developed access. And I was wrong about that. So that's what I assumed generally was in place until we became aware that they weren't.

But on this particular day, I just had an instinct that maybe whatever the rules were, that we didn't maybe know enough about these folks to know whether there should be a picture there. I didn't assume anything negative about them; I just thought that we just didn't know.

Now, with regard to the memo about Mr. Chung, I can't answer that question because I never saw it, and no one ever told me it had been written, and I don't know who did

see it. So I really can't answer that whole cluster of questions because the first I ever knew such a memo had been written was when it was discussed in the public domain. I did not know that. I had no reason to believe that there was any problem there.

Q. And what was your relationship with Mr. Chung? How did you come to know him? How did he get into your office and write you letters that you replied to? There is lots of record of that.

The President. Well, I like to think we're pretty good about replying to our letters, and I don't think there is anything wrong with that. I don't remember how I met him, but I think I met him at some Democratic Party event. I'm sure that's where I met him. I didn't have a relationship with him prior to my becoming President, to the best of my knowledge.

Wolf.

Decision on an Independent Counsel

Q. Mr. President, early in your administration, when you were faced with a similar round of pressure for a special prosecutor to investigate Whitewater, you made it easy on Janet Reno by preempting her and saying, "Yes, it's time for a special prosecutor"—Robert Fiske, in that particular case—"to go forward." And ever since—you know, the history of Whitewater. Why not make it easy for Janet Reno this time and similarly preempt her and say, "Yes, there's enough of a threshold, enough of the law has been met to go forward and get to the bottom of this"?

The President. For one thing, there was no law at the time. And I might point out that if there had been a law, either the previous law or this law, there would have been no special prosecutor because the threshold of the law was not met. And you know, the American people will have to make a judgment about whether all of this has been worth it when the facts come out. But the threshold of the law was not met, and I doubt very seriously if one ever would have been called if any law had been in place.

Now there is a law in place. It is a legal question. I do not think it should become a political question. And I have been very rigorous in dealing with this and saying it in just that way, and I'm going to stick with my position.

Peter [Peter Maer, NBC Mutual Radio].

1996 Campaign Financing

Q. Mr. President, you again today, Vice President Gore the other day, and your staffs have repeatedly told us that no laws were broken in the Lincoln Bedroom issue, in the phone calls for donations, in Maggie Williams accepting and then passing along the donation to the DNC. But cumulatively, Mr. President, what are your thoughts on the propriety and the appearance of all of these various actions?

The President. Well, let's take them one at a time. The Vice President has said that he believes he should—if he makes further fundraising calls as opposed to attending fundraising events, he should not make them from his office even if it is paid for with a political credit card.

I have said that I believe Maggie Williams thinks, in view of the environment in which we now are, that even though there is an explicit regulation on this—right on point on this—that what she probably wishes she had said and what I expect future employees to say is, "Look, I can take this; it is legal. But we're not going to do it this way. You have to mail it in, or you have to take it in yourself."

On the third thing, I just have a different view of this than you do. We have—I have done something no President has ever done. I mean, I gave you a list of the people that spent the night in the White House. And it shows that a relatively small percentage of them, about one in nine, were people that I met in the course of running for President, who supported me for President, who either gave me contributions or also helped to raise money for me.

The people that did that, I'm grateful to them for doing that. I appreciate the fact that they helped me in the campaign in '92. And the document which was released, which most of you reported on, which showed the note I had sent back to Nancy Hernreich, makes it clear that I wanted to get back in touch with those people. I appreciated what they had done. I didn't want them to feel estranged from me. And I don't think there is anything wrong with a President—me or anyone else—reaching out to his supporters.

And some of them, including—let me just give you—I mean, I can give you lots of examples, but there have been a lot of different kinds of people who spent the night here. But one of the newspapers made an issue of B. Rapoport from Texas. Well, he was my friend 25 years ago. When I was a defeated candidate for Congress with a campaign debt that was almost twice my annual salary, he was my friend. When I was the youngest former Governor in the history of the Republic and nobody felt I had any political future, he was my personal friend. I don't think there is anything wrong with having people like that spend the night with you.

So you can make your own judgments about this. But I have tried to be very forthright with you about this. I've given you all of this information, and you can make your own judgments. But I just simply disagree that it is wrong for a President to ask his friends and supporters to spend time with him.

And let me remind you of one problem. A lot of you who have to travel around with me are acutely aware of this. This job, even when you're traveling, can be a very isolating job. Usually when you travel someplace, you go someplace; you stay a little while; you turn around and leave. If you go to these fundraisers—on the coffees, for example, I'm the one that's most responsible—or for the dinners out, the fundraising dinners—I get frustrated going to meetings and goings where all you do is shake hands with somebody or you take a picture, no words ever change. You never know what somebody's got on their mind, or they never get a chance to talk to you. You never have any real human contact. I look for ways to have genuine conversations with people. I learn things when I listen to people.

But I can tell you this: I don't believe you can find any evidence of the fact that I have changed Government policy solely because of a contribution. It's just that I don't think I should refuse to listen to people who supported me or refuse to be around them or tell people, "Well, you contributed to the campaign. Therefore, even though I'd love to have you come see me at the White House, I can't do it anymore." And you will just have to sort through that and evaluate whether you agree with that or not. But that's how I feel.

Q. Are those who question the propriety off base? Is that what you're saying?

The President. Well, no, I'm saying that I do not believe that inviting people to spend the night with me at the White House, the overwhelming majority of whom were personal friends of mine of long standing, family members, friends of family members, friends of my daughter's, dignitaries, public officials, former public officials—some of whose connection with me really did begin in 1991 when I started running for President and that involved their willingness to give me money or to raise money for me—I don't think that that is a bad thing.

What I think is a bad thing is to say—and again, this may not be illegal either, and you know the documents also show that I stopped this—I don't think a political party should say, "If you give this amount of money, we'll guarantee you this specific access. If you give that amount of money, we'll guarantee you that specific access." I don't think that a political party should say or a President should say, "If you want access to us, you have to contribute. And if you want access to us, you not only have to contribute to us, you can't contribute to them." I never did any of that.

As I have said before, one of the most important meetings I had about China policy was one organized by Republicans; as far as I know, none of them had ever done anything in my behalf before. But it was important.

I just don't think you should eliminate contacts with your supporters. And I don't think that anyone else—if you really think about it, I don't think you will think that, either.

John [John Donvan, ABC News].

Q. Mr. President, in listening to many of your supporters and aides respond to these questions over the last several weeks, one note that I think I hear is one of frustration, a sense that these questions are unfair and the focus on the Democrats is unfair. But I also find something unsatisfactory in that response, and my question to you as somebody who has enormous power to lead by example, is it good enough to say that everybody else does it?

The President. No, no, and I'm not trying to say that. I'm going to try to get through this whole press conference and never talk about the practices of the Republicans. [*Laughter*] I'm going to do my best to get all the way—I don't think that's a good example.

And I also don't think it's good enough to say it is legal. I think we should be held to a higher standard than just, "It is legal." But what I do want you to know is, when it is obvious that we have a disagreement—when I read reports or see them on television and I think—you see this in a certain way, and I just honestly see it in a different way—I think it's helpful to the American people and to you and

to me for me to tell you how I see it, that's all.

But I think there are things that when we see them in the light of day, even if we've been given guidance about what the limits of what the law are, it seems that it's not a prudent thing to do. I thought the Vice President gave a very upfront and forthright statement about that the other day. So I don't believe it's enough to say everybody does it.

On the other hand, I don't believe either that we can afford to run the risk of having one party just kind of disappear from the scene because they don't do what—they're unwilling to do what is necessary to be competitive in raising funds in the system that exists, which is why I say to you, in the end, we should set a high standard. But if I honestly disagree with you about what's right and wrong, I should be free to say that. But in the end, the answer to this is to pass a reasonable campaign finance reform bill this year. That's what I really believe.

Yes, go ahead.

Q. Mr. President, you have—you and your officials have given us a number of explanations over the past several months about what you thought was legal. You said you got clear legal advice and gave us the impression that the dividing line on solicitations for contributions—that the dividing line between right and wrong was whether or not that solicitation took place at the White House. But when we learned that the Vice President did just that, then we were told that that wasn't the standard after all. Which is right?

The President. Well, let me just say on the—I think that's one the Vice President—first of all, I think they're both right, and let me explain why. Because it's clear that what the law is on this, going back a long time, is that it's as if he'd written a letter to somebody from the White House. Did the solicitation occur when he wrote the letter or when the letter is received? And the law is clearly that the solicitation is consummated, if you will, when the person is solicited and where the person is solicited.

And the Vice President thought that as long as he was not using taxpayer money to make the call, that it was legal. I think he was right about that. He also thought about it and said, "If I ever do this again"—in terms of calls—"I'm not going to do it in my office because it doesn't look right. We ought to have a higher standard." And I was proud of him for saying that.

But I think that's what—that goes back to the question that John said. There is a difference between—sometimes there is a difference between what is legal and what ought to be done, and this is a place where I think there is a difference, and I think we've made that clear. And I was proud of the statement that he made.

Q. Mr. President, your Press Secretary this week left open the possibility that you, too, had made calls like the Vice President did. Did you ever make those calls?

The President. I told him to leave that possibility open because I'm not sure, frankly. I don't like to raise funds in that way. I never have liked it very much. I prefer to meet with people face to face, talk to them, deal with them in that way. And I also, frankly, was very busy most of the times that it's been raised with me. But I can't say, over all the hundreds and hundreds and maybe thousands of phone calls I've made in the last 4 years, that I never said to anybody while I was talking to them, "Well, we need your help," or "I hope you'll help us."

So I told him not to flat out say that I'd never done it because I simply can't say that I've never done it. But it's not what I like to do, and it wasn't a practice of mine. And once I remember in particular, I was asked to do it, and I just never got around to doing it.

But I don't believe the Vice President did anything wrong in making the calls. I know some people have advanced the proposition that the Vice President should not ever ask anybody for funds, at least unless he's looking at them face to face as opposed to on the telephone. I just disagree with that. I do think he made the right decision about not doing it in the office.

So I asked that that be—that Mike McCurry do it in that way, not to mislead you or to be cute but just simply because I don't want to flat out say I never did something that I might, in fact, have done, just because I don't remember it.

Susan [Susan Feeney, Dallas Morning News].

Q. You said that you've operated within the parameter of the laws, but in retrospect, do you have any regret about the quantity of campaign activity that happened in the White House?

The President. You mean—I do not regret the friends that I have asked to come and stay with me here. And in terms of the coffees, based on what I knew the facts to be and what I still believe they were, that no one was going to be solicited at the meeting and that there was no specific price tag on coming to the coffees, which is what my understanding was, I don't regret doing that.

As I said—again, this is a matter of perception. I really was—I mean, I think I was more upset maybe than some of you were when I found out that my party was not checking the checks that were coming in. I was livid and stunned that in 1996, after all we'd been through in the last 20 years, that could have happened. It took my breath away. I was upset when I saw a proposed brochure that says, "This is the access you get to the President in the White House if you have this amount of money. If you give that amount of money you get guaranteed a certain amount of other access." I thought that was wrong.

But on the other hand, I have a different take on some of this than you do. I am, as I said—I want to take personal responsibility for this. If you find the coffees offensive—I can't say if somebody did something around the coffees they shouldn't have done, but if you find the fact of the President having coffee at the White House with people who either have supported him in the past or who he hopes will support him in the future—I am personally responsible for that, and I take full responsibility for it, because I enjoyed them enormously. I found them interesting. I found them valuable. I found that all these people, many of whom had been active in elections for years and they'd done all kinds of different things with their lives, were given the first chance they'd ever had to just sort of say, "Here's my idea, and I hope you'll consider it," or "Here's what I think you should do," or "Here's where I think you're wrong." And I genuinely enjoyed them, and I did not believe they were improper.

And I still believe as long as there was no specific price tag put on those coffees, just the fact that they would later be asked to help the President or the party does not render them improper. That's what I believe.

Mara [Mara Liasson, National Public Radio].

Q. My question really was, if you had it to do all over again, would you have moved these things outside of the White House or had stricter standards about what political things would be done in the White House?

The President. Well, if I had it to do all over again, we would fix what we have now fixed. We would have stricter standards about admission to the White House. And the answer to your other question—I hesitate to give you a general answer because there may be some facts about a particular coffee or another that I don't know. All I'm saying is that based on what I thought the facts were, which is these were people that we hoped would help us, some of whom had helped us in the past, some of whom had never helped us, and they were going to be invited here, and I was going to have coffee with them, and we're going to talk about things, after which some or all of them—not all of them, as it turned out, but many of them would be solicited to help in the campaign—I do not believe that was wrong, and I feel comfortable about what I did there.

I wish—I've said this a million times—I almost wish that one of you had been in all of these coffees, because they were, frankly, fairly pedestrian events in the sense that nothing very juicy was discussed, but people got to come out with their ideas, state their convictions. And maybe there ought to be some way of dealing with that. Maybe at least you ought to have some assurance that, if these sort of things were done like this on a regular basis, at least, that you ought to have some knowledge of what goes on in them, and that might make you feel better about it.

Mr. Cannon [Carl Cannon, Baltimore Sun].

Access and Economic Issues

Q. Mr. President, you said a moment ago that no decision or policy made here was solely because of a contributor. But should that be a factor at all in U.S. foreign policy and who gets Government contracts and who goes on trade missions? Should that even be considered at all?

The President. Well, what I think should— let me just say this. This is the nub; this is the difficulty. Every public official—this is a problem or an issue that the President, Members of Congress, Governors, mayors all face. People who help you, people who try to help you put your program in, you try to stay in touch with them, so you're more likely to know if they want to do something than you are people who didn't help you and people who weren't involved in it. The instructions that I gave were, if someone who helped us wants to be considered for an appointment, they ought to be considered for the appointment, but they shouldn't get it unless they're qualified for it. They shouldn't be disqualified because they have been a supporter of ours.

That's the way I felt about the trade missions. If someone wanted to go on a trade mission and was qualified and could make a contribution, then they ought to get to go. But if they would never get to go in a thousand years, that no one would think they should have any business on the trade mission and the only reason they were going to get to go was because they contributed to us, I didn't think they should go.

But I think it's disingenuous for anybody in public life to say that it doesn't help you to be considered for these things if you help the person who happens to win an election, because you have to stay in touch with the people that helped you. And it is a good thing to do. That's the way the political system works. That's the way—I would expect that of a Republican or a Democrat or an independent who got elected to any office, that people that helped you and people that you know, people you have confidence in, you ought to listen to them. But you should never make a decision and do something solely because they have helped you before or solely in anticipation of something they might do for you in the future.

And what we have to do is to have our decisions open enough and transparent enough that the American people can see that that is being done. And I can tell you, people come to you in all different kinds of ways. For example— let me just give you one example. It's not a trade mission, but I'll just give you one example. There was a huge amount of money at stake in the private sector in the legislation involving the telecommunications reform. It was the first time we had reformed telecommunications in 60 years. You all are in it. You know better than I do how much it's changing—all the competition issues, massive amounts of money.

The Vice President has been interested in this issue forever. In our weekly lunches, we spent endless amounts of time talking about the telecommunications act, what it should look like, and we took a position. We then found we had all these people who came to us and supported us, many of whom had been Republicans their whole lives, who were independent long distance telephone operators. And they came to us because the majority party had decided to take a position favored by the larger telephone companies.

We had a clear public position beforehand. Should we not have accepted their contribution? Should we not have accepted their support and help? I think we did the right thing. Now, flip it around. If they had been helping us all along, but we agreed with them, should we have weakened in our advocacy just because they were supporting us?

In other words, I think the whole reason for the first round of campaign reform—let's go back to that—is that all these contributions should be made public and you should be free to evaluate them and you should be free to determine and to speculate and to probe about whether the money we received from such and such a group has affected a decision we made and does it undermine or support the public interest. You should be free to do that. That's why full disclosure is important. But I think that unless we're going to a completely publicly financed system, contributors will always have access to public officials, then other kinds of people will who helped them. That's the way it is.

Mara, go ahead.

Q. Mr. President, you say that there is no evidence that you've ever changed a policy because of someone you met with. But what does appear to have occurred is that certain people traded on their access. In other words, access to you became a valuable business commodity to get new clients or impress their current clients. Do you think that that meets the higher standard that you want the White House to adhere to?

The President. Well, what I think about that is that we need to evaluate whether we did anything which would give the impression that we were trying to help someone get business. In other words, I can't say who, beyond the reach of our personal contacts, would be impressed with people who had their picture taken with me. After today, it may be that everybody will go broke unless they take the pictures off the wall. I don't know. But I can't say that.

What I can say is that the White House should not knowingly permit the White House or the Presidency or the Vice Presidency to

be used to advance some private economic interest. And that—you've put your finger on something that is troubling to me, and we have to evaluate that more. And it's one of the reasons that I wanted to make sure that we had a system in place on access and on all of these things that will meet that standard in the future, and I believe we've done that. But I think that's a legitimate problem.

Jim [Jim Miklaszewski, NBC News].

Q. Mr. President——

The President. Just a minute, I'll come back to you.

1996 Campaign Financing and Partial Birth Abortion

Q. Mr. President, when you vetoed the ban on partial birth abortion, you said you did so to protect the lives of the mothers and because they were fairly rare. Well, it's since been revealed that there are approximately 5,000 of these so-called partial birth abortions performed every year, 90 percent of them in the 5th and 6th month. Would you now support a ban if it included provisions to protect the mother but would ban the procedure also in the 5th and 6th month?

And one second unrelated question, did the White House discover if there were any other checks or money passed besides the $50,000 to Maggie Williams? [*Laughter*]

The President. That's fair. No, that's a fair question. As far as I know, that did not happen. As far as I know, any other checks that came in, we really didn't—were things that came in the mail and were just routinely referred. And I don't even know if there were any of those or how many there were. But as far as I know, there was no other instance like the one involving Maggie.

Now, let me answer the other question as clearly as I can. The admission by the gentleman in question, that, you know, he thought he was misrepresenting the facts to the Congress in the last debate, has caused a lot of stir here. But I believe—and I tried to be clear about this at the time—I was under the impression that the facts are just as we all said they were, more or less what you've said. I don't know that we have exact numbers.

What I said before was, and let me restate it, I sought to get a bill I could sign that would ban this procedure when it was inappropriate, because there would be other avenues available if an abortion was otherwise legal. What I was concerned about again—and you said 500, I think, so let's just take your number. We don't really know.

Q. Actually, I think it's 5,000.

The President. Five thousand total, of whom a small proportion, maybe 10 percent or so, are like those five women that I had in the White House. I will say again, they are my concern. They are my only concern. And I would remind you that three of those five women identified themselves to me as pro-life voters. And they were told that unless they had a procedure which would be banned under the law that I vetoed, after it was over, the babies they would be carrying would be dead and their bodies would never be able to have another baby. That is my only concern. I have made that as clear as I can.

So I can't answer the question that you asked me any clearer than that because I want to see the language of any proposed bill. I think you can make a very compelling case that for the small number of people I'm trying to protect, this is the biggest issue in their entire lives and that for them my position is the pro-life position. And I believe that it would be a mistake for us to pass this bill one more time without taking care of those folks. When—because, as you just pointed out, Mr. Miklaszewski, because anybody that's in the first two trimesters that has an elective procedure will still have access to another one in a different way after the bill passes.

So, in a funny way, this might not work to reduce the overall number of abortions at all. But in the end, what it could do is every year to take a few hundred women and wreck their lives and wreck the possibility that they could have further children. That's why I was working on this. And if we can solve that problem, I will happily sign this bill. This thing is a real—it has hurt the American people, dealing with this. And I don't mean it's harmed physically; I mean, this has been a great emotional trauma for the American people trying to come to grips with this issue and deal with it. It's a deep thing out there around the country, and it goes way beyond the traditional pro-life/pro-choice fight or disagreement.

I would like to see us bring some harmony to this and put it behind us. But every time anybody mentions this, I remember so vividly the faces of those five women and their life stories and what happened to them afterward. And a few hundred people a year, they don't have much votes or influence, but they're the people I'm concerned about, and they're the people I'm going to try to protect right down to the end.

Let's take one from Sarah [Sarah McClendon, McClendon News Service]. And then I've got to take one from Jill Dougherty [Cable News Network] because she's about to go to Moscow, and she needs to have her parting shot. Go ahead.

American Sovereignty

Q. Sir, this is on another subject. We have a very great problem in this country today, and I wonder if you would use your leadership to counteract the rumormongers that are abroad in the land who are spreading all these rumors that are scaring people to death; large segments of our citizens believe that the United Nations is taking over whole blocks of counties in Kentucky and Tennessee. [*Laughter*]

The President. Yes.

Q. And some of them, they believe that——

The President. Now, you all are laughing, but——

Q. ——you're going to put us in a concentration camp and you're going to give our Army to Russia and all that baloney. Could you do something about this, because it's hurting the unity of the United States.

The President. I don't know, because the people who believe that think I'm the problem. [*Laughter*] We're all laughing about it, but there is not an insubstantial number of people who believe that there is a plan out there for world domination and I'm trying to give American sovereignty over to the U.N. There was a—I read in our local Arkansas newspaper, one of them the other day had a letter to the editor saying that there I go again, there's Clinton out there trying to give American sovereignty over to the United Nations.

Let me just say this: For people that are worried about it, I would say, there is a serious issue here that every American has to come to grips with—including Americans that don't much think about foreign policy until some great problem occurs—and that is, how can we be an independent, sovereign nation leading the world in a world that is increasingly interdependent, that requires us to cooperate with other people and then to deal with very difficult circumstances in trying to determine how best to cooperate?

That's the issue that you will all be reporting on for the next week in the Mexico certification issue. Did I do the right thing to certify Mexico? Are the Members of Congress who disagree with me right when they say we should have decertified Mexico and then given a national interest waiver so we could continue to cooperate economically and in others ways?

I strongly believe I was right. But we don't— if you want to go into that, we can later, but the issue is, we live in an interdependent world. We have to cooperate with people. We're better off when we do. We're better off with NATO. We're better off with the United Nations. We're better off when these countries can work together. So I just think for folks that are worried about this out in the country, they need to be thinking about how—we're not going to give up our freedom, our independence, but we're not going to go it alone into the 21st century either. We're going to work together, and we have to.

Jill?

Russia and NATO Expansion

Q. Thank you very much, Mr. President. Speaking of Russia and NATO, yesterday we heard President Boris Yeltsin saying that the purpose of the motivation by the West for NATO expansion is to squeeze Russia out of Europe and politically marginalize it. And in a couple of weeks, you'll be sitting down with Mr. Yeltsin again. We've heard similar things from the Russians many times. Are you making any progress in changing the Russians' position on this?

The President. Well, I hope so. Let me answer the—I'd like to make two points about it. First of all, this meeting that we're going to have in Helsinki, President Yeltsin and I, it will be very important. And yet it's important to recognize that it's part of a regular pattern of meetings over the last several years which have changed the nature of U.S.-Russian relations forever, I hope, so that it will be a meeting that will be extremely candid, extremely straightforward, and I hope it will deal with not only the question of Russia's relationship to Europe but also what we can do with the Russians to continue to reduce the nuclear threat and what we can do with the Russians to help them to build their economy, because I'm convinced that

they have the capacity, if they can make certain changes, to enjoy a phenomenal amount of economic growth in a relatively short time, which I think would help a lot of things in their country.

Now, on the merits, I have said since 1993 that one of my dreams for the 21st century world is a Europe that for the first time is united, democratic, and free. Since the dawn of nation-states, about the beginning of the last millennium in Europe, it has never been so. There has never been a single time when Europe was united, democratic, and free. The final capstone to that, I think, is working out a security relationship with NATO, a European Union that is expanding and still tied—a Europe still tied to the United States and to Canada, to North America, not only economically and politically but also in terms of our security alliance, but also has a special relationship with Russia and does not rule out even Russian membership in a common security alliance.

The best answer I can give to President Yeltsin is, what are we doing with NATO today and with whom are we doing it? What we are doing today is Bosnia. We together ended the bloodiest war in Europe since World War II, and we are doing it with Russia. And there are lots of other things we can do with Russia.

The final point I want to make is, among the great questions—there are five or six great questions which will determine what the world will look like 30 or 40 years from now. One of those great questions is, how will Russia and China, the two great former Communist powers, define their greatness in the next century? Will they define their greatness as we try to do, in terms of the achievements of our people, our ability to protect ourselves, and our ability to relate to other people? Or will they define— and I think that's a more modern definition, if you will—or will they define their greatness in terms of their ability to influence, if not outright dominate, the people that live around them as well as to control the political debate of people who live within their borders to a degree that I think is not helpful?

If that debate is resolved in the proper way, the 21st century is going to be a very good time for the American people. And I think when you hear all this stuff about NATO, you have to understand that there's two things going on. The Russians want to know, are we aggressive in NATO expansion or defensive, and looking at other targets like Bosnia? Then they're having to define in themselves, "Where do we want to be 25 or 30 years from now?"

And when they say things that we find offensive, I would ask the American people to understand their sensitivities. We were never invaded by Napoleon or Hitler, and they were. So they're a little sensitive about the prospects of their borders. And we're trying to work together for a better, brighter world.

I think that we're going to get there. I expect that the Helsinki meeting will be positive. But you should understand, this is a tough debate

and that they have reasons in their own psyche and circumstances that make it a difficult one.

Thank you.

NOTE: The President's 137th news conference began at 2:02 p.m. in the East Room at the White House. In his remarks, he referred to Nancy Hernreich, Deputy Assistant to the President and Director of Oval Office Operations; Bernard Rapoport, member, Advisory Committee for Trade Policy and Negotiations; and Ron Fitzsimmons, executive director, National Coalition of Abortion Providers.

Statement on the National Economy
March 7, 1997

Today we learned that the economy is continuing to generate good jobs, almost 600,000 jobs in the first 2 months of this year alone. That's good news for American workers and their families. The American economy has now created nearly 12 million new jobs since I took office. Now it's time to keep this American job engine on the move by passing a balanced budget plan that invests in education and our future.

Our 1993 economic plan has helped spur this strong job growth, while cutting the deficit by 63 percent, from $290 billion in 1992 to $107 billion in 1996. Now we must cut the deficit to zero while investing in our people. My budget will do just that. I look forward to working with the Congress to get the job done by passing a balanced budget plan.

Letter to Congressional Leaders Reporting on Iraq's Compliance With United Nations Security Council Resolutions
March 7, 1997

Dear Mr. Speaker: (Dear Mr. President:)

Consistent with the Authorization for Use of Military Force Against Iraq Resolution (Public Law 102-1) and as part of my effort to keep the Congress fully informed, I am reporting on the status of efforts to obtain Iraq's compliance with the resolutions adopted by the United Nations Security Council (UNSC). This report covers the period from January 7 to the present.

Saddam Hussein remains a threat to his people and the region. The United States successfully responded to the increased threat resulting from Saddam's attack on Irbil in late August 1996, but he continues to try to manipulate local rivalries in northern Iraq to his advantage. The United States and our coalition partners con-

tinue uninterrupted enforcement of the no-fly zone over northern Iraq under Operation Northern Watch, the successor mission to Operation Provide Comfort. France chose not to participate in Operation Northern Watch, but the United Kingdom and Turkey remain committed to the same enforcement of the no-fly zone above the 36th parallel that existed under Operation Provide Comfort. Enforcement of the southern no-fly zone also continues, and France remains engaged with our other coalition partners in conducting Operation Southern Watch.

Besides our air operations, we will continue to maintain a strong U.S. presence in the region in order to deter Saddam. U.S. force levels have returned to approximate pre-Operation Desert

Strike levels, with land- and carrier-based aircraft, surface warships, a Marine amphibious task force, a Patriot missile battalion, and a mechanized battalion task force deployed in support of USCINCCENT operations. On February 20, 1997, an air expeditionary force consisting of 30 F–16s and F–15s deployed to Doha, Qatar, to further strengthen the U.S. deterrent in the region. On February 22, an F–117 squadron deployed to Kuwait since last autumn was redeployed to the United States upon the completion of its mission. USCINCCENT has completed the initial phases of Operation Desert Focus, with the relocation and consolidation of all combatant forces in Saudi Arabia into more secure facilities throughout Saudi Arabia. To enhance force protection throughout the region, additional military security personnel have been deployed for continuous rotation. USCINCCENT continues to closely monitor the security situation in the region to ensure adequate force protection is provided for all deployed forces.

United Nations Security Council Resolution (UNSCR) 949, adopted in October 1994, demands that Iraq not utilize its military forces to threaten its neighbors or U.N. operations in Iraq and that it not redeploy troops or enhance its military capacity in southern Iraq. In view of Saddam's reinforced record of unreliability, it is prudent to retain a significant U.S. force presence in the region in order to maintain the capability to respond rapidly to possible Iraqi aggression or threats against its neighbors.

Regarding northern Iraq, we have conducted three rounds of talks, along with our British and Turkish partners, with the major Kurdish parties in northern Iraq—the Kurdistan Democratic Party (KDP) and the Patriotic Union of Kurdistan (PUK). Our immediate goal is to strengthen the U.S.-brokered cease-fire of October 23, which continues to hold, and to encourage political reconciliation between the PUK and KDP. This Administration continues to warn all concerned that internecine warfare in the north can only work to the advantage of Saddam Hussein and Iran, which we believe has no role to play in the area. In this connection, we remain concerned about Iraqi Kurd contacts with either Baghdad or Tehran.

The United States is providing political, financial, and logistical support for a neutral, indigenous Peace Monitoring Force (PMF) in northern Iraq that has demarcated the cease-fire line and will monitor the cease-fire. The PMF likely will be fully deployed in the next few weeks. Our support is being provided in the form of commodities and services in accordance with a drawdown directed by me on December 11, 1996, and in the form of funds to be used to provide other non-lethal assistance in accordance with a separate determination made by former Secretary of State Christopher on November 10, 1996.

We also are encouraging both Kurdish groups to take steps toward reconciliation. At the latest round of higher-level talks in Ankara on January 15, the Iraqi Kurds agreed to establish joint committees to cooperate in such areas as education, health, and transportation. Local representatives of the two Kurd groups, the three countries and the PNF continue to meet biweekly in Ankara and move forward on other confidence-building measures. All our efforts under the Ankara process, like all our efforts concerning Iraq, maintain support for the unity and territorial integrity of Iraq.

The United States, working through the United Nations and humanitarian relief organizations, continues to provide humanitarian assistance to the people of northern Iraq. We have contributed more than $15 million this fiscal year to programs in the north administered by the United Nations International Children's Fund (UNICEF) and the World Food Program (WFP). Security conditions in northern Iraq remain tenuous at best, with Iranian and Kurdistan Workers Party (PKK) activity adding to the ever-present threat from Baghdad.

The oil-related provisions of UNSCR 986, which authorized Iraq to sell up to $2 billion of oil during an initial 180-day period (with the possibility of UNSC renewal of subsequent 180-day periods), went into effect on December 10, 1996. This resolution requires that the proceeds of this limited oil sale, all of which must be deposited in a U.N. escrow account, will be used to purchase food, medicine, and other materials and supplies for essential civilian needs for all Iraqi citizens and to fund vital U.N. activities regarding Iraq. Critical to the success of UNSCR 986 is Iraq's willingness to follow through on its commitments under 986 to allow the U.N. to monitor the distribution of food and medical supplies to the Iraqi people. While Iraq has already sold nearly 80 percent of the oil allowed for the first 90-day period, Iraqi efforts to impose restrictions on the access and freedom of movement of the U.N. monitors tasked with overseeing the equitable distribution of humanitarian supplies have slowed such distribution.

Since my last report, the Government of Iraq has continued to flout its obligations under UNSC resolutions in other ways. Under the terms of relevant UNSC resolutions, Iraq must grant the United Nations Special Commission on Iraq (UNSCOM) inspectors immediate, unconditional, and unrestricted access to any location in Iraq they wish to examine, and access to any Iraqi official whom they wish to interview, so that UNSCOM may fully discharge its mandate to ensure that Iraq's weapons of mass destruction program has been eliminated. Iraq continues, as it has for the past 5 years, to fail to live up either to the letter or the spirit of this commitment.

On February 23, UNSCOM Chairman Rolf Ekeus obtained permission from the Iraqi regime to remove more than 130 SCUD motors from Iraq for extensive testing in the United States and France. Iraq agreed to this action after 3 months of stalling, and only after a December 30 Security Council Presidential Statement deplored Iraq's failure to comply with its obligation to cooperate with UNSCOM. Ekeus continues to believe that Iraq maintains significant numbers of operational SCUD missiles, possibly with CBW warheads. As long as Saddam refuses to cooperate fully with U.N. weapons inspectors, UNSCOM will be impeded in its efforts to fulfill its mandate. We will continue to fully support the mandate and the efforts of UNSCOM to obtain Iraqi compliance with all relevant U.N. resolutions.

Implementation of UNSCR 1051 continues. It provides for a mechanism to monitor Iraq's efforts to reacquire proscribed weapons capabilities by requiring that Iraq notify a joint unit of UNSCOM and the International Atomic Energy Agency in advance of any imports of dual-use items. Similarly, countries must provide timely notification of exports to Iraq of dual-use items.

Iraq continues to stall and obfuscate rather than work in good faith toward accounting for the hundreds of Kuwaitis and third-country nationals who disappeared at the hands of Iraqi authorities during the occupation. It has also failed to return all of the stolen Kuwaiti military equipment and the priceless Kuwaiti cultural and historical artifacts, which were looted during the occupation.

Iraq's repression of its Shi'a population continues with policies that are destroying the Marsh Arabs' way of life in southern Iraq as well as the ecology of the southern marshes. The human rights situation throughout Iraq remains unchanged. Saddam Hussein shows no signs of complying with UNSCR 688, which demands that Iraq cease the repression of its own people.

The Multinational Interception Force (MIF) has been increasingly challenged in the last few months. In the first 6 weeks of the year, 12 merchant vessels were diverted for sanctions violations. This represents the highest volume of smuggler traffic we have seen since maritime sanctions enforcement began. Most of these smugglers take gas oil illegally from Iraq via the Shatt Al Arab waterway and sell it on the spot market for enormous profit. As I have noted in previous reports, these smugglers use the territorial waters of Iran to avoid the MIF inspection in the Northern Gulf. With the help of the Iranian government, which profits from these activities by charging protection fees, these smugglers are able to export between 40,000 and 65,000 metric tons of gas oil through the Gulf each month.

To counter the efforts of those who engage in illegal trade with Iraq, we have taken a number of steps to minimize the smuggling activity. We have adjusted the positioning of our naval forces to take maximum advantage of known trade routes. We are working closely with our friends in the Gulf Cooperation Council to develop greater cooperation in border patrol and customs inspection procedures. We have publicized the involvement of the Iranian government at the United Nations and in press reports.

It is important to remember that these sanctions violations not only aid Saddam and his policy of resisting U.N. mandates, but also slow the flow of humanitarian aid to the Iraqi people who are in such great need. Committing scarce MIF assets to counter the smuggling trade results in fewer ships available to process the legal humanitarian shipments that bring food to Iraq under the provisions of UNSCR 986 and the humanitarian exceptions to sanctions.

We continue to work closely with our maritime partners in the MIF. Recently, The Netherlands informed us that they will send a frigate and an aircraft to join the MIF in the near future. Canada will also soon be sending a ship to join the MIF. The continuing support of the international community is critical to the success of this multinational operation.

Since the implementation of UNSCR 986 in December, the MIF has not encountered any serious problems in processing the maritime traffic involved in lifting oil from the Mina Al Bakr offshore terminal. While it is still too early to tell if the inbound shipments will go as smoothly, we are hopeful that our advance planning and preparation in this area will pay off.

The United Nations Compensation Commission (UNCC), established pursuant to UNSCR 687, continues to resolve claims against Iraq arising from Iraq's unlawful invasion and occupation of Kuwait. The UNCC has issued over 1 million awards worth approximately $5.2 billion. The UNCC has authorized to date only limited payments for fixed awards for serious personal injury or death because additional funds to pay awards have been unavailable due to Iraq's refusal to comply with all relevant UNSC resolutions. With the advent of oil sales

under UNSCR 986, however, 30 percent of the proceeds will be allocated to the Compensation Fund. These proceeds will be used to make installment payments on awards already made and to finance operations of the UNCC.

To conclude, Iraq remains a serious threat to regional peace and stability. I remain determined to see Iraq comply fully with all of its obligations under United Nations Security Council resolutions. My Administration will continue to oppose any relaxation of sanctions until Iraq demonstrates its peaceful intentions through such compliance.

I appreciate the support of the Congress for our efforts and shall continue to keep the Congress informed about this important issue.

Sincerely,

WILLIAM J. CLINTON

NOTE: Identical letters were sent to Newt Gingrich, Speaker of the House of Representatives, and Strom Thurmond, President pro tempore of the Senate.

The President's Radio Address
March 8, 1997

Good morning. This week we learned that America's economy continues to grow steady and strong, creating almost 600,000 new jobs in the first 2 months of this year alone and about 12 million in the last 4 years. We can make this time one of enormous promise for America, but only if we make sure that all Americans who are willing to work have the chance to reap the rewards of our prosperity.

This morning I want to talk to you about what we can do to lift the permanent underclass into a thriving and growing middle class and to announce new steps the National Government will take to move people from welfare to work.

Four years ago when I became President, I pledged to end welfare as we know it. We worked with States to launch welfare reform experiments to require work. We cracked down on child support enforcement, increasing child support payments by 50 percent. We required teen mothers to stay at school and live at home

if they wanted to receive welfare. Today I'm pleased to report that due to these efforts and our growing economy, we've already moved 2.6 million people off the welfare rolls, a record number.

Last summer we took the most dramatic step of all when I signed the bipartisan welfare reform legislation that imposed time limits, required work, and extended child care and health care so that people can move from welfare to work without hurting their children. The new law ended the old welfare system when we said to those on welfare: Responsibility is not an option; it must be a way of life.

Now, all the rest of us have our responsibility, indeed, our moral obligation, to make welfare reform work, to make sure that those who now must work, can work. We must move another 2 million more people off the welfare rolls in the next 4 years. And frankly, we must recognize that many of these people will be harder to reach and will need more help than those who moved off the rolls in the past 4 years. This cause must engage the energy and the commitment of everyone in our society, of business, houses of worship, labor unions, universities, civic organizations, as well as government at every level.

Above all, we must harness the private sector to bring jobs and hope to our hardest pressed neighborhoods. We are working with leaders of American business to help mobilize other businesses to hire people off welfare. My balanced budget plan would give businesses tax incentives to hire people and would give job placement firms a bonus for every person they place from welfare into a job.

States can do more, too. I have called upon every State to use the power that has now been given to them under the new welfare law, to turn welfare checks into private sector paychecks.

And the National Government must do its part and set an example. Our National Government is now the smallest it has been in three decades, but it is still the Nation's largest employer. We must do our part. So today I am committing a National Government action plan to hire people off welfare. I am formally directing the heads of each agency and department of our Federal Government to do everything they can to hire people off the welfare rolls into available jobs in Government, consistent with the laws already on the books for hiring Federal workers. Because this effort is so important, I am asking Vice President Gore, who has led our reinventing Government effort and done so much to make our Government work better as it costs less, to oversee this endeavor.

I want these agencies to use the worker-trainee program which the Government already has in place to train workers quickly and move them into entry-level jobs. Then if the people do well for 3 years, they can join the civil service. And I am asking every member of my Cabinet to prepare a detailed plan for hiring welfare recipients, what jobs they will fill, how they will recruit welfare recipients, how they will make sure these people have the chance to work hard, perform well, and, thereby, deserve to keep their jobs. The members of the Cabinet will present these plans to me in one month at a special Cabinet meeting.

The job of moving people from welfare to work as the law requires will not be easy. But we must help them as they help themselves. And we need to help all low income Government workers. We need to make sure they take advantage of the earned-income tax credit, the tax cut that already has helped 15 million of our hardest pressed working families. We should give these workers help with transportation to work, and we must help them to find affordable child care.

Government can help to move people from welfare to work by acting the way we want all employers to act, demanding high performance from workers but going the extra mile to offer opportunity to those who have been on welfare and want to do something more with their lives. If we all do that, we can move into the 21st century strong, united, and with the American dream alive for all our people.

Thanks for listening.

NOTE: The President spoke at 10:06 a.m. from the Oval Office at the White House.

Memorandum on Government Employment for Welfare Recipients
March 8, 1997

Memorandum for the Heads of Executive Departments and Agencies

Subject: Government Employment for Welfare Recipients

Since I signed the historic welfare reform law, I have urged businesses, nonprofit organizations, and religious groups across the Nation to help

make its promise of opportunity real by offering jobs to welfare recipients. We are making great progress, but there is more to do. And today, I take action to ensure that the Federal Government, as the Nation's largest employer, contributes to the greatest extent possible to this national effort.

I therefore direct each of you, as head of an agency or department, to use all available hiring authorities, consistent with statute and prior executive memoranda, to hire people off the welfare rolls into available job positions in the Government.

In particular, I direct you to expand the use of the Worker-Trainee Program and other excepted service hiring authorities. The Worker-Trainee Program allows agencies to quickly and easily hire entry-level persons for up to 3 years, with the ability to convert the appointment to career status if the employee has performed satisfactorily. Though recently underutilized, the program allows agencies to bypass complex Federal personnel hiring rules and procedures to bring people into the junior grades of the work force.

I further direct you, in recognition of the different characteristics of the various agencies' work forces, to prepare an individualized plan for hiring welfare recipients and to submit that plan to me within 30 days. This plan should have three principal components:

- The plan should contain a survey indicating in which divisions and for which categories of positions your agency can most easily hire welfare recipients, both in the Washington, D.C. area, and in the field.
- The plan should describe in detail how the agency intends to recruit and hire qualified welfare recipients. This description should include a proposed local outreach program, and utilize Federal Executive Boards and Federal Executive Agencies to bring Federal job opportunities to the attention of welfare offices, State and private employment offices, nonprofit organizations, and others that work with welfare recipients on a regular basis. This program should build upon the Government's existing nationwide employment information systems.
- The plan should describe in detail how the agency will assist welfare recipients, once hired, to perform well and to keep their jobs. The agency should include in this aspect of the plan proposals for on-the-job training and/or mentoring programs.

I expect each agency head to report to me about his or her plan at a special cabinet meeting called for that purpose. Following this meeting, I also expect monthly reports on implementation.

To ensure deep and continuing involvement in this issue by the White House, I ask the Vice President to oversee this effort. Based on his expertise in Federal workplace issues, he will assist all agencies in carrying out their commitments.

Finally, I direct appropriate agencies to take three steps that will help bring welfare recipients into the Federal work force while assisting all other low-income Federal employees.

- I direct each agency head to notify all employees eligible for the Earned Income Tax Credit (EITC) of both their eligibility and their ability to receive EITC monies each month in their paychecks. Currently, not all agencies inform qualifying employees of their eligibility and options for payment. To insure uniform implementation, I direct the Secretary of the Treasury to issue to each agency within 15 days a statement of EITC eligibility rules which agencies can use to inform their employees.
- I direct the General Services Administration (GSA) to issue within 30 days guidelines regarding use of the Federal Fare Subsidy Program. These guidelines should address whether agencies may offer fare subsidies based on employee income, which would enable more agencies to participate in the Fare Subsidy Program.
- I direct the GSA, after consultation with all Federal agencies, to report back to me within 30 days on plans to assist low-income Federal workers in finding affordable child care. This report shall include information on agency-sponsored child care centers and agency contracts with local child care resource and referral services, as well as recommendations on any appropriate expansion of these arrangements to provide assistance to low-income Federal workers.

WILLIAM J. CLINTON

Remarks Prior to Discussions With President Hosni Mubarak of Egypt and an Exchange With Reporters
March 10, 1997

President Clinton. Let me say that I'm very glad to welcome President Mubarak back to Washington. The United States and Egypt have been partners in the quest for peace in the Middle East for two decades now. Nothing positive has happened except when we work together, and I think it's important that we continue to do so. And I'm looking forward to this meeting to discuss that as well as what we can do to improve the relations between our two countries.

Welcome, Mr. President. I'm glad to see you.

President Mubarak. Thank you very much.

U.S. Veto of U.N. Resolution on Jerusalem Settlements

Q. President Mubarak, you're the leader of the first nation to begin a peace process with Israel. Do you buy President Clinton's rationale that he is preserving the peace process by, in effect, sanctioning the building of settlements in East Jerusalem?

President Mubarak. It is said in the memo that the President did change his mind concerning the settlements, but the statements coming out from the State Department and from the White House concerning the settlements—the President is a full partner in the peace process. Without the United States, it would be very difficult to continue the peace process. So it's very important to have his influence, his leadership, his activity——

Q. But he gave a green light with his veto.

President Clinton. We're going to have a press conference later.

President Mubarak. Yes.

President Clinton. And we're going to answer all the questions. But I don't think it's fair to say I've sanctioned that. We'll have a press conference later. I'll answer more questions.

Q. Are you prepared to explain the veto, Mr. President—Clinton?

President Clinton. Sure. Yes, we'll have a press conference, and I'll answer all those questions. I'll be happy to answer that. And if no one gets to ask it, I will voluntarily answer it later.

[At this point, one group of reporters left the room, and another group entered.]

President Clinton. Let me begin by saying that it's a great honor for the United States to have President Mubarak back at the White House. His leadership for a comprehensive peace in the Middle East has been absolutely essential to any progress which has been made for 20 years now. We have worked closely together, and I'm looking forward to having this meeting.

Let me also say that we're going to have a press conference afterward, and we'll do our best to answer whatever questions you have.

Do you have anything you would like to say, Mr. President?

President Mubarak. Usually, I come to the United States to meet Mr. Clinton, for the United States is a full partner for the peace process, making tremendous efforts so the process will continue, so as to reach a comprehensive settlement and peace could prevail in the whole area and cooperation will continue among the countries in the Middle East. I thank the President for his efforts, and we are going to discuss other issues now.

Thank you.

NOTE: The President spoke at 11:11 a.m. in the Oval Office at the White House. A tape was not available for verification of the content of these remarks.

The President's News Conference With President Hosni Mubarak of Egypt
March 10, 1997

President Clinton. Good afternoon. I was glad to have the chance to welcome President Mubarak back to the White House. He has been a valued friend of the United States for 16 years now, one of the very first leaders to visit me in 1993 and also one of the first now to come to Washington during my second term.

Through this meeting and through consultations with other leaders from the region, including Prime Minister Netanyahu, Chairman Arafat, and King Hussein, who will be here next week, we are working to help the parties find common ground through progress toward lasting peace. We know that these efforts cannot succeed without the leadership of Egypt.

Since the Camp David accords in 1979, Egypt has been a powerful force for peace in the Middle East. That has continued to be true through the last 3½ years, a time of extraordinary progress toward peace and repeated challenges. Now, as Israel and the Palestinians embark on the difficult task of permanent status negotiations, as we look to revive negotiations between Israel and Syria and then bring Lebanon into the process to complete the circle of peace, we know that Egypt's leadership will be vital to finish the job.

In January Israelis and Palestinians once again demonstrated that even though the challenges are great, the will to create peace is there. An agreement on difficult issues can be achieved through genuine negotiations. But we've also been reminded recently of how difficult it is to maintain the momentum toward peace. Clearly, we're at a moment when all those with a stake in the peace process must rededicate themselves to building confidence and making progress.

Today the United States and Egypt have deepened our own understanding in our partnership, our determination to coordinate our efforts even more closely and to encourage the parties to tackle the tough questions ahead. We also discussed how we can increase our cooperation on issues of regional security and expand the ties of commerce between our people. Stability and security in the region demands that the people of Egypt and all the peoples of the Middle East are rewarded in their efforts by greater prosperity.

I congratulated President Mubarak on the strong economic advances Egypt has made in the last 2 years, the work that he and Vice President Gore have done. And the U.S.-Egypt partnership for economic growth and development has made a real difference by promoting privatization and tariff reduction.

The President's Council, a group of business leaders from the United States and Egypt, has achieved dramatic success, increasing trade and investment between our nations and deepening support for necessary economic reforms. Now Egypt is creating new growth and opportunity, building a better future for its people and for others throughout the Middle East.

Mr. President, you and I have been together here at the White House, in Cairo, at the Summit of the Peacemakers at Sharm al-Sheikh, and elsewhere, working for a just and lasting peace and a new day in the region. Now we're in a new phase, and we have to protect the hard work and achievements of the last 3½ years, and we know we'll have to work hard to fulfill the hopes for the Middle East and for peace. I know we can look to you as a friend and partner, and I look forward to being your friend and partner on this historic mission.

Welcome.

President Mubarak. Ladies and gentlemen, I was very pleased to meet once again with President Clinton and exchange with him views and ideas of matters of common concern. Let me first seize the opportunity to congratulate the President on the reaffirmation of the American people's confidence in his wise and inspiring leadership. It is most reassuring for many to know that they have a knowledgeable and farsighted friend in the White House.

In our discussion today, we had the opportunity to review several issues of special interest to us. First, we reviewed recent developments of the Middle East peace process. While we are pleased by the progress which has been attained on the Israel-Palestinian track, we were alarmed by the differences and the complications that have appeared lately. Such developments make the peace process a fragile and vulnerable one. I'm referring here specifically to the Israeli settlement activities, particularly in Jerusalem.

We all know that the issue of Jerusalem is as sensitive to Muslims and to Christians as it is to Jews. Hence, the rights and sentiments of all these people should be fully respected.

It was for this reason that I urged Prime Minister Netanyahu to reconsider the decision taken by the Israeli Cabinet to authorize the construction of thousands of housing units for Israelis in East Jerusalem. I urged him also not to close the Palestinian office there. Our purpose here is to eliminate all potential sources of tension and violence. It is equally important to avoid any violation of the interim agreement and related documents. We view such actions as flagrant violations that would not serve any useful purpose.

At any rate, I agreed with the Prime Minister to stay in touch and deal with these and other issues with an open mind, in light of their sensitivity. We are looking forward to the carrying out of further redeployments in good faith. On the other hand, we hope that the two parties engage in the final status negotiations without delay. Time is of essence. Every day that goes by without attaining meaningful progress hurts the chance of peace.

Our commitment to a comprehensive peace requires us to exert maximum effort in order to get the negotiations resumed on the Syrian and the Lebanese track. I have discussed the matter at length with President Asad and found him positively inclined. He reiterated serious commitment to a just and comprehensive peace settlement on the basis of the Madrid formula. He believes, not without justification, that the talks should be resumed from the point where the parties had left off a year ago.

There is no reason why we should waste the progress which was achieved through the strenuous negotiations in Washington and Wye plantation. I discussed the issue with Prime Minister Netanyahu, and it is my earnest hope that we can work out an acceptable formula for the resumption of talks with the help of the United States. I need not emphasize the importance of the Syrian and Lebanese track. We should never miss another opportunity for making progress and peace.

President Clinton has assured me of the fact that the U.S. position on these various issues remains unchanged. That's very reassuring, indeed. It reinforces confidence in the U.S. as a reliable sponsor and a promoter of peace in the Middle East. We are determined to pursue our joint efforts in the months ahead with zeal and hope. Together, we shall achieve our goal.

Mr. President, we are both pleased with the progress that has been achieved in our bilateral relations. In recent years, U.S.-Egyptian relations have entered a new era, expanded into new spheres of cooperation, and reached greater depth and warmth.

Today I can say with confidence that we have an economy that is moving toward the future on solid ground. We have established the infrastructure to growth, and we have instituted the necessary reforms and the policies that have placed Egypt in the forefront of the emerging economies, attracting substantial capital flows. We now look forward to years of sustainable high growth, greater investment, and a steady increase in the standard of living of all Egyptians. As we did in the previous stages, we regard the U.S. as one of our most trusted partners in peace and socioeconomic progress.

In conclusion, I would like to thank President Clinton and the American people for their continued support and help. You are undertaking an historic mission at this crucial crossroads. And thank you very much.

U.N. Resolution on Jerusalem Settlements

Q. Mr. President, in casting a veto on a new Israeli settlement in the U.N., the U.S. went against the conscience and the consensus of the world. The general assumption is that Israel is trying to force, with military backing, a preemptive solution to the status of Jerusalem rather than going through negotiations as promised. Is that your read on it?

President Clinton. Well, let me answer the two questions at once there. We made it very clear that the decision to build in the Har Homa neighborhood, in our view, would not build confidence, would not be conducive to negotiations, would be seen by the Palestinians and others as an attempt to, in effect, precondition some of the final status issues. And that's why we said that we thought it was a complication we would prefer strongly that it not have been made.

On the other hand, we felt that the resolution of the Security Council was also ill-advised for the general reason that we generally prefer that the Security Council resolutions not be injected into the peace negotiations, first, and second, because there was specific language in this resolution that we have previously vetoed because we also feel it attempts to shape the final status negotiations.

I think that we have seen—we have learned one thing, I have, in the last 4 years plus, and that is when the parties get together and negotiate in good faith and take risks for peace, good things happen. When they attempt to preclude the process of negotiations or preempt it or are insensitive to the needs and the feelings of people in the negotiating process, more destructive things happen and it becomes more difficult to make peace.

So I feel that we did the right thing from the point of view of the United States and the United Nations. But that should not be interpreted as an approval of the decision that was made by the Israeli Government.

Q. You don't think the U.N. has a role in peacemaking?

President Clinton. Oh, yes, I do think the U.N. has a role. But I think—again, I say, go back and read the language of the resolution. Look at the position we've taken in previous votes with the same kind of language. And remember that we believe it's our job to try to protect the final status issues for the final status negotiations.

You know, I had this same issue on completely the other side last year and the year before when there was a big move in Congress to move the Embassy to Jerusalem. And I opposed it because I thought it was a way by indirection of our taking a position on the final status, which I don't think we should do, I don't think any of us should do. We have got to force these parties to—and to help to work to create an environment in which they make the decisions together in an atmosphere of genuine negotiations. And that's the position that I hold.

Would you like to call on an Egyptian journalist?

President Mubarak. Yes.

Q. A question to both heads of state. Under the fourth Geneva Convention of August 12, 1949, concerning the protection of civilians under occupation, the Palestinians of East Jerusalem should be protected from confiscation of land. In Cairo, when Prime Minister Netanyahu came, he boiled down the problem of the East Jerusalem settlement to a mere housing problem and made the dangerous claim that settlements

are built on Jewish land, ignoring the fact that he is building on occupied territory. Can you then blame the Palestinians if they should sort of revolt, each in his own way?

President Clinton. Who's going first, Mr. President? [*Laughter*]

President Mubarak. Please, Mr. Clinton.

President Clinton. First of all, it's obvious that who owns the land is disputed and that—but the reason that I took the position that it would be—that notwithstanding whatever housing needs do or don't exist, it would be better if the houses not be built in the neighborhood, the Har Homa neighborhood—that I knew that it would be perceived by the Palestinians in just the way you have stated. And what I think is important is—on the other hand, if I were to answer the question in the way that you have established it, it would also seem that we were deciding a final status issue the other way.

That's why the people who set up the Oslo agreements and the people who signed the Israel-PLO accord here in September of 1993, they were very smart. They knew how explosive all these issues were, and they knew that a lot of confidence had to be built up first. And they knew that, for example, the land transfers had to be worked out in the West Bank and Gaza and other issues had to be worked out before the issue surrounding Jerusalem could be resolved. And that is why I think all these things are so terribly difficult and why the best thing is, insofar as both parties can do so, to let them be resolved by negotiations and final status issues without interference by anyone from the outside.

Now, having said that, yes, I still believe it would be a terrible mistake for the Palestinians to resort to violence. Every time they have done it, they wind up losing. They wind up getting hurt. They have a democratically elected leader. They have made dramatic progress in self-government. We are urging always on the Israelis more opportunities to let them progress more economically. We are urging on Mr. Arafat more reforms that will allow them to progress economically and politically. So I think that is the direction to go in. That's the direction that I support.

Do you want to answer the question, Mr. President?

President Mubarak. When Prime Minister Netanyahu was in Cairo last week, I opened this issue with him, and I discussed the issue of building new settlements in the area of Jerusalem. And I commented on his answers in the press conference, telling that this is illegal and this may create problems and we shouldn't touch the area of Jerusalem until the negotiations for the final status, as is the spirit of the Oslo agreement.

But he told me that "I'm building for both sides." But this is not satisfactory to persuade the Palestinians to accept this. We shouldn't build anything in the area of Jerusalem, although there is expansion and increase of population, until the negotiation of the final status come to an end. It will be much more convenient to both sides.

Alleged Chinese Efforts To Influence the 1996 Election

Q. Mr. President, two officials of the White House National Security Council were briefed by the FBI last June about suspicions that China was trying to influence the outcome of U.S. congressional elections, but supposedly this warning wasn't passed up the chain of command. Shouldn't the President be told when a foreign power is trying to influence U.S. elections, and isn't this the type of information you would want to know? And would this have raised a red flag about foreign contributions?

President Clinton. There are basically three things you've asked there. Let me try to—first of all, yes, the President should know. And I can tell you, if I had known about the reports—and again, these are reports; these are allegations; we have not reached a—as far as I know, no one in the Government has reached a conclusive decision about this. So it's very important not to accuse people of something that you don't know they have done. But had we known about the reports, the first thing I would have done is I would have given them to Leon Panetta and to Tony Lake and to Sandy Berger, and I'd say, "Listen, look at these, evaluate them, and make recommendations about what, if any, changes we ought to make or what should we be alert to." So it would have provoked at least to that extent a red flag on my part.

Now, let's go back to the first question. I absolutely did not know it was done. It is my understanding that two members of the National Security Council were briefed by the FBI, and then the agent, for whatever reasons, asked that they not share the briefing, and they honored the request. And we did not know at any time

between—for the rest of the year. We just didn't know, and certainly during the election period we did not know. And why that is, I don't know. But anyway, that happened.

So Mr. Berger has discussed this with the White House Counsel, and they are reviewing the whole episode to try to see what, if any, action is appropriate and what should have been done. But yes, I believe I should have known; no, I didn't know. If I had known, I would have asked the NSC and the Chief of Staff to look at the evidence and make whatever recommendations were appropriate.

Q. Are you going to ask Director Freeh why you weren't told?

President Clinton. I'm going to wait for the National Security Council and the White House Counsel to get back to me on the whole episode and tell me what the facts were and what they think should have happened. And then I'll make whatever decision is appropriate then.

U.N. Resolution on Jerusalem Settlements

Q. The question is for President Bill Clinton. The American administration has always been voicing its concern over the settlement issue. I want to revisit this issue again, if you will allow me. And you first described it as illegal and then as an obstacle to peace and as building mistrust and now dubbed it as a mere difficulty to peace. And a couple of days ago you vetoed a moderate decision by the United Nations over that issue.

Well, you've explained the position of the U.S. administration, but it looks—it's a little bit puzzling for us in the Arab world to understand that position, because don't you think that such a position places the U.S. credibility as an honest peace broker in question? And secondly, doesn't such a position also make the United States interests in the Arab world in jeopardy?

Thank you.

President Clinton. Well, let me say, first of all, in all candor, I'm very concerned about that. I'm concerned about—and I was very aware of how the veto might make the United States look in the Arab world, because I have worked very hard, as I told Mr. Arafat when he was here, to be fair to the Palestinians and fair to all the parties in the Middle East peace process and to see that their legitimate interests are advanced. And I worked hard to avoid, frankly, having a Security Council resolution. We were prepared to support a rather strong statement,

Presidential statement, as an alternative. But I think it's important—and I would say to the people in the Arab world who are looking at this and wondering what we're up to here, I'd like to say, you have to remember a couple of things.

Number one, if you go back and read that resolution, we have had a consistent position. Even though I have abstained in some resolutions—I haven't vetoed all the resolutions criticizing Israel, but even though I have abstained in some, we've had a consistent position that we can never achieve peace through U.N. Security Council resolutions, number one.

Number two, there is language in this particular resolution which is identical to language that we have felt constrained to veto in the past because we felt that it, too, prejudged the final status.

And number three, I would say, just the way you asked the question makes my point. For the Arab world, the building in Har Homa is a settlement and, therefore, a violation. For the Israelis, they are building in a neighborhood that is already a part of their territory. So they are—they strongly dispute that it is a settlement in the sense that they admit other settlements exist.

Now, that very point makes a point I tried to make, which is why I believe the decision should not have been made. This should be part of the final status negotiations. Everything surrounding Jerusalem is of immense emotional, political, and religious significance to all the parties involved here. That's why they wisely put it as a final status issue. And the only thing I can say to you is that you may disagree with this decision, but if you look at what I've done for the last 4 years and what I intend to do, I am trying to get to a point where the parties themselves can honestly make a just, fair, and lasting peace. And I will not do anything that I think undermines the ability of the United States to stand for that.

Gene [Gene Gibbons, Reuters].

Alleged Chinese Efforts To Influence the 1996 Election

Q. Mr. President, you don't seem particularly angry with the information about what's—the allegations that a foreign power was trying to subvert the U.S. elections was not brought to your attention. You're the person ultimately in charge of U.S. national security. I'm just won-dering why you wouldn't pick up the phone and demand of Director Freeh why you weren't told. You certainly were the one person who probably should have known that information.

Thank you.

President Clinton. Well, what I seem and what I feel may be two different things. [*Laugh-ter*] The older I get, the more I become aware of the fact that there's some things that there's no point in expending a lot of energy on. It didn't happen. It should have happened. It was a mistake.

But what I want to do now is—first of all, let's go back to the beginning here of when this came up—whenever it did, several weeks ago. The first thing we have to do is to allow the investigation to proceed, to find out—this is a very serious allegation, but as far as I know, it is only that. And it would be very serious if it were true. But it would also be a foolish error. Anyone who understands the sort of inter-play of American politics, the scope and scale of the issues, the amount of investment involved, I mean, it just wouldn't make much sense. But it's a very serious thing.

The first and foremost thing we have to do is—now let's find out what the truth is, if we can, first. Second, let's find out exactly how this happened—which is why I asked the Counsel and the NSC to look into it—that is, what did these agents say? Were they instructed to say that? Did they just think it would be a good idea? Why did they do that? What was involved? We don't know the answers to a lot of questions.

So, Gene, until I know the answers to these questions, I think it's better for us to be calm, to be disciplined, to be firm, to be straight-forward. There's no point in shedding more heat than light on this. I'm interested in light being shed on this situation, and then as we know the facts, we'll all be able to make our judg-ments then about what should have been done and what we should do from here forward.

Final Status Negotiations

Q. Both of you have spoken about Jerusalem and how it should be only discussed in the final status negotiations. But these negotiations are supposed to start in 4 days, in fact. Do you believe that this deadline will be met, and if not, how will this affect the peace process?

President Mubarak. You're asking me? Both of us. You start, Mr. President.

President Clinton. I went first last time. That's not fair. [*Laughter*] Let me say, the deadline may not be met, but the important thing is to find the basis on which the parties can resume negotiations. I have been very impressed by how gifted the Palestinian negotiating team has been and how gifted the Israeli team has been. For anyone to just even look at the maps on Hebron, it's a stunning achievement, really, that they could come to grips with all this, the complexity of it.

But whether they're prepared to go on right now or whether we're going to have to figure out some way to build the confidence back to jump-start it, we'll see. But if they don't start in 4 days, they're going to have to start sooner or later, or there won't be peace. So I would just bear down and keep working hard to try to get them back together, if they don't meet in 4 days.

President Mubarak. Concerning the Palestinians?

President Clinton. Yes. The Palestinians and the Israelis, yes.

President Mubarak. I know the problem between the Palestinians and the Israelis is so complicated, anyway at least for this specific period of time, especially the rate of redeployment in Area C, which has been declared yesterday about 2.1 percent. I think it needs much more effort from the United States and Egypt to just persuade the two parts and find the solution for this so the negotiation could resume, especially the negotiation for the final status, which is very important, which could decide the whole thing at the end.

Welfare Reform

Q. Mr. President, with the welfare reform issue that you've been dealing with lately, and that's one of your main focuses, are you looking to hire welfare recipients here at the White House in the very near future, because you've gotten a lot of flak from civil rights groups as well as from the business community?

President Clinton. Well, let me just say the rules—the White House will be covered like everybody else, with the instruction that I sent out, which is that everyone will—each unit of Government under the various departments will have to send back a plan for what they might be able to do to hire welfare recipients. And then we will have our approach that will include every department in the Government, including

the White House. So it depends. Here, it depends upon whether vacancies occur and in what area. But if they do, I certainly wouldn't rule it out, and I would want to rule it in. That is, I'd like to see us set an example, if we have a chance to do so.

Keep in mind, we have reduced the size of the Federal Government by about 285,000 now from the day I took office. But there are still enough vacancies every year that we can make a substantial contribution to the Nation's goal of having a million people move into jobs from welfare over the next 4 years. And yes, I'd like it very much if one of them was in the White House.

Jerusalem Settlements

Q. Mr. President Mubarak, you announced yesterday on CNN that you are going to ask Mr. Clinton to use his influence in Israel to stop carrying out the building of more settlement in Jerusalem. Did you raise this matter with His Excellency, and what is his reaction about that?

President Mubarak. I think I raised the question of the problem of the Middle East as such and as a whole, and we discussed the issue of the settlement activities. And it is well-known that the United States didn't change its mind, contending that building more settlements, changing the situation is illegal, runs against—creating a problem in the Middle East. We didn't differ in that issue.

President Clinton. We have to take a couple of more, because President Mubarak and I promised this lady she could have—Trudy [Trudy Feldman, Trans Features], do you have a question? And then we'll call on you.

Egypt's Economy

Q. For President Mubarak. May I? President, since you began privatizing your economy, foreign investors have shown increased interest in Egypt. So are you now a convert to free market economics—[*inaudible*]—private sector?

President Mubarak. Oh, sure. I'm inviting any of us who could come. We have changed the laws. We have market economy. We are open to any investors to come and work with us. And mind you, a couple of days ago we have about 17 or 18 businessmen from Israel and other places. And they ask of me if I could give green light to the business people to help there. I told them the green light has already been given years ago, and this depends only on the political atmosphere. But we never prevent anybody to work here or there, or we will not stop and stand against any of us to come to invest in Egypt. And we welcome them at any time.

Q. So you've become a convert?

President Clinton. I think we have just heard the Egyptian version of "Show me the money." [*Laughter*] There's a movie that was made in the United States about a sports agent, Mr. President, and they were always saying, "Show me the money."

Now, this lady, we promised her she could ask a question, didn't we?

President Mubarak. Yes, of course.

U.N. Resolution on Jerusalem Settlements and Syria

Q. A question for both Presidents, please. The whole Arab world was disappointed by the veto. Don't you think, first, that this policy pursued by the U.S. could encourage Israel to build more settlements inside Jerusalem which would make an obstacle—new obstacles to the peace process? And if you have discussed any new Syrian—any new ideas to push forward the Syrian track?

President Clinton. Yes, the answer to your first question is, it would—it might be seen as encouraging the present Israeli Government to do that if we had stated that we were vetoing the resolution because we agreed with Israel's decision. But we've made it clear we do not agree with Israel's decision and we—that we have to go back to the negotiations. So for that reason, I do not believe so.

Second question is, yes, we did. We had a very long, good detailed discussion about what we might do together to get the Syrian negotiations back on track. And we've both agreed now to go out and do a few things to try to see if we can't make that happen. Whether we can, of course, is up to President Asad and Prime Minister Netanyahu. But we believe it's important, and we believe that there is at least a potential there that the parties could reach across the ground that divides them.

President Mubarak. I may say concerning the veto that it's unfortunate that the resolution was not adopted because it might have given a signal to the Israelis to stop any settlement activities, especially in the area of Jerusalem, which is illegal. But I hope in the future we could avoid this.

President Clinton. Okay, one more from each. Go ahead.

Narcotics Certification for Mexico

Q. Thank you very much, Mr. President. It seems like the Congress is trying to reverse your decision to certify Mexico. What are you going to do about it? And are you trying to ask Mexico some gesture in their part to strengthen your hand in Congress?

President Clinton. Well, first let me say, what we're going to do about it is we're going to make a full-court press to bring the administration's position and perspective to the Members of Congress before they vote at large. In fairness to the committee, which voted overwhelmingly against my position last week in the House, we really hadn't had much of a chance to have a discussion with them. And I don't think that there is a great difference about the facts here. The question is, which action by the United States, number one, is required by the law, and number two, is most likely to reduce the drug problem in the United States and in Mexico?

Now, the law says that we should certify Mexico if the government is fully cooperating and if there is some evidence of progress being made. Now, does the fact that the President announced that the drug czar was being dismissed for corruption mean that the government has not been cooperating or the government has been cooperating? I believe it's evidence that the government is cooperating. Secondly, they have dismissed 1,200 other public officials in the last year because of corruption or suspected corruption.

And then let's look at the other issue. Have they gotten results? We have record numbers of eradications, arrests, and seizures of drugs. We have the first extraditions in history of suspected criminals, charged criminals, from Mexico to the United States. We have an agreement between Mexico and General McCaffrey to work together to design a strategy.

I think what we need to do is find a way to work with the Congress to see what the next steps are going to be. I think if Congress says, "If you want us to certify, we've got to know what the next steps are going to be," I think it's legitimate for the Congress to know that. And I think that President Zedillo and I both want to demonstrate—and I hope we will on my trip to Mexico—that we've got a plan to do this that's good for America, good for Mexico, and basically good for our entire region.

But I strongly feel we should certify them. That's the recommendation Secretary Albright has made to me. I think she was right, and I'm going to do my best to persuade the Congress that we're right.

Thank you.

NOTE: The President's 138th news conference began at 2:36 p.m. in the East Room at the White House. In his remarks, he referred to Prime Minister Binyamin Netanyahu of Israel; Chairman Yasser Arafat of the Palestinian Authority; King Hussein I of Jordan; President Hafiz al-Asad of Syria; and President Ernesto Zedillo of Mexico.

Statement on Senator Wendell H. Ford's Decision Not To Seek Reelection
March 10, 1997

Senator Wendell Ford has served his home State of Kentucky with pride and distinction for four terms as a Member of the U.S. Senate. He has been a leader in the Democratic Party and a personal friend for many years. Senator Ford's tireless efforts as a veteran, businessman, Lieutenant Governor, and Governor before coming to Washington have earned him the admiration of all who know him. I will miss his leadership and advice on Capitol Hill but know that he will continue to find ways to improve the lives of the constituents he has served so well for so long. Kentucky and the Nation are better for his dedication and service. Hillary and I wish him, his wife, Jean, and their family well in the years to come.

Letter to Congressional Leaders Transmitting the Report on Peacekeeping Operations
March 10, 1997

Dear Mr. Chairman:

Enclosed is a copy of the 1996 Annual Report to the Congress on Peacekeeping, pursuant to section 407(d) of the Foreign Relations Authorization Act, Fiscal Years 1994 and 1995 (Public Law 103–236).

Once again in 1996, multilateral peacekeeping operations proved their worth in helping to defuse conflict and alleviate humanitarian crises around the world. Our support for the United Nations and other peacekeeping options allows us to protect our interests before they are directly threatened and ensures that others share with us the risks and costs of maintaining stability in the post-Cold War world.

The concerted efforts we have made over the past few years have brought greater discipline to peacekeeping decision-making in national capitals and at the United Nations. Tough questions about the mandate, size, cost, duration, and exit strategy for proposed missions are asked and answered before they are approved. Careful attention is also given to ensuring that those responsible for leading the mission—whether the United Nations, NATO, or a coalition of concerned states—are capable of doing the job at hand.

I hope you will find the enclosed report a valuable and informative account of how the United States uses peacekeeping to promote stability and protect its interests. It is important that peacekeeping remain a viable choice when we face situations in which neither inaction nor unilateral American intervention is appropriate. To that end, I look forward to working with you on my proposal to continue our reform efforts at the United Nations and to pay off our peacekeeping debt.

Sincerely,

WILLIAM J. CLINTON

NOTE: Identical letters were sent to Jesse Helms, chairman, Senate Committee on Foreign Relations; Strom Thurmond, chairman, Senate Committee on Armed Services; Ted Stevens, chairman, Senate Committee on Appropriations; Benjamin A. Gilman, chairman, House Committee on International Relations; Robert L. Livingston, chairman, House Committee on Appropriations; and Floyd Spence, chairman, House Committee on National Security.

Remarks to the Conference on Free TV and Political Reform and an Exchange With Reporters
March 11, 1997

The President. Thank you. What a gift. [*Laughter*] Thank you, Walter Cronkite. Thank you, Paul Taylor, for your passion and your commitment. Thank you, Senator McCain, Chairman Hundt, Ann McBride, Becky Cain. And thank you, Barry Diller, for what you have said about this important issue. I am delighted to have the chance to come here today, and I thank the sponsors of this event.

Again, let me say that I participated in the last election in the free television offered by the networks. Thanks to the efforts of Paul Taylor and Walter Cronkite and the members of the Straight Talk Coalition, Senator Dole and I were given a unique opportunity to talk directly to the voters—no gimmicks, no flashy graphics—a full minute or two at a time. And I really enjoyed it. I put a lot of effort into those opportunities, and I'm sure that Senator Dole did as well. I felt that they were a great gift.

And Walter and I had a talk backstage before we came out about how it might even be done better in the next round of elections. Maybe my opinions will carry more weight on such matters since I never expect to run again for anything. And I do believe that the free television was a very important thing. I think if it could be done, as we were discussing, at the same time every evening on a given network and back to back so that the candidates can be seen in a comparative context, I think it would be even more valuable.

We have to do some things to improve the way our political system works at election time and the way it communicates, or its leaders communicate, to people all year around. This should not be surprising to anyone. The Founding Fathers understood that we were an experiment. We're still around after all of these years

because we have relished the idea that we are an experiment, that America is a work in progress, that we're constantly in the making. We always have to change.

A lot of good things have happened to expand participation in the political system from the time we were a new nation, when only white male property owners could vote, and we have to make some more changes now. But if you look at the changes which have been made in the last 200 years, we should be hopeful.

Television has the power to expand the franchise or to shrink the franchise. Indeed, that is true of all means of communications and all media. We know that television is a profound and powerful force. We know that we don't fully understand all of its implications—even what you said, Walter, we don't really know what the connection is between television and a diminished voter turnout. It could be because there is a poll on television every night that tells people about the election, so some people think that there's no point in their voting, because the person they're for is going to win anyway or the person they're for can't win anyway.

We need to think about that, and that's not the subject of this meeting, but we need to—we really need—all of us need more information, more research, about why people vote and why they don't vote. There was a very—I've seen one survey, done I believe for the Democratic Leadership Council, of the nonvoters. It's a poll that doesn't pay off. You know, it was done, after the election, of the nonvoters. But it was very interesting, and some of the findings were quite counterintuitive about why people did or didn't vote. But I would urge those of you who are interested in it to get that, look at it, and think about what new work could be done to look into that.

Today we want to talk about whether the medium of free television could be used to diminish the impact of excessive money in politics and about whether it can be used, therefore, to reform our system in a way that makes it better and, ultimately, that leads to better decisions for the American people. It is now commonplace—everybody will tell you—that campaigns cost too much and it takes too much time to raise the money and the more money you raise from a larger number of people, the more questions will be raised about that.

Major party committees spent over 3 times as much in this last election cycle as 4 years before. And that doesn't count the third party expenditures, both the genuinely independent third party committees and those that weren't really independent although they claimed to be. Spending in congressional campaigns has risen sixfold in the last two decades. That's over 3 times the rate of inflation. The biggest reason for this is the rise in the cost of television. But of course, there is also now more money being spent on mail, on telephoning, on radio, and on other print advertising as well.

In 1972 candidates spent $25 million for political ads; in 1996, $400 million. Presidential campaigns now routinely spend two-thirds or more of their money on paid ads; Senate candidates, 42 percent of their money on television; House races, about a third. Interestingly enough, that's often because there is no single television market which just overlaps a House district and often the cost is prohibitive, particularly in the urban districts. But you get the drift; it's the same everywhere.

We are the only major democracy in the world where candidates have to raise larger and larger sums of money simply to communicate with voters through the medium that matters most. Every other major democracy offers candidates or parties free air time to speak to voters, and we can plainly do better, building on the big first step urged by this group in 1996. We have an obligation to restore our campaign finance system to a system that has the broad confidence of the American people but also of the American press that comments on it. In order to do that, television has to be part of the solution. I have said before and I will say again, everybody who has been involved in this system has to take responsibility for it and for changing it.

Those of us in public life know better than anybody else what the demands of prevailing in the present system are, and those who control the airwaves understand it well also. First and most fundamentally, I came here to support Senator McCain. We have to take advantage of this year to pass campaign finance reform. The campaign finance laws are two decades out of date. They have been overtaken by events, by dramatic changes in the nature and cost of campaigns and the flood of money that has followed them. The money has been raised and spent in ways that simply could not have been imagined when the people who fashioned the last campaign finance law in Congress did it.

They did the best they could, and I will say again, I believe that they did a good thing and that that law did improve the financing of our campaigns and restored a level of confidence to our politics and made things better. It is simply that time has changed, and we need new changes to reflect the things that have happened in the last 20 years.

It will not be easy to do this, but the situation is far from hopeless. After all, the first thing I want to say is, the American people do care about this, and our politics, I think, in terms of traditional honesty, is getting better, not worse. I have asked over a dozen people, just in the last 2 years, who have been living in Washington for the last 30 years, who have been in politics—the most recent person I asked was Senator Dole—whether politics was more or less honest today than it was 30 years ago, and all 12 or 15, however many I asked, all gave the same answer. They said it's more honest today than it was 30 years ago. I think that's where we have to start.

It is important to put this in the proper perspective, if you want people in Congress to vote to change it. They cannot be asked to admit that they are doing something that they're not or that they are participating in dragging the country down the drain, because anybody who knows what went on 30 years ago and what goes on today would have to say that the system is still better than it was then. On the other hand, anybody who denied that, at an exponential pace, changes are occurring which imperil the integrity of the electoral process and the financing of campaigns would also be badly amiss.

The second thing I'd like to say is, we should be hopeful because we have seen over the last 4 years, in other contexts, real bipartisan processes to improve the way politics works, not in campaign finance reform, but there was bipartisan support for the motor voter law, for the lobby disclosure overhaul, that was the first one in 50 years, in which Congress banned meals and gifts from lobbyists to lawmakers but also required much more disclosure. And that's the most important thing. When you get 100 percent disclosure of an area where there hasn't been any before, then that offers all of you in the press the opportunity to communicate to the American people what the activities of lobbyists are and to let them and you draw your own conclusions in terms of the results produced by decisionmakers. We required Congress to live under the same laws that they impose upon the private sector.

Every single one of these things has happened in the last 4 years with broad, bipartisan support. So I think it is very, very important that we recognize this will not happen unless there is bipartisan support. But there is evidence that if the environment is right, if the support is deep enough, if the calls are strong enough and positive enough, we can get this kind of change.

Now, let me also say that I think it's important to make this point, because I see all these surveys that say that campaign finance reform is important to people, but if you rank it on a list of 10 things, it will always rank 10th behind balancing the budget, education, and all this. That can be used by politicians as an excuse, if you will, not to deal with it. They say, "Well, look at all these surveys. Campaign finance reform—sure, people like it, but it's not as important to them as whether we'll have national standards for reading and math," for example, one of my passions.

What we have to do is to make a connection between the two for the American people. What we have to argue is, yes, we really need to be up here doing the public's business. We need to be balancing the budget, improving education, reforming welfare, expanding health care coverage to children who don't have it, passing a juvenile justice reform, the kinds of things that I'm passionately interested in.

But having the right kind of campaign finance reform system and having the right kind of straight talk on television and having issues be more—elections be more issue-oriented and

having the debates of both sides heard clearly by all people and increasing voter interest and voter turnout, all these things will increase the likelihood that this laundry list of good things will be done and will be done in better fashion than would otherwise be the case. I think it is very important that those of you who care about this make this connection because that's how to build broad and deep support for this endeavor.

It seems to me that we do have an historic opportunity to pass campaign finance reform. And I think the public owes a lot of gratitude to Senator McCain and Senator Feingold and Congressman Shays and Congressman Meehan and all of their supporters for the legislation they have offered. It is real and tough. It would level the playing field and reduce the role of big money in politics. It would set voluntary limits on campaign spending and ban soft money, all corporate contributions, and the very large individual ones. It would restrict the role of political action committees and lobbyists and make needed reforms within the confines of the Constitution as defined by existing Supreme Court case law.

In all these ways, it would set ceilings on money in politics, and just as important, it would also provide a floor. And I think that is very important; it would also provide a floor. You actually have some Members in Congress who come from districts where there's a very low per capita income, for example, who are very afraid of campaign finance reform because they're afraid, among their own constituents, they'll never be able to raise enough money in their district to compete the first time a multimillionaire runs against them.

So the law has to give a floor. And McCain-Feingold does that by giving candidates free air time to talk directly to the voters if they observe the spending limits of the law. And we need to emphasize that any ceiling law should have a floor to guarantee that people have their say and are heard. It gives candidates deeply discounted rates for the purchase of time if they observe the limits of the law. In all these ways, it will level the playing field, giving new voices a chance to be heard and being fair to both parties.

I have supported the idea of free TV time for many years. When the Vice President was in Congress, he actually introduced legislation to require it. It was first proposed by President

Kennedy in 1962. It has been around long enough. We now tried it in the last election more than ever before, and we know that it advances the public interest.

In my State of the Union Address, I asked Congress to pass the McCain-Feingold bill by July 4th, the day we celebrate the birth of our democracy. I pledge to you that I will continue to work with Members of both parties to do this. I will be mustering more support out in the country—and that will be announced over the next few weeks—for this endeavor.

We have to use the present intense interest in this, as well as the controversy over fundraising in the last election and all the publicity on it, as a spur to action. We cannot let it become what it is in danger of becoming, which is an excuse for inaction.

And that again is something that I challenge all of you on. Do not let the controversy become an excuse to do nothing and to wallow around in it. Use it as a spur to changing the system, because until you change the system, you will continue to have controversies over the amount, the sheer amount, of money that is raised in these elections.

The second thing I'd like to discuss is what Walter talked about in some detail, and that is how broadcasters can meet their public interest obligations in this era. Ever since the FCC was created, broadcasters have had a compact with the public. In return for the public airwaves, they must meet public interest obligations. The bargain has been good for the industry and good for the public. Now startling new technologies are shaking and remaking the world of telecommunications. They've opened wider opportunities for broadcasters than ever before, but they also offer us the chance to open wider vistas for our democracy as well.

The move from analog signals to digital ones will give each broadcaster much more signal capacity than they have today. The broadcasters asked Congress to be given this new access to the public airwaves without charge. I believe, therefore, it is time to update broadcasters' public interest obligations to meet the demands of the new times and the new technological realities. I believe broadcasters who receive digital licenses should provide free air time for candidates, and I believe the FCC should act to require free air time for candidates. The telecommunications revolution can help to transform our system so that once again voters have

the loudest voice in our democracy. Free time for candidates can help free our democracy from the grip of big money. I hope all of you will support that.

There are many ways that this could be done. Many of you here have put forward innovative plans. I believe the free time should be available to all qualified Federal candidates. I believe it should give candidates a chance to talk directly to the voters without gimmicks or intermediaries. Because campaign finance reform is so important, I believe it should be available especially to candidates who limit their own spending. It is clear under the Supreme Court decision that this can be done, and I believe that is how it should be done.

Candidates should be able to talk to voters based on the strength of their ideas, not the size of their pocketbooks, and all voters should know that no candidate is kept from running simply because he or she cannot raise enormous amounts of funds.

Last month the Vice President announced that we would create an independent advisory committee of experts, industry representatives, public interest advocates, and others to recommend what steps to take. Before I came over here today, I signed an Executive order creating that committee. The balanced panel I will appoint will advise me on ways we can move forward and make a judgment as to what the new public interest obligations of broadcasters might be. But today, let us simply agree on the basic premise. In 1997, for broadcasters, serving the public should mean enhancing our democracy.

Finally, let me challenge the broadcasters as well. Broadcasters are not the problem, but broadcasting must be the solution. The step the broadcasters took in this last election, as I have said over and over again in other forums, with the encouragement of Straight Talk for TV, was a real breakthrough. Now I ask broadcasters to follow up on this experiment in democracy, and I'm especially pleased that a leader in the industry, Barry Diller, has challenged his colleagues to open up the airwaves to candidates. He has made clear, forcefully and very publicly, that he and all of his colleagues have an obligation to society, and his presence here today makes it clear that he is willing to assume the mantle of leadership. But surely there are others—I know there are—who will gladly join in and take up this cause as well.

There are many questions about political reform. Many skeptics will look at all proposed reform measures and ask whether they'll work and whether there will be unintended consequences. The truth is that they will work and there will be unintended consequences.

But if we use that for an excuse not to change, no good change in this country would ever have come about. There will always be something we cannot foresee. That's what makes life interesting and keeps us all humble, but that must not be an excuse for our refusing to act in this area. We know—we know—when we work to expand our democracy, when you give people a greater voice and advocates of all political views a firm platform upon which to stand, we are moving forward as a nation. By passing campaign finance reform, by renewing the compact between broadcasters and the public to better serve in this new era, we can do that again.

And I will say again, I will do all I can on both these fronts, on campaign finance reform legislation and on requiring free use, free availability of the airwaves to public candidates. We need your support for both, and we need broader and more intense public support. And again I say, that has to be built by demonstrating to the public that this is not an inside-the-Beltway exercise in both parties trying to find ways to undermine each other but a necessary way of opening our democracy so that we can better, more quickly, and more profoundly address the real challenges facing the American people in their everyday lives. These two steps will help, and together I hope we can make them this year.

Thank you very much.

1996 Elections

Q. Mr. President.

The President. Hello, Sarah [Sarah McClendon, McClendon News Service].

Q. I want to know—you said that you would not have been reelected had you not raised that money——

The President. I think—no, I think I probably—I might have been, because I'm the President and a President has unusual access to the public. And you have the Presidential debates, which are unique in terms of their viewership and their potential impact. But I believe that if you just look at the races for Congress and the number of votes that changed just in the last 5 days and how the votes were counted when the votes changed and the movement changed, there is no question that the amount of money deployed in an intelligent way can have a profound impact on the outcome of these elections. And what you want to do is to make sure that everybody has the same fair chance at the voters and nobody has an excessive chance. And given the Supreme Court cases, the way the McCain-Feingold bill is drawn up, plus the effort to get more free air time, are the best responses to overcome the undue influence of excessive money.

Thank you very much.

NOTE: The President spoke at 11:12 a.m. at the National Press Club. In his remarks, he referred to Walter Cronkite, chair, and Paul Taylor, executive director, Free TV for Straight Talk Coalition; Ann McBride, president, Common Cause; Becky Cain, president, National League of Women Voters; and Barry Diller, former chairman, Fox Broadcasting. The Executive order of March 11 establishing the Advisory Committee on the Public Interest Obligations of Digital Television Broadcasters is listed in Appendix D at the end of this volume.

Remarks Announcing the Economic Plan for the District of Columbia
March 11, 1997

Thank you. Thank you very much. Mr. Vice President, Representative Norton, Representative Moran, members of the administration, Mr. Mayor, Chairman Brimmer, Mr. Evans, and especially all the citizens of the District of Columbia who are here today.

You know, every year millions of visitors come here, but even those who don't come know a good deal about our Capital. America's eyes and the eyes of the world constantly focus on Washington. They see the good, and there is much good. There is history here, everywhere, tremendous resources, and talent from all over the world. But there is more as well. There are the people of the District, some of whose families have lived here for generations. They are hardworking, and they are committed to making the community and their neighborhoods better. There are businesses which strive to make it, sometimes under very difficult conditions. There is much dedication and much heart.

In my State of the Union Address, I said that we have to renew our Capital City, to make it the finest place to learn, to work, and to live, because people here deserve no less and because the District matters beyond the city limits. The city is every American's home, and it should be every American's pride. Our Capital City must reflect the best of who we are, what we hope to become, and where we are going.

Washington started as a planned city. George Washington, Thomas Jefferson, and a soldier and architect named Pierre L'Enfant shared a vision of order and beauty. The boulevards, the museums, the monuments reflect their vision. But this is a different time, and our city needs a new and different vision, one that reaches where the magnificent vistas end; one that touches our schools, where too often books and teachers are in short supply; our streets, where too often children are robbed of their futures, their freedom, and law-abiding citizens too often live in fear of the few who break the law; one that touches the lives of those who want to be responsible in work but lack the opportunity to do so; one that makes businesses want to locate here, to create jobs here, to give the community new economic life and spirit and vitality.

Our strategy must begin to reset the course for a better life for all who call the District home. Our challenge is to revitalize the city as the Nation's Capital, to improve the prospects of self-government to succeed, and to make it a place where people really want to live, to work, to do business. We can clearly do this.

From New York to Chicago to San Francisco, we have seen new life brought to urban areas. Unemployment is down. Crime is down. Things are looking up. We know that if we empower people and we help them within the economic framework, they will do the rest, and that is the heart of our strategy.

Of course, our Capital City faces enormous challenges. Of course, these challenges are, to

some extent, unique to DC and have been a long time in the making. But at least now we have a plan, and we are committed. More of you, in more ways than I have ever seen before, are committed. We at the Federal level must help our Capital City to lift itself to the point where it can be a model for the Nation for revitalization. Working together, we can and we must make Washington once again the proud face America shows to the world.

As the Vice President said, there are steps which have been taken already, but now it's time for the next step, our economic plan for the District of Columbia, an important piece of a larger strategy to build on the work begun and on what we have learned from success stories in other cities about what actually is working there. It reflects our agenda to revitalize urban America. It addresses the unique needs of the District. It recognizes that only the people of the District can lift it up in the end, so it gives people the tools to do the job.

Our $300 million plan has two parts. First, it will provide $250 million in Federal tax incentives for jobs and capital to strengthen the economic base in our Capital City. Second, it will provide $50 million in Federal commitment to help capitalize a new, non-Federal public-private partnership, the DC Economic Development Corporation.

The corporation will develop an economic development strategy, coordinate large-scale development projects, support efforts to create jobs and business opportunities. It will have broad powers to facilitate many existing plans such as the Monumental Core, the Downtown Interactive, and the New York Avenue plans. The Economic Development Corporation will be authorized to allocate a new DC capital credit, which will provide $95 million in tax credits for investors in and lenders to DC businesses. These credits will be worth up to 25 percent of the amount invested or borrowed. This will help to bring and keep businesses where jobs are needed, and they will be given on a competitive basis to investors and lenders who can do the most for the District and its people.

The corporation will also have authority to issue tax-exempt private activity bonds to finance businesses in hard-hit areas. And it will be able to receive transfers of land or development rights from the Federal Government and from others. It will work with the National Capital Infrastructure Commission we're creating to make certain that infrastructure and economic development build on each other.

The corporation will be a driving force for our Capital's renewal, for it to take its rightful place in the fast-growing economy of this region and in our Nation. The Federal Government's investment of $50 million in the corporation is just a start. Our goal is to involve all sectors of the economy in helping the District.

Our plan also includes a new DC jobs credit, available to businesses in the District that hire low- or moderate-income residents living in economically distressed areas. It would provide a 40 percent tax credit on the first $10,000 of eligible wages in the first year of employment. This jobs credit builds on the work opportunity tax credit passed last year and my proposed welfare-to-work tax credit. Our plan will also allow small businesses in distressed areas to deduct up to $20,000 in additional expenses for certain equipment costs. Just as we are committed to seeing that self-government works as it should, we have a commitment from the District government to cooperate fully in the Economic Development Corporation.

This is important, but we need more. I challenge business and community leaders to give their unqualified support to bringing back the District. If you're a business or an association in the District, don't give up on it. I commend the members of the National Association of Home Builders, who decided to keep their headquarters here, because that's important for a truly national organization, and it's important for a truly international organization as well. I thank MCI for its decision to keep their offices in the District.

If you're a business making money in the District, then invest here. Follow the lead of Ford Motor Company, which is providing a line of credit to repair emergency, police, fire, and other vehicles. And Ford has set up an automotive program with three District schools.

I want to mention another example of good citizenship as well, and good business. Tomorrow Secretary Cuomo will be on hand as Safeway opens a large supermarket in Southeast DC. It sounds so basic to have access to a grocery store, but that area has not had one in 20 years. Safeway will create 200 new jobs. And we thank you, sir. Thank you very much.

I want to thank all the businesses who are here today for everything you do to support the District. I hope you will work with Director Raines and Secretary Rubin to develop concrete ways to participate with the Economic Development Corporation and the District and report back to me within 60 days.

The Government will honor its commitment to the District. We know the Federal presence here is critical to the local economy. We know that we must do more, and that is why I have issued a directive to ensure that agencies do all they can to stay here and to contribute here. We want to build on our presence wherever possible. For example, the Navy will boost employment at the Southeast Navy Yard by doubling its current levels by 2001, adding 5,000 jobs here in the District.

As District residents, the First Lady, the Vice President, Tipper, and I will continue to do our part. Recently, the First Lady presented a check for $18 million to repair our city schools coming from the privatization of Connie Lee, the institution that insures college and university bonds. And our public-private partnership will now benefit District schoolchildren. The First Lady also challenged law firms—I thought that was good—we don't have any shortage of law firms in DC—[*laughter*]—to expand their efforts to adopt DC schools, to visit with students, to develop relationships with them and mentor them.

I'm proud of all the departments and agencies in the Federal Government that have adopted DC schools. And I would like to say a special word of thanks to my Secret Service detail who gave that to the First Lady and me as a Christmas present not very long ago. I couldn't imagine a better gift. And the work they do at the Kramer School is something that I am particularly proud of.

As the Vice President said, our administration has worked hard to be a good neighbor. But I've asked the Cabinet to do more. You will hear and see a lot of our Cabinet Secretaries in the District. You will see them doing things. In the next 2 weeks, for example, Secretary Albright and Ambassador Richardson will adopt local schools to teach children about diplomacy and geography. Secretary Glickman will announce a renewed effort to glean surplus food from cafeterias at Federal buildings to feed the hungry here in the District. And I'm asking all the Secretaries to report back to me within 90 days with a targeted plan of action for each department to do all it possibly can to help the District.

It has been said that Americans didn't think much of their Capital until they had to defend it during attack in the War of 1812 when, as all of you know, in 1814 the White House was burned. In a way, history is repeating itself, because for too long, Americans have not thought enough about our Capital City. But Washington is still worth fighting for. In fact, it's more worth fighting for than ever.

The people I have seen who live in this city, who do miraculous things every day to try to help people make more of their own lives, to try to help kids in trouble, to try to turn things around and see people live up to their potential, deserve more than the rest of us have done. And I am determined that even though the solu-tions will not come overnight, we will provide our part of the effort. And together, with local government and business, with the involvement of every citizen, we can have a strategy and implement a strategy that makes Washington the city we all know it ought to be and that we must believe it will be.

Thank you very much.

NOTE: The President spoke at 4:40 p.m. in the East Room at the White House. In his remarks, he referred to Mayor Marion S. Barry, Jr., of the District of Columbia; Andrew F. Brimmer, chairman, DC Financial Responsibility and Management Assistance Authority; and District of Columbia Ward 2 Councilman Jack Evans.

Remarks at a Reception for Senator Byron L. Dorgan
March 11, 1997

Thank you. I'm delighted to be on the stage with 40 percent of all the Democrats from North Dakota. [*Laughter*] You know, in 1974 it took three of them to lose the race for Congress; I did it at home all by myself. [*Laughter*] And I now know why they lost. The only person who should have been talking up here was Kim. [*Laughter*] And she hasn't said a word. I made her go out first tonight so I knew we'd get an applause instead of a boo. [*Laughter*]

I am delighted to be here. I am honored to be here with Senator Dorgan and Senator Conrad and Congressman Pomeroy. The three of them represent what I hope and believe, philosophically and in terms of their commitment to public service and the way they do their work, is not just the future of our party but the future of our country, because they have repeatedly been willing to stand up and make tough decisions, some of which are popular with the electorate back home in North Dakota and may not be so popular with people here in Washington, some of which are not popular anywhere, but they just think they're right.

And I have a special feeling for Byron Dorgan. I followed his career long before he became a Senator, and I admired mightily what he did in North Dakota. Kent said he was voted the most powerful politician in North Dakota, and he said that he was sure that the person handling the revenues in Arkansas wasn't the most powerful person in the State. Actually, he was; I just had sense enough to make sure the folks didn't know that. [*Laughter*] I don't know how he got out of that box.

I really admire him. He deserves to be reelected. I'm glad you're here to help him. And I'd just like to remind you of a couple of things that often get lost in the hurly-burly of daily events around here. Thanks in no small measure to the leadership that he has exerted and the support that he has given, we reversed more than a decade of trickle-down, supply-side economics and replaced it with invest-and-grow economics. And by the narrowest of margin, thanks to his strong support and his vote, we reduced the deficit 63 percent, and this economy has produced 11½ million jobs for the first time ever in 4 years and the lowest combined rates of unemployment and inflation since the 1960's. That's enough to get him reelected. You deserve that.

In 1992 people talked about problems like crime and welfare as if they would always be with us in the same way that they were. But we have reversed; trends have declined—working with people all over this country—putting 100,000 police on the street; working with States to move people from welfare to work, 2¼ million people. Now it will be 2½ million when we get the last total in 4 years, the largest number of people ever to move off the welfare rolls. And we have more to do. But that's something to be proud of. The crime rate going down every year, that's something to be proud of.

We have reasserted the importance of the family in our social policy, with the family and medical leave law, with special tax breaks for families with modest incomes, by raising the minimum wage, by passing the V-chip legislation and taking on some of these other very tough issues. I think it's very important. That's the kind of pro-family policy that Senator Dorgan has fought for.

We have fought for free and for fair trade for America. We're the number one exporter in the world again. We had record exports for the last 4 years. We've reasserted the leadership role of our country in reducing the nuclear threat and taking advantage of the opportunities that are out there.

Now, we've got a lot left to do. We still have to balance the budget. People tell me all the time, "Well, can we keep this recovery going?" The answer is, we can if we do the right things but only if we do the right things. The American people are more than doing their part. They're willing to keep working. They're willing to keep starting small businesses, keep expanding businesses. They're dying to improve their education and skills and to become more productive. We have to create the conditions and give people the tools to make the most of their own lives. If we do it, we'll keep going forward.

That's what is at stake when Byron Dorgan presents himself to the people of North Dakota again. And no one should forget that on the major policy questions of the last 4 years, no matter how controversial, no matter how tight, no matter how tough, he stood up and cast the right vote. And this is a better, stronger country, and his State is better and stronger because of it. And he deserves to be rewarded for the leadership he's exercised and, most important, for the potential he has in the future for balancing the budget, for putting education first among our priorities, for doing the right thing to finish the work of welfare reform, for dealing with the problems that rural States have that are so easy to overlook here in Washington unless you have the kind of strong, clear voice that he has exhibited.

So you're doing a good thing being here for him tonight. And I'm glad to be here with him. I am honored to be his friend, honored to work with him every day. And I trust that I will have the chance to do that until I am term-limited out and he goes on to his just reward. [*Laughter*]

Thank you, and God bless you all.

NOTE: The President spoke at 7 p.m. in the John Hay Room at the Hay-Adams Hotel. In his remarks, he referred to Senator Dorgan's wife, Kim.

Remarks at a Democratic National Committee Dinner
March 11, 1997

Thank you. Please sit down. Thank you. First of all, I want to thank Roy Romer for his willingness to go back and forth across America, from here to Colorado and back several times every week to try to help us do what all of us need to do with our party. I thank in his absence Steve Grossman. We're all thinking about him and Barbara. Nothing hurts worse than cracking your elbow, I don't think, and we've got to be thinking about them. And I thank Alan Solomont for his work. And I thank all of you for your support.

I have just come from an event for Senator Byron Dorgan of North Dakota. It was a fascinating event. You know, North Dakota is a State that's so small, I felt like a sophisticate from Arkansas being there. [*Laughter*] And it's one of the few delegations that's completely Democratic, even though the State always votes Republican in Presidential elections. They have two Democratic Senators and a Democratic Congressman.

And the first time Byron Dorgan ran for Congress was in 1974, the first year I ran for public office. And Senator Conrad was his campaign manager, and Congressman Pomeroy was his driver. And I told him that it took all three of them to lose that race, and I lost mine all by myself. [*Laughter*] But it was a very interesting and heartening event, because I was thinking about Byron Dorgan and Kent and Earl, and I was thinking that if any of those three had either not been there or had not been willing to put their necks on the line, we would not have passed the budget in 1993. And we would have not reversed trickle-down economics, or in a less pejorative term, we would not have reversed supply-side economics.

And because we did, in an economic plan that invested in our children and our technology, in a fairer tax system for working people, 4½ years later—or 4 years later, we've got 11½ million jobs, the first time any administration, period, had produced that much; 63 percent decline in the deficit; lowest rates of unemployment and inflation combined since the 1960's. That's what this party is about, and don't ever forget that. That's one big thing.

I'll tell you a little thing. Today I got a letter from a woman that I know from Iowa. I met her in Cedar Rapids in 1992. She was offering to defend me from the attacks that we're only interested in people like you. And she reminded me of this story of how I met her. I met her in a rally in 1992, and she was holding a child of another race in her hands. I said, "Where did you get that baby?" She said, "This baby is my baby." I said, "Well, where did you get it?" She said, "In Miami." I said, "Where in the world—how did you get a baby from Miami? You're from Iowa." She said, "Well, nobody else wanted this baby. This baby has got AIDS."

And later in the campaign, my staff actually went out of their way to try to help this lady in a difficult situation. She adopted a child when she had been left by her husband. She was raising two children on her own, her own children. She had barely enough money to put body and soul together. And she was at a political rally because she thought it was important for her future. And she has struggled to keep that little baby alive for 4 years. And that child is coming up to the National Institute of Health now, because a lot of the things that are now keeping adults with AIDS alive for very long periods of time, they're not quite sure how to do that with children.

So she wrote me a letter because, she said, "You've always welcomed us. You've always tried to help us, and we'd like to come by and see you." And I love this little kid, and I've kept up with her all these years. And I thought to

myself, that is also what this administration and what this party is about, giving people like that little girl a chance to live the fullest life she can, recognizing the dignity of people like that woman who took what only—you could characterize as a truly heroic stand to do something most of us in far more comfortable circumstances have never done. And all those things in the middle, that is really what this is all about. And we can never forget that what we do affects real people in real lives.

So when we replaced trickle-down economics with invest-and-grow economics, we gave Americans a chance to have a better future.

When we got away from hot rhetoric and got down to concrete action on social problems and we reversed the social decline, working with people all over America to get the crime rate down and the biggest drop in welfare rolls in history, we helped to give people a better future.

When we restored family, not just in rhetoric but in fact, at the center of our social concerns, with things like the Family and Medical Leave Act and the V-chip and the television ratings and the regulations to protect children from tobacco and the earned-income tax credit, those things changed people's lives.

When we reaffirmed the leadership of the United States for peace and freedom in the world and reduced the nuclear threat, that makes our future better. That's what I'm going to try to do when I go to meet with President Yeltsin next week in Helsinki. What can we keep doing to reduce the nuclear threat? What can we do to build a Europe that's united and free, so in the 21st century we don't have the hundreds of thousands, indeed, the millions of young Americans going over to Europe and risking losing their lives, as happened in World War I and World War II. This is about big things. And I want you to think about that.

And Roy talks about 1995 and '96—we had—I found that experience sometimes exhausting but ultimately exhilarating, because we were fighting about real things, and the American people had to make a decision, huge, big differences in how we should move into the future, what is the role of Government in our lives. And I think the election pretty much resolved that.

And we decided we would no longer try to have our daily bread by demonizing our Government in a democratic, free society. I can say that this administration has done more to reduce the size of Government and the number of regulations and the burden of it than our Republican predecessors, but we never could figure out how to use the rhetoric to convince the American people that the Government that they elected and paid for was their enemy inherently. And I think what we see now is that people want it to work better, and they want it to be effective.

Today I had the privilege of appearing with Walter Cronkite and Paul Taylor, who spearheaded the coalition last year to try to get the networks to give free television time to the candidates for President as the opening salvo of what they hope will be a broad campaign finance reform effort that will actually open up the airwaves to all qualified candidates. And I said to them that I felt very strongly that now that we were switching from—we were switching to digital channeling, which will give the networks far more options to communicate with people, that we ought to require as a part of the public interest more free TV time. And at least one executive, Barry Diller, has challenged his colleagues to do that. And it sounds like a lot of money—let's say we just equal what is about spent on television that's funded now, about $55 million in the off-years; let's say $400 million in election years; that's still less than 2 percent of the total revenues of these operations.

And when you get a monopoly on the airwaves, I think you ought to act in the public interest. All of us know that we cannot—those of us who've followed the campaign laws—under the decisions of the Supreme Court, the only way we can ever control the aggregate spending in political campaigns is to offer something to those who voluntarily observe the limits. And the only thing that's worth it is access to the voters in a free and unfettered way, principally through television. So we were talking about that today. That's something that's important to do.

There are a lot of other things that we have to do here. We've got to balance the budget. We've got to pass the education reform proposals that I have recommended, both to raise standards and to open college. We've got to take more seriously this juvenile justice issue. Even with the crime rates dropping dramatically, juvenile crime rates are too high almost everywhere. But we know we can do something about it.

I was in Boston the other day; I spent a day in Boston. There has not been a single child killed in Boston in a year and a half, not one, zero, because—and it is not an accident—because of all the things that they have done there that we have now put into a bill and tried to give the tools to the rest of the country to do, which is exactly what we did with the crime bill.

So we have all these things out there to do, and that's what you're fighting for. But I want you to be proud of the fact that this country is in much better shape than it was 4 years ago because of specific changes that were made as a direct result of the efforts made not only by the President and the Vice President but by the people who supported us in the Congress and throughout the country. This country is better because of that, and I thank you for that.

And I ask you for your support for all the things we're trying to do now. Stay with us. We have so much more to do. As I said, this is not a time, just because things are going well, that the country can afford to relax. We have to finish the job of balancing the budget, if you want the economy to continue to grow. We have to finish the job of raising educational standards and opening opportunity, if you want everybody to participate in economic growth. And ultimately, our economic growth will be retarded unless we dramatically improve the education of our people. Because of the job mix, the good new jobs we're creating, virtually all of them now require something more than high school.

If you expect everybody to be treated fairly in this society, we have got to find a way to give jobs to those people on welfare. We've told them they've got to go to work. Who are we to say that unless they have work that they can go to every day?

So there's a lot out there. Let me say again, I am proud of what Governor Romer and Steve Grossman have done in putting the Democratic Party foursquare on the side of passing campaign finance reform this year. And I hope that some of the decisions that are being taken now in the Senate will help us to do that.

But I want all the Democrats to stay out there for that. We need to be on the side of positive change. We have rescued—I believe we have rescued the debate from a sterile, meaningless debate over whether Government is the problem or Government is the savior. We know it is neither now. What we now have to do is to create a Government for the 21st century that will command the support of the American people and do the job that needs to be done to give people the tools to make the most of their own lives.

That's what we're going to do for 4 more years, thanks to you. And I want you to be happy about it, proud of it, and determined to continue to do it.

Thank you very much.

NOTE: The President spoke at 7:35 p.m. at the Sheraton Carlton Hotel. In his remarks, he referred to Democratic National Committee officials Gov. Roy Romer of Colorado, general chair, Steve Grossman, national chair, and his wife, Barbara, and Alan Solomont, national finance chair; President Boris Yeltsin of Russia; and Walter Cronkite, chair, and Paul Taylor, executive director, Free TV for Straight Talk Coalition.

Remarks Announcing Proposed National Transportation Efficiency Legislation
March 12, 1997

Thank you very much. Secretary Slater, Mr. Vice President, members of the administration, the Department of Transportation. Senator Moynihan, thank you for being here. Mayor Schwartz, thank you for being here.

I spent a lot of time in the last few years talking about the need to build a bridge to the 21st century. And usually I'm talking in metaphorical terms that involve—[*laughter*]—balancing the budget, improving education for our children, preserving the environment as we grow the economy. Today we're talking about building bridges and roads and transit systems and highways in more literal terms. But I think it's important also to point out that as we invest in these bridges and roads and transit systems, we are also building a bridge to a cleaner environment. We're building a bridge from welfare to work. We're building a bridge to sustainable communities that can last and grow and bring people together over the long run. And that is the importance of the legislation that we submit to Congress today. It does the old-fashioned work of investing in America's infrastructure in a very important way, but it also ties those investments to the challenges we face today and tomorrow.

I am proud that even as we have moved toward a balanced budget and cut our deficit by 63 percent in the last 4 years, we have still increased our Federal investment in transportation infrastructure, and I thank the Members of Congress who have supported that. [*Applause*] I feel compelled to disclose that I did not plant the person in the middle of the audience over here who started the applause. [*Laughter*] But if he's a Federal employee, he will immediately get a raise. [*Laughter*]

Compared to 4 years ago, our highways and bridges are stronger, 100 miles of new transit lines are under construction, and that is just part of the story. But it is a big part of why our economy has produced almost 12 million jobs in the last 4 years and one month, including over one million new jobs in construction.

Today we're taking the next big step to maintain and modernize our transportation system and to make sure it is the best in the world. The "National Economic Crossroads Transportation Efficiency Act," as Secretary Slater said, known as NEXTEA, authorizes $174 billion over the next 6 years to improve our bridges, highways, and transit systems. It will create tens of thousands of jobs for our people, help move people from welfare to work, protect our air and water, and improve our highway safety.

I'm especially proud that as we build our infrastructure, we are going to help build better lives for people who are moving off welfare. One of the biggest barriers facing people who move from welfare to work is finding transportation to get to their jobs, their training programs, their children's day care center.

There was recently a study of Atlanta, Georgia, employment and the community surrounding Atlanta, pointing out that in entry-level jobs, an overwhelming percentage of those jobs—for example, in fast food restaurants—were held full time by inner-city adults who were low income people, if they were in Atlanta. If they were in the surrounding communities, it was just a little over 50 percent. Why? Because the people who wanted the full-time jobs had no way to get there. And you see that repeated over and over and over throughout the country.

This bill provides $600 million over 6 years to help provide and pay for transportation, so that those who have been told by the Congress in the last session that they have to go to work are, in fact, able to reach the jobs that are out there. And I ask for the support of everyone for that.

For too long, too many people have believed that strong transportation and a clean environment could not go hand in hand. This bill proves that that is not true. NEXTEA provides more than $1.3 billion a year to reduce air pollution and millions more to preserve wetlands and open space. By helping communities to invest in cleaner methods of transportation, by supporting recreational trails, bike paths, and pedestrian walkways, by investing in scenic byways and landscaping, this bill strengthens our infrastructure while protecting and enhancing our precious natural resources. Make no mistake about it, this is one of the most important pieces of environmental legislation that will be considered by the Congress in the next 2 years. And I think it should be thought of in that way.

This legislation also builds on our progress in making roads safer, increasing highway traffic safety funds by 25 percent, expanding our aggressive campaign to crack down on drunk and drugged driving.

At its heart, therefore, as you can see and as Secretary Slater said, this bill is about more than our roads and our bridges. It's about cutting-edge jobs in commerce. It's about the infrastructure we need to prepare for them. It's about the responsibility of those moving from welfare to work and our responsibility to help them get there. It's about the community we share and the steps we have to take to make it both safer and cleaner for our children.

The chance to reshape America's infrastructure comes along only once every 6 years. That means that this transportation bill literally will be our bridge into the 21st century. That's why we must work together to pass this legislation, to build on a long bipartisan position of cooperation in transportation policy to move our Nation forward. Together we can keep our economy on the right track and ensure that the track itself is strong enough for the enormous challenges and opportunities that lie ahead.

I am excited about this legislation. I applaud all the people in the Department who put it together, and I'm very much looking forward to working with the Congress to make it a reality.

Thank you very much.

NOTE: The President spoke at 9:55 a.m. in Room 450 of the Old Executive Office Building. In his remarks, he referred to Oklahoma City Councilman Mark Schwartz, president, National League of Cities.

Remarks in ABC's "Straight Talk on Drugs" Radio Townhall Meeting
March 12, 1997

[*ABC News anchor Peter Jennings opened the program and introduced the President.*]

The President. Good morning, Peter.

Mr. Jennings. Thank you for being with us, sir. The President has already had a chance to talk to the kids here just a little bit. Tell the folks at home why you think it's important for them and you to be here together.

The President. I think it's important because we know that while overall drug use in America is still going down, drug use among people under 18 is, in fact, going up. And that's a very troubling thing because all of you represent our future. And I'm concerned about what happens to you as individuals, and I'm concerned about what happens to your communities and what happens to our country.

And ABC has been good enough not only to do this little townhall meeting for us but also to run a public service campaign with ads telling our young people and telling their parents and their friends and their mentors that, in effect, we have to talk about this, that silence about this problem is like accepting it. And I think that we all owe ABC a debt of gratitude for good citizenship here, and I appreciate what they're trying to do. We're here because the number one goal of our antidrug strategy is to persuade young people to stay away from drugs in the first place.

And I just want to thank especially our Olympian, Dominique Dawes, who is here with us today, who has agreed to be the spokesperson for our Girl Power campaign. And she's taped a lot of public service radio ads telling young girls to go for the gold, to stay off drugs, to make the most of their own lives. And that's why we're here, and I'm glad we are. I'm glad you're here, too, Dominique.

[*At this point, Olympic gymnast Dominique Dawes thanked the President and said that young people should stay busy and stay off drugs. Mr. Jennings then introduced Mickisha Bonner of Garnet-Patterson Middle School in Washington, DC, who described a drug market across the street from her school.*]

The President. Well, Mickisha, are these drug sellers in the same place every day?

Participant. The same place every day.

The President. And how long have they been there?

Participant. Since I've been going to school there.

The President. And have the school officials asked the police to move them——

Participant. Yes.

The President. ——get rid of them, to arrest them? Have they ever been arrested?

Participant. I don't really know. I just see them every day.

The President. I'll see what I can do about that.

Mr. Jennings. Talk to the President after the—he's very good, I've seen him do this before.

The President. I'll see what I can do about that. That's not right.

Mr. Jennings. But even though this is radio, I want to try a show of hands. How many of you have seen drugs being traded——

The President. Or sold.

Mr. Jennings. ——or sold around your school? We've got maybe 30 kids with us here, for those of you at home, and we've had more than a dozen kids go up.

There are, by the way, so many drugs for kids to abuse, it's almost mind boggling at times. But again for you at home, to get some sense of what we're talking about here, here briefly is ABC's Jim Hickey to tell us what is available for kids to abuse.

[*Following a report by Mr. Hickey on effects of various drugs, Mr. Jennings introduced Brandon Power of Woburn, MA, who had nearly died of a muscle relaxant drug overdose in February. Brandon explained that an acquaintance had offered him prescription pills taken from a neighbor's mail.*]

The President. Well, let me ask you this. Did you know they were muscle relaxants when you took them?

Participant. Nobody really knew exactly what they were, but not like anything big.

The President. Was there one person who had them all who then gave them to the rest of you?

Participant. Yes, there was one girl that had a bottle of them.

Mr. Jennings. Under some pressure, do you think, because the other kids were taking them?

Participant. I don't think it was really pressure, but in some cases—I can't speak for everyone, but there were other groups of kids that, like, I'm not totally friends with that may have felt pressure. But I didn't at all.

The President. Do you believe that in this case that if people had understood how dangerous they were, that they wouldn't have done it?

Participant. I don't really know, but I think that if they had found out about what would have happened and how they could have died and how close they came, they wouldn't have taken them.

The President. This is a big problem for us. This is why it's so important that people talk about this and that we educate children at a very young age about what they can do, because it's not a bad thing to have legal drugs being shipped through the mail. It helps a lot of senior citizens, for example, who are not mobile, who have a hard time getting around. If they have a legal prescription and they can get it through the mail, that's a good thing. It makes their lives easier and better.

Inhalants—virtually everything people inhale is legal and performs some sort of function in our society. And I think what you're saying, it's kind of another important piece of evidence for me that we need to have more conversations just like this in every home in America, in every school in America. We need to talk about it, because those muscle relaxants are—if you think about it, I don't know if you've ever had a muscle spasm, but I have. If you ever had a muscle spasm, it takes something pretty powerful to unlock that muscle. And so if you—even someone as big as I am, you can't take more than a couple of those pills within a period of time without having an adverse reaction.

[*Brandon asked about improving mail security.*]

The President. Well, I don't know what we could do about that because she probably took it out of the neighbor's mailbox. And so, once that happens, I don't know what we could have done. There may be something that can be done to label them more clearly.

Now, we do have—the Postal Service is on the alert for illegal drugs being shipped in the mail. That also sometimes happens. But when you've got a legal prescription drug, about all I can think of you could do is maybe have the post office try to deliver it to the door. Maybe that's one thing you could do, and maybe not leave it in the mailbox. And I'll talk to them about it and see if there's anything else we can do.

[*Another participant suggested special deliveries for prescription drugs as a means to prevent thefts.*]

The President. I think that's a good idea.

[*Following a commercial break, a participant commented that Brandon should not have taken pills, even from a friend, if he didn't know what they were.*]

The President. I was just wondering—I see someone has got a comment back there, but I was wondering—this raises a question about what obligations young people have to each

other, because no matter how—let's assume that we can fix this mail problem and say, okay, you'll have certain dangerous drugs, or potentially dangerous, and they'll only be delivered direct to people. There will always be some opportunity. You can't get all the inhalants off the market because they're legal. What obligations do you all have to each other? If you have a friend you know is doing drugs, what do you do about that? What are your obligations to each other?

[*A participant responded that as a recovering drug abuser, he would preach to friends about the negative aspects of drug use. Another participant said she would point out the health risks involved. Another commented that some kids use drugs to be cool and to get attention.*]

The President. Do people believe it's dangerous? You had your hand up back there.

[*A participant said that a friend's obligation would be greater when there was the possibility of harm to other people, rather than only to the drug user.*]

The President. What about these guys? Michael, what were you going to say?

[*A participant noted that marijuana had become so accepted that the users had more arguments for drug use than he had arguments against them.*]

The President. You said—this is very important because the biggest increase in drug use among children under 18 by far has been marijuana. You believe it's because they simply don't believe it's dangerous or they don't believe it will hurt them?

[*The participant said that kids did not believe it was dangerous, especially in light of the California law allowing medicinal use of marijuana, and that they thought medicines would not harm them.*]

The President. Well, Brandon can prove that's not true.

Participant. Exactly.

[*A participant from Los Angeles, CA, discussed the drug problem there, saying that he was a former gang member and drug user, and that the counseling he received after being arrested had helped him to see a broader world beyond his immediate surroundings.*]

The President. Had anybody tried to talk you out of using drugs in the first place, before you did? At home, at school?

[*The participant said that his parents were drug abusers and he first accepted it but later viewed it as part of a bad environment. Participant Matthew Migliore then described his alcohol overdose at the age of 10, saying that a variety of drugs were available and that he had seen antidrug public service announcements but just never believed them.*]

The President. So how can we be more effective about this? Let me just give you one example, because you talked about this. We know a lot about marijuana, for example, we didn't know 20 or 30 years ago. We now know that it is roughly 3 times as toxic as it used to be, number one, and number two, that it does have bad health effects on your heart, your lungs, and your brain. And specifically, for young people—this is very important for young people—sustained use of it makes it more difficult for people to concentrate, to learn, and to retain. It has a—we know this now.

So how can we—you may be right, Matt, maybe we've overdone it. But what can we do to communicate it in a way that's effective?

[*Following a commercial break, a participant discussed the importance of parents talking to their children about drugs. Another participant said that having positive role models would help children avoid using drugs.*]

The President. And tell me—give me an example.

Participant. Well, I don't have any examples because I don't do drugs. But a lot of my friends do, and they do a lot of pot. And they have—that's the most—the worst thing they've done. But they don't have anyone to look up to.

The President. So like somebody in the Big Brother/Big Sister program.

Participant. Yes, or a mentor.

The President. Or a mentor of some other kind.

[*A participant stated that teens who didn't use drugs could be good role models for their peers.*]

Mr. Jennings. Mr. President, we were all talking with Chelsea before you got here. She recently turned 17. When did you start talking to her about drugs, and what did you talk to her about?

The President. Well, I think probably when she was probably 7 years old, 6 or 7, something like that, very young. And then she had—she went through the D.A.R.E. program at her school—which is one thing I think Philip mentioned—the D.A.R.E. officer. She loved her D.A.R.E. officer. He had a profound effect on the young people.

But we began when she was very, very young, talking to her, basically saying that this is wrong. This can cause you great damage. It can wreck your life. It can steal things from you. It costs money. It costs you your ability to think. It costs your self-control. It costs you your freedom in the end. So we talked to her about it quite a lot when she was very young.

Mr. Jennings. A lot of people at home know we have a baby boomer President, and a lot of people in the baby boomer generation are nervous, apprehensive; some even think it's hypocritical to talk to their kids because of their own experience. What did you tell her about yours?

The President. Well, I basically told her what I've told everybody in America, which is when I was 22 years old in England and I thought there were no consequences, I tried marijuana a couple of times. But if I had known then what I know now about it, I would not have done it. And I think that—I feel the same way Dan does. I think that if you have done something that you're not especially proud of, but that you know more about it, you have almost a bigger obligation to try to prevent other people from getting in trouble.

I think this business about how the baby boomers all feel too guilt-ridden to talk to their kids is the biggest load of hooey I ever heard. They have a bigger responsibility to talk to their children. Most of us did not—most of us—first of all, most of us were much older when the experimentation started. And secondly, we did not know what we know now. We have no excuse. We have a greater responsibility, not a smaller one. So it hasn't bothered me to tell her that she shouldn't make the same mistakes I did.

I think all parents, by the way, hope their children won't make the same mistakes they did in many areas of life, not just this. And so that's part of what being a parent is all about.

[*A participant described his experience with inhalants, explaining how easily they could be obtained and the adverse effects of using them. Mr. Jennings asked why he had started, and the participant responded that his troubled homelife contributed to his drug use. He then explained that he sought help at a treatment center, but after his release, he started using crack and returned to the center.*]

The President. Do you think that you can have an impact on other people because of what you've been through?

Participant. Yes.

The President. Can you talk to other people and get through to them in a way that someone else couldn't because of what you've been through?

[*The participant replied that he hoped to help at least one person learn from his experiences with drugs. Another participant described his continuing battle with crack addiction. The next participant said he thought drugs were destroying the country and asked the President if the United States could institute effective sanctions against drug producing countries.*]

The President. Well, let me tell you a little about that. Let me just talk for a couple minutes.

First of all, I agree with that. We require countries where drugs are grown to cooperate with us in trying to destroy them and arrest the people who are selling them, if they want to keep getting any kind of aid or any help with trade from us. And I think that's a good thing.

But let me tell you what they say. I'll tell you what they say back. They say, "Okay, we have a poor little country here, and I'm a little farmer. And I can grow coca to make cocaine or I can grow bananas and pineapples, and I'll go broke if I do that and I'll make money if I do the other thing." The police officers in these poor countries where the drugs are shipped through—last year we know there was something like $500 million spent in Mexico alone to make payments to police officers that like tripled or quadrupled their annual salary. And so these countries that try to help us that are poor, where the drugs are grown, they say, "If the Americans didn't buy—the American people have 5 percent of the world's population and buy 50 percent of the world's drugs. And if they didn't want the drugs and weren't willing to pay these outrageous prices for them, we

wouldn't have a market, and we'd have to go do something else for a living."

In other words, I think you're right. We have to be tougher on them. And last year we had record numbers of destruction of drugs in foreign countries and arrests and all that. But as long as there is as much money as there is, and as long as Americans are just dying to have it, it's going to be impossible to completely eradicate. And we need to do more.

But all of us have to take responsibility, too. If we didn't have a drug problem in this country, they would go broke, and they would go do something else. Now, I'm not saying we shouldn't do more in other countries, but we have to take a lot of responsibility here, too.

Mr. Jennings. A show of hands—radio, again—a show of hands from the kids only, is he convincing? Well, you didn't do too badly. Okay, so we'll continue in just a moment.

The President. It's better than I did in the election. That's great. [*Laughter*]

[*Following a commercial break, Mr. Jennings asked what role the media played in educating children about the dangers of drugs. A participant said that the media did have an influence and suggested that the President support an increase in antidrug public service announcements.*]

The President. More of the antidrug commercials?

Participant. Antidrug commercials.

Mr. Jennings. But now somebody said earlier——

The President. What about what Matt said——

Mr. Jennings. ——there were too many of them.

The President. ——that if you overdo it, people won't believe it? What's the answer to that? Matt?

Participant. A lot of kids are—they don't believe it. You know, it's just not the right message.

The President. So what is the right message? Go ahead.

[*Several participants explained how television programming sent mixed messages on drug use and gave examples from daytime programming and situation comedies where drug use was treated lightly. Other participants indicated that their friends were not influenced by public service announcements. Mr. Jennings then invited the President to speak for the remaining 2 minutes of the program.*]

The President. Well, I'm going to give you back the 2 minutes. I'm going to give you 2 minutes to tell me anything specific you think I could do to help more kids stay off drugs.

Mr. Jennings. Okay. You're going to have to make it very quick.

The President. Very quick, though. Real quick. One line, everybody.

Participant. What you need to do is make more mentorship programs, more after-school programs where kids could keep themselves busy right after school.

Participant. There should be more treatment centers and more education.

Participant. People who are in jail should have more learning while they're in jail and not just getting out and learning more while they're in the system.

Participant. You should have more police officers out on the street, make sure nobody is selling drugs.

Participant. I think you need more of a firsthand look from people who have experience with this problem to—that's it.

Participant. I think you should cut back on the cartooning commercials and make there be more live-action commercials that get to the point about drugs.

The President. Give evidence.

Participant. More education programs for kids and younger kids about the harmful effects.

Participant. Well, I think that the cartoons they really don't believe because it's just—if they do it then they think it's cool anyway.

Participant. I also think that you should open up more after-school programs where kids have sports to do after school, keep them active.

Participant. I think the parents need to get really, really involved with their kids, no matter how many times their kids try to make them stay away from them.

Mr. Jennings. Boy, don't you wish you could get such fast, cogent advice from your Cabinet members? [*Laughter*]

The President. It's great, and I think—first of all, I agree with the after-school arguments, the mentoring arguments, the treatment, all the things you have said. But I think it's a good thing that we ended with Ally, because we know that children that have parents who work with them and deal with this issue are much less likely to be in trouble.

NOTE: The townhall meeting began at 11:06 a.m. in the East Room at the White House.

Statement on Senate Confirmation of Federico Peña as Secretary of Energy
March 12, 1997

I want to applaud the Senate today for its strong vote of support for Federico Peña to serve as our Nation's new Energy Secretary. As Transportation Secretary, Federico Peña built consensus among communities, business, and Government and streamlined operations to reap benefits for all taxpayers.

With this record, I am confident that Secretary Peña has the skill, experience, and dedication to lead the Energy Department to meet its central challenges—to broaden America's energy resources, to promote a safer, more secure world, and to help to create a brighter economic future for all Americans.

Remarks on the Attack on Israeli Schoolchildren and an Exchange With Reporters
March 13, 1997

The President. Today along the normally peaceful border between Israel and Jordan, we have seen an inexcusable and tragic act of violence against schoolchildren. I condemn this act in the strongest possible terms. I offer to Prime Minister Netanyahu, the Israeli people, and the families and friends of the innocent children who died or were wounded my profound condolences and those of the American people.

As I travel to North Carolina today to speak to people about our own schoolchildren, the senseless denial of a future for these young Israeli children will bear heavily on my mind. There is no justification or excuse for these acts. Now the leaders in the region must work hard to calm the situation, to do everything in their power to create an atmosphere in which violence is rejected rather than embraced.

I call on the leaders and the people of the region to reject violence, to redouble their efforts toward peace and reconciliation. I was encouraged by the statement which King Hussein issued not long ago—just a few moments ago—and I am very hopeful that the leaders and the people will respond in an appropriate manner.

Thank you.

Jerusalem Settlements

Q. Mr. President, do you believe the Israelis have to halt the settlements in East Jerusalem at this point? Do you think that might help calm the situation there?

The President. Let me first say that there is no evidence at this moment that this terrible incident is related to the tensions in the area over the issues. For all we know, this may have been just a deranged person. And I think it is important, given King Hussein and Jordan's long record of reaching for peace and reconciliation, that no one jump to any undue conclusions.

We don't have the facts. None of us have any facts other than we know this incident occurred. But we have no reason to believe that this was politically motivated by any larger group or anything. We just don't know that.

But you know what I believe. I believe that this is a time when we need to be building confidence and working together and there needs to be a certain mutuality of action in the Middle East to get this peace process well underway. That is what I had hoped would happen after the Hebron agreement, and that is still what I believe has to happen if we're going to succeed.

So we'll be talking to all the parties, and I'm in more or less constant contact with them. And we'll continue to be hopeful. But for right now, I think we need to give the people of Israel the time to absorb this terrible shock.

Thank you.

Q. Have you had a chance to talk to King Hussein?

The President. No.

NOTE: The President spoke at 8:36 a.m. on the South Lawn at the White House, prior to his departure for Raleigh, NC. In his remarks, he referred to Prime Minister Binyamin Netanyahu of Israel and King Hussein I of Jordan.

Remarks to a Joint Session of the North Carolina State Legislature in Raleigh
March 13, 1997

Thank you very much. Lieutenant Governor Wicker, Speaker Brubaker, Senator Basnight, the other State elected officials who are here, my good friend Governor Hunt, Mayor Fetzer.

I'd like to thank those who came down here with me today. I brought some of the Members of your congressional delegation home. They don't need to hear this speech, they've heard it before, but I was glad to have them here in moral support: Congressman David Price; Congressman Bob Etheridge, your former superintendent of education; Congressman Mike McIntyre; and Congresswoman Eva Clayton. I thank them for coming.

I also want to say I'm glad to be joined today by your neighbor, the Secretary of Education, Richard Riley, former Governor of South Carolina, and by our new Secretary of Defense, Bill Cohen of Maine. We're glad to have him with us today, too. Thank you, Secretary Cohen, for coming.

I was glad that you mentioned my Chief of Staff, Erskine Bowles. He wouldn't come here with me today because he was afraid all of you would think that he was shirking his duties and not at work. But let me tell you, he is doing a magnificent job. I'm very proud of him. I couldn't believe it when he agreed to come back to Washington and take this job, especially because I knew it would cost him a small fortune. And he reminded me that his father used to tell him, "Once you have the tools, you've got to spend some time to add to the woodpile." So he's up in Washington adding back to the woodpile. And you should all be very proud of him. He is a remarkable man. He's doing a good job.

I'd also like to thank the other North Carolinians on my staff. Two of the three of them are here today. Doug Sosnik, my former political director and senior counselor, is not here, but my Director of Communications, Don Baer, is here, and Charles Duncan, the Associate Director of Presidential Personnel. They both came home with me, and they were glad to have the excuse to come home. And I appreciate their being here and their service.

I was told that this was the first time a sitting President has addressed the North Carolina State Legislature. If it's not true, don't disabuse me now, because I'm about to say something good. [*Laughter*] And I am very honored to be here. Even more important, I've spent a little time here over the years, and I am honored and mildly surprised that you are here, because it's tournament time and you've got four teams, as usual, in the tournament.

You may know that I am something of a basketball fanatic. And you may know that one of my most memorable basketball experiences—I once saw North Carolina and Kentucky play in the Dean Dome, and the car that I came in

was towed. [*Laughter*] But I had so much fun at the ballgame, I would have walked all the way back to Arkansas after it was over. [*Laughter*] I make it a point never to take sides in basketball games unless my home team in Arkansas or my alma mater, Georgetown, are playing. But I am looking forward to the day when the great Dean Smith breaks Adolph Rupp's record.

There is much for the rest of the Nation, and especially the rest of the South, to admire in North Carolina, the determined and visionary leadership that has characterized this State for many decades in education and economic development, in bringing harmony among peoples of different backgrounds.

When I was a young man, I followed the work here of then-Governor Terry Sanford, who later became my friend and colleague. Eighteen years ago, when I first started my career as Governor of Arkansas, my best mentor and friend was Jim Hunt. And he is still my mentor and friend. Dick Riley and I were laughing with Jim Hunt—we were together 18 years ago as the Governors of Arkansas, South Carolina, and North Carolina, and we were laughing that Jim was probably the only one of us who could still get elected Governor in our home States after 18 years. [*Laughter*] And I applaud him on that.

It was in Chapel Hill that the cornerstone was laid at our Nation's first publicly funded university, in Kitty Hawk where man first took to the skies. And today, North Carolina is an aeronautics and an air travel hub center for millions of people. Your State universities receive the highest level of funding for research and development in the Nation. You have connected more of your communities than any other State in the country to the information superhighway, something I'm trying to do for every classroom and library in America by the year 2000. The Research Triangle has one of the highest per capita concentrations of Ph.D.'s in the world, and you are clearly one of America's most dynamic centers of economic activity.

The most important thing about all this is not for me to brag on you, you know that already, but to emphasize the main point: These things do not happen by accident. They are the product of vision and disciplined, long-term effort.

Now our country faces the challenges of a new century, a whole new economy, a whole new way in which people will work and live and relate to each other here at home and around the world. It is driven by information and by technology. Its best hopes may be undermined by its darkest fears, by the old demons of racial and religious and ethnic hatreds, by terrorism and narcotrafficking and organized crime.

This new time that we're moving into, that coincidentally will be part of a new century and a new millennium, will give more people in this State and this Nation the chance to live out their dreams than at any period in human history, if we take advantage of it to seize our opportunities and deal with our challenges.

There is unprecedented peace and prosperity now, and it has been very rare in our country's history. You can go back and find maybe a couple of other examples when we've had real security, a feeling of prosperity, and yet, a whole lot of challenges before us. Usually when people feel secure and relatively prosperous, one of two things happens—neither of them very laudable, but it's part of human nature—we either get sort of happy and self-satisfied and don't do anything, or because we are not gripped by big differences, we fall out with each other over small things, and petty things make us less than we ought to be.

The point I want to make today is that we cannot afford either to be complacent or to be divided among ourselves about small things. For we have been given an opportunity almost unique in American history to fashion a future that will embrace everybody. And we cannot and dare not blow that opportunity.

If you look at where we are now, you can see the vistas of the future. Our economy produced 12 million jobs in 4 years—never happened before in a 4-year period. We've had constant decline in crimes. We've had the biggest drop in the welfare rolls in American history in the last 4 years. In North Carolina, you've seen the unemployment rate drop to 4.2 percent, 75,000 people off the welfare rolls, 350,000 new jobs. That's going on all over America. But you know that we have more to do.

I have been going around the country, to the Michigan and the Maryland State legislatures—today the Vice President is in California speaking to the State legislature as I am here with you—because I know that to achieve the vision that we share for America, we all have

to do our part. I've said many times that the era of big Government is over. Your Federal Government is now 285,000 people smaller than it was the day I took office. It's the smallest it's been since President Kennedy was in office, in real terms. As a percentage of the civilian work force, the Federal Government is now as small as it was when Franklin Roosevelt was sworn into office the first time, before the New Deal.

But the challenges we face are still very big indeed. If they cannot be solved by government alone, and especially by the Federal Government, obviously, a new partnership is required. And new efforts, new activity, new responsibility is required of people at the State level, at the local level, and in their private lives. The biggest challenge we face today, I believe, is the challenge of creating a world-class education system that embraces every child that lives in this State and in this Nation. And this must not be a political football.

In the cold war, because we knew that communism threatened our existence, it became commonplace that politics would stop at the water's edge, and the Democrats and the Republicans would fight like cats and dogs over whatever it was they were fighting about, but when it came to standing up to the threat of communism, we were together. If the President of one party went abroad on a mission of world peace, he was never criticized back home by members of the other party because politics stopped at the water's edge.

I think we understand today, intuitively, that education holds the key to our future in the 21st century. And I believe politics must stop at the schoolhouse door.

When I was Governor, a long time ago now, North Carolina already had the highest percentage of its adults in institutions of higher education of any State in the South. The economy was growing, and it was diversifying, and yet you still had more success in maintaining manufacturing jobs than any State in our region and, indeed, in the country. You know all this. Last year you had the biggest increase in eighth grade math scores, I noticed, in the country. I was in Michigan, and I said that they had the second biggest increase in math scores, and the minute I got in the car, Governor Hunt made sure I knew who was number one. [*Laughter*] So I knew that.

The Governor chose to be sworn in at the Needham Laughton High School, his old school, to make clear that school standards and teaching excellence will be his top priorities. But with all the progress that we have made, you know we've got a lot more to do.

Between 1992 and the year 2000, 89 percent of the new jobs created in this economy will require more than a high school level of literacy and math skills—89 percent. Today, even though over 80 percent of our children are graduating from high school, more than half—or about half the people entering the work force are not prepared with these skills. We all know that is true.

For 20 years, inequality among working Americans grew. In the last few years it started to shrink—in the last couple of years—as we've gotten—more and more of our new jobs are becoming higher wage jobs and as growth and productivity are permitting wages to rise again.

Many people just a couple of years ago were saying, "Well, is the middle class vanishing in America? Will it always be squeezed? Are we going to create a country with a huge number of people that are very well off and an even much larger number of people that are poor, with a smaller middle class?" We've seen in the last few years that that does not have to happen. We can begin to grow the middle class again with productivity and growth and the right kinds of new jobs, but we have to be able to provide the people with the skills to hold those jobs if we're going to maintain a high-wage, high-growth, high-opportunity society in America in the 21st century. And our schools are still turning out millions of young people who simply cannot do that.

That is why our number one priority has to be to make America's education the best in the world. We have to have a nation in which every 8-year-old can read independently, every 12-year-old can log on to the Internet, every 18-year-old can go on to college, and every adult American can keep on learning throughout an entire lifetime.

In my State of the Union Address, I laid out a 10-point call to action for American education that describes the steps we have to meet. First, we have to make sure that all of our children come to school ready to learn. Our balanced budget will expand Head Start to a million children.

But we all must do more, and a lot of that has to be done at the State level. And I hope every State in the country is looking closely at the Smart Start program in North Carolina. The idea of having all elements of a community in a community nonprofit environment working on not only education but health care and parenting skills and child care, trying to give our poorest children a coherent early childhood, is terribly important. Scientists have discovered that learning begins in the earliest days of life. And now we have to explore how parents and educators can best use these findings. On April 17th the First Lady and I will host the White House Conference on Early Childhood Development and Learning in Washington, and I want Smart Start to be an important part of what is considered there.

Let me just give you one simple example of the scientific findings. Over half of the capacity of the brain to absorb and to learn and to grow—the capacity is developed in the first 4 years of life. In the first 4 years of life, if a child has parents who understand this and who constantly—whether they have a Ph.D. or they were high school dropouts, but who constantly work at nourishing the child's learning capacities, that child will get 700,000 positive contacts. But in the typical experience of a child with a single parent, let's say, with very little education and no self-confidence about parenting and no training and no understanding and a sense that no difference can be made, and the child is left in front of the television in the first 4 years, that child will get 150,000 positive contacts, a more than four-to-one difference.

Now, you tell me what the future is going to be like for them. Smart Start can change that. And our cooperative efforts can change that. But we have to understand that we have totally underestimated the impact of this whole thing. And the new scientific findings impose upon all of us a heavier responsibility than we have ever had for developing the capacities of our children in their earliest years. So I look forward to that.

I believe we have to do more to give constructive alternatives, creative alternatives for our young children in our public schools. I favor public school choice. I've been a pioneer supporter of the charter school movement. I think that it's important to open schools that stay opened as long as they do a good job, but only as long as they do a good job. And I know that this afternoon, your State board of education has the opportunity to open more charter schools than any State has ever opened at one time, to foster innovation and competition and renewal. I hope the board will take that step today, and one more time, North Carolina will be in the vanguard of a movement you can be proud of.

We have got to have a commitment to rebuild our schools and give our children the facilities they need to learn in. We have the largest number of children in public schools in history. The Secretary of Education never gets tired of reminding me, since I am the oldest of the baby boomers, that our generation has finally been eclipsed in numbers by the people that are in the public schools today. We also have the physical facilities in many of our schools deteriorating at a rapid rate. So, for the first time in history, I have proposed a program that will enable us at the national level to support local efforts to increase their investment in the physical facilities of the schools by making sure that the interest rates are lower and the costs are lower in the places where the need is most critical.

I'm going to Florida after I leave you, and tomorrow morning I will be at a school where there are 17, I understand, according to my briefing, 17 trailers for classroom space around the existing school facility in a modest-sized community in Florida. That is not an atypical experience in many of our States.

We have to meet our national goal of connecting every classroom and library to the Internet by the year 2000. We have to open the doors of college to all. North Carolina pioneered, with your network of 4-year and 2-year higher educational institutions, pioneered the idea that education ought to be a lifetime experience and that the doors ought to be open to everyone.

In the last 4 years, we have lowered the cost and improved the reach of the student loan program, added 200,000 slots to work-study, opened up almost 70,000 slots for college through the national service program, AmeriCorps. We have worked very, very hard, but I think we have to do more.

It is clear to me, if you look at the job profile, where 89 percent of the new jobs will require more than a high school education, we have to make 2 years of education after high school, the 13th and 14th grades, just as universal in

America by the year 2000 as a high school diploma is today, every bit as universal.

To achieve that, our balanced budget plan proposes a $1,500 HOPE scholarship, a tax credit that reflects the cost of the typical community college tuition in America, modeled on Governor Zell Miller's HOPE scholarship program in Georgia. We propose to give people a tax deduction of up to $10,000 a year for the cost of any education after high school, an expanded IRA that you can withdraw from tax-free if the money is used to pay for higher education, and the largest increase in Pell grants in 20 years, along with another 100,000 work-study slots. That will help North Carolina, and it will help America.

Finally, let me say on this subject, we know we have to make sure learning continues throughout a lifetime. We know that we have older and older students going back to community colleges, changing their careers and getting new careers and opening up new vistas. We have a Federal response which I think is totally antiquated. There are at least, conservatively speaking, at least 70 different Federal programs that were developed with the best of intentions, to try to help to pay for various training programs for people who lose their jobs or people who are grossly underemployed.

I have proposed for 4 years, with a Democratic Congress and with the Republican Congress, getting rid of these programs and putting the money in a pot and sending a skills grant to an unemployed person or an underemployed person who has qualified for any of them and let them go to the nearest community college or 4-year college if it's the appropriate one, whatever is nearest and best to get their education. We do not need a lot of Government intermediaries here. People know—people know what they need. They're capable of making a judgment.

In a State like North Carolina and most places in the country, nearly everybody's within driving distance of a community college that works. I call that my "GI bill" for America's workers. And if you could prevail upon your legislators to support it, I would appreciate it. I've been trying for 4 years to pass that thing. I would appreciate it.

I think the most important thing we have to do is to make sure that our children have met certain national standards in basic courses.

In 1989, when President Bush and the Governors met at the University of Virginia, I had the honor of being the Democratic Governor chosen to try to write the Nation's education goals. And at the time, we always assumed that out of those goals there would come national standards and a system, a nationally recognized system of testing our children to see if they met those standards.

Well, that hasn't happened yet. And as a result, we still don't know. We don't really know whether every child in every classroom knows what he or she needs to know when he or she needs to know it in math and in basic language skills. I have challenged every State in this country to adopt high national academic standards, not just in math and language but in other areas as well, to participate nationally by 1999 in an examination of fourth graders in reading and eighth graders in math, so that we can see how every child is doing in meeting those basic standards.

Now, this is, I know, somewhat controversial. There are people who have actually argued that you couldn't possibly have a national examination reflecting national standards in a country as diverse as America, as if it's some sort of plot, as if math is different in Raleigh than Little Rock or any board of education could rewrite the rules of algebra for Alaska as opposed to Florida. I think that is inherently implausible.

When you compete here in North Carolina for a new high-tech plant, when the Research Triangle finds some new breakthrough, you do it based on an international competition; you have to win based on standards that are imposed. We have to be willing to hold our children to the same standards and to hold ourselves to the same standards.

Governor Hunt told me today that he will endorse our call for national standards and a testing plan. North Carolina, therefore, would be the third State to do so. The Republican Governor of Michigan joined in, along with his legislative leaders, just a few days ago.

But let me say what I think we need to do. A lot of you know a lot about this. We have some standardized tests in America, but we don't have any test to nationally accepted standards. The closest we have is the so-called NAEP test, the National Assessment of Education Progress. But as all of you know, it only is given to a sample of students in various districts. There is no examination in America which says,

here are the standards that everyone should know in language or math, and here is a test which reflects those standards, and it doesn't matter whether you're first or last in your class, it matters whether you get over this bar. If you're first in your class and nobody is over this bar, nobody knows what they need to know. If you're last, but you're over the bar, you're still going to do okay in this old world. I think that is very important. We all need to know that. We all need to know that.

And let me also say that I know it won't be easy, because some of our kids won't do all that well at first. If you saw the State of the Union Address, you know that I introduced two students from 20 school districts in northern Illinois who took the Third International Math and Science Survey, and the 20 school districts up there tied for first in science and second in math in the survey, with Singapore for first. But if they had finished dead last I would have been equally proud of them because they were willing to actually hold themselves to international standards of achievement and measure themselves.

And this is where we need all of your help. I'm convinced that one of the reasons that we've never done this in America is that we were afraid if the news was bad, we wouldn't know what to do about it. And I think that in so doing, we have sold our children short. All the evidence is, all the scientific evidence is, all the anecdotal evidence is that almost all of our children, without regard to their race, their income, and where they live can learn what they need to know to compete and win in the global economy. And when we do not hold them to high standards because we are afraid that in the beginning they won't meet them, we are selling their futures down the drain and we are insulting them, because they can meet these standards.

What we have to be willing to do is to say, "Okay, we'll have these exams. We'll hold people to high standards. Some people won't make it at first. We don't want to punish people. We want to lift everybody up, but we can't know how to lift people up unless we know where we start."

When I go around the world, people find it unbelievable that we have no national standard in America to tell our parents and our school leaders whether our children know what they're supposed to know in the basic skills that are necessary to learn all the other more sophisticated things we want people to know.

And I tell you, I believe in the kids of this country. I have been in schools in circumstances where it would be unthinkable that people could learn because of crime in the neighborhoods and because of poverty in the neighborhoods. And I have seen children performing at very high levels, meeting standards that would be acceptable in anyplace in the entire world. And I am tired of people telling me that there is some reason we shouldn't have that opportunity given to every American child. We are not protecting our children by denying them the chance to develop their God-given capacities to measure up to what they need to know and do, to do well in the future. And we ought to stop it and do better.

Now, on a lighter note, you may wonder why the Secretary of Defense is here with me today. [*Laughter*] Before I came down here, Senator Helms asked me to tell you that he is not the guard that Jesse once said I would need to come to North Carolina. [*Laughter*] Ever since I got a Chief of Staff that does not speak with an accent, we've been getting along a lot better, Senator Helms and I. [*Laughter*]

There is another reason that the Secretary of Defense is here today. We want to set an example. We think we ought to start the standards movements with the schools that we run at military bases. At 66 schools across our country and 167 more around the world, our Department of Defense educates 115,000 of our children every year. The Department of Defense runs a school system as big as that of the State of Delaware. And I met some of the children, some of the teachers, and some of the parents out at the airport when I came in today.

Sixteen of those schools are at Camp Lejeune and Fort Bragg, right here in North Carolina, and nearly 8,000 students attend them. It's important that we give these children the best possible education, too, especially these children, because their families sacrifice. They live far from home. They often risk their lives for their country. It's important, too, because these students come from every racial and ethnic background. They move from place to place as their parents are transferred from base to base.

Because of this mobility, no group of students better underscores the need for common national standards and a uniform way of measuring

progress than this group. If standards can work in these schools, they can work anywhere.

So I am pleased to announce today that, with the strong support of the Secretary of Defense, the Department of Defense schools have stepped forward to ask that their students be among the first to take the new tests when they become available. The Secretary of Defense and the Secretary of Education Riley have both committed their work.

Starting in 1999, students and classrooms, from Wiesbaden Air Force Base in Germany to Kadena Air Force Base in Okinawa, to Camp Lejeune will learn the same rigorous material and take the same national tests as students throughout this State and, I hope, throughout our entire Nation. We can make our public schools, just like our military, the best on Earth if, like our military, we are willing to adhere to high, rigorous standards for all people, regardless of their background. That's what we ought to do. And I thank you, Mr. Secretary, for being here today.

Let me also say that we know we have to do more work to prepare all of our students. And the Department of Defense is being directed today, through its school system, to use every resource to prepare the students for 1999 when the new math and science tests—or math and reading tests are ready.

Let me mention one other thing that I think is very important, and it goes well with a lot of what you are doing here with your preschool years and your early years. It is appalling to me that 40 percent of America's 8-year-olds cannot read a book on their own, but it's true. And the rest of this stuff is just sort of whistling the breeze, if people can't read. So we have launched the America Reads initiative, through the Department of Education, to mobilize an army of a million reading tutors, properly trained, to help make sure that by the year 2000 every 8-year-old can read independently.

Thirteen North Carolina college presidents have pledged to commit a portion of their work-study students to serve as tutors, and I thank them for that. We're going to have 300,000 new work-study students over a 4-year period. If we can put at least a third of them into reading instruction for our young children, we'll be a long way toward those million volunteers.

We ought to be clear about something else, too, and here's something that I really take my hat off to Governor Hunt for. We cannot expect our children to meet high standards unless we demand that our teachers meet high standards. We have to do whatever is necessary to make sure that they do.

Last year the report of Governor Hunt's National Commission on Teaching and America's Future laid out a blueprint for the road ahead. And all of you have come together across party lines to develop a comprehensive legislative agenda that implements the report's recommendations. We have to start by recognizing and rewarding our best teachers. We all know what a difference a good teacher can make in the life of a child. I know what a difference my teachers made in mine.

The National Board for Professional Teaching Standards, led by Governor Hunt, has encouraged teachers all over the country to improve their skills and seek certification as master teachers. North Carolina already has more certified national teachers—master teachers—than any other State in the country. And the Governor was kind enough to bring five or six of them out to the airport to meet me, and they were not ashamed of the fact that they had been board-certified master teachers.

Over 20 percent of all the teachers that have been certified are here in North Carolina. That's the good news. The bad news is that only about 500 teachers have been certified. In our balanced budget plan, there's enough money to help 100,000 teachers achieve this important credential. Now the States need to do things like North Carolina has and offer to pay. The Governor's plan would pay master teachers another 12 percent more. You have to encourage people. But we need 100,000 at least, because what we really want is at least a board-certified master teacher in every single school building in America. If you get one in every single school building in America, we know from the research that they will change the education environment and help lift the standards that other teachers achieve and help to lift the quality of teaching in all the classrooms.

So that is one of the things that we're trying to do in our budget. But again, I'd say that we are following your lead and especially the years and years and years that Governor Hunt has put into this. In April Secretary Riley will hold a national forum on attracting and preparing teachers with 50 of our Nation's best teachers and thousands of others. And we are going to have to do more to encourage our brightest young people to become teachers.

Finally, we also have to make sure, as the Governor said, that while good teachers get a raise, the truly bad teachers who can't measure up should get a pink slip. We have to do that in an expeditious and fair way. Today, that is too time consuming and costly. In some States it can cost hundreds of thousands of dollars. That same money could be and should be used to reward good teachers and to train those who are trying to improve their skills. We can change this, as they have in Cincinnati where school boards and teachers unions have worked together in partnership to find more efficient and fair ways to remove teachers who should leave the classroom. Encouraging teachers is not easy or cheap, but again, I say, we know what a phenomenal difference it makes.

Finally, to elevate teaching, I think we have to reform the way we spend money in our schools and give parents the tools to demand more accountability. Today the Vice President is discussing that at the State legislature in Sacramento, California. His reinventing Government initiative has helped us to shrink the National Government to the smallest it's been in three decades and to take that money and invest it in education, invest it in technology, invest it in transportation, invest it in growing the economy and building a better future. We have to have the same sort of national effort to analyze the way expenditures are made in public education throughout America, so that we can support those who are committed to reducing unnecessary bureaucratic expenditures and increasing expenditures on children and teachers and learning.

Yesterday I did a townhall meeting with 35 children, on drugs. And I asked all these kids—and some of these kids had been on drugs and were off drugs, a couple of these kids were in treatment, some of them had been in families of gang members who had been involved in drugs, and then some of them had never used drugs. It was a whole panoply of kids. But I went through child after child after child, and I asked them to tell me about their circumstances. And they all said, "We need mentors. We need programs we're interested in." And one after another they kept telling me about how their school had had to abandon its music program or its art program, its physical education programs, its intramural athletic programs, all the things that happen after school or on weekend that keep kids involved in positive things.

We have to understand that however much money we have for our schools, we have to make sure we are spending it first and foremost on instruction and, secondly, on ways designed to give the children the best chance to live productive, wholesome, good, constructive lives, and that ought to be a national effort as well. We have found phenomenal amounts of money that we could redirect in the Federal Government to reducing the deficit or investing in our future simply by slowly but deliberately eliminating hundreds of unnecessary programs, thousands of unnecessary regulations, and reducing, without running people off, just slowly reducing the size of Government until we have got it to the point where I mentioned to you earlier.

And we have to work on that in our schools because we cannot afford to waste a single dollar when it comes to these children's future. And it is folly to ˙believe that we're not paying for it when we take these kids away from a chance to have a full, wholesome experience and to be in those schools after school hours or before school hours and doing things in addition to their academic learning. So I hope you will support that. [*Applause*] Thank you.

Let me just say one final word in closing about another big job we have to do together. We have to finish the work of welfare reform. In the first 4 years of my Presidency, we gave waivers from Federal rules to 43 States to do all kinds of things to help move people from welfare to work. We now know that partly because of the growing economy, partly because of State welfare reform efforts, and partly because of a 50 percent increase in child support collections nationwide, the welfare rolls went down by 2.6 million in 4 years, a record number.

Then the Congress passed and I signed the welfare reform bill, which says there will still be a national guarantee for poor children for food and medicine, but there's a limit to how long an able-bodied person can be on welfare without going to work. And we're going to give it to the States and let the States decide how to design their plans to move people from welfare to work.

Well, what I want to tell you folks is that this is like that old country singer Chet Atkins, who used to say, "You've got to be awful careful what you ask for in this old life, because you might get it." And now you've got it. And here is what you have. In order to meet the demands of the law that was supported by almost every Governor and every State official in the country, we must move about another million people from welfare to work. Now keep in mind when we reduced the welfare rolls by 2.6 million, some of those were children; only about a million of those were people moving from welfare into the work force. So we moved a million people in 4 years when the economy created almost 12 million jobs. We have to move another million in the next 4 years because of what the law says, whether the economy creates the jobs or not. And it is your responsibility to design a plan to get that done.

Now, I want to help. And I have proposed Federal legislation to give a tax credit of 50 percent for up to $10,000 in salaries for people who hire people specifically off welfare. I have proposed to give extra cash to high-impact, high-unemployment areas so people can do public service work, community service work, if necessary.

But there are more things you can do. Your Work First program here in North Carolina is encouraging private employers by subsidizing paychecks and holding job fairs. These are the kinds of things we have to do everywhere. But you really need to look at how your program works. And you need to look at whether you have a system for challenging private employers to look at the incentives that are available. And you need to figure out how many people every county is going to have to move from welfare to work in order for you not to have a train wreck at the end of the next 4 years.

Every State has to do this. And it's going to have to be done county by county, community by community. Because I'm telling you, everybody that ever said people who are able-bodied on welfare ought to have to work now has a moral obligation to make sure that the people who have been told they have to work actually have jobs so they can work. We have to do that.

Let me just say, I have been to a lot of States and looked at a lot of programs. In Missouri, they go to employers and say, "We'll give you the welfare check for up to 4 years if you need it, but you have to pay people $1.75 over the minimum wage, and we'll give you the welfare check as an employment and training supplement. And you can have it for a slot, but not for a particular individual, for up to 10 years, if you'll just keep being part of our program." So they've got a lot of employers, small, medium, and large, who are part of that.

You have to do something like that to do something for the employers who are not taxed. Community nonprofits and religious organizations can hire a lot of people from welfare into their ranks and have a lot to do with integrating their families into the mainstream of life in North Carolina. But they have to have some incentive to do so.

The second thing I would urge you to do is to make sure that as you realize savings from people moving from welfare to work, I think you can meet your goals better if you turn around and invest at least the initial of those savings back into the transition. We did a good job of adding $4 billion to child care for people moving from welfare to work. But we still may not have enough child care to do the job. And we know that is a huge barrier. You cannot ask people to hurt their kids when they go to work. And a lot of folks entering these entry-level jobs don't make much money. Now we can carry them over with Medicaid health insurance for their kids for a while. They've got to have the child care.

This bill gives you a lot of flexibility, and now you have to design this program. I would just implore you to really get down to brass tacks, get the facts: How many people does North Carolina have to move from welfare into jobs in 4 years? How many is that per county? How many is that per community? What are the tools we have? Who have we asked to do the job?

I believe that the private sector is anxious to be asked to participate in this. I believe they want to end the permanent under class in America and help people move into the thriving, growing middle class. But we have to do it in an organized, disciplined way, State by State. We're going to do our part, but we need you to do yours.

Finally, let me say that it is obvious from looking at education that we have to have a new partnership in America. Washington can lead the way, but the work has to be done by all Americans. North Carolina has led the way for a long time.

I was smiling today when I got up and I thought about coming down here, and I thought about the first time I was ever in a meeting with Governor Hunt and Governor Riley—18 years ago; we were all much younger then. And we had this idea that all the Southern States would reach the national average in per capita income and have all these great opportunities for our people if only we could have an education system that was as good as anyplace in the country and it would reach everybody, without regard to race or income.

And ironically, the mission that many of us who are southerners have carried for 20 or 30 years in our hearts is now the mission of America in a global society dominated by information and technology. And it is within our reach, literally, to give every single child in America the greatest future in human history, if we create the conditions in which we can flourish—that's partly our job, through national defense and meeting the security challenges and providing a good economy, but also having the tools.

We cannot guarantee the future for any child, but we can give every child the tools to make the most of his or her own life. That is now America's mission. It is a mission this State has pursued for a long time. If you will lead the way, America's best days are still ahead.

Thank you, and God bless you all.

NOTE: The President spoke at 11:09 a.m. in the House of Representatives Chamber. In his remarks, he referred to Gov. James B. Hunt, Jr., and Lt. Gov. Dennis Wicker of North Carolina; Harold Brubaker, speaker, North Carolina House of Delegates; Marc Basnight, president pro tempore, North Carolina State Senate; Mayor Tom Fetzer of Raleigh; Dean Smith, men's basketball coach, University of North Carolina; and Gov. John Engler of Michigan.

Memorandum on National Testing in Defense Department Schools
March 13, 1997

Memorandum for the Secretary of Defense

Subject: Participation of Department of Defense Dependents Schools and Domestic Dependent Elementary and Secondary Schools in National Testing

The Department of Defense Dependents Schools overseas and the Domestic Dependent Elementary and Secondary Schools here at home play an important role in enhancing the quality of life and overall readiness of the Armed Forces of the United States. They provide military families deployed overseas and within the United States with outstanding educational opportunities, and they play a vital role in preparing the children of military and civilian personnel in the Armed Forces for the future.

Students in these schools deserve the best we can offer, starting with the highest expectations and most challenging academic standards available. Drawn from all racial and ethnic backgrounds, located in 15 countries throughout the world and in seven States and Puerto Rico here at home, all highly mobile, no group of students better underscores the need for common national standards and a uniform way of measuring progress.

That is why I am pleased the Department of Defense Dependents Schools and Domestic Dependent Elementary and Secondary Schools have accepted the challenge of benchmarking the performance of their students against widely accepted national standards in fourth grade reading and eighth grade math, using voluntary national tests aligned with these standards. This step will ensure that students, parents, and teachers in the Department of Defense Edu-

cation Activity (DoDEA) schools will have honest, accurate information about whether students are mastering the basic skills. Along with the States of Maryland, Michigan, and North Carolina, the DoDEA schools are among the first in the Nation to commit to participate in this testing program, beginning in 1999.

Accepting this challenge of meeting national standards means much more than administering new tests. It means beginning immediately to prepare students to meet these standards. This will require steps such as providing parents with the information and assistance they need to be their child's first teacher, upgrading the curriculum, implementing proven instructional practices and programs, making accessible new technologies to enhance teaching and learning, supporting and rewarding good teaching, and providing students who need it with extra help and tutoring.

The DoDEA schools have already begun this task, but much more needs to be done. And the lessons the DoDEA schools learn from these efforts can be valuable for other schools throughout our Nation.

Therefore I direct you to ensure that the DoDEA schools take these and other steps as appropriate, and use all available resources to prepare every one of their students to meet these standards, in 1999 and each year thereafter, and to report annually on the progress being made toward this objective, and on the effectiveness of the strategies and approaches the DoDEA school system uses to achieve it.

WILLIAM J. CLINTON

Statement Announcing the White House Conference on Early Childhood Development and Learning
March 13, 1997

Today Hillary and I are pleased to announce that on April 17, 1997, we will host the White House Conference on Early Childhood Development and Learning: What New Research on

the Brain Tells Us About Our Youngest Children. The conference, which will take place at the White House, will spotlight exciting new findings about how our children develop, and explore how we can make the most of this information to give our children what they need to thrive.

We hope that this one-day conference will make the latest scientific research, nearly all supported by the Federal Government, more accessible and understandable to America's families. The research clearly indicates the importance of children's first few years to their later success in school and in life. This conference is a continuation of my administration's commitment to children, and in particular, it follows Hillary's work over the years on issues relating to early childhood development.

The conference will examine how we can use this new research in practical ways—to be better parents, more informed caregivers, and more responsive members of our communities. It will also explore how this information can be used by all members of our society—from corporate executives to pediatricians, from ministers to elected officials—to help strengthen America's families.

Parents desperately want to do right by their children, and we all have a role to play in making sure they have the tools they need to do the best job they can. We believe this conference can make a valuable contribution.

Statement on House of Representatives Action on Narcotics Certification for Mexico
March 13, 1997

Today's vote by the House of Representatives on Mexico is the wrong way to continue and deepen the unprecedented cooperation we are getting from Mexico in the war on drugs and the wrong way to protect the interests of the American people.

We all seek the same goal: to keep drugs out of America's neighborhoods and away from our children. Accomplishing that goal requires that we work closely with nations that share our objective of halting the flow of illegal narcotics, especially with the one country in the hemisphere whose 2,000 mile border with the United States makes it a ready target of the traffickers seeking to smuggle their contraband into the United States.

I certified Mexico because in the last year, we have achieved an unprecedented level of cooperation on counternarcotics, because Mexico has taken concrete steps on its own to fight drug trafficking, and because certification is the best way to make sure that Mexico's cooperation and antidrug efforts grow even stronger.

Under President Zedillo's leadership, Mexico broke new ground by extraditing two of its citizens to the United States and expelling drug kingpin Juan Garcia Abrego, who is now behind bars in an American prison for life. Our military cooperation has improved dramatically as we have expanded antidrug training and assistance on drug interdiction.

Moreover, Mexico has taken the initiative by itself: Drug seizures, arrests, crop eradication, and the destruction of drug labs and runaways in Mexico have all increased. New laws to combat organized crime and money laundering have been enacted. And the Zedillo administration immediately arrested and prosecuted its drug czar when they discovered he had been corrupted by a major drug ring.

President Zedillo recognizes the enormity of the problem Mexico faces, and he has been courageous in carrying this battle forward. He deserves our support, not a vote of "no confidence" that will only make it more difficult for him to work with us and defeat the scourge of drugs.

I will continue to work with Congress to ensure that legislation that would undermine progress we have made with Mexico does not become law.

Remarks at a Democratic Senatorial Campaign Committee Dinner in Aventura, Florida
March 13, 1997

Thank you very much. I have these elaborate notes I just wrote out. [*Laughter*] I am so glad to be here. I believe Senator Graham and Lieutenant Governor MacKay and Senator Torricelli. I tried to get Bob to say that so many of you were glad he was here so you could hear someone speak without an accent. [*Laughter*] I believe this is the first time I have been to Florida to give a public speech since the election, and so let me begin by saying, thank you, thank you, thank you.

This has been a wonderful day for me. I began by going to North Carolina to speak to the North Carolina Legislature about education and welfare reform. And Governor Jim Hunt of North Carolina was the Governor of North Carolina in 1979, when Bob Graham was the Governor of Florida, and the Secretary of Education, Dick Riley, was the Governor of South Carolina, and I was the Governor of Arkansas. And we had all these wonderful ideas, and we were very young. And I have been friends with Bob and Adele for a long time, and I'm honored to be here in their behalf tonight.

I thank Senator Torricelli for being here. Senator Harkin, I thank him for coming. Lieutenant Governor MacKay, thank you very much. Somebody told me Bill Nelson was here. I don't know if he is or not, but if he's not, tell him I mentioned his name. And if he is, he'll know I did. [*Laughter*]

It's wonderful to see Elaine Bloom and Ron Silver again. And Dante, they told me you were 80 years old, but I don't believe it. It's just another one of your lies, the way politicians are. [*Laughter*] It looks good on you. It looks great on you. You should have been—they had this great story in the New York Times Sunday Magazine—I don't know if you saw it—about how old isn't old anymore. And it really was about, I hope, all of us. And I don't know anyone who is younger in heart and spirit than Dante Fascell.

Let me also say that I'm very proud of all of you who have helped Bob Graham and helped Buddy MacKay and helped a lot of us. And I'm proud of those of you who have helped

me and have stood with me. And I hope you're proud of it, too.

Well over a year ago, we had a meeting talking about the 1996 campaign. And a lot of these so-called experts said in this meeting in Washington that we had to target the States we won last time and just try to hold most of them, that we certainly couldn't expect to expand our base and we couldn't—I said, "Oh yes we can. There's two places we lost last time we're going to win this time." And they said, "Where?" And I said, "We're going to win in Arizona, where no Democrat has won since 1948." And they thought I had lost my mind. And I said, "We're going to win in Florida." And they said, "You're nuts." They said, "You know, Lawton Chiles won in Florida, but he has all that she-coon language and all that stuff"—or he-coon. [*Laughter*] And I said, "I can talk like that." They said, "Yeah, but they won't believe you anymore. You've been living in Washington 4 years." [*Laughter*]

And I said—I swear this is true—we had this big argument, and it was that great story about how Abraham Lincoln had a meeting of his Cabinet and the vote was seven to one. And he said that seven of them wanted to do one thing, and he wanted to do the other thing, and he said, "The ayes have it." [*Laughter*] "Seven no's, one 'I,' the I's have it." That's the way it was.

And I told them all—over a year before the election, I said, "Here's what's going to happen on election night. We will win Florida. And it's on the East Coast and it will come up early and they will gasp and they will say, 'This thing is over. Turn out the light.'" And that's exactly what happened, thanks to you, and I thank you for it. And I told them it was going to happen.

And it happened not just because of the campaign but because of the work that we were able to do together with Bob Graham and Governor Chiles and Lieutenant Governor MacKay and so many others, the work we were able to do with the Summit of the Americas, with moving the Southern Command, with dealing with the aftermath of the hurricane, with promoting the economy, with dealing the issues that so gripped us for 4 years on and off around our relations with Cuba and with the importance of the Cuban-American community here, with the restoration work we have begun and that we intend to finish on the Everglades, and any number of other issues. This administration built a partnership with the people of Florida for the future, and you were good enough to reward us with your votes in November, and I am very, very grateful.

And let me say quickly, Bob Graham is very important to this country, not just to the Democratic Party but to the country. I have told many people this, so I'm not saying this out of school. I was a Governor forever. Most people thought that I just couldn't get a promotion—I was Governor forever. I was Governor in the seventies, Governor in the eighties, Governor in the nineties. I served with 150 people. And I found something to learn from all of them, and I enjoyed knowing them all. But if I had to name the 5 best Governors out of the 150 I served with, Bob Graham would be on the list and near the top.

You know what he's doing with all these little notes that he—you see him make all these little notes. I'm surprised Mitchell Berger hadn't quit supporting him. He's destroyed more trees with those note pads than any single person in America. [*Laughter*] But he'll be writing notes now before the thing's over. And there's probably vaults full of Graham's notebooks after all these years.

But I'll tell you what he's doing is—he's doing with those notes—is the same thing he's doing with his work days that he's done with such discipline and faithfulness over all these years. He has this crazy idea that politics is about more than words and rhetoric, it's about people and action and change and moving forward and making things better.

And there are lots of folks who can give good speeches but not so many people who can give good service along with good speeches. And Bob Graham is constantly striving to understand what is going on and where we ought to be going and how to put together what is going on with where we ought to be going. And he does it in a way that is almost unique in public life. And so I'm glad you're here for him, but I want you to know we need him. And I was afraid he wouldn't run for Senator again because Washington is—MacKay said, "So was I." [*Laughter*]

You might as well have a laugh here, because the further you get away from where people live in American politics—now I gave you a laugh; now be serious. [*Laughter*] And this is serious. I was afraid he wouldn't run again, because the further you get away from where people live in American politics and the more distance there is between where you work and where people live and the more intermediaries there are between you and the people you represent, the more likely it is that words and rhetoric will matter more and deeds will matter less.

And I can say that as someone who was a Governor for many years of what my opponent in 1992 affectionately referred to as a "small Southern State," where people expected me to run my office like a country store. If somebody called up, they expected me to call them back; if somebody walked in, they expected to see me; if somebody had a problem, they expected me to deal with it. It was an action-oriented job. And you got graded at election time based on whether you actually produced anything or not.

And we have to struggle always in Washington against the temptation to make the day's work about ourselves and what we can say about each other in political parties and across the kind of rhetorical walls that exist there, instead of about you. And Bob Graham is a daily breath of fresh air, because he gets up every day, and he thinks about you and what he can do to change things for the better for you.

And he is an inspiration to everybody who really knows him, who understands after a few years of observation what the work days are about and what all those little notebooks are about. They're about a guy that does not want to live his life in vain and is not running to get a lot of votes just to have his ego stroked. He actually wants to use the power of the job he holds to change things for the better. And that is a great and good thing, and we need more of it in Washington, not less. And so you need to send him back.

The second point I want to make is that the results are fairly satisfactory for what we've been working on the last 4 years. We reversed trickle-down economics and installed an economic theory based on investment in our people, reducing the deficit, and expanding trade. And to show for it, the country has produced 11½ million jobs in 4 years for the first time in any Presidential term. Bob Graham cast the decisive vote to make sure that we could pass that plan. And we did a good thing.

We reversed decades of social decline. We had the biggest drop in welfare rolls in the history of the country in the last 4 years, and in each of the last 4 years, the crime rate went down. We had a tough crime bill, and we had a sensible approach to welfare reform. We restored family and community at the center of our social policy with things like the family and medical leave law and the effort to deal with the damaging effects of advertising and selling and marketing tobacco to children.

We reasserted the leadership of the country in the cause for peace around the world. I don't know how many of you tonight came up to me and had detailed conversations with me about the Middle East peace process. I think it's a good thing that you can talk to your President about the Middle East peace process. I think it's a good thing that Monday, when we have the annual St. Patrick's Day celebration in the White House, that Irish-Americans, both Protestant and Catholic, will be able to talk to the President about the peace process in Northern Ireland.

I think it's a good thing that I am going to meet President Yeltsin in just a few days in Helsinki to talk about what we can do to build stronger relations with each other, to have a strong and united and free Europe, and to reduce the threat of nuclear war more. I think these are good things, and I'm glad that the United States is a leading force for peace and freedom and a better future for the world.

And I might say, I think it's a good thing that my supporters feel free to talk to me about issues relating to the United States and their relationships with Cuba, with the Middle East, with Northern Ireland, with the Everglades, or anything else you've got on your mind. That's the way the democratic system works, and I'm proud you're here and glad you talked to me about these things. I think it's one of your better programs.

And finally, let me say, I think we've resolved this fight over the role of Government and the role of our community in our common life. You don't hear any of that rhetoric we lived with through '95 and early '96 that the Government's inherently the enemy of the American people, that we're better off on our own, and that we don't have more in common than we do that divides us. And that's a good thing.

And so now, we're in a position to really build that bridge to the next century in the next 4 years. And that is the last thing I leave you with and the final point. We've got a lot left to do. We still have to balance the budget. We've got to fix this welfare reform law and stop punishing legal immigrants who through no fault of their own need and deserve the help of the United States as well as the State of Florida. You need it to keep from having your State budget go bankrupt. But it is the morally right thing to do, and I want you to help us get it done.

We have a lot to do around the world, but the last thing I want to say is, we have got to make education the most important domestic issue in this country in the next 4 years. I am striving to get every State in the country to agree that we should establish national standards first in reading and math and then expand it to other things in education. It's unbelievable to me; here we are in a global economy, and we've never had that. We have never had national education standards in America, as if somehow school boards with different student bodies could legislate differences in algebra or math or reading, and it's wrong. And we're going to do that. And we're going to open the doors of college to all Americans. And we're going to be able to go into the next century together because we're going to have the best educated citizens in the world, and that way, our diversity will be an asset instead of a liability. And I want every one of you committed to that.

The last thing I'll say is this. Democracy requires vigorous involvement by people, and you have been vigorously involved. Some of you apparently have been paying for it lately, but I appreciate it, and I hope that you will always be proud of what you did for me but, more importantly, for your country and for your children and for your grandchildren. And when you get involved in these races in the next 2 years, in 1998, and when you send Bob Graham to the Senate and you hold the Governor's office for someone who believes that we can grow Florida together and preserve the environment, even as we grow the economy and have a balanced and good and whole future, you'll be doing it not for yourselves primarily but for your children and your grandchildren.

And that's why this country is still around here after 220 years. A friend of mine who is a newspaper publisher from out West was in town the other day, and he was saying to me that he thought Abraham Lincoln and all of our forebears would be pretty happy if they looked at America now and saw that we had a vigorous, vital, two-party political system where people could participate, the country was doing well by any standard, our political system was cleaner than it was 30 years ago or 50 years ago or 100 years ago, and more importantly, our country was producing results for the people and for the future.

And that's what I want you to think about tomorrow when you wake up, determined to keep the people in office and elect people to office that will make it so, and even better, for our children and our grandchildren.

Thank you, and God bless you.

NOTE: The President spoke at 8:55 p.m. at Turnberry Isle Resort. In his remarks, he referred to Gov. Lawton Chiles and Lt. Gov. Buddy MacKay of Florida; Senator Bob Graham's wife, Adele; Bill Nelson, Florida State insurance commissioner; Elaine Bloom, Florida State representative; Ron Silver, Florida State senator; Dante Fascell, former U.S. Representative; Mitchell W. Berger, finance chair, Florida State Democratic Party; and President Boris Yeltsin of Russia.

Remarks to the Saxophone Club in Miami, Florida
March 13, 1997

Thank you. Thank you, Buddy MacKay. Thank you, Elaine Bloom. I want to thank all the people here from the Saxophone Club, and Merry Morris and Mr. Berger, the co-chairs of tonight's event. I want to thank Ed Kia and his trio who played earlier, and Albita and John Secada and these wonderful musicians. They were fabulous at the Inaugural, and they were great here tonight. I only wish they had sung about 10 more minutes. I love that song.

Let me say, first and foremost, this is my first trip back to Florida since the election. It has been 60 years since a Democrat was re-elected President and 20 years since a Democrat carried the State of Florida in any election. And I came to say, more than anything else, thank you, thank you, thank you.

And it is true what Buddy MacKay said, my whole odyssey, the whole struggle that I have waged these long years, not just to be President but to change the direction of our country, got its first big boost in the State of Florida in December of 1991, in the straw poll. And Buddy was there, Elaine Bloom was there, and a number of others were, and we won it. And it was the beginning of a terrific personal adventure for Hillary and for me, but more importantly for a different direction for our country.

And I want all of you to be proud who are here at this Saxophone Club event. You know, the Saxophone Clubs really started with the campaign of '92 with some young people who wanted to find a way for people who couldn't give a lot of money but wanted to give some money and work and to be a part of the political process and to be valued and to have their voices heard to do that. And that gave birth to these Saxophone Clubs. And they've spread all across the country now. And I always say, wherever I go, I don't want to do any kind of event unless we also have something for the Saxophone Club because I especially want to see the young people who come out to these events. And I want them to know that we're working every day for them and their future in Washington to make this country better in the years ahead. And I thank you for that.

I want all of you who have helped us these last few years to be proud of the fact that we have the lowest combined rates of unemployment and inflation in over 30 years, that we just had an economy that produced more jobs in one Presidential term than any before in history, that we've had 4 years of declining crime rates and the biggest reduction in welfare rolls in history, that our country is leading the world toward reducing the nuclear threat, dealing with the new threats of biological and chemical weapons, working for peace from the Middle East to Northern Ireland, working—I'm going to meet with President Yeltsin next week in Helsinki to try to work on making sure that Europe will be free and democratic and it will have a positive relationship with Russia and that we can get rid of the nuclear problems that are still out there overhanging us from the cold war. We are moving ahead.

And as Buddy MacKay said, I'm also going around the country on what has become a personal crusade for me and for Hillary and for the Vice President. Today I spoke in the North Carolina Legislature; Al Gore spoke in California. In a couple of weeks, Hillary and I are going to sponsor a conference in Washington on early childhood learning. And all of this is designed to make sure that for the next 4 years, we commit ourselves to making sure that in the 21st century every person in this country, without regard of their racial or ethnic background, will have access to world-class education and a chance to live out their dreams by developing their goals.

Make no mistake about it, that's what all this is about. You are part of a movement to build this country and move it into a new century with the American dream alive for everyone, where we reject the divisions that so many try to impose on us at political times for political reasons and come together as one country, and where we continue to lead the world for peace and freedom and prosperity. That is the world I'm determined to leave to you in 4 years when I go out of office and a new century and a new millennium come into our lives. And together that's exactly what we're going to do.

Thank you, and God bless you all.

NOTE: The President spoke at 10:15 p.m. at the Sheraton Bal Harbour Hotel.

Telephone Remarks to Lighthouse Elementary School in Jupiter, Florida
March 14, 1997

Dr. Joan Kowal. Good morning, Mr. President.

The President. Good morning, Joan.

Dr. Kowal. And good morning—I know that the President is saying good morning to all the boys and girls here that are gathered at Lighthouse. We're very pleased to at least have you on the phone. And we wish you were here in person, and we know you do, too.

The President. Oh, I really wish I were there. I wanted so much to come and visit because I've heard so much about the school. And I know about the problem of growth and crowding in Florida, and I wanted to use the work you're doing there as a strong argument for passing this program in Congress to help school districts like this one and throughout the State of Florida to do the building they need to do.

And I'm very grateful—and I also wanted to thank all the students and the educators for showing up. I know the student body president there, Marcy Haylett—I've been told this is her birthday. I hope you will tell her happy birthday for me.

Dr. Kowal. I will tell you she also has the title of president. I was going to get to introduce that president this morning. And she is, indeed, celebrating an 11th birthday at this time. And I think one of the things—we know you didn't choose Lighthouse quite by accident. When we think of the symbol of a lighthouse and the fact that what it offers is a real symbol of hope on the horizon and helps navigators, and we know that one of the things that as you're looking for growth, that it's a real sense of hope for us. And we're very pleased that you've recognized the challenge here as we talk about rebuilding America's schools.

Can you tell us just a little bit more—and let me just say, Marcy wants to—she had a long introduction here, but I'm going to ask her just to say a couple of words out of her introduction, because she wanted the opportunity to do that. Is that okay?

The President. Sure, I want to hear her.

Marcy Haylett. Hey, Mr. President. It is an honor and a privilege to have the 42d President to come to Lighthouse Elementary School to speak to us and to help us to solve our problem of overcrowded schools.

The President. Thank you, Marcy.

Ms. Haylett. You're welcome.

The President. And happy birthday again.

Ms. Haylett. Thank you.

The President. Hope you have a great day.

Ms. Haylett. Hope you feel better.

The President. Oh, I'll feel better, and I hope I get to come and visit you later, okay?

Ms. Haylett. Okay.

The President. That's great.

Dr. Kowal. Mr. President, can you give us a few words—you are now on loudspeaker, and let me just mention that standing here with me is Commissioner Brogan, and he's grabbing the phone out of my hand. But I'll tell you what, he is one of the most visible commissioners we've had here in Florida. He just wants to say howdy.

The President. Hello, Frank.

Commissioner Frank Brogan. Mr. President, how are you?

The President. I'm great. I heard you and Joan talking on the television a few moments ago. It was very good, and I appreciate what you had to say.

Commissioner Brogan. Well, Mr. President, we are certainly sorry to hear about your accident. The good news is they'll have to give you two strokes a side in the future, I suppose.

The President. Right. I saw Greg Norman this morning; I told him my handicap is going up by the minute.

Commissioner Brogan. Well, we are disappointed, as I'm sure you're well aware, but I told all of the wonderful children and teachers and parents here at Lighthouse Elementary that I'm sure you're considerably more disappointed, having had the accident and not being able to visit this great school.

The President. I'm so disappointed because I really looked forward to coming. As soon as I heard about the school and how the principal, Una Hukill, and all the teachers were working hard to cope with the growth, and I really wanted to come there because I thought that Lighthouse would be a symbol of what we need to do, of the best in our education system and how we need to respond to the growth issue.

We have more young people in school today than ever before in the history of America, and we don't have enough facilities. And in many places, the facilities that are there are deteriorating. And what my proposal would do is simply say to the local community, if you're out there trying to do your part to build or repair facilities, we want the National Government to put some money aside, to lower the interest rates so that you can get more money for building for less

effort as long as you're making an appropriate effort on your own.

It's a way of using our national funds, which are more limited, to leverage far more money all across America to help deal with this growth issue. And I'm looking forward to passing it, and I just want to encourage everyone there to talk to the Members of Congress and the Senators from Florida and ask them to support this.

Commissioner Brogan. Well, Mr. President, we appreciate that. And I've spoken personally with both Senator Graham and Senator Mack, who obviously recognize some of the overcrowding that we're facing in what we believe is a very special State, with 2.3 million schoolchildren who come to us not just from around the country but all over the world. And we believe that facilities is an issue for both the local and the State government. But we also believe because of our special circumstances, as do Senators Mack and Graham, that we need some special consideration from the Federal level.

Your proposed visit here today has really made a statement. We're sorry that you couldn't be here personally, but believe me, it has made a statement. And we're working in Tallahassee right now, in the legislative session, drawing some attention to this issue of overcrowding. They're working on it at the local level. And we thank you for bringing some national attention to a very special State with very special problems.

The President. Thank you. I was glad to do it. I talked to Congressman Foley today—he came by the hospital to see me—I was glad to see him. And I think if we can get all the legislators from Florida behind this in Washington, we've got a good chance to pass the program.

Commissioner Brogan. Well, you take care of yourself. I had surgery similar to that when I was a little bit younger, and I seemed to have come through it. I run every day, and I know you'll be back on the golf course very soon.

The President. I want to be back running soon, and that's encouraging. And again, I want to thank Joan Kowal and all the people from the school there. Please forgive me for not being there, and give me a raincheck. I can't wait to see you, and believe me, you've done a lot of good for this program today, just by the national publicity you've achieved. Perhaps you'll even get more, in addition—than I heard that you would have had otherwise.

Commissioner Brogan. Well, that's very possible. You know how these things work. I'm going to turn, very quickly, the telephone over to the chairman of the school board here in Palm Beach County, and also the principal, because I know they want to say a quick "hello" and "get well soon" to you, Mr. President.

Thank you. Take care of yourself. Fly safely.

Paulette Burdick. Good morning, President. My name's Paulette Burdick from the school board.

The President. Good morning.

Ms. Burdick. Well, we certainly wish you well. We're sorry that you're not here, but all the children wish you a speedy recovery. They're all busy addressing and making get-well cards for you.

The President. Oh, great.

Ms. Burdick. And we thank you for bringing a national recognition to the fact of school overcrowding. I've just returned from Tallahassee, and your visit down here to south Florida certainly has increased the dialog up in Tallahassee and also at our local level. And certainly, on behalf of the nearly 135,000 students in Palm Beach County, we do want to extend another invitation to come back to our glorious county.

The President. Thank you very much. I'll try to do it without incident next time. [*Laughter*]

Ms. Burdick. Well, okay. Thank you. I'm going to turn you over to our wonderful principal here, Ms. Hukill.

Ms. Una Hukill. Good morning, Mr. President. This is Una Hukill, the principal of Lighthouse Elementary. And on behalf of all of our students and our staff and our parents, we wish you a very, very speedy recovery. All of our thoughts and prayers are certainly with you this morning.

The President. Thank you. Thank you for all the effort you put into this visit. I'm so sorry I can't be there. I'm looking at the children on television now. They look wonderful. And I hope I get a chance to visit with you in the future.

Ms. Hukill. Well, I truly want to extend that offer to you. Anytime that you happen to be anywhere near our area, our door is always open and welcome to you, and any impromptu time, we would be happy to have you here with us.

The President. Thank you very much.

Ms. Hukill. And have a very speedy recovery, and you'll be receiving packages from us very soon.

The President. I can't wait. I'll need it.

Ms. Hukill. I need to just tell you that we have some wonderful lemon cake and your Diet Coke in sterling silver waiting for you, and we'll keep it.

The President. Just save them all. I'll be there.

Ms. Hukill. We'll save it. We're hoping that we'll be able to just put it on hold for a very brief time.

The President. Hi, kids. I can see them waving on the television. That's great.

Ms. Hukill. Let me give this to Superintendent Kowal who will also introduce to you Congressman Mark Foley. Okay, I guess he just spoke at you. I'll give you back to the superintendent. Thank you so much, and for a speedy recovery.

The President. Thank you. Goodbye.

Dr. Kowal. One more time we want to let Marcy, who introduced you, say goodbye. We really appreciate—I know when you are in pain it's sometimes hard to have a smile on your face, but everybody tells us you do right now.

The President. Thank you. I'm doing fine.

Dr. Kowal. That's really good. Just reechoing what the commissioner said, we have a school board that has been committed to doing the right things for children in providing the very best in teaching and learning. And I know that you would have liked to have seen that, classroom to classroom. But you're certainly here in our spirits.

I'm going to let President Haylett say goodbye to you. Okay? Hello?

The President. Yes, I can hear you.

Ms. Haylett. Hi, hope you feel better.

The President. Thank you, Marcy. I'll feel better. And you tell all your classmates that I'm sorry I missed them, and I thank them for their good wishes, okay?

Ms. Haylett. Okay. Hope to see you next Friday in Washington.

The President. Oh, great. I'd like that.

NOTE: The President spoke at 9:06 a.m. from Air Force One. The President canceled his scheduled visit to the school after injuring his knee during a visit to professional golfer Greg Norman's residence on the evening of March 13. The following persons participated in the telephone conversation: Joan P. Kowal, superintendent, Palm Beach

County schools; Florida Commissioner of Education Frank Brogan; Marcy Haylett, student body president, and Una Hukill, principal, Lighthouse Elementary School; and Paulette Burdick, chair, Palm Beach County School Board.

Message to the Congress Reporting on the National Emergency With Respect to Iran
March 14, 1997

To the Congress of the United States:

I hereby report to the Congress on developments concerning the national emergency with respect to Iran that was declared in Executive Order 12957 of March 15, 1995, and matters relating to the measures in that order and in Executive Order 12959 of May 6, 1995. This report is submitted pursuant to section 204(c) of the International Emergency Economic Powers Act, 50 U.S.C. 1703(c) (IEEPA), section 401(c) of the National Emergencies Act, 50 U.S.C. 1641(c), and section 505(c) of the International Security and Development Corporation Act of 1985, 22 U.S.C. 2349aa-9(c). This report discusses only matters concerning the national emergency with respect to Iran that was declared in Executive Order 12957 and does not deal with those relating to the emergency declared on November 14, 1979, in connection with the hostage crisis.

1. On March 15, 1995, I issued Executive Order 12957 (60 *Fed. Reg.* 14615, March 17, 1995) to declare a national emergency with respect to Iran pursuant to IEEPA, and to prohibit the financing, management, or supervision by United States persons of the development of Iranian petroleum resources. This action was in response to actions and policies of the Government of Iran, including support for international terrorism, efforts to undermine the Middle East peace process, and the acquisition of weapons of mass destruction and the means to deliver them. A copy of the order was provided to the Speaker of the House and the President of the Senate by letter dated March 15, 1995.

Following the imposition of these restrictions with regard to the development of Iranian petroleum resources, Iran continued to engage in activities that represent a threat to the peace and security of all nations, including Iran's continuing support for international terrorism, its support for acts that undermine the Middle East peace process, and its intensified efforts to acquire weapons of mass destruction. On May 6, 1995, I issued Executive Order 12959 to further respond to the Iranian threat to the national security, foreign policy, and economy of the United States.

Executive Order 12959 (60 *Fed. Reg.* 24757, May 9, 1995) (1) prohibits exportation from the United States to Iran or to the Government of Iran of goods, technology, or services; (2) prohibits the reexportation of certain U.S. goods and technology to Iran from third countries; (3) prohibits dealings by United States persons in goods and services of Iranian origin or owned or controlled by the Government of Iran; (4) prohibits new investments by United States persons in Iran or in property owned or controlled by the Government of Iran; (5) prohibits U.S. companies and other United States persons from approving, facilitating, or financing performance by a foreign subsidiary or other entity owned or controlled by a United States person of certain reexport, investment, and trade transactions that a United States person is prohibited from performing; (6) continues the 1987 prohibition on the importation into the United States of goods and services of Iranian origin; (7) prohibits any transaction by a United States person or within the United States that evades or avoids or attempts to violate any prohibition of the order; and (8) allowed U.S. companies a 30-day period in which to perform trade transactions pursuant to contracts predating the Executive order.

At the time of signing Executive Order 12959, I directed the Secretary of the Treasury to authorize through specific licensing certain transactions, including transactions by United States persons related to the Iran-United States Claims Tribunal in The Hague, established pursuant to the Algiers Accords, and related to other international obligations and United States Government functions, and transactions related to the export of agricultural commodities pursuant to preexisting contracts consistent with section 5712(c) of title 7, United States Code. I also directed the Secretary of the Treasury, in consultation with the Secretary of State, to consider authorizing United States persons through specific licensing to participate in market-based swaps of crude oil from the Caspian Sea area for Iranian crude oil in support of energy projects in Azerbaijan, Kazakstan, and Turkmenistan.

Executive Order 12959 revoked sections 1 and 2 of Executive Order 12613 of October 29, 1987, and sections 1 and 2 of Executive Order 12957 of March 15, 1995, to the extent they are inconsistent with it. A copy of Executive Order 12959 was transmitted to the Speaker of the House of Representatives and the President of the Senate by letter dated May 6, 1995.

2. On March 5, 1997, I renewed for another year the national emergency with respect to Iran pursuant to IEEPA. This renewal extended the authority for the current comprehensive trade embargo against Iran in effect since May 1995. Under these sanctions, virtually all trade with Iran is prohibited except for information and informational materials and certain other limited exceptions.

3. The Iranian Transactions Regulations (the "Regulations" or ITR), 31 CFR Part 560, were amended on October 21, 1996 (61 *Fed. Reg.* 54936, October 23, 1996), to implement section 4 of the Federal Civil Penalties Inflation Adjustment Act of 1990, as amended by the Debt Collection Improvement Act of 1996, by adjusting for inflation the amount of the civil monetary penalties that may be assessed under the Regulations. The amendment increases the maximum civil monetary penalty provided in the Regulations from $10,000 to $11,000 per violation.

The amended Regulations also reflect an amendment to 18 U.S.C. 1001 contained in section 330016(1)(L) of Public Law 103–322, September 13, 1994; 108 Stat. 2147. The amendment notes the availability of higher criminal fines pursuant to the formulas set forth in 18 U.S.C. 3571. A copy of the amendment is attached.

Section 560.603 of the ITR was amended on November 15, 1996 (61 *Fed. Reg.* 58480), to clarify rules relating to reporting requirements imposed on United States persons with foreign affiliations. Initial reporting under the amended Regulation has been deferred until May 30, 1997, by a January 14, 1997, *Federal Register* notice (62 *Fed. Reg.* 1832). Copies of the amendment and the notice are attached.

4. During the current 6-month period, the Department of the Treasury's Office of Foreign Assets Control (OFAC) made numerous decisions with respect to applications for licenses to engage in transactions under the ITR, and issued 13 licenses. The majority of denials were in response to requests to authorize commercial exports to Iran—particularly of machinery and equipment for the petroleum and manufacturing industries—and the importation of Iranian-origin goods. The licenses issued authorized the export and reexport of goods, services, and technology essential to ensure the safety of civil aviation and safe operation of certain commercial passenger aircraft in Iran; certain financial and legal transactions; the importation of Iranian-origin artwork for public exhibition; and certain diplomatic transactions. Pursuant to sections 3 and 4 of Executive Order 12959 and in order to comply with the Iran-Iraq Arms Non-Proliferation Act of 1992 and other statutory restrictions applicable to certain goods and technology, including those involved in the air-safety cases, the Department of the Treasury continues to consult with the Departments of State and Commerce on these matters.

The U.S. financial community continues to interdict transactions associated with Iran and to consult with OFAC about their appropriate handling. Many of these inquiries have resulted in investigations into the activities of U.S. parties and, where appropriate, the initiation of enforcement action.

5. The U.S. Customs Service has continued to effect numerous seizures of Iranian-origin merchandise, primarily carpets, for violations of the import prohibitions of the ITR. Various enforcement actions carried over from previous reporting periods are continuing and new reports of violations are being aggressively pursued. Since my last report, OFAC has collected a civil monetary penalty in the amount of $5,000. The violation underlying this collection involves the unlicensed import of Iranian-origin goods for transshipment to a third country aboard a U.S.-flag vessel. Civil penalty action or review is

pending against 21 companies, financial institutions, and individuals for possible violations of the Regulations.

6. The expenses incurred by the Federal Government in the 6-month period from September 15, 1996, through March 14, 1997, that are directly attributable to the exercise of powers and authorities conferred by the declaration of a national emergency with respect to Iran are approximately $800,000, most of which represent wage and salary costs for Federal personnel. Personnel costs were largely centered in the Department of the Treasury (particularly in the Office of Foreign Assets Control, the U.S. Customs Service, the Office of the Under Secretary for Enforcement, and the Office of the General Counsel), the Department of State (particularly the Bureau of Economic and Business Affairs, the Bureau of Near Eastern Affairs, the Bureau of Intelligence and Research, and the Office of the Legal Adviser), and the Department of Commerce (the Bureau of Export Administration and the General Counsel's Office).

7. The situation reviewed above continues to involve important diplomatic, financial, and legal interests of the United States and its nationals and presents an extraordinary and unusual threat to the national security, foreign policy, and economy of the United States. The declaration of the national emergency with respect to Iran contained in Executive Order 12957 and the comprehensive economic sanctions imposed by Executive Order 12959 underscore the United States Government opposition to the actions and policies of the Government of Iran, particularly its support of international terrorism and its efforts to acquire weapons of mass destruction and the means to deliver them. The Iranian Transactions Regulations issued pursuant to Executive Orders 12957 and 12959 continue to advance important objectives in promoting the nonproliferation and antiterrorism policies of the United States. I shall exercise the powers at my disposal to deal with these problems and will report periodically to the Congress on significant developments.

WILLIAM J. CLINTON

The White House,
March 14, 1997.

Remarks Following Treatment at the National Naval Medical Center in Bethesda, Maryland
March 14, 1997

Press Secretary Mike McCurry. Since we're talking about him, I thought maybe you'd like to hear from the President. So he just wanted to say hello, so we connected him in here.

The President. Mike, can you hear me?

Press Secretary McCurry. Yes, sir, we can hear you fine. Go ahead.

The President. Well, I'm enjoying this press conference. [*Laughter*]

Press Secretary McCurry. First one in a long time you probably enjoyed.

The President. It's wonderful not to be answering the questions. But I want you guys to quit giving my doctor a hard time about letting me go to Helsinki. We're all going to Helsinki; we have to go to Helsinki. [*Laughter*]

Press Secretary McCurry. Thank you, sir.

The President. I feel great. They did a terrific job. And let me say, I just had an unlucky break. But I've had almost no injuries in my life. In 25 years of running and a lot of other athletic activity, I've been remarkably free of injuries. I had one skiing accident once, and this was just an accident. Accidents happen to people. But I was very fortunate that Greg Norman, being a better athlete than I am, immediately heard my knee pop and turned around and caught me before I fell on the ground. And then the hospital down in Florida did a wonderful job, Dr. Cohen and the other people. And my team did a good job here. I feel great.

And don't worry about it; I'll just spend a little time here and get home and go back to work.

Thank you.

NOTE: These remarks were included in the transcript of a press briefing by the President's attending physicians which began at 5:50 p.m. The President spoke from the Medical Evaluation and

Treatment Unit at the National Naval Medical Center, following surgical treatment for a knee injury he sustained on March 13 when he lost his footing on a staircase at the home of professional golfer Greg Norman. In his remarks, the President referred to Comdr. David P. Adkison,

USN, chair, orthopedic surgery, National Naval Medical Center; and Joel E. Cohen, orthopedic surgeon, St. Mary's Medical Center, West Palm Beach, FL. A tape was not available for verification of the content of these remarks.

Letter to Congressional Leaders Reporting on the Deployment of United States Forces to Albania
March 15, 1997

Dear Mr. Speaker: (Dear Mr. President:)

In February 1997, civil unrest broke out in Albania after a nationwide pyramid investment scheme destroyed the life savings of tens of thousands of investors unaware of the fraudulent nature of those investments. Protesters took to the streets and later joined political opponents of President Sali Berisha in demanding his removal. By March 13, much of Albania, including the capital city of Tirana, had fallen into widespread disorder. Looting and gunfire was reported throughout the country as sympathetic police and military officials refused to enforce the law. While there was no evidence that Americans were being directly targeted, the disorder and violence sweeping the country subjected American citizens and property to risks ranging from criminal acts to random violence.

On March 13, due to the rapidly deteriorating security situation and the potential threat to American citizens and the American Embassy, U.S. military personnel were deployed to provide enhanced security for the American Embassy in Tirana and to conduct the evacuation of certain U.S. Government employees and private U.S. citizens. Approximately 25 U.S. Marines entered the capital city on March 13 and immediately took up positions in and around the American Embassy compound. Evacuation operations began concurrently as U.S. CH–46 helicopters operating from the USS *Nassau* amphibious ready group transported approximately 50 U.S. citizens to U.S. Navy ships at sea. Evacuation efforts resumed on March 14 and are expected to continue for several days. The res-

cue helicopters are escorted by AH–1W Cobra helicopters, which came under fire but were not damaged during separate, sporadic incidents on March 14. In addition, a 150-member Marine rifle company has also been inserted near the American Embassy to provide additional security for the evacuation.

The Marines involved in this operation are from the Marine Expeditionary Unit currently operating in the Adriatic Sea. Although U.S. forces are equipped for combat, the evacuation is being undertaken solely for the purpose of protecting American citizens and property. United States forces will redeploy as soon as evacuation operations are complete and enhanced security at the American Embassy is no longer required.

I have taken this action pursuant to my constitutional authority to conduct U.S. foreign relations and as Commander in Chief and Chief Executive.

I am providing this report as part of my efforts to keep the Congress fully informed, consistent with the War Powers Resolution. I appreciate the support of the Congress in this action to protect American citizens and the American Embassy in Tirana.

Sincerely,

WILLIAM J. CLINTON

NOTE: Identical letters were sent to Newt Gingrich, Speaker of the House of Representatives, and Strom Thurmond, President pro tempore of the Senate.

Exchange With Reporters
March 16, 1997

Recovery From Knee Surgery

Q. How are you feeling, sir?

Q. Good morning, Mr. President. How are you feeling, sir?

The President. I feel fine today. I was a little sore yesterday, you know, the first day after the operation when the pain started to wear off—I mean, the painkiller, you know, the anesthesia. But I feel fine today, and I've done 2 days of therapy, learned to use my crutches.

Hillary wanted me to come home before she left for Africa. She and Chelsea wanted me well settled, so that's what I'm doing.

Q. Is that going to be difficult for you to use crutches for the next few months?

The President. I just want to do it well. It will be an interesting experience. I just want to be careful and not make any mistakes and do it well. But I think I'll be perfectly mobile and perfectly fine.

I also want to say that the medical team I had at the Bethesda Naval Medical Center did a magnificent job. They really were wonderful, and I feel very fortunate. And the American people should know that that military medical center is a very good place, not just for the President but for everybody who is treated there.

President's Planned Travel

Q. Did they have to twist your arm to get you to delay the trip to Helsinki for a day?

The First Lady. No twisting of arms—or any other limb. [*Laughter*]

The President. No, because I can go back to Copenhagen and do that probably when we do the NATO meeting.

Recovery From Knee Surgery

Q. Sir, does it hurt every time you move?

The President. No.

Q. It doesn't?

The President. No. You just have to learn to use a few different muscles. But it's quite interesting. I mean, it will be a learning experience. It's like going back to school and learning some new things.

Q. Do you think this will get you any sympathy votes in Congress for any of your bills? [*Laughter*]

The President. I don't know, but if it does, I'll take them any way I can get them. [*Laughter*] I'd be very grateful if it did.

Q. Glad to have him home, Mrs. Clinton?

The First Lady. Yes, I'm very glad to have him home.

The President. Goodbye.

NOTE: The exchange began at 11:46 a.m. on the South Lawn at the White House, following the President's return from the National Naval Medical Center in Bethesda, MD, where he underwent knee surgery on March 14. A tape was not available for verification of the content of this exchange.

Statement on the Murder of John Slane in Northern Ireland
March 17, 1997

I am deeply saddened by the murder last Friday of John Slane in Belfast. Our sympathy goes out to Mr. Slane's family and friends. This horrific killing deserves universal condemnation. I hope the British authorities will quickly identify who is responsible.

As I have said so many times, nothing worth having in Northern Ireland can be achieved by killing and maiming, terror and threats. The people of Northern Ireland deserve a future of peace and prosperity unmarred by brutality and fear in their daily lives. I urge the people of both communities to make known in every way they can their repudiation of violence by any group, for any reason. I will continue to stand with those who stand for peace, today as we commemorate the saint who brought the message of peace to Ireland, and every day.

Remarks on Withdrawal of the Nomination of Anthony Lake To Be Director of Central Intelligence and an Exchange With Reporters
March 18, 1997

The President. Let me begin by saying that while I do understand his reasons, Tony Lake's decision to withdraw from consideration as Director of Central Intelligence is a real loss to our country and to me. He would have been an outstanding CIA Director because of his intelligence, his unquestioned integrity, his extremely valuable experience. I respect his decision because nobody should have to endure what he has endured in the course of this nomination. But make no mistake about it, it's a loss for the country.

For 4 years, Tony Lake was one of my closest advisers and one of my most trusted ones. He was an integral part of every foreign policy decision we made, and his legacy can be seen around the world, from an end to the war in Bosnia to a fresh start for peace in Haiti, from real hope for peace in the Middle East and Northern Ireland to real progress on arms control. He is a patriot, a professional, and a statesman. Our Nation will miss his service very much, and so will I.

This episode says a lot about how so much work is done in our Nation's Capital. For too long, we have allowed ordinary political processes and honest disagreements among honorable people to degenerate first into political sniping, then into political revenge. And too often, that results in political destruction that absolutely builds nothing for the American people and is not worthy of our responsibilities to them. It is past time for all of us to stop remembering who shot first and why, and instead, to start remembering why we are here and the fact that the American people sent us here to work on their concerns and their future.

The cycle of political destruction must end. And I hope we will let it end today. We can't let partisan bickering stop us from doing the work we were sent here to do. I sense that more and more Democrats and Republicans believe that and believe as I do that we have to seize this opportunity to pass a bipartisan agreement to balance the budget.

There are now some new and hopeful signs that we are in a position to do that. Last month I proposed a balanced budget plan that secures

Medicare and Medicaid, extends health care coverage to more children, strengthens education, gives working families tax relief, and protects the environment. I believe that's the best way to balance the budget. As you know, as part of that plan, the day after my Inauguration I made an offer to the Republican Congress on Medicare, proposing savings that moved halfway toward those envisioned in the most recent Republican plan. Yesterday the Republican leaders showed me flexibility on tax cuts and economic assumptions. This new flexibility is a very positive sign, and I applaud their comments. They move us closer than ever to the point where we can reach an agreement on a balanced budget that is good for the American people.

I'm also encouraged by the extensive work being done by people of good will on both sides of the aisle throughout the Congress. Now it is time to build on all this momentum and make this a season of bipartisan cooperation on the budget. I want a balanced budget plan that can win the support of majorities in both parties in both Houses in Congress.

To that end, I am announcing three steps. First, I'm asking the leaders of the Budget Committees to meet with me tomorrow before I leave for Helsinki to give me their assessment of progress in Congress and the prospect of reaching a bipartisan balanced budget agreement. Second, I'll ask my budget team to meet with the congressional budget leaders over the congressional recess. I'll instruct them to be open-minded and flexible and to work in the spirit of bipartisanship. Third, I will ask these budget officials to report back to me and to the congressional leadership at the White House after the congressional recess on the progress they have made and the best means for reaching the bipartisan agreement we all seek.

This balanced budget plan must be tough and credible. It must strengthen education and protect the environment and protect health care while extending coverage to more children. But let us recognize, balancing the budget will require cooperation from all sides. No one will achieve everything he or she wants. Everyone must be prepared to compromise if we're going to break the gridlock and finally balance the budget. And that is true for the President as well as for the Congress.

I am determined that we will seize this moment to end the political stalemate and to show the American people how we should do our work here in the Nation's Capital. If we work together in the right spirit, we can achieve what both parties clearly want, a balanced budget that reflects our values, helps our economy, and preserves and strengthens our future.

So let me say with that, also I'm looking very much forward to my trip to Helsinki, and I'm looking forward to coming back, making a positive report to the American people, and getting on with this work on the budget. I'm very hopeful because of what was said yesterday.

Director of Central Intelligence Nomination

Q. Mr. President, have you thought of a successor to your nomination of Mr. Lake? And in doing so, what will you demand of Senator Shelby in that process to avoid what you have stated Mr. Lake has gone through?

The President. Well, first of all, all I want from any Member of Congress and any committee chair is to give any nominee of mine a fair hearing, a reasonable benefit of the doubt, a respectful listening, and a prompt disposal of the matter, one way or the other. So that's all I want for anybody that I send up there. I support the senatorial review process, but like anything else, it has to be run in an efficient and forthright manner if it's going to be effective.

In answer to your first question, yes, I have given some thought to it, and I expect that quite soon I will have a name for you. But I would ask you to respect the fact that, you know, we have to do some review of our own before we send a name up there, and it's really not fair to put someone out on the line on this until we know that the President has, in fact, determined to nominate him or her.

Q. Mr. President, Mr. Lake said he had enough votes to get confirmed. Why not just stick with it, fight the good fight, and go all the way to a vote?

The President. Well, that was, of course, my preference. I told them that I was deeply disappointed and that I wanted to fight. I know Tony Lake. I have seen him operate. I know how tough-minded he is and how confident he is. I know what a role he played just in the

Bosnian matter, just to cite one example. I know how he kept us working on many different fronts for 4 years in national security. And just yesterday I talked to one Republican Senator— I called him about another matter, but I talked to him about Tony Lake, and he is a strong supporter of Tony Lake, and he talked what an able man he was and how much he regretted how politicized this process had become.

I think Tony felt two things. First of all, that he did have the votes to get out of the committee if he could ever get a vote. I think he was convinced after he even went so far as to let the leaders of the committee look at FBI data, which was really an unprecedented thing to do in that kind of forum and, although it was apparently very appropriate and positive toward him, that there still was—there's always something else, always something else to delay. I think he believed that they might have the ability to delay his hearings for another month or two or three. Already, this is very late for any kind of nomination to be stuck in hearings by any kind of historical standard. And I think he was afraid that there might never be a hearing.

And secondly, I think he was afraid that the longer this went on with delay, the more it would damage the Agency. He was very concerned—all the time he worked for me, he was very concerned about the integrity, the strength, the effectiveness of the intelligence agencies— all of them of the Government—and especially the CIA, and he didn't want to do anything that would further weaken the Agency.

So that's what he said to me, and I accept his reasons. But if it had been up to me, I'd be here a year from now still fighting for it because I think he's a good man.

Q. We're told there were some personal accusations, Mr. President. Did anyone on the Hill cross the line in your view?

The President. Well, let me say, I don't believe that I can contribute to the public interest by getting into what I think has already been an example of what's wrong with Washington, not what's right with it. What I wanted to say is that we need to put this hearing process in a proper context. Hearings need to be scheduled properly, matters need to be resolved. When questions are asked, everybody involved needs to be able to believe and see and sense that they're being asked in good faith and not simply for the purpose of trying to undermine someone or delay a process forever. That's what I think needs to be done. But I don't want to contribute to the difficulties of this particular moment, and neither does Tony Lake.

And personal recriminations are not important here. The public's interest is all that matters. And we are not serving the public interest here when we waste our energies on trying to undermine each other. That's the point I—we're not doing that. That does not serve the public interest. And all of us are up here to do that and only that. So we can have these honest disagreements in a proper context without doing it. And nearly everybody I know understands where the balance is and knows when it's gone too far.

Helsinki Summit

Q. Mr. President, what tone does it set for the Helsinki summit when President Yeltsin is quoted yesterday as saying he'll give no more concessions and your Secretary of State says today that's inappropriate language?

The President. Well, let me say, first of all, I'm glad to see President Yeltsin up and around and healthy, and I appreciate, in light of my condition, that he agreed to move the meeting from Moscow to Helsinki so it will be a little closer to me than it otherwise would have been.

We have never had a meeting that didn't result in constructive progress in the relations between the United States and Russia and in matters of our common concern. And I believe this will be such a meeting. There's been a lot going on in Russia in the last several weeks, and I would just caution everyone not to overreact too much to any particular event or statement. Let us get in there. I have always had a good, honest, open relation with President Yeltsin. I expect we will continue to do that.

And let me remind you of the stakes involved in Helsinki. Number one, we're going to talk about our shared desire for a Europe that is free and democratic, secure and united, and my hope that we can achieve an agreement between Russia and NATO that will be part of that. We do have some evidence that Russia and NATO can have a positive, not a negative, relationship in our remarkable partnership in Bosnia.

Number two, the United States and Russia still have a heavy responsibility to lead the world further away from the nuclear issue. And we've got to go forward with START II; we've got

to go forward with what happens after that. We've got a whole range of issues around nuclear issues that have to be dealt with.

And number three, there are a lot of economic issues that have to be dealt with. Russia has the potential of having terrific economic growth in ways that would, I think, alleviate a lot of these other anxieties that are there and a lot of other questions people have, if we do the right things from here on out.

So we've got a broad, tough agenda. We're going to have to do a lot of work in a day and an evening before. But I'm very optimistic about it, and I just wouldn't overreact to any particular thing that's said or done between now and then. Let us have the meeting, do the work, see what kind of product we can produce, and discuss it.

Recovery From Knee Surgery

Q. How's your health? How's your health, are you getting around all right?

The President. I'm getting around all right. I'm doing two sessions of therapy a day of, more or less, an hour each. And I'm trying to, number one, continue to get more flexibility and strength in this leg to keep it from atrophying and also to just get the flexibility back. And then I'm trying to make sure that I know how to use the rest of my body to keep it protected. Some of it's sort of embarrassing. I had to learn how to get in and out of a shower again, you know, with a walker and all that kind of stuff—but just using the crutches properly, getting up and down stairs with crutches, when I should use the wheelchair. We're using the wheelchair more now, before Helsinki, because we want to minimize the chance of any kind of injury, and I want to keep my energy level as high as possible. So I'm using the wheelchair more. And when I get back I'll probably use my crutches relatively more. So I'm dealing with all that.

But basically, it's been an interesting learning experience—rather humbling. I've been very blessed. I've got a great team of sports doctors and therapists who have helped me, and I'm hoping that I can avoid gaining a lot of weight and that I can stay in reasonably good shape during this period of convalescence and repair. But it's been good.

Efforts To Balance the Budget

Q. Mr. President, you praised the Republicans for flexibility. Are you willing to forgo the tax cuts you sought yourself?

The President. Well, let me say, first of all, I've actually produced a budget that does give the tax cuts that I believe—that are much more limited than they had previously proposed and are sharply targeted toward education and childrearing. That's first. Secondly, I consider those education investments and the children's investments a part of advancing America's family and education agenda. But in terms of all the details of the budget, I think all of us have to be willing to show some flexibility. They have shown some flexibility here, and their recent comments by the leaders were really quite forthcoming. And we all need to recognize that, and all of us need to be flexible as we go into these negotiations.

There are all kinds of things that each of us will care about more than other things. But I think that I have to say that on all these issues I have to show flexibility; they have to show flexibility. We'll put our heads together, and we'll come out with an agreement. And I think that if we do that it will be in the best interests of the American people.

Thank you.

NOTE: The President spoke at 4:25 p.m. in the Residence at the White House. In his remarks, he referred to President Boris Yeltsin of Russia.

Statement on Legislation To Reauthorize the Export-Import Bank and the Overseas Private Investment Corporation
March 18, 1997

Today my administration is transmitting to Congress legislation to reauthorize both the Export-Import Bank of the United States and the Overseas Private Investment Corporation (OPIC). I am also asking that my requests for these agencies and for the U.S. Trade and Development Agency (TDA) be fully funded.

These three specialized agencies play important complementary roles in helping U.S. firms compete for valued export markets. Never in our recent history have exports been more critical to American economic growth and to the creation of high-paying U.S. jobs. Other major trading countries rely heavily on government trade and finance agencies to help their companies compete in the world's fastest growing economies. Because of our efforts over the past 4 years, the United States has signed more than 200 new trade agreements and is once again the world's leading exporter. We need Ex-Im Bank, OPIC, and TDA to help maintain that position and continue to create good jobs for our people.

The appropriations for these agencies are relatively modest, particularly compared to the benefits of increased export growth that ripple throughout the entire U.S. economy. Each of these programs delivers public benefits by expanding U.S. commercial opportunities abroad, helping meet competition from other countries, and broadening the base of U.S. export-oriented businesses. Each has taken steps to streamline its own operations and improve its coordination with other agencies. My administration stands ready to work with Congress on ideas for further improvements that will yield even greater benefits for the American economy.

Telephone Remarks to a National Center on Addiction and Substance Abuse Dinner
March 18, 1997

The President. Hello, Joe. Can you hear me all right?

Joseph A. Califano, Jr. Yes, sir.

The President. Well, thank you, ladies and gentlemen, for the applause. And I'd like to be there with you tonight, you know, but I'm not particularly mobile at this time. I want to congratulate all of you who have had anything to do with the National Center on Addiction and Substance Abuse on the fifth anniversary. Hillary and I are pleased to be the special honorary chairs for CASA's anniversary dinner. And I'm delighted to join you in paying tribute to Nancy Reagan, to Peter Lund, and to Sandy Weill as they're honored for extraordinary achievements in our common crusade against substance abuse.

All of you know very well that alcoholism, teen smoking, drug addiction, and other forms of substance abuse are claiming the lives of thousands of people every year and fueling crime, domestic violence, disease, and death. But because of the efforts of the National Center on Addiction and Substance Abuse and so many other people throughout our country, we have reason to hope for a better future.

In just 5 short years, CASA has established itself as one of our Nation's premier institutions in the field of substance abuse. In communities all across our Nation, concerned individuals and groups from all parts of our society are coming together under the leadership of CASA to empower our people with the information and services they need to lead productive and drug-free lives.

I especially want to commend Joe Califano and the board of directors, the staff, and the special supporters of CASA for your vision and your leadership in this crusade to protect our families, our friends, our neighbors, and our future from the ravages of substance abuse. Your knowledge and professionalism and hard work will make our Nation stronger and our future brighter.

Our administration is taking forceful measures to help our citizens in this crucial endeavor. We're attacking the supply of illegal narcotics at its source, sending a strong message to our Nation's young people about the dangers of alcohol, tobacco, and drug abuse to prevent it before it begins, including a $175 million national antidrug media campaign directed toward our youth that's part of our budget proposal, and doing everything we can, finally, to have the right kind of law enforcement that focuses on prevention as well.

We want to be good partners with you. But everyone in America has to recognize the unique role that the National Center on Addiction and Substance Abuse has played in concentrating our attention and making us know that we have to keep working on this problem. And we cannot tolerate the trends of recent years in increased substance abuse among our young people. We're going to turn that around, and we're going to take our Nation where we need it to go, thanks in no small measure to your leadership.

I give you my best wishes for a memorable anniversary celebration tonight and, even more important, for continued success. And once again, let me personally thank Nancy Reagan and Peter Lund and Sandy Weill for all that they have done.

Thank you, Joe, and thank you, ladies and gentlemen.

NOTE: The President spoke at 9:05 p.m. from the Residence at the White House to dinner participants at the Waldorf-Astoria Hotel in New York City. In his remarks, he referred to Joseph A. Califano, Jr., president, National Center on Addiction and Substance Abuse; and former First Lady Nancy Reagan, Peter A. Lund, president and chief executive officer, CBS, Inc., and Sanford I. Weill, chairman and chief executive officer, The Travelers Group, Inc., recipients of the CASA Distinguished Service Award.

Remarks Announcing the Nomination of George J. Tenet To Be Director of Central Intelligence and an Exchange With Reporters
March 19, 1997

The President. Good afternoon. I have just completed a very productive meeting with the Senate and House chairs and ranking minority members of the Budget Committee, and all of you know I'm about to leave in a few hours for Helsinki for my meeting with President Yeltsin. But before we discuss those things, I want to announce my intention to nominate George Tenet, who is standing here with me with his family, currently the Acting Director of the CIA, as the Director of Central Intelligence.

He brings a wealth of experience and skill to the challenge of leading our intelligence community into the 21st century. Beginning in 1995, he served with real distinction as Deputy Director under John Deutch. Prior to that, he was my senior aide for intelligence at the National Security Council. He did a superb job of helping to set out our intelligence priorities for new challenges. And at the CIA, he has played a pivotal role in putting these priorities into place and leading the intelligence community in meeting the demands of the post-cold-war world.

As the longtime staff director of the Senate Select Committee on Intelligence, George Tenet understands the essential role Congress must play in the intelligence community's work. Since joining our administration, he has maintained a strong relationship in Congress. He knows well the concerns of the intelligence community as well. He knows that I must have the unvarnished truth. He knows how critical timely, reliable intelligence is to our Nation's security. I'm proud to nominate him for this vital job and very grateful for the service that he has rendered to our administration and to our country. George.

[*At this point, Director-designate Tenet thanked the President and made brief remarks.*]

The President. Thank you.

Mr. Tenet. Thank you.

The President. Congratulations. Thank you.

Q. Do you think he will be confirmed?

The President. I do.

Q. Why?

The President. Well, because he's well-known to the Senate and well-respected by Republicans as well as Democrats.

Q. Mr. President——

Efforts To Balance the Budget and Summit in Helsinki, Finland

The President. Let me finish my statement. Our first order of business when I get back from Helsinki must be to finish the job of balancing the budget. We have to do it this year. Recent statements by the leaders of the Republican Party in both the Senate and the House have given new impetus to this hope, and today we began to build on that momentum.

When I met with the Republican chairs and the ranking Democratic members of the Senate and House Budget Committees, along with our budget team, including Erskine Bowles, Secretary Rubin, Director Raines, NEC Chair Sperling, Legislative Director Hilley, and the Council of Economic Advisers Chair, Janet Yellen—of course, along with the Vice President—we agreed that, during the recess, they will begin an effort to reduce the differences among us in topics including Medicare and Medicaid, other entitlements, national defense, domestic spending, revenues, and other issues relevant to the budget, so that when I meet with the bipartisan leadership after Congress' Easter recess, we will be ready to make rapid progress until we reach a balanced budget agreement.

We agree on the goal. We have agreed on a schedule to start discussion. Now comes the hard work of writing the agreement, dollar by dollar, program by program, issue by issue. We have circled these issues long enough. It's time now to give the American people a balanced budget, and I believe we will do it and do it this year.

Tonight I'm leaving for Helsinki for my 11th meeting with Boris Yeltsin, Russia's President. Not too long ago, it was historic whenever the President of the United States and the leader of Russia met. Today, our meetings have become almost routine as we work through problems and build cooperation. The increasing normalcy of our ties make it easy to lose sight of the great opportunity that lies before us now. We will focus on three important areas: first, on moving forward with our work to build a Europe that is undivided, democratic, and at peace for the first time in the history of the Continent; second, on continuing to reduce the danger of weapons of mass destruction; and third, on expanding the economic partnership that is good for Americans and Russians alike.

In Europe, we can complete the work that was only half-finished a half-century ago by bringing stability and prosperity to all the people on that continent. That work begins with NATO, the anchor of Europe's security. We are adapting NATO to take on new missions, enlarging NATO to take in new members, strengthening NATO's partnership with nonmembers, and seeking to build a robust partnership between NATO and Russia, a relationship that makes Russia a true partner of the alliance.

In Helsinki, we'll discuss the outlines of a NATO-Russia charter that NATO Secretary General Solana and Foreign Minister Primakov are negotiating. I believe NATO and Russia should consult regularly and should act jointly whenever possible, just as we are doing today in Bosnia.

Our two nations have a responsibility also to continue to lead the world away from the nuclear threat. We have already made remarkable progress, from signing the Comprehensive Test Ban Treaty to extending the Non-Proliferation Treaty to bringing START I into force. Now we hope to see the Russian Duma ratify START II. Together with START I, it will cut arsenals by two-thirds from their cold war height. Just think about it; we will, with START I and START II, cut our arsenals by two-thirds from their cold war height. But we also want to do more. President Yeltsin and I will discuss possible guidelines for further reductions under START III.

Finally, we will focus on Russia's efforts to build a stable and prosperous market economy. The Russian people have made remarkable strides in a short time. They have created a private sector where once there was none. They've slashed inflation and stabilized the ruble.

Now the challenge is to create a climate that actually attracts more investment and promotes more trade so that Russia will have real economic growth and that that real growth will reach ordinary citizens. President Yeltsin and I will discuss the steps both of us will take to create that climate.

I'm encouraged by the new economic team President Yeltsin announced this week. It underscores Russia's commitment to continued reform. This is a time of extraordinary opportunity for America and for Russia, indeed, for the entire world.

I look forward to my meetings with President Yeltsin and to our common efforts to build a broad foundation for progress, prosperity, partnership, and peace in the 21st century. I look forward to balancing the budget, and I look forward to George Tenet becoming the next Director of Central Intelligence. This is a good day.

Director of Central Intelligence Nomination

Q. Mr. President, your decision to move so quickly with this announcement—is that a sign that you are concerned about the morale within the intelligence community?

The President. No, but it is a sign that I believe that we should not leave these positions vacant long, particularly in the national security area, but throughout the Government. You know, the Vice President and I have worked very hard to reform and to reduce the size of Government, and the Federal employees have taken on increasing responsibilities. But we believe where there is a mission, it ought to be done and done well, and we ought to keep the morale high and keep the direction clear.

You can't have a ship without a captain, and we need to get after it. And I think George Tenet is clearly the best qualified person to move quickly into the. leadership. He has been the Acting Director, he did an outstanding job as John Deutch's deputy, he did a terrific job here for us in the National Security Council on intelligence matters, and he has the confidence of many, many in the Congress in both parties. So I didn't see any point in waiting around. We need to get this done and go on.

Russia and NATO

Q. Mr. President, if you want an undivided Europe, why are you leaving Russia out? Why don't you take her into NATO and make it all one big, happy family?

The President. First of all, I have never left Russia out. I have explicitly said in every speech that I have made about this subject that I do not believe Russia should be excluded from NATO membership. I'm not sure that Russia would not prefer a special charter between Russia and NATO; that's what we're trying to achieve now. But I would be the last person to try to exclude them. I don't believe anybody should be excluded.

Q. Do you think she would join?

The President. I don't know. As I said, it's my belief that at this moment in time, Russia would prefer to have a charter setting out a relationship between NATO and Russia. But I would never exclude them from membership.

Look, I am trying to build a world for our children and grandchildren that will not repeat the worst of the 20th century and will take advantage of the best that the future offers.

Q. That's my point, that the two World Wars were started by nations being isolated, Versailles, Yalta, and so forth.

The President. That's why we've tried to get— right now, it's so hard to have a special charter between Russia and NATO, that's why we have made it clear that NATO is not an aggressive organization trying to limit, restrict, or undermine anyone who wants to treat their neighbors with respect and work in concert the way Russia and NATO and the United States particularly are working together in Bosnia.

I'll see you in Helsinki.

The Vice President. Mr. President, Helen [Helen Thomas, United Press International] played Madeleine at the Gridiron, and I think she's still in the role. [*Laughter*]

The President. Just come get on the plane. Believe me, I missed you, and I missed him, and I'm really sorry I missed you both.

Q. He was fabulous.

The President. I ought to——

Q. And you did pretty good.

NOTE: The President spoke at 4:49 p.m. in the Red Room at the White House. In his remarks, he referred to NATO Secretary General Javier Solana and Minister of Foreign Affairs Yevgeniy Primakov of Russia.

Letter to Speaker of the House Newt Gingrich on Proposed Compensatory Time Legislation
March 19, 1997

Dear Mr. Speaker:

America's working families find it increasingly difficult to balance the demands of work and family. Our nation's workers and their employers deserve responsible compensatory time legislation that gives working people the flexibility they need to meet their obligations at home and in the workplace, while upholding three fundamental principles: real choice for employees, real protection against employer abuse, and preservation of fair labor standards such as the 40 hour work week and the right to overtime pay.

The legislation currently pending House consideration, H.R. 1, the Working Families Flexibility Act of 1997, does not meet these principles. As a result, I strongly oppose H.R. 1 and will veto this bill if passed in its current form.

We should enact comp time legislation this year that meets the needs of working families and U.S. businesses. Last year, I proposed employee-choice flex-time legislation and included expansion of the Family and Medical Leave Act (FMLA) so that workers could take leave for parent-teacher conferences or attend to the routine medical needs of their families. With these objectives in mind, I encourage you to support a substitute amendment to be offered by Representative George Miller. Unlike H.R. 1, the Miller amendment allows comp time without endangering fair labor standards, and without burdening business with greater costs or risks.

It is time for us to work together to give America's working families the help they need to succeed in an increasingly demanding environment. Although I am prepared to support and sign a responsible comp time bill, I intend to veto any legislation that fails to guarantee real choice for employees, real protection against employer abuse, and preservation of fair labor standards such as the 40 hour work week and the right to overtime pay. To that end, I hope that you can support the Miller amendment—a good step toward responsible comp time reform.

Sincerely,

BILL CLINTON

Message to the Congress Transmitting a Report on Environmental Quality
March 19, 1997

To the Congress of the United States:

I am pleased to transmit to the Congress the Twenty-fifth Annual Report on Environmental Quality.

As a nation, the most important thing we can do as we move into the 21st century is to give all our children the chance to live up to their God-given potential and live out their dreams. In order to do that, we must offer more opportunity and demand more responsibility from all our citizens. We must help young people get the education and training they need, make our streets safer from crime, help Americans succeed at home and at work, protect our environment for generations to come, and ensure that America remains the strongest force for peace and freedom in the world. Most of all, we must come together as one community to meet our challenges.

Our Nation's leaders understood this a quarter-century ago when they launched the modern era of environmental protection with the National Environmental Policy Act. NEPA's authors understood that environmental protection, economic opportunity, and social responsibility are interrelated. NEPA determined that the Federal Government should work in concert with State and local governments and citizens "to create and maintain conditions under which man and nature can exist in productive harmony, and fulfill the social, economic, and other requirements of present and future generations of Americans."

We've made great progress in 25 years as we've sought to live up to that challenge. As we look forward to the next 25 years of environmental progress, we do so with a renewed determination. Maintaining and enhancing our environment, passing on a clean world to future generations, is a sacred obligation of citizenship. We all have an interest in clean air, pure water, safe food, and protected national treasures. Our environment is, literally, our common ground.

WILLIAM J. CLINTON

The White House,
March 19, 1997.

Message to the Congress Transmitting a Budget Rescission
March 19, 1997

To the Congress of the United States:

In accordance with the Congressional Budget and Impoundment Control Act of 1974, I herewith report one proposed rescission of budgetary resources, totaling $10 million.

The proposed rescission affects the Department of Energy.

WILLIAM J. CLINTON

The White House,

March 19, 1997.

NOTE: The report detailing the proposed rescission was published in the *Federal Register* on March 26.

Statement on Signing the Victim Rights Clarification Act of 1997
March 19, 1997

Today I have signed into law H.R. 924, the "Victim Rights Clarification Act of 1997," to ensure that victims of crime and their families will not be prevented from attending a criminal trial in Federal court simply because they intend to exercise their right to give a statement during a sentencing hearing, once guilt has been decided. I commend the Congress for responding to the initiative led by crime victims and their families, and by a bipartisan group of State attorneys general. As I have said before, when someone is a victim, he or she should be at the center of the criminal justice process, not on the outside looking in. The Act, of course, does not limit the courts' authority and obligation to protect the defendant's right to a fair trial under the due process clause.

WILLIAM J. CLINTON

The White House,
March 19, 1997.

NOTE: H.R. 924, approved March 19, was assigned Public Law No. 105–6. This statement was released by the Office of the Press Secretary on March 20.

Exchange With Reporters Prior to Discussions With President Martti Ahtisaari of Finland in Helsinki
March 20, 1997

Summit With President Boris Yeltsin of Russia

Q. Mr. President, what did you think of President Yeltsin's conciliatory remarks on his arrival here?

The President. I was quite encouraged. I felt good about it. I'm looking forward to the meeting. And I thank President Ahtisaari for making it possible for us to be here.

Q. Are you finding—how are you finding a bum knee? Is that compatible with international diplomacy?

The President. So far we're doing all right. My knee and I are getting around pretty well.

NOTE: The exchange began at 5:48 p.m. in the Yellow Room at the Presidential Palace. A tape was not available for verification of the content of this exchange.

Statement on the Tentative Agreement in the Dispute Between American Airlines and the Allied Pilots Association
March 20, 1997

I am pleased by the announcement yesterday that the negotiating teams for American Airlines and the Allied Pilots Association have reached a tentative agreement on their longstanding labor dispute. This tentative agreement will be presented on Friday to the APA board of directors for approval and subsequent ratification by the union membership.

I want to commend the management of American Airlines and the leadership of the Allied Pilots Association for their commitment to each other and to the traveling public. I think it speaks well of the parties and their intentions that this tentative agreement was reached more than 5 weeks before the April 28 "cooling off" deadline. When labor and management work together, as they did here, U.S. industries are better able to maintain their prominent positions in the global marketplace.

I also want to thank Presidential Emergency Board Chairman Robert Harris and the other members of the panel, Helen Witt and Anthony Sinicropi, for their dedication and hard work. This settlement would not have been possible without their leadership and oversight.

Statement on Senate Action on Narcotics Certification for Mexico
March 20, 1997

I welcome the Senate action endorsing greater cooperation with Mexico and other nations in our hemisphere in the common fight against the scourge of drugs. The resolution approved today represents bipartisan cooperation at its best. Senators reached across the aisle in a way that supports our work with Mexico to keep illegal narcotics out of America's neighborhoods and away from our children.

The Senate and I share a common goal: We both want to improve cooperation with Mexico, Latin America, and the Caribbean in the fight against drugs. I certified Mexico because of the unprecedented level of counternarcotics cooperation we have achieved in the last year and because of the positive steps Mexico has taken on its own to fight drug trafficking. But as I said when I made that decision, much more needs to be done by everyone in this battle. This certification reinforces our ongoing efforts and will foster increased U.S.-Mexico cooperation and strengthen Mexico's own antidrug initiatives. This approach, not confrontation, is the right way to get the results we all want.

The Senate's resolution adopts a clear stand that will support our efforts. It also makes a constructive contribution by emphasizing that solving the problem of drugs requires work on both sides of the border. For example, the bill requires reporting on steps that my administration is taking, such as strengthening border enforcement and improving antidrug education for our youth. I welcome the Senate's farsighted approach, and I urge the House to take up this bill and pass it as quickly as possible.

Statement on the Anniversary of the Sarin Gas Attack in Tokyo, Japan
March 20, 1997

Two years ago terrorists launched a cowardly chemical attack in Tokyo's subways that took 12 lives and injured thousands more. Today we join with the people of Japan in remembering their pain and loss.

This tragic anniversary also reminds us that we must do everything possible to protect Americans from the threat of a similar terrorist outrage. That includes ratifying the Chemical Weapons Convention, a step that Japan's Diet took within a month of the attack in Tokyo. And just this week, the treaty was submitted to Russia's Duma for ratification. We still have not ratified. It would be harmful to our national interests if the United States, which led the way in developing this treaty, was on the outside, not the inside, when it comes into operation on April 29.

The Chemical Weapons Convention will help to thwart chemical terrorists in several important ways. It will eliminate their largest potential source of chemical weapons by mandating the destruction of existing chemical weapon stockpiles. It will make it more difficult for terrorists to gain access to chemicals that can be used to make chemical weapons. It will tie the United States into a global intelligence and information network that can help provide early warning of terrorist plans for a chemical attack. It will give our law enforcement new authority at home to investigate and prosecute anyone seeking to acquire chemical weapons or to use them against innocent civilians.

Just as no law prevents every crime, no treaty is foolproof. But the Chemical Weapons Convention will help make our citizens more secure. It will also help protect our soldiers by requiring member nations to destroy their chemical weapons, a step that we are already taking under U.S. law.

These overwhelming benefits explain why America's military leaders and Presidents of both parties have strongly supported the ratification of this treaty. As we remember the terrible toll that sarin gas took in Tokyo 2 years ago, I urge the Senate to help protect our citizens and soldiers and strengthen our fight against terror by ratifying the Chemical Weapons Convention now.

Exchange With Reporters Prior to a Dinner Hosted by President Martti Ahtisaari of Finland in Helsinki
March 20, 1997

Summit With President Boris Yeltsin of Russia

Q. President Clinton, what are the prospects for common ground on this NATO issue?

The President. I'm looking forward to the meeting. I think we'll work something out; I hope we will. We have had 11 meetings. We've worked hard together, and I'm glad to see President Yeltsin looking so fit and well.

Q. How are you doing, President Clinton?

The President. Great.

NOTE: The exchange began at 7:05 p.m. in the Yellow Room at the Presidential Palace. A tape was not available for verification of the content of this exchange.

Exchange With Reporters on Greeting President Boris Yeltsin of Russia and President Martti Ahtisaari of Finland in Helsinki
March 21, 1997

Helsinki Summit

Q. Mr. President, do you expect to be able to find a way to agree to disagree with President Yeltsin on NATO expansion?

President Clinton. I think we'll have a good meeting. And we'll have a press conference this afternoon to answer your questions.

Q. Do you expect any surprises?

President Yeltsin. During the discussions there may be some surprises, but I'm confident that we'll be able to find a way out, a solution out of these surprises. We have a good will to try to accommodate each other and remove all the disagreements that we still have today. And we grow convinced that our most ardent desire— and then we know that skeptics in the past have always proved that wrong, saying that it's not possible to reach agreement on an issue; in the final analysis we did come to agreement on most thorny issues. And the two Presidents, heads of the two great powers, are duty bound to act in this way. And I think Bill would agree with me that each of us will be prepared to cover his own part of the way.

NOTE: The exchange began at 9:38 a.m. at Mantyniemi, the residence of President Ahtisaari. President Yeltsin spoke in Russian, and his remarks were translated by an interpreter. A tape was not available for verification of the content of this exchange.

Exchange With Reporters Prior to Discussions With President Boris Yeltsin of Russia in Helsinki
March 21, 1997

Russia and NATO

Q. President Yeltsin, do you consider NATO a threat to Russia, or are you convinced otherwise by now?

President Yeltsin. Well, I'm not convinced otherwise.

President Clinton. We'll have a press conference later, guys.

Q. You guys always give us a surprise when you meet, Mr. President. Do you expect any surprises today?

President Yeltsin. Perhaps through the course of the discussions we may have some surprises. We won't have any surprises at the end of the discussions.

NOTE: The exchange began at 9:43 a.m. at Mantyniemi, the residence of President Martti Ahtisaari of Finland. President Yeltsin spoke in Russian, and his remarks were translated by an interpreter. A tape was not available for verification of the content of this exchange.

The President's News Conference With President Boris Yeltsin of Russia in Helsinki
March 21, 1997

President Clinton. Please sit down, everyone. Don't make me all alone. [*Laughter*] Let me say that President Yeltsin and I will have opening statements, and then we'll begin alternating questions, first with a question from the Russian press and then the American press and then back and forth.

I would like to begin by thanking President Ahtisaari, Prime Minister Lipponen, all the people of Finland for their very gracious hospitality to President Yeltsin and to me and for the extremely constructive role that Finland plays in a new era for Europe.

This is my first meeting with President Yeltsin in each of our second terms, our 11th meeting overall. At each meeting we have strengthened our nations' relationship and laid a firmer foundation for peace and security, freedom and prosperity in the 21st century.

Here in Helsinki we have addressed three fundamental challenges: first, building an undivided, democratic, and peaceful Europe for the first time in history; second, continuing to lead the world away from the nuclear threat; and third, forging new ties of trade and investment that will help Russia to complete its remarkable transformation to a market economy and will bring greater prosperity to both our peoples.

A Europe undivided and democratic must be a secure Europe. NATO is the bedrock of Europe's security and the tie that binds the United States to that security. That is why the United States has led the way in adapting NATO to new missions, in opening its doors to new members, in strengthening its ties to nonmembers through the Partnership For Peace, in seeking to forge a strong, practical partnership between NATO and Russia. We are building a new NATO, just as the Russian people are building a new Russia. I am determined that Russia will become a respected partner with NATO in making the future for all of Europe peaceful and secure.

I reaffirmed that NATO enlargement in the Madrid summit will proceed, and President Yeltsin made it clear that he thinks it's a mistake. But we also have an important and, I believe, overriding agreement: We agreed that the relationship between the United States and Russia and the benefits of cooperation between NATO and Russia are too important to be jeopardized.

We didn't come here expecting to change each other's mind about our disagreement, but we both did come here hoping to find a way of shifting the accent from our disagreement to the goals, the tasks, and the opportunities we share. And we have succeeded.

President Yeltsin and I agree that NATO Secretary General Solana and Russian Foreign Minister Primakov should try to complete negotiations on a NATO-Russian document in the coming weeks. It would include a forum for regular consultations that would allow NATO and Russia to work and to act together as we are doing today in Bosnia. It would demonstrate that a new Russia and a new NATO are partners, not adversaries, in bringing a brighter future to Europe.

We also agreed that our negotiators and those of the other 28 participating states should accelerate their efforts in Vienna to adapt the CFE Treaty to the post-cold-war era by setting new limits on conventional forces.

The second area of our discussion involved our obligation to continue to lead the world away from the dangers of weapons of mass destruction. We have already taken important steps. We signed the Comprehensive Nuclear Test Ban Treaty. We extended the Non-Proliferation Treaty. We stopped targeting each other's cities and citizens. We put START I into force. And we're both committed to securing ratification of the Chemical Weapons Convention before it goes into force next month, so that we can finally begin to banish poison gas from the Earth.

Today President Yeltsin agreed to seek the Duma's prompt ratification of START II, already ratified by the United States Senate. But we will not stop there. The United States is prepared to open negotiations on further strategic arms cuts with Russia under a START III immediately after the Duma ratifies START II. President Yeltsin and I agreed on guidelines for START III negotiations that will cap at 2,000 to 2,500 the number of strategic nuclear warheads each of our countries would retain, and to finish the reductions of START III by the year 2007. Now, think about it. This means that within a decade we will have reduced both sides' strategic nuclear arsenals by 80 percent below their cold war peak of just 5 years ago.

We also reached agreement in our work to preserve the Anti-Ballistic Missile Treaty, a cornerstone of our arms control efforts. Distinguishing between ballistic missile systems restricted by the ABM Treaty and theater missile defenses that are not restricted has been a very difficult issue to resolve. Today, after 3 years

of negotiations, we agreed to preserve the ABM Treaty while giving each of us the ability to develop defenses against theater missiles.

Finally, we discussed our economic relationship and the fact that the strong and secure Russia we welcome as a full partner for the 21st century requires that the benefits of democracy and free markets must be felt by Russia's citizens.

President Yeltsin recently demonstrated his determination to reinvigorate economic reform in his State of the Federation Address and with the appointment of a vigorous new economic team. His bold agenda to improve the investment climate and stimulate growth includes comprehensive tax reform, new energy laws, and tough anticrime legislation.

To help American companies take advantage of new opportunities in Russia, we will mobilize support to help finance billions of dollars in new investment. We will work with Russia to advance its membership in key international economic institutions like the WTO, the Paris Club, and the OECD. And I am pleased to announce, with the approval of the other G–7 nations, that we will substantially increase Russia's role in our annual meeting, now to be called the Summit of the Eight, in Denver this June.

Here in Helsinki, we have proved once again that we can work together to resolve our differences, to seize our opportunities, to build a better future.

Before I turn the microphone over to President Yeltsin, let me say one word about the bombing today in Tel Aviv, which we have both been discussing in the last few minutes. Once again, an act of terror has brought death and injury to the people of Israel. I condemn it, and I extend my deepest sympathies to the families of those who were killed or injured.

There is no place for such acts of terror and violence in the peace process. There must be absolutely no doubt in the minds of the friends or of the enemies of peace that the Palestinian Authority is unalterably opposed to terror and unalterably committed to preempting and preventing such acts. This is essential to negotiating a meaningful and lasting peace. And I will do what I can to achieve that objective.

Mr. President.

President Yeltsin. Esteemed journalists, ladies and gentlemen, the first meeting of the Presidents of Russia and the United States has been held after our reelection. Naturally, it was a difficult one because difficult issues were under discussion. But as always, our meeting was quite frank, and on the whole, it was successful. And I am completely in accord with what the President of the United States, Bill Clinton, just said.

We have opened a new stage of Russian-American relations. We discussed in detail the entire range of Russian-American issues—issues of Russian-American partnership, which is quite broad in scale. After all, our countries occupy such a position in the world that the global issues are a subject of our discussions.

Both sides defended their national interests, and both countries did not abandon them. However, our two great powers have an area—a vast area—of congruent interests. Chief among these is the stability in the international situation. This requires us to develop our relations, and there has been progress in that direction.

Five joint statements have been signed as a result of our meeting—President Bill Clinton and I just concluded signing these—on European security, on parameters of future reductions in nuclear forces, concerning the ABM missile treaty, on chemical weapons, and we also signed a U.S.-Russian economic initiative. But we have not merely stated our positions. We view the signed statements with the U.S. President as a program of our joint action aimed to develop Russian-American partnership.

I would say that emotions sometimes get the upper hand in assessing Russian-American partnership. This is not the approach that Bill and I have. Let's not forget that establishing the Russian-American partnership relations is a very complex process. We want to overcome that which divided us for decades. We want to do away with the past mistrust and animosity. We cannot accomplish this immediately. We need to be decisive and patient, and we have both with Bill Clinton.

I firmly believe that we will be able to resolve all issues which, for the time being, are still outstanding. Today's meeting with Bill convinced me of this once again. We will be doing this consistently, step by step. We will have enough patience and decisiveness.

And now I ask you to put questions to us.

Russia and NATO

Q. Boris Nikolayevich, our first impression is that there was no breakthrough on NATO here in Helsinki. Tell me, can there be some kind

of movement forward before the Madrid summit?

President Yeltsin. I don't agree with you. It was today that we had progress, very principled progress, and they consist of the following—that, yes, indeed, we do maintain our positions. We believe that the eastward expansion of NATO is a mistake and a serious one at that. Nevertheless, in order to minimize the negative consequences for Russia, we decided to sign an agreement with NATO, a Russia-NATO agreement. And this is the principal question here. We've agreed on the parameters of this document with President Bill Clinton.

This is the non-proliferation of nuclear weapons, to those new members of NATO to not proliferate conventional weapons in these countries. We agreed on non-use of the military infrastructure which remained in place after the Warsaw Pact in these countries of Central and Eastern Europe. The decision of joint actions with Russia alone, this, too, will be included in the agreement with NATO.

And finally, we've come to an agreement that this document will be binding for all. For that reason, everyone will sign this, all heads of state of all 16 member nations of NATO. This is a very principled issue, and we came to agreement on this with President Bill Clinton. That is, all states, all nations—and this will take place before Madrid—all heads of state will sign this document we sign together with Bill Clinton. And then there will be a signature of the General Secretary of NATO. And we believe that this document indeed is binding for NATO, for Russia, for all states whose leaders signed this document. So this is a very principled progress.

We didn't talk about this just yesterday and the day before. We couldn't have. We can only talk about this now, during these minutes, once we've signed the statements with the President of the United States.

President Clinton. Terry [Terence Hunt, Associated Press].

NATO Expansion

Q. President Yeltsin, after all that you've been told about how the world has changed and that there will be no nuclear weapons in Eastern Europe, do you still regard NATO's enlargement as a danger to Russia?

And to President Clinton, this exclusion of nuclear weapons from Eastern Europe and the promise that there will be no big troop buildup in the new states, does that mean that NATO's new members will be second-class citizens, second-class members?

President Yeltsin. No, of course not, no one will think of these as being secondary states. No one is calling that. That's not what's involved here. However, I believe and Bill believes the same thing, Bill Clinton believes the same, that these decisions that can be taken, they will be taken by all leaders of these nations, which is extremely, extremely important. I already mentioned this.

President Clinton. Let me say, Terry, in answer to the question you raised to me, emphatically no, this does not mean any new members would be second-class members. That's one of the things that we have committed ourselves to. There are no second-class members.

What are the two most important things that you get if you're a member? One is the security guarantee, the mutual security guarantee. The other is a place in the military command structure. These will be available to any new members taken in.

Now, we also want to make it clear that in addition to the security guarantee and participation in the military command structure, NATO is a different organization today than it was. We have a different mission. What is the most important thing NATO is doing today? Working in Bosnia. NATO has a major partnership with Russia in Bosnia. And a partnership, I might add, with a number of other nonmember nations who are in our Partnership For Peace, where we've done joint military exercises and other things.

Now, on the two questions you mentioned— on the nuclear question, the NATO military commanders reached an independent judgment that, based on the facts that exist in the world today, they have no reason, therefore, no intention and no plan to station any nuclear weapons on members' soil. Look, we just announced an agreement here that will reduce nuclear weapons, if we can implement it, within a decade by 80 percent below their cold war height, number one.

Number two, the NATO members have just tabled a proposal on conventional forces in Europe which would put strict limits and would freeze the conventional forces we could have in Europe now, along with having strict limits in the Visegrad countries themselves, which

would be the areas where you'd might expect an old difficulty to arise in new circumstances.

So I think we are doing the right thing, the sensible thing. If it is reassuring to Russia, so much the better. We have a clear, new, and different mission for NATO in the 21st century, but clearly not second-class membership.

Anti-Ballistic Missile Treaty

Q. President Clinton, it is known that in your Congress there's some criticism frequently that you are a supporter of the ABM Treaty. Today's meeting, did that convince you to strengthen the ABM Treaty?

President Clinton. Some people have criticized me in my Congress because I do support the ABM Treaty. Yes, that's accurate; they have. I do support the ABM Treaty. I think it's important. I believe in it. And we have, I believe, strengthened the chances that the ABM Treaty will survive by the agreement we have made today and the distinctions we have drawn between the missiles that are covered by the ABM Treaty and by theater defense missiles. I believe that very strongly.

There are those in the Congress of the United States, but they are not a majority—let me emphasize, they are not a majority—who would undermine the ABM Treaty because they don't believe it's in our interest. I believe they're wrong. I believe that the ABM Treaty has served us well and will continue to serve us well, especially in view of the questions that we have clarified today between us.

Laurie [Laurie Santos, United Press International].

Terrorist Attack in Israel

Q. In light of today's attack on Tel Aviv, sir, you just said the Palestinian Authority is unalterably opposed to terror. Are you saying that there was no green light for terrorist attacks like Prime Minister——

President Clinton. No, no. What I said is— let me clarify what I said. What I intended to say, what I believe I said was that the Palestinian Authority has to make it clear to the friends and to the enemies of the peace process that it is unalterably opposed to terror and must take all possible steps to make that clear and to prevent any terror from occurring. This is a formulation that has frequently been used in the Middle East, but everyone knows that no one in the Middle East can guarantee 100 percent protection against terror. But all the people who participate in the peace process should guarantee 100 percent effort against terror.

Q. What about what Prime Minister Netanyahu—[*inaudible*]?

President Clinton. Well, I can't—first of all, I can't comment decisively, one way or the other, on exactly what was or wasn't done because I don't think any of us know. What I think is very important is that no matter how strongly Mr. Arafat and the Palestinian people feel about the Har Homa decision, nothing—nothing—justifies a return to the slaughter of innocent civilians. It cannot be justified. And we have to have a clear and unambiguous position.

And in the past, when Mr. Arafat has taken that position, I believe it strengthened him. I also believe that acts of terror undermine him because he, in the end, is the popularly elected leader trying to lead the Palestinian people to a peaceful resolution of these differences.

So I have made that very clear just in the last couple of days, and we will continue to work to that end.

Russia-U.S. Relations

Q. The question is to the Russian President. Boris Nikolayevich, you said that this meeting started a new phase for these U.S.-Russian relations. What precisely new was introduced into these relations?

President Yeltsin. Well, first of all, we finally were able to determine our positions on issues of European security. We've come to settle our position on NATO, and we have described for ourselves the parameters of the NATO-Russia agreement.

Secondly, there's an unprecedented reduction of nuclear weapons, that is, of START III—that's 85 percent of the overall arsenal of warheads is being reduced in connection with that. That is significant. This is a very principled issue, and this encompasses the interests of not only our two countries but of the entire European Continent and the whole world.

And the question on economics reflects a completely different approach. We won't conceal this. And I think that Bill Clinton will excuse me if I perhaps am incorrect here, but I think that a certain restriction on questions, holding back on the American side on the Russian economic relations—there was, along the lines of

the Ministry of Energy, on antidumping laws and also the Jackson-Vanik amendment, and many other items speak of the fact that the United States has not been that interested in developing a strong economic Russia or that trade would grow in a healthy way between Russia and the United States. Finally a breakthrough has been made. A joint statement has been signed. We've discussed these issues in great deal with President Bill Clinton.

And on chemical weapons, that, too; any issue we handled, we've been able to manage a major breakthrough. We didn't discuss small issues. We talked only about strategic issues, and on all five issues we were able to find an answer, we were able to find our common point of view. And that's what is reflected in our joint statements.

President Clinton. If I might just support that question, because I think that's a question all the Americans and all the Russians and others will be interested in. What came out of this meeting that was different? One, the idea that there will be a NATO-Russia agreement that all the leaders will support. That's a significant thing. We agreed to disagree about the question of expansion, but we agreed that there must be a partnership between NATO and Russia going forward into the future.

Two, the notion that Russia should play a larger role in international economic institutions and that if certain internal changes are made, which President Yeltsin has already announced his support for, then the United States will make a more vigorous effort to facilitate investment in Russia.

And third, and I think almost unexpected even among us—we were working along here hoping this would happen—we resolved a number of roadblocks relating to START II and other related issues which permitted us to say that President Yeltsin would seek prompt ratification of START II and we would together support guidelines for START III, which we would hope could be negotiated quickly after that, which would reduce the cold war arsenals by over 80 percent from the cold war height, to more or less 80 percent. These are dramatic and very substantial results, and I'm very pleased with them.

Wolf [Wolf Blitzer, Cable News Network].

President Yeltsin. Just a moment, I'd like to continue for a second longer. You've touched on a very current issue which has to be clarified all the way.

Well, you understand, of course, why it is that the State Duma has not yet ratified START II—because ABM was suspended. There was no belief that the treaty from '92 on ABM is not only being complied with by the Russian administration but in the future, conditions are being created which would not allow circumvention of the treaty. In other words, we, for the State Duma, were able to prepare grounds so that the Duma could positively look at the issue of ratifying START II.

President Clinton. Wolf.

Russia-NATO Agreement

Q. Mr. President, Mr. President, one of the most contentious aspects of a potential agreement or charter between NATO and Russia was whether or not it would have to be legally binding on the 16 members of NATO or would simply be a political statement of intent. This agreement that you hope to forge with NATO, do you expect that the legislatures, the U.S. Senate, for example, would have to ratify this agreement, or it would simply be a statement that President Clinton would support?

President Yeltsin. As far as Russia is concerned, we intend to send this treaty and send this agreement to the State Duma for ratification. That's what our intention is.

At the same time, we understand that if 16 states will have to coordinate this issue with their parliaments, this will take up many, many months. And therefore, we've come to an agreement that, given these conditions, it will be quite enough, of course, given the good will of these states, simply a signature of the leaders of these countries that would be affixed to this agreement. How the U.S. would act in this regard, let President Bill Clinton respond.

President Clinton. If you look at the language, President Yeltsin has basically said it accurately. We think it's important to get this agreement up, get it signed, and get it observed—have it observed. And there are so many of the NATO countries. What we have called for is for each and every member country to make—and I believe the exact language of our agreement is—an enduring commitment at the highest political level. And President Yeltsin described to you how we will manifest that.

If our Secretary General, Mr. Solana, and Foreign Minister Primakov succeed in negotiat-

ing this agreement within the timeframe that we all anticipate they will be able to, then we would expect to all meet somewhere and publicly affix our signatures and reaffirm our commitment to the terms of the agreement.

Changes in NATO

Q. The question is to the U.S. President. Mr. President, you, both today and on earlier occasions, said that you intend to transform in some way the North Atlantic Treaty Organization. After today's meeting with President Yeltsin, what specifically do the United States plan to do to change the current structure of NATO? Thank you.

President Clinton. Well, first let me point out we have already transformed NATO. When I became President there was no Partnership For Peace, for example. There were no joint exercises where you had Russian troops, American troops, Polish troops, French troops, others. We didn't have these sorts of things. We didn't have a Partnership For Peace with more than two dozen other countries regularly participating with us now in military planning and training and sharing and working together. And we certainly had nothing like our cooperation in Bosnia.

I believe that the old NATO was basically a mirror image of the Warsaw Pact, and that's why I've been very sensitive to why the Russian people or the Russian leaders would wonder about what the new NATO is . There is no Warsaw Pact. There is no cold war. We just made an agreement to work to cut our nuclear arsenals by 80 percent from their cold war height, which I would remind you existed just 5 years ago.

And what we need to recognize is there will be new security threats to Europe. And you can see them. You have dealt—we've seen them in Bosnia. We've seen them in the other ethnic, religious, and racial traumas that you have dealt with along your borders. You see it in the continuing disputes between nations within the European community.

What we want to do is to provide a way for more and more countries, either as members or as members of the Partnership For Peace— Finland is a good example of an active member of the Partnership For Peace—or because of the special relationship of Russia and the special role Russia will play in the future of Europe and security in the context of the Russia-NATO agreement, we want to provide an opportunity within which all of us can deal with the security aspects of trying to create a Europe that is undivided and democratic for the first time in history.

I would remind you, go back and read from the dawn of nation-states on the Continent of Europe, there has never been a time when all the people were living under democratic governments and were free of foreign domination. That has never happened. So we are simply trying to create the conditions in which we can grow together.

Will there be questions? Will there be skepticism along the way? Will there be uncertainty? Of course, there will be. But we are not attempting to draw a different dividing line in Europe, just somewhat further to the East. What we are trying to do is to develop structures that can grow and evolve over time so that there will be a united effort by free people to join their resources together to reinforce each other's security, each other's independence, and their common interdependence. And I believe we will succeed at that.

Let's see, someone else in the back row here. Alison [Alison Mitchell, New York Times].

Ratification of Agreements

Q. To both Presidents, both of you have had problems with your individual parliaments, and yet——

President Clinton. Seems to be a curse of democracy.

Q. Yes. You each have made arms control agreements here that, you know, the parliaments will want a say in. To Mr. Yeltsin, can you guarantee that the Duma will follow your lead and ratify this? And to Mr. Clinton, how can you assure Mr. Yeltsin that you won't have a rebellion in the Congress over the antimissile defense agreement?

President Yeltsin. As far as Russia is concerned, I expect that the State Duma will make a decision based on my advice. [*Laughter*]

President Clinton. Boy, I wish I could give that answer. [*Laughter*] Let me answer—you give me an opportunity, actually, to point out the full elements of this timetable on START III. And for those of you—if you haven't had time to study it, I want to make full disclosure here.

Number one, I expect that our Congress, those who believe in the ABM system but who

want us to be able to develop theater missile defenses, which may someday protect all of our friends in different circumstances, including our friends in Russia—who knows what use we will put to theater missile defenses when we have troops that have to be protected in the future— I would think that the Members of Congress who believe in the ABM Treaty but want us to be able to develop theater missile defenses will be quite pleased by this agreement. I think that that is not where the problem could come.

Let me explain what we agreed to today— and I did it, I might say, with the full concurrence of General Shalikashvili and Secretary of Defense Cohen, who is not here today, but we checked with him. In order to implement START II in a way that is economically feasible for Russia but does not in any way compromise the security of the American people, what we agreed to do in this framework is to set a date of 2007 for the full implementation of the reductions in START III but to delay the date of all the destructions in START II to 2007. We also agreed to move from the beginning of 2003 to the end of 2003 the time that Russia would have to deactivate the warheads covered by START II.

Now, since our Congress ratified START II based on different target dates for the deactivation of the warheads, on the one hand, and the destruction—ultimate destruction of the missiles, on the other, we will have to go back to them, either separately or in the context of a START III agreement, and ask them to ratify that. And they will have a full opportunity to debate and discuss this.

But I have to tell you, when the Russians advanced this possibility—when President Yeltsin advanced this possibility with me today, the thought that the American people might be able to live in a world, within a decade, where the nuclear arsenals had been reduced by 80 percent, and the thought that, in addition to that, accelerating the time we had anticipated it would take us to meet the START III targets would save our Department of Defense precious dollars that we need to secure our defense in other ways and will therefore enhance our national defense as well as reducing the threat, caused General Shalikashvili to recommend this to me, caused Secretary Cohen to sign off on it, and made me think it was a very good arrangement, indeed, for the Russian people and for the American people and, indeed, for anybody else who would be affected by what we do on this issue.

So, yes, I've got to go back to the Congress. I believe they will, once they have a chance to fully review this, support the decision I have made today. It may take us a little longer than President Yeltsin indicated it would take him with the Duma, but I think we will both get a favorable result because this is so clearly in the interests of the Russian and the American people.

Would you like to take one more?

Russia-U.S. Economic Initiative

Q. Boris Nikolayevich, what's your thought on the version that the Russian giving way on the issue of NATO's expansion to the East will be paid by financial generosity of the West?

President Yeltsin. First of all, I don't see it that way at all. I don't see this generosity at all. If in the statement on economic issues which we had just signed, if there are formulas in there that investments will be supported, investments going to Russia, and certain sums of money will be appropriated by the American side, that does not mean that this is assistance to Russia. This is assistance to the private sector for making investments in Russia. This is assistance to American citizens, not to Russia. Why do you see an exchange here? There's no exchange. And I categorically disagree with that formulation that in place of one we sort of bartered here and as a result of that we have come up with these ideas. I don't agree with that.

I should say that even the order of looking at these issues—and we've held four tours lasting from 45 minutes to an hour and a half each—the order of looking at these issues was as follows: First, we looked at Europe security and NATO. Secondly, the ABM issue. Then we took up chemical weapons. Then we talked about START III, that is, the reduction of further strategic weapons. And only after that, we started talking of economic issues. I did not know that the American side was preparing this. But you see, first we resolved and discussed all of these issues, and only then we approached the economic question. This should tell you that this was not a case where we used this as a poker chip.

President Clinton. I'd just like to support that. And let me say, first of all, what President Yeltsin said about the order in which we took these issues up is absolutely right, first. Second, I believe that the economic announcements which were made today are in the interest of the American people, both directly and indirectly. Let me deal with the indirect question first.

Russia, in the end, cannot be the strong partner that we seek in the 21st century and cannot be free to help create a very different future for Europe and for itself—a future in which we define our greatness by the way we treat other people and by our success in our free dealings, rather than our ability to dominate them—Russia cannot build that kind of future unless ordinary Russian citizens receive the benefit of free markets and democracy. That will not happen.

Secondly, I believe that Russia has the potential to have enormous economic growth in a short period of time by attracting large flows of investment from around the world, if the elements that President Yeltsin outlined in economic reform and the legal changes which he has proposed to the Duma can be embraced. I would be irresponsible as President of the United States if I did not bring into play the Export-Import Bank and our other mechanisms for investing our money to make American investors competitive with investors from around the world for new economic opportunities in Russia. It would be irresponsible of me.

If we do that and we put a lot of money in Russia, billions of dollars, will your people have more jobs and higher incomes? Yes, but so will Americans. And all the time I have to be looking at—it would be just like I can't walk away from Latin America. I would be irresponsible if we didn't try to invest in our neighbors in Latin America in the future. So that's the way I feel.

A lot of the areas where you're going to grow in Russia—in the energy sector, just for example, just to take one area—are areas where American businesses have enormous expertise and literally decades of experience. We would be foolish if we walked away from the opportunity that you present to make money and have opportunity.

So I entirely agree with what the President said, but I want to reinforce it from our perspective.

The lady in the back there in the red dress, go ahead.

Finland's Nonaligned Status

Q. I would like to ask something from both of you. How would you react, sir, if Finland would express its willingness to join NATO?

President Clinton. Maybe I should—you asked both. Since I discussed this with the President—he brought it up with me. President Ahtisaari said to me that he thought Finland had made the right decision to be a member of the Partnership For Peace and to maintain its independence and its ability to work constructively with Russia and with NATO nations and not be a member of NATO and that he had no intention of asking that Finland be considered for membership. But he thought that the policy of being able to be considered was a good one because it reinforced the feeling of independence and the security that Finland and other nations who decide to maintain relative independence and membership in the Partnership For Peace had. So I can do no more than to support the statement that your own President has made about this.

President Yeltsin. I, too, would like to respond on this issue. I should say that the reason we respect Finland as a state—its nation, its people, and leadership—is the fact that Finland is implementing a course of a neutral state, of non-aligning itself to any bloc. This is very important. This creates a very stable and calm balance within the country. This facilitates good neighborly relations with Russia.

We, with Finland, have a turnover of trade of 4.7 billion U.S. dollars. This is 40 percent of the entire turnover of trade. Find me another country that could equal this sort of turnover in trade with Russia. There is no other country. And for that reason, I believe—and, of course, this is the matter entirely of the people of Finland and its government, but that which the President of the Finnish Republic, President Ahtisaari, stated very clearly that he is not joining any blocs. This calls for the feeling of respect for him.

President Clinton. Let me say, since we took an equal number of questions from the Russian and the American journalists but we took a Finnish question, let me, in the interest of fairness—Mr. Donvan [John Donvan, ABC News], you have a question. We ought to take one more question from an American so we'll be even here.

Russia-NATO Agreement

Q. Thank you. I'll make it two questions, one very focused and one somewhat broader. [*Laughter*]

President Clinton. No good deed goes unpunished here.

Q. The focus question is this: In the Russia-NATO agreement, as envisaged, if there is disagreement—Russia disagrees with something NATO wants to do—does Russia have a veto power? The broader question is this. In the Second World War, it was very simple: We were enemies—we were allies, I meant to say. During the cold war, it was very simple: We were enemies. Today, what word describes this relationship where the situation is not so clear and not so simple?

President Yeltsin. I can respond by saying that the way we solve these issues is by consensus. That's how it is today, indeed, among the NATO countries. And that's how it will be once we conclude an agreement between Russia and NATO, already with the participation of Russia.

President Clinton. The short answer to your question is, a voice but not a veto. And the answer to your second question is that we are partners, and like all partners in any partnership, starting with a society's most basic partnership, a marriage and a family, and going to business partnerships, there are sometimes disagreements. But partnerships are bound together by shared values, shared interests, and the understanding that what you have in common is always more important than what divides you.

And so you work for the consensus that President Yeltsin outlined. And that's where we are, and I think that's exactly where we ought to be. And that's why we are not going to have the kind of cataclysmic bloodshed in the 21st century that we saw through three world wars, the cold war, and countless others in the 20th century. If we can stay with that attitude and work on it, we will have a Europe that's not only peaceful but free and undivided.

Thank you very much.

Presidents' Health

Q. How are you both feeling?

President Yeltsin. Thank you. [*Laughter*]

President Clinton. Great. I can tell you he feels great. He looks great, and he feels great. And I feel fine.

NOTE: The President's 139th news conference began at 6:45 p.m. at the Kalastaja Torppa Hotel. In his remarks, President Clinton referred to President Martti Ahtisaari and Prime Minister Paavo Lipponen of Finland; NATO Secretary General Javier Solana; Foreign Minister Yevgeniy Primakov of Russia; and Chairman Yasser Arafat of the Palestinian Authority. A reporter referred to Prime Minister Binyamin Netanyahu of Israel. President Yeltsin spoke in Russian, and his remarks were translated by an interpreter.

Russia-United States Joint Statement on Parameters on Future Reduction in Nuclear Forces
March 21, 1997

Presidents Clinton and Yeltsin underscore that, with the end of the Cold War, major progress has been achieved with regard to strengthening strategic stability and nuclear security. Both the United States and Russia are significantly reducing their nuclear forces. Important steps have been taken to detarget strategic missiles. The START I Treaty has entered into force, and its implementation is ahead of schedule. Belarus, Kazakstan, and Ukraine are nuclear-weapon free. The Nuclear Non-Proliferation Treaty was indefinitely extended on May 11, 1995 and the Comprehensive Nuclear Test Ban Treaty was signed by both the United States and Russia on September 24, 1996.

In another historic step to promote international peace and security, President Clinton and President Yeltsin hereby reaffirm their commitment to take further concrete steps to reduce the nuclear danger and strengthen strategic stability and nuclear security. The Presidents have reached an understanding on further reductions in and limitations on strategic offensive arms that will substantially reduce the roles and risks of nuclear weapons as we move forward into the next century. Recognizing the fundamental significance of the ABM Treaty for these objectives, the Presidents have, in a separate joint statement, given instructions on demarcation between ABM systems and theater missile defense systems, which will allow for deployment of effective theater missile defense and prevent circumvention of the ABM Treaty.

With the foregoing in mind, President Clinton and President Yeltsin have reached the following understandings.

Once START II enters into force, the United States and Russia will immediately begin negotiations on a START III agreement, which will include, among other things, the following basic components:

- Establishment, by December 31, 2007, of lower aggregate levels of 2,000–2,500 strategic nuclear warheads for each of the parties.
- Measures relating to the transparency of strategic nuclear warhead inventories and the destruction of strategic nuclear warheads and any other jointly agreed technical and organizational measures, to promote the irreversibility of deep reductions including prevention of a rapid increase in the number of warheads.
- Resolving issues related to the goal of making the current START treaties unlimited in duration.
- Placement in a deactivated status of all strategic nuclear delivery vehicles which will be eliminated under START II by December 31, 2003, by removing their nuclear warheads or taking other jointly agreed steps. The United States is providing assistance through the Nunn-Lugar program to facilitate early deactivation.

The Presidents have reached an understanding that the deadline for the elimination of strategic nuclear delivery vehicles under the START II Treaty will be extended to December 31, 2007. The sides will agree on specific language to be submitted to the Duma and, following Duma approval of START II, to be submitted to the United States Senate.

In this context, the Presidents underscore the importance of prompt ratification of the START II Treaty by the State Duma of the Russian Federation.

The Presidents also agreed that in the context of START III negotiations their experts will explore, as separate issues, possible measures relating to nuclear long-range sea-launched cruise missiles and tactical nuclear systems, to include appropriate confidence-building and transparency measures.

Taking into account all the understandings outlined above, and recalling their statement of May 10, 1995, the Presidents agreed the sides will also consider the issues related to transparency in nuclear materials.

NOTE: An original was not available for verification of the content of this joint statement.

Russia-United States Joint Statement Concerning the Anti-Ballistic Missile Treaty
March 21, 1997

President Clinton and President Yeltsin, expressing their commitment to strengthening strategic stability and international security, emphasizing the importance of further reductions in strategic offensive arms, and recognizing the fundamental significance of the Anti-Ballistic Missile (ABM) Treaty for these objectives as well as the necessity for effective theater missile defense (TMD) systems, consider it their common task to preserve the ABM Treaty, prevent circumvention of it, and enhance its viability.

The Presidents reaffirm the principles of their May 10, 1995 Joint Statement, which will serve as a basis for reaching agreement on demarcation between ABM systems and theater missile defense systems, including:

—The United States and Russia are each committed to the ABM Treaty, a cornerstone of strategic stability.

—Both sides must have the option to establish and to deploy effective theater missile defense systems. Such activity must not lead to violation or circumvention of the ABM Treaty.

—Theater missile defense systems may be deployed by each side which (1) will not pose a realistic threat to the strategic nuclear force of the other side and (2) will not be tested to give such systems that capability.

—Theater missile defense systems will not be deployed by the sides for use against each other.

—The scale of deployment—in number and geographic scope—of theater missile defense systems by either side will be consistent with theater ballistic missile programs confronting that side.

In this connection, the United States and Russia have recently devoted special attention to developing measures aimed at assuring confidence of the Parties that their ballistic missile defense activities will not lead to circumvention of the ABM Treaty, to which the Parties have repeatedly reaffirmed their adherence.

The efforts undertaken by the Parties in this regard are reflected in the Joint Statement of the Presidents of the United States and Russia issued on September 28, 1994, as well as in that of May 10, 1995. Important decisions were made at the United States-Russia summit meeting on April 23, 1996.

In order to fulfill one of the primary obligations under the ABM Treaty—the obligation not to give non-ABM systems capabilities to counter strategic ballistic missiles and not to test them in an ABM mode—the Presidents have instructed their respective delegations to complete the preparation of an agreement to ensure fulfillment of this requirement.

In Standing Consultative Commission (SCC) negotiations on the problem of demarcation between TMD systems and ABM systems, the United States and Russia, together with Belarus, Kazakstan and Ukraine, successfully finished negotiations on demarcation with respect to lower-velocity TMD systems. The Presidents note that agreements were also reached in 1996 with respect to confidence-building measures and ABM Treaty succession. The Presidents have instructed their experts to complete an agreement as soon as possible for prompt signature on higher-velocity TMD systems.

Neither side has plans before April 1999 to flight test, against a ballistic target missile, TMD interceptor missiles subject to the agreement on demarcation with respect to higher velocity TMD systems. Neither side has plans for TMD systems with interceptor missiles faster than 5.5 km/sec for land-based and air-based systems or 4.5 km/sec for sea-based systems. Neither side has plans to test TMD systems against target missiles with MIRVs or against reentry vehicles deployed or planned to be deployed on strategic ballistic missiles.

The elements for the agreement on higher-velocity TMD systems are:

- The velocity of the ballistic target missiles will not exceed 5 km/sec.
- The flight range of the ballistic target missiles will not exceed 3500 km.
- The sides will not develop, test, or deploy space-based TMD interceptor missiles or components based on other physical principles that are capable of substituting for such interceptor missiles.
- The sides will exchange detailed information annually on TMD plans and programs.

The Presidents noted that TMD technology is in its early stages and continues to evolve. They agreed that developing effective TMD while maintaining a viable ABM Treaty will require continued consultations. To this end, they reaffirm that their representatives to the Standing Consultative Commission will discuss, as foreseen under the ABM Treaty, any questions or concerns either side may have regarding TMD activities, including matters related to the agreement to be completed on higher-velocity systems, which will be based on this joint statement by the two Presidents, with a view to precluding violation or circumvention of the ABM Treaty. These consultations will be facilitated by the agreed detailed annual information exchange on TMD plans and programs.

The Presidents also agreed that there is considerable scope for cooperation in theater missile defense. They are prepared to explore integrated cooperative defense efforts, inter alia, in the provision of early warning support for TMD activities, technology cooperation in areas related to TMD, and expansion of the ongoing program of cooperation in TMD exercises.

In resolving the tasks facing them, the Parties will act in a spirit of cooperation, mutual openness, and commitment to the ABM Treaty.

NOTE: An original was not available for verification of the content of this joint statement.

Russia-United States Joint Statement on Chemical Weapons
March 21, 1997

President Clinton and President Yeltsin discussed issues relating to the entry into force of the Convention on the Prohibition of the Development, Production, Stockpiling and Use of Chemical Weapons and on Their Destruction. They stressed the commitment of the United States and Russia to full and effective accomplishment of the tasks and objectives of the convention.

The Presidents reaffirmed their intention to take the steps necessary to expedite ratification in each of the two countries. President Clinton expressed his determination that the United States be a party when the Convention enters into force in April of this year, and is strongly urging prompt Senate action. President Yeltsin noted that the Convention had been submitted to the Duma with his strong recommendation for prompt ratification.

Mindful of their special role and responsibility in the matter of chemical disarmament, the United States and Russia understand that their participation in the Convention is important to its effective implementation and universality.

The Presidents noted that cooperation between the two countries in the prohibition of chemical weapons has enabled both countries to enhance openness regarding their military chemical potential and to gain experience with procedures and measures for verifying compliance with the Chemical Weapons Convention. The Parties will continue cooperation between them in chemical disarmament.

The United States will seek appropriation of necessary funds to build a facility for the destruction of neuroparalytic toxins in Russia as previously agreed.

NOTE: An original was not available for verification of the content of this joint statement.

Russia-United States Joint Statement on European Security
March 21, 1997

Presidents Clinton and Yeltsin discussed the present security situation in the Euro-Atlantic region. They reaffirmed their commitment to the shared goal of building a stable, secure, integrated and undivided democratic Europe. The roles of the United States and Russia as powers with worldwide responsibilities place upon them a special requirement to cooperate closely to this end. They confirmed that this cooperation will be guided by the spirit of openness and pragmatism which has increasingly come to characterize the U.S.-Russian relationship in recent years.

Recalling their May 1995 Joint Statement on European Security, the Presidents noted that lasting peace in Europe should be based on the integration of all of the continent into a series of mutually supporting institutions and relationships that ensure that there will be no return to division or confrontation. No institution by itself can ensure security. The Presidents agreed that the evolution of security structures should be managed in a way that threatens no state and that advances the goal of building a more stable and integrated Europe. This evolution should be based on a broad commitment to the principles of the Organization for Security and Cooperation in Europe as enshrined in the Helsinki Final Act, the Budapest Code of Conduct and other OSCE documents, including respect for human rights, democracy and political pluralism, the sovereignty and territorial integrity of all states, and their inherent right to choose the means to ensure their own security.

The Presidents are convinced that strengthening the OSCE, whose potential has yet to be fully realized, meets the interests of the United States and Russia. The Presidents expressed their satisfaction with the outcome of the Lisbon Summit of the OSCE and agreed on the importance of implementing its decisions, both to define further the goals of security cooperation and to continue to devise innovative methods for carrying out the growing number of tasks the OSCE has assumed.

They underscored their commitment to enhance the operational capability of the OSCE as the only framework for European security cooperation providing for full and equal participation of all states. The rule of consensus should remain an inviolable basis for OSCE decision-making. The Presidents reaffirmed their commitment to work together in the ongoing OSCE effort to develop a model for security in Europe which takes account of the radically changed situation on the eve of the 21st century and the decisions of the Lisbon Summit concerning a charter on European security. The OSCE's essential role in Bosnia and Herzegovina and its ability to develop new forms of peacekeeping and conflict prevention should also be actively pursued.

In their talks in Helsinki, the two Presidents paid special attention to the question of relations between the North Atlantic Treaty Organization and the Russian Federation. They continued to disagree on the issue of NATO enlargement. In order to minimize the potential consequences of this disagreement, the Presidents agreed that they should work, both together and with others, on a document that will establish cooperation between NATO and Russia as an important element of a new comprehensive European security system. Signed by the leaders of the NATO countries and Russia, this document would be an enduring commitment at the highest political level. They further agreed that the NATO-Russia relationship, as defined in this document, should provide for consultation, coordination and, to the maximum extent possible where appropriate, joint decision-making and action on security issues of common concern.

The Presidents noted that the NATO-Russia document would reflect and contribute both to the profound transformation of NATO, including its political and peacekeeping dimension, and to the new realities of Russia as it builds a democratic society. It will also reflect the shared commitment of both NATO and Russia to develop their relations in a manner that enhances mutual security.

The Presidents recalled the historic significance of the Treaty on Conventional Armed Forces in Europe in establishing the trust necessary to build a common security space on the continent in the interest of all states in Europe, whether or not they belong to a military or political alliance, and to continue to preclude any destabilizing build-up of forces in different regions of Europe.

The Presidents stressed the importance of adapting the CFE Treaty. They agreed on the need to accelerate negotiations among CFE parties with a view to concluding by late spring or early summer of 1997 a framework agreement setting forth the basic elements of an adapted CFE Treaty, in accordance with the objectives and principles of the Document on Scope and Parameters agreed at Lisbon in December 1996.

President Yeltsin underscored Russian concerns that NATO enlargement will lead to a potentially threatening build-up of permanently stationed combat forces of NATO near to Russia. President Clinton stressed that the Alliance contemplates nothing of the kind.

President Yeltsin welcomed President Clinton's statements and affirmed that Russia would exercise similar restraint in its conventional force deployments in Europe.

President Clinton also noted NATO's policy on nuclear weapons deployments, as articulated by the North Atlantic Council on December 10, 1996, that NATO members have "no intention, no plan and no reason" to deploy nuclear weapons on the territory of states that are not now members of the Alliance, nor do they foresee any future need to do so. President Clinton noted NATO's willingness to include specific reference to this policy in the NATO-Russia document. President Yeltsin spoke in favor of including such a reference in the document.

The Presidents agreed that the United States, Russia and all their partners in Europe face many common security challenges that can best be addressed through cooperation among all the states of the Euro-Atlantic area. They pledged to intensify their efforts to build on the common ground identified in their meetings in Helsinki to improve the effectiveness of European security institutions, including by concluding the agreements and arrangements outlined in this statement.

NOTE: An original was not available for verification of the content of this joint statement.

Joint Statement on United States-Russia Economic Initiative
March 21, 1997

President Clinton and President Yeltsin have committed to a joint initiative to stimulate investment and growth in Russia, deepen U.S.-Russian economic ties and accelerate Russia's integration with global markets. In so doing, the Presidents underscored the vital importance of bold measures to complete Russia's historic transformation to a market economy. This transformation is in the mutual interest of the United States and Russia—to meet the aspirations of the Russian people for a more secure and prosperous future, and to encourage trade, investment and new jobs in both countries. Both Presidents affirmed their commitment to achieve

the vast potential of U.S.-Russian economic cooperation.

The Presidents discussed recent economic developments in their countries and objectives for the future. The process of unprecedented transformation of Russia into a democratic nation that respects private ownership and the principles of a free market is continuing. In the past five years, a once non-existent private sector has emerged to produce 70 percent of Russia's national income and employ 55 percent of the Russian work force. With basic market structures now formed, markets, not the state, increasingly allocate resources and drive prices and business decisions. Private banks, capital markets and commodity exchanges are emerging as the new institutions underpinning Russian economics. Inflation has been sharply reduced, and Russia has begun to enter international capital markets. Taking into account these changes, the United States and Russia will consider problems connected with the regulation of trade between the two countries, take steps to increase access to each other's markets, and establish the appropriate conditions to extend Most Favored Nation status to Russia on a permanent and unconditional basis.

President Yeltsin outlined Russia's plans to enact and implement a new legal regime that convincingly demonstrates Russia's commitment to attracting foreign and domestic investment. His highest economic priority is a tax regime that both meets the revenue needs of the Russian government and stimulates legitimate business, including actions on the value-added tax, excise tax, and both corporate and individual income taxes. Russia will act to pass a new tax administration law that clarifies authorities, responsibilities, fines and the ability to resolve disputes. In the energy sector, measures will be taken to pass legislation that brings into full force Russia's Production Sharing Agreement law and provides the authority to develop PSA fields. New efforts will be made to ratify the U.S.-Russia bilateral investment treaty. The Presidents committed to deepen cooperation to fight economic crime. President Yeltsin highlighted his plans to consolidate the rule of law and to strengthen Russian legislation aimed in particular at combating money laundering and organized crime. President Yeltsin stressed the importance of the quick adoption of a new criminal procedure code. He will pursue the substantial completion of this agenda by the end of 1997. Further, the Presidents committed to work together to meet the challenge of attracting investment in order to utilize the vast human and natural resources that Russia possesses.

President Clinton stated that U.S. Government agencies will maximize support under their programs to finance American investment in Russia. U.S. efforts will include intensified efforts for project finance, political risk insurance and investment funds through the Overseas Private Investment Corporation; expanding financing for transactions involving equipment exports through the Export-Import Bank that will result in capital investments in the Russian economy;

and additional investments through the U.S.-Russia Investment Fund.

The Presidents applauded plans announced by Vice President Gore and Prime Minister Chernomyrdin to launch a regional investment initiative that will attract resources to key regions, including the Russian Far East, to demonstrate the impact of joint efforts on policy reform and investment finance and to create new channels of commercial cooperation between regions in both countries. The United States and Russia recognize that Russian action on its economic agenda is key to building investor confidence and creating the demand needed to translate American financing into real investments in Russia. Toward this end, President Clinton is seeking additional funding in 1998 to expand U.S.-Russian economic cooperation, with a focus on tackling barriers to investment and doubling exchange programs between Americans and Russians, including the introduction of a new program to forge long-lasting connections between young, highly qualified individuals likely to emerge as influential leaders in future U.S. and Russian societies. The Presidents looked forward to the work of the joint Capital Markets Forum, which will bring together public and private sector participants to support the rapid development of Russia's capital markets.

Presidents Clinton and Yeltsin affirmed that cooperation to integrate Russia's economy into the global economic system represents one of their most important priorities. The United States and Russia will intensify their efforts to accelerate Russia's integration into the international economic community. The Presidents set as a target that both sides would undertake best efforts for Russia, on commercial conditions generally applicable to newly acceding members, to join the World Trade Organization in 1998, and to join the Paris Club in 1997 assuming agreement on conditions of membership. Together, the United States and Russia will define tasks which need to be accomplished and set targets for their completion in order to achieve this objective. They also count on making considerable progress toward Russia's accession to the Organization for Economic Cooperation and Development.

The Presidents agreed that Vice President Gore and Prime Minister Chernomyrdin should broaden and intensify the work of the U.S.-Russian Commission on Economic and Technological Cooperation. The Presidents welcomed the Commission's efforts to move beyond cooperation between federal governments to foster regional and local ties between the peoples of their countries. They noted the Commission's important achievements in the fields of trade and investment, energy, environment, health, defense conversion, agriculture, space, and science and technology. They recognized the Commission's leadership role in carrying forward bilateral relations into the twenty-first century.

Presidents Clinton and Yeltsin expect that as the century turns, their joint initiative will result in a strategic economic partnership between the United States and Russia that will decisively strengthen bilateral ties and positively shape changes in the world economy. They look forward to a prosperous and market-oriented Russia as a full partner in the premier organizations that will define economic and trade relations for the twenty-first century. This will allow Russia to take its place among the community of nations contributing to a new international economic order where open markets and free trade foster global prosperity and the well-being of American and Russian citizens alike.

NOTE: An original was not available for verification of the content of this joint statement.

The President's Radio Address
March 22, 1997

Good morning. I'm glad to be back at the microphone this morning after relying on the Vice President to fill in for me last Saturday. My knee is healing just fine, and I'm happy to report that I've just completed a successful summit meeting with President Boris Yeltsin of Russia in Helsinki, Finland. Together we're building a strong United States-Russia relationship to meet the challenges of the 21st century: building a democratic, undivided Europe at peace; leading the world away from the nuclear threat; forging new ties of trade and investment that will benefit all our people.

Today I want to talk with you about how we can work together to strengthen America's working families and to help them meet their responsibilities both at work and at home. We have made significant progress in this area with the Family and Medical Leave Act of 1993. That was landmark legislation, and I was very proud that it was the first bill I signed as President. But I'm even more proud of the impact this law has had on the everyday lives of working families.

Since its enactment, millions of Americans have been able to take unpaid leave to care for a newborn child or to be with a family member who's sick. I know that many Americans would have lost their jobs if it weren't for the family leave law.

With new pressures on families in the way they work and live, we have to do even more to give people the chance to be good workers and good parents. That's why I proposed expanding the Family and Medical Leave Act so that workers can take time off to attend teacher conferences or to take a child for a medical checkup. I have challenged the Congress to pass legislation that will do just that this year, and I have high hopes that they will.

This morning I want to talk about another way to strengthen our working families. I have a plan that offers employees this simple choice: If you work overtime, you can be paid time and a half, just as the law now requires, or if you want, you can take that payment in time, an hour and a half off for every hour of overtime you work. Simply put, you can choose money in the bank or time on the clock. Comp time can be used for a vacation, an extended maternity leave, or to spend more time with your children or your parents.

We can give employees in American business more flexibility. That serves everyone's interests. But we must make sure that as we give greater flexibility, we do it in a way that's good for both business and employees.

Unfortunately, a version of comp time legislation that is moving through Congress now would take the wrong approach. It could actually leave working families worse off than today. Strong comp-time legislation gives employees the choice of when to take their overtime pay in money or in time off from work. But under the congressional majority's proposal, employees aren't really guaranteed that choice. There are no effective safeguards to stop an employer from telling an employee who needs a paycheck more than family time that he or she has no choice: "You work overtime this week, then I'll give you less time next week."

Strong comp-time legislation would give employees the choice of when they take time off. That's the best way to strengthen families and to give parents more flexibility. But the congressional majority's plan would make it simply too easy for employers to tell workers they cannot take the comp time they have earned.

Under strong comp-time legislation, the time off you have earned is just that, time off. But under the congressional majority's plan, employees who take comp time could be forced to work extra hours at night or on the weekend to make up the time without any overtime pay. That means if you take off a Friday that you have earned by working overtime, your employer could simply make you work Saturday without paying overtime because you haven't worked your full 40-hour week.

Above all, strong comp-time legislation preserves the protection of our 40-hour week, which has been the law now for most of this century. Today the law says if you are an hourly worker and you work longer than 40 hours, you get paid time and a half for overtime. Our plan would give you the choice of taking an hour and a half off for every hour you work instead. But under the congressional majority's plan, some employees who work an extra hour would get only an hour off, less overtime than they would be eligible for today. That's money out of their pocket.

The vast majority of our employers will be fair to their workers under any system. But as we modernize our laws to fit a changing workplace, we have to uphold historic safeguards for all our employees. Giving workers the real choice of taking time off as overtime pay is good for our families. It will help all Americans balance the demands of home and work. But it's employees and their families, not employers, who should choose if, when, and how they take and use comp time.

Congress should pass expanded family leave and a strong comp-time bill. The moment a responsible comp-time bill hits my desk, I will gladly sign it. It will be good for workers, good for business, good for the economy, and strong in the building of our families. But let me also be clear: I will have to veto any legislation that fails to guarantee real choice for employees, real protection against employer abuse, and real preservation of fair labor standards including the 40-hour week.

It's time for us to join together to give America's families the help they need to succeed on the job and in the home. Let's pass comp-time legislation, but let's do it right.

Thanks for listening.

NOTE: The address was recorded at 2:10 p.m. on March 21 at Mantyniemi, the residence of President Martti Ahtisaari of Finland in Helsinki, for broadcast at 10:06 a.m. on March 22.

Remarks Announcing Proposed Medicare and Medicaid Fraud Prevention Legislation and an Exchange With Reporters
March 25, 1997

The President. Thank you very much, Governor Chiles. And thank you, Secretary Shalala. Ladies and gentlemen, I also want to thank the representatives of the AARP who are here and others who have been very interested in this program.

As all of you know, and as I have given further evidence of here today, I was recently reminded the hard way that our doctors and medical care are the best in the world. That is certainly true. I can vouch for the doctors and nurses in the hospital in Florida that cared for me when I was recently injured. I've worked hard to give all America's families access to quality health care, and as Governor Chiles and the Secretary have made clear, a critical part of that mission has to be to make sure that our system is free of fraud.

Over the past 4 years, we have made real progress in our efforts to expand access to health care. Last year we made it possible for people to move from job to job without fear of losing their health insurance. Our balanced budget plan will provide health care coverage for up to 5 million of the 10 million children who don't have it. It preserves and strengthens the Medicare system, ensuring the life of the Medicare Trust Fund for another decade.

Today we are taking the next steps to end the waste, fraud, and abuse in health care that threatens our ability to provide high-quality and affordable health care for America's citizens. Medicare fraud costs us billions of dollars every year. It amounts to a fraud tax that falls on all of our taxpayers but most heavily upon our senior citizens. Because of fraud they have to pay higher premiums and higher out-of-pocket costs that otherwise they would not have to pay.

Medicare and Medicaid are more than just programs, they are the way we do honor to our parents, the way we strengthen our families, the way we care for our poorest and most vulnerable children. We cannot tolerate fraud that robs taxpayers even as it harms those of us to whom we owe a great duty.

The law enforcement partnership described by Governor Chiles and Secretary Shalala has made real strides in the fight against health care fraud. Over the past 4 years, we have assigned more Justice Department prosecutors and more FBI agents to fight health care fraud than ever before. We've won a record number of convictions and settlements in fraud cases. All told, since 1992, the number of health care fraud convictions has increased by 241 percent. Operation Restore Trust, which Secretary Shalala described, has the potential to save $10 for every dollar invested in it.

All of these efforts together have helped us save over $20 billion in health care claims. Money that would have been wasted has gone instead to help provide quality health care and peace of mind for America's families.

Today I am pleased to announce that I will send to Congress legislation to continue and toughen our crackdown on fraud and abuse in the Medicare and Medicaid programs. First, the best way to prevent fraud is to keep dishonest doctors and other scam artists out of the Medicare system in the first place. Under this bill, a provider or supplier who's been convicted of fraud or another felony could be barred from joining the Medicare and Medicaid programs.

For example, in Florida, our investigators found a medical equipment supplier previously convicted of securities fraud, and they found that supplier was bilking the Medicare program. He was ordered to pay $32 million in restitution, and he's back in jail serving a 9-year sentence. But people like this should not be allowed to join Medicare in the first place. With this legislation, it's less likely that they will be able to do that.

Second, our reform would improve safeguards against fraud by requiring anyone who wants to do business with Medicare to register with the Government and give us their Social Security number. This will help track and stop fraudsters who try to repeat their crimes setting up shop under phony names with dummy corporations or in new States.

Third, the legislation will toughen sanctions so that those who cheat pay the price. The Government will have a stronger hand in imposing larger and newer civil monetary fines.

And finally, it will close loopholes in the law that today let Medicare and Medicaid providers pocket overpayments from the Government simply by declaring bankruptcy. Under this bill, Medicare providers will no longer be able to avoid accountability by declaring bankruptcy.

These steps are important. They will save the Government and the American people a great deal of money. They will also buy something that money cannot alone buy, a greater sense of security and peace of mind for our parents, our most vulnerable families, and children. We can and will preserve Medicare. We can and will make the Medicaid system work better and serve more children. The steps we take today will protect and strengthen those systems that mean so much to our families and to our future. And thank you all for your contributions to the effort. Thank you very much. [*Applause*] Thank you.

And let me just say one other thing. This is my first public statement, I think, since coming back from Helsinki. We had a terrific meeting there. It was good for the United States, good for the people of Russia. And again, I'd like to thank my medical team for making it possible for me to make the trip so soon after my surgery. But it went fine, and it was a remarkable thing, not only the progress we made on NATO but especially on our commitment to slash the nuclear arsenals of both the United States and Russia by 80 percent from their cold war highs, within decades. So I'm very excited about it. It was a good meeting, and I'm glad to be back.

Former President George Bush

Q. Mr. President, what do you think about your predecessor's venture into skydiving? [*Laughter*] President Bush is supposed to be parachuting even as we speak. [*Laughter*]

The President. I am mightily impressed. [*Laughter*] And I wish him well. I'm excited. I can't wait to see him get down and give us the story. [*Laughter*]

President's Travel Plans

Q. Are you going to have to postpone your Mexico trip because of your injury?

The President. What we have decided to do, and I think we've announced it—we will announce it today—is to postpone the Mexico trip for about a month and put it where I was going to do my full Latin American trip to the other countries, to Central America, to South America, and the Caribbean. And what we're going to do is to make the trip to Mexico, to Costa Rica, and to Barbados, to do Central America and the Caribbean and Mexico during that timeframe. And then later in the year, we're going

to go to South America and do that trip when I'm somewhat more mobile, because, among other things, we're going to Argentina and Brazil. They're big countries. There's going to be a lot of moving around, and I need a little more physical mobility. Besides, I'm hoping to ride horses and do some other things, and I'm not quite ready for that, as you can see.

Medicare Fraud Initiative

Q. Mr. President, the cornerstone of the Florida program is the surety bond and the on-site inspections, both of which are missing from your proposal. Why is that?

The President. Do you want to comment on that?

Secretary of Health and Human Services Donna Shalala. Yes. The on-site inspection is in it. On the surety bond, it's one of the things that we have the authority under our regulatory authority, and we'll have a later announcement on that.

The President. Thank you all.

NOTE: The President spoke at 12:32 p.m. in the Roosevelt Room at the White House. In his remarks, he referred to Gov. Lawton Chiles of Florida.

Statement on Campaign Finance Reform Legislation
March 25, 1997

In my State of the Union Address, I challenged Congress to pass bipartisan campaign finance reform by July 4th, the date we celebrate the birth of our democracy. The only way that political reform will become law is if citizens raise their voices to demand change. I strongly support the bipartisan legislation introduced by Senators John McCain and Russ Feingold, and Representatives Chris Shays and Marty Meehan. It is real, it is fair, it is tough, and it will curb the role of big money in our politics.

We know the pressing need for reform. The campaign finance laws are two decades out of date and have been overwhelmed by a flood of money that rises with every election. Above all, campaign finance reform will help us to

meet our Nation's fundamental challenges. It will help us balance the budget, fight crime, extend health care to our children, protect our young people from the dangers of tobacco. Reform will help make sure that our political system stands for ordinary Americans and helps them in their daily lives.

At Faneuil Hall, the "Cradle of Liberty," and at Independence Hall, our Founders forged our democracy. Now it is up to all of us, in a new time, to renew that democracy and to make sure that our Government represents the national interest, not just narrow interests. I thank those who are fighting for reform and who are gathered at Faneuil Hall for their leadership and urge all citizens to join in this effort. This year can be the year that we finally pass campaign finance reform.

NOTE: This statement was read at the Project Independence rally for campaign finance reform at Faneuil Hall in Boston, MA.

Remarks Prior to Discussions With President Alija Izetbegovic of Bosnia-Herzegovina and an Exchange With Reporters
March 26, 1997

President Clinton. Let me say that it's a real pleasure for me to welcome President Izetbegovic back to the White House. I'm looking forward to this meeting and to getting an update on his efforts to complete the implementation of the Dayton accord. The United States remains committed to that and committed to supporting those in Bosnia who are working for that.

And we still have an awful lot of work to do in the time remaining for our mission there on the security front, and then even beyond there will be a lot more to do. So I'm pleased to have him here, and I'm looking forward to our visit.

Middle East Peace Process

Q. Mr. President, why did you send Dennis Ross to the Middle East?

President Clinton. Because I'm concerned about the peace process, and we have been talking among ourselves here intensely over the last several days about whether there are some ideas we ought to advance with the Israelis and the Palestinians, and particularly what we can do to minimize the violence and to get the negotiations back going. So that's what—Dennis' trip is the product of our deliberations here, and we'll see what it produces.

Q. What are you suggesting?

FBI and Alleged Chinese Efforts To Influence the 1996 Election

Q. Mr. President, we never had a chance to ask you yesterday about your response to the possibility that FBI Director Louis Freeh withheld information that you might actually have needed to conduct policy. I was wondering if you have a response to that and what you're doing, if anything, to look into whether that actually occurred.

President Clinton. Well, first of all, obviously I have no way of knowing—you don't know what

you don't get. But if you look at the last several years, or just the last couple of years, we have worked with the FBI in areas that have both national security implications and the question of a crime that violates the criminal laws of the United States. The two most obvious and most recent cases are the Khobar Towers and the Atlanta bombing during the Olympics. And we worked with them on both cases.

Now, they have dual obligations to share with the White House and with the State Department—the Secretary of State, where appropriate, information we need to protect and advance national security and to preserve the integrity of criminal investigations. And ultimately, those things almost have to be resolved on a case-by-case basis, where there is a doubt, by the Attorney General.

And I'm confident that that is what has been and will continue to be done in this case. And that's really the best answer I can give you here.

Q. Do you still have strong confidence in Louis Freeh to run the FBI?

President Clinton. Yes, I have no basis—on the basis of this incident, I don't have any information at this time which would call into question that confidence. These are not always easy questions. And that's why the Attorney General has to resolve them when there is a real doubt. I just wanted—I wanted to make sure that the national security interests of the country have been fully taken into account and that there's really been an honest effort to look at all the evidence and to resolve it.

I can't say that—to go back to your original question, since I don't know what was not given, I can't make a judgment about it.

Q. Well, why——

President Clinton. But I do know that the Attorney General was sensitive to it, and I believe will continue to make an effort to resolve the matters in the appropriate way.

Q. But there seems to be a—Mr. President, there seems to be a disconnect with what you get. I mean, it seems to me that they are not telling you a lot of things that you should know.

President Clinton. Well, I'm concerned about that, as I said, but the only way we have of resolving that is through the Attorney General. And again, I've seen these suggestions in the press, but I don't know what the facts are. I think everyone understands that there are significant national security issues at stake here and that the White House, the National Security Council, and the Secretary of State, as well as the President, need to know when the national security issues are brought into play.

And I have no reason—I have no evidence on which I could say that, that we have not been able to get the information we need. I know what I read in the press story, and I know that we have raised it with the Attorney General, and I believe that she will do the best she can to make the right decision.

Vice President's Visit to China

Q. Mr. President, have you talked to Vice President Gore since he's been in China, sir?

President Clinton. I haven't talked to him because of—I think he hasn't wanted to bother me because of my knee and the time differences, but I've gotten daily reports at least once and sometimes more than once a day on the Vice President's trip. And so far, I'm quite pleased with what I hear and what I have seen.

And I've obviously gotten my daily reports and sometimes more on the First Lady's trip. And I'm quite pleased by what I have seen there as well.

Middle East Peace Process

Q. Would you consider another emergency summit with the Mideast leaders?

President Clinton. I don't want to comment anymore about anything I would consider on the Middle East until I hear back from Mr. Ross. He has very explicit instructions that he is implementing as a result of our meeting on this. And I want to see what happens as a result of that.

But I'm concerned about it. I think everybody in the world who's worked for peace in the Middle East is concerned about it. We're all going to put our heads together and do the best we can.

One more Bosnia question, yes.

Bosnian Peace Process

Q. Mr. President, the peace process seems to be in trouble in Bosnia. Could you comment on that?

President Clinton. Well, I'm going to talk to the President about what we can do to push it along. It's obviously going to take an effort on behalf of all parties. But the things that we knew from the beginning would be difficult, have been difficult. The resettlement issues, the return issues have been difficult.

But I think it's important not to lose sight of what has been done and not to lose sight of the fact that there will be an international security presence there for quite some time yet, during which time we have to work hard to do as much as we possibly can to implement the Dayton agreement. And that's going to be my commitment and what I look forward to discussing with President Izetbegovic.

Q. But you fully still expect U.S. troops to be out by June '98 as scheduled?

President Clinton. I do. I think that in the— I think we all understood that we couldn't have an international security presence in a country forever. But on the other hand, I think we have to—we shouldn't focus so much on that now, as I have pleaded with everyone. We should focus on what's going to happen tomorrow and next week and next month and between now and the end of this year and in the months in 1998 that we have. We have—there is a lot of very specific work to be done that, if done and done right, will make it possible for the nation to succeed and for the people to be brought back into a more constructive cooperation and existence when we're gone.

Q. How does the President of Bosnia—do you feel that way too? Do you feel hopeful?

President Izetbegovic. Yes, I hope. First, I have to thank Mr. President for receiving me twice because of his leg.

And we have some problems with the process of the Dayton—implementation of Dayton, especially civil part of it is going slowly. And the implementation operation also is going slowly. We know that it is—that is—all that is our job firstly, primarily our job, but we need help of the States to push on the—and I am going to talk about this problem with Mr. President.

Q. Do you think your country will be ready in a year and a half to exist on its own?

President Izetbegovic. I believe yes on condition—maybe on four conditions: If civil part of the Dayton agreement would be implemented, first; secondly, equip and train program also would be implemented; then, if—protocol about disarmament would be done; and an additional condition, maybe if Bosnia would be received in the Partnership of Peace. That's—on these four conditions, I believe that SFOR forces or foreign forces can leave Bosnia without big problems.

President Clinton. Thank you all.

President Izetbegovic. Some problems, maybe, but——

President Clinton. Thank you.

NOTE: The President spoke at 11:29 a.m. in the Oval Office at the White House. In his remarks, President Clinton referred to Ambassador Dennis B. Ross, Special Middle East Coordinator. A tape was not available for verification of the content of these remarks.

Remarks on the Advisory Commission on Consumer Protection and Quality in the Health Care Industry
March 26, 1997

Thank you very much. Thank you, Secretary Shalala, Acting Secretary Metzler. Thank you both for the work you've done on this. I thank the Commission members for their willingness to serve, those who are here and a few who could not be here with us today. And I thank all of you here in this audience for your interest in this profoundly important matter.

The Advisory Commission that I announced today will help to chart our way through a time of profound change in health care. Their task will be focused and urgent: to find ways to ensure quality and to ensure that the rights of consumers in health care are protected.

Since I took office, we have been committed to improving our health care system, to making it more affordable, more accessible, while preserving its high quality. You have heard Secretary Shalala mention some of the things we have done together. We've worked with States to expand Medicaid to more than 2 million Americans who previously had no insurance. We reached across party lines to enact the Kassebaum-Kennedy law that provides that working families will not lose their insurance when they change jobs, increased the health care tax deduction for 3 million self-employed Americans. And now in our budget plan, we have funds sufficiently targeted to extend coverage to as many as half of our 10 million American children who still don't have medical coverage.

We've worked to constrain costs. Just yesterday, I announced a new effort to combat the multibillion dollar problem of fraud and abuse in Medicare and Medicaid. Our balanced budget proposal also strengthens Medicare through savings and overdue structural reforms.

Of course, we're not alone in this. The private sector has found ways to rein in costs, sometimes dramatically. And in many cases, changes in the health care delivery system have, frankly, also improved its quality. For example, the growing recognition of the value of preventive care, such as mammography screening, is saving and extending lives and the quality of life. This is all very encouraging. Step by step we have been working to expand access to health care, and today we take the next step.

In this time of transition, many Americans worry that lower costs mean lower quality and less attention to their rights. On balance, however, managed health care plans, HMO's, PPO's, and others, give patients good care and greater choice at lower cost. Still, we must make sure that these changes do not keep health professionals from offering the best and the most medically appropriate services to their patients. Managed care managed well can be the best deal for our families. Whether they have traditional health care or managed care, none of our people should ever have inferior care.

I am proud that the Medicare and Medicaid programs have taken the lead in responding to the quality concerns of both patients and health care providers, as Secretary Shalala has just described. But we're learning the defining, measuring, and enforcing quality is far from a simple task. There are many complicated issues. They require thoughtful study. And not surprisingly, there are many areas where broad-based consensus on how best to proceed does not yet exist.

That is why I decided late last year to establish the Advisory Commission on Consumer Protection and Quality in the Health Care Industry. Today I am happy to introduce the members of that Commission to the American people. They are a highly distinguished, broad-based, and diverse group. They represent consumers, business, labor, health care providers, insurers, managed care plans, State and local governments, health care quality experts. Their specialties are wide-ranging, including care for children, the elderly, women, people with disabilities, mental illness, or AIDS. This Commission includes some of the best health care policy minds in our Nation and a lot of people with hands-on experience. Its task will be as challenging as it is critical.

Today, to assure that they get busy right away, I am charging the Commission to develop a consumer bill of rights so that health care patients get the information and care they need when they need it. Let's assure that patients and their families—first, that the health care professionals who are treating them are free to provide the best medical advice available; second, that their providers are not subject to inappropriate financial incentives to limit care; third, that our sickest and most vulnerable patients, frequently the elderly and people with disabilities, are receiving the best medical care for their unique needs; fourth, that consumers have access to simple and fair procedures for resolving health care coverage disputes with plans; fifth, and perhaps most important, that consumers have basic information about their rights and responsibilities, about the plans—the benefits the plans offer, about how to access the health care they need, and about the quality of their providers and their health care plans.

I'm delighted that the Secretary of Health and Human Services and the Secretary of Labor will take on the task of being the Commission's Cochairs. I look forward to reviewing their first report at the end of the year and their final report next March.

The need for this Commission is real. It is urgent. It will give us a roadmap to help us make our way through the time of rapid change we now see in our health care system. There are few people in the Nation better suited to the task than the members of this Commission. And again, let me say, I want to thank them for their commitment to serve.

And to all the rest of you let me say, one of the things, one of the many things I have learned in the last 4 years as President is that a distinguished commission, broadly based with a clear mandate, can make a profound positive difference for our country. In the health care related areas, I ask you to think of only two. Think of the work done by the Gulf War Commission and what we now know that we did not know when they started to meet and work. Think of the remarkable work done by the Commission that dealt with those who were exposed to human radiation experiments just a few decades ago here and the work that they have done. There is a peculiar way in which the citizens of the United States, when brought together around a clear mandate, interfacing with their Government and with the private sector, can do more than either the Government or the private sector could do alone.

And so again, let me say, I'm very hopeful about this Commission. I look forward to their progress on the consumer's bill of rights. I look forward to all the work that they do. And I ask you to join me in thanking them for their willingness to serve.

Thank you very much.

NOTE: The President spoke at 2:32 p.m. in the East Room at the White House. In his remarks, he referred to Acting Secretary of Labor Cynthia Metzler.

Remarks on National Cancer Institute Recommendations on Mammography and an Exchange With Reporters
March 27, 1997

The President. Secretary Shalala has just briefed me on the National Cancer Institute's new recommendations on mammography. These recommendations, based on the latest and best medical evidence, give clear, consistent guidance to women in our national fight against breast cancer. Breast cancer is the most commonly diagnosed cancer among women. It affects one in eight women in their lifetimes and has touched the families of nearly every American, including my own.

We may not yet have a cure for breast cancer, but we do know that early detection and early treatment are our most potent weapons against this dread disease and we know that mammography can save lives. That is why it's important to send a clear, consistent message to women and to their families about when to start getting mammograms and how often to repeat them.

After careful study of the science, the National Cancer Advisory Board has now concluded that women between the ages of 40 and 49 should get a mammography examination for breast cancer every 1 or 2 years, in consultation with their doctors. The National Cancer Institute has now accepted these recommendations. Now women in their forties will have clear guidance based on the best science, and action to match it.

Today I am taking action to bring Medicare, Medicaid, and the Federal employee health plans in line with the National Cancer Institute's recommendations. First, in the Medicare budget I am sending to Congress today I am making annual screening mammography exams, beginning at age 40, a covered expense without coinsurance or deductibles. Second, Secretary Shalala is sending a letter to State Medicaid directors urging them to also cover annual mammograms beginning at 40 and assuring them that the Federal Government will pay its matching share if they do so. And today I am directing the Office of Personnel Management to require all Federal health benefit plans to comply with the National Cancer Advisory Board's recommendations on mammogram screenings, beginning next year.

The Federal Government is doing its part to make sure women have both coverage and access to this potentially lifesaving test. I want to challenge private health insurance plans to do the same. They, too, should cover regular screening mammograms for women 40 and over.

Finally, we know there has been much discussion on this issue and a lot of confusion. That is why we are launching a major public education campaign to make sure every woman and every health care professional in America, that all of them are aware of these new recommendations. This is a major step forward in our fight against breast cancer.

In addition to Secretary Shalala, I want to thank National Cancer Advisory Board Chairperson Dr. Barbara Rimer and all the members of the Board, along with the NCI Director, Dr. Richard Klausner, for the fine job that they did in producing these recommendations.

I also want to thank the First Lady, who could not be with us here because of her visit to Africa. She has devoted countless hours to educating women about the importance of mammography, and this is a happy day for her. She has especially tried to educate older women to take advantage of the Medicare coverage of mammograms, because we know that too few of them still do. And that's the last point I would like to make. These guidelines and this coverage, it's all very good, but unless women are willing to actually take advantage of the coverage, we won't have the full benefit of the recommendations and the findings that have been made.

Now I'd like to turn the microphone over to Secretary Shalala to make a few comments.

[At this point, Health and Human Services Secretary Donna Shalala made brief remarks.]

Heaven's Gate Cult Mass Suicide

Q. Mr. President, do you have any comment on the mass suicide in California?

The President. Well, of course, all I know is what I read about it this morning and what I saw last night reported. But it's heartbreaking; it's sickening; it's shocking. I think it's important that we get as many facts as we can about this and try to determine what, in fact, motivated those people and what all of us can do to make sure that there aren't other people thinking in that same way out there in our country, that aren't so isolated that they can create a world for themselves that may justify that kind of thing. It's very troubling to me. But I don't think I know enough to make a definitive comment about it.

Democratic Party Finances

Q. Mr. President, switching gears on another subject, the Democratic Party emerged from this most recent election in the aftermath of all of these fundraising problems—it seems to be in pretty bad shape financially—enormous debt that they can't repay. What, if anything, can you do about this, and how much responsibility do you have to try to get the Democratic Party back into shape?

The President. Oh, a lot, and I have been doing a lot, and I will do more. We knew that we would have to spend—last year when it became obvious that our congressional candidates were going to be outspent massively, we did everything we could to raise a good deal of money at the end. But the committees and the Democratic Committee went into debt with money that they could legally borrow in the hope of trying to be competitive. They actually did a pretty good job. They were still outspent, I figure, in the last 10 days, 2 weeks, probably 4 or 5 to 1 in all of the contested races. But we knew that would happen, and we knew it would take some time to pay it back. But I'm not particularly concerned about it. I think we will pay it back. And it was, I thought, important.

Keep in mind, we were at the bottom of the barrel in November of '94, and in 1995 we did a good job, I think, of building our party back and showing what the clear differences were between the two parties. And the previous leadership of the party deserves a lot of credit. We got up to a million small donors, and they're coming back now. They're beginning to make their contributions, and that's very encouraging. So I think we'll get there. I'm not particularly concerned about it.

We made a deliberate decision to kind of downplay the Inaugural and not to try to tie too much of that to fundraising, so we're going to have to work harder this year. But I've been doing some work, as you know, and I will continue to do more.

Q. Do you think Governor Romer has second thoughts about some of the changes that previously—eliminating contributions from subsidiaries of foreign companies and also non-U.S. citizens—he seems to be having some second thoughts about some of those proposals you made over the past few months.

The President. Well, let me say, I still don't believe—I think, on balance, it's better policy to say that people who can't vote shouldn't contribute. In terms of the subsidiaries, the real problem there is the law says if the money is made in the United States, it can be given in the United States. The problem is, how do you ever know that? And so I think that he was trying to bend over backwards to get us off on the right foot.

But I'd be willing to talk to him about it. But the main thing is we're just going to have to get together and work hard and rally our troops and remind them of what we're trying to do here, how we're trying to balance the budget, what we're trying to do for education, what we're trying to do to move the country forward and get the efforts going. We've had several successful events this year. We just have to do more. And we knew—what you have to do after an election, when we saw all this third party money and all these other things coming down the pike, we wanted to give our Members of Congress a chance to be competitive, and so we undertook to do so. And I'm glad we did, but we're just going to have to work double hard now to pay the money back, and we'll do that. We'll pay our debts, and we'll make our budget this year.

Middle East Peace Process and China

Q. Have you received any updates from Ambassador Ross or the Vice President?

The President. Yes.

Q. And what have they been?

The President. Well, Ambassador Ross had a very good meeting with Chairman Arafat, and he's proceeding now on his trip. And I don't have anything else to tell you, but he was encouraged by the response of Chairman Arafat to the matters that we discussed here before he left.

I started the day this morning with physical therapy and a talk with the Vice President in China, which was also good therapy. [*Laughter*]

And he said to me that in every aspect, his trip had gone quite well and better than he had anticipated, and he was anxious to get back and give me a report on all the issues that we're concerned about. But I think the trip has been a real validation for our strategy of engagement with China, of taking our agreements, our disagreements, our matters of common interest, our matters of concern directly to them. And he is very pleased with the results so far, and I certainly am very pleased with the work he's done, with the speech he gave on human rights and with all the work that he's done in China so far. I'm encouraged about it. I think the trip has been well worth making.

FBI and Alleged Chinese Efforts To Influence the 1996 Election

Q. Have you seen that Janet Reno gave Louis Freeh a ringing endorsement this morning—every confidence in his leadership at the FBI?

The President. Well, as I said—of course, she works with him every day, and that's why I said yesterday what I did. I was troubled by the headline in the New York Times story, but I did not know the facts. And I think it's important for me not to assume that someone has done or failed to do something that's adverse to the national interest before I know it's true. And she's the one that has to make those calls. And as she said in her comments, the system that we have—the President appoints the Director of the FBI, but the FBI is a part of the Justice Department. It's a part of the justice system. And whenever you have dual responsibilities in the Government, you're going to have some time when you've got to make a close call.

And I still don't know—as I said, I just literally don't know—I could actually tell you whether I agreed or disagreed, if I knew what—if and what information had not been forthcoming to the National Security Council. I do believe that there should be a—that doubt should be resolved in favor of disclosure to the National Security Council of essential national security information. But the Attorney General has to resolve those things. And I trust her to do it. And so, what she said is fine by me.

Q. Is there a problem if the President of the United States—a lot of Americans simply don't understand—the President of the United States says, "I don't know that there's a problem because I haven't necessarily been given"——

The President. Well, I think there is. Yes, I think there is. If I knew that one existed, I would agree that there was a problem. But I don't know it. And I'm still not sure that there was. I just have to—I have to trust the Attorney General to make sure that the National Security Council gets the information that we need to make good national security judgments here. I think, for example, in the Khobar Towers incident, there is absolutely not a shred of evidence that there's anything that we have been denied. And so, if I knew that there was and I knew what it was and I thought there was a mistake, I'd be happy to say that there's an honest disagreement here, but I just don't know that there is one.

Ambassadorial Nominations

Q. Has your administration been hamstrung in terms of ambassadorial appointments, appointments at the State Department and so forth because of all of these investigations on the campaign?

The President. No, not at all. As a matter of fact, we've been working on getting ready for the next round of ambassadorial appointments. I approved a small number of them, oh, probably a couple of weeks ago so we could move in critical countries. But the others we're trying to do on a schedule which at least guarantees that all the Ambassadors now serving will do the traditional 3-year tour of duty. So we have some time on them. But we've worked very hard for the last month or so on that, and I don't see those two things as in conflict or a problem at all.

Thank you.

President's Health

Q. How do you feel today?

The President. I feel fine. Every day I'm getting a little more mobile, and I'm getting able to, you know, do a little more. I'll tell you one thing, I wouldn't wish this on anyone. But it's been a very enlightening experience, a very humbling experience. And the respect that I feel now for people who spend all day every day in a wheelchair or people who spend all day every day in braces and on crutches is enormous.

The dignity and the strength of character that it takes to kind of organize your life and carry it out if you're always subject to some sort of significant physical disability is enormous. These are things that we all sometimes see, but when you've felt just a little taste of it, when you realize what it means to be able to just navigate and do the basic things in life—just to dress yourself for the first time when you couldn't do it, for example—it just makes you understand that the rest of us in society who have been fortunate enough to have full use of our physical facilities owe an enormous amount of respect and sensitivity to people who don't.

It's just been a stunning experience for me. I mean, I will never again see a person who has to deal with a disability in the same light again. I mean, it's just—it's had a profound impact. It's nothing I didn't know before, but feeling it and knowing it are two different things.

Q. Thank you, Mr. President.

The President. Thank you.

Q. Like your doctor after you all the time?

The President. Yes. She just wants to make sure I don't blow it.

Q. I see her—we see her right here.

The President. There she is.

Q. She's watching.

The President. These crutches are quite good. This way you can walk by putting your bad leg down and keeping the weight here. Otherwise, you have to just do this and then kind of do that. But if you can walk, it's a lot easier; the chances of falling are less.

Q. They're better than the traditional crutches.

The President. Yes, much better.

NOTE: The President spoke at 12:17 p.m., in the Oval Office at the White House. In his remarks, he referred to Gov. Roy Romer of Colorado, general chair, Democratic National Committee; Ambassador Dennis B. Ross, Special Middle East Coordinator; and Capt. Connie Mariano, USN, the President's physician.

Remarks to the NCAA Football Champion University of Florida Gators
March 27, 1997

The President. Thank you very much. Please be seated. President and Mrs. Lombardi, Athletic Director Foley, Mayor Jennings, Congresswoman Thurman—I know what a happy day this is for you. Senator Breaux, we're glad to see you here. Senator Breaux thinks he represents anyplace that's perpetually warm. [*Laughter*] We're honored to have you here.

Let me say, when Coach Spurrier and Danny and I walked in I was hoping, when I hobbled in, that one of you might mistake me for a member of the team who just had a rough time in the bowl game. [*Laughter*] But I remembered that a few years ago Danny had a little knee injury, and if I come back from mine as well as he did from his, my future is secure, I think.

I am delighted to be here with you. I look forward to these occasions every year, but I especially want to congratulate you on a wonderful season and an astonishing championship game. The 32-point margin of victory, I'm sure all of you know, against the number one ranked team is the largest in bowl history and something that the University of Florida can always be very proud of.

I'd also note—it's somewhat difficult for me to note this, being from Arkansas, but every year I've been President, Florida has won the Southeastern Conference championship. [*Laughter*] I was impressed not only by the stars on the team—by Danny Wuerffel and Ike Hilliard, and by the fact that Terry Jackson joined his brother, Willy, in Sugar Bowl history by rushing for over 100 yards—I was impressed by the teamwork of this team. And I have followed college football very closely for nearly 40 years now, and I really believe that the University of Florida, in the last 5 or 6 years, has written a whole new chapter in college football, in much the way that Oklahoma did a few decades ago with the wishbone. You have changed football forever and for the better. It is more exciting than it has ever been before, and you do it better than anyone else.

I know that this national championship was a special triumph for Steve Spurrier because when he played for the Gators, he won the Heisman Trophy. He came back as a coach to have many successes, but there is no success like winning the national championship. And doing it for your alma mater after so many efforts and so many fine performances and, frankly, when it doesn't come so easily, when you have to keep fighting for it, even sometimes when you think it's not quite fair, must make it all the sweeter.

I've also been in a position of having to try to defeat someone who once beat me for something I cared a great deal about, and that makes it a little better, too. [*Laughter*] So again, let me say it's a great honor to have you in the White House. I know I'm too old to play for this team, but don't hold my injury against me.

Coach Spurrier, the floor is yours.

Thank you.

[*At this point, head coach Steve Spurrier and quarterback Danny Wuerffel made brief remarks and presented the President with a jersey.*]

Coach Spurrier. I don't know if you can wear that jogging or not.

The President. Yes, I can. Thank you. Move that out of here so we can take a good picture of this.

Thank you very much.

NOTE: The President spoke at 5:55 p.m. in the East Room at the White House. In his remarks, he referred to John V. Lombardi, president, University of Florida, and his wife, Cathryn; Jeremy Foley, Athletic Director, University of Florida; and Mayor Edward Jennings of Gainesville, FL.

Letter to Congressional Leaders Reporting on the Situation in Zaire
March 27, 1997

Dear Mr. Speaker: (Dear Mr. President:)

The Republic of Zaire has been embroiled in an internal conflict for several months. Rebels seeking to oust ailing President Mobutu Sese Seko have captured more than one-fifth of the country. While there is no evidence that Americans are being directly targeted, the potential for civil disorder and general unrest in Kinshasa may subject American citizens and property to a range of risks, including those from criminal acts and random violence.

On March 25, 1997, a standby evacuation force of U.S. military personnel from the U.S. European Command and the United States deployed to Congo and Gabon to provide enhanced security for the more than 300 American private citizens, government employees, and selected third country nationals in Kinshasa, should their evacuation become necessary. We do not anticipate that the more than 200 remaining American citizens outside Kinshasa will be at risk. These forces augment the noncombat-equipped enabling forces that deployed to Congo on March 21, 1997, to prepare for a possible evacuation operation.

The enabling and evacuation forces based in Brazzaville, Congo and Libreville, Gabon are prepared for a possible evacuation. These forces include a forward deployed Joint Task Force Headquarters, fixed-wing and rotary aircraft, airport control and support equipment, and medical and security personnel and equipment. In addition, USS *Nassau*, with a Marine Battalion Landing Team and a helicopter squadron reinforced with fixed-wing AV–8 Harrier aircraft embarked, is moving into the area.

Although U.S. forces are equipped for combat, this movement is being undertaken solely for the purpose of preparing to protect American citizens and property. United States forces will redeploy as soon as it is determined that an evacuation is not necessary or, if necessary, is completed.

I have taken this action pursuant to my constitutional authority to conduct U.S. foreign relations and as Commander in Chief and Chief Executive.

I am providing this report as part of my efforts to keep the Congress fully informed, consistent with the War Powers Resolution. I appreciate the support of the Congress in this action to prepare to protect American citizens in Zaire.

Sincerely,

WILLIAM J. CLINTON

NOTE: Identical letters were sent to Newt Gingrich, Speaker of the House of Representatives, and Strom Thurmond, President pro tempore of the Senate.

Statement on Protections for Human Subjects of Classified Research
March 28, 1997

When I accepted the Advisory Committee's report in October of 1995, I promised that it would not be left on the shelf to gather dust. I made a commitment that we would learn from the lessons the committee's report offered and use it as a roadmap to lead us to better choices in the future. We have actively worked to respond to the Advisory Committee's recommendations to make the record of these experiments open to the public, to improve ethics in human research today, and to right the wrongs of the past.

The report we are releasing today is an important milestone in our progress, but we are by no means at the end of our journey. Much work remains to be done. I am confident that all of us—the eminent committee that produced the original report, the Federal officials who worked so hard to support the committee's efforts, and most importantly, the citizens of this great country from whose experiences we have learned so much—can together help ensure a better world for our children.

NOTE: Secretary of Energy Federico Peña read the President's statement in a briefing announcing the report entitled "Building Public Trust: Actions To Respond to the Report of the Advisory Committee on Human Radiation Experiments." The related memorandum of March 27 is listed in Appendix D at the end of this volume.

Message on the Observance of Easter, 1997
March 28, 1997

Warm greetings to everyone celebrating Easter.

For almost two millennia, Christians around the world have celebrated this sacred and joyous season as a time of promises fulfilled. It is the promise that a long, harsh winter will dissolve into the warmth and beauty of spring. It is the promise that hearts can be changed and lives renewed by God's love and forgiveness. It is the promise that the sufferings of Good Friday will be transformed into the glorious triumph of Easter morning.

Now, as we swiftly approach the dawn of a new millennium, let us strive together to fulfill our own promise, both as individuals and as a nation. By strengthening our families and communities, bringing hope and help to those in need, and creating a climate of peace and reconciliation where hatred and violence and prejudice have no place, we can each play a vital role in carrying out God's loving plan for humanity. As Saint John's Gospel so eloquently reminds us, ". . . God sent not his Son into the world to condemn the world; but that the world through him might be saved."

As you gather with family and friends to share the joys of this holy season, Hillary and I extend best wishes to all for a wonderful Easter.

BILL CLINTON

Letter to Congressional Leaders Reporting on Payments to Cuba
March 28, 1997

Dear Mr. Speaker: (Dear Mr. President:)

This report is submitted pursuant to 1705(e)(6) of the Cuban Democracy Act of 1992, 22 U.S.C. 6004(e)(6) (the "CDA"), as amended by section 102(g) of the Cuban Liberty and Democratic Solidarity (LIBERTAD) Act of 1996, Public law 104–114 (March 12, 1996), 110 Stat. 785, 22 U.S.C. 6021–91 (the "LIBERTAD Act"), which requires that I report to the Congress on a semiannual basis detailing payments made to Cuba by any United States person as a result of the provision of telecommunications services authorized by this subsection.

The CDA, which provides that telecommunications services are permitted between the United States and Cuba, specifically authorizes the President to provide for the issuance of licenses for payments due to Cuba as a result of the provision of telecommunications services. The CDA states that licenses may provide for full or partial settlement of telecommunications services with Cuba, but does not require any withdrawal from a blocked account. Following enactment of the CDA on October 23, 1992, a number of U.S. telecommunications companies successfully negotiated agreements to provide telecommunications services between the United States and Cuba consistent with policy guidelines developed by the Department of State and the Federal Communications Commission.

Subsequent to enactment of the CDA, the Department of the Treasury's Office of Foreign Assets Control (OFAC) amended the Cuban Assets Control Regulations, 31 C.F.R. Part 515 (the "CACR"), to provide for specific licensing on a case-by-case basis for certain transactions incident to the receipt or transmission of telecommunications between the United States and Cuba, 31 C.F.R. 515.542(c), including settlement of charges under traffic agreements.

The OFAC has issued eight licenses authorizing transactions incident to the receipt or transmission of telecommunications between the United States and Cuba since the enactment of the CDA. None of these licenses permits payments to the Government of Cuba from a blocked account. For the period June 30, 1996, through December 31, 1996, OFAC-licensed U.S. carriers reported payments to the Government of Cuba in settlement of charges under telecommunications traffic agreements as follows:

AT&T Corporation (formally, American Telephone and Telegraph Company)	$19,162,032
AT&T de Puerto Rico	227,709
Global One (formerly Sprint Incorporated)	2,589,706
IDB WorldCom Services, Inc. (formerly, IDB Communications, Inc.)	561,553
MCI International, Inc. (formerly, MCI Communications Corporation)	5,354,423
Telefonica Larga Distancia de Puerto Rico, Inc.	104,498
WilTel, Inc. (formerly, WilTel Underseas Cable, Inc.)	2,913,610
WorldCom, Inc. (formerly, LDDS Communications, Inc.)	1,687,896
Total	32,601,427

I shall continue to report semiannually on telecommunications payments to the Government of Cuba from United States persons.

Sincerely,

WILLIAM J. CLINTON

NOTE: Identical letters were sent to Newt Gingrich, Speaker of the House of Representatives, and Albert Gore, Jr., President of the Senate.

The President's Radio Address
March 29, 1997

Good morning. Spring is a season of renewal, not just of the world around us but of the ideals inside us, those that bind us together as a people. Millions of families will come together to celebrate Easter this weekend and Passover in the coming weeks, to reaffirm their faith in God and their commitment to our sacred values.

And in this season of renewal, I ask all Americans to reaffirm their commitment to this central ideal, that we are many people but one nation, bound together by shared values rooted in the essential dignity and meaning of every American's life and liberty. That is the root of the American idea of a community of equal, free, responsible citizens and the American dream to build the best possible future for our children.

The divide of race has been America's constant curse in pursuit of our ideals. The struggle to overcome it has been a defining part of our history. Racial and ethnic differences continue to divide and bedevil millions around the world. And as we become an ever more pluralistic society with people from every racial and ethnic group calling America home, our own future depends upon laying down the bitter fruits of hatred and lifting up the rich texture of our diversity and our common humanity.

We're not there yet, as we often see in the tragic stories in the news. Just last week in Chicago, a 13-year-old boy, riding his bike home from a basketball game, was brutally attacked and almost beaten to death, apparently for no other reason but the color of his skin. Lenard Clark is black; the young men accused of attacking him are white. This weekend, I hope all Americans join Hillary and me in a prayer for Lenard and his family.

There is never an excuse for violence against innocent citizens. But this kind of savage, senseless assault, driven by nothing but hate, strikes at the very heart of America's ideals and threatens the promise of our future, no matter which racial or ethnic identity, the attackers' or the victim's. We must stand together as a nation against all crimes of hate and say they are wrong. We must condemn hate crimes whenever they happen. We must commit ourselves to prevent them from happening again. And we must

sow the seeds of harmony and respect among our people.

And let's be honest with ourselves: racism in America is not confined to acts of physical violence. Every day, African-Americans and other minorities are forced to endure quiet acts of racism, bigoted remarks, housing and job discrimination. Even many people who think they are not being racist still hold to negative stereotypes and sometimes act on them. These acts may not harm the body, but when a mother and her child go to the grocery store and are followed around by a suspicious clerk, it does violence to their souls. We must stand against such quiet hatred just as surely as we condemn acts of physical violence, like those against Lenard Clark.

At the same time, black Americans must not look at the faces of Lenard Clark's attackers and see the face of white America. The acts of a few people must never become an excuse for blanket condemnation, for bigotry begins with stereotyping—stereotyping blacks and whites, Jews and Arabs, Hispanics and Native Americans, Asians, immigrants in general. It is all too common today, but it is still wrong.

In Chicago, we see leaders of different races and political philosophies coming together to decry the crime against Lenard Clark. That is good, and it is reason for hope.

The holidays of this season teach us that hope can spring forth from the darkest of times. Those of us who are Christians celebrate a risen God who died a painful, very human death to redeem the souls of all humanity without regard to race or station.

So as families come together to celebrate Easter and Passover, as parents reunite with their children, their brothers and sisters, and friends with each other, let us all take time to search our souls. Let us find the strength to reach across the lines that divide us on the surface and touch the common spirit that resides in every human heart.

And let us also remember there are some Americans who feel isolated from all of the rest of us in other ways, sometimes with truly tragic consequences, like the events just outside San

Diego which have so stunned us all this week. Our prayers are with their families as well.

In this season of reflection, we must find kinship in our common humanity. In this season of renewal, we must renew our pledge to make America one Nation under God. In this season of redemption, we must all rise up above our differences to walk forward together on common ground, toward common dreams.

Thanks for listening.

NOTE: The address was recorded at 11:50 a.m. on March 28 in the Roosevelt Room at the White House for broadcast at 10:06 a.m. on March 29. In his address, the President referred to the mass suicide of Heaven's Gate cult members discovered on March 26.

Remarks at the White House Easter Egg Roll
March 31, 1997

Good morning. Let me say, first of all, it's getting warmer. [*Laughter*] And I want to thank all the sponsors who make this possible this year and the more than 500 volunteers. A lot of them worked here all weekend. I went down and visited with them. Let's give them all a big hand. [*Applause*] Thank you very much.

This is the 119th year we've had the White House Easter egg roll, and every year it gets a little better, I think, and a little different. We've worked hard to make this a good time not only for children but for their parents and family members, so that we could have fun together and we could learn together.

There is a Learn Big Things tent, which I hope you'll all visit. For many of the young people, it will give them a first chance to log on to the Internet or even to visit our White House home page. There is a Learning Adventures tent where children can learn to use CD–ROM's and learn about things like nutrition. Then there is the opportunity to do Easter egg painting and to listen to storytelling.

And I want to thank all the people who have been willing to be part of this, especially one of our special guests today who is down here with us along with two of her four children, "Dr. Quinn, Medicine Woman," Jane Seymour. Thank you, Jane, for coming. We're glad to have you here.

And now, are they ready over there at the Easter egg roll? Are you all ready? Now, you can't start until I blow the whistle. On your mark—are you ready? Come on, line up. Shape up here. One of us needs to be able to run. [*Laughter*] On your mark, get set, go.

[*At this point, the President blew the whistle to start the egg roll.*]

Thank you, and God bless you. Happy Easter.

NOTE: The President spoke at 11:20 a.m. from the South Portico Balcony at the White House. In his remarks, he referred to actress Jane Seymour.

Remarks on Action To Protect Pension Programs
March 31, 1997

Thank you very much, Marian Jones, for that fine introduction. Acting Secretary Metzler, Secretary Daley, thank you for your good work at the Pension Benefit Guaranty Corporation.

I'd like to welcome Congressman Pomeroy and former Congressman Jake Pickle, from Texas, who had so much to do with the success

of our administration's endeavors in this area; AFL–CIO President John Sweeney; the Acting Director of the Pension Benefit Guaranty Corporation, John Seal; Olena Berg, from the Department of Labor. And I'd also like to thank all the other members of the Department of Labor who are here today for the work that you have done in this and in so many other areas. And I'd like to acknowledge that we have two Department of Labor alumni, at least two, at least—maybe three—working in the White House; Ann Lewis and Maria Echaveste have just come there, and we're thankful for that.

Since we're having the annual Easter egg roll at the White House today, I didn't know if anyone would be here when I showed up—[*laughter*]—but I do appreciate your coming.

As Cynthia Metzler has said, the Department of Labor has done a remarkable job in the last 4 years in advocating for the interests of working people and their families and their future. I am confident that Secretary-designate Alexis Herman and her future Deputy, Kitty Higgins, both of whom have strong roots at the Department of Labor, will build on that record when they're confirmed.

We know that one of our biggest challenges moving into the 21st century is to help people to build strong work lives and strong family lives and to do that in a time when the labor force is ever more dynamic. One of the critical elements of the success of that endeavor must be to make sure that the pension dollars Americans work so hard to build throughout their working lives are there when they need them.

First of all, we have to have a strong economy. With 4 years of growth, we have done that. A strategy of investing in our people, reducing the deficit, and expanding trade is working. Our country has produced more than 11.7 million new jobs. Unemployment is low. Wages are beginning to rise. And you see it in so many other ways. That's having a helpful impact on our efforts to reduce the welfare rolls, down by over a 2.25 million, the largest drop in American history. It's very helpful in the efforts that law enforcement community leaders have undertaken to reduce crime, which has been going down several years in a row now.

There is a new spirit of community and possibility in this country, but it all begins with giving people the ability to succeed at home as parents and in the workplace. That's why things like the family and medical leave law, the minimum wage law, the passage of the Kennedy-Kassebaum health reform bill were so important and why we have to do more of that.

Last year, especially, I am proud of the work we did to raise the minimum wage and to put in place new measures to expand pension coverage, to increase pension portability, to protect workers' pensions. We made it easier for small businesses to offer pension plans by creating a new small business 401(k) plan. We made it possible for more Americans to keep their pensions when they change jobs without having to wait before they can start saving at their new jobs.

And you and I know that when it comes to securing the benefits of pensions, no organization has done more than the Pension Benefit Guaranty Corporation, the agency that guarantees traditional pension plans.

Just before I came here today, I read an article which appeared in one of our major newspapers in December of 1992, chronicling the dire straits of the Pension Benefit Guaranty Corporation, talking about what a great financial crisis it had. When I took office, it was facing a $3 billion deficit. Millions of Americans' pensions were in jeopardy. Literally millions and millions of Americans' pensions were in jeopardy.

Thanks to the actions of the last 4 years, the Corporation has made a remarkable recovery. The passage of the Retirement Protection Act of 1994, legislation we all worked so hard for, helped to make retirement more secure, literally for 40 million Americans. Today I am pleased to announce that the Pension Benefit Guaranty Corporation has gone for the first time in its 22-year history from being in the red to being in the black. It has the first surplus ever—that's what this chart means—last year. So you can see from 1976 to the dropping point in '92 and '93—look what's been done in just 4 short years. To every single one of you who's been involved in that, you should be very, very proud.

Let me say, when I look at that chart it is a bittersweet experience for me, because a great deal of the credit for turning the Pension Benefit Guaranty Corporation around goes to my friend, the late Marty Slate. Hillary and I first met him—well, she knew him before, but I first met him when we were in Yale law school together. He spent almost his whole life working to make sure that our laws were fair and applied justly. We saw him put that commitment on the line time after time, as a freedom rider in the South, as a visionary creating a scholarship program for minority lawyers at the IRS, as a dear friend in so many ways. Marty Slate was the quintessential public servant. I'm proud that I appointed him to direct the Pension Benefit Guaranty Corporation in its hour of crisis and need. It's one of the best decisions that I have made as President. Thanks to him, millions of workers like Marian here can sleep better at night knowing their pensions are safe and secure. I really wanted to have a chance to say that one more time in public, and I'd like to thank Marty's wife, Cookie, for being here today. Thank you, and God bless you.

We have made great strides in protecting the pensions of a growing number of workers who are now saving for their own retirement in 401(k) plans. While the vast majority of those plans are safe, we've stepped up our enforcement against employers who spend or borrow their employees' pension contributions. In just 2 years, the Pension and Welfare Benefits Administration 401(k) enforcement project has recovered over $20 million for more than 40,000 employees.

New rules we've put in place for faster deposit of 401(k) contributions will result in increased earnings—listen to this—increased earnings just by faster deposit, averaging $70 million a year over the next 10 years to stabilize the pension plans and benefit the workers who are saving.

But we have to do more. We're going back to Congress this year with a proposal that didn't quite make it into law last year, reforms that will ensure that our pensions are audited thoroughly. The audit reform proposal will do three things. First, it will address the fact that, today, more than $950 billion in pension plans assets are not meaningfully audited, leaving more than 22 million workers in the dark about the health of their pensions. Our proposal closes the loophole that permits these cursory audits. Second, it will require prompt reporting if criminal acts

are discovered during an audit. And third, it will assure that only qualified professionals conduct audits of ERISA plans. I urge Congress to pass the audit reform this year so that our workers can have the peace of mind they deserve.

Finally, we are putting more power for protecting pensions in the hands of employees themselves. Today the Labor Department is activating a toll-free pension hotline that workers can call to get publications about their rights and to help them identify the early warning signs of pension problems. The toll-free number is 1–800–998–7542. I love to do this. [*Laughter*] That's 1–800—[*laughter*]—998–7542.

All the steps we announced today—getting the Pension Benefit Guaranty Corporation in the black, fighting for audit reform, and giving employees better tools to protect their pensions— are part of our overall commitment to achieving basic retirement security for America's working families. Our people deserve to know that if they work hard throughout their lives, the money they work for and that they saved is not being squandered or left unprotected.

Thomas Jefferson once said, "In matters of style, swim with the current. In matters of principle, stand like a rock." Today we affirm our common commitment to stand like a rock for our working families and their right to a secure retirement they have saved for, paid for, and earned.

Thank you all very much.

NOTE: The President spoke at 1:54 p.m. in Room 450 of the Old Executive Office Building. In his remarks, he referred to Marian Jones, employee, Anchor Glass Container Co., Salem, NJ, and glass workers union local president; and Acting Secretary of Labor Cynthia Metzler.

Statement on the Nomination of General Wesley K. Clark To Be Supreme Allied Commander, Europe
March 31, 1997

I am pleased to announce that I have nominated General Wesley K. Clark, United States Army, to succeed General George A. Joulwan as Supreme Allied Commander, Europe. This nomination is subject to the approval of the

North Atlantic Council. I also intend to send forward to Congress General Clark's nomination to serve as Commander in Chief, United States European Command.

General Clark has had a long and distinguished career spanning three decades, with significant policy and diplomatic experience as well as impeccable credentials as a military commander. He has vast experience in armored and mechanized forces, including a combat tour in Vietnam, service in two armored units in Germany, and command of the 1st Cavalry Division. This experience is enhanced by his tours at the Army's National Training Center, and the Army Training and Doctrine Command, all of which focused on training and preparing the Army for the future. Additionally, while assigned to the Joint Staff as the Director for Strategic Plans and Policy, he served as the senior military member of the U.S. negotiating team that crafted the 1995 Dayton peace accords, which ended the fighting in Bosnia. In these postings, as well as in his current role as Commander in Chief of the U.S. Southern Command, Panama, he has demonstrated both the military expertise and political acumen needed to fill one of our most important security postings.

General Clark will assume the post of Supreme Allied Commander, Europe at a time when NATO is demonstrating its important role in European security by helping bring security and stability to the people of Bosnia, as well as during a time of profound adaptation within the alliance as NATO contributes to building a secure and undivided Europe. NATO's ongoing adaptation includes further streamlining of the NATO military command structure, the establishment of a European security and defense identity (ESDI) within the alliance, the integration of new NATO members and, we expect, the development of a strong NATO-Russian partnership. I look forward to General Clark's continuing the work of General Joulwan as SACEUR takes on the challenge of guiding NATO military forces through this important period of transition and the completion of the work of NATO's Stabilization Force (SFOR) in Bosnia. I have the utmost trust and confidence in his ability to do so.

Remarks Prior to Discussions With King Hussein I of Jordan and an Exchange With Reporters
April 1, 1997

President Clinton. Let me say, it's always an honor to have His Majesty, King Hussein, back in the White House. I believe this is our 15th meeting since I became President. I want to have the chance to thank him for his continuing devotion to peace, the particularly courageous trip he recently took to Israel. And I want to discuss with him what our next steps are.

I think it's clear that we would not have gotten the agreement in Hebron had it not been for his leadership, and his leadership is essential as we go forward. So this is a difficult time for the peace process, and we have a lot to talk about. We also have a lot to talk about in terms of the relationships between the United States and Jordan, and I'm looking forward to that.

Middle East Peace Process

Q. Mr. President, I think you would agree that——

Q. Mr. President——

President Clinton. One at a time, one at a time.

Q. I think that you would agree that the establishment of the—or attempt to establish a settlement in East Jerusalem, with soldiers and bulldozers, is the real cause of violence, in contradiction to the Oslo agreements. So what are you going to do to restore that faith, that confidence in the agreements?

President Clinton. Well, that's what we're going to discuss here today, and we'll have a——

Q. I mean, this is not—I think you'd agree it wasn't——

President Clinton. As you know, I just sent Dennis Ross out to the region. We've just—we've had two meetings, one yesterday—an extended meeting yesterday and an extended meeting this morning about it. What I think we have to do is to restore the environment of security and of confidence so we can go forward with the negotiating process. And we've got some ideas about it, but I want to talk to the King about it first.

And you may be sure we're working on it. It's an urgent thing for me and for the whole peace process.

Q. Mr. President, there was an incident in Gaza today, and the U.S. line—I don't mean that in an unfavorable way—last week was that you needed a clear signal from Yasser Arafat that he disapproves of violence, terrorism as an instrument. Did you get that clear signal? Because there has been no public statement.

President Clinton. He's made several moves in the last few days which are encouraging in that regard. But let me say that, unambiguously, a precondition of going forward is a commitment to zero tolerance for terrorism, for making the best effort.

All the parties have acknowledged that no one can promise that there will never be a violent incident, that you could control every last thing that every person does. But there has to be an attitude of zero tolerance, a determination to do all that can reasonably be done to maintain the peace so that then negotiated progress can be made. And that's what the United States expects, and that's what we will continue to press for.

Q. Do you think the Palestinians have no right to defend their land?

President Clinton. I think that the subjects that are clearly identified as to be negotiated in the final status should be negotiated in that way. And I've made that clear whether any side likes it or not. But I don't believe there is an excuse for terrorism in any case. I believe terrorism is always wrong.

Q. Can we ask the King a question? Sir, Your Majesty, what more do you think the United States can do to try to get the peace process back on track?

King Hussein. I think the United States has taken the lead over many years, and I've had the privilege of working with the President for the establishment of peace, not only between Jordan and Israel but a comprehensive peace in the region. And I hope to have the chance to discuss with the President what further steps all of us can take to achieve our goal.

Q. Would you like to see the Secretary of State go to the region? Do you think that would help at this point?

King Hussein. I suppose at some point in the future at an appropriate moment that, sure,

the Secretary of State could probably visit the area, and she'd be most welcome.

Q. [*Inaudible*]—to support Israel as it seeks peace? Is it time to ask Israel to do certain gestures or to support them or to press them to make issues?

Q. Are you sending Albright to the Middle East?

President Clinton. At the right time. I certainly want her to go, but I want it to be part of a clear strategy designed to produce progress. And I will make the decision in consultation with—obviously with Secretary Albright and my entire team but also with King Hussein and our other friends in the region. We want it to—I couldn't say it better than His Majesty did, that we want it to be a trip that will actually be part of a strategy designed to move the process forward.

Thank you.

[*At this point, one group of reporters left the room, and another group entered.*]

Q. The Jordanian press would like to share with you our wishes for a speedy recovery.

President Clinton. Oh, thank you so much. Well, it's just an unfortunate accident, but I'm making good progress.

Let me make a statement first, if I might. I believe this is my 15th visit with His Majesty, King Hussein, and I welcome him back to the White House. I am eager to have this opportunity to discuss the peace process, as well as issues relating to our bilateral relations. And I cannot express how much I continue to admire the role he has played and the courage he has displayed consistently, in very personal terms, including after the unfortunate incident recently along the border and his trip to Israel.

I do not believe we can have a comprehensive peace in the Middle East without the powerful influence of King Hussein. The United States believes that we have more to do now. We've been talking about some other steps we could take, and that's what I want to visit with the King about. So I'm looking forward to it.

Q. Mr. President, you just mentioned the role that His Majesty has played, and he has invested all of his personal credibility and prestige to bring the parties together and rescue the peace process. But recently, the U.S. veto of two U.N. resolutions on settlement was seen by many Arab countries as a departure from longstanding policy. What are you, Mr. President, willing to do to change that image and to help His Majesty put the peace process back on track without seeing any more of the violence we've seen in the past few weeks?

President Clinton. Well, first of all, let me say that the vetoes did not evidence support in the United States for the decision for the building to go forward at Har Homa. And I made that clear at the time. We were very clear about our position on that.

We vetoed the resolutions for two reasons. One is, we don't think that they're very helpful to the peace process. And second is, there were other—there was language in both resolutions which we believe prejudiced the final status negotiations against the Israelis in the same way that we favor—we felt that some of the actions prejudiced final status negotiations in their favor. We don't want to do either one.

What we want to do is to see these final status issues, as envisioned by the Oslo agreement, actually and honestly negotiated without prejudice. I think that is the clear thing that I want to drive home here.

And I want to discuss with His Majesty what are the next steps we can do. How can we create a sense of both security and confidence in the Middle East, that is, that the Israelis will believe there is a commitment on the part of the Palestinians to security and the Palestinians will have confidence that the Israelis will not attempt to prejudge the issues that should be negotiated in good faith between them? And we have some ideas. We'll be discussing them. And perhaps together we can get this peace process back on track. We'll do our best.

Q. Mr. President, how do you envisage—*[inaudible]*—cooperation and support Jordan in your second term, please?

President Clinton. Well, I'd like to do more. I think that Jordan has done as much to keep the Middle East peace process alive and moving forward as any nation, without much—frankly, without much assistance from the outside for doing it. And I believe that we should do more, and that's another thing I want to discuss with His Majesty, what other steps we can take and how we might go about getting that done. But I think that's something that ought to be a part of our private discussions until I have more to say on it.

Iraq

Q. Mr. President, is the Iraqi situation going to be one of the issues discussed with His Majesty? And what can be done to alleviate the Iraqi suffering, of the Iraqi people?

President Clinton. Well, the reason we supported the U.N. Resolution 986 is so that the oil could be sold to alleviate the suffering of the Iraqi people. So Saddam Hussein can use that money now to alleviate that suffering, and we certainly hope that he will. That's why we supported the United Nations resolution all along. So I think that's the first thing that needs to be said.

However, from my point of view, we still see no evidence that he has changed his fundamental attitude toward his neighbors or his fundamental way of operating. And so I still believe that our position is right on that. But we supported 986 in the hope that the suffering of the Iraqi people, and especially the children, could be alleviated by that income coming in for that purpose.

Q. Your Majesty, how could——

President Clinton. Should the King answer one question? You want to ask him one question? One question, one question; go ahead.

Middle East Peace Process

Q. Your Majesty, how could Jordan and the United States of America work together to advance the peace process and build confidence again between the Arab partners and Israel?

King Hussein. I believe that we are working together. We have worked together as partners and friends totally committed to the cause of peace, and I certainly hope this will be another opportunity for me to speak with the President and our friends here and to discuss what needs to be done beyond this point.

Q. President Mubarak said this morning that the peace process reached its low point—that the peace process reached its low point in 20 years, is what President Mubarak said this morning.

King Hussein. Well, we are certainly passing through a difficult stage, but I wouldn't like to say that all the ground we have covered right now should be considered as nothing. I think we have covered a long way, and certainly conditions today are not what they were 20 years ago.

NOTE: The President spoke at 11:55 a.m. in the Oval Office at the White House. In his remarks, he referred to Ambassador Dennis B. Ross, Special Middle East Coordinator; Chairman Yasser Arafat of the Palestinian Authority; and President Saddam Hussein of Iraq. A reporter referred to President Hosni Mubarak of Egypt.

Remarks on the Advertising of Distilled Liquor and an Exchange With Reporters
April 1, 1997

The President. Thank you very much.

The Vice President and I have worked very hard for the last 4 years to help parents protect the health and the safety of their children. Our parents face enormous pressures today, greater than ever before, and they need our help as they try to guard their children from harmful influences.

That's why we fought to impose appropriate regulation on the sale and distribution of cigarettes and smokeless tobacco and on the advertising of these products in a way that appeals to young people, why we're working to make our schools and children safe and drug-free, to combat gangs and youth violence.

It's a fact that popular culture is not always popular with parents, because it's not always good for their children. That was the thinking behind the V-chip and the television rating systems, which together will help parents to better control which programs their children watch. You need only to turn on the television for an evening to know there are some things that children should not be watching.

We're here today because parents now face a new challenge in protecting their children, the advertising of liquor on television. For half a century, for as long as television has been around, this has not been an issue. The distilled spirit industry voluntarily did not advertise on television. The reason was simple: It was the responsible thing to do. Liquor has no business with kids, and kids should have no business with liquor. Liquor ads on television would provide a message of encouragement to drink that young people simply don't need. Nothing good can come of it.

Today our message to the liquor industry is simple: For 50 years you have kept the ban; it is the responsible thing to do. For the sake of our parents and our young people, please continue to keep that ban.

I want to thank the television networks and the many television stations all across America which have shunned these new liquor ads. They have acted responsibly. I urge them to remain steadfast. I also want to thank Reed Hundt, the Chairman of our Federal Communications Commission. He has spoken out strongly and plainly to broadcasters to keep the voluntary ban on TV advertising.

I agree with Chairman Hundt that the FCC has an obligation to consider any and all actions that would protect the public interest in the use of the public airwaves. So today I urge the FCC to take the next step. I want the Commission to explore the effects on children of the hard liquor industry's decision to advertise on television. And I want the FCC to determine what action is appropriate in response to that decision.

Let me say directly again to the makers of distilled spirits: It should not require a Federal action to encourage you to continue to act responsibly. I have asked that liquor ads be kept off the air for the same reasons you yourself have kept them off the air for 50 long years. We must do nothing—nothing—that would risk encouraging more of our young people to drink hard liquor. That is simply common sense. Alcohol is a drug most abused by adolescents and teenagers. Studies show a strong connection between underage drinking and youth crime, including murder and rape. Year after year, underage drinking causes thousands of deadly car crashes.

As a nation, we've worked to bring down those numbers by increasing the drinking age to 21 and passing and enforcing zero-tolerance legislation for underage drinking and driving.

We've taken that further. I've asked the Transportation Secretary, Rodney Slater and our drug czar, General McCaffrey, to develop an initiative to further reduce drug use and drunk driving by young people.

All these actions are aimed at helping parents to protect their children better and to help young people deal better with the temptation of bad influences. Now I think we should move urgently to save parents, young people, and our Nation from the unavoidable bad consequences of liquor advertising on television. I urge the manufacturers again to rethink their decision to break from their tradition of being responsible on this front. If they remain responsible, it will be easier for our young people to do so, and parents will have one less thing to worry about.

Barring that, we will work to find ways to respond to the decision by the distilled spirits industry. We will do what we must do to support our parents, to help them do their jobs. We dare not do anything less.

Thank you.

Q. Mr. President, the industry is saying, why not beer and wine, also?

The President. Well, for one thing, let's just focus on where we are now. The FCC is going to look at this whole issue, if they respond positively to my suggestion. But at a minimum, there should be no backsliding. Look at the evidence. If the evidence is as I suspect it will be, that a great deal of problem is caused by hard liquor ingestion already among young people and that advertising would cause it to be worse, then I think the FCC has grounds to act. But I think we ought to start with the principle of no backsliding. Let's don't make it worse.

Q. Sir, the industry, in a sense, considers this a solution in search of a problem, because they have done so very little advertising on television at this point. How would you respond to that?

The President. That's right, they have. And that's what we're trying to do; we're trying to nip it in the bud. We're trying to make it a dog that does not bark, if you will. It's not a solution in search of a problem; there was no problem before the announced intention to abandon the 50-year ban. And what we're trying to do is to nip it in the bud, hopefully and most importantly, by persuading them to stay with their policy.

This is an area where—you know, the liquor industry has really been remarkably responsible

for five long decades when it would have been easy for financial reasons for them to try to take another course. And I understand the financial pressures they're under, but I hope that they will agree to go back and embrace their original position. If they don't, I think it's only responsible for the Federal Communications Commission to explore what the likely impact of this is and if it is appropriate for the FCC to take action. That's what I've asked them to do in my letter today.

Q. Mr. President, both the liquor industry and the advertising community say that you are wrong, that they are opposed to this. Don't you expect a major fight from them?

The President. Sure. I mean, I guess I do expect a major fight if they've changed their position. And I would expect them to take the opposite position, but that's why we have—that's why we have public debate, and that's also why we have institutions like the FCC to try to determine what the public interest is here.

Q. Mr. President, how was your meeting with King Hussein?

The President. One at a time.

Q. Alcohol is alcohol. If it sends a bad message to put ads on television that kids will see urging them to drink Seagrams, why wouldn't it send just as bad a message—the ads that they're seeing to urge them to drink Coors Lite or——

The President. Well, again I will say, first of all, let's—there's something to be said for not making matters worse. And most of us, every day, make decisions in an imperfect environment in which we make responsible decisions. This is one thing adults have to do for their children all the time, in which you say, "Well, I'm not going to make a perfect decision here, but at least we're not going to make things worse." And that's the position we have taken.

I think the liquor industry itself once thought that there was a distinction to be drawn if, for no other reason than alcohol content, between beer and wine and hard liquor, which is why they observed this distinction for 50 years. They thought there was a distinction for 50 years; otherwise, they would not have observed it. That was their opinion for 50 years, and I think they were right. And so I would say, the FCC— if there is no difference, if there are problems— the FCC can evaluate whatever evidence comes in, and the liquor industry would be free to present that information to the FCC.

But I believe there is a distinction, and I think there is a very powerful argument for doing no harm. Why make things worse? Why backslide?

Meeting With King Hussein of Jordan

Q. How was your meeting with King Hussein? What was his response to your ideas on ways of reviving the Middle East peace process? And having met with him, are you in a position to now give us more detail on what those ideas are?

The President. The meeting was good. He responded well to the things that I suggested; I responded well to the things that he suggested. And no, I'm not in a position to be more specific, because—let me just say—all of you know this—this is a very difficult time in this process. We have got to reestablish the sense of—on the part of the Israelis that the Palestinian Authority has committed to security. We have to reestablish on the part of the Palestinians that the Israelis are committed to continuing to build confidence by doing concrete things as contemplated by the Oslo agreement.

This is not an easy time. The more I say about it specifically, the more difficult it will be for me to succeed over the long run. I can tell you this: The United States is prepared to take significant efforts—I am prepared personally to do anything I can to get this process back on track and to move it forward. But I think the less I say about it, the more likely I am to have some success in doing that, particularly in the next 2 to 3 weeks when we have got to try to keep the lid on things over there.

As you know, we had some other incidents this morning. We've just got to work at it. It is not going to be easy, but I am encouraged by what I would have to call creative thinking on the part of all the parties involved, and I would include the Israelis and the Palestinians in that right now.

Prime Minister Binyamin Netanyahu of Israel

Q. [*Inaudible*]—Netanyahu when he is here this weekend?

The President. Yes, he—I understand he's coming, and I certainly hope to see him. I expect to see him. If he is able to keep his travel plans and come on over for the AIPAC meeting, then I will certainly clear some time to see him. I think it's important for us to talk, and I'm glad he's coming.

NOTE: The President spoke at 1:24 p.m. in the Roosevelt Room at the White House.

Letter to the Chairman of the Federal Communications Commission on the Advertising of Distilled Liquor
April 1, 1997

Dear Chairman Hundt:

I write to ask your assistance in addressing a new and emerging challenge to parents struggling to raise safe, healthy children: the decision by manufacturers of hard liquor to advertise on television.

For half a century, these companies voluntarily refrained from such advertising. They understood that advertising over the uniquely powerful and pervasive medium of broadcasting could reach children inappropriately, encouraging them to drink before it is even legal for them to do so. Until now, these companies have shown appropriate restraint. For as long as there has been television, they have known that a voluntary ban was right and they lived by it.

Now, some companies have broken ranks and started placing hard liquor ads on TV. I was greatly disappointed by their decision. I have previously expressed my dismay at this action and called on the industry to urge all its members to return to their long-standing policy and stand by the ban. I am gratified to learn that, according to one survey, the vast majority of television stations are declining to air these advertisements. I applaud that stand.

I firmly believe that we have a national obligation to act strongly to protect our children from threats to their health and safety. That's why I have fought so strongly to impose appropriate regulations on the sale and distribution of cigarettes and smokeless tobacco and tobacco advertising that appeals to adolescents, to ensure that our schools and children are safe and drug-free, and to combat gangs and violence afflicting our youth.

I applaud your public remarks calling on the industry and broadcasters to reactivate the voluntary ban. I also commend your comments that the Federal Communications Commission has an obligation to consider any and all actions that would protect the public interest in the use of the public airwaves.

I urge the Commission to take all appropriate actions to explore what effects might ensue in light of the decision by manufacturers of hard liquor to abandon their long-standing voluntary ban on television advertising, specifically the impact on underage drinking.

We have made tremendous progress in recent years reducing the incidence of deaths due to drunk driving among our youth. We have taken

important steps including the increase in the 1980s in the drinking age to 21 and the passage of zero tolerance legislation for underage drinking and driving. But there is more to be done. Too many of our young people are dying in car crashes, and too many young people are starting to drink at an early age, leading to alcohol and other substance abuse problems.

I would appreciate your help and the help of the Commission in exploring the possible actions you could take to support our parents and children in response to the manufacturers' decision to break with the long and honorable tradition of not advertising on the broadcast medium.

Sincerely,

WILLIAM J. CLINTON

NOTE: This letter was sent to Reed E. Hundt, Chairman of the Federal Communications Commission. An original was not available for verification of the content of this letter.

Remarks on April Fool's Day and an Exchange With Reporters
April 1, 1997

The President. I came here today because I thought I should personally deliver some disturbing news. Mike McCurry has just made a fool of himself by taking an unfortunate fall on dimly lit steps here at the White House. We believe he may have torn a tendon in his upper right thigh, which could get him a 6-inch incision above the place where he's torn it, but we won't know for sure until he's been thoroughly examined. And so until we can bring him back to full health, Kris Engskov is going to do the daily briefing today. [*Laughter*] And he will be my Press Secretary during Mike's absence, and he has some truly disturbing things to comment on. And frankly, I do not have the courage to stand here and listen to what he's about to tell you. But I am responsible for all of it. [*Laughter*]

Q. Will his accent get in the way of his job?

The President. I thought we should have a Press Secretary that did not have an accent for the first time in 4 years. [*Laughter*]

Q. Is there a danger of Mr. McCurry getting his old job back?

The President. I think McCurry's job is in real danger now. [*Laughter*]

Q. Will he be taking narcotics, pain—[*laughter*]——

The President. Yes. And under the 25th amendment he has already signed his authority over to Kris Engskov. [*Laughter*]

Q. How come the pool wasn't notified earlier about this accident?

The President. It's because we're pretty sneaky around here. [*Laughter*]

Q. Was he using alcohol before he fell? [*Laughter*]

The President. And beer and wine. [*Laughter*] But only after he watched 4 hours of advertisements on television. He was shaking beyond all belief.

Q. What about controlling legal authority here?

The President. Well, Kris Engskov is, I'm reliably informed, still underage. [*Laughter*] I first met this man when he was 3 years old, in his grandfather's store. And he still looks like he's 3 years old to me. [*Laughter*]

Q. Sometimes acts like it.

The President. That's right. Which makes him a perfect choice for the Presidential Press Secretary. [*Laughter*]

Mr. Engskov, this is your big chance. Don't blow it. [*Laughter*]

NOTE: The President spoke at 2:20 p.m. in the Briefing Room at the White House. In his remarks, he referred to Press Assistant Kris Engskov.

Remarks in a Roundtable Discussion on Education
April 2, 1997

The President. Let me welcome all of you here to the East Room of the White House today for this very important announcement and this important roundtable. And by extension, let me welcome Mayor Susan Hammer and the CEO of Netscape, Jim Barksdale, and others who are with us via satellite today from the Stonegate School in San Jose, California.

In my State of the Union Address, I said that the greatest step our country must take to prepare for the 21st century is to ensure that all of our people have the best education in the world, that every 8-year-old can read, that every 12-year-old can log on to the Internet, that every 18-year-old can go on to college, that every American adult can continue to learn for a lifetime.

But the most important thing of all is that we know whether we are learning what we need to know. And that requires something America has put off doing for too long, the embracing of a genuine commitment to national standards of learning for our young people. I have challenged every State to embrace national standards and to participate in 1999 in an examination to see whether our children have met those standards for fourth graders in reading and eighth graders in math.

Today, America's largest school system and leaders of its most forward-leaning high-tech industries have joined together to put California alongside Maryland, Michigan, North Carolina, and our military schools in the support of the national standards movement. I thank Delaine Eastin. I thank the 200 high-tech executives who have supported this. And I thank them for their pledge not just to announce their support today but to write every Governor, every school board, every State education leader and ask them to participate in the standards crusade.

It has been less than 2 months since I called on every State to adopt high national standards. Today, with California's endorsement, States and school systems that educate nearly 20 percent of America's schoolchildren are now on the road to measuring their students against those high standards. If any State understands the challenges we face in the 21st century in the global economy in an information age, it is surely California, our gateway to much of the world and the home of many of the industries that will shape our future.

California and all of you who are here today and all of those in California today have given powerful new momentum to the crusade for national education standards—education and business leaders, Republicans and Democrats and independents, people all committed to seeing politics stop at the schoolhouse door and America have no stopping place in tomorrow's world.

I want to thank everyone who has made this possible. I thank especially Secretary Riley for his work and the Vice President in particular for the work he did to put this group together today. This is a very, very happy day for me personally but, more importantly, for the cause of educational advancement and reform and standards.

And now I'd like to call on the California Superintendent of Public Education, Delaine Eastin, for any remarks you might like to make. Delaine.

[*At this point, the discussion began.*]

The President. Jim, it's President Clinton. I'd like to thank you for being there and thank Congresswoman Lofgren and my good friend Mayor Susan Hammer.

I'd like to ask you to amplify just a moment on a point that John Doerr made when he was introducing you, when he pointed out that just the 240 companies who have endorsed this national standards movement today have created 130,000 jobs in the last 4 years and have thousands of job openings now waiting to be filled.

We have tried very hard in this administration to create a climate and an environment and to pursue policies which would permit us to increase the number of high wage, good future jobs so that we could raise incomes, average incomes, in America again.

I think it would be helpful if you would just state explicitly from your point of view what the relationship is in having citizens, young people educated according to high national standards and filling those jobs with young Americans and raising our average income, because I think that's one thing the American people haven't clearly focused on, the extent to which our ability to create high-wage jobs in the end depends upon our ability to produce people who can fill those jobs once they're created. And I wish you would talk about it just a little bit.

[The discussion continued.]

The President. Thank you very much. Let me just make one other brief point about this and put it against one of our other big national challenges, our effort to reform the welfare system and to limit the amount of time that able-bodied people spend on public assistance and to maximize their movement into the work force.

You have this unbelievable situation today where in some of our cities—St. Louis and Chicago come to mind because we've had studies there in the last 18 months—there are six to nine applicants for every entry level job that opens up. And yet, you look around the country and there are tens of thousands of the kinds of jobs that the industries represented in this room and out in San Jose have opened and made available right now that cannot be filled.

So it is obvious, to take this one step further, that we'll never really answer the whole welfare reform challenge and move people from dependence to independence until we can demonstrate to employers that we have educated all of our young people, even our poorest young people, at a level of international acceptance.

I'd like to go on now and talk to two people here who really represent our children and give them a chance to make a couple of remarks. Let me begin with Carmen Cortez, who is a first grade teacher from the Olive Street School in Porterville, California. She's been a reading

specialist and an elementary school teacher for 30 years—I find that hard to believe—[*laughter*]—but—ever since she was 8 years old she's been an elementary school teacher. [*Laughter*] And she's a member of California's statewide coordinating committee on standards.

I'd like to begin by asking her the question that we often get asked, which is that—is it realistic for us to expect that we can set standards that are at once high and meaningful and secondly, that can be achieved by virtually all of our students in a country with such a diverse student body, not only diverse racially and ethnically but also economically? Is that realistic? And I'd like for you to talk about it based on your experience.

[The discussion continued.]

The President. Let me just—I'd like to emphasize what Carmen said—the most important thing she said. Keep in mind now, here's somebody who has been teaching our children for 30 years. I am so sick and tired of people assuming on the front end that children's learning is limited because of their racial, their ethnic, or their income background or whether they live in some poor rural area or some isolated inner city.

Their conditions create greater hurdles for them. We should clear away the hurdles, but we should not lower our expectations. When we lower our expectations of those kids, we're selling them down the river; we are not doing our jobs as adults. It is our job to be the shepherds for their future, to bring them into a better future.

To me, the most important thing that's been said here today by anybody is a person who has been an educator for 30 years saying that "When I have high expectations for these children, I find that they meet those expectations." And I think that's important.

I think we ought to hear from the parent who is here, too. We have Lydia Perez-Howard, parent of a third grade daughter who attends Cleveland Elementary School in Pasadena, California. She's the vice president of the PTA and active on the school advisory council and the neighborhood strengthening project. And I'd like to ask her to talk about how she feels about this whole standards movement and her daughter's future and how it will affect it.

[The discussion continued.]

The President. Let me say why I think Lydia's comments are so important. In the end, whatever we do in the schools needs to be reinforced by what the children hear at home. And we learned a lot over the last, oh, 12 or 13 years, since the issuance in 1984 of the "Nation At Risk" report.

But one of the most important things that I learned in all these years I was working as a Governor on standards and educational improvement is that in the United States there were too many parents who tended to believe that their children's performance in school was largely due to their income or their racial or ethnic background or whether English was their first language. And in a lot of other cultures that we're competing with, they believe their children's performance in school is directly related to effort and the level of support they get from the parents at home.

And it seems to me that you can have a debate if you want about what you think is right, or is it 90 percent one and 10 percent the other, but there is only one attitude likely to produce positive results for the children, and that is to believe that what children learn is largely the function of effort and the level of support they get in the home. So when the parents say something like what Lydia has said, it seems to be profoundly important.

The other thing I'd like to say—you say you came up in the schools of the Bronx in a different time. It put me in mind of something else that's especially important to California. This country has been built by generation after generation of immigrants who came to this country and believed that their children would do better than they did and would fully participate in the American dream. I would argue there were two elements to that: One is the immigrants worked like crazy, saved, and gave their kids a better life; second, their kids had a good education and were assimilated into the mainstream of American life.

We are becoming an ever more pluralistic society. And more and more of our immigrants are people who desperately need not only for the working age parents to have the chance to get good jobs and build a good future but for those children to have that future, too. We cannot become the country we ought to become, as a multiethnic, multiracial democracy in a world that will value that enormously, in the absence of a good educational system.

And again I say, having teachers who believe in high expectations and having parents who believe that if their schools work properly and have high expectations, they will support that and they will tell their children that what they learn will be a function of effort more than IQ, those two things will count more than anything else the rest of us will do. Then all of us have to do is show up, do our part, and create the system that will enable those kinds of teachers, those kinds of parents, and those kinds of children to succeed. So I think we ought to give our teacher and our parent another hand. I think they did a great job. [*Applause*]

I'd like to ask the Secretary of Education, who has been my friend and colleague on this for nearly 20 years now, to talk a little bit about what we're doing to try to work with the States to get the standards movement up and going and, specifically, to prepare the fourth grade reading and the eighth grade math examination by 1999 so that it meets the standards that Delaine Eastin and others in other States would expect it to.

Mr. Secretary.

[*The discussion continued.*]

The President. I'd like to leave everyone with this one final point—and then I'd like to call on the Vice President to close the meeting—to tie something together that Secretary Riley talked about and what Lydia Perez-Howard and what Carmen Cortez said about the students, and obviously what Delaine said earlier, and going back to something Jim Barksdale said about how everything that he's involved in, he has to meet standards.

I think it's important to make a distinction over and over again about what the difference is between what we propose here and what tests are in the classroom normally. We are striving for what you would call in manufacturing a zero-defect result, which means we want to set high standards that will guarantee 100 percent of the children, whether they graduate at the top of their class or at the bottom or somewhere in the middle, that they'll still have what they need to go on with their lives and make a success of it and to make our country strong. Which means that, in a given class, a student could make the highest grade in the class, but if the student doesn't achieve the standards, it's still not good enough. And in another class, even a student who might have the lowest grade in the class would still be a good, successful, performing learner and know that he or she can have a good future and has been given a good education. That is the important thing.

Furthermore, these examinations are not being given to label anybody a failure but to give everybody a benchmark on which they can build to success. Of course, not everybody will do well the first time they're given, but we have to know what the benchmark is. We have to know what the roadmap is.

But I just want to emphasize that again. If parents have the attitudes that we heard from Lydia, if teachers have the attitude we heard from Carmen, and States have the leadership that we heard from Delaine, from John Doerr, from all the folks out in San Jose today, we can achieve virtually a zero-defect society from an educational point of view and give our children the future they need. And especially States that are on the cutting edge of the future, both in terms of being highly pluralistic and having those new jobs of tomorrow, places like California, will be the greatest beneficiaries.

So I think it's important that we go out there and talk about this, so that everyone understands exactly what we mean. These are different from what most people think of as classroom tests, and we need to hammer that home. We believe all these kids can clear the bar, and we're determined to see that they do it.

NOTE: The President spoke at 2:48 p.m. in the East Room at the White House, with a satellite connection to a group of educators and high-tech corporation chief executive officers meeting in San Jose, CA. In his remarks, he referred to Mayor Susan Hammer of San Jose, CA; and John Doerr, partner, Kleiner, Perkins, Caulfield, and Byers.

Statement on the Resignation of Eljay B. Bowron as Director of the United States Secret Service
April 2, 1997

Eljay Bowron has done a superb job as Director of the United States Secret Service, and I am accepting his resignation with regret. I have great admiration for what he has accomplished during his service to our country.

For 23 years, Eljay Bowron has focused his intelligence, judgment, and deep professionalism on implementing, improving, and reforming the critical national missions of the United States Secret Service. Following his tenure with the Detroit Police Department, Eljay began his career as a special agent in the Chicago field office. From there, he engaged successfully in a series of assignments investigating crimes, especially counterfeiting and financial crimes, serving in the Secret Service's intelligence division, and finally participating in the Secret Service's protective mission.

As Director, Eljay has been fond of saying, "When you stop changing, you stop growing," and this reformist instinct marked a tenure of great accomplishment. Before strategic planning initiatives were a regular part of Government management, Eljay formed teams to examine every Secret Service function. He changed the way Secret Service agents are trained; he consolidated the agency's forgery and financial crime investigative units; he made a powerful case for closing Pennsylvania Avenue; and he led the production of the new currency with anticounterfeiting improvements. For these reasons and more, his tenure as Director will long be remembered by admirers of law enforcement and the Secret Service.

I want to take this opportunity to thank Eljay's wife, Sandy, and his son, Brandon, for accepting the pressures and difficulties that arise from being a part of the Secret Service family. They endured a number of moves, as many Secret Service families do, from one great American city to another. I hope that Eljay's decision to join Ameritech will mean greater freedom for Eljay to enjoy Brandon's interest in baseball and development as a pitcher. Family means so much to Eljay—you can see that with the pride he exhibits in carrying and keeping his father's badge from the Detroit Police Department. Eljay's father would be very proud of his accomplishments, especially on this day.

On behalf of my family, the Vice President and his family, the former Presidents and their families, indeed on behalf of everyone who has felt the reassurance of being in the care of the Secret Service agents led by Eljay Bowron, let me thank the distinguished Director of the U.S. Secret Service for his remarkable devotion to duty and our country. He will be missed.

Remarks at a Democratic Business Council Dinner
April 2, 1997

Thank you. I wonder if you were just clapping because you were surprised I could stand up. [*Laughter*] Let me say I'm delighted to see all of you here tonight. I want to say a special word of thanks to Carol Pensky for her willingness to lead this group and for her leadership ability, and to my good friend Alan Solomont for agreeing to come on as the finance director of the Democratic Party when he knew it would be such an easy job just now, to Roy Romer for what he said and for what he's been and for the friendship we've enjoyed over so many years. And I'd also like to say a word of thanks to Steve Grossman, who is not here tonight because they've had 24 inches of snow in Boston. Now, Solomont didn't use that for an excuse, and I haven't quite figured out how. But anyway, I thank them all.

I'd like to thank Secretary and Mrs. Peña and Secretary and Mrs. Slater and Frank Raines for coming tonight, as well as the people from our staff in the White House and the Vice President's staff. We're glad to have this opportunity to visit with you and to talk tonight.

You know, this was an interesting day for me at the White House for more reasons than one. But you may have seen reported in the news that today we had an event in which the secretary of public instruction for the State of California—which has over 10 percent of the schoolchildren in the country—and the heads of 240 different high-tech companies jointly endorsed the national standards movement in education that I have been advancing and that I talked about in the State of the Union and agreed that the children of California would participate in 1999 in the examination of fourth grade students in reading and eighth grade students in math to see if they had met those standards. And that meant that within a period of only 2 months since the State of the Union, we now have 20 percent of all the schoolchildren in the country already committed to be a part of that.

And we had—the most moving thing to me was we had a teacher of 30 years and a parent who was the vice president of her local PTA, both of them from different California communities, both of them, as it happened, Hispanic-Americans, who said that they strongly believe that all of our children should be held to high standards. And the teacher said, "If there's one thing I've learned about kids, it's if you have high expectations, they rise to meet them, and if you don't have high expectations of them, they don't. And we owe it to them to have high expectations." And then the parent said that she had been educated at a time when everyone just assumed that, and she didn't know how we lost our way, and that she wanted to see the country come back.

Then Jim Barksdale, the CEO of Netscape, talked about how everything that was done in the high-tech community had to meet high international standards, and it was amazing that America had escaped applying those kinds of standards to our system of education for as long as possible. Then the head of the California School Board Association came up to me. And I thought, well, this is interesting because the reason America has never had national standards in schools is that we have local control of our schools and every time we try to do something like this—and Governor Romer and I have been working at this for a very long time now—they would say, "Well, this ends local control." So the head of the California School Board Association, who is herself a member of the local school board, said, "I finally figured out that we couldn't have local control without national standards." She said, "What kind of control is it if—what are you controlling for? The only reason I wanted to be on the school board is to improve the education of the children in the school district, and how could I do this unless I knew what the measure was, unless I could tell whether I was succeeding or not?" And I thought to myself, we are doing something really important here. This is going to change America. This is going to give people opportunities that they would not have otherwise had. And it has ramifications in other ways.

I want to talk a little more about this in a moment, but you know we've got this new welfare reform law that I signed, which requires us to move 40 percent of the eligible people on welfare from welfare to work over the next 4 years, which is about another million people. And we moved about a million people from welfare to work in the last 4 years, but the economy produced 11½ million jobs, and that had never happened in a 4-year period before. This time, under the law, we have to move that many people whether the economy produces 11½ million jobs or not.

And this was the anomaly: Last year in St. Louis, there were nine job applications for every entry-level job opening. In Chicago, there were six. The 240 companies, however, represented in this press conference today have created, just themselves, 130,000 jobs in the last 4 years and today have thousands and thousands of job openings. So there is a mismatch between the people we're trying to move into the work force and the skills required to get there. This is a huge deal.

I say that to make this point. I see what we are all doing as part of the seamless web of moving America into the 21st century, and I want you to know that I'm proud that you have decided to help support us, support these policies. If the election did not come out the way it did last November, that meeting would not have been held in the White House today. We would not be doing this. This would not be America's great national priority now. And you helped to make it possible, and you ought to be proud of it. You ought to be proud of it. So I thank you for that.

Now let me give you just a quick rundown on where we are. Number one, on the budget, I have submitted my budget by the—the budget resolution requires the congressional majority to submit at least the outline of a budget by April 15th. That may or may not happen. But for whatever it's worth, I really believe we'll get a bipartisan balanced budget agreement this year. I think it is the right thing to do for

the country. And because it's the right thing to do for the country, it is by definition good for the Democratic Party to do. But it is clearly the right thing to do for the country.

And I want to say a special word of thanks to Frank Raines, who came into OMB at a difficult time and has helped us to produce a fine budget, and we're going to get there. And I hope that you will encourage your Members of Congress and your friends in the Congress, whether they represent you directly or not, to support this. If it's the right thing for the country it, by definition, is the right thing for our party. And we need to keep this economic expansion going, and we need to get an agreement for a balanced budget that protects our investments in the future and in our people. And ours does, and we can get that kind of agreement through Congress if we all work on it.

The second thing I want to say is we need to continue to expand trade. I'm going to Latin America later this year. I have to go—because of my injury now, I have to go in two legs. I'm going to Mexico, Central America, and the Caribbean; then I'm going to go back to South America later in the year. There's some controversy, I know, still, about whether we did the right thing in NAFTA or not. All I can tell you is our exports are at an all-time high as a percentage of our economy. And export jobs, on the whole, pay better. And for whatever our difficulties with Mexico are, if you look back at the last time the Mexican economy collapsed before NAFTA 10 years previously, they were 2 or 3 times as rough then. We have been in much better shape because we have created a trading bloc with Canada and Mexico. And we have to do more trade with our neighbors in Central and South America. We have to do it.

Last year for the first time, while we're still debating what we want to do, the MERCOSUR countries in South America did more trade with Europe than the United States. And it is time— we've got to take a serious look at this. And again I would say, from the time of Franklin Roosevelt the Democratic Party has been on the side of free and fair trade, and we can achieve both. And I think any of you who've worked with Mickey Kantor, when he was our trade ambassador, or Charlene Barshefsky know that we have worked hard and we have fought hard for fair trade for the American workers and the American businesses. And we will continue to do that.

But in a world growing ever more interdependent, when uncertainties abound, we need to be tied as closely as we can to our democratic neighbors who are willing to work with us and build a common future with us. So especially with regard to the important countries in South America and Latin America, I think we have to do more, and that will be a big issue in this year.

On the social front, let me say one of the things I'm proudest of is that we've proved to ourselves as Americans in the last 4 years that we don't have to put up with social conditions we know are unconscionable. People now know they don't have to put up with a crime rate that's unconscionable. We have the crime rate now going down every year, and we have before the Congress a juvenile justice proposal that I believe will find strong bipartisan support and will enable us to keep lowering the crime rate.

But I would just say again—and I hope we'll have your support in this—while the crime rate is going down, the juvenile crime rate is still too high. While drug use is going down, drug use among juveniles is still going up. Still too many kids out there who are disconnected, don't feel connected to the future, don't feel connected to their neighborhood, their families, their schools, or anything else. And while we need a juvenile crime bill that is tough, we also need one that is compassionate, intelligent, and gives these young people something to say yes to. And that's one of the reasons that I'm proud to be a member of this party, that we believe in the human potential of everybody. And I am determined that before I leave this job, we will have put a stake in the ground that proves that we do not have to lose the thousands and thousands and thousands of our young people we continue to lose every year. And if we do the right thing, we won't lose them.

Let me just mention two other things. We've taken a lot of steps to strengthen family life and work life for families in this country in the last 4 years, whether it was in the family and medical leave law or raising the minimum wage or passing the Kassebaum-Kennedy health care bill or the V-chip bill, the television rating standards, the anti-teen-smoking initiative. But one of the biggest problems we still have is that there are still 10 million of our children who don't have health insurance. And a lot of them don't have health insurance because their parents lose jobs or change jobs. We have a proposal before the Congress that we believe would provide insurance to half of those children in the next 4 years. There are bipartisan proposals on that. I am very, very hopeful that we will do something in this Congress which will take a long step toward providing health insurance for all the children in this country. And that's important.

We have also proved that we could lower the welfare rolls quite a bit and far more than the economy alone can account for. The welfare rolls have gone down by about 2½ million now in the 4 years and 2 months that I've been in office. And we know from the patterns of the past that about half this decline would have occurred just because the economy got better. But we also know that about half the decline occurred because people were working at it, States, communities, people believing in welfare reform, people believing that able-bodied people who wanted to go to work ought to have the chance to go to work.

Now, this welfare reform law, as I said, requires us to do more. And I will have more to say about this later. But I've asked every State in the country to take the welfare check and make it available to employers as a wage and training subsidy, if that will help. I'm trying to get the Congress to pass a very tightly targeted tax credit that's worth up to half of the wage of a welfare recipient who goes into a new job for an employer at a pay of up to $10,000 a year. But we are going to have to have help from the private sector and every community in this country to meet these goals. We cannot let welfare reform become an excuse for hurting children. It's got to be an excuse—or the pretext or the lever by which we liberate families from dependency. And we can do this. It is clear that we can do it. But we're going to have to work at it with great discipline. And I hope all of you will be willing to help. There are some people in this audience tonight who've already hired people from welfare to work and I want to—you know who you are, and I thank you for doing that. But that will be a big part of what we're up against.

With regard to the work that the Vice President and I have been doing on reinventing Government and changing the way the Government works, you should know now that the Government has 285,000 fewer people than it did on the day I became President in 1993—dramatic downsizing. And yet I'm confident that we are providing better service to more people in different ways, because we've worked at it very hard. We will continue to do that.

We passed lobby reform legislation. We passed legislation to require Congress to live under the laws it imposes on others. The next thing we have to do is to pass a campaign finance reform. I believe that the McCain-Feingold bill should pass. I am strongly supporting it. But there are some other things that I think ought to be done as well, and I would like to ask all of you to think about this. You've been involved in this deeply. You know as well as I do that the exponential rise in the costs of communicating with the voters is what has led the exponential rise in the costs of the campaign.

There is a coalition in America today working to get free television time for candidates. And if we could get that free television time for candidates, only those candidates who agree to observe certain spending restraints, that would do more to change the incentives and to change the framework in which we all operate and to give everybody a fair chance to get their message across than anything else.

I have just seen an interesting analysis of the unprecedented amount of time—free television time that was given to Senator Dole and to me in the last election. And while it shows that only about 22 percent of the American people saw our spots that we did—your know, we did spots for—several of the networks gave us time to talk—1 minute, 90 seconds, 2 minutes—on various issues. Sometimes we were both asked the same questions, and our answers were run back to back on successive nights. Sometimes we were given the opportunity just to talk about certain subjects. But the analysis showed that, on the whole, there was more policy information in these free timeslots than either in our paid ads or in the news coverage of the campaign—more policy information—that they tended to be less negative, less personal, but they tended to draw out the legitimate issue differences between the candidates. I believe that would happen in the races for Congress as well.

And so what I think we need to be thinking about is, how are we going to improve the way this thing works? I also would urge all of you

to think about what we could do to make voting more accessible, to change the—to think about this campaign reform as a way of giving the country more and more to the people who have to live with the decisions that are made in the elections. But there are a lot of exciting opportunities out there that I hope you will help us to pursue.

Finally, let me say that I think this will be a very big year in our country for charting our role in the world ahead. We had a very good summit with President Yeltsin in Helsinki. We have agreed to try to reach agreement within a short period of time to lower our respective nuclear arsenals to 2,000 to 2,500 warheads, which would be an 80 percent reduction from the cold war high of just 5 years ago, by 10 years from now. That's a very important thing, an 80 percent reduction.

I am going to have this week a bipartisan event to try to highlight the importance of our passing the Chemical Weapons Convention this year, which is absolutely imperative. The United States cannot afford not to be in the forefront of banishing chemical weapons from the Earth. We are trying to do something to restrict severely and eventually ban landmines. We are working hard on that. We hope to have some progress to report on that this year.

You know what we've been doing on the Middle East peace. The only thing I can tell you is, the one thing I've learned about those folks is don't give up. Don't give up on it. No matter how bad the headlines are, don't give up. And we've got some very good ideas; we're working on that.

I believe the Vice President had an extremely successful trip to China. He was able to spend some high-level time that we had not spent—our country had not been able to spend since our differences over Tiananmen Square—just making sure they understood how we looked at the world and we understood how they looked at the world and charting the areas where we could work together, particularly in the areas of nuclear proliferation where the Chinese supported us with the Comprehensive Nuclear Test Ban Treaty last year and dealing with the problems on the Korean Peninsula, in trying to resolve some of our economic disputes. And he also gave a very powerful human rights speech while he was there, of which I was very proud. I think it was a very good trip.

And I believe that by the end of the year, you will see with that, the expansion of NATO, the other things that are going on, we will be a lot closer to a world which has more democracy, more free market economics, more cooperation, and where we're making progress in trying to beat back the new security threats of our time.

In short, this really is an age of great possibility, and it requires us to work together. But in the kind of country we have where the public sector is limited and the private sector is large, which I like, you have to play a role in public decisions, and it's good citizenship. And that's what you're doing. And again, let me say I'm proud of you. I appreciate what you've done, and I hope that you will continue to make your voices heard on the things that we are doing.

We have a lot of other decisions I haven't even gone into tonight. Secretary Slater's here;

we're going to redo the transportation bill this year. Secretary Peña has got a lot of our most important research going on in the Department of Energy. We've got a lot going on. We want you to be a part of it. But we want you to be proud of the fact that what you have done has made America a better place. In 4 more years, it'll be a much better place, indeed.

Thank you, and God bless you.

NOTE: The President spoke at 8:28 p.m. at the Sheraton Carlton Hotel. In his remarks, he referred to Carol Pensky, treasurer, Alan Solomont, national finance chair, Gov. Roy Romer of Colorado, general chair, and Steve Grossman, national chair, Democratic National Committee; Secretary of Energy Federico Peña's wife, Ellen Hart Peña; and Secretary of Transportation Rodney Slater's wife, Cassandra Wilkins Slater.

Remarks to the 1996 National Basketball Association Champion Chicago Bulls
April 3, 1997

The President. Good morning. Please be seated. Just think of me as another injured basketball player. [*Laughter*]

Congressman Rush; Congressman Jackson; Mr. Cedric Dempsey, the executive director of the NCAA; Richard Lapchick, who is with the Center for Sport in Society; to the young athletes who are here with us today, who have been recognized for their academic achievements and their personal heroism as well as their achievements in athletics. We're all delighted to be here with our Secretary of Commerce, Bill Daley, and half the city of Chicago has come. [*Laughter*] Will everybody from Chicago please raise your hand, be recognized, stand up. [*Applause*] That's good.

As all of you know, the First Lady is from Chicago, and it's sort of become my adopted big city. And around here, we like it when the Bulls are doing well, which means that no matter what's in the newspaper in Washington every day, I can nearly always find some reason to be happy. [*Laughter*] And believe me, some days we need it more than others.

On behalf of all of us here and people around the Nation, I want to congratulate Jerry Reinsdorf, Phil Jackson, and the entire team on winning the 1996 championship and on winning four of the last six championships.

The '96 championship was the first one captured at the United Center, and I had that in mind when we picked it for the site of the Democratic National Convention last summer. We wanted the home court advantage. I think we got it.

Last year, the Bulls had a record of 72 and 10. And I checked this morning; I think it's 63 and 9 now. I'd say that's pretty good. The individual Bulls stars are well-known to America, all of them, but I'd like to point out that this is a team that plays great defense as well as great offense and a team with a great sense of teamwork, a team that plays together and works together and tries to win together. It seems to me that that's something that we'd all do well to remember. That's one of the things I like about the city of Chicago. Whenever I go there, I think that it's a city that tends to work because it works together with coherent teams of people and neighborhoods and all walks of life.

So let me say again, the Chicago Bulls have given America a lot of thrills. They've given Chicago a lot of pride. They've produced perhaps the greatest basketball dynasty ever and perhaps the greatest basketball individual feats ever. But more than anything else, they've given us the sense that when people do things together, a lot more is possible.

Now, I'd like to introduce now Jerry Reinsdorf so we can go on with the rest of the program. And meanwhile, I want you to know that in 6 months I'll be as good as new and available for the next draft. [*Laughter*]

Thank you.

[*At this point, team owner Jerry Reinsdorf made brief remarks and presented the President with a championship watch and Bulls jacket.*]

The President. Think I'll be safe in this in Washington? [*Laughter*] Thank you.

[*Mr. Reinsdorf then introduced coach Phil Jackson and cocaptains Scottie Pippen and Michael Jordan.*]

The President. Look at those shoes.

[*Mr. Jackson made brief remarks and presented a Bulls jersey to the President.*]

The President. Do I have your permission? [*Laughter*]

Thank you.

Mr. Jackson. Thank you.

The President. You guys aren't going to speak? You got to say something. Come here, Scottie, say something. [*Laughter*] Everybody from Arkansas talks. You have to. [*Laughter*]

[*Mr. Pippen made brief remarks.*]

The President. Thank you.

[*Mr. Jordan made brief remarks.*]

The President. I want to thank again all the people from Chicago for coming. I want to say how proud—I can't help but say that all the people that I know, and I know half the town from the little community in southeast Arkansas where Scottie Pippen grew up, are still wildly proud of him. So it's okay for somebody outside Chicago to like that.

And I want to say to Michael Jordan, I like your two-tone shoes. [*Laughter*] When I was growing up, all well-bred young Southern boys learned to wear two-tone shoes in the springtime—[*laughter*]—and I'm glad you kept up the tradition.

And finally, I'd like to thank the Bulls for being so good to Hillary when she visited them at the United Center recently. And that night, she got Dennis Rodman's jersey. It is now freshly washed and hanging in the White House in a place of honor.

Thank you very much.

NOTE: The President spoke at 11:02 a.m. at the South Portico at the White House.

Remarks Prior to Discussions With Prime Minister Antonio Guterres of Portugal and an Exchange With Reporters
April 3, 1997

President Clinton. Let me say it's a great honor for the United States to have Prime Minister Guterres here from Portugal. We are immensely grateful to Portugal for many things and our partnerships. But I would especially mention their peacekeeping role as a nation in Bosnia and Africa, the work we've done together in the United Nations, the work we are going to discuss today regarding NATO. And we appreciate the very progressive and strong leadership the Prime Minister has given to his nation.

So I'm looking forward to this, and it's been too long coming, but I'm very glad to have you here. Would you like to say anything?

Prime Minister Guterres. Well, first of all, let me say how happy and proud I am to accept the invitation of President Clinton. Portugal, as you know, is very much in favor of a united Europe, but we want a Europe that preserves its Atlantic character. And for us, the relationship between Europe and the United States is an extremely important part of our own way of life. And this is relevant in economics, in culture, in people-to-people contacts, and also in defense and security.

We want NATO to go on as the basic framework for European security, and we consider that the United States has an irreplaceable role in the guarantee of European security. And we are very happy with the partnership that we have been able to establish in the past, and we are looking forward to improve as much as possible our bilateral relations that have been excellent, as a matter of fact, in the past.

President Clinton's ideas have been very inspiring to our own programs, and we hope to go on doing our best to take profit of your initiatives, your ideas, your policies.

Russia and NATO Expansion

Q. And you also are in favor of expansion of NATO, and what kind of an agreement, charter are you going to have with Russia?

Prime Minister Guterres. Well, I think that the expansion of NATO is—as the expansion of the European Union, it's a basic condition for democracy, for peace and stability in Central and Eastern European countries.

And as for Portugal, it has been extremely important 10 or 15 years ago to consolidate our democracy. I think the same right must be granted to those new democracies in Eastern Europe. Of course, we understand that it is very important to preserve the very special relationship with the new Russia.

I once heard Vice President Al Gore telling me that he looked at the enlargement of NATO and relations with Russia like the coupling of two space ships and the need to put them in the same orbit. I think this is a very good idea, and I think it's what effectively is being done now with the recent contacts in Helsinki and all the preparatory work that is going on.

I hope that one day in the future NATO and Russia can be allies, defending the values of enlightenment against all the irrational behaviors in the modern world, irrational behaviors based on extreme nationalism, religious fundamentalism, and all other things that should not exist in a modern world.

Webster Hubbell

Q. Mr. President, earlier this year when asked about the $100,000 Lippo payment to Webb Hubbell, you said, "I can't imagine who could have ever arranged to do something improper like that, and no one around here knows about it." Were the phone calls——

President Clinton. That's not what I said.

Q. Let me ask this question——

President Clinton. I don't believe that's exactly what I said.

Q. Let me ask you this, Mr. President. Were the phone calls made by Mack McLarty and Erskine Bowles proper or improper? And if you knew about them, should you have put a stop to them?

President Clinton. Well, first of all, let's go back to what you said before. I believe what I said was that I was unaware of the Lippo contract until it became public. And I believe that's all I said. I rendered no judgment on it one way or the other.

Secondly, I do not believe they were improper. From what I know about them, they were just—they were people who were genuinely concerned that there was a man who was out of work, who had four children. And as I understand it, they were trying to help him for no other reason than just out of human compassion.

Secondly, let me remind you of the critical fact. At the time that it was done, no one had any idea about whether any—what the nature of the allegations were against Mr. Hubbell or whether they were true. Everybody thought there was some sort of billing dispute with his law firm. And that's all anybody knew about it. So, no, I do not think they did anything improper.

Campaign Documents

Q. Mr. President, Harold Ickes took a carload of documents away from the campaign. National Archives says it was your call. Did you give him permission to take all of those papers from the campaign?

President Clinton. I don't remember being asked about it one way or the other. I don't remember being asked about it.

Q. Do you care?

President Clinton. Well, I didn't know it was my call to care. I don't remember being asked about it. I'd have to know more about it before I could answer that question.

[At this point, one group of reporters left the room, and another group entered.]

Visit of Prime Minister Guterres

President Clinton. Let me begin by saying it's a great honor for the United States and for me personally to have the Prime Minister here today. We are very proud of our friendship with Portugal. Our partnership, our alliance is very important to us. We are especially grateful for the leadership that Portugal has evidenced in peacekeeping in Bosnia, in Africa, in the United Nations, in our discussions about the role of NATO in the future and the expansion of NATO. And I have looked forward to this meeting for a long time, and I'm anxious to have it with the Prime Minister.

And I think I'd like to give the Prime Minister a chance to make a few remarks, and then if you have a question or two, we'll try to answer them.

Prime Minister Guterres. Well, first of all let me say how happy and proud I am to have been able to accept this kind invitation of President Clinton. This is a very exciting moment for the Atlantic community, and we have many things to discuss about our common interests in regards to the relations between Europe and the United States, at the level of the European Union, NATO, NATO's enlargement, relations with Russia, and also doing our best to improve the excellent bilateral relations that we have between the United States and Portugal. So it's really a very good opportunity for us also to discuss some of the very inspiring ideas that President Clinton has introduced in the world political debate.

East Timor

Q. Mr. President, do you plan to review the United States position on the incorporation of its East Timor at any stage, sir?

President Clinton. What about East Timor?

Q. At the moment, the U.S. recognizes the incorporation of East Timor without maintaining that legitimate act of self-determination took place. Do you plan to review this position once it has about, I think, about quite a couple of years?

President Clinton. Well, my main concern now is to make sure that we have done everything we can possibly do to respect the political and human rights of the people in East Timor. And the United States has been—particularly since I became President, has been very forthright on that subject. And I know that Portugal has as well and has a longer attachment than we do there. So that's one of the things I want to talk to the Prime Minister about, about what we can do to further the cause of human rights for the people of East Timor.

Q. But Mr. President, you told Senator Feingold, regarding a proposal for a referendum in East Timor for self-determination, that you would take his idea into consideration in a letter you sent him late last year. What does that mean exactly? Does that mean that a review of that position is possible? Could you explain the meaning of it?

President Clinton. It means that I think we should do whatever is most likely to give us sufficient influence to guarantee basic human rights protections for the people of East Timor. And we have to do what we think is most likely to achieve our overriding objective, which is to give those people a chance to have the lives of decency and integrity. And sometimes what seems obvious is maybe not the best course, and we're reviewing what our options are. That's what it means.

Q. Isn't self-determination the ultimate human right?

President Clinton. Well, that depends. That's a very complicated question. We fought a civil war over it.

NOTE: The President spoke at 12:20 p.m. in the Diplomatic Reception Room at the White House. A tape was not available for verification of the content of these remarks.

Remarks on the Anniversary of the Aircraft Tragedy in Croatia
April 3, 1997

Thank you very much. Mr. Vice President, Mrs. Gore, Mr. Prime Minister, Mr. Ambassador, to all the members of the Cabinet and the administration who are here, all of our distinguished guests from Croatia, including the wonderful musicians, members of the diplomatic corps, Mrs. Brown, members of the Brown family, and all of you who come here as family and friends.

A year ago, when so many of us gathered in grief at that airplane hangar at the Dover Air Force Base, it was one of the longest days of my life. And yet I can only imagine how much worse it was for so many of you. Well, now it's another April and another springtime. The dogwood tree we planted on the South Lawn of the White House last year in memory of your loved ones has grown a whole foot taller, and soon it will bloom. And so we gather here today, going on in celebration but clearly not free of sadness—grateful for the lives of those who were lost, yes, mindful of our obligation to them to live on as they would want us to live, but still a little sad.

I was searching all of you today, remembering those of you whom I saw a year ago, wondering what had been most difficult for you in the last year and what you missed and how once the moment of tragedy passes, the little things become so important. It's springtime, and I can't go play golf with Ron Brown. We will never shoot baskets again, and he's not here making fun of me because I had that stupid accident with my leg. And I miss that. I miss seeing the smiles of those young people that worked here at the Commerce Department, who believed in this country and were totally unjaded by the cynical veneer that grips too many people. I miss that. I see the children out here and the spouses, and I wonder of all those little things that you miss.

But I can say, we should be heartened by the missing because the people we lost enriched our lives with their gifts of love, with their gifts of talent. As the Vice President said, they greatly enriched our country through their patriotism and their service. And they certainly enriched the world through their sacrifice for the cause of peace. As Secretary Daley indicated, they have inspired those who are left behind in this Department to continue on.

When Ron Brown became Secretary of Commerce, he revolutionized the role of the Commerce Department in our lives, going from rhetoric to reality. And every person, public and private and citizen alike who was a part of that should feel proud of what happened. He made our passion for trade a force not only in our

economic life but in our foreign policy. He identified not only those 10 great emerging economies that we all ought to visit and work with and build bridges to but, as a distinguished American columnist noted just a couple of days ago, even in places where crises had not passed, he sought to bring the benefits of American ingenuity and entrepreneurialism and to prove that you could do good and do well at the same time, whether it was in South Africa or Northern Ireland or the Middle East, where I note that when Mr. Arafat was here just a few days ago, he took some time out to celebrate the opening of a business development center in Gaza named after Ron Brown. They thought our trade missions were pretty great, and they thought the people that went on them were pretty great.

And of course, the Balkans. Every person on that plane shared a common vision: They all loved America, they all believed in America's mission in the world, and they certainly believed in America's mission to the Balkans. The dream for which they gave their lives is now slowly and surely being realized by people who have, too, lost a very great deal. In a country where almost every family, every springtime, can remember the terrible pain that so many of you now feel, the divided families have been reunited; marketplaces are full of life, not death; the lights are on; the water runs; homes and businesses are being restored; playgrounds belong to children again.

So a year later, with your dogwood growing and people in the Balkans returning to a more normal life, I cannot ask you to give up your pain, but I can ask you to celebrate the lives of those who died on that mountain a year ago, to celebrate them in all the ways we do, through personal tributes paid by families and communities.

The Commerce Department has set up a scholarship fund to help the children of Commerce employees. There is a high school in White Plains, New York, named in honor of Lee Jackson. A scholarship has been established for Christina Kaminski, the 13-year-old daughter of Stephen Kaminski. The William E. Morton Library opened last fall at the Geneva Kent Elementary School in West Virginia. The Monterey Bay Export Assistance Center was dedicated to young Adam Darling. The Naomi Poling Warbasse Memorial Fund was established at George Washington University by her family and friends. The University of Wisconsin has established a Charles F. Meissner Memorial Scholarship for students from the Washington, DC, area. The New York Times has established the Nathaniel Nash Memorial Foundation to support children's education. A New Jersey church and YMCA has teamed to create the Walter Murphy Memorial Fund. Riggs National Bank has set up a worldwide scholarship for the Buckley School in New York in honor of Paul Cushman. And of course, the Ronald Brown Foundation was established by Ron's family as a means of carrying on his vision of a more compassionate, cooperative, and just world.

And these are not all the tributes which have come in honor of those whom we lost. We also can celebrate our loved ones by knowing that the mission of peace and reconstruction they undertook in Bosnia and Croatia is being carried on. When they fell, so many of you here, even those of you who had experienced painful personal losses, took up a fallen standard. Today, with the great outpouring of reconstruction aid from around the world, with dozens of American companies working to restore the currents of commerce, with the Department of Commerce preparing to open the door of its new office in Zagreb next week, the habits of peace are taking on. And that's something to celebrate.

Above all, we can celebrate them by striving to live our lives in a way that honors their lives. Whether we're in Government or in our military, in journalism or business, let us resolve to serve. When we see a child in need, a community in distress, a nation struggling to be free, let us resolve to act. Let us resolve to learn from this tragedy and work, as so many of you have done, to make our airplanes and our airports and air travel safer. Let us resolve to

honor those business leaders who perished by celebrating the best of American business and saying, yes, it can be a good and noble thing, and we should work to expand its reach.

Earlier today, the Conference Board and our administration announced that we are creating the Ronald H. Brown Award for Corporate Leadership. Each year that award will honor America's finest corporate citizens, those who do well and do good by serving.

Above all, let us resolve always to shine a light of hope and freedom in the darkness, for the people we lost a year ago did not die on a distant mountain because they did not care or did not believe in the possibility of tomorrow being better than today. And if we owe them anything at all, we owe them our best efforts to make tomorrow better than today and to spread hope among our people and throughout the world.

Tomorrow will be 29 years since Martin Luther King was killed in Memphis. When you think of your loved ones, remember him and what he said: "All inhabitants of the globe are now neighbors. The large house in which we live demands that we transform this worldwide neighborhood into a worldwide brotherhood." The people we celebrate today gave their lives building that worldwide brotherhood. For the men and women, the boys and girls alive all over the world, and those yet to come, it is up to us to celebrate them by continuing that noble work.

Thank you, and God bless you all.

NOTE: The President spoke at 3:04 p.m. at the Commerce Department. In his remarks, he referred to Prime Minister Zlatko Matesa and Ambassador to the United States Miomir Zuzul of Croatia; and Alma Brown, widow of former Secretary of Commerce Ronald H. Brown.

Letter to Congressional Leaders Reporting on the National Emergency With Respect to Angola (UNITA)
April 3, 1997

Dear Mr. Speaker: *(Dear Mr. President:)*

I hereby report to the Congress on the developments since my last report of September 19, 1996, concerning the national emergency with

respect to Angola that was declared in Executive Order 12865 of September 26, 1993. This report is submitted pursuant to section 401(c) of the National Emergencies Act, 50 U.S.C. 1641(c), and section 204(c) of the International Emergency Economic Powers Act, 50 U.S.C. 1703(c).

On September 26, 1993, I declared a national emergency with respect to the National Union for the Total Independence of Angola ("UNITA"), invoking the authority, *inter alia,* of the International Emergency Economic Powers Act (50 U.S.C. 1701 *et seq.*) and the United Nations Participation Act of 1945 (22 U.S.C. 287c). Consistent with United Nations Security Council Resolution 864, dated September 15, 1993, the order prohibited the sale or supply by United States persons or from the United States, or using U.S.-registered vessels or aircraft, of arms and related materiel of all types, including weapons and ammunition, military vehicles, equipment and spare parts, and petroleum and petroleum products to the territory of Angola other than through designated points of entry. The order also prohibited such sale or supply to UNITA. United States persons are prohibited from activities that promote or are calculated to promote such sales or supplies, or from attempted violations, or from evasion or avoidance or transactions that have the purpose of evasion or avoidance, of the stated prohibitions. The order authorized the Secretary of the Treasury, in consultation with the Secretary of State, to take such actions, including the promulgation of rules and regulations, as might be necessary to carry out the purposes of the order.

1. On December 10, 1993, the Department of the Treasury's Office of Foreign Assets Control (OFAC) issued the UNITA (Angola) Sanctions Regulations (the "Regulations") (58 *Fed. Reg.* 64904) to implement my declaration of a national emergency and imposition of sanctions against UNITA. The Regulations prohibit the sale or supply by United States persons or from the United States, or using U.S.-registered vessels or aircraft, of arms and related materiel of all types, including weapons and ammunition, military vehicles, equipment and spare parts, and petroleum and petroleum products to UNITA or to the territory of Angola other than through designated points of entry. United States persons are also prohibited from activities that promote or are calculated to promote such sales or supplies to UNITA or Angola, or from any transaction by any United States persons that evades or avoids, or has the purpose of evading or avoiding, or attempts to violate, any of the prohibitions set forth in the Executive order. Also prohibited are transactions by United States persons, or involving the use of U.S.-registered vessels or aircraft, relating to transportation to Angola or UNITA of goods the exportation of which is prohibited.

The Government of Angola has designated the following points of entry as points in Angola to which the articles otherwise prohibited by the Regulations may be shipped: *Airports*: Luanda and Katumbela, Benguela Province; *Ports*: Luanda and Lobito, Benguela Province; and Namibe, Namibe Province; and *Entry Points*: Malongo, Cabinda Province. Although no specific license is required by the Department of the Treasury for shipments to these designated points of entry (unless the item is destined for UNITA), any such exports remain subject to the licensing requirements of the Department of State and/or Commerce.

There has been one amendment to the Regulations since my report of September 19, 1996. The UNITA (Angola) Sanctions Regulations, 31 CFR Part 590, were amended on October 21, 1996 (61 *Fed. Reg.* 54936, October 23, 1996), to implement section 4 of the Federal Civil Penalties Inflation Adjustment Act of 1990, as amended by the Debt Collection Improvement Act of 1996, by adjusting for inflation the amount of the civil monetary penalties that may be assessed under the Regulations. The amendment increases the maximum civil monetary penalty provided in the Regulations from $10,000 to $11,000 per violation.

The amended Regulations also reflect an amendment to 18 U.S.C. 1001 contained in section 330016(1)(L) of Public Law 103–322, September 13, 1994; 108 Stat. 2147. The amendment notes the availability of higher criminal fines pursuant to the formulas set forth in 18 U.S.C. 3571. A copy of the amendment is attached.

2. The OFAC has worked closely with the U.S. financial community to assure a heightened awareness of the sanctions against UNITA—through the dissemination of publications, seminars, and notices to electronic bulletin boards. This educational effort has resulted in frequent calls from banks to assure that they are not routing funds in violation of these prohibitions. United States exporters have also been notified of the sanctions through a variety of media, including via the Internet, Fax-on-Demand, special fliers, and computer bulletin board information initiated by OFAC and posted through the U.S. Department of Commerce and the U.S.

Government Printing Office. There have been no license applications under the program since my last report.

3. The expenses incurred by the Federal Government in the 6-month period from September 26, 1996, through March 25, 1997, that are directly attributable to the exercise of powers and authorities conferred by the declaration of a national emergency with respect to UNITA are about $61,000, most of which represent wage and salary costs for Federal personnel. Personnel costs were largely centered in the Department of the Treasury (particularly in the Office of Foreign Assets Control, the U.S. Customs Service, the Office of the Under Secretary for

Enforcement, and the Office of the General Counsel), and the Department of State (particularly the Office of Southern African Affairs).

I will continue to report periodically to the Congress on significant developments, pursuant to 50 U.S.C. 1703(c).

Sincerely,

WILLIAM J. CLINTON

NOTE: Identical letters were sent to Newt Gingrich, Speaker of the House of Representatives, and Albert Gore, Jr., President of the Senate. This letter was released by the Office of the Press Secretary on April 4.

Remarks Calling for the Ratification of the Chemical Weapons Convention and an Exchange With Reporters
April 4, 1997

The President. Thank you. Thank you very much, Senator Boren, for your words and your presence here today. We were laughing before we came out here. Senator Boren and I started our careers in politics in 1974 together, but he found a presidency that is not term-limited—[*laughter*]—and I want to congratulate him on it.

Mr. Vice President, Secretary Albright, Secretary Cohen, Secretary Baker, Senator Nancy Kassebaum Baker, General Shalikashvili. Let me thank all of you who have spoken here today for the words you have said, for you have said it all. And let me thank all of you who have come here to be a part of this audience today to send a clear, unambiguous, united message to America and to our Senate.

I thank General Colin Powell and Senator Warren Rudman, former arms negotiators Paul Nitze, Edward Rowny, and Ken Adelman; so many of the Congressmen who have supported us, including Senator Biden and Senator Levin who are here; the truly distinguished array of military leaders, leaders of businesses, religious organizations, human rights groups, scientists, and arms control experts.

Secretary Baker made, I thought, a very telling point, which others made as well. This is, in the beginning, a question of whether we will continue to make America's leadership strong

and sure as we chart our course in a new time. We have to do that, and we can only do that if we rise to the challenge of ratifying the Chemical Weapons Convention.

We are closing a 20th century which gives us an opportunity now to forge a widening international commitment to banish poison gas from the Earth in the 21st century. This is a simple issue at bottom, even though the details are somewhat complex. Presidents and legislators from both parties, military leaders, and arms control experts have bound together in common cause because this is simply good for the future of every American.

I received two powerful letters recently, calling for ratification. One has already been mentioned that I received from Senator Nancy Kassebaum Baker, Senator Boren, and former National Security Adviser General Brent Scowcroft. The other came from General Powell, General Jones, General Vessey, General Schwarzkopf, and more than a dozen other retired generals and admirals, all of them saying as one: America needs to ratify the Chemical Weapons Convention, and we must do it before it takes effect on April 29th.

Of course, the treaty is not a panacea. No arms control treaty can be absolutely perfect, and none can end the need for vigilance. But no nation acting alone can protect itself from the threat posed by chemical weapons. Trying to stop their spread by ourselves would be like trying to stop the wind that helps carry their poison to its target. We must have an international solution to a global problem.

The convention provides clear and overwhelming benefits for our people. Under a law Congress passed in the 1980's, we were already destroying almost all our chemical weapons. The convention requires other nations to follow our lead, to eliminate their arsenals of poison gas and to give up developing, producing, and acquiring such weapons in the future. By ratifying the Chemical Weapons Convention, as Secretary Cohen said, we can help to shield our soldiers from one of the battlefield's deadliest killers. We can give our children something our parents and grandparents never had, broad protection against the threat of chemical attack. And we can bolster our leadership in the fight against terrorism of proliferation all around the world.

If the Senate fails to ratify the convention before it enters into force, our national security and, I might add, our economic security will suffer. We will be denied use of the treaty's tools against rogue states and terrorists. We will lose the chance to help to enforce the rules we helped to write or to have Americans serve as international inspectors, something that is especially important for those who have raised concerns about the inspection provisions of the treaty.

Ironically, if we are outside this agreement rather than inside, it is our chemical companies, our leading exporters, which will face mandatory trade restrictions that could cost them hundreds of millions of dollars in sales. In short order, America will go from leading the world to joining the company of pariah nations that the Chemical Weapons Convention seeks to isolate. We cannot allow this to happen.

The time has come to pass this treaty, as 70 other nations already have done. Since I sent the Chemical Weapons Convention to the Senate 3½ years ago, there have been more than a dozen hearings, more than 1,500 pages of testimony and reports. During the last 3 months, we have worked very closely with Senate leaders to go the extra mile to resolve remaining questions and areas of concern. I want to thank those in the Senate who have worked with us for their leadership and for their good-faith efforts.

Ratifying the Chemical Weapons Convention, again I say, is important both for what it does and for what it says. It says America is committed to protecting our troops, to fighting terror, to stopping the spread of weapons of mass destruction, to setting and enforcing standards for international behavior, and to leading the world in meeting the challenges of the 21st century. I urge the Senate to act in the highest traditions of bipartisanship and in the deepest of our national interest.

And let me again say, the words that I have spoken today are nothing compared to the presence, to the careers, to the experience, to the judgment, to the patriotism of Republicans and Democrats alike and the military leaders who have gathered here and who all across this country have lent their support to this monumentally important effort. We must not fail. We have a lot of work to do, but I leave here today with renewed confidence that together we can get the job done.

Thank you, God bless you, and God bless America.

[At this point, the President greeted the guests and later took questions from reporters.]

Q. What about King Hussein—that the very terrorists who Secretary Cohen was talking about are the ones who are most likely to get hold of these weapons and who really are not going to be prohibited by this treaty?

The President. But this will require—I have two responses. Number one, this will require other countries to do what we're already doing and destroy their stockpiles, so there won't be as much for them to get ahold of. Number two, it will make it much more difficult for the component parts that make bigger—are used to make chemical weapons to get into the hands of terrorists, because we'll have much stricter controls on them. So those are the two answers there. That's why all these people are for this.

Q. They really are the people, though, who can get these without being regulated. I mean, you know——

The President. Yes, but as Madeleine Albright said, that's the argument you make against drug trafficking. In other words, criminals will always make an effort to evade the law; that's what they do. But if you have—if you destroy the chemical stockpiles, and you make it more difficult for the agents to make the chemical weapons to get into the hands of terrorists, you have dramatically improved the security of the world. Yes, there will still be people who will try to do it. Yes, there will still be people in home laboratories who can make dangerous things. This does not solve every problem in the world, but it will make the world much safer.

Q. Why do you think you had to do this today? Why did you have to come out and do it today?

The President. Because we're going to have to work like crazy to pass the thing.

Q. You don't have the votes right now?

The President. No, but we'll get there. I don't know yet, but we'll get there. I feel very much better because of this broad bipartisan support, but I've been working with Senator Lott since the first of the year on this. He knows how important it is to me, and he's dealt with us

in good faith. And we've worked with Senator Helms. We've worked with everybody, and we agreed that we would start the highly public, visible part of this campaign at about this time. So we're getting after it. We've got a month to deliver. We're going to try to do it.

NOTE: The President spoke at 11:01 a.m. on the South Lawn at the White House. In his remarks, he referred to former Senator David L. Boren, president, University of Oklahoma; and retired generals Colin L. Powell, David C. Jones, and John W. Vessey, Jr., former Chairmen, Joint Chiefs of Staff, and H. Norman Schwarzkopf, former Commander in Chief, U.S. Central Command. The exchange portion of this item could not be verified because the tape was incomplete.

Remarks to the Women's Economic Leadership Forum
April 4, 1997

Welcome to Humility 101. Thank you, Betsy, Maria, Linda. Thank you, Senator Landrieu, all of you. I'm delighted that you're here for this first ever Women's Economic Leadership Summit. Linda, I want to especially thank you and the Center for Policy Alternatives for your role in this meeting.

I couldn't help thinking, when Betsy was introducing me, that I—of all the things that I have done to try to elevate the status, the visibility, and the success of women, the most difficult one for me to do was just this week when I permitted Secretary Albright to represent me in throwing out the first ball—[*laughter*]—of the baseball season. It was very difficult. But you see, she got a lot more publicity for it than I would have. [*Laughter*] She throws hard, straight, and low when necessary—[*laughter*]—that's good.

I'm delighted to see all of you here. When I came into office, one of the things that I wanted most to do was not only to fashion a new economic policy for our country that would move the economy forward but to do it in a way that would address two problems that I saw really eating away at the heart of America: one, the fact that all Americans didn't have a chance to participate in our economy, even

when it was doing well, and I wanted to change that; and second, the fact that more and more Americans were having genuine difficulty fulfilling their responsibilities to their children and their responsibilities at work, principally lower income working people but not exclusively lower income working people, a lot of others as well.

So we attempted not only to have a big economic strategy on the big issues, focusing on cutting the deficit, eventually balancing the budget, continuing to invest in education and technology and research, expanding trade—all of those things that I think are so important— but also to specifically target people and places that had been left out of the economic mainstream with initiatives like the empowerment zones, the community development financial institutions initiative, the microenterprise initiative—which I imagine Hillary will talk a little bit about when she comes over in a few minutes—but also with a lot of initiatives specifically directed toward women, the things that we've done in the Small Business Administration, increasing by 300 percent the number of loans to women from the SBA, and a number of other things. And of course we have done a lot in the area of work and family.

And I think the results have been, conservatively speaking, pretty impressive. Just this morning the new unemployment figures were announced. Unemployment dropped to 5.2 percent. I now think we have persuaded most economists that we could actually have 5 percent or lower unemployment in this country without having inflation if we do it with discipline. I'm going to do everything I can to get a balanced budget agreement this year so that it will send a signal to the markets that they can keep interest rates modest, we can keep the markets strong, and we can keep creating jobs and bring more and more people into the work force.

Because, keep in mind, this 5.2 percent unemployment rate is misleading. There are lots and lots of States that have unemployment rates at 4 percent or less now; there are huge numbers of areas in States that have unemployment rates of 4.5, 4 percent, or less; and then there are places that have unemployment rates of 10 percent or more. So it's very important that we keep this effort going. It's also very important on the question of whether we can move the number of people from welfare to work that are prescribed in the welfare reform bill, and I'll say a little more about that in a minute.

But the point I want to make to you is, number one, it's very important to do the big things right. And we have to continue to do that. If the overall economy is doing well because more and more women are well-educated and well-versed in business and because there are more and more groups out there trying to support each other and bring people into the economic mainstream, a lot of good things will happen if nothing else is done. So it's important to do the big things right.

But secondly, it's also important to have specific, targeted initiatives that open up economy opportunity for everybody. The average pay of women is still only 71 cents on the dollar of what men make; for minority women it's about 60 cents. It's still more difficult on the whole for women to start a business. It's still more difficult on the whole for women to rise above certain levels in corporations. And we can't stop until we have this whole thing done. That's really the thing I want you to focus on today.

And what I'd like to do is just to summarize very quickly some of the things that we've tried to do that directly or indirectly bear on this, the major initiatives outstanding that we're trying to implement in this Congress, and then

again say that I hope that one of the things that will come out of the summit is that you will give us some more ideas about the road from here and where we go.

If you look at the world we are living in and the one we are certain to live in for the next few decades, it will be a world in which the flexibility of all human potential in a country will determine its capacity for success—the ability to learn, the ability to work, the ability to change, and the ability to reconcile competing obligations. The biggest competing obligation for any great society as a whole is, how do you balance the need to be highly competitive with the need to adequately reward work and provide a decent amount of security, without which people feel so disoriented it's hard for them to be productive? How do you strike the right balance? That requires us to forge a whole new synthesis in economic policy and to break out of old ways of thinking.

At a very personal level, we have to do the same thing with work and family. How do you enable people to succeed in the work place, to find personal fulfillment, whether it's in a for-profit or a not-for-profit or a public environment? How do you get the maximum number of able-bodied people in the work force and never forget that any society's most important task is raising good children who are successful and wholesome and happy and able to grow into successful people?

And so when we look at the future, we have to analyze every issue in terms of those two things. So that, if you take, for example, the struggle that I've waged here for the last 4 years to get people to accept, respect, and indeed rejoice in the fact that we are becoming an ever more multiracial, multiethnic society—that also, parenthetically, is necessary if we're going to reconcile these economic issues properly and if we're going to reconcile work and family properly, because we're not going to be able to raise successful children unless they fell comfortable not only with their own heritage but in respecting and dealing with people of different heritages. So this is very, very important.

I'd just like to start with that, because it's very important that, you know, when anybody brings something to me and they say, "Mr. President, we ought to do this," or "We shouldn't do that," or "We should try to stop the other thing," I try to see it through that framework. And I try to ask myself more and more, how will this affect America when our daughter is my age? What will this country look like in 30 years? How will we maintain the American dream? How will we maintain a sense of one America with genuine respect for our differences? How will we maintain the leadership of this country?

Just this morning I had a wonderful event with a number of leading Republicans and Democrats who have worked in arms control for years, endorsing the ratification of the Chemical Weapons Convention, which, by the way, is a very big thing not only in terms of national security but in terms of our economic well-being that we do this. But the most important thing to me is, it will help to provide the right balance between change and security for the American people 30 years from now if we do it. And if we don't, we'll pay a terrible price for it. And I think every one of you—we all need a kind of a framework for the future that we think about.

I'll just say this one other example. I had a very successful summit meeting in Helsinki with President Yeltsin. But the only way it succeeded was that he was able—not just me but he was able to think about a future that is very different from the immediate past and not to be imprisoned by the categories of the past but to think about, you know, "What do I want Russia to look like in 30 years? What do I want the men and women coming of age in Russia to be like? What kind of life do I want them to live? How should they relate to the United States and to the rest of Europe?" And this sort of courageous thinking is really required of all of us. And we may have to give up some things we'd just as soon not give up in the short run, but we're going to be able to embrace a much richer future if we do it.

Now, to come back to the subject of the meeting, it seems to me that we have to stay with the proposition that in the near term, that small business will be the most powerful engine of opportunity for the largest number of women who are trying to move into the economic mainstream, either as employees or owners. When I became President—I think this is right—I believe that woman-owned businesses contributed about $1.6 trillion to our gross national product. It's up to $2.3 trillion now. One in five employees in the country are working for a business owned by a woman. That's a stunning statistic.

It also means that we have to do more to try to help women have access to the credit markets, to move in, to succeed. And we have tried to do that with the SBA and with other things. But secondly, it means that we have to be sensitive to the fact that if more women work in small businesses, they will be more vulnerable unless we have other mechanisms to enable them to succeed.

That's one of the big reasons I thought it was important to raise the minimum wage. It's one of the big reasons that one of the most important provisions of the 1993 deficit reduction act in our economic plan was a huge expansion in the earned-income tax credit for working families. So it's a very good thing to do. By the way, what that means is now that all families with two children with incomes of under $30,000 a year are now paying markedly lower taxes than they would have been paying if that bill hadn't passed. So it has made a difference.

It's one of the reasons that I was proud that the Family and Medical Leave Act was the first bill I signed. We have millions of people who have now taken advantage of that, and we know that it has not hurt our economy. And again I will say, I know that it is somewhat inconvenient for some businesses on occasion, even though the surveys show that way over 80 percent of the businesses say there's been literally no cost. But in the end it has to increase the productivity of a society when people feel that they can do a good job at work and they're not worried sick at work about either their children, their parents, their spouses, or someone else because they can't even have a basic amount of time with them when they need it. So these are things it seems to me we need to focus on in the future.

We changed the pension laws in the last couple of years in ways that I think are very important, especially to a lot of women workers who have been employed by companies that were vulnerable. When I became President, they told me that the pension system of the country was going to be the next S&L crisis. And the Pension Benefit Guaranty Corporation was in terrible trouble and had been in debt for 16 years. Well, now it's running a surplus for the first time in over 20 years, and over 40 million workers have had their pensions secured. We made it easier for millions and millions of people to take out 401(k) plans and to keep them when they move from job to job and made nonprofits eligible for 401(k) plans, hospitals, educational institutions, other health care institutions. This affects 4 million women.

And we now know that while we have to be determined to preserve the stability and the integrity of the Social Security system, it is really not adequate to maintain the lifestyle of people when they get in their retirement years. We have to have higher savings rates for people in the work force. And since more and more retirement plans that are funded by employers are going to define contribution plans instead of define benefit plans, it is absolutely essential that we continue to move forward with both the integrity and the accessibility of savings plans for retirements for women in the work force. And we have some more things that we will propose to the Congress this year to try to strengthen the integrity as well as the accessibility of retirement. I think it is very, very significant.

In addition to that, we have tried to improve, as Betsy said, the operation of the Federal child care programs and how they interface with those at the local level. And in the welfare reform bill, one of the best things about it was we put up $4 billion more for child care. But let me say, I still believe in some ways that's the most underfunded employee support program in the United States. And I urge you to take a look at that—about the delivery system and how it works.

One of the things that I think should be done intensely in every State—and I'm going around to State legislators, along with the Vice President and the First Lady, to talk to them about education reform and welfare reform, and one of the things that I think every State should do is to target the establishment of child care centers and the training of child care workers for moving people from welfare to work and then giving people on welfare who do become certified child care workers either free or discounted service for their own children in the child care centers where their parents work.

If you look at it, we have a window here of significant opportunity, because the States got a block grant under the welfare reform bill, targeted to how much they were getting when the welfare rolls were at their highest. The welfare rolls have now dropped by about 2.5 million, the biggest drop in history. So they have some extra money here until the next economic recession comes along.

And I believe that one of the most significant things that can be done—and I urge all of you to ask your States to consider doing this and to lobby at the State level to do this—is to focus very sharply on the opportunity this welfare reform bill plus this extra cash to the States gives us to set up for the first time a genuinely comprehensive, well-trained, well-staffed, properly funded child care network in the country in a way that will move people from welfare to work and make child care available to lower wage working people who have never been on welfare in their lives but can't afford decent child care for their kids. It's a terrific opportunity, and we should be doing it.

Let me also say that we've done a lot of other things here that only—at least indirectly impact the economy, but have a huge impact on women: the Violence Against Women's Office, which I think has done a great job in the Justice Department; the Women's Health Office; the White House Women's Office that Betsy heads; the White House Interagency Committee on Women's Business Enterprise. We have dramatically increased medical research in areas that disproportionately affect women and involve women in testing protocols in a way they were not involved before I became President, which dramatically compromised the medical research effort of the country in terms of how it affected women. And I think that has been changed substantially, and I'm very proud of that.

Now, there is still a lot to do, and let me just mention some of the things that are my priorities. First of all, in the health care area. While the Kennedy-Kassebaum bill did a good thing saying that you couldn't be denied health insurance if someone in your family got sick or when you changed jobs, it's only good if you can still afford to buy your health insurance. And we know there are 10 million children who still aren't insured and that a huge percentage of them aren't insured because their parents lose their insurance when they lose their jobs or when they're between jobs.

We have a proposal on the table which we think, with the money we now have available, will cut that number to 5 million. There are other proposals which have been offered in this Congress by both Republicans and Democrats alike. I would just urge you to do whatever you can and say whatever you can to whomever you can to tell us to do the best we can. I mean, we do have a sense that—I think a sense—there's a majority I think in the Congress now committed to doing as much as we can on this. And if we could get the kids of this country insured, it wouldn't be long before we'd figure out how to fill the rest of the gaps. That's what I believe. And so I hope that we can make progress there.

With regard to welfare reform, the problems that I see in the bill are as follows. Number one, the biggest problem has nothing to do with welfare reform, and that is that they cut aid to legal immigrants too much. And I'm not talking about people who come here and don't tell the truth when they come to America and immediately try to get on welfare. I'm talking about people who work, pay taxes, have children. Many of them are women and, through no fault of their own, get sick, are victims of crime, have accidents, and now won't be able to claim any access to Medicaid or any other public benefits. Our budget corrects that, and I hope you will support that.

Furthermore, and right on point here, I believe that women business owners are more likely than men business owners to be sensitive to the extra effort that will have to be made to move people from welfare to work. But we know that most of these jobs are going to have to come from the private sector.

Now, let me just describe to you what the dimension of the problem is in welfare reform. In the last 4 years, our economy produced 11½ million jobs. We had never done that before. That's the most we ever produced. In that 11½ million jobs, there were one million people who moved from welfare to work. Of that one million people who moved from welfare to work, my Council of Economic Advisers estimates that about half of them moved from welfare to work because the economy got better and if nobody had lifted a finger, they would have moved from welfare to work because people don't like to be on welfare. They want to go to work if they can.

The other half—of the other half, most them moved from welfare to work because of special efforts that had already been made in the States and localities under welfare reform initiatives that were already underway. Some of them moved off the welfare rolls because we had a 50 percent increase in child support collections in 4 years, something that I'm very proud of.

And we have provisions to do better even, and we're going to do better.

But here's the rub: under this new law, 40 percent of those who are able-bodied and able-minded enough to be in the work force have to move from welfare to work some time in the next 4 years. And to cut to the chase, that's about 900,000 more. But that's 900,000 more that have to move from welfare to work whether we can produce 11.5 million jobs for another 4 years or not. If we did it back to back, it would be wonderful, and we might. But if we do, we will sure enough set some records. It has not ever been done before.

That means two things: One, we should give some extra help to communities with high unemployment to hire people to do community service related jobs, and there's something in our budget for that; but second, most of these jobs are going to have to come from the private sector and from welfare reform efforts. And there are—in my budget, there is a special credit which you can get only if you can demonstrate (a) that you've hired someone from welfare to work and (b) that they got a new job, they didn't replace someone else. But the credit is substantial. It's 50 percent of the salary up to $10,000 a year. So that is, in effect, an education and training supplement because we know that some of these folks who have never had work experience are going to be hard to place.

In addition to that, every State can—and I've been going around challenging them to do, and several are starting—can give the welfare check to an employer as an education and training supplement. In Kansas City, if you pay $1.75 over the minimum wage, they'll give you the welfare check. Kansas City will give it to you for up to 4 years. But most States would be more like a year.

But the point is, even if as a private employer, you couldn't hire someone for more than the length of the subsidy, if you hired somebody for a year, they'd have something on a resume. It would be that much easier to get another job. That would be 1 year on their 5 year lifetime limit on welfare that wouldn't be used up. So it would be worth doing, even if it could just be done for a year.

And the women business owners of America can have a huge impact in doing something that, by the way, will also help the economy if you create that many more consumers, bring that many more people into the work force, have that many more people being productive, that many more people being a positive role model for their own children. This is a huge thing. So I hope that you will, all of you, do what you can to try to mobilize the women business people of America to try to take an active and aggressive role in this effort.

I have asked the Congress to pass what I think is a good flextime bill to give people more options to take their overtime in time or money. But I think the important thing is that the employee ought to have the choice. It shouldn't be a way around the 40 hour work week. [*Applause*] Thank you.

I have asked the Congress—I think—I've asked the Congress to expand family and medical leave in a very narrow way just to give some time off to go to children's conferences at school and to take their children or their parents to regular doctor's appointments in a very limited fashion. I hope that will pass and find favor. And as I said, we've also proposed some other things in the retirement security area.

The last thing I would say is, I think that there are a lot of women who are outside their regular school years who deserve a second chance, who could make a major contribution to the economic life of this country. And the education proposals that are on the table in this Congress would be really helpful. If we pass the $1,500-a-year tax credit for the first 2 years of college, it would in effect make community college education as universal as high school is today.

I also proposed a tax deduction of up to $10,000 a year for the cost of any high school—any tuition after high school, easier access to an IRA that you could withdraw from tax-free to pay for education, and the biggest increase in Pell grants in 20 years.

But I think these things are important. We need to remind ourselves that the average age of people in our educational institutions is going higher and higher and higher. Even in the 4 year colleges now, it's up to 25—26 in some of our 4 year colleges in America. Most of our community colleges, it's higher than that. And so having universal access so people can get a second chance, I think, is profoundly important. And I hope that you will support that. It's a big deal for our economy and a big deal for women's economic opportunity.

So these are the things that we're going to be pushing. If you have other ideas, I hope you will do that and give them to us.

And the last thing I want to say is I hope you will continue to participate as partners with us. I went to a memorial service yesterday over at the Commerce Department for Ron Brown and the other people who were killed a year ago in Croatia, and I think one of the more important things that Secretary Brown did was to make sure that he emphasized women business leaders in these trade missions and reaching out to the rest of the world and trying to build ties. So I hope you will look for other opportunities to participate in that way and to continue to be a part of the partnership that we're trying to establish with America to create the kind of country we want for the 21st century.

Thank you very much. Thank you.

NOTE: The President spoke at 12:41 p.m. in the Indian Treaty Room at the White House. In his remarks, he referred to Betsy Myers, Deputy Assistant to the President for Women's Initiatives and Outreach, and Maria Echaveste, Assistant to the President and Director of Public Liaison, White House; and Linda Tarr-Whelan, president and chief executive officer, Center for Policy Alternatives.

The President's Radio Address
April 5, 1997

Good morning. I want to talk with you today about how we can make this glorious spring a season of service all across America. As I have said many times, the era of big Government may be over, but the era of big challenges for our Nation is surely not. Citizen service is the main way we recognize that we are responsible for one another. It is the very American idea that we meet our challenges not through heavy-handed Government or as isolated individuals but as members of a true community, with all of us working together.

On April 27th through 29th, at Independence Hall in Philadelphia, we will be convening an historic Presidents' Summit on Service. I will be joined by President Bush, General Colin Powell, by every living former President or his representative, by other prominent Americans, including former HUD Secretary Henry Cisneros and Lynda Robb. Every person, business, or organization represented at the summit will have already committed to take specific steps to help to serve our children and to rebuild our communities. Our mission is nothing less than to spark a renewed national sense of obligation, a new sense of duty, a new season of service.

I hope that many activities in the weeks leading up to this wonderful event will make all Americans think about the duty all of us owe to one another. Citizen service can take many shapes. It can mean volunteering nights or on weekends in a religious group or neighborhood association or devoting full years of your life to service like those the Peace Corps or the Jesuit Volunteer Corps members do.

Over the past 4 years, we have worked to harness this citizen energy in so many ways. I am especially proud of AmeriCorps, the national service program I proposed when I ran for President, that we launched the very next year. Since its creation, 50,000 young people have earned college tuition by serving their communities, with the basic bargain of getting the opportunity to go to college in return for giving something back to their friends and neighbors.

The success of AmeriCorps shows that service can help to meet our most pressing social needs, from renewing our cities to protecting our environment, to immunizing poor children, to giving them mentors and someone to look up to. And that service often leads to more service; a typical AmeriCorps member trains or recruits a dozen or more community volunteers.

To focus the American people on the importance of this summit and the urgency of service, I'll issue a proclamation designating the week of April 13th through 19th as National Service Week in America. During that week, over a million young people will participate in 3,000 events across our Nation, cleaning up neighborhoods and working with children.

I've asked the thousands of AmeriCorps alumni and returned Peace Corps volunteers to participate as well, reaching out to youth in their communities, speaking in schools, recruiting volunteers, and teaching a new generation about the power of service. I'm very pleased that some of them have joined our Peace Corps Director, Mark Gearan, here with me today.

I hope that they will teach that citizen service cannot be a pursuit for just a week or a month, that the ethic of service must extend throughout a lifetime. No one is too young to serve. As a recent study by Brandeis University shows, when you begin to serve at a young age, schoolwork improves, and there is a good chance you will continue to serve in the years to come. It's a good habit that's hard to break. And no one is too old to serve, either. But we must find even more ways to encourage our young people to begin to serve.

I'm joined here today by some young men and women from Maryland, along with that State's Lieutenant Governor, Kathleen Kennedy Townsend, who has been a leader in making Maryland the first State in our Nation to require that every student perform some service as a condition of high school graduation. One of the students meeting with me gathered food and clothing for the needy; another, dyslexic herself, taught disabled students; another tutors young children at a Head Start center.

Today I challenge schools and communities in every State to make service a part of the curriculum in high school and even in middle school. There are many creative ways to do this, including giving students credit, making service part of the curriculum, putting service on a student's transcript or even requiring it, as Maryland does. This week, the National Association of Secondary School Principals agreed to introduce service learning to more than 2 million students, and I hope they'll work to find even more creative ways to involve service. States and schools, of course, should be free to decide this for themselves. But every young American should be taught the joy and duty of serving and should learn it at the moment when it will have the most enduring impact on the rest of their lives.

Two weeks ago, applications went out to high school principals all around our Nation, inviting them to select a student in that school who has performed outstanding service, thereby making them eligible for a $1,000 scholarship.

Under this new initiative, which we launched last year, our National Government will put up $500 for each student if it is matched by local communities. Already, a host of civic organizations, including the Veterans of Foreign Wars, Moose International, the Lions Clubs, the U.S. Jaycees, have accepted our challenge to work with their local chapters to provide matching funds for these scholarships. And public servants from agencies like the Agriculture Department will continue to work as partners with these schools, sending volunteers to work with teachers and acting as mentors to the students.

I hope all of you will join in the spirit of the Presidents' Summit on Service and take part in the National Week of Service beginning April 13th. Service is in our deepest national tradition.

Millions of young Americans in my generation were inspired by the call to service issued so often from this very office by President Kennedy. Now it is up to all of us to take up President Kennedy's challenges, remembering, as he said, that every person can make a difference, and every person must try.

Thanks for listening.

NOTE: The President spoke at 10:06 a.m. from the Oval Office at the White House. In his remarks, he referred to Gen. Colin L. Powell, USA (ret.), former Chairman, Joint Chiefs of Staff; and Lynda Robb, wife of Senator Charles S. Robb. The National Service and Volunteer Week proclamation of April 11 is listed in Appendix D at the end of this volume.

Exchange With Reporters Prior to Discussions With Prime Minister Binyamin Netanyahu of Israel
April 7, 1997

Middle East Peace Process

Q. Mr. President, how dangerous is the standoff between Israel and the Palestinians?

President Clinton. Well, I think it's very important to get this peace process back on track. The Prime Minister is coming here at a very good time. As you know, he saw King Hussein the other day; I did, too. And I want to have this chance to spend an hour with him to discuss what we can do to get it going again.

Q. Mr. President, will you be amenable to hosting a peace conference at Camp David, as the Prime Minister has suggested?

President Clinton. Well, I think it's important not to jump the gun on that. The first thing we have to do is get the process going again. There is a preexisting process. There are a whole lot of agreements. And the Prime Minister has got some ideas about what we can do to get the substance working.

Obviously, I've been heavily involved in this from the day I became President. I continue to be heavily involved, and I wouldn't rule out any reasonable opportunity for me to make a positive contribution. But we have to have the conditions and the understandings necessary to go forward. That's the most important thing, is to get the thing going again.

Q. Mr. President, are the Palestinians entitled to a concession in order to make a statement against terrorism, the kind of zero-tolerance statement you want? Does Israel have to trade something for that, or is that just an obligation under the Oslo agreement?

President Clinton. I think under the Oslo agreement and under any sense of human rights and human decency, we ought to have zero tolerance for terrorism.

Q. Mr. Prime Minister, how was your visit with King Hussein?

Prime Minister Netanyahu. It was very good. I wanted very much to see him. He had paid a visit to Israel under very difficult times and, I think, expressed his humanity and his concern for peace, and I wanted to come there. And I wanted very much to come here as well. It's always, for me, a pleasure to meet President Clinton. He is the world leader, who is also taking tremendous efforts and tremendous pains to assist us in the quest for peace with security. I think both of us see eye to eye on the need to fight terrorism, and we'll explore these and other subjects, I'm sure.

Q. Mr. President, you've said that your role is to support Israel as it takes risks for peace. Has the time come to exert more influence or pressure, as some would say, to get certain concessions from Israel?

President Clinton. I think the important thing is to create the environment in which the steps can be taken which will make peace possible. And one precondition of that, obviously, is the absence of terrorism; the other is the presence of a certain confidence on the part of both sides that peace is possible. And I think that I will do whatever I think is most appropriate to achieve that. But you all need to let us go to work here and try to get something done.

Q. Thank you.

[At this point, one group of reporters left the room, and another group entered.]

Q. The Prime Minister said this morning that Israel will not pay with concessions for the right of not being terrorized. Just how badly concessions and gestures are needed now, or maybe the best one is a unity government in Israel to ignite and restart the peace process again?

President Clinton. Well, of course, the form of government in Israel is for the people of Israel to determine and, in this case, for the leaders of Israel to determine, not for me.

I agree that freedom from terrorism is something which no one should have to purchase. I think it should be—it's a precondition. We have to have a secure environment, and terrorism is wrong. Having said that, I think then the question is, how do we actually have an honorable negotiating process which will lead to a peace that the parties can fully and, indeed, wholeheartedly embrace? And that will require constructive steps. That's what we want to talk about today.

But it shouldn't be ever seen as a bargain to be free from terrorism. No one should have to bargain to be free from terrorism. But we do need to continue the peace process in an honorable way that will bring it to an honorable conclusion.

Q. Mr. President, what would be your position on the idea of having some sort of a Camp Clinton for the Middle East?

President Clinton. Well, I think the important thing, if I might, is to get the process going again and to have some idea in the minds of all of us who are part of it about where we're going, an agreed-upon destination, and then to reestablish the confidence necessary for the parties to go forward. I think it's premature for us to commit to that until we can get this thing back on track again.

I've been very active in this from the day I became President and deeply, personally committed to it and will remain so. So I wouldn't rule out anything. But I think it's important that we not put form over substance here. We need to know where we're going, and that's—I need to talk to the Prime Minister about that.

Q. Mr. President, are you going to ask the Prime Minister to stop or to freeze the building in Har Homa near Jerusalem?

President Clinton. I'm going to have a conversation with the Prime Minister, if I can end the press conference. That's what I want to do.

NOTE: The exchange began at 12:05 p.m. in the Oval Office at the White House. In his remarks, the President referred to King Hussein I of Jordan. A tape was not available for verification of the content of this exchange.

Remarks Announcing the Appointment of Sandra L. Thurman as Director of the Office of National AIDS Policy and an Exchange With Reporters
April 7, 1997

The President. Thank you very much. Thank you. Please be seated. Thank you, Mr. Vice President. I'd like to join the Vice President in thanking Eric Goosby for his work as the Acting Director of the Office. And thank you very much, Patsy Fleming, for the fine job that you've done. We miss you. Thank you, Scott Hitt and all the members of the council, for

the good work that you have been doing, and thank you especially for the meeting we had together not so very long ago and the candor and passion of your recommendations.

America has not beaten AIDS yet, but we are getting closer, and we remain committed to the fight and to winning it. More than ever, we need a strong advocate for people with

AIDS, and of course that's why we're here today. Let me begin by reiterating our goal: We want to find a vaccine against the AIDS virus and a cure for those who have the HIV infection. They have eluded researchers so far, but we are committed. The work goes on, and it will go on until we are successful. Until that day comes when HIV and AIDS no longer threaten our people, we must continue to do all we can to hit the epidemic hard with a coordinated effort of research, treatment, and prevention.

When I took office, I established the Office of National AIDS Policy because America had been turning its head away from the problem. Many Americans had not come to grips with HIV and AIDS and their consequences. Now we're learning AIDS strikes in the best of families, and from this disease no community has immunity, gay or straight, black or white, male or female, old or young. Anyone can get AIDS, and if we're going to win this fight, we must begin with the acceptance of that fact.

It was clear 4 years ago, as it is now, that it is only with an aggressive campaign against AIDS that we will win the battle. That is what we have begun. In the first 4 years, we increased overall spending by about 60 percent. In FY 1997 alone, $167 million will go to State AIDS drug assistance programs which provide access to medication, including protease inhibitors for low-income individuals with HIV who don't have prescription drug coverage.

We speeded the time needed to approve drugs to treat AIDS, leading to the approval of 8 new AIDS drugs and 19 for AIDS-related conditions. This has allowed many people simply to go on with their lives, to live with this disease, not worry-free but not in despair either.

We should all take heart that for the first time there has been a marked decrease in deaths among people with AIDS. With new treatment therapies, we hope to see even greater life expectancy. And with education and prevention, the number of estimated new HIV infections has slowed dramatically.

In our war against AIDS, the Office of National AIDS Policy plays an important role. The Office is charged with coordinating all our Federal policy and programs regarding AIDS. It also builds our partnerships with other levels of government and with private-sector communities and organizations. Our Office is charged with keeping us on track in treatment and in education and to keep our focus on research for ways to prevent and cure this disease. An AIDS vaccine could save millions of lives around the world. And we must help those who are already infected. Make no mistake, a cure has been and always will be our very first priority.

The Director of this Office must be an individual with a clear understanding of AIDS as a disease and as a social issue in America, someone who knows the scientific front as well as the human center of AIDS, someone who knows how to fight to cut through redtape to get the job done.

I have found that person in the woman I nominate today to fill this office, Sandy Thurman. She is no stranger to those who know this issue. She's a member of our Advisory Council on HIV and AIDS. She's worked on the frontlines in the AIDS epidemic for more than a decade. She's been an advocate and a catalyst at the State, local, and national levels. She transformed AID Atlanta, the oldest and largest AIDS service organization in the South, into one of the most successful projects of its kind anywhere in the country. As executive director from 1988 to 1993, she tripled its size, beefed up its budget, and made it a direct-service agency with a staff of 90 workers and 1,000 volunteers.

Her experience in running a large community-based organization makes her especially well-equipped to build the partnerships we need throughout our country, for beating the AIDS epidemic will take this kind of teamwork everywhere. I am pleased that she has agreed to serve as the Director of the Office of National AIDS Policy. I've worked with her, and I can attest, she tells it like it is. She speaks the truth unvarnished. She won't hold back in this office. [*Laughter*] She is passionate. She is committed. She is difficult to say no to. [*Laughter*] And I have already assured her that she will have the support and the resources she will need, including my personal support, to succeed in this all-important task. My door is open to her.

And now I'd like for us to all hear what she has to say.

Sandy Thurman.

[*At this point, Ms. Thurman thanked the President and made brief remarks.*]

The President. Thank you very much.

Q. Mr. President, how do you see this czar being different from your two previous czars?

What would you like to see changed? And have you given up on the so-called Manhattan-style project that you promised in '92?

The President. Well, first of all, I think if you look at—let me answer the second question, first. If I had told you in 1993, in January, when I was inaugurated, that we would have 8 new AIDS drugs, 19 new drugs for AIDS-related conditions, that the number of AIDS-related deaths would be going down, and that the quality and length of life expectancy would expand as much as it had, you would think that we had put a pretty good amount of effort in here with a 60 percent increase in our investment.

So I think we're moving forward. What I would like to see is to rely on the President's Advisory Council and the AIDS Office even more heavily to mobilize even more people to have support for the work we're doing in research to find a cure and also to do more at the grassroots level and to tie the efforts at the community level to what we're trying to do nationally. And I think that Sandy will do a very good job of that because of her personal experience in Atlanta.

Q. Mr. President, when you read——

Middle East Peace Process

Q. Mr. President, do you think you've made any progress, sir, in your meeting with Prime Minister Netanyahu? Do you think that you've been able to move the peace process closer to being back on track, as you put it earlier?

The President. Well, we had quite a long meeting, as you know. What are we, an hour late starting here? [*Laughter*] And I apologize to you for that, but it was necessary that we continue the meeting. It was a long and very thorough meeting. Now it's important for us to visit with the Palestinians, and we'll try to get this thing up and going again.

But you know how these things are—it's— I need to say not too much about it and work very hard on it. And that's what I'm going to do. I'm going to do my best to get it back on track.

Q. But Mr. President, Mr. President, did anything—part of the Palestinian frustration is that the Prime Minister says he wants to speed up final status talks. His position, according to them, appears to be final. I was wondering if you saw any change in that position?

The President. Well, I'm—again, I think the problem is the more I comment, the more I undermine the chances of success. We had a very specific, frank, candid, and long talk. And now we're going to talk to the Palestinians and see whether there is something we can do to get this thing going again. And we'll do our very best, and I'll do my best. That's all I think I should say right now.

Q. Thank you.

The President. Thank you.

NOTE: The President spoke at 2:25 p.m. in the Roosevelt Room at the White House. In his remarks, he referred to Patricia Fleming, former Director, Office of National AIDS Policy; H. Scott Hitt, Chairman, Presidential Advisory Council on HIV/AIDS; and Prime Minister Binyamin Netanyahu of Israel.

Message to the Senate Transmitting the Flank Document of the Conventional Armed Forces in Europe Treaty With Documentation
April 7, 1997

To the Senate of the United States:

I transmit herewith, for the advice and consent of the Senate, the Document Agreed Among the States Parties to the Treaty on Conventional Armed Forces in Europe (CFE) of November 19, 1990, which was adopted at Vienna on May 31, 1996 ("the Flank Document"). The Flank Document is Annex A of the Final Document of the first CFE Review Conference.

I transmit also, for the information of the Senate, the report of the Department of State on the Flank Document, together with a section-by-section analysis of the Flank Document and three documents associated with it that are relevant to the Senate's consideration: the Understanding on Details of the Flank Document of 31 May 1996 in Order to Facilitate its Implementation; the Exchange of Letters between the

U.S. Chief Delegate to the CFE Joint Consultative Group and the Head of the Delegation of the Russian Federation to the Joint Consultative Group, dated 25 July 1996; and, the Extension of Provisional Application of the Document until May 15, 1997. I take this step as a matter of accommodation to the desires of the Senate and without prejudice to the allocation of rights and duties under the Constitution.

In transmitting the original CFE Treaty to the Senate in 1991, President Bush said that the CFE Treaty was "the most ambitious arms control agreement ever concluded." This landmark treaty has been a source of stability, predictability, and confidence during a period of historic change in Europe. In the years since the CFE Treaty was signed, the Soviet Union has dissolved, the Warsaw Pact has disappeared, and the North Atlantic Alliance has been transformed. The treaty has not been unaffected by these changes—for example, there are 30 CFE States Parties now, not 22—but the dedication of all Treaty partners to achieving its full promise is undiminished.

The CFE Treaty has resulted in the verified reduction of more than 50,000 pieces of heavy military equipment, including tanks, armored combat vehicles, artillery pieces, combat aircraft, and attack helicopters. By the end of 1996, CFE states had accepted and conducted more than 2,700 intrusive, on-site inspections. Contacts between the military organizations charged with implementing CFE are cooperative and extensive. The CFE Treaty has helped to transform a world of two armed camps into a Europe where dividing lines no longer hold.

The Flank Document is part of that process. It is the culmination of over 2 years of negotiations and months of intensive discussions with the Russian Federation, Ukraine, our NATO Allies, and our other CFE Treaty partners. The Flank Document resolves in a cooperative way the most difficult problem that arose during the Treaty's first 5 years of implementation: Russian and Ukrainian concerns about the impact of the Treaty's equipment limits in the flank zone on their security and military flexibility. The other Treaty states—including all NATO Allies—agreed that some of those concerns were reasonable and ought to be addressed.

The Flank Document is the result of a painstaking multilateral diplomatic effort that had as its main goal the preservation of the integrity of the CFE Treaty and achievement of the goals of its mandate. It is a crucial step in adaptation of the CFE Treaty to the dramatic political changes that have occurred in Europe since the Treaty was signed. The Flank Document confirms the importance of subregional constraints on heavy military equipment. More specifically, it revalidates the idea, unique to CFE, of limits on the amount of equipment particular nations in the Treaty area can locate on certain portions of their own national territory. Timely entry into force of the Flank Document will ensure that these key principles are not a matter of debate in the negotiations we have just begun in Vienna to adapt the CFE Treaty to new political realities, including the prospect of an enlarged NATO.

I believe that entry into force of the CFE Flank Document is in the best interests of the United States and will contribute to our broader efforts to establish a new European security order based on cooperation and shared goals. By maintaining the integrity of the CFE flank regime, we take a key step toward our goal of ensuring that the CFE Treaty continues to play a key role in enhancing military stability into the 21st century. Therefore, I urge the Senate to give early and favorable consideration to the Flank Document and to give advice and consent prior to May 15, 1997.

WILLIAM J. CLINTON

The White House,
April 7, 1997.

Message to the Senate Transmitting the International Grains Agreement, 1995, With Documentation
April 7, 1997

To the Senate of the United States:

With a view to receiving the advice and consent of the Senate to ratification, I transmit herewith the Grains Trade Convention and Food Aid Convention constituting the International Grains Agreement, 1995, open for signature at the United Nations Headquarters, New York, from May 1 through June 30, 1995. The Conventions were signed by the United States on June 26, 1995. I transmit also for the information of the Senate, the report of the Department of State with respect to the Conventions.

The Grains Trade Convention, 1995, replaces the Wheat Trade Convention, 1986, and maintains the framework for international cooperation in grains trade matters. It also continues the existence of the International Grains Council.

The Food Aid Convention, 1995, replaces the Food Aid Convention, 1986, and renews commitments of donor member states to provide minimum annual quantities of food aid to developing countries.

The International Grains Council and the Food Aid Committee granted the United States (and other countries) a 1-year extension of time in which to deposit its instruments of ratification, and have permitted the United States in the meantime to continue to participate in the organizations.

It is my hope that the Senate will give prompt and favorable consideration to the two Conventions, and give its advice and consent to ratification so that ratification by the United States can be effected and instruments of ratification deposited at the earliest possible date.

WILLIAM J. CLINTON

The White House,
April 7, 1997.

Letter to the Speaker of the House of Representatives on Supplemental Funding for the Federal Election Commission
April 7, 1997

Dear Mr. Speaker:

I ask the Congress to consider the enclosed requests for an FY 1997 supplemental and an FY 1998 budget amendment for the Federal Election Commission (FEC).

The FEC is charged with guarding the integrity of our election process. I have sought to strengthen this important agency; its budget has increased from $21 million per year in 1993 to $28 million per year today. But the agency plainly lacks the resources it needs to keep pace with the rapidly rising volume of campaign spending and electoral activities. In fact, over the past 2 years, the Congress has appropriated for the FEC substantially less than I requested.

Today, commissioners of both parties have testified that the FEC is overworked, underfunded, and unable to address the many issues raised in recent elections. Campaign spending by candidates, soft money expenditures by parties, independent expenditures, and issue advocacy expenditures have exploded. As part of a bipartisan effort to restore the public trust in the way we finance elections to the Congress and the Presidency, I urge you to provide these additional funds for the FEC.

In addition, I urge the Congress to enact legislation that would strengthen the FEC as part of comprehensive campaign finance reform. The bipartisan campaign finance reform legislation introduced by Representatives Chris Shays and Marty Meehan and Senators John McCain and Russell Feingold includes several critical steps to strengthen the FEC, strengthening the agency's ability to stop improper practices and allowing random audits of campaigns.

The details of my budget requests are set forth in the enclosed letter from the Director of the Office of Management and Budget. I concur with his comments and observations.

Sincerely,

WILLIAM J. CLINTON

NOTE: An original was not available for verification of the content of this letter.

Remarks Welcoming Prime Minister Jean Chretien of Canada
April 8, 1997

Prime Minister and Mrs. Chretien, members of the Canadian delegation, distinguished guests, it is a great honor and personal pleasure for me to welcome to Washington the Prime Minister of Canada, Jean Chretien, leader of a land of great beauty and bounty and a great and good people.

When Hillary and I visited Ottawa in 1995, the Prime Minister and the Canadian people made us feel as if we were family. The personal working relationship I have established with the Prime Minister for nearly 4 years now has made us good friends.

Today we celebrate one of history's most remarkable partnerships, for if nature has made us neighbors, we are friends and allies by choice. The close cooperation between our two nations should be a model for the world in the 21st century. Every day, 250,000 people and nearly $1 billion in trade cross our border. From the snowy Yukon to the shores of eastern Maine, our border does not divide our people; it joins us as partners and friends, with more and better jobs, cleaner air and water, the comforting knowledge that our freedom is jointly guarded and defended. Together we are working to shape the force of change to serve our region

and our world, expanding trade throughout the Americas, exploring the mysteries of space, speaking out for freedom, and standing up for peace from Bosnia to Haiti. In a world where suffering too often results because people cannot live with others different from themselves, Canada's compassionate, tolerant society inspires us all with hope.

A Canadian Ambassador to Washington once said that summits between our nations are a time to set the beacon jointly. Under your wise leadership, Mr. Prime Minister, relations between the United States and Canada have never been closer or more constructive. As we stand on the threshold of a new millennium, let us raise our beacon high. Let us build a future of peace and prosperity, of freedom and dignity for our continent and beyond.

Mr. Prime Minister, welcome to the United States.

NOTE: The President spoke at 10:22 a.m. on the South Lawn at the White House, where Prime Minister Chretien was accorded a formal welcome with full military honors. In his remarks, the President referred to Prime Minister Chretien's wife, Aline.

Remarks Prior to Discussions With Prime Minister Jean Chretien of Canada and an Exchange With Reporters
April 8, 1997

President Clinton. Good morning, everybody. I'm delighted to have the Prime Minister here, and we're just about to start a conversation about NATO expansion, which is something of importance to both of us, and about some trade issues and a number of other matters. We have

a lot of good agreements that we're going to have signed during this trip, so we're excited about that.

And we're going to have a press conference afterwards, so we'll be able to answer questions about it all.

Chemical Weapons Convention

Q. Jesse Helms called the Chemical Weapons Convention today destructive and defective and dangerous. The hearing is not off to a good start.

President Clinton. Well, I know he's not for it. All I want to do is try to get it on the floor of the Senate and persuade two-thirds of the Senators to be for it.

I think it's obvious that it's the right thing to do for the world and critical for America's leadership that we do it. I do not believe that all those military leaders who were here with us earlier this week and the Republican leaders, including Senator Kassebaum Baker and former Secretary of State Jim Baker, would do something that was dangerous for America. I think it's critically important for America.

If we don't ratify it, then the rest of the world will be compelled to treat us like they treat the rogue states, and it will—just basically to ostracize us and impose trade sanctions on our chemical companies. And we'll deserve it if we don't ratify it, because we won't be good citizens in the world.

Q. Will you speak with Senator Helms between now and——

President Clinton. We're working with him. We've worked hard with him, and we've worked through a lot of his objections, and we'll keep working. But I'm going to focus hard on trying to—not only to persuade him but we have to have 67 votes. We've got to get it out of the committee, and then we've got to have 67 votes. That's what we've got to do. We're going to try to do it.

Middle East Peace Process

Q. Any further words—[*inaudible*]—Prime Minister Netanyahu?

President Clinton. No, I don't have anything to add to what I said yesterday. We had a long, thorough, very frank conversation. I want these parties to do what they have to do to get this process up and going again. We've got to have an atmosphere of zero tolerance for terror, but we also have to have the kind of confidence-building necessary to make peace. And he's got some good ideas, and I think we have some good ideas, and we want to talk to the Palestinians this week and see if we can get this going again. But the parties have got to do what it

takes to get it going, and I think if we work together we can do it.

Q. Did you ask him to stop building at Har Homa?

President Clinton. I don't want to say any more about what I did or didn't say.

Q. [*Inaudible*]

President Clinton. The incident in Hebron? Well, all those things are troubling. But the main thing is we can't let them get in the way of moving the path toward peace forward. That's the ultimate resolution of all these things. We've just got to keep going. They have to decide they're going to keep going, and they've got to do it.

[*At this point, one group of reporters left the room, and another group entered.*]

Prime Minister Chretien's Visit

President Clinton. Let me say again how pleased I am to have the Prime Minister here. We're going to have a chance to talk about our mutual interests in NATO expansion, in Bosnia, in Haiti, and a number of bilateral issues between us. And of course, we're going to have some good agreements signed on this trip, so I think this will be a very useful and productive trip. I know it will be for me, and I hope it will be for the Prime Minister and for Canada. And again, I want to welcome you.

Prime Minister Chretien. Thank you very much. I'm happy to be here. I think it's going to be a very good meeting.

You know, our relations are—you know, terms of trade, for example—the biggest in the world. And when we look at it, we manage to solve most of the problems in a very nice way. And I hope that if the world were to work the way that Canada and United States manage to work together, there would be more prosperity around the world. So you have to keep setting the example. We have to talk to each other to achieve it.

Extraterritorial Impact of Sanctions

Q. Mr. President, what about the issue of Helms-Burton? Do you think there's any common ground to be found there?

President Clinton. Well, I think we have a difference of opinion. I think the real issue is how we manage our differences right now. And we'll talk about that.

The Cuba issue is a difficult issue, but Canada has had a very solid position on human rights, generally. And we just have a different approach here, and we'll try to find a way to manage our differences. I think that's the best way we can do it.

Prime Minister Chretien's Visit

Q. Mr. President, how unusual is it for you to invite a leader from another country to an unscheduled meeting the night before the scheduled meeting?

President Clinton. Well, fairly unusual, but we're friends, and besides that, I owed him a golf match, which I now cannot provide. So I thought, since we couldn't play golf together, we ought to visit and talk about golf and other things together.

[*At this point, a question was asked and answered in French, and a translation was not provided.*]

Q. Mr. Prime Minister, is there a reason why you didn't want people to know about your first visit to the White House last night?

President Clinton. You're wrong—[*laughter*].

Prime Minister Chretien. [*Inaudible*]—called me and said, "Come and have coffee with me," and I went. But he didn't invite you. [*Laughter*] But Moscovitz [Jason Moscovitz, Canadian Broadcasting Corporation] was there with his crew, and he filmed that, and I waved at them. I didn't hide anything. You were not there; where were you?

Q. I was looking for you, sir. [*Laughter*]

President Clinton. It wasn't his fault——

Prime Minister Chretien. But I was not in a bar downtown; you were at the wrong place. [*Laughter*]

President Clinton. It was unscheduled, you see.

Q. Have you rescheduled the golf game?

President Clinton. Well, I have about a minimum—a minimum—of 4 months and probably a couple more weeks before I can play golf. So it's a long way away.

Q. Can you tell us, Mr. Prime Minister, what you talked about last night——

Prime Minister Chretien. Oh, we talk about a lot of things. We talk about our relations and, as I mentioned earlier, that we have managed to resolve most of the difficulties. When we started we had 5 percent of our trade involved in dispute, and now it's down to 1 percent. And the fact that we have managed to talk to each other and very good relations, because we know and we believe—and we might discuss that—that the growth in the world will come if we have more free trade around the world.

And we're talking about the progress in APEC. I will be the host of APEC in November. And we're talking about the expansion of free trade in the Americas as we decided, I think, in December '94 to ratify. And now we hope that they will be able to proceed quickly with the fast track, because when we met at that time, we had a goal to have an agreement with all these countries by the year 2005. But we have to—and Chile was to be the first one, and it was blocked. But now is the time to resume with them. We have signed a bilateral agreement with them. And look at free trade between the two of us—you know, 45 percent increase in the trade between Canada and United States. So we look at that, and we're both benefiting from that.

And when we look at Asia, we know that this is the market of tomorrow. Imagine, you know, more than a billion—200,000 million people in China and India next door. And so when they start to become consumer, they will buy a lot of goods and services from America and I hope proportionately more from Canada. [*Laughter*] But it's fair competition.

President Clinton. Keep in mind, we'll have a press conference later, too. We'll answer more.

NOTE: The President spoke at 10:51 a.m. in the Oval Office at the White House. In his remarks, he referred to Prime Minister Binyamin Netanyahu of Israel. A tape was not available for verification of the content of these remarks.

The President's News Conference With Prime Minister Jean Chretien of Canada
April 8, 1997

President Clinton. Good afternoon. Let me say again that it is a very great pleasure for me to welcome Prime Minister Chretien to the White House. It's an especially important day in his life, because this is the 34th anniversary of Jean Chretien's first election to the Canadian Parliament. In the years since, he has held virtually every high office in the Canadian Government. He has traveled to Washington on countless missions. But this is his first official visit as Prime Minister, and I'm delighted that he's here.

It's fair to say that there has never been a relationship between two nations like the one that exists today between the United States and Canada. We have the most comprehensive ties of any two nations on Earth. Every day, our Governments work together to improve the lives of our people in ways no one could have imagined just a few years ago. We trade goods and services on an unprecedented scale and share ties of friendship that are unique.

We've worked hard today and made progress on important issues. We discussed our common efforts to create an open and more competitive trading system throughout our hemisphere. The benefits of this effort will be tremendous. Since NAFTA took effect, trade between our nations has grown by more than 40 percent, a remarkable achievement for what was already the world's preeminent trade partnership. United States exports to Canada have grown over $133 million and now support more than 1½ million jobs in our Nation. As partners in the Summit of the Americas process, our efforts to expand trade in our hemisphere not only increase prosperity, they also reinforce democratic values, which have made such extraordinary progress in the Americas in our time.

Today we've made concrete progress on key issues involving our two nations. We've agreed on new measures to crack down on criminals who use cross-border fraudulent telemarketing schemes to prey on the elderly and others. We're stepping up our cooperation to stop those who would abduct children and transport them across our borders. We agreed to modernize our border crossing so that by the year 2000,

22 pairs of towns will be equipped with remote video systems and new technologies to give them 24-hour service, and residents won't have to drive hours out of their way to the next border crossing. We're streamlining import and export processing, cutting freight costs, reducing truck backups.

We're working together to protect, clean, and manage the natural heritage we share. Twenty-five years ago, our nations signed the Great Lakes Water Quality Agreement, which has helped to revive the ecosystem of the Great Lakes Basin. Yesterday, Minister Marchi and EPA Administrator Browner signed an agreement to work for the virtual elimination of toxic pollutants in the Great Lakes. This unprecedented environmental effort will involve the public and private sectors at all levels. There are some other areas, like Pacific salmon fisheries, where further progress is needed. But we're working on it.

Beyond our borders, we discussed the preparations for the July NATO summit in Madrid, where the Atlantic alliance will take a major step toward creating security for the 21st century.

I also want to salute the Prime Minister for his government's determination to support peace in Bosnia and Central Africa and other troubled places of the globe and especially for his nation's steadfast engagement in Haiti. Canada's efforts to help democracy put down strong roots in Haiti will long be remembered as a hallmark of the commitment to principle of the Canadian people.

Our work together spans the globe. It reaches into the heavens. I'm pleased that the Prime Minister has brought with him today a model of the remarkable 11-foot Canada Hand that will be used to build the international space station. I have personally seen it in its full size, Mr. Prime Minister, and it is a dramatic and important contribution. This instrument will perform delicate assembly work essential for the space station's construction. And I thank you and your Cabinet for voting last month to fund this important project.

Soon, Canada and the United States will be joined at the elbow in space, and that is a perfect symbol of the cooperation between our nations. Here on Earth, this cooperation has been a beacon of hope for countries on every continent. Today we've made that light brighter by reaffirming the ties between our nations and carrying forward our work together.

Mr. Prime Minister, I thank you, your government, and all of Canada for your dedication to this extraordinary partnership.

Prime Minister Chretien. Thank you, Mr. President. As I said earlier, I'm delighted to be in Washington, and I'm very satisfied and pleased with the discussions we had this morning. They were very frank, friendly, and very productive.

We are neighbors who work together, and I think we're working quite well. The President and I discussed our partnership in the economy, the environment, fisheries, in managing our border, in space, and in promoting world peace.

As you all know, our economies are performing very well, and that means more jobs and growth. Our trading relationship is the largest in the world. It's a real success story. And it is an example to the world. As you said, our trade has increased since 1993 by more than 40 percent, and most of our trade is problem-free. And when we have problems, we sit down and we work them out. Yesterday we announced a series of environmental agreements. We want to ensure that our citizens breathe clean air and drink clean water. Today we are announcing new ways to improve our shared border, all that based on the agreement that we signed 2 years ago on open sky.

But what is very important is our cooperation on peace and security. [*Inaudible*]—with the partnership we have had in Haiti and in Bosnia. We are in agreement on NATO enlargement. We all agree on U.N. renewal, and it's very important that this problem be resolved.

Once again, our cooperation is extending beyond the globe itself with the new Canada Hand, the next generation of Canada Arm. This gave a new meaning, Mr. President, to the term "hands across the border," and it's a symbol of our relationship as we enter a new century. By lending a hand to the American space program, we will be creating new jobs and opportunities in Canada in the high-tech sector of the future.

Sometimes our approaches are different. Sometimes in foreign policy, it's a matter of different means of achieving common goals; sometimes it is because our national interests are different. But we approach these differences with the honesty and mutual respect that a relationship like ours deserves. But the areas that bring us together are much greater than those that divide us. Working together, we are creating jobs, opportunities, and prosperity for the people in both countries, and we are setting an example of international cooperation for the world.

[*At this point, Prime Minister Chretien repeated a portion of his remarks in French.*]

And I would like to say that the Canadian people are very proud to be your neighbor. We have been able to work together, and we will do that in the future because together we can achieve a lot. And for you, Mr. President, as I said earlier, it's extremely important to carry on the leadership that you have shown in the last years because the United States is now the biggest and almost the unique power, compared to the situation that existed a few years ago. And I salute your leadership. And I know that you face some difficult problems, but you'll always have Canada on your side because we are both for peace around the world and prosperity around the world.

And thank you very much for your kind reception. And it has been fantastic so far. And the weather is well-organized. In Canada, I say that it is a federal responsibility. I don't know if it is the case here, but you've done a good job on that, Mr. President. [*Laughter*]

President Clinton. Thank you.

Helen [Helen Thomas, United Press International]?

Middle East Peace Process

Q. Mr. President, you seem to have struck out in getting the Mideast peace talks back on track at this moment. Does the U.S. lack any diplomatic leverage with Israel despite 50 years of assistance and support? And where do you go from here?

President Clinton. Well, first of all, I wouldn't assume that, based on the comments that have been made so far. Where I go from here is that we're waiting for the Palestinian delegation to come in. We're going to review the ground that we went over with Prime Minister

Netanyahu, and we're going to do our best to get this thing going again.

There are clearly two preconditions: One is zero tolerance for terror; the other is a genuine commitment to build confidence and to make progress and to do the things required by the Oslo agreement. And the parties are going to have to decide whether they're willing to let the peace process go forward.

We are prepared to do whatever we can, but I would not conclude from the fact that I'm giving very noncommittal answers that I think there's no chance that we'll get it going again. I think that there is a fairly decent chance that we can, but I think it's important now not to say things which will undermine whatever prospect we have of success later.

In the end, it still depends on what it always has depended on, and that is the parties taking responsibilities to take the risks for peace.

President's Relationship With Prime Minister Chretien

[*The following question was asked in French and translated. Prime Minister Chretien answered in French and then repeated his answer in English.*]

Q. Mr. Prime Minister, the nice words you had with President Clinton plus what you said last night at the White House, would they reassure us in thinking that your relationship with President Clinton is as good or even better than that of your predecessor—Brian Mulroney had with Presidents Reagan and Bush?

Prime Minister Chretien. Perhaps I should translate; there will be an interest in English, I guess. [*Laughter*]

Yes, we are good friends. The President and I, we are politicians since a few years. [*Laughter*] And we can share a lot of debate together and spent a good time together last night talking about the problems of the world and a bit about the political problems that we all face on a daily basis. He gave me advice. I gave him advice. And it's free, so no problem. [*Laughter*]

It's a good relation, but he knows that we will disagree. And I'm—and I know that he will disagree with me. But we have shown that it is possible to tackle a problem at a time. And today we realize that the number of the problems that exist between United States and Canada today are very small, very few. And we explain each other, but sometimes our national interests are not the same. But I have to tell you that he's a good guy, and I enjoy to be with him. [*Laughter*]

President Clinton. Let me say, the biggest threat to our friendship is this injury of mine because it has precluded our indulging our mutual passion for golf. I don't think that—I don't know if any two world leaders have played golf together more than we have, but we meant to break a record, and I've had to take a 6-month respite. But I'll be back in the arena before long.

Anybody else? Mr. Hunt [Terence Hunt, Associated Press].

Terrorist Attack in Dhahran, Saudi Arabia

Q. Mr. President, are you asking Canada to extradite the Saudi man who is being held in Ottawa and is suspected of being involved in the bombing of the U.S. barracks in Saudi Arabia? Is the Prime Minister agreeable to doing that?

President Clinton. Well, let me say we have discussed this. It's being handled in accordance with Canadian law. But I believe the FBI put out a statement about it today, and we are fully satisfied with our cooperation with Canada at this point, and I think we have to let the Canadian legal process play itself out.

Canadian Unity

Q. Mr. President, you came out strongly in favor of Canadian unity during the last Quebec referendum campaign. Can the Prime Minister count on your support again, given the fact that in all likelihood there will be another Quebec referendum in your second term?

President Clinton. Well, the United States—it's not just my position; we have long felt that our relationship with a united Canada was a good thing and that people of different cultures and backgrounds live together in peace and harmony with still some decent respect for their differences in both our two countries. And I would be—I haven't changed my view about that, and I haven't changed my relationship with the Prime Minister, so I don't know what else to tell you. My feelings have not changed.

Mr. Bloom, [David Bloom, NBC] you're new here. Maybe we ought to let you get a question here. Welcome.

Affirmative Action

Q. Thank you, Mr. President. Mr. President, today a California Federal appeals court upheld Proposition 209. If the State proceeds with dismantling affirmative action programs, will that help or hinder efforts to ease racial tensions in America?

President Clinton. Well, I believe if States are precluded from trying to take appropriate steps that are not quotas and that do not give unqualified people a chance to participate in whatever it is—the economic or educational life—but do recognize the disadvantages people have experienced, I think that will be a mistake. And I think we'll all have to regroup and find new ways to achieve the same objective.

I think—as you know, my position on affirmative action is that a lot of the things that we had been doing should be changed. I've worked hard to do that at the national level. But my formulation of "mend it, don't end it" I still think is the best thing for America. And so— and that's what I said in California during the election that people disagreed with me. But I think that we will see that, for example, universities are better, more vital places if they are racially and ethnically diverse. I believe that. And I think that it ought to be a legitimate thing for any university to be able to seek an appropriate amount of diversity among people who are otherwise qualified to be there.

Cuba

Q. Mr. President, on the Helms-Burton issue, Canada has insisted that its policy of engaging Fidel Castro is more effective than your policy of isolating the dictator. Have you seen any evidence that Canada's policy is paying off when it comes to human rights and jailed prisoners?

President Clinton. No, but neither one of us has succeeded yet. I mean, the evidence doesn't—since there hasn't been appreciable change in the Cuban regime, neither of our policies can claim success. But this is an area where I think we have an honest political disagreement. The Prime Minister characterized it earlier: We have the same objectives; we differ about how to pursue it. And since neither one of us has succeeded, we really can't know.

Russia and NATO Expansion

Q. Mr. Prime Minister, a number of experts at Harvard and elsewhere in the world say that the risk is increasing every day of nuclear leakage or nuclear smuggling out of Russia, which conceivably could lead to a nuclear terrorist attack somewhere in North America. In view of that mounting risk, wouldn't it be better to postpone NATO enlargement for a couple of years, continue with the Partnership For Peace, and make sure that denuclearization has taken full root in Russia with START II and START III?

Prime Minister Chretien. I don't think that you can link the two. I think that the expansion of NATO is something that is on the table since a long time, because when those countries decided to become democracy- and market-oriented, we told them that we were to accept them in NATO. And we have to deliver on the word we gave to them, and I compliment the President for the work he has done on that. He has had—he approached Mr. Yeltsin in a very practical way, in a very firm way, but in an understanding way, and we're very hopeful that NATO will be expanded this summer.

President Clinton. I'd also like to comment on that, because I believe that Russia has a big interest in preserving the security of its nuclear stockpiles, and they have worked with us in good faith hard now for years to try to dismantle the nuclear arsenals. One of the important agreements we've made here to try to get the START III agreement in force was also to make sure that we were actually destroying the weapons as well as dismantling them, and we have been working since I've been here very hard in a mutual and cooperative way with the Russians to ensure the security of those nuclear materials.

Yes, as long as they're in existence, I suppose there is some risk that someone will try to pilfer them. We've had instances of that before in the last few years, but if we work at it and we work together with them, I think we're likely to succeed. But I do not believe that the Russians have any greater desire than we do to see any of this material stolen or put into the hands of the wrong people. I think they have a deep, vested interest in them.

Canadian Unity

Q. In meetings yesterday with President Clinton, have you called attention to the international situation, and have you talked about the national unity issue? Has Mr. Clinton asked questions about it, and what were your general observations on the topic?

[*The Prime Minister answered the question in French, and a translation was not provided.*]

Q. Mr. President——

President Clinton. Gene [Gene Gibbons, Reuters].

Middle East Peace Process

Q. Mr. President, in his election campaign, Prime Minister Netanyahu was very critical of the Oslo accords. At one point, I believe he described them as a knife in the back of Israel. And since then, he has taken a number of preemptive actions that have created a series of crises in the peace process. How does that square with your statement that one of the requirements is a genuine commitment to build confidence in the peace process?

President Clinton. I have so far not disclosed anything that has passed between us, but I will say that both—because he said it publicly—the Prime Minister has said repeatedly publicly, and said again to me when he was here, that even though he did not agree with everything about Oslo, he felt that the Israeli Government was bound by it, and he thought that he ought to honor it. And that's been his public statement, and I believe it remains his position.

Free Trade in the Americas

Q. Mr. Prime Minister, in light of all of the discussion and talk about free trade and the possibility of expanding free trade, did you ever think you would be this comfortable as a free trader?

Prime Minister Chretien. Yes. [*Laughter*] Because one of my problems at the time, I was afraid that the free trade agreements with the United States were to be a series of bilateral agreements, one with Canada, a bilateral with Mexico, a bilateral with something else. And I thought that we had to have a system where it will engage at the same time many countries to have a kind of counterweight to the might of the United States. And if we were to be alone, it was to be difficult.

And at that time, I was afraid that they—they worked to be the hub and make deals with everybody. Now that we have the concept of NAFTA, and now that we're looking and I hope that the President will convince the Congress to proceed on the fast track for Chile because we want to have by the year 2005 all the Americas together. And it's urgent that we

move, because some are getting impatient in South America.

For example, MERCOSUR is working very well, and they are lobbied very strongly by the Europeans. And I would rather have them in the Americas than to be oriented elsewhere. So it's why I believe—and I will mention that to the leaders in the Congress this afternoon and in the Senate—that it's urgent to have a fast track to carry on to the commitment that we made in December '94 in Miami.

President Clinton. Let me say, I think it's very important that the Prime Minister has said this here in the United States and intends to continue and follow through with it. I am very concerned that we have not passed fast-track authority in this country. I think we have to do it. It's clear that expanding trade will strengthen democracy in Latin America and will strengthen our hand in the second fastest growing area of the world.

Last year, the MERCOSUR countries in South America did more business with Europe than the United States for the first time, simply because we have not had as aggressive a posture as we need. We had better go on and complete the work of the Summit of the Americas and create a free trade agreement area of the Americas if we expect to succeed.

Wolf, [Wolf Blitzer, CNN] and then I'll answer Sarah's [Sarah McClendon, McClendon News Service] question.

Relax, Sarah, I'm going to call on you.

Alleged DNC Access to Intelligence Information

Q. Thank you, Mr. President. There's a report, as you probably noticed in the Washington Post today, not only suggesting that there's an allegation of improper, unethical behavior on the part of the White House and the Democratic Party but perhaps even a crime, a violation of national security, that sensitive intelligence information was perhaps illegally passed on to the Democratic National Committee in order to prevent a fundraiser from getting someone into a dinner with you in 1995. I wonder if you've looked into that allegation, if you could tell us if there's any merit to it?

President Clinton. Well, this morning the Counsel's office held a series of conversations, which to the present time do not reveal any basis for believing that any sensitive information was improperly transmitted to the DNC. But because it's nonetheless a serious allegation, I met with my Counsel this morning, and I asked him to give me some advice about what next steps should be taken to look into it further. But based on the conversations so far, there's— we have no basis to believe that it was done.

Prime Minister Chretien. Yes, in the back there.

Arms Sales and Illegal Immigration

Q. Mr. Prime Minister—[*inaudible*]—about the United States trying to sell arms to Latin American countries like Chile? And I have a second question for President Clinton. What's your response to the—[*inaudible*]—of Mexico and other Latin American countries about the change in the immigration law in the United States?

Prime Minister Chretien. Is it to you or to me?

President Clinton. They want to know—I think he—you want to know if he objects to the sale of arms to Chile by the United States?

Q. Yes.

Prime Minister Chretien. I don't know what kind of arms you're talking about. This is a problem with—every government has an army, and they have to have equipment. We buy equipment for our army, too, so I don't know if there is some materials that should not be sold. No problems have been mentioned to me in that possibility of United States selling arms to Chile.

President Clinton. Let me just respond to both those questions. First of all, the United States policy is to reduce tensions between our Latin American allies. We've worked very hard, for example, on the border dispute between Peru and Ecuador and even sent our soldiers there to help to resolve the matter in a way that was mutually agreeable to both parties.

And we have made no final decision about what to do with regard to arms sales to any country. But all the militaries there have to continue to modernize their forces. So the question is, you want to help the modernization process in a way that will not spark an arms race. That's how the line has to be drawn.

With regard to the immigration law, the immigration law—I think the fears of the most extreme consequences have been exaggerated. But the law is tougher on illegal immigration and tries to speed up the process by which people who come to this country illegally leave. We have very high immigration quotas. We take a lot of immigrants in every year. I have strongly supported that, and I have strongly opposed attempts to discriminate against legal immigrants. But for all the people who wait their turn and come into this country legally, I think that they, too, are entitled to an immigration system that has as much as integrity as possible, which means we should be fair and generous to our legal immigrants and treat them in a fair way, but we should not countenance illegal immigration, and we should reduce it however we can within the limits of our law and constitution.

John [John Donvan, ABC News]?

Q. Mr. President——

1996 Campaign Financing

Q. Mr. President, there's a perception that, as a result of all the questions and anguished debate about the campaign finance issue, that your administration is in some areas of—other areas of government becoming somewhat bogged down. For example, it is said to be a factor in the delay in appointing ambassadors. It is said to have made the administration less sure-footed in its dealings with China. How accurate is this perception?

President Clinton. Oh, I disagree with that. I can't comment on what others are concentrating on or doing, but what I'm working on is how to balance the budget, how to get my education program through and get the national standards movement going all the way to success, how to complete the business of welfare reform. And dealing specifically with the Vice President's trip to China, he did and said exactly what he should have done and said, and he would have done it anyway in exactly the way that he did. So I just disagree with that.

With regard to the appointments process, the appointments process generally is always more political when you have the President of one party and the Senate of another. I don't think there's any question about that. But we're working very hard. We spent—I spent a lot of time on the ambassadors in the last 10 days, on both the career and the noncareer ambassadorial posts. And with the Secretary of State, the National Security Adviser, the Vice President, we've signed off on a large number. And we're trying to finish the process so we can send a great big group to the Senate and they can all be considered at one time.

So the work of this White House is going right on and will continue to go right on.

Q. Mr. President——

Middle East Peace Process

[*The following question was asked in French and translated. Prime Minister Chretien answered in French, and then repeated his answer in English.*]

Q. Mr. Prime Minister, have you and President Clinton talked about the situation—the peace process in the Middle East? And did you discuss about your position, about the new settlements by Israel?

Prime Minister Chretien. We have discussed, yes, the Middle East problem with the President. I agree with the President that only cooperation between the Israelis and the Palestinians will permit a solution to the problem. We consider that building new settlements in places that were not contemplated by preexisting agreements cannot be supported, because there will be a difficulty to achieve peace.

President Clinton. Sarah, what were you going to ask?

Cross-Border Drug Trafficking

Q. Sir, this is a question for both of you. The records show that there are far more drugs coming over the border from Canada into the United States now than ever before. Can you look into that and maybe do something about it, both of you?

Prime Minister Chretien. It's more trade. [*Laughter*]

Q. More drugs coming in from Canada to the United States.

President Clinton. More drugs, she said.

Prime Minister Chretien. More drugs—I heard "trucks." [*Laughter*] I'm sorry.

President Clinton. I'm glad we clarified that, or otherwise he'd have to delay calling the election. [*Laughter*]

Prime Minister Chretien. But we discussed the problem, and we have a good collaboration between the two groups who enforce the laws in Canada and in the United States. And of course, we're preoccupied by the level of drug trafficking in North America, and we are working as close as possible with the administration to control this problem because, of course, it's very devastating socially in both our countries.

President Clinton. One of the important things we did as a part of this meeting was to take steps to deepen our law enforcement cooperation generally. This is a difficult problem, but the only answer is to more closely cooperate and do the best we can and make the best use we can of our officials and our technology.

Thank you all very much.

NOTE: The President's 140th news conference began at 1:31 p.m. in the Rose Garden at the White House. In his remarks, he referred to Minister of Environment Sergio Marchi of Canada. Prime Minister Chretien referred to President Boris Yeltsin of Russia.

Message to the Congress Transmitting the Report of the Department of Transportation
April 8, 1997

To the Congress of the United States:

As required by section 308 of Public Law 97–449 (49 U.S.C. 308(a)), I transmit herewith the Annual Report of the Department of Transportation, which covers fiscal year 1995.

WILLIAM J. CLINTON

The White House,
April 8, 1997.

Message to the Congress Transmitting the Report of the National Endowment for Democracy
April 8, 1997

To the Congress of the United States:

Pursuant to the provisions of section 504(h) of Public Law 98–164, as amended (22 U.S.C. 4413(i)), I transmit herewith the 13th Annual Report of the National Endowment for Democracy, which covers fiscal year 1996.

The report demonstrates the National Endowment for Democracy's unique contribution to the task of promoting democracy worldwide. The Endowment has helped consolidate emerging democracies—from South Africa to the former Soviet Union—and has lent its hand to grass-roots activists in repressive countries—such as Cuba, Burma, or Nigeria. In each instance, it has been able to act in ways that government agencies could not.

Through its everyday efforts, the Endowment provides evidence of the universality of the democratic ideal and of the benefits to our Nation of our continued international engagement. The Endowment has received and should continue to receive strong bipartisan support.

WILLIAM J. CLINTON

The White House,
April 8, 1997.

Message to the Congress Transmitting a Report on Radiation Control for Health and Safety
April 8, 1997

To the Congress of the United States:

In accordance with section 540 of the Federal Food, Drug, and Cosmetic (FDC) Act (21 U.S.C. 360qq) (previously section 360D of the Public Health Service Act), I am submitting the report of the Department of Health and Human Services regarding the administration of the Radiation Control for Health and Safety Act of 1968 during calendar year 1995.

The report recommends the repeal of section 540 of the FDC Act, which requires the completion of this annual report. All the information found in this report is available to the Congress on a more immediate basis through the Center for Devices and Radiological Health technical reports, the Center's Home Page Internet Site, and other publicly available sources. Agency resources devoted to the preparation of this report should be put to other, better uses.

WILLIAM J. CLINTON

The White House,
April 8, 1997.

NOTE: An original was not available for verification of the content of this message.

Remarks at a State Dinner Honoring Prime Minister Jean Chretien of Canada
April 8, 1997

Prime Minister and Mrs. Chretien, Ambassador and Mrs. Chretien, distinguished Canadian guests and my fellow Americans: It has been a real honor for me to welcome the Prime Minister and Mrs. Chretien to Washington and to do our best to return the warm hospitality that Hillary and I received in Ottawa 2 years ago.

The whole state visit has gone exactly as planned, except we didn't get to play golf.

[*Laughter*] Now, the last time the Prime Minister and I played, we played exactly to a tie. The press corps had a field day trying to figure out how long it took the Ambassadors to negotiate that result. [*Laughter*] But we wanted to give some truly symbolic, ego-overriding manifestation of the equal partnership between the United States and Canada.

From the start of his career in public life—and for those of you who were not here earlier, Jean Chretien was elected to Parliament at the age of 29, exactly 34 years ago today. Throughout those years, he has brought passion and compassion to every endeavor. He has held almost every post in the Canadian Government at one time or another. As I said in Ottawa when I first read his resume, I wondered why he couldn't hold a job. [*Laughter*] Now as Prime Minister, he seems to be doing impressively well at that, leading his nation's remarkable economic success: his deficit down to balance this year, the lowest interest rates in four decades, growth rates near the top of those of the industrialized nations.

Under his leadership, relations between our two nations are stronger and better than ever. Of course, close neighbors sometimes disagree. Family members sometimes disagree. But united by democratic values and our long border and rich friendship, we've always found a way to work through those disagreements with patience and mutual respect, even back in the War of 1812 when, as Ambassador Chretien admitted tonight when I showed him the burn marks that are still on the White House from that war, our people were officially on opposite sides. Nonetheless, the residents of St. Stephen, New Brunswick, actually lent gunpowder to their neighbors across the river in Calais, Maine, so they could celebrate the Fourth of July.

Our relationship works. We measure its merit in the difference it makes in the daily lives of Americans and Canadians. Today we've worked to strengthen our law enforcement cooperation to protect our most vulnerable citizens. We've taken new action to protect our environment and the environment especially of the Great Lakes our two nations are blessed to share.

We've made it even simpler to cross the borders so neighbors can visit each other with greater ease and traffic jams become a thing of the past. We've set our sights on new horizons in space. I thank the people of Canada for providing the special purpose dexterous manipulator, otherwise known as the Canada Hand—[*laughter*]—for the international space station. This 11-foot machine is so precise, it can pick up an egg without breaking it. And now, Mr. Prime Minister, if you could supply us sometime in the very near future a "Canada knee," I for one would be very grateful. [*Laughter*]

The Canada Hand is practical, sophisticated, smart, and strong. Therefore, it is a fitting symbol of the helping hand the people of Canada have always extended to the world. From the days you helped runaway slaves to freedom to the battles we've fought together in Europe, Korea, and the Persian Gulf in this century, to the hope your sons and daughters represent to the people of Bosnia and Haiti, Canada stands for the best of humanity. And every day, Canada leads by example.

Prime Minister and Mrs. Chretien, we are proud to honor the great and good partnership between our nations. And let me also say on a personal note, I thank you for your friendship to Hillary and me, and we applaud your own remarkable partnership as you celebrate your 40th wedding anniversary this year.

To you both, to your nation, to the people of Canada, long live our mutual friendship. *Vive la Canada.* I ask you to join me in a toast to the Prime Minister and Mrs. Chretien.

[*At this point, the President offered a toast.*]

Mr. Prime Minister.

NOTE: The President spoke at 8:27 p.m. in the State Floor at the White House. In his remarks, he referred to Prime Minister Chretien's wife, Aline; and Raymond Chretien, Canadian Ambassador to the United States, and his wife, Kay.

Remarks Following the Entertainment at the State Dinner Honoring Prime Minister Jean Chretien of Canada
April 8, 1997

Let me say to all of you, first, I have wanted Denyce to sing here for a very long time, and I have patiently waited for the chance to get all this worked out. And I heard her sing not very long ago at the annual prayer breakfast here in Washington. And I came home, and I said, "I'm impatient. I'm tired of this. I want this woman at the Canadian state dinner." [*Laughter*] I don't know whether she had to cancel something else to be here tonight or not.

Thank you, Warren, for your wonderful playing and your artistry. I thought they were a fitting end to a wonderful evening.

Now, let me again say to Jean and Aline and to all the Canadians who are here, we're de-lighted to have you. There will be music and dancing in the hall for those of you who are capable. [*Laughter*] And the rest of us will creep off into the sunset. [*Laughter*] But you may stay as long as you like.

And again, please join me in expressing our appreciation to Warren Jones and Denyce Graves. [*Applause*]

Thank you very much.

NOTE: The President spoke at 10:34 p.m. in the East Room at the White House. In his remarks, he referred to Prime Minister Chretien's wife, Aline.

Remarks at a Memorial Service for Albert Shanker
April 9, 1997

Thank you very much to all of you, but especially to Eadie and the members of Al's family, to the members of the family of the AFT, the other labor leaders who are here, and other friends and admirers and those who are indebted to Al Shanker.

I'd like to begin simply by thanking everyone who has already spoken and all the people at the AFT who put together that wonderful film at the beginning. I think if Al were here and were whispering in my ear, he would say, "This has been very nice, Mr. President, but keep it short, we're getting hungry." [*Laughter*]

I have to say also that Hillary very much wanted to be here with me today. She worked with Al on a number of things over the last 15 years, and a long-standing commitment in New York kept her away. But I want to speak for both of us today in honoring a person we considered a model, a mentor, and a friend, a union leader, a national leader, a world leader. But first, last, and always, as the film began today, Al Shanker was our teacher and clearly one of the most important teachers of the 20th century.

In 1983, in April, when the "Nation At Risk" report broke like a storm over America and resonated deeply in the consciousness of the country, that our country was at risk because we weren't doing right by our children and our schools—one month before, I had signed a law passed by my legislature establishing a commission to study our schools and to improve them, and I had appointed my wife to chair the commission. And we were eagerly reading this report and the reactions to it, and we noticed that there was Al Shanker, the first leader of a union to come out and say, "This is a good thing. We need to do this. We've got to raise these standards. We've got to hold ourselves to higher standards. We've got to be accountable. We owe our children more."

That began what was for me one of the most remarkable associations of my entire working life. Hillary and I had occasion to be with Al on so many different occasions, and one of the previous speakers said, "You know, if you go to enough of these education meetings, the usual suspects are rounded up, and after a while we could all give each other's speech, except for Al." [*Laughter*] And it really did make a huge difference. After a while you get tired—you get off the plane; you're spending the night in another strange hotel room; you're showing up at another meeting—but if he was there, I always kind of got my energy flowing, my juices were running, and I knew it was going to be an interesting time. He was always saying that the students he taught wanted to know, "Well, does it count?" I can tell you, whenever he talked, it counted. It counted.

Over all the years, it counted for me. In 1989, when President Bush called the Governors together in this education summit in the University of Virginia and I was the designated Democrat to stay up half the night and try to write those education goals, I was always consulting Al, who was there, trying to draw out of him exactly how we ought to write this so that in the end we could actually wind up with not just goals but standards that would apply to our schools and students across the country. And we thought we had done a pretty good job.

It didn't work out exactly as we wanted. So, in 1993, when I became President, we were working together again, and we drafted this Goals 2000 legislation. And we thought, well, this will get it done because the States will be developing their standards, but we'll have a national measure of testing whether we're meeting those standards, which is what we agreed to do way back in 1989 because Al Shanker wanted us to do that. He knew it was the right thing to do. But it never quite worked out because people always could find some excuse for it not to count.

So, in my State of the Union Address this February, I announced the plan that is what Al Shanker wanted us to do all along, that we would develop national standards and that we would begin to make sure they counted, and we would begin with a fourth grade reading test and an eighth grade math test but that we ought to go on and do more after that. And after the speech, I called Al, as I had been calling him since he'd gotten sick periodically, and I said, "You know, I hope you feel good now, because you've been telling us to do this for years and years and years, and finally your crusade will be America's crusade." Well, he only lived a couple of weeks after that, but he had to know that what he did counted.

You know, I have to tell you that one of the things that I valued most about him and one of the reasons that he had such a big impact

on me is that I always felt that I could say whatever was on my mind to him without thinking about how I would say it. You know how we all relate to each other? You know, when teachers talk to administrators—it's not that you're not honest with them, but you have to think about how you have to be honest with them, right? [*Laughter*] Or school board members talk to teachers or politicians talk to union leaders or union leaders talk to politicians—it's not that we don't say what's on our mind, but we think, well, we have all these sort of preconceptions that we've learned over a lifetime about how people who are in some other group view the world. So it's not that you're not honest with them, but you know you've got to talk to them a certain way or you won't even be heard.

I never gave a second thought to that with Al Shanker. I never thought, here's this guy who grew up in New York City and I'm some rube from the country, and I'm a politician and he's a labor leader, and he's got all this stuff, I've got to think about—after about the second time I was with him, I never thought about it anymore. It's like a huge burden lifted off your shoulders to realize you can say any outrageous thing that comes to your mind if you believe it, and here's a person you can trust to absorb it with a level of self-confidence and integrity that will permit an honest conversation to ensue. And I see a lot of you nodding your heads. You know I'm telling the truth, don't you? You felt the same thing. [*Laughter*]

And if we could all achieve that with each other, if somehow we could give each other the confidence to think and be who we are, the way he did to all of us, what a better world we could build. And he did it not to let us off the hook but to put us on the spot. That was the interesting thing that I thought was so important. He thought that this whole standards movement was essential for democracy to work, that it was the only way we could ever give every child, without regard to their background, a chance to live up to his or her God-given capacity. It was the only way we could ever avoid the kind of false elitism that always creeps into every society, was to give everybody a chance to reach high and achieve high and find dignity and meaning in life.

He did not believe that how you learn depended upon accident of birth. And he thought all the arguments used to deny the need for some sort of national standards for measuring ourselves were ridiculous. I'm very sensitive to that now because one of the things I heard him say over and over again was he would compare standards. When people would say, "Well, standards will tie the hands of teachers," or "They won't be fair to poor kids"—and I heard all these arguments a thousand times—he would equate it to surgery. Now, I'm sensitive to that now. [*Laughter*] And I thought to myself, how would I feel if Al Shanker—I never realized it—how would I feel if I had heard my surgeon just before my recent surgery making all those arguments about "There really is no uniform standards here." [*Laughter*] "Well, there is, but I'm not going to observe it because I have my own way to do it." I'd say, "Please, I'd like to have another doctor." [*Laughter*]

We're laughing about this now, but this was a profoundly wise man who lived with us. And because he was also a good man and a self-confident man and he wanted us to be fearless and thinking, he made us feel that we could say what was on our minds but that we had to keep being honest and reaching higher and going further.

Al Shanker once said something about Bayard Rustin that he should have said about himself. He said the great thing about Rustin was that he didn't put up his finger to see which way the wind was blowing. He had the guts to say what he felt was right, no matter how unpopular it was.

Al Shanker would say something on one day that would delight liberals and infuriate conservatives. The next day, he would make the conservatives ecstatic and the liberals would be infuriated. He really—even though he came out of the, if you will, the left wing of our society in the sense that he was a passionate union leader, when he thought about the future, he never thought about what wing he was seeking; he thought about how he could seek the truth and synthesize the facts and move us all forward. And that, too, is a great gift that we will sorely miss.

And again, I say, he let no one off the hook—no one—not politicians, not administrators, not the public, not the students, and certainly not the teachers.

In the last years of his life, he worked hard to bring people all over the world together around democracy and freedom and dignity. And he wanted teachers to lead the way. As the son of Russian immigrants, he had a deep interest in the work of the United States Information Agency, which has been sending American teachers abroad and bringing foreign teachers to America to support the development of democracy, especially in Central and Eastern Europe and the Newly Independent States of the former Soviet Union.

I want to announce that today, from now on, teachers who participate in these international programs in civic education will be designated Shanker Fellows. Some of them are here with us today, and we thank them for their presence.

In 1999, when the first fourth graders take the reading exam and the first eighth graders take the math exam, they, too, will be part of Al Shanker's legacy. And if, God willing, our budget passes, instead of 500 of those board-certified teachers, like the wonderful woman we heard just before the Vice President and I came up here, that Al Shanker worked so hard for, we'll have 100,000—100,000.

He really believed if we could get one in every school, they would be magnets; they would change the whole culture of American education. If this national certification movement, the standards movement for teachers, could just get one of those board-certified teachers in every schoolhouse in America, it would change the culture of education forever and change the whole way we thought about teaching. And we are determined to do that, and that, too, will be part of his legacy, along with his love of life and music and art and bread, along with all the energy that he put into his family and his friends.

Al Shanker's life fully reflected the wisdom of the words of Herman Melville—I bring out this quote from time to time, and I don't think I know anyone it applies to better. Herman Melville said, "We cannot live only for ourselves. A thousand fibers connect us with our fellow men. And among those fibers, as sympathetic threads, our actions run as causes, and they come back to us as effects."

Al Shanker's cause was education. And through his lifelong devotion to it, he lifted up our children, our schools, our teachers, and others who work in our schools, our Nation, and our world. He was truly our master teacher.

Today, education is the number one priority of the American people. Al Shanker helped to make it so. His life was full of tumult and controversy, of growth and triumph. But what I think he would want to know is, does it count? You bet it does. It counts, Al, and we thank you. We love you, and we bid you Godspeed. Thank you.

NOTE: The President spoke at 12:12 p.m. at the Lisner Auditorium. In his remarks, he referred to Albert Shanker's widow, Eadie.

Message on the Rollout of the F–22 *Raptor* Fighter
April 9, 1997

Today marks a major milestone in the defense of our nation. The introduction of the F–22 *Raptor* air superiority fighter culminates over 10 years of dedicated hard work by thousands of people across the country, the vision and long-range planning of congressional leaders, and the leadership of three Presidents. But perhaps more than anything else, it is proof positive of the know-how and can-do spirit of America's most valuable asset—the American work force.

Today's ceremony is more than just the "rollout" of a new fighter aircraft. It is a tribute to the American worker and testimony to the skill, training, and dedication of our people.

Across 46 states and in hundreds of companies, large and small, these men and women have come together to produce this catalyst for a revolution in air power. I'm proud to salute all those who have gathered for this event and to wish everyone associated with the F–22 much success as it moves into the flight test phase of its development program.

BILL CLINTON

NOTE: This message was read at the rollout ceremony for the aircraft at Dobbins Air Force Base in Marietta, GA.

Message to the Congress Transmitting a Report on Science and Technology
April 9, 1997

To the Congress of the United States:

A passion for discovery and a sense of adventure have always driven this Nation forward. These deeply rooted American qualifies spur our determination to explore new scientific frontiers and spark our can-do spirit of technological innovation. Continued American leadership depends on our enduring commitment to science, to technology, to learning, to research.

Science and technology are transforming our world, providing an age of possibility and a time of change as profound as we have seen in a century. We are well-prepared to shape this change and seize the opportunities so as to enable every American to make the most of their God-given promise. One of the most important ways to realize this vision is through thoughtful investments in science and technology. Such investments drive economic growth, generate new knowledge, create new jobs, build new indus-

tries, ensure our national security, protect the environment, and improve the health and quality of life of our people.

This biennial report to the Congress brings together numerous elements of our integrated investment agenda to promote scientific research, catalyze technological innovation, sustain a sound business environment for research and development, strengthen national security, build global stability, and advance educational quality and equality from grade school to graduate school. Many achievements are presented in the report, together with scientific and technological opportunities deserving greater emphasis in the coming years.

Most of the Federal research and education investment portfolio enjoyed bipartisan support during my first Administration. With the start of a new Administration, I hope to extend this partnership with the Congress across the entire science and technology portfolio. Such a partnership to stimulate scientific discovery and new technologies will take America into the new century well-equipped for the challenges and opportunities that lie ahead.

The future, it is often said, has no constituency. But the truth is, we must all be the constituency of the future. We have a duty—to ourselves, to our children, to future generations—to make these farsighted investments in science and technology to help us master this moment of change and to build a better America for the 21st century.

WILLIAM J. CLINTON

The White House,
April 9, 1997.

Remarks on the Implementation of Welfare Reform and an Exchange With Reporters
April 10, 1997

The President. Welcome to the members of the Cabinet and their representatives as well as to the members of the press. One month ago, I directed the members of the Cabinet to do everything they can to hire people off the welfare rolls into available jobs in Government. And I asked the Vice President to lead and coordinate this effort. Today we are here to receive each agency's specific plans to do that.

We have the good fortune to begin with some encouraging news. Today I am pleased to report that over the last 4 years, from January of '93 to January of '97, America's welfare rolls declined by 2.8 million people. The welfare rolls have now declined by as much in the past 4 years as they increased in the previous 25 years. And that's a great tribute to all of those who worked on welfare reform as well as to the strength of the American economy.

In the next 4 years, we have to move another 2 million people off welfare to meet the targets of the welfare reform law. We have all got to take responsibility to see that the jobs are there so that people can leave welfare and become permanent members of the work force. Of course, the vast majority of these jobs will have to come from the private sector. And I will convene a meeting of business leaders here at the White House next month to talk about what more can be done to aid that endeavor. I also want to say that the members of the Cabinet that have special responsibility there will be doing more. And I'm glad to announce today that, at the initiative of Aida Alvarez, Betsy Myers, the Director of Women's Outreach here

at the White House, will leave the White House and move to the Small Business Administration to coordinate a new effort there to encourage small- and women-owned businesses to hire people from welfare to work.

But the Government must do its share as well. The Federal Government, after all, is a large employer in the United States. We employ a little over one percent of the total work force of our country. Today I'm pleased to announce that we will hire at least 10,000 welfare recipients over the next 4 years, and we will urge private contractors that work with Government to hire people off welfare as well.

I'm especially pleased that six of those who will be hired from the welfare rolls will work right here in the White House. Now, let me be clear: These will not be make-work jobs. These will be jobs that actually need to be fulfilled, work that needs to be done for the American people. We will demand the highest performance from the new employees and insist that they live up to their responsibilities. But we will also offer them a chance at a new beginning.

Today we have with us two former welfare recipients who have found that new beginning. The Vice President and I just had the honor of meeting with them in the Oval Office. They are on my left. To my far left is Rebecca Wilson of Clinton, Iowa. That has a nice ring to it. [*Laughter*] She is a single mother of two who was on welfare, working and attending and—then while she was attending Clinton Community College. Last year, she got a part-time job as a clerk in her local Social Security office.

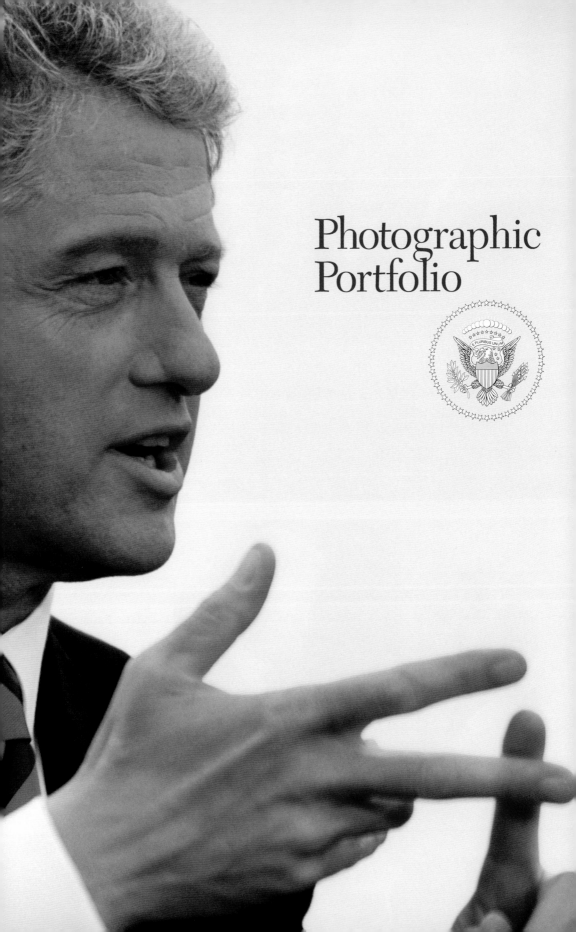

Photographic
Portfolio

Overleaf: Responding during an interview in La Jolla, CA, June 14.
Above: Hosting the Presidents' Summit for America's Future with former Presidents Gerald Ford and George Bush and former First Lady Nancy Reaga in Philadelphia, PA, April 28.
Left: Congratulating Medal of Honor recipient Vernon Baker in the East Room, January 13.
Right: Meeting with President Martti Ahtisaari of Finland and President Boris Yeltsin of Russi in Helsinki, March 21.

Above left: Receiving a Jackie
Robinson 50th anniversary
commemorative baseball cap
from Rachel Robinson in Queens,
NY, April 15.
Above: Touring an area of tornado
damage in College Station, AR,
March 4.
Left: Being sworn in for a
second term by Supreme Court
Chief Justice William H.
Rehnquist at the West Front of
the Capitol, January 20.

Above: With Prime Minister Tony Blair of the United Kingdom and President Jacques Chirac of France at the NATO-Russia Founding Act signing ceremony in Paris, May 27.
Left: Reading to students at Garrison Elementary School, February 21.
Right: With Prime Minister Jean Chretien of Canada and Mrs. Chretien at the North Portico, April 8.
Overleaf: Touring the newly dedicated Franklin Delano Roosevelt Memorial, May 2.

That enabled her to leave the welfare rolls while she finished school. With her supervisor's encouragement, she's now on her way to a business degree. She just got a raise and a promotion 2 days ago. Congratulations.

Rebecca Wilson. Thank you.

The President. And she's been offered a permanent job with the Social Security Administration after she graduates.

Tonya Graham of Plainview, Texas, had a child when she was 16, went on welfare while attending college part-time. She found out about a job at the Social Security Administration through one of her professors. She left welfare the very month she was hired, finished her degree, and is now working full-time as a Social Security claims representative.

These two women are examples that, not just for the Government but for the private and nonprofit sectors as well, if we give people who are on welfare the opportunity, they will do the rest, helping us to break the cycle of dependence and make responsibility a way of life.

The decisions we make in this room today will enable thousands of more American families to remake their lives as Rebecca and Tonya have done. Together, we have already reduced the welfare rolls by 2.8 million; that is the greatest reduction in our history. Now we have to finish the job, and the Federal Government has to do its part by offering jobs to at least 10,000 more welfare recipients over the next 4 years.

We can elevate our most fundamental values of family and work and responsibility and make welfare reform work.

Now I'd like to ask the Vice President, who has done so much to reinvent our Government and who spearheaded this effort to get all the agencies together around this number, and ask him to say a few words.

[At this point, the Vice President made brief remarks.]

Q. Mr. President, if people want to get these jobs, if they think they're eligible for them, how are they going to find out about it? How do they learn whether they can qualify?

The President. Do you want to answer that?

The Vice President. They will find out from the Federal departments in their area. We also have a job bank on the Internet and you can, from a library or from a friend who has a personal computer or if you have an Internet connection in some other way, you can plug into the job bank, and they will be listed there, and you can go to the Federal office building in your area.

The President. But the main thing is, you see, the Federal departments will all be trying to meet their targets. And the people who are placing the welfare workers who will be working for the State, people who interview the people on welfare, will be able to tell them, "Look, the Federal Government's got a program here, and they're trying to hire people, and we'll check around at all of these different agencies in your community and see if there's an opening there." That's how welfare workers—welfare workers at the State level actually interview these people, but they will all know now what our national goals are, and then they'll be able to determine quickly whether, by department, there's an opening in the area. And the welfare recipients will be coming in under the new welfare reform law to these workers, and they will be working together to try to help them get a job within the time prescribed.

Q. Can we ask Ms. Wilson and Ms. Graham if they are making ends meet with their job? The Vice President mentioned child care being a problem. As a single mother of two, are you able to make enough money?

Ms. Wilson. I have a lot of support from my family and friends and all the people around me. So it's been rough, but they're there for me if I need them.

Ms. Graham. And I do not have any small children that are not in school.

Q. What about all the people that do?

The President. We put $4 billion more into child care, keep in mind. But one of things that we have to work on here is we gave the money to the States. Keep in mind that the States are in a unique position now to provide even more for child care than we appropriated in the bill, because their block grant is tied to the moment—the highest—the peak of the welfare rolls. If I make a mistake, Secretary Shalala, correct me. The block grant is tied to the peak population of welfare rolls, which we reached sometime in early '94. So they're getting money now that's more money than they would otherwise get, because the welfare rolls have gone down so much.

Plus, there's a $4 billion add-on in the welfare reform bill to the States to help them provide affordable child care. What we have to do— and that's one of the reasons that this process has been so important—is we've had to work through with each department, since they don't get part of that block grant, whether there's some way they can be a part of it, or the recipient, at least, if it's out in the States as opposed to DC, could get some benefit from it. And we'll have to work through all that.

But I think that there won't be any problem with that, and at least—I think one of the things that will happen as a result of welfare reform, by the way, that will be one of the ancillary benefits is that there will be a lot more child care slots opened up in the country, and that will make available more affordable child care to people who aren't on welfare and haven't ever been on welfare. That's one of the goals that I have, and I believe it will occur.

Q. Mr. President, the two women who are with you are living proof that it can be done, in a sense, without a special program or a special idea. I imagine the critics would say, we don't necessarily need all of this special push.

The President. But you do if you want everybody to be like them. That is, let me—remember what I said all along, from the day I got here and we started these welfare reform experiments over 4 years ago, I said all along, look, the system we have works fine for about 40 to 45 percent of the people because they are like these women. And nearly everybody on welfare wants to get off, wants to be self-supporting, wants to be an independent member of society, would rather pay taxes than draw from the public treasury.

But the system we have—the way it works, especially for people with very young children made it actually—it was a disincentive for a lot of people to get off welfare. So all we tried to do is to create a set of circumstances now where 100 percent of the able-bodied people on welfare will be able to do what these two women have done on their own under the old system.

If we didn't do anything, about 4 in 10 people on welfare would continue to be on a while, get the help they need, get right off, and go on with their lives. What we're trying to do is to get to the other 60 percent. That's what welfare reform is all about.

And the reason we had—let me remind you—the reason we had the biggest drop ever in the last 4 years, according to a study done by Janet Yellen and the Council of Economic Advisers. They say about a third of the drop in the welfare rolls was due directly to specific welfare reform efforts. And a quarter of the drop was due to other efforts like the 50 percent increase in child support collections. And a little over 40 percent was due to the improvement in the economy. And that corresponds with a little over 40 percent who always do—who did well under the old welfare system.

So we're working on the other 60 percent. But the other 60 percent had become a significant problem for America because you were having generational dependence on welfare.

Webster Hubbell

Q. Mr. President, I have to ask you a question about another topic because this is the only time I will see you today, but——

The President. Go ahead.

Q. ——just a little while ago, Mrs. Clinton was asked about questions that keep coming up about efforts—whether the White House knew of or was behind or whether there were any efforts to pay hush money to Webster Hubbell. And she called it "part of the continuing saga of Whitewater, the never-ending fictional conspiracy that honest-to-goodness reminds me of some people's obsession with UFO's and the Hale-Bopp comet." [*Laughter*] And I was wondering——

The President. Did she say that? [*Laughter*] That's pretty good. [*Laughter*]

Q. I was wondering if you share that sentiment? And also, we haven't had a chance to— [*laughter*].

The President. Well, if I didn't, I wouldn't disagree with her in public. [*Laughter*]

Q. We haven't had a chance to hear what your comment is to the apology that Webb Hubbell made and his claim that he was a con artist who fooled people here at the White House. Are you angry at him now? He seems to have caused you a whole lot of trouble, and he seems to be causing it——

The President. Well, no, I'm not angry at him anymore because he's paid a very high price for the mistake he made. And, you know, if he hadn't come up here and he'd stayed home and tried to work it through, he would have paid a price, but it would have been a smaller one.

But let me remind you that everybody pays in life. There's—somehow we all wind up paying for whatever we do, and he paid a very high price. And he's apologized, and I accept his apology. He's got four wonderful children and a fine wife, and he's done a lot of wonderful things in his life, and I hope he'll be able to go on and do some more wonderful things. And as far as I'm concerned, that's why we have a criminal justice system: people get punished; they pay their price; and they're supposed to be able to go on. He got punished and paid quite a high price, and I hope he'll be able to go on with his life now.

President's Health

Q. How are you getting along on those crutches?

The President. I'm doing great. These are my stealth crutches. [*Laughter*] I think really they were developed as an offshoot of B–2 technology, see, and I like them quite a lot. [*Laughter*]

Thank you.

NOTE: The President spoke at 1:48 p.m. in the Cabinet Room at the White House, prior to a Cabinet meeting.

Remarks at the Radio and Television Correspondents Association Dinner
April 10, 1997

The President. Thank you. Thank you very much. Thank you very much, ladies and gentlemen. Members of Congress, members of the press, fellow sufferers—[*laughter*]—I would like to thank the Radio and Television Correspondents Association for inviting me this evening. I want to give Terry Murphy a special thanks for the kind introduction, and also, given my condition, I'd like to give a special thank-you to the Ridgewell Catering Company for bringing me here tonight. [*Laughter*] Enough laughs.

I have come here tonight to speak about a topic of perennial concern in Washington, something we never get around to doing anything about. And that is the close, some would even say cozy relationship, between the rarified elite who make public policy and those who report on it. And on that topic, just let me say this: Congratulations, Andrea. [*Laughter*] You know, that fella standing next to you in the newspaper photos a few days ago—[*laughter*]—he looked exactly like Alan Greenspan, only exuberant. [*Laughter*]

I want all of you to know that, until recently, I had planned out a really dramatic entrance to this dinner. [*Laughter*] And then, George Bush stole my thunder. [*Laughter*] I mean, look at this: This guy is 72 years old; he jumps out of a plane at 12,000 feet; he lands without a scratch. [*Laughter*] I fall 6 inches, and I'm crippled up for 6 months. It's ridiculous.

Now, as you might imagine, my injured knee adds complications to my schedule. In fact, you know, just when I was on the way over here tonight—[*laughter*]—as you have seen, my Press Secretary, Mike McCurry, just handed me a note. According to wire reports, former President Bush has just bungee jumped off the Seattle Space Needle. [*Laughter*]

That reminds me—I was supposed to make another announcement tonight. Mr. Murphy has asked me to tell you that the Radio and Television Correspondents Association has decided to adopt the practices of the Democratic National Committee. [*Laughter*] That means you can all pick up your $1,000 refund checks on the way out tonight. [*Laughter*]

You know, I'm getting a little sick of these fundraising stories. [*Laughter*] But here I am, I'm doing the best to do the job the American people sent me here to do. But with all this ruckus in Washington these days, we have to work harder and harder to sort of be heard through the din. So my staff worked up a few new ideas that we thought might break through. I want you to be the judge. After all, it's your din. [*Laughter*]

Here are the suggestions: Take a cue from the TV show "Ellen." Start a rumor that in the last Presidential press conference of the season, my character will become a libertarian. [*Laughter*] Announce that we've discovered signs of life on Mars. We already tried that, and some of you bought it; I couldn't believe it. [*Laughter*] Announce that I will fight

Evander Holyfield—anytime, anyplace. [*Laughter*] Here's the Vice President's suggestion. Sign an Executive order hiring people on welfare to install computers in our Nation's classrooms, to E-mail messages to neighborhood watch volunteers, to use their cell phones to call 100,000 community police officers, to remind the one million literacy tutors to show up for work. [*Laughter*] If all else fails, push myself down a flight of stairs. [*Laughter*] As you know, that's the one we decided to go with. [*Laughter*] It worked for a while, and I would do it again. I may have to. [*Laughter*]

Thank you very much, Mike. [*Laughter*]

Ladies and gentlemen, you will be pleased to learn that former President Bush—[*laughter*]—has just successfully jumped the Snake River Canyon on a rocket-powered motorcycle. [*Laughter*] Now he's just taunting me. [*Laughter*]

You know, one of the results of being bummed up for awhile is that I've gotten to watch a lot more television than normal, and I spent a day in the hospital just sort of channel-flipping, "surfing," that's what you call it now. And I was amazed at the way all these different channels struggled to accurately but uniquely cover my surgery. [*Laughter*] C–SPAN, of course, provided live, uninterrupted coverage of my injured knee—[*laughter*]—while C–SPAN 2 devoted full coverage to my other knee. [*Laughter*] Within an hour of the accident, CNN had composed ominous theme music—[*laughter*]—and put up a graphic, "Breaking News, Breaking Knees." [*Laughter*] I knew it was going to be a major story when their "Headline News" devoted a full 5 seconds to it. [*Laughter*] MSNBC immediately proclaimed itself the state-of-the-art global interactive command center for all leg-related news. [*Laughter*] ESPN broke into the North Carolina-Colorado basketball game with a breathless bulletin that Greg Norman was just fine. [*Laughter*] PBS kept interrupting coverage of my knee for pledge drives. [*Laughter*] For every $100 donation, you got a commemorative X-ray of my leg. [*Laughter*] Bob Novak went on "Crossfire" to argue the positive aspects of debilitating knee injuries for Democrats. [*Laughter*] And then, there was MTV. All they wanted to know was, did I wear a hospital gown or pajamas? [*Laughter*]

Press Secretary Mike McCurry. Another one.

The President. Thank you, Mike. [*Laughter*] Ladies and gentlemen, President Bush has just

had himself manacled, placed inside a padlocked trunk—[*laughter*]—and submerged off the coast of Kennebunkport. [*Laughter*] The clock is ticking. [*Laughter*] Our prayers are with him. [*Laughter*]

Anyway, I'm back on my feet, and I'm working for the American people. Congress is back in session this week. That came as a surprise to people in Washington who didn't know it was away. [*Laughter*] Things have been so slow this year, C–SPAN is actually showing reruns of the 104th Congress.

We can't get agreement to change the consumer price index; that's the hangup on this whole budget deal. And there are Democrats and Republicans in the House—they're scared to death of it. But you know, a small change in the CPI could shave billions of dollars from the deficit, add years and years to the life of the Social Security Trust Fund.

Now, I know this is a complicated issue for some people, and I've been looking for some simple way to explain it. And so, consider how we might re-index some other statistics. For example, a report said last month that we Americans are the heaviest people in the world. Working together, reaching across party lines, we can change all that. [*Laughter*] Instead of 16 ounces to a pound, we'll say there's 20 ounces. [*Laughter*] That way, a person who weighs 200 pounds would weigh 160 pounds. Think about it: overnight, Democrats and Republicans can make America the thinnest nation in the world. [*Laughter*]

Let me tell you, I'm doing the best I can, but actually I'm kind of hurting. The worst thing about this injury is it's hard to stand for long periods of time, and about this time I start to get tired. So I'm going to sort of sit down with a confession. When I signed that Executive order banning cloning research, it was too late to do anything about an experiment or two that had already been started. [*Laughter*] But one of them has come in handy in moments like this.

"Bill," would you mind? [*Laughter*]

[*At this point, "Saturday Night Live" comedian Darrell Hammond joined the President at the dais and made brief remarks impersonating the President.*]

The President. I have to take this over before it gets out of hand. [*Laughter*] God knows, I can't afford to jeopardize my relationship with the press corps. [*Laughter*] But I want to thank you, "Bill" or "Mr. President." By the way, I wrote up a to-do list for you for the next couple of days. As usual, there's the morning jog; you have to do that now. [*Laughter*] Tomorrow at 3:30 p.m., I have a conflict. I have a root canal appointment and a press conference in the East Room. I know it's going to hurt, but would you mind doing the press conference? [*Laughter*] No, wait a minute. I couldn't ask anybody else to do that, even me.

Actually, I enjoy these press conferences, and I enjoy coming here every year. I thank you all for what you've done to sustain our democracy for nearly 225 years. Our country is still a work in progress, and I look forward to building on that progress with you. I even look for-

ward to these dinners, and I really wouldn't want to send anyone else in my place. So I want to thank all of you for having Hillary, me, and me here this evening. [*Laughter*]

In closing, let me say, we must find common ground. [*Laughter*] We are going to build that bridge to the 21st century. [*Laughter*] I do have to refer you to Lanny Davis on that one. Ya-da, ya-da, ya-da.

Good night, and thank you very much.

NOTE: The President spoke at 8:28 p.m., at the Washington Hilton Hotel. In his remarks, he referred to Terry Murphy, chairman, Radio and Television Correspondents Association; and newly-weds Andrea Mitchell, NBC News, and Alan Greenspan, Chairman, Federal Reserve Board.

Remarks and a Question-and-Answer Session With the American Society of Newspaper Editors
April 11, 1997

The President. Thank you very much. And thank you, Bob, for reminding me of my best line from the speech last night. [*Laughter*] George Bush got the last laugh—[*laughter*]—12,000 feet, not a scratch. I fell 6 inches; I'm hobbled for 6 months. [*Laughter*]

I'm delighted to be here. I want to thank you for having me and congratulate this year's writing award winners. I missed last year, and I'm sorry I couldn't come, but the Vice President told me all about it. And because he came here, I had to listen one more time and look one more time at all those pictures from his days as a long-haired reporter for the Nashville Tennessean. [*Laughter*] This is what it's really like. I don't mind learning about global warming and high technology and everything, but I had to learn all about the newspaper business all over again. [*Laughter*] I hear that speech about once every 3 months from him.

You know, times have changed remarkably since Will Rogers said, "All I know is what I see in the papers." Today, we live in a world with 500 channels, literally hundreds of thousands of web sites exploding all the time—we're trying to develop the Internet, too—but still, the role that you play in informing and educat-

ing Americans and in helping them to make the right kind of choices is terribly important.

I want to talk today about one of those choices that will have a profound effect on all of our lives and the lives of our children in the next century, and that is the choices we must make to sustain America's leadership in the world.

Four years ago I came into office determined to renew our strength and prosperity here at home. But I also believed that in the global society of the 21st century, the dividing line between foreign and domestic policy was increasingly an artificial distinction. After all, our national security depends on strong families, safe streets, and world-class education. And our success at home clearly depends on our strength and willingness and our ability to lead abroad.

The conviction that America must be strong and involved in the world has really been the bedrock of our foreign policy for the last 50 years. After World War II, a generation of far-sighted leaders forged NATO, which has given us a half century of security and played a strong role in ending the cold war. They built the United Nations so that a hard-won peace would not be lost. They launched the Marshall plan to rebuild a Europe ravaged by war. They created the World Bank and other international financial institutions to pave the way for unprecedented prosperity for American people and others around the world. They did this throughout a half century, Republicans and Democrats together, united in bipartisan support for the American leadership that has been essential to the strength and security of the American people for half a century now.

Now we stand at the dawn of a new century and a new millennium—another moment to be farsighted, another moment to guarantee America another 50 years of security and prosperity. We've largely swept away the blocs and barriers that once divided whole continents. But as borders become more open and the flow of information, technology, money, trade, and people across the borders are larger and more rapid, the line between domestic and foreign policy continues to blur.

And we can only preserve our security and our well-being at home by being strongly involved in the world beyond our borders. From fighting terrorism and drug trafficking to limiting the proliferation of weapons of mass destruction, to protecting the global environment, we stand to gain from working with other nations, and we will surely lose if we fail to do so.

Just as American leaders of both political parties did 50 years ago, we have to come together to take new initiatives and revitalize and reform old structures so that we can prepare our country to succeed and win and make the world a better place in this new era.

You know, it is commonplace to say that since the end of the cold war, America stands alone as the world's only superpower. That is clearly true, but it can be dangerously misleading because our power can only be used if we are willing to become even more involved with others all around the world in an increasingly interdependent world. We must be willing to shape this interdependent world and to embrace its interdependence, including our interdependence on others. There is no illusory Olympus on which the world's only superpower can sit and expect to preserve its position, much less enhance it.

In my State of the Union Address, I set out six key strategic objectives for America's prosperity, security, and democratic values in the 21st century: first, a Europe that is undivided, democratic, and at peace for the first time in its history; second, strong and stable relations between the United States and Asia; third, our willing continuation of America's leadership as the world's most important force for peace; fourth, the creation of more jobs and opportunity for our people through a more open and competitive trading system that also helps others all around the world; fifth, increasing cooperation in confronting new security threats that defy borders and unilateral solutions; and sixth, the provision of the tools necessary to meet these challenges, from maintaining the world's strongest, most modern, and most adaptable military to maintaining a strong, fully funded, and comprehensive diplomacy.

On that last point, let me just point out that Secretary Albright often says that our whole diplomatic budget is only about one percent of the budget. We devote less of our resources to that than any other major country in the world. And yet, about half of America's legacy will be determined by whether we have the adequate resources to do that. That's a very important thing, because I think most of your readers don't know that. They think we spend more and get less out of our foreign policy investments when, in fact, we spend less and get more than almost any other area of public endeavor.

Each of these six goals is vital to realizing the promise of our time and to guarding against its perils. Together, they provide a blueprint for our future, not just for the next 4 years but for the next half-century.

In the next 3 months we'll face critical choices that will determine whether we have the vision and will to pursue these objectives. We have to seize the opportunity to complete the mission America set out on 50 years ago and to push forward on the mission of the next 50 years.

We will begin by strengthening the foundation for security and prosperity in our own hemisphere. In the first of my three trips to the Americas over the next year, I will meet with our closest neighbors in Mexico, Central America, and the Caribbean to help our democracies and economies grow together and to intensify our shared fight against crime, drugs, illegal immigration, and pollution.

Just before the 50th anniversary of the Marshall plan, I will hold a summit with the European Union to affirm our transatlantic ties even as we expand our global partnership.

I will host the world's leading industrial democracies at what we used to call the G–7 but now call the Summit of the Eight in Denver, which will give us an opportunity to deepen our cooperation with Russia for peace and freedom and prosperity.

At the NATO summit in Madrid this July, we will continue to adapt NATO to the demands of a new era and invite the first—but not the last—new members to join history's most successful alliance.

And I will continue America's efforts to bring the parties together at this very difficult moment for peace in the Middle East.

Like the larger agenda they support, each of these initiatives calls for American leadership that is strong and steadfast. The powerful trend toward democracy and free markets is neither inevitable nor irreversible. Sustaining it will take relentless effort. But leadership brings its rewards. The more America leads, the more willing others will be to share the risks and the responsibilities of forging the future we want.

In the last 4 years, we have seen that over and over again. We've seen it in Bosnia. We've seen it in Haiti. We've seen it in the Summit of the Americas and in the APEC leaders forum, where we have agreed with our partners to build a free and open trading system early in the next century.

Our leadership also faces two other pressing tests now and in the coming months: first, immediately ratifying the Chemical Weapons Convention; and then, giving the United States the means we need to continue our growth by making trade more open and fair in the global economy.

Let me deal with the first issue. For the last 50 years, Americans have lived under the hair-trigger threat of mass destruction. Our leadership has been essential to lifting that global peril, thanks in large measure to the efforts of my predecessors and during the last 4 years also, when we have made remarkable progress.

The collapse of the Soviet Union left 3,400 nuclear warheads in Ukraine, Kazakhstan, and Belarus. Today, there are none. North Korea was accumulating material for nuclear weapons when I became President. Now its nuclear program is frozen, under international supervision, and eventually will be dismantled.

We helped to win the indefinite extension of the Nuclear Non-Proliferation Treaty, a powerful global barrier to the spread of nuclear weapons and their technology. We led in concluding the Comprehensive Test Ban Treaty, which will bring to life a decades-old dream of ending nuclear weapons testing. President Yeltsin and I agreed in Helsinki to a roadmap through the START treaties to cut our nuclear arsenals over the next decade by 80 percent from their cold war peaks and actually to destroy the warheads so they can never be used for destructive ends.

Now America must rise to the challenge of ratifying the Chemical Weapons Convention and doing it before it takes effect on April 29th, less than 3 weeks from today.

This century opened with the horror of chemical warfare in the trenches of World War I. Today, at the dawn of a new century, we have the opportunity to forge a widening international commitment to begin banishing poison gas from the Earth, even as we know it remains a grave, grave threat in the hands of rogue states or terrorist groups.

The Chemical Weapons Convention requires other nations to do what we decided to do more than a decade ago, get rid of all chemical weapons. In other words, the treaty is about other nations destroying their chemical weapons. As they do so and renounce the development, production, acquisition, or use of chemical arms and pledge not to help others acquire them or produce them, our troops will be less likely to face one of the battlefield's most lethal threats. As stockpiles are eliminated and the transfer of dangerous chemicals is controlled, rogue states and terrorists will have a harder time getting the ingredients for weapons. And that will protect not only military forces but also innocent civilians.

By giving us new tools for verification, enabling us to tap a global network for intelligence and information, and strengthening our own law enforcement, the treaty will make it easier for us to prevent and to punish those who seek to violate its rules.

The Chemical Weapons Convention reflects the best of American bipartisanship, negotiated under President Reagan and President Bush, supported by a broad and growing number of Americans, including every chairman of the Joint Chiefs of Staff since the Carter administration. Last week at the White House, I was proud to welcome a remarkable cross-section of these supporters, including former Secretary of State

James Baker, General Colin Powell, other military leaders, legislators, arms control experts, and representatives from small and large businesses, religious groups, and scientists.

I urge the Senate to do what is right and ratify this convention. If we fail to do it, we won't be there to enforce a treaty that we helped to write, leaving our military and our people more vulnerable to a silent and sudden killer. We will put ourselves in the same column with rogue nations like Libya and Iraq that reject this treaty, instead of in the company of those that set the norms for civilized behavior in this world. We will subject our chemical companies, among our leading exporters, to severe trade restrictions that could cost them hundreds of millions of dollars in sales and cost many Americans good jobs. And perhaps most important, we will send a clear signal of retreat to the rest of the world at the very time when we ought to be sending the opposite signal.

America has led the effort to establish an international ban against chemical weapons. Now we have to ratify it and remain on the right side of history. If we do, there will be new momentum and moral authority to our leadership in reducing even more the dangers of weapons of mass destruction.

Within my lifetime we've made enormous strides, stepping back from the nuclear precipice, from the bleak time of fallout shelters and air-raid drills. But we have so much more to do. We have to strengthen the world's ability to stop the use of deadly diseases as biological weapons of war. We have to freeze the production of raw materials used for nuclear bombs. We must give greater bite to the global watchdogs responsible for detecting hidden weapons systems and programs. Continuing this progress demands constant work, nonstop vigilance, and American leadership.

There is a second matter that demands bipartisan cooperation in the coming months. For 50 years, our Nation has led the world not only in building security but in promoting global prosperity. Now we have to choose whether to continue to shape the international economy so that it works for all our people or to shrink from its challenges. The rapidly growing and ever-changing global economy is an inescapable fact of our time. In the last 50 years, global trade has increased 90 fold. Over the next decade, it is expected to grow at 3 times the rate of the American economy. Nations once divided

by great gulfs of geography and military rivalry are now linked by surging currents of commerce.

Now, the world marketplace does pose stiff challenges. But it offers us great opportunity. In each of the last 3 years, the United States has been ranked the world's most competitive economy. Our exports have surged to record levels; our budget deficit is now the smallest as a share of national income of any major economy in the world; basic industries have revived. Our auto industry is number one in the world again for the first time since the 1970's. From semiconductors to biotech to Hollywood, American firms lead the industries that are remaking the world. Our economy produced 11½ million jobs in the last 4 years for the first time ever. Our unemployment today is 5.2 percent; that's 1½ percent lower than the 25-year average before I took office.

We can make the most of this new economic era. We do not need to be afraid of global trade. But in a world where we have only 4 percent of the population and where the fastest growing markets for our products and services are Asia and Latin America, where export-related jobs pay 13 to 16 percent more than other American jobs, we don't have a choice; we have to export. To do that, we have to have higher skills, stronger productivity, deeper investment. That's why we have to balance the budget—to keep our interest rates down, our investment up, and to keep the economy going.

We have to give our people the best education in the world. That's why we need the new national school standards. We must open the doors of college to all. We ought to pass the "GI bill" for America's workers I've proposed that would give every unemployed and underemployed person a skills grant to use and get into training that he or she needs.

We must continue to expand research and development in both the public and private sectors. And in every opportunity, we have to press forward for more open international trade.

Our administration has concluded more than 200 separate trade agreements, each of which opens someone else's markets wider to American business. We fought for NAFTA, which created the free market with our neighbors, and today, in spite of its economic crisis, our exports to Mexico are up 37 percent over pre-NAFTA levels. We broke 7 years of global gridlock and successfully negotiated the new round of GATT, which has lowered average tariffs on Americans goods around the world by one-third. We have broken down barriers and boosted exports to Japan, up 41 percent since 1993 and 85 percent in the areas where we have negotiated specific trade agreements.

This is a record to build on, not to rest on. When the momentum for open market falters, the world can easily slide backward. And when America falters, our relative position will certainly slide backward. It is unacceptable for us to sit on the sidelines while other nations forge bonds of trade. Only American leadership can create the prosperity for our people and for the world in the next 50 years. And America cannot lead if we don't act.

And here's what the issue is: Every American President since 1974, Democrat and Republican alike, has had the authority to negotiate new trade agreements, called fast-track negotiating authority, which permits the agreements to be presented in a package to the Congress to be approved up or down. Every time this has been extended with the support of Members of Congress of both parties. That is how we have exercised our most fundamental economic leadership. That authority has expired. And today I renew my call to Congress to give me the authority to negotiate new trade agreements that will create opportunities for our workers and our businesses in the global economy and will maintain our leadership in creating the kind of world we want the young people who are here in this audience to live in.

We have seen in the past 6 months what a strong trade agreement can do for our people and our businesses. The information technology agreement that we reached with 37 other nations in December will eliminate tariffs and unshackle trade on $500 billion of trade in computers, semiconductors, and telecommunications. This amounts to a $5 billion cut in tariffs on American products exported to other nations. It can lead to hundreds of thousands of high-wage jobs for Americans.

Now, if Congress grants fast-track authority, I can use it to open trade in areas where American firms are leading and where our future lies. We lead the world in high technology. In years to come, we must press to tear down barriers that keep that technology, products like computer software, medical equipment, environmental technology out of other markets.

We lead the world in agricultural exports. We have to negotiate trade agreements to open even more markets. We will negotiate a comprehensive free trade agreement with Chile and follow through on our leadership to determine the future of trade in our own hemisphere with our own neighbors, all of whom but one are democracies. And we have to keep them that way and keep them strong.

We will press aggressively to open markets in Asia as well. We must also continue to open opportunities in the world's newest market economies. In particular, I urge Congress to support my new partnership for freedom, to expand trade and investment, entrench free markets in democracy, and promote stability in Russia and the New Independent States.

If we don't seize these opportunities, our competitors surely will. Let me just give you one example. Last year, for the first time ever, Latin American nations had more trade with Europe than the United States. There is no reason to think that others will wait while we sit idle. These nations, in Latin America especially, are our friends; they're our partners. They have done an enormously important thing in moving to freedom and democracy in the last few years all over Central and South America. We dare not let this opportunity pass us by.

I am determined that the new trade agreements we seek will be good for our working people. After all, we've got 11½ million more jobs and 5.2 percent unemployment; we know we can make it good for the American people. And I am determined that they will be good for the environment. More and more, in the future, we will see nations negotiating environmental partnerships for the sake of their economies and the stability of their society and the future of their children.

I have asked the United States Trade Representative, Charlene Barshefsky, to work with Members of Congress of both parties, with labor and business and environmental groups to try to reach consensus on these issues. But let me be clear: There is one consensus we cannot avoid. We cannot shrink from the challenges of leadership in the global economy.

Trade and communications are remaking our world. They're bringing it closer together. They're bringing a revolution in global trade. Because in the long run we know that it's going to happen, we ought to lead it. We have to lead it. And if we do, it will increase our buying power and expand our exports. American workers and businesses, given the chance, can outcompete anyone, and I hope Congress will help me let them do just that.

The larger question we face is as old as America: whether to turn inward or reach outward, whether to fear change or embrace it. Over the past 50 years, over the past 4 years, I believe we've made the choices that have served America well.

Now we face another moment of choice. While we no longer face a single implacable foe, the enemy of our time is inaction. It is so easy to be inactive when things seem to be going well and so easy to believe a new choice will cause more trouble than it will do good. But we did not get where we are today by being inactive or by sitting on the sidelines. The decisions we make in the next few months will set America's course in the world for the next 50 years. We have to make them together, and they must be the right ones.

Thank you very much.

Security Classified Information

[*A participant asked if the President would support legislation proposed by the Commission on Protection and Reduction of Government Secrecy to place restraints on security classification of Government documents and to create a declassification center to report to the Congress on progress in that area.*]

The President. Well, first of all, let me say, the short answer to your question is: I think there has to be—we have to do something about it to respond to the commission's report and to respond to the fact that there are too many people who can make too many things classified in the Government. And we are reviewing the report. We have also started conversations with Members of Congress about it. And I'm—we're attempting to fashion what we think is the appropriate response. But let me remind you that I believe that we ought to unearth more documents and not keep so many secrets for so long.

I've worked very hard to open up documents since I've been President. We did it with the human radiation experiments. We have conducted a relentless effort to find out what really happened in the Gulf war, in terms of whether our people were or were not and to what extent exposed to dangerous chemicals. And in any

number of other ways, I support the general thrust for the commission's report.

I have asked my staff to study it. I have not received a specific recommendation on the specific points in the report, but generally I think there is too much secrecy in the Government, and I think too many people have too much unfettered discretion just to declare documents secret, and I think that you will see some significant progress coming out of this.

Domestic Chemical Weapons Stockpiles

[*A participant asked about more intensive scrutiny of the Nation's aging chemical weapons stockpiles, suggesting accelerated disposal and highway infrastructure improvements to decrease risks to the public.*]

The President. You've asked me a question no one's ever asked me before, but I can tell you the answer to the first question is, does it make more sense to bring more attention to the country about it? The answer to that is yes, if for no other reason, not just because of what your people may be exposed to but because one of the reasons we decided to destroy all this before I ever came along—my predecessors made that decision, it was the right one—is that you don't want even small amounts of these kinds of chemicals in the · wrong hands—can be used for very bad things.

And let me also say—now, on the second question, I will have to go back and see what the facts are and see what we can do to accelerate it. I don't know enough now to give you a sensible answer, but you've asked a good question, and I will get an answer, and I'll get back to you. And let me just make one other point on this. Some of the opponents of the Chemical Weapons Convention say, "Well, you know, you can't protect everybody against everything." Well, if that were the standard, we'd never have any treaties, and we wouldn't pass any laws.

You know, still, some people may be able to cook up chemical weapons in laboratories in their garages. But if you look at what happened to the Japanese people, for example, when the extremist sect unleashed the sarin gas in the Tokyo subway, it was a devastating thing. Now, maybe they could or could not do that once the chemical weapons regime is fully in force and we have much tighter restrictions on what can cross national lines. But one thing we know for sure: Japan has already ratified this treaty because they have suffered through this, and they know even if somebody who has got a half-cocked idea and a home-baked laboratory can go out and do something terrible like this, there will be fewer incidents like this if we pass the Chemical Weapons Convention.

And I think it's very interesting—a lot of the objections that have been raised to this convention in America were totally dismissed out of hand in Japan, a country that has genuinely suffered from chemicals like this in the hands of terrorists. But that goes back to the question the gentleman from Alabama asked, and it's one of the reasons we want to destroy our stockpiles as quickly as possible, because, in addition to the risks that people in the area are exposed to, we want to minimize the chances that anybody ever can get their hands on any of this for mischievous, evil purposes.

Access to Chemical Weapons Technology

[*A participant requested a response to the argument that the Chemical Weapons Convention might allow some rogue states access to U.S. chemical weapons technology and asked if the President could change the treaty to ensure its ratification.*]

The President. Well, first of all, it is—let me answer the second question first, and then I'll go back. In general, obviously no one country can change the body of a treaty which has already been ratified by other countries; we can't do that, and lots of other countries have ratified it. But every country is empowered to, in effect, attach a set of understandings as to what the treaty means, and as long as they're not plainly inconsistent with the thrust of the document and don't vitiate it, they can go forward. And one of the things we've been doing with a lot of the opponents and the skeptics of the treaty—Senator Helms, for example, and others raised, I think, 30 different questions in the beginning, and we have reached agreement, I believe, in 20 of those 30 areas, and we've offered alternatives that we believe are reasonable in the other areas.

Let me just say for those of you who may not understand this, Iran is a signatory of the—they have ratified the Chemical Weapons Convention. Iraq and Libya have not and will not. The concern is that if a country is attacked by chemical weapons, and they are part of the treaty, that all the rest of us have pledged to

do something to help them. And the concern would be, well, what if Iran is attacked by Iraq, and the United States and Germany, for example, give them a lot of sophisticated defense technology on chemical weapons, and they turn around and use the chemical weapons against someone else—in other words, if they turned out to have lied about their promise in the treaty? That's the argument.

We have made it clear that, as regards other countries, we will not do anything to give them our technology—not Iran, not anybody—and that's what our response will be, will be limited to helping them deal with the health effects of the attack. We will help people in medical ways and with other things having to do with the health consequences.

So I believe that the compromise we have reached on that, once it becomes fully public and the language is dealt with, will be acceptable to at least most of those who have opposed the treaty on that ground.

Cuba

[*A participant asked about the difference between the U.S. policy of engagement with such countries as China, Vietnam, and North Korea, and the policy of embargo for Cuba, suggesting it would be better to open up Cuba.*]

The President. Well, I think, first of all, as a practical matter, with each of these countries, we do what we think is in our interest and what is most likely to further our interest. Secondly, the other three countries you have mentioned have not murdered any Americans lately.

We had a law that I strongly supported, the Cuba democracy act. I strongly supported it. I thought it was absolutely the right policy. It strengthened the economic embargo but also gave us a chance to open up relations to Cuba and to take care of humanitarian problems, to facilitate travel, to do all kinds of things. And we were implementing that law. It gave the Executive requisite flexibility. And in return for the Cuba democracy act, the Castro government illegally shot down two planes and murdered Americans. And so we changed our policy. Congress was outraged. They passed the Helms-Burton law, and I signed it regretfully but not reluctantly.

And our policy toward Cuba, therefore, today is one that was dictated by Cuba, not by the United States. And until I see some indication of willingness to change, it's going to be very difficult to persuade me to change our policy. And I would have a different attitude toward China or Vietnam or North Korea if they murdered any Americans. And I would hope you would want me to have a different attitude toward them if they did.

President's Legacy and Aspirations for the Future

[*A participant said his son's class would vote for the first time in 2004 and asked what the President's legacy would be for them and what they could do to prepare themselves for the future.*]

The President. Let me answer the second question first. I think the following things I would recommend to the fifth graders to prepare themselves for the 21st century. Number one, first and foremost, be a good student. Learn all you can. Learn the hard things as well as those that aren't hard for you. And stay out of trouble. Don't do something dumb, like get involved with drugs or alcohol or something that will wreck your life. Learn. Be a good student.

Secondly, get to know people who are your age but who are different from you, people of a different racial or ethnic group, people of a different religion, because you're going to live in the most multiethnic, multiracial, multireligious democracy in human history. And how we handle that will determine whether the 21st century is also an American century—still somewhat of an open question, although I'm encouraged about it.

The third thing I would say is, learn as much as you can about the rest of the world, because it will be a smaller world and you will need to know more about it.

And the fourth thing I would say is, start to take the responsibilities of citizenship seriously and find some way—even at the age of 10—to be of service in your community, whether it's helping some student in your school that's not learning as well as he or she should or doing something on the weekends to help people who are unfortunate. I think that we need to build an ethic of citizen service into our young people.

Those are the four things I would advise him to do.

In terms of what I hope the legacy will be, I hope people will look back on this period and say that while I was President, we prepared America for the 21st century basically in three ways: that we preserved the American dream of opportunity for everybody who is willing to work for it; number two, that we preserved America's leadership for peace and freedom and prosperity in the world, and the world is a better place because of it; and number three, that Americans are living in greater harmony with one another as one America because we passionately advocated a respect for people's differences and respect for our shared values, and we made real progress in overcoming these divides and extremist hatreds that have not only weakened our democracy but are virtually destroying countries all around the world.

Or in a more pedestrian way, I hope at least people will say, "Well, after Bill Clinton was President, at least we had a new set of problems to deal with." [*Laughter*]

In 1983, I was in Portland, Maine, at a Governors conference. And the former Senator and former Secretary of State, Edmund Muskie, who recently passed away—a remarkable man—was there. And we were having a visit, and he said, "You know, I loved being a Governor. In some ways I liked it even more than being a Senator or Secretary of State. I liked running something." And I said, "How did you keep score, Senator Muskie? How did you know whether you had succeeded or not?" He said, "I knew I had succeeded if my successor had a new set of problems." [*Laughter*]

And you think about it: We will always have problems. It's endemic to the human condition and to the nature of life. The way you define progress is if you get a new set of problems and if you get over it.

And particularly, I feel, on this whole issue of how we deal with our racial diversity—it's something, of course, that's dominated my whole life because I grew up as a Southerner, but it's a very different issue now. It's more than black Americans and white Americans. The majority of students in the Los Angeles County schools are Hispanic. And there are 4 school districts in America—4—where there are children who have more than 100 different racial, ethnic, or linguistic backgrounds within the school districts already.

So this is a big deal. And every issue that we debate, whether it's affirmative action or immigration or things that seem only peripherally involved in this, need to be viewed through the prism of how we can preserve one America, the American dream, our shared values, and still accord people real respect and appreciation for their independent heritages. It will be a great, great challenge. It's a challenge that, by the way, I think the newspapers of the country can do a lot to help promote in terms of advancing dialogue, diversifying your own staffs, doing the things that will help America to come to grips with what it means not to be a country with a legacy of slavery and the differences between blacks and whites but to have grafted onto that not only the immigration patterns of the early 20th century but what is happening to us now.

It is really potentially a great thing for America that we are becoming so multi-ethnic at the time the world is becoming so closely tied together. But it's also potentially a powder keg of problems and heartbreak and division and loss. And how we handle it will determine, really—that single question may be the biggest determinant of what we look like 50 years from now and what our position in the world is and what the children of that age will have to look forward to.

National Economy

[*A participant said his area had been devastated by downsizing of the military and asked how the President's trade policies would help revive its citizens' spirits and its economy.*]

The President. Well, let's talk about the downsizing of the military and the trade policy. The trade policy alone won't necessarily revive a place with a stagnant economy, because very often the trade policy increases jobs in the places that are already doing well, because success will build on success. So the only way it can help is if the people in the Mohawk Valley can identify companies that are going to have to expand because of expanding trade and try to get the expansions to locate there.

But what I think is important—and I believe the United States, first of all, has an extra obligation to communities that have been adversely affected by military downsizing. And we have worked very hard to accelerate the rate at which we work with communities that have had military downsizing, to give them back the resources that they can use to rebuild their communities. In many places, we've had a lot of success; in some places we haven't.

Secondly, I think it's important that in areas like yours the United States gives greater economic incentives for new investment to diversify the economy. One of the things that I have asked the Congress to do in my balanced budget plan is to more than double the number of empowerment zones and enterprise communities from the numbers we have now in the new plan, so we can give real incentives for people to invest their money and to create good, stable, long-term jobs in areas with high unemployment rates.

If there's anything else you can think of I can do, I'll be happy to do it. If there's anything we should have done in the defense downsizing to benefit your area that we haven't done, I'll be happy to look into that. But I think the main thing we have to do at the national level is to keep the economy strong and then to create extra incentives for people—like people we're trying to move from welfare to work where I proposed some special incentives—or for places with high unemployment rates, so that we can more uniformly spread economic opportunity.

When you see that America has a 5.2 percent unemployment rate, that's very misleading. We have a lot of States with unemployment rates below 4 percent now. We have within States a lot of communities with unemployment rates below 5.2 percent. But we still have places with unemployment rates of 7, 8, 9, 10, 12 percent. And so the trick is to create the economic incentives that will even out the investment patterns. And that's what I'm trying to do. And if you can think of anything specific I can do to help you, I hope you'll feel free to contact me and let me know.

Thank you very much.

NOTE: The President spoke at 12:17 p.m. at the J.W. Marriott Hotel. In his remarks, he referred to Bob Giles, board president, American Society of Newspaper Editors.

Statement on the District Court Decision Striking Down the Line Item Veto
April 11, 1997

I firmly believe that the lower court has ruled incorrectly in striking down this landmark line item veto legislation. I continue to believe that the line item veto—a power exercised by 43 Governors—is an important tool for the President to strike wasteful spending and tax items from legislation. The last Congress took the right step in enacting this important tool, and I was very pleased to sign it into law.

The Solicitor General has reviewed the decision and has authorized an immediate appeal to the United States Supreme Court. The Solicitor General intends to ask the Supreme Court to expedite the consideration of the appeal and to schedule argument in June so that the case can be decided before the conclusion of the Court's term at the end of June.

This action has my strong support. It is my hope that it will result in an expedited ruling that clears up any confusion.

Memorandum on Expanded Family and Medical Leave Policies
April 11, 1997

Memorandum for the Heads of Executive Departments and Agencies

Subject: Expanded Family and Medical Leave Policies

I have strongly supported meeting Federal employees' family and medical leave needs through enactment of the Family and Medical Leave Act of 1993 (FMLA) and the Federal Employees Family Friendly Leave Act of 1994 (FEFFLA). However, Federal employees often have important family and medical needs that do not qualify for unpaid leave under the FMLA or sick leave under the FEFFLA. I ask you to take immediate action to assist Federal workers further in balancing the demands of work and family.

Last year I proposed to expand the Family and Medical Leave Act of 1993. My legislation would allow Federal and eligible private sector workers 24 hours of unpaid leave during any 12-month period to fulfill certain family obligations. Under the legislation, employees could use unpaid leave to participate in school activities directly related to the educational advancement of a child, including early childhood education activities; accompany children to routine medical and dental examinations; and tend to the needs of older relatives.

In furtherance of my proposed policy, I ask that you take immediate action within existing statutory authorities to ensure that Federal employees may schedule and be granted up to 24 hours of leave without pay each year for the following activities:

(1) *School and Early Childhood Educational Activities*—to allow employees to participate in school activities directly related to the educational advancement of a child. This would include parent-teacher conferences or meetings with child-care providers, interviewing for a new school or child-care facility, or participating in volunteer activities supporting the child's educational advancement. In this memorandum, "school" refers to an elementary school, secondary school, Head Start program, or a child-care facility.

(2) *Routine Family Medical Purposes*—to allow parents to accompany children to routine medical or dental appointments, such as annual checkups or vaccinations. Although these activities are not currently covered by the FMLA, the FEFFLA does permit employees to use up to 13 days of sick leave each year for such purposes. Agencies should assure that employees are able to use up to 24 hours of leave without pay each year for these purposes in cases

when no additional sick leave is available to employees.

(3) *Elderly Relatives' Health or Care Needs*—to allow employees to accompany an elderly relative to routine medical or dental appointments or other professional services related to the care of the elderly relative, such as making arrangements for housing, meals, phones, banking services, and other similar activities. Although Federal employees can use unpaid leave or sick leave for certain of these activities under the FMLA or FEFFLA, such as caring for a parent with a serious health condition, agencies should ensure employees can use up to 24 hours of unpaid time off each year for this broader range of activities related to elderly relatives' health or care needs.

This new policy will assure that Federal employees can schedule and receive up to 24 hours away from the job each year for these family and medical circumstances. I also urge you to accommodate these employee needs as mission requirements permit, even when it is not possible for employees to anticipate or schedule leave in advance for these purposes. In addition, I ask that you support employees' requests to schedule paid time off—such as annual leave, compensatory time off, and credit hours under flexible work schedules—for these family activities when such leave is available to these employees. The Office of Personnel Management shall provide guidance to you on the implementation of this memorandum.

I encourage you to use a partnership approach with your employees and their representatives in developing an effective program that balances the employees' needs to succeed both at work and at home. I ask agencies, unions, and management associations to continue to work together to assess and improve the use of family-friendly programs and to make certain that employees are aware of the expanded family and medical leave policy.

WILLIAM J. CLINTON

NOTE: This memorandum was embargoed for release until 10:06 a.m. on April 12.

The President's Radio Address
April 12, 1997

Good morning. Today I want to talk about the toughest job any person can have. It's not a job you can quit, show up late for, or do just enough to get by. In every way, it's a lifetime commitment: It's being a parent.

In our times, parenting has become an even greater challenge. The world moves faster, and parents rightly worry more about how to protect their children's health, their safety, and their future. Jobs place more demands on mothers and fathers. Finding a balance between home and work takes more effort than ever.

Parents can use some help. And while Government doesn't raise children, it can sometimes give parents the tools they need to make their jobs easier. That's why we fought for and won the V-chip and a ratings system for TV, so parents can better protect their young children from unsuitable shows. That's why we fought to keep the tobacco industry from advertising their products to children and why we're fighting to keep streets safer and to reduce juvenile crime. All these help parents to do a better job with their children.

But there is still work to be done. Parents want to do the right thing by their children from the very start. And giving our youngest children what they need to thrive from the very first days of life is something the First Lady has studied for a long time. In her book, "It Takes a Village," Hillary called on our Nation to give its attention to new findings about the early years of children's lives that so often are overlooked in intellectual, social, and emotional development.

Our administration has worked hard to better understand these early years. Since 1993, we've increased funding for children's research at the National Institutes of Health by 25 percent, or

$322 million, and my balanced budget plan promotes further increases in funding. We've expanded and improved Head Start, and we created an Early Head Start program for children age 3 or younger so that they could get the stimulation they need at those critical times.

From our research, we know that from the very first days of life a child is developing emotionally and intellectually, and how he or she does in those first 3 years of life will help to determine how a child does later in school and in life. That's why we need to begin teaching and nurturing our children before they go to school.

We want to sort through our research and get it to parents and to caregivers who work with children. So next week Hillary and I will bring together researchers, parents, and other experts for the White House Conference on Early Childhood Development and Learning: What New Research on the Brain Tells Us About Our Youngest Children.

We will meet for a full day at the White House, with satellite hookups to 60 more sites around our Nation. This conference is an exciting and an enormous undertaking. It is a call to action to parents, to businesses, to caregivers, the media, the faith community, and the Government each to do their part to enhance the earliest years of life. It grows out of our commitment to find new ways to support parents and to help their children reach their God-given potential.

As part of that commitment, I also want to call today on the Members of Congress to do their part to come to the aid of our families. They can do that very simply by passing my expansion of the Family and Medical Leave Act.

This bill would allow workers up to 24 hours of unpaid leave each year to fulfill certain family obligations. It could allow a worker to attend a parent-teacher conference or to take a child to the pediatrician or to find quality child care or to care for an elderly relative.

Families occasionally need these small pieces of time to take care of their own. More than 12 million American workers have taken leave for reasons covered by the Family and Medical Leave Act since it became the very first bill I signed into law in 1993. It was needed then, it's needed now, and we need to improve on it. So I urge Congress to act soon on this legislation. Don't ask people to choose, ever, between being good workers and good parents. We can help them to do both. Pass the expanded family and medical leave act.

I believe this bill is so important that today I am asking all Federal departments and agencies to make expanded family and medical leave available to their workers immediately. Wherever possible, I want workers to have access right now to essential time off for family obligations.

I am committed to doing all we can to support families as they struggle to do right by their children. We know that the very earliest years will decide whether children grow up to become healthy and happy people. That's why we're giving parents time off to care for them, why we should extend the family leave law so millions more parents can have that opportunity, and why we must focus all our science, education, and public efforts to give our children the very best start in life.

Almost a century and a half ago, Oliver Wendell Holmes said a child's education should begin at least 100 years before he was born. What we do now can benefit generations of Americans to come. We can start with the smallest community, the family, and from there we can rebuild and renew the best in America by beginning with the best of America, our children.

Thanks for listening.

NOTE. The address was recorded at 6:55 p.m. on April 11 in the Roosevelt Room at the White House for broadcast at 10:06 a.m. on April 12.

Statement on the Decline in Violent Crime Statistics
April 11, 1997

Today the Department of Justice reported that violent crime dropped 12.4 percent in 1995.

Four years ago, we made a commitment to take our streets back from crime and violence.

We had a comprehensive plan: to put 100,000 new community police officers on the street and tough new penalties on the books; to steer young people away from crime, gangs, and drugs; and to keep guns out of the hands of criminals with the assault weapons ban and the Brady bill.

Today we learned that the first full year of our crime bill produced the largest drop in violent crime in 22 years. Earlier this year we learned that the Brady bill has already stopped 186,000 felons, fugitives, and stalkers from purchasing handguns.

Our plan is working. Now we must press forward. Fighting the scourge of juvenile crime and violence is my top law enforcement priority for the next 4 years. In February I submitted my Anti-Gang and Youth Violence Strategy to Congress. This bill declares war on gangs, with new prosecutors and tougher penalties; extends the Brady bill so violent teenage criminals will never have the right to purchase a handgun; and provides resources to keep schools open late, on weekends, and in the summer, so young people have something to say yes to.

I am hopeful that Congress will pass it without delay. We must keep the crime rate coming down and every child's prospect of a bright future going up.

NOTE: This statement was embargoed for release until 4:30 p.m. on April 13.

Remarks on the Apparel Industry Partnership
April 14, 1997

Thank you very much. I would like to begin, first of all, by thanking all the members of this partnership, the cochairs, Paul Charron of Liz Claiborne and Linda Golodner of the National Consumers League, Jay Mazur of UNITE. I thank Kathie Lee Gifford, who has done so much to bring public attention to this issue. I thank the Members of Congress who are here: Congressman George Miller, Congressman Bernie Sanders, Congressman Lane Evans, Congressman Marty Martinez, and especially I thank my good friend Senator Tom Harkin, who first brought this issue to my attention a long time ago. Thank you very much, sir, and thank all of you for your passionate concern. I thank the former Secretary of Labor, Bob Reich, and Acting Secretary Cynthia Metzler and Secretary-designate Alexis Herman, who is here. And I thank Maria Echaveste and Gene Sperling for their work.

The announcement we make today will improve the lives of millions of garment workers around the world. As has now been painfully well documented, some of the clothes and shoes we buy here in America are manufactured under working conditions which are deplorable and unacceptable—mostly overseas, but unbelievably, sometimes here at home as well.

In our system of enterprise, which I have done my best to promote and advance, we support the proposition that businesses are in business to make a profit. But in our society, which we believe to be good and want to be better, we know that human rights and labor rights must be a part of the basic framework within which all businesses honorably compete.

As important as the fabric apparel workers make for us is the fabric of their lives, which is a part of the fabric of our lives, here at home and around the world. Their health and their safety, their ability to make a decent wage, their ability to bring children into this world and raise them with dignity and have their children see their parents working with dignity, that's an important part of the quality of our lives and will have a lot to do with the quality of our children's future.

Last August, when the Vice President and I brought together the leaders of some of our Nation's largest apparel and footwear companies and representatives of labor, consumer, human rights, and religious groups, I was genuinely moved at the shared outrage at sweatshop abuses and the shared determination to do something about it. That led to this apparel industry partnership. This partnership has reached an agreement—as already has been said—that will significantly reduce the use of sweatshop labor over the long run. It will give American consumers greater confidence in the products they buy.

And again, I say they have done a remarkable thing. Paul Charron said it was just the beginning because even though there are some very impressive and big companies represented on this stage, there are some which are not. But I would like to ask all the members of the partnership here to stand, and I think we ought to express our appreciation to them for what they have done. [*Applause*]

Now, here's what they agreed to do: first, a workplace code of conduct that companies will voluntarily adopt, and require their contractors to adopt, to dramatically improve the conditions under which goods are made. The code will establish a maximum workweek, a cap of 12 hours on the amount of overtime a company can require; require that employers pay at least the minimum or prevailing wage, respect basic labor rights. It will require safe and healthy working conditions and freedom from abuse and harassment. Most important, it will crack down on child labor, prohibiting the employment of those under 15 years of age in most countries.

It will also take steps to ensure that this code is enforced and that American consumers will know that the tenets of the agreement are being honored. The apparel industry has developed new standards for internal and external monitoring to make sure companies and contractors live up to that code of conduct. It will also form an independent association to help implement the agreement and to develop an effective way to share this information with consumers, such as labels on clothing, seals of approval in advertising, or signs in stores to guarantee that no sweatshop labor was used on a given product line.

Of course, the agreement is just the beginning. We know sweatshop labor will not vanish overnight. We know that while this agreement is an historic step, our real measure of progress must be in the changed and improved lives and livelihoods of apparel workers here at home and around the world. That is why we need more companies to join this crusade and follow its strict rules of conduct.

One of the association's most important tasks will be to expand participation to as many large and small companies as possible. And I urge all of America's apparel companies to become part of this effort. If these people are willing to put their names, their necks, their reputations, and their bottom lines on the bottom line of America, every other company in America in their line of work ought to be willing to do the very same thing.

We have spent a lot of time trying to find jobs for everybody in America who wants to work, and we have spent a lot of time saying that people who are able-bodied, who can work, should be required to work. Now, we are also reminding ourselves that no one, anywhere, should have to put their safety or their dignity on the line to support themselves or their children. This is a great day for America, a great day for the cause of human rights, and I believe a great day for free enterprise. And I thank all of those who are here who made it possible.

I'm proud that this agreement was industry-led and wholly voluntary. Like the TV industry's decision to rate its programming, like the new private sector effort to help move people from welfare to work, like the high-tech industry's efforts to wire our schools and our classrooms to the Internet, all of them, by the year 2000—which we will continue this Saturday—this is further evidence that we can solve our problems by working together in new and creative ways.

The apparel industry understands that we all share a stake in preparing our country for the 21st century and preparing the world to be a good partner. Reaching across lines that have too often divided us in the past, this new partnership will create more opportunity for working families. It will demand more responsibility for working conditions. It will build a stronger community here in America and bind us to the community of people all around the world who believe in the value of work but who also believe in the importance of its dignity and sanctity.

Thank you, and God bless you all.

NOTE: The President spoke at 1:05 p.m. in the East Room at the White House. In his remarks, he referred to entertainer Kathie Lee Gifford and the Union of Needletrades, Industrial and Textile Employees (UNITE).

Message to the Congress on the Generalized System of Preferences
April 11, 1997

To the Congress of the United States:

The Generalized System of Preferences (GSP) program offers duty-free treatment to specified products that are imported from designated developing countries. The program is authorized by title V of the Trade Act of 1974, as amended.

Pursuant to title V, I have determined that Argentina fails to provide adequate and effective means under its laws for foreign nationals to secure, to exercise, and to enforce exclusive rights in intellectual property. As a result, I have determined to withdraw benefits for 50 percent (approximately $260 million) of Argentina's exports under the GSP program. The products subject to removal include chemicals, certain metals and metal products, a variety of manufactured products, and several agricultural items (raw cane sugar, garlic, fish, milk protein concentrates, and anchovies).

This notice is submitted in accordance with the requirements of title V of the Trade Act of 1974.

WILLIAM J. CLINTON

The White House,
April 11, 1997.

NOTE: This message was released by the Office of the Press Secretary on April 15. The related proclamation of April 11 is listed in Appendix D at the end of this volume.

Remarks on Kick Butts Day in Brooklyn, New York
April 15, 1997

The President. Thank you. Good morning. Let me, first of all, say that I am delighted to be here. And I thought Ayana gave a wonderful introduction, didn't you? Give her a hand. [*Applause*]

I'm delighted to be here with all of the young people at the Hudde School, not only those who are here but those who are outside this room listening to us and looking at us over closed-circuit television. There are young people around New York and all across America participating in this second annual Kick Butts Day. But I am glad to be here.

I thank your principal, Julia Bove, for making me feel so welcome. I am delighted to be here with Congressman Chuck Schumer, my longtime friend who has worked so hard on this tobacco issue, and also he's worked hard on the assault weapons ban and the Brady bill and other things to make the streets of New York safer for children.

I'm glad to be here with Major Owens who was a very early supporter of mine here and who has been a great champion for education. You heard him talking about education—we're trying to get this Congress to really focus on the education needs of our children. And if it does happen in this Congress and we get the kind of progress that I think we will, it will be in no small measure due to Major Owens. I thank you, Major, for your leadership.

And I want you to think about Mark Green's title a minute because I'm going to talk to you about my job, their jobs, your jobs in a minute. Mark Green's title is the public advocate. I don't know if there's another city in America that has an elected public advocate. But think about what that means. What would it mean for you to be a public advocate? Someone who is standing up for people at large, right? For the public. Now, it was in that connection that Mark Green created this day, Kick Butts Day, all across the United States; he was the first official to ask to ban cartoon figures in tobacco ads—to his fight for at-risk and uninsured children. He's been fighting for children, but just think about it, because he was advocating for the public in New York, we now have a national Kick Butts Day involving, as you heard, about 2 million people. That's an incredible thing, and we thank Mark Green for his leadership for that.

I also want to thank Bill Novelli and the Campaign for Tobacco-Free Kids. I thank the others who are here on the platform with me today:

the president of the New York City Board of Education, Bill Thompson; and Rudy Crew, the chancellor of the board of education; and I'm glad to see Sandy Feldman and the American Federation of Teachers representatives, out here in this group.

And I'm glad to be at this school. I've heard a lot about this school. Congressman Schumer says, "My daughter goes to this school." I actually have—one of the press people who travels with me, Mark Knoller of CBS Radio, graduated from this school. And I hate to admit it, but he got a good education, too. He's done a good job. [*Laughter*] He's also very popular with the press corps, as you can hear. [*Laughter*]

Now, let me ask you to think about my job and your job. How many of you saw something in the news about Tiger Woods winning the Masters? How many of you thought it was a good thing? How many of you know that we're going to celebrate tonight at Shea Stadium the 40th anniversary of Jackie Robinson—the 50th anniversary of Jackie Robinson breaking into baseball? You all know that? And how many of you know who Jackie Robinson played for? Who did he play for? The Dodgers. When they were in——

Audience members. Brooklyn.

The President. ——Brooklyn. And how many of you think it was a good thing that Jackie Robinson broke the color line in baseball and gave everybody a chance to play baseball? [*Applause*] Okay, now, to do things that are great, you have to be able to imagine that you can do them. You have to be able to dream your dreams and actually imagine that you can be there. But you also have to pay the price. You have to develop good character and a good mind and good habits. And those are things that no one can do for you.

And I came here today for a specific reason. Because I think all the time about my job as President, I'm sort of the country's public advocate. You think about my job and what I can do and what I cannot do. Where does my job as President end and your job as a student and a citizen begin? That's what I want you to think about, because that's really what this is about. That's what all these T-shirts are about. That's what this slogan is about. It's about your future, your life, what all of us on this stage can do, and what only you can do.

Now, if you think about my job—this morning, I got up early this morning and read the newspapers and talked to my wife and daughter and read my security briefing to see what was going on in the rest of the world. And I got on Air Force One, the special plane that the President flies in, and I flew to New York and then came over here. And I thought about on the way over here, how much do these young students know about my job?

My job is to protect the United States, to promote world peace and the interest of the United States around the world. My job is to try to give you a strong economy so those who are willing to work can find a job; to commit to giving Americans the best education in the world so everybody has the chance to develop their minds; to try to make our streets safer; to try to make our environment cleaner; to try to make sure that the health and welfare, especially of our children, are in better shape for the future; and maybe more than anything else now—and look around at this student body— to try to make sure that we in America can learn to live together in harmony and peace and genuine affection and respect across our racial, ethnic, and religious differences, to have a true democracy that's blind to the differences in terms of prejudice but respects the fact that we are different and says, that's a good thing. It's a better thing that this country has people from many different racial and ethnic and religious backgrounds. It makes us stronger, not weaker, for the 21st century. That's my job.

Now, what does that mean? That means, in specifics, that I'm down in Washington now; I'm trying to work with the Congress to do the public's business to balance the budget, because it will make our economy stronger and guarantee that we'll have more growth and your parents will have more opportunities for good income. I'm trying to do it in a way that invests in education because unless we have the best education system in the world, we won't do as well as we should in the future and you won't have the opportunities you deserve. Those are just two examples.

But think about where what I do ends and what you do begins, because in the days when Jackie Robinson broke into baseball, someone had to make the decision that this racial prejudice was a stupid, dumb thing, right? And the owner of his club made that decision and give him a chance to play. That's a good thing, right? But just think what a downer it would have been if he couldn't play baseball. He still had to play baseball, right? He had to believe he could play baseball. He had to train himself to play baseball. He had to deal with all the prejudice and all the insults and all the hatred and all the rejection, and he had to maintain his dignity, all the time waiting for that chance and never knowing for sure it would ever come.

Now, think about Tiger Woods. He grew up in a time when there was—legal segregation by and large was illegal, unless it was in private clubs. And he had a wonderful father and mother who believed in him and gave him love and discipline and opportunities, right? But he still wouldn't have won that golf tournament unless he could hit the ball—a long way. [*Laughter*] Straight, right?

So all of us, we can get together. What's that got to do with you and Kick Butts Day? We can get together, and I can tell you, like they did, 3,000 kids start smoking every day, and 1,000 of them are going to die sooner because of it. I can say that. I can tell you that more people die from cigarettes every year than die from all of the other problems that you heard Congressman Schumer talking about. And I can tell you that; it's really true—more than from AIDS, more than from cancer, more than from car wrecks, more than from all that stuff. I can tell you that advertising has a disproportionate impact on young people.

How do we know that? We actually know that. How do we know that? Because younger people who buy cigarettes are far more likely to buy the advertised brands of cigarettes than the so-called generic brand, you know, where there's no advertising, no brand, just plain cigarettes. They're cheaper, but you never see them advertised. Older people are more likely to buy them, and younger people are more likely to buy the advertised brands even though they're more expensive.

So I can tell you all that. I can tell you that tobacco companies are getting more clever now. Virginia Slims is now sponsoring concerts because kids love music and CD's. Joe Camel cartoons are now on the packets of cigarettes, not just in the ads. Toy race cars are still emblazoned with tobacco brand names, even though we know adults don't buy many toy race cars.

Now, just last month, one of the tobacco companies finally changed its story. The president of the tobacco company Liggett said—and this is a quote from him—he can tell you this. This is a guy that ran a tobacco company. He can

say, "We acknowledge that the tobacco industry markets to youth, which means those under 18 years of age." And he also admitted that nicotine is addictive. Now, that's what he said. I hope the other tobacco companies will follow his lead and tell the truth and stop trying to sell their products—to adults and not to kids.

Now, all this is my problem and their problem and the other people that are in this. We're supposed to do this. We're supposed to do everything we can do to stop them from advertising to you and to stop this, and I have done everything I know to do. Last August, we put out these rules, and we said they have got to stop this. But after we do all that, there's still you. Right?

Think about it like Jackie Robinson. And so all of us, we're like the guys that own the ballteam, right? We're supposed to make everything all right so you have a chance to play baseball, except what we're trying to do is make everything all right so that the chances are very high that you won't be tempted to smoke.

But it's still up to you. That's why I'm here today, because I can sit in Washington and work all day and all night long and make this speech until I'm blue in the face, and unless the children of this country band together and show solidarity with each other and help each other resist peer pressure and stand up for your future and understand that your body is the most prized gift you've been given along with your mind and your spirit, nothing I do will amount to a hill of beans. That's why I'm here, because you have to take responsibility for your future. We can give you the opportunity. You have to seize it. And I want everybody in America on the news tonight and anybody who hears about this to know that in this school, you children are setting an example for the rest of America's young people. I am proud of you, and I want you to remember it tomorrow when you're not wearing that T-shirt.

And I want you to remember this, too. Even with no barriers, not everybody's going to be able to play baseball like Jackie Robinson did. I still remember when I was—I was 10 years old before I ever got a television. But Jackie Robinson had 2 years left in baseball and I got to watch him on television. I still remember that.

Even with golf more open to more and more kinds of people, with 2,500 minority children in a golf program in Houston, Texas, for example, very few people are going to be able to drive the ball 320 yards consistently. But you can all have some dream. And everybody's life has real meaning and every one of you has to figure out what that dream is going to be for you. But no matter what it is, you've got to do just what the champions do: You have to believe you can do it and think about it and visualize it. You have to work for it. You've got to get a good education, and you've got to take care of your mind and your body. And if you do, you'll be a champion, no matter what you do and no matter whether you're famous or not.

You think about it. This country has one President, for example, and 260 million other people. Now, if tomorrow we had to do without one President or all 260 million other people, it would be a pretty easy choice, wouldn't it? You'd say, "I like you, President Clinton, but I'm sorry, you'll have to go." [*Laughter*] "The rest of us are going to stay."

The greatness of America is in all the people. It's in the billions and billions and billions of decisions they make every day. And you're making them for your life and your future and your country. I am very proud of you. But don't you ever forget this: Have your dreams and live for them, but take care of yourselves. Take care of yourselves. Your body is a precious gift. And you have set an example today that I can only hope and pray that every young person in this country, that all of them will follow.

Thank you, and God bless you.

NOTE: The President spoke at 11:10 a.m. in the gymnasium at Andries Hudde Junior High School. In his remarks, he referred to student Ayana Harry; Representative Major R. Owens; William D. Novelli, president, Campaign for Tobacco-Free Kids; Sandra Feldman, president, American Federation of Teachers; and 1997 PGA Masters' winner Tiger Woods.

Remarks at a Democratic Congressional Campaign Committee Luncheon in Brooklyn
April 15, 1997

Thank you very much. Congressman Rangel said, "I guess I can't say 'break a leg,' can I?" [*Laughter*] Actually you could. They told me if I had broken my leg, I would have healed quicker.

Ladies and gentlemen, I want to thank all of you for being here. I want to thank Martin Frost for his tireless work on behalf of the Democratic Congressional Campaign Committee. I thank Dick Gephardt for the wonderful work that he has done with me over the last 4 years and few odd months as majority leader, as minority leader, and I hope in January of 1999, as the Speaker of the House of Representatives, with your help.

To give you an idea of what this Democratic Congressional Campaign Committee did and what our candidates did in 1996, it is worth noting that even though they were out-spent often by breathtaking margins in the last 10 days—unimaginable amounts in some of the seats—with only 9,759 votes spread across 10

congressional districts, the Democrats could be in the majority today. That's how close that election was. And therefore, your presence here today and your support for them is very important.

I am proud of the things that Mr. Gephardt mentioned. I'm proud of the fact that in 1992 we said we would turn this country around and change the direction of the country, and we did. I'm proud of the fact that we changed the economic philosophy that dominated Washington for a long time, that we reversed trickle-down economics and instead said, "We're going to reduce the deficit and invest in our future. We're going to expand trade and make it more fair."

And the results, I think, are pretty impressive. We've got an unemployment rate today that's the lowest it's been in many, many years, and the unemployment rate today is a full percent and a half below the average—the average of the two decades before I took office. So we're working together; we're moving forward.

I am proud of the fact that with the leadership of a lot of the Members of the Congress in this room we've taken a serious step instead of just hot-air talk in trying to make our streets safer and our futures brighter for our young people. We had the biggest drop in crime the year before last that we've had in over two decades. We haven't gotten the 1996 statistics yet, but all the indications are that they continue to go down. We are moving in the right direction on that.

And I am very proud of the fact that, again, with the leadership with a lot of New Yorkers in this room, we have put education first on America's domestic agenda again. And I'm very proud of that.

I'm going to do my best to keep doing the public's business, and I will do my best to do it in a fair and open way with the Members of both parties in the Congress. But I can tell you, if you look around the room at the people who are here, and you ask yourself, what are the great challenges of the 21st century for America? Can we keep the American dream of opportunity for all who are willing to work for it alive; can we give our children a world-class education; can we deal with the health care and the safety needs of all the poor children who come from different cultures who are in our country and give them a chance to make their full contribution; can we preserve an American community that's one America and still have an enormous amount of respect for the racial and ethnic and religious differences we have among ourselves? Because if we can, then we are clearly the best positioned country in the world for the new century.

You have to ask yourselves, who would I like to take the lead in answering those questions and in fashioning the answer? And I know what that answer is for me; I know what that answer is for you. And your presence here today will help the American people make a good decision in 1998.

I'd also like to thank the Members of Congress from Brooklyn and the people of Brooklyn for hosting us here today. I have consistently done very well in Brooklyn, as the Members never forget to tell me, and I am very grateful for that. And I am honored to be in this beau-tiful, beautiful place, and I hope to stay and look around a little bit.

I'm going to Queens tonight to Shea Stadium to watch the Mets and the Dodgers play and to commemorate the 50th anniversary of Jackie Robinson's breaking the color line in baseball. And I'd just like to say one final word about that. It's all the more appropriate, I think, coming as it does right after Tiger Woods' record-shattering performance in the Masters. But it's important to remember that you had, I think, the two great ingredients of a good society at work in both places. In the case of Jackie Robinson, you had people who were willing to end discrimination and an owner who was willing to give him a chance. But you also had a highly disciplined, profoundly dignified, greatly talented ballplayer who was prepared not only physically but also emotionally and mentally to do what had to be done. The same thing happened in the Masters last week.

And I often believe—have said this and I will say it again because I believe it—I think that the elections that really matter in this country are genuinely determined by questions people ask not only about us but about themselves and how they view themselves in the world in the future we're going into.

And I will say this in closing: I believe that the efforts of Martin Frost and Leader Gephardt and all the members of the New York delegation in 1998 will be successful. If we can get the right kind of balanced budget passed in the Congress, if we can continue to stand up for what's right for America, and if we can make sure the American people are asking the right questions in 1998 of our society and of themselves—if that happens, I am not worried about the outcome of the elections, and more importantly, I'm not worried about the future of our country.

Again, let me say I'm profoundly grateful to New York and grateful to Brooklyn and glad to be here, and thank you for helping the DCCC.

Thank you very much.

NOTE: The President spoke at 1:24 p.m. at the Brooklyn Botanical Garden. In his remarks, he referred to Representative Martin Frost, chairman, Democratic Congressional Campaign Committee.

Statement on the Fire in Mina, Saudi Arabia
April 15, 1997

I was deeply saddened to learn today of the tragic loss of life in Saudi Arabia among the pilgrims performing the Hajj. I have sent condolences to King Fahd on behalf of the American people and extend our deepest sympathy to the families of those who were killed or injured in the fire.

Exchange With Reporters in Queens, New York
April 15, 1997

Jackie Robinson Commemorative Coins

The President. Mark [Mark Knoller, CBS Radio], did you give out any autographs today over at the school?

Q. Thank you, sir, that was very kind of you.

The President. It's a great school, isn't it? Very impressive.

You all know this is the design for the Jackie Robinson coin. And Mrs. Robinson and her family consulted on it—do you want to just tell them?

Rachel Robinson. Yes. The gold coin represents the total man, and we wanted that because we have been trying to impress people with Jack's life in its totality. And we think that's going to be a very rare piece. We're very excited about it. We love the design, and we love the concept, and we're very happy to have it. The silver coin will represent the baseball period and that, of course, he's had an illustrious career. So of course we're proud of that. But we wanted to commemorate both aspects of him—or total aspects of him. And we will sell out. [*Laughter*] We are already marketing and——

The President. We're hawking the coin. Anybody in our press corps would like to buy one, we can make one available. [*Laughter*]

Q. What denomination is it? How much money is it worth? What is the face value of it?

The President. What's the sale price?

Mrs. Robinson. The final price hasn't been determined. It's around $250 on the gold and about $35 on the silver. And the Jackie Robinson Foundation will receive surcharges from the coins, which we will invest in our permanent endowment fund.

1996 Campaign Financing

Q. Mr. President, what do you think of all the attacks on your Attorney General? What do you think of all the attacks on your Attorney General for the decision she made yesterday on the independent counsel? Newt Gingrich said today he likened that position to something that John Mitchell would do.

The President. That cries out for an answer, I guess. Let me say, I think that—I don't have anything to add to what I've already said. She had to make a legal decision on a legal question. And as I understand it, she consulted her career staff people there and made a decision. And that's all I know. So I don't have any other comment about it. It should not be a political matter; it should be a legal matter. And that's the way everybody ought to leave it.

Q. Thank you.

Jackie Robinson 50th Anniversary Cap

Mrs. Robinson. On behalf of the Jackie Robinson Foundation, we would like to present you with our anniversary cap, since we know that you wear caps——

The President. I do.

Mrs. Robinson. ——we hope to see this on your head. [*Laughter*]

The President. I hope you see me running and playing golf.

NOTE: The President spoke at approximately 6:40 p.m. at Shea Stadium during a meeting with Rachel Robinson, widow of Jackie Robinson, and other family members. A tape was not available for verification of the content of this exchange.

Interview With Chris Berman of ESPN in Queens
April 15, 1997

[The President's remarks are joined in progress.]

The President. And if he hadn't done what he did and Branch Rickey hadn't done what he did, PeeWee Reese hadn't run the team like he did, it would have been a very different world. But Jackie Robinson—you know, someone—maybe fate has a way of doing that in history, but he was—he had the unique blend of talent and character to do what he did. And it's made a real difference.

It made a real difference to the way people thought about race. I think that's more important than the fact that he was a great baseball player because baseball really was our national pastime then, too, and there was no competition from highly televised pro basketball or pro football or anything else. It was the thing. And so it was—as important as it was, and 3 years later basketball was integrated and other things happened—this was a huge deal. Most Americans now can't even imagine how big a deal it was.

This was the year before President Truman signed the order to integrate the Army. This was a huge deal.

Mr. Berman. It was really 15 years plus before marches in the sixties. I mean, it was so far ahead of its time——

The President. Almost a decade before Rosa Parks. And it was baseball, so it was a statement about America. Anything you said about baseball in the forties and the early fifties, it was a statement about America.

Mr. Berman. By the way, Olerud is at first base with a single; one out. But Bernard Gilkey is up.

The President. He's doing better in New York, isn't he, although——

Mr. Berman. Well, he's in another——

The President. But he's hitting well again, and it's good. It's been a good move for him.

Mr. Berman. It kind of got a little stale for him in Toronto.

The President. Yes. It's good for him.

Mr. Berman. Did you ever get up to see Jackie Robinson play? I don't know how many Cardinal games you went to. Arkansas was a good drive from there.

The President. Only one time when I was a child. My father took me on a train to St. Louis to watch a game, but they weren't playing the Dodgers. But we didn't get a television until 1956, but it was right after the '55 season, right after the Boys of Summer. So for 2 years I sat transfixed in front of my television set. And tonight we had a contest in the place where I'm sitting to see how many people could remember the names of people on the '55 team— how many names you could remember. I quit at seven. And I hadn't even thought about it since. And I still remember the first time I saw Jackie Robinson, with that hitch in his swing and the way he ran sort of almost—on television it looked almost like he was bent over. It was an amazing thing. I remember just being transfixed by it.

Mr. Berman. Well, you have these images all—the old crystal set, right, which was how you followed your baseball. And so many people did, certainly, in the fifties. When you finally saw him, or now that you've seen him afterwards on the old newsreels, et cetera, was that the image you had of him as a boy listening on the radio, or was he more impressive in person?

The President. More impressive in person. But I used to do my homework at night listening to the Cardinals games on the radio. So I— I probably shouldn't say, it's a bad example for students of today.

Mr. Berman. We all did it; we all did it.

The President. But I did. And so, he was better than I thought he would be. He was beautiful. He was fabulous, watching him.

Mr. Berman. You're excited about this evening, aren't you?

The President. I am, it's very important. I think that it's also good for baseball. This night will capture the attention of America and make everybody forget about some of the things they didn't like that happened the last 2 years and make people fall in love with baseball again, I hope.

Mr. Berman. As we did the night of the Cal Ripken thing.

The President. Yes, we did.

Mr. Berman. I have to ask you this. It's April 15th. Are your taxes done?

The President. Yes. Paid them all.

Mr. Berman. Because I might be able to get you an extension.

The President. I don't think I ought to. I've got to set a good example, you know. [Laughter] I'm surprised all these baseball players shook hands with me tonight. They make more money than Jackie Robinson did, so they probably weren't very happy to see me tonight. [Laughter]

Mr. Berman. Oh, I think they were. I think you honored everybody with your presence. Thank you for joining us.

The President. Thank you. I'm glad to be here. Thanks.

NOTE: The interview began at 8:45 p.m. at Shea Stadium. In his remarks, the President referred to civil rights activist Rosa Parks. He also referred to Executive Order 9981 of July 26, 1948 (13 FR 4313). The press release issued by the Office of the Press Secretary did not include the complete opening remarks of the President.

Remarks in Queens Celebrating the 50th Anniversary of Jackie Robinson's Integration of Major League Baseball
April 15, 1997

Thank you very much. Ladies and gentlemen, Mrs. Robinson, members of the Robinson family. It is hard to believe that it was 50 years ago at Ebbets Field that a 28-year-old rookie changed the face of baseball and the face of America forever. Jackie Robinson scored the go-ahead run that day, and we've all been trying to catch up ever since.

Today I think every American should say a special word of thanks to Jackie Robinson and to Branch Rickey and to the members of the Dodger team who made him one of their own and proved that America is a better, stronger, richer country when we all work together and give everyone a chance. And today I think we should remember that Jackie Robinson's legacy did not end with baseball, for afterward he spent the rest of his life trying to open other doors and keep them open for all kinds of people. He knew that education, not sports, was the key to success in life for nearly everyone, and he took that message to young people wherever he went. I congratulate Rachel Robinson for continuing that mission through the work of the Jackie Robinson Foundation, which has given hundreds of young people a chance to build the life of their dreams.

I can't help thinking that if Jackie Robinson were here with us tonight, he would say that we have done a lot of good in the last 50 years, but we can do better. We have achieved equality on the playing field, but we need to establish equality in the boardrooms of baseball and throughout corporate America. And we need to make sure that, even as we celebrate his brilliant successor Tiger Woods' victory in the Masters, we need even more of our young people from all walks of life to get their master's degrees and help to make more of their lives in this country.

And he would remind us—look around this stadium tonight—that as we sit side by side at baseball games, we must make sure that we walk out of these stadiums together. We must stand for something more significant even than a grand slam home run. We ought to have a grand slam society, a good society where all of us have a chance to work together for a better tomorrow for our children. Let that be the true legacy of Jackie Robinson's wonderful, remarkable career and life.

Ladies and gentlemen, please welcome Mrs. Rachel Robinson.

NOTE: The President spoke at 9:39 p.m. at Shea Stadium. In his remarks, he referred to Branch Rickey, owner of the Brooklyn Dodgers in 1947, and professional golfer Tiger Woods.

Remarks at the Opening of the White House Conference on Early Childhood Development and Learning
April 17, 1997

Thank you very much, and welcome to the White House. I was relieved to hear Hillary say that the brain is the last organ to fully develop. It may yet not be too late for me to learn how to walk down steps. [*Laughter*] Or maybe I was thinking it was because I was always hugged when I fell down as a child, I did this subconsciously on purpose. [*Laughter*]

Let me begin by thanking the members of the Cabinet who are here. I see Secretary Riley and Secretary Glickman. I thank Governor Romer and Governor Chiles for being here. I think Governor Miller is coming. There are many others who are here. Congresswoman DeLauro is either here or coming. Thank you, Governor Miller. I see I was looking to the left there. [*Laughter*] He's from Nevada—he just went up five points in the polls when I said that. [*Laughter*]

Let me say, first of all, the first time I met Hillary, she was not only a law student, she was working with the Yale Child Study Center, and she began my education in these issues. And for that, I am profoundly grateful. And I thank her for bringing the scientists, the doctors, the sociologists, the others whose work is the basis for our discussion today here. And I, too, want to thank the thousands of others who are joining us by satellite.

This unique conference is a part of our constant effort to give our children the opportunity to make the most of their God-given potential and to help their parents lead the way and to remind everyone in America that this must always be part of the public's business because we all have a common interest in our children's future.

We have begun the job here over the last 4 years by making education our top domestic priority, by passing the family leave act and now trying to expand it and enact a form of flextime which will give parents more options in how they take their overtime, in pay or in time with their children, by the work we have done to expand the Family and Medical Leave Act, and by the work we've tried to do to give parents more tools with the V-chip and the television rating system and the work we are still carrying on to try to stop the advertising and marketing and distribution of tobacco to our children and other work we've done in juvenile justice and trying to keep our kids away from the dangers of alcohol and drugs.

All these are designed to help our parents succeed in doing their most important job. Now, it seems to me maybe the most important thing we can actually do is to share with every parent in America the absolutely stunning things we are learning from new scientific research about how very young children learn and develop. In that regard, I'd like to thank Rob Reiner and others who are committed to distributing this information, and I'd like to thank the media here in our Nation's Capital and throughout the country for the genuine interest that they have shown in this conference.

I think there is an instinctive understanding here that this is a very, very big issue that embraces all of us as Americans and that if we learn our lessons well and if we're patient in carrying them out, as Hillary said, knowing that there is no perfect way to raise a child, we are likely to have a very positive and profound impact on future generations in this country. So I want to thank, again, all of you for that.

Let me say there are some public programs that bear directly on early childhood development: the Head Start program, which we've expanded by 43 percent over the last 4 years; the WIC program, which we've expanded by nearly 2 million participants. I have to say that I was a little disappointed—or a lot disappointed—to see a congressional committee yesterday vote to underfund the WIC program. I hope that if nothing else happens out of this conference, the results of the conference will reach the members of that congressional committee and we can reverse that before the budget finally comes to my desk.

I would also like to remind all of you that this conference is literally just a start. We have to look at the practical implications of this research for parents, for caregivers, for policymakers, but we also know that we're looking at years and years of work in order to make the findings of this conference real and positive in the lives of all of our children. But this is a very exciting and enormous undertaking.

This research has opened a new frontier. Great exploration is, of course, not new to this country. We have gone across the land, we have gone across the globe, we have gone into the skies, and now we are going deep into ourselves and into our children. In some ways, this may be the most exciting and important exploration of all.

I'm proud of the role that federally funded research has played in these findings, in discovering that the earliest years of life are critical for developing intellectual, emotional, and social potential. We all know that every child needs proper nutrition and access to health care, a safe home, and an environment, and we know every child needs teaching and touching, reading and playing, singing and talking.

It is true that Chelsea is about to go off to college, but Hillary and I have been blessed by having two young nephews now—one is about 2, and one is about 3—and we're learning things all over again that, I must say, corroborate what the scientists are telling us.

We are going to continue to work on this, and I know that you will help us, too. Let me just mention two or three things that we want to work on that we think are important. We've got to do a lot more to improve the quality, the availability, and the affordability of child care. Many experts consider our military's child care system to be the best in our country. I'm very proud of that, and not surprised.

The man responsible for administering the Navy's child care system, Rear Admiral Larry Marsh, is here with us today. He leads a system that has high standards, including a high percentage of accredited centers; a strong enforcement system with unannounced inspections; parents have a toll-free number to call and report whatever concerns they may have; training is mandatory; and wages and benefits are good, so, staff tends to stay on.

I am proud that the military places such importance on helping the families of the men and women who serve our country in uniform. But it's really rather elementary to know that they're going to do a lot better on the ships, in the skies, in faraway lands if they're not worried about how their children are faring while they're at work serving America.

To extend that kind of quality beyond the military, I am issuing today an executive memo-

randum asking the Department of Defense to share its success. I want the military to partner with civilian child care centers to help them improve quality, to help them become accredited, to provide training to civilian child care providers, to share information on how to operate successfully, and to work with State and local governments to give on-the-job training and child care to people moving from welfare to work.

I think this is especially important. Let me say, in the welfare reform bill, we put another $4 billion in for child care. In addition to that, because the States are getting money for welfare reform based on the peak caseload in welfare in 1994 and we've reduced the welfare rolls by 2.8 million since then, most States, for a period of time until an extra session comes along, will have some extra funds that they can put into more child care. This gives States the opportunity they have never had before to train more child care workers, to use funds to help even more people move from welfare to work, and perhaps even to provide more discounts to low-income workers to make child care affordable for them.

This welfare reform effort, if focused on child care, can train lots of people on welfare to be accredited child care workers and expand the availability of welfare in most of the States of the country. It's not true for every State, because some of them have had smaller drops in the caseload and three have had no drops. But by and large, the welfare reform bill, because of the way it's structured, gives all of you who care about child care about a year or two to make strenuous efforts, State by State, to create a more comprehensive quality system of child care than we have ever had before. And I certainly hope that what we can do here, plus the support of the military—we'll see dramatic advances in that regard.

I'd like to thank the people here who have done that work. And I'd like to say that we are going to hold a second conference, this one devoted exclusively to the child care issue, here at the White House in Washington this fall. And I hope all of you who care about that will come back.

The second thing we want to do is to extend health care coverage to uncovered children. The budget I have submitted will extend coverage to as many as 5 million children by the year 2000 with the children's health initiative in the budget proposal, to strengthen Medicaid for poor children and children with disabilities, to provide coverage for working families through innovative State programs, to continue health care coverage for children of workers who are between jobs. There is an enormous amount of interest in this issue in both parties, I'm happy to say, in the Congress in this session. And I am quite confident that if we'll all work together, we can get an impressive expansion in health care coverage for children in this congressional session.

I'm pleased that Dr. Jordan Cohen, the president and CEO of the Association of American Medical Colleges, is with us today to lend his association's strong support to these efforts. With the support of leaders in medicine, again I say, I am convinced we'll have a bipartisan consensus that will extend coverage to millions more uninsured children.

The third thing we want to do is this: Because we know the great importance of early education, we're going to expand Early Head Start enrollment by at least one-third next year. Early Head Start was created in 1994. It's been a great success in bringing the nutritional, educational, and other services of Head Start to children aged 3 and younger and to pregnant women. It has been a real success, and we need to expand it.

Today we are requesting new applications for Early Head Start programs to accomplish the expansion. And to help parents to teach the very young, we developed a toolkit called, "Ready, Set, Read," part of our America Reads challenge, designed to make sure that every child can read independently by the third grade. This kit gives tips on activities for young children. It's going out to early childhood programs all across the country along with a hotline number for anyone else who wants the kit.

The fourth thing we're going to do is to protect the safety of our children more. In particular, we have to help young children more who are exposed to abuse and violence.

Let me tell you, as you might imagine, I get letters all the time from very young children. And my staff provides a significant number of them for me to read. The Secretary of Education not very long ago gave me a set of letters from children who were quite young—a couple of years ago gave me a set of letters from children who were in the third grade. But sometimes I get them from kindergarten children

and first grade children, talking about what they want America to look like. And it is appalling the number of letters I get from 5- and 6-year-olds who simply want me to make their lives safe, who don't want to worry about being shot, who don't want any more violence in their homes, who want their schools and the streets they walk on to be free of terror.

So today the Department of Justice is establishing a new initiative called Safe Start, based on efforts in New Haven, Connecticut, which you will hear about this afternoon. The program will train police officers, prosecutors, probation, and parole officers in child development so that they'll actually be equipped to handle situations involving young children. And I believe if we can put this initiative into effect all across America, it will make our children safer. And I'm glad we're announcing it today during Victims of Crime Week.

We all know that it's going to take a partnership across America to help our children reach their full potential. But the toughest job will always belong to our parents, first teachers, main nurturers. Being a parent is a joy and a challenge. But it's not a job you can walk away from, take a vacation from, or even apply for family leave from. [*Laughter*] The world moves too fast, and today, parents have more worries than ever. Work does compete with family demands, and finding a balance is more difficult than before. That's why this must always be part of the public's business.

Let me come now to the bottom line. The more we focus on early years, the more important they become. We know that these investments of time and money will yield us the highest return in healthier children, stronger families, and better communities.

Now, let me say, finally, I know that none of us who are in politics, none of us who are just parents, will ever know as much as the experts we're about to hear from today. But what they're going to tell us is the most encouraging thing of all, which is, they have found out that we can all do the job. No matter how young, a child does understand a gentle touch or a smile or a loving voice. Babies understand more than we have understood about them. Now we can begin to close the gap and to make sure that all children in this country do have that chance to live up to the fullest of their God-given potential.

Again, I thank you all for being here. I thank our experts. I thank the First Lady. And I'd like to ask Dr. David Hamburg to come up and sit there and take over the program.

David.

Thank you.

NOTE: The President spoke at 10:45 a.m. in the East Room at the White House. In his remarks, he referred to Gov. Roy Romer of Colorado; Gov. Lawton Chiles of Florida; Gov. Bob Miller of Nevada; Rob Reiner, founder, I Am Your Child campaign; Rear Adm. Larry R. Marsh, Assistant Chief of Naval Personnel for Personnel Readiness and Community Support; and David A. Hamburg, president, Carnegie Corporation of New York.

Memorandum on Improving the Quality of Child Care in the United States
April 17, 1997

Memorandum for the Secretary of Defense

Subject: Using Lessons Learned from the Military Child Development Programs to Improve the Quality of Child Care in the United States

We now know that children's earliest experiences, including those in child care, have significant effects on learning and development. I believe we all have a role to play in making sure that all of our children have a strong and healthy start in life.

The Military Child Development Programs have attained a reputation for an abiding commitment to quality in the delivery of child care. The Department of Defense's dedication to adequate funding, strict oversight, improved training and wage packages, strong family child care networks, and commitment to meeting national accreditation standards is laudatory. I believe that the military has important lessons to share with the rest of the Nation on how to improve the quality of child care for all of our Nation's children.

I therefore direct you, consistent with existing statutory authority, to share the expertise and lessons learned from the Military Child Development Programs with Federal, State, tribal, and local agencies, as well as with private and nonprofit entities, that are responsible for providing child care for our Nation's children. I further direct you, in doing so, to consult with the Secretary of Health and Human Services, the Administrator of General Services, and the heads of other Federal departments or agencies with statutory authority over child care programs. I ask that you provide me with a preliminary report within 6 months, and with a final report within 1 year on actions taken and further recommendations, including recommendations on any needed or appropriate legislation. I urge you to consider the following:

I. In consultation with States, encourage military installation child development facilities in the United States to partner with civilian child care programs in their local communities to improve the quality of service offered. The Department of Defense staff could provide assistance with local accreditation efforts, offer training as available, assist with State and local child development credentialing processes, and provide models of effective child development practices.

II. Establish military Child Care Programs of Excellence, to the greatest extent feasible, to offer training courses to civilian child care providers. These training courses could demonstrate model practices for child care centers, family child care homes, and school-age facilities.

III. Make widely available to the civilian child care community information on the model approaches and designs that the military uses for training and compensation, accreditation and evaluation, playground and facility design, support systems linking individual family child care providers, as well as overall financing strategies.

IV. Establish partnerships with State or county employment and job training programs to enable Military Child Development Centers and Family Child Care Homes to serve as training locations for welfare recipients moving from welfare to work. The

448

Department of Defense programs could provide on-the-job training, work experience, and an understanding of best practices for the delivery of child development services.

WILLIAM J. CLINTON

Statement on the Death of Chaim Herzog
April 17, 1997

I was informed this morning that former Israeli President Chaim Herzog had died after a long illness. I offer my heartfelt condolences to his family and to the people of Israel. Chaim Herzog not only served the Israeli people with distinction as their President for 10 years, he was a courageous soldier in the liberation of Europe and a distinguished leader in the Israeli armed forces. He will long be remembered for his years as a statesman and scholar—he personified a vibrant, emerging Israel, taking its place in the community of nations.

Statement on the Senate Decision To Bring the Chemical Weapons Convention to a Vote
April 17, 1997

I welcome today's unanimous agreement by the Senate to bring the Chemical Weapons Convention to a vote next week. This treaty—initiated by the Reagan administration, completed and signed by the Bush administration, submitted to the Senate by my administration—has been bipartisan from the beginning. Now, thanks to the good-faith efforts of Majority Leader Lott and Minority Leader Daschle—working closely with my national security team and key members of the Senate from both sides of the aisle—the Senate will be able to vote on the treaty before it goes into effect on April 29.

Over the past 2½ months, we have all gone the extra mile to work through outstanding concerns about the treaty. As a result of negotiations Senator Lott and I established and discussions led by Senators Biden and Helms, we now have agreement on 28 conditions that will be included in the treaty's resolution of ratification when it goes to a vote, resolving virtually all of the issues that have been raised about the CWC.

Just today, our negotiators reached agreement concerning the use of riot control agents like tear gas and to require warrants for any involuntary searches of an American business or facility under the treaty's inspection provisions. We still have five issues on which we fundamentally disagree, but we are now assured, thanks to today's agreement, that they will be decided by votes of the full Senate.

These important developments reflect widespread, bipartisan, and growing support for the Chemical Weapons Convention. Yesterday, former Presidents Bush and Ford joined Secretary of State Albright in making a special appeal for ratification. Today at a congressional hearing, former Chairman of the Joint Chiefs of Staff Colin Powell strongly reiterated his endorsement of the treaty, which also has the support of every other Chairman of the Joint Chiefs of Staff for the past two decades. And three former Secretaries of Defense—Harold Brown, Elliot Richardson, and Bill Perry—released a joint statement calling for the Senate to ratify the Chemical Weapons Convention.

All of these distinguished American leaders agree that by requiring countries around the world to destroy their chemical weapons stockpiles—as the United States already has decided to do—and to renounce developing or trading in chemical weapons in the future, the Chemical Weapons Convention will help make our troops safer while making it harder for rogue states and terrorists to acquire chemical weapons.

449

This treaty literally was "made in America," and it also is right for America. I urge every Member of the Senate to support the Chemical Weapons Convention when it comes to a vote next week.

Teleconference Remarks on the Opening of the Newseum
April 18, 1997

The President. Thank you, Al and Charles and Peter. Thanks a lot for asking me an easy question that can only get me in trouble. Whatever I say, I'll be behind the curve ball, which is, of course, where all of you try to keep me. [*Laughter*] Nonetheless, I'm glad to be with you today. And I am glad the Vice President was able to officially open the Newseum, and I'm glad he told you the stories that I hear about once a week about his days as a reporter. [*Laughter*] He says he was always accurate, vigorous, and totally fair. [*Laughter*]

Thanks to the technological wizardry that you've built into this wonderful Newseum, I'm able to join you on your video news wall for the grand opening. It's amazing to me that this is happening. You know, when I was growing up, I got my news from my local paper or watching the 6 o'clock news on my family's black and white TV, and I suppose I never imagined the incredible array of ways people would someday get their news and their information, from all-news radio and TV to the Internet and all the sort of "near-news" programs.

And I think that's why this Newseum is so important, because it will remind us that we've come a long way, but no matter how it's packaged or delivered, news has always fulfilled mankind's most basic need to know. And it also reminds us that democracy's survival depends upon that need to know and the free flow of ideas and information.

I congratulate you on giving our children and their parents an opportunity to learn about the role news media has in protecting our freedoms and helping us to build the most robust and open society in human history.

This Newseum is not only a tribute to the news profession, it's also a tribute to the men and women who have dedicated their lives to it, who know that, always, there are going to be people who will work hard to struggle, sometimes at real personal risks to themselves, to get the news and hopefully to be fair, honest, and critical in their reporting of it. America is stronger and freer because of them, and I thank them. This Newseum is really a great addition to the Washington area. And I know it will attract a lot of visitors, not only from every State but also from all around the world.

Now, the question you asked me is a fair one and a good one. I think that the fundamental role of the news media and the reporting today is what it has always been—is to give people information in a fair and accurate way. But the context is far different. There are, first of all, more sources of news. There is more information that people have to process, and people get their news in more different ways. And as I said, there are all these sort of "near-news" forces bearing down on you and offering competition.

I sometimes wonder what it's like to put together an evening news program or a morning newspaper when the main story has been playing every 5 minutes on CNN for 6 hours, and whether you really—whether that affects what you do or not. I would say that from my perspective, the most important thing is that while we're being inundated with this glut of information, that we try to make sure that people have a proper context within which to understand the information. I think that the fact that we can have more facts than ever before is important, but if you don't have any framework within which to understand those facts, it seems to me it poses an enormous challenge.

The other thing that I think we have to do is to be careful when we report the stories about things that might be true, not to say that they are, particularly if to say that they are or to imply that they are could cause real damage to people in their reputations and, indeed, in their own lives.

But I think that the competition to which you're subject makes it more difficult both to keep down excessive hype in some stories and to take the time and the effort to put it in proper context. I think in some ways it is much more difficult to be a member of the news media than in years past. It's a great challenge. And all the benefits of this communications explosion impose new challenges on you to meet the old-fashioned duty of being accurate, thorough, tough, and fair.

Q. [*Inaudible*]—once you're off your crutches, you and your family will come over and browse

through the Newseum with us. Thank you very much, Mr. President.

The President. I'd love to do it. Thank you, and bless you all. Congratulations.

NOTE: The President spoke by satellite at 11:24 a.m. from the Roosevelt Room at the White House to the Newseum in Arlington, VA. In his remarks, he referred to Allen H. Neuharth, chairman, and Peter S. Prichard, executive director, Newseum; and Charles Overby, chief executive officer, Freedom Forum.

Remarks at the Award Ceremony for the National Teacher of the Year
April 18, 1997

Thank you very much to our Teacher of the Year and all the teachers of the year and their friends and supporters and family members who are here. Senator Glenn, Congressman Chabot, Secretary Riley, and Vice President Gore, thank you for being such wonderful partners to me.

Next year, Dick Riley and I will have been working together for 20 years in one way or another, and we're about to get the hang of it. [*Laughter*] And I really think he's done a wonderful job as our Secretary of Education.

I want to tell you, this NetDay idea that the Vice President developed—we were just sitting around talking one day, and I was bemoaning the fact that he was doing some elaborate thing on his computer screen in his office and I still can hardly figure out how to turn mine on. [*Laughter*] And we were all laughing about how our children were leapfrogging us in their capacity to deal with computers and one thing led to another and before you know it, we have a goal that we'll hook up every library and classroom in the country by the year 2000, and then there's going to be a NetDay and, all of a sudden, one day we hook up 20 percent of the classrooms in California. And I never met anybody that was any better at taking an idea and turning it into reality than Al Gore. And this NetDay thing, it's going to revolutionize education in this country, because we're not going to stop until we bring the benefits of technology to every single child in this country, and I think it's a wonderful thing.

I could have done without Secretary Riley telling that story that my—[*laughter*]—my second grade teacher did. But I was sitting here— I have no notes on this, so if I mess it up you'll have to forgive me, but the truth is that Sister Mary Amata McGee, whom I found after over 30 years of having no contact with her— she was my second and third grade teacher. I found her in Springfield, Missouri, one night when I came there near the end of the 1992 campaign. I had no idea what had become of her. I didn't know what had happened. So I reestablished my relationship with her. But she was a little too generous. The truth is, I think she gave me a D in conduct—[*laughter*]—and I think she gave me a D not because I raised my hand but because I spoke whether I was called on or not. [*Laughter*]

But if ever you wonder whether what you do matters, after Sister Mary Amata McGee in the second and third grade, there was Louise Vaughn, Mary Christianus, Kathleen Scher, my sixth grade teacher, who was my steady pen pal until she died just a few days before she became 90 years old, when I was Governor. And then in the seventh grade, my homeroom teacher was Ruth Atkins. And then there was Miss Teague, my civics teacher in the eighth grade. And Mary Broussard, my ninth grade English teacher, who was the only person in our class besides me that supported John Kennedy over Richard Nixon. [*Laughter*] In the ninth grade!

451

And I could go through my whole high school list of teachers, through my college list of teachers. All the people around here have to put up with stories that I forget that I've already told once about specific verbatim things I remember that my teachers in college said in lectures over 30 years ago.

Now, don't ever think what you do does not matter. I remember them all as if I were sitting with them yesterday. And there are things that each of them gave to me that I am not even aware of today, after all these years of having had a chance to think about it.

Every one of you made a decision that you would never be wealthy. [*Laughter*] You made a decision that you would give yourselves to the next generation. You made a decision that you would do at work what we're all supposed to do in our families—that you would always be thinking about tomorrow.

On New Year's Eve, someone asked me, in this meeting I was at, if I had to write a legacy on my tombstone, what would it be? And I would say—I said something like—I don't remember exactly what I said, but something like that I had the privilege of leading America into a new century and keeping the American dream alive for everyone, having our very diverse country live together as one America, and maintaining our leadership as the world's greatest force for peace and freedom and prosperity. If you think about that, every single one of those tasks requires that we do a better job of educating more of our people, every single one.

You look around America today, we have 5.2 percent unemployment. It's a great thing. And it's also entirely misleading. Unemployment is virtually zero for people who have the skills necessary to meet the demands of the emerging economy if they live in a place where investment is coming in. What we have to do is to close the gaps and the skill levels. How do you do that? Give people better education and then provide incentives to invest in the places that have been left behind.

The Vice President was in Detroit a few days ago, promoting our empowerment zone concept of trying to build communities and give incentives for people to invest where people are there willing to work and there is no investment. But the unemployment rate is absolutely meaningless if you're unemployed. If you're unemployed, the unemployment rate is 100 percent. [*Laughter*] It's not one or zero or five or—you know, that's

what it is. So we can't create opportunity for all Americans unless everybody first has the educational skills.

We certainly can't learn to live together as one America, with all this rich diversity we have, without being educated to it, because for thousands of years, people have lived in tribal patterns that taught them to be suspicious of those that were different from themselves. Among the Teachers of the Year here today, we have an immigrant from Taiwan making a great contribution to the United States. Among the Teachers of the Year today we have a Japanese-American whose parents were interned during World War II. My State had one of those internment camps. I've been down there to see it, and I still can't believe my country ever did that. We have African-Americans and Hispanic-Americans. We have people from different religious backgrounds.

You know that what unites us is more important than what divides us, and, once having recognized that, you know that what divides us makes us more interesting and far better positioned to do well in the world of tomorrow than countries that are less diverse than we are. But we can't learn to do this right unless we can not only feel our way out of this but think our way out of this. We have to know more than we now know.

And we certainly—we certainly—cannot take advantage of the opportunities that are there for us at the end of the cold war to create a whole new order of peace and freedom and prosperity without much higher levels of understanding.

Or let me put it in another way. The American Society of Newspaper Editors were here the other day, and one of the editors from out in the country stood up, and I thought, you know, I'm going to get a question on whatever is going on in Washington. He said, "I got a 10-year-old son in the fifth grade, and he wants to know what your advice is for him for the future." And it was the hardest question I got asked all day.

And I said, he should study hard. He should stay out of trouble and not defile his body with drugs or anything else. He should seek out people who were of different racial and religious backgrounds and get to know them and understand them. He should try to learn more about the rest of the world as early as possible, as soon as possible. And he should begin right now taking some time to serve in his community to help people who needed help. Those are the five things I said. Why? Because I think that will give him a good education and give him opportunity, help us to come together as one America and appreciate our differences, and help us to maintain our leadership in the world. And you're doing that every day. The kindergarten teachers here are doing that.

Now, that's why I look so forward to this every year. Because most of the time, frankly, we just sort of take you for granted, unless we get mad because we don't like the way the test scores come out or the comparative test scores or whatever else. And I think it is very important that we not lose the enormous significance of your collective impact. And I thought I'd stand up here today and try—and I didn't know if I could do it, but I thought I could—just remember all my teachers, just to show you the personal impact you have. See, I'll bet you a lot of you could do the same thing I just did, and that's probably why you're doing what you're doing today.

We do have some changes to make, and we do have to recognize that we have to keep moving to lift the standards and we have to realize that there are some senses in which we do what we do very well and some senses in which we have challenges because we have so much diversity among our children that others don't have. But we can't use that as an excuse. We have to just deal with the facts and believe every child can learn.

At this brain conference yesterday that the Vice President mentioned that the First Lady and I hosted, I was stunned when we had these scientists there talking about one trillion networks being developed in the brain.

We've known for a long time—I was taught in school that we only use a small part of our brain's capacity, but I never understood the extent to which the brain keeps developing all during childhood and how we interrelate to it. But what it convinced me of was what I already believed by conviction, which is that nearly everybody is fully capable of learning whatever they need to learn to get where they need to go.

And that's to me what this whole standards business is about and what the encouragement of all the States to develop standards that are nationally and internationally sound, challenging all the States to join in the fourth grade reading

and the eighth grade math tests in 1999 is all about. It's not about another test. It's about saying, we believe all our children can learn, and we believe children learn according to the expectations placed on them, and our expectations are going to be high. That's what this is about. And I hope every one of you will support that, because I think it is terribly important.

So far, in only a couple of months, the educational leadership of California has joined Maryland, Michigan, North Carolina, and the schools of the Defense Department system in endorsing—in saying they will participate in this standards movement. And I hope every State in the country will say yes before the time comes.

Because we have a record number of students in our schools and they're growing rapidly, and now we've got for the first time—it's rather humbling for me and the Vice President—we finally have more kids in school than we had during the baby boom. [*Laughter*] We're going to have to find in the next 10 years 2 million new teachers, and that's going to be quite a challenge. And we have to train them for the challenges that they'll face today and the world their children will face tomorrow.

So I want to thank you for your willingness to think about that and for helping to encourage teachers to achieve new levels of excellence. I know many of you are participating in Secretary Riley's national forum, which gives you a chance to share ideas with educators all across the country about the best way to train teachers. This is an issue that is very hard. It will never make the front page on any day. There will always be something more immediate. But there are very few things that are more important than how we train our teachers and how we continue to learn as teachers in the classroom and in the schools and how we can all learn from each other. That's one of the reasons I encourage teachers all over the country to seek board certification from the National Board for Professional Teaching Standards.

And we now have 500 of these teachers, nationwide. Governor Hunt from North Carolina, who is well-known to many of you, has been working on this as an obsession for years. But in our balanced budget plan we've got $105 million that would put 100,000 master teachers in our Nation's classrooms. And the idea is not really—it's just like you. You're the Teacher of the Year, but you know, you're really standing in the shoes of every other good teacher in your State. But if you can put this training in the hands of one teacher in every school building in America, which we ought to be able to do with this, it will upgrade the performance of all the teachers in the schools and it will change the culture of the schools. So I hope you will support that as well.

There are a lot of other things in our education program, but I wanted to focus on those two things, plus our efforts to wire the schools, to focus just on the public schools today. We're also trying to help the schools that are terribly overcrowded get some financial help to reduce the cost of new construction or repair work when the local districts are willing to do their part, and I hope that initiative will pass.

But the main thing I want to tell you is, what you do really matters. It matters to the country as a whole, it matters to individual kids, and if any—if at all possible, it matters even more now to our society at large than it did when I had all those teachers whose names and faces and voices and manners and stern rebukes I still remember. [*Laughter*]

Today we honor, especially, Sharon Draper. She happens to be one of our Nation's first master teachers and a member of the National Board for Professional Teaching Standards, and I'm especially pleased about that.

For 27 years, she has inspired students with her passion for literature and life. The standards

to which she holds her students at the Walnut Hills High School in Cincinnati are legendary, so much so that seniors wear T-shirts that proclaim, "I survived the Draper Paper"—[*laughter*]—when they finish their senior thesis. I was intrigued when I read that, and I asked her for one of those T-shirts. And I was denied because I haven't yet survived it. [*Laughter*]

Her gifted teaching has not gone unrecognized. She received both the National Council of Negro Women Excellence in Teaching Award and the Ohio Governors Educational Leadership Award. She is an accomplished author in her own right. She was honored with the American Library Association's Coretta Scott King's Genesis Award and its annual Best Books for Young People Award. She has devoted her career not only to teaching and to writing but to helping other teachers improve their skills as well.

Sharon Draper is more than a credit to her profession; she is a true blessing to the children she has taught. And it gives me great pleasure now to present her with the National Teacher of the Year Award and ask her to come forward and say whatever she'd like to say. Congratulations.

NOTE: The President spoke at 2:10 p.m. in the East Room at the White House. In his remarks, he referred to Gov. James B. Hunt, Jr., of North Carolina.

The President's News Conference
April 18, 1997

The President. Good afternoon. Less than 2 weeks from today, the Chemical Weapons Convention goes into effect, with or without the United States. The bottom line is this: Will the United States join a treaty we helped to shape, or will we go from leading the fight against poison gas to joining the company of pariah nations this treaty seeks to isolate?

With this treaty, other nations will follow the lead we set years ago by giving up chemical weapons. Our troops will be less likely to face poison gas on the battle field. Rogue states and terrorists will have a harder time acquiring or

making chemical weapons, and we'll have new tools to prevent and punish them if they try. But if we fail to ratify, other countries could back out as well. We won't be able to enforce the treaty's rules or use its tools, and our companies will face trade sanctions aimed at countries that refuse to join.

As the Senate prepares to vote next week, I'm encouraged by the great progress we have made but mindful of the hurdles we still must overcome in order to gain approval of the CWC. I welcome yesterday's unanimous agreement by the Senate to bring the treaty to a vote, and

I thank Majority Leader Lott, Senator Daschle, Senator Helms, and Senator Biden, and all the Members of the Senate from both parties for their efforts. By going the extra mile, we've reached agreement on 28 conditions that will be included in the treaty's resolution of ratification, for example, maintaining strong defenses against chemical attacks, toughening enforcement, allowing the use of riot control agents like tear gas in a wide range of military and law enforcement situations, and requiring search warrants for any involuntary inspections of an American business.

These agreed-upon conditions resolve virtually all of the issues that have been raised about this treaty. But there are still a handful of issues on which we fundamentally disagree. They will be voted on by the full Senate as it takes up the treaty next week. We should all understand what's at stake. A vote for any of these killer amendments will prevent our participation in the treaty. Let me quickly address four of them.

The first would prohibit the United States from joining the treaty until Russia does. That is precisely backwards. The best way to secure Russian ratification is to ratify the treaty ourselves. Failure to do so will only give hardliners in Russia an excuse to hold out and hold on to their chemical weapons.

A second killer condition would prohibit us from becoming a party until rogue states like Iraq and Libya join. The result is we'd be weaker, not stronger, in our fight to prevent these rogue states from developing chemical weapons because we would lose the ability to use and enforce the treaty's tough trade restrictions and inspection tools. No country, especially an outlaw state, should have a veto over our national security.

A third killer condition would impose an unrealistically high standard of verification. There is no such thing as perfect verifiability in a treaty, but this treaty's tough monitoring, reporting, and onsite inspection requirements will enable us to detect militarily significant cheating. Our soldiers on the battlefield will be safer. That, clearly, is an advance over no treaty at all.

Finally, the opponents would force us to reopen negotiations on the Chemical Weapons Convention to try to fix two concerns that have already been resolved. First, they claim that a treaty expressly devoted to eliminating chemical weapons somehow would force its parties to facilitate the spread of chemical weapons. This

interpretation is totally at odds with the plain language of the treaty. I have committed to the Senate that neither the United States nor our allies share this interpretation and that we will reaffirm that fact annually.

The opponents also misread the treaty to require that we share our most advanced chemical defensive technology with countries like Iran and Cuba, should they join the Chemical Weapons Convention. I have committed to the Senate that in the event such countries are threatened by chemical attack, we would limit our assistance to providing nothing more than emergency medical supplies.

America took the lead in negotiating the Chemical Weapons Convention, first the Reagan administration, then the Bush administration. Every Chairman of the Joint Chiefs of Staff for the past 20 years supports it, as do the overwhelming majority of our veterans, the chemical industry, and arms control experts. Now we must lead in bringing this bipartisan treaty to life and enforcing its rules. America should stand with those who want to destroy chemical weapons, not with those who would defy the international community. I urge every Member of the Senate to support the convention when it comes to a vote next week.

Now, let me take this opportunity also to say a few words about the budget. Yesterday my economic team briefed me extensively on the full range of issues that are now being discussed as we continue serious high-level talks on the balanced budget. The progress we've made so far is encouraging, and I'm hopeful that a bipartisan balanced budget agreement can be reached.

We're working closely with Senate and House Democratic leaders and budget committee leaders as we move forward on this issue. I want to thank Senators Domenici and Lautenberg, and Congressmen Kasich and Spratt for working so hard and in such good faith with our economic team. There is no question that serious differences remain, but if each of us is willing to compromise our sense of the perfect, I know we can reach an agreement that advances the greater good. And we can both do so without compromising our deeply held values.

Based on the progress that we've made so far, I'm asking the bipartisan negotiators to continue their work. I hope that in the near future we can—they can recommend ways to bridge the remaining differences. This can be a victory for all Americans. Over the past 4 years, we have shown that with hard work and strong resolve, we can make significant progress toward balancing our budget while still investing in our people and that both those things will lead us to the strong economy we have today and an even stronger economy tomorrow.

Neither side can have everything it wants. But we know that a good agreement must include at a minimum that our children will have the best education from the first days of life through college to prepare for the 21st century, that more children will have access to quality health care, that our environment will be protected, that we are living up to our obligations to the most vulnerable among us, and that Medicaid—Medicare will be strengthened while ensuring the solvency of its Trust Fund well into the next decade. This is what we can achieve and what I think we must achieve and why we all have to stay at the table until the job is done.

Chemical Weapons Convention and State Department Reorganization

Q. Mr. President, what is your outlook for ratification of the treaty? And how much of a quid pro quo was there with Senator Helms on reorganizing the State Department? Will the Voice of America still have its autonomy? All of these things are kind of worrisome.

The President. Well, yes, the Voice of America will still have its independent voice. It will still be the Voice of America. There was no linkage.

Senator Helms came to see me personally at the White House last year sometime—I don't remember when—and we met up in my office in the Residence for an extended period of time, with just a few of his staff members, a few of mine. He was going over his plan for reorganization of the agencies and why he thought it was right. I promised him that I would seriously consider the issue, that I thought there ought to be some reorganization. I had a slightly different take on it. And actually, since that time, but especially in the last few weeks, we have been working very, very hard to reach a consensus within the administration on an alternative proposal. I think it is warranted, and I think it's good on the merits.

I can tell you that there was no linkage between these two issues. I do not expect Senator Helms to vote for the Chemical Weapons Convention. I would be elated if he did. We have,

as I said, resolved, I think, to his satisfaction, 27 of the 30 issues that we made.

Q. All of these were concessions on your part, weren't they, all the conditions?

The President. No, all these—well, they were—I didn't consider them concessions because I agree with them. There is nothing in any of these conditions that I think is bad for the treaty, bad for the system, or bad for the national security. But they do clarify questions that Senator Helms and other Senators had about the meaning of the treaty. But they all can be attached to the treaty without in any way undermining its integrity, its fundamental meaning, or its rules of enforcement and inspection, and that is the critical thing.

So I consider that the things that we've agreed to in good faith are really a tribute to the work that Senator Lott and Senator Helms and Senator Biden and a number of others did to really clarify what this convention will mean. I think it's a positive thing.

Bill [Bill Plante, CBS News].

Whitewater Investigation

Q. Are you concerned, Mr. President, by the statement of Mr. McDougal and the independent prosecutor that there is new evidence, new documents which, according to the suggestions that seem to be coming out of there, might cause you or Mrs. Clinton further trouble?

The President. No.

Q. Why not?

The President. For obvious reasons. I mean, go back, look at the RTC report; look at all the evidence that's ever come out on this. We did not do anything wrong. We had nothing to do with all these business matters that were the subject of the trial. No, I'm not worried at all.

Peter [Peter Maer, NBC Mutual Radio].

Bob Dole's Loan to Speaker Newt Gingrich

Q. President Clinton, what do you think about the deal worked out between Bob Dole and Newt Gingrich? Is this the right arrangement when you consider that it's not the kind of arrangement that most Americans could get in similar circumstances if they faced a fine?

The President. Actually, I was thinking of calling Senator Dole this afternoon—you know, Chelsea is about to go off to college, and it's pretty expensive. [*Laughter*] I——

Q. Where is she going?

The President. Let me say that this is a matter that has to be decided by the House. They have certain rules, certain standards, and they will have to decide whether it complies with those rules and standards.

John [John Donvan, ABC News].

Israeli Politics and the Peace Process

Q. Mr. President, the Prime Minister of Israel is having domestic troubles now, and occasionally, these sorts of issues can leak into the large international arena, particularly in regard to this peace process. Are you concerned about that sort of spillage, and have you had any conversations with him about it since the news was announced or during his visit here?

The President. He didn't say anything to me during his visit here which is inconsistent with what he's said in public since then. He made the same general statements to me. We have had no conversations since then. As you know, Dennis Ross has been there and helped to broker this meeting between the Palestinians and the Israelis on security. It's obviously an internal matter for Israel to deal with. They're a great and vibrant democracy, and they'll deal with that in their way. But I think that the important thing is that we get the security cooperation up and going, and then we just keep plugging ahead here. We cannot allow anything—anything—to derail the peace process, and I don't believe we will.

Hong Kong

Q. Mr. President, could you tell us a little bit about your meeting today with Mr. Lee? And one of the concerns since the day that— once Hong Kong is turned over to the Chinese, if there's any kind of erosion of liberties, is there much the United States could do?

The President. Well, let me say this: I think the United States has to make it clear that Hong Kong is important to us, the people of Hong Kong are important. The agreement made in 1984 by China and Great Britain, which they sought the support of the United States on when President Reagan was here, clearly commits China to respect not only the economic liberties but also the political and civil liberties of the people of Hong Kong. And our policy is that the agreement was a good one when we said we supported it in 1984; it's a good one in 1997, and it ought to be honored.

Wolf [Wolf Blitzer, Cable News Network].

Q. But, sir, do you—are you prepared to do something if you thought the Chinese were not living up to the agreement?

The President. Well, that's a hypothetical question. Let me say at this time, it's very important to us. We believe it's an important matter, and we expect that they will live up to their agreement. And it's our policy—strong policy—that they should.

Wolf.

Aberdeen Trials

Q. Mr. President, a lot of Americans have been shocked by the Aberdeen trial of the U.S. Army drill sergeant and the allegations that this is part of a much bigger problem that has developed in the U.S. military. I wonder if you'd share with us your thoughts on how serious a problem that this kind of alleged sexual harassment is? Is it a pervasive problem throughout the military?

The President. Well, as you know, there's now an inquiry going on, and the instructions that I have given on this are the same instructions I gave on the Gulf war issue, which is to get to the bottom of it, find the facts, tell the truth, and take appropriate action. And I think we ought to let that play out.

Domestic Terrorism

Q. Sir, in light of tomorrow's anniversaries of the Oklahoma City bombing and of the fiery end to the Waco standoff, first of all, are there any credible security threats that Americans ought to be worried about? And secondly, is this a date that Americans ought now view with trepidation?

The President. Well, my answer to the first question is that we are mindful of the issues and we have taken the actions that I think are appropriate. I don't think that I should say more than that.

I would hope that tomorrow, rather than viewing these actions with trepidation, the American people would be thinking about two things: First, with regard to Oklahoma City, as Hillary and I saw last year when we were there, some of the surviving victims and the families of victims who survived and who did not survive are still hurting and face some continuing difficulties, and I would hope that they would be in our prayers. And I hope that we would, as I said at the time, all take a little time to express appreciation, rather than condemnation, for people who serve the public in the way they did. They were targeted solely because they work for the United States.

With regard to Waco, in light of what happened with the Heaven's Gate group out in San Diego, which was an entirely different thing but came to an equally tragic end, I would hope that the American people would say, "We really value the freedom of religion and the freedom of political conviction, and we want people to have their own convictions, but we need to all be sensitive and to be aware of what can happen to people if they develop a kind of a cult mentality which can push them off the brink." And we ought to do what we can to try to avoid that.

Terry [Terence Hunt, Associated Press].

James Riady and Webster Hubbell

Q. Mr. President, in the summer of 1994, you met at the White House with James Riady, and then just a little bit later, you met at Camp David with Webb Hubbell. And about the same time, the Lippo Group started paying Mr. Hubbell $100,000. What do you recall about the conversations with those two gentlemen?

The President. I don't have anything to add to what I've already said about both of them. Mr. Riady was there in the White House for 5 or 10 minutes, basically a social call. We had exchanged a few comments, and he said nothing about Mr. Hubbell that I can remember. I don't believe he did.

And when Mr. Hubbell came to Camp David, my recollection is we played golf and I took a walk with him and asked him point blank if he had done anything wrong. And as he has said now in public, he told me that he hadn't and that he had a billing dispute with his law firm and he expected it to be resolved. And I have really nothing to add to that. There was no correlation between the two.

Q. There was no discussion about——

The President. No.

Q. ——efforts to—for him, any assistance for Mr. Hubbell?

The President. No, I don't remember anything about that, and he didn't—we didn't talk about the Lippo Group at all.

Federal Bureau of Investigation

Q. Mr. President, the problems with the FBI crime lab are only the latest controversy involving the FBI. What is your current view of the performance of the FBI and its Director, Mr. Freeh?

The President. Well, let me say about the crime lab, obviously, I'm concerned about the lab, but I think that you have to give the Justice Department, the Attorney General, and Mr. Freeh credit for doing what I think should be—in any organization, you're always going to have some problems. I, frankly, think—I was impressed with the fact that they did what I want the Pentagon to do on the sexual harassment issue—I mean, the matter was looked into, the facts were laid honestly before the public, and now I think it's important that all appropriate corrective action be taken.

Budget Agreement

Q. One more on the budget. Do you share the view of many in Washington that the next week or maybe 2 weeks is really a make-or-break period on the budget, and if a deal is going to happen, it's going to become apparent in this next window?

The President. Well, let me say, as you know, there is also a view directly contrary to that.

Q. What's your view?

The President. There are people—well, I think it's important—there are people who think that all the various positions are so unsettled that even the budget leaders and the leaders of the Senate and House and White House acting in good faith can't put together an agreement that will hold up and produce significant bipartisan majorities in both Houses.

My view is, I don't believe in saying "make or break" because I don't believe in ever saying "never." I've seen too many things come back again and again. And I believe we'll get a balanced budget agreement this year because it is so important to the country and to our future.

We've got this unemployment rate down to 5.2 percent. Inflation seems to be dropping again. If we passed a balanced budget, I think it would remove a lot of other lingering fears about inflation out there. I think it would give a new jolt of confidence to the economy. I think it would keep the recovery going. And I think it would be very good for the long term, especially if it also protected the Medicare Trust Fund for significant numbers of years in the future, and if it—[*inaudible*]—investment.

Now, I am in the camp of people who believe it would be better to do it sooner rather than later if we can do it. But I don't believe for a minute that it's an easy task, and I don't believe that an agreement at any price is worth doing it in the next 4 or 5 days. And I don't believe the Republicans do. I wouldn't ask them to do that either. You know, we have strong convictions. And you saw in 1995 and until the end in 1996, when we made a remarkable amount of progress there just right before the Congress adjourned for the election, that we have different and deeply held views, and they're honestly different.

But I do believe that if we could do it sooner rather than later and it would be good for the country and consistent with our principles and theirs, an honorable compromise—which I think is there—I think sooner rather than later is better. But I certainly won't give up if it doesn't happen. I'm going to keep on working until we get it done. I expect it to happen this year. I'm very optimistic. And I am hopeful that it can happen sooner rather than later. And I am committed personally to doing everything I can to put it together.

Thank you.

NOTE: The President's 141st news conference began at 3:40 p.m. in the Briefing Room at the White House. In his remarks, he referred to Kenneth Starr, independent counsel; former Senator Bob Dole; Prime Minister Benjamin Netanyahu of Israel; Ambassador Dennis B. Ross, Special Middle East Coordinator; and James Riady and Webster Hubbell of the Lippo Group. A reporter referred to Martin Lee, head of the Hong Kong Democratic Party.

Letter to the Oklahoma City Memorial Foundation
April 14, 1997

Dear Friends:

Our nation will never forget that tragic day, almost two years ago, when we first learned of the bombing of the Alfred P. Murrah Federal Building in Oklahoma City, and we will always remember the courage shown by the citizens of your strong and united city during that dark time. All Americans continue to support your recovery efforts, and our prayers are with you.

With the destruction of the Murrah Federal Building, we learned once again that America is a family, and that such a brutal attack on any American is an attack on us all. In uniting around the citizens of Oklahoma City, our nation proved once again that no force of hatred or terrorism can ever defeat the American spirit.

I want to express my support for your efforts to establish a memorial on the site of the bombing. This memorial will be a fitting tribute not only to those who died, but also to those whose lives were changed forever on April 19, 1995. I know that, by honoring our fellow Americans in this way, we can help to further the healing and restore hope for a brighter, more secure future.

Hillary and I will always remember the time we spent with the families and survivors. Please know that we are keeping them, and all the people of Oklahoma City, in our thoughts and prayers.

Sincerely,

BILL CLINTON

NOTE: This letter was released by the Office of the Press Secretary on April 19. An original was not available for verification of the content of this letter.

Memorandum on Expanding Access to Internet-based Educational Resources for Children, Teachers, and Parents
April 18, 1997

Memorandum for the Heads of Executive Departments and Agencies

Subject: Expanding Access to Internet-based Educational Resources for Children, Teachers, and Parents

My number one priority for the next 4 years is to make sure that all Americans have the best education in the world.

One of the goals of my Call to Action for American Education is to bring the power of the Information Age into all of our schools. This will require connecting every classroom and library to the Internet by the year 2000; making sure that every child has access to modern, multimedia computers; giving teachers the training they need to be as comfortable with the computer as they are with the chalkboard; and increasing the availability of high-quality educational content. When America meets the challenge of making every child technologically literate, children in rural towns, the suburbs, and inner city schools will have the same access to the same universe of knowledge.

I believe that Federal agencies can make a significant contribution to expanding this universe of knowledge. Some agencies have already launched a number of exciting projects in this area. The White House has a special "White House for Kids" home page with information on the history of the White House. NASA's K–12 initiative allows students to interact with astronauts and to share in the excitement of scientific pursuits such as the exploration of Mars and Jupiter and with experiments conducted on the Space Shuttle. The AskERIC service (Education Resources Information Center), supported by the Department of Education, has a virtual library of more than 900 lesson plans for K–12 teachers, and provides answers to questions from educators within 48 hours—using a nationwide network of experts and databases of the latest research. Students participating in the Vice President's GLOBE project (Global Learning and Observation for a Better Environment) collect actual atmospheric, aquatic, and biological data and use the Internet to share, analyze, and discuss the data with scientists and students all over the world. With support from the National Science Foundation, the Department of Energy, and the Department of Defense's CAETI program (Computer-Aided Education and Training Initiative), the Lawrence Berkeley Laboratory has developed a program that allows high school students to request and download their own observations of the universe from professional telescopes.

We can and should do more, however. Over the next 3 months, you should determine what resources you can make available that would enrich the Internet as a tool for teaching and learning, and produce and make available a new or expanded version of your service within 6 months.

You should use the following guidelines to support this initiative:

- Consider a broad range of educational resources, including multimedia publications, archives of primary documents, networked scientific instruments such as telescopes and supercomputers, and employees willing to serve as tele-mentors or answer student and teacher questions.

- Expand access not only to the information and other resources generated internally, but by the broader community of people and institutions that your agency works with and supports. For example, science agencies should pursue partnerships with professional societies, universities, and researchers to expand K–12 access to scientific resources.

- Update and improve your services in response to comments from teachers and students, and encourage educators to submit curricula and lesson plans that they have developed using agency material.

- Focus on the identification and development of high-quality educational resources that promote high standards of teaching and learning in core subjects. Of particular importance are resources that will help students read well and independently by 4th grade, and master challenging mathematics, including algebra and geometry, by 8th grade.

• Make sure the material you develop is accessible to people with disabilities. Earlier this month, I announced my support for the Web Accessibility Initiative, a public-private partnership that will make it easier for people with disabilities to use the World Wide Web.

I am also directing the Department of Education to develop a "Parents Guide to the Internet," that will explain the educational benefits of this exciting resource, as well as steps that parents can take to minimize the risks associated with the Internet, such as access to material that is inappropriate for children.

The Department of Education will also be responsible for chairing an interagency working group to coordinate this initiative to ensure that the agency-created material is of high quality, is easily accessible, and promotes awareness of Internet-based educational resources among teachers, parents, and students.

WILLIAM J. CLINTON

NOTE: This memorandum was released by the Office of the Press Secretary on April 19.

The President's Radio Address
April 19, 1997

The President. Good morning. Vice President Gore and I are here in the Oval Office on the second national NetDay, when citizens and communities all across America come together to help us meet the goal of connecting every classroom and library in the United States to the Internet by the year 2000. With us today are three AmeriCorps members, two local high school students, and two Communication Workers of America volunteers, all of whom are contributing to this effort.

NetDay is a great example of how America works best when we all work together. It's like an old-fashioned barnraising, neighbor joins with neighbor to do something for the good of the entire community; students, teachers, parents, community groups, government, business, unions, all pulling together to pull cable, hook up our schools, and put the future at the fingertips of all our young people.

Once we reach our goal of linking our schools to the Internet, for the first time in history, children in the most isolated rural schools, the most comfortable suburbs, the poorest inner-city schools, all of them will have the same access to the same universe of knowledge. That means a boy in Lake Charles, Louisiana, can visit a museum halfway around the world, a girl in Juneau, Alaska, can visit the Library of Congress on-line.

Since the first NetDay just over a year ago, nearly a quarter million volunteers have wired 50,000 classrooms around our country. Today NetDay activities are occurring in more than 40 States. In a few minutes, Vice President Gore and I will have a chance to use a new video and computer technology set up for the first time right in the Oval Office to meet with volunteers in south central Los Angeles and children in Hartford, Connecticut. I want to thank them and all the NetDay volunteers for their service to our country.

We have to do everything we can to make technology literacy a reality for every child in America. That's why I asked the Federal Communications Commission to give our schools and libraries a discount, a special "E-rate," or education rate, to help them connect classrooms to the Internet and to stay on-line. On May 6th, the FCC will vote on a plan to provide more than $2 billion in yearly E-rate discounts for schools and libraries. This can make all the difference for communities struggling to make sure their students are ready for the 21st century. So today, again, I call on the FCC to approve this plan and give our children access to this new world of knowledge.

Now, more than ever, we can't afford for our children to be priced out of cyberspace. But connecting young people to the Internet is not enough. We have to make sure that when they log on they have access to the information that will prepare them for the world of the future. And Government has a vital role to play in all this. For instance, NASA lets students talk to astronauts on the Internet. And Vice President

Gore's GLOBE project gives tomorrow's environmental scientists a chance to interact with the scientists of today. Today I am directing every department and agency in our National Government to develop educational Internet services targeted to our young people. With this action, we are one step closer to giving young people the tools they need to be the best they can be in the 21st century.

We owe much of our progress thus far to the efforts of the Vice President. He has led our national campaign for technology literacy, and I'd like him to say a few words now.

Mr. Vice President.

[*At this point, the Vice President made brief remarks describing Technology Literacy Challenge Fund grants.*]

The President. Thank you, Mr. Vice President. Both of us encourage all of you to visit the White House home page. And once again, let me thank all the NetDay volunteers. We are going to meet our goal. We're going to get every classroom and every library in this country hooked up by the year 2000.

Have a great day, and thanks for listening.

NOTE: The President spoke at 10:06 a.m. from the Oval Office at the White House.

Teleconference Remarks to Students on NetDay
April 19, 1997

The President. Hi, students!

Students. Hi, Mr. President!

The President. Now, is that Mr. Contreras with you?

Precious Robinson. Yes, this is Mr. Contreras.

The President. Hello, Miguel, how are you?

Miguel Contreras. Buenos dias, Mr. President.

The President. Buenos dias. Now, why don't you tell us why you're volunteering this weekend?

Mr. Contreras. Well, we've got quite a number of union members here in Los Angeles as part of the national AFL–CIO NetDay, that are coming together here to help wire 38 schools and empowerment zones in Los Angeles. And we're going to kick it off today. We think that educational opportunities is equivalent to civil rights here, and we want to make sure that all our students have the necessary tools to bring them into the 21st century.

So we're glad that you're supporting this effort. And the unions here—in particular, the International Brotherhood of Electrical Workers, Local 11; we have the CWA, Communication Workers of America; and the United Teachers of LA all have turned out today to ensure that the wiring is a success. So we're going to move forward today.

The President. Thank you.

And Ms. Robinson, what benefits do you expect to flow from this to the students at your school?

Ms. Robinson. Well, we want to be prepared for the 21st century, and we want our children to be familiar and to be competent and to be ready to use the Internet. So we expect a great deal—great many benefits from this. We want the super-information highway. We know that is the way of the future, and we want all of our students to be prepared for that.

We have a lot of our staff members here also, my teachers, my parents, my superintendent. And so we're all very excited about the work that's going to take place today.

The President. Well, thank you.

How many of the young people behind us know how to use a computer? Raise your hand if you can use a computer.

Mr. Contreras. Quite a number of them.

The President. Good for you. Well, good luck.

Mr. Contreras. Don't ask the adults. [*Laughter*]

The President. Well, don't ask the adults on this side of the screen, either. [*Laughter*] The Vice President can raise his hand; I'm not so sure about me. [*Laughter*]

Have a good day. Thank you.

Students. Thank you, Mr. President.

The President. Now we want to go to Hartford. There's Hartford. Good morning!

Students. Good morning!

The President. I want to thank all the young people who are there participating in the Youth

Tech Corps. The Vice President and I just announced that Connecticut will be getting some more funds from the Department of Education to make sure that every child in Connecticut will have access to educational technology. So I want you to tell me about what the Youth Tech Corps is doing and how that relates to getting technology out to everybody.

Student. The Youth Tech Corps, first of all, is a program that is designed to match students who have strong interests with technology with other students and use businesses to enhance this program.

The President. So those of you who have good skills are helping those who need it, right?

Student. All who are interested.

The President. Yes, well, maybe you could send me a volunteer. I need some help down here. [*Laughter*]

Student. No problem.

The President. I see a couple of volunteers in the back of the room there. They're laughing. [*Laughter*]

What have you done on NetDay? What does it mean for Connecticut and for you?

Student. Well, basically the Youth Tech Corps is—basically, we're trying to continue on the process of Connect '96 and just take it the next step to getting the schools connected—all the schools connected and make sure that they can use the computers once they have computers and they're connected to the Internet.

The President. Do you find that in your own experience that once the computers are there and they're hooked up to the Internet that they are widely used?

Student. I think they're widely used if the people using them know how to. I know, like, a lot of students—there are some that probably don't know how to. But I think—I feel that they're widely used.

The President. What about the teachers? Do all the teachers know how to make maximum use of it?

Student. No. [*Laughter*]

The President. Some yes and some no, right? [*Laughter*]

Student. Yes. Some do and some don't, you know, because some teachers actually put their grades on computer, not for—[*inaudible*]—but those who calculate it.

The President. So it's important that we don't let the connecting of the schools and the classrooms get ahead of training the teachers and the students about how to use the computers.

Student. Right.

Student. Exactly.

The President. Because otherwise they're useless just sitting there, right?

Student. Right.

The President. Now, is everybody in the room a member of the Tech Corps?

Student. This is the corps; this is the beginning of it. Hopefully, they will continue to be a part of the Youth Tech Corps.

The President. Good for you.

Do you want to say anything, Al?

The Vice President. Well, I just want to congratulate all of you. It's an exciting day. It makes you feel good to be a part of this, doesn't it?

Student. Yes.

The Vice President. Well, congratulations, and keep up the wonderful work.

Student. Thank you.

The President. You've reminded us of something very important today about what you're doing, too, because we sometimes get so focused on making sure all the classrooms in the country are hooked up that we forget that the hookup is worthless unless the teachers and the students are trained to use it——

Student. That's right.

The President. ——and have the time and ability to use it.

So I thank all of you for what you're doing, and I hope that this conversation we're having today will lead to some greater publicity for your Tech Corps so that maybe every community in the country will have one to make sure that the students and the teachers can use the computers and the hookups that we're providing.

Thank you, God bless you, and good luck. Hang in there.

Students. Thank you.

The President. Bye-bye. Have a good day.

NOTE: The President spoke by satellite at 10:40 a.m. from the Oval Office at the White House to students in Los Angeles, CA, and Hartford, CT. In his remarks, the President referred to Miguel Contreras, executive secretary-treasurer, Los Angeles County Federation of Labor; and Precious Robinson, principal, Barrett Elementary School in Los Angeles.

Remarks to the United Auto Workers
April 20, 1997

The President. Thank you.

Audience member. We love you, man!

The President. Thank you. I love you, too. And I appreciate you.

President Yokich, Secretary Treasurer Wyse, to the officers and the ladies and gentlemen of the United Auto Workers. I came here, more than anything else, to say two things. Number one, thank you very much for helping me and the Vice President become the first Democratic ticket to be reelected in 60 years. Thank you very much. [*Applause*] Thank you. The second thing I came here to say is that if we do the right things, we can build that bridge to the 21st century together.

You know, we've had a lot of monumental fights in Washington in the last 4 years. That's not all bad, and it was to be expected. You have lived through, in the last few years, the biggest economic change to occur in the United States and in the world since the global Depression of the 1920's and the 1930's. And this one, thank goodness, has not led to global depression, but you know how much things are changing.

And when I became President, there were a lot of assumptions here in Washington that had come to dominate our country's thinking and politics, during the years when the Presidents of the other party dominated the White House. People believed that you could talk about the deficit, but you didn't really have to do anything about it, that if there was anything done to help labor it was, by definition, bad for business. People believed that Government was always the enemy. And they believed that the only kind of tax cuts that were any good were ones that cut taxes on the very wealthiest Americans because they would somehow benefit everyone else by trickling down.

I came here believing we could balance the budget in a way that was fair to all Americans, get interest rates down, and help grow the economy, which would help people who have capital and invest it, but it would also help to lower car payments and home mortgages and college loan payments and make this country strong in the world again. I came here believing that the only long-term way to strengthen the American economy was to build the middle class, and that

meant we had to be pro-worker and pro-business, and we could do both.

I came here believing that in a country that now has only about 4 percent of the world's population, if we want to continue to enjoy about 20 percent of the world's wealth, we're going to have to get some other people to buy our goods, but we could only have free trade if it was also fair trade. And we have 200 separate trade agreements to show for our efforts in that in the last 4 years. All of these things you helped to make possible.

And if you think about the debates going on in Washington today—if you think about the fights we had in '95 and '96, which the American people were heard loud and clear on—they said, "We don't believe the Government is always the enemy." They said, "We do think we have a responsibility to protect education and the environment and the integrity of our health care programs." They said, "You can balance the budget without hurting ordinary Americans or trampling on the poor."

And I think that message is out there. I agree with President Yokich; you came about 10,000 votes short of having our party win the House of Representatives again because they outspent us 4, 5, or 6 to 1 the last 10 days. But we did a pretty good job. And by the way, I'm proud of the fact that you invested in our campaigns and helped us and fought for us and stood up for us and stood with us.

You hear all this talking today. You know, people forgot what was at stake there. In 1993 when we passed that economic plan, our opponents said it was the end of civilization as we know it. Remember all the things they said? "Unemployment will go up. The deficit will go up. The world's going to just go to pieces in America because of the President's economic plan."

Well, in 4 years this country produced over 11½ million new jobs for the first time in any Presidential term. They were wrong, and you were right. You were right—107,000 of them were in the auto industry. Unemployment now is down to 5.2 percent, a 9-year low. In 1995, average wages started to rise again for the first time in 20 years. And last year, over half of the new jobs were in higher wage categories, in dramatic contrast to most of the new jobs we got in the years before we took office. We are moving in the right direction. You have supported the right policies. You should be proud of it, and you should make sure the American people know it.

In 1992, the year before I took office, Japan produced 28 percent more autos than American workers. By 1994, America had passed Japan for the first time since 1979, and you're still ahead of them. And I'm proud of you. In 1995, we finally got an auto agreement. And I'm proud to report that last year, in the first full year of that agreement, American auto sales went up by 34 percent in Japan, European sales went up by 10 percent, overall car sales only went up by 3 percent. If you give people the chance to buy American, even in Japan, they will buy American because you're putting out the finest cars in the world today. Auto parts sales went up 20 percent last year. They're now double what they were in 1992 in Japan.

We have a long way to go, and we made that clear yesterday, and we intend to keep working. But it makes the point I want to make: If we can open these markets to American products—the American people paid the price and you paid the price in the tough and difficult years of the 1980's and the early 1990's to dramatically increase quality and productivity. And you deserve the chance to sell your products anywhere in the world, and if you can, you're going to do very well.

Over 4 million more Americans own their own home. More than 10 million Americans have refinanced their homes with lower interest rates. The welfare rolls in 4 years dropped a record 2.8 million. We moved more people from welfare to work in the last 4 years than went on welfare in the first 25 years of the program. Don't tell me we can't reform the welfare system; we can—we can—move people from welfare to work if we do it right.

And that is just the beginning. We have got to do more. And as I said, I never believed that being pro-growth, pro-private sector, and pro-business meant being anything other than pro-worker, pro-union, and pro-family. I believe they are consistent, and I believe that the record proves that when we work together and when we're fair to everybody, we produce more, people feel better, and they're more productive. And I think it's time that everybody understood

that we don't want to be a hard-work, low-wage economy, we want to be a hard-work, smart-work, high-wage economy in which we all work together.

That's why I worked with you to defeat attempts to repeal the prevailing wage laws, to bring back company unions, to weaken workplace health and safety laws. That's why I fought for a tax cut that used to be supported also by members of the other party, the earned-income tax credit. Since 1993, we've ratcheted it up now so that the average family of four with an income of $30,000 or less and two kids in the home has a $1,000 lower tax bill than they did 4 years ago. Now they can go out and buy cars again. I think that's the right sort of tax cut to have in America to reward working people, and I think we're stronger because of it.

And I thank you for your support for the minimum wage increase. No person who works 40 hours a week in a country that preaches that people who are on welfare ought to go to work should live in poverty when they're working full time and trying to support their children. And we don't have to tolerate it.

On July 1st the historic legislation you helped to enact to make sure workers don't lose their health insurance if they lose their jobs takes effect. We've made pensions more affordable, and we've cracked down on pension fraud and abuse. Today, the fund that guarantees 42 million private sector pensions has saved the pensions of 8½ million Americans that were in danger when I took office and now has a surplus for the first time in its over 20-year history. We are moving to make work rewarded in this country and get the kind of security and support it deserves.

As Steve said, since I took office I have vetoed every piece of anti-worker legislation that has landed on my desk. And I will continue to do just that. [*Applause*] Thank you.

Now, I want to ask you for help on some other things as well. First of all, I want you to help me get Alexis Herman confirmed as Secretary of Labor. Now, listen to this: She was voted out of the committee unanimously. Every Republican in the committee voted for her. She gets to the floor, we're assured she's going to be brought to a vote, and all of a sudden they decide that maybe they can get me to change some of the executive actions I have taken to try to prevent anti-union activities when it comes to Government contracts by saying, "We just won't give you a Secretary of Labor. We'll show you we don't agree with what you're doing. You got elected. You have the power to do it. The people voted for you. We voted your nominee out of committee unanimously." Some of her strongest support came from Republicans who knew her well and knew that she was a good and able woman and tried to be fair to business as well as labor. They knew she had a history in the Labor Department, a history of experience, and they said, "Okay, she's qualified. We all voted for her in committee. You won the election. You have the power to do this. But if you do it, we might not ever give you a Secretary of Labor."

Now, I don't think that's a very good way to run a railroad. You know, I don't refuse to work with them because they won the election. I know they wouldn't have voted for me, and that goes two ways. The American people made this decision. They put us both in the boat, and they told us to row. And we've got to figure out how to get the oars going in the same direction. That's what we've got to do. And we're working hard to do that.

We're working hard on this chemical weapons treaty to try to reduce the dangers of chemical warfare to our soldiers. Every Chairman of the Joint Chiefs of Staff in our major military organizations have endorsed this—every Chairman of the Joint Chiefs of Staff since President Carter's administration. And we're going to have to do it together. We'll never get a balanced budget unless we do it together.

Now, this is something we have to do together. And I'd like to say to them and to say to you: If they think I'm wrong about something I've done, we ought to sit down and talk about it. But we've got a qualified person, and Labor has been out a Secretary too long. Let's have a Secretary of Labor and confirm Alexis Herman. And I ask for your help to do it.

Twelve million people have taken advantage of the family and medical leave law since I signed it in 1993, the first bill I signed. Many people who have good jobs have family and medical leave through their contracts, but a lot of people don't. And we've proved now that if you help people succeed at home, so they're not worried sick at work about their children or their parents, you let them take a little time off for that, actually workplace performance goes up. We haven't lost jobs or lost small businesses

since the family and medical leave law came into effect. In fact, we've had a record number of new businesses started in every single year I've been President.

That's why I want to expand the family and medical leave law, to give people a little time off every year to go to regular doctor's appointments with their children and with their parents if they're sick or to go to regular parent-teachers conferences at the school. We've got to have the parents if we're going to improve the quality of education, and I think it will be a good thing to do.

I also would like to say to you that we have more work to do on this budget. Now, in the last 4 years—when I came here, people laughed at me when I said we could reduce the deficit and increase our investment in education, in medical research, in technology, in fighting crime, and in our future. Well, now we've got 4 years of declining welfare rolls, 4 years of declining crime rates. Every expert in America now admits we were right when they fought us in trying to put 100,000 more police on the street. We know we can do this.

But we also see that people are saying, "Well, maybe this recovery can't go on. Maybe interest rates are going up. Maybe if they don't, inflation will come back." You've seen all this. We need to go on and balance this budget to keep this recovery going. That will remove any question about inflation coming back in the economy and will keep interest rates down. It will make cars more affordable here and abroad. It will keep UAW members working. It will keep America strong. But we have got to do it in a way that protects the integrity of the things we fought 2 long years for in 1995 and 1996, for education, for the environment, for the integrity of these health programs. We have got to do that.

This balanced budget of mine does exactly that. It provides tax cuts for education and health care, to help raise a child and buy and sell a home. It protects Medicare and Medicaid but adds a lot of years to the Medicare Trust Fund. It is something that I'm very proud of in terms of what it does for medical research and for protecting the environment. And it is also very, very good for education. If you look at the future, we know that we have got to improve the performance of our schools if we want all of our children to have good jobs with growing incomes. We know that. We know that most of this has to be done at the local level with support from the States, but we know the national level and we in the National Government have a responsibility as well.

My budget makes an unprecedented commitment of $51 billion to make sure that by the year 2000, every 8-year-old will be able to read on his or her own, every 12-year-old can log on to the Internet, every 18-year-old can go on to college, and every adult can continue to learn for a lifetime and get the skills necessary to get good jobs.

I've laid out a 10-point plan for education; I just want to mention 3 to you. Number one, we have got to quit hiding behind the idea that we have local control of our schools and using that for an excuse not to have national standards in education. All of our competitors have national standards in education. And I am not talking about Federal Government standards; I'm talking about national standards. But I have challenged all the States to meet them and to give all of our children a test in reading at the fourth grade level and a test in math at the eighth grade level by 1999. And I hope you will support me in that wherever you come from in every State in America. It is the right and moral thing to do for our country.

We ought to open the doors of college to everybody who's prepared to work for it. I want to give a $1,500 tax credit, modeled on the HOPE scholarship in Georgia, America's HOPE scholarship. That's about what it costs at any community college in the country. I want to give it for 2 years to open the doors of college for at least 2 more years to make them just as universal as a high school diploma is today by the year 2000. And we can do that. I think we ought to give people a $10,000 tax deduction for the cost of any college tuition after high school, any higher education. It will help a lot of people in this room, I would imagine. And because we can never forget the people who don't make enough money to take tax deductions, I've also proposed the biggest increase in the Pell grant scholarships for needy students in 20 years, so we can all have the chance to go on.

The average age of people in college is going up steadily every year. It will continue to go up. You probably all know friends of yours in their thirties, in their forties, maybe in their fifties, who had to go back and get retrained. And we ought to have a system that makes it possible for every American who wants to work, who's willing to work, who needs an education, to get it for a lifetime. It is simple, and it is good for the American economy. We ought to do it.

The last thing I want to say about that is, I've been trying for 4 years through Democratic and Republican Congresses to get the Congress to adopt my "GI bill" for America's workers. And I know there have been a lot of questions about it. Essentially, what I want to do is take 70 separate training programs, put them in a grant, and just give a chit, give a skills grant to people who are unemployed or underemployed and say, "You take it to the place nearest you which will be most likely to get you a job." Almost every American is within driving distance of a community college. This would include union-sponsored training programs, anything else, just whatever is necessary and whatever is most handy to get a job—the "GI bill" for America's workers.

I think we've wasted a lot of money on intermediaries and Government employees. We've got all this money here; give it to the people who are unemployed and you can go after them, everybody else can who wants to train them. But I believe a "GI bill" for people—I think most people have enough sense to figure out on their own, in their own communities, what would be most likely to put them back in the work force at a higher wage. And I hope you'll help me pass the "GI bill" for America's workers.

And just because we got beat on our attempt to say that everybody in America who works for a living and all their children ought to have access to health care, I hope you won't quit trying to expand health care access to the American people who need it. [*Applause*] Thank you.

I have proposed new legislation to crack down on Medicare fraud. I've appointed a new commission on health care quality to make sure that the lower costs of today's managed plans doesn't dilute the quality of them. We've moved to help fight breast cancer by making women 40 and over eligible for mammograms who are covered by Federal programs, which I think is important.

In my balanced budget plan, we are moving to try to stop the sort of drive-by mastectomies, where women with breast cancer are basically operated on and put out of the hospital in a matter of a few hours. We are moving to cover respite care for Alzheimer's victims, because there are so many families who care for a family member with Alzheimer's. And having lost an aunt and an uncle to Alzheimer's, I know it's a 7-day a week, 24-hour a day job. We can actually save a lot of money over the long run if we help give those families a little help for respite care if they're willing to take care of those folks in their homes. It's so much less expensive, and if families want to do it, we ought to help cut them a little slack, I think.

We also want to give people access to health insurance when they temporarily are between jobs or lose their jobs. We want to make it easier for them, affordable for them to keep their health insurance. Nearly half of the children who lose their insurance do so because their parents lose or change a job. And my budget would provide coverage for up to half of the 10 million children today who do not have health insurance. I think it's very important to do more to try to cover children and to cover people who are between jobs.

Well, these are just a few of the things that I could be talking to you about tonight. They are big things. This will affect the way people live for generations to come. And while you're here, I want to ask you to think about that. We've had a lot of fun tonight. We've cheered, and we're glad we won the election—sorry we lost a few Congress seats. We're proud of the fights we fought, and we're awfully glad America is in better shape than it was 4 years ago. But what I want you to think about is what kind of America have you worked all your life for? What do you want this country to look like in 20 years, 25 years, when your children are your age, when your grandchildren are your age? I think about it every day—every day.

When I look at these kids out in this audience, I know if we do the right things, they will have more chances to live out their dreams

than any generation of Americans. That's the first thing I want. The second thing I want is for America to be the world's leading force for peace and freedom and prosperity a generation from now, just like it is today, because I know the whole world will be better off if that is the case. And the third thing I want, that I see as I look at all of you from your different backgrounds, is I want us to be one America.

We're going to become more and more diverse, racially, ethnically, religiously. If we can keep the democratic culture the values of America, if we can overcome our own prejudices and fears, if we can learn to respect each other's differences and enjoy our own difference but be bound together by what unites us, then in a world that is every day consumed by the problems of the Middle East or Africa or Northern Ireland or Bosnia, America will surely be the light of the world. And the labor movement has always stood for the proposition that anybody that was willing to work hard for a living ought to be given a fair chance to make it in the United States of America, always.

I love being with you. I'm very grateful. I'm glad you reelected me. I'm having a good time, limp and all. [*Laughter*] But remember, you can't stop thinking about what you want it to be like in a generation, because the world is changing in profound and fast ways. And we have to do a good job now and a good job for all these children who are here. I think we're going to do it together.

Thank you. God bless you.

NOTE: The President spoke at 6:05 p.m. at the Sheraton Washington Hotel. In his remarks, he referred to Stephen P. Yokich, president, and Roy Wyse, secretary-treasurer, United Auto Workers.

Message on the Observance of Passover, 1997
April 21, 1997

Warm greetings to everyone observing Passover.

Commemorating God's liberation of the Israelites from Egyptian slavery, Passover is the story of a people who, sustained by their faith in God and strengthened by their own courage

and determination, broke free from oppression to seek a new life in a new land. Their journey was long and full of peril, and their resolve sometimes shaken by doubt; but ultimately the Jewish people reached the Promised Land, where they could live and worship and raise their children in the sweet air of freedom.

The ageless festival of Passover holds profound meaning for Americans. We began our nation's journey to freedom more than two hundred years ago, a journey that is still not complete. Now we look forward to a new century and a new millennium, strengthened by the knowledge that we, too, have been blessed by God with the vision of a land of great promise set aside for those who cherish freedom.

As we mark the observance of another Passover, let us renew our commitment to America's promise. Let us continue our journey to a land where all our people are free to pursue our common dreams—to live in peace, to provide for our families, and to give our children the opportunity for a better life.

Hillary joins me in extending best wishes for a joyous Passover celebration.

BILL CLINTON

Remarks on Earth Day and the Community Right-To-Know Law and an Exchange With Reporters
April 22, 1997

The President. Thank you very much, Mr. Vice President. Good morning, ladies and gentlemen. As all of you know I am about to leave for North Dakota, where the people are quite literally in the fight of their lives. What they have endured is enormous; how they are enduring it is remarkable. I am going to view the flood damage to pledge our Nation's support to see that we are doing everything we can do to help them.

You know, Americans have a habit of joining together at times like this, and I think all Americans have been very deeply moved by the pictures we have seen of a town being flooded and burning at the same time, the people in North Dakota losing everything they have. I personally can't remember a time when a community that large was entirely evacuated. And we have to stay together.

I think it is appropriate, for the reasons the Vice President said, that coincidentally this trip is occurring on Earth Day, because since 1970, the first Earth Day, Americans have stood side by side against a rising tide of pollution and for the proposition that we have to find a way to live in harmony with and grow our economy in a way that is consistent with preserving our environment.

Earth Day started at the grassroots. Soon the force of neighbor joining with neighbor grew into a national movement to safeguard our air, our land, and our water. The movement led national leaders of both parties to put in place the environmental safeguards that protect us

today: the Clean Air Act, the Clean Water Act, the Environmental Protection Act. In 1995, an attempt to reverse this consensus and to radically weaken our environmental laws was strongly rebuffed here in Washington and, even more importantly, all across America. And in 1996, that consensus began to be restored again.

These environmental protections have done an awful lot of good. But one of the best things we can do in Washington to protect the environment is to give people in communities all across our country the power to protect themselves from pollution. That is the mission of the community right-to-know law. This law tells citizens exactly what substances are being released into their neighborhoods. In the decade it's been on the books, citizens have joined with government and industry to reduce the release of toxic chemicals by 43 percent. Under our administration, we strengthened right-to-know, nearly doubling the number of chemicals that must be reported, making it easier for Americans to find out what toxics, if any, are being sent into the world around them.

In 1995, I directed EPA Administrator Carol Browner to find ways to expand community right-to-know even further. Today we are making good on that pledge. Today we increased by 6,100—30 percent—the number of facilities that need to tell the public what they are releasing into our environment. Today seven new industries, including mining, electric utilities, and hazardous waste treatment centers that use substances like mercury, lead, and arsenic, will now be subject to the community right-to-know law. Today more information will be required from 700[1] companies already providing information under the law. It will be more accessible to Americans. And today we set in motion a process that will guarantee that all the stakeholders, including citizens, community groups, environmental groups, and businesses, will have opportunities to work together from now on to continue to improve this law.

By expanding community right-to-know, we're giving Americans a powerful, very powerful early warning system to keep their children safe from toxic pollution. We're giving them the most powerful tool in a democracy: knowledge. We are truly living up to the promise of Earth Day.

I also want to say a special word of thanks to Katie McGinty for the work that she has done on this in the White House. And I want to thank the Vice President for taking my place at the Earth Day celebration at Anacostia today to talk about community right-to-know and for all of his work on the environment.

And just let me say in closing, with regard to the comments he made about climate change and the possible impact it may have had on the enormous number of highly disruptive weather events that have occurred just since we've been here in the last 4 years and a few months, I think it is very important that we continue to intensify our Government's research efforts in this regard and that we take the very best knowledge we have and bring it to bear on a lot of the decisions we'll be having to make together as a country over the next 4 years. We do not know, as the Vice President said, for sure that the warming of the Earth is responsible for what seems to be a substantial increase in highly disruptive weather events, but many people believe that it is, and we have to keep looking into it. We have to find the best scientific evidence we have, and we have to keep searching for the answers to this. I think every American has noticed a substantial increase in the last few years of the kind of thing we're going to see in North Dakota today. And if there is a larger cause which can be eased into the future, we ought to go after that solution as well.

Thank you very much.

---

[1] White House correction.

North Dakota Floods

Q. Is a "Marshall plan" appropriate? Your Chief of Staff suggested yesterday it may take a "Marshall plan" to help North Dakota.

The President. You know, we've had—I suppose because North Dakota is not highly populated we may—we've had disasters which have affected more people. But I believe that probably this is the highest percentage of people in any State or community that I have seen affected by this. And you know, if you look at Grand Forks, you see a place that literally has to be completely rebuilt or people have to reconstitute their lives elsewhere. So I do believe that we're going to have to be prepared to be very creative here.

The Congress has shown in the past, even when it was quite costly, after the earthquake in California, for example, that we can unite across party lines to do what has to be done. We need to take a hard look at this. This situation in North Dakota is virtually unprecedented in many, many ways, and I want to go out there, make sure that I have read all the information available, talk to the people there, see for myself. And then I'll come back and, along with the congressional delegation with Senator Dorgan and Senator Conrad and Congressman Pomeroy, we'll put our heads together and see where we go from here.

Q. Any idea, Mr. President, on how much money it might take, and will it be there when you need it?

The President. I think, as I said, my experience in dealing with the flood in the Middle West and all the disasters in California, the Pacific Northwest, the floods in the Southeast, is that Congress finds a way. And I think everybody in America has been totally overwhelmed by what we have seen on television and seen in the news reports—these pictures of buildings completely surrounded by water, burning down. You know, I think it's been an overwhelming experience. I think the American people are with the people of North Dakota, and I think we'll do what we have to do.

Chemical Weapons Convention

Q. Mr. President, are you making any tangible headway on the chemical weapons treaty, on getting the votes for the chemical weapons treaty?

The President. Well, I hope so. We're working hard on it. We are working very, very hard on it. I am; the Vice President is; everyone in our administration is. I worked over the weekend some on it. We're doing the best we can to put together a strong case. I think the fact that we have come up with a package of 28 clarifying amendments that respond to 90 percent of the objections, even of the strongest opponents of the treaty, I think shows the good faith in which we have proceeded. And we've worked very hard on this, and I'm actually quite optimistic.

Iraq

Q. Do you have a message for Saddam Hussein and honoring the no-fly zone?

The President. Well, my message is that we support people in exercising their religious liberties and in living out their religious convictions everywhere in the world. And we certainly support that in the Muslim world. But we don't want to see religion, in effect, used and distorted in a way to try to avoid the international obligations that are imposed. And we intend to continue to observe the no-fly zone and continue to support the embargo until he lives up to the conditions of the United Nations resolutions.

Thank you.

NOTE: The President spoke at 9:05 a.m. on the South Lawn at the White House, prior to his departure for Grand Forks, ND. In his remarks, he referred to President Saddam Hussein of Iraq.

Remarks in a Roundtable Discussion on Flood Damage in Grand Forks, North Dakota
April 22, 1997

The President. Well, first of all, let me say to all of you that I'm honored to be here with the people from our administration. Thank you, Mayor Owens and Mayor Stauss, the other mayors that are here. I thank Senator Conrad and Senator Dorgan, Senator Daschle, Senator Johnson who came in with me, and Senator Wellstone and Senator Grams who met us, and Congressman Pomeroy and Congressman Peterson who met us here, Governor Schafer, Governor Carlson. I also want to thank all the people who came with me from my administration: the Secretary of Agriculture, Dan Glickman; the Secretary of Health and Human Services, Donna Shalala; the Secretary of Housing and Urban Development, Andrew Cuomo; the Secretary of Transportation, Rodney Slater; Aida Alvarez, our Small Business Administration; and Togo West, the Secretary of the Army. I want to thank the Air Force, the National Guard, the Red Cross, the Corps of Engineers, the Coast Guard, the Salvation Army, and all the people at the State and local government and the community groups that have worked so hard on this endeavor.

Today we saw, obviously, these two communities that have been so devastated, but we know that there is a lot of other loss in North and South Dakota and Minnesota. We're going to meet with people now, and I'm going to get a briefing from people who have, unbelievably, dealt with blizzards, floods, and fires all at the same time. I have never seen that before. And when I saw pictures of some of you stacking sandbags in a blizzard, I thought that I had bad reception on my television at first. It was an amazing thing. I don't recall ever in my life seeing anything like this. And I've been very impressed by the courage and the faith that all of you have shown in the face of what has been a terrible, terrible dilemma.

I want to say before we start this roundtable discussion that we are going to do everything we can to move as quickly as possible to do as much as can be done to help. I want to be briefed by everyone here at the table. And James Lee Witt has already talked to me quite extensively about this over, as you might imagine, a long period of time now. But I wanted to say that there are three things I'd like to announce first.

First of all, before I left the White House this morning, I authorized FEMA to provide 100 percent of the direct Federal assistance for all of the emergency work undertaken by Federal agencies in the 149 counties where disasters have been declared. We will do this retroactively from the moment that the counties were recognized as disaster areas, which I hope will relieve the State and local governments from the worry of whether or not they'll be able to actually afford to help citizens and the communities through the cleanup. We do this only in the most difficult of circumstances. Normally the reimbursement rate is 75 percent. But anyone who has been here and seen the destruction, as I have, knows that this is not an ordinary disaster, if there is such a thing. The people here are giving 100 percent, and we should, too.

Second, we are dramatically expanding FEMA's public assistance grant program. We'll add 18 counties in Minnesota and 53 counties in South Dakota today. And these counties also will be eligible for funds for repair and restoration of their communities after the waters subside. Let me also say that we expect to make additional counties in North Dakota and Minnesota eligible for this assistance as soon as we can fully assess the damage that they have sustained.

The third thing I'd like to say is that today I'm asking Congress to approve an additional $200 million of contingency emergency funds for North and South Dakota and for Minnesota. I've asked that these funds be made available both for short-term emergency response activities and for long-term efforts to help the region to rebuild in the aftermath of the flood. If approved, this action will bring to $488 million the total amount of disaster assistance we've requested for the people of these States.

Finally, I'm directing our FEMA Director, James Lee Witt, to lead an interagency task force to develop and direct a long-term recovery plan for North Dakota, South Dakota, and Minnesota. We know that this is going to be a long-term effort.

And when we were coming in today, one of the things that I was just noting based on my now 20-plus years of experience in dealing with things like this—although I have never seen a community this inundated by flood, this large a community—we have to deal with the long-term problems. And you have to know that we can be relied on to be there in all these communities over the long run.

The only other thing I'd like to say, Madam Mayor, to you and the other officials—you know

this already, but a lot of people are still almost in shock, I'm sure, and have not had time to focus on some of the things which will make the losses most painful, the things that have been lost in these homes, the records of family occasions, the letters from World War II, the letters from the kids that go off to college, all the things that people will have to come to grips with in the days ahead. And I know that $488 million or $4 billion wouldn't make that go away. But at least we want you to know that we are going to be there over the long run.

And the rest of America has, I think, looked with great compassion and pain but also enormous admiration at the heroic conduct of the people of this community and of all these States in the last several days when they've gone through things that most of the rest of us can't imagine. We could never imagine facing a flood and a fire and a blizzard all at the same time. And we admire you greatly, and we're going to do what we can to be there with you over the long haul.

Thank you.

Mr. Witt.

[At this point, the discussion began.]

The President. First of all, Mayor, and to all of you who've spoken, I thank you for what you said and for how you said it and for what you've done. And the pain with which you spoke, I think, only showed the rest of us that you're speaking for all the people in these communities. And I thank you for that.

I wonder if, Mr. Witt, if you could comment, or any of the people that we brought with us can comment on the question of the immediate needs—the immediate need for housing, even for basic toilet facilities, for these things—these basic immediate needs. How are we going to deal with that?

[The discussion continued.]

The President. We've got the entire congressional delegation from North Dakota and from South Dakota, and they came to see me as one a couple of weeks ago. And I really appreciated it. I don't think even they were prepared for what's happened since then here, but they did come and made me aware of what was going on.

And of course, we have Senator Wellstone, Senator Grams, and your Congressman, Collin

Peterson, here from Minnesota. And I wonder if any of them, or Governor Schafer or Governor Carlson, would like to either make a comment or ask a question.

Senator Dorgan, Senator Conrad, either one of you have anything you want to say?

[*The discussion continued.*]

The President. Well, let me just say this. I think one of the things that we need your input in, to go back to this sort of "Marshall plan" characterization that Senator Conrad and Senator Dorgan used and that my Chief of Staff, Erskine Bowles, used yesterday, we need to try to design this aid package so that it gives maximum flexibility to people at the grassroots level to do what needs to be done in these communities. This is an unprecedented thing, and I will work with you on it.

As I said, my sense is that the rest of the country has been profoundly moved by this. And if your colleagues in the Congress, in both parties, will really help us with this—we just need to—we need your guidance. You've been out here since Thursday; you know a lot more about it than we do. We need to try to structure what we're going to do in the Congress in the next few days in a way that deals with it. I think that's why Senator Daschle mentioned the community development block grant program or some other programs that gives the maximum flexibility to the people at the community level.

Governors, would you like to say anything?

[*The discussion continued.*]

The President. After years and years of dealing with things of this kind, my instinct is that what Governor Carlson said is right, that what Minnesota learned and what we learned in all the Midwestern States that were engulfed in the flood of '93 will give us some very valuable lessons about what to do in the rebuilding in all the communities affected here, with the exception of these two where you've had the total destruction of communities of this size. In my experience, we've not gone through anything like this. So I do think we're going to have to be creative and flexible.

I just want to make two brief points, but I want to—before I do, we have some other mayors here, and I know we can't hear from everybody, but Mayor Stauss, would you like to say anything?

[*The discussion continued.*]

The President. Before we break this up, I just want to make two points. The first thing I wanted to ask is a question. Is there an estimated time for when the water and sewer will be hooked up again? Do we even know? Do we have any way of—anyone know?

[*A participant responded that it would be at least a month before the normal water supply was restored.*]

The President. Well, one of you—I think maybe it was Curt—said you were worried it might take 3 or 4 weeks before people could be back on their homesites.

Let me say—Mr. Witt said something about the trailers, on-site trailers, which we have found work best. As soon as we know how many people want to go back there and live under those circumstances and how many people—the quicker we can do that inventory the better because even if we have to have these made, which typically we do in numbers this large, you can get incredibly rapid turnaround. You can turn one around—you can order, make, and deliver up here probably within less than 2 weeks. They can make a large number on order at any of these sophisticated manufacturing places in 10 days.

So I think we can do our part of that, but it depends on what kind of other arrangements you can make for water and sewer and when you tell us. Isn't that about right?

[*Director James Lee Witt of the Federal Emergency Management Agency responded affirmatively to the President's question.*]

The President. Yes, but we've also got to have the inventory ready simultaneously. We could be—we can order these things before the water and sewer is back on so that they happen together. That's the point I'm trying to make. You can—and that can save people at least a couple of weeks. And I know right now, any day, people say, means something to them.

The second point I want to make is to my—basically a request to the Members of Congress who are here and for help from the Governors. Believe me, everybody in Congress—I think virtually everybody will be sympathetic to this request. On the other hand, the thing that bothers me that could delay this some, and I don't want to see it happen, is sometimes in Congress, when something that is so important, so popular like this comes along, other people, for perfectly legitimate reasons, think, "Well I've got something I care about; maybe I can tack that on there, too." And there may be some other agendas that get caught up in this.

So I would just ask, on a completely bipartisan, or, if we will, nonpartisan basis—this is an American issue—if we can get this supplemental request through the Congress on its own terms or, at most, only with other emergency-related expenditures in other parts of the country, so that none of us—and the administration included—we all resist whatever temptation we might have to get something else done. I think that is the moral and the right thing to do. These people deserve help now, and that's the only way to make sure we won't have any extraneous debates and won't fool around and waste a lot of time.

And I will do whatever I can. But we need—and again, believe me, I don't know anybody who is going to do this, I've just seen it happen over and over and over again where it seems like it's just an irresistible temptation when you think some interest you represent can ride along on the train that deserves to go out of the station in a hurry. We all need to resist that and do what's right by these folks and get it done now. And if we can do that, I think that, from what I've seen here today, they'll take care of the rest.

Thank you.

NOTE: The President spoke at 1:58 p.m. in the Enlisted Club at Grand Forks Air Force Base. In his remarks, he referred to Mayor Patricia Owens of Grand Forks, ND; Mayor Lynn Stauss of East Grand Forks, MN; Gov. Edward T. Schafer of North Dakota; Gov. Arne H. Carlson of Minnesota; and Curt Kreun, a resident of East Grand Forks.

Remarks to the Community in Grand Forks
April 22, 1997

The President. Thank you. Wait a minute, folks, I've got to get these crutches right here. [*Laughter*] Thank you, General Hess. Let me begin by thanking everyone who is a part of the Grand Forks Air Force Base for what you do for our national security and especially for what you have done to support the people of the Grand Forks communities in these last few days. I'm very proud of you. Thank you.

As I think all of you know, I have just come from touring the devastation of the floods as well as a very moving community meeting, presided over by Mayor Owens, attended by Mayor Stauss and other mayors, the entire congressional delegation from North Dakota and from South Dakota, Senator Grams and Senator Wellstone from Minnesota, Congressman Collin Peterson from Minnesota, and the Governors from North Dakota and Minnesota.

It has been a very moving experience for all of us. Five members of my Cabinet are here, the Secretaries of Agriculture, Health and Human Services, Housing and Urban Development, Transportation, and the Administrator of the Small Business Administration. The Secretary of the Army is here. We have all come,

first of all, to see firsthand what it is you've been going through; secondly, to pledge to do our part to help make you whole; and thirdly, to tell you that we're here for you. We have hardly ever seen such a remarkable demonstration of courage and commitment and cooperation and basic human strength, and we are very impressed and proud to be Americans when we see what you have done in the face of this terrible disaster.

We know that this rebuilding is going to be a long-term prospect, and we also know that there are some very immediate and pressing human needs that many people have. Before I left this morning, I took some steps I wanted to tell you about. First, I authorized James Lee Witt and the Federal Emergency Management Agency to provide 100 percent of the direct Federal assistance for all the emergency work going to be undertaken here.

The second thing we did was to add to the counties already covered another 18 counties in Minnesota and 53 in South Dakota who need help.

The third thing I did was to ask Congress to approve another $200 million in emergency funds for North Dakota, South Dakota, and Minnesota. These funds will be available for both short-term emergency response activities and for long-term efforts to help you rebuild. If approved, this action will bring to $488 million the total amount of disaster assistance that I have requested for the people of these three States.

Now, let me say there are—I say again, I know there are short-term, immediate concerns, people who need a place to sleep, people who don't know where their next check is coming from, even people who don't have access to basic sanitary facilities except here on the air base. We are working to restore those things with your local community folks. And we had some specific talks about what we could do to get proper housing available while you're rebuilding your communities.

[At this point, there was a disturbance in the building.]

The President. That's up there. Anybody hurt? Well, we've had a fire, a flood, a blizzard—[laughter]—I guess we can take a—[applause].

So anyway, we'll have our folks here, and there will be lots of them. And let me just say, this is going to be—these next few days—our FEMA Director, James Lee Witt, and I have been working on these things a long time. He was my emergency director when I was Governor of Arkansas. I know what's going to happen. I've been through floods and tornadoes and terrible losses. The next few days are going to be very, very hard on a lot of people. A lot of you who have been very, very brave and courageous, helped your friends and neighbors, are going to—it's going to sink in on you what you have been through and what has been lost. And I want to encourage all of you to really look out for each other in the next few days and be sensitive to the enormous emotional pressures that some of you will feel and also kind of be good to yourselves. Understand you don't have to be ashamed if you're heartbroken. But it's going to be tough in the next few days.

But I also want you to feel very resolute about the long run. I have asked Director Witt to head an interagency task force to develop a long-term plan for what our responsibilities are to help you rebuild and be stronger and better than ever. And believe me, it may be hard to believe now, but you can rebuild stronger and better than ever. And we're going to help you

do that. And we want you to keep your eyes on that future.

Let me also say, as I go back to Washington to ask the Congress to approve this emergency package, I will never forget what I have seen and heard here. Four of your community leaders who played various roles in the last several weeks, Ken Vein, Jim Shothorst, Randy Johnson, and Curt Kreun, talked to me and to others in the meeting a few moments ago. I have seen the pictures of people battling the flames of the fire in the rising floods. I have seen rescue workers working around the clock even as they lost their own homes. I have seen people pitching in to rescue books from the University of North Dakota library. I have read the last 3 days' editions of this newspaper. How in the world they kept producing the newspaper for you is beyond me. And you ought to be very proud of them for doing that. I read this morning that there's a message board right here that's covered with offers for free housing all around. And that's the kind of spirit that will get everyone through this.

With all the losses, I hope when this is bearing down on you in the next few days, you will remember the enormous courage and shared pride and values and support that all of you have given each other. You have shown that when we think of our duties to one another, our own lives are better, that we're all stronger when we try to make sure our friends and neighbors are safe and strong as well. And no matter what you have lost in this terrible flood, what you have saved and strengthened and sharpened and shown to the world is infinitely better. And you should be very, very proud of that.

I saw something your mayor said the other day that struck me in particular. She said, "What makes a community a place to live in is not the buildings. It's the people, the spirit, and faith that are in those people. Water cannot wash that away, and fire cannot burn that away, and a blizzard cannot freeze that away." And if you don't give it away, it will bring you back better than ever. And we'll be there with you every step of the way.

Thank you, and God bless you.

NOTE: The President spoke at 2:50 p.m. in Hangar

Two at Grand Forks Air Force Base. In his re-marks, he referred to Brig. Gen. Kenneth Hess, USAF, Base Commander, Grand Forks Air Force Base.

Statement on Investment Sanctions Against Burma
April 22, 1997

Today I am announcing my decision to impose a ban on new U.S. investment in Burma.

I have taken this step in response to a constant and continuing pattern of severe repression by the State Law and Order Restoration Council (SLORC) in Burma. During the past 7 months, the SLORC has arrested and detained large numbers of students and opposition supporters, sentenced dozens to long-term imprisonment, and prevented the expression of political views by the democratic opposition, including Aung San Suu Kyi and the National League for Democracy (NLD).

I have therefore imposed sanctions under the terms of the "Cohen-Feinstein" amendment, a bipartisan measure that I fully support. As contained in the Burma policy provision of the Consolidated Appropriations Act for Fiscal Year 1997 (Public Law 104–208), this amendment calls for investment sanctions if the Government of Burma has physically harmed, rearrested for political acts, or exiled Aung San Suu Kyi, or has committed large-scale repression of, or violence against, the democratic opposition. It is my judgment that recent actions by the regime in Rangoon constitute such repression.

Beyond its pattern of repressive human rights practices, the Burmese authorities also have committed serious abuses in their recent military campaign against Burma's Karen minority, forcibly conscripting civilians and compelling thousands to flee into Thailand. The SLORC regime has overturned the Burmese people's democratically elected leadership. Under this brutal military regime, Burma remains the world's leading producer of opium and heroin, and tolerates drug trafficking and traffickers in defiance of the views of the international community. The regime has shown little political will to stop the narcotics exports from Burma and prevent illicit drug money from enriching those who would flaunt international rules and profit by destroying the lives of millions.

The United States and other members of the international community have firmly and repeatedly taken steps to encourage democratization and human rights in Burma. Through our action today, we seek to keep faith with the people of Burma, who made clear their support for human rights and democracy in 1990 elections which the regime chose to disregard. We join with many others in the international community calling for reform in Burma, and we emphasize that the U.S.-Burma relationship will improve only as there is progress on democratization and respect for human rights.

In particular, we once again urge the authorities in Burma to lift restrictions on Aung San Suu Kyi and the political opposition, respect the rights of free expression, assembly, and association, and undertake a dialog on Burma's political future that includes leaders of the NLD and the ethnic minorities.

NOTE: The related Executive order of May 20 prohibiting new investment in Burma is listed in Appendix D at the end of this volume.

Remarks on the Chemical Weapons Convention and an Exchange With Reporters
April 23, 1997

The President. Thank you. Thank you very much. Thank you, Mr. Wallace, for your remarks and for your service; Mr. Vice President; General Shalikashvili. Thank you, General

Scowcroft, for being here. Thank you, Admiral Zumwalt, for being here and for being on this issue for so long. General Jones, Admiral Arthur, to all the distinguished veterans and veterans groups who are with us today and to the men and women in uniform who are here today. And I'd like to say a special word of thanks to General Powell and to Senator Dole for being here.

You have witnessed today, I believe, an example of America at its best, working as it should, putting the interests of the American people and the interests of the men and women of America in uniform first. And it is something for which I am very grateful.

This treaty will make our troops safer. It will make our Nation more secure. It will at least reduce the likelihood that innocent civilians here and around the world will be exposed in the future to horrible chemical weapons. That is why every Chairman of the Joint Chiefs for the last 20 years and all the military leaders and political leaders and veterans you have heard today have supported it.

All the arguments have been made, so I would like to tell you a story. We now know that chemical weapons have bedeviled Americans in uniform from Belleau Wood in World War I to Baghdad in the Gulf war. We know that thousands were injured or killed by chemical warfare in World War I. And I thought it would be a wonderful thing today to show what this treaty is all about, to have one remarkable American veteran of World War I who survived such an attack. And he is here with us today, Mr. George Clark. Thank you for coming, sir. God bless you.

Mr. Clark was just in the Oval Office with all of us. And Senator Dole apparently asked him if he was a contemporary of Senator Thurmond, and he said he thought Senator Thurmond was a little young for the heavy responsibilities that he has enjoyed. [*Laughter*]

As a 16-year-old marine, almost 80 years ago, George Clark fought in the Battle of Soissons in July of 1918. Taking cover in a ditch during fierce fighting, his squad came under artillery attack by mustard gas. Every man except him was either killed or wounded as the poisonous fog settled on the ground. But Corporal Clark, who received the Purple Heart for what he endured that day—and he's wearing it here today, 80 years later—refused medical treatment even though, as he said, "It hurt my lungs bad." This man went on to serve our country in World

War II and the Korean war in the Army and in the Air Force, retiring after 32 years of active duty.

Sir, I thank you for your extraordinary record of service and sacrifice to our Nation. I thank you for caring about all the young people who will follow in your footsteps and for taking the effort and the trouble to be here today to support the ratification of the Chemical Weapons Convention. God bless you, sir, and thank you.

All the arguments have been made, and the vote is about to come in. But let me just restate a couple of points I think are very important that the opponents of this treaty cannot effectively rebut. We have decided—as General Powell said, we have decided to give up our chemical weapons. We decided to do that a long time ago.

Now, as more and more nations eliminate their arsenals and they give up not only their arsenals, but they give up developing, producing, and acquiring such weapons, our troops will be less likely to face attack. But also as stockpiles are eliminated and as the transfer of dangerous chemicals—including chemicals which can be put together to form chemical weapons for that purpose—as that is controlled, it will be more difficult for terrorists and for rogue states to get or make poison gas. That is why it is not a good argument that we don't have some countries involved in this treaty. That's not an argument against ratification. This commits everybody else not to give them anything that they can use to make chemical weapons to use against our forces or innocent civilians.

We also have now tough new tools on short notice, on-site inspections; we create a worldwide intelligence and information sharing network; we strengthen the authority of our own law enforcement officials. That is also very important. That's one of the reasons the Japanese were so supportive of this, because of what they have endured in their country. All these things together are going to help us make America's men and women in uniform and American citizens safer.

During the last 2 months, as Senator Dole said so clearly, we have worked hard with Senate Majority Leader Lott, Senator Helms, Senator Lugar, Senator Biden, and others. We've resolved virtually all the concerns that some Senators have raised, and those resolutions will be embodied tomorrow in an amendment with the

28 understandings to which Senator Dole referred.

Now, we can't let the minor and relatively small number of disagreements that remain blind us to the overwhelming fact, to use the words of Admiral Zumwalt, that at the bottom line our failure to ratify will substantially increase the risk of a chemical attack against American service personnel. None of us should be willing to take that. As Commander in Chief, I cannot in good conscience take that risk. I'm very proud of the work that's been done under the two predecessor administrations to mine of the opposite party. And I'm very proud that we're all standing here together today as Americans in support of a good and noble and tremendously significant endeavor. And all working together, maybe tomorrow it will come out all right.

Thank you, and God bless you.

Q. Mr. President, at his briefing today, Senator Lott appeared to be leaning toward supporting this treaty—that's sort of my analysis—because of the so-called 28 conditionalities, as he says. If there are so many provisos—if this passes with so many provisos, what is the rest of the world going to think of this treaty? And can we just—the United States say, because we're putting so much in the bill—can we just say, "You accept it the way we like it?"

The President. If you read the provisos tomorrow, every one of them is consistent with the overall treaty and would clearly be a clarification of it. I think the rest of the world will applaud what we have done. And I believe that in very important respects they will say, "That's the way we read the treaty all along." So I believe it will be reinforcing it. And I think you'll see the differences over the debate tomorrow, where the line falls. I think it will be clear that this will strengthen and enhance the meaning of the treaty, not only for ourselves but for others all around the world.

Thank you.

NOTE: The President spoke at 11:25 a.m. in the Roosevelt Room at the White House. In his remarks, he referred to Robert Wallace, executive director, Veterans of Foreign Wars; Gen. Brent Scowcroft, USAF (ret.), former National Security Adviser; Adm. Elmo R. Zumwalt, Jr., USN (ret.), former Chief of Naval Operations; Gen. David C. Jones, USAF (ret.), former Chairman, Joint Chiefs of Staff; Vice Adm. Stanley R. Arthur, USN (ret.), former Deputy Chief of Naval Operations, Logistics; Gen. Colin L. Powell, USA (ret.), former Chairman, Joint Chiefs of Staff; and former Senator Bob Dole.

Statement on the Supreme Court Decision To Expedite Review of the Line Item Veto
April 23, 1997

I am pleased that the Supreme Court has granted the Solicitor General's request to provide an expedited review of a lower court ruling on the line item veto. The line item veto provides a critical tool for the President to strike wasteful spending and tax items from legislation.

Congress took the correct step giving the President this authority, and I was pleased to sign the line item veto into law. It is my hope that this expedited ruling will clear up any confusion on this matter.

Message on the Observance of Take Our Daughters to Work Day
April 23, 1997

Warm greetings to everyone participating in "Take Our Daughters to Work Day." We dedi-

cate this special day each year to empowering girls with the encouragement and practical work experiences that will enable them to become leaders in the workplace of the future.

Young girls must never believe that there are limitations on what they can do or become in this country. That's why all of us have a responsibility to renew our commitment to gender equality not only at work, but also in our homes, schools, and communities. It is time to treat our children the same, to embrace their unique gifts, and to allow them to utilize their God-given talents as they choose.

As parents, family members, mentors, and teachers, we also have an obligation to introduce our children to new experiences and to extend their education beyond the boundaries of the classroom. If we are to fulfill the exciting promise of the twenty-first century, we must instill in our girls and boys a deep appreciation for lifelong learning and the confidence and self-esteem to live out their dreams.

I commend the thousands of families, businesses, schools, and communities participating in "Take Our Daughters to Work Day" for showing America's young women that we believe in them and in their ability to lead us in the years to come. You are making a lasting investment in America's future.

Hillary joins me in extending best wishes for a memorable observance.

BILL CLINTON

NOTE: This message was made available by the Office of the Press Secretary on April 24 but was not issued as a White House press release.

Statement on Proposed Employment Non-Discrimination Legislation
April 24, 1997

Today Vice President Gore and I met with a bipartisan delegation from Congress, representing the lead House and Senate sponsors of the "Employment Non-Discrimination Act" ("ENDA")—an important piece of civil rights legislation which would extend basic employment discrimination protections to gay and lesbian Americans. At our meeting, I underscored my strong support of the bill, which will soon be reintroduced in Congress, and our intention to work hard for its passage.

As I said in my State of the Union Address this January, we must never, ever believe that our diversity is a weakness, for it is our greatest strength. People on every continent can look to us and see the reflection of their own great potential, and they always will, as long as we strive to give all of our citizens an opportunity to achieve their own greatness. We're not there yet, and that is why ENDA is so important. It is about the right of each individual in America to be judged on their merits and abilities and to be allowed to contribute to society without facing unfair discrimination on account of sexual orientation. It is about our ongoing fight against bigotry and intolerance, in our country and in our hearts.

I applaud the bipartisan efforts of Senators Jeffords, Kennedy, and Lieberman and Con-

gressmen Shays and Frank to make the "Employment Non-Discrimination Act" the law. I also thank the members of the Human Rights Campaign and the Leadership Conference on Civil Rights, whose executive directors joined in our meeting, for their early support and hard work on behalf of this bill. It failed to win passage by only one vote in the Senate last year. My administration worked hard for its passage then, and we will continue our efforts until it becomes law.

Discrimination in employment on the basis of sexual orientation is currently legal in 41 States. Most Americans don't know that men and women in those States may be fired from their jobs solely because of their sexual orientation, even when it is has no bearing on their job performance. Those who face this kind of job discrimination have no legal recourse in either our State or Federal courts. This is wrong.

Individuals should not be denied a job on the basis of something that has no relationship to their ability to perform their work. Sadly, as the Senate Labor and Human Resources Committee has documented during hearings held in the last Congress, this kind of job discrimination is not rare.

The "Employment Non-Discrimination Act" is careful to apply certain exemptions. It provides an exemption for small businesses, the Armed Forces, and religious organizations, including schools and other educational institutions that are substantially controlled or supported by religious organizations. This later provision respects the deeply held religious beliefs of many Americans. The bill specifically prohibits preferential treatment on the basis of sexual orientation, including quotas. It does not require employers to provide special benefits.

As I indicated when I originally announced my support of this legislation in October of 1995, the bill in its current form appears to answer all the legitimate objections previously raised against it, while ensuring that Americans, regardless of their sexual orientation, can find and keep their jobs based on their ability and the quality of their work. It is designed to protect the rights of all Americans to participate in the job market without fear of unfair discrimination. I support it, and I urge all Americans to do so. And I urge Congress to pass it expeditiously.

Remarks on Senate Ratification of the Chemical Weapons Convention and an Exchange With Reporters
April 24, 1997

The President. Ladies and gentlemen, the United States Senate has served America well tonight. Because they have ratified the Chemical Weapons Convention, our troops will be less likely to face poison gas on the battlefield, our hand will be strengthened in the fight against terrorists and rogue states. We will end a century that began with the horror of chemical weapons in World War I much closer to the elimination of those kinds of weapons. And once again, America has displayed the leadership that we must demonstrate as we build a safer world for the 21st century.

Two and a half months ago, Majority Leader Lott and I put together a process to work through the concerns that some Senators had about the treaty. Our negotiating teams held 30 hours of meetings; so did groups led by Senator Biden and Senator Helms. At the end of the day, because we went the extra mile, we resolved the problems that had been raised by the vast majority of the Senators.

I thank the Majority Leader for guiding these efforts so successfully. I applaud the efforts of Senators on both sides of the aisle, including Minority Leader Daschle, Senator Biden, Senator Lugar, and Senator McCain. And I've been so gratified that in these past few weeks, so many have put politics aside to join together behind this treaty, as we saw yesterday when Senator Dole and General Powell, Brent Scowcroft, and other Republicans joined me, as they had previously.

I thank the Vice President, the Chairman of the Joint Chiefs of Staff, and so many of our military leaders, past and present, who also came out strongly in support of this treaty.

This vote is an example of America working as it should, Democrats and Republicans together, putting our country first, reaching across party lines, reaching for the common good. This vote is vivid proof that we are stronger as a nation when we work together. It's true when it comes to our leadership in the world; it's also true when it comes to dealing with our challenges here at home: strengthening our education system, finishing the job of reforming welfare, fighting crime, defending the environment, and finishing the job of balancing the budget.

The Chemical Weapons Convention truly was made in America, under two of my predecessors. It is right for America. Now it has been ratified in America, and it will make our future more secure. For that, on behalf of the American people, I am profoundly grateful to the United States Senate.

Budget Agreement

Q. Mr. President, Senator Lott said today that, in light of his support of this treaty, that you should show, quote, "similar courage against your base and make budget concessions that might upset Democrats." Are you willing to anger Democrats to balance the budget, if that's what it takes?

The President. Well, first of all, a majority of Republicans supported this treaty and all the Democrats. And I think we can get a balanced budget supported by a majority of Republicans and a majority of Democrats in both Houses if we work together in good faith. This was not some unilateral move. This was an honest, good-faith negotiation. We put 28 clarifying conditions on to the treaty that we worked very hard with Senator Lott and others with.

I am—what I am willing to do, I'm willing to work through this process on the budget just the way we worked through this. I'm very encouraged by it, and I think that America should be encouraged by it. If we work together in a very practical way to do what's in the national interest, I think we can get there.

Q. Mr. President, how far apart are you right now with the Republican leadership and the Democrats in Congress in achieving a balanced budget agreement?

The President. I don't want to characterize it. They're working hard, and they're working in good faith. And I want to leave it like that.

I'm going to—we're going to talk tomorrow. It's late. Let's go to bed.

Missing Military Trucks in Texas

Q. Mr. President, we're told that two military trucks are missing tonight, one carrying four unarmed Air Force missiles, the other said to be carrying machine guns and mortar. Mr. President, we're told that they are overdue 3 to 4 days. What's being done to find these trucks, and is foul play suspected?

The President. I've just been briefed on it. The FBI is working on it—working hard on it. It's my understanding that one of the trucks has been recovered, and that the other one has weapons that are inert and cannot cause any harm. But we're working on it. We'll have more reports tomorrow.

NOTE: The President spoke at 10:51 p.m. in the Briefing Room at the White House. In his remarks, he referred to former Senator Bob Dole; Gen. Colin Powell, USA (ret.), former Chairman of the Joint Chiefs of Staff; and Gen. Brent Scowcroft, USAF (ret.), former National Security Adviser.

Remarks Prior to Discussions With Prime Minister Ryutaro Hashimoto of Japan and an Exchange With Reporters
April 25, 1997

President Clinton. Everybody in? Let me say it's a great honor for me to host my friend Prime Minister Hashimoto here at the White House. We had a nice visit last night, and he was here at the time the Chemical Weapons Convention passed, so we shared a moment of celebration. And we have a busy agenda today, and of course we'll have a press conference later and we'll do our best to answer your questions.

But I think it's important to reaffirm that the relationship the United States has with Japan is unique and comprehensive and profoundly important to our future and to the stability and prosperity and peace of the world. And we intend to keep working on it and make it better.

Mr. Prime Minister.

Prime Minister Hashimoto. I find myself being a very lucky man. I was lucky enough to be invited by Bill last night, after arriving here in the evening, and I could share the greatest moment with Bill for the wonderful passage of the splendid Convention in the Senate. The fact that I was able to share that wonderful moment together with the President, itself, makes my trip to Washington worthwhile.

I see all the familiar and very inquisitive faces in this room, so there will be many questions asked of me, but even with that fact, I'm very happy that I was able to share the moment with the President last night. And last night I was very appreciative of the kindness of Bill because he got Mickey Kantor on the phone without any fighting between us. [*Laughter*]

President Clinton. He tried to get him to switch sides, but he didn't do it. [*Laughter*]

China-Russia Relations

Q. Mr. President, does the U.S. or Japan have any reason to be concerned about the treaty between China and Russia?

President Clinton. Well, my view is that the United States should have a partnership over the long run for stability in the Asia-Pacific region that includes our longstanding alliance with Japan and a positive relationship with both Russia and with China. And as long as any agreement they make is consistent with that kind of positive partnership and is not directed in any negative way toward their neighbors, I think that we don't have anything to worry about.

Mr. Prime Minister.

Prime Minister Hashimoto. I wonder if there's anything I could add to that wonderful statement. That was a splendid answer to the question, I believe. If I may add, I think that the summit between the President and President Yeltsin in Helsinki was a great contributor not just to the stability in Europe but also the stability for the entire world.

I think the President gave a succinct answer describing the situation of the moment. It's very important that Russia and the European countries have a stable relationship. We are in the transitional period of great change. We are trying to engage, for example, China as a constructive partner in international society, and we're transforming the G-7 summit to the Summit of Eight. So in that context, I think the President gave an excellent answer to your question.

Q. Thank you, Mr. President.

President Clinton. We'll answer the others later. We're going to have a press conference later.

Q. ——Governor Weld as Ambassador to Mexico?

President Clinton. We're going to have a press conference later, and I'll answer all the questions. We have to work.

[At this point, one group of reporters left the room, and another group entered.]

Discussions With Prime Minister Hashimoto

Prime Minister Hashimoto. I guess we have to shake hands again. *[Laughter]*

President Clinton. Yes. Let me say very briefly, it's a great honor for me to have my friend Prime Minister Hashimoto here in the Oval Office. He made Hillary and me feel very welcome in Japan not so very long ago, and we're glad to have him back here.

We just had his daughter and son-in-law and grandchild in here. We were playing with the baby, so we're a little late in getting our work started. And we had—but we had a very good visit last night, and he was here at the moment that the Chemical Weapons Convention passed the Senate, which was a happy coincidence for me and, I think, for him. And we have a lot of business to transact today, and I'm looking forward to this meeting and also to the press conference that we will have together after our meeting.

Mr. Prime Minister.

Prime Minister Hashimoto. *[Inaudible]*—when the Senate was just passing the Chemical Weapons Convention. We were able to share that joy. It was all the more pleasing for me to share that great moment with the President.

I expressed my sympathies for the damage caused by the flooding in the State of North Dakota and Minnesota. Also, I expressed my gratitude to the—cooperation by the United States up to the solution of this incident in Peru. It was a wonderful moment between the two of us. And I'm sure that we will have very meaningful discussions in our meeting.

Q. Mr. President, do you think Japan should go ahead with the additional food aid, putting aside——

President Clinton. We need to discuss that.

Q. ——Prime Minister on trade and particularly the current account trade surplus, sir?

President Clinton. Obviously, we don't want it to go back up. We've made some real progress. But we'll discuss that. We'll have a press conference later.

NOTE: The President spoke at 11:10 a.m. in the Oval Office at the White House. Prime Minister Hashimoto spoke in Japanese, and his remarks were translated by an interpreter. A tape was not available for verification of the content of these remarks.

The President's News Conference With Prime Minister Ryutaro Hashimoto of Japan
April 25, 1997

President Clinton. Good afternoon. Before we begin the discussion of my meetings with the Prime Minister, let me say that I have just come from signing the instrument of ratification to the Chemical Weapons Convention, along with the Vice President and the Secretary of State and others who worked very hard for it.

Last night's strong bipartisan vote in the Senate will keep our soldiers and our citizens safer, and it will send a clear signal that Americans of both parties are united in their resolve to maintain the leadership of our Nation into the next century.

It is very appropriate that the vote took place last night when I was visiting with the Prime Minister and that the signing took place a moment ago while Prime Minister Hashimoto was here, because Japan set a very strong example for the world by ratifying this treaty more than a year ago.

I am particularly pleased on this historic day to welcome the Prime Minister to Washington. Over the last 2 years, Ryu and I have met many times. We've built a good friendship that reflects the shared values and interests of the world's two strongest democracies and leading economies. Today's discussions were no exception. The Prime Minister and I continued our work to make sure that our partnership meets the challenges of the new century.

Our security alliance remains the cornerstone of peace and stability in the Asia-Pacific region. Building on the joint declaration we signed in Japan last April, we are strengthening our cooperation while reducing the burden of our bases on the Japanese people. Today we reviewed recent progress in consolidating some of our bases in Okinawa in ways that reflect our continuing sensitivity to their effect on the lives of the Okinawan people. I particularly appreciate the strong leadership and support for our alliance the Prime Minister showed in passing legislation to enable our forces to continue using these important facilities.

We also discussed regional security, including our joint interest in promoting peace and stability on the Korean Peninsula. The United States and Japan are united in urging North Korea to accept the standing offer for four-party peace talks. I want to thank the Prime Minister for Japan's role in the Korean Energy Development Organization that has helped to keep North Korea's dangerous nuclear program frozen.

The Prime Minister and I agreed on the critical importance of cooperative relations with China. We also agreed on the need for the international community to stand firmly behind the progress of democracy in Cambodia.

We both recognize the importance of keeping our economic relationship moving in the right direction. Over the last 4 years we've worked hard to open markets and achieve a better balance in our trade and investment ties. I told Prime Minister Hashimoto we need to build on this success to create new opportunities in key sectors for both the workers of our country and broad benefits for the consumers of Japan. We both want to promote strong domestic demand-led growth in Japan and to avoid a significant increase in Japan's external surplus. These are essential to sustaining the progress that has been made.

I welcome the Prime Minister's commitment to restructuring Japan's economy, including his support of far-reaching deregulation. An ambitious reform program should bring economic benefits to Japan and improve market access for American and other foreign firms. To this end, we have agreed to intensify talks on deregulation under our framework agreement.

Among the global issues we discussed were preparations for this June's Summit of the Eight in Denver and how we can work together to strengthen reform in the United Nations. Tomorrow the Vice President and the Prime Minister will discuss our common agenda to fight disease, protect the environment, and meet other important common challenges.

Finally, let me say I had the opportunity to thank the Prime Minister for Japan's efforts to bring our young people closer together. The new Fulbright Memorial Fund will send 5,000 American high school teachers and administrators to Japan over the next 5 years. We welcome the Prime Minister's initiatives to send high school students from Okinawa to study in the

United States and will increase our funding for American students to do the same there. These ties of friendship reflect the shared values that underpin our vital alliance.

If you will permit me to quote a haiku poem:

Old friends standing tall—
Spring sunlight on their shoulders
Makes them move as one.

Moving as one in this time of challenge and change, that's what Prime Minister Hashimoto and I are committed to see the United States and Japan do.

Mr. Prime Minister, welcome.

Prime Minister Hashimoto. Well, I am pleased to be able to make this official visit to Washington, DC, and to have had a thorough exchange of views with President Clinton.

Last night the President invited me for drinks, and we had an enjoyable evening at the White House. There I conveyed to him my sympathies for the damage caused by the flood in the Midwest. I also was able to express joint pleasure at the approval of the Chemical Weapons Convention by the Senate.

I had 3 hours of frank discussion with Bill, as friends and as leaders of the two countries. I believe we have the following four points as the main themes.

The first theme is the security relationship, which is the foundation of a Japan-U.S. friendship and alliance. We fully agreed that we must further enhance the security relationship and based on the Japan-U.S. Joint Declaration on Security issued last April. I explained to President Clinton the efforts my administration has been making on issues concerning Okinawa and its top priority task to secure a solid basis for the stable security relationship. President Clinton made it clear that he will continue to be sensitive to and cooperative on issues concerning Okinawa, including the steady implementation of the SACO final report.

With regard to the review of the guidelines for Japan-U.S. defense cooperation, we'll intensify this joint task as we head towards this fall. I'd also like to ensure full transparency, both at home and abroad, of the review process. We also reaffirmed our commitment in the joint declaration that in response to changes which may arise on the international security environment, we'll continue to consult closely on defense policies and military postures, including

the U.S. force structure in Japan which will best meet the requirements of the two Governments.

The second theme is the economic relationship. I gave to the President updates on the reforms now being undertaken in Japan by the Government and political parties in unison, especially on structural reforms, including the fiscal reform and consolidation, deregulation, and financial system reform.

I must say that these reforms do have great relevance to maintaining and enhancing the good bilateral economic relationship we enjoy today. The President welcomed my commitment to restructuring Japan's economy, including far-reaching deregulation. We both support the common objective of avoiding a significant increase in Japan's external surplus by promoting strong domestic demand-led growth in Japan. Furthermore, we have decided to have the officials of the two Governments start discussions on how we could enhance the Japan-U.S. dialog on deregulation under our framework.

The third theme is furtherance of peace and prosperity in the Asia-Pacific region under Japan-U.S. cooperation and joint leadership. In this context, the President and I agreed on the special significance of establishing constructive, cooperative relations with China. We reaffirmed that Japan, the United States, and the Republic of Korea will continue to deal with issues concerning the Korean Peninsula, including early realization of the four-party talks and promotion of the activities by the Korean Peninsula Energy Development Organization, or KEDO, under tripartite coordination.

On Cambodia, there was concurrence of views that the international community needs to send out a political message for the stability of Cambodia under consolidation of democracy. I have dispatched Mr. Komura, the State Secretary for Foreign Affairs, to Cambodia to fulfill this task.

The last and the fourth theme is Japan-U.S. cooperation on global issues. It was reconfirmed in our meeting that we will further coordinate our policies on such wide-ranging issues as the Denver summit, antiterrorism and anticrime measures, United Nations reforms, cooperation with Russia, and the Middle East peace process.

I'd like to note here that the seizure of the Japanese Ambassador's residence in Peru recently came to an end, with the three unfortunate casualties, yet with a vast majority of the hostages freed without serious injuries. Today

our two nations renewed their resolves and resolved to condemn and fight terrorism without
succumbing to it, hand in hand with the international community.

I would also like to welcome the approval
of the Chemical Weapons Convention in the
Senate yesterday, as I mentioned at the outset.
And I certainly welcome the fact that this document was also ratified today.

The President and I agreed to strengthen our
efforts to promote common agenda towards the
21st century. I proposed to vigorously promote
environmental education, and I'm happy to have
President Clinton's agreement. As the President
mentioned just now, it gave the two of us much
delight that people-to-people exchanges between
Japan and the United States have been steadily
widening, as exemplified by the teacher exchange through the Fulbright Memorial Program and the high school student exchange between Okinawa Prefecture and the United
States.

There is no other bilateral relationship in the
world that has any semblance to the Japan-U.S.
relationship in the present and fundamental importance. In closing, I would like to reiterate
my determination to further enhance the Japan-
U.S. relationship for the benefit of not only the
two peoples but also for the Asia-Pacific region
and the world as a whole, on the solid basis
of my close cooperation with President' Clinton.

Thank you very much.

President Clinton. What we will do is, I will
call on an American journalist, and then the
Prime Minister will call on a Japanese journalist.
And we'll begin with Mr. Fournier [Ron
Fournier, Associated Press].

Tobacco Regulation Ruling

Q. Let me ask you a couple questions about
an important domestic development today. The
court said that the FDA cannot restrict tobacco
advertising, which is a cornerstone of your crackdown against teenage smoking. Other than an
appeal, is there any other recourse? For example, regulating advertising—[*inaudible*]—would
the White House be less likely to push forward—[*inaudible*].

President Clinton. Well, first of all, this is,
on balance, a great victory for the fight we have
been waging for our children's health, because
the fundamental legal issue was, did the FDA
have jurisdiction over tobacco companies? And
they said yes. And since we believe strongly

that for young people, access equals addiction,
the fact that the yes includes the ability of the
FDA to deal with access of young people to
tobacco is a huge victory. And we started out
against overwhelming odds, a very powerful interest group; no administration had undertaken
this before. And so I feel a great deal of reassurance today.

Now, the court also held, as you pointed out,
that that statute which gave the FDA authority
to regulate tobacco and regulate access, among
other things, did not cover, by its express terms,
advertising. So we will appeal that part of it.
But this is a day that—I know Dr. Kessler has
already been out celebrating about this. We're
very pleased by the court's decision, especially
coming as it does out of North Carolina, and
we are determined to proceed on this course.
We think it's a great victory for us.

Q. Could the FCC regulate advertising—[*inaudible*]—slow down your push for—[*inaudible*]?

President Clinton. I don't know the answer
to the FCC question. I presume, but I don't
really know the answer. I can't—and in terms
of the settlement, let me say that we have been
involved in the settlement, the White House
has, only in a monitoring capacity. The parties
are involved in the settlement. And my concern
was twofold only: One is to protect the integrity
of the FDA's efforts and to protect our children,
and the second was to make sure that the larger
public health issues were put front and center.

So I don't have an opinion about that. I
don't—I'm not the expert here about the inter-
section of the legal discussions and the protection of the public health. But I can tell you
that my opinion about any proposed settlement,
should one ever be agreed to, would be determined solely on what I thought was good for
kids and good for the public health.

Japan-U.S. Defense Guidelines

Q. I would like to ask a question of Prime
Minister Hashimoto. You'll be completing the
review process of the Japan-U.S. defense guidelines, and I wonder if this will require new
contingency legislation. In case such new legisla-
tions are required for emergency cases, what
happens to the consistency with the Japanese
Constitution?

Prime Minister Hashimoto. Well, first of all,
this review will be conducted solely within the
confines of the Japanese Constitution, and I

would like to make that point clear first. Having said that, let me say that we are working very diligently with this review process of the guidelines. The purpose of reviewing the guidelines is to consider the Japan-U.S. defense cooperation a new era and make that evident to the entire world. And also, we are trying to establish smooth cooperation and promote cooperation between Japan and the United States vis-a-vis various and new and unexpected circumstances that were not considered in the past.

When the review process is completed, what sort of response will be needed domestically— what sort of laws might become necessary domestically? That is a matter I would not like to make any presumptions about. But security is a matter that—or this is a matter that touches on the fundamental security of Japan, and we also would like to proceed with this review process in a totally transparent manner both at home and abroad. And sometime in May, we would like to announce the various views that are expressed in the process of the Japan-U.S. joint review and the items that are being considered, and by so doing we would like to avoid undue concerns on the part of other countries and also avoid undue disruptions.

And should there be any pieces of wisdom that we could take advantage of, we certainly would like to receive them. And I sincerely hope that it will be conducive to building up strengthened security relations between the two countries.

China-Russia Relations

Q. Mr. President, Mr. Prime Minister, you both earlier today said that the China-Russia agreement should not be worrisome as long as it's not directed in any negative way toward its neighbors. I'm wondering, given the high profile irritants in the U.S. relations toward both Russia and China, how can you be sure what the motivation is behind that agreement, and specifically, how can you be sure it isn't directed toward either the United States or any of its neighbors?

President Clinton. Do you want me to go first?

Well, first of all, let me say, if you look at the map and you look at the history of the 20th century, Russia and China have a lot of things that they need to deal with between themselves. They have a rich history; they have a history of both cooperation and significant conflict. And if they have a good cooperative

partnership in the future that is part of a larger balance of forces working toward security, open trade, genuine respect for borders not only of the parties to any agreement but of any other parties in the neighborhood, I think that's a positive thing.

If you look at, for example, the extent to which the politics of India have been dictated partly by the tensions between Russia and China in the past, and how important India is—soon to become the largest country in the world, already with the largest middle class in the world—and how important our relationships with India will be, and then with Pakistan, there is so much of what goes on between Russia and China that affects our relations, not only directly but indirectly, that I think it's a very positive thing that they're talking and working together.

And again I will say, as long as they are not making an agreement that is designed to somehow undermine the security or the prosperity or the integrity and freedom of any of their neighbors, I think it is a positive thing. And I look forward to having the same sort of constructive relations with both parties, and I think that the Prime Minister does as well.

Q. Do you know that's true, or do you——

President Clinton. No I don't know. But I don't know that it isn't, either. I have no reason to believe it's not, and I don't think we should approach these things with paranoia. We have no basis on which to conclude that there is some negative connotation to the fact that the Russians and the Chinese are trying to get along. In the periods when they didn't get along, it was more difficult for both of them.

Prime Minister Hashimoto. Well, a very good, model answer has already been provided, so if there is anything that I could add to this exemplary response: Well, countries that have adjacent borders between those countries, it is better that cooperation and harmony continue, rather than confrontation. That will be in the benefit of the human society as a whole. Should there be any problems, then of course, the two countries concerned should cooperate with each other so that the situation or any problem that has arisen will proceed in a better direction. That is my view.

Japan-U.S. Security Relationship and Okinawa

Q. I'd like to ask this question of both the Prime Minister and President.

Mr. Prime Minister, you mentioned earlier that—[*inaudible*]—reaffirmation of the joint declaration that you will be cooperating with each other with regard to North Korea—[*inaudible*]. When do you think the reduction of U.S. marines stationed in Okinawa will become possible, whether that is difficult, and in the shorter term, is it possible to relocate U.S. military drills from Okinawa to other parts of Japan as a short-term measure to reduce the burden on the Okinawan people?

Prime Minister Hashimoto. Well, I think I should start off first on this point. So following my response, I would like to ask the President to supplement.

First, at the present stage, I believe that the U.S. forces that are deployed in the Asia-Pacific, including those stationed in Japan, we have no intention of asking for the reduction of these forces. In maintaining the stability and safety of the entire region, we very much cherish the present commitment that we have, and this is a matter of great importance for the President in terms of maintaining security as well.

Now, I need not tell you that there are many spots of instability and uncertainties in the Asia-Pacific today. Now, if the U.S. forces in the Asia-Pacific, not just stationed in Okinawa, are to be reduced, then we'd very much like to, in fact, create an Asia-Pacific region that can allow that reduction, discussing that possibility with smiles. And to that end, we'd like to cooperate with each other.

Now, as I have mentioned earlier, there is no doubt that we are causing burdens on the Okinawan people, and in order to reduce those burdens, we would like to say that the first step is to steadily realize the recommendations of the SACO final report. Thanks to all the efforts, the live fire drills across the prefectural Route 104 will be relocated. And the KC-130 aircraft now will be relocated to Iwakuna Base on Honshu Island.

President Clinton. The only thing that I could add to what the Prime Minister has already said is just to reaffirm my strong support for the SACO process. The United States is very aware that our presence, while it has enhanced the security of our country and Japan and the stability of the Asia-Pacific region, has imposed burdens on the people of Okinawa. We have been very sensitive to it. Since I have been President, I have done what I could to change that. We now have a SACO final report and a process

underway which will lead to significant changes designed to reduce the burden on the people of Okinawa while permitting us to do what we need to do together to maintain stability in the region.

And I'd like to let that process play itself out. I think that you will see we are proceeding in good faith, and we will work hard to make that process end in a success for the people of Okinawa.

Wolf [Wolf Blitzer, Cable News Network] and then——

FBI and Alleged Chinese Efforts To Influence the 1996 Election

Q. Mr. President, Prime Minister Hashimoto made the case for the United States and for Japan to maintain stronger relations with China. But now there is apparently some evidence that the FBI has that top Chinese officials were trying to influence the U.S. political process. The question for you, Prime Minister Hashimoto, would be, if you had evidence that China was trying to influence politics in Japan, would that affect your relationship with China?

And to you, Mr. President, are you confident that what the FBI briefed members of the Senate Intelligence Committee, that that information is being made available to you and to your senior national security advisers?

Prime Minister Hashimoto. Well, I can't say anything about the U.S.-related part, but speaking of Japan and China relations, the latter half of last year, due to my own mismanagement as well, the Japan-China relations since then have been somewhat awkward. But in the run-up to the APEC summit meeting on Manila, I had meetings with Mr. Jiang Zemin, and we were able to more or less resolve the problem. And the Japanese Foreign Minister has visited Beijing since, and most likely I will be visiting China later this year, in the fall. And following that, I think that Mr. Li Peng, the Chinese Premier, will visit Japan. And we are also inviting Mr. Jiang Zemin to visit Japan.

So through this process we, on both sides—Japan and China—we're trying to further improve our bilateral relations.

What I couldn't quite get from your question was, I think you said, are the Chinese leaders attempting to exercise influence on Japanese politics? Well——

Q. If the Chinese Government, were attempting to influence politics in Japan, would that affect your relationship with China?

Prime Minister Hashimoto. If the Chinese Government, in fact, does behave that way and if the Japanese are pliable, then, of course, that end result will happen. But I don't think that the Chinese leaders are attempting to do that with the Japanese politics. And we certainly have no intention of imposing our own views on the Chinese. Well, this year, as I said, happens to be the 25th anniversary of normalization of diplomatic relations, so it was with this mindset that we would like to make this year a fruitful year in terms of Japan-China relations.

President Clinton. I'd like to answer the questions, if I might, in reverse order, and as carefully as I can.

First of all, I believe that the President and Secretary of State and the National Security Adviser should have access to whatever information is necessary to conduct the foreign policy and to protect the national interest of the country.

Secondly, especially in light of some of the allegations which have been made, I have made it clear that to resolve all questions, I expect every piece of information the Justice Department gives me to be shared with the Congress. I not only do not object to it, but I expect it to be done. That will be reassuring to everybody who's covering other stories, and I think it's important.

Now, in response to your question, I do not know the answer to that because I don't know precisely what the briefing was. But my policy is clear. And we have received some information from the Justice Department. Whether we have received everything they have, I have no way of knowing, because I don't know what they got. But whatever—the important thing for me, for you to know, and for the American people to know is that as long as these questions are out there, I also expect anything that I am given to conduct the foreign policy of the country should be shared with the Intelligence Committees of the Congress so you'll know that it is shared in that way.

Now, to go to the second point, I have said before, and I will just simply reiterate what I have said before: If there was any improper attempt to influence the workings of the United States executive or legislative branches, obviously that would be a matter of serious concern. But I think it is important that we not accuse people of something that we don't know for sure that they have done, number one.

Number two, let's keep in mind—and I would encourage all of you to think about this yourselves—think about what you would define as improper influence. A lot of our friends in the world, countries with whom we are very closely allied, have friends in the United States that advocate for the policies of the governments all the time.

It's true—to take two obvious examples—it's true of Israel; it's true of Greece. And it's not—I would not consider that improper. It's publicly done. There's nothing secret or covert about it; we know that it's done. It's part of the political debate in America, and we don't take offense at it.

So we have to—but if there were some improper attempt to influence this Government, would it affect our relations? Of course, it's something we'd have to take seriously. But meanwhile, we have very large interests in a stable relationship with China and having China be a stable force in the Asia-Pacific region, just as Japan does. And so I think it is important that we not assume something we do not know and act in a way that may not be warranted. We need to get the facts here before we do that.

Japan-U.S. Economic Relations

Q. In your meeting, I believe you discussed bilateral economic relations, and I think you agreed that both would hope there would not be any significant increase in Japan's surplus. More specifically, did you discuss what measures ought to be taken in order to avoid such a significant increase?

Also, in the coming days, there will be the finance ministers meeting of the two countries, and there will be G–7 finance ministers meetings, and I think the markets are very much interested about the developments on the exchange front. I wonder if you had any discussions on that aspect as well.

Prime Minister Hashimoto. Well, let me first say that what we discussed today was that we would not like to see any significant increase in Japan's external surplus, and we're not assuming a situation where there will be absolutely no increase in Japan's surplus.

Now, it is true that we discussed this question, and I also tried to explain that the Japanese economic situation is not at all like the situation that many worry it to be in. In fact, in fiscal '96, its growth rate is certain to reach 2.5 percent per annum.

Of course, the discontinuation of the special tax cut measures at the end of last fiscal year would have some negative effects. And yet, we would expect a 1.9 percent real economic growth rate for fiscal '97. And I also communicated to the President that it is with confidence that we expect Japan's economy will grow with the strength of domestic demand.

Of course, strong imbalances are not good, but we've indicated that we are concerned about this. And as far as the exchange rate question is concerned, we believe that having touched on this matter between ourselves, it is more proper to leave the matter to Secretary Rubin and Minister Mitsuzuka.

Budget Agreement

Q. Mr. President, some of your top advisers clearly believe that next week is a crucial one in the budget talks. Some of them have suggested that it might be a make-or-break-it week as far as getting a balanced budget. Number one, do you share that belief? Number two, if so, why? And number three, is there anything that you can hold onto, concrete, that says yes, we might get a balanced budget this year?

President Clinton. Well, first of all, I was heartened by the process by which we reached agreement on the chemical weapons treaty because it really was a process with a lot of integrity. It was very specific, very problem oriented—problem-solving oriented, and it resulted, as you know, in getting a majority of both caucuses in the Senate to vote for the treaty. And that's an indication of what we can do if we put the country first.

Secondly, as I have said before, we have had some days now of quite intense talks between the Republican and Democratic budget leaders of the Senate and House. And they have worked, I'm convinced, with us in complete good faith. You know what the differences are; they're clear. We want a balanced budget that protects what we think are the most important values and interests of the country, including investing more in education, expanding coverage to children for health care, protecting the environment, cleaning up 500 toxic waste dumps, continuing to invest in technology and things of that kind. They would favor more cuts in

those programs and bigger tax cuts. We have differences between us.

Now, can we bridge the differences? If we proceed just as we did with the Chemical Weapons Convention, in the same sort of way, I'm convinced we can. Do I favor an early agreement? Yes, I do, if it's a good one and if it protects those things that I care about. Do I believe that there will be no balanced budget this year if the early agreements cannot be realized? No, I don't believe that.

I think it is so manifestly in the interest of the United States to do this—it would be so good for our economy; it would keep interest rates down; it would keep job growth going—that we will do it. Just that same reason I believed, when we didn't have the votes on the Chemical Weapons Convention, eventually we'd find a way to do it because it was manifestly in the interests of the United States to do it.

And we want to keep this long expansion going. We want to keep these jobs coming into our country. We want to keep the higher wage jobs being created. And if we want to do that, we're going to have to balance this budget.

Now, it would be better to do it earlier rather than later, if both sides can agree in good conscience. It will be more difficult to do—when you fail, it's harder to kind of pick yourself up and try again. But I still believe it will get done sometime this year if we don't get it done now. But I favor an early agreement, if possible.

Korean Peninsula

Q. Mr. President, the Korean Peninsula is vital to U.S. interest in Northeast Asia. What is the U.S. position for establishing a peaceful regime on the Korean Peninsula?

President Clinton. Well, first of all, we had hoped very much that the North Koreans would follow up on their agreement in principle to the four-party talks and actually come to New York and participate in the talks. It was a big disappointment to me when they did not come, because I think it is clearly in their interests. And they, I think, are better off having agreed to freeze their nuclear program and getting an alternative source of energy. And I think they ought to go the next step now and resolve all their differences with South Korea in a way that will permit the rest of us not only to give food aid and emergency food aid because people are terribly hungry but to work with them in restructuring their entire economy and helping to make it more functional again and giving a brighter and better future to the people of North Korea.

So from my point of view, both because of the security problems inherent in the tension of the two armies facing each other across the 17th parallel and because of the capacity of North Korea to produce missiles and other kinds of mischief and because there are a lot of people living in North Korea who are in distress now, I would very much like to see these talks resume.

And the Prime Minister and I talked about it in some detail, and we know that our interests would be advantaged if the talks could be brought to a successful conclusion. And I would urge the North Koreans to reconsider and to enter the talks as soon as possible.

We'll take one more—[*inaudible*].

FDR Memorial

Q. Mr. President, how strongly do you feel about having the new memorial to Franklin Roosevelt give prominent attention to his disability? The reason I ask the question is some of the disabled groups fear, because of the congressional politics on the issue, the legislation going forward now will not contain an ironclad guarantee of such a display. If it did not, would that be a violation of your commitment to them?

President Clinton. I can't give you an honest answer to that because—I mean, a good answer because I never thought about it in those terms before. I never thought about it as a legislative fight or making a deal with the groups. As far as I know—I've gotten some letters on this— I don't think anyone is coming to see me about it. I just have always felt—I'll tell you why I feel this way, that there should be constructed at an appropriate time a statue of—a sculpture of President Roosevelt in his wheelchair.

The genius of Roosevelt was that he had a flexible, imaginative mind that permitted us to preserve our fundamental values and principles and systems under great assault. And he knew that in the time he lived he would have had great difficulty getting elected President if people had thought of him as a "polio" or a "cripple," to use the words that were prevalent in the early thirties. And so he went to these enormous lengths to construct this deception. You know, he had two strong people who would carry him up stairs with his elbows held straight to pretend that he was walking up the stairs.

And to a movie camera from a distance, it looked as if he was. He did all kinds of other things to create this deception. Why? Because he knew it was necessary at the time. He knew that he had the capacity to be President, and he didn't want some artificial perception to keep him from being President.

However, if he were alive today, my belief is just as strong that he would insist on being shown in his wheelchair because he would see all the progress we have made in the last 65 years on this issue—more than 65 years—and he would insist that we keep making progress. He would want this to be a living memorial, if you will, that would be part of America's thrust into the future, not just a musing on the past. That's what I believe.

And I've read a lot about Roosevelt. Sometimes I feel like I'm talking to him instead of Hillary talking to Eleanor. [*Laughter*] That's what I honestly believe. And I know even some of his family members differ with me, so I'm very respectful of people who have a different opinion than me about this. But I have thought about this a lot, and I believe if he were here he would say, "Look at what we have done. Look at how we have changed attitudes toward disabilities. Look at all the doors we're trying to open for people with disabilities. For God's sake, tell everybody I did this and I was disabled, so that all those disabled kids can know they can grow up to be President, too, now, and they don't have to hide it like I did."

President's Knee Injury

Q. But didn't you give up your wheelchair too early? [*Laughter*]

President Clinton. No. No, actually, Sarah [Sarah McClendon, McClendon News Service], I put myself at greater risk giving up the wheelchair. The reason I went to Helsinki in the wheelchair is so I wouldn't—because I was new on my crutches. But this is better for my therapy. And I went to Helsinki—because they didn't want me to go at all, and I said I was determined to go, and they said the only safe way to go was to go in a wheelchair. But I don't think I did give it up too early.

Q. The White House corridors are so long; you have to walk so far.

President Clinton. I'm building up my arm strength.

Let's take one more question. Would you like to take one more question, and then I'll take

Mr. Donvan [John Donvan, ABC News] and Bill [Bill Plante, CBS News]. Go ahead. We're having a good time. [*Laughter*]

North Korea

Q. On food aid, during the flight to Washington, DC, Mr. Prime Minister, I think you expressed a view that as Governor of Japan you wished to maintain a very careful attitude, cautious attitude. I wonder how you explain Japan's position to the President, and I wonder if the President understood Japan's position.

Prime Minister Hashimoto. Yesterday, during the flight, I met with the press reporters traveling with me, and I touched on this question. We certainly are aware of the situation in North Korea that requires humanitarian food aid. At the same time, if we speak of humanitarian circumstances, there are certain things we would like the North Koreans to do for us. And one of them relates to Japanese nationals, Japanese women who got married to North Koreans. And those people who went to North Korea have not been able to send letters to Japan, whereas North Koreans visiting Japan could always go back and forth between Japan and North Korea. These Japanese women who married North Koreans have not even been allowed to return to their families for temporary visits. So, speaking of humanitarian issues, we would like the North Koreans to allow these Japanese women, Japanese wives, to write letters back home or pay temporary visits to their families in Japan.

And also, according to information that we have gleaned, several mysterious incidents took place, one after another, in a rather limited time period. Some of them junior high school students, or lovers—these people suddenly disappeared from Japanese shores. And North Korean spies who later have confessed in South Korea, and it is so reported, that they have said these people were abducted. So there is a high possibility that these Japanese who disappeared from Japanese shore were abducted by the North Koreans. And probably, there is no doubt about that. And yet, we cannot really determine that is the case. But we have to remember that these people have disappeared in a mysterious manner.

In the process of Japan-North Korea normalization talks, we discussed the problem of Nai Unya, who was originally a Japanese. But we raised the issue of having the person recognized and returned to Japan. As soon as we raised the issue, the talks were discontinued.

So we understand it is a humanitarian situation in North Korea, but likewise, if we are to speak of humanitarian problems, there are humanitarian problems in Japan as well. There are, as I said, Japanese women who are married to North Koreans, and they surely wish to write to their families in Japan. They surely wish to visit their families back home. And we hope they, the North Koreans, will give humanitarian considerations to these people.

So these are, in fact, what I explained to President Clinton as well.

President Clinton. Let me say, I personally am very grateful for the Prime Minister's support and for Japan's support for the program to end the North Korean nuclear efforts, to freeze it and dismantle it, and for Japan's generosity in so many areas around the world where Japan spends a higher percentage of its income than the United States on humanitarian efforts.

We have devoted a significant amount of money and have pledged more to feed the people of North Korea. But the real answer here is, we can—the world will find a way to keep the people of North Korea from starving and from dealing with malnutrition. But they need to lift the burden of a system that is failing them in food and other ways off their back, resolve their differences with the South. That will permit them the freedom to reconcile the problems they have still with Japan.

So what I think is so important—again I say, I implore the North Koreans to return to the talks. We have set these talks up, these four-party talks, with the Chinese, the people who were involved in the armistice at the end of the Korean war. We have given them every opportunity to come with honor and to be treated with fairness. And it is time to bring this long divide to an end, as well as to alleviate the misery of so many of their people.

Get Bill, then John. Go ahead.

China and Campaign Finance Reform

Q. Mr. President, following up on your answer about China, you seem to be suggesting almost that China's mistake may have been that it didn't approach advocacy in the American system in the American way, which is to say, by hiring a high-powered lobbying firm here in Washington to do its advocacy work rather than possibly trying these back channels.

And I also wanted to ask about campaign finance reform, and that is, how in the world do you expect to persuade very many of the people who were elected under the old system to ever give it up? Isn't this kind of a chimera?

President Clinton. Well, let me answer the second question first, and then I'll answer the first question.

I think that the only way I can persuade them to give it up is to believe that they—if they're on equal terms with their opponents, to have the confidence that since they're already in, if they're serving well and doing a good job, they should be able to persuade a majority of the people to reelect them. And I would never support any kind of campaign reform that did not at least guarantee some sort of equal footing to the competitors.

Now, I know what you're saying. You're saying, once you get in, you can normally raise more money than your competitor. But the only way we can do it—let me tell you, the only way we can do it, since you have a lot of people from rural States who cannot raise what it costs to campaign, all of the money, in their own States—we have a lot of people from poor congressional districts who can't do that, and then you have people who just because—as I said, this is a harder sell for the Republicans than the Democrats because they could raise more money, and now that they're in the majority in Congress, they can raise a lot more money. So let's be fair to them. It's harder for them to buy this than it is for us.

But one reason they ought to do it is, it takes too much of their time, and it raises too many questions. And they would get more sleep at night; they would have more time to read; they would have more time to spend with their families; they would have more time to do the job of being in Congress. They could also spend time with people they know who have money and influence and not be asked if they were spending it for the wrong reasons, and they could actually solicit people's opinion without somebody worrying about whether they had actually purchased a Congressman's vote on something.

So, for all these reasons, I think that, besides the fact that it's right for America, I think they ought to do it.

Now, let me answer your first question. I do not know the facts. That's the only thing I'm saying. I just don't want to see people tried and convicted before we know the facts. I don't know the facts. But I didn't just mean having lobbyists. What I mean is, we're comfortable in America. If an Irish-American friend of mine from Boston says to me before we got involved in the Irish peace talks, "I think it's time that America changed their policy and got involved in this and tried to bring peace and harmony in Northern Ireland," and that Irish-American has direct contacts with people in the Government in the Republic in Ireland and people in the Parliament in Northern Ireland, no one thinks that it's inappropriate because it's a comfortable, open part of the way we are as Americans.

If a Jewish-American friend of mine happens to also be a friend of Prime Minister Netanyahu or Prime Minister Peres—former Prime Minister Peres or former Prime Minister Rabin, no one thinks anything is wrong with it because it's the way things are. That's the only point I was trying to make, that we have a multiethnic society where people have different ties, different contacts, different feelings. And some of it we're comfortable with because we understand it. Other things we're uncomfortable with because it's new and different and jarring. And before we accuse people of wrongdoing, we at least need to know what are the facts. The only point I'm trying to make, the bottom line and significant point I'm trying to make is, I do not know what the facts are here, and I do not want to condemn without the evidence.

Let's take one more from each side. You want to take one more? And then John, we'll—and then Karen [Karen Breslau, Newsweek].

Strength of the Dollar and Trade

Q. I have a question for President Clinton. I understand that the United States is in favor of a strong balance, and at the same time the United States doesn't want any kind of increase in U.S. trade deficit with Japan. I think that the strong dollar—[*inaudible*]—Japan's exports to the United States, thus, an increase in U.S. trade deficit with Japan. Do you want a weaker dollar to help cut—to help prevent U.S. trade deficit to Japan from increasing significantly?

President Clinton. You have asked an excellent question and one to which I must give a careful answer; otherwise I will affect the value of the dollar, which I don't want to do.

Here is our position. We do not want a weak dollar simply to improve our trade position. We think that would be—that is not our economic policy, to go out and seek a weak dollar. We want our dollar to be healthy and strong because we have a good, strong economy and good economic policies.

But neither do we want any other actions to have the effect of throwing the exchange rate system out of whack in order to gain undue advantage in international trade. So what we would like to see is, and what we have campaigned for—what I have personally campaigned around the world for 4 years are good, coordinated, balanced economic policies among all the strong economies of the world, and a commitment among all of us to expand into a global trading system that will give other countries the chance to grow wealthier on responsible terms. That is what I think is the best policy over the long run.

John. And then I'll take one from Karen.

Tobacco Regulations Ruling

Q. Mr. President, a followup to today's news. You have said, in regard to the talks the tobacco companies are involved in for a possible global solution, that your goal would be a solution that protects the health of children. My question is, does today's news not put the tobacco companies more on the run than ever before, at least more on the defensive? And does that not in some way weaken their hand in these negotiations and make the outcome you're looking for all the more likely?

President Clinton. Well, I certainly hope it makes the outcome I'm looking for all the more likely. Of course, just as we intend to appeal the advertising portion of the decision in North Carolina, I'm doubtless they will appeal the other portion of it. So we've got some time to go, and we'll have some other legal steps to go through. But I hope this will strengthen the hands of the public health advocates.

The only point I was trying to make earlier, John, is I simply do not know. I'm not the house expert here, and I don't know that we even have an expert in-house about where the right balance is in these negotiations with the public health at large. We originally began to monitor the negotiations with a very limited purpose, to ferociously protect what we had fought so hard for to get the FDA to do. But we know there is a larger public health interest here. And I hope that today's decision enhances the likelihood that the public health of the

United States can be advanced, not only for children but for our country as a whole.

Let's take one more. We're having a good time, let's do one more. [*Laughter*] Karen, you're next. Otherwise I'll get blasted for having all men I called on today—properly blasted, properly blasted.

Japanese Deregulation

Q. Mr. President, you mentioned—[*inaudible*]—are you confident that Hashimoto's package of deregulation will be strong enough and timely enough to sustain growth in Japan without any kind of help from the fiscal side?

President Clinton. Well, I hope so. He's confident that it will be. And you know, he has to make the call. But we had a very good and, I thought, pretty sophisticated conversation about it today. I understand why Japan also wishes to cut its deficit, increase its savings rate. And I understand—we have similar long-term demographic challenges in Japan and the United States. You will face them before we will. And I understand that. But it's also important to keep our systems open, to keep opening them up and to not let the trade balance get out of whack. And we're committed to working on it. And I think we'll be reasonably successful if we work at it.

Go ahead.

Press Secretary Mike McCurry. Last question.

President Clinton. All right.

Press Secretary McCurry. The Prime Minister has to go——

President Clinton. I know.

Initiative on Race Relations

Q. Mr. President, your aides have said that in coming weeks you plan to announce a major initiative on the state of race relations in this country. Why now? And what do you expect a blue ribbon panel or commission or task force, whatever you decide, to produce in terms of tangible results that will make a difference in people's lives?

President Clinton. Well, first of all, let me say, I have not yet settled on a final form of an initiative. But what I think we need to do is to examine the nature of our relations with one another as Americans and what America is going to be like in this new century. I think it is time for a taking of stock.

We've been through some huge upheavals over race in America. We fought a civil war over slavery and race, and then we had a series of constitutional amendments that gave basic citizenship rights to African-Americans. Then we had a long civil rights struggle which was marked by steady, explicit forbidding of various kinds of discrimination. And then we had the Kerner Commission report in '68, which basically said, even if you eliminate all these negative things, there are certain affirmative things you have to do to get people back to the starting line so they can contribute to our society. And then we had 25 years of affirmative action which is being rethought now, reassessed, and argued all over again.

But America has changed a great deal during that time. The fastest growing minority group now are the Hispanics. There are four school districts in this country, including one right across the river here in Virginia, that have children from more than 100 different racial and ethnic groups in one single school district. And I personally rejoice at this. I think this is a huge asset for the United States as we go into the 21st century, if we learn how to avoid the racial and ethnic and religious pitfalls that are bedeviling the rest of the world today.

So that's what I want to do. I want to take stock, see where we are, and see how we can get into the 21st century as one America, respecting our diversity but coming closer together. I think—by the way, I think this Summit of Service will have a lot to do with making it better.

But I'm making the final policy decisions, and I'll have some announcement to make before too long.

Thank you very much. Thank you, Mr. Prime Minister.

NOTE: The President's 142d news conference began at 2:36 p.m. in the East Room at the White House. Prime Minister Hashimoto spoke in Japanese, and his remarks were translated by an interpreter. During the news conference, the following persons were referred to: Vice Minister for Political Affairs Komura Nasahiko and Finance Minister Hiroshi Mitsuzuka of Japan; and President Jiang Zemin and Premier Li Peng of China. The leaders also referred to the Special Action Committee on Okinawa (SACO).

Statement Announcing an Appeal of the District Court Decision on Tobacco Regulations
April 25, 1997

This is a historic and landmark day for the Nation's health and children. With this ruling, we can regulate tobacco products and protect our children from a lifetime of addiction and the prospect of having their lives cut short by the diseases that come with that addiction. This is a monumental first step in what we always knew would be a long, tough road, and we are ready to keep pushing on.

This is a fight for the health and lives of our children. Each day, 3,000 children and young people become regular smokers, and 1,000 of them will have their lives cut short as a result of smoking. This is a fight we cannot afford to lose. It is a fight we cannot afford to stop waging. The Vice President and I are committed to protecting our children.

Our commonsense approach is aimed at limiting the appeal of these products and making

it harder for children to buy them. Retailers have the responsibility to make certain that they are not selling tobacco products to anyone under 18. Asking them for a photo ID is just plain common sense. Keeping tobacco billboards away from schools and playgrounds is just plain common sense.

Senior attorneys from the Department of Justice, the Department of Health and Human Services, and the Food and Drug Administration have carefully reviewed the District Court's opinion. On the basis of that review, the Solicitor General has informed me that an appeal would be appropriate for that part of the rule not upheld, and I have directed that an appeal be filed.

We will continue to work to protect our children and our children's children. We will not stop until we succeed. Where our children's health and safety are concerned, we cannot, and we will not, rest.

Message to the Senate on the Chemical Weapons Convention
April 25, 1997

To the Senate of the United States:

I am gratified that the United States Senate has given its advice and consent to the ratification of the Convention on the Prohibition of the Development, Production, Stockpiling and Use of Chemical Weapons and on their Destruction (the "Convention").

During the past several months, the Senate and the Administration, working together, have prepared a resolution of advice and consent to ratification of unusual breadth and scope. The resolution that has now been approved by the Senate by a strong, bipartisan vote of 74–26 contains 28 different Conditions covering virtually every issue of interest and concern. I will implement these provisions. I will, of course, do so without prejudice to my Constitutional authorities, including for the conduct of diplomatic exchanges and the implementation of treaties. A Condition in a resolution of ratification cannot alter the allocation of authority and responsibility under the Constitution.

I note that Condition (2) on Financial Contributions states that no funds may be drawn from the Treasury for payments or assistance under the Convention without statutory authorization and appropriation. I will interpret this Condition in light of the past practice of the Congress as not precluding the utilization of such alternatives as appropriations provisions that serve as a statutory authorization.

I am grateful to Majority Leader Lott, Minority Leader Daschle, and Senators Helms, Biden, Lugar, Levin, McCain and the many others who have devoted so much time and effort to this important ratification effort. It is clear that the practical result of our work together on the Convention will well serve the common interest of advancing the national security of the United States. In this spirit, I look forward to the entry into force of the treaty and express my hope that it will lead to even more important advances in United States, allied, and international security.

WILLIAM J. CLINTON

The White House,
April 25, 1997.

Message to the Congress on the Chemical Weapons Convention
April 25, 1997

To the Congress of the United States:

In accordance with the resolution of advice and consent to ratification of the Convention on the Prohibition of the Development, Production, Stockpiling and Use of Chemical Weapons and on Their Destruction, adopted by the Senate of the United States on April 24, 1997, I hereby certify that:

In connection with Condition (1), Effect of Article XXII, the United States has informed all other States Parties to the Convention that the Senate reserves the right, pursuant to the Constitution of the United States, to give its advice and consent to ratification of the Convention subject to reservations, notwithstanding Article XXII of the Convention.

In connection with Condition (7), Continuing Vitality of the Australia Group and National Export Controls: (i) nothing in the Convention obligates the United States to accept any modification, change in scope, or weakening of its national export controls; (ii) the United States understands that the maintenance of national restrictions on trade in chemicals and chemical production technology is fully compatible with the provisions of the Convention, including Article XI(2), and solely within the sovereign jurisdiction of the United States; (iii) the Convention preserves the right of State Parties, unilaterally or collectively, to maintain or impose export controls on chemicals and related chemical production technology for foreign policy or national security reasons, notwithstanding Article XI(2); and (iv) each Australia Group member, at the highest diplomatic levels, has officially communicated to the United States Government its understanding and agreement that export control and nonproliferation measures which the Australia Group has undertaken are fully compatible with the provisions of the Convention, including Article XI(2), and its commitment to maintain in the future such export controls and nonproliferation measures against non-Australia Group members.

In connection with Condition (9), Protection of Advanced Biotechnology, the legitimate commercial activities and interests of chemical, biotechnology, and pharmaceutical firms in the United States are not being significantly harmed by the limitations of the Convention on access to, and production of, those chemicals and toxins listed in Schedule 1 of the Annex on chemicals.

In connection with Condition (15), Assistance Under Article X, the United States shall not provide assistance under paragraph 7(a) of Article X, and, for any State Party the government of which is not eligible for assistance under chapter 2 of part II (relating to military assistance) or chapter 4 of part II (relating to economic support assistance) of the Foreign Assistance Act of 1961: (i) no assistance under paragraph 7(b) of Article X will be provided to the State Party; and (ii) no assistance under paragraph 7(c) of Article X other than medical antidotes and treatment will be provided to the State Party.

In connection with Condition (18), Laboratory Sample Analysis, no sample collected in the United States pursuant to the Convention will be transferred for analysis to any laboratory outside the territory of the United States.

In connection with Condition (26), Riot Control Agents, the United States is not restricted by the Convention in its use of riot control agents, including the use against combatants who are parties to a conflict, in any of the following cases: (i) the conduct of peacetime military operations within an area of ongoing armed conflict when the United States is not a party to the conflict (such as recent use of the United States Armed Forces in Somalia, Bosnia, and Rwanda); (ii) consensual peacekeeping operations when the use of force is authorized by the receiving state, including operations pursuant to Chapter VI of the United Nations Charter; and (iii) peacekeeping operations when force is authorized by the Security Council under Chapter VII of the United Nations Charter.

In connection with Condition (27), Chemical Weapons Destruction, all the following conditions are satisfied: (A) I have agreed to explore alternative technologies for the destruction of the United States stockpile of chemical weapons in order to ensure that the United States has the safest, most effective and environmentally sound plans and programs for meeting its obligations under the convention for the destruction of chemical weapons; (B) the requirement in section 1412 of Public Law 99–145 (50 U.S.C. 1521) for completion of the destruction of the United States stockpile of chemical weapons by December 31, 2004, will be superseded upon the date the Convention enters into force with respect to the United States by the deadline required by the Convention of April 29, 2007; (C) the requirement in Article III(1)(a)(v) of the Convention for a declaration by each State Party not later than 30 days after the date the Convention enters into force with respect to that Party, on general plans of the State Party for destruction of this chemical weapons does not preclude in any way the United States from deciding in the future to employ a technology for the destruction of chemical weapons different than that declared under that Article; and (D) I will consult with the Congress on whether to submit a request to the Executive Council of the Organization for an extension of the deadline for the destruction of chemical weapons under the Convention, as provided under Part IV(A) of the Annex on Implementation and Verification to the Convention, if, as a result of the program of alternative technologies for the destruction of chemical munitions carried out under section 8065 of the Department of Defense Appropriations Act of 1997 (as contained in Public Law 104–208), I determine that alternatives to the incineration of chemical weapons are available that are safer and more environmentally sound but whose use would preclude the United States from meeting the deadlines of the Convention.

In connection with Condition (28), Constitutional Protection Against Unreasonable Search and Seizure: (i) for any challenge inspection conducted on the territory of the United States pursuant to Article IX, where consent has been withheld, the United States National Authority will first obtain a criminal search warrant based upon probable cause, supported by oath or affirmation, and describing with particularity the place to be searched and the persons or things to be seized; and (ii) for any routine inspection of a declared facility under the Convention that is conducted on an involuntary basis on the territory of the United States, the United States National Authority

first will obtain an administrative search warrant from a United States magistrate judge.

In accordance with Condition (26) on Riot Control Agents, I have certified that the United States is not restricted by the Convention in its use of riot control agents in various peacetime and peacekeeping operations. These are situations in which the United States is not engaged in a use of force of a scope, duration and intensity that would trigger the laws of war with respect to U.S. forces.

In connection with Condition (4)(A), Cost Sharing Arrangements, which calls for a report identifying all cost-sharing arrangements with the Organization, I hereby report that because the Organization is not yet established and will not be until after entry into force of the Convention, as of this date there are no cost-sharing arrangements between the United States and the Organization to identify. However, we will be working with the Organization upon its establishment to develop such arrangements with it and will provide additional information to the Congress in the annual reports contemplated by this Condition.

WILLIAM J. CLINTON

The White House,
April 25, 1997.

The President's Radio Address
April 26, 1997

Good morning. Tomorrow I will be in Philadelphia at the Summit for America's Future. Together with Presidents Bush, Carter, and Ford, and General Colin Powell, I will issue a call to citizen service to all Americans. For 3 days we'll explore how we can all play a role in helping America's young people build a better future and, just as important, how all our young people can help to build a better America.

This is the right time to enlist in America. We're on the verge of a new century filled with promise and challenge. But to make the most of it, we must ensure that all our people, and especially all our children, have the opportunity to reach their highest potential. And we must understand that we can do that only if we all

join hands, reaching across the lines that divide us, to build one America together. That's an enormous job, but it's a job we'll have to do if we really want to prepare our country for the 21st century.

Citizen service is neighbor helping neighbor. It's part-time volunteers and full-time community service workers. It's communities coming together to solve common problems. And it is an essential part of what it means to be an American. We all have to promote it.

That's why I was so proud to launch our AmeriCorps program 4 years ago. Since then, 50,000 young people have taken a year or two to work full-time, mobilizing hundreds of other volunteers, helping the old and the young, the environment, helping communities afflicted with disaster, as I saw in North Dakota just a couple of days ago. And in the process, they also earn some money for college tuition, as they give back to their country.

But one of the important ways our AmeriCorps volunteers have found to give back is to help our children learn to read. Their success has been remarkable. To give just one example, 25 young AmeriCorps members went to work in Simpson County, Kentucky, where second graders' reading scores were disturbingly low. With the help of AmeriCorps volunteers, second graders all across that county jumped three full reading levels in just one year. The AmeriCorps volunteers made all the difference in those students' lives, and the service changed the lives of the AmeriCorps volunteers.

We know that intensive tutoring like this works. Now we have to do for all America's children what the AmeriCorps volunteers did for the children of Simpson County. That's what our America Reads challenge is all about. It's spearheaded by our Secretary of Education, Dick Riley, and Carol Rasco, my former Domestic Policy Adviser here in the White House. The America Reads challenge marshals the resources of entire communities—schools and libraries, religious institutions, universities, college students and senior citizens, all working together with teachers and parents to teach our children to read.

We need America Reads, and we need it now. Studies show that students who fail to read well by the fourth grade are more likely to drop out of school and less likely to succeed in life. But 40 percent of our fourth graders still can't read at a basic level. We can, and we must, do better than this.

With me today are AmeriCorps members, tutors, and parents from four different organizations who are helping to make a real difference in our children's lives: First, the Home Instruction Program for Preschool Youngsters, or HIPPY, an early learning program involving parents and children; second, Hands On Atlanta, from Georgia; then, Reading One on One from Texas; and Oregon's SMART. All help to recruit volunteers and teach our children to read. Together these groups reach thousands of children every year. America Reads will help them and others to reach millions more.

This Monday I will send my America Reads legislation to the Congress so that we can mobilize the citizen army of one million America Reads tutors I called for in my State of the Union Address, to make sure that every 8-year-old child in America can pick up a book and say, "I can read this all by myself." This legislation is part of my balanced budget. It will fund 25,000 reading specialists and tutor coordinators, including 11,000 AmeriCorps members and many others. They will recruit and train our America Reads citizen army, bringing reading help to the 3 million children who need it the most.

It will also help parents to instill a lifelong learning of reading in children. Parents are our children's first teachers, and we have to do everything we can to make their jobs easier. Community groups like HIPPY, which Hillary and I worked hard to bring to Arkansas, are doing exactly that. The plan I'm sending to Congress will expand their ability to reach more families. My balanced budget also increases Head Start funding to reach one million 3- and 4-year-olds, and expands title I to aid teaching and learning in classrooms and the Even Start Family Literacy Program.

But it will take more than money to make sure that all our children can read. It will take a commitment from our entire community. That's why I'm pleased to announce that as part of the Service Summit, many of our major corporations and nonprofit organizations will help us to recruit tens of thousands of additional tutors for America Reads. One hundred sixty-six colleges all across America already have answered the challenge I issued in December and pledged thousands of their students to be reading tutors. I thank them for their support.

Last summer in Wyandotte, Michigan, when I announced the America Reads program, I sat with two young children and read "The Little Engine That Could," a book that has taught countless children that they can do anything they think they can. I want every child in America to know that he or she can read. And America Reads will make sure that all those children can.

I hope some of you who are listening will consider being part of America Reads. After all, we need a million citizen servants, and we're not there yet. If you're interested, call 1–800–USA–Learn, the Department of Education's hotline, or just contact your local elementary school or library.

All of us can help. All you really need to do is roll up your sleeves, sit with a child, and open a book together. And remember, you'll be doing more than just reading, you'll be writing an exciting new chapter in America's progress.

Thanks for listening.

NOTE: The President spoke at 10:06 a.m. from the Oval Office at the White House.

Remarks at the White House Correspondents' Association Dinner
April 26, 1997

Thank you very much. Mr. Hunt, thank you so much for reading the notes that I wrote you. [*Laughter*] Just like every other journalist, make all my memos public. [*Laughter*] To Larry McQuillan, Arlene Dillon, Jon Stewart, who will make us glad we came in a few moments, to all the distinguished head table guests, and ladies and gentlemen.

I tried to fulfill Terry Hunt's agenda as President. Those are real notes I wrote him. And I will try to fulfill Larry's agenda. I think it's terrible the conditions in which the White House press corps labor. It really is. It reminds me of Nurse Ratched's office in "One Flew Over the Cuckoo's Nest." [*Laughter*] And it's really a tribute to the futility of a politician pandering to the press, because that used to be an indoor swimming pool that brought joy to FDR and JFK and Presidents in between. Richard Nixon gave it to you. [*Laughter*] And he got such good press in return. [*Laughter*] Maybe this is his final revenge, the miserable conditions of it. We could uncover it, but let you keep it. [*Laughter*] I could build a cabana. Well, you think about it.

Before I get into my jokes, I have some important, serious news. [*Laughter*] Senator Lott and I have broken the gridlock over the budget. A deal now appears imminent. Miraculously, the $56 billion—[*applause*]—thank you—the $56 billion gap that has separated Democrats and Republicans has been bridged. And ladies and gentlemen, we owe Senator Dole a huge debt of gratitude. [*Laughter*] And the best part is, we don't have to start paying it back until 2005. [*Laughter*] And that's outside the budget window. Bigger tax cuts, more money for the Justice Department, whatever—just sign up, you can have it. [*Laughter*] You know, if I had known

Bob Dole was that generous, I'd have invited him over for coffee. [*Laughter*]

I want to congratulate awardees tonight: Byron Acohido, who has come from so far away and did such good work; and then there are the local winners, Ron Fournier, Mara Liasson, Todd Purdum. Of course, I'm not familiar with any of your work, but I'm sure it's very good. But this Purdum guy's name sounds familiar. Purdum, Purdum—I think I read it in the engagement announcements recently. Hillary and I congratulate Todd and Dee Dee on their marriage next month.

You know, Dee Dee and I started together on a little plane in New Hampshire, and we made it all the way to the White House. Then she sort of strayed over to your side for a while, and I was kind of disappointed. Now she's getting on a 747 and going to Beverly Hills. They grow up so fast, don't they? [*Laughter*]

Oh, I got another serious thing I want to talk about. Something that I know—really, you all are on me about all the time. Many of you are distressed that you're not notified in a timely fashion about breaking news, like my knee breaking. And that's valid, and I've been doing some work to make sure it never happens again. In fact, in the spirit of reinventing Government that the Vice President has so indoctrinated me with, starting tonight we have decided to give you advance notice of upcoming mishaps. [*Laughter*]

Mike McCurry has asked me to inform you of the following. While engaging in some volunteer work tomorrow in Philadelphia, I will be on the receiving end of a painful encounter with a ball-peen hammer. [*Laughter*] And I will do my best to do it before your filing deadline at 5. On May 22d, I will be visiting the home of Tiger Woods to celebrate his recent victory in the Masters. Please be advised: There is a loose brick on the patio. [*Laughter*] On July 8, during the fifth inning of the All Star game in Cleveland, I will attempt to catch a foul ball from Rafael Palmeiro. Stay tuned. [*Laughter*] Look, Mark Knoller is running out to call his editor now. [*Laughter*]

I know we're here to honor you tonight because of the work you do, but this dinner is a pittance compared to the testament to your profession last week which opened its doors, called the Newseum—the Newseum, the Newseum. What really surprised me, for any event in Washington, this opening actually got a lot of favorable press coverage. [*Laughter*] Evidently, you journalists have a lot of friends in the media. [*Laughter*]

But there are a bunch of exhibits I'm dying to see. I want to see the portrait gallery of unnamed sources—[*laughter*]—the Gergen and Shields retrospective—[*laughter*]—the museum's crown jewel, the hall of pundits. [*Laughter*] Modeled after the Hall of Presidents at Disneyland, it features mechanized mannequins mouthing contentious blather. No wait, that's the McLaughlin Group. [*Laughter*]

There is also an absolutely amazing collection of historical artifacts: C–SPAN's gavel-to-gavel etchings of the Constitutional Convention; CNN's very first "Crossfire"—from the left, Alexander Hamilton, from the right, Aaron Burr, topic, gun control. [*Laughter*] There is an actual press corps travel manifest from Stage Coach One. Guess what, the film they showed was "Fargo." [*Laughter*] The 30 people in the White House press corps are laughing at that. [*Laughter*]

There are artifacts of contemporary Washington journalism as well. There is the stack of Bibles upon which Joe Klein swore. [*Laughter*] There is Johnny Apple's expense reports, a transcript of Anne Rice's interview with Bob Novak, the contract where Bob Woodward insists on Robert Redford being cast as him. [*Laughter*] There is a haunting photograph from the 1961 White House Correspondents' dinner of young Brian Williams shaking hands adoringly with Chet Huntley. [*Laughter*]

And then there is a whole wing dedicated to historic scoops. For example, did you know that Helen Thomas broke the story about the Lincoln Bedroom—while Lincoln was still sleeping in it. [*Laughter*]

However, the most important part of the museum is an exhibit which poses an utterly fascinating question, both contemporary and historical: How would current White House correspondents and columnists have covered past Presidential administrations? Have you seen this? I mean, this is an incredible thing. In the exhibit, everyone in the current press corps is making fun of Millard Fillmore's name—that's everyone except Wolf Blitzer. [*Laughter*] David Letterman keeps calling William Howard Taft "Tubby" and Teddy Roosevelt "Old Four Eyes." [*Laughter*] Maureen Dowd writes a column dismissing the first Presidential election as politics as usual. [*Laughter*] Sam Donaldson makes fun of George Washington's wooden teeth but completely ignores the obvious fact that he's wearing a wig. [*Laughter*] The New York Times calls for a special counsel to look into George Washington's winning campaign in the Revolutionary War—because Lafayette was French. And Barbara Walters asks the Father of our Country, "If you could chop down a tree, any tree at all, what kind of tree would it be?" [*Laughter*]

All right, now we're going to tell some stuff on us. I know you give me grief from time to time, but really we work around the clock trying to help you do your job. I mean, really, what other administration would make thousands and thousands of internal memos and official documents available for your daily enjoyment? [*Laughter*]

But you did miss a couple of good stories. Roll it in, boys; come here. Where are they? Where are my documents? [*Laughter*] Come here! I hope no one is in contempt for ignoring these. This is just a representative sample. You'll have them all tomorrow. [*Laughter*]

Here's a memo from Harold Ickes to Leon Panetta: "Leon, FYI, Maxwell House coffee is on sale this week for $3.49 a pound." [*Laughter*] Here's a copy of a check we mistakenly thought was a small campaign contribution from AT&T. It turns out that by cashing it, I authorized a switch in our long distance service. [*Laughter*] Here's a memo outlining the DNC's high donor program. It's pretty embarrassing—business class upgrades for Air Force One. Mr. Speaker, it could have been you. [*Laughter*] And let's see, here's one: For $10,000, you can have a private meeting with Vice President Gore to discuss reinventing Government. And for $20,000, you don't have to go. [*Laughter*] And this is the most embarrassing one of all, from the White

House visitor log last year. I can't believe any of you missed this. It seems that during the period of time when the First Lady was recording her Grammy Award winning album, Milli Vanilli came to the White House 32 times. [*Laughter*]

Now, I don't know how this got in here. This is a letter of acceptance to Chelsea, saying that she will—from Chelsea, saying that she will attend—no, that's privileged. [*Laughter*] But look, the bad news is, our only child is going off to college. The good news is, it opens up another bedroom. [*Laughter*]

But now look, you all know I want a bridge to the future, not the past. I'm interested in the future, so I want you to just forget about the documents. [*Laughter*]

Now, we know how important technology is to our future, and the White House has always been the center of new technological developments, ever since John Adams occupied it. There was the electric lights, the telephone, the telegraph, the tape recorder—[*laughter*]—and the Clapper—[*laughter*]—and, most recently, the computer.

Now, just last week the Vice President and I used a computer in the Oval Office. I felt like a kid who first got to drive; he actually let me do some things on it. [*Laughter*] And it's clear that we are once again at the threshold of a new era that will forever change the way Presidents conduct matters at home and abroad. As of this week, I have been working around the clock trying to balance the budget with Quicken. [*Laughter*] And I want you to consider this. In the post-cold-war era, the introduction of the computer has raised a profound question: Whose finger do you want on the control-alt-delete button? [*Laughter*]

You know what my favorite button is? F2, search and replace. [*Laughter*] I have enjoyed the daily press clips so much more since I discovered F2. [*Laughter*] I read them on-line now, and then I search and replace. Thanks for showing me that, Al. I mean, after all—look, your news reports are just the first rough draft of history anyway, and I'm just doing the F2 thing to do a little editing. Let's take some of the news stories you've written just in the last month: F2, search for "budget standstill";

replace with "prosperity at home and peace abroad." [*Laughter*] It's better, isn't it? It is. Search for "beleaguered"; replace with "Lincoln-esque." [*Laughter*] Search for "independent counsel"; replace with "the ice cream man." [*Laughter*]

I'll never forget how I found out about this incredible device, search and replace. I walked into the Vice President's office not very long ago, and he was there working on his computer—F2, search for Bill Clinton—[*laughter*]—I got there just in time.

James Thurber said that humor is one of our greatest and earliest national resources that has to be preserved at all cost. Well, I hope we've saved a little up tonight and enriched it. I thank you and come here to honor your indispensable part in our lively 225-year-old experiment in democracy. May we work together so that it continues to light and lead the world.

Tomorrow I'm going to Philadelphia, where this great experiment began, to open the Presidents' Summit for America's Future. We'll gather there to renew the spirit of service that built this country. Each of us must serve; you in your way, me in mine. You can start right now—by busing your own tables and helping with the dishes. [*Laughter*] Now, when Jon finishes, I'm going home.

Thanks, and good night. [*Laughter*]

NOTE: The President spoke at approximately 10:05 p.m. in the International Ballroom at the Washington Hilton Hotel. In his remarks, he referred to White House Correspondents' Association outgoing president Terence Hunt, Associated Press, and incoming president Larry McQuillan, Reuters; Arlene Dillon, CBS News; comedian Jon Stewart; Byron Acohido, Seattle Times; Ron Fournier, Associated Press; Mara Liasson, National Public Radio; Todd Purdum, New York Times; former Press Secretary Dee Dee Myers, Vanity Fair; Mark Knoller, CBS Radio; Joe Klein, author, "Primary Colors"; Johnny Apple, New York Times; author Anne Rice; syndicated columnist Bob Novak; Bob Woodward, Washington Post; actor Robert Redford; Brian Williams, NBC News; Helen Thomas, United Press International; Wolf Blitzer, Cable News Network; and Sam Donaldson and Barbara Walters, ABC News.

Remarks at the Kickoff of the Presidents' Summit for America's Future in Philadelphia, Pennsylvania
April 27, 1997

The President. Thank you. Thank you very much. Good morning!

Audience members. Good morning!

The President. Are you ready to go to work?

Audience members. Yes!

The President. Are you warmed up?

Audience members. Yes!

The President. Have you heard all the speeches you want to hear?

Audience members. Yes!

The President. I want to just say—let me say, first of all, how grateful I am to be here with all the people who have made this possible and with all of you. I thank the people of Philadelphia for being so good to me since 1992 and for being my friends and for giving me a chance to work with you to bring Philadelphia back. Thank you so much. I thank all your officials. I thank your wonderful Mayor.

General Powell told me when he retired from the United States Army as Chairman of the Joint Chiefs of Staff that the one thing he wanted to do more than anything else was to find a way to give every child in this country a chance at a good future, and I thank him for doing that.

I thank Colin and Alma. I thank George and Barbara Bush for their examples, Mrs. Bush with her literacy program, President Bush for A Thousand Points of Light. I thank President and Mrs. Carter for caring about the children of this country, for the work they've done with Habitat for Humanity and for going all over the world to rid the children of the world of dread diseases, to give them food to eat and a decent, humane place to grow up in. I thank all of you.

But let's face it—I want everybody to face it. Why are we here? We know that a lot of us would be doing a lot of this anyway. There are a lot of wonderful volunteers in America. Here's why we're here. This country has produced a lot of jobs in the last 4 years. The crime rate is going down; the welfare rolls are going down. But we're still losing too many kids to crime, to drugs, to not having a decent income in their home, and to not having a bright future. And we're here because we don't think

we have to put up with it, and we believe together we can change it. Isn't that right? [*Applause*]

I'm here because I want the young people out here to grow up in an America that is even greater than the America I grew up in. That is the eternal dream and promise, and every one of you deserves that. I'm here because, frankly, I believe that as children of God, we can never fulfill our own ambitions until we help our brothers and sisters to fulfill theirs.

I'm here because I want to redefine the meaning of citizenship in America. I want the children here, starting next week, and all over America—if you're asked in school, what does it mean to be a good citizen, I want the answer to be, "Well, to be a good citizen, you have to obey the law. You've got to go to work or be in school. You've got to pay your taxes, and, oh, yes, you have to serve in your community to help make it a better place."

And General Powell, since we're going to keep this going and we all have to make an account of ourselves, I'll go first. Here's my commitment to you and your project.

In the next 4 years, the Department of Defense will mentor, tutor, and teach one million children. In the next 4 years, the Department of Transportation and the private businesses who work with them will do that for one million more. We will adopt a total of 2,000 schools in the Federal agencies of this country. We will find one million reading tutors in the America Reads program, to make sure every child can read independently by the third grade. And our AmeriCorps volunteers will go across this country to recruit at least a dozen more volunteers for every one of them, to make sure that all of the items on your agenda succeed. That is our commitment.

Are you ready to keep your commitment?

Audience members. Yes!

The President. After today is over, do you promise to keep working tomorrow?

Audience members. Yes!

The President. And next year?

Audience members. Yes!

The President. And the year after that?

Audience members. Yes!
The President. Until the job is done?
Audience members. Yes!
The President. I promise. Say it!
Audience members. I promise!
The President. Let's go to work.
God bless you.

NOTE: The President spoke at 11:05 a.m. at Marcus Foster Stadium. In his remarks, he referred to Mayor Edward Rendell of Philadelphia; Gen. Colin L. Powell, USA (ret.), former Chairman, Joint Chiefs of Staff, and his wife, Alma; and former First Lady Rosalynn Carter.

Remarks on Presenting the President's Service Awards in Philadelphia
April 27, 1997

The President. Thank you. I like that version of "Hail to the Chief." Maybe the Marine Band could pick it up. [*Laughter*]

Ladies and gentlemen, these President's Service Awards are traditionally presented at the White House every year, but Hillary and I are profoundly honored to be here this evening with President and Mrs. Bush, General Powell, and all others who are part of this very important ceremony.

As all of you know, we're here along with President Ford, President and Mrs. Carter, Mrs. Reagan, here in Philadelphia where our great democracy began, for the first Presidents' Summit for America's Future, to mobilize every community and challenge every citizen, to give our young people a chance to live up to their God-given potential, and to ask our young people to become citizen servants, too.

So tonight we're going to give these awards, very appropriately, in the categories that have been set out for the challenge to America, the categories that General Powell talked about in his moving opening remarks. And I'm going to have the honor of recognizing the caring adults. I'm pleased to be joined tonight by a man who has dedicated his entire life to meeting the challenge of service, Harris Wofford.

[*At this point, Harris Wofford, Chief Executive Officer, Corporation for National and Community Service, made brief remarks.*]

The President. You know, you might have guessed that before he headed our Nation's citizens service effort and the corporation for national service, Harris Wofford was in politics— [*laughter*]—the Senator from Pennsylvania. But before that, he was a college president; before that, a founder of the Peace Corps; a top aide to President Kennedy; a friend and ally of Dr.

Martin Luther King. Hardly any American living today better personifies citizen service than Harris Wofford, and I thank him for that.

As I said, we begin by recognizing that every single child needs a caring adult in his or her life to teach and guide them. Every child needs to know that he or she is profoundly important to some grownup. The three Americans we honor now have devoted themselves to meeting this challenge.

Marjorie Klein knows that parents are our children's first teachers, and she's doing everything she can to help them. At 20 inner-city schools throughout the Philadelphia area, PACT, or Parents And Children Together, the organization Marjorie founded, brings parents into the classroom to read to the children and to help their children learn to read. At the same time, parents can improve their own literacy and tutoring skills, and they can even earn college credit. We salute Marjorie Klein and PACT for their tremendous commitment to families and our children.

[*The President presented the award to Ms. Klein.*]

The President. Earl Phelan deeply believes that mentoring is the key to young people's success. Through B.E.L.L., or Building Enterprises for Learning and Living, the organization he helped to found, he has given hundreds of African-American young adults the chance to be role models and tutors to inner-city elementary school students throughout the greater Boston area. Under their tutelage, those children are thriving, their futures are brighter, and therefore so are ours. Tonight we honor Earl Phelan for his remarkable contribution to our American community.

[*The President presented the award to Mr. Phelan.*]

The President. Pat Esparza learned early in life that confidence and pride can make all the difference to a young girl's future. A single mother of three by the age of 19, she worked her way through school and devoted herself to helping at-risk girls. She founded Las Mariposas as a dance studio, but for the people of El Paso, Texas, it is a community treasure. At Las Mariposas hundreds of young girls have learned to dance and to value themselves and their culture. We honor Pat for giving the young girls of her community the confidence and pride they need to succeed in life.

Congratulations.

[*The President presented the award to Ms. Esparza.*]

All of them have helped to make sure that more of our young people do, in fact, have a caring adult to give them the support they need to build positive futures. Your work is an inspiration to all of us. I thank you for doing it, and I hope all of us will now be more willing to follow your lead. God bless you.

[*Former First Lady Barbara Bush, assisted by actor John Travolta, presented the second group of awards. Former President George Bush, assisted by actress Brooke Shields Agassi, presented the third group of awards. Hillary Clinton, assisted by movie director Rob Reiner, presented the fourth group of awards. Following the award presentations, singer Patti LaBelle performed.*]

The President. Thank you, Patti LaBelle, for giving us all a second wind. [*Laughter*] I want to apologize to all of you for having to spend so much time tonight watching me walk up and down stairs. But as you know, I need the practice. [*Laughter*]

I want to say that this last award in some ways may be the most important, because we're recognizing young people who, themselves, are serving in an extraordinary way. And one of the elements of this summit is the proposition that every young person should serve, and that, in so doing, we hope to expand the definition of what it means to be a good citizen in this country so that when we ask young people in years to come, what does it really mean to be a good American, they'll say, "Well, you have

to be in school or work, you have to obey the law, and you have to serve."

I'm joined now on stage by a young public servant, Jahi Davis, an AmeriCorps volunteer from north Philadelphia. Like a lot of high school students, this young man paid more attention to his social life than to his future. Then he nearly lost his life in a serious accident. He says now he wouldn't have finished high school without the guidance of a tutor who helped him keep his grades up while he was in the hospital. When he recovered, he decided to do for others what had been done for him. He joined AmeriCorps in 1995, and since then, he has tutored children, started a mentoring program in his own neighborhood, and rehabilitated houses for low income families. He's planning to attend Temple University, where I know he'll continue to give back. Please welcome him up here with me. [*Applause*]

When 21-year-old Na'Taki Osborne learned that Carver Hills, Georgia, a low income African-American community, was the most environmentally polluted area in Fulton County, she didn't just become concerned, she got involved. She got 200 community volunteers involved, too. And together they spent hundreds of hours cleaning up Carver Hills, making it a safer and more beautiful place for the entire community to enjoy.

Thank you, Na'Taki Yatascha Osborne, for caring enough to change your community for the better.

[*The President presented the award to Ms. Osborne.*]

The President. Amber Lynn Coffman is only 15 years old, but she's been volunteering to help disadvantaged people since she was 8. Her mother taught her that even one person can make a real difference, and for most of her still-young life, she has tried to be that one person and to encourage her friends and schoolmates to do the same. Working together as a group called Happy Helpers, they make over 600 box lunches every week for the homeless and the hungry. Thank you, Amber Lynn, for your wonderful commitment to your community.

[*The President presented the award to Ms. Coffman.*]

Across America, more and more businesses believe that good citizenship is also good business. More and more, they're encouraging their employees to give something back. Target Stores is a perfect example. Through the Family Matters Program, started by Points of Light, Target Stores is the first national company to involve its employees and their families in community service.

Last year, nearly 5,000 Target employees and their families volunteered. Working alongside their parents, young people learned firsthand about the importance and the joy of giving back. We thank Target stores for helping so many young children start early on a lifetime of service.

With us tonight to represent Target is Julie Hennessy.

[*The President presented the award to Ms. Hennessy.*]

The President. As Oprah said earlier, the 16 award winners with us tonight represent volunteers all over our country who are committed to helping us all build a better and stronger future. In honoring their contributions, we celebrate the spirit of service that has sustained America in times of trouble and united us with common hopes and dreams.

At the dawn of a new century, let us all resolve to join hands to do it more. Remember what this summit is all about. These people were doing all this before we gathered. Ninety-three million Americans already volunteer. What we're saying is that in every community in America, more people must do it in a systematic way, and everyone must do it if America is going to have the future it deserves and our children are going to all be like those whom we honor here tonight.

Thank you, and God bless you all.

NOTE: The President spoke at 9:10 p.m. in Exhibit Hall A of the Convention Center. In his remarks, he referred to Gen. Colin L. Powell, USA (ret.), former Chairman, Joint Chiefs of Staff; former First Ladies Rosalynn Carter and Nancy Reagan; and television talk show host Oprah Winfrey.

Remarks at the Opening Ceremony of the Presidents' Summit for America's Future in Philadelphia
April 28, 1997

Thank you very much. Ladies and gentlemen, I want to begin by thanking Matthew and Teevee and Christina and Jamil and Christy for introducing the Presidents and Mrs. Reagan. They reminded us of what this summit is all about.

I thank President and Mrs. Bush, President and Mrs. Carter, President Ford, Mrs. Reagan, Vice President and Mrs. Gore for their devotion to this endeavor. I thank Harris Wofford and Bob Goodwin, the president of the Points of Light Foundation; Henry Cisneros and Lynda Robb; and all the others who have worked for this day. I say a special word of thanks to all the public officials who have come from all over our country, Members of Congress, Governors, Lieutenant Governors and others.

But particularly, I want to thank General Colin Powell. At our last meeting, when he was about to retire as Chairman of the Joint Chiefs of Staff, I asked him if there was another mission which might bring him back into public life. He said he wanted to help children who didn't have what they needed to succeed in life and who needed the chance to serve America. Well, General, this may be your most important mission, and I want to thank you for reenlisting. Thank you.

I thank my friend Mayor Rendell and the wonderful people of Philadelphia, Governor Ridge and the people of Pennsylvania who have made us feel so welcome.

We come here before the house where America was born, the place where we, the people, took the first step on our centuries-old journey to form a more perfect Union. On the last day of the Constitutional Convention, Benjamin Franklin walked out of this hall and encountered a woman anxious to know what had gone on inside. She asked him, "Well, Doctor, what have we got, a monarchy or a republic?" Mr. Franklin replied, "A republic, if you can keep it."

For more than 200 years, we have struggled to keep this Republic. It is an enduring and endless challenge, for endemic in human nature and human frailty are successive generations of problems. But we have always succeeded in making our Union more perfect. Consider how imperfect it was when we had people in this country who weren't even treated as people but slaves. Consider how imperfect it was when children could be forced to work long hours into the night in dangerous conditions. Consider how imperfect it was when women, now more than half the population of America, could not even vote.

So when you get discouraged, remember: We have succeeded in over 200 years in forming a more perfect Union. We have succeeded because we've had a brilliant free enterprise system. We have succeeded because we had a flexible, constitutional, evolving, effective government at every level. But we have succeeded mostly because, in the gaps between what is done by Government and what is done by the private economy, citizens have found ways to step forward and move our country forward and lift our people up. Citizen service is the story of our more perfect Union.

Now we live in one of the great moments of change in our history, more full of promise, as President Ford said, than any period of America's past. More of these children behind me and more of these children out here on these streets of Philadelphia will have more chances to live out the future of their dreams than any generation of American children in history if the citizens of this country step forward to fill the gaps in their lives and in our national life to form a more perfect Union.

But let us not be blind to the facts. Even with all the progress that together we have made, with 12 million new jobs and a record drop in welfare rolls and years of dropping crime rates, you and I know that millions of our children are being left behind in lives of too much danger, too many drugs, too little hope, and not enough opportunity. You and I know that too many people are out there doing the very best they can and still not keeping up, much less moving forward.

Yes, there are things that the Government should do. None of us stand here, President and former Presidents, to say that we must not do our responsibility. Of course, we should do better with our schools. Of course, we should open the doors of college to everyone. Of course, all our children should have health care

coverage. Of course, we can do more to make our streets safer. But even if we do everything we should, you and I know that a lot of the problems facing our children are problems of the human heart, problems that can only be resolved when there is a one-on-one connection, community by community, neighborhood by neighborhood, street by street, home by home, with every child in this country entitled to live out their God-given destiny. You know it is true.

I am proud of the fact that because of the computer and micro solutions to problems we don't need big Government bureaucracies to do some of the things that used to be done. But as I have said repeatedly, the era of big Government may be over, but the era of big challenges for our country is not, and so we need an era of big citizenship. That is why we are here, and that is what we should promise ourselves we will do.

Let me say one other thing, too. Look at these kids behind me. They're America's future, all of them. And when you think of what is tearing the world apart today, the racial, the ethnic, the religious hatreds, from Bosnia to Northern Ireland to the Middle East to Africa, and you look at the children behind me and you realize what a gift from God our diversity is, you know that if we know each other, if we serve each other, if we work with each other, one of the things that will happen is, we will make sure that our diversity is a rich resource to make our Union more perfect, not an instrument of our national undoing in the 21st century.

We cherish our citizen volunteers. There are already more than 90 million of us, and after this summit there will be more, especially because General Powell, Ray Chambers, and others have organized a followup to this. And the really important work of this summit will begin after my talk's over, when you go into the workshops and the meetings and make a commitment that in every community there will be a systematic, disciplined, comprehensive effort to deal with the five areas outlined as the challenges for our young people. That is what really matters here.

Young people above all, however, have the time, the energy, and the idealism for this kind of citizen service. Before they have their own families, the young can make a unique contribution to the family of America. In doing so, they can acquire the habit of service and get a deeper understanding of what it really means to be a citizen. That is the main reason, perhaps, we are here.

In Philadelphia, the superintendent of schools is working to make service the expected thing in elementary and middle school. Maryland has required it in high school. And I challenge every State and every school in this country at least to offer in a disciplined, organized way every young person in school a chance to serve. A recent survey said if they were just asked, over 90 percent of them would do it. We ought to be ashamed of ourselves if we don't give them the chance to do that.

Let me also say, of course, that we need some of them to serve full-time. They do, you know, in the Peace Corps. [*Applause*] And we have some former Peace Corps volunteers out there applauding. But we should all applaud them because they have helped to change the world for the better—[*applause*]—and they do in AmeriCorps, the national service program that was started in our administration. The idea behind AmeriCorps was to instill an ethic of mutual responsibility in our children so that young people could improve their own lives in return for improving the life of America.

Since its creation, 50,000 young Americans have earned college tuition by serving their communities in many ways. And we know that the typical full-time community servant recruits at least a dozen more volunteers. I saw that in North Dakota when I went to see what the Red River had done to Grand Forks and to the rest of North Dakota and Minnesota. I saw our young AmeriCorps volunteers, and I knew that because they were able to serve full-time, they'd be there when the waters receded, the mess was there, the people had to put their lives back together, and the cameras were gone. I saw it again yesterday when we were working on the streets and on the stadium and on the schools.

The will to serve has never been stronger, and more of our young people want to serve full-time. But there's a limit to what we can do now. And yet, there is a solution—ironically, one I came to right here in Philadelphia, for here in Philadelphia, a minister who is a friend of mine, Reverend Tony Campolo, is helping to organize a movement among churches to get churches to sponsor 10,000 full-time youth volunteers to take a year off from college or defer a year from college under the sponsorship of their churches.

The churches will do what we do in AmeriCorps, helping to provide for the living expenses of the young people. But I think we ought to say to them, at the very least, it shouldn't cost you any money to serve. And so if you've got a college loan and you take a year off to serve under the sponsorship of a religious organization, I'm going to propose legislation to say during that year no interest should accrue on that college loan. It should not cost you any money to serve your country.

But we can do more. We can double the impact of AmeriCorps with the help of our religious and charitable institutions. I want to challenge every charity, every religious group, every community group, and their business supporters to give young people the support they need to do a year of community service. If you do that, then in our budget now we will be able to give every one of them the scholarship that AmeriCorps volunteers get for their year of community service. Work with your churches, work with your community organizations, and we can provide that to young people. Put them to work as mentors, as teachers, as organizers of other volunteers, and we can double the number of full-time youth volunteers by adding another 50,000. By the year 2000, that would mean that in 8 years, more children will have served full-time on our streets than have worked in the entire history of the Peace Corps around the world. We can change America, folks, if we'll do it together, hand in hand, community by community.

The same thing is true of the police corps, which offers young people a chance to pay for their college education if they'll be police officers for 4 years. We can triple the number of young people who do that, and I intend to try. We need more young people going as teachers into our schools. And we must support them in that.

We have to understand that we need a balance between volunteers on a part-time basis, volunteers on a full-time basis, and there is no conflict between the two. We have to understand that we value America's free enterprise system. We know we need our Government, but there will never be a time when we need citizen servants more than we need them today, because these children have got to be saved one by one.

And let me say to all of you, the most important people here today are not the Presidents or the generals or the Governors or the Senators. The most important people are those who teach the student to read, who save the health of the infant, who give help to families when all help seems gone. The most important title today is not Senator, Vice President, general, Governor, or President; it is—as Harry Truman reminded us so long ago, the most important title any of us will ever hold in this country is the title of citizen. This is our Republic. Let us keep it. [*Applause*] Thank you.

And now, I would like to call upon Mrs. Reagan and my fellow Presidents to join me in signing this summit declaration, "A Call to Citizen Service To Fulfill the Promise of America." We do this in the hope that in the weeks and months to come, millions and millions and millions of you will join us in putting your names to the declaration, devoting your lives to the mission, and beginning the era of big citizenship for the United States.

Thank you, and God bless you all.

NOTE: The President spoke at approximately 10:30 a.m. at Independence National Historical Park. In his remarks, he referred to Henry Cisneros and Lynda Robb, vice chairs, Presidents' Summit for America's Future; Mayor Edward Rendell of Philadelphia; Gov. Tom Ridge of Pennsylvania; Raymond G. Chambers, cofounder, Points of Light Foundation; and David Hornbeck, Philadelphia superintendent of schools.

Remarks at the Presidents' Summit for America's Future Luncheon in Philadelphia
April 28, 1997

Thank you, ladies and gentlemen. I've had a great time here, and I want to thank all of you for being so patient while I lumber around with my temporary disability. Can you imagine how bad I would look if I had actually jumped out of an airplane? [*Laughter*] I'm looking forward to not being President. You know, if I can jump out of an airplane and look like Jerry Ford does in 30 years, I'll be one happy guy. That's a great thing.

I want to thank President Bush for all of the people that he mentioned and thanking them—I join with that—and especially Ray Chambers and Stuart Shapiro and General Powell for their extraordinary efforts. I'd also like to thank the leaders of the corporate and nonprofit sector who are here today, including my longtime friend Millard Fuller, Bob Allen, Doug Watson, and Gerry Greenwald and so many others. We've all been washed in the warm glow of lots of words and music and the powerful examples. And I must say, I will live with the stories that the young people told last night at that event for the rest of my life.

I would just like to make two points here, because I really want this to make a difference. I think there are two keys to whether, when people look back on this moment 10 years from now, they say, "These people really did something special; they changed America." The first is what General Powell and Ray Chambers and others are doing with the followup on America's Promise. And everything you can do to support that, you should, making those promises. We're going to try to do our part.

I said yesterday that the Department of Defense will tutor or teach a million children in the next 4 years. The Department of Transportation and the contractors with whom it works have committed to reach another million kids with tutoring or teaching. We are going to go from 1,500 to 2,000 schools we've adopted. Going back to what Eli said—we'll have more to say about that later—we're going to hire 10,000 people to move from welfare to work so they can support their children better. We're going to try to extend health insurance to 5 million kids and try to at least make the first 2 years of college as available as a high school education is today. We'll try to do our part, and we'll try to do it in very personal ways.

The last Christmas and the last birthday I had were some of the best I ever had in my life because my gift from the White House staff was a notebook of personal pledges for community service. My Secret Service detail adopted a junior high school in Washington, DC, where those young people are getting the role models that they need. We'll try to do our part.

And the followup—one reason I wanted to do this summit so badly was that I thought we could find a completely nonpartisan way to embrace this issue, and then I knew I could trust Colin Powell and Ray Chambers and the others to do good followup. That's the first thing.

Here's the second thing. Let me just tell you a brief story. Before I came to Philadelphia, I asked a man in Washington, DC, named Kent Amos, a lot of you know, to come in and see me. I met him when my friend Ron Brown died in a plane crash, and he was Ron's next-door neighbor. And a lot of you know he and his wife, Carmen, kind of got into this volunteer work by just taking in kids that their children went to school with who came from dysfunctional backgrounds. And they wound up having 20 or more at a time that were, in effect, living with them. And now he's tried to take the model that he—I thought he perfected in his own home and kind of took it into neighborhoods and communities.

But I asked him to come see me. And I said, "What do you want me to do now? What can I do to help you, and what do we have to do now?" He said, "Go to that summit and tell them the breakout sessions are the most important thing that's going to occur, because unless every community gets organized, community by community, we will not have the maximum benefit of this, because essentially the problem is we have an unacceptably high percentage of people living in dysfunctional environments. And you can do a number of good things for them sporadically, but until you completely change the environment, we won't have the success rate we need."

That's essentially what General Powell said in our last conversation before he took his uni-

form off, that all the troubled young people that he knew who came into the military had gone from whatever dysfunctional environment they had into a completely functional environment. Now, you can't guarantee that, any of you individually. But collectively, community by community, we can. So, in that sense, the Governors and the mayors who are here are profoundly important people. And the people who run community-based nonprofits are important people.

But the only other thing I would say is, let's really pay attention to these breakout sessions, and let's promise ourselves that in addition to running up the numbers that we all promised—and since I've got a big organization, I can promise big numbers—but we're, honest to goodness, going to promise ourselves that we will try to change the culture in these communities from dysfunctional environments to functional ones. You saw these kids. They're great. They're going to make it. They're going to do just fine if we just give them what they need in a systematic way, place by place.

Thank you, and God bless you all.

NOTE: The President spoke at 1:05 p.m. in the Ballroom at the Benjamin Franklin Hotel. In his remarks, he referred to Raymond G. Chambers, cofounder, Points of Light Foundation; Stuart Shapiro, president and chief executive officer, Presidents' Summit for America's Future; Gen. Colin L. Powell, USA (ret.), chairman, America's Promise—the Alliance for Youth; Eli Segal, Board of Directors member, Corporation for National and Community Service; Millard Fuller, founder, Habitat for Humanity; Robert E. Allen, chairman and chief executive officer, AT&T Corp.; Douglas Watson, president and chief executive officer, Novartis Corp.; and Gerald Greenwald, chief executive officer, United Airlines.

Remarks to Students, Teachers, Parents, and AmeriCorps Volunteers in Philadelphia
April 28, 1997

Thank you. Thank you very much. I am so pleased to be here. Thank you for making me feel so welcome. I want to say to all of you, I have looked forward to coming to this school since I knew I was coming to Philadelphia, because I knew when I came here the people who come with me, including the press corps, would see what we're talking about when we talk about service and we say that everyone can serve, everyone can make a difference, and if all young people serve, we can turn this country around and put it in the right direction for every single child in America.

I want to thank so many people. I thank your principal, John Krauss; the superintendent and my longtime friend, David Hornbeck. And thank you, Harris Wofford, for doing a wonderful job with the Corporation for National Service. I kind of hated to hear David Hornbeck say we had more AmeriCorps volunteers in the Philadelphia schools than anywhere else because now somebody will think that he was doing the home folks a little home cooking. [*Laughter*] But I'm glad you're here. And you ought to be here in Philadelphia, where our country got started.

I want to thank the young AmeriCorps volunteers I just saw inside who work with Youth Build, Antoine Jackson and William McBride. I saw them in the school there. I'd like to thank your wonderful Congressman, Tom Foglietta, and Congressman Don Payne from New Jersey and Congressman Sam Ford who came all the way from California to be here with us today. We're glad to see them. I'd like to thank Latifah Beard and the other students here at the student council—the student body—who gave Hillary and me the gifts. And I'd like to say that I thought Tiffany and Daryl did a very good job introducing the First Lady, didn't you? [*Applause*] And finally, I'd like to thank Jahi Davis for speaking on behalf of all the AmeriCorps volunteers. He helped me with the President's Service Awards last night, and he said what he had to say today better than I ever could.

I just want to say to all of you that when I ran for President for the first time, starting now more than 5 years ago, I had a dream that I could give young people in this country a chance to serve in their communities, to help children, to make places safer, to make the schools work better, to deal with the health problems and the worries and the fears of our children and build up their hopes and, at the same time, earn a little money for a college education. That's how AmeriCorps was born.

I really dreamed that someday I could walk into a school like Nebinger Elementary and see what I saw today, two young people tutoring

5-year-olds, talking to them about their lives and their future. One of the young men actually dropped out of high school before joining AmeriCorps, but now, because of AmeriCorps, he wants to be able to help young people from now on and to go on with his own education. We learn that by giving and serving other people, we're actually helping ourselves.

I told somebody the other day that if we could get everybody in America to serve, we'd have the happiest country on Earth and people would see that service is selfish. Did you ever see an unhappy person who was really helping somebody else? Aren't you all happier because you're in Youth Build, because you're in the National School and Community Corps?

And that's what the Presidents and General Powell and others have come together to do here in Philadelphia at this Presidents' Summit of Service. We want to try to help guarantee that our children have a better future. And what I want to do is to challenge every young person in America to serve as a volunteer or as a full-time community service person.

Let me tell you, since AmeriCorps opened its door just 4 years ago, we've had 50,000 young people—and some not so young—50,000 serve in communities the way these young AmeriCorps volunteers are today. And it's making a difference for America's future. More importantly, the average AmeriCorps volunteer helps to generate another 12 part-time volunteers who come along and help. That, too, makes America strong.

And what I asked America to do today was to support me in making it possible for many more young people to serve, like Jahi and the other AmeriCorps volunteers have done, because I found out that here in Philadelphia there's another movement going on spearheaded by a minister who's a friend of mine named Tony Campolo. He's going around to churches and saying, "You ought to support young people the way AmeriCorps supports young people and pay for them to have living expenses so they can serve a year in community service work."

Today I said, if those young people do that through their churches or their synagogues or their mosques, through their community organizations, we will make sure, number one, if they're in college and they've got a student loan, that they don't have to pay any interest on the student loan during the year that they're working and no interest builds up. And number two, if they're willing to go out and meet the same standard of hard work and long hours that the AmeriCorps volunteers meet, they will also become eligible for the scholarship. That could bring 50,000 more young people into the kind of community service we see with Youth Build and with the National School and Community Corps.

And finally, let me say, you know what the project was that kids were working on in the class I just visited? Every one of them was talking about how they like to serve. Every one of those young children had to say, "I like to help. I like to do something," and then draw a picture of what they like to do. No one is too young to serve. No one is too old to serve.

We are the most diverse country in the world with a big democracy. We have people from all different races, all different ethnic groups, all different religions. But when we live together and work together and reach across the lines that divide us, we are the most interesting, the most powerful, the most vital country in human history. If we serve, that's the kind of country we'll be in the 21st century for all these children. That's my promise to you, and I want it to be your promise to yourselves.

God bless you, and keep it up.

NOTE: The President spoke at 2:46 p.m. at the George Washington Nebinger Elementary School. In his remarks, he referred to students Latifah Beard, Tiffany Way, and Daryl Way.

Letter to Congressional Leaders Transmitting a Report on Cyprus
April 25, 1997

Dear Mr. Speaker: (Dear Mr. Chairman:)

In accordance with Public Law 95–384 (22 U.S.C. 23732(c)), I submit to you this report on progress toward a negotiated settlement of the Cyprus question. The previous submission covered progress through November 30, 1996. The current submission covers the period December 1, 1996, through January 31, 1997.

As I noted to you in my last report, we have been very concerned about the decision by the Government of Cyprus to purchase the SA–10 anti-aircraft missile system and the resulting threats of a military strike by Turkey. The United States and its allies tried hard to persuade Cyprus that purchasing these missiles was a step leading away from negotiations, which remain the only way to solve the Cyprus problem. In the context of the already excessive levels of armaments on Cyprus and last summer's intercommunal violence, the government's decision to go forward with the purchases was doubly regrettable. Additionally, I remain disappointed that the parties have not implemented alternative measures to reduce tensions along the cease-fire lines. Despite these clear setbacks, I believe the decision by Cyprus, at our urging,

to defer importation of components of the SA–10 system for 16 months is a step in the right direction and provides us with a window of opportunity to make progress in resolving the Cyprus issue.

As Secretary Albright noted at her confirmation hearings, the parties need to take further steps to reduce tensions and improve the climate for negotiations. The United States remains committed to promoting a Cyprus settlement but needs the full cooperation of the parties, including Greece and Turkey, to achieve our mutual goals. We continue to see that the only way forward is direct, good faith negotiations between the parties themselves. The United States will continue to work toward bringing these negotiations about.

Sincerely,

WILLIAM J. CLINTON

NOTE: Identical letters were sent to Newt Gingrich, Speaker of the House of Representatives, and Jesse Helms, chairman, Senate Committee on Foreign Relations. This letter was released by the Office of the Press Secretary on April 29.

Statement on U.S. Sentencing Commission Action on Penalties for Drug Offenses
April 29, 1997

I commend the Sentencing Commission for moving forward with recommendations to Congress to reduce the disparity between crack and powder cocaine penalties. My administration will give them very serious consideration. I have asked Director McCaffrey and Attorney General Reno to review the recommendations and to report back to me in 60 days. I look forward to working with the Congress on this issue.

In October 1995, I signed legislation disapproving the Sentencing Commission's recommendation to equalize penalties for crack and powder cocaine distribution by dramatically reducing the penalties for crack. I believe that was the wrong approach then and would be the wrong approach now.

Current law creates a substantial disparity between sentences for crack and powder cocaine. This disparity has led to a perception of unfairness and inconsistency in the Federal criminal justice system.

The sentencing laws must continue to reflect that crack cocaine is a more harmful form of cocaine. The Sentencing Commission's new recommendations do so. Trafficking in crack, and the violence it fosters, has a devastating impact on communities across America, especially inner-city communities. Any change in penalties must ensure that more dangerous offenders receive tougher sentences.

As I have stated before, however, some adjustment to the cocaine penalty structure is warranted as a matter of sound criminal justice policy. Federal prosecutors should target mid- and high-level drug traffickers, rather than low-level drug offenders. An adjustment to the penalty scheme will help ensure this allocation of resources and make our Federal efforts in fighting drugs more effective. That is why the legislation I signed directed the Sentencing Commission to undertake additional review of these issues and to report back with new recommendations.

I am also pleased that the Sentencing Commission has increased penalties for methamphetamine offenses pursuant to the legislation which I signed into law last year. This law asked the Commission to toughen penalties on this emerging drug to prevent the kind of epidemic we saw in the 1980's with cocaine use. We will carefully study these new penalties.

My administration has fought to stop drug abuse and its destructive consequences. Overall, drug use in the United States has fallen dramatically—by half in 15 years. And cocaine use has dramatically decreased since the high point in 1985—the number of current cocaine users is down by 74 percent over the last decade. While these are encouraging figures, I am fully committed to doing more to keep bringing drug use down—particularly among our children.

Remarks Prior to Discussions With President Jose Aznar of Spain and an Exchange With Reporters
April 30, 1997

President Clinton. Well, let me begin by welcoming President Aznar and his group of leaders from Spain. Spain has set an example for the world now for quite a few years in its transition to a remarkable and healthy and vibrant democracy, which produced your recent election, and has been a very valuable ally and partner of the United States in Bosnia and now in Guatemala and, of course, is going to be the host of our summit on NATO in July. So we're looking very much forward to being there. And we appreciate you very much.

Yes, we have our fingers crossed. [*Laughter*]

Budget Agreement

Q. Have you got a budget deal, Mr. President? And why did Chelsea pick Stanford? [*Laughter*]

President Clinton. Not yet, but if you look at the economic news this morning, it is one more clear example that we did the right thing in '93 and that the right strategy is to bring the deficit down, expand trade, and invest in education and training and science and technology. And so, if we can get an agreement that does all that—that is, balances the budget but also continues to invest in the areas that our people need to grow the economy—then I will support it. And we're working hard. We worked hard yesterday. And perhaps it will happen.

Q. Before you go to Mexico?

President Clinton. Oh, I don't know about that.

Chelsea Clinton's College Selection

Q. Tell us about why Chelsea chose Stanford—why you think she did?

President Clinton. I don't know. She looked at all these schools, she had wonderful choices, and she made her own decision. And her mother and I are proud of her, and we support her.

You know, the great thing about America is that there are literally a few hundred world-class educational institutions in this country. And she didn't have a bad choice; she just picked the decision she though was best for her.

Q. How do you feel about her going so far away?

President Clinton. Well, the planes run out there, and the phones work out there. [*Laughter*] And the E-mail works out there. So we'll be all right.

Q. What was your role, sir, in the decision?

President Clinton. None, except I listened, asked questions, and attempted to have no influence whatever.

Hong Kong

Q. Mr. President, did you get any assurances from the Foreign Minister of Hong Kong that Hong Kong would enjoy greater autonomy under Chinese rule? Did you get any assurances?

President Clinton. Well, we had a good discussion about Hong Kong, and he assured me that China intended to observe the terms of the agreement of 1984 that they made with Great Britain and that the United States supported back then. I was quite satisfied with what

he said. And I certainly hope that it will reflect Chinese policy.

The Vice President. Thank you. *Muchas gracias.*

Extraterritorial Impact of Sanctions

Q. Do you consider the conflict on Helms-Burton completely finished, sir?

President Clinton. I hope so.

[*At this point, one group of reporters left the room, and another group entered.*]

Visit of President Aznar

President Clinton. Is everybody in?

Let me begin by welcoming President Aznar here to visit us. We have had a wonderful partnership with Spain for many years and have admired the vibrant democracy that the Spanish people enjoy, and have appreciated the partnership we have had with Spain in NATO, working together in Bosnia, most recently in Guatemala.

And I want to say a special word of appreciation, obviously, to the President for hosting the NATO summit in Madrid this July. I'm looking forward to that and hoping I can come a day or two early and look around Spain again, for the first time in 30 years.

President Aznar. You're invited; you know that. I hope to see you there.

[*At this point, President Aznar continued his remarks in Spanish, and a translation was not provided.*]

Role of Spain in NATO

Q. Mr. President, what do you expect from Spain with the new role that NATO has to play?

President Clinton. Well, first of all, I expect an important leadership role. We want Spain integrated fully into the NATO command structure. We're very fortunate in having a Secretary-General of NATO from Spain. And having Madrid be the site of this historic summit when we will vote for the first time to take in new members and hopefully be in a position to celebrate a new arrangement with Russia—we're working on that now; we hope we can achieve that—I think symbolizes the role that Spain will play in the years ahead in NATO.

Also, we look to the Spanish to lead in NATO, to be willing to do what has to be done, to have a say in situations which may not be immediately popular but which are profoundly important.

Again, let me say, I'm very grateful to the support we've received in Bosnia, to the work we're doing in Guatemala. The influence that Spain has in Latin America is something that's especially important to the United States because we seek to integrate ourselves more closely into Latin America and in partnership with Spain. So we're very hopeful there.

Q. [Inaudible]—petition for—taking a bigger role, more important role in the NATO?

President Clinton. Well, the details of all that have to be worked out by the command structure. But we want Spain integrated into the structure, yes.

President's Upcoming Visit to Spain

Q. [Inaudible]—will you come next?

President Clinton. I don't know. Since I've been President, I've only been really to Madrid, and for brief periods. But 30 years ago—28 years ago this month, I had a vacation as a very young man in Spain. And I've always wanted to go back, and I've always wanted to have a chance to see it with Hillary. My daughter was able to come to Spain for an extended period a couple of years ago. So we're hoping that we can take just a couple of days off before the summit to see some more things in Spain. I'll follow the President's lead; I won't sketch out my itinerary here because I don't really have one. *[Laughter]*

NOTE: The President spoke at 12:45 p.m. in the Oval Office at the White House. In his remarks, the President referred to Minister of Foreign Affairs Qian Qichen of China; and Javier Solana, Secretary-General of the North Atlantic Treaty Organization. A tape was not available for verification of the content of these remarks.

Statement on Economic Expansion and Job Creation
April 30, 1997

Today we have received positive news about the Nation's economy—more strong growth with moderate inflation. In the first quarter of this year, the economy grew 5.6 percent on an annualized basis—the highest in a decade. That means more jobs and better wages for American workers and stronger profits for businesses—both large and small. Our sound fiscal policies, together with the hard work of the American people, have sparked a remarkable period of economic expansion and job creation. It is imperative that we pass a bipartisan balanced budget agreement to continue this solid economic progress.

Just more than 4 years ago, we inherited a deficit that was nearly $300 billion, and we have cut it by 63 percent already. While it is still too early to know for certain, our economic policies and this year's healthy growth may help us cut the deficit for the 5th straight year—for the first time in 50 years. Now, it's time to finish the job and balance the budget.

Statement on the Senate Resolution Establishing National Erase the Hate and Eliminate Racism Day
April 30, 1997

I applaud the leadership of Senator Baucus, along with Senator Burns and all Members of the United States Senate who have joined together to designate today as a national day to erase the hate and eliminate racism. America is the world's most diverse democracy, and the world looks to us for leadership in building on that diversity and showing that it is our greatest strength. Today's resolution shows that the Senate is determined to reach across party lines to help achieve that promise.

We must do all we can to fight bigotry and intolerance, in ugly words and awful violence, in burned churches and bombed buildings—including efforts such as today's resolution. The only way we can meet our challenges is by meeting them together—as one America—and giving all of our citizens, whatever their background, an opportunity to achieve their own greatness.

Statement on Senate Confirmation of Alexis Herman as Secretary of Labor
April 30, 1997

I want to thank the Senate for its strong show of support for Alexis Herman. There was never any question that she was highly qualified to be Secretary of Labor. She understands the needs of workers and understands the challenges they face as we approach the 21st century.

This is an important time for the Labor Department. The Department must reform and manage programs that will help prepare America's working men and women for the challenges of our changing economy. Alexis Herman is fully prepared to lead the Department in this effort. She will be an outstanding Secretary of Labor.

Statement on House of Representatives Action on Adoption Promotion Legislation
April 30, 1997

I congratulate the House of Representatives on the passage of H.R. 867, the Adoption Promotion Act of 1997. This bipartisan legislation will further our efforts to give the children waiting in the foster care system what ever child in America deserves—loving parents and a healthy, stable home.

The First Lady and I have had a continuing commitment to uniting these waiting children with families to teach, guide, and care for them. In December, I directed the Department of Health and Human Services to come up with a strategy to simplify the adoption process and move more children more quickly from foster care into permanent homes. In response to this directive, HHS submitted Adoption 2002, a report which takes its name from one of its central goals—to double by the year 2002 the number of children adopted or permanently placed each year.

The Adoption Promotion Act of 1997 incorporates many of the recommendations made in the administration's report. I urge Congress to keep this important legislation moving forward.

Statement on Signing the Assisted Suicide Funding Restriction Act of 1997
April 30, 1997

Today I am signing into law H.R. 1003, the "Assisted Suicide Funding Restriction Act of 1997," which reaffirms current Federal policy banning the use of Federal funds to pay for assisted suicide, euthanasia, or mercy killing.

This is appropriate legislation. Over the years, I have clearly expressed my personal opposition to assisted suicide, and I continue to believe that assisted suicide is wrong. While I have deep sympathy for those who suffer greatly from incurable illness, I believe that to endorse assisted suicide would set us on a disturbing and perhaps dangerous path. This legislation will ensure that taxpayer dollars will not be used to subsidize or promote assisted suicide. The Act will, among other things, ban the funding of assisted suicide, euthanasia, or mercy killing through Medicaid, Medicare, military and Federal employee health plans, the veterans health care system, and other Federally funded programs.

Section 5(a)(3) of the Act also assures that taxpayer funds will not be used to subsidize legal assistance or other forms of advocacy in support of legal protection for assisted suicide, euthanasia, or mercy killing. The restrictions on the use of funds contained in this section, properly construed, will allow the Federal Government to speak with a clear voice in opposing these practices. The Department of Justice has advised, however, that a broad construction of this section would raise serious First Amendment concerns. I am therefore instructing the Federal agencies that they should construe sec-

tion 5(a)(3) only to prohibit Federal funding for activities and services that provide legal assistance for the purpose of advocating a right to assisted suicide, or that have as their purpose the advocacy of assisted suicide, and not to restrict Federal funding for other activities, such as those that provide forums for the free exchange of ideas. In addition, I emphasize that section 5(a)(3) imposes no restriction on the use of nonfederal funds.

WILLIAM J. CLINTON

The White House,
April 30, 1997.

NOTE: H.R. 1003, approved April 30, was assigned Public Law No. 105–12.

Memorandum on Excused Absence for Employees Affected by the Flooding of the Red River and Its Aftermath
April 30, 1997

Memorandum for the Heads of Executive Departments and Agencies

Subject: Excused Absence for Employees Affected by the Flooding of the Red River and its Aftermath

I am deeply concerned about the devastating losses caused by the flooding of the Red River and the impact on the well-being and livelihood of our fellow Americans who have been affected by this disaster. Elements of the Federal Government have been mobilized to respond to this disaster.

As part of this effort, I request the heads of executive departments and agencies, who

have Federal civilian employees in Minnesota, North Dakota, and South Dakota in areas designated as disaster areas because of the flooding of the Red River and its aftermath, to use their discretion to excuse from duty, without charge to leave or loss of pay, any such employee who is faced with a personal emergency because of this flood and who can be spared from his or her usual responsibilities. This policy should also be applied to any employee who is needed for emergency law enforcement, relief, or clean-up efforts authorized by Federal, State, or local officials having jurisdiction.

WILLIAM J. CLINTON

Remarks Commemorating the Centennial of the Thomas Jefferson Building at the Library of Congress
April 30, 1997

I ask you tonight to listen to these words as if you had never heard them before and try to imagine what it was like when they broke across the landscape of America and the world, arguably the most important words ever written

by an American because out of them all the rest flowed:

"When in the Course of human events, it becomes necessary for one people to dissolve the political bonds which have connected them to another, and to assume among the powers of the earth, the separate and equal station to which the Laws of Nature and of Nature's God entitle them, a decent respect to the opinions of mankind requires that they should declare the causes which impel them to the separation.—We hold these truths to be self-evident, that all men are created equal, that they are endowed by their Creator with certain unalienable Rights, that among these are Life, Liberty and the pursuit of Happiness.—That to secure these rights, Governments are instituted among Men, deriving their just powers from the consent of the governed . . . . But when a long train of abuses and usurpations, pursuing invariably the same Object evinces a design to reduce them under absolute Despotism, it is their right, it is their duty, to throw off such Government, and to provide new Guards for their future security. . . . We, therefore, the Representatives of the United States of America, in General Congress, Assembled, appealing to the Supreme Judge of the world for the rectitude of our intentions, do, in the Name, and by the Authority of the good People of these Colonies, solemnly publish and declare, That these United Colonies are, and of Right ought to be Free and Independent States; . . . And for the support of this Declaration, with a firm reliance on the protection of Divine Providence, we mutually pledge to each other our Lives, our Fortunes and our sacred Honor."

Mr. Chief Justice, Mr. Speaker, Senator Daschle, Congressman Thomas, and other Members of Congress, the Joint Commission on the Library, Mr. Kluge, and the James Madison Council. Mr. Allaire, thank you all for what you have done to make this night come to pass. I thank Michael Ryan for singing the national anthem and making us feel so patriotic. He has served our country, as many of you know, for many years. I thank Jim Billington for his brilliant job and all the staff here for what they have done.

Those words were Thomas Jefferson's words, with edits by John Adams and Benjamin Franklin. I learned something tonight looking at the Thomas Jefferson draft: Ben Franklin gets credit for saying that these truths are self-evident. And that's a pretty good edit. [*Laughter*] Would that we all had such an editor.

As the Speaker said, now every American will be able to have access to these treasures, not only in this magnificent building with its glorious reading room and its American treasures exhibition but also through the Internet. Think of it, everything from the rough draft of the Declaration of Independence, from which I just read, to George Washington's letter on the importance of religious freedom, to the first known autobiography of a slave, to the first kiss captured in a movie, to Groucho Marx talking to Johnny Carson, to the magical music of Washington's Duke Ellington.

But it is fitting that the books from Mr. Jefferson's library are at the core of the American Treasures Collection, for he above all understood that democracy and liberty depend upon the free flow of ideas and the expansion of knowledge, upon the remembrance of history and the imagining of the future.

To pursue those objectives, our young Nation, at great cost, established this Library. From those first volumes, the Library of Congress has become the world's largest library, visited by 2 million people every year in person and millions more every week on the Internet Web site, with more to come as we work together to enable every school and library in the United States to connect to the Internet. In the most modern way, children in the most isolated rural districts, the poorest inner-city districts, the most comfortable suburbs, now will be able to share that rough draft of the Declaration of Independence and all the other wonderful resources of the Library.

Mr. Jefferson, who looked to the future more than the past, even at the end of his days, would surely be very proud, Mr. Billington, of what his library has become.

As we walk through these beautifully restored rooms and hallways on this 100th anniversary, you can almost feel the exuberance and optimism of the United States at the turn of the century. And now, at the dawn of a new century, we face yet a new age of possibilities, full of new challenge and hope. Yet in a sense, we are back where we were in the beginning. For of all our challenges, ignorance is the most threatening, and of all our riches, knowledge is the most enduring, except this will be even more true in the years ahead.

That is why the opening of this exhibit and the restoration of this building is so significant. By renewing the Founders' commitment to the Library of Congress, we ensure that future generations will continue to be inspired and guided by the ideals, the values, and the thirst for knowledge that are at our beginning core. We are giving all of our people, especially our children, what they will need to realize their dreams and our ever-unfolding destiny as a nation.

As these exhibits show, we are, and have ever been, a nation of creators and innovators. We are all Jefferson's heirs, and we are doomed sometimes to succeed and sometimes to fail. I was amused at the picture of the massive double circular kite that Alexander Graham Bell thought might compete with the Wright brothers. He would do very well on the Frisbee circuit today, I think, but it wasn't much of an airplane. But if he hadn't had the courage to try that, well, we might not have had the telephone. We must always maintain that spirit, and we must remember the words of Jefferson.

President Lincoln invoked the Jeffersonian ideal to heal a wounded nation as he stood at Gettysburg. President Roosevelt looked toward the world that would follow World War II, and he too called upon Jefferson for inspiration and courage. The words that he wrote then are as relevant today as they were in 1945, and I would like to close with them.

"We must do all in our power to conquer the doubts and the fear, the ignorance and the greed, for today science has brought all the different quarters of the globe so close together that it is impossible to isolate them one from another. Today we are faced with the preeminent fact that if civilization is to survive, we must cultivate the science of human relationships, the ability of all peoples of all kinds to live together and work together in the same world at peace. And to you and to all Americans who dedicate themselves with us to the making of an abiding peace, I say the only limit to our realization of tomorrow will be our doubts of today. Let us move forward with strong and active faith."

That was the speech Franklin Roosevelt was working on in this month, 52 years ago, when he died in Warm Springs. Though unspoken, his words, like those of Jefferson, come down to us today with a freshness, a vitality, and a fundamental truth that must forever guide us as a nation.

On Friday, we will gather to dedicate the memorial to President Roosevelt, the very first Presidential memorial since President Roosevelt dedicated the one to Thomas Jefferson in 1943. Together we will renew our commitment to fight tyranny with liberty, ignorance with knowledge, fear with hope and confidence.

Thomas Jefferson and Franklin Roosevelt, I believe, would be quite proud of America today—still eager to right its wrongs and seize its new opportunities. And I might say, I think they'd be a little impatient with those among us who, finding America at the pinnacle of its power, influence, and success, and therefore at the pinnacle of the responsibility outlined by President Roosevelt so long ago, would seek to walk away from what are our plain obligations to engage the rest of the world. For in the course of human events, it has fallen to us, for our own benefit and because it is right, to extend to a waiting world the ideals to which Thomas Jefferson and his friends pledged their lives, their fortunes, and their sacred honor.

Thank you, and God bless America.

NOTE: The President spoke at 8:10 p.m. In his remarks, he referred to John Kluge, chairman, James Madison Council; Paul Allaire, chairman and chief executive officer, Xerox Corp.; MGySgt. Michael Ryan, USMC, United States Marine Band; and James H. Billington, Librarian of Congress.

Interview With the San Antonio Express News, the Los Angeles Times, and the Dallas Morning News
May 1, 1997

The President. Hello?

Elizabeth Shogren. Mr. President, good morning. This is Elizabeth Shogren with the L.A. Times.

The President. Hi, Elizabeth.

Ms. Shogren. How's it going?

The President. Fine, thank you.

Mexico-U.S. Antidrug Efforts

Ms. Shogren. I spoke with Senator Feinstein a couple minutes ago, and she mentioned to me some particular evidence of progress on drug issues that she'd like to see from your trip—in particular, indications from the Mexicans that they're going ahead with money-laundering law and will give DEA agents permission to carry sidearms. I wondered if you are going to press for measurable indications from Mexico of progress on the drug issues or if you have some other strategy?

The President. Well, first of all, as you know because it's reported in the press today, the Mexicans have announced significant reorganization of their antidrug effort, which I think is very encouraging. And they have cooperated with us in a number of ways. As you know, we do have DEA agents assigned to our Embassy in Mexico City in a liaison capacity. We are committed, both of us, to increasing our law enforcement, counter-drug cooperation, and we're committed to the safety of our law enforcement personnel, and we're working with the Government of Mexico to make sure we can assure their security. So I feel that we will be able to resolve that.

But our participation in task forces, in terms of being detailed to Mexico, will have to require some resolution of this safety issue, but we're working on it. They have done—in almost every other area, they have continued to cooperate with us and have produced a lot of results, and money laundering is the next thing we're working on.

But I believe you'd have to say that Zedillo's government has worked with us. Now, we know what the problem is in a lot of these countries that are dealing with poor people, often living in reasonably remote areas and with unlimited amounts of money to try to corrupt local officials. But I believe that Zedillo and his team are committed to trying to work with us, not because they want to work with us any more than they want to clean up Mexico and have Mexico be a good place for the people who live there.

We both have a huge stake in this anti-drug effort. Obviously, for us, we're trying to keep drugs from being imported into the United States; for them, they're trying to keep the narcotraffickers from undermining the integrity of their democracy and the long-term success and stability of their society.

So I'm—that's why I've strongly supported continuing their certification status. I think they want to work with us, and we're going to keep doing it.

Kathy Lewis. Mr. President, this is Kathy Lewis [Dallas Morning News].

The President. Hi, Kathy.

Ms. Lewis. Hi. There was a report this weekend that the U.S. has quietly been debating proposals to impose economic penalties against Mexican drug traffickers. How seriously are you considering freezing U.S. assets and blocking traffickers' access to their bank accounts? And have you made a decision?

The President. Well, we work on that all the time. And if we can identify people whose assets—who are narcotraffickers and whose assets we can legally freeze, we would do that without hesitation. We have—I'm very encouraged that we have increased our capacity to identify, for example, Colombian companies that are essentially fronts for drug money and are able to freeze their assets and limit their activities in the United States. So we would do that for companies from anywhere, and we're working on it all that time.

Mexico-U.S. Trade

Gary Martin. Mr. President, this is Gary Martin with the San Antonio Express News.

The President. Hi, Gary.

Mr. Martin. Hi. Your administration has been criticized in Texas, by Texas officials, for banning organized labor and delaying the implementation of NAFTA accords that would allow Mexican and U.S. truckers to haul cargo into border States. What's being done to resolve that issue? And will we see an announcement lifting the ban made in Mexico City?

The President. Well, we're working hard on that. But let me just say, we think there are some legitimate questions which we raised. And we believe that we're committed and duty bound to allow Mexican motor carriers and drivers to operate in the United States if they are safe. And we're trying to identify steps that we can agree upon between the United States and Mexico to jointly take to benefit the motor carriers and the customers and enhance public safety and security at the same time.

Our trade—U.S.-Mexico trade came to $130 billion in 1996. If you have a relationship this broad, there is going to be some areas of disagreement, just like we have continuing areas of disagreement with our neighbor to the north, Canada. But that represents a very small portion of our bilateral commerce. And we have to try to resolve it.

We've had a couple of other disagreements. We're trying to work through these things. But they're going to—we knew from the beginning that there would be some areas of disagreement, that no comprehensive agreement like this is perfect. But I think it's clearly been best for both Mexico and the United States.

Antidrug Efforts

Ms. Shogren. Mr. President, this is Elizabeth Shogren again. Given that the certification process, as it stands now, has given you and the Congress and the Mexican people so much trouble each time it comes up—it's a huge hassle—do you have any plans to change that process? And will you speak about these plans with President Zedillo or others in Mexico?

The President. Well, I don't expect that we will discuss that since that decision is behind us now, assuming we continue our cooperation here. But I believe that the question of whether this whole certification system is the best way of dealing with the fight against drugs and securing cooperation is a legitimate question. There's a lot of debate about it in the Congress now. Congressman Lee Hamilton made a public statement about it just a couple of days ago. I know that the Speaker and others have voiced their questions about it. And what I have tried to do here is to set in motion a little bipartisan discussion in the Congress about it, try to evaluate whether we should keep the system we have and, if we change it, what we put in its place, what they believe the best alternatives are.

It's the sort of thing that it's easy to demagog if you seek to change it, but if it's not working, we at least ought to—or if there's serious reason to doubt whether it's the most effective way to fight drugs, then we ought to have an honest evaluation of it. I know General McCaffrey has some questions about it. So what I've asked our people to do is to try to get knowledgeable people in the Congress together on both sides and really take a hard look at this and make a recommendation to us and see if we can't make a bipartisan decision here and move forward with that.

You don't want to do something which appears on the surface to be tough but actually undermines the ultimate objective. The ultimate objective is to reduce the volume of drugs coming into the United States.

Ms. Shogren. Right.

The President. So, yes, we're looking at it.

Mexico-U.S. Relations

Ms. Lewis. Mr. President, U.S.-Mexico relations are always delicate, but you're traveling there at a particularly sensitive time because of drugs and immigration and the concern about it on both sides. Will you be able to address that with both the people of Mexico and those in the United States having their concerns eased? And also, do you feel the trust has been recovered that was lost since the decertification debate and the arrest of Mexico's drug czar?

The President. Well, first of all, I think we ought to see this in the larger context. I mean, if you compare our relationship with Mexico today, for example, with several years ago, there's no question that we're stronger today, that when NAFTA was passed it brought us closer together commercially, that we were growing closer together anyway, that the fact that we came to Mexico's aid when the economy was teetering and threatening to destabilize the economies of many other Latin American countries, and that, in turn, they paid their loan back to us ahead of schedule and with $500 million profit in interest. I think those things ought to be seen as enormous positives, bespeaking a new partnership. They were also— Mexico is a very active part of the Summit of the Americas, and we know that a lot of our common future is tied up with Mexico.

Secondly, with regard to immigration, keep in mind that the United States is now the fifth largest Hispanic nation in the world, with 22 million legal residents. And obviously, they're from many, many different countries, but the largest source is Mexico.

So I think that we have a positive trend here toward economic reform in Mexico, toward political reform with a third of Mexico's people living, at the State and local level, under opposition party leaders to the governing party, freely elected in free elections. And now I think there's a serious effort being made to deal with the drug issues.

So the framework, I think, is quite positive, especially if you look to the years ahead. Now, what we have to do is just to continue to work on our economic relationship, continue to work on the narcotrafficking. And what I think for our part in the United States we have to do is to make—on the immigration issue, I think it is absolutely imperative that the provisions that were tacked onto the welfare bill—they're not part of the welfare reform bill, they were tacked onto the welfare reform bill—hostile to legal immigrants already living in this country be changed.

And I think it's important for us to be sensitive in the way that we implement the new law dealing with illegal immigration. But after all, what that law requires us to do, it seems to me, is eminently sensible. It gives us the tools to strengthen border control, to toughen worksite enforcement, and to increase the removal of criminal aliens and others who are deportable and come in contact with the Government in some way.

I think that this is not an anti-immigrant country. We let in 960,000 immigrants legally last year. But we do have to do our very best to see that any immigrant who comes into this country, comes in legally. And if there are no consequences to coming in illegally, it will be impossible to do that.

So we have to do this in a humane and decent way. We have to continue to show that we're a nation of laws. We have to respect human rights and not have any kind of discriminatory treatment or massive deportations. But this new law will give us tools we need to try to increase the integrity of our immigration system so that we can continue to maintain support for legal immigration but be more effective in deterring illegal immigration.

Murderer of DEA Agent

Mr. Martin. Mr. President, what do you plan to say to President Zedillo about the Mexican judicial system's decision to vacate a killer's conviction for the slaying of DEA agent Enrique Camarena, which many Americans believe smacks of official corruption itself?

The President. Well, it's my understanding that he's seeking to use a procedure that's similar to our habeas corpus procedure to appeal the conviction. And furthermore, it's my understanding that even if he were to win his appeal, he'll still be subject to 35 more years in jail in Mexico.

In any case, we have a standing immediate-arrest request in Mexico for the purpose of extraditing him to the United States as soon as he's released from confinement in Mexico for whatever reasons. So, if he's going to serve 35 more years in jail, that's one thing. If for some reason we're wrong about our understanding of the facts and a court would release him, we would expect his immediate extradition to the United States so that he could be prosecuted here.

Deputy Press Secretary Mary Ellen Glynn. OK, thanks everyone.

Mr. Martin. Thank you.

Ms. Shogren. Thank you, Mr. President.

Ms. Lewis. Thank you.

The President. Goodbye. Thank you.

NOTE: The President spoke at 11:22 a.m. by telephone from the Oval Office at the White House. In his remarks, he referred to President Ernesto Zedillo of Mexico and Rafael Caro Quintero, who was convicted of the murder of DEA agent Enrique Camarena.

Interview With Jacobo Goldstein of CNN Radio Noticias
May 1, 1997

Mexico-U.S. Antidrug Efforts

Mr. Goldstein. Mr. President, let's start with Mexico. You're going down there on Monday. The news today is that Mexico just dismantled its antidrug agency and has put a new agency in place with new trainees. Will this stop the corruption that has been so rampant?

The President. Well, I think there's a good chance that it will improve things. Keep in mind the Mexicans have a big challenge. This is not just something they—this cooperation we're undertaking in the antidrug area from Mexico's point of view is not primarily for the United

States. Of course, we want to reduce the number of illegal drugs coming into America. Primarily, it's for Mexico. It's to preserve the social, political, and economic integrity of the country.

And I think this is a very good first step. I've had a good relationship with President Zedillo and with Mexico since I became President. I've done everything I could do to try to make sure America is a good neighbor and a good partner for the future. And I think this will enable us to work more closely together in that area.

Elections in Mexico

Mr. Goldstein. Mr. President, Mexico is going to have midterm elections that are going to be watched throughout the world. And I know President Zedillo has been trying to change some of old time and change the structure of his party. What are your expectations of these midterm elections? It's the first time the mayor of Mexico City is going to be elected.

The President. I don't know. My only expectations are that they'll be free and fair and that they will express the will of the Mexican people and that we will support that, whatever that is.

NAFTA and Trade Expansion

Mr. Goldstein. Mr. President, NAFTA, according to the numbers, seems to be working. Do you expect the U.S. Congress to help push NAFTA to Chile fast-track? And you have spoken, and your people have spoken, how important Latin America is as far as a trading partner, but does Congress share your view, sir?

The President. I believe a majority do. I am, frankly, disappointed and surprised that there is still so much opposition to expanding fast-track. NAFTA has been a big success for us, with Canada and with Mexico. It has helped the Mexican economy to grow. It has brought our two countries closer together. When Mexico had a difficult time economically, the United States made the loan that—I made the decision to make a loan to Mexico, and they paid the loan back early with interest and a profit. And it's working well. It's creating more jobs for Mexico, more jobs for the United States.

And I think we would be very, very, very shortsighted if we did not extend fast-track, go down and involve Chile, and then eventually complete the promise of the Summit of the Americas—involve the Andean nations, the

MERCOSUR nations, all the nations, Latin America, Central America, Caribbean in the trade area of the Americas. That's what I want to do, and I'm going to keep pushing for it.

Nomination for Ambassador to Mexico

Mr. Goldstein. Mr. President, you placed great importance on the relations with Mexico, personal relation between you and President Zedillo. And now the word is out, you're going to be naming a very famous politician of the other party, the Governor of Massachusetts, Governor William Weld. How will this create better relations between you and Mexico?

The President. Well, if Governor Weld's appointment goes through, I would expect it to greatly strengthen our relationships because I think that they will have a lot in common and that the three of us will all have a good relationship, which will facilitate our countries growing closer together and working better together.

Mr. Goldstein. Will he have direct access to you and Madeleine Albright?

The President. Oh, absolutely. I know him well. I mean, he is a member of the other party, and when he ran against Senator Kerry last year, I worked very hard for Senator Kerry. But we have a good personal relationship. He's a highly intelligent man, and he and I are clearly on the same wavelength in terms of what we believe our policy toward Mexico and, indeed, toward all Latin America should be.

Human Rights

Mr. Goldstein. Finally, Mr. President, I want to touch slightly the issue of human rights. There has been some criticism of violation of human rights in Mexico. Will the subject of human rights be broached during the bilateral meeting, or will you deal—with President Zedillo?

The President. I expect we will discuss everything that is out there to be discussed in our relationship. We have a very open and candid relationship. If he has some problems with the United States, he feels free to raise them with me. And we'll talk through everything I think we should talk through.

Immigration

Mr. Goldstein. Migrations—the new migration laws have created a huge stir in Mexico and Central America, also—the issue, that will come up?

The President. It will come up, and it should. I would like to make three points. First of all, there were provisions dealing with legal immigrants tacked onto the welfare reform bill that had nothing to do with welfare reform, that I strongly opposed, and that will have to be significantly changed if we are going to get a budget agreement here with the Republican Congress. I have told them that, and we're working hard on it.

Secondly, with regard to the law dealing with illegal immigration, I know that there are some questions about that law in Latin America. But let me point out, the main thing the law does is to give us extra tools to control our borders, to deal with illegal immigrants in our workplaces and who come into the criminal justice system.

We are going to work very hard to avoid any draconian interpretation of the law that would lead to any kind of mass deportations or anything of that kind. But keep in mind, the United States admitted last year 960,000 legal immigrants. We are now the fifth largest Hispanic country in the world, with 22 million Hispanic-Americans here. So we are committed to open immigration and to having more people here from the Americas, but we have to do it in a legal way that has some discipline and order and integrity to it. And we will try to do it in a fair and balanced way.

Mexico-U.S. Trade and NAFTA

Mr. Goldstein. Mr. President, there was some concern in Mexico when Mexican trucks were not allowed—truckers to drive in this country. I'm sure that issue will also come up.

The President. It will come up. President Zedillo would bring it up if I didn't. We will—we're trying to work that out. Our concerns here are basically safety concerns, and we have an obligation under NAFTA, the United States does, to permit Mexican truckers into the United States if they meet the standards that we apply to our people. And we're trying to work out exactly how we define that and resolve it with the Mexicans.

There have been actually relatively few trade disputes. This is now a $130 billion trade relationship. It's a huge relationship. And we have two or three relatively minor matters—[*inaudible*]—all but one. And I think we have to work very hard to try to rectify the economic harm done to the Caribbean countries inadvertently by Congress when they adopted NAFTA but

wouldn't go along with my suggestion to give the same treatment to the Caribbean countries.

Mr. Goldstein. Excuse me, by Caribbean you mean Central America and the Caribbean Basin?

The President. Caribbean Basin, absolutely. All the Caribbean Basin countries. We did not—I don't think the Congress meant to hurt them by passing NAFTA, but I told them what I was afraid would happen. I asked them to at least maintain the status quo, so that they wouldn't lose any ground compared to Mexico because Mexico's great gains have come from the labors of the Mexican people and from the transfer of some production from Asia back to Mexico. They never intended to take anything away from the Central America and Caribbean countries.

So we have to rectify that because those countries have to have a chance to grow. Otherwise, the more successful Mexico is in its antidrug efforts, the more vulnerable the Caribbean countries will be—especially the Caribbean, even more than Central America. They will become even more vulnerable to drug traffickers because they won't be able to make a living there. So we've got to rectify this, and I'm hoping to resolve it with this session of Congress.

Immigration

Mr. Goldstein. Mr. President, the Central American countries will also bring up the immigration issue because El Salvador, Guatemala, Nicaragua, Honduras—they were all deeply affected in the eighties during the liberation or revolution, the civil wars of the eighties.

The President. They—because of the unique status that they bore when they came into this country, they are in a position different from legal immigrants or plainly illegal immigrants. They are in a different position. And we've already had one discussion, interestingly enough, about that today. We're trying to work that out in a way that seems fair and humane and balanced, and I hope we can.

Hostage Situation in Peru

Mr. Goldstein. Mr. President, I would like to ask you two questions as they're pushing me out. One has to do with Peru. You were very much involved, your country was, with Japan during the hostage crisis, which came to a conclusion a few days ago.

The President. Yes.

Mr. Goldstein. There seems to be some rumblings about some possible human rights violations when the army barged in and saved the hostages. Do you know anything about it or——

The President. No.

Mr. Goldstein. ——have you had any conversations with Mr. Fujimori?

The President. I do not know what the facts are on that. I do know that the Government of Peru was very patient for a long time, that the people who took the hostages were terrorists who threatened their lives, and that it was a good thing and remarkable that only one of them was—life was lost in the rescue attempt. But I do not know what the facts were about what happened on the compound.

Extraterritorial Impact of Sanctions

Mr. Goldstein. Mr. President, finally, you know Cuba is an issue. Helms-Burton has created a rift—between Latin America and the United States because of Cuba and Helms-Burton. Do you visualize any circumstances under which Helms-Burton could be lifted? And do you feel this will not threaten your commercial relations and political relations with the Latin American nations?

The President. Well, first of all, I think the biggest problem with Helms-Burton, vis-a-vis Latin America, may well have been solved by the resolution we made with the European Union about the interpretation of Helms-Burton. And I think if we look at what happened with the European Union, what we want the other democracies of Central America and Caribbean and South America to do is to work with us on promoting openness, human rights, and freedom in Cuba, and we need to do that every way we can.

Now, under the statute, the Helms-Burton statute, about the only agreements I can work out are the ones that—like we worked out with Europe. That law supplanted a bill that I liked very much, the Cuba Democracy Act, which gave the United States the flexibility to be both more open and tougher with Cuba, depending on the facts. But that law was passed by Mr. Castro himself. He passed the law as surely as if he'd been here voting on it when he shot down those planes and killed those innocent people.

So we're doing the best we can with the law we have, but we all need to keep working for greater openness in Cuba. I think the only prospects for a change in the law would be those that are, again, completely within the control of the Cuban Government and of Mr. Castro. I mean, if he were to evidence some changes, then he might get some changed attitudes here. But we've got to see what happens.

NAFTA and Trade Expansion

Mr. Goldstein. Finally, Mr. President, you—during your first term, you fought very hard for NAFTA against your own party. You fought very hard to save Mexico—the economic bailout—against people of your own party including. Will you fight as hard now that you don't need to run for reelection? Political considerations aside, will you fight just as hard to make sure that Latin America has a free trade agreement?

The President. Oh, sure.

Mr. Goldstein. It may take about a year or two. And are you optimistic you can do it by the year 2005, as they said in Miami at the Summit of the Americas?

The President. Well, yes, I will fight just as hard. And I will certainly—there are no political considerations for me one way or the other now. I would like to point out we did get quite a large number of Democrats who supported NAFTA and that the leadership in both parties supported me with the Mexican loan.

I'm quite concerned that there may have been an erosion of support for the free trade concept in the Americas, not just in the Democratic Party but in the Republican Party as well. And I find this surprising. Here we are now at the pinnacle of our economic success, political influence in the world, but the only way we can exercise our political influence for good is to become involved with other countries. And it disappoints me when I hear Americans who seemed to be reluctant to do that. I think that's a mistake. And so I'm going to try to persuade them to do the right thing from my point of view, and I believe we'll win.

Budget Agreement

Mr. Goldstein. And will you get a budget agreement? Everybody in the basement asked me to ask you——

The President. I don't know. I hope so.

Mr. Goldstein. Thank you, sir.

NOTE: The interview began at 11:42 a.m. in the Oval Office at the White House. In his remarks, the President referred to President Ernesto

Zedillo of Mexico; President Alberto Fujimori of Peru; and President Fidel Castro of Cuba. A tape was not available for verification of the content of this interview.

Statement on the Interim Report of the Presidential Advisory Committee on Gulf War Veterans' Illnesses
May 1, 1997

I appreciate the ongoing, rigorous work of the Presidential Advisory Committee on Gulf War Veterans' Illnesses, and I welcome their interim letter report.

The care and well-being of our Gulf war veterans is a national duty and a national priority. That is why I appointed the Committee in May 1995, extended its mandate in January 1997, and directed its attention in February 1997 to the recently released intelligence documents concerning possible chemical exposures.

I am determined that my administration will do everything necessary to uncover all the facts and act on any relevant information, to provide our Gulf war veterans with the quality medical care they need, and to make sure that in any future troop deployments, we draw on lessons learned in the Gulf war to better protect the health of our troops and their families.

This interim report, like those that preceded it, will help us meet that responsibility in an increasingly effective way. I have asked the Secretaries of Defense, Veterans Affairs, and Health and Human Services, as well as the Acting Director of Central Intelligence, to study the report and, 2 weeks from today, provide me their proposals for implementing the Committee's recommendations.

To further strengthen our search for the facts, Secretary Cohen and Acting DCI Tenet have asked former Senator Warren Rudman to review the results of their ongoing investigations related to Gulf war illnesses and to offer appropriate recommendations. Senator Rudman brings solid expertise and sound judgment to this important job. I am confident he will assist the Department of Defense and the Central Intelligence Agency in ensuring their investigations are thorough and will also enhance our ability to integrate Gulf war intelligence "lessons learned" into our future planning.

I am grateful for the PAC's dedication and persistence, and look forward to their continued, indispensable efforts to make sure no stone is left unturned on behalf of America's Gulf war veterans. We will not rest in our determination to find the answers our service men and women need and ensure that they receive the care and benefits they deserve.

Remarks at a Democratic National Committee Dinner
May 1, 1997

Thank you very much. Mr. Vice President, thank you for that overly generous introduction. I loved every word of it. [*Laughter*] That 5 minutes was the best 5 minutes I ever lost in my Presidency. He hasn't been the same person since.

I want to thank Tipper and Al and Hillary, all of them in their various ways for being unique parts of our rather unique team. I want to thank Tommy Lee Jones for coming here tonight and for giving that fine speech and being loyal to his old friend Al Gore.

You know, I'm not as mobile as I normally am, and I've been in this big old awkward chair, and I heard Tommy Lee's voice sort of booming out, you know, and I couldn't decide whether I was the fugitive and I ought to be on the run, whether I was Batman and I should duck— I didn't know what I should do. [*Laughter*] You know, I really enjoyed watching Tommy Lee and Al's friendship; they have a lot in common.

They sort of like to shoot the bull, and when they get around each other—they've been friends so long—their accents get thicker, you know, and the stories get more embellished. Just like any other two rednecks from Harvard you ever met. [*Laughter*]

I want to thank our distinguished leaders, Governor Romer and Steve Grossman, and the dinner chairs: Abe Pollin, Tommy Boggs, Morty Bahr, Janice Griffin, Bob Johnson. Thank you, Alan Solomont and Dan Dutko and Carol Pensky. Thanks to the entertainers. But I'd like to ask you all to give a special hand to our dinner chairs; they worked like crazy to bring this off for us tonight and I thank them for it very much.

I won't take long tonight, but I want to just reinforce a couple of things the Vice President said. Tomorrow we're going to dedicate this memorial to Franklin Roosevelt, a man who believed in bold, persistent experimentation; a man who became President at the country's lowest ebb in this century and whose faith and optimism and determination carried us a very long way. When Al Gore and I sought your support and the votes of the American people in 1992, we were, thankfully, in nowhere near that much trouble. But it was clear that we were in the midst of drift and division and deadlock. It was clear that we were going through a period of profound change, moving into a new century, a new millennium, and a new way of living together, and that we had, as a nation, no clear strategy to pursue.

And I had a simple idea that I wanted my daughter and her children to grow up in an America in the 21st century where everyone willing to work for it had opportunity; where all citizens recognized that there were no rights without responsibility; where we cherish our diversity, instead of being torn asunder by it, and we grew together, closer as one America; and where we embrace the world, instead of running away from it, and we're glad to be still the leading force for peace and freedom and prosperity. That is what I want, that is what I wanted, and that is what we are going to have in the 21st century, thanks to you and millions of Americans like you all across this country.

And I thought to do it, we would have to experiment. I had some ideas that people said were nutty, and they weren't appropriately pure. They were not perfectly liberal or perfectly conservative. I had this crazy idea that you could reduce the deficit and still increase investment in people, in education; that you could actually reduce the size of Government but put more money into the things people needed; that you could actually help business and labor; that you could actually grow the economy and preserve and even improve the environment.

Now, we started this economic program, and all of our friends in the other party voted against it and said it was crazy and it would never work. Well, sooner or later, the posturing has to not count nearly as much as the results. We've had a record number of new jobs, a record number of new businesses. We have the strongest, healthiest economy in 30 years, and wages are going up and inequality in this country is going down among working families for the first time in over 20 years. And you should be proud of that because you made it happen. I'm proud of it, and I want you to be proud of it.

I had this idea that crime was not a political football that you should position yourself around in Washington with a bunch of rhetoric, that it really would make a difference if we put community policing back into America's streets, and we put more police on the street. Not just Dwayne and Eddie, the two that Al put when he was President, but—[*laughter*]—99,998 more. And we're well on the way.

And I thought it was silly to say that an American citizen couldn't favor the right of sports people and hunters to use their weapons and not be for sensible restraints on gun ownership and acquisition by criminals, and dangerous people and people who were incompetent should not have them. I thought that was wrong.

When we passed the crime bill, they said, well, it didn't fit into anybody's little box. All I know is crime is still going down every year; there are more police on the street; America is a safer place today because we were interested in what would work to fulfill our values. And if people are not secure in America, they are not fully free. We were right, and you should be proud of that. I want you to be proud of it.

Well, I could go through a lot of other issues. I'm proud of what we did in Haiti and Bosnia and the Middle East and Northern Ireland. I'm proud of the way we reached out to Russia and to expand NATO. I'm proud of the fact that we said we are going forward as one country, and we started the AmeriCorps program to give young people a chance to serve their country and earn some money to go to college.

And as I look back on it, I would have to say that, thanks to all those things and the family and medical leave law, the initiative on tobacco, and a lot of other things, this country has more opportunity, more responsibility, a closer knit community, and is stronger in the world in its leadership role than it would have been if we'd stayed the course that was dominant in 1992—you were right, and you should be proud of it—and a whole lot better off than we'd have been if the "Contract With America" had not been stopped in 1995.

Now, in the first 100 days of this administration, Democrats and Republicans are working in good faith in the hope that we can reach a budget agreement. But what we want is simple and clear: We want to balance the budget and invest more in education, extend health care to children. Yes, we didn't win the health care fight, but Franklin Roosevelt was for experimentation. I'm glad I tried to give the hard-working families in this country health insurance. I'm not sorry I tried to do that. I think we were right to try, and we ought to at least give it to the children of America in this term. We can do that.

We ought to continue to clean up the environment. Now that we're requiring people on welfare who are able-bodied to go to work, we ought to make darn sure the jobs are there for them. And we ought to stop the punishment—unjust—of legal immigrants in this country who work hard and do their part to make our country strong.

We've got that kind of budget, and I hope we've got that kind of budget negotiations going. We've got 20 percent of the country committed already in the first 100 days to embracing national standards for learning, and for the first time ever in America, having an examination of fourth and eighth graders in reading and math. We have got hundreds of businesses—hundreds and hundreds—committed to helping us move a million people from welfare to work.

We had Hillary's conference on early childhood and the brain and the magnificent Summit of Service in Philadelphia last weekend. That embodies what I think America is at its best, putting people first, putting our country's future first, not taking cheap shots. And after a long fight, we also ratified the Chemical Weapons Convention, which will take us a long way toward eradicating the threat of chemical weapons from the face of the Earth. We are moving in the right direction.

What I want to say to you tonight in closing are two brief points: First of all, it bothers me that members of both parties, at this moment of America's greatest influence, most profound economic and social renovation, when we are in the greatest position of all to try to bring the people of the world together in economic cooperation and competition, advancing democracy and human rights, finding ways globally to preserve our little planet's environment—that people in both parties somehow feel afraid of the future and afraid of the rest of the world and don't want to eagerly embrace it.

If you believe for a moment that we can fulfill the legacy of Franklin Roosevelt and continue to lead the world by hunkering down, withdrawing, turning our backs on a waiting world that longs for what we now almost take for granted, that is wrong. The Democratic Party at the end of World War II, under Franklin Roosevelt and Harry Truman, said to the rest of the world, "Come on, we'll all get together and go forward together." And I want you to be a part of that kind of Democratic Party for the 21st century.

And the last thing I want to say is that Franklin Roosevelt was an awfully good politician. After all, he managed to get himself elected 4 times. He managed to always look happy and strong and confident no matter what personal pain he might have endured. And he was marvelously successful because he liked people and he liked politics.

And I hope you're here tonight because you like politics. And I hope you never stop liking politics. And I wish that we could have had this event tonight in the Lincoln Bedroom, but we did not have enough coffee in the White House. [*Laughter*]

Now, the next time somebody asks you why you're helping us, tell them the stories I told you tonight and think about the people you know whose lives have been changed by what we have done in moving the AIDS drugs more rapidly to market, in coming out for the family leave law, in making college more affordable for people, in creating all these jobs to give people the chance to work in dignity, and having the biggest drop in welfare rolls in the history of the country. Now, you think about that. All that was made possible by the American political system.

I am proud of you. I want you to be proud of you. And I want you to get up tomorrow and say, "I'm glad I was part of that. America is better than it was 4 years ago. It's going to be better 4 years from now. And the most important thing is my grandchildren will live in a 21st century that is worthy of American's glorious past."

Thank you, and God bless you all.

NOTE: The President spoke at 9:20 p.m. at the D.C. Armory. In his remarks, he referred to actor Tommy Lee Jones; Gov. Roy Romer of Colorado, general chair, Steve Grossman, national chair, Alan D. Solomont, national finance chair, and Carol Pensky, treasurer, Democratic National Committee; Abe Pollin, owner, NBA Washington Bullets and NHL Washington Capitals; Tommy Boggs, attorney; Morton Bahr, international president, Communications Workers of America; Janice Griffin, vice president, Prudential; Robert L. Johnson, chairman and chief executive officer, BET Holdings, Inc.; and Dan Dutko, chair, Victory Fund.

Remarks to the Saxophone Club
May 1, 1997

The President. I was sitting there pondering—standing there pondering—[*laughter*]—giving the Vice President a standing ovation with my stiff leg—[*laughter*]—how he had so much energy at 10:30 at night. [*Laughter*] And then I realized, well, he is a younger man. [*Laughter*]

Let me say to all of you who helped to make this evening possible tonight, I thank you, and I thank Tipper and Al for being there with Hillary and me for the last 4 years and 2 months—not only politically but also personally, in a remarkable and perhaps unique way. I thank the Vice President for being the most important adviser I could have on a whole range of issues. There's very little he doesn't know a lot about, and now he knows more than he even did when he showed up here. [*Laughter*] And this country is much better off because Al Gore's been the Vice President of the United States.

When Tipper and Al and Hillary were talking, I thought to myself, I love these Saxophone Club events, and I love to look out at the sea of eager faces thinking about the future. "Don't stop thinking about tomorrow." [*Laughter*] And I was looking at Billy Baldwin, and then when Al said he was handsome and articulate and committed——

The Vice President. Suave.

The President. Suave. [*Laughter*]

The Vice President. Charming.

The President. Charming. [*Laughter*] What I was thinking is "and young," and I really resent it. [*Laughter*]

And Tracy and her band, I'm glad they were here, and I thank them for performing and for being in such good humor tonight. I hope we all are. But I really appreciate—I want to tell you a story about Billy Baldwin. He also came to New York once during the campaign and introduced us at an event—you may have been there or—[*laughter*]—or you're just stirred by the very thought of it. [*Laughter*] He does have that effect on some people. [*Laughter*] And he actually—I mean, I felt like I should write him an excused absence because he missed his anniversary to be there with us one night, because he cared so much——

Audience members. Aw-w-w.

The President. Well, he celebrated it the next day. [*Laughter*] That's something you can do when you're young. You think there will always be a next day, so it's good. But the thing that struck me about that was that here is this man who is doing this—who does not have to do this—because he believes it.

And I saw his brother the other night, and he came up and started talking to me about a whole other set of issues. And I thought, just what he said tonight in his remarkable speech—I thought those guys must have had a remarkable upbringing because they're not just going off and living with their money and living with the stars and forgetting about everybody else in this country. And they care about things that affect all of us, and somehow they understand that their identity is tied up with all of us.

And if I could just make one very brief point tonight about what this whole thing is about. I really believe that the significant choice that we have to make as a people now on the edge of this new millennium is really what we think it means to be an American and what we think it means to be a member of a community and who is in our community. And so much of what we have done that really mattered was rooted in my conviction—our conviction, if you will—that none of us can be completely fulfilled individually unless we are connected to others and unless we have respect for them, unless we have concern for them, and unless we are prepared to take some steps to make sure that everybody has a chance to live up to their God-given capacities and that we conserve, preserve, and protect those things that we share in common, whether it's a common environment or the public safety.

And that's what I want you to think about. Because when you hear all these debates—you go back and replay the debates, the political debates of the last 15 years, you'll see that when you strip it all away, it's really about whether you believe that we're out there on our own and a good thing, or whether you believe that by definition to live in this country at this time and to live in this world at this time means that you have to recognize communities and you have to want to be a part of them, embrace them, and want to raise your children in a better one.

And if you think about it, the reason I want to balance the budget is I don't want this young man here to have to worry about that. I want him to have a new set of problems. I mean, it's endemic to human nature. I can't make all the problems go away for the future, but at least we can give you a new set of problems. [*Laughter*] And the reason I want to do it in a way that honors the integrity of our health care programs is because I don't want to abandon the elderly and the disabled. And the reason that I believe in education is that I think it's the greatest gift we can give to people now, not only the young but the not-so-young who have to learn for a lifetime.

But I think it all comes back to us. When Hillary goes around the world and has these meetings in Africa and Latin America and Beijing and everyplace—South Asia—and talks to these little groups of women and girls—and the girls may not even get to go to college, or get to go to high school, get to go to grade school, maybe have lived in places where girls and women are still oppressed—I realize that the liberation of their talents will not only strengthen their families and their own lives and enrich their own lives, it will make their countries better partners for us in the years ahead and make our future better.

And that's why—we fought for things like the Religious Freedom Restoration Act, the Employment Nondiscrimination Act, mending but not ending affirmative action—all these things are a way of trying to define an American community in a way that would say, you can be a part of our community if you share our values and you work hard and you're responsible and you want to be a part of something that's good.

This whole world today is absolutely being tormented by people who can't bear the thought of someone else's existence or happiness and it's because they're different from them. I mean, this whole world is being tormented by people who believe that their lives only make sense if they're kicking somebody else's brains out or who believe that if they don't kick somebody else's brains out, they will be killed in turn or they will be oppressed in turn, so they have to do it as a defensive mechanism.

Now, if you think about the whole world, here we are—we're talking about how we can connect every school and library in America to the Internet. Last night, I went to the dedication of the Thomas Jefferson Building at the Library of Congress, and we talked about how we can share all these treasures with kids all over the world. And yet we are still plagued by almost primitive impulses, making us less than we ought to be, and by people who almost seek to make a moral virtue out of our walking away from each other.

So if you ask me what it is that's sort of that central idea that I think will determine what America will look like 50 years from now, it is whether or not we really do believe we are part of a community, that we are one Nation under God, that we are one world under God, that we have—we are entitled to individual rights but we have common responsibilities and we'll be a whole lot happier if we just recognize them.

And I want you to be proud of what we've done, and I want you to be proud of what we're doing, and I want you to be proud of where we're going. And if all goes well, when these 8 years are over, this country will start a new century and a new millennium a lot better than it was 8 years ago but, more importantly, with a philosophy, an attitude, a way of looking at living together that will carry us a very long way and make the 21st century more peaceful, more prosperous, more happy than the 20th, yet still very much an American century.

That's what I want for you and why I'm glad you're here.

Thank you, and God bless you all.

NOTE: The President spoke at 10:30 p.m. at the Hyatt Regency Hotel. In his remarks, he referred to actors William and Alec Baldwin and musician Tracy Bonham.

Remarks on the National Economy
May 2, 1997

The President. Good morning. As all of you know, I'm on my way to the dedication of our Nation's memorial to President Franklin Roosevelt. It will be a celebration of our century's greatest leader, someone whose faith in our country and our people helped us to conquer challenges in a very difficult time. Today, if we have the same faith and confidence in ourselves, we can clearly move into the 21st century stronger and more confident, with the American dream alive, with the American community more united, with America's leadership in the world secure.

Before I go, I want to comment on the very good news we have received on the economy today and what it means for our present work in Washington. The new employment report has just been issued. I'm pleased to report that the unemployment rate has dropped to 4.9 percent; 4.9 percent is the lowest it has been in 24 years.

Our economy has now created over 12 million jobs since the beginning of 1993. Inflation remains low. Our economy is now the strongest it has been in a generation. This is a great tribute to the efforts of the American people and to the validity of the new economic policy that we brought here in 1993.

In late 1992, when we were putting this economic policy together in its final details, we were determined to move away from the failed policies of trickle-down economics to a policy of invest and grow: to bring the deficit down, but to invest more in our people's education and training and technology and science, and to expand trade dramatically so that we could create new jobs at higher wages. This strategy is working. We know now that the deficit will be down, probably by more than two-thirds what it was when I took office by the end of this year. With 4.9 percent unemployment, we know what works. This strategy works.

We need to finish the job now. We need to balance the budget while continuing to invest in our people and in our future. I've been working hard with the leaders of Congress to do just that. I am hopeful that we can get an agreement that will balance the budget and continue our commitments to invest in education and in the health care of our children and in environment and in technology. I am hopeful that we can do this in a way that preserves, enhances, reforms Medicare and protects Medicaid, and deals with the problems of legal immigrants, which I feel so strongly about, and also gives appropriate but disciplined tax relief.

The one thing I am determined to do is to keep on this economic course which has brought us to the lowest unemployment rate in 24 years. Therefore, we have to be very careful not to set conditions in motion which could explode the deficit again because of the way the tax cut is written or other provisions are written after this budget period ends.

So we changed the course of the Nation. This is profoundly important. And we now have to finish the job, not undo it. I'm very optimistic. I'm very hopeful. We've had good conversations late last night and early this morning. But I want to make it clear that we're moving in the right direction, and this budget agreement must continue that movement, not reverse it, not undermine it but continue it and give more Americans the chance to participate in the prosperity that our Nation is enjoying.

Thank you very much.

Q. Mr. President, do you think you'll have a budget deal today?

The Vice President. We're late for the dedication, so questions later.

NOTE: The President spoke at 9:40 a.m. on the South Lawn at the White House, prior to his departure for the Franklin Delano Roosevelt Memorial dedication ceremony.

Remarks at the Dedication of the Franklin Delano Roosevelt Memorial
May 2, 1997

Thank you very much, Senator Inouye; Senator Hatfield; Your Highness; my longtime friend David Roosevelt and the members of the Roosevelt family; Mr. Vice President; to all those who have worked to make this day a reality. Let me begin by saying to Senator Inouye and Senator Hatfield, the United States proudly accepts the Franklin Delano Roosevelt Memorial.

Fittingly, this is the first occasion of its kind in more than 50 years. The last time the American people gathered near here was in 1943 when President Franklin Roosevelt dedicated the memorial to Thomas Jefferson. Today we honor the greatest President of this great American Century.

As has been said, FDR actually wanted no memorial. For years, none seemed necessary, for two reasons. First, the America he built was a memorial all around us. From the Golden Gate Bridge to the Grand Coulee Dam, from Social Security to honest financial markets, from an America that has remained the world's indispensable nation to our shared conviction that all Americans must make our journey together, Roosevelt was all around us. Second, though many of us never lived under his leadership, many who did are still around, and we have all heard about him from our parents or grandparents—some of us, as we pass by WPA or CCC projects along country roads, some of us as we looked at the old radios that our parents and grandparents kept and heard stories about the fireside chats and how the people felt.

Today he is still very real to millions upon millions of Americans, inspiring us, urging us on. But the world turns, and memories fade. And now, more than a half-century after he left us, it is right that we go a little beyond his stated wishes and dedicate this memorial

as a tribute to Franklin Roosevelt, to Eleanor, and to the remarkable triumphs of their generation.

President Roosevelt said—[*applause*]—thank you. President Roosevelt said, "We have faith that future generations will know that here, in the middle of the 20th century, there came a time when men of good will found a way to unite and produce and fight to destroy the forces of ignorance and intolerance and slavery and war." This memorial will be the embodiment of FDR's faith, for it will ensure that all future generations will know. It will ensure that they will all see the "happy warrior" keeping America's rendezvous with destiny.

As we stand at the dawn of a bright new century, this memorial will encourage us, reminding us that whenever America acts with certainty of purpose and FDR's famous flexibility of mind, we have always been more than equal to whatever challenges we face.

Winston Churchill said that President Roosevelt's life was one of the commanding events in human history. He came from privilege, but he understood the aspirations of farmers and factory workers and forgotten Americans. He electrified the farms and hollows, but even more important, he electrified the Nation, instilling confidence with every tilt of his head and boom of his laugh. His was an open, American spirit with a fine sense for the possible and a keen appreciation of the art of leadership. He was a master politician and a magnificent Commander in Chief.

And his partner was also magnificent. Eleanor Roosevelt was his eyes and his ears, going places he could not go, to see things he would never see, to come back and tell him how things actually were. And her reports were formed as words in his speeches that touched little people all across America who could not imagine that the President of the United States knew how they lived and cared about them. She was his conscience and our Nation's conscience.

Franklin Roosevelt's mission was to change America to preserve its ancient virtues in the face of new and unprecedented challenges. That is, after all, America's mission in all times of change and difficulty. The depth and sweep of it was unprecedented, when FDR asked a shaken nation to put its confidence in him. But he had no doubt of the outcome.

Listen to what he said in September 1932, shortly before he was elected for the first time. He proclaimed his faith: "Faith in America, faith in our tradition of personal responsibility, faith in our institutions, faith in ourselves demanded we recognize the new terms of an old social contract. New conditions imposed new requirements upon government and upon those who conduct government." That was his faith. He lived it, and we are here as a result.

With that faith, he forged a strong and unapologetic Government, determined to tame the savage cycles of boom and bust, able to meet the national challenges too big for families and individuals to meet on their own. And when he restored dignity to old age, when he helped millions to keep their farms or own their homes, when he provided the simple opportunity to go to work in the morning to millions, he was proving that the American dream was not a distant glimmer but something every American could grasp. And then that faith of his infused all of his countrymen.

With that faith, he inspired millions of ordinary Americans to take responsibility for one another, doing their part, in his words, through the National Recovery Administration, reclaiming nature through the Civilian Conservation Corps, gathering scrap, giving up nylons, and eventually storming the beaches at Normandy and Okinawa and Anzio.

With that faith, he committed our Nation to lead the world, first as the arsenal of democracy and then at the head of the great crusade to free the world from tyranny. Before the war began, the four freedoms set the foundation for the future and made it clear to the whole world that America's goal was not domination, but a dominion of freedom in a world at peace.

With that faith, as the war neared an end he would never see, he traced the very architec- ture of our future, from the GI bill to the United Nations. Faith in the extraordinary potential of ordinary people sparked not only our victory over war, depression, and doubt, but it began the opening of doors and the raising of sights for the dispossessed in America that has continued down to the present day.

It was that faith in his own extraordinary potential that enabled him to guide his country from a wheelchair. And from that wheelchair and a few halting steps, leaning on his son's arms or those of trusted aides, he lifted a great people back to their feet and set America to march again toward its destiny.

He said over and over again in different ways that we had only to fear fear itself. We did not have to be afraid of pain or adversity or failure, for all those could be overcome. He knew that, of course, because that is exactly what he did. And with his faith and the power of this example, we did conquer them all, depression, war, and doubt.

Now we see that faith again alive in America. We are grateful beyond measure for our own unprecedented prosperity. But we must remember the source of that faith. And again, let me say to Senator Inouye and others, by showing President Roosevelt as he was, we show the world that we have faith that in America you are measured for what you are and what you have achieved, not for what you have lost. And we encourage all who face their difficulties and overcome them not to give in to fear but to believe in their possibilities.

And now, again, we need the faith of Franklin Roosevelt in an entirely different time, but still no ordinary time, for in this time, new livelihoods demand new skills. We have to fight against the enormous destructive influences that still grip the lives of too many of our young people. We must struggle to make our rich racial, ethnic, and religious diversity a source of strength and unity when such differences are the undoing of millions and millions around the world. And we must fight against that nagging old doubt.

It is a strange irony of our time that here, at the moment of our greatest prosperity and progress in so many years—in 1932, one in 4 Americans was out of work; this morning we learned that fewer than one in 20 Americans are out of work for the first time in more than 2 decades. And at this time, where the pinnacle that Roosevelt hoped America would achieve in our influence and power has come to pass, we still, strangely, fight battles with doubts, doubts that he would treat with great impatience and disdain, doubts that lead some to urge us to pull back from the world at the very first time since Roosevelt's time when we actually can realize his vision of world peace and world prosperity and the dominance of the ideals for which he gave his life.

Let us honor his vision not only with this memorial today but by acting in the way he would tell us to act if he were standing here giving this speech, on his braces, looking at us and smiling at us and telling us we know what we have to do. We are Americans. We must have faith, we must not be afraid, and we must lead.

The great legacy of Roosevelt is a vision and a challenge—not a set of specific programs but a set of commitments—the duty we owe to ourselves, to one another, to our beloved Nation, and increasingly, to our fellow travelers on this small planet.

Now we are surrounded by the monuments to the leaders who built our democracy: Washington, who launched our great experiment and created our Republic; Jefferson, who enshrined forever our creed that it is self-evident that we are all created equal, with unalienable rights to life, liberty, and the pursuit of happiness; Lincoln, who gave his life to preserve Mr. Washington's Republic and to make real Mr. Jefferson's words; and now, Franklin Roosevelt, who saved freedom from tyranny, who restored our Republic, who defined Mr. Jefferson's creed to include freedom from want and fear. Today, before the pantheon of our democracy, let us resolve to honor them all by shepherding their legacy into a new century, into a new millennium.

Our mission is to prepare America for the time to come, to write a new chapter of our history, inspired always by the greatest source of hope in our history. Thomas Jefferson wrote the words, but Franklin Roosevelt lived them out every day. Today I ask you to remember what he was writing at Warm Springs when he died, that last speech: "The only limit to our realization of tomorrow will be our doubts of today. Let us move forward with strong and active faith."

My fellow Americans, every time you think of Franklin Roosevelt, put aside your doubts, become more American, become more like him, be infused with his strong and active faith.

God bless you, God bless America, and may God always bless the memory of Franklin Delano Roosevelt.

NOTE: The President spoke at 10:50 a.m. at the memorial. In his remarks, he referred to David B. Roosevelt, cochair, FDR Memorial Capital Campaign; and Princess Margriet of The Netherlands, President Roosevelt's goddaughter.

Remarks Announcing the Budget Agreement and an Exchange With Reporters in Baltimore, Maryland
May 2, 1997

The President. For more than 4 years now, I have worked hard to pursue a strategy that would keep our economy growing and creating opportunity for the American people, giving people a chance to be rewarded for their labors, and also imposing upon ourselves the discipline necessary to prepare for the future and to relieve ourselves of a lot of the problems that had been accumulated over the last several years, especially the deficit.

Now, we have reached agreement, in broad but fairly specific terms that I am satisfied will do that, with the Republican leaders today that would balance the budget by 2002, continue to increase our investment in education, in science and technology and medical research, require us to continue to show great discipline in other areas and to continue to downsize some Government operations. It would invest in doing what I think is important, to be sure that we can move people from welfare to work who are going to be required to go to work. It would expand coverage to millions of children who presently do not have health insurance. It would restore cuts to benefits for legal immigrants who are in this country who have sustained injuries and other problems for which they would otherwise be eligible for benefits. It will extend the life of Medicare and secure the integrity of the Medicaid program between now and 2002. It will be the first balanced budget in three decades.

It's a good thing that it's coming today, when we learned that our employment rate had dropped to 4.9 percent for the first time in 24 years. We know that we have the biggest decline in inequality in our work force since the 1960's, and we've seen our economy produce the largest number of new jobs since 1993 ever produced in a 4-year period. That happened because a lot of the people standing up here with me right now had the courage to vote for a plan to bring the deficit down in 1993 and get interest rates down and investments up.

This agreement will help us to finish the job. I have spoken several times over the last several days with Senator Lott and with Speaker Gingrich. I want to thank them personally for negotiating with me openly, candidly, and I'm convinced, in complete good faith.

I have also had occasion to speak with the representatives of the Democratic caucus, obviously, who were in this budget negotiation, Senator Lautenberg for the Democrats and Congressman John Spratt from South Carolina, and the Republicans who were represented by their chairs, Senator Domenici and Congressman Kasich. I want to thank them all. I want to thank Senator Domenici and Congressman Kasich; they worked very hard. And we know there are significant differences between us in how we look at what is the best way to balance the budget, and they tried to bridge these gaps. Congressman Spratt and Senator Lautenberg did, as well, and I'm very proud of all four of them. They served America well. They put the interests of the country first in trying to work through to get us as close as we are today. And so I appreciate that very much.

Now, let me say again—let me give you just some of the details very quickly. The plan will protect Medicare, extending the life of the Trust Fund for a decade, extending new benefits for annual mammograms and diabetes screening. Home health will be shifted from Part A to Part B, and there will be a modest premium for home health services being phased in at one dollar per month, a year.

Second, and perhaps most important, this budget meets my goal of making education America's number one priority on the edge of the 21st century. It will have the largest increase in education funding in 30 years. It will have the largest increase in Pell grant scholarships in 20 years. It will help us to make sure that every 8-year-old will be able to read, every 12-year-old can log on to the Internet, every 18-year-old can go into college. I am very, very pleased that it will also include in a tax cut, per person, aid to help people go on to college and to finance college education.

Third, as I said, it will extend health insurance to 5 million uninsured children. This is a major breakthrough in our efforts to move toward coverage for all Americans.

Fourth, it will give businesses incentives and work with mayors to hire people from welfare to work. It will also, as I said, address the concerns I raised in last year's welfare law—restoring benefits to disabled legal immigrants and moderating excessive cuts in food stamps, along with giving the States a reserve, so that if people would be unjustly cut off food stamps because they simply cannot go to work, the States will be able to avoid malnutrition and real harm to those people in these cases.

Fifth, it will protect the environment, providing funds to clean up 500 of our most dangerous toxic waste sites, cleaning up toxic sites in urban areas, and adding resources for environmental enforcement.

Sixth, it includes tax relief for the American people, but thanks to the rules of the Senate and the agreement of the leaders, the tax relief will be limited. And we'll know the dollar amount not only for the first 5 years but for the second 5 years following, so that we will not run the risk of having an explosion in the deficit as a result of unintended leaks in a tax program, so that when we tell the American people we're going to balance the budget, we know we can keep it balanced and we won't get ourselves back into the difficulties we've seen over the last 15 years.

Like Americans of all political views, I have been deeply committed to this, but I wanted a balanced budget with balanced values. I believe we have got it today. There are things in this budget that—everyone will find something that he or she disagrees with; everyone could find something that he or she wishes were in the budget. There is no perfect agreement, but as I said, we know America is more prosperous when we have fiscal discipline, when we invest in our future, and when we do it in the right way. We have evidence of that.

It will never get any easier to do this job. Senator Lott made that point to me on the phone the other night. He said, "You know, when you're doing well, it's easier to balance the budget than it is when you're not. This is not going to get any easier. We have to do it now." And I said, "I agree with you, and we are going to do it."

So I ask Americans of all political parties and all philosophies to look at this plan, give it your support. Let's balance the budget and get on about the new business of preparing America for a new century.

And I thank you, and I'd like to ask Senator Daschle now and come up and say a word.

[*At this point, Senators Tom Daschle and Frank Lautenberg, Representatives Charles Stenholm and Steny Hoyer, and Vice President Al Gore each made brief remarks.*]

The President. Thank you. I just can't help saying, there for a moment I thought the Vice President was sad he's not going to get to cast another tiebreaker in this vote. [*Laughter*]

The Vice President. Right.

Medicare and Medicaid

Q. Mr. President, during the campaign, you repeatedly expressed concern about cuts—potential cuts in Medicaid and Medicare. Are you satisfied that no one will be hurt——

The President. Yes.

Q. ——in the changes?

The President. Yes, I am. Let me say, first of all, I think we have improved the Medicaid program in this budget agreement—and I want to make full disclosure here—with the full support of the Republican negotiators, over and above what it was in the budget I presented. Now, that's been made possible partly because we know the economy is getting better, but we have.

The Medicare program, I'm convinced—first of all, the savings in Medicare which I proposed, meeting the Republicans halfway between our differences last time, are, by and large, rooted in policy, which I believe is good policy, designed not only to save money for 5 years but to save money over the long run. We need to change some of the policies to show appropriate

discipline. They don't hurt people, but they will impose more rigor in the system.

The modest one-dollar-a-month premium for home health services, I think, is an appropriate contribution, given the fact that people, I believe, at 120 percent of the poverty line and down are exempted. I think it's an appropriate contribution for what is the fastest growing element of the Medicare program and something that—150 percent, they just told me, are excluded, and below. The home health part is the fastest growing part of Medicare and has not been subject to any premium, and I think it should. There should be some contribution there, just as is associated with other elements of Part B. But it will not be burdensome, and the aggregate premium will still be much lower than would have been the case if I hadn't vetoed the budget in '95.

So I think we've reached out to the health care experts in our caucus and in the Republican caucus. We've reached out to interest groups throughout the country that would be affected by this. I believe they will support this. I believe there will be broad support for this, and I think it will be seen for just what it is. It will preserve and strengthen the integrity of the Medicare program for a decade. We can't responsibly let this Trust Fund get down to a year or two and just kick it down the road for another year or two. We need to keep it a decade or more out all the time.

Budget Negotiations

Q. Senator Daschle described this as an agreement that was tentatively reached 24 hours ago. Can you give us an idea of what transpired between that point and now? [*Laughter*]

The President. I don't think it would be——

The Vice President. Sausage. [*Laughter*]

The President. Let me just say, I think what Senator Daschle said is accurate, but let me try to recast it a little bit. We had some broad outlines 24 hours ago. We went back to our folks; they went back to theirs to talk about some details. We came back with some details; they came back with some details. We got some of the details we wanted, and some we just had to abandon—and knowing that there will still be disagreements within various categories as this budget comes up.

Keep in mind, this is an agreement. Then it has to be embodied in law. Then it has to be embodied in specific appropriation bills and tax bills this year and in the years to come. So there is still some room for some debate between the two parties and within the two parties over some issues. But the framework is pretty specific—guarantees the essential elements that were necessary to get the Democrats and the Republicans to support it and to get the President to support it.

So we did get some more specifics in and had to leave some more specifics out in the last 24 hours, but I think, in fairness to the Republicans with—as I said, I am convinced they negotiated with me and with Senator Lautenberg and Mr. Spratt in complete good faith. And in fairness to them, without talking to them about it, I don't think I should characterize exactly what happened in the last 24 hours.

Tax Cuts

Q. Mr. President, how big is the tax cut in the package? Can you give us any indication? Who will get tax relief?

The President. It is a tax cut of a net of $85 billion, which is—over 5 years—which is considerably smaller than we were—they were discussing. And then in the second 5 years, it must not exceed about a hundred and—what is it? About $170 billion, $165 billion, something like that.

And you'll get briefings on that; back at the White House they'll explain it. But also, we have gone as far as we could, keep in mind, the tax-writing committees were not part of this negotiating process, the budget committees were. So let me finish. We have gone as far as we could also in discussing what the components are. You know the thing the Republicans want in it. You know we want an education tax cut as well as some environmental relief for brownfields and some other very specific things, and we want to protect the tax cuts that are progressive in our Tax Code, particularly the earned-income tax credit for low income people, the low income housing credit, and we want to try to protect the pension programs from being raided. And we've gone about as far as we can in doing that in an agreement that does not include the leaders of the tax-writing committee.

And Secretary Rubin, who is our guardian on that, finally signed off and said, "Well, this is the best we're going to be able to do."

Budget Negotiations and Reaction

Q. Mr. President, the Republicans are happy they got their tax cut; you're happy you got your investments. It can't all be win-win. What did you have to give up? Where will Americans feel a pinch? Where's the sacrifice?

The President. Well, first of all, they're taking a smaller tax cut than they had originally sought. We're providing larger savings in this budget than previously in Medicare and in other areas. But the growth in the economy has made it easier than it otherwise would have been. And we've all acknowledged that. I think we have to acknowledge that.

So, for example, the difficult questions that had been raised around the CPI—the cost of living adjustment for benefits—the sense of both sides is that that should continue to be handled in the ordinary course of business, that there will be an adjustment of some kind coming out of the Bureau of Labor Statistics in the process, that we have a fairly good idea of what it is. But even if it's not sufficient to cover everything—and they acknowledge they can't analyze all the relevant factors—that is an issue which now can be handled outside of these budget negotiations. And that is an issue which would have been very difficult here.

Q. Mr. President, how big a selling job do you still have?

The President. Well, I don't know. We're going to have to see how the Democrats and Republicans react to it. The Democrats will think that the tax cuts are too big and too skewed to people with high incomes. The Republicans will think that we're investing too much in education and other things; I think many of them may think that. And I'm sure that there will be some on both sides who won't vote for it.

And then some people will be disappointed that even though we did some good reform in the Medicare program, that without a consumer price adjustment that's larger, some will say we're not doing enough to save Social Security. My argument is we can look at saving Social Security independent of this; let's balance the budget. We don't have to mix the two, and we can take that on its own merits.

But there will be a lot of things in here that—as I said, no one will look at this budget and say, "This is perfect. It has everything in it I want, and there's nothing in it I don't like."

So everybody will say, "I wish something were in it that isn't." I wish that there were things that are in it that weren't. But I think we've got a good shot at getting the majority of both parties in both Houses, which has been my goal from the day one. And if it happens, America will be much better off.

Keep in mind, the bottom line is, if we show discipline here and keep interest rates down by balancing the budget, the American people in the private sector will grow the economy for us. That solves a lot of problems. If we show discipline in continuing to invest in our future,

then we will grow the economy in a way that will give us high-wage jobs, higher incomes, and greater equality, which will solve our problems for us. And meanwhile, we'll have a little honest—an honorable compromise; that's part of the way the process works.

Thank you. There will be a briefing on more specifics down at the White House shortly.

NOTE: The President spoke at 3:58 p.m. while attending a Democratic senatorial retreat at the Harbour Court Hotel.

Exchange With Reporters on the Budget Agreement
May 2, 1997

Q. Mr. President, have you got all the Democrats on board now?

The President. A lot of them. I feel good about it.

Q. Do you need to do a selling job to the American people? Do you think you need to sell this at all?

The President. Oh, sure. We need to talk about it. We will. It's a good agreement, a good thing for America.

Q. [*Inaudible*]

The President. We're having them over here for a while.

NOTE: The exchange began at 6:05 p.m. on the South Lawn at the White House, on the President's return from Baltimore, MD. A tape was not available for verification of the content of this exchange.

Statement on the Department of Justice Appeal of the District Court Decision on Tobacco Regulation
May 2, 1997

Today the Department of Justice filed a notice in the Greensboro U.S. District Court appealing the part of Judge Osteen's order that invalidated the Food and Drug Administration's tobacco advertising restrictions. The Department is asking for an expedited appeal, because every day of delay matters to our children's health. Each day, 3,000 children and young people become regular smokers, and 1,000 of them will

have their lives cut short as a result of their smoking. And this problem of youth tobacco use is getting worse. The percentage of 8th and 10th graders who smoke has risen for 4 consecutive years. The FDA's commonsense access and advertising restrictions would reverse this trend. We will continue to work to protect our children from tobacco, and we will not stop until we succeed.

Message to the Congress Transmitting a Report on Proliferation of Weapons of Mass Destruction
May 2, 1997

To the Congress of the United States:

The National Defense Authorization Act for Fiscal Year 1997 (Public Law 104–201), title XIV, section 1443 (Defense Against Weapons of Mass Destruction), requires the President to transmit a report to the Congress that describes the United States comprehensive readiness pro-gram for countering proliferation of weapons of mass destruction. In accordance with this provision, I enclose the attached report.

WILLIAM J. CLINTON

The White House,
May 2, 1997.

The President's Radio Address and an Exchange With Reporters
May 3, 1997

The President. Good morning. Yesterday we took a dramatic step to prepare America for the 21st century, and we got the best evidence yet that the new economic policy we adopted in 1993 is working for our people. Yesterday morning, we learned the unemployment rate has dropped to 4.9 percent, the lowest in 24 years. And yesterday afternoon, I reached an historic agreement with the leaders of Congress to balance the budget by 2002, with a plan that ensures we will balance the budget, invest in our future, protect our values and our obligations to our children, our parents, and those in need.

Four years ago when I took office, the economy was stagnating; job growth was sluggish; the budget deficit threatened to drown our economy. I believed it was time to change course with a new economic strategy: Invest and grow, cut the budget deficit, sell more products overseas through tough trade agreements, and invest in the skills of our people. In 1993, we put our economic plan in place. It wasn't easy; it required hard choices. But now, the deficit has been cut for 4 years in a row, falling from $290 billion in 1992 to about $80 billion this year—more than two-thirds of the way home to our first balanced budget since the 1960's. All this has spurred lower interest rates, more investment, and stronger growth.

And the good news goes beyond low unemployment: Economic growth is at its highest in a decade; core inflation at its lowest in three decades; the largest decline in income inequality since the 1960's; and thanks to the hard work of the American people, 12 million new jobs. It is now clear that our economy is the strongest it's been in a generation.

Now we have to keep this economic growth going. We have a great opportunity to build a world for our children better than any America has ever known. But my fellow Americans, we must prepare. We have to give Americans the education and skills they need to compete in the global economy. We have to invest in science and technology. We have to continue to get and keep our economic house in order.

To keep our economy growing, we must stay on the path of fiscal responsibility. To make sure all our people can share in this prosperity, we must make sure that a balanced budget also invests in their future. Balancing the budget, investing in our people: we must do both these things. In 1993, many people doubted that it could be done. We have shown that it can be done. And with this budget agreement, a bipartisan budget agreement, we will prove that we can actually balance the budget and continue to invest in our future.

It took weeks of intense negotiations to lead to an agreement that protects our values. A balanced budget with unbalanced values and priorities would not have been enough. There were times when it seemed that we perhaps would never reach this agreement, times when it appeared that we could not secure a balanced budget true to the principles and priorities essential to our future and bringing Democrats and Republicans together across all their differences. But everyone understood that the stakes were too great and the cost of failure too severe to give up.

So, yesterday, we reached an agreement on just such a plan. It is a significant breakthrough for our country. And it proves that our political system can work when we put our partisan differences aside and put the American people and their future first.

This budget honors our duty to our parents and to those in need by securing Medicare and Medicaid and extending the life of the Medicare Trust Fund for a full decade. It honors our duty to our children, expanding health coverage to children who don't have it, up to 5 million more of them. It keeps my pledge to continue the job of welfare reform by providing tax incentives to businesses to move people from welfare to work and restoring some of the unwise and excessive cuts included in last year's welfare bill. It cleans up 500 toxic waste dumps and strengthens enforcement for a clean environment. It gives the American people tax relief for education, for help in raising their children, and to spur investment in our future.

And perhaps most important of all, this bipartisan agreement reflects our commitment to make education America's top priority on the edge of a new century. Here are our goals: Every 8-year-old can read; every 12-year-old can log on to the Internet; every 18-year-old can go on to college; every adult can keep on learning for a lifetime.

This balanced budget is a breakthrough toward those goals. It's the best education budget in three decades. It will give families tax cuts to pay for college, and it will include our HOPE scholarship, a tax credit for tuition for the first 2 years of college to make those first 2 years as universal as a high school diploma is today. The budget also includes the biggest increase in Pell grant scholarships for deserving students in 30 years. It funds our America Reads challenge, which will mobilize a million volunteer reading tutors to make sure that all our 8-year-olds will be able to read independently. It will help to connect all our classrooms and libraries to the information superhighway. And it will support our move to develop genuine national standards in education and, by 1999, to test every fourth grader in reading and every eighth grader in math to make sure we can compete in the world of tomorrow.

This balanced budget plan is in balance with our values. It will help to prepare our people for a new century. It will help to propel our country into that century stronger than ever. I urge Members of Congress in both parties to pass it.

Yesterday morning, I had a chance to think about our country, its history, and its destiny, when I was privileged to join in the dedication of the new memorial to Franklin Delano Roosevelt here in Washington. It is a tribute to him, to Eleanor Roosevelt, and to the generation that changed America, conquering depression at home, defeating tyranny abroad. We've come a long way since then, and we can go much, much further if we work with the same faith, commitment, and confidence that FDR's generation showed as they met the challenges of their time.

In words from his last speech, which he wrote shortly before he died, President Roosevelt said, "The only limit to our realization of tomorrow will be our doubts of today. Let us move forward with strong and active faith."

My fellow Americans, the news on the economy, the balanced budget agreement, they should give us confidence; they should validate our faith; they should erase our doubts. Let us now reach across party lines and seize our chance to balance the budget and maintain that strong and active faith that will ensure that our best days as a nation lie still before us.

Thanks for listening.

[At this point, the radio address ended, and the President took questions from reporters.]

President's Visit to Mexico

Q. [Inaudible]—with our requests on drug enforcement, their policies with immigration and trade, as you know. And some are characterizing your trip as kind of a visit of reconciliation. How would you characterize it, and how is the cooperation, specifically on drugs?

The President. First of all, I don't see it as a visit of reconciliation. I see it as building on an ongoing partnership between two great nations that share a huge border and a common future, have some common problems, and inevitably some disagreements. We should look at this as a regular part of our building a common future. We will have some disagreements, but we've got an awful lot in common. But I think that the people of Mexico and the Government of Mexico know that the United States and that our administration wish them well and want to help them build a better future.

We also know we have some common problems. This drug problem is as big or bigger a problem for Mexico as it is for the United States. They will, in the end, not be able to maintain the fabric of an orderly, democratic, free society if the narcotraffickers come to dominate huge sections of their country. On the other hand, we have to understand the pressures that they are under, and we have to help them to beat back those pressures. And we'll work through it as well as we can.

On immigration, we will continue to have some tensions because what we have done as a country is to have a very broadminded view of legal immigration. I would remind you—all those that think that we somehow have a narrowminded view—we let in almost a million people legally into this country last year. But if we're going to have a broad attitude toward legal immigration, we have to increase our intolerance for illegal immigration. We can—if we have laws and people wait in line, sometimes for years, to come to this country, it is wrong not to try to be tough to stop those who seek to evade those laws and come in ahead of their ordinary time. That's not right. So we'll work through that. I think our policy is right, and I think it will be a productive trip.

Q. Mr. President, what's your reaction to the British election?

Budget Agreement

Q. It seems that the budget deals hinge on this $225 billion windfall from the new economic forecast. What if that doesn't pan out? What does that do to you?

The President. Well, first of all, let me remind you that—and I want to compliment both sides here—we have known for some time that—even before the last figures came in—that economic growth was at 5.6 percent in the last quarter, which is extraordinary, and that—then these new unemployment figures. We have known that the economy was performing well enough that our outlays would be lower, because more people would—fewer people would depend on Government assistance, and our revenues would be higher. The CBO's preliminary estimates— they don't file their final report until August— was that over a 5-year period, that might generate about $226 billion in new revenues.

There were some problems in this budget; there still are some discipline problems in this budget. Keep in mind, we're still going to have to downsize the central Government. We're still going to have a lot of agencies that will grow at less than the rate of inflation. We are concentrating our new money in education, in science and technology and research, in environmental cleanup, in things that will build our future.

But what I want to compliment the budget negotiators on is, they didn't try to spend that money. They only spent about 11½ percent of the money that we're now pretty sure will come in. All the rest of the money will go to reducing the deficit. So, if they're wrong, even quite a bit wrong, this budget will still balance in 2002 because they spent just a little over 10 percent of the money. If they're right, it will balance before 2002 because of the work and the growth and the productivity of the American people.

So the real story here is not that they've spent $26 billion to stop what could have been a terrible problem in the Medicaid program for States with high disability costs or large numbers of poor people and poor children especially; or that they want to invest a little more money in infrastructure, which is good for our long-term economic growth; or that we're going to alleviate some of the extreme cuts in the food stamp program last year—that's not the real story. The real story is, they looked at this pot of money that appeared before them and said, "We're going to leave nearly 90 percent of it there for deficit reduction and try to balance the budget even quicker." And to me, that is the real story. And they deserve a lot of credit for that.

And that's the way I look at this. Yes, we took a little of the money. It gets us a few more votes for the plan. But it's also good things to do. We also put a little money back into the last year of defense, especially in the authorizing funds, simply so we could plan, because the Defense Department has to be able to plan long-term for the continuing restructuring of the military but increase reliance again on research, development, new technologies, and new weapons.

So that small amount of a big pie shows, in fact, that we probably will balance the budget even sooner. But we don't intend to spend money that hasn't been realized yet.

Elections in the United Kingdom

Q. Mr. President, what's your reaction to the British election?

The President. Well, I think it's obviously a big vote for change. I think it's a validation of the themes that Mr. Blair struck. I think it once again proves that the people do not want political parties and political leadership tied to the rhetoric of the past. If you go back to the section of President Roosevelt's speech to the Commonwealth Club that I quoted—in 1932—yesterday, he said that if you have new times, you have to have new policies. You don't have new values, but you do have new directions. And so I thought it was a case where the people made that decision.

I must also tell you though that this is my first chance to comment on this, and I'm looking forward to serving with Prime Minister Blair. He's a very exciting man, a very able man. I like him very much. But I also think that the people of the United States and the people of Great Britain should know that John Major represented that nation very well in the world. I have obviously no experience and no judgment about what happened domestically, because I wasn't there and I'm not a British citizen, but in all of our dealings over these last 4 years

and several months, I was profoundly impressed by his patriotism, by his willingness to take tough decisions, especially in Bosnia where they were with us all the way. And so the British people can be proud of this stewardship.

And the Conservatives had a good, long run. Nothing lasts forever, and they were in for a very long time. But I hope that Prime Minister Major and I hope the British people will always feel a great deal of pride in what they did in the way they related to the rest of the world in his stewardship because I was very impressed by it. And I also was impressed by the fact that he had the courage to start the peace process in Northern Ireland. And I hope and pray, now that the British election is over, that Prime Minister Blair will take up the torch, that the IRA will declare a cease-fire, and that we can get back on the road to resolving that problem. It is high time, and I can tell you, that's what the people of Northern Ireland want.

Thank you.

Note: The President spoke at 10:06 a.m. from the Oval Office at the White House. In his remarks, he referred to newly elected Prime Minister Tony Blair of the United Kingdom.

Remarks on Departure for Mexico and an Exchange With Reporters
May 5, 1997

The President. Good afternoon. As you all know, I'm about to leave on a weeklong visit to our closest southern neighbors, Mexico, Central America, and the Caribbean. It's the first of three trips I'll take in our hemisphere over the next year. I'd like to say a few words about what I hope to accomplish and why the Americas are so important for our own security and prosperity in the 21st century.

Little more than a decade ago, our neighbors were plagued by civil wars and guerrilla insurgencies, coups and dictators, closed economies and hopeless poverty. Now we face a far different moment, a moment of truly remarkable possibility. Every nation in our hemisphere but one has embraced both free elections and open markets. The region's growing economies have become our largest trading partners. Already we

export twice as much to the Americas as to Europe and nearly half again as much as to Asia.

A partnership is emerging between the United States and the Americas based not only on history, geography, and culture but increasingly on shared interests and values and a shared commitment to a common future. More than ever before, we are working with our neighbors on the basis of mutual respect to make a difference on issues that matter most to people in their daily lives: creating good new jobs by opening markets and spurring growth, improving education to prepare our people to succeed in the global economy, making our water clean and the air clean for our children, facing up to problems we cannot defeat alone like drugs, crime, and corruption.

But while the trend in the Americas is positive, clearly the transition is not complete. If we want citizens to make a lasting commitment to democracy, peace, and open markets, we must support them in gaining confidence that they have made the right choice.

Three years ago, at our historic Summit of the Americas in Miami, the leaders of this hemisphere mapped out a concrete plan to lock in the democratic gains the Americas have made and to see that they work for all of the people. This week we will continue to advance that plan. Together, we can strengthen the institutions of democracy and promote respect for human rights. We can broaden the benefits of open and fair trade. We can shore up the stability of nations that have renounced war. We can combat the drugs and crime and environmental degradation that threaten all our futures. And we can open the doors of education to more, so that they can have the skills they need to make the most of their own lives.

It is fitting that this trip should begin in Mexico. We share one of the broadest and deepest relations of any two nations on Earth. Beyond the 2,000-mile border that joins us, beyond the strong bonds of trade that benefit both our people, we must cooperate as never before to find common solutions to common problems.

Our partnerships with Mexico and with the other nations should be the foundation of our own freedom, stability, and prosperity in the 21st century, an engine for economic growth and jobs, a sword in the fight against transnational threats that respect no borders, an example to the world that democracy and open markets actually deliver for those who embrace them. If we continue to shape the future of our hemisphere, the Americas will prosper and so will America.

Thank you.

Director of Central Intelligence Nomination

Q. Mr. President, given the frustrations of what Tony Lake went through for his nomination, are you confident that George Tenet will sail through on his nomination—confirmation process?

The President. I believe he will be confirmed. I sure do.

Flood Aid Legislation

Q. Mr. President, while you are gone, the House and Senate are going to take up the legislation regarding the flood aid. Are you still threatening to veto that? Do you still feel a need to, especially with the budget deal?

The President. I have no reason to change the position I adopted.

Q. But people are waiting for that aid.

The President. That's right, and that's why Congress ought to pass it unencumbered.

NOTE: The President spoke at 3:21 p.m. on the South Lawn at the White House.

Message on the Observance of Cinco de Mayo, 1997
May 5, 1997

Warm greetings to everyone celebrating Cinco de Mayo.

The life of our nation has been continually renewed and strengthened by the many different people who choose to come here and become our fellow citizens. Each brings a part of his or her own heritage, which over time becomes part of our common heritage. As we seek to become a more united people, we must not forget our roots, for they remind us of who we are and of what we have to share with others.

This year, as we celebrate the 135th anniversary of the Mexican Army's triumph at the Battle of Puebla, we realize anew how much our nation has been enriched by the people and culture of Mexico and how closely our futures are intertwined. The U.S.-Mexican relationship is one of the closest our nation has today, and it is most appropriate that my visit to Mexico should begin on Cinco de Mayo.

On this day devoted to victory, pride, and independence, let us rededicate ourselves to strengthening the bonds of friendship and partnership between Mexico and the United States.

Let us work together to ensure that the legacy of courage and freedom we commemorate on Cinco de Mayo will continue to inspire us as we look forward to the promise of the twenty-first century.

Hillary joins me in extending best wishes for a wonderful holiday.

WILLIAM J. CLINTON

Statement on the Resignation of Cynthia A. Metzler From the Department of Labor
May 5, 1997

From the time she assumed the role of Acting Secretary of Labor in January, Cynthia A. Metzler provided leadership and vision for the 16,000 employees of the Department of Labor. As a result of her unique blend of skills, the Department did not miss a beat in fulfilling its mission for America's working families. As Ms. Metzler departs for the private sector, the Department of Labor is positioned for a smooth and effective transition to Alexis Herman's leadership.

During her tenure as Acting Secretary, Ms. Metzler continued and accelerated the Department's initiatives on behalf of working families. Low wage workers now have better protections as a result of Ms. Metzler's efforts to expand the Department's sweatshop initiative, as well as new initiatives launched in other low wage

industries. Ms. Metzler has also assured that workers' pensions are better protected.

In addition, Acting Secretary Metzler kicked off this year's Washington, DC, summer jobs program earlier than any other year. She doubled the number of summer youth the Department will hire, and she led the Department's effort to create more job opportunities for DC residents in furtherance of this administration's DC initiative. She also provided outstanding leadership in our effort to train and employ welfare recipients.

As Cynthia Metzler starts a new chapter in her exceptional career, Hillary and I wish her the very best and thank her for her outstanding service to this administration and to the American people.

Message to the Senate Transmitting the Hong Kong-United States Mutual Legal Assistance Agreement With Documentation
May 5, 1997

To the Senate of the United States:

With a view to receiving the advice and consent of the Senate to ratification, I transmit herewith the Agreement Between the Government of the United States of America and the Government of Hong Kong on Mutual Legal Assistance in Criminal Matters, with Annex, signed in Hong Kong on April 15, 1997 (hereinafter referred to as "the Agreement"). I transmit also, for the information of the Senate, a related exchange of letters, with attached forms, signed the same date, and the report of the Department of State with respect to the Agreement.

The Agreement is one of a series of modern mutual legal assistance treaties that the United States is negotiating in order to counter criminal activities more effectively. The Agreement should be an effective tool in our continued cooperation with Hong Kong after its reversion to the sovereignty of the People's Republic of China on July 1, 1997, to assist in the prosecution of a wide variety of modern criminals, including members of drug cartels, "white-collar" criminals, and terrorists. The Agreement is self-executing.

The Agreement provides for a broad range of cooperation in criminal matters. Mutual assistance available under the Agreement includes: (1) taking evidence, testimony, or statements of persons; (2) providing information, documents, records, and items; (3) locating or identifying persons or items; (4) serving documents; (5) transferring persons in custody and others to provide assistance; (6) executing requests for search and seizure; (7) confiscating and forfeiting the proceeds and instrumentalities of crime and otherwise assisting in relation thereto; (8) delivering property, including lending exhibits or other items; and (9) any other form of assistance not prohibited by the law of the Requested Party.

I recommend that the Senate give early and favorable consideration to the Agreement and give its advice and consent to ratification so that the Agreement can enter into force no later than July 1, 1997, when Hong Kong reverts to the sovereignty of the People's Republic of China.

WILLIAM J. CLINTON

The White House,
May 5, 1997.

Message to the Senate Transmitting the Hong Kong-United States Agreement on the Transfer of Sentenced Persons With Documentation
May 5, 1997

To the Senate of the United States:

With a view to receiving the advice and consent of the Senate to ratification, I transmit herewith the Agreement Between the Government of the United States and the Government of Hong Kong for the Transfer of Sentenced Persons signed at Hong Kong on April 15, 1997. I transmit also, for the information of the Senate, the report of the Department of State with respect to this Agreement.

At present, transfers of sentenced persons between the United States and Hong Kong (in either direction) are conducted pursuant to the 1983 multilateral Council of Europe Convention on the Transfer of Sentenced Persons, which is in force for both the United States and the United Kingdom, and which the latter has extended to Hong Kong. Effective July 1, 1997, however, when Hong Kong reverts to the sovereignty of the People's Republic of China, the Council of Europe Convention will no longer provide a basis for such transfers.

The agreement signed on April 15, 1997, will provide a basis for such transfers to continue after Hong Kong's reversion. The agreement is modeled after both the Council of Europe Convention and other bilateral prisoner transfer treaties to which the United States is a party. It would establish essentially the same procedures as are now followed with respect to transfers of prisoners between the United States and Hong Kong, and would continue the requirement that all transfers be consented to by the sentencing state, the sentenced person, and the receiving state. When the sentenced person has been sentenced under the laws of a State of the United States, the consent of the authorities of that State will also be required.

I recommend that the Senate of the United States promptly give its advice and consent to the ratification of this Agreement.

WILLIAM J. CLINTON

The White House,
May 5, 1997.

Remarks at the Welcoming Ceremony in Mexico City, Mexico
May 6, 1997

President and Mrs. Zedillo, members of the Mexican Government, citizens of Mexico, *saludos, amigos.* I am delighted to be in Mexico, rich with history, culture, and beauty, and most of all, a great and good people who have given so much to the world.

In 1943, the Presidents of our countries exchanged visits in Monterrey and Corpus Christi, launching a tradition of Presidential meetings we carry forward today. President Roosevelt noted, in that dark night of war, that our people had found they had common aspirations and could work for a common objective. Today, at the dawn of a new century, in a very different time, we still have common aspirations and we must work for a common objective, for the partnership between our two great nations has never been more important.

Powerful currents of commerce and culture pull us closer together. A growing convergence of values and vision gives our friendship new force. Mexico is opening democracy's doors, embarking on bold economic reform, decentralizing power, and giving new voice to its citizens, communities, and regions.

The success of Mexico's endeavors matters to the United States of America. Our nations share far more than a common border; we share common challenges and common opportunities as we move toward a new century. We must meet the future together, respecting each other's uniqueness but knowing that in today's world, cooperation is the surest path to security, prosperity, and peace.

We are reaping the benefits of more open trade and working toward a wider community of stable, free-market democracies throughout the Americas. We want a 21st century where economic growth creates more and better jobs, where a good education and a clean environment are the birthright of every child, where we conquer our common enemies of drugs and crime, where accountable governments provide the tools for people to make the most of their own lives. Our challenges are great, but so is our resolve.

President Zedillo, I thank you for taking some time last night to show me through the remarkable museum containing the ancient heritage of Mexico. Here in the heart of modern Mexico, the remnants of a remarkable ancient civilization rise up through the city's foundations. Your great writer Carlos Fuentes has written, "The greatness of Mexico is that its past is always alive."

But, Mr. President, just as alive and just as great is the vitality of Mexico's present and the promise of its future. I have seen it in the bold leadership you have exerted, in the vibrant debate going on in your country, in the strong efforts made by the ordinary citizens of Mexico. Mexico's promise for the future is seen in the hands of its working people, in the efforts of those working to deepen democracy, in the talent of its writers and artists, and most of all, in the faces of the children here today.

Mr. President, our histories and our destinies are forever joined. Let us reach across our common frontier to embrace our tomorrows together, to enter the 21st century as valued partners and trusted friends.

Again, thank you for making Hillary and me and our party feel so welcome. And thank you for the future we are building together.

NOTE: The President spoke at 9:28 a.m. at Campo Marte. In his remarks, he referred to President Ernesto Zedillo of Mexico and his wife, Anilda Patricia.

Exchange With Reporters Prior to Discussions With President Ernesto Zedillo of Mexico in Mexico City
May 6, 1997

Mexico-U.S. Antidrug Efforts

Q. President Zedillo, could you——

President Zedillo. The press conference will be later on, and I'll be delighted to answer there any questions.

Q. Well, while we've got this opportunity, let me just clarify what the Mexican Government's position is on DEA agents being allowed——

President Zedillo. No, we'll talk about that in the press conference. Now we have to have our private conservation, and I have spoken about that before.

Thank you.

Q. Do you want DEA agents to stay here——

President Zedillo. We'll speak about all of those issues later.

President's Visit

Q. Mr. President, are you sorry you waited until the 5th year of your Presidency to come to Mexico?

President Clinton. I'm just glad to be here now. You know, we've had—I'm coming to Latin America 3 times in less than a year, and in the first term I did a lot of work on it. You know, we had the Summit of the Americas, and we had a lot of involvement with Mexico with NAFTA and the difficulty with the peso, so I think we've had a lot of very close contact. And I'm glad to be here. I like it here.

Mexico-U.S. Antidrug Efforts

Q. Mr. President, can you assure DEA agents that they'll be safe here?

President Clinton. We're going to have a press conference later. We'll answer all—on all of the decisions and stuff.

Stock Market

Q. What do you think of the stock market soaring past 7,000?

President Clinton. Americans are happy. They ought to be. The country's doing well. We're going to do better.

Q. Do you think your budget deal is responsible?

President Clinton. It didn't hurt. [*Laughter*]

NOTE: The President spoke at approximately 10:10 a.m. on the Veranda of the Residence at Los Pinos Presidential Palace. A tape was not available for verification of the content of this exchange.

Remarks on Receiving the Binational Commission Report in Mexico City
May 6, 1997

Well, thank you very much. Members of the Mexican Cabinet and the American Cabinet, thank you for your reports and for the specific concrete efforts that you are making to move our relationship forward and to help our peoples.

Secretary Albright commented that the work of the Binational Commission was so broad because our relationship is so broad. This is a truly extraordinary thing to have this many people in our Cabinet, this many people in your Cabinet all working together on a broad range of issues.

Let me say, Mr. President, as you know, I'm particularly gratified also to be joined here by strong bipartisan delegations from the United States Congress that are here from many States along the border, as well as Governor Miller of Nevada, the chairman of the Governors' association in the United States. So we're here because we know that we have to make this relationship work together beyond party politics, within our countries and across our borders.

In the 21st century, we want our border to be our bond, and we want it to be rooted in a mutual commitment to the exchange of people and commerce across the border and to our fidelity to the rule of law. The reports we have heard today are fully consistent with that objective.

With regard to narcotics, I was very impressed by the drug threat assessment done jointly; by the proposal for an alliance, and I think the word is well taken—it must be an alliance undertaken in good faith and mutual respect; by the news that the alliance will actually articulate a strategy and specific tactics for implementing the objectives of the alliance by the end of the year.

For our part, we in the United States know that we have to reduce our demand, and General McCaffrey will tell you we've presented the largest counternarcotics budget ever, but we also think we're doing more of the right things. The Attorney General is working very hard to pass the right kind of juvenile justice legislation. And as perhaps many of you in Mexico know, we have been quite successful in reducing drug use among people whom we thought were the biggest problem, young Americans aged 18 to 34. Drug use in our country is going up among Americans even younger, under 18. So we are devoting an enormous amount of time and effort to that problem, and we hope we can show progress on our side.

I am confident, from the efforts which have been made and the statements which were made to me by the President earlier, that Mexico is equally committed to making progress on this side of the border.

With regard to the migration report, I think it strikes the right balance. The Attorney General has explained what we are trying to do in the United States on this issue. I think we all know we have a deep stake in making the border crossings work, and we in the United States, in our Government, have no interest in causing any unfair or undue harm to immigrants in our country. We are a nation of immigrants. We have been deeply enriched by them. They have made us the fifth largest Hispanic country in the world, with 22 million Americans now of Hispanic descent. But we know that we also have to enforce the integrity of our immigration laws at the border, in the workplace, in the criminal justice system, and we are attempting to strike the right balance.

As regard to the other issues, let me just say very briefly, I welcome the specific announcement on clean wastewater. We are trying to show our good faith by committing more funds to the environmental projects. We are concerned that the joint commission has approved something like 16 projects, of which only 4 have been approved for financing by the North American Development Bank, and we're committed to doing something about that.

I'm especially pleased by the educational exchange comments and the commitment to increased educational exchange. I think that is very important. I'm very pleased that there will be a report back to us within 90 days from the relevant Cabinet officers on what we can do more to implement the labor and environmental accords.

And finally, let me say, Mr. President, I'm glad to see that our Cabinet members are reaffirming the fact that NAFTA has worked. There are some people, still, who assert in the United States that it has not, but it has. If you compare what has happened in the last 3 years with what happened the last time Mexico had some economic distress, you see that American exports have fared much better, and the Mexican economy has come back much quicker and much stronger, and NAFTA is clearly partly responsible for that. So I'm glad to see that our Cabinet members are hanging in there and trying to get the evidence out because I think it's clear that we did the right thing.

No one issue defines this relationship. The scope of it presents us with unique challenges and opportunities. It's vital that we work together, but I feel much better about our shared future because of the work that our Cabinet ministers are doing in this unprecedented forum. And I thank them for it, and I thank you for hosting us today.

NOTE: The President spoke at approximately 11:30 a.m. in the Lopez Mateos Room at Los Pinos Presidential Palace. In his remarks, he referred to President Ernesto Zedillo of Mexico and Gov. Bob Miller of Nevada, chairman, National Governor's Association.

The President's News Conference With President Ernesto Zedillo of Mexico in Mexico City
May 6, 1997

President Zedillo. President Clinton, ladies and gentlemen from the media from the United States and from Mexico, once again I would like to express the satisfaction of my government and the people of Mexico for the visit of President Clinton. We are truly very pleased that President Clinton is beginning his tour here in Latin America, starting in Mexico. We are also especially pleased by the results of the work of the Mexico-U.S. Binational Commission and by the agreement that will be materialized today.

President Clinton and I have heard the report of the trade relations between Mexico and the United States. It is very encouraging that from the beginning of NAFTA, our trade has increased over 60 percent and now accounts for close to 150 billion U.S. dollars per year. And this represents, above all, more and improved economic opportunities and more and improved jobs for Mexicans as well as for U.S. citizens.

This is very encouraging in intensifying our efforts in order to reach agreements in the fields that are still pending. This effort has also encouraged us to reaffirm the commitment to NAFTA and to work so that at the summit meeting in Chile next year we will provide an important impulse to a creation of free trade in the American Continent.

The Mexican Government is very pleased with the agreements we have reached in order to promote educational, scientific, and cultural exchanges, as well as to protect the environment and nature, particularly along the border area, our common border. These agreements prove that we are united by interest in the conditions in which our communities live, the conditions of the health and the safety of the families.

We are particularly satisfied that President Clinton and I will be signing the Declaration of the Mexican-U.S. Alliance Against Drugs. Our alliance will be based on mutual trust and on our commitment as heads of state that the collaboration between our countries will progress in keeping with fundamental principles. These principles include the absolute respect of sovereignty and territorial jurisdiction of Mexico and of the United States; shared responsibility

in facing the problem of illegal drugs and related crimes such as money laundering and weapons trafficking; a comprehensive fight against drugs, attaching the same priority to all aspects of the problem; balance and reciprocity in actions, programs, and guidelines to take on the threat of drugs in both countries; and effective law enforcement in both nations.

Based on these principles and based on the joint assessments we received today—President Clinton and I both received this—Mexico and the United States now has a shared vision of the magnitude of the problem, and we share the will to combat the problem with all of the resources within our reach.

The declaration we will be signing contains specific objectives. We have given instructions to our Governments to prepare a common strategy in order to follow through with the objectives and to prepare plans for reciprocal implementation. A particularly pleasing aspect is that the declaration includes the intention to work together, jointly, in order to have a hemispheric agreement against illegal trafficking of weapons, and also an agreement for the extraordinary U.N. assembly on drugs next year.

The Mexican Government appreciates the sensitivity of President Clinton in terms of the Mexicans' rights and the dignity of Mexicans in his country. Thus, it is very pleasing that today we will also sign a joint declaration on migration. For the past 2 years, our Governments have made important progress in dealing bilaterally with issues such as consular protection and the human rights of migrants as well as the efforts to combat trafficking in human beings. Today we have reaffirmed the commitment of both Governments to strengthen bilateral cooperation in order to deal with the migration phenomenon.

We have agreed to base our work on three basic principles: One, the sovereign right of every nation to apply its migration laws however it deems most appropriate for its national interests, always in keeping with international law and in a spirit of bilateral cooperation; the second principle is that of absolute compliance with the objectives of the memorandum of understanding on consular protection of Mexicans in the United States, which was signed almost one year ago, particularly in the respect of human rights of migrants; and the third principle is to deal with the migration phenomenon in a comprehensive view which is mutually beneficial and will make it possible to conserve family unity and to protect the dignity of human beings.

Based on these principles, this establishes the commitments of our Government to protect the rights of migrants and to promote the procurement of justice for migrants as well as the respect of due legal process in the application or the enforcement of migration laws. There is also a shared commitment to ensure safe repatriation and orderly repatriation of migrants and apply new measures to reduce violence along the border and to combat trafficking in human beings and falsification of documents. In order to ensure a comprehensive view on migration, we will examine scientific analysis which will be the result of binational cooperation.

This reflects the cooperation and the good will of our Governments to create a border whose communities are joined by friendship and cooperation, not by conflict. We want appropriate, just, and harmonious development. The visit of President Clinton and the agreements signed and to be signed are a firm step in our relationship of friendship, respect, and cooperation which will benefit both Mexico and the United States.

Once again I would like to thank President Clinton for his visit and also ask him to address you at this time, before we take the questions from our friends from the media.

President Clinton. Thank you. Thank you, Mr. President. To all the members of the Mexican Government here and our hosts, the members of the American delegation, the members of the Cabinet administration, and the Members of Congress. This is my first trip to Mexico as President, my fifth occasion to be in your country in my lifetime, and I'm very pleased to be back. As you know, I had planned to be here a month ago, but I literally got a bad break and couldn't come. So I'm very happy that we're able to consummate this trip today.

As President Zedillo has said just a short while ago, we heard the reports of the United States-Mexico Binational Commission, a remarkable Cabinet-level group that oversees the day-

to-day interaction of our Governments. The presentations demonstrate vividly the remarkable depth and breadth of our relationship. No two countries are working together on more important issues, with a more direct effect on the lives of their people, than Mexico and the United States.

The reports demonstrate that, for the most part, we do agree on the opportunities and the problems before us. And in a few moments, the President and I will sign joint declarations on drugs and migration. They demonstrate that, more than in the past, we also agree on solutions and that we are prepared to carry forward our cooperation to a higher level.

We share more than a 2,000-mile border and, more importantly, we also share a vision of what the border should be in the 21st century: a safe, clean, efficient model of prosperity and cooperation joining our people, not a barrier that divides them.

The joint declaration on migration makes clear that we both see our border as a dynamic living space with complex problems, to be sure, and real opportunities, both of which require a comprehensive approach. The declaration commits both our Governments to improve how we manage the border. We will ensure that the human rights of all migrants are respected, regardless of their status; expand public information campaigns warning migrants of dangerous crossings; reduce violence and criminality at the border; and combat the terrible practice of alien smuggling.

The issue of immigration raises passions on both sides of our border. I'm proud of our tradition of generous legal immigration. I will do everything I can to preserve it. I deeply believe that America's diversity is our greatest source of strength for the future. There is no more powerful proof of that than the remarkable contributions Mexican-Americans have made to our country in every walk of life and to my administration.

But to maintain safe and orderly immigration and to do justice by the hundreds of thousands of people who legally immigrate to the United States every year, we must take effective action to stop illegal immigration. Our new immigration law will help us to do that. In applying the law and in our overall approach to immigration, we must balance control with common sense and compassion.

I am very pleased that the balanced budget agreement I reached with our Congress last week restores certain benefits to some legal immigrants. I will continue to work with Congress to correct some aspects of the immigration law. We will ensure respect for human rights and seek to apply the law humanely, with special concern for children and for families. There will be no mass deportations and no discrimination. But I am also determined to help our southern neighbors make the most of their rich economic and social potential, because, ultimately, that's the best way to give people the confidence they need to make their futures at home.

President Zedillo and I will also sign a joint alliance against drugs. With this alliance, we recognize the dangers we both face, the responsibilities we both share. Illegal narcotics are not simply a Mexican problem—far from it—but neither are they simply an American problem. They are our common problem, and we must find a common solution.

The alliance takes our already unprecedented cooperation to a new level. It respects the laws and sovereignty of our countries, while committing us to 15 concrete goals, to put in place a shared strategy by the end of this year. We've agreed to intensify our work on money-laundering investigations, to increase our cooperation on extraditions, to facilitate trials on both sides of the border, to apply profits seized from drug traffickers directly to law enforcement purposes, and to step up our fight against gun-running, including a hemispheric agreement outlawing the trafficking in illegal arms.

These two declarations prove that we can work through our problems in ways that work for both of us. But this relationship is about far more than resolving our problems. It's about seizing the real opportunities to make our people more prosperous and more secure on the edge of a new century. That's what we did with NAFTA, which has helped to raise our exports to Mexico to an all-time high and helped Mexico to bounce back from a wrenching recession that caused great hardship to people here.

Now, as President Zedillo and I agreed, we must push forward on NAFTA's promise to help us clean up the environment, especially along the border, and to improve working conditions and safeguard worker rights on both sides of the border.

I'm especially pleased with the new steps we have taken to protect the environment and to promote education. The United States will provide $170 million in Environmental Protection Agency funds for border water projects. We will work with Mexico to attract private sector investments in pollution prevention. We will work to preserve endangered species and natural forests.

We have also agreed to expand the Fulbright scholarship program, a favorite one of mine because it was named for my mentor and one of the most outstanding people ever to come from my home State. This will double the number of Fulbright scholars for Mexicans studying in the United States, with a special focus on science and technology.

Our partnership with Mexico for opportunity, security, and prosperity is fundamental to the future of both our peoples. Today we have strengthened that partnership. Our prospects for shaping that future for the children are brighter, and I feel very, very good about what we have done and quite optimistic about what we will do in the days and years ahead.

Thank you, Mr. President.

[At this point, President Clinton and President Zedillo signed the Joint Statement on Migration Adopted by the President of the United States and the President of Mexico, and the Declaration of Mexican and United States Alliance Against Drugs.]

Upcoming Elections in Mexico

Q. I would like to address my question to President Clinton. President Clinton, are you concerned by the elections which will take place here in Mexico next June, and particularly, can you imagine a Congress in Mexico without a PRI majority?

President Clinton. I'm actually more concerned about the American Congress. [*Laughter*] Let me say, I applaud the movement toward political reform and electoral reform in Mexico just as I have applauded and supported the movement toward economic reform.

The judgments in the election are for the Mexican people to make and for all the rest of us who support democracy and freedom and human rights to support. I welcome the fact that so many observers have been invited here to watch it take place, and I respect President Zedillo for supporting this process.

Mexico's Social Policies

Q. President Zedillo and President Clinton, a U.N. report out last month, just last month, said that the extensive focus on free-market economic reforms by themselves have failed to lift much of Latin America, including Mexico, out of poverty—the population out of poverty—and it suggests that more attention needs to be spent on social spending as at least a complementary action.

I'm wondering if you agree with that assessment, if you feel that maybe your extensive focus on free-market reforms need to be balanced in any degree, and if you can offer any kind of prediction on how many years into the future it will be before the countries of Latin America and Mexico specifically reach the level of society-wide economic prosperity, that issues that you've been dealing with such as immigration and drug-trafficking largely dry up on their own or begin to dry up on their own.

Thank you.

President Zedillo. Thank you very much. I will let others talk about the situation of other sister nations in Latin America, and I'll refer to the case of Mexico. One of the reasons why we Mexicans have been reinforcing our economic structure—and this has taken place for just over 10 years—is precisely being able to have a material base which arises from vigorous and sustained economic growth so as to be able to support more ambitious social policies which will make it possible to more effectively combat poverty and inequality, which are the problems that our nation is suffering from.

I think it's very important to underscore the fact that many social problems, many of the problems of inequality and poverty in Mexico today—and I think that there are other countries of Latin America suffering them as well—their basic source is found in government policies which in past decades stressed government control over economic processes too much. The long period of stagnation in our economy cannot be tied to nor should it be tied in any way to the processes of economic liberalization—quite the contrary.

I think that thanks to these policies of opening up towards foreign countries and the internal liberalization of our economies and also adjusting the size of the Mexican Government, as far as the control of the economy is concerned, means that we will now be able to open

up a period of sustained growth, dynamic growth which will make it possible for us to expand the reach, the objectives, the sense, and the results of our social policies.

Extradition Treaty

Q. President Clinton, are you familiar with a list of Mexicans that are extraditable, and would you be willing to review the extradition treaty?

President Zedillo, does this new relationship imply a new concept of sovereignty?

President Clinton. Well, let me say that we have enjoyed an unprecedented amount of cooperation related to common criminal and drug problems in a way designed to strengthen our sovereignty, not to undermine it. So we have worked with Mexico in grievous cases on extraditions, and I appreciate that, just as we are trying to work with Mexico in providing helicopters to support eradication, or computer technology to help Mexico work with us on money laundering, or working on the preventive aspects of the narcotics problem. So I believe that extradition partnerships that are fair, equal, and balanced reinforce a nation's sovereignty; they don't weaken it. And it's an important part of our long-term strategy to work together on the drug issue.

Terry [Terence Hunt, Associated Press].

Whitewater Investigation

Q. Mr. President, I'd like to ask you about a question back in the United States. The Whitewater prosecutors assert that Mrs. Clinton's testimony on several issues has changed over time or differs from that of other witnesses. Do you have any idea of what the discrepancies might be? And what does this suggest to you about the course of the investigation? Is it becoming more troublesome for Mrs. Clinton?

President Clinton. No and no.

Q. Why is that, sir?

President Clinton. Well, you've been watching it for years. If you don't know, I can't help you.

North American Free Trade Agreement

Q. President, 4 years after NAFTA was signed, are the terms fully enforced, or do you believe that it is necessary to carry out any changes, amendments, or are some of the clauses obsolete?

Thank you.

President Zedillo. I believe that the North American Free Trade Agreement has performed very clearly in keeping with the objectives that the three countries participating in the agreement had decided on. And proof of this are the figures of the three countries, the trade figures of the three countries. Just a moment ago I mentioned that in bilateral trade alone between the United States and Mexico during NAFTA trade has grown over 60 percent; that is, almost close to 70 percent. And that is despite the fact that in 1995 in our country we had an economic recession.

Thus, I believe that the terms under which NAFTA was negotiated were very good terms. And I think that within the agreement we have very clear and transparent mechanisms to deal with any kind of dispute, and I believe that at this time there is no significant reason from the Mexican perspective to review the contents of NAFTA.

If you'll allow me, because just a moment ago one question went unanswered, the second part of—[*inaudible*]—question. I would merely like to say that under no circumstances does this new understanding based on respect between Mexico and the United States—in no way does it mean that the concept of sovereignty has changed; on the contrary. It is very pleasing for me as a President and as a representative of the people of Mexico that in a document which we just signed, that President Clinton and I just signed, respecting this alliance against drugs, the first principle which we mutually recognize is—and I will read it—is "the absolute respect for the sovereignty and territorial jurisdiction of both Mexico and the United States of America."

Wreath Laying Ceremony and Whitewater Investigation

Q. Mr. President, as has been discussed a great deal in the last 2 days, the two nations have a long history together and sensitivities have grown up as a result of involvement with one another, including involvement during war. Later today, you will be laying a wreath at the tomb of Mexican cadets who were actually boys at the time that they died at the hands of American troops. This is one of those issues in which the Mexicans have been very sensitive. These boys are heroes and are seen basically as children who died in war.

My question is, are you going there and laying that wreath in any way as a gesture of apology or atonement for action by the U.S. military?

President Clinton. I'm going there as a gesture of respect, not only respect for their lives but respect for the patriotism and the integrity of the people who have served this country.

President Truman went there as well when he was here, and it's my understanding that no one has gone since. But I think other heads of states regularly go there, and I do not believe the President of the United States should decline to go because of what happened between our two countries a long time ago.

You know, we are trying to heal the wounds of war with nations with whom we fought even more recently. I'm sending Pete Peterson, who was a prisoner of war in Vietnam for over 6 years, to Vietnam as the new Ambassador. It seems to me that if the United States wants to lead the world in the direction we say we do, then it is imperative for us to respect our friends and neighbors especially, in countries around the world, and honor their symbols of national honor. And I'm proud to be able to do this.

Let me just say, since the President clarified an answer he gave, let me say to Mr. Hunt I did not mean to be flippant. What I meant to say was I know of no factual discrepancy, period. I am unaware of one. But if you took the four of you sitting there together on the front row and got you all together again 13 to 19 years later and asked you precisely what happened on this day, you might have slightly different memories. I have no idea that there is any such discrepancy, but I have no reason to be concerned about it whatever. We've both done our best to answer all the questions that were asked of us, and already tens of millions of dollars have been spent on this, and I am just perfectly comfortable with where we are.

Immigration Law

Q. President Clinton, the question is regarding what you just mentioned, that is that you would be working with your Congress on some aspects of the migration law. What aspects would these be, and how would they benefit our citizens in the United States?

President Clinton. Well, let me just say, first of all, we've cleared a big hurdle, I think, in the budget agreement, dealing with the eligibility of legal immigrants for public assistance when, through no fault of their own, they're put into some distress. And then there are a number of other issues which have been raised about the administration of this law and the extent to which it might prompt, in a way that Congress never really intended, the virtual permanent breakup of families, especially the people who maybe had visas even there to come into the country in the first place.

So I'm working with Congress on it. But I hope you will understand when I tell you that since this is such a terrifically emotional issue, until we have a clear approach and I understand who is on what side here, the more I say about it, I might be endangering my chances to succeed. I think we all know what the most significant potential problems of the law are. I still support its fundamental traditions. I support—I'm glad I—I would sign the law again tomorrow if I had to because it gives us the ability to control our borders better, to get illegal immigrants out of the workplace, and to take illegal immigrants who come into the criminal justice system and remove them quicker. So I think that's all to the good.

I'm concerned about undue family breakup and disqualifying people who may not deserve it virtually permanently from applying for citizenship.

Mexico-U.S. Antidrug Efforts

Q. A question for both men. Have you resolved the issue of whether American drug agents operating in Mexico can carry sidearms for their own protection? And if you have, given the level of trust—or distrust—between our two countries, such that it takes a Presidential meeting to resolve an issue like that, why should anyone believe that the United States and Mexico would be able to cooperate, exchange highly sensitive intelligence information on drug trafficking or drug smuggling, or is the talk of cooperation just that—talk?

President Zedillo. If you will allow me, in the declaration that we've just signed, that President Clinton and I have just signed, it is very clear on two aspects. The first aspect, having to do with the principles—and I referred to them a moment ago, but I will refer to them again—and that is the absolute respect for the sovereignty and territorial jurisdiction of both Mexico and the United States.

And the other aspect, which is very important for the Mexican Government and is expressed

as one of the specific tasks to be undertaken by both Governments, and it reads, literally, "The Governments will do whatever necessary to ensure the protection of the officials in charge of enforcing the law." And this naturally is on both sides of the border, applicable for both sides of the border.

This principle and this recommendation which we've made to our Governments must be translated into practical measures which obviously are in keeping with both of the previously mentioned principles. I have already answered this question, the question that you've put me, in the past, and I can assure you that we will comply both with the principles that both Governments have agreed to, as well as with the objective of providing these people with safety.

Naturally, it would not be appropriate for us to refer to the specific mechanisms with which, within the principle for the respective sovereignty, we will be protecting these law enforcement agents. I am sure that President Clinton nor myself would ever make public the details which might jeopardize the safety of these people. Yet our commitment in both areas is very clear.

President Clinton. This is in response to the second half of your question. You said, why should anyone believe that we can work together? And let's be frank here among friends. On the American side the problems are, we have less than 5 percent of the world's population, and we consume about half the drugs. And we're more than happy every year, American citizens, to give billions of dollars that winds up in the hands of narcotraffickers. That's our big problem. Our second problem is that while we are increasing our capacity to deal with it, we have not succeeded in reducing the demand or completely controlling the border on our side.

Now, the Mexican problem is that narcotraffickers can destroy the fabric of civil society. They can undermine the integrity of any society. And they go after places with open spaces and a vulnerability to organized money and violence. And so they also have to worry about corruption, as anyone would targeted with that kind of money.

But you say, how can we rely on them to cooperate? Let me talk about some facts that we never—that we under-report. And I don't mean that as a criticism; I mean we do, too, we in public life. We now have 202 cooperative money-laundering ventures going now; 54 of them are complete, joint investigations. Last year, 200 law enforcement officers in Mexico lost their lives in the line of duty—200. And extraditions, seizures, prosecutions, and eradications are all up in the last year.

So I believe that this Government is trying to work with us. And I believe that the chances of our succeeding in dealing with our problems, and the chances of their succeeding in dealing with their problems are dramatically heightened if we work together and be honest about our problems but also not deny good-faith efforts when they exist. All those 200 people had families that grieved for them. They laid down their lives trying to fight—roll back the narcotraffickers, roll back corruption, roll back crime. And it seems to me that their lives alone are evidence that we ought to be working to cooperate.

President Zedillo. In view of the time constraints, we will take one last question.

Q. Thank you. Good afternoon. President Zedillo, in view of the magnitude of the fight against drug trafficking, is it possible that Mexico will accept the $6 million in cash offered by the United States to combat drugs as an additional resource to combat drug trafficking?

And President Clinton, how did your view or your vision of Mexico change when you arrived here after your meeting with President Zedillo, and particularly, what was your concept after having visited the Museum of Anthropology?

Thank you.

President Zedillo. In terms of the principle of mutual respect and cooperation that the United States of America and Mexico have developed in fighting drug trafficking, there have been different occasions on which we have received material support for this struggle, which is a struggle that we all participate in.

I am not informed of the details of the resources that you've mentioned. I am sure that within the context of the agreement that we have reached we will examine in all detail this offer, and in keeping with the principles and objectives that I've mentioned we will reach a decision in this regard.

Mexico-U.S. Relations and President's Visit to Museum of Anthropology

President Clinton. Let me briefly say that I don't know that my view of our relationship has changed since I got here yesterday after-

noon, but I have been reinforced in my conviction that we can make progress on all these fronts as long as we do it in a genuine atmosphere of mutual respect, and as long as we're completely honest about our differences and willing to work hard to overcome them, and we tell the people the facts about the progress we are making and the problems we have. So I feel very much reassured.

And in terms of going to the Anthropological Museum, I haven't been there since the 1970's. I was a young man in a different line of work back then. And I think the President can tell you that I think I kept him about an hour longer than I was supposed to, and I would probably still be there if it were up to me. But I hope the Mexican people are very proud of that because it shows, even to an outsider like me, the remarkable cultures which were the foundation of modern Mexico. And it certainly gave me a deeper appreciation for the richness and depth of this country's history and the incredible talents and gifts of its people.

President Zedillo. Muchas gracias.

President Clinton. One more—equal time? [*Laughter*]

Mexico-U.S. Antidrug Efforts

Q. Mr. President, you mentioned the responsibilities that the United States bears for the international drug problem because of the massive demand in the United States. Can you give us some of your ideas of new efforts that you might have to help to combat this big demand?

The President. First of all, let me say, I have—we could talk all day about this, and I have to be brief. But the first thing I would urge you to do is to never forget the plan that General McCaffrey has filed now, because General McCaffrey is a military man and when he files a plan, that's his mission, and he intends to follow it. And if you look at our budget and if you look at our priorities, we're trying to implement it.

But let me just mention two points, if I might. Number one, we are trying, with the work of the Attorneys General of the two countries and our drug operations, to intensify our cooperation with Mexico and to work more effectively with other countries to prevent drugs at their source or in transit. Number two, we are focusing on our young people. We know that we have—and we thank God for it—we know we've had a big decline in drug use among people between the ages of 18 and 34. So now we have to focus on the young. And that means more education, more testing, more treatment. And it means that we have to have a comprehensive juvenile justice youth development program in every community in the United States.

That's one of the reasons I strongly supported the Summit of Service in Philadelphia, because I believe if they really want to do the things that we all said we wanted to do, there will have to be a community-based initiative that the Federal Government supports in every community to keep our kids alive and keep them off drugs.

So we have to do our part. And I'm firmly committed to doing it.

Thank you.

President Zedillo. Muchas gracias.

NOTE: The President's 143d news conference began at 1:47 p.m. in the Residence at the Los Pinos Presidential Palace. President Zedillo spoke in Spanish, and his remarks were translated by an interpreter. In his remarks, President Clinton referred to Attorney General Jorge Luis Madrazo of Mexico. A portion of the news conference could not be verified because the tape was incomplete.

Joint Statement on Migration Adopted by the President of the United States and the President of Mexico
May 6, 1997

The issue of migration of Mexican nationals to the United States is a priority on our bilateral agenda. We, the Presidents of the United States and Mexico hereby politically commit our respective governments to strive to ensure a proper and respectful management of this complex phenomenon taking into consideration its diverse causes and economic and social consequences in both countries.

During the last two years, our governments have engaged in consultations and exchange of information through many mechanisms and have produced significant progress in the bilateral treatment of issues such as human rights and consular protection of migrants and efforts to combat migrant trafficking. This constructive dialogue should serve as a first step leading to specific proposals to manage migration between our nations in a mutually beneficial manner.

In pursuing these proposals, our governments reaffirm a commitment to enhanced bilateral cooperation in the management of migration. We will be guided by the following principles:

- The sovereign right of every State to formulate and enforce its immigration laws in a manner that addresses its national interests, always in accordance with the rules of international law and in pursuit of a spirit of bilateral cooperation;
- Full compliance with the objectives of the memorandum of Understanding on Con-

sular Protection of United States and Mexican Nationals, signed on May 7, 1996, especially the respect for human rights of all migrants; and,

- Dedication to a comprehensive vision of managing migration and our shared border that turns differences between our nations into sources of strength, and that leads to mutually beneficial economic and social development that preserves family reunification and protects human dignity.

On the basis of these principles, we, the Presidents of the United States and Mexico commit our governments to intensify dialogue and to accelerate efforts to achieve the following goals:

- Explore ways to strengthen mechanisms and fora for consultation and cooperation on migration and consular protection that the two governments have established at the national and local level;
- Protect the rights of migrants, pursue vigorously the administration of justice in situations in which migrants and border communities register complaints concerning unlawful actions, and respect due process and constitutional guarantees in the implementation of immigration laws;
- Ensure the implementation of safe and orderly procedures for the repatriation of migrants;

- Design and implement new ways to reduce violence along the border and to protect innocent victims of traffickers from the dangers of crossing in mountainous and desert terrain, including a vigorous educational and public information campaign to advise families on both sides of the border of the hazards of crossing in those areas;
- Combat trafficking in migrants and forging of documents and, to that end, develop effective mechanisms of exchange of information and cooperation, with full respect for the sovereignty of each country;
- Achieve a comprehensive approach on the migration phenomenon between the two countries through scientific and cooperative studies that contribute to a bilateral understanding of this issue.

We, the Presidents of the United States and Mexico, affirm our governments' political will to strive to fulfill a vision of our shared border in the twenty-first century as a place that supports and depends on building communities of cooperation rather than of conflict. In pursuance of this vision, our governments will work together to expand upon the foundation of progress made through joint planning and cooperation during the last two years in certain border areas. Both administrations will intensify efforts to achieve the following goals:

- Encourage binational strategic planning activities that seek to design new integrated approaches to mutually beneficial economic, social, environmental, and cultural development in border communities;
- Support and expand public and private partnerships in developing cross border interests and activities, and in pursuing shared interests on either side of the border;
- Intensify the dialogue on financing mechanisms that promote and implement cross border development projects;
- Test new ways to design infrastructure and community development projects that provide a dignified approach to public safety in border communities;
- Explore new approaches to managing temporary travel between border communities, consistent with the laws of each nation, recognizing the economic, social and family benefits of vigorous cross border exchange; and,
- Promote effective management of ports of entry to foster orderly movement of traffic of goods and people, and to reduce the waiting times for daily commuters and other commercial vehicles.

We, the Presidents of the United States and Mexico, call on the relevant agencies of both administrations to report to us in one year, through the Binational Commission, on the progress made towards the better management of the migration phenomenon and the transformation of our border into a model area of bilateral cooperation.

WILLIAM J. CLINTON	ERNESTO ZEDILLO PONCE DE LEÓN
President	President
The United States of America	Federal Republic of Mexico

NOTE: An original was not available for verification of the content of this joint statement.

Declaration of Mexican and United States Alliance Against Drugs
May 6, 1997

Drug abuse and drug trafficking are a danger to our societies, an affront to our sovereignty and a threat to our national security. We declare our nations united in an alliance to combat this menace.

With trust in one another and in our commitment as Chiefs of State, our collaboration will go forward based on the following fundamental principles: a) absolute respect for the sovereignty and territorial jurisdiction of Mexico and the United States; b) shared responsibility for confronting the problem of illegal drugs and related crimes, such as illegal arms trafficking and money laundering; c) adoption of an integrated approach against illegal drugs, which will confront the problem from the demand and supply side simultaneously; d) balance and reciprocity in the actions, programs and rules developed to confront the drug threat in both countries; and e) effective application of the laws in both countries.

Our governments have issued a joint threat assessment detailing the nature of illegal drug use in both our societies, and the extent of drug trafficking and related crimes as they threaten both our peoples. Mexico and the United States are fully agreed on the magnitude of the problem in both countries, and are determined to combat it with all resources at our disposal.

Accordingly, we have instructed our responsible Cabinet Officers, acting through the U.S./ Mexico High Level Contact Group for Drug Control, to work out a common counterdrug strategy, and to develop mutually reinforcing implementation plans for this common strategy, consistent with each other's National Drug Control Programs.

Acting together in accordance with this political commitment, and working to enhance trust, mutual support and confidence, Mexico and the United States will:

- Reduce the demand for illicit drugs through the intensification of anti-drug information and educational efforts, particularly those directed at young people, and through rehabilitative programs.
- Reduce the production and distribution of illegal drugs in both countries, particularly marijuana, methanphetamine, cocaine and heroin.
- Focus law enforcement efforts against criminal organizations and those who facilitate their operations in both countries.
- Strengthen U.S./Mexican law enforcement cooperation and policy coordination, and assure the safety of law enforcement officers.
- Ensure that fugitives are expeditiously and with due legal process, brought to justice and are unable to evade justice in one of our countries by fleeing to or remaining in the other. To this end, we agree to negotiate a protocol to the extradition treaty that, consistent with the legal system in each country, will allow, under appropriate circumstances and conditions, individuals to be tried in both countries prior

to the completion of their sentence in either country.
- Identify the sources of, and deter the illegal traffic in firearms.
- Work together to conclude a hemispheric agreement outlawing illegal traffic in firearms.
- Work together for the success of the Special Session of the U.N. General Assembly on Illicit Drugs in June 1998.
- Increase the abilities of our democratic institutions to attack and root out the corrupting influence of the illegal drug trade in both countries.
- Enhance cooperation along both sides of our common border to increase security.
- Control essential and precursor chemicals to prevent chemical diversion and illicit use, and improve information exchange on this subject.
- Implement more effectively the laws and regulations to detect and penalize money laundering in both countries, and enhance bilateral and multilateral exchanges of information and expertise to combat money laundering.
- Seize and forfeit the proceeds and instrumentalities of drug trafficking, and direct these to the use of drug prevention and law enforcement, in accordance with legal procedures in force in and between our countries.
- Improve our capacity to interrupt drug shipments by air, land, and sea.
- Implement training and technical cooperation programs to ensure that anti-drug personnel acquire needed capabilities and perform with the highest level of professionalism and integrity.
- Enhance and facilitate exchange of information and evidence to prosecute and convict criminals and deter drug trafficking; and ensure the security and appropriate use of the information and evidence provided.

Our Alliance's counterdrug strategy, along with respective plans of operations for its implementation shall be completed by the end of the year. Prior to that we will meet again with our respective responsible Cabinet Officers to resolve any outstanding issues, and review the progress in our cooperation.

In pursuance of this Alliance Against Drugs, we hereby pledge the fullest support of ourselves and of our governments to construct drug free societies for the twenty-first century.

WILLIAM J. CLINTON

President
The United States of America

ERNESTO ZEDILLO
PONCE DE LEÓN

President
Federal Republic of
Mexico

NOTE: An original was not available for verification of the content of this declaration.

Statement on the Election of Sandra Feldman as President of the American Federation of Teachers
May 6, 1997

In electing Sandra Feldman president, the American Federation of Teachers has chosen someone who has already proven herself as a dynamic leader and superb educator. I've visited schools with her in New York and have seen first-hand the respect that teachers and students have for her. I share that respect.

Like her predecessor, Al Shanker, Sandra Feldman is an outstanding advocate for our Nation's students. I look forward to working with her on a variety of issues that will improve the quality of education our children receive, including making high standards a reality in every American public school.

Message to the Congress Transmitting a Report on the Lapse of the Export Administration Act of 1979
May 6, 1997

To the Congress of the United States:

As required by section 204 of the International Emergency Economic Powers Act (50 U.S.C. 1703(c)) and section 401(c) of the National Emergencies Act (50 U.S.C. 1641(c)), I transmit herewith a 6-month periodic report on the national emergency declared by Executive Order 12924 of August 19, 1994, to deal with the threat to the national security, foreign policy, and economy of the United States caused by the lapse of the Export Administration Act of 1979.

WILLIAM J. CLINTON

The White House,
May 6, 1997.

Exchange With Reporters Prior to Discussions With Andres Manuel Lopez Obrador of Mexico's Democratic Revolutionary Party in Mexico City
May 6, 1997

Q. Mr. President, why did you decide to be the first American President to meet with opposition leaders?

The President. Because we support the political reform process in Mexico, and I do this in other countries, in Russia, Israel, other countries I visit. So I thought it was important.

NOTE: The exchange began at 7:10 p.m. at El Presidente Intercontinental Hotel. A tape was not available for verification of the content of this exchange.

Remarks at the State Dinner in Mexico City
May 6, 1997

Mr. President, Mrs. Zedillo, members of the Mexican Cabinet and other distinguished public servants, citizens of Mexico, on behalf of Hillary, of all the members of our delegation from the administration and the Congress, I first thank you for the graciousness and warmth with which you have welcomed us. We live side by side as neighbors, we work together day-in and day-out as partners, but the warmth of your reception has reminded us today that we are also close friends.

Just before the dinner began, President and Mrs. Zedillo took Hillary and me to see the magnificent murals of Diego Rivera that adorn this great palace. They are very moving works. Along with the paintings of Orozco and Siqueiros, they represent the peak of artistic achievement in this century and one of the many contributions of Mexico to the culture of the world. Anyone who has seen it knows that the power of Rivera's "Epic of the Mexico People in Their Struggle for Freedom and Independence" comes from more than mere technical skill. In this grand work we see the proud spirit of Mexico's revolution and Mexico's heart.

Instantly, I saw Rivera's extraordinary love of the Mexican people, the same passion which then and now inspires Mexico's journey toward a better and freer society. Rivera never actually finished his epic, and perhaps that is fitting because the journey of every nation to increase the freedom of its people, the labor at the very heart of democracy, never ends.

I am delighted to be in Mexico at another time when this struggle is making a dramatic stride forward. Mexico's leaders and political parties are opening the doors of democracy wider than ever. New citizen groups have sown the seeds of a vibrant civil society that promises to deliver to all Mexicans a better and freer future.

Mr. President, you reminded us that it was in this palace where Benito Juarez corresponded with Abraham Lincoln. Our President, Mr. Lincoln, who many of us consider to be our greatest President, called in the United States in his time for a new birth of freedom. The murals here remind us here that the birth of freedom is more than a matter of improving our political systems. We must also strive to see that our citizens are free from want and hunger, free from the dangers our new age brings, and free to make the most of their own lives.

The partnership we seek with Mexico is one that will advance that kind of freedom, here and throughout the Americas. We want to work together to lay the foundation of an enduring prosperity. We want to join together to improve the air and water we share. We want to work to turn our border into a region of growth, to defeat disease, to defeat the threat of drugs, organized crime, and corruption.

Mr. President, we can succeed because we have forged a relationship as broad and deep as that which exists between any two nations. And today we have made important progress. We are answering the demands of our time, advancing the common goals of our people, serving a friendship that is at the heart of what we all want for our future. In so doing, we honor the legacy of Benito Juarez and Abraham Lincoln and the constant quest for a new birth of freedom.

Ladies and gentlemen, I ask you now to join with me in toasting President and Mrs. Zedillo and their family, to partnership of our nations and the new day of freedom it will bring to the friends and neighbors of our shared continent.

NOTE: The President spoke at 10:09 p.m. at the Presidential Palace. In his remarks, he referred to President Ernesto Zedillo of Mexico and his wife, Anilda Patricia. A tape was not available for verification of the content of these remarks.

Address to the People of Mexico in Mexico City
May 7, 1997

Thank you, Mr. President, for the wisdom of your words, for the warmth of your personal expression, and for the great generosity with which the people of Mexico have received my wife and our delegation, the members of the administration and the Members of Congress. We thank all those who have been a part of that in the Mexican Government, throughout the political system, and citizens at large.

I am honored to speak today in the heart of this magnificent capital, where Teotihuacan and Aztec civilizations flourished, where one of the world's greatest cities grew up centuries before the first English tents were pitched in Jamestown, Virginia, or Plymouth, Massachusetts. I'm frankly a little envious that Hillary got to spend an extra day here, and I want to thank those who are responsible for the wonderful welcome she received in the Yucatan. Almost 22 years ago now, Hillary and I came to Mexico for our honeymoon. Mexico won our hearts then, but now as then, *mi encanta Mexico.*

I come here today to celebrate the ties that bind the United States and Mexico and to help set a course to strengthen them for the age of possibility before us as we enter the 21st century. Our nations and our hemisphere stand at a crossroads as hopeful as the time when Hidalgo and Morelos lit the torch of liberty for Mexico almost two centuries ago.

Democracy has swept every country but one in the Americas, giving people a vote and a voice in their future. Decades of coups and civil wars have given way to stability, to peace, to free markets, and to the search for social justice and a cleaner environment. The electricity of change is surging throughout our hemisphere and nowhere more hopefully than Mexico.

I congratulate the Mexican people for carrying forward bold political reforms that will lead in July to the most intensely contested elections in your history. We know from our own 220-year experiment that democracy is hard work. It must be defended every day. But it is worth the effort, for it has produced more opportunity for people to make the most of their own lives than all its rivals.

Four years ago, in this very place, we began a grand common effort to secure democracy's gains in our hemisphere for all our people. On behalf of my administration, Vice President Gore here invited the nations of our hemisphere to the Summit of the Americas in Miami. There we set an ambitious agenda to create free trade throughout the hemisphere and to cooperate on a host of other issues with the goal of fulfilling the age-old dream of building a truly democratic and prosperous family of the Americas in the 21st century.

Revolutionary forces of integration and technology and trade and travel and communications are shaping our times and bringing us all closer together. The stroke of a computer key sends ideas, information, and money across the planet at lightening speed. Every day we use products that are dreamed up in one country, financed in another, manufactured in a third, with parts made in still other countries, and then sold all over the world. Like it or not, we are becoming more interdependent. And we see that, too, on the negative side, as when a stock market crash, an environmental disaster, or a dread disease in one country sends shock waves deeply felt far beyond its borders.

While economic integration is inevitable, its shape and its reach depend upon our response to it. In both our countries, there are some who would throw up walls of protection to ward off the challenge of change. But more and more, people here, in the United States, and throughout the Americas understand that openness, competition, and the flow of ideas and culture can improve the lives of all our people if we ensure that these forces work for and not against all our people.

With our long border, rich history, and complex challenges, Mexico and the United States have a special responsibility to work together to seize the opportunities and defeat the dangers of this time. Our partnership for freedom and democracy and for prosperity and our partnership against drugs, organized crime, environmental decay, and social injustice is fundamental to the future of the American people and to the future of the Mexican people.

To succeed, this partnership must be rooted in a spirit of mutual respect. Your great leader Benito Juarez, whose statue stands not far from the White House in Washington, said, "Respect for the rights of others is peace." Today I reaffirm to the people of Mexico: We embrace the wisdom of Juarez. We seek a peaceful, prosperous partnership filled with respect and dignity.

Four years ago, together, we led the fight for NAFTA. Many people in both our countries painted a dark picture of lost jobs and boarded-up factories should NAFTA prevail. Well, they were wrong. NAFTA is working, working for you and working for the American people.

In 3 short years, and despite Mexico's worst recession in this century, trade between our nations has grown nearly 60 percent, as President Zedillo said. Mexico is our third largest trading partner, just behind Japan, which has an economy 15 times larger. Our exports to Mexico are 37 percent higher than before NAFTA, an all-time high in spite of the economic difficulties here.

But for Mexico, NAFTA's benefits are just as great. Two and a half years ago, the financial crisis that struck Mexico wrought real and profound hardship to your people as jobs vanished and inflation skyrocketed. The storm hit only days after President Zedillo took office. He might have simply complained that he got a big dose of bad luck, but instead he responded with vision and courage. By keeping to the path of reform and the blueprint of NAFTA, he lessened the impact of the recession. Though real hardships remain, Mexico has made a remarkable turnaround. Since the crisis, you have created one million new jobs, cut inflation by more than half, and regained the confidence of international investors.

Now, compare this with the economic crisis of 1981 and '82, when Mexico sharply raised its tariffs and followed a different course. Then, it took 7 long years for Mexico to return to the financial markets; this time, only 7 months. Then, it took 4 years for your economy to recover the lost ground; this time, only a year after the crisis, Mexico grew by more than 5 percent and is expected to grow strongly this year, too.

You have endured punishing setbacks, but America is proud to have worked with you from the very beginning, enlisting international support for a loan package that safeguarded hundreds of thousands of jobs in both our countries, calmed emerging markets throughout Latin America and the world, and when Mexico paid the loan back, earned the respect and admiration of the entire world. I congratulate you on this course.

Of course, the ultimate test of our economic partnership is not in big numbers but in human impact: the electronic workers of Mexico's Baja Peninsula whose new jobs mean better health care and pensions and more education for their children; the hundreds of thousands of Mexican women who now have mammograms because American-made diagnostic equipment has become more affordable to you; and all the American workers with good high-wage jobs based on our trade with you.

NAFTA has also become an important tool for improving the environment and the well-being of workers. Its institutions are working to clean up pollution in the border region, with four treatment plants already under construction and more to come. Its labor agreements have created a new awareness of workers' rights and labor conditions in both our countries.

We must accelerate the pace of these efforts to reach more people and more communities. And we must include more nations in our partnership so that we can achieve the goal we set out at the Summit of the Americas of a free trade area of the Americas. That is why I'm working with Congress to gain support for fast-track authority and why I'm coming back to Latin America twice in the next few months.

As we celebrate these accomplishments, we must also do everything in our power to assure that the benefits and the burdens of change are fairly shared. The most powerful tool for doing that, plainly, is education, giving our people the skills they need to compete and succeed.

At the Miami summit, Mexico took the responsibility of leading a hemispheric education initiative. Working with Brazil, Chile, and the United States, you have set our sights on lifting standards and bringing new methods and technologies to classrooms throughout the hemisphere. We can rekindle the passion for education that swept this country after your revolution. Your great poet Alfonso Reyes described that moment as "a grand crusade for learning that electrified the people. Nothing equal to it has ever been seen in the Americas."

Let us see something equal to it and greater. Let us renew this crusade. And let us remember—as my wife has said to citizens on every continent, in distant villages and large cities—this crusade for education must include young women as well as young men, on equal terms. And let us resolve to make this crusade a shining light of our next Summit of the Americas next year in Santiago.

In Miami, at the first summit, we also reaffirmed that we cannot be responsible stewards of freedom unless we are also responsible stewards of our natural resources, our hemisphere's land and air and water as well as the rich texture of plant and animal life they support.

Over the long run, the development of democracy and a prosperous economy requires the sustainable development of our natural resources. That is why we have put the protection of the environment right where it belongs, at the heart of our hemispheric agenda. That is the course we charted together in Rio, in Miami, in Santa Cruz, and one we must pursue further in Santiago.

Trade, education, and the environment are critical pieces of the greater mosaic of our relationship, designed to turn our 2,000-mile border into a vibrant source of growth and jobs and open exchange. We're also building a bridge between Brownsville and Matamoros and roads to connect our people, streamlining cargo transit with high-tech scanners, improving water supplies for the area's inhabitants, and through our Border 21 initiative, giving local communities a strong voice in the future of the dynamic living space they share.

As our cooperation grows closer, so do our people. For America, that means pride in the fact that we are one of the most diverse democracies in the world. That diversity will be one of our great strengths in the global society of the 21st century. And Mexican-Americans are a crucial part of our diversity and our national pride. Now more than 12 million strong, they have helped to make the United States the fifth largest Hispanic nation in the world.

Mexican-Americans are contributing to every dimension of American life. In Congress, they have written the laws of our land. Just yesterday, Ambassador Bill Richardson, whose mother came from this city, was working to bring peace in central Africa, and every day he is America's voice at the United Nations. Our administration draws strength from many other remarkable Mexican-Americans, including several who are here with me, our Energy Secretary, Federico Peña; my Director of Public Liaison, Maria Echaveste; my Congressional Liaison, Janet Murguia. I am also pleased to have in our party two distinguished Members of Congress who are Mexican-Americans, Xavier Becerra of California and Silvestre Reyes of Texas and four other distinguished elected officials who represent large number of Mexican-Americans and who care deeply about our partnership, Senator Kay Bailey Hutchison of Texas, Senator Jeff Bingaman of New Mexico, Representative Jim Kolbe of Arizona, and Governor Robert Miller of Nevada.

Last year nearly 160,000 Mexicans immigrated legally to America, bringing their talents, their energies, their aspirations. They've played by the rules. And we, for our part, must make sure that the system treats them fairly and gives them the chance to live up to their hopes and dreams.

But to maintain an immigration policy that is generous, fair, safe, and orderly, we must also take effective action to stop illegal immigration. We are a nation of immigrants and of laws. Just as those who obey our laws are welcome, those who break them must face the consequences. Our new immigration law will help us to achieve these goals. In applying it and in our overall approach to immigration, we will balance control with common sense and compassion.

I am very pleased that the balanced budget agreement I reached with our Congress last week includes a significant restoration of welfare benefits to legal immigrants. I will continue to work with Congress to correct some aspects of our immigration law. We will ensure respect for human rights and seek to apply the law humanely, with special concern for children and families. There will be no mass deportations or no discrimination. And we will continue to support Mexico's efforts to create new opportunities here, so that no one feels compelled to leave home just to earn a living for his or her family.

In the end, that is the answer. But I ask you to remember and work with us on the central premise. We have a generous immigration policy, perhaps the most generous in the world, but to make it work we must be a nation of laws.

This moment of great promise for us is, frankly, also one of peril. The great irony of this time is that the forces of global integration have also unleashed powerful sources of disintegration that use open borders and technology and modern communications to strike at the very heart of civilized societies, our families, our institutions, our very lives.

For us, the greatest of these scourges is that of illegal drug trafficking. The costs to both of us of illegal drugs are staggering. In America, every year drugs kill 14,000 people and cost our country almost $70 billion for crime, prisons, lost work, wounded bodies, and ruined lives. Every year, our law enforcement officials arrest one million people on drug charges. In Mexico, President Zedillo has called narcotics trafficking the greatest threat to national security, the biggest hazard to social health, and the bloodiest source of violence.

Throughout our hemisphere, we see how drug cartels threaten the fabric of entire societies. They corrupt or murder law enforcement officials and the judiciary, take over legitimate businesses and banks, spread violence to offices and homes, to streets and to playgrounds.

Drugs are not simply a Mexican problem or an American problem; they are our common problem. The enormous demand for drugs in America must be stemmed. We have just a little less than 5 percent of the world's population, yet we consume one-third of the world's cocaine, most of which comes from Mexico. The money we spend on illegal drugs fuels narcotraffickers who, in turn, attack your police and prosecutors and prey on your institutions. We must face this curse together, because we cannot defeat it alone. My friends, the battle against drugs must unite our people, not divide them.

We must fight back together, and we must prevail. In the United States we have begun the largest antidrug effort in our history. More than two-thirds of its $16 billion budget will go to attacking our domestic drug problem. We've cut casual drug use by 50 percent in America, but tragically, among young people under 18 drug use has doubled. We're reaching out to young people with an unprecedented effort, a public education campaign to teach that drugs are wrong, illegal, and deadly. We're supporting successful neighborhood strategies like community policing that are making our streets and schools safer and more drug-free. We're punishing drugpushers with tougher sentences and working with our partners abroad to destroy drugs at the source or stop them in transit.

Here in Mexico, you must continue your brave fight against illegal drugs. Already you have shown real advances in drug eradication. You've enacted strong new measures to combat money laundering and organized crime. You've destroyed more drug labs and landing strips and seized more drugs, including more than 10 tons of cocaine just days ago. And last week, you resolved to rebuild your drug enforcement agency on a firmer foundation.

I know the hardship and sacrifice this has caused. More than 200 Mexican police officers died last year because of drug violence. As terrible as this toll is, the price of giving up and giving in would be higher. Let us resolve to redouble our efforts, not by pointing fingers but by joining hands.

Yesterday, President Zedillo and I took an important step forward when we declared the U.S.-Mexican alliance against drugs. Based on mutual respect and common sense, we will strengthen our attack on drug production, trafficking, and consumption. We will crack down harder on the key problems of money laundering and arms trafficking. The future of our children depends upon these efforts and depends more on our determination to continue the fight. We must not let our children down.

Our alliance against drugs is but one of many elements in our cooperation for the coming century. Yesterday, the President and I received the report of our Binational Commission. From wiping out tuberculosis in our border States to protecting endangered species in the Pacific, to increasing educational opportunity with more Fulbright scholarships, the scope of our joint efforts has become as large as the continent we share.

Fifty years ago, President Harry Truman came to Mexico. His visit was a turning point between our people. He spoke of the difficulties in our past and of the need for us to work more closely. He said, "I refuse to be discouraged by apparent difficulties. Difficulties are a challenge to men of determination." In the face of our difficulties, we must be men and women of determination. We can bridge the divides of culture, history, and geography to achieve Juarez's noble vision of respect and peace.

Rooted in the rule of law, rooted in prosperity for all who will work for it, rooted in good health and a clean environment, rooted in modern education and timeless values, the bright promise of a new century lies before us. Let us embrace it together.

Thank you.

NOTE: The President spoke at 11:21 a.m. at the National Auditorium, and his remarks were broadcast live on Mexican television. In his remarks, he referred to President Ernesto Zedillo of Mexico.

Remarks to the Community in Tlaxcala, Mexico
May 7, 1997

Buenos dias, Tlaxcala. President and Mrs. Zedillo, Governor and Mrs. Alvarez-Lima, to all of our friends from Mexico and the United States. Mayor Teroba, thank you for welcoming us to this wonderful city. It is great to be here. I thank you for coming out to say hello.

President Zedillo and I have been working hard, as he said, and now we have come just to celebrate Mexico's people and culture with you. This is an especially important day for my wife and for me because we were married about 22 years ago, and we came to Mexico on our honeymoon. And so we always love to come back. And this is a very romantic setting to be in today, and we thank you for that.

The partnership between Mexico and the United States, the friendship between Mexico and the United States is important to the future of the American people and the Mexican people. It must be pursued in a genuine spirit of respect, equality, and dignity.

We are moving into a world with great changes in the way we work and live, and the world grows smaller because of technology and rapid communications. But some things do not change. This beautiful city, founded nearly 500 years ago, reminds us that even in times of great change, some things are meant to last: our heritage, our love of family, community, our devotion to work, our respect for the land we are blessed to inhabit.

It is my purpose to work with you to preserve the things that we want to preserve, to change as we must so that the people of Mexico and the people of the United States will have more and better jobs, good health care, all our children, boys and girls alike, will have good education, and we will be able together to beat back our common enemies of drugs and crime; so that as we move into the new century, we will know we have preserved our community, our values, our integrity, and we have prepared the way for our children's future.

In closing, I would like to say a special thank-you to the Mexican people for the many contributions that Mexican-Americans have made to our life in the United States. Two members of my Presidential Cabinet, many people in my administration, many Members of our Congress, people successful in all walks of life have their roots here in Mexico. They are proud of it, and so am I. And we are going to work hard to make sure that in the years ahead we draw closer together, we work together, we maintain a spirit of pride in our own heritage but a genuine partnership for a better future.

Thank you. Thank you, Mexico. Thank you for a wonderful visit.

NOTE: The President spoke at 1:41 p.m. in the town square. In his remarks, he referred to President Ernesto Zedillo of Mexico and his wife, Anilda Patricia; Gov. Jose Antonio Alvarez-Lima of Tlaxcala and his wife, Veronica; and Mayor Cesareo Teroba of Tlaxcala. A tape was not available for verification of the content of these remarks.

Remarks on Arrival in San Jose, Costa Rica
May 7, 1997

President Figueres, Mrs. Figueres, members of the Costa Rican delegation, and let me say a special word of thanks to the students and to the National Youth Symphony for giving us such a warm welcome. Thank you very much. I am pleased and honored to be in Costa Rica for the very first time and to experience firsthand your unique tradition of greeting foreign leaders not with a military salute but with the cheers of your wonderful young people.

Costa Rica's steadfast devotion to peace and democracy and your commitment to education and to the preservation of your marvelous environment have long been a model for the stable, democratic, and prosperous hemisphere we are working to build together.

This is a moment of great opportunity and hope for all the Americas, but especially here in Central America where decades of conflict and division have given way to peace and cooperation. That new reality helps to open a new era of partnership between the United States,

the nations of Central America, and the Dominican Republic. Over the next 2 days, I look forward to working with President Figueres and our fellow leaders to strengthen democracy, expand the reach of free and fair trade, and improve the life of all of our people.

Mr. President, I honestly believe the young people here and in my country and throughout our region will have more opportunities to live out their dreams than any generation of young people in history, if we do our jobs.

On behalf of Hillary and myself and our entire American delegation, let me thank you again for making us all feel so at home. *Muchas gracias. Nos vemos mañana.* [Thank you very much. We'll see you tomorrow.]

NOTE: The President spoke at 10:26 p.m. at Juan Santa Maria International Airport. In his remarks, he referred to President Jose Maria Figueres of Costa Rica and his wife, Josette Altmann de Figueres.

Remarks at the Central American Summit Welcoming Ceremony in San Jose
May 8, 1997

Thank you very much. President Figueres, thank you for bringing us all together. And to my fellow leaders from Central America and the Dominican Republic, thank you for coming. To all of you, to our distinguished guests, to all Ticos and all the people of Central America, let me say, *Es realmente un nuevo dia.*

Less than a decade ago, much of the Americas was still dominated by civil war, repression, and hopeless poverty. Today, we celebrate the advance of peace, growing prosperity, and freedom across our hemisphere. And we honor the remarkable men and women of Central America who helped to lead the way.

When the history of our region and our time is written, it will record your courage and your strength in ending four decades of conflict, braving the threat of bombs and bullets to cast ballots, embracing the challenge of economic re-

form, and opening the door to a new era of partnership among all our nations.

President Figueres, in that epic struggle, Costa Rica, this nation of brothers, has been a wise leader and set a powerful example. Waging peace as tenaciously as others have waged war, Costa Rica has shown that a country does not need an army to be strong. We thank Costa Rica and its leaders for building a vibrant democracy that takes care of its citizens and shoulders its responsibilities in the world.

Three years ago, our hemisphere's 34 democracies met in Miami at the historic Summit of the Americas to secure the hard-won gains our nations have made and to make them work for all our people. Today in San Jose, in the first summit between the leaders of the United States, Central America, and the Dominican Republic in almost three decades, we stand before you united in our course, determined to advance together to help the daily lives of our people in better jobs, safer streets, cleaner air, brighter hopes for our children and their future.

We are here to help our economies grow and to grow closer by opening our markets, protecting our workers, and sharing more fairly the benefits of prosperity. We are here to give all our people the tools to succeed in the global economy by making good education the birthright of every citizen of every country here. We are here to strengthen our democracies by standing against the criminals, the drug traffickers, the smugglers who exploit open borders to threaten open societies. And we are here to protect our future by launching new efforts to prevent pollution and protect our precious natural environment.

When President Kennedy came to Costa Rica more than three decades ago, he said, "Every generation of the Americas has shaped new goals for democracy to suit the demands of a new age. Our generation must meet that challenge, and we must do it together. We know that we must not be just neighbors but real partners, working together in a spirit of friendship, equality, and mutual respect."

My fellow citizens of the Americas, that is the partnership we have come here to build. Here in the heart of our hemisphere, let us go forward into a bright new century full of unlimited possibilities for our young, knowing that to realize those possibilities we must go forward together.

Thank you.

NOTE: The President spoke at 10:27 a.m. at the National Theater Plaza. In his remarks, he referred to the following summit participants: President Jose Maria Figueres of Costa Rica; Prime Minister Manuel Esquivel of Belize; President Leonel Fernandez of the Dominican Republic; President Alvaro Arzu of Guatemala; President Carlos Roberto Reina of Honduras; President Arnoldo Aleman of Nicaragua; and President Armando Calderon of El Salvador.

The President's News Conference With Central American Leaders in San Jose
May 8, 1997

President Figueres. Good afternoon, friends. I wish to express on behalf of the heads of state and of government of Central America and the Dominican Republic how pleased we are with the results of the extraordinary work session we have had this morning with President Clinton. It has been a very sincere dialog, a very realistic dialog, a very human dialog, and especially, a very friendly dialog.

I would like to share with you four main conclusions which are the outcome of our discussions and which are reflected in the joint declaration which we have just signed. First of all, we've inaugurated a new phase, a new stage in the relations among our countries. We attach a very special importance to this alliance. It reflects a new visional mood, a more optimistic one, a more mature one, and a more propositional one. And it also demonstrates the existence of a shared agenda, the fundamental objective of which is the well-being of our peoples through the consolidation of economies which are more and more open and integrated. And we have ratified this will.

Secondly, we wish to emphasize the brotherly spirit, the friendship and the understanding which have prevailed in our discussion of topics which we knew were sensitive and complex. We have made a special effort to reach agreements, to compromise and to understand the realities which our Governments face. Beyond those realities, we found a will to work together, and we have opened areas for this dialog to continue and for our collective action.

Third, we underlined the importance of having maintained, as a constant concern of this meeting, the social issues, the importance of which for Latin America and for our region is more vital today than ever before. We share a special concern with the more needy, a concern which reflects solidarity, not charity, as a means to generate opportunities for productive employment and to ensure the dignified life which our peoples demand.

I especially wish to recognize the contribution of women to the developing of economic democracy and how urgent it is to guarantee nondiscriminatory treatment for them in the workplaces, in political life, and in social relations generally. All this should have a significant impact in the improvement of the quality of life of the coming generations.

Finally, we wish to stress the significant role which environmental issues continue to have on our agenda. We have deepened and expanded the scope of the joint declaration of Central America and the United States, CONCAUSA, and in doing so, we have helped our region move even further forward as one of those regions which are noted throughout the world for their commitment to the rational use and intelligent use of our natural resources. In this regard, we can state that the decisions we've adopted in this field in this declaration can be characterized as revolutionary at a hemispherical level.

An essential element to attain institutional strengthening and to ensure good governance of our countries has to do with the possibility of expanding our markets and stimulating investments which generate employment and improve the quality of life. I believe that with respect to both topics, free trade and investment, we have moved forward in an impressive manner in attaining a better understanding and in acceptance that reciprocity should be the new byword in the establishment of all our discussions.

Ladies and gentlemen, the President and the Prime Minister of Belize and the Dominican Republic would like to make a special mention to the democratic circumstance that prevails in all the region: We are committed to strengthen and perfecting it.

We are aware that, at the threshold of the 21st century, it is not enough to guarantee access to free, fair, and transparent elections for our citizens. Threatened by formidable enemies such as narcotrafficking and organized crime, it is indispensable to fortify democratic institutions and to ensure ways in which civil society can participate more effectively in the decision-making process.

Nonetheless, it is through the development of dynamic economies and more equitable social structures that we will be able to fully grasp the benefits of democratic governance. To this regard, we are convinced that one indispensable element to ensure such democratic governance

has to do with the possibility to expand our markets and, with it, stimulate investments that generate employment and improve the quality of life of our populations.

Both issues, trade and investment, were positively reinforced during our meeting with President Clinton, and we would like to emphasize our satisfaction as the new criteria that will guide our next steps towards the construction of free-trade zones in the Americas.

In closing, let me emphasize the warmth of this meeting. You, President Clinton, with your insight and your thoughtfulness, have come to Central America and with our friends from the Dominican Republic have given a new dimension to our relations. We all came here with high expectations, We had the opportunity to share our thoughts but express the feelings of our hearts. And we all part full of optimism, ready to continue our work, work that is circumscribed by the need we all have to continue bettering the conditions of living of our people.

Thank you very much.

President Clinton. President Figueres has given an excellent statement. I will just make a few brief comments. First of all, I know I speak for all of us who are guests here in thanking the President and the people of Costa Rica for their warmth and hospitality.

This is truly a new day for Central America. The transition from conflict to cooperation has changed the relationship among the Central American countries and between the United States and Central America. A decade ago, we focused on civil wars. Now, together, we are fighting against poverty and fighting for prosperity, stronger democracy, and the sustainable development of our precious resources.

It is this new reality, this new agenda that we share which brings us here to San Jose for the first summit meeting between the leaders of the United States, Central America, and the Dominican Republic in 30 years. The people of Central America have chosen peace and democracy. We must help them to prove that they made the right choice, that democracy delivers.

Today, we agreed to an intensified ongoing dialog between the United States, Central America, and the Dominican Republic to work together on issues that will make a real difference to the lives of all our people with a high level, follow-on structure to make sure that our commitments are realized.

Together we looked at ways to strengthen our democracies and to combat the drugs, crime, and corruption that threaten to undermine them. I'm encouraged by the growing cooperation among Central American law enforcement authorities, including the creation of a joint center for police studies in El Salvador. To advance it further, the United States plans to establish an international law enforcement academy in Latin America by the end of this year, modeled on our successful academy in Budapest. We also agreed to modernize extradition treaties and to apply them vigorously. Those who commit a crime in one nation in our region should know that they will have no place to run and hide elsewhere in the region.

We took important steps to broaden the benefits of open and competitive trade. Our trade with Central America exceeded $20 billion last year. That is a 120-percent increase since 1990. This dramatic increase is the direct result of the progress the nations of this region have made toward improving their economies and opening their markets.

To identify concrete actions we can take to expand commerce even more, and to explore ways to move toward our common goal of a free trade area of the Americas by 2005, we created a ministerial level trade and investment council.

The open skies agreement we signed today—the first in our hemisphere—are a powerful example of how we can move forward together. They will allow our air carriers greater freedom to increase passenger and cargo services, to lower prices for travelers and shippers, and literally to bring the Americas closer together.

Today, we also agreed that our labor ministers will meet later this year to exchange ideas on promoting respect for worker rights and improving working conditions. And we discussed the issue of immigration. I'm proud that the United States has a tradition of generous legal immigration. Last year, over 900,000 people legally immigrated to the United States. I will do what I can to preserve it because I believe America's diversity is one of our greatest strengths as we move into a new century in an increasingly global society.

But to maintain that tradition and to do what is right by people who immigrate to the United States legally, it is also necessary that we be more effective in stopping illegal immigration. Our new immigration law is designed to accom-

plish that objective. I appreciate the decision by several Central American nations to criminalize the terrible practice of alien smuggling, which is also a scourge to all of us.

I do want you to know that enforcing our laws, I am determined to balance the need for firm controls against illegal immigration with common sense and compassion. Our country has greatly benefitted from the talents and the energies of Central Americans who came to our shores because they were fleeing civil war. Today, the remarkable progress in that region means that many can return home. But we want that to occur in a manner which avoids destabilizing the nations and the economies of Central America, or creating enormous hardships for children and families.

There will be no mass deportations and no targeting of Central Americans under this law. I am working with Congress to implement the new law so that it does not produce these unintended results.

Finally, we explored ideas to make a good education the birthright of every child in this region. We agreed that education should be a centerpiece of next year's Summit of the Americas in Santiago, for which today's summit is an important building block.

This has been a full and a productive session. Again, let me thank my colleagues for the passion and the depth of commitment they bring to this enterprise, and to our shared vision for a new partnership between the United States and Central America on the brink of a new century. Thank you very much.

Extradition Policy and NAFTA Membership

Q. Good afternoon. Thank you very much, Mr. President. I have two questions. For you, Mr. President Figueres, I'd like to know, within the declaration, in the chapter on strengthening democracy and good governance, I'd like to know what should be understood in the paragraph that says that we take on the commitment to update our extradition treaty and apply it vigorously to make sure that criminals are taken to justice, where the effects of their crime are felt more severely.

If we are dealing here with a paragraph that is somehow suggesting for the future any possibility of extraditing our citizens—[*inaudible*]— that the Central American contingency meet in order to be considered by your country to be part of the free trade agreement and if so, if we are, after Chile, the next one—[*inaudible*].

President Clinton. I was listening—[*inaudible*]—you started talking in Spanish.

Q. Okay, so here again. My question is—[*inaudible*]—[*laughter*].

President Clinton. It's been a long day. [*Laughter*]

Q. Thank you. What do you think the conditions that Central American countries should meet in order to be considered by your country to be part of the Free Trade Agreement, and if we do meet those requirements, are we the next after Chile? Thank you.

President Figueres. The biggest—[*inaudible*]—is that respecting our constitutions and the independence of the branches of government in our countries, the judiciary and the legislative. We will continue cooperating in these areas which have to do with ensuring citizen security. And in accordance with our responsibility as Presidents with respect to our population, I think we should work out together combating drug trafficking, money laundering, and these modern scourges which have been developing in our societies and which can only cause harm to our societies.

This is a reaffirmation of our will to continue working in that direction, with respect to our constitutions and to our legal provisions. We are all states under the rule of law, fortunately.

President Clinton. I would like to make one comment about that from the point of view of the United States. We do not believe that our sovereignty is undermined by extraditing people through our countries as long as they follow the same rules with us, so that we both respect each other's criminal justice system.

Now, let me answer your question. First of all, I believe that the nations of Central America have already gone a long way toward becoming part of a free-trade area by embracing democracy, open markets, and committing themselves to expanded trade, and committing themselves to increasing international cooperation. After all, we have the President of the Inter-American Development Bank here, we have the Secretary General of the OAS here. We are all working together more. We are committed already, the United States is, to working with all the nations that are here present to establish a free-trade area of the Americas by 2005, which is not so very far away.

Now, in between now and then, can we do more to have reciprocal open trade with the Central American countries? I believe we can, and I have agreed to two steps. The first is that we have set up a ministerial trade and investment council here, as a result of this communique, to identify what the next concrete steps are. But, before that, I have proposed in my budget an expansion of the Caribbean Basin Initiative, and I have funded it over the next 5 years, which would permit us to reduce or eliminate tariffs on a large number of other items coming from Central America that would further deepen our trade relations.

So, I'm strongly supportive of it. I think the big steps have already been taken. The next steps are subject to agreement by our trade negotiators and people who are concerned about investment. And they can be worked out if we stay on the path we're on.

Terry [Terence Hunt, Associated Press]

Central America-U.S. Relations

Q. Mr. President, some of the leaders here today and some other prominent Central American figures have complained in recent days that the United States pays attention to this region only in times of war and in times of natural disaster. Do you think that that has been a valid criticism?

And to President Figueres, what, if anything, has President Clinton said today that makes you think that that attitude would change?

President Clinton. Well, first of all, I think there is some validity to that criticism—that is, I think there are some sectors of our society that may have been more interested in Central America when it was a battleground in the cold war or when it could at least be interpreted to have been a battleground in the cold war. But I don't think it's a fair characterization of America as a whole or of the attitude of this administration.

After all, we convened the Summit of the Americas including all the democratically elected leaders of Central America and the Caribbean and the rest of Latin America in 1994. We have worked diligently since then in meeting with and working with various leaders in this area. We have worked for the cause of peace in Central America and applauded it when it prevailed.

And this meeting here, which as I said, is the first time since 1968 when President Johnson met with the leaders of Central America, the Dominican Republic that such a meeting has occurred, and this one has a different agenda. This is designed to send the message that we believe it is in the interest of the United States and the people of the United States, as well as the right thing to do, to have an economic and a political partnership with Central America as we move into the new century.

President Figueres. I—[inaudible]—to this meeting with a completely different perspective of what our relationship should be. The old relationship that we have had in the past is no longer the one that can most benefit us in the world of a globalized economy. And today, we have all come as true partners to share the responsibilities of our development and to look for common paths through which we can develop. Central America today, fully democratic and in peace, is willing to pull its own weight, and we are perfectly well aware of the responsibilities in that respect that we have as leaders of our nations. This is truly the beginning of a great new partnership.

Q. Good afternoon, Presidents. For President Clinton. The countries of Central America have been complaining—complaining that the United States has abandoned Central America lately. Aside from progressively, steadily liberalizing trade, in what other way could the United States help the people of Central America—for meetings such as this not be considered as social events with rather rhetorical results that have nothing to do with reality?

President Clinton. Well, I think there are lots of specific ways we can work with Central America apart from trade, and I mentioned one in my remarks. We intend to establish a law enforcement academy in Latin America that will serve the people of Central America in helping them to develop professional police forces that are effective and respects human rights and effective judicial systems.

We did this in Central Europe, with one in Budapest, and we have worked with a lot of former communist countries in the area of law enforcement cooperation in a way that has been extraordinarily well received there, and I believe will be here.

Last night when President Figueres and I had a chance to meet, and again today in our larger meeting, I reaffirmed our willingness to work with countries of Central America to help to expand educational opportunities and to bring the benefits of educational technology to all students. And I think there are great opportunities there. I think there are enormous opportunities for us to cooperate in the environmental areas in ways that will be helpful to the long-term stability of the nations that are represented here.

So those are just three areas in which I expect there to be significantly increased cooperation in the years ahead. In addition to that, as you know, we still have some modest aid programs. The Peace Corps is active in many of these nations, doing very constructive things. So I expect that there will be other things which will be done in the years ahead.

Keep in mind, the United States has finally voted for the first time since 1969—at least we have an agreement with the leaders of the Congress—to balance our budget. And that will permit us the freedom and the economic stability, I think, to be a better partner with our neighbors in a whole range of other areas. But the most important thing is for you to prove that your economy will work. And I think the plan we're following will enable you to do that.

Paul [Paul Basken, United Press International].

Immigration Law

Q. Mr. President, Central American leaders before this meeting were saying the new U.S. immigration laws are causing major economic and political headaches. A State Department official was quoted today as saying that, given the situation in Congress, all you have been able to offer them today was "words and promises and hot air." Did that turn out to be true, and what do you realistically expect to get from Congress on immigration between now and the date of September 30th, set out in the statement today?

And, for President Figueres, if you could, are the Central American leaders overreacting to the situation?

President Clinton. Well, first of all, let's describe what the situation is. There are a lot of immigrants living in the United States from the countries that are represented here today who came to the United States primarily because of upheaval caused in their countries during wars. Some of those immigrants are there legally, but not as legal immigrants. That is, there is a separate category of our immigration law which says if you're, in effect, fleeing political disruption in your own country, you can stay in our country but you don't become a legal immigrant with the right to apply for citizenship after 5 years. But many of them have been there quite a long while. Some of them are not legal under that status but they've been there quite a long while, and they did come because of the political upheaval.

There are two real problems with just shipping all of them up and sending them home, aside from the practical problems of whether it can be done or not. One is that a lot of them have been in the United States so long that they have families there, they have children in school, they have lives that are intertwined with their communities. And it would be significantly disruptive and unfair to the families and the children.

The other is that a lot of—such a dislocation would rob a lot of these countries of cash remittances that a lot of these folks are sending back home to their families which take the place of a lot of foreign aid or domestic economic activity in keeping the country going. And also, that level of influx would destabilize them.

So I think it's fair to say that everyone who studied this understands that the Central American countries—a number of them are in a very special category when it comes to dealing with the immigration laws.

The immigration law that we passed was designed to help us stop illegal immigration at the border, in the workplace, and in the court system. And it will achieve that. But we have to implement it in a way that is humane and recognizes the special problems created here.

So what I have said is that, number one, for the immigrants that are there legally, but not as legal immigrants—that is, they're in the category of people fleeing political problems at home—the law says that I can only exempt 4,000 people from being sent back to their countries. I will not trigger that law until September, the end of September, during which time I will work with Congress to try to figure out how to implement it.

As to people who are generally not in America legally, there will be no mass deportations and no targeting of any citizens from any country. They will have to be dealt with on a case-by-case basis.

And again, I will say, I'm not so sure, as whoever your anonymous source was, that the Congress will be unwilling to recognize the fact that these Central American countries are in a rather special category. After all, the United

States Government was heavily involved with a lot of these countries during the time of all this upheaval. And just as we were quite generous—and we should have been—in welcoming Vietnamese people to our shores after the termination of our involvement in Vietnam, where our country did not prevail, in these nations where democracy has prevailed and we want to work with them to succeed, it seems to me we ought to be sensitive to the disruptions that were caused during those tough years that we were involved in as a nation. So I'm not so sure we can't get some treatments.

But the law itself, I want to say, as I said in Mexico, it's a good thing that we try to stop illegal immigration because if we don't, we won't be able to keep the American people in support of legal immigration. So we have to stop it as much as we can. But we have to understand, these Central American countries are in a different category because of what they went through in the 1980s.

President Figueres. I feel that we have advanced a lot on this subject, which is certainly important to the Central American nations for many of the reasons that President Clinton has just mentioned. But on this issue of immigration, your question was, has there been an overreaction in Central America. I don't believe that there has been an overreaction, and I believe that we have achieved substantial progress.

If I may, on that, I would like to call perhaps on President Armando Calderon Sol, because he is really the one that, in terms of Central America, with President Arnoldo Aleman, led the conversation.

President Calderon. I would just like to add that, for us, this new relationship that we have begun between Central America and the United States, at the time of President Clinton's visit is profoundly significant. It represents a recognition by the United States, a recognition of the contribution that our people make to their economy, a recognition of the human drama that our people are experiencing in the United States because of what happens here, because this was the theater of operations of the cold war, here in Central America, to hear this from the President of the United States and to hear the profoundly humane position that he adopts when he looks at the people which have had so much pain, for us is very encouraging. And he has stated very clearly that there will not be mass deportations, that they will seek to work more flexibly with the new immigration law, that there is time from now until September for a joint initiative with the Congress and to awaken more awareness within the Congress concerning this issue which is so important for Central America.

Today is a very important day, a day of great hope for all Central Americans who, because of some of the tragic conditions of violence, had to leave to seek new shores, to find refuge in the United States.

President Figueres. One last question.

Central America-U.S. Trade

Q. Thank you, Mr. President. The question first for President Figueres, don't you think there's very little scope in having the support of the U.S. Government for a draft that would provide to expand the benefits of the Caribbean Basin Initiative when the countries of the region would like to have something more specific than that before the year 2005?

And President Clinton, don't you think that mere support of good will for a draft is actually a very small guarantee for the Central American countries when there is a Congress which is actually against anything that has to do with free trade or unions or even the Democrats, themselves?

President Figueres. With respect to trade, I feel that we have made major progress. These countries have benefitted from the Caribbean Basin Initiative for a number of years now. And this program is the basis on which we have been able to expand our exports from the entire region into traditional markets and also into new markets.

The program that the executive branch of the United States is submitting to the Congress differs from the situation of the past. It contains funds to be able to counteract the loss of tariff income, which would mean expanding the list of products and the exemptions for many of the products coming from this region.

Moreover, I think it is vitally important that we have agreed here to ask our ministers, the ministers who are involved in foreign trade, to task them with finding new ways, new creative ways to continue working together as a region with an eye to the year 2005, the date for which our continent plans to integrate. So the idea would be that we could advance even more in the field of trade before that date comes.

With respect to trade, Laura [Laura Martinez, Television 7, Costa Rica], we need to stress investment. I think this meeting, this summit meeting, in many ways, is a stamp of approval for the profound reforms that have been led by the Presidents of the area in the different countries. Today, the economies are much more open and much more competitive. They are true democracies and, of course, this opens up our doors to greater flows of investment. And ultimately, this is the way for us to integrate better.

President Clinton. I would like to try to respond to your question with two points. First of all, this is not a—from our point of view— a vague commitment. I think you should see this in three steps—the question of how we might expand our trade between the United States and Central American countries.

Number one, I have presented a budget to the Congress which, if the Congress will go along, provides for the reduction of tariffs over the next 5 years on a lot of other goods which would increase trade with both Central America and the Caribbean. It is fully paid for in my budget. And therefore, I think we will have— we have some chance of passing it, perhaps a good chance. And I certainly intend to fight hard for it. So there's that step.

Then the second step is that we have agreed to bring our trade and investment ministers together to identify what we do after that, what more can we do. Then the third step is adopting the free-trade area of the Americas by 2005.

I know 2005 sounds like a long time away, especially if you're very young, but it's not so very long. And if you think about what will then be a trading area of over a billion people, it is a stunning achievement if we can pull it off. So I am not excluding the possibility that we can do more than expand the Caribbean Basin Initiative, nor am I taking for granted that it will be done, but that is the three-step process I see.

Now, the larger point you made is that the Congress of the United States is opposed to free trade. That may not be true. There are strong opponents of expanded trade in the Congress, but there are also very strong supporters. Some people are just against trade because they think it gives the United States a bad deal. I think the evidence is squarely against them. The more we open our markets, the better our economy does. And we have wages going up for the first time in 20 years, and last year, more than half the new jobs, for the first time in many years, coming into our economy were above average wage. So trade is good for us, not bad.

Secondly, we can get a lot of people in my party—you mentioned my party specifically—we can get a lot of people in my party to vote for a fast-track authority if our trading partners will give serious attention to the question of making sure that all people in our country get to participate in the benefits of expanded trade and wealth. That's why I have advocated that we set up a labor forum to go with the business forum that will meet as we work toward a free-trade area of the Americas. The more Americans believe that all ordinary working people in other countries will benefit from expanded trade, the more likely we are to find support for it in the Congress.

Yes, ma'am.

Q. Thank you, Mr. President. I have a question for you and one question for the Presidents of Central America. Regionally, Central America was looking for NAFTA parity, and then later they changed things, that they preferred to have a free trade agreement. Given the sentiments in Congress, what do you personally believe is the best venue, the most effective to get that free trade agreement? And also, when do you expect to have a fast-track authority with Congress?

And also, for the Presidents of Central America—President Figueres or any of the other Presidents that you are going to seek an amnesty with regard to immigration. I don't know if you asked for that amnesty of President Clinton, and if so, what was his response?

President Clinton. Let me answer your question quite succinctly. I think the best course is for me first to try to pass my budget which contains an expansion of the Caribbean Basin Initiative; and second, to try to pass fast-track authority in the Congress this year, which I fully intend to do my best to do. We're going to work very hard on that. And at the same time, then, to consult with leaders of the Congress in both parties who favor this approach about what they believe the best way to proceed is, because we're all going to have to work together on this.

While we're consulting with Congress, there will be this meeting of our ministers, all of our ministers, identifying what they think the next step should be to continue to expand trade. So

I think that our road map is quite clear, and that is the one I intend to pursue.

President Figueres. With respect to the question of immigration, it has already been covered by Armando Calderon Sol, but I would like to go back to your question with respect—that, first, Central America wanted parity an then later on began to look for other ways to acquire more investment and how do we think is the best. Don Alvaro Arzu discussed this issue extensively this morning in the forum, and I would like to invite him to answer your question.

President Arzu. Thank you. What we have stressed and tried to demonstrate is that the region of Central America is prepared, is ready. It's no longer time for us to be reaching out our hands to ask for support, although we are grateful for the support we have received. But instead, we have a desire for a more longstanding, a more permanent relationship of partnership, and more than that, we want a free trade agreement. This is our aspiration.

We need to follow certain parameters, which are requirements, with Congress for example; also with public opinion, the press—[*inaudible*]—in communication. But what we mostly want to tell the American union is that we are ready. In Central America, we are ready to compete. We are ready to receive investment. We are ready to generate production. And we are ready to diversify the results and the profits that we attract among the large mass of impoverished people in our region in order to begin shrinking the very profound socioeconomic gap that we still have. So we want to go beyond that, and I think we can do it.

Thank you.

President Figueres. Thank you. This concludes the press conference.

NOTE: The President's 144th news conference began at 1:20 p.m. at the National Theater. President Jose Figueres of Costa Rica spoke in Spanish and English, and his Spanish remarks were translated by an interpreter. President Armando Calderon of El Salvador and President Alvaro Arzu of Guatemala spoke in Spanish, and their remarks were translated by an interpreter. In his remarks, President Clinton referred to Inter-American Development Bank President Enrique V. Iglesias and Organization of American States Secretary General Cesar Gaviria.

Declaration of San Jose
May 8, 1997

We, the Presidents of Costa Rica, El Salvador, the United States of America, Guatemala, Honduras, Nicaragua, the Dominican Republic and the Prime Minister of Belize, meeting in San Jose, Costa Rica on May 8, 1997, hereby reaffirm the remarkable democratic transformation in Central America. Central America is now a region of peace, liberty and democracy, profoundly committed to a process of integration, in which a spirit of harmony, cooperation, pluralism and respect for human rights prevails. This spirit marks an unprecedented era of stability in Central America's history.

We hold the conviction that the resources and potential of Central America and the Dominican Republic can now be focussed so as to ensure that our peoples are able to develop to their full potential within the framework of just and democratic societies. We are determined to march toward the future in a partnership based on friendship, understanding and ever stronger cooperation. This meeting marks the inauguration of a new stage in our relations, based on mutual respect and reciprocity which will give our nations greater advantages with which to successfully meet the challenges of the next millennium.

We recognize that there are great challenges that we must jointly assume and that there are many opportunities which favor the creation of a great region of shared prosperity among Central America, the Dominican Republic and the United States, as well as the creation of a visionary and creative association among our nations.

Inspired by the principles and goals of the Summit of the Americas and guided by the Central American Alliance for Sustainable Development, we recognize as the cornerstones of this renewed relationship the promotion of prosperity through the strengthening of democracy and good governance; dialogue on immigration and illegal migrant trafficking; economic integration and free trade; the continued development of just and equitable societies that provide opportunities for all people; and the development of responsible environmental policies as an integral element of sustainable development; all of which must be undertaken within a framework of mutual cooperation.

Strengthening of Democracy and Good Governance

We reaffirm our profound conviction that only democratically elected governments can guarantee the full existence of the rule of law, an indispensable prerequisite for the preservation of peace and harmony.

We reaffirm our belief in the dignity of our people and our commitment to the rule of law. We maintain that crime is one of the principal threats to the democracy, public security and social stability of our countries. For this reason, we will redouble our efforts to combat crime and improve security for our people. Consistent with our constitutional provisions and recognizing the independence of our legislative and judicial branches, we are committed to the modernization of extradition treaties and their vigorous application to help ensure that criminals are brought to justice where the effect of their crime is felt most severely.

We resolve to intensify our national efforts and to increase bilateral, multilateral and regional cooperation to combat drug consumption, drug trafficking, money laundering and illegal drug activity in all its manifestations. We reaffirm our commitment to fight corruption through mutual cooperation and the strengthening of oversight institutions and we agree to seek ratification of the Organization of American States' Interamerican Convention Against Corruption. We instruct our Ministers responsible for public security and law enforcement, and other appropriate authorities, to work together to develop a plan of action this year to combat these threats to the welfare of our people.

The Presidents of the United States and the Dominican Republic, and the Prime Minister of Belize express their support for the progress achieved by the Central American Presidents in redefining regional security within a framework of the rule of law, the enhancement of democratic institutions by strengthening civilian authority, the limiting of the role of the armed forces and public security forces to their constitutional mandates, and the fostering of a culture of peace, dialogue, understanding and tolerance based on common democratic values. The strong commitment to these principles serves as an important example to other parts of the world seeking transparency and mutual confidence in their relations.

Dialogue on Immigration and Illegal Migrant Trafficking

We are aware of the serious impact of new immigration provisions on groups that come from the region and who live and have roots in the United States. We therefore undertake to maintain an open, ongoing dialogue at the highest levels to find humane and adequate solutions to address the complexities of the immigration situation, and to ensure that each person's case is evaluated individually and fairly, taking into account his or her valuable contribution to the host country.

Having expressed their concerns to the President of the United States, the Presidents of Central America, the Dominican Republic and the Prime Minister of Belize welcome the United States Government's initiation of consultations with its Congress on the scope, implementation and consequences of the recent immigration legislation approved by the United States, and are confident that the dignity and human rights of the individuals it may affect will be fully respected.

We believe trafficking in migrants is an affront to human dignity and we are committed to increase cooperation to combat this degrading practice.

Promotion of Prosperity through Economic Integration, Free Trade and Investment

At the Summit of the Americas, we decided to move toward a hemisphere united through free trade by the year 2005. We reiterate our resolve to take all necessary actions to make this "spirit of Miami" a reality. With this in mind, we call for the commencement of negotiations at the Santiago Summit of the Americas that will lead to the establishment of the Free Trade Area of the Americas (FTAA). We reiterate our intention to work cooperatively throughout these negotiations.

The Presidents of Central America, the Dominican Republic and the Prime Minister of Belize welcome the decision of the Government of the United States to support the expeditious passage of a bill which enhances the benefits granted under the Caribbean Basin Initiative. We recognize that unilateral concessions have been of great importance in the initial phases

of the process of economic liberalization. We now believe that it is necessary to move toward a commercial relationship which offers all parties mutually beneficial conditions.

We are convinced that to promote and maintain democratic stability and to contribute to our joint prosperity it is necessary to have sound and dynamic economies. With this in mind and recognizing the advances that Central America has made in economic liberalization, we have resolved to deepen our economic and commercial relations. We will work jointly and expeditiously, consistent with the World Trade Organization (WTO) agreements and the FTAA process, to identify specific steps, including bilateral, multilateral and regional reciprocal trade agreements, that will intensify the economic relationships among our nations. To achieve these common trade objectives, we instruct our Ministers of Trade to constitute themselves as a Trade and Investment Council with a mandate to make specific recommendations. In support of these goals, our governments will continue efforts to conclude bilateral investment treaties and intellectual property rights agreements. In addition, under the aegis of the WTO, we will seek to liberalize our telecommunications, information technology and financial services sectors.

The signing of Open Skies Agreements between the United States and Costa Rica, El Salvador, Guatemala, Honduras and Nicaragua during our meeting in San Jose is a significant manifestation of this commitment and these agreements will serve to enhance our commercial relations and tourism among our people and productive sectors. In this regard, it is necessary to undertake additional actions that will strengthen and broaden technical cooperation in aviation matters.

We underscore the importance of free market economies and private sector initiatives as a source of prosperity for our people and we reaffirm our goal of promoting business events and other complementary activities that expand trade and investment relations between the private sectors of our countries.

We recognize that there are important challenges in this process that we must face to maintain suitable conditions for our economic and social growth, taking into account the particular circumstances of each country. Among these challenges are the need to maintain open markets for trade and investment, to ensure the participation of all our people in the benefits of economic growth, and to maintain a stable macroeconomy and financial system. Within the framework of a market economy, the use of debt can supplement scarce domestic savings and support high rates of investment and growth. With this in mind, we declare our intention to utilize more fully modalities that allow for better management of debt burdens and the cost of external debt.

Continued Development of Just and Equitable Societies that Provide Opportunities for All People

We express our determination to continue making necessary social investments in order to improve the quality of life in our countries. We are convinced that the training of our labor forces, combined with access to health, education and basic housing services improves the well-being of our societies, while at the same time increasing the productivity and competitiveness of our economies. We are committed to share ideas, human resources and programs within mutually agreed guidelines to promote development and democracy.

We underscore the importance of placing greater emphasis on the full participation of women in all political, social and economic spheres of development, especially in areas such as access to credit, community organization, and in the commercial sector and decision-making bodies.

We reaffirm our commitment to human rights as stipulated in the Universal Declaration and to international and interamerican human rights instruments, to which we are parties, respectively. In particular, we recognize the importance of economic, social and cultural rights, and within these we underscore the rights of workers, and reaffirm our commitment to ensure compliance with the Constitution and Conventions of the International Labor Organization, as respectively ratified by our governments. We welcome the input of the labor sector in the hemispheric economic integration process.

We recognize the efforts by interested parties such as employers and workers organizations to work together to promote respect for workers rights and enhance working conditions. We have asked our Labor Ministers to meet to exchange ideas with interested parties on this issue.

The Presidents of Central America and the Dominican Republic and the Prime Minister of Belize note with interest the recent announcement by the President of the United States of the Apparel Industry Partnership.

We agree that micro-, small- and medium-sized businesses are important for the social development of our countries. These entrepreneurial undertakings make it possible for a wide range of social sectors to expand productively and make a decisive contribution to the democratization of capital and the equitable distribution of wealth. We will broaden our efforts to promote such businesses and to increase their capabilities. We also request that the Interamerican Development Bank, the World Bank and other institutions and donors continue and strengthen their support of these activities.

The Development of Responsible Environmental Policies as an Integral Element of Sustainable Development

We renew our commitment to the promotion of the environmental principles and objectives of the Alliance for Sustainable Development, which inspired the signing of the Joint Central American-United States Declaration (CONCAUSA) and influenced the Conference on Sustainable Development in Santa Cruz de la Sierra. Within this framework, we recognize the goals we have reached, the support we have received and are in agreement on the need to expand cooperation to new areas of action.

We recognize the leadership of Central America in the protection of the environment and the preservation of biodiversity, in particular, the recovery and beneficial use of ancestral knowledge from our indigenous cultures, as well as innovative use of public-private sector joint ventures. In this context, we will renew our efforts to protect endangered species and make sustainable use of flora and fauna.

We note actions already underway in Central America in the area of climate change, especially those which include the participation of our private sectors and will grant credit for Joint Implementation projects and other initiatives to limit and reduce greenhouse gas emissions. In this regard, we urge the parties to the UN Framework Convention on Climate Change to make a determined effort to address these issues during the Third Conference.

In this spirit, we resolve to support the promotion of investment in environmental projects such as ecotourism, the development of renewable energy sources, recycling, the transfer of clean technologies on terms mutually agreed by all parties, and trade in organic products, among others. In particular, we highlight the importance of our joint efforts in the sustainable generation and use of energy in projects which, by combining our efforts with those of other nations, allow for taking greater advantage of our resources while at the same time fostering regional integration.

Follow-Up Mechanisms

In order to strengthen our relations as friends, neighbors and partners and to ensure an increasing and effective level of communication, coordination and follow-up among our governments, we have resolved to establish a consultative mechanism which will include periodic meetings at the highest level; an actual meeting of our Foreign Ministers, who will meet next during the October 1997 regular session of the United Nations General Assembly; a ministerial-level Trade and Investment Council, which will hold its inaugural session in Washington, D.C.; and

an ongoing dialogue on immigration issues at the highest level.

In addition, our Ministers responsible for public security and law enforcement and our Ministers of Labor will convene meetings in their respective areas this year.

JOSE MARIA FIGUERES OLSEN	ARMANDO CALDERÓN SOL
President	President
Republic of Costa Rica	Republic of El Salvador
WILLIAM J. CLINTON	ALVARO ARZÚ IRIGOYEN
President	President
The United States of America	Republic of Guatemala
CARLOS ROBERTO REINA IDIÁQUEZ	ARNOLDO ALEMÁN LACAYO
President	President
Republic of Honduras	Republic of Nicaragua
LEONEL FERNÁNDEZ REYNA	MANUEL ESQUIVEL
President	Prime Minister
Dominican Republic	Belize

NOTE: An original was not available for verification of the content of this joint statement.

Statement on Juvenile Crime Legislation
May 8, 1997

Today, the House of Representatives missed an important opportunity to fight and prevent the scourge of juvenile crime. I oppose passage of H.R. 3, the Juvenile Crime Control Act, because it fails to provide a comprehensive plan to crack down on youth and gang violence.

As I began my second term as President, I made juvenile crime and gangs my top law enforcement priority over the next 4 years. I called on every police officer, prosecutor, and parent in America to work together to keep our young people safe and to keep young criminals off our streets.

America's Anti-Gang and Youth Violence strategy must declare war on gangs; target funding for additional local prosecutors to pursue, prosecute, and punish gang members; extend the Brady law so violent teen criminals will never have the right to purchase a gun; require Federal dealers to sell a child safety lock with every gun, to protect our kids from using guns to hurt each other or themselves; and target resources to keep schools open late, on week-

ends, and in the summer, to keep young people off the street and out of trouble.

The legislation passed in the House today fails to provide any of these necessary measures to give law enforcement, prosecutors, and parents the tools they need to combat gangs and youth violence in their communities.

Four years ago, we made a commitment to take our streets back from crime and violence. We had a comprehensive plan of 100,000 new community police officers on the street, tough new penalties on the books, and steps to keep guns out of the hands of criminals with the assault weapons ban and the Brady bill.

Our plan is working. Last year, violent crime came down for the 5th year in a row. And for the first time in 7 years, the rate of young people arrested for violent crime and murder has gone down. But we cannot waste this opportunity to bring down violent juvenile crime even further. I will continue to work with Congress to ensure passage of legislation that will give our children the safest and most secure future possible.

Letter to Congressional Leaders Reporting on Iraq's Compliance With United Nations Security Council Resolutions
May 8, 1997

Dear Mr. Speaker: (Dear Mr. President:)

Consistent with the Authorization for Use of Military Force Against Iraq Resolution (Public Law 102–1) and as part of my effort to keep the Congress fully informed, I am reporting on the status of efforts to obtain Iraq's compliance with the resolutions adopted by the United Nations Security Council (UNSC). This report covers the period from March 7 to the present.

Saddam Hussein remains a threat to his people and the region and the United States remains determined to contain the threat of Saddam's regime. Speaking on behalf of the Administration on March 26, 1997, in her first major foreign policy address, Secretary of State Madeleine Albright stated that the United States looks forward to the day when Iraq rejoins the family of nations as a responsible and law-abiding member and that, until then, containment must continue. Secretary Albright also made clear that Saddam's departure would make a difference and that, should a change in Iraq's government occur, the United States would stand ready to enter rapidly into a dialogue with the successor regime.

In terms of military operations, the United States and our coalition partners continue enforcement of the no-fly zones over northern Iraq under Operation Northern Watch, the successor mission to Operation Provide Comfort, and over southern Iraq through Operation Southern Watch. On April 22, 1997, Saddam Hussein announced that Iraqi military helicopters would be flown through the southern no-fly zone for the purpose of transporting Iraqi pilgrims from the vicinity of the Iraqi-Saudi border to various areas in Iraq, publicly disregarding the prohibition against operating Iraqi rotary and fixed wing aircraft south of the 33rd parallel. The next day, 10 helicopters crossed the southern no-fly zone and arrived at a ground staging base in western Iraq, just north of the Iraqi-Saudi border, to await the arrival of the pilgrims. Because of the possible danger to innocent Iraqi civilians, the non-threatening nature of these flights, and the religious sensitivity of the situation, the United States and our coalition partners agreed not to take military action to intercept the helicopters.

On April 25–27, the same Iraqi helicopters returned the pilgrims to their homes in various locations throughout Iraq, transiting the northern and southern no-fly zones in the process. Again, the United States and its coalition partners decided not to act against these flights for humanitarian and policy reasons. We have made clear to the Government of Iraq and to all other relevant parties, however, that the United States and its partners will continue to enforce both no-fly zones, and that we reserve the right to respond appropriately and decisively to further Iraqi provocations.

In addition to our air operations, we will continue to maintain a strong U.S. presence in the region in order to deter Saddam. United States force levels include land- and carrier-based aircraft, surface warships, a Marine amphibious task force, a Patriot missile battalion, and a mechanized battalion task force deployed in support of USCINCCENT operations. To enhance force protection throughout the region, additional military security personnel have been deployed for continuous rotation. USCINCCENT continues to closely monitor the security situation in the region to ensure adequate force protection is provided for all deployed forces.

United Nations Security Council Resolution (UNSCR) 949, adopted in October 1994, demands that Iraq not utilize its military or any other forces to threaten its neighbors or U.N. operations in Iraq and that it not redeploy troops or enhance its military capacity in southern Iraq. In view of Saddam's accumulating record of unreliability, it is prudent to retain a significant U.S. force presence in the region in order to maintain the capability to respond rapidly to possible Iraqi aggression or threats against its neighbors.

Since my last report, the Government of Iraq has continued to flout its obligations under UNSC resolutions in other ways. Under the terms of relevant UNSC resolutions, Iraq must grant the United Nations Special Commission on Iraq (UNSCOM) inspectors immediate, unconditional, and unrestricted access to any location in Iraq they wish to examine, and access to any Iraqi official whom they wish to interview, so that UNSCOM may fully discharge its mandate to ensure that Iraq's weapons of mass destruction (WMD) program has been eliminated. Iraq continues, as it has for the past 6 years, to fail to live up either to the letter or the spirit of this commitment. Of particular concern is UNSCOM's report to the Security Council of serious incidents involving repeated Iraqi threats to shoot down UNSCOM aircraft, an Iraqi escort helicopter flying dangerously close to the Commission's aircraft to force it to change direction, and Iraqi personnel aboard an UNSCOM helicopter attempting to wrest control of the aircraft.

On April 11, UNSCOM Chairman Rolf Ekeus reported to the Security Council that resolution of the remaining questions about Iraq's WMD programs would require a "major political decision" on the part of Iraq's leadership to "give up, once and for all, all capabilities and ambition to retain or acquire the proscribed weapons." The UNSCOM continues to believe that Iraq instead maintains significant numbers of operational SCUD missiles, possibly with CBW warheads. In early April, UNSCOM also asked Iraq to withdraw its "full, final, and complete declaration" regarding its biological weapons programs because it contained obvious inaccuracies and fabrications, and to submit a new one. As long as the Iraqi leadership refuses to cooperate fully with U.N. weapons inspectors, UNSCOM will be impeded in its efforts to fulfill its mandate. We will continue to fully support the mandate and the efforts of UNSCOM to obtain Iraqi compliance with all relevant U.N. resolutions.

Implementation of UNSCR 1051 continues. It provides for a mechanism to monitor Iraq's effort to reacquire proscribed weapons capabilities by requiring that Iraq notify a joint unit of UNSCOM and the International Atomic Energy Agency in advance of any imports of dual-use items. Similarly, countries must provide timely notification of exports to Iraq of dual-use items.

Regarding northern Iraq, the United States continues to lead efforts to increase security and stability in the north and minimize opportunities for Baghdad or Tehran to threaten Iraqi citizens there. Acting Assistant Secretary of State for Near Eastern Affairs David Welch led a U.S.

delegation to northern Iraq on April 3 and 4, the first visit to the north by a U.S. official since Saddam's attack against the region in September 1996, and the first visit at this level in several years. Welch met with leaders of the two main Iraqi Kurd groups, Massoud Barzani of the Kurdistan Democratic Party (KDP) and Jalal Talabani of the Patriotic Union of Kurdistan (PUK). Both Iraqi Kurd leaders reaffirmed their support for U.S. policy and their commitment to cooperate with us through the Ankara reconciliation process. Welch also met with Iraqi Assyrian and Turkoman political leaders, PMF personnel, and U.N. officials.

Regarding the Ankara process to help the PUK and the KDP resolve their differences, we have facilitated three rounds of higher-level talks, along with our British and Turkish partners. Our immediate goals in the process are to focus on strengthening the U.S.-brokered cease-fire of October 23, 1996, which continues to hold, and on encouraging political reconciliation between the PUK and KDP.

The United States is providing political, financial, and logistical support for a neutral, indigenous Peace Monitoring Force (PMF) in northern Iraq that has demarcated the cease-fire line and monitors the cease-fire. Our support is being provided in the form of commodities and services in accordance with a drawdown I directed on December 11, 1996, and in the form of funds to be used to provide other non-lethal assistance in accordance with a separate determination made by former Secretary of State Christopher on November 10, 1996. The PMF began full deployment in mid-April, and has already succeeded in resolving several troublesome incidents in violation of the cease-fire.

The PMF has also helped the groups move forward on several other confidence-building measures, including a mutual release on April 14 of approximately 70 detainees from each Kurd group. The two Iraqi Kurd groups also continue to work on reconciliation efforts, including an initial meeting on March 12 of a joint Higher Coordination Committee to improve cooperation on civilian services such as electricity and health. Local representatives of the two Kurd groups, the three countries, and the PMF continue to meet biweekly in Ankara and move forward on other confidence-building measures.

Security conditions in northern Iraq nonetheless remain tenuous at best, with Iranian and

PKK (Kurdistan Workers Party) activity adding to the ever-present threat from Baghdad. All our efforts under the Ankara process, like all our efforts concerning Iraq, maintain support for the unity and territorial integrity of Iraq.

Implementation of UNSCR 986 is proceeding. The oil-related provisions of UNSCR 986, which authorized Iraq to sell up to $2 billion of oil during an initial 180-day period (with the possibility of UNSC renewal of subsequent 180-day periods) went into effect on December 10, 1996. The first shipments of food and humanitarian goods purchased with Iraqi oil proceeds started to arrive in Iraq on March 20.

UNSCR 986 requires that the proceeds of this limited oil sale, all of which must be deposited in a U.N. escrow account, will be used to purchase food, medicine, and other materials and supplies for essential civilian needs for all Iraqi citizens and to fund vital U.N. activities regarding Iraq. Critical to the success of UNSCR 986 is Iraq's willingness to follow through on its commitments under 986 to allow the United Nations to monitor the distribution of food and medical supplies to the Iraqi people.

During the first 90 days since implementation, Iraq sold just over $1 billion worth of oil in accordance with the terms of UNSCR 986. Significant delays in implementing distribution of humanitarian goods—caused, in part, by Iraqi efforts to impose new restrictions on the freedom of access and movement of U.N. monitors—made it impossible for the U.N. Secretary General to report on the adequacy of distribution and monitoring procedures during the first 90 days. We will continue to monitor the situation closely.

Iraq continues to stall and obfuscate rather than work in good faith toward accounting for the hundreds of Kuwaitis and third-country nationals who disappeared at the hands of Iraqi authorities during the occupation. It has also failed to return all of the stolen Kuwaiti military equipment and the priceless Kuwaiti cultural and historical artifacts that were looted during the occupation.

The human rights situation throughout Iraq remains unchanged. Iraq's repression of its Shi'a population continues with policies that are destroying the Marsh Arabs' way of life in southern Iraq, as well as the ecology of the southern marshes. Saddam Hussein shows no signs of complying with UNSCR 688, which demands that Iraq cease the repression of its own people.

On April 16, the U.N. Human Rights Commission passed a resolution strongly condemning the Baghdad regime's continued human rights abuses. That same day, the Administration announced support for an effort by various Iraqi opposition groups and non-governmental organizations to document Iraqi war crimes and other violations of international humanitarian law. This effort, known as INDICT, seeks ultimately to ensure that Saddam Hussein and other members of his regime are brought to justice before an international tribunal. We are in touch with organizers of INDICT and other parties to discuss the best means to move forward.

The Multinational Interception Force (MIF) is facing an increased challenge from smugglers and Iran. As I have noted in previous reports, these smugglers use the territorial waters of Iran to avoid the MIF inspection in the Northern Gulf. With the help of the Iranian government, which profits from these activities by charging protection fees, these smugglers are able to export over 70,000 metric tons of gas oil through the Gulf each month. This represents a significant increase from the amount included in my last report. We are working closely with our allies in the Gulf and with our MIF partners to develop new strategies to curb these violations of the sanctions regime.

Although MIF exchanges with the regular Iranian naval units have been professional and courteous, Iranian Revolutionary Guard Corps naval units have been much more aggressive in confronting the MIF and are actively involved in aiding the smugglers. The MIF is acting with good judgment and caution in its encounters with Iran. Our objective is to enforce sanctions—not to engage in unproductive encounters with Iran.

We regularly provide detailed briefings regarding developments in MIF sanctions enforcement to our MIF partners and Gulf Cooperation Council allies. We also are working closely through our mission in New York with the U.N. Sanctions Committee and like-minded allies on our approach toward Iran and sanctions violators, generally.

The MIF continues to process the maritime traffic involved in lifting oil from the Mina Al Bakr offshore terminal and the delivery of much-needed humanitarian supplies to Umm Qasr in Iraq. So far, those operations are proceeding smoothly. The smuggling trade, however, continues to force the MIF to devote scarce resources to sanctions enforcement. This has resulted in fewer ships available to process the legal humanitarian shipments that bring food and other supplies to Iraq under UNSCR 986.

The United Nations Compensation Commission (UNCC), established pursuant to UNSCR 687, continues to resolve claims against Iraq arising from Iraq's unlawful invasion and occupation of Kuwait. The UNCC has issued over 1 million awards worth approximately $5.2 billion. With the advent of oil sales under UNSCR 986, 30 percent of the proceeds are being allocated to the Compensation Fund to pay awards and finance operations of the UNCC. Initial payments out of the Compensation Fund are currently being made on awards in the order in which the UNCC has approved them, in installments of $2,500.00. In January 1997, the United States Government submitted claims totaling approximately $8.8 million for expenses incurred in the efforts to assess and respond to environmental damage in the Persian Gulf region caused by Iraq's unlawful invasion and occupation of Kuwait.

To conclude, Iraq remains a serious threat to regional peace and stability. I remain determined to see Iraq comply fully with all of its obligations under U.N. Security Council resolutions. My Administration will continue to oppose any relaxation of sanctions until Iraq demonstrates its peaceful intentions through such compliance.

I appreciate the support of the Congress for our efforts and shall continue to keep the Congress informed about this important issue.

Sincerely,

WILLIAM J. CLINTON

NOTE: Identical letters were sent to Newt Gingrich, Speaker of the House of Representatives, and Strom Thurmond, President pro tempore of the Senate.

Remarks at the Central American Summit Dinner in San Jose
May 8, 1997

President Reina, President and Mrs. Figueres, to my colleagues and friends at this table, and to all of you at this wonderful dinner: The day has been long and the hour is late, and most of what needs to be said has been said. I would like to begin briefly by simply thanking President and Mrs. Figueres and all the people of Costa Rica for their wonderful reception, including the magnificent music we heard this evening. Thank you very much, Mr. President.

I think you could tell by the remarks of President Reina and President Figueres that there was a wonderful spirit in our meeting today, a real desire to meet each other on terms of equality and respect, an understanding that we should seize the future together. And it left us all feeling larger and better than we came. I believe in Costa Rica you say that is *pura vida*. [*Laughter*]

As we rejoice tonight in the new hope and opportunity that is sweeping across the Americas, it would be wrong of us not to also remember and applaud the brave struggles of countless Central Americans in forging the peace we now celebrate. Because of the price they paid, today we find former guerrillas and ex-officers sitting side by side in legislatures. Central America's jaguars are second only to Asia's tigers in their rates of growth. Our nations are working together no longer to strip and exploit the land but instead to use our resources wisely, with future generations in mind.

Tonight I would like to especially salute President Arzu for all he has done to end four decades of conflict in Guatemala.

We are among the 34 democracies that committed in Miami 3 years ago to build a free trade area of the Americas by the year 2005. Today we issued the San Jose Declaration in that same spirit. Both are based on a fundamental conviction that we cannot build the future we seek unless we build it together.

I also want all of you to know that we resolve to actually work together to make these words real. We have had specific discussions about what we do next to expand trade, what we do next to improve education, what we do next to advance the environmental agenda. And just before I left the hotel to come here tonight, when Hillary and I were talking about the evening and the day, I received a call from General McCaffrey, who heads our efforts against illegal narcotics. He was full of excitement because he had been meeting with all of his counterparts from the countries here represented. He said, "Mr. President, this is the best meeting I ever had. These people really care about their children getting involved with drugs. They really want to defeat this. They're going to help us. We're going to work together. I feel better about this than I did the first day I took office." That is the spirit we intend to bring to every one of our endeavors.

Perhaps most important, we leave here with deeper ties as friends and partners. President Franklin Roosevelt said this 60 years ago in a speech to the Pan American Union; it's still true today: "Your Americanism and mine must be a structure built of confidence, cemented by a sympathy which recognizes only equality and fraternity." My fellow citizens of the Americas, we stand on the edge of a bright new century. Let us bring that spirit to its work, and let us live with a dream that is worthy of our children.

I ask you now to join me in a toast of salute and gratitude to President and Mrs. Figueres for bringing us together here in Costa Rica.

NOTE: The President spoke at 10:15 p.m. in the Hotel Herradura. In his remarks, he referred to President Carlos Roberto Reina of Honduras; President Jose Maria Figueres of Costa Rica and his wife, Josette Altmann de Figueres; and President Alvaro Arzu of Guatemala. A tape was not available for verification of the content of these remarks.

Remarks at Braulio Carrillo National Park, Costa Rica
May 9, 1997

Thank you very much. Thank you, Mr. President, for delivering on the rainforest. [*Laughter*] You know, in my part of the United States, the children are raised with an old proverb that has come true today. The proverb is, you must be very careful what you ask for in life because you might get it. [*Laughter*]

Well, Dr. Macaya, to Joaquin Viquez—didn't that young man do a great job? You should be very proud of him. He was terrific. [*Applause*] Thank you.

To all of those who have spoken before and who have come here, and let me thank the members of my Cabinet and administration who are here, and also the members of the National Park Service. Hillary and I try to make sure we're at at least one of our national parks every year. And I think it's fair to say that they are the most popular public servants in the United States, so it's nice to see them—in the case of Mr. Findley, someplace besides Yellowstone. I'm glad you're all here. Thank you all very much for what you do.

Most of what needs to be said has been said. I come here to emphasize the importance of the forest that surrounds us to the chain of life, not only in Costa Rica and Central America but to all the world. We know that the rainforests of the world provide us with a good deal of our oxygen and enormous resources coming out of the plant and animal life they contain. We know that the forest helps us to keep our climate stable, to preserve our soils, to protect our rivers. It nurtures plants that provide food and clothing and furniture and medicine. And from the stunning quetzal bird to the stealthy jaguar, we know that the marvelous animals must be preserved for all to see.

There is a new understanding today in the world between the bonds that connect human beings and their natural environment. We know we have to preserve them, and we know that in the end economic development itself cannot occur unless the environment is preserved. That is the lesson of the Rio Earth Summit 5 years ago, the driving force behind the CONCAUSA Alliance between the United States and Central America that President Figueres discussed, and also the driving notion behind the way we want to integrate this hemisphere—not just in trade and economics but also in education and health and, finally, in common cause to sustaining the treasures we see around us here today.

Costa Rica is showing the way. You heard, President Figueres says that now more than one-quarter of its land is being protected. The unique natural resources are generating jobs and income. Just before I came up here, Secretary Babbitt gave me the figures on Costa Rica's tourism income because of the commitment the people of this country have made to preserving and protecting the natural environment. We now know we have to do this not only in our hemisphere but around the world.

You know, the examples that the President cited I thought were quite important. We are pursuing ways to reduce greenhouse gases. There is some doubt about exactly what increased greenhouse gas emissions are doing to the climate, but no one doubts that they're changing the climate, and no one doubts that the potential consequences can be very profound and severe.

Almost 3 years ago, the Vice President of the United States, Al Gore, and President Figueres signed an agreement that will help United States companies to cut greenhouse gas emissions by investing in environmental projects in Costa Rica. Today, there are more than a dozen of these joint projects all across Central America, promoting solar energy in Honduras, geothermal energy in Nicaragua, forest management in Belize. Now the carbon certificates created by the Government of Costa Rica and the United States companies will provide a new way to finance these investments. Proceeds will go to clean powerplants, protecting or planting forests, launching other programs that pay environmental dividends. This is a long way from the philosophy which prevailed in this country, in our country, and indeed throughout the developed and the developing world just a few years ago.

From electric buses, which the President pointed out, to wind-driven power plants, Costa Rica's ambitious plans prove that we can have clean air and renewable energy in ways that create jobs here and in our country. That bus, I believe, was made in the Vice President's home State of Tennessee. And he asked me to say he appreciates it. [*Laughter*]

Third, let me say a special word of appreciation for something the President mentioned, and that is the work that is being done with the rainforest and with the space program by Dr. Franklin Cheng Diaz to deal with Chagas disease, which kills 20,000 people in Latin America

every year. The idea of combining what we know about space and what we find in the rainforest to make people have better and healthier lives is another stunning reminder that we destroy these resources at our peril.

Last, let me say, we're finding new ways to preserve our natural heritage. Once, our National Park Service worked with Costa Rica to help to set up your incredible network of parks. Now the Costa Rican Park Service is returning the favor by helping us to use your computer software in ways that will enable our park rangers at Yellowstone, which is the shining diamond of our park system, to catalog and preserve its natural wonders.

Soon after we complete this moment, Secretary Babbitt and Minister Castro will sign an agreement strengthening our cooperation for the next century. We're also working together to help other countries take better care of their wildlife, train professionals to manage fisheries in Argentina, run national parks in Paraguay, teach conservation in Guatemala. Now we have to work across national lines to protect the habitat of the songbirds, the sea turtles, the other creatures that migrate between our shores, and to stop the illegal and deadly trade in endangered species.

Yesterday in San Jose, President Figueres, our fellow leaders, and I pledged to make sustainable development a cornerstone of our relations. It will be part of the 1998 Summit of the Americas in Santiago and, eventually, the foundation of a larger global effort.

We must ban leaded gasoline everywhere, not just in Costa Rica, and control pesticides in our hemisphere, and reach a global agreement to phase out the most dangerous toxic chemicals. We have to protect our own forests and work with the United Nations to develop a strategy for the sustainable management of others around the world. And we must meet the challenge of climate change, regionally and beyond our hemisphere.

Together, we can make this a very historic year, Mr. President. As you know, the United Nations is having a special session next month on the environment. I am pleased to be leading America's delegation to the U.N. I hope many other world leaders will be there. Together, we need to reaffirm the spirit of Rio and lay out the concrete steps we're going to take to move ahead to make the preservation of the global environment and sustainable development the policy of every nation on Earth.

We are seeking to build a world where people live in the 21st century in harmony, not at war with each other; when they recognize that they have more in common than what divides them; when they no longer seek to elevate themselves by demeaning other people. That kind of world will only occur if we are also generous, wise, and good to our natural environment, and where we do not expect today's growth to threaten tomorrow's survival. That is my commitment. That is Costa Rica's commitment. Let us make sure we realize it.

Thank you, and God bless you all.

Before the paper is too wet, we have to ask Secretary Peña, Secretary Babbitt, and Minister Castro to come sign our agreements on electric transport and parks on behalf of our two nations. And we hope that the pens still work. [*Laughter*]

NOTE: The President spoke at 11:07 a.m. In his remarks, he referred to Dr. Gabriel Macaya, rector, University of Costa Rica; Mike Findley, superintendent, Yellowstone National Park; student Joaquin Viquez, who introduced the President; Dr. Franklin Cheng Diaz, director, Laboratorio de Propulsion Avanzada Especial de la NASA; and Costa Rican Minister of Natural Resources, Energy, and Mines Rene Castro.

Remarks at a Reception for Caribbean Leaders in Bridgetown, Barbados
May 9, 1997

Governor General, Madam, Prime Minister and Mrs. Arthur, leaders of the Caribbean, distinguished guests. First I'd like to thank our hosts for their hospitality and the weather. [*Laughter*] And I'd like to thank all of you for agreeing to join in this meeting here in beautiful Barbados.

I'm deeply honored to be the first American President to hold a summit with Caribbean heads of government here in the Caribbean. But it is high time; America, after all, is a Caribbean nation. Puerto Rico and the American Virgin Islands lie in the heart of this region. The bonds of commerce among us and the bonds binding our people are strong.

Today, millions of my fellow Americans trace proud roots to the Caribbean. These people have enriched and strengthened the United States. We can all be proud that our leadership as a Caribbean community, supported by nations around the world, along with the determination of the Haitian people, have given Haiti another chance to build a democratic future. And we are delighted to have President Preval with us here tonight.

The last time we met as a group was in the White House 3½ years ago on the eve of Operation Uphold Democracy in Haiti. This hopeful moment gives us another chance to meet together and work together. It demands that we work together because there are great forces

of change sweeping our world and our region. We must harness them to our benefit. We must meet the host of new challenges before us. And frankly, none of us can make the most of the opportunities or deal with the dangers alone.

That's what our meeting tomorrow is all about. We need to ensure that the galloping global economy does not trample small economies or leave them behind. We must ensure that economic growth and environmental protection go forward hand in hand. We must band together to defeat the criminal syndicates and drug traffickers that prey on open societies and put our children and our very social fabric at risk.

No nation is so strong that it needs no help from its friends, and none is too small to make a real difference. Together we must build a new partnership for prosperity and security in the Caribbean, based on our common values, aimed at our common dreams. I look forward to the work we will do tomorrow and even more to the days of closer and more productive partnership ahead.

Thank you. And thank you for welcoming Hillary and me tonight. Thank you very much.

NOTE: The President spoke at 9:10 p.m. at the Government House. In his remarks, he referred to Barbados Governor General Sir Clifford Husbands and his wife, Lady Ruby Husbands; Prime Minister Owen Arthur of Barbados and his wife, Beverley; and President Rene Preval of Haiti.

The President's Radio Address
May 10, 1997

Good morning. This morning I want to talk about the responsibility we share to protect our children from the scourge of violent crime and especially from crime committed by other young people. We've all worked hard over the last 4½ years to prepare America for the 21st century, with opportunity for all, responsibility from all our citizens, and a community that includes all Americans. Because of these efforts, America's children face a brighter future. Economic growth is the highest it's been in a decade. Unemployment is at its lowest level in 24 years, with over 12 million new jobs. Last Friday we reached an historic agreement to finish the job of balancing the budget, to keep our economy thriving, with the biggest investment in education in 30 years, tax cuts to help pay for a college education for all Americans, and health care coverage for 5 million children who have no insurance now.

But with all these advances, our children cannot live out their dreams if they are living in fear of gangs and guns. That's why I have worked so hard to reverse the tide of crime. We passed a tough crime bill that's putting 100,000 new community police on our street. We passed the Brady bill, which has stopped over 186,000 felons, fugitives, and stalkers from buying handguns. We banned deadly assault weapons. We initiated the biggest antidrug effort ever to make our children's schools and streets safe, drug-free, and gun-free.

This strategy is working. Serious crime has dropped 5 years in a row. But sadly, crime among young people has been on the rise. According to a report by the Justice Department's juvenile division, unless we act now, the number of juveniles arrested for violent crimes will more than double by the year 2010. That means we must launch a full-scale assault on juvenile crime based on what we know works.

This February I sent legislation to Congress that would declare war on gangs, with new prosecutors and tougher penalties. It would also extend the Brady bill so that someone who commits a violent crime as a juvenile is barred from buying a gun as an adult. It would require that child safety locks be sold with guns to keep children from hurting themselves or each other. It would help keep schools open after hours, on weekends, and in the summer to keep children off the streets and out of trouble.

This is a tough and balanced approach based on what is actually working at the local level. In Boston, where many of these efforts are already in place, youth murders have dropped 80 percent in 5 years, and not one child has been killed with a gun in over a year and a half.

Unfortunately, this Thursday the House of Representatives passed the juvenile justice bill that falls far short of that promise. The House bill is weak on guns, and it walks away from the crime prevention initiatives that can save a teenager from a life of crime. And as drafted, it would actually only reach a few States with the good it does do.

The House bill does not ensure the new antigang prosecutors we desperately need to pursue and punish violent juveniles. It does not support efforts such as Boston's Operation Night Life, where police and probation officers make nightly visits to the homes of young probationers to make sure they live up to the strict rules of their probation. The bill does not fund anticrime initiatives to keep our schools open later and on weekends so young people can stay under the watchful eye of parents, educators, and community leaders instead of on street corners where the most common influences are bad ones. We know juvenile crime peaks right after the schoolday ends. We've got to engage our children during those hours, to steer them away from gangs.

You know, just a couple of weeks ago, I sponsored the Service Summit in Philadelphia, along with all our former Presidents and General Colin Powell. The summit was dedicated to giving every young American a chance to make

585

the most of his or her life, enlisting millions and millions of volunteers to guarantee children a healthy start, access to basic skills, a mentor, a safe environment, and the chance to serve themselves. Republicans and Democrats alike applauded this summit. It highlighted successful efforts to guarantee children a safe environment.

Now, this bill the House passed ignores the real spirit of the summit, its bipartisanship and its focus on what works. The plain evidence of what is working right now to save our children is nowhere apparent in this bill. It's the same old tough rhetoric without any prevention, without any change in the environment to make it harder for gangs to function, or without real toughness in every State in America. Perhaps most troubling, the House bill rejects my call to cut off young people's access to guns, now the third leading cause of death for young people between the ages of 13 and 24. We must begin with the simple precaution of child safety locks. It's heartbreaking when a gun owned by a law-abiding parent is used by a child to hurt themselves or others. According to a National Institute of Justice survey, 185 children died in 1994 because of accidental shootings. Now, if we can have safety precautions to prevent children from opening bottles of aspirin, surely we can have the same safety precautions to prevent children from using guns.

Extending the Brady bill is critical as well. If you commit a violent crime as a 17-year-old, you should not be able to buy a gun on your 21st birthday. I challenge Congress to pass a real juvenile justice bill, one that's tough on gangs and tough on guns and is serious about the kind of prevention efforts we know will work.

To me, a juvenile justice bill that doesn't limit children's access to guns is a bill that walks away from the problem. Not a single hunter would lose a gun because of child safety locks. Not a single law-abiding citizen would be denied a gun if we extend the Brady bill to those with violent juvenile records. But countless young lives would be saved if stolen guns became useless guns and if lawless juveniles became gunless adults.

If Congress really wants to get tough on juvenile crime, then it's time to get tough on guns and take them out of the hands of violent juveniles. We've come a long way in the last 4½ years. But to really make sure we prepare our children for the 21st century, we have got to give them a safe and orderly environment where they can make the most of their future and of the world they will soon inherit.

Thanks for listening.

NOTE: The address was recorded at 2:50 p.m. on May 9 aboard Air Force One for broadcast at 10:06 a.m. on May 10.

Address to the People of Central and South America
May 10, 1997

Good morning. I'm speaking to you today from Bridgetown, Barbados. I'm proud to be the first American President to meet with Caribbean leaders in the heart of the Caribbean. This was not a meeting between Caribbean nations and the United States, it was a meeting among Caribbean nations including the United States.

We are charting a roadmap for how we can work together for the benefit of all of our people as we move into a new century. Today, every nation in the Americas but one has embraced free elections and open markets. This hopeful moment gives us real opportunities to improve the lives of all our people, but it also demands that we work together to bring the benefit of change to all our citizens and to band together to meet the transnational threats that respect no borders.

That's what the Partnership for Prosperity and Security in the Caribbean that we signed today is all about. It lays out an ambitious action plan to expand trade with the Caribbean; to launch the Caribbean clean energy initiative to better protect the environment; to create a Caribbean scholars program so students have access to specialized training; to support the banks that make low-interest loans readily available to workers, farmers, and women's groups; and to deepen our cooperation to fight drugs and organized crime.

Working as partners, we can help build a future of peace and prosperity for all our children to enjoy. That's what we've committed to do at our summit in Barbados; that's what we'll continue to do as neighbors, friends, and partners.

NOTE: The address was recorded at approximately 3 p.m. on May 9 aboard Air Force One for later broadcast by Voice of America to Latin American outlets. A tape was not available for verification of the content of this address.

Remarks at a Welcoming Ceremony With Caribbean Leaders in Bridgetown
May 10, 1997

To our host, Prime Minister—if I had known earlier in my life that George Washington came here as a young man, I would have been here before. [*Laughter*] I thank you for the warm welcome that you have given to me and to my wife, to Secretary Albright, and our delegation.

I wanted to make the important point last night, and I would like to make it again, that while we have gathered as a group before in the White House and in Port-au-Prince, this is the first time an American President has actually held a summit with the Caribbean heads of Government in the region itself. But the point I wish to make is that this is not a meeting between Caribbean nations and the United States, but rather a meeting among Caribbean nations including the United States.

Puerto Rico and the American Virgin Islands lie at the heart of this region. We are joined today by the Governor of the Virgin Islands, Governor Roy Schneider; the congressional delegate from Puerto Rico and former Governor, Carlos Romero-Barceló; last night the delegate from the Virgin Islands, Donna Christian-Green, was here with us; and we also have Congresswoman Maxine Waters from California here.

The United States is very much aware that millions of our fellow citizens trace their heritage to these islands and that we have benefited immeasurably from them. More than ever before, we are linked economically and politically. Every nation but one in the Caribbean has chosen free elections and free markets. I am proud that the United States has long been a beacon for freedom in this hemisphere. But I am proud

that so many of the other nations represented around this table have also been long beacons for freedom.

And like all the rest of you, we are especially gratified to be joined by the second democratically elected President of Haiti. And President Preval, we're glad you're here and we wish you well and we're with you all the way.

We have a lot of work to do today, and I will try to be brief. We have to work on means to expand the quality of our lives by expanding trade, by helping small economies compete in a global economy, by strengthening the education of our children, and deepening our cooperation against crime and drugs. If we work together, we can bring the benefits of change to our citizens and beat back the darker aspects of it. We can meet the new threats to our security and enhance our prosperity.

I want this summit to be the start of an ongoing and deeper process of Caribbean cooperation. We have worked very hard, all of us have, to make this summit productive. We have a rich and full document to which we are all going to commit ourselves. But still, we must be committed to working over the months and years ahead for our people and our Caribbean community, and that is my commitment to you. This summit should be the beginning, not the end of this process.

Thank you.

NOTE: The President spoke at 10:13 a.m. in the North West Plenary Conference Room at the Sherbourne Center.

The President's News Conference With Caribbean Leaders in Bridgetown
May 10, 1997

Prime Minister Arthur. Mr. Chairman, President of the United States of America, fellow Caribbean heads of state and government, Secretary General of CARICOM, distinguished delegates, members of the press. First, I should like to say that my wife and I are pleased that you could find it possible to come to share the residence with us. It is my pleasure to inform you that the just concluded Caribbean-United States summit has been a great success.

The signing of the Bridgetown Declaration of Principles is tangible expression of the new partnership between the Caribbean States and the Government and the people of the United States of America. Equally important is a plan of action which gives concrete expression to the commitment of the Caribbean States and the United States of America to cooperate on trade, development, finance, the environment, as well as on justice and security.

The summit has afforded our region the opportunity to present as one its perspectives on several concerns which we share with the United States of America. History and shared traditions already unite us. As technology and globalization bring us closer together, it is inevitable that meetings of this type will be necessary to share perspectives, coordinate actions, and to find solutions to common problems.

On this historic occasion, we have been able to undertake a detailed review and analysis of critical aspects of the relationship between the Caribbean nations and the United States of America. We have also been able to lay the foundations for future cooperation and consultation.

This summit is but the first step in a process of reaffirming and redefining a partnership between our two societies. We have come a long way in a short time from our first meeting at Sam Lord's castle through the meeting of the working groups and subcommittee in Tobago and St. Lucia, to a just concluded summit at Sherbourne and here at Ilaro Court.

Through these discussions, Mr. President, your Special Envoy, Mr. Richard Clark, has been a valuable and critical advocate in advancing our discussions. The need for an accessible contact between us cannot be overstated. It is my hope that any arrangement of this type will not end with the summit activities but will continue to allow future consultations between the Governments of the Caribbean and United States to prosper.

In the preparatory stages for the summit, the States of the Caribbean have been ably represented by the Foreign Minister Ralph Maraj of Trinidad and Tobago; Foreign Minister, Mr. Rohee of Guyana; Attorney General David Simmons of Barbados; and Ambassador Richard Bernal of Jamaica. I wish to place on record as well our appreciation for the magnificent contribution of the Secretary General of CARICOM and his staff and the advisers.

Barbados is proud and honored to host this summit, the first of its kind between the Caribbean States and the Government of the United States of America. I am confident that history will recall this summit as having forged a new and a lasting bond between the people of our nations and those of the United States of America. It is in this spirit, therefore, that I now have the greatest pleasure in introducing the Prime Minister of Jamaica, the Right Honorable P.J. Patterson, Chairman of the Conference of Heads of Governments of the Caribbean Community to address you. I thank you.

Prime Minister Patterson. Presidents of the United States of America, Haiti, Suriname, and Guyana, colleague heads of government, ladies and gentlemen. In the closest of families, difficulties are bound to arise from time to time in their relationships. For those relationships to endure, it is essential that they must have the capacity from time to time to meet within the bosom of the family and to sort out whatever difficulties may have arisen.

Today is one such occasion. And as a result of the family meeting we have had among all the nations that are a part of the Caribbean, including the United States, we have agreed to chart a course that will enable us to move forward and together in the days ahead. We have discussed matters relating to democracy, development, and security, recognizing the considerable interlinkages which necessarily exist between all these important subjects.

Today we have signed the Bridgetown declaration and a plan of action which charts a course for progress and for unity and for integrated development within our region. We were very pleased at the firm and unequivocal commitment given by the President of the United States and his administration of the priority which is to be attached to the question of NAFTA parity. And we are pleased at the prospect of that legislation being presented to the consideration of the Congress of the United States and will do everything in our power to make representations that will ensure its favorable consideration and early passage.

Not surprisingly, we spent some time on the issue of bananas. And I have the authority of the Prime Minister of St. Lucia, Dr. Vaughn Lewis, to quote something he said to us today: "For many of our countries, bananas is to us what cars are to Detroit."

Here in Bridgetown, we have reaffirmed our resolve to fight crime, violence, corruption, trafficking in drugs and illegal weapons by a seamless alliance between the United States of America and the sovereign nations of the Caribbean. We cannot allow the drug cartels and international criminal organizations operating in or across our borders to threaten our democratic institutions, to pervert our system of justice, and destroy the health and well-being of our citizens, young or old.

We have also raised the need, if we are to be engaged in partnership, for there to be a process of collective evaluation and decision-making, rather than unilateral assessments. And we have established some machinery that will enable us to facilitate this.

We are committed to the notion of a trans-Caribbean community which would embrace all the countries washed by the Caribbean Sea. This we see as a major plank in the new partnership which today's summit is intended to forge between the sovereign nations of the Caribbean and the United States.

We see here in Bridgetown the opening of a new chapter, the start of a meaningful dialog. It was good for us to be here, and together we intend to do it the Caribbean way.

President Clinton. Good afternoon. Prime Minister Arthur, Prime Minister Patterson, fellow Caribbean leaders, let me begin by thanking our Barbadian hosts for their hospitality and all the leaders for their hard work in making this summit a success.

I'm honored to be here with the Secretary of State and several members of my Cabinet, as well as a distinguished delegation interested in the Caribbeans from the Congress: Congresswoman Maxine Waters, the Chairman of the Congressional Black Caucus; Congressman Carlos Romero-Barceló, the delegate from Puerto Rico; and Governor Roy Schneider from the Virgin Islands.

The partnership for prosperity and security in the Caribbean that we signed today is a broad and ambitious plan of action. It can make a real difference for our people's lives and livelihoods, promoting open and fair trade, protecting the environment, strengthening education, spreading telecommunications, extending loans to small businesses, and combating international crime and drug trafficking.

Just as important as the commitments we've made is our determination to see them through with an ongoing, intensified process of Caribbean cooperation. The followup structures we've put in place, including an annual meeting among our foreign ministers and high-level working groups on justice and security and on development, finance, and the environment, will help us to turn our action plan into actions.

I want to highlight two areas where our cooperation is especially important: helping our people to thrive in the global economy and fighting crime and drugs. The move toward open and competitive trade around the world and in our hemisphere is bringing new opportunities for people to prosper. But rapid change is disruptive as well, as people struggle to acquire new skills and nations strive to compete. The United States is working to ensure that the transition to free trade in our hemisphere is fair to our Caribbean partners.

When I return to Washington, I will submit a Caribbean Basin trade enhancement act to Congress. When passed, this legislation will increase trade for all the Caribbean nations and help them to prepare to take part in a free-trade area of the Americas.

We're also committed to help the Caribbean nations diversify their economies and become more competitive. I discussed with my fellow leaders their concern for the Caribbean banana industry. In pursuing and winning our case at the World Trade Organization, our target was a discriminatory European system, not the Caribbean nations. I made it clear that as we work toward a solution with our European partners, we will continue to support duty-free access for Caribbean bananas in the European market, and we will seek ways to promote diversification of the Caribbean economies.

When economies are strong, they can better resist the pressures of organized crime, the drugpushers, the gunrunners, the alien smugglers, the criminal gangs. But to truly conquer them, we must work together. That's why I'm pleased we've been able to conclude agreements for maritime law enforcement cooperation with more countries in the region, including most recently Jamaica and Barbados. Today the United States committed to help our Caribbean partners strengthen their fight against drug trafficking, providing aircraft and Coast Guard cutters to patrol the sky and the sea. We will participate in international negotiations to outlaw and prevent traffic in illegal arms, and we will help to establish a Caribbean institute to train investigators and prosecutors to combat money laundering so that criminals will no longer be able to scrub the fingerprints off their profits.

Working together, we can build a future of prosperity and security for our people. But the scope is broad, and a commitment is deep as the waters that link our shores.

Thank you very much.

Cuba and Caribbean-U.S. Relations

Q. Mr. President, I wonder, first of all, if you could comment on the tone of your discussions and your reception here today, given the admitted lack of U.S. attention to the region in the past. And specifically, given the political baggage that accompanies U.S. policy toward Cuba, were the Caribbean leaders able to offer you any constructive suggestions on how you could shift your handling of Havana more from the negative to the positive? And I'd also like to extend that question to any Caribbean leader who would like to take it.

President Clinton. Well, first of all, we did not discuss Cuba. We talked about what those who are represented here could do together. And secondly, I believe that I have demonstrated my good faith and the good faith of this administration toward the Caribbean in many ways. We have already been together in Washington, right before our operation to restore democracy in Haiti. Most of us were gathered in Haiti when we celebrated that restoration. And I think it is well-known that at the time we fought for and succeeded in passing

NAFTA in Congress, I made a strong plea that we make sure that the Caribbean nations not be discriminated against.

I think we have now found a formula that will permit us to do that, that I believe has a good chance of passing in the Congress, and it is included in my budget. And so I feel quite good about the legislation I'm going to introduce, and I'm going to work hard to pass it and to establish a closer, more ongoing relations with all these nations.

Do you want one of them to reply?

Prime Minister Patterson. Our working sessions included a business session this morning, which we have just concluded, and a working lunch, to which we will now embark. There are a number of matters that could not be covered in the business session, and the opportunity of a working lunch among the heads will afford us an opportunity of discussing those subjects in the intimacy of that setting.

The views of the Caribbean leaders are well known, insofar as Cuba is concerned. Cuba is a Caribbean territory. We would like to see steps taken that would integrate Cuba fully not only in the Caribbean family but into the hemispheric family of nations. And we would certainly want to use the opportunity to indicate to the President over lunch the steps which we think would be possible to secure that objective.

Prime Minister Arthur. If I may, quickly. It should not escape your attention that this is the first-ever summit between the Government of the United States of America and the Caribbean that has ever been held on Caribbean soil. And that, in and of itself, should represent the sense of partnership that we are trying to build on matters of crucial importance to the two sets of societies. This spirit has not only been parlayed in the diplomatic sense of the word but has been constructive to the extent that it has sought to address matters of immediate consequence, as well as to lay a framework for the long-term development of the relationships between the two sets of societies.

We have approached this summit with a sense of pragmatic optimism. We do not believe that all of the concerns between our two sets of societies will be dealt with in one swoop. But we feel that the putting in place of a partnership and a mechanism for the followup of actions will allow us to be able to redress some of the imbalances in the relationship of the past and chart new directions for the future.

Haiti

Q. In the just-signed document, partner for prosperity, the chief of states and government at the summit pledged to give priority consideration to technologies such as the Internet. President Clinton, if asked by President Preval, will your administration tangibly support a plan to link all public schools in Haiti to the Internet by the year 2004, on the 200-year anniversary of Haiti's independence?

President Clinton. Well, this is the first I have heard about this specific proposal, so I hate to answer a question "yes" when I don't know whether I can do it or not. But let me say, you may know that we are attempting to link all of our classrooms and libraries to the Internet in the United States by the year 2000, and then we want to move aggressively to try to establish those kinds of interconnections with our allies elsewhere. And I believe that with Haiti struggling to both preserve democracy and overcome economic adversity, the nation and the children would benefit immensely if that could be done.

So I would certainly be willing to try to help. If I know I can do it, I will tell you, yes, I can do it. But I haven't had time to be briefed on it. But I am very open to the suggestion, trying to help.

U.S. Arms Embargo Against Latin America and Whitewater Investigation

Q. Thank you very much, Prime Minister Arthur—Wolf Blitzer from CNN. I wonder if all of you would be interested in reacting to the open letter from Oscar Arias that was written to President Clinton while he was in Costa Rica, appealing to him not to lift the U.S. arms embargo to sell sophisticated warplanes to countries in Latin America, which is on the agenda right now.

And President Clinton, I wonder if you've made up your mind whether or not you're going to sell F–16's and other sophisticated warplanes and hardware to these countries, at a time when he says—former President Arias—that they need their money for more productive purposes as opposed to weaponry. And with the indulgence of your host, I wonder if I could ask you a parochial question. Kenneth Starr, the Whitewater independent counsel, at this hour is

scheduled to be delivering a speech in which he says the White House is an impediment to his investigation, and I wonder if you have any reaction to his comment. Thank you.

President Clinton. I don't object to the Prime Ministers commenting on—is this on? Now can you hear? I'll just speak up. I don't object to the Prime Ministers commenting on the arms decision, but on that I can tell you that no decision has been made yet.

The United States will not knowingly do anything that will spark a new arms race or divert funds from defense to—from nondefense to defense areas in Latin America. The real question is whether or not the armies in question, where the militaries have discussed this with our country, are going to upgrade their militaries anyway and whether it would be better in fending off future conflicts and controlling defense spending for the United States, their hemispheric partner, to be the main supplier or someone else to be the main supplier.

We have no interest in doing this for purely economic reasons, and we have no interest in promoting an arms race in Latin America. So the judgment that I'm trying to make—and I haven't received a final recommendation on it from my administration top personnel—is whether or not, given the facts in the various countries, it would be better for them and better for us and better for peace over the long run in Latin America for these airplanes essentially to be supplied by the United States as opposed to someone else.

Now, on the other issue, I think that Mr. Starr must be—I haven't seen the speech, but I think he must be referring to the eighth circuit case, the facts of which have now been made public, and I don't have anything to add to what my counsel said. I think that it's obvious that for several years now we've been quite cooperative, and we'll continue to be. The White House Counsel made his statement, and I think it's clear and self-evident what he said and why.

Would you like to say anything about the arms issue, either one of you?

Prime Minister Patterson. I would say very simply that I have participated in a gathering at the conference center a few weeks ago at which the proposal conveyed by former President Arias to President Clinton was fully discussed and endorsed. Jamaica as a government supports the appeal.

Immigration

Q. President Clinton, what guarantees can you give us here in the Caribbean that your new immigration laws won't lead to mass repatriation of illegal Caribbean immigrants in the United States?

And my second question is for Mr. Patterson. Can you tell us if you've got any assurance from the President that criminals in the United—Caribbean criminals in the United States won't be sent back home without any information being conveyed to you, without any mechanisms being put in place to deal with them when they arrive here?

President Clinton. First of all, let me point out that I believe the United States has the most generous immigration policy of any large nation in the world. Last year, over 900,000 legal immigrants were admitted to the United States.

In order to sustain a policy that generous, it also has to have some integrity. And looking at it, I suppose you could say we had two choices. We could just lower the legal immigration target dramatically to take account of all those who are entering illegally, or instead we could reward those who wait, play by the rules, and obey the law, and try to strengthen our capacity to stop illegal immigrants from coming into the country, which we propose to do by stiffening our controls primarily at the border, in the workplace, and when people get into the criminal justice system.

Now, having said that, I can assure you, as I told the leaders of the Central American countries, no one nation or region will be targeted, and there will be no mass deportations. We are increasing our capacity to deal with people we find in the workplace, at the borders, in the criminal justice system.

Finally—Prime Minister Patterson and Prime Minister Arthur might want to comment on this—I do not believe it is right for the United States to send people back to their native lands, who have been in our criminal justice system, without appropriate advance warning and notice. And I pledged to them that I would set up such a system. It is not right for us to do it otherwise.

Would you like to say something?

Prime Minister Patterson. By recognizing the right of each state to determine its policies on deportation, subject to international law, the plan of action to which we agreed set out a number of specific measures that should be put in place. The President has referred to one of them, the provision of adequate advance notice to designated authorities prior to the deportation of anyone. We also think that adequate information should be provided regarding the persons to be deported and, of course, it must be established that the person being deported is a national of the receiving state.

Let me say very frankly why the problem is so acute. We have found in several cases people being deported who have lived in the United States not only for all their adult life, but have gone there from the days of early childhood with their entire families, and they have no family connection back in the Caribbean and no social contact to the communities to which they are being returned. And we, therefore, think if it is not to fuel the criminal problem, it is a matter that we have to address within the gambit of the cooperation to which we have pledged ourselves.

Prime Minister Arthur. I wish to add, please, that on the matter of the possible effects of U.S. law on Caribbean immigrants was a matter that was frankly discussed at our summit today. We represented the concerns of our nationals, and we have impressed on the President need for any legislation to be applied in a manner that is not discriminatory, nor is unfair, and nor that—undue—put at risk the security and prosperity of legal immigrants in the United States of America.

And I just want to add on the second matter that as regards the matter of deportees, Barbados has managed to work out a comprehensive framework with United States of America on all matters pertaining to the fight against drugs. And I'm pleased to say that I'm advised by my Attorney General that included in that comprehensive framework is a protocol establishing the rules that will be applied in the return of Barbadians to Barbados. And we regard this as a substantial advance. And I'm also pleased that our plan of action sets out a multilateral approach to dealing with this potentially vexatious issue.

Immigration and Trade

Q. You promised—on every stop of this trip, including today, you have promised to try to soften the new immigration law and try to extend trade preferences. But you can't get any of that done without congressional approval and, in the case of bananas, without cooperation with the European Union. What happens to these relationships here in Central America and in Mexico if you can't deliver on your rhetoric?

President Clinton. Well, first of all, with regard to the immigration law, the only thing that I was attempting to change in the immigration law, the congressional leadership has agreed to change. They've agreed to restore benefits to legal immigrants, which I thought was important.

We can, under the existing law, have the kind of protocols that Prime Minister Arthur discussed, where we pledge not to violate the human rights of any particular group of people, we pledge not to target any particular group, we pledge not to engage in mass deportations. That is not required under our law, nor was it contemplated.

To say that a country should and must have the capacity to enforce its immigration law is not the same thing as saying that there's going to be some huge roundup here. We just want to be able to enforce the law when we come in contact with people who have plainly violated it. So I don't agree that we need congressional cooperation there, although I believe it's consistent with what Congress intended when they passed the law.

Now, on this trade issue and on the question of getting fast-track authority from Congress, generally, I think that everyone understands, and I made it clear in our meetings, that all I could do was ask the Congress for its support, that there was opposition in both parties to expanded trade, but there was strong support in both parties to expanded trade. We've been through these arguments before in the last few years, but I would say the last time we had the debate back in '93, the American economy was not in nearly the shape it's in now and the Congress did the right thing for the future of America and the future of the Americas, and I believe it will be inclined to do so again.

Haiti

Q. My question is directed to President Clinton. To fight the high cost of living, the Government of Haiti has put in place a program of agrarian reform to provide Haitian farmers with technical means and rural credit to increase their capacity of production. I would like to know if the United States is ready to help in

realizing this agrarian reform in Haiti, because it is important for agriculture and for the people to find something to eat. That's number one.

But number two, I would like to mention that in Haiti, there is a sense of profound gratitude toward you, personally, President Clinton, and toward the U.S.A. for the role played in the restoration of constitutional order in Haiti after the military coup d'etat that overthrew the first democratically elected President of Haiti, Jean-Bertrand Aristide. And following that, there were a lot of promises that gave hope to the Haitian people. But since then, except for some very limited contributions, there is a sense that the American administration, under your leadership, has not done enough to help meet the expectations and the most crucial needs of the Haitian people. My question is, what are the next steps that the United States intends to take to show that democracy can bring prosperity as promised in Haiti?

President Clinton. Well, first of all, that is a complicated question because it requires significant actions on behalf of the Haitian people as well as those around the world who wish to support Haiti.

I am going to have a meeting with President Preval later this afternoon, after lunch, and we are going to discuss that, and I will have some other examples of specific things the United States intends to do. But I can tell you that I believe that we should be involved, over the long run, in trying to help to restore the economy and to restore the environment of Haiti—without which the economy cannot be sustained—and to maintain the integrity of the democracy. So we will be working hard on all those issues within the limits of our ability to do it. We will do as much as we can. It's very important to me.

Whitewater Investigation

Q. I know you answered Wolf's [Wolf Blitzer, Cable News Network] question, but you didn't go very far, and Ken Starr really came out quite strongly today. I wonder if you have begun to take this a little bit personally. And also today he said very strongly that he believes that White House lawyers are paid by the Federal Government, they represent the Federal Government, and as such, they are duty-bound to disclose relevant information to a Federal grand jury. As President, do you agree with that? And again, as I asked before, do you feel that this has become a little personal?

President Clinton. Well, not on my part. Perhaps on—you know, you said he's the one that came out strongly. I'm just over here doing my job in the Caribbean. [*Laughter*]

I can only say what I have said before. Chuck Ruff, whom I believe has a reputation as a lawyer of impeccable integrity and who is an expert in these kinds of processes, came to me and said that the effect of the decision would be not confined to the President, the First Lady, the Chief of Staff at the White House, any group of people, that the position that the Special Counsel was arguing for would, in effect, abolish the lawyer-client privilege between a Federal Government lawyer and a Federal employee at any level under any circumstances.

Now, the law firms in America might be ecstatic about that because it would certainly make a lot more private business for lawyers. But he came to me and said, "I cannot tell you how emphatically I believe that this case must be appealed." He said, "I'm your lawyer; I know

you haven't done anything wrong, I know you've made all the evidence available to them. This is a major constitutional question, and Mr. President, you do not have the right to go along with saying that every Federal employee in America should lose the attorney-client privilege under these circumstances if the Federal employee has a lawyer in the Federal Government." Now, that's what he said to me. I cannot enlighten you any more. If you want to know any more about it, you've got to ask him.

NOTE: The President's 145th news conference with Prime Minister Owen Arthur of Barbados and Prime Minister Percival James (P.J.) Patterson of Jamaica began at 1:33 p.m. at Prime Minister Arthur's residence, following the signing of the Bridgetown Declaration of Principles. In his remarks, President Clinton referred to Counsel to the President Charles F. Ruff and President Rene Preval of Haiti. Prime Minister Patterson referred to former President Oscar Arias of Costa Rica.

Caribbean/United States Summit: Bridgetown Declaration of Principles
May 10, 1997

We, the Heads of State and Government of the Caribbean nations of Antigua and Barbuda, the Commonwealth of the Bahamas, Barbados, Belize, the Commonwealth of Dominica, the Dominican Republic, Grenada, the Co-operative Republic of Guyana, the Republic of Haiti, Jamaica, the Federation of St. Christopher and Nevis, Saint Lucia, St. Vincent and the Grenadines, the Republic of Suriname and the Republic of Trinidad and Tobago and of the United States of America, meeting in Bridgetown, Barbados on May 10, 1997, pledge to strengthen our cooperation in responding to the challenges of the coming millennium, in a spirit of partnership and mutual respect.

2. We affirm our unswerving commitment to the norms of international law and the principles enshrined in the Charter of the United Nations and in the Charter of the Organization of American States and our respect for the sovereignty of states, multilateral approaches, democratic

traditions, human rights, good governance, human dignity and the rule of law.

3. We recognise the heterogeneity and diversity yet shared identity of our family of nations and people bonded by historic and ethnic origins, cultural ties and affinity and close social and economic links. We remain appreciative of the significant contribution of our respective nationals as immigrant communities to the development of each other's societies.

4. We also recognise the inextricable link between trade, economic development, security and prosperity in our societies. We therefore declare our intention to act in concert to improve the economic well-being and security of all our citizens, to defend and strengthen our democratic institutions and to provide for social justice and stability.

5. As we enter a new century marked by rapid expansion and globalisation of finance and investment, production and commerce, driven by revolutionary developments in technology, we acknowledge the need for a new era in our

partnership. In this context, we re-affirm our support for the Declaration of Principles and Plan of Action adopted by the 1994 Summit of the Americas of Miami. We recall that this process undertook to consider the special needs of small economies, with a view to enhancing their level of development and preparing them to meet the challenges posed by the inexorable trends of globalisation and liberalisation of the world economy, and the creation of the Free Trade Area of the Americas. We note the increasing role of the human, technological and communication capacities required for operating in this new competitive international environment and the current reality in most Caribbean States and accept the need for systematic, cooperative initiatives to strengthen the quality of their human resources and technological capacity.

6. Firm in our conviction that stable and prosperous economies, buttressed by the rule of law, are bulwarks against the forces of transnational crime, we are concerned by the growing strength and capabilities of transnational criminal organisations and drug cartels, their attempts to distort and weaken our free economies and democratic systems, and the effects which their activities and presence have on levels of violence and basic public order. We declare our resolve to collaborate in combatting both organised transnational crime and the threat posed to our peoples and the foundations of our nations by illegal firearms and ammunition trafficking. We are acutely concerned by the increasing incidence of alien smuggling and commit ourselves to search for creative and innovative ways to improve our justice systems and the cooperation between them, in order to provide our societies with that sense of security and stability so necessary to freely pursue sustainable social and economic development.

7. We recognise that despite the substantial progress in dealing with debt problems, high foreign debt burdens still hinder the development of some of our countries. We therefore affirm the importance of appropriate debt management measures including those in the programmes of the International Financial Institutions.

8. We affirm our strong commitment to internationally recognised labour standards and worker rights, especially freedom of association and collective bargaining. We underscore the importance of the empowerment of women to permit their full participation in the political and economic spheres, through fair access to education, health care and credit and recognise that addressing and preventing violence against women is an important step toward our goal of strengthening democracy. Vibrant, sustainable and equitable development requires the contribution of all members of society.

9. To achieve these objectives and maintain our process of consultation, we agree that all Ministers/Secretaries of State of the nations of the Caribbean responsible for Foreign Affairs and the Secretary of State of the United States of America will meet to oversee and report to us on an annual basis on the implementation of the Plan of Action appended hereto. In addition, we hereby establish Joint Committees on Justice and Security and on Trade, Development, Finance and Environmental Issues, the latter to work in close collaboration with the CARICOM/U.S. Trade and Investment Council, to facilitate an increasing and effective level of communication, coordination and follow-up among our Governments.

10. Towards these ends, we adopt and issue this *Bridgetown Declaration of Principles*, detailing our beliefs and uniting our efforts to strengthen the ability of our States to pursue sustainable development and to preserve our democracy, peace, economic and social progress and to which we hereby affix our signatures.

NOTE: This joint statement was embargoed for release until the conclusion of the President's 145th news conference. An original was not available for verification of the content of this joint statement. The Caribbean/United States Summit Plan of Action was attached to the release.

Statement on House Action To Reauthorize the Individuals With Disabilities Education Act
May 13, 1997

I am pleased that the House today took a major step toward ensuring high quality educational opportunities for all students with disabilities by voting to reauthorize the Individuals with Disabilities Education Act (IDEA). I am hopeful that the Senate will do the same shortly.

Over the last 20 years, the IDEA has made it possible for young people with disabilities to reach their full potential. This legislation strengthens and reaffirms our commitment to these children and their parents, and I look forward to signing it into law.

This legislation is the result of a bipartisan process that involved hard work not only by both Democrats and Republicans in the Congress but also by the Department of Education and representatives of the education and disability communities. I hope that we can continue in this bipartisan spirit and move forward on the rest of our agenda to improve education and prepare America for the 21st century.

Message to the Congress Reporting on the National Emergency With Respect to Iran
May 13, 1997

To the Congress of the United States:

I hereby report to the Congress on developments since the last Presidential report of November 14, 1996, concerning the national emergency with respect to Iran that was declared in Executive Order 12170 of November 14, 1979. This report is submitted pursuant to section 204(c) of the International Emergency Economic Powers Act, 50 U.S.C. 1703(c) (IEEPA). This report covers events through March 31, 1997. My last report, dated November 14, 1996, covered events through September 16, 1996.

1. The Iranian Assets Control Regulations, 31 CFR Part 535 (IACR), were amended on October 21, 1996 (61 Fed. Reg. 54936, October 23, 1996), to implement section 4 of the Federal Civil Penalties Inflation Adjustment Act of 1990, as amended by the Debt Collection Improvement Act of 1996, by adjusting for inflation the amount of the civil monetary penalties that may be assessed under the Regulations. The amendment increases the maximum civil monetary penalty provided in the Regulations from $10,000 to $11,000 per violation.

The amended Regulations also reflect an amendment to 18 U.S.C. 1001 contained in section 330016(1)(L) of Public Law 103–322, September 13, 1994, 108 Stat. 2147. Finally, the amendment notes the availability of higher criminal fines for violations of IEEPA pursuant to the formulas set forth in 18 U.S.C. 3571. A copy of the amendment is attached.

2. The Iran-United States Claims Tribunal (the "Tribunal"), established at The Hague pursuant to the Algiers Accords, continues to make progress in arbitrating the claims before it. Since the period covered in my last report, the Tribunal has rendered eight awards. This brings the total number of awards rendered to 579, the majority of which have been in favor of U.S. claimants. As of March 24, 1997, the value of awards to successful U.S. claimants from the Security Account held by the NV Settlement Bank was $2,424,959,689.37.

Since my last report, Iran has failed to replenish the Security Account established by the Algiers Accords to ensure payment of awards to successful U.S. claimants. Thus, since November 5, 1992, the Security Account has continuously remained below the $500 million balance required by the Algiers Accords. As of March 24, 1997, the total amount in the Security Account was $183,818,133.20, and the total amount in the Interest Account was $12,053,880.39. Therefore, the United States continues to pursue Case A/28, filed in September 1993, to require Iran to meet its obligation under the Algiers Accords to replenish the Security Account. Iran filed its Rejoinder on April 8, 1997.

The United States also continues to pursue Case A/29 to require Iran to meets its obligation of timely payment of its equal share of advances for Tribunal expenses when directed to do so by the Tribunal. The United States filed its Reply to the Iranian Statement of Defense on October 11, 1996.

Also since my last report, the United States appointed Richard Mosk as one of the three U.S. arbitrators on the Tribunal. Judge Mosk, who has previously served on the Tribunal and will be joining the Tribunal officially in May of this year, will replace Judge Richard Allison, who has served on the Tribunal since 1988.

3. The Department of State continues to pursue other United States Government claims against Iran and to respond to claims brought against the United States by Iran, in coordination with concerned government agencies.

On December 3, 1996, the Tribunal issued its award in Case B/36, the U.S. claim for amounts due from Iran under two World War II military surplus property sales agreements. While the Tribunal dismissed the U.S. claim as to one of the agreements on jurisdictional grounds, it found Iran liable for breach of the second (and larger) agreement and ordered Iran to pay the United States principal and interest in the amount of $43,843,826.89. Following payment of the award, Iran requested the Tribunal to reconsider both the merits of the case and the calculation of interest; Iran's request was denied by the Tribunal on March 17, 1997.

Under the February 22, 1996, agreement that settled the Iran Air case before the International Court of Justice and Iran's bank-related claims against the United States before the Tribunal (reported in my report of May 17, 1996), the United States agreed to make *ex gratia* payments to the families of Iranian victims of the 1988 Iran Air 655 shootdown and a fund was established to pay Iranian bank debt owed to U.S. nationals. As of March 17, 1997, payments were authorized to be made to surviving family members of 125 Iranian victims of the aerial incident, totaling $29,100,000.00. In addition, payment of 28 claims by U.S. nationals against Iranian banks, totaling $9,002,738.45 was authorized.

On December 12, 1996, the Department of State filed the U.S. Hearing Memorial and Evidence on Liability in Case A/11. In this case, Iran alleges that the United States failed to perform its obligations under Paragraphs 12–14 of the Algiers Accords, relating to the return to Iran of assets of the late Shah and his close relatives. A hearing date has yet to be scheduled.

On October 9, 1996, the Tribunal dismissed Case B/58, Iran's claim for damages arising out of the U.S. operation of Iran's southern railways during the Second World War. The Tribunal held that it lacked jurisdiction over the claim under Article II, paragraph two, of the Claims Settlement Declaration.

4. Since my last report, the Tribunal conducted two hearings and issued awards in six private claims. On February 24–25, 1997, Chamber One held a hearing in a dual national claim, *G.E. Davidson* v. *The Islamic Republic of Iran*, Claim No. 457. The claimant is requesting compensation for real property that he claims was expropriated by the Government of Iran. On October 24, 1996, Chamber Two held a hearing in Case 274, *Monemi* v. *The Islamic Republic of Iran*, also concerning the claim of a dual national.

On December 2, 1996, Chamber Three issued a decision in *Johangir & Jila Mohtadi* v. *The Islamic Republic of Iran* (AWD 573–271–3), awarding the claimants $510,000 plus interest for Iran's interference with the claimants' property rights in real property in Velenjak. The claimants also were awarded $15,000 in costs. On December 10, 1996, Chamber Three issued a decision in *Reza Nemazee* v. *The Islamic Republic of Iran* (AWD 575–4–3), dismissing the expropriation claim for lack of proof. On February 25, 1997, Chamber Three issued a decision in *Dadras Int'l* v. *The Islamic Republic of Iran* (AWD 578–214–3), dismissing the claim against Kan Residential Corp. for failure to prove that it is an "agency, instrumentality, or entity controlled by the Government of Iran" and dismissing the claim against Iran for failure to prove expropriation or other measures affecting property rights. Dadras had previously received a substantial recovery pursuant to a partial award. On March 26, 1997, Chamber Two issued a final award in Case 389, *Westinghouse Electric Corp.* v. *The Islamic Republic of Iran Air Force* (AWD 579–389–2), awarding Westinghouse $2,553,930.25 plus interest in damages arising from the Iranian Air Force's breach of contract with Westinghouse.

Finally, there were two settlements of claims of dual nationals, which resulted in awards on agreed terms. They are *Dora Elghanayan, et al.* v. *The Islamic Republic of Iran* (AAT 576–800/801/802/803/804–3), in which Iran agreed to pay the claimants $3,150,000, and *Lilly Mythra Fallah Lawrence* v. *The Islamic Republic of Iran* (AAT 577–390/391–1), in which Iran agreed to pay the claimant $1,000,000.

5. The situation reviewed above continues to implicate important diplomatic, financial, and legal interests of the United States and its nationals and presents an unusual challenge to the national security and foreign policy of the United States. The Iranian Assets Control Regulations issued pursuant to Executive Order 12170 continue to play an important role in structuring our relationship with Iran and in enabling the United States to implement properly the Algiers Accords. I shall continue to exercise the powers at my disposal to deal with these problems and will continue to report periodically to the Congress on significant developments.

WILLIAM J. CLINTON

The White House,
May 13, 1997.

NOTE: This message was released by the Office of the Press Secretary on May 14.

Remarks on the NATO-Russia Founding Act and an Exchange With Reporters
May 14, 1997

The President. Good afternoon. Today in Moscow, we have taken an historic step closer to a peaceful, undivided, democratic Europe for the first time in history. The agreement that NATO Secretary General Solana and Russian Foreign Minister Primakov have reached and which we expect to be approved by NATO's governing council this week, forms a practical partnership between NATO and Russia that will make America, Europe, and Russia stronger and more secure. The agreement builds on the understandings that I reached with President Yeltsin in Helsinki. It helps to pave the way for NATO, as it enlarges to take in new members, to build a new relationship with Russia that benefits all of us.

In this century, Europe has suffered through two cold wars—through two World Wars and a cold war. And America has also paid a heavy price. Three years ago at the NATO summit in Brussels, I laid out a vision for a new, different Europe in the 21st century, an undivided Continent where our values of democracy and human rights, free markets and peace know no boundaries; where nations know that their borders are secure and their independence respected; where nations define their greatness by the promise of their people, not their power to dominate or destabilize.

For 50 years, NATO has been at the core of Europe and America's security. From the start of my first administration, the United States has worked to adapt NATO to new missions in a new century, to open its doors to Europe's new democracies, to strengthen its ties to nonmembers through the Partnership For Peace, and to forge a strong, productive relationship between NATO and a free, democratic Russia. These are goals Republicans and Democrats alike share, building on the legacy of bipartisan leadership in Europe, begun after the war between President Truman, Secretary of State Marshall, and Senator Arthur Vandenberg.

Today's agreement sets out a sustained cooperative relationship between NATO and Russia. NATO and Russia will consult and coordinate regularly. Where they all agree, they will act jointly as they are doing today in Bosnia. Russia will work closely with NATO but not within NATO, giving Russia a voice in but not a veto over NATO's business.

I congratulate NATO Secretary General Solana and Russian Foreign Minister Primakov. I look forward to personally thanking Secretary General Solana for his remarkable work when he visits here next week.

This agreement opens a way for a truly historic signing in Paris next month—or excuse me, it will be later this month now. Let me say that NATO's relationship with Russia is a part of a larger process to adapt NATO to new circumstances and new challenges in the 21st century. Just 8 weeks from now in Madrid, NATO will invite the first new members to join our alliance. Its doors will remain open to all those ready to shoulder the burdens of membership. The first new members will not be the last.

NATO, working with Russia and other friends of freedom, will see that we work to prevent a return to national rivalries, to defeat new threats to peace and freedom and prosperity, like the ethnic rivalries that have torn Bosnia asunder, terrorism, and weapons proliferation.

This March in Helsinki, President Yeltsin and I agreed that despite our differences over NATO enlargement, the relationship between the United States and Russia and the benefits to all of cooperation between NATO and Russia were too important to be jeopardized. And we set out the principles for how NATO and Russia could cooperate. Those form the basis for today's agreement, an agreement that proves that the relationship between NATO and Russia is not a zero-sum game and that the 21st century does not have to be trapped in the same assessments of advantage and loss that brought death and destruction and heartbreak to so many for so long in the 20th century.

It is possible to enlarge NATO, to maintain its effectiveness as the most successful defense alliance in history, to strengthen our partnership with Russia, and to do all this in a way that advances our common objectives of freedom and human rights and peace and prosperity. We can build a better Europe without lines or gray zones but with real security, real peace, and real hope for all its citizens. A more secure, peaceful, and hopeful Europe clearly means a better world for Americans in the 21st century.

Thank you.

Russian Cooperation and NATO Expansion

Q. Mr. President, what do you think finally brought the Russians around, if there was one deciding factor? And how much of a problem is it going to be, now that you've got the Russians sort of on board, to convince Congress that NATO should, in fact, be expanded?

The President. Well, let me answer the first question. I think what brought the Russians to this agreement was a sustained effort at dialog between Russia and NATO and between Russia and the United States and other friends of democratic Russia, making it clear that NATO

has a new mission, that there was no attempt to be more threatening to Russia but instead to build a common partnership for democratic values and democratic interests.

Yesterday President Havel of the Czech Republic had a very compelling article in one of our major newspapers, laying out that case. We are not going to define NATO in the 21st century in the same way we did in the 20th century. And we are trying to change the realities that caused so much grief in the last century. I think he understood that, in other words, that a democratic, free, nonaggressive—that is, in a destructive sense—nonaggressive Russia is not threatened by an expanded NATO, particularly now that there's going to be a partnership to work in areas which are in our common interests to work. So that's the first thing.

The second thing I would say is, in terms of the Congress, now that the partnership has been solidified between NATO and Russia, which I think is an important thing on its own merits, it would seem to me to be a great mistake to deny countries that are clearly able and willing and anxious to take on the responsibilities of NATO membership the opportunity to do that. The understandings that we have reached among ourselves about the process of expansion mean that the members themselves are ready to expand. And I believe that in the end Congress will support that, particularly since all of our NATO allies will be voting on to whom new membership will be offered.

Russian Domestic Acceptance

Q. How tough a sell does President Yeltsin have at home with this?

The President. Well, I would hope that the clarifications that were hammered out, first at Helsinki but then the excellent work that Secretary General Solana did, will help President Yeltsin to demonstrate that he has secured an agreement which shows that, while they don't have a veto over NATO actions, that NATO has no plans, no intentions, and has made clear that its mission is not to threaten, confine, or in any way undermine Russia; that we're looking for a partnership here between a democratic Russia and the democracies that are in NATO; and that this, in fact, will strengthen Russia's security and reduce the sense of anxiety that it might have otherwise felt, I believe. And I believe he'll be in a position to argue that to the Russian people now in a forceful way.

But keep in mind, all of us are trying to change the—not only the facts on the ground, if you will, but the whole pattern of thought which has dominated the international politics of Europe for 50 years. And even though the cold war is over, a lot of people want to go back to the kind of—kind of an analysis that was more typical even before World War II, in the late 19th and early 20th century.

And we're trying to change all that. We're trying to prove that democracies can reach across territorial lines to form partnerships that commit themselves not only to preserve freedom within each other's borders and the integrity of those borders but to face these new transnational threats like terrorism, ethnic convulsions, and weapons proliferation.

Military Installations in New Member States

Q. Mr. President, President Yeltsin said that you have made a precise commitment in this document to guarantee that there will be no military installations in the new member states. Have you given those guarantees?

The President. I would urge you, first of all, to look at the language that Secretary General Solana has agreed to and that our representatives have provisionally agreed to just in the last couple of hours. What the language does is to make it clear that there are no plans and there are no reasons to, in effect, activate old Warsaw Pact military installations for what you might call traditional NATO aggressive forward-posturing but that we will have to use—there is an explicit understanding in the agreement that we will have to use some infrastructure for the agreed-upon operations that are an integral part of being a NATO member.

So all we're doing in the understanding is to recognize, yes, there will be some use of military infrastructure so that the requirements of membership can be met by any new members, but, no, we are not moving the dividing line of Europe from its old dividing line between NATO and the Warsaw Pact further east. So I think we got just exactly the right kind of understanding. And again, I think Secretary General Solana did it right.

Thank you.

NOTE: The President spoke at 2:29 p.m. in the Rose Garden at the White House. In his remarks, he referred to NATO Secretary General Javier Solana; Foreign Minister Yevgeniy Primakov and President Boris Yeltsin of Russia; and President Vaclav Havel of the Czech Republic. The agreement was formally entitled "Founding Act on Mutual Relations, Cooperation and Security Between NATO and the Russian Federation."

Message to the Senate on Conditions to the Flank Document of the Conventional Armed Forces in Europe Treaty
May 14, 1997

To the Senate of the United States:

I am gratified that the Senate has given its advice and consent to the ratification to the CFE Flank Document and I look forward to the entry into force of this important agreement. It will reaffirm the integrity of one of the CFE Treaty's core provisions and will facilitate progress on CFE adaptation and, thus, NATO enlargement, key elements for advancing United States and European security.

I must, however, make clear my view of several of the Conditions attached to the resolution of advice and consent to ratification, including Conditions 2, 3, 4, 6, 7, 9 and 11. These Conditions all purport to direct the exercise of authorities entrusted exclusively to the President under our Constitution, including for the conduct of diplomacy and the implementation of treaties. The explicit limitation on diplomatic activities in Condition 3 is a particularly clear example of this point. As I wrote the Senate following approval of the Chemical Weapons Convention, a condition in a resolution of ratification cannot alter the allocation of authority and responsibility under the Constitution. I will, therefore, interpret the Conditions of concern in the resolution in a manner consistent with the responsibilities entrusted to me as President under the Constitution. Nevertheless, without prejudice to my Constitutional authorities, I will implement the Conditions in the resolution.

Condition (9), which requires my certification that any agreement governing ABM Treaty succession will be submitted to the Senate for advice and consent, is an issue of particular concern not only because it addresses a matter reserved to the President under our Constitution, but also because it is substantively unrelated to the Senate's review of the CFE Flank Document. It is clearly within the President's authorities to determine the successor States to a treaty when the original Party dissolves, to make the adjustments required to accomplish such succession, and to enter into agreements for this purpose. Indeed, throughout our history the executive branch has made a large number of determinations concerning the succession of new States to the treaty rights and obligations of their predecessors. The ABM Succession MOU

negotiated by the United States effectuated no substantive change in the ABM Treaty requiring Senate advice and consent. Nonetheless, in light of the exceptional history of the ABM Treaty and in view of my commitment to agree to seek Senate approval of the Demarcation Agreements associated with the ABM Treaty, I have, without prejudice to the legal principles involved, certified, consistent with Condition (9), that I will submit any agreement concluded on ABM Treaty succession to the Senate for advice and consent.

WILLIAM J. CLINTON

The White House,
May 14, 1997.

NOTE: This message was released by the Office of the Press Secretary on May 15.

Message to the Congress on Conditions to the Flank Document of the Conventional Armed Forces in Europe Treaty
May 14, 1997

To the Congress of the United States:

In accordance with the resolution of advice and consent to ratification on the Document Agreed Among the States Parties to the Treaty on Conventional Armed Forces in Europe of November 19, 1990 ("the CFE Flank Document"), adopted by the Senate of the United States on May 14, 1997, I hereby certify that:

In connection with Condition (2), Violations of State Sovereignty, the United States and the governments of Belgium, Canada, Denmark, France, Germany, Greece, Iceland, Italy, Luxembourg, the Netherlands, Norway, Portugal, Spain, Turkey and the United Kingdom have issued a joint statement affirming that (i) the CFE Flank Document does not give any State Party the right to station (under Article IV, paragraph 5 of the Treaty) or temporarily deploy (under Article V, paragraphs 1 (B) and (C) of the Treaty) conventional arms and equipment limited by the Treaty on the territory of other States Parties to the Treaty without the freely expressed consent of the receiving State Party; (ii) the CFE Flank Document does not alter or abridge the right of any State Party under

the Treaty to utilize fully its declared maximum levels for conventional armaments and equipment limited by the Treaty notified pursuant to Article VII of the Treaty; and (iii) the CFE Flank Document does not alter in any way the requirement for the freely expressed consent of all States Parties concerned in the exercise of any reallocations envisioned under Article IV, paragraph 3 of the CFE Flank Document.

In connection with Condition (6), Application and Effectiveness of Senate Advice and Consent, in the course of diplomatic negotiations to secure accession to, or ratification of, the CFE Flank Document by any other State Party, the United States will vigorously reject any effort by a State Party to (i) modify, amend, or alter a United States right or obligation under the Treaty or the CFE Flank Document, unless such modification, amendment, or alteration is solely an extension of the period of provisional application of the CFE Flank Document or a change of a minor administrative or technical nature; (ii) secure the adoption of a new United States obligation under, or in relation to, the

CFE Treaty or the CFE Flank Document, unless such obligation is solely of a minor administrative or technical nature; or (iii) secure the provision of assurances, or endorsement of a course of action or a diplomatic position, inconsistent with the principles and policies established under conditions (1), (2), and (3) of the resolution of advice and consent to ratification of the CFE Flank Document.

In connection with Condition (7), Modifications of the CFE Flank Zone, any subsequent agreement to modify, revise, amend or alter the boundaries of the CFE flank zone, as delineated by the map entitled "Revised CFE Flank Zone" submitted to the Senate on April 7, 1997, shall require the submission of such agreement to the Senate for its advice and consent to ratification, if such changes are not solely of a minor administrative or technical nature.

In connection with Condition (9), Senate Prerogatives on Multilateralization of the ABM Treaty, I will submit to the Senate for advice and consent to ratification any international agreement (i) that would add one or more countries as States Parties to the ABM Treaty, or otherwise convert the ABM Treaty from a bilateral treaty to a multilateral treaty; or (ii) that would change the geographic scope or coverage of the ABM Treaty, or otherwise modify the meaning of the term "national territory" as used in Article VI and Article IX of the ABM Treaty.

In connection with Condition (11), Temporary Deployments, the United States has informed all other States Parties to the Treaty that the United States (A) will continue to interpret the term "temporary deployment", as used in the Treaty, to mean a deployment of severely limited duration measured in days or weeks or, at most, several months, but not years; (B) will pursue measures designed to ensure that any State Party seeking to utilize the temporary deployments provision of the Treaty will be required to furnish the Joint Consultative Group established by the Treaty with a statement of the purpose and intended duration of the deployment, together with a description of the object of verification and the location of origin and destination of the relevant conventional armaments and equipment limited by the Treaty; and (C) will vigorously reject any effort by a State Party to use the right of temporary deployment under the Treaty (i) to justify military deployments on a permanent basis; or (ii) to justify military deployments without the full and complete agreement of the State Party upon whose territory the armed forces or military equipment of another State Party are to be deployed.

WILLIAM J. CLINTON

The White House,

May 14, 1997.

NOTE: This message was released by the Office of the Press Secretary on May 15.

Remarks at the Peace Officers Memorial Ceremony
May 15, 1997

Thank you. Thank you very much. President Gallegos, Auxiliary President Lippe, to all the distinguished law enforcement representatives who are here; Senator Thurmond, Senator Biden, Senator Leahy, Congressman Stupak; members of our Cabinet administration. I'd like to thank all of those who support this endeavor every year, and especially this year Tommy Motolla and Gloria Estefan and most importantly, to the family members of those who have lost their lives in the service of our country.

In just 2 weeks, on Memorial Day, the American people will pause to pay tribute to the fallen military heroes who died to preserve the liberties upon which our Nation was founded and which have enabled it to endure for more than 200 years. Today we stand here on Peace Officers Memorial Day to pay tribute to a sacrifice no less great and no less critical to our liberties.

The police officers whose names are carved on the memorial are also our fallen heroes. And in the hearts of their families and the people whose lives they touched, their heroism will always shine.

Officer Lauretha Vaird was a 9-year veteran on the Philadelphia Police Department, a single, working mother. She often said that her two greatest loves were her boys and her badge, and she dedicated her life to them both. She was a community police officer who walked the streets of her beat with pride. One day she responded to a silent alarm at a local bank. And as she tried to prevent an armed robbery, a gunman's bullet took her life and left her children with only the memory of their heroic mother.

Officer Brian Gibson was a community police officer who grew up on streets he would later patrol. A native of this city, he served our country as a United States Marine in the Persian Gulf before joining the DC police force, a decorated officer who pounded the pavement to fight drugs and the people who sell them. One night he was killed at point-blank range by a raging gang member as he simply sat in the police car just a short ride from that memorial where his name will be carved. He, too, left behind a grieving family and friends and a legacy of courage.

Today we honor the service and take pride in all the stories of the 116 men and women who gave their lives to protect our safety. Our safety was their purpose and passion. And while we can never repay them for their ultimate sacrifice, we can, and we must, honor their memory not only in words but in actions that do justice to their lives and to the great loss their families and loved ones have suffered.

For too many years in our country, crime seemed destined to keep rising regardless of citizen outrage or law enforcement frustration. Then, slowly, you in law enforcement began to turn the tide, building bridges to concerned citizens and needy children and troubled neighborhoods, but losing brothers and sisters along the way.

Four years ago, we joined you as a nation to reclaim our streets, our schools, and our society with a commitment to a comprehensive approach to crime based on what you told us— what you told us would work. You told us we needed more police on the street, tougher penalties and better prevention. You told us especially we needed more community police officers. Today, we're putting 100,000 more of them on the street to join with you.

You told us illegal handguns and deadly assault weapons were undermining your efforts to fight gangs and drugs, so we banned them with the Brady bill and the assault weapons ban. Just since the Brady bill was enacted in 1993, 186,000 felons, fugitives, and stalkers have been denied the right to buy handguns. Today we take another step—[*applause*]—thank you. Today we take another step to protect our communities from gun violence by dangerous drifters who threaten our safety.

Two months ago, after the terrible tragedy at the Empire State Building, I directed the ATF to require people who buy guns from federally-licensed dealers simply to prove they were not just passing through. Today, we're releasing a new application to make sure that certification of residency is an unavoidable step for gun purchases. Those who can't prove it, can't purchase.

These efforts—[*applause*]—thank you. And thanks to you, these efforts are working. Crime is dropping, and all over America, neighborhood by neighborhood, hope for a safer future is slowly but surely being restored. It is all the more bittersweet that as crime has dropped in this country 5 years in a row for the first time in more than two decades, we must still gather to carve new names into the hard stone of the National Law Enforcement Officers Memorial.

In 1996, we added 116 names. While the loss of even one of those officers' lives is one too many, that is the smallest number of police officers to lose their lives in the line of duty since 1959. Today, in honor of those 116 officers, let us pledge to redouble our efforts so that every year, there will be fewer and fewer names, until one year we will gather with not a single name to add to that roll of heroes. Let that be our goal and our solemn obligation.

I ask you all now to move with us to our most pressing priority—to take back our streets from violent gangs. Once again, we known what to do because you have told us what to do. You have proven in place after place that it can be done, in cities like Boston where youth murders have dropped by 80 percent in 5 years and not a single child has been killed with a gun in a year and a half. If we can do it in one community in this country, we must be able to do it in every community in America.

In February, I sent legislation to the Congress that follows law enforcement's advice and Boston's lead, to declare war on gangs and youth violence with more prosecutors, tougher penalties, and better prevention programs for at-risk young people. For as tough as we must be on violent juvenile crime, we also must ensure a safer environment and positive opportunities and role models for our children in the most vulnerable communities.

Statistics show that half of juvenile crime at least occurs in the 3 hours after school is closed and before the parents come home. My bill will help to launch 1,000 after-school initiatives. Who can be against allowing a child to stay in school instead of on a street corner? Who can be against teachers as children's role models instead of thugs? Who can be against adults to supervise children instead of a lawless world of gangs to guide them?

Finally, we know we must cut off young people's access to guns that can cut off their lives. And I believe someone who commits a violent crime at 17 should not be able to turn around and buy a gun for a birthday present at 21. I want a juvenile crime bill to extend the Brady bill to violent juvenile offenders.

I also believe that these guns should be sold with child safety locks. We protect aspirin bottles in this country better than we protect guns from accidents by children.

In March, I directed Federal agencies to provide their agents with such child safety devices, and I'm pleased to say that today every FBI and ATF agent has a child safety lock. By October 15th, every agent from the DEA to the U.S. Marshal to the Border Patrol to the Park Police will have one, as well. If a child safety lock is good enough for law enforcement, it ought to be even better for the general public.

In the last 4 years we have proved that we can work together and learn from each other and that when we do, we can restore hope and improve safety in our communities. Now we have a chance to build on that progress by passing a smart, balanced juvenile justice bill that does more than talk tough. The American people deserve that. A juvenile crime bill that doesn't crack down on guns and gangs, that doesn't guarantee more prosecutors, probation officers, and after-school hours is a crime bill in name only.

Today I ask the Members of the Congress to work with me, without regard to party, to pass a juvenile crime bill that will help us to work toward year-in and year-out fewer and fewer people to honor here, until there is no one new to add to the wall.

To the family members of the victims who are here, I know and I must say again that nothing we can do or say can bring them back or ease your sorrow. Only God and the time and comfort you give to each other can do that. But I ask you this: to know that the cause in which your loved ones died, right against wrong, law against lawlessness, hope against fear, is a worthy and noble cause. And because of their efforts and the efforts of others who wear our uniforms, it has now become a winning cause.

It is our job, those of us who remain, to make sure that we press on and on and on until such tragedies are a stunning exception, not a numbing statistic. As we go forward into that future, that is our most solemn obligation to you.

Thank you, and God bless you.

NOTE: The President spoke at 1:30 p.m. on the West Grounds of at the Capitol. In his remarks, he referred to Gil Gallegos, president, and Karen Lippe, auxiliary president, Fraternal Order of Police; Thomas Motolla, president and chief operating officer, Sony Music Entertainment; and entertainer Gloria Estefan. The Peace Officers Memorial Day and Police Week proclamation of May 7 is listed in Appendix D at the end of this volume.

Message to the Congress Transmitting a Report on the National Security Strategy
May 15, 1997

To the Congress of the United States:

As required by section 603 of the Goldwater-Nichols Department of Defense Reorganization Act of 1986, I am transmitting a report on the National Security Strategy of the United States.

WILLIAM J. CLINTON

The White House,
May 15, 1997.

Remarks on the Budget Agreement and an Exchange With Reporters
May 16, 1997

The President. Good morning. Less than 2 weeks ago, the Vice President and I joined with leaders of Congress in announcing a truly historic agreement, a bipartisan agreement to balance the Federal budget for the first time in nearly three decades. We knew that only by finishing the job of putting our fiscal house in order could we keep our economy thriving for all Americans. And I knew that because of all the progress we've made in the last 4½ years, we could balance America's books while protecting America's values and preparing the American people for the 21st century. Last night we took the next significant step toward writing the spirit and substance of that agreement into the law.

I want to begin by thanking Chairman Domenici, Chairman Kasich, Senator Lautenberg, and Congressman Spratt for their hard work and their earnest commitment to sticking with this very difficult process to put our balanced budget agreement in writing. I know from my own negotiating team that we would not be here today without their good faith and good efforts, and I am deeply grateful to them.

I also want to thank the congressional leadership who supported this process. And I'd like to thank the people who are here: the Vice President; Erskine Bowles, who's still a pretty good negotiator even though he's left his beloved private sector; Secretary Rubin; Deputy Secretary Summers; OMB Director Frank Raines; NEC Director Gene Sperling; our CEA Chair, Janet Yellen; and John Hilley, who handles our congressional relations and had one of the most difficult and demanding jobs of his life in the last few weeks; OMB Deputy Director Jack Lew.

I'd like to also thank all the people who are here from OMB, Treasury, and perhaps from other agencies who were the team that put the numbers together, that made this agreement possible. Thank you. You ought to give yourselves a hand. [*Applause*] You did a great job. Thank you.

We have finalized a detailed description of the agreement reached 2 weeks ago. The document is already before the relevant congressional committees who are now moving the balanced budget resolution through the legislative process at an expedited pace. This agreement will keep in place the economic strategy that has served our Nation so well for the last 4½ years.

When I took office, I was determined to reverse the failed policies of the past. Back then, we faced growing deficits as far as the eye could see. It was a time of economic stagnation and high unemployment. We moved quickly in 1993 to put in place a policy of invest and grow: cut the deficit, invest in our people, open new markets around the world through tough trade agreements.

We are now in the 4th year of the disciplined, tough, 5-year economic strategy we put in place in 1993. The results of the strategy are now clear and no longer subject to reasonable debate: 12 million new jobs, the highest economic growth in a decade, the lowest unemployment in 24 years, the lowest inflation in 30 years, the largest decline in income inequality since the 1960's. And the deficit has been cut already by 77 percent. Our economy is now the envy of the world.

That progress has brought us to this rare moment in history and made it possible for us to balance the budget in a way that balances our values. America needs a balanced budget that is in balance with our values, that protects Medicare and Medicaid, education and the environment, that gives tax relief to working families, and that prepares our people for the 21st century. That is exactly what this budget does.

What is important about the agreement is not only what it does on a spreadsheet but what it will do for our families and our future. It keeps our fundamental commitments to our parents, preserving and protecting Medicare for at least a decade, without steep premium increases. Because of this agreement, 5 million American children will have health care who do not have it today. The agreement protects our air, our water, and our land for future generations. I'm especially pleased that it includes the funds to clean up 500 of our most dangerous toxic waste sites and to go forward with our commitment to preserve and restore the Florida Everglades.

It helps to move people from welfare to work by providing tax incentives to businesses to hire welfare recipients and support for community service jobs in areas of high unemployment. It restores unwise cuts made last year and restores fair treatment to immigrants who legally come to America for the promise it provides. It gives middle class families tax relief to help sell a home, raise their children, and send those children to college. In each of these ways, it honors our values.

At the very heart of this agreement, however, is its historic investment in education. This agreement includes the most significant increase in education funding in 30 years. Even more important, it provides the largest single increase in higher education since the GI bill in 1945, more than 50 years ago.

That landmark legislation gave opportunity to millions of Americans and gave birth to the American middle class. That was my goal for this budget, to dramatically expand opportunity through education and give all our children the tools they need to succeed in a new economy in a new century.

That is why I insisted that this balanced budget also be America's education budget. It not only puts our fiscal house in order, it opens the schoolhouse door wider than ever before, with $35 billion in tax relief for higher education, including our HOPE scholarship tuition tax credit to make 2 years of education after high school as universal as a high school education is today, and tax deductions for all the costs of tuitions after high school.

It includes the largest increase in Pell grant scholarships for deserving students in three decades. It helps to raise standards in our schools. It funds our America Reads challenge to make sure every 8-year-old can read independently. It helps to bring the information age to our schools so that we can meet the goal that the Vice President has worked so hard for, to connect all of our schools and libraries to the Internet by the year 2000.

All across America last year, I said I wanted a nation in which every 8-year-old would be able to read, every 12-year-old could log on to the Internet, every 18-year-old could go to college, every adult could keep on learning for a lifetime. This balanced budget takes a major stride toward these goals. This is not only the first balanced budget in a generation, it is an American balanced budget that protects our values for future generations.

So I say to all Members of Congress of both parties, take this balanced budget agreement and write it into law. If we stay true to this historic agreement, if we have the courage to eliminate the deficit while dramatically expanding opportunity through education, we will enter the 21st century stronger and better prepared for the challenges and the opportunities that lie ahead.

Thank you very much.

Budget Agreement

Q. Mr. President, 2 weeks ago we were told that there was a deal, and there was much hoopla. We came to find out at that point that, if I may use the egg analogy, that the shell was relatively thin. How much thicker is the shell now, and can this egg still crack up, so to speak?

The President. Well, first of all, I think we did have a deal 2 weeks ago. And I think the fact that we've reached agreement in writing on the details is evidence that there was one.

But when you agree on broad principles and you have long hours of negotiations, there's still some difficulties involved in writing the details of the agreement down, making sure everybody remembers it the same way, that you've got the kind of accord you need. So this is a huge step forward because now we have a much more detailed agreement committed to writing.

Wolf [Wolf Blitzer, CNN].

Late-Term Abortion Legislation

Q. Mr. President, I wonder now that the Senate has rejected Senator Daschle's compromise proposal on the late-term abortion procedure, I wonder if there is any way that you think language could be crafted that would avoid your having to veto Senator Santorum's legislation once again?

The President. Well, of course, I have nothing to add to what I have said on this all along. What I need to do is to be convinced that no woman will be grievously harmed by this legislation and that no woman will be put in the position, for example, of being so harmed that she will never be able to have further children because of this legislation. You know what my concerns are; I've made them abundantly clear.

I must say, I regret that Senator Daschle's legislation did not pass because it would have reduced the number of abortions by far, far more—light-years more than the Santorum bill. The Santorum bill may not reduce the number of abortions by one.

So what we don't want to do is to, in effect, not reduce the number of abortions in the third trimester, which the Supreme Court permits us to do and which I've invited the Congress to do ever since I got here, and at the same time put a lot of women's health at risk in a way that is unwise and unconstitutional.

Zaire

Q. Mr. President, what are you thoughts on Mobutu losing power in Zaire?

The President. Well, I want to make a couple of points on it. It does appear that he has left Kinshasa. The United States position is clear: We want to see a transition to a genuine democracy. The second point I want to make is that President Mandela of South Africa has done a superb job of exercising leadership in this area, and the United States is supporting him and his efforts. And I want the whole world to get behind the leadership that Nelson Mandela is showing there and to do what we can to support Africa in taking one of the largest and most important nations in Africa and promoting a democratic transition. That is what I think is important.

Thank you very much.

NOTE: The President spoke at 11:25 a.m. in the Rose Garden at the White House. In his remarks, he referred to President Mobutu Sese Seko of Zaire and President Nelson Mandela of South Africa.

Remarks in Apology to African-Americans on the Tuskegee Experiment
May 16, 1997

Ladies and gentlemen, on Sunday Mr. Shaw will celebrate his 95th birthday. I would like to recognize the other survivors who are here today and their families: Mr. Charlie Pollard is here; Mr. Carter Howard; Mr. Fred Simmons—Mr. Simmons just took his first airplane ride, and he reckons he's about 110 years old, so I think it's time for him to take a chance or two. [*Laughter*] I'm glad he did. And Mr. Frederick Moss, thank you, sir. I would also like to ask three family representatives who are here—Sam Doner is represented by his daughter, Gwendolyn Cox. Thank you, Gwendolyn. Ernest Hendon, who is watching in Tuskegee, is represented by his brother, North Hendon. Thank you, sir, for being here. And George Key is represented by his grandson, Christopher Monroe. Thank you, Chris.

I also acknowledge the families, community leaders, teachers, and students watching today by satellite from Tuskegee. The White House is the people's house; we are glad to have all of you here today. I thank Dr. David Satcher for his role in this. I thank Congresswoman Wa-

ters and Congressman Hilliard; Congressman Stokes; the entire Congressional Black Caucus; Dr. Satcher; members of the Cabinet who are here, Secretary Herman, Secretary Slater; a great friend of freedom, Fred Gray, thank you for fighting this long battle all these long years.

The eight men who are survivors of the syphilis study at Tuskegee are a living link to a time not so very long ago that many Americans would prefer not to remember but we dare not forget. It was a time when our Nation failed to live up to its ideals, when our Nation broke the trust with our people that is the very foundation of our democracy. It is not only in remembering that shameful past that we can make amends and repair our Nation, but it is in remembering that past that we can build a better present and a better future. And without remembering it, we cannot make amends, and we cannot go forward.

So today America does remember the hundreds of men used in research without their knowledge and consent. We remember them and their family members. Men who were poor and African-American, without resources and with few alternatives, they believed they had found hope when they were offered free medical care by the United States Public Health Service. They were betrayed.

Medical people are supposed to help when we need care, but even once a cure was discovered, they were denied help, and they were lied to by their Government. Our Government is supposed to protect the rights of its citizens; their rights were trampled upon—40 years, hundreds of men betrayed, along with their wives and children, along with the community in Macon County, Alabama, the City of Tuskegee, the fine university there, and the larger African-American community. The United States Government did something that was wrong, deeply, profoundly, morally wrong. It was an outrage to our commitment to integrity and equality for all our citizens.

To the survivors, to the wives and family members, the children, and the grandchildren, I say what you know: No power on Earth can give you back the lives lost, the pain suffered, the years of internal torment and anguish. What was done cannot be undone. But we can end the silence. We can stop turning our heads away. We can look at you in the eye and finally say, on behalf of the American people: What the United States Government did was shameful, and I am sorry. The American people are sorry—for the loss, for the years of hurt. You did nothing wrong, but you were grievously wronged. I apologize, and I am sorry that this apology has been so long in coming.

To Macon County, to Tuskegee, to the doctors who have been wrongly associated with the events there, you have our apology, as well. To our African-American citizens, I am sorry that your Federal Government orchestrated a study so clearly racist. That can never be allowed to happen again. It is against everything our country stands for, and what we must stand against is what it was.

So let us resolve to hold forever in our hearts and minds the memory of a time not long ago in Macon County, Alabama, so that we can always see how adrift we can become when the rights of any citizens are neglected, ignored, and betrayed. And let us resolve here and now to move forward together.

The legacy of the study at Tuskegee has reached far and deep, in ways that hurt our progress and divide our Nation. We cannot be one America when a whole segment of our Nation has no trust in America. An apology is the first step, and we take it with a commitment to rebuild that broken trust. We can begin by making sure there is never again another episode like this one. We need to do more to ensure that medical research practices are sound and ethical and that researchers work more closely with communities.

Today I would like to announce several steps to help us achieve these goals. First, we will help to build that lasting memorial at Tuskegee. The school founded by Booker T. Washington, distinguished by the renowned scientist George Washington Carver and so many others who advanced the health and well-being of African-Americans and all Americans, is a fitting site. The Department of Health and Human Services will award a planning grant so the school can pursue establishing a center for bioethics in research and health care. The center will serve as a museum of the study and support efforts to address its legacy and strengthen bioethics training.

Second, we commit to increase our community involvement so that we may begin restoring lost trust. The study at Tuskegee served to sow distrust of our medical institutions, especially where research is involved. Since the study was halted, abuses have been checked by making informed consent and local review mandatory in federally funded and mandated research.

Still, 25 years later, many medical studies have little African-American participation and African-American organ donors are few. This impedes efforts to conduct promising research and to provide the best health care to all our people, including African-Americans. So today I'm directing the Secretary of Health and Human Services, Donna Shalala, to issue a report in 180 days about how we can best involve communities, especially minority communities, in research and health care. You must—every American group must be involved in medical research in ways that are positive. We have put the curse behind us; now we must bring the benefits to all Americans.

Third, we commit to strengthen researchers' training in bioethics. We are constantly working on making breakthroughs in protecting the health of our people and in vanquishing diseases. But all our people must be assured that their rights and dignity will be respected as new drugs, treatments, and therapies are tested and used. So I am directing Secretary Shalala to work in partnership with higher education to prepare training materials for medical researchers. They will be available in a year. They will help researchers build on core ethical principles of respect for individuals, justice, and informed consent, and advise them on how to use these principles effectively in diverse populations.

Fourth, to increase and broaden our understanding of ethical issues and clinical research, we commit to providing postgraduate fellowships to train bioethicists especially among African-Americans and other minority groups. HHS will offer these fellowships beginning in September of 1998 to promising students enrolled in bioethics graduate programs.

And finally, by Executive order I am also today extending the charter of the National Bioethics Advisory Commission to October of 1999. The need for this commission is clear. We must be able to call on the thoughtful, collective wisdom of experts and community representatives to find ways to further strengthen our protections for subjects in human research.

We face a challenge in our time. Science and technology are rapidly changing our lives with the promise of making us much healthier, much more productive, and more prosperous. But with these changes, we must work harder to see that as we advance, we don't leave behind our conscience. No ground is gained and, indeed, much

is lost if we lose our moral bearings in the name of progress.

The people who ran the study at Tuskegee diminished the stature of man by abandoning the most basic ethical precepts. They forgot their pledge to heal and repair. They had the power to heal the survivors and all the others, and they did not. Today all we can do is apologize. But you have the power, for only you, Mr. Shaw, the others who are here, the family members who are with us in Tuskegee—only you have the power to forgive. Your presence here shows us that you have chosen a better path than your Government did so long ago. You have not withheld the power to forgive. I hope today and tomorrow every American will remember your lesson and live by it.

Thank you, and God bless you.

NOTE: The President spoke at 2:26 p.m. in the East Room at the White House. In his remarks, he referred to Tuskegee Experiment survivors Herman Shaw, who introduced the President, and Frederick Moss; and Fred D. Gray, attorney for participants in the Tuskegee Experiment, which was formally entitled "Tuskegee Study of Untreated Syphilis in the Negro Male." The Executive order of May 16 extending the National Bioethics Advisory Commission is listed in Appendix D at the end of this volume.

Statement on Strengthening International Safeguards on Proliferation of Nuclear Weapons
May 16, 1997

On May 15 the international community took a major step toward significantly reducing the danger that any nation can secretly acquire a nuclear arsenal. Last September, in my speech at the United Nations, I called on the international community to strengthen the Nuclear Non-Proliferation Treaty and improve our ability to identify and isolate those states that seek to violate its rules. In the most dramatic strengthening of nuclear inspections in the last quarter-century, the International Atomic Energy Agency (IAEA) and its member states have agreed in Vienna to develop strong new tools to assist

in tracking the use and location of nuclear materials around the world.

During the last 4 years, we have made significant progress in curbing the proliferation of nuclear weapons and ending the dangerous legacy of cold war weapons stockpiles. But as the clandestine efforts of nations such as Iraq to acquire nuclear weapons have made clear, we must reinforce our ability to find and stop secret nuclear weapons programs. Only in the aftermath of the Persian Gulf war were we able to discover the full scope of Iraq's activities and intentions.

The strengthened safeguards system adopted by the IAEA will give international nuclear inspectors greater information and access to nuclear and related facilities worldwide. By accepting a new legally binding protocol, states will assume new safeguards obligations that will make all their nuclear activities more transparent—including by allowing inspections at all suspicious sites, not just at declared sites.

I urge all nations to adopt as soon as possible appropriate protocols to their own safeguard agreements or to make other legally binding arrangements that will put this new system of safeguards in place. And I call on all nations that have not already signed the Nuclear Non-Proliferation Treaty to do so without delay.

Reducing the threat of nuclear and other weapons of mass destruction is one of our highest obligations. Since I took office, we have made the Nuclear Non-Proliferation Treaty permanent, dramatically cut existing nuclear arsenals under the START treaties, and ratified the Chemical Weapons Convention that will outlaw poison gas forever. I look forward to working with the Senate as we seek ratification of the Comprehensive Nuclear Test Ban Treaty and as we seek congressional approval of this protocol and other arms control measures. Together, we must continue our efforts to provide the American people with real and lasting security.

Statement on the Northern Ireland Peace Process Initiative by Prime Minister Tony Blair of the United Kingdom
May 16, 1997

I welcome Prime Minister Blair's statement today on Northern Ireland as a balanced and constructive step toward restoring momentum to the peace process. His words offer hope and reassurance to the people of both of Northern Ireland's traditions.

The Prime Minister has made clear that this British Government, like its predecessor, wants to see inclusive talks, but it will invite Sinn Fein to the negotiating table only on the basis of an unequivocal cease-fire. And he has taken the initiative in offering to meet with Sinn Fein, at the official level, to assess whether inclusive talks are possible on that basis. I urge Sinn Fein to take up this offer, and I pray it will bring about an end to the violence for good. Now is the time to open a new chapter in the history of this tragic conflict and achieve through dialog and negotiation the lasting settlement the people of Northern Ireland want and deserve.

Remarks Prior to Discussions With President Leonid Kuchma of Ukraine and an Exchange With Reporters
May 16, 1997

President Clinton. Let me say, I'm delighted to have President Kuchma back at the White House. He and the Vice President have worked hard today. They've made a lot of progress on economic issues and on security issues, and I'm quite encouraged by the report I have received and quite hopeful about our future partnership with Ukraine and Ukraine's role in a united, democratic Europe.

NATO

Q. President Kuchma, are you interested in having Ukraine join NATO as a formal member?

President Kuchma. First of all, I understand the situation nowadays in Europe, and I'm well aware of the configuration of political forces. And I understand that Ukrainian application to NATO would not be timely, though Ukraine has proclaimed its aim to integrate with European and transatlantic structures.

Q. President Clinton, President Yeltsin seems to have a pretty different interpretation of the charter, the NATO charter with Russia, than what was described here. Is that the way you read what he's been saying and his advisers have been saying?

President Clinton. I think that the agreement is clear and will be clear from the details as they're published. And I also believe it's a good agreement for NATO and a good agreement for Russia. And let me further say I hope now that the Russian Duma will proceed to ratify START II because it's very much in Russia's interest as well as the United States and in the interest of world peace. It will enable us to go on to START III, which will reduce the nuclear arsenals 80 percent from their cold war high and relieve Russia of an enormous financial burden while maintaining its strategic interests.

[*At this point, one group of reporters left the room, and another group entered.*]

President Clinton. I am delighted to have President Kuchma back in the White House. The United States values its partnership with Ukraine and believes that we cannot have a successful, undivided, democratic Europe without a successful, democratic, progressive Ukraine. And I appreciate the hard work that President Kuchma and Vice President Gore have done in their commission all day and the results they have achieved, which they will announce, I think, at a press conference.

President Kuchma. It was a pleasure for me to hear the words by President Clinton, that European security is impossible without a prosperous Ukraine and an independent Ukraine. In fact, this was the thrust, the direction of the efforts of the Vice President and my efforts. And I should say that we spared no efforts.

Summit of the Eight

Q. How do you think—will Ukraine take part in the discussion of the Chernobyl issue in the summit of G–7 in Denver in some form—maybe in a conference, in another form?

Vice President Gore. It will be a subject of discussion among the eight.

President Clinton. I don't know the answer to that, I'm sorry to say, but I know that it will be a subject of our discussions because all of the seven have made clear their commitment for years to helping Ukraine to come to grips with Chernobyl and the aftermath and making sure that consequences can be dealt with and also that the country has the supplies necessary and energy to grow and to prosper.

NATO

Q. Mr. President, aren't there reasons to fear that Ukraine might fear that a NATO-Russian agreement might divide Europe into spheres of influence?

President Clinton. No, quite the contrary. The argument that I made to President Yeltsin when we met at Helsinki was that we had to create a united Europe and that we should not view the mission of NATO in the future as we viewed the mission of NATO in the past. We have to create a world in the 21st century where people do not define their greatness by their ability to dominate their neighbors but instead define their greatness by their ability to maximize the achievements of their own citizens and band together with others to defeat common problems like terrorism and weapons proliferation.

You can see that in the partnership that NATO has had with both Ukraine and Russia in Bosnia. All people who want to be free and who want their neighbors to be free have an interest in banding together to fight problems like that.

NOTE: The President spoke at 4:34 p.m. in the Oval Office at the White House. In his remarks, he referred to President Boris Yeltsin of Russia. A tape was not available for verification of the content of these remarks.

The President's Radio Address
May 17, 1997

Good morning. This morning I want to talk about our new balanced budget agreement and the way it expands opportunity through education so that we can keep the American dream alive for all our children. When I took office 4½ years ago, America faced growing deficits as far as the eye could see. It was a time of economic stagnation and high unemployment, in spite of the fact that our businesses and working people had done so much to compete in the global economy.

We moved quickly back then to put in place a new policy, a policy of invest and grow, cutting the deficit, investing in our people, opening new markets around the world through tough trade agreements. The results of that strategy are now clear: We've had 12 million new jobs, the highest economic growth in a decade, the lowest unemployment in 24 years, the lowest inflation in 30 years, the largest decline in income inequality since the 1960's, and the deficit has already been cut by 77 percent, from $290 billion a year when I took office, to $67 billion this year.

We proved that we could make the tough decisions to put our fiscal house in order and still protect America's values, especially through education. While we were cutting that deficit by 77 percent, we were expanding Head Start; supporting States and schools and raising academic standards; increasing scholarships and student loans; and lowering the cost of repaying back those loans.

To keep our economy strong, we have to keep that strategy in place and finish the job. That's why I'm so proud that we've reached a bipartisan agreement to balance the Federal budget for the first time since 1969, when President Johnson was in the White House. Thanks to leaders in Congress in both parties who led the way, along with my negotiators, we have crafted an historic accord.

What is truly important about this budget agreement is not just what it does on the spreadsheet but what it does for our families and our futures. It brings the deficit down to zero over the next 5 years while reflecting our values and preparing our people for the 21st century: preserving and protecting Medicare and Medicaid; extending the Medicare Trust Fund for at least a decade without steep premium increases; expanding health care coverage to 5 million children who don't have it today; protecting our environment, including cleaning up 500 of our most dangerous toxic waste dumps, and going forward with our project to preserve and restore the Florida Everglades; helping move people from welfare to work with tax incentives to businesses to hire people from welfare and support for community service jobs in those areas with high unemployment; providing tax relief for parents to raise their children and send their children or themselves to college; restoring unfair cuts in support for legal immigrants who come here lawfully in search of the American dream.

All of those values are important. But to me, the heart of this balanced budget agreement is its historic commitment to education. This agreement includes the most significant increase in education funding in 30 years. Even more important, it provides the largest single increase in higher education since the GI bill in 1945, more than 50 years ago.

That landmark legislation gave opportunity to millions of Americans and gave birth to our great middle class after World War II. And that was my goal for this budget, to dramatically expand opportunity through education, to give all our children the tools to succeed in the new economy and the new society of the new century.

Education has always been at the heart of opportunity in America. It's the embodiment of everything we have to do to prepare for the 21st century. Nothing will do more to open the doors of opportunity for exciting new working careers to every American, nothing will do more to instill a sense of personal responsibility in every American, and nothing will do more to build a strong, united community of all Americans. For if we all have the tools we need to succeed, and if we all know enough to understand each other and respect, not fear, our differences, we can move forward together, as one America, an America in which every 8-year-old can read, every 12-year-old can log on to the Internet, every 18-year-old can go on to college, and every adult can keep on learning for a lifetime.

This agreement will fund our America Reads challenge, which will mobilize an army of volunteer reading tutors to ensure that every 8-year-old can pick up a book and say, "I can read this all by myself." It includes our technology literacy initiative, to help us finish the job of wiring every classroom and school library to the Internet by the year 2000 so that children in the poorest inner-city schools, in the most remote rural schools can have access to the same vast store of knowledge in the same time and the same way as children in the wealthiest schools in America.

It includes $35 billion in tax relief for higher education, including our HOPE scholarship for tuition tax credit to make the first 2 years of college as universal as high school is today and a tax deduction for the cost of any tuition after high school. It includes the largest increase in Pell grant scholarships for deserving students in two decades. At the same time, it expands Head Start, increases job training, preserves our commitment to school-to-work initiatives to help the young people who don't go on to college get the skills they need to succeed when they finish school, and supports our efforts to achieve national standards of academic excellence.

The bipartisan agreement we have reached not only gives us the first balanced budget in a generation, it also helps millions of children learn to read. It gives millions of Americans tax cuts to pay for college. It gives hundreds of thousands more students Pell grant scholarships and helps tens of thousands of schools to wire their classrooms to the Internet to prepare their children for the world of work and raise academic standards to national and international norms.

This agreement is moving through Congress at an expedited pace. I urge the Congress, Members of both parties: Pass the balanced budget and pass the biggest and best education bill in America's history. If both parties stay true to this historic agreement, if we have the courage to eliminate the deficit while significantly expanding education, we will enter the 21st century stronger and better prepared for the challenges and the exciting opportunities that lie ahead. I ask all Americans for your support for our future.

Thanks for listening.

NOTE: The address was recorded at 12:09 p.m. on May 16 in the Roosevelt Room at the White House for broadcast at 10:06 a.m. on May 17.

Commencement Address at Morgan State University in Baltimore, Maryland
May 18, 1997

Thank you. Dr. Richardson, Judge Cole, Governor Glendening, Lieutenant Governor Kennedy-Townsend, Mr. Mayor, City Council President, other elected officials, Mr. Speaker, Senator Miller, Senator Sarbanes, Congressman Cardin, and Congressman Cummings, my great partners, to the board of regents, to the faculty, staff, to distinguished alumni, to the magnificent band and choir; I thought it was a great day when I got here, but I know it is now. Thank you very much.

To the members of the class of 1997, your family, and your friends, congratulations on this important day in your lives, the lives of your Nation, and the life of this great institution. Your diploma reflects a level of knowledge that will give you the chance to make the most of the rapidly unfolding new reality of the 21st century. It gives your country a better chance to lead the world toward a better place, and it reaffirms the historic mission of Morgan State and the other historically black colleges and universities of our great land.

When the doors of college were closed to all but white students, Morgan State and the Nation's other historically black institutions of higher education gave young African-Americans the education they deserved and the pride they needed to rise above cruelty and bigotry. Today, these institutions still produce the lion's share of our black doctors and judges and business people, and Morgan State graduates most of the black engineers and scientists in the great State of Maryland.

I am here today not because Morgan State is just a great historically black university; it is a great American university. You have produced some of our Nation's finest leaders: your grads like Parren Mitchell, Kweisi Mfume, and Earl Graves; judicial leaders like Judge Bell and Judge Cole; public servants like State Treasurer Dixon; and on a very personal note, my fine assistant, Terry Edmonds, class of 1972, the first African-American ever to serve as a speechwriter for the President of the United States. There he is. [*Applause*]

Now—you're getting too much applause now, Terry. [*Laughter*]

You graduate today into a world brimming with promise and rich with opportunity. Our economy is the strongest in a generation, our unemployment the lowest in 24 years, with the largest decline in income inequality since the 1960's.

On Friday we finalized the details of an historic agreement with the leaders of Congress to balance the Federal budget for the first time in nearly three decades, in a way that will keep our economy going and in balance with our values, caring for those in need, extending health care to 5 million more children, cleaning and preserving and restoring our environment, helping people to move from welfare to work, and most important, funding the largest investment in education in a generation and the largest increase in higher education since the GI bill in 1945, more than 50 years ago.

It will open the doors of college to all, with the largest increase in Pell grant scholarships in three decades, $35 billion in tax relief to help families pay for higher education, including tax deductions for the cost of all education after high school, and our HOPE scholarship tuition tax credits to make the first 2 years of college as universal by the year 2000 as a high school diploma is today.

And this agreement contains a major investment in science and technology, inspired in our administration by the leadership of Vice President Gore, to keep America on the cutting edge of positive change, to create the best jobs of tomorrow, to advance the quality of life of all Americans.

This is a magic moment, but like all moments, it will not last forever. We must make the most of it. In commencement addresses across the

Nation this year, I will focus our attention on what we must do to prepare our Nation for the next century, including how we can make sure that our rich diversity brings us together rather than driving us apart and how we must meet our continuing obligation to lead the world away from the wars and cold war of the 20th century through the present threats of terrorism and ethnic hatred, weapons proliferation and drug smuggling, to a more peaceful and free and prosperous 21st century.

But today, here, I ask you simply to imagine that new century, full of its promise, molded by science, shaped by technology, powered by knowledge. These potent transforming forces can give us lives fuller and richer than we have ever known. They can be used for good or ill.

If we are to make the most of this new century, we, all of us, each and every one of us, regardless of our background, must work to master these forces with vision and wisdom and determination. The past half-century has seen mankind split the atom, splice genes, create the microchip, explore the heavens. We enter the next century propelled by new and stunning developments.

Just in the past year, we saw the cloning of Dolly the sheep, the Hubble telescope bringing into focus dark corners of the cosmos never seen before, innovations in computer technology and communications, creating what Bill Gates calls "the world's new digital nervous system," and now cures for our most dreaded diseases, diabetes, cystic fibrosis, repair for spinal cord injuries. These miracles actually seem within reach. The sweep of it is truly humbling. Why, just last week we saw a computer named Deep Blue defeat the world's reigning chess champion. I really think there ought to be a limit to this. No computer should be allowed to learn to play golf. [*Laughter.*] But seriously, my friends, in science, if the last 50 years were the age of physics, the next 50 years will be the age of biology.

We are now embarking on our most daring explorations, unraveling the mysteries of our inner world and charting new routes to the conquest of disease. We have not and we must not shrink from exploring the frontiers of science. But as we consider how to use the fruits of discovery, we must also never retreat from our commitment to human values, the good of society, our basic sense of right and wrong.

Science must continue to serve humanity, never the other way around. The stakes are very high. America's future, indeed the world's future, will be more powerfully influenced by science and technology than ever before. Where once nations measured their strength by the size of their armies and arsenals, in the world of the future, knowledge will matter most. Fully half the growth in economic productivity over the last half-century can be traced to research and technology.

But science is about more than material wealth or the acquisition of knowledge. Fundamentally, it is about our dreams. America is a nation always becoming, always defined by the great goals we set, the great dreams we dream. We are restless, questing people. We have always believed, with President Thomas Jefferson, that freedom is the first-born daughter of science. With that belief and with willpower, resources, and great national effort, we have always reached our far horizons and set out for new ones.

Thirty-six years ago, President Kennedy looked to the heavens and proclaimed that the flag of peace and democracy, not war and tyranny, must be the first to be planted on the Moon. He gave us a goal of reaching the Moon, and we achieved it, ahead of time. Today, let us look within and step up to the challenge of our time, a challenge with consequences far more immediate for the life and death of millions around the world. AIDS will soon overtake tuberculosis and malaria as the leading infectious killer in the world. More than 29 million people have been infected, 3 million in the last year alone, 95 percent of them in the poorest parts of our globe.

Here at home, we are grateful that new and effective anti-HIV strategies are available and bringing longer and better lives to those who are infected, but we dare not be complacent. HIV is capable of mutating and becoming resistant to therapies and could well become even more dangerous. Only a truly effective, preventive HIV vaccine can limit and eventually eliminate the threat of AIDS.

This year's budget contains increased funding of a third over 2 years ago to search for this vaccine. In the first 4 years, we have increased funding for AIDS research, prevention, and care by 50 percent, but it is not enough. So let us today set a new national goal for science in the age of biology. Today let us commit our-

selves to developing an AIDS vaccine within the next decade. There are no guarantees. It will take energy and focus and demand great effort from our greatest minds. But with the strides of recent years, it is no longer a question of whether we can develop an AIDS vaccine, it is simply a question of when. And it cannot come a day too soon. If America commits to find an AIDS vaccine and we enlist others in our cause, we will do it. I am prepared to do all I can to make it happen. Our scientists at the National Institutes of Health and our research universities have been at the forefront of this battle.

Today I'm pleased to announce the National Institutes of Health will establish a new AIDS vaccine research center dedicated to this crusade. And next month, at the summit of the industrialized nations in Denver, I will enlist other nations to join us in a worldwide effort to find a vaccine to stop one of the world's greatest killers. We will challenge America's pharmaceutical industry, which leads the world in innovative research and development to work with us and to make the successful development of an AIDS vaccine part of its basic mission.

My fellow Americans, if the 21st century is to be the century of biology, let us make an AIDS vaccine its first great triumph. Let us resolve further to work with other nations to deal with great problems like global climate change, to break our reliance on energy use destructive of our environment, to make giant strides to free ourselves and future generations from the tyranny of disease and hunger and ignorance that today still enslaves too many millions around the world. And let us also pledge to redouble our vigilance to make sure that the knowledge of the 21st century serves our most enduring human values.

Science often moves faster than our ability to understand its implications, leaving a maze of moral and ethical questions in its wake. The Internet can be a new town square or a new Tower of Babel. The same computer that can put the Library of Congress at our fingertips can also be used by purveyors of hate to spread blueprints for bombs. The same knowledge that is developing new life-saving drugs can be used to create poisons of mass destruction. Science can enable us to feed billions more people in comfort, in safety, and in harmony with our Earth, or it can spark a war with weapons of mass destruction rooted in primitive hatreds.

Science has no soul of its own. It is up to us to determine whether it will be used as a force for good or evil. We must do nothing to stifle our basic quest for knowledge. After all, it has propelled from field to factory to cyberspace. But how we use the fruits of science and how we apply it to human endeavors is not properly the domain of science alone or of scientists alone. The answers to these questions require the application of ethical and moral principles that have guided our great democracy toward a more perfect union for more than 200 years now. As such, they are the province of every American citizen.

We must decide together how to apply these principles to the dazzling new discoveries of science. Here are four guideposts. First, science and its benefits must be directed toward making life better for all Americans, never just a privileged few. Their opportunities and benefits should be available to all. Science must not create a new line of separation between the haves and the have-nots, those with and those without the tools and understanding to learn and use technology. In the 21st century, a child in a school that does not have a link to the Internet or the student who does not have access to a computer will be like the 19th century child without school books. That is why we are ensuring that every child in every school, not matter how rich or poor, will have access to the same technology, by connecting every classroom and library to the Internet by the year 2000.

Science must always respect the dignity of every American. Here at one of America's great black universities, let me underscore something I said just a few days ago at the White House. We must never allow our citizens to be unwitting guinea pigs in scientific experiments that put them at risk without their consent and full knowledge. Whether it is withholding a syphilis treatment from the black men of Tuskegee or the cold war experiments that subjected some of our citizens to dangerous doses of radiation, we must never go back to those awful days in modern disguise. We have now apologized for the mistakes of the past; we must not repeat them, never again.

Second, none of our discoveries should be used to label or discriminate against any group or individual. Increasing knowledge about the great diversity within the human species must not change the basic belief upon which our ethics, our Government, our society are founded.

All of us are created equal, entitled to equal treatment under the law. With stunning speed, scientists are now moving to unlock the secrets of our genetic code. Genetic testing has the potential to identify hidden inherited tendencies toward disease and spur early treatment. But that information could also be used, for example, by insurance companies and others to discriminate against and stigmatize people.

We know that in the 1970's some African-Americans were denied health care coverage by insurers and jobs by employers because they were identified as sickle cell anemia carriers. We also know that one of the main reasons women refuse genetic testing for susceptibility to breast cancer is their fear that the insurance companies may either deny them coverage or raise their rates to unaffordable levels. No insurer should be able to use genetic data to underwrite or discriminate against any American seeking health insurance. This should not simply be a matter of principle but a matter of law. Period. To that end, I urge the Congress to pass bipartisan legislation to prohibit insurance companies from using genetic screening information to determine the premium rates or eligibility of Americans for health insurance.

Third, technology should not be used to break down the wall of privacy and autonomy free citizens are guaranteed in a free society. The right to privacy is one of our most cherished freedoms. As society has grown more complex and people have become more interconnected in every way, we have had to work even harder to respect the privacy, the dignity, the autonomy of each individual. Today, when marketers can follow every aspect of our lives from the first phone call we make in the morning to the time our security system says we have left the house to the video camera at the toll booth and the charge slip we have for lunch, we cannot afford to forget this most basic lesson.

As the Internet reaches to touch every business and every household and we face the frightening prospect that private information, even medical records, could be made instantly available to the world, we must develop new protections for privacy in the face of new technological reality.

Fourth, we must always remember that science is not God. Our deepest truths remain outside the realm of science. We must temper our euphoria over the recent breakthrough in animal cloning with sobering attention to our most cherished concepts of humanity and faith.

My own view is that each human life is unique, born of a miracle that reaches beyond laboratory science. I believe we should respect this profound gift. I believe we should resist the temptation to replicate ourselves. But this is a decision no President should make alone. No President is qualified to understand all of the implications. That is why I have asked our distinguished National Bioethics Advisory Commission, headed by President Harold Shapiro of Princeton, to conduct a thorough review of the legal and ethical issues raised by this new cloning discovery. They will give me their first recommendations within the next few weeks, and I can hardly wait.

These, then, are four guideposts, rooted in our traditional principles of ethics and morals, that must guide us if we are to master the powerful forces of change in the new century: one, science that produces a better life for all and not the few; two, science that honors our tradition of equal treatment under the law; three, science that respects the privacy and autonomy of the individual; four, science that never confuses faith in technology with faith in God. If we hold fast to these principles, we can make this time of change a moment of dazzling opportunity for all Americans.

Finally, let me say again, science can serve the values and interests of all Americans, but only if all Americans are given a chance to participate in science. We cannot move forward without the voices and talents of everyone in this stadium and especially those of you who are going on to pursue a career in science and technology.

African-Americans have always been at the forefront of American science. This is nothing new. Nothing, not slavery, not discrimination, not poverty, nothing has ever been able to hold back their scientific urge or creative genius. Benjamin Banneker was a self-taught mathematician, surveyor, astronomer, who published an annual almanac and helped to design the city of Washington. George Washington Carver was born a slave but went on to become one of our Nation's greatest agricultural scientists. Ernest Everett Just of Charleston, South Carolina, is recognized as one of our greatest biologists. Charles Drew lived through the darkest days of segregation to become a pioneer in blood preservation. And today you honor an African-American doctor at Johns Hopkins University who is truly one of the outstanding physicians of our time.

All these people show us that we don't have a person to waste, and our diversity is our greatest strength in the world of today and tomorrow. Now, members of the class of 1997, it is your time. It is up to you to honor their legacy, to live their dreams, to be the investigators, the doctors, and the scholars who will make and apply the discoveries of tomorrow, who will keep our science rooted in our values, who will fashion America's greatest days. You can do it. Dream large. Work hard. And listen to your soul.

Thank you, and God bless you all.

NOTE: The President spoke at 10:30 a.m. at Hughes Field. In his remarks, he referred to Earl Richardson, president, and Harry Cole, chairman, board of regents, Morgan State University; Gov. Parris Glendening, Lt. Gov. Kathleen Kennedy-Townsend, and Treasurer Richard N. Dixon of Maryland; Mayor Kurt Schmoke of Baltimore; Lawrence Bell, president, Baltimore City Council; Casper R. Taylor, Jr., speaker, Maryland House of Delegates; Thomas V. Miller, Jr., president, Maryland State Senate; former Representative Parren Mitchell; Kweisi Mfume, president, National Association for the Advancement of Colored People; Earl Graves, chief executive officer, Black Enterprise magazine; Robert M. Bell, chief judge, Maryland Court of Appeals; and James Terry Edmonds, Deputy Assistant to the President and Deputy Director for Speechwriting.

Remarks Prior to Discussions With NATO Secretary General Javier Solana and an Exchange With Reporters
May 19, 1997

President Clinton. Let me say that the United States is very, very appreciative of the leadership that Secretary General Solana has shown in negotiating this NATO-Russia Founding Act. We are excited about the partnership. It is consistent with what we believe NATO should be doing. It is consistent with our plans to expand NATO. And I think the Secretary General has done a marvelous job, and I'm looking forward to having this chance to talk with him about our meeting, I guess a week from today in Paris, to celebrate the NATO-Russia partnership and then, of course, the Madrid summit this summer.

Secretary General Solana. Thank you very much, Mr. President, for your kind words. What you did is a prudent thing. [*Laughter*]

President Clinton. Go ahead.

NATO

Q. Mr. President, not to put too much of a damper on your enthusiasm, but some people are quite critical of the—questioning this NATO expansion. They're saying it will create more tension and cost more money and give us less security in the long run. Can you give assurances that this is not the case?

President Clinton. Well, it's a question of what you believe. I believe that we have had a long cold war and two world wars in the 20th century and a 19th century full of heartache and bloodshed because people were arguing over territory in Europe. And we now have a chance to create a European Continent where nation-states, for the first time, say they're going to respect each other's borders and work together on common security problems, as we are all doing together in Bosnia. And it seems to me, to find a framework which accomplishes that and which also keeps the United States and, I might add, Canada tied to the security and the freedom and the territorial integrity of Europe is an extraordinary achievement and gives us a chance to write a whole new chapter in the 21st century different from the one we have just written.

So I just simply disagree with those; it's a difference of opinion. I think that we're right and I believe history will prove us right and I'm prepared to take the decisions and live with the consequences.

Base Closings

Q. Mr. President, do you feel, as the Secretary of Defense does, that more bases need to be closed, more military bases? That is a politically, of course, unpopular idea.

President Clinton. I believe that the Secretary of Defense has done a good job on this quadrennial review. And what he has shown is the following: If we're going to keep a defense budget that is modest and take care of the men and women in uniform and continue to modernize our weapons system so we will maintain the kind of technological superiority we enjoyed in the Gulf war—and hopefully, never even have to fight a Gulf war again in the near future—to do that within the dollars available, we're going to have to continue to reorganize the military. And he's going to present that to the Congress and we will debate it and discuss it, but I think there are going to have to be some difficult decisions in the future. We can't balance the budget and continue to invest in the things that we need, whether it's new weapons systems or education, without continuing to restructure the underlying governmental support system.

Let me remind you that on the civilian side we've reduced the size of the Federal Government by 300,000 since 1993, and as a percentage of the civilian work force, it's now as small as it was in 1933 when President Roosevelt took office before the New Deal. So this is a restructuring that you see going on all over the world; it has to be done in America in the Government, and the Defense Department can't be fully exempt from it. They've managed it brilliantly, and I think they've done a good job. And it's not just the Secretary of Defense; it's also the Joint Chiefs. They've all worked on this. They believe it's in our national security interests, and I'm going to do my best to be supportive.

Most-Favored-Nation Trade Status for China

Q. Mr. President, supporting MFN for China, how will you reconcile that support with the human rights record of China?

President Clinton. I think we're more likely— as I've said repeatedly, I think we're more likely to have a positive influence on China by engaging them than we are by trying to isolate them. I think it's a simple judgment.

Russia-NATO Agreement

Q. Boris Yeltsin said today that he would reconsider his agreement with NATO if former republics like the Baltic States were to join NATO. Is it of concern to you?

President Clinton. I think—look, let's just take this—we're moving in the right direction. We've got an agreement that speaks for itself with Russia. And if we can continue to work with a democratic free Russia led by a man like Boris Yeltsin, I think you'll see a more peaceful world. And I think we'll harmonize these things as we go along. You can't resolve every issue at every moment. We're moving in the right direction, and I'm quite comfortable that we're going to get there.

NOTE: The President spoke at 1:15 p.m. in the Oval Office at the White House. In his remarks, he referred to President Boris Yeltsin of Russia. A tape was not available for verification of the content of these remarks.

Remarks to Young Presidents and World Presidents Organizations
May 19, 1997

Thank you very much. Please be seated. First of all, welcome back to Washington. I'm delighted to see you. I always enjoy meeting with this group. I think a lot of you know that at least—I've identified at least three errant members of my administration who have been associated with YPO, Erskine Bowles, Mack McLarty, and Phil Lader. There may be more, and if there are, they'd probably like to be back with you instead of over here with me. [*Laughter*]

I will try to be succinct about what I want to say. I know that the Treasury Secretary and others are coming on in a few moments to talk about the details of our budget agreement and some of the other issues that are cooking around here in Washington today. But I'd like to use this opportunity to make an official announcement about China. And let me just sort of set the stage by saying I think that our country has three huge questions that we are in the process of answering as we move into a new century and a very different time.

One is, how are we going to preserve a structure of opportunity for the next generation to keep the country going and growing? The second is, what kind of society are we going to be? Is this country going to work as a whole? Can we deal with problems of crime and welfare and the intergenerational responsibilities as the baby boom generation retires? And can we learn to live in what is rapidly becoming the world's most rapidly multiracial, multireligious, multiethnic democracy? There are four school districts in America now where the children come from more than 100 different ethnic groups in one school district. And the third great question is, are we prepared to do what it takes to see the United States continue to be the world's leading force for peace and freedom and prosperity? Because ironically, at the end of the cold war, because we are not in two armed camps in the world, all of our economic and military strength can only be brought to bear if we're willing to become more interdependent with the rest of the world and recognize our linkages.

In some ways, the decision that we have to make every year about China reflects elements of all three of those great questions, our prosperity, the kind of society we are, and how we're going to deal with the rest of the world. The United States has a huge stake in the continued emergence of China in a way that is open economically and stable politically. Of course, we hope it will come to respect human rights more and the rule of law more and that China will work with us to secure an international order that is lawful and decent.

I have decided, as all my predecessors have since 1980, to extend most-favored-nation status to China for the coming year. Every Republican and Democratic President since 1980 has made the same decision. This simply means that we extend to China the same normal trade treatment that virtually every other country on Earth receives from the United States. We believe it's the best way to integrate China further into the family of nations and to secure our interests and our ideals.

But as we have had controversies and differences with China over the years, this decision itself has become more controversial, because there are those in both parties in the Congress who believe that if we hold our trade relationship hostage to China because of our differences on human rights, our weapons technology, or the future of Hong Kong, we will have more influence since we buy about 30 percent of China's exports every year—sometimes we buy even more.

But I believe if we were to revoke normal trade status, it would cut off our contact with the Chinese people and undermine our influence with the Chinese Government. This is a big issue this year because, as many of you know, under the agreement signed more than a decade ago between Great Britain and China, Hong Kong is reverting to China shortly.

I think it's interesting that Hong Kong, which has the world's most open trading system, has vociferously argued to the United States that we should extend most-favored-nation status. Even those people in Hong Kong that have been most passionately identified with the cause of freedom and human rights and have been most in conflict with the Chinese have argued that we have to maintain an open trading relationship with them so that we can continue to work with them. I might also say that if we were to revoke their normal trading status, it would close one of the world's most rapidly growing, emerging markets, one that already supports 170,000 American jobs and doubtless will support more in the years ahead.

So our broad policy is engagement. That doesn't mean that we win every point, but it means we work together when we can and we're honest in our disagreements when they exist. For example—and I think it's important to point this out—we actually work together with China quite a lot. We worked with them to extend the nonproliferation treaty indefinitely. That

means that we've got over 170 countries in the world that say they will never develop any kind of capacity to proliferate nuclear weapons around the world in other countries, and they agreed to be tested for it.

We worked with China to get a historic accord on the comprehensive ban of nuclear testing. We worked with them to freeze North Korea's nuclear weapons program, which, when I became President 4 years and 4 months ago, I was told was the most immediate major security concern of the Nation at the time. We work with them now to advance the possibilities that there will actually be a lasting peace on the Korean Peninsula, which is the last frontier of the cold war.

We also work with them on drug-trafficking, terrorism, alien smuggling, and environmental decay. And when we don't agree with them, we have found ways to say so without cutting off all of our contacts. We pressed them to stop assistance to unsafeguarded nuclear facilities in other countries. We insisted that they protect the intellectual property rights of American videotape and compact disc makers. That's a huge economic issue for America. And so far China has done what they said they would do in closing down its facilities that were essentially stealing money and jobs from America's businesses. That's still an ongoing problem; it will continue to be one, as it has been in every emerging country a long way from the United States that can copy things that we do here. But we have certainly fought to reduce the problem. We also took action to show our displeasure with provocative military actions in the Taiwan Straits last year, and we stood up for human rights at the Human Rights Commission meeting of the United Nations.

So we have ways to deal with our differences. There are those who believe that our differences are so profound they would—we would get our way more, if you will, or our position would be more likely to prevail, if we cut off all trade contact. I believe that is wrong. And we're going to have a big debate about it in the Congress. But today, in front of you, I thought I would make this formal announcement that I do intend to extend most-favored-nation status. The way it works under the law is, now Congress has a chance to try to undo this, and we will have a big debate in the Congress. While you're here, if you have an opinion on it, I hope you'll express it to your Senator or Member of Congress.

But how we deal with this goes back to the larger question: What is our role in the world? Do you believe we should continue to be the world's leading force for peace and freedom and prosperity? If so, how? What kind of society are we going to create? Are we going to be one nation, or are we going to become more divided by race, by generation, by income? And how are we going to preserve a structure of opportunity?

Now, let me say when I came here, I felt very strongly that we would have to change the economic policy, the social policy of the country, the way the Government worked—the Federal Government worked—and we would have to have a much more aggressive and comprehensive approach to the world. On the economic policy, when I came here, we had a $290 billion annual deficit with no end in sight. I was told it would be way over $300 billion by this year. It's going to be $67 billion this year, 77 percent less than it was the day I took office.

And we also have been very aggressive about trade. Again, there are people in both parties who seem to believe that America is disadvantaged by open trading systems because we pay higher wages than other countries and because many other countries, especially developing countries, have more closed economies than ours. Well, now we have some evidence to judge which theory is right.

I've always believed that open trading was good for us because it kept us on our toes. It also helps to keep inflation down and productivity up. We've got some evidence now, because in the last 4 years we've had 200 new trade agreements as well as the big NAFTA agreement and the World Trade Organization being set up and an agreement in principle with the Asian-Pacific countries to go to a free-trade area there by early in the next century and an agreement with the Latin American countries to go to a free-trade area of the Americas early in the next century.

In the midst of the welter of all that activity, we can see what the consequences were. We also downsized the Government and increased our investment in education, technology and science, and medical research. Now, after 4½ years, the deficit's come down by 77 percent, we have the lowest unemployment rate in 24 years, the lowest inflation rate in 30 years, the highest business investment in 35 years, the smallest Federal Government in 35 years, and

as a percentage of the civilian work force, it is the same size it was in 1933 when President Roosevelt took office before the New Deal.

So I think it's hard to argue that we're not moving in the right direction. We've also, parenthetically, had the biggest decline in inequality among classes of working people in over 30 years. So America does not have to be afraid of competition. America can balance the budget and increase investment where we need to increase investment, and we can do this in a disciplined way.

In the area of social policy, we've passed a new crime bill, took a different approach to welfare, basically tried to put the family back at the center of social policy and reconcile a lot of the emerging conflicts between family and work, which is bedeviling most working families throughout the country, including people in rather high-income brackets. It is a general problem of our society. And we have had the biggest drop in welfare rolls in 50 years in America in the last 4 years, before the impact of the new welfare reform law. And I'll say more about that in a minute.

The crime rate has gone down 5 years in a row in America for the first time in 22 years. And we now know exactly what to do about it. It's just a question of whether we will. Not only that; on the more troubling problem of youth and gang violence, the city of Boston, the city of Houston, and a few other big cities in America have seen big declines in youth crime. And in Boston, Massachusetts, not a single child under the age of 18 has been killed with a gun in a year and half now.

So there is a lot of confidence in this country now that we can actually make sense out of our common life, that we can actually deal with these problems. And that's very important. And for the rest of us, it's great because we don't have to think up something to do. We've got a roadmap out there; we can just try to replicate it, community by community, to make it work.

In the area of our relationships with each other and our diversity, I would say that we have made some significant progress. We now—I think as a country we're still debating a lot of these things, like affirmative action, and I have my own views about that. But I would hope that the American people at least understand that if you look at how big the world is getting and the fact that our population is relatively smaller as a percentage of the whole than it used to be, less than 5 percent, and our economy is not as big as it once was as a percentage of the whole, although still over 20 percent, the fact that we have people in the United States from everywhere else is an enormous asset to us in a global economy.

But we have to learn to find a way to respect our differences and be bound together by our shared values. And it sounds so simple, it may sound almost trite, but when you consider what people do with differences in Bosnia, in Northern Ireland, in the Middle East, and in countless other places around the world, you sometimes wonder whether there is not some primitive urge in all of us that, unless it's consistently tended to, can cause enormous difficulties. And so I think that we cannot spend enough time on figuring out a way to make sure that we're a very different country but we're still one America.

Finally, let me say I'm quite determined that we have got to fight through all these successive issues here about America's role in the world. I've tried to be very careful not to send our troops into harm's way and in an indiscreet way, not to pretend that we could solve all the problems of the world. But I know that we have an opportunity here and a responsibility unlike any ever imposed on a nation in history. Because of the way the cold war ended with a victory for freedom and for free markets, because other countries are willing to work with us and even give higher percentages of their income that we do to the work of development and expanding the capacity of people in other countries, we have a significant responsibility here to try to fulfill these incredible opportunities.

And every one of you needs to spend some time thinking about this. Because historically, our country—historically—has been relatively isolationist. If you go through the whole history of America—George Washington told us that we should beware of foreign entanglements, and all of our—we've always been somewhat reluctant to get involved in the world.

I think the only reason we did it after World War II is the Soviet Union was there. There was a cold war; the threat was clear and apparent. And now, sometimes I think we don't see our own best interests. We're going to have another big trade issue coming up after MFN, and that's the question about whether the President should be given what is called fast-track authority. And for those of you who aren't famil-

iar with the trade lingo, all that means is that we can negotiate a trade agreement with another country and present it to Congress, and they have to vote it up or down instead of, in effect, being able to amend it 100 times so that, in effect, it would no longer be the agreement that we made with another country—treats it almost like a treaty, except it just requires a majority vote.

I can't see why we wouldn't want to do that when we got 4.9 percent unemployment. And another statistic I didn't give you is for the last 2 years more than half of the new jobs in this country have paid above average wages. So I think we should feel good about these things. And I certainly do, and I want you to.

Now, let me just say in closing, they're going to come on and tell you a little about the budget agreement. But in the last 4½ months, in the categories I gave you, if you look, it's creating a structure of opportunity for America. We've agreed to the first balanced budget in over three decades. And it is a compromise agreement between the Republicans and the administration and the Democrats in Congress and the leadership; it is a principled one. Does it solve all of America's problems? No. Will it get us to a balanced budget? Yes, it will.

And I might say, when I got here, a lot of times there were overly optimistic economic assumptions used in putting these budgets together, especially by the executive branch, in both parties. Every year I've been here, the deficit's been lower by several billion dollars than we estimated it would, every single year. So I want to assure you that we didn't cook up a bunch of numbers. Now, if we have a horrible recession, will the deficit be bigger? Yes, it will. But at least we've been quite responsible in the numbers that we've used here to try to make sure we were not misleading the American people about this.

So we got a budget agreement, which is important. We had a new telecommunications agreement, which will open 90 percent of the world's markets to American producers of telecommunications services and create hundreds of thousands of good jobs in this country over the next several years. We have had—we got the Chemical Weapons Convention ratified, which is a huge problem because we've got to stop the proliferation of chemical weapons, and it could affect you and your life and your community. The guy that blew up the Federal building in Oklahoma City, in that truck was fertilizer, a chemical weapon. But in Japan, a lot of people died in the subway because they had a laboratory that made sarin gas. So this is a major issue. Can we guarantee that there will never be anybody in a laboratory making chemical weapons? No. But we can dramatically reduce the chances that terrorists can get them in ways that make Americans safer all across the country.

We have reached this historic agreement between NATO and Russia to expand NATO and have a partnership with Russia which will enable us to have a unified Europe and, hopefully, avoid what destroyed millions and millions of people in the last century, in the 20th century, which was all these fights in Europe.

So the country is in good shape. We're moving in the right direction. We're dealing with all these issues. Are there things that still have to be done? Yes. Have we made adequate provision for the retirement of the baby boomers and not imposing undue burdens on our children? Not yet. Will we do so? I'm absolutely convinced we will. But you have to understand this system will only accommodate so much change at one time. I've thought about that a lot in the last 4 years. And the fact that we have a budget that will balance the budget, meet our national security needs, have the biggest increase in investment in education in a generation, continue our progress in the environment and medical research and technology, I think is a very significant thing and, parenthetically, provide health care coverage to 5 million kids that don't have it is very encouraging.

The last point I want to make is this. The biggest near-term problem we have in the country is that 20 percent of the kids who are born in this country are born below the poverty line, and many of them are still living in completely dysfunctional environments. When the Presidents, all of us, the living Presidents, and General Powell sponsored that Summit of Service in Philadelphia, it was about more than trying to get everybody to do more community service. It was about trying to focus attention on having every community in the country develop a strategy to make sure every child has a healthy start, a decent education, a safe place to live, a mentor, and a place to serve the community and feel worthwhile. That is the biggest near-term problem of the country.

You live in a nation where drug use is dropping dramatically among young adults and still

going up among juveniles, where crime is going down dramatically around the country but still going up among juveniles, except in the instances that I cited and others like that.

So as you look ahead to your own responsibilities, I would just mention two things. Number one, every community needs to develop a system of dealing with the children of the community. Number two, the welfare reform bill in the budget that we just agreed to will include tax incentives that are very tightly targeted to move people from welfare to work. And States have the power actually to give employers what used to be the welfare check as an employment and training subsidy.

I would hope that the members of the YPO would consider whether or not there is a role for you to play in your States and your communities, because under the welfare reform law, we have to move almost a million people from welfare to work in the next 4 years. We moved a million people from welfare to work in the last 4 years, but over 40 percent of that was the growth of the economy, and we produced 12.5 million new jobs. Maybe we can do it again. It's never happened in the history of the country before that we've had 8 years that good, back to back. Maybe we can do it again.

But under the law, we have to move that many people from welfare to work, whether the private economy produces 40 percent of those jobs or not, in the ordinary course of growth. There will be incentives there, but we had to do this—I would argue we had to do something like this to break the cycle of dependency that so many people were trapped in. But having now told people, most of whom are single mothers with very small children, that there is a limit to how much public assistance you can have, and you have to go to work at the end of a certain amount of time, period, we have to make sure that there are jobs there for them.

The communities of our country are going to get about $3 billion that will go into the high unemployment areas to do community service work when there's no way the private sector could do it. But for the rest, it will have to be done by the private sector. So I hope that while you're here and after you go home, you will be willing to consider whether there's something you could do to help us deal with this problem. Because if we can break the cycle of dependency and all people who are out of work who are adult, able-bodied, and otherwise have the capacity to work begin to be treated the same, instead of having some people disaggregated over here as being on welfare as if they couldn't work, we will have gone a long way toward changing the future of children in America and, therefore, changing the future of the country.

Thank you very much.

NOTE: The President spoke at 2:48 p.m. in Room 450 of the Old Executive Office Building.

Remarks at a Democratic Business Council and Women's Leadership Forum Dinner
May 19, 1997

Thank you. Please be seated. Thank you, Tom, and thank you, Cynthia, for your wonderful work. And I want to thank Steve Grossman and Alan Solomont and all the folks at the DNC for what they have done. I thank Secretary Babbitt and Ambassador Babbitt for coming tonight. And mostly, I want to thank you for being a part of these two very important components of our party's effort to take our country into a new century.

As you might imagine, I'm feeling pretty good about things right now. I'm very happy about the budget agreement, very happy for our country. But I think it's worth pointing out that where we are today is a function of the work of tens of millions of Americans, in their own lives, making the most of those lives, and also a direct function of the changes that we brought to Washington 4½ years ago.

I was convinced in 1992, when I sought the Presidency, that we had to change the economic policy of the country if we wanted to build a structure of opportunity that would keep the American dream alive for all Americans. I was convinced that we would have to change the social policy of the country if we wanted to have an American community that really worked instead of being divided by race and region and religion and paralyzed by crime. And I was convinced we would have to change the role of Government and that we needed a very expansive view of what our responsibilities in the world are.

And in so many ways, the conditions we enjoy in America today are the direct result of our country moving forward in all three of those areas. And I'd just like to say that we changed the economic policy to go from running deficits as far as the eye could see to bringing down the deficit but continuing to invest more in education, research, development, technology, science, while we were cutting back on the rest of Government and expanding trade throughout the world. And a lot of people said it wouldn't work.

But 4 years later, the deficit has been reduced. Before this balanced budget package is ever voted on, we will have a deficit that is 77 percent lower than it was the day I took office. And I'm proud of that, and you should be, too.

And our economy produced a record 12 million new jobs in the last 4 years. The unemployment rate is the lowest it's been in 24 years, the inflation rate the lowest in 30 years, the business investment rate the highest in 35 years. I'm proud of those things. I'm also proud as a Democrat that income inequality last year dropped by the largest amount since the 1960's, so that more and more ordinary Americans are beginning to participate in the benefits of a growing economy. And that is important, because we've had 20 years in which, because of competitive problems and a lot of other things, inequality among working people has increased in times where the economy is expanding and shrinking.

So these things are important, and we should feel good about them. I am proud of the fact that crime has gone down for 5 years in a row for the first time in about a quarter of a century, that we had the biggest drop in welfare rolls, before the welfare reform bill passed, in 50 years—50 years. And I'm proud of that. And you should be proud of that.

I'm proud of the fact that the world has moved closer toward peace and freedom than it was 4 years ago, in spite of all the problems we have. And in the last 4 months and a couple of weeks, since the Inauguration, we can take some genuine pride in what has happened. In terms of creating opportunity, we negotiated a telecommunications agreement with the rest of the world which will open up 90 percent of the world's markets to American sellers and producers of telecommunications services and equipment. It will create hundreds of thousands of high-wage jobs in America over the next few years.

This balanced budget agreement will keep the deficit coming down; it will keep interest rates down; it will lengthen the economic recovery. It also contains almost everything that I advocated in the campaign of 1996. You heard Cynthia say that it has the biggest increase in educational investment in a generation. It also has the biggest expansion of aid for people to go to colleges since 1945, since the GI bill came in. It has the biggest increase in Pell grant scholarships for poor students in 20 years and will provide tax deductions and tax credits to make the first 2 years of college as universal as a high school diploma is today and to put college within reach of all Americans. I think that is very important, and I hope you do, too.

With the Secretary of the Interior here, I can't help noting that it also has a very strong environmental budget. It protects our parks and enables us to continue our historic work of rescuing the Florida Everglades from destruction and will enable us to clean up 500 toxic waste dumps, the most dangerous ones in this country, in the next 4 years. The plan will extend—[*applause*]—that's worth clapping for.

The plan will extend health coverage to half of the 10 million children in America who don't have any health insurance. And these are in working families; these children are in working families.

The plan will restore, as I pledged to do in 1996, a lot of unfair cuts in assistance to legal immigrants and their children who come here lawfully and have misfortunes visit them. It will also provide funds to help cities in our high unemployment areas hire people who run out of their welfare benefits and have to go to work. And it will provide tax incentives for businesses to hire people from welfare to work.

So it is a good budget. There are tax provisions in this budget. The budget will contain some form of capital gains tax, some form of estate tax relief, the entire education tax package

I generally described to you, and some tax relief for families with children, minor children in the home, to help them deal with their child care and other costs. But the cost of this package is sharply circumscribed, and by agreement with the leaders of the Congress, it will—to give you some idea of it, in today's dollars it will only be about one-tenth as costly as the huge tax cut that was passed in 1981.

So don't let anybody tell you that we have agreed to blow a big hole in the deficit. We have not done so, and we will not do so. And I will not permit such a bill to become law. The bill we agreed to is a good-faith compromise reached by Republicans and Democrats, but it validates the economic direction this administration took. And it would not have been possible—none of this would have been possible if we hadn't passed the economic package back in 1993, with only Members of our party supporting it and with no votes to spare—the Vice President broke the tie in the Senate, and as he says, "Whenever I vote, we win." [*Laughter*]

So this is a happy day. This budget is good for America. The telecommunications agreement is good for America. We're moving forward economically. We're also moving forward to try to come together more. I'm trying to pass a juvenile justice bill in the Congress which will give communities the resources and the help they need to try to restore civility and calm and order to the lives of our young people.

In most of America, while crime is going down precipitously, the crime rate among people under 18 is continuing to rise, leveling off only last year. But in some places in America, it's a different story. In Boston, Massachusetts, there has not been a single child killed with a gun in 18 months, not a single child. In Houston, Texas, where the mayor opened an inner-city soccer program and an inner-city golf program—pre-Tiger Woods—[*laughter*]—he had 3,000 kids in the soccer program, 2,500 kids in the golf program, and the crime rate among juveniles went down.

So I'm doing my best to pass a juvenile justice bill that will follow up with what the crime bill did in 1994 and keep the crime rate coming down. Tomorrow I'll have an important announcement on welfare reform, to try to move more people from welfare to work. There is a lot to do out there, but we are moving in the right direction, and you should feel good about your country.

On the world front, we've ratified the Chemical Weapons Convention, which will make every community in America safer from terrorism and crime in the future, from poison gas. We have reached an agreement between NATO and Russia that will have a partnership instead of enmity between NATO and Russia. And we will, in July, expand NATO for the first time. We are moving toward a more peaceful, more stable, more democratic world.

I just got back from a very successful trip to Mexico and Central America and the Caribbean, and I just have to tell you that I'm convinced that the direction we're taking is the right one. But we still have some tough decisions to make, and we can't rest on our laurels.

First of all, we've got to pass the budget, and then we have to see that the terms of the agreement become law in the appropriations bills. Secondly, we have to deal—now that we've dealt with the structural deficit in American life, in the years ahead, we're going to have to deal with the generational deficit. That is, we have to make sure that the burden of us baby boomers retiring does not bankrupt our children, number one. And number two, we have to do something about the fact that while we have the lowest poverty rate ever recorded among senior citizens in America last year—something I am proud of, that's a good thing, and America should be proud of it—the poverty rate among children under 18 was almost twice the poverty rate among Americans over 65. So we have challenges still out there awaiting us.

But what I want to say to you is, we can look at the last 4 years and we can look at the last 4 months and understand that as a country, our problems are like the problems of any other human endeavor, they yield to effort. When you move away from the rhetoric and you move away from the hot air and you sit down in good faith and you say, "What do we have to do to keep opportunity alive in America; what do we have to do to be a stronger American community; what do we have to do to preserve our leadership role in the world," we can do these things.

Just one last issue that I'm very concerned about, and that is—and as I look around this room, I'm proud of this room for many reasons, but I think the fact that we are becoming the world's most diverse democracy, in terms of race and ethnicity and religion, is a huge asset in a world that's getting smaller and smaller and

smaller. And having worked in Bosnia, Northern Ireland, the Middle East, and in the Aegean, I am mindful of the fact that racial and ethnic conflicts are difficult and thorny things. Having pleaded with my friends in Pakistan and India to try to resolve their difficulties—I'm glad to see them talking now—I'm mindful to the fact that these are difficult things.

But we should be able to see, both from the heartbreak of other countries in the world and from the enormous opportunities we are creating for ourselves, that if we can find a way to respect our differences and be bound closely together by our shared values, it is, I think, very likely that the United States in the next 50 years, even though we will be a smaller percentage of the world's population and a smaller percentage of its overall economy, I think it is very likely that we will have even more positive influence in the next 50 years that we did in the last 50 years.

But the number one question that will determine that—mark my words—is not an economic question or a Government budget question, it is whether we can learn to live together across the lines that divide us. That is the single most significant thing, in my judgment, along with whether we are willing to exercise our leadership in the world, that will determine the shape of the next 50 years. So I intend to work hard on the that, and I want you to help me.

The last thing I would like to say is that, again, regarding your presence here tonight, what you have done is to invest in the work of America. The purpose of political parties, in my judgment, is not only to win elections but to give people a forum within which they can become organized to express their views and to have people who represent their views act in the public interest. Because you are here, because you have supported us, because we won the last election, because we are moving forward, this country is a better place. And you made a contribution to that. You continue to do it. And I hope tonight when you go home, you will be very proud of it.

Thank you, and God bless you.

NOTE: The President spoke at 8 p.m. in the Colonial Room at the Mayflower Hotel. In his remarks, he referred to dinner cochairs, C. Thomas

Hendrickson, chair, Democratic Business Council, and Cynthia Friedman, chair, Women's Leadership Forum; and Alan D. Solomont, national finance chair, and Steve Grossman, national chair, Democratic National Committee.

Remarks at a Democratic National Committee Dinner
May 19, 1997

Thank you very much. Thank you, ladies and gentlemen. And thank you, Steve, for that very eloquent introduction. I almost wish you'd just stay up here and give the rest of the speech. It was beautiful.

Ladies and gentlemen, thank you for being here tonight. I will be quite brief because I want us to have a chance just to sit around the table and visit, but I thought it might be helpful for me to just say a few things that everyone would hear, and it might inform our discussions going forward.

The first thing I want to say is that your country is moving in the right direction, and we should be glad of that. When I came here after the 1992 election, I had a simple strategic notion of what I wanted to do to prepare America for the new century. I wanted to change the economic policy of the country to create opportunity for everybody who was willing to work for it and get away from the endless deficits and go back to reducing the deficit, increasing investment in education and research and technology and the things we needed more of, and expanding trade.

I wanted to change the social policy of this country in ways that would bring us together instead of driving us apart, focusing on bringing the crime rate down, reducing the welfare rolls, putting family at the center of social policy and helping people juggle family and work, and bringing us together across the racial and religious and other differences that we have in this country.

And the third thing I wanted to do was to chart a course that would keep America's leadership in the world alive and well for peace and freedom and prosperity.

Now, we have pursued that for 4 years now. And I believe the wisdom of the economic course, the course on crime, the course on welfare, the course of our leadership in the world is no longer open to serious debate. We have the lowest unemployment rate in 24 years, the lowest inflation rate in 30 years, the highest business investment rate in 35 years. We have the smallest Government in 35 years, and as a percentage of the civilian work force, the Federal Government is the smallest it's been since 1933, when Franklin Roosevelt took office, before the New Deal.

But we continue to invest more in education, more in science, more in technology, more in environmental protection, more in children. We're moving in the right direction. The welfare rolls have seen their biggest drop in 50 years. The crime rate has gone down 5 years in a row. We are moving in the right direction. The country has plainly done a great deal to expand trade and to promote democracy and freedom and peace throughout the world. I'm proud of that.

Just in the last 4½ months, we've seen the Chemical Weapons Treaty. We now have an agreement between NATO and Russia to try to work together for a democratic, undivided Europe. We had a telecommunications trade agreement which will open 90 percent of the world's markets to America's telecommunication services and products and will create hundreds of thousands of high-wage jobs in this country.

We had a Summit of Service in Philadelphia in which all the former Presidents and I and General Powell challenged every community in America and every citizen in America to give every child in America a good education, a safe place to grow up, a healthy start, a mentor, an adult role model, and the chance to serve for themselves. And I think we have a chance to make that work in a profoundly positive way.

And of course, finally, we got this great budget deal. The budget deal, in brief, would provide that the budget would be balanced in 5 years. It contains the largest increase in educational investment since the sixties and the biggest expansion of higher education opportunities since

627

the GI bill in 1945. It would insure half—5 million of the 10 million kids in this country who are in working families who don't have access to health insurance. It would restore virtually all of the cuts made—wrongly, I think—by the Congress last year in aid to legal immigrants who come here and, through no fault of their own, have misfortunes. It would provide funds to clean up 500 of the worst toxic waste dumps in the country and to do other important environmental projects, including preserving the Florida Everglades, which is a profoundly important endeavor for the United States. It contains, in short, 99 percent of the investments I recommended myself in the budget I sent to the Congress and is better—better now than the one we started with for poor children.

It also contains—as it had to if we were going to have any kind of agreement—a provision for tax cuts that include some things that we wanted, like a tax cut for children and working families to pay for child care and other costs, and a tax credit and a tax deduction for the cost of education after high school, which I believe will make it possible for us to say we're making

2 years of college as universal as high school is today. And it contains some form of capital gains tax relief, some form of estate tax relief, which were the things that the Republicans cared about.

But we also will not refight 1995 because they have pledged not to try to reduce the earned-income tax credit—which is a tax benefit that low-income working people get—not to try to repeal the low-income housing tax credit, and not to raid workers' pension funds to pay for any of these tax programs.

This is a good deal. It's a good thing for Democrats. It's a good thing for Republicans. But most importantly, it's a good thing for America. It will keep interest rates down and growth going in a way that also will promote long-term growth.

So I am very happy about it. I hope you're very happy about it. And I hope Congress will be happy enough about it to pass it quickly.

Thank you very much.

NOTE: The President spoke at 8:23 p.m. in the East Room at the Mayflower Hotel.

Letter to Congressional Leaders Transmitting a Report on the Korean Peninsula Energy Development Organization
May 19, 1997

I transmit herewith the 6-month report required under the heading "International Organizations and Programs" in title IV of the Foreign Operations Appropriations Act, 1996 (Public Law 104–107), relating to the Korean Peninsula Energy Development Organization (KEDO).

Sincerely,

WILLIAM J. CLINTON

NOTE: Identical letters were sent to Ted Stevens, chairman, and Robert C. Byrd, ranking member, Senate Committee on Appropriations; and Robert L. Livingston, chairman, and David R. Obey, ranking member, House Committee on Appropriations. This letter was released by the Office of the Press Secretary on May 20.

Remarks Launching the Welfare to Work Partnership
May 20, 1997

Thank you, George Stinson, for your wonderful introduction, your remarks, and most importantly, for your very, very powerful example. I thank the Governors, Tom Carper and Tommy

Thompson, my former colleagues and friends, for being here and for the power of their example. I thank the Members of Congress, and most of all, I thank all the business leaders who are here, Gerry Greenwald and the leaders of the other companies that were with us when we just had 5, and all of you who are part of our first 105. Thank you all.

And I want to say a special word of thanks to my friend Eli Segal. He'd be a lot richer man if he'd never met me. [*Laughter*] But I have made him America's reigning expert in public startups. [*Laughter*] He is truly the father of AmeriCorps, the national service program that I love. And I can say, as I've been around the country now for nearly 4½ years, more people have come up to me and said of AmeriCorps, "That changed my life for the better," than anything I have done as President, except now this will be more numerous.

Because now—you know, Eli and I were just sitting around talking one day, and he said, "Now, what can I do for you now?" And I said, "Well, we passed this welfare reform law," and I said, "I really believe in it, but I mean, you know, there's no way in the world we're going to get there. We've got the deficit, we've got to balance the budget, and we can't possibly meet the hiring targets of the welfare reform law unless we can organize the private sector and maximize in every State all the options to give people incentives to hire people in the private sector to move people from welfare to work. Oh, we can get a little money to put into the very high unemployment areas for the community service jobs, and Congress has agreed to do that, but we've got to have the private sector." And he said, "We can do that." Then he found Gerry and the other first 4 that were here, who are here in the audience, and then there were 100, and soon there will be 1,000. And I thank you all very much.

I would like to talk about this today, a little bit, from my perspective as President, but first let me say that I respect the fact that those of you who come here, come here as Americans. You come here primarily as business people. Some of you are Republicans; some of you are Democrats; some of you probably wish you had never met a politician. [*Laughter*] But you all recognize that this is not a partisan issue, that it is a moral obligation for our country. It is America's business, and therefore, it must be the work of American business.

How did we get this goal of moving a million people from welfare to work by the year 2000? How did you get here to make a difference, as you can, as you saw from the young women

who have been introduced here, to help people to move from a lifetime of dependence to one of independence, to move from burdening their children with a legacy of despair to leaving their children with an inheritance of hope? Well, it all goes back to the effort we have made now as a nation. Some of us, as you heard the Governors talking, have been involved with this welfare reform issue a long time.

But when I became President, I was convinced that we had to change both the economic policy and the social policy of the country if we wanted America to work again for everyone; that we had to do something to get the deficit down and expand trade and, at the same time, invest more money in education and science and technology and research and the things that would grow the economy; but that we had to prove that America could work again in a fundamental human way. So we had to deal with crime. We had to deal with our great diversity and get people to come together across the lines that divide us and a stronger community. We had to deal with the conflicts people feel with family and work, that working people are having trouble raising their kids too and meeting their obligations at work.

And a big part of this mosaic was to change the culture of dependency that had arisen around our welfare system. There was lots of evidence that nobody really liked the welfare system very much, especially the people that were on it. There was also, frankly, a lot of evidence that, for about half the people that were on it, it worked reasonably well, just because for those people, you'd have to practically throw them up against a wall to stop them from doing all right in life—people that hit a rough patch in life, and they'd be on public assistance and they'd go on. But increasingly, to the point where we wound up with slightly more than half of the people on welfare were long-term dependents who felt it literally unable to come back into the mainstream of American life.

Well, we've seen a lot of progress in the last few years, and a lot of it's been helped by the fact that we've got the lowest unemployment rate in 24 years, and for the first time ever, our economy produced about 12 million jobs in a 4-year administration period. In that time, the welfare rolls had their biggest reduction ever in that short a period of time. And so I began to think, well, maybe we can make the welfare reform targets. And then I realized—I asked the Council of Economic Advisers to study this, and I said, "How much of this welfare decline is due to the economy doing better, and how much of it is due to the fact that most States now are really working hard on welfare reform with us? They've gotten waivers from the Federal Government to get out from under rules and regulations and move people to work."

And the study indicated that about 40 percent—a little more—of the people moved from welfare to work because the economy got better and just—the labor markets got tighter. About over a third, more or less, got there because most States were aggressively working with us either statewide or in parts of their States on welfare reform, and about a quarter got there for some other reason. But one of the reasons was that child support collections were increased by 50 percent in the last 4 years.

So then we said, "Okay, let's change. Let's go another step. Let's tell people that if they're able-bodied, they can only have 5 years of welfare over the course of a lifetime and no more than 2 years at one time, and let's give the States responsibility and the power and the money to design, State by State, a welfare reform system that will work and, in effect, will have to be designed community by community." That was the import of the welfare reform law. And in that law, as the Congressman here will tell you, they set up very strict targets. But essentially, about 40 percent of the population has to be fully into this law over the next 4 years. That's how we got to this burden you're undertaking, because I want all of you who signed on to understand what is at stake here.

Now, what that means, bottom line, is that we have to move about another 900,000 to one million people in the work force in the next 4 years to meet the requirements of the law, which will move about 2½ million people off welfare, because the average welfare family is about 2.5, 2.6, something like that.

Now, if we produce another 12 million jobs, we'll get close anyway. But it would be the first time in history that we ever did it 8 years in a row, since we've only done it once 4 years in a row, and we just came out of that. Maybe we can do it. And I'd be the last to say we couldn't. But even if we did that—here's the point I want to make—even if we did that, if we don't have people like this man and like all of you, the people who would come off would be those who might make it off under

any circumstances. And what we are trying to do here, the import of the reform welfare law, was to change, challenge, and end the culture of poverty, which means you have to find people who don't think they can make it, who have no idea what a resume is, who never had to show up on time before. There are people in this audience today who have helped find people like that before, and I wish all of you who have actually hired people from welfare to work were up here speaking today.

But what this is about is saying that we are going to go beyond what the normal economy would produce; we're going to make an extra effort. And the Government will do its part, but it has to be led by the private sector.

Now, in April the Vice President and I announced that we would hire at least 10,000 welfare recipients in the next 4 years without replacing anybody, just through job turnover, in an area where we will expand employment, which I think is a pretty good thing in a Federal Government that's 300,000 people smaller than it was 4 years ago when I took office. We'll do 10,000. And with the help of Secretary Slater and some of our other Cabinet Secretaries, we're going to work with our private contractors, the people that do direct business with us, to hire 10,000 more. And we believe we can do that.

When we reached the budget agreement—historic budget agreement with the leaders of Congress to balance the budget, it not only will give us the first balanced budget in almost 30 years, it contains the elements that we agree jointly should be a part of our contribution to your welfare reform effort. So let me mention them.

First, it provides, as I said earlier, $3 billion to help cities and States to create jobs and subsidize jobs, either community service jobs or subsidized private sector jobs. That money will be targeted to very high unemployment areas where you cannot reasonably expect any effort to deal with the time deadlines.

Second, it encourages employers to hire and retain welfare recipients by giving a 50 percent tax credit over 2 years for up to $10,000 in wages for every long-term welfare recipient hired that does not displace someone else.

Now, these two things will help. But in addition to that, we have other big problems. One of the biggest problems that we think we need to get more help on is transportation. You heard

Governor Carper talking about child care. There's $4 billion more in the welfare reform bill for child care. But there was a study that came out of Georgia recently which said that of the entry-level jobs in the inner city in fast food establishments, for example, something like, I don't know, 80 percent of the jobs were held by people who were low-income adults. In the suburbs, just a little more than half of those jobs were held by people who were low-income adults. The transportation barrier kept them from maximizing their ability to move from dependence to independence.

So since two out of three new jobs are created in the suburbs and a significant percentage of people on welfare live in urban centers, it is very important that we do more on that. Today, we're awarding seed grants to 24 States to develop transportation schemes to help people go and get the jobs where the jobs are. And the legislation that we proposed in the new transportation bill would provide $600 million to help States and local communities put these plans into action. It also was approved in the budget agreement, so that's a very, very good thing.

And let me just say one other thing since we've got two very innovative Governors here, and Governor Thompson, as you've seen—they've had a huge drop in Wisconsin and a sizeable drop in Delaware. If you look around the country, there's still a lot of unevenness in how much the welfare rolls have dropped. Part of it is due to underlying economic conditions. But part of it is due to how comprehensive the efforts are.

One of the things that I think is important is that the States really do get together and steal the best ideas from each other. You should know that among other things, the States now have the power under this new law to take what was the welfare check and give all or part of it to an employer for a period of time as an employment or training subsidy. And a lot of States are doing that as well. There are lots of options out there.

So I want to say to all of you who are part of this first hundred, you have to work with the Governors and with the State legislators, too, and with the mayors and the community-based operators. We've got to have a system here that's community based.

Finally, let me say that if you look at the numbers, a million people sounds like a huge amount over 4 years, but in an American econ-omy that has well over 100 million people in the work force, that produced 12 million new jobs in the last 4 years, with these extra incentives around the edges, with committed private sector employers, small, medium, and large businesses, this is not a problem. This is a startup enterprise that can be stunningly successful. But as far as I know, there is no exact precedent for it in our history. There has never been anything quite like this, and this is something we're trying to do together. I will do my best to do my part, but I thank all of you from the bottom of my heart, starting with Eli and Gerry and encompassing all of you, for doing your part.

You know, I've tried to learn about what a lot of you are doing. And Mr. Marriott here has this Pathways to Independence program that supports the transition from welfare to work. I've seen that. Then I meet a man with a small business, and more than half his employees are people who were on welfare. We were in Kansas City not very long ago, and I met a man who stores data for the Federal Government, way out in Kansas City—that's what computers do for you these days—and he had 25 people in his business, in this data storage business, and 5 of them were people that he had hired from the welfare rolls. Every time he expands now, he tries to hire somebody from welfare.

I know we can do this. I just want to say to you, when you leave here today I want you to imagine what it is you would like your country to look like when we enter the 21st century. There will always be people who, for one reason or another, are out of work. There will always be people who, for one reason or another, have a rough spot in life. And as long as we're a nation of immigrants, there will always be people who start out below whatever the federally established poverty line is. But we do not have to have a country with an intolerable crime rate, with an intolerable failure rate among young people in poverty and addiction and violence. And we do not have to have a country with a permanent culture of dependence. We do not have to have that.

We just had this Service Summit in Philadelphia where we said, "We're all going to get together, without regard to party, try to give every child in America five things, a healthy start in life, a safe place to grow up, a decent education, a mentor with a caring adult, and a chance to serve and give something back, no matter how modest the child's resources are."

I'll tell you, we could do more to get that done by liberating their parents from the culture of dependence than anything else. You are making the America we ought to have for the 21st century. And I hope when you leave here today, you'll be even more dedicated to it, because the future of our children is riding on it.

Thank you, and God bless you.

NOTE: The President spoke at 2:50 p.m. in the East Room at the White House. In his remarks, he referred to George R. Stinson, chairman and president, General Converters and Assemblers, Inc.; Gov. Tom Carper of Delaware; Gov. Tommy G. Thompson of Wisconsin; Gerald Greenwald, chief executive officer, United Airlines; Eli Segal, president, Welfare to Work Partnership; and J.W. Marriott, Jr., chairman, president, and chief executive officer, Marriott International, Inc.

Remarks to the Super Bowl Champion Green Bay Packers
May 20, 1997

Thank you very much. Please be seated. I want to welcome the Green Bay Packers and their fans here and send a special welcome to the congressional delegation from Wisconsin, Senator Kohl, Senator Feingold, the Members of the House. And I see we also have some interlopers from Michigan and Minnesota who claim to be the—[*laughter*]—fans of the Packers. It's still snowing in all those places, according to the coach, so—[*laughter*]—you guys have got to stick together.

I want to thank Robert Harlan and Ron Wolf and Coach Holmgren for being here and, of course, Brett and Reggie and the whole team. I got a lot of good advice when we were up in the White House having our pictures taken from the players about my knee therapy, and I appreciate that. What I need is some advice about how to make sure it never happens again. [*Laughter*]

Congratulations on bringing the Lombardi Trophy back to Green Bay, for the first time in almost 30 years. I had two indications that this was going to happen. The first was my very early visit with the Packers at the stadium; I could see that this was a team on a mission. The second was that the Secretary of Health and Human Services, who used to be president of a little school in Wisconsin, told me that they were bound to win. And I'm glad to see you here, Secretary Shalala. Thank you.

Let me say that, for all of us who are football fans, this was a great year because of all the things that the Packers did, including having the best Packer defense in 35 years and the best in the NFL. I'd like to congratulate Fritz Shurmur and his whole team and say that we're glad that you recovered from the injury that you sustained during last year's playoffs. And if you want to come here and teach us how to play defense in the White House, we need it as bad as the Packers do.

I congratulate Reggie White on his sacks in the Super Bowl and on being the all-time NFL leader in sacks. And I also think the Packers offense deserves a lot of credit. Brett Favre won his second consecutive NFL MVP award. And I congratulated Antonio Freeman on that 81-yard record touchdown catch when I saw him in the line. It was a very exciting time, that long pass, the long pass to Andre Rison. And also, even though he's not here today, I don't think any of us will ever forget that Desmond Howard was the first special teams player ever to be a Super Bowl MVP. It was a great Super Bowl by a great team and a team effort, and I congratulate you.

I would also like to say something not just as President but as a citizen. In a world where professional athletics becomes, it seems in sport after sport, more and more transient, where players, quite properly, have to look out for themselves in what may be a relatively short lifespan as professional athletes and people move from team to team and then teams move from town to town, the Green Bay Packers are something special, unique, old-fashioned, and heartwarming. The team is owned by ordinary citizens from all walks of life. The profits get poured back into the team. The players and the coaches have a unique relationship with the fans, which all of us who watch the games even on television can tell. Whether the fans are lining up in the winter to shovel snow so the games can be played or the players are volunteering in the community, it really means something to the rest of the country to see the relationship between Green Bay and the Packers and to know, that come what may, it will be there next year and the year after that and the year after that. And I thank you for that. It's a good example that the rest of us should remember in all forms of human contests and endeavor.

Let me say, finally, I want to express my admiration for Coach Mike Holmgren. He has one of the toughest coaching jobs in the world. Green Bay is a wonderful place to be, but the expectations are reasonably high. [*Laughter*] I can't think of anybody who could have done a better job in fulfilling the legacy of Vince Lombardi, meeting the expectations of the people of Green Bay, and creating the kind of atmosphere on this team that is palpable even to an outsider: mutual support, teamwork, and

always looking out for the ultimate goal and the welfare of the team and its success. This championship has earned him and his team their rightful place in history.

And coach, I hope that you will always, always be proud not only of the team but of what you were able to do to infuse the kind of spirit that it takes to get people to work together and play together through the tough times as well as the good times.

Congratulations to all of you, and welcome again to the White House.

NOTE: The President spoke at 5:35 p.m. on the South Portico at the White House. In his remarks, he referred to team president Robert Harlan; executive vice president and general manager Ron Wolf; head coach Mike Holmgren; quarterback Brett Favre; defensive end Reggie White; defensive coordinator Fritz Shurmur; wide receivers Antonio Freeman and Andre Rison; and punt return specialist Desmond Howard.

Message to the Congress on Prohibiting New Investment in Burma
May 20, 1997

To the Congress of the United States:

Pursuant to section 570(b) of the Foreign Operations, Export Financing, and Related Programs Appropriations Act, 1997 (Public Law 104–208) (the "Act"), I hereby report to the Congress that I have determined and certified that the Government of Burma has, after September 30, 1996, committed large-scale repression of the democratic opposition in Burma. Further, pursuant to section 204(b) of the International Emergency Economic Powers Act (50 U.S.C. 1703(b)) (IEEPA) and section 301 of the National Emergencies Act (50 U.S.C. 1631), I hereby report that I have exercised my statutory authority to declare a national emergency to respond to the actions and policies of the Government of Burma and have issued an Executive order prohibiting United States persons from new investment in Burma.

The order prohibits United States persons from engaging in any of the following activities after its issuance:

—entering a contract that includes the economic development of resources located in Burma;

—entering a contract providing for the general supervision and guarantee of another person's performance of a contract that includes the economic development of resources located in Burma;

—purchasing a share of ownership, including an equity interest, in the economic development of resources located in Burma;

—entering into a contract providing for the participation in royalties, earnings, or profits in the economic development of resources located in Burma, without regard to the form of the participation;

—facilitating transactions of foreign persons that would violate any of the foregoing prohibitions if engaged in by a United States person; and

—evading or avoiding, or attempting to violate, any of the prohibitions in the order.

Consistent with the terms of section 570(b) of the Act, the order does not prohibit the entry into, performance of, or financing of most contracts for the purchase or sale of goods, services, or technology. For purposes of the order, the term "resources" is broadly defined to include such things as natural, agricultural, commercial, financial, industrial, and human resources. However, not-for-profit educational, health, or other humanitarian programs or activities are not considered to constitute economic development of resources located in Burma. In accordance with section 570(b), the prohibition on an activity that constitutes a new investment applies if such activity is undertaken pursuant to an agreement, or pursuant to the exercise of rights under an agreement that is entered into with the Government of Burma or a non-governmental entity in Burma, on or after the effective date of the Executive order.

My Administration will continue to consult and express our concerns about developments in Burma with the Burmese authorities as well as leaders of ASEAN, Japan, the European Union, and other countries having major political, security, trading, and investment interests in Burma and seek multilateral consensus to bring about democratic reform and improve human rights in that country. I have, accordingly, delegated to the Secretary of State the responsibilities in this regard under section 570(c) and (d) of the Act.

The Secretary of the Treasury, in consultation with the Secretary of State, is authorized to issue regulations in exercise of my authorities under IEEPA and section 570(b) of the Act to implement this prohibition on new investment. All Federal agencies are also directed to take actions within their authority to carry out the provisions of the Executive order.

I have taken these steps in response to a deepening pattern of severe repression by the State Law and Order Restoration Council (SLORC) in Burma. During the past 7 months, the SLORC has arrested and detained large numbers of students and opposition supporters, sentenced dozens to long-term imprisonment, and prevented the expression of political views by the democratic opposition, including Aung San Suu Kyi and the National League for Democracy (NLD). It is my judgment that recent actions by the regime in Rangoon constitute large-scale repression of the democratic opposi-

tion committed by the Government of Burma within the meaning of section 570(b) of the Act.

The Burmese authorities also have committed serious abuses in their recent military campaign against Burma's Karen minority, forcibly conscripting civilians and compelling thousands to flee into Thailand. Moreover, Burma remains the world's leading producer of opium and heroin, with official tolerance of drug trafficking and traffickers in defiance of the views of the international community.

I believe that the actions and policies of the SLORC regime constitute an extraordinary and unusual threat to the security and stability of the region, and therefore to the national security and foreign policy of the United States.

It is in the national security and foreign policy interests of the United States to seek an end to abuses of human rights in Burma and to support efforts to achieve democratic reform. Progress on these issues would promote regional peace and stability and would be in the political, security, and economic interests of the United states.

The steps I take today demonstrate my Administration's resolve to support the people of Burma, who made clear their commitment to human rights and democracy in 1990 elections, the results of which the regime chose to disregard.

I am also pleased to note that the Administration and the Congress speak with one voice on this issue, as reflected in executive-legislative cooperation in the enactment of section 570 of the Foreign Operations Act. I look forward to continued close consultation with the Congress on efforts to promote human rights and democracy in Burma.

In conclusion, I emphasize that Burma's international isolation is not an inevitability, and that the authorities in Rangoon retain the ability to secure improvements in relations with the United States as well as with the international community. In this respect, I once again call on the SLORC to lift restrictions on Aung San Suu Kyi and the political opposition, to respect the rights of free expression, assembly, and association, and to undertake a dialogue that includes leaders of the NLD and the ethnic minorities and that deals with the political future of Burma.

In the weeks and months to come, my Administration will continue to monitor and assess action on these issues, paying careful attention to the report of the U.N. Special Rapporteur appointed by the U.N. Human Rights Commission and the report of the U.N. Secretary General on the results of his good offices mandate. Thus, I urge the regime in Rangoon to cooperate fully with those two important U.N. initiatives on Burma.

I am enclosing a copy of the Executive order that I have issued. The order is effective at 12:01 a.m., eastern daylight time, May 21, 1997.

WILLIAM J. CLINTON

The White House,
May 20, 1997.

NOTE: The Executive order is listed in Appendix D at the end of this volume.

Remarks to the United States Conference of Mayors
May 21, 1997

Thank you very much, Mr. Mayor. Mayor Helmke and other officers of the Conference of Mayors, General McCaffrey, Mr. Vice President, to members of the Cabinet and the administration, all of you who are here. First, let me thank you for participating in what, as Mayor Daley said, is a fairly unprecedented, long-term, consistent effort at cooperation with all these Federal agencies to try to work through a united approach to this issue.

It occurred to me as I was coming here that one of the things I ought to say is that all the objectives that all of us have for our country depend in part on our being able to give our children a drug-free future. I came here saying that I wanted to be President because we needed to change America for the 21st century, to make sure opportunity would be available for all people—it's by definition not there for people who are too paralyzed to take advantage of it—to make sure that all citizens would be responsible contributors to a community becoming more united. Drugs divide America in all kinds of ways that you're very familiar with and, by definition, represent irresponsibility.

And I wanted our country to be a leader in the world for peace and freedom and prosperity. And it's hard for America to lead when we're fighting all the time over the drug issues. And we certainly do. I just got back from a trip to Mexico, Central America, and the Caribbean, and each stop along the way, it was a big point of our discussions.

So it's important that you're here. A lot of you were just at the Presidents' Summit of Service in Philadelphia. We said we were going to try to create communities in which every child in this country by the year 2000 would have a safe place; a decent, healthy start in life; access to a good education and marketable skills; a mentor trying to help him or her; and have a chance to serve themselves—our children. We can't do any of that unless these kids have a drug-free future. So this is very, very important.

Before I get into the substance of my remarks, I'd also like to say a special word of thanks to someone who has worked with you on our behalf for over 4 years now. This is Marcia Hale's last day on the job, and I think we ought to say to her she has done a magnificent job representing the mayors. [*Applause*] Thank you. She leaves for London tomorrow. She's going to work for a great American company, and as nearly as I can tell, she will soon be in a position to support me in my old age. [*Laughter*] And so we wish her well.

Let me say that, also, I want to thank all of you for the work you've done with the Attorney General and with our other law enforcement officials in trying to drive down the crime rate. We can be very pleased with what has happened when we've had more police, more punishment, more prevention in our communities with a community-based strategy. One of the chiefs of police I met today said that the COPS program had been the best thing the Federal Government had done in his 37 years in law enforcement, and I appreciate that.

You all know that the crime rate has dropped for 5 years in a row, and we learned last week at the annual observance at the Law Enforcement Memorial that we had the fewest number of police officers killed last year in the line of duty in 35 years. And all those are good signs.

We've also had some success in the fight against illegal drugs. Monthly drug use today is about half of what it was 10 years ago. But what we have to face is—and I was glad General McCaffrey said what he did—is that we have had this anomalous situation in America for the last several years where crime is going down but crime among juveniles is going up; drug use among young adults, which used to be— that used to be the biggest problem category— 18 to 35, going down, drug use among juveniles going up. And that is the thing, I think, that is plaguing all of us.

This report you have given, I think, is very, very instructive about what we can do, and I want to talk a little more about what we can do together. But I think it's also important to point out that this problem is the problem of every American citizen. It goes beyond the responsibilities of even the President and the Attorney General and the drug czar and the DEA and the mayors and even the people who are involved in prevention and treatment. Our society cannot say on the one hand we want to have a tough and tolerant attitude toward drugs and on the other hand send a very different message every time there might be a little money to be made out of it.

And I want to say specifically, there have not been consistent and unwavering messages. You know, a lot of you have experienced in your communities the increasing allure of heroin among young people. We've seen a lot of communities where cocaine use goes down, heroin use comes up. For most people in our generation—a lot of you are younger than I am, but most of you are about my age—we all grew up thinking heroin was the worst thing in the world, and there were these horrible images associated with it, strung-out junkies lying on street corners in decidedly unglamorous ways. But we now see in college campuses, in neighborhoods, heroin becoming increasingly the drug of choice. And we know that part of this has to do with the images that are finding their way to our young people.

In the press in recent days, we've seen reports that many of our fashion leaders are now admitting—and I honor them for doing this—they're admitting flat out that images projected in fashion photos in the last few years have made heroin addition seem glamorous and sexy and cool. And if some of the people in those images start to die now, it's become obvious that that is not true. You do not need to glamorize addiction to sell clothes. And American fashion has been an enormous source of creativity and beauty and art and, frankly, economic prosperity for the United States, and we should all value and respect that. But the glorification of heroin is not creative; it's destructive. It's not beautiful; it is ugly. And this is not about art; it's about life and death. And glorifying death is not good for any society. And I hope that we have all come to recognize that now, because none of us are going to succeed unless all of us work together on this problem.

Let me say that I also recognize that we have more to do here. The balanced budget agreement that we have reached with the Congress, and which received overwhelming support from Members of both parties in the House of Representatives last night—I am very, very proud of it—will allow us to continue to increase our efforts to work with you to do our part of the job. And I agree with what Mayor Daley said; we have a lot of things to do here, including improving the coordination between what we do and what you do.

Among other things, General McCaffrey has succeeded in making the case for a $175 million advertising campaign which will be leveraged with private sector resources to give our children the hard facts about drugs. I think that is very important. We have a lot of evidence that drug use does go down or up depending upon the absence or presence of certain messages and a certain cultural environment about it.

There are also two other things I'd like to mention because they were mentioned specifically, Mr. Mayor, in your plan. First, we have some good news to report in our progress about methamphetamines. Last year, we targeted this increasingly popular drug as a special focus for our efforts. Meth has a devastating effect on those who use it. It is produced in clandestine labs which carry an enormously high risk of fire and explosion. The Congress supported our efforts by enacting the Comprehensive Methamphetamine Control Act, establishing new controls over the chemicals used to make meth and strengthening penalties for trafficking in those chemicals.

Now a year later, we are releasing a one-year progress report. First, seizures of dangerous drug labs used to manufacture meth are up 170 percent in one year alone. Second, the use of methamphetamine is down in key western cities. In 8 of the 10 cities where meth use had been skyrocketing, it's dropped between 7 and 52 percent. So this shows you that if we work together, we can actually turn the tide in problem after problem after problem.

A second focus of our efforts—and again, one that you mentioned in your report—involved a vigorous crackdown on money launderers. We know that without a steady stream of laundered cash, the drug trade will wither. Today the Treasury Department will take three steps to further cut off the cash. We will require currency exchanges, check cashers, and other money services to register with the Treasury Department. We will require more businesses to report suspicious activity under penalty of law and will require the transfer of funds overseas above $750 to be reported to Federal law enforcement. We know this will cut back on money laundering. It will require some efforts at compliance, but it is worth doing. We know if we can get to the money, we can get to the problems very often.

Finally, let me ask your help in trying to get the Congress to pass the kind of juvenile justice bill we all know that we need. Organized gangs, armed to the teeth, prowl too many of our streets and threaten too many of our communities and are part of the drug problem. I have proposed comprehensive legislation, modeled on what is working in Boston and many other cities present in this room and around the country, that will protect our children better from violence and give local communities the capacity to have safe streets again.

The plan will add prosecutors and probation officers, keep schools open longer to keep children off the streets. And we know an awful lot of the problems young people have occur in the first few hours after they get out of school and before they can be home with their parents.

It will also require child safety locks on guns. Right now, we protect aspirin bottles better than we protect guns. And it would extend the provisions of the Brady bill to juveniles who commit serious violent crimes; they wouldn't be able to buy a gun when they turn 21.

The legislation passed in the House of Representatives contains tougher penalties and more prosecutors, but only about a dozen States qualify. It does not do anything on prevention. It does not make all States available for extra prosecutors and probation officers. And it does not deal with the child safety locks or extending the coverage of the Brady bill to juveniles who commit serious crimes.

Now, I believe we ought to get a good juvenile crime bill here that can be actually used in the way the crime bill of 1994 and the COPS program are being used by you on the streets. We want to give you something you can use. This bill, like the other ones, was largely written by local officials telling us what should be in the bill. So I do not want this to be a political issue; I do not want this to be a partisan issue. I tried to do this in a very straightforward way, based on what those of you who labor in this vineyard every day told me was the right thing to do.

So I hope that you will help us do that, continue to make progress on meth, continue to make progress on money laundering. I assure you we will review your plan and your recommendations very closely. And again, let me say I also hope you will help us remind the people in your communities that if we want our kids to be drug-free, we've got to work hard to send the right signals.

Thank you very much.

NOTE: The President spoke at 10:30 a.m. in the State Dining Room at the White House. In his remarks, he referred to Mayor Paul Helmke of Fort Wayne, IN, and Mayor Richard M. Daley of Chicago, president, U.S. Conference of Mayors.

Remarks at a Democratic Senatorial Campaign Committee Reception
May 21, 1997

Thank you very much. Senator Kerrey, thank you so much for what you said. I certainly hope someone taped that; I may need it later. [*Laughter*] Thank you, Senator Torricelli, for your tireless efforts, your great energy. I thank all the other Senators who are here from our party. I have seen Senators Harkin, Dodd, Mikulski, Breaux, and Rockefeller. I'm sure I've missed someone. Who else is here? Senator Graham, Bryan. Bumpers is not here, is he? Dale Bumpers came to a fundraiser? My Senator is here. Give him a hand. [*Applause*] That's great. [*Laughter*]

Anyway, I want to say a special word of appreciation to Senator Daschle, who took on the leadership of our party and the Senate at a difficult time. And I think that every single Member of the United States Senate would have to say that he has performed with incredible skill and discipline and leadership and humanity. And we are very grateful to him.

Ladies and gentlemen, I thank you for being here tonight. I'm here because I want to see the Democrats who are running for reelection win. I want to see Senator Biden have a chance to chair the Judiciary Committee. I want Senator Hollings—I know he's here—to be reelected, and Senator Boxer, Senator Murray, Senator Carol Moseley-Braun.

I'm here because even though we have had occasional well-publicized disagreements, the last time I checked, the Democratic Congress has supported me more frequently than the Democrats supported my last three Democratic predecessors. So I am very grateful for the partnership that we have had. It means a lot to me, and I thank them for that.

And I'm here because I wanted to tell all of you who contributed to us so that we could all be here tonight, I am proud of you. You are doing what it takes to make the American political system work. And you ought to be proud of yourselves, because if it hadn't been for you, a lot of us would not be here doing the things which have been done to advance the cause of the American people. And I hope you will always be proud to be here among your friends who agree with you and who are trying to move this country forward. And thank you, Dale Chihuly, for your support and your artistic gifts to all of us. God bless you, sir.

Ladies and gentlemen, for almost 4½ years now we have worked hard to lead this country into a new century with a different way of governing America. In 1992, our country was drifting and divided, and I had a new idea, that we could bring the American people together and move us forward if we thought about what it would take to essentially preserve the American dream for everyone in the 21st century. Opportunity for all, responsibility from all, everybody is part of our community, and we're prepared to lead the world toward peace and freedom and prosperity—a very simple program.

At the time, Democrats had had a hard time commanding national trust because people said, well, we couldn't be trusted because we'd spend every dollar we got our hands on; we couldn't be trusted with the deficit; we couldn't be trusted to manage the economy; we couldn't be trusted with defense; we couldn't be trusted with foreign policy; we couldn't be trusted with crime. You remember all that whole litany that our friends on the other side used to say, about us.

Well, now we have 4½ years of experience. Yes, we're going to pass a balanced budget plan; but don't you forget, 77 percent of the work has been done, done entirely by Democrats who voted in 1993 for the economic program that represented the philosophy the voters ratified in 1992. And we were right, and that's why we can balance the budget today and continue to invest in our country and move us forward.

Senator Daschle talked about a record number of new jobs. We've also got the lowest employment rate in 24 years, the lowest inflation in 30 years, the highest business investment in 35 years. And here's something important to Democrats, the biggest decline in inequality in incomes of working families in over three decades. That's what we came here to do; that's what we're doing; and that's what we're going to do more of if you help us keep these people in the Senate and bring some friends along so that we can have a majority and continue to move this country forward.

Crime has gone down 5 years in a row for the first time in over two decades. We've had the biggest drop in welfare rolls, before the welfare reform bill was signed, in 50 years. The Democrats have a lot to be proud of. And we have a lot to do. And all elections are about the future.

Now when this agreement passes, it will provide for a balanced budget that has the biggest increase in education in a generation; enough funds to continue protecting the environment and close 500 of the worst toxic waste dumps and continue our work to try to preserve our national parks, to try to save the Florida Everglades, to try to move this country forward environmentally. It contains funds that are adequate to restore almost all of the cuts in—wrongful cuts in aid to legal immigrants that were imposed last year by the Congress. And it provides funds to help us make sure that all those people we are telling, "You have to move from welfare to work," will actually be able to get from welfare to work and will be able to have a job when they get there.

Yesterday we announced a new partnership with 100 companies, that will soon grow into 1,000, who are committing to hire people to move from welfare to work. We are going to move another million people into the work force from welfare in the next 4 years. That is our approach: Don't cut people off and walk away from them; give them a chance to raise their children and succeed in the workplace.

Let me just say that we have a lot of challenges ahead. We have cured the structural deficit in our country, but we have to attack the generational deficit. That means that we have to recognize that while poverty is at an all-time low among senior citizens, and we're proud of that, it's twice that high among our children. And we can't let it get worse as those of us in the baby boom generation move toward our retirement years. We have to literally carry out a crusade to take care of the future of the children of this country. Part of the things that I like about this budget is that it's got funds in there—$16 billion worth of funds—to extend health insurance to half the kids in this country who don't have it. And we shouldn't quit until we finish that job.

And finally, let me say, we have one big debate still raging in our party and in our country. And I'm clearly on one side, and I'm here to plead guilty. I believe it's good for America to

lead the world to a more open economy, to more peaceful arms arrangements, to more cooperation, to more democracy. And I believe we did the right thing in the last 4 years to conclude over 200 trade agreements, the largest trade record of any administration in the history of the country. That's one of the reasons in the last 2 years more than half of the new jobs coming into our economy have paid above average wages.

I believe we're doing the right thing to make an agreement between NATO and Russia, which I'm going to Paris to celebrate next week. I believe we're doing the right thing to open NATO membership to new members so that we can avoid having a 21st century like the 20th century and, frankly, virtually every century before it where wars were fought and people were killed on the soil of Europe.

I believe it's a good thing for the United States to try to make peace in the Middle East and Northern Ireland and Bosnia, to try to ask our friends in Greece and Turkey to work with us to resolve their problems. I believe it's a good thing for us to care about what's going on between India and Pakistan and hope that it can be worked out. I believe it's a good thing for us to believe that here at home our incredible racial and ethnic diversity should be seen as an asset. And I am proud of the fact that I have consistently opposed the dismantlement of all affirmative action programs. I think it is a terrible mistake, and you can see it in the enrollment figures in these colleges and universities in Texas and California now.

So that's what I believe. And it's hard to quarrel with the results now. If you can help us with your ideas and your contributions and with recruiting good candidates in all these States, we now have a record. It is no longer open to serious debate that when we said in 1993 you could shrink the deficit, cut the size of Government, and increase investment in education, technology, and science and research, they laughed at us and said, "All you're going to do is bring on a recession and make the deficit worse." The deficit's been cut by 77 percent. You heard Tom Daschle say we produced 12 million jobs for the first time in history in a 4-year period and the lowest unemployment rate in 24 years. Our approach was right, and they were not, and that's why we got a budget agreement today that will enable us to balance the budget. All we have to do is to stay on the good issues, run on the high road, and be able to find good candidates and finance them, and we can keep moving this country forward.

Don't you ever forget—you go home tonight—12 million people have jobs because we changed the economic policy of the country; 186,000 felons, fugitives, and stalkers did not buy handguns in the last 4 years because we changed the policy of the country; 12 million working families got to take a little time off from their jobs when they had a sick parent or a sick child without losing their jobs because we changed the direction of the country. And I could go on and on and on.

What you do makes a difference in the lives of people you will never meet, you will never know, who could never afford to be here tonight. That is the unique role you occupy in American democracy. I am very proud of it and very grateful to you and deeply determined to keep this country and our party moving in the right direction.

Thank you for your support. Thank you, and God bless you.

NOTE: The President spoke at 9:23 p.m. at the Corcoran Museum of Art. In his remarks, he referred to glass artist Dale Chihuly, whose work was displayed at the museum.

Remarks at a Townhall Meeting on Education in Clarksburg, West Virginia
May 22, 1997

The President. Thank you very much. Thank you, Mary Helen. She said she was nervous, but I thought she did a great job, didn't you? Terrific.

Thank you, Bob Kittle, for hosting us here, Leon Pilewski, the principal, and all the faculty here at Robert Byrd High School. I thank Governor Underwood, Mrs. Underwood, Governor Caperton, the other State officials for being here, the legislative leaders, the local school officials.

The congressional delegation did want to come, but the Senate is voting today on the balanced budget amendment. I'll have a little more to say about that in a minute. But I kind of wish Senator Byrd had been able to come here, especially to this school, but he and your other legislators have put their duty first, and I respect that, and they're where we all want them to be.

I'd like to thank your State superintendent of education, Hank Marockie, for being here, and recognize the president of the State board of education, Cleo Mathews, who's here because not only is she the president of the State board of education but her daughter, Sylvia, is the Deputy Chief of Staff to the President. And that's a nice little walk from Hinton, West Virginia, so I thank them for being here. Cleo, thank you.

I thank Mayor Flynn and others for making me feel so welcome in Clarksburg and all the communities along the way where the people came out to say hello. But mostly I want to thank all of you in this audience for joining me to talk about education, about the plans that you have and the plans that I have to make education better, and especially the importance of high standards, to give our children the knowledge and skills they will need to seize the opportunities and meet the challenges of the 21st century.

I came here in part because of the great progress you are making in the national movement to raise academic achievement. In 1996, the State of West Virginia tied for third in the Nation in improvement since 1992 in the mathematics performance of fourth and eighth graders. You should be very, very proud of that.

I want to thank Governor Underwood for supporting this educational effort, and I want to thank my former colleague, with whom I served for many years, Gaston Caperton, for making education his top priority here in West Virginia, among other things, making West Virginia the Nation's leader in putting technology in schools.

I believe you either now have or soon will have computers in every single one of your elementary schools in West Virginia. That is something you can be very proud of—that, the distance learning work you've done. And I want to tell you all, if you don't know, in addition to being on public broadcasting here in West Virginia and whatever else the networks choose to pick up tonight, we are live on the Internet in West Virginia and across the country. So you're in cyberspace, and I hope you're having a good time there.

For the last 4 years we have worked very hard to advance our goals in education to make sure all our children are ready to learn; to make sure that they have good basic skills, from expanding Head Start to the Goals 2000 program, which West Virginia has used; to have grassroots efforts to raise academic performance; to our school-to-work program, to help the learning of young people who don't go on to colleges but do deserve to have good access to further training after high school; to open the doors of college to all Americans.

The balanced budget agreement that I reached with the leaders of Congress provides for the largest increased investment in education in a generation. If the Senate adopts it—the House has already adopted it by a better than 75 percent vote; if the Senate adopts it, that's what it will do. It expands Head Start, moving toward our goal of a million kids in Head Start by 2002. It funds our America Reads program, designed to mobilize a million volunteer reading tutors across America to ensure that every 8-year-old in this country can read independently by the end of the third grade—very important in a country that is as diverse as ours is becoming.

We have 4 school districts in America where there are more than 100 different native ethnic linguistic groups. That's a stunning statistic. But everybody has to be able to read in our common language of English, so this is very important.

We also have the largest increased investment in higher education since the GI bill was passed at the end of World War II; a HOPE scholarship tax credit for families, designed to make 2 years of education after high school as universal as a high school diploma is today; tax deductions for the costs of all tuition after high school; and the biggest increase in Pell grants in 20 years. It will add 300,000 more people who are eligible for the Pell grant program, something which will be especially helpful in a State like West Virginia.

In addition to that, we have funding to try to follow your lead to make sure that we can connect every classroom and library in the United States to the Internet by the year 2000. But the most important thing of all in our education program, I believe, is the effort to develop national standards and a national measure of whether those standards are being met, because from West Virginia to Nevada, from Washington State to Florida, from Maine to Arizona, math is the same; the need for basic reading skills are the same.

I called in my State of the Union Address for national standards of excellence in basic learning, not Federal Government standards but national standards, starting with fourth grade reading and eighth grade math and reflected in examinations which I would challenge every school, every State, every student to participate in by 1999.

I have proposed that these exams be based on the only widely accepted national standards-based test we have today, called the National Assessment of Education Progress. When I just said that West Virginia ranked third in the country in progress and performance in math tests, that is based on your students' performance on the so-called NAEP test, the National Assessment of Education Progress. But today we only give those tests to a sampling of students in States, and we only know what either the State scores are or in some cases the district or regional scores are. So we have to do this for the whole Nation.

Today I am pleased to announce that Governor Underwood, along with the State board of education and the State superintendent of education, has agreed that West Virginia should participate in these examinations in 1999. And I'm grateful to him, and you should be proud of it.

In addition, Massachusetts and the National Alliance of Business are endorsing our call for national tests. West Virginia, Massachusetts, the National Alliance of Business joined several other States and other groups in the growing national consensus for standards. And I am very, very encouraged.

Let me also say that, you know my native State of Arkansas has a lot in common with West Virginia. In the 1980 census, we were the two States with the highest percentage of people living in the States who were born there. And we also have had to struggle with low incomes and an economy that was not easily changeable to meet the demands of the modern world. And

I'd like to think that we believe that our children are as gifted as children anywhere and that if we give them high standards, good teaching, and good parental support and good support in the schools, they can do as well as students anywhere in the world. So again, Governor, thank you. And thank you to all the educators. We're going to do this, and it's important.

Now, before we open the floor to questions, I thought you might be interested in just seeing what these exams are like. So we'll go through a question or two, just so you'll get the feeling for what a fourth grade—we'll start with the fourth grade reading exam, and you'll see why this is important. If you have a standards exam—it's not like giving an exam in class where somebody might grade on the curve and two people can make an A and everybody else has to make something lower. Standards-based exams are designed to assure that everybody can pass, but to pass, it means something. It means you know what you need to know. So no one is supposed to fail, and this is not designed to put any school, any student, any group down but to lift us all up. The tests are designed so that if they don't work out so well the first time, you'll know what to do to teach, to improve and lift these standards.

But it's very important to understand the difference between a standards-based test and normal grading, where you expect somebody to make 100, somebody to make 60, and everybody to be in between. With the idea of standards, you want everybody to clear at least the fundamental bar.

So let's look at the charts here. Chart one describes the fourth grade reading test, and the standard performance is divided into three categories. Basic performance means that a reader can recognize most of the words, identify the most important information. The next level is proficient; in addition to that, you can summarize the passage, find specific information, and describe the way it's presented. Then an advanced understanding would be that you could provide a more detailed and thoughtful explanation. And I'll give you an example of that by asking one of your students to join me. Hannah Galey, who is a fourth grader from Nutter Fort Intermediate, is going to come forward. Hannah is going to read us a passage from "Charlotte's Web," a wonderful book I'm sure a lot of the adults here read with your children when they were little.

Hannah? Give her a hand. [*Applause*]

[*At this point, Hannah Galey read the passage.*]

The President. That's wonderful. That's great. Give her a hand. [Applause] You were great. If we were giving a read score, she would be double advanced, you know. [*Laughter*] Thank you.

Now, here's the way the question would work for a fourth grader: "Based upon the passage you just read, how would you describe Charlotte to a friend?" And then these are three possible answers, and you see how they would be graded, based on what I just said. A basic proficiency would be, "Charlotte keeps her promise." That's basic standards. A proficient answer would be, "Charlotte works hard to keep her promise," describing that she hasn't kept it yet, she's working to keep it. And then, an advanced understanding would just explain in one sentence what the whole paragraph was about. "She plans to keep her promise to save Wilbur's life"—what the promise is—"by tricking Zuckerman"—how she plans to keep it—all three things. But you can see if you give—and obviously there are various variations, but the test would be—the answers would be aggregated in three categories like that, so that you would have some sense of how the children were reading.

Now, let's look at chart four, which will show how our fourth graders are doing. Again, this is the National Assessment of Education Progress. This is the reading version of the math test that I just quoted that West Virginia was third in the country in improvement on. Given to a representative sample of fourth graders in America, 40 percent did not do as well as saying, "Charlotte keeps her promise"—could not say that's what this was about.

Now, you know, some of these young people may not have English as a first language, but a lot of them do and still are not reading at an advanced enough level. That is why it is so important that we provide in every community an army of trained reading tutors to help support the parents and support the literacy efforts under way and support the schools.

Thirty percent cleared the first hurdle: "This is about Charlotte keeping a promise." Twenty-three percent were more proficient; they knew it was her plan, she was outlining her plan. Only 7 percent of the fourth graders went as far as saying, "She plans to keep her promise to save the life by tricking the man." You see?

So it shows you that ideally we would like 100 percent at advanced, but at least we need 100 percent at basic or above. And so the idea of giving the exam would not be to identify failures but to show schools and school districts how well children are reading based on what they understand so that everybody would reach a certain understanding. That way their performance in all subsequent grades would improve. A lot of children have the mental capacity to do very well in school and fall further and further behind because they didn't get the comprehension they needed early on.

Now, I want to show you one other chart, and we'll come back to this at the end of the program. This is a sample eighth grade math test, so ask yourself this question—no answer forthcoming now: A car has a fuel tank that holds 15 gallons of fuel. The car consumes 5 gallons of fuel for every 100 miles. A trip of 250 miles was started with a full tank of fuel. How much fuel remained in the tank at the end of the trip? And there are four answers: 2½ gallons, 12½ gallons, 17½ gallons, 5 gallons. We'll come back to that at the end of the show. That's designed to hold viewer interest out there. [*Laughter*]

So that's basically what these standards tests are designed to do. I wanted to come here and talk about that because West Virginia has not only proved that you can have a big increase in teachers' salaries, which is wonderful; one of the best student-teacher ratios in America, which is wonderful; the most aggressive plan to put computers in elementary schools in the country, which is terrific and helps to reinforce standards learning; but you're also showing that you can raise standards and today, with the Governor's statement, that you want to do more.

So with that, I'd like to hear from about any of these educational matters you would like to discuss, questions you'd like to ask, statements you'd like to make, and we'll go back to our leader here, Mr. Kittle.

Thank you.

Mr. Kittle. We're ready now to do the town-hall meeting, so we're ready to open for questions for the President.

The President. Here's some over here.

Mr. Kittle. Over here?

The President. Yes, over there. And there's some there.

[*David Hardesty, president of West Virginia University, asked the President to identify the impediments to the adoption of national standards.*]

The President. I think there are two major barriers, from what I've heard. The first is a political one; the second one is a deeply personal one, almost.

The political one is sometimes when people say "national standards"—and Secretary Riley and I have to deal with this all across America— when people say "national standards," they say, "I don't want the Federal Government setting standards for my school." That is not what this is about. All the Federal Government proposes to do is to fund the development of the tests to measure whether the standards are being met.

The National Assessment of Education Progress tests, which you participate in, was developed by educators, academics, and other experts. The Federal Government is not running this test. We are not telling you that you have to participate in it. The whole thing is voluntary. But I believe every State will want to be a part of it when it is obviously a process that has integrity, that will help our children.

So the first thing is we have to tell people, this is not some attempt of the Federal Government to take over your schools. We have done a lot in our administration to get rid of a lot of the Federal rules and regulations associated with grant programs, to try to give local school districts more flexibility as long as they were developing academic standards that they could hold themselves accountable for. That's the first thing.

The second thing—big problem, I think, is it's scary. It's personal. You're afraid. What happens if you take it, and you don't do very well? And I think the important thing there is that we are not—we want all of our children to take it, but we're not necessarily trying to identify the specific score of every student, but we want the schools and the classes to see how they're doing so they can lift the students up. I don't want anybody's score published in the paper or anything like that. This is not an instrument of failure; it's an instrument of accountability and a pathway to success.

But I can tell you, when you look at other countries with which we're competing for the high-wage jobs of tomorrow—huge issue in

West Virginia, now, for years—I was looking at the topography of West Virginia, which looks like about half of Arkansas, you know, all these mountains and how beautiful it is. For years, it made it hard for you to diversify your economy. You had coal in the ground, but it was hard for people to get here and do other things, and it slowed up the diversification of your economy and kept your wage levels too low.

The explosion of technology will mean that many kinds of work can be done anywhere in America and anywhere in the world. And it both gives you an enormous new opportunity but a much higher responsibility to lift your education level. So we've got to get people over the idea that they have to be scared of how this thing comes out.

No matter how bad it is, once you get a roadmap, it will be better next year, and it will be better the year after that. And all the evidence is that children do better with higher expectations. To me those are the two things. If you can confront those two things head on, go out here and tell the citizens of West Virginia the Government is not trying to run a testing program and take over your schools, number one; and number two, don't be scared of how it comes out, because it's going to make us better in the long run.

Mr. Kittle. Okay. Time for the next question. Let's take one from this group over here.

[A participant asked if schools would receive increased funding for reading specialists at the elementary school level.]

The President. What's the answer to that, Secretary Riley? Yes? Yes, he doesn't have a microphone. Secretary, just tell him what you just said. [*Laughter*] This is something I'm very proud of. I'll give you the intro. In addition to the million volunteers we're going to try to get to support you, those of you who do this at a higher level of skill on a full-time basis, we are also going to provide—that's what he was about to say.

[Secretary of Education Richard W. Riley responded that the President's America Reads initiative provided Federal funding for reading specialists to work with selected students.]

The President. Twenty-five thousand extra reading specialists, so that should put one in every school.

Now, let me ask you something. You say you're a reading recovery teacher, and have you had great results with it? You know, the reading recovery program revolutionized literacy in the whole nation of New Zealand——

Secretary Riley. Absolutely.

The President. ——and is probably the most consistently effective reading program that any of us know about. It's more intensive, and it's more expensive. And what we're trying to do is to create a network where, in effect, people like you can be at the center of a hub that reaches out, that included reading specialists and all the volunteers, so we'll have enough hopefully to cover what every child needs.

[Donna Rose, a teacher at Lost Creek Elementary School, described the reading program at Lost Creek, its emphasis on parental involvement, and the long-term improvement in student scores. She gave credit to the Title I funding and the flexibility permitted by the program and asked if the President was working on similar programs for the future.]

The President. Let me say, first of all I thank you for what you are doing because I think it's very important. It's the most important thing, especially with the parents being involved. One of the things that we have done that I'm most proud of is the way we redid the Title I program, because when we got here, Secretary Riley and I got here and we had been Governors living with the Title I program for years, we thought it was really selling our lower income children in our poorer school districts short, basically creating a two-tiered system of education. And instead, we tried to organize it so that you grassroots teachers could use it to lift the performance level of children who were covered by Title I, and I think that's what you've done, and I'm very thrilled by it.

What we're trying to do now, in addition to what we've just been talking about, on the standards—first we want to increase the availability of preschool education so that more kids will come to school prepared to learn. Secondly, we want to try to do what we can to support the literacy programs in the schools. We explained that.

And then we've taken the basic education programs that we have on the books now in this balanced budget plan and tried to continue or dramatically increase the funding of as many of them as we could. We are particularly interested in trying to help enhance math and science education and, as I said earlier, trying to accelerate the movement of computers and connection to the Internet and good educational software and trained teachers in every classroom in America. And that's a big part of this program.

So I hope that all those things together will make a significant difference when we finish this work over the next 4 to 5 years.

Mr. Kittle. Let's take a question from one of the students now.

The President. You've got a bunch of them. Your choice.

Mr. Kittle. Let's take the one here on the front row, on the left.

The President. We'll take both of them. Go ahead.

[Jennifer Brown, a fifth grade student at Simpson Elementary School, voiced her concern that funding for art, music, and theater programs had been cut, and asked if the President would ensure that the programs remain in schools.]

The President. Wonderful. Well, first of all, let me say that historically, the main support for arts and education out in the country from the National Government has come through programs like the National Endowment for the Arts, the National Endowment for the Humanities, because most of the big money coming from the National Government to the schools has come to schools that have basically low tax bases because of low income, or to students with special needs. And the idea was that if the Federal Government gave extra money to poor schools or gave extra money to students with special needs because their costs were higher, then the States and the localities would be able to keep up the rest of the programs.

There has been an alarming decline all over America in the arts and music programs and, I might say, in the athletic programs, apart from the big school teams. And I think it's a serious mistake, because we now know that a lot of young people develop their intellectual capacities in different ways, different kids learn in different ways, and that we really are significantly eroding the future of certain segments of our children if we deprive them of access to the arts and music and, even if they're not varsity football or basketball players or baseball players, to other sports.

But we don't—except through the National Endowment for the Arts, we've done some things that benefit public schools. We don't have direct programs to do that because we spend all our money on other things. But I must say, I personally believe it's a mistake for schools to cut back on it. And when I was a Governor, I tried to dedicate enough funding to these purposes, to try to offset it, even though usually the decisions about the curriculum are made completely at the local level. I think that may be the problem, that all schools from time to time have financial problems. And it may be that because there's not a specific funding stream for a lot of these programs, they're more likely to be left undefended.

I think the best way to keep them is for you and students like you to point out that you think it's an important part of your education.

Ashby Hardesty. Mr. President, my name is Ashby Hardesty, and I'm a fifth grader from Nutter Fort Elementary School. I was wondering if you use the Internet in the White House.

The President. We do.

Secretary Riley. All right.

The President. But my daughter uses it more than I do. [*Laughter*] We access the Internet in the White House, and we also have extensive E-mail. But my speechwriters use the Internet. They can do research on the Internet; they pull up articles and things. We use the Internet for all kinds of things.

When I become curious, I can always go down to the Vice President's office, because he's a bigger expert than I am, and we have interesting environmental discussions based on things he pulls up for me on the Internet. But the White House uses the Internet quite a lot.

Mr. Kittle. Okay, let's hear from one of the parents over in this section.

Jim?

Jim McCallum. Mr. President, welcome to West Virginia.

The President. Thank you.

[Mr. McCallum, a member of the West Virginia Board of Education, asked the President's opinion on extending the school year.]

The President. I have always thought if you could afford it, it was a good thing to do. I think that the only major industrial country with a shorter school year than we have, that I'm aware of is Belgium, and I'm not quite sure what the historic reasons for it are. But Belgium does have a shorter school year than we do. Every other nation in the world with an advanced economy has a longer school year.

And as you know, basically the American school year was developed around an agricultural society when all of the children had to get off and help their folks in the fields. A lot of our more overcrowded school districts now are now open year-round. They just operate on three trimesters, and the students have to go to two of three trimesters. And obviously that reduces by a third the amount of new school construction they have to do, although it costs more, obviously, to operate the schools and pay the personnel.

I think on balance it's a good thing to do. I think that—let me just say what we're learning already from the NAEP tests and other things. In math—what we're learning in mathematics for example in the higher years is that our students may skip over a large number of subjects and touch a large number of subjects, for example, in advanced mathematics. But our competitors in East Asia and in Germany, for example, may study slightly fewer subjects, but because they're in school longer, they go into much greater depth, which means when they get out of high school, they carry a higher level of capacity with them.

So if you are going to lengthen the school year, I would say the first thing you ought to do is bring educators and others in and say, "Well, if we went to school longer, what would we do with the time?" I mean, you don't want the kids to get bored. In a lot of States like our home State, every time we talked about lengthening the school year, they would tell me about how many schools weren't properly air-conditioned and we would have the teachers and the kids passing out and all that kind of stuff. It's very unpopular, lengthening the school year, but I was always for it. I just think you need to analyze—and I think you get more support if you say, "Here is what we would do if we went to school a week longer. Here is what we would do with that time. If we went to school 2 weeks longer, here is what we would do with that time." And then, of course, you have to figure out how you're going to pay for it and what kind of offset you get with questions like the young lady asked here about already having cutbacks in other things.

On balance, do I think it would be better if we had a slightly longer school year? I do.

[*Bill Sharpe, president pro tempore of the West Virginia Senate, asked the President if the national standards would emphasize the importance of writing.*]

The President. First of all, let me say I do not—if I were in a different line of work, for example, if I were the superintendent of schools here like Mr. Kittle, or if I were the State superintendent of public education, I would not say that we should only have high standards in reading for fourth graders and math for eighth graders. It's just that this is the—we have to make a beginning somewhere as a nation, so I'm trying to get us to make a beginning as a nation with this in 1999.

I would have—we already have an enormous amount of work that's been done, for example, by the science teachers to have national standards in science. And National Geographic has spent a fortune to work with geography teachers to develop national standards in geography and teaching materials for it. And there are national standards in civics. And there should be standards in reading and language, generally, that go from the fourth grade to the eighth grade. And there ought to be—and one in high school, perhaps 10th grade. And in my dream world, before too long, we would have this fourth grade reading test and this eighth grade test replicated in elementary, junior high, and high school in several areas, and then all the schools in the country could pick and choose about what they would participate in.

Obviously, if you went to the eighth grade, and certainly in the high school, you would want a writing sample as well. I'm interested in—more and more of the college application forms you see a lot of you—I'm sort of into this now, as a lot of you know—[*laughter*]—are requiring young people to write an essay to get into college. And I think it's a very good thing. So I would agree that writing and the measurement of writing capacity should be a very important part of a national standards program once you move beyond the fourth grade into junior high and then on into high school. It's very important that young people be able to express themselves.

Mr. Kittle. Let's move back to this side.

The President. What were you going to say? Secretary Riley wants to say something. Talk to him about our summer program, Dick.

[*Secretary Riley discussed Read Write Now, a summer program designed to encourage young people to read and write every day in the summer.*]

Mr. Kittle. Let's move on to the back row.

The President. While she's taking the microphone back there, Senator, let me say one other thing.

Senator Sharpe. You have the floor, sir. [*Laughter*]

The President. There is a lot—and you probably know this—there is a lot of educational research that shows just as some young people learn better when they're exposed to music and the arts, there are some young people whose learning increases exponentially, even if they're not particularly literate at the time, when they begin to write, and they begin to write stories of their own life and stories of how they want to—so it triggers their imagination in a way that nothing else quite can. So I think it's very important that this be taught, even before it's tested.

[*Parent Jim Eschenmann asked what additional measures could be taken to protect students from the harmful areas of the Internet, while guaranteeing full access and protecting freedom of speech.*]

The President. Well, you know, I signed a bill—when I signed the telecommunications bill, which I believe will create hundreds of thousands of jobs in our country along with the agreement we've made to open telecommunication competition in the world to American products and services—I had a provision in there to try to protect against young people being exposed to some of the harmful things that are on the Internet, not just pornography but, as I'm sure a lot of you know because of the events in the news in the last couple of years, there are even instructions on how to build bombs and things like that. There are a lot of things on there that we wouldn't want our children to see.

That provision has been thrown out by a court and is still in the courts, I think. So it may be that what we have to do is try to develop something like the equivalent of what we're developing for you for television, like the V-chip, where it's put in the hands of the parents or the educators. And then if it were in the hands of the educators, the school board could approve certain guidelines.

It's technically more difficult with the Internet. As you know, there are hundreds of new services being added to the Internet every week. It's growing at an explosive capacity, and we're in the process actually of trying to develop an Internet II. But I think that is the answer. Something like the V-chip for televisions. And we're working on it. I think it's a serious potential problem myself.

But let me say it would be a serious potential problem if they were not in the schools. I think putting them in the schools, because the kids are normally under supervision, you have a far less likelihood that the Internet will be abused or that the children will be exposed to something they shouldn't see during the school hours, in all likelihood, than at home. But I do think you need guidelines in both places, and we're doing our best to try to figure out if there's some technological fix we can give you on it.

[*Jeremy Thompson, a national merit scholar finalist from Bridgeport High School, asked if the President thought students should have to pass a national exam to graduate from high school and what would be the minimum levels in English, math, and science.*]

The President. Well, New York, for many years, has had a Regents exam that you actually had to pass to get a full-fledged high school diploma. And I believe that Louisiana, several years ago, adopted an 11th grade exam that you had to pass to go into high school. When I was Governor of our State, we passed a requirement that you had to pass an exam in the eighth grade to be promoted to high school.

I basically believe that it would be a good thing if you had a standard—an exam like this, not one you have to make a certain score on but one you have to show certain competence on, to move to different levels of education. If one were being given in high school, I would like to see it be given in the 11th grade so it could be given again in the summer so young people can go on to their senior year. Or if it were a condition of a diploma, it should be given very early so it can be taken at least twice more. Because if you give an exam that you have to make a certain score on or show certain competencies on to get a diploma after you've been put through 11 years of school, I think you ought to be given more than one shot.

But I think that generally, if we can move to standards-based education so that every young person in America can stand up and make the statement about their early education that you just made, then it would be a good thing to have certain benchmarks along the way so you would make sure that if you were sending somebody to that next level, they really could do the work.

Otherwise, you can really, I think, hurt a lot of young people. There are so many young people—there's lots of evidence that a lot of young people have difficulty in high school years because they never got the basic skills they needed in the early years. And they get sort of typed as being inadequate, as if they don't have the intellectual capacity to do it, and the truth is that way over 90 percent of us can do way over 90 percent of what we need to do in any given field of endeavor, given a proper level of preparation, the proper level of support, and a proper level of effort. So I would like to see something like that, but if you did it in the high school before graduation, I think we would have to start it early and give everybody more than one chance to pass.

[Janet Dudley-Eshbach, president of Fairmont State College, indicated that college presidents have difficulty devoting 50 percent of their work-study dollars to the America Reads program and asked if the President would be open to alternatives such as community service learning programs.]

The President. Number one, absolutely; and secondly, let me make it clear what we asked to be done with work-study. We have not asked anybody to devote half of their work-study students to America Reads. What we did do is to say, last year we increased the number of work-study students by 100,000 over the next couple of years, in our budget last year—by 200,000, excuse me. In my new budget, we put another 100,000 in there so that within a matter of 3 years, we'll go from—nationwide from 700,000 work-study students total to a million. What we really were shooting for is to get 100,000 of the next 300,000 into reading tutoring. We were urging the colleges, if they could, to, in effect, give up that number of hours of students working on campus to work in reading.

So we're not trying to get anybody to give up half their work-study students. And so you could more easily calibrate kind of what your share was, if you wanted to participate, but there is no mandate on that.

Secondly, I would love it if you did it that way, because another thing I'm trying to do, that we emphasized at the Summit of Service in Philadelphia with the former Presidents and General Powell and I sponsored at the volunteer summit, is that I hope that every college in America will start giving a credit for community service and will try to channel all of its students into community service. So if you did it that way, I would be elated.

You just have to make sure—let me just say, you just have to make sure, and I'm sure our reading teacher over here would say that you just have to make sure that you've got enough time to give the minimal training to do what needs to be done, and that in this—whatever you have to do to get the credit, they'll be spending enough time with one student or two students or however many to really do the kids some good that they're helping.

But I would love that, because I think every— I'd like to see every college in America follow your lead and give students credit for doing community service.

[Parent Patricia Schaeffer asked how the utilization of technology could ensure access to quality education for all children.]

The President. Well, I can tell you what we're doing. What we are doing is to—let me get my brace out of the way here. Let me tell you what we're doing. We have provided some money in each of the next 5 years in our budget to go to States to try to put, with help we get from the private sector and any money that the States want to put in, to try to make sure that all the schools get covered.

Frankly, the principal beneficiaries of this should be the most rural schools and the poorest inner-city schools, because of a lot of the other schools are going to get computers just in the normal course of events. And the whole program will be a failure if we don't hook it up to all the rural schools.

When we started this, when the Vice President and I started this, we went out to California a couple of years ago and hooked up 20 percent of the classrooms in California in one day. And we got all those high-tech companies in Silicon Valley to do that. And then we went to New Jersey and highlighted what they had done there to turn around a district that was in trouble.

My whole idea was that this would make it possible, if we did it right, for the first time in the history of the country for kids in the poorest urban districts and the most remote rural districts to have access to the same information in the same way in the same time as the students in the wealthiest public and private schools in America. I mean, if we do this right, it could revolutionize access to learning.

So I think you've got to get the computers out there, but secondly, we have to make sure the teachers are trained, and third, we have to make sure that the software is good.

So the answer to your question is, my goal is going to be to see that—every State is going to have to have a plan, and that's how we put the money out.

Go ahead.

[Secretary Riley noted the administration's support of the Federal Communications Commission decision to approve a discounted Internet rate for schools in low-income areas.]

The President. You understand what he's talking about? The poorest schools can have—we'll make it as close to free as we can to hook on to the Internet, which will make a big difference, because a lot of our schools were worried about getting the equipment, the software, and everything else and just not being able to afford to stay hooked up. But the E-rate that the Federal Communications Commission approved will be a 90 percent discount for the poorest schools in the country and an average 60 percent discount. So that should mean that everybody out in the hills and hollows of north Arkansas and West Virginia should be able to afford to keep wired up.

[Pina Price, owner of a tax business, mentioned the President's plan to give parents a tax credit for the cost of their children's college tuition.]

The President. That's right.

[Ms. Price asked if it was going to happen and if the President had considered giving new graduates a tax break for student loans.]

The President. The answer to your question is, yes, it is going to happen. And the only question is—we haven't actually passed the actual tax bill through the Congress yet, but we have allocated roughly $35 billion over a 5-year period to provide tax relief against the cost of college education.

And we know that, among other things, there will be a tax credit, that is a dollar-for-dollar reduction off your taxes, for the first 2 years of college for an amount that will be roughly equal to the cost of a typical community college. So you can take that just off your taxes as a tax credit. Because our goal is to try to make 2 years of education after high school as universal as a high school diploma is today.

If you look at—the last census figures we have in 1990 show that young people who have 2 years of—younger workers, now, it's not the same for older workers—but younger workers who have 2 years of education or more after high school tend to get jobs with rising incomes. Young people who have less than 2 years of education after high school tend to get jobs with stagnant incomes. Young kids who are high school dropouts tend to get jobs with declining incomes. So it would be a tax credit.

In addition to that, there will be a tax deduction from your taxable income for the cost of any tuition after high school, not just the first 2 years, any tuition—the second 2 years, postgraduate, vocational, any tuition after high school.

Now, beyond that, what we tried to do to help young people when they come out is for the schools that are in the Department of Education's direct college loan program, young people have the option of choosing to pay back their loans—they have big loans—either on a regular repayment schedule, which would be hard for them, particularly if they have become school teachers or police officers or nurses or something else where they're not making a lot of money. They have the option of paying that back as a percentage of their income, which lifts a huge burden off of them in the early years. So we've tried to do that. But the main focus of our efforts in this tax bill will be the tax credit and the tax deduction. But the details of it are still somewhat open because, obviously, Congress hasn't acted. And Secretary Riley and I talked about it on the way up here today, what we could do that would do the most good for the largest number of people.

[Parent Katherine Folio asked what the President planned to do for the gifted student programs, under the new education program.]

The President. Support them. You want to talk any more about that, Secretary Riley? Support them. I think they should be supported.

[*Secretary Riley stated that the goal of the standards process is aimed at educating students in the same way that gifted kids have been taught. He noted that one of the advantages of gifted student programs was to offer advanced placement courses and college credits.*]

The President. The more factually accurate answer to your question is the one Secretary Riley gave. Just about all we do for gifted education is to support advanced placement, and we're going to promote more of that. But philosophically, I strongly support it. I do believe—and let me say when I was Governor of my State, we actually put it into our academic standards that every district had to offer special opportunities for gifted students. And we actually had a funding stream in our education formula for it. So I'm strongly committed to it.

But I think the larger problem in American education is that we've given up on too many of the other students. Because I believe—I'll say again, I believe more than 90 percent of the students are capable of learning way over 90 percent of what they need to know to keep this country in the forefront of the world and keep their opportunities the richest in the world in the 21st century and that what we really need to focus on is lifting our sights so that everybody can stand up and make the speech this young man did when they get out of high school.

I do strongly support gifted programs, but I think as a nation, what we need to do is to say the school districts and the States should fund those gifted programs, we should support nationally advanced placement, but the main thing we ought to do is be lifting the sights of all of our children.

[*Jim Archer, a production manager at Northrup Grumman, asked the President what steps could be taken to help parents and teachers be more open to vocational and technical education.*]

The President. The first thing we should be doing, in my opinion, is asserting that the dividing line between vocational education and academic education in the world of the future is an artificial dividing line. If anybody doubts that, they ought to just take a random tour of factories in America today and see how many factory workers there are running very complex machines with computer programs and a thousand other examples that you well know.

I can only tell you what we have tried to do and what I think we should do. The reason I pushed the development of this school-to-work program when I became President is that I had seen the same sort of thing you were talking about, on the one hand, and on the other hand, I had seen young people who were in vocational programs very often not getting the level of vocational training they needed because it's much more sophisticated now.

So what we decided we ought to do is to bring the business community, in effect, into the schools and bring the students into the businesses and let young people make up their minds and let young people who chose, in effect, a kind of vocational option to do it in a way that they would know was not closing future doors. If they decided they wanted to go to a 4-year college later on or they decided they wanted to pursue a different career later on, they could do it.

That's the whole idea of school-to-work, is to set up a partnership between the employers in the community and the schools so that the idea of working and learning are—these ideas are compatible, not two different things, and so that if young people decide they want to go into the workplace, they will have an adequate amount of training to be worth enough to you so that you will give them a decent income and they can earn more as they go along and they're not foreclosing the option of taking a different path if, after a few years, they want to go back and go to school.

I think that a lot of the things that I have to do involve, well, do we have the right program, you know, do we have the right kind of incentives to go to college? Well, a lot of it is just making sure we're thinking right about this, because most of the decisions made every day by Americans are not made by anybody in Government, they're made by all the rest of you. So it's the way we think about these problems very often that determines whether we accomplish them.

And if you look at the level of work being done at Northrup Grumman and any number of other companies today, it is a very foolish and outdated idea to have this old-fashioned dividing line between this is academic and respectable and this is vocational and not quite as good. We need to abolish the line, and that's what our school-to-work program has tried to do.

Mr. Kittle. Mr. President, in closing, would you like to go back to that sample math question, give us the answer, and explain how the United States students are compared to students in other countries?

The President. I think that means we're out of time. [*Laughter*]

Let me tell you what we always do at these town meetings. I love these. I have not done one in a couple years, but if any of you have questions that you would like to have answered, if you will provide them to the superintendent here, he'll load them all up, send them to me, and I'll write you back, because I think if you come here with a question, you're entitled to get an answer. I wish we had more time.

But let's do the question, let's go back to this. Here's the eighth grade question, okay. If the car has a fuel tank that holds 15 gallons, and it uses 5 gallons every 100 miles, and it goes 250 miles, obviously it uses 12½ gallons of fuel and there is 2½ gallons left, and that was question A.

But here is the stunning thing. Let's look at the results. Let's go to the next slide. Only 34 percent of American eighth graders got that question right. Fifty percent of Korean eighth graders got it right. Seventy percent of eighth graders in Singapore got it right. So if you lengthen the school year, maybe you should work on specific math skills.

This has nothing to do with IQ. Nearly 100 percent of all the brains in the world will process this problem. Do not worry about whether we can do this. This is not an issue of whether we can achieve this level of excellence. We can easily do this. We just haven't.

And when we deprive our children of the capacity to do this, then there are all kinds of other processes that they can't absorb, and it blunts their capacity to learn later. So I want to see that number up at about 90, and the only way to do it is to try and to test it. And we can do it.

Thank you very much.

NOTE: The President spoke at 1:12 p.m. in the gymnasium at Robert C. Byrd High School. In his remarks, he referred to Mary Helen Shields, senior at Robert C. Byrd High School, who introduced the President; Robert Kittle, superintendent, Harrison County schools; Gov. Cecil H. Underwood of West Virginia, and his wife, Hovah; Gaston Caperton, former West Virginia Governor; and Mayor Robert T. Flynn of Clarksburg.

Remarks to High School Students in Clarksburg
May 22, 1997

The President. Thank you very much. Well, did you see it?

Audience members. Yes!

The President. On the screen and the Internet?

Audience members. Yes!

The President. Well, you may have had the better deal, because it's cooler in here. [*Laughter*] Let me thank Danny Phares for his introduction. And I want to say I'm glad to be here with Governor Underwood and with Secretary of Education Dick Riley and with Cleo Mathews, the president of the State board of education. And you may have heard me say that her daughter, Sylvia, who is here today, is my Deputy Chief of Staff in the White House and she graduated from high school in Hinton, West Virginia.

So I think that's a pretty good statement of West Virginia's education quality. And I have to tell you, I did not have an auditorium this nice when I was in high school. I love this school. Congratulations on having a beautiful, beautiful school.

You heard the townhall meeting—I'm just going to come down here and shake hands with anybody who wants to come down and say hello. But I just want to say one thing to all of you. We are about to enter not only a new century but a new millennium, literally a time which happens once every thousand years. By coincidence, you are also entering a period in our history which will be very different from the past, different in the way people work, different in the way people learn, different in the way people relate to each other. And it can be the greatest moment of human promise in all history. It may be, if we do everything as we should, that young people your age and those coming along behind you will have more opportunities to live their dreams than any group of people who ever lived.

But none of this will happen unless we continue to put top priority on education, continue to believe that all young people can learn, and continue to be dedicated to the proposition that everybody should have a maximum opportunity to learn as much as possible. So when you leave this high school, I hope you will keep that conviction with you for the rest of your lives and be dedicated to the proposition that not only you but all the young people coming behind you should have those opportunities.

Thank you. God bless you, and good luck.

NOTE: The President spoke at 2:50 p.m. in the theater at Robert C. Byrd High School. In his remarks, he referred to Danny Phares, student body president.

Remarks to the Clarksburg Area Community in Bridgeport, West Virginia
May 22, 1997

Thank you, West Virginia. Thank you for coming out today. It's wonderful; thank you. I want to thank Governor Underwood and my former colleague and good friend Governor Caperton, Mayor Furbee, Mayor Flynn, Secretary of State Hechler, Attorney General McGraw, Treasurer Perdue, Auditor Gainer, your Agriculture Secretary Douglass, and to the speaker of the house, the president of the senate, the majority leader of the senate, and all of the people who are here who made my stay in West Virginia so wonderful today.

I have to tell you, I have had a terrific time. The townhall meeting on education we had at Robert Byrd High School was a wonderful testament to the dedication to education and excellence and opportunity for every child of the people of West Virginia. And I hope all of you get a chance to see the program and that you're as proud of the people from your State as I was today when we did it. It was an amazing event, and we thank you.

I'd also like to thank Mary Frances Smith for singing the national anthem. I thank the ROTC unit and the band from Robert Byrd High School, thank you; the Lincoln High School Young Professionals; and all the others who came here today to make this rally a success.

Ladies and gentlemen, I will be very brief. I want to take a little time to get out here and shake a few more hands. But I came here today with a simple message. First, I want to thank the people of West Virginia for twice placing their confidence in me in giving me the chance to serve as President of the United States.

Second, I want to say that our country is moving in the right direction. And we can be proud of that, but we have more to do. If you compare where we are now to where we were 4 years ago, we have a record 12 million new jobs and, nationally, the lowest unemployment rate in 24 years, the lowest inflation. rate in 30 years, and the biggest decline in inequality among working Americans in more than 30 years. I'm proud of that, and you should be too.

The crime rate has been going down every year. The welfare rolls have dropped by the largest amount in 50 years in the last 4 years. We are moving in the right direction, and we're coming together as a country. But you and I know that in the world we're moving into, where information travels around the world in the flash of a second, where the borders of countries no longer can protect us from common problems like terrorism and weapons of mass destruction and no longer can keep us from opportunities unimagined just a few years ago—we know that if West Virginia, if every little hill and hollow in this State and every child growing up in this State is going to have an opportunity to make the most of the 21st century, a new century in a whole new millennium, it will depend more than anything else on whether we can give every child in West Virginia a world class education, on whether every 8-year-old can read well, every 12-year-old can log on to the Internet, every 18-year-old, without regard to their family's income, who's willing to work for it, can go on to college, every single one of them who wants to go. It will depend upon whether every adult can keep on learning for a lifetime.

These are the things that are driving my administration in these 4 years. We are about to conclude debate in the Senate today on a balanced budget amendment that will give our country the first balanced budget we've had since the 1960's. And it's high time, and I'm proud of it. But I want to say to you that the deficit has already been cut by more than 75 percent, thanks to the work that Senator Byrd and Senator Rockefeller, Congressman Mollohan and Congressman Rahall did back in 1993. Now, we're going to finish the job, and we're also going to increase our investment in education, even as we cut the deficit, because we want to fix the deficit today but fix the future of the young people of this country and this State for tomorrow.

So let me say, today I was deeply touched—the drive from here to the high school—to see all the people along the way. I stopped a couple of times to say hello to the children coming back and it made us a little late and I hope you'll forgive us. But there were thousands of people along the way, all of you here—it makes me very happy personally, but more than that, as your President, it makes me happy to see you supporting the future of this country and the future of our children.

So I ask you this. You gave me a chance to serve again; now let's get behind a common goal: to raise our standards to the highest in the world in education and to believe that every one of our children can learn and to commit ourselves to a future more brilliant than our glorious past and to know that the way we're going to do it is one child at a time. I'll do my part. You do yours, and we'll all be celebrating when 2000 rolls around.

God bless you, and thank you all.

NOTE: The President spoke at 4:05 p.m. at Benedum Airport. In his remarks, he referred to Gaston Caperton, former West Virginia Governor; Mayor Carl E. Furbee of Bridgeport; Mayor Robert T. Flynn of Clarksburg; West Virginia Secretary of State Ken Hechler; State Attorney General Darrell McGraw, Jr.; State Treasurer John Perdue; State Auditor Glen Gainer III; State Agriculture Secretary Gus Douglass; Speaker of the House of Delegates Robert Kiss; State Senate President Earl Ray Tomblin; State Senate Majority Leader H. Truman Chafin; and Mary Frances Smith, who sang the national anthem.

Statement on Supplemental Emergency Legislation for Disaster Assistance
May 22, 1997

I urge the Congress not to leave for Memorial Day recess without sending me a clean emergency supplemental bill that provides the disaster assistance upon which hundreds of thousands of Americans are depending. The people of 33 States are waiting for the Congress to act. In recent weeks, we have witnessed extraordinary destruction in the Dakotas and Minnesota matched only by the courage with which residents of these States have faced their plight. The Congress owes it to them to pass a clean bill and send it to me for my signature.

The President's Radio Address
May 24, 1997

Good morning. This past week, the House and the Senate voted by overwhelming bipartisan majorities to endorse an historic, bipartisan agreement to balance the Federal budget by

2002. This agreement brings us closer to putting our fiscal house in order, and it represents a huge downpayment toward America's future prosperity.

Already, our economy is the envy of the world. In the last 4 years, it's created 12 million new jobs. We've had the highest economic growth in a decade, the lowest unemployment in 24 years, the lowest inflation in 30 years, the largest decline in income inequality since the 1960's. The deficit has been cut already by 77 percent, thanks to the historic 1993 budget and economic package passed by the Congress at that time.

And now, with a balanced budget agreement, our economy can continue to thrive. We'll balance our books while we protect Medicare and Medicaid, invest in education and environmental protection, and give our people a tax cut. It's a balanced budget that's in balance with our values. Now I urge all Members of Congress of both parties to take the next step, to finish the job and write this agreement into law.

This is a proud moment. Our balanced budget agreement shows what we can accomplish when we work together, across party lines, in the interest of the American people. This is how our Government should work.

But today I have to talk about an example of how it should not work and how it's not working. Our Government is not working for our citizens in the Dakotas and Minnesota, who are still waiting for the Congress to act so that they can begin the long road back from the floods that destroyed their homes and devastated their lives.

Tens of thousands of people suffered losses in these floods. Now they're trying to reclaim their lives and their communities. But they can't do it alone. Some have depended on the kindness of neighbors they didn't even know. The town of Thompson, North Dakota, doubled its population when residents opened their homes and their churches and took in 1,000 people from flooded Grand Forks, 11 miles away. Private citizens became angels, volunteering and donating everything from essential supplies to evening dresses, so that a flooded high school could still have its prom. One woman quietly donated millions of dollars for distribution to victims.

All that is welcome help. But recovering from a large natural disaster takes more; it takes the combined resources of our Nation. That was the only way back after the earthquakes and fires in California, the flooding in the Mississippi Valley and the Pacific Northwest, the tornadoes in the South, the hurricanes in Florida. Right now, people in 33 States need some degree of disaster assistance. Just imagine being in their shoes, having your life's work swept away, your home gone, often in an instant. Think of your concern for your family and your home. That's why we need quick and effective governmental action, from rescue efforts by the National Guard to financial and other assistance from our Federal agencies. They've all done well by our people, and I am especially proud of the work of our Federal Emergency Management Agency, FEMA, and its Director, James Lee Witt. Now FEMA is a model for responding to disasters. When I took office, it was often criticized; now I think it's the most often complimented Federal agency.

After I visited North Dakota with the congressional delegation, including the Senators from North Dakota, Kent Conrad and Byron Dorgan, who join me here today, and saw the impact of the floods last month, I asked James Lee Witt to chair a task force of our Federal agencies and come up with a plan for the region's long-term recovery. Now we have that plan to deliver help quickly while we get maximum results for every Federal dollar spent.

But to get that long-term relief to our people, we must have action from Congress. I asked congressional leaders for just that, in an emergency supplemental spending bill, the kind that we have had before when we had disasters. Many Members, led by lawmakers from the flooded States, worked hard to get a bill to me, but I'm sorry to say, some Members of the majority tried to use this important bill for different purposes. And without taking action, Congress left town, and our people were left in the lurch.

Hundreds of thousands of our citizens are depending on this aid so they can get on with their lives. Even without action from the Congress, we're doing all we can to get immediate help to the victims. FEMA is using all the resources and authority it has to help with food, shelter, and emergency services. But these funds are limited. They will eventually run out, and they won't start the job of long-term recovery.

Unless Congress approves these disaster relief funds, the victims cannot begin their long-term recovery; they can't rebuild homes and businesses; farmers can't dig out their fields to plant crops. These people are in dire need, and Congress has failed to act for them. That is unconscionable. It flies in the face of the spirit of bipartisan cooperation we saw in our budget negotiations, and it's not how we treated other Americans when they were in similar dire straits over the last 4 years.

In North Dakota, I saw not only the devastation of the floods, I saw the determination of the people, proud people doing their level-best to survive and get on with their lives. They don't expect free rides or handouts, but they do have a right to expect us to do the right thing by them, as we have by their fellow Americans when they were down and out.

The wrath of nature can be random, swift, and unforgiving. That's where human nature must provide a balance. We should act out of compassion, as many Americans have, to help the victims. And in Government, we must act because that is our duty as Americans. We cannot leave the victims without the help they need and deserve. We have to act.

I urge Congress to do its part and to do it quickly. Disaster doesn't take a holiday. Let's work together to bring relief to people who need it—now.

In closing, I want to wish you all a happy Memorial Day weekend. Drive safely, drive slowly, and buckle up.

Thanks for listening.

NOTE: The address was recorded at 7:08 p.m. on May 23 in the Roosevelt Room at the White House for broadcast at 10:06 a.m. on May 24.

Remarks at a Memorial Day Ceremony in Arlington, Virginia
May 26, 1997

Thank you very much. General Foley, Chaplain Schwartzman, Mr. Metzler, to the members of the Cabinet, General Shalikashvili and the leaders of our Armed Forces, to Members of Congress, and especially to the members of the Armed Forces who are here, the leaders of our veterans organizations, all of you who are veterans and your families, and all of you who are family members of those who have given their lives in the service of our country.

My fellow Americans, we gather here today, as we do faithfully every year, to pay tribute to our country men and women who fell in the line of duty, who gave their lives to preserve the liberties upon which our Nation was founded and which we have managed to carry forward for more than 200 years now. All across America, our grateful Nation comes together today to honor these men and women, some celebrated, others quite unknown, each a patriot and a hero.

For many of our schoolchildren who have known no war, today may seem to be little more than a day off from school or a welcome start to the summer. But on this day, and all that we pause to remember, there are essential lessons for the young and, indeed, for all the rest of us as well: Appreciate the blessings of freedom; recognize the power and virtue of sacrifice; respect those who gave everything on behalf of our common good.

This day reminds us of what we can achieve when we pull together as one nation, respecting each other with all of our myriad differences, but coming together, we can fight any battle and face any challenge.

It reminds us of our duty to honor not only those we have lost in freedom's cause but also, through attention and care, the service men and women who came back home and are now our veterans, as well as the families of those for whom there tragically has never been a final accounting.

It reminds us of our obligation to take care of those who have taken care of us and those who take care of us today. That means ensuring that our men and women in uniform have the best training and equipment and preparation possible to do their jobs for freedom, because even in times of peace, we must remain vigilant in a very new and still uncertain world.

And above all, it reminds us of America's responsibility to remain the world's leading force for peace and prosperity and freedom as we enter the 21st century, so that future generations of young Americans who wear our uniform will never have to endure the losses in battles that our predecessors did in the 20th century.

Behind me, just a few yards from where we gather today, lies the grave of General George Marshall, an heroic soldier in war and a visionary statesman for peace after the Second World War. He built the armies that enabled freedom to triumph over tyranny in World War II. And after the war, along with President Truman, Senator Arthur Vandenberg, and others, he inspired America to make the investments and forge the institutions that built the peace, reached out to former adversaries, spread democracy and prosperity, and ultimately won the cold war. General George Marshall was the very first full-time soldier ever to win the Nobel Prize for Peace. A half-century ago, he knew that in order to be strong at home and safe at home, we had to lead the world to a more secure and better place.

Now, at the end of the cold war, when there appears to be no looming threat on the horizon, we must rise to Marshall's challenge in our day. We must remember the lessons of those who gave their lives in World War II and those who worked so hard to make sure that we would prevail in the cold war and not have to go back to war again. We must create the institutions and the understandings that will advance the security and prosperity of the American people for the next 50 years.

This great endeavor must begin in Europe. Twice in this century—indeed, twice within a period of a few decades—Americans went over there and gave their lives in defense of liberty. Many more stood sentry with our European allies through the long night of the cold war. Today, our generation has been given a precious chance to redeem that sacrifice and service, to build an undivided, democratic European Continent at peace for the very first time in history.

Over the course of this week, beginning this evening, I will travel to Europe to advance this goal. Tomorrow in Paris, President Yeltsin of Russia, my fellow NATO leaders, and I will join an historic signing of the Founding Act of the NATO-Russia partnership, opening a new era of cooperation in Europe to bridge the historic divisions there. Then I will have the great honor to represent you in The Netherlands, joining with leaders from all over Europe to celebrate the 50th anniversary of the Marshall plan, the

plan that helped Europe to recover its prosperity and secure its liberty. I will challenge Europe's people to work together with America to complete the work that General Marshall's generation began, extending the reach of security and prosperity to the new democracies in Europe that once were on the other side in the cold war. Finally, I will have a chance to meet with the new Prime Minister of Great Britain to celebrate our unique partnership with our old and close ally.

My fellow Americans, if you look at all the gravestones here today, you will see that they have not died in vain, when you see what we enjoy today and that we stand at the pinnacle of our power, our success, and our influence as a nation. But that means we stand at the pinnacle of our responsibility.

At the end of World War II, General Marshall could make that case to America. We fought a bloody war because we did not assume that responsibility at the end of World War I. Today it is perhaps more difficult because we feel no impending threat as we did from the Communist forces in the cold war.

But I ask you when you leave this place today to ask yourself, as an American, what can I do to honor the sacrifices of those we honor here today? For what did George Marshall dedicate his life? For what did these people fight and die? And how can we make sure that we have a new century in which we do not repeat the mistakes of the last one?

I will say, the only way that can happen is if America refuses to walk away from the world and its present challenges. We must learn the lessons General Marshall and his generation left us. Their sacrifice and their spirit call upon us to seize this moment, to shape the peace of the present for future generations, to turn the hope we share into a history we can all be proud of.

And so on this day when we remember those who gave everything for our Nation and its freedom, let us resolve to honor them by renewing our commitment, on the edge of a new century and a new era, to lead the world toward greater peace and security, freedom and prosperity. In doing that, we will make Americans safer. We will allow our men and women in uniform to stand sentinel for our freedom with less risk to their lives.

May God always bless the American heroes we honor today. May He bless those fallen and those who still stand at the ready. May He always bless the United States, and may He always give us the wisdom to do what is right for tomorrow.

Thank you, and God bless you all.

NOTE: The President spoke at 11:30 a.m. in the Amphitheater at Arlington National Cemetery. In his remarks, he referred to Col. Joel R. Schwartzman, USAF, Chief of Chaplains, Bolling Air Force Base; John Metzler, Superintendent, Arlington National Cemetery; President Boris Yeltsin of Russia; and Prime Minister Tony Blair of the United Kingdom.

Remarks at the Signing Ceremony for the NATO-Russia Founding Act in Paris, France
May 27, 1997

President Yeltsin gave me this cane; now he's giving it to me twice. [*Laughter*]

Ladies and gentlemen, on this beautiful spring day in Paris, in the twilight of the 20th century, we look toward a new century with a new Russia and a new NATO, working together in a new Europe of unlimited possibility. The NATO-Russia Founding Act we have just signed joins a great nation and history's most successful alliance in common cause for a long-sought but never before realized goal: a peaceful, democratic, undivided Europe.

The United States feels a great deal of gratitude today. The world my predecessors dreamed of and worked for for 50 years is finally within reach. I want to thank President Chirac for his strong leadership in making this day possible and for hosting us. I thank President Yeltsin for his courage and vision, for his unbelievable capacity to imagine a future that is different from the past that imprisoned us. I thank his Foreign Minister, Mr. Primakov, for his negotiations in good faith to make this day possible. I especially thank Secretary General Solana for his brilliant and persistent and always good-natured efforts that made this founding act a reality. I thank my fellow leaders of the North Atlantic Treaty Organization and especially our senior leader, Chancellor Kohl, who has worked longer and paid a higher price for the dream of a united Europe than any other leader.

For all of us, this is a great day. From now on, NATO and Russia will consult and coordinate and work together. Where we all agree, we will act jointly, as we are in Bosnia where a Russian brigade serves side by side with NATO troops, giving the Bosnian people a chance to build a lasting peace. Deepening our partnership today will make all of us stronger and more secure.

The historic change in the relationship between NATO and Russia grows out of a fundamental change in how we think about each other and our future. NATO's member states recognize that the Russian people are building a new Russia, defining their greatness in terms of the future as much as the past. Russia's transition to democracy and open markets is as difficult as it is dramatic. And its steadfast commitment to freedom and reform has earned the world's admiration.

In turn, we are building a new NATO. It will remain the strongest alliance in history, with smaller, more flexible forces, prepared to provide for our defense but also trained for peacekeeping. It will work closely with other nations that share our hopes and values and interests through the Partnership For Peace. It will be an alliance directed no longer against a hostile bloc of nations but instead designed to advance the security of every democracy in Europe, NATO's old members, new members, and nonmembers alike.

I know that some still see NATO through the prism of the cold war and that especially in NATO's decision to open its doors to Central Europe's new democracies, they see a Europe still divided, only differently divided. But I ask them to look again, for this new NATO will work with Russia, not against it. And by reducing rivalry and fear, by strengthening peace and cooperation, by facing common threats to the security of all democracies, NATO will promote greater stability in all of Europe, including Russia. And in turn, that will increase the security of Europe's North American partners—the United States and Canada—as well.

We establish this partnership because we are determined to create a future in which European security is not a zero-sum game, where NATO's gain is Russia's loss and Russia's strength is our alliance's weakness. That is old thinking; these are new times. Together, we must build a new Europe in which every nation is free and every free nation joins in strengthening the peace and stability for all.

Half a century ago, on a continent darkened by the shadow of evil, brave men and women in Russia and the world's free nations fought a common enemy with uncommon valor. Their partnership, forged in battle, strengthened by sacrifice, cemented by blood, gave hope to millions in the West and in Russia that the grand alliance would be extended in peace. But in victory's afterglow, the freedom the Russian people deserved was denied them. The dream of

peace gave way to the hard reality of cold war, and our predecessors lost an opportunity to shape a new Europe, whole and free.

Now we have another chance. Russia has opened itself to freedom. The veil of hostility between East and West has lifted. Together we see a future of partnership too long delayed that must no longer be denied. The founding act we signed captures the promise of this remarkable moment. Now we must implement it in good faith, so that future generations will live in a new time that escapes the 20th century's darkest moments and fulfills its most brilliant possibilities.

Thank you very much.

NOTE: The President spoke at 10:20 a.m. at the Elysee Palace. In his remarks, he referred to President Boris Yeltsin and Minister of Foreign Affairs Yevgeniy Primakov of Russia; President Jacques Chirac of France; NATO Secretary General Javier Solana; and Chancellor Helmut Kohl of Germany.

Statement on the Resignation of Reed E. Hundt as Chairman of the Federal Communications Commission
May 27, 1997

It was with regret that I learned today that Reed Hundt, Chairman of the Federal Communications Commission, intends to leave before the end of his term, upon appointment of his successor.

Chairman Hundt has been a strong and visionary leader of the FCC during this historic period in telecommunications policy. His steadfast commitment to the public interest and to bringing the benefits of competition to consumers is evident in his many accomplishments during his tenure, including the successful launching of spectrum auctions and the Commission's ontime implementation of the Telecommunications Act of 1996. His expertise and counsel were indispensable in bringing home this year's

World Trade Organization agreement on telecommunications, which will open markets abroad as never before.

Perhaps most importantly, Chairman Hundt helped make the FCC an advocate for our children. He reinvigorated children's broadcasting, and he took pathbreaking steps to ensure that every classroom and library in America will be linked to the information superhighway.

Chairman Hundt's leadership has opened opportunity to businesses here and abroad, while ensuring that all Americans share in the benefits of the telecommunications revolution. The Vice President and I are sorry to see him go and extend to him thanks on behalf of the American people for his excellent service.

Statement on the National Economy
May 27, 1997

Today's Conference Board release, along with the University of Michigan's release earlier this month, indicate more good news on the economy. Today's report shows that Americans are more confident about their current and future economic conditions than they have been in 28 years. With consumer confidence, unemployment, and inflation the best they've been in decades, America's economy is more than ever the envy of the world.

Unemployment is at its lowest level in 24 years, economic growth is the highest it has been in a decade, and inflation is the lowest since John F. Kennedy was President. We have already cut the deficit 77 percent since 1992, helping spark this remarkable period of strong growth and low inflation. The bipartisan budget agreement—which will balance the budget for the first time since 1969—will help to continue this solid economic performance.

The President's News Conference With European Union Leaders in The Hague, The Netherlands
May 28, 1997

Prime Minister Kok. Ladies and gentlemen, I'm very glad to say that President Clinton and President Santer and I have had very productive and fruitful discussions this morning in the framework of our semiannual EU–U.S. summit on the new transatlantic agenda, including the transatlantic marketplace and a wide range of other issues. We have been making very good progress in implementing the new transatlantic agenda since its adoption, now 1½ years ago.

We achieved a number of concrete results. I'll mention a few of them. This morning an agreement will be signed on the control on chemical precursors for drugs. This means an important step towards better controlling substances that are used for the production of synthetic drugs. We decided to step up our operation in the fight against drug trafficking in the Caribbean. This included joint studies on maritime cooperation, exchange of information and equipment, and training of police and judicial authorities.

Negotiations have been concluded for the EU to join the U.S., Japan, and South Korea in the Korean Peninsula Energy Development Organization, KEDO, underlining our global responsibilities and shared commitment to strengthen nonproliferation efforts.

In the context of the transatlantic marketplace, we will sign an agreement on customs cooperation that will facilitate trade and contrib-

ute to the fight against fraud and corruption. We also reached agreement on veterinary inspections, thus preventing a trade conflict that might otherwise have arisen on the export of meat products. And furthermore, we are very close to a common understanding with regard to the mutual recognition of norms and standards of products, the so-called mutual recognition agreements. I hope that we will be able to tie up these discussions in a few days' time.

We have implemented the small-business initiative which bridges European and American small- and medium-sized enterprises by means of linking better business and organizing joint events. We agreed on an awards program to encourage democracy in civil society across the Continent of Europe. And apart from these agreements, we discussed a number of specific foreign policy issues.

We looked back briefly on our historic meeting in Paris yesterday where we signed the NATO-Russia Founding Act, and we looked at some important meetings ahead of us, firstly, the G–7 meeting—or G–8—in Denver, the special session of the U.N. General Assembly on the environment in New York, and the NATO summit in Madrid, which is 2 months from now. And I informed President Clinton yesterday already about the main elements of the upcoming European summit in Amsterdam.

We have had a brief meeting with representatives of the Transatlantic Business Dialogue. They presented us with an interim report that provides us with useful building blocks and inspiration to explore further possibilities of liberalizing trade and investment flows.

In my view, ladies and gentlemen, this summit not only signifies a strong reconfirmation of the close ties between the United States and the European Union, it also provides a new impetus to our relationship both economically and politically. There is a lot that binds us and little that divides us. President Clinton has been very clear in reconfirming the strong American bonds with Europe.

This morning we have carried forward our transatlantic partnership, a partnership that we will celebrate this afternoon during the commemoration of the 50th anniversary of the Marshall plan. It has been very inspiring, indeed, to find once again that we share common agendas, common values, and common goals in preparing the international community for the 21st century.

So I am grateful, after the session we had, both for the substantial progress we have been making and for the atmosphere, the climate of cooperation between the United States and the European Union, because we know sometimes there are some minor or major problems we have to solve, but the positive agenda—the positive agenda—in order to shape the future together in the benefit of our children and grandchildren, is of key importance for the two of us. So I'm grateful to President Clinton for his presence, his contribution, and this is the end of my presentation.

Thank you very much.

President Clinton. Thank you very much, Prime Minister. Let me begin by thanking you and the people of The Netherlands for the warm welcome you have given to Hillary, to me, to our entire delegation, including the Secretary of State, Secretary of Commerce, three Members of the United States Congress who are with me and are sitting there on the front row, Senator Smith and Congresswoman Pelosi and Congressman McHugh. We are all delighted to be here.

And I think it is very fitting that our summit is taking place in The Netherlands as we commemorate the 50th anniversary of the Marshall plan. In many ways, The Netherlands sets the model for helping fellow nations secure freedom and prosperity.

Two hundred years ago, the Dutch extended loans that saved the young United States from bankruptcy. By the end of that decade, 200 years ago, fully half our national debt was owed to you. [*Laughter*] I trust we have paid it since then. [*Laughter*] In our century, the United States was proud to return the gesture. The Marshall plan, about which I'll have more to say later today, helped to lay the foundation for an Atlantic community of democracies. It planted the seeds of institutions that reconciled enemies and brought Western Europe together, from NATO to the OECD to the European Union, today one of our most valued partners.

The Netherlands, as current president of the European Union, once again is leading the way as the EU carries forward its historic mission: building the union between its members and reaching out to expand to Central and Eastern Europe. A more prosperous, a more united Europe will not only be a stronger Europe, it will be a stronger partner for the United States in the 21st century.

Through our work here, we have taken another step on the path that began with General Marshall's vision, working with the people of Bosnia to help peace take root, recognizing that we must do more to speed up the pace of economic reconstruction, increase funding for police training and monitors, work to ensure successful municipal elections and to ensure the ultimate effectiveness of the War Crimes Tribunal located here in your nation, in this city. The Dayton agreement was a good one; we have to make sure that it works.

Under our new transatlantic agenda, the newest offspring of the Marshall spirit, which was created 18 months ago in Madrid, we're cooperating on a broad range of common challenges, bringing down trade barriers, fighting international crime and terrorism and nuclear proliferation and drug trafficking. Today we agreed to intensify our cooperation against a new problem that we face, the increasing practice of trafficking in women, which re-creates, in an entirely different context, almost a new kind of modern day slavery. And we intend to do what we can to stop it.

I'm pleased that we're advancing on our goal of reducing trade barriers. The Prime Minister has already commented, but I'd like to point out that just in the last 6 months we have completed agreements on information technologies and telecommunications that lower trade barriers on over $1 trillion in goods and services in a way that will cut the costs of living, increase the productivity of business, and create huge numbers of new, good-paying jobs in both Europe and the United States.

We've made progress on virtually all the outstanding issues, in difficult negotiations, on mutual recognition of each other's standards and testing requirements. This is very important, and I can't add to what the Prime Minister has said. We feel we have a breakthrough, and we hope it will lead to an agreement in the next few days. That would abolish redundant testing and inspection on a broad range of products worth $40 billion in annual trade.

I thank the European Union for the work we have done today to strengthen our fights to keep illegal drugs out of our neighborhoods by agreeing to control the chemicals used to make a broad range of these drugs. This is a terribly important agreement.

And we've also agreed to increase our customs cooperation to fight fraud, to streamline trade. And again, Mr. Prime Minister and President Santer, let me thank you for the decision by the EU to join in the Korean Peninsula Energy Development Organization. This will help us to make good on our commitment to freeze and eventually to dismantle North Korea's dangerous nuclear program.

Today we're also announcing a joint U.S.–EU awards program for communities, individuals, and nongovernmental organizations that promote grassroots democracy in Central and Eastern Europe. This will help to deepen the commitment to freedom as we work to build an undivided continent.

Finally, let me say the United States is grateful to the leaders of the European Union for making this progress possible, for building on the legacy that General Marshall began, for strengthening our partnership for democracy and prosperity as we confront the challenges of the 21st century.

Thank you very much.

President Santer. Prime Minister, Mr. President, ladies and gentlemen, I am happy to note that today's meeting has seen further progress in cementing the relationship between the European Union and the United States. Our trade and investment partnership is the largest in the world. Our stock of investment in each other's markets stands at $650 billion. Annual two-way trade in goods and services between us counts for some $400 billion. This is a formidable asset, and we are determined to develop it even further.

We have made good progress since our last meeting in December. We have worked successfully together in the WTO to ensure the conclusion of two major multilateral agreements, the information technology and basic telecommunications agreements. We have together liberalized trade in goods and services worth approximately $1 trillion dollars. In the same spirit of joint leadership, we should now work towards a successful conclusion of a financial services agreement by the agreed deadline.

We shall be signing two important agreements this morning. The chemical precursor agreement is designed to curb the diversion of chemicals used in the manufacture of illicit drugs. The customs cooperation agreement will facilitate trade and help combat fraud. We have also noted good progress in our negotiations on a mutual recognition agreement which will bring enormous trade benefits to both sides. We hope to be able, as the President expressed also, to conclude the agreement within the next few days.

These are concrete examples of what we set out to achieve when we agreed on our new transatlantic agenda in December 1995. But the picture of our enhanced cooperation and joint action is even richer. Whether on foreign policy issues, multilateral trade, ties in many areas, social, scientific, educational, cultural, as well as in global challenges like terrorism, we are determined to make further progress under each of those, and we will take stock at our next summit at the end of the year.

Our meeting has taken place against the background of commemorations which I consider to be of great significance. This afternoon we will commemorate the 50th anniversary of the Marshall plan. The United States helped Western Europe to get back on its feet and regenerate after a devastating war. We Europeans have not forgotten this invaluable support given by the United States.

Last month in Rome, we commemorated the start, 40 years ago, of the European Economic Community. The original community of six member states decided in 1957 that they had to help themselves by rooting out war among them and by pledging a closer integration and solidarity. The 6 have become today's European Union of 15, a strong and dynamic partner of the United States. And together, we have on many occasions shown the way forward.

And yesterday in Paris, with the signing of an agreement between NATO and Russia, we have entered a new era of hope, of cooperation, of peace and security. The United States has played a crucial role in achieving this result. The European Union is making its own contribution to the reconstruction of Central and Eastern Europe and the former Soviet Union through massive help, some $160 billion for the period between 1990 and the end of the century, almost twice what was given under the Marshall plan, but its most significant contribution will be the welcoming Central and Eastern European countries as members of the European Union.

I believe that these reminders show the essential importance of the relationship between the European Union and the United States. For each of us and for the world at large, let's not forget that whenever we have to deal with bilateral difficulties, they are inevitable in such a vast relationship. We have solved them in the past; we will in the future.

Thank you.

Single European Currency

Q. A question, if I may, for President Clinton. Mr. President, you've referred in your reference to the 50th anniversary of the Marshall plan, the impetus it gave towards the beginnings of greater European unity. How important, in your view, is the planned move to a single European currency to help achieve that goal, even foreseen 50 years ago, to achieve that goal of a closer European Union?

President Clinton. Well, first of all, the decision to do that and the mechanics of how to do it is a decision that has to be left to the members of the Union. The United States position—let me restate it because I feel it very strongly, and I tried to clarify it as soon as I got elected and assumed office—is that a more integrated, more closely cooperating Europe with fewer barriers to trade, to communications, to travel, to working together is a good thing for Europe and a good thing for the United States and, therefore, a good thing for the world.

How to do that, in what order, and by what steps, I think still should be decisions for the

Europeans to make, and I think it would be, frankly, not appropriate for the United States to go much further than I have gone in this. I think it's clear that I support European integration, and I've wanted to make that clear because we not only are not threatened by it, we are excited by it and want to support it. But beyond that, I think it's up to you to decide how to do it and on what timetable.

New Marshall Plan for Eastern Europe

Q. Mr. President, do you support the initiative of the Dutch Prime Minister for a more or less new Marshall plan for Eastern Europe, and do you see a specific role for the U.S. in this?

President Clinton. Well, we have together seen in the last few years—I believe this is roughly accurate—about $50 billion in various kinds of funds go into the Central and Eastern European nations, mostly through international financial institutions, and nearly that amount now in private investment. And I believe it is very important that we continue this process.

We can't simply say to these countries, "We want you to be for democracy and we want you to have a democracy and we want you to support economic reform, and good luck," because there is an enormous gap between the poorest countries on the Continent and those that aren't, and between their infrastructures and, therefore, their capacity to grow. And I think that's one thing that's easily overlooked. If you compare this time, say, to 50 years ago—and the Prime Minister might want to comment on this—but, yes, Europe was in ruins, but Europe had also been at the pinnacle of the global economy with lots of people who knew how to rebuild economies and lots of people who understood how to put in place the building blocks. That was wiped away from a lot of these countries in Central and Eastern Europe for half a century.

So do I think we need to do more? Yes, I do. And am I prepared to support that? Of course I am. You know, we'd have to get into the details, but basically I think the Prime Minister is wise in trying to make sure that we don't just walk away from these nations with an encouragement toward economic reform and democracy and just assume that everything is going to be all right. We're going to have to continue to be engaged.

Q. A question for President Clinton and for Mr. Kok. Are there already—can we talk about a new Marshall plan for Eastern Europe? Are there already rough lines? Is there any frame? I mean, are we now on a point which goes further than general ideas?

Prime Minister Kok. Well, could I say, perhaps, a few words on this? First of all, we should not underestimate what has been done and what is done nowadays in the multilateral institutions. We have the European Bank for Reconstruction and Development, where not only European countries but also the United States participates. We have the World Bank and IMF activities. We have a lot of EU financial and political and economic activities giving support to the development in the Central and Eastern European economies. So it would be a mistake to think that until now, never has been done and that we just create an idea here. That would be wrong.

But taking the experience of the Marshall plan into account 50 years ago—50 years ago and the period afterwards—we see that perhaps on top of what is already done, new initiatives can be taken also to bring more private investment capital to the development of the Eastern and Central European countries. We are not just for mainly talking about taxpayers' money; we are also talking about bringing private capital in order—for example, to have huge infrastructural projects. Infrastructure connects people.

We see that bringing the new countries in closer to Europe, to the countries of the European Union, it is in their and our benefits to make an effort to organize creativity. And on top of what is done, I think new initiatives should be taken, but it could be a terrible mistake to think that this is only a new idea. I mean, you are already bringing it, to a large extent, into pass.

President Clinton. I would just like to support what the Prime Minister has said. I believe the numbers I'm about to give you are right; if they're wrong, I'll stand corrected. I think in today's dollars, in today's dollars the value of the Marshall plan investments in Europe were about $88 billion. I think that's right. Now, we have seen the international financial institutions commit about $50 billion already to the former Communist countries, plus about $45 billion in private investment.

I think that most of what still needs to be done is to accelerate the pace of private investment. And it's very different in different coun-

tries. If you look at Poland, for example, I think their growth rate must be about the highest in Europe now, and about 9 in 10 of the retail projects in Poland, retail outlets, are already in private hands. Russia has largely privatized huge chunks of its economy.

But what I think we have to do is to work with each country and look at, first of all, what are the laws, have the laws been changed so that we can float private capital into these countries and have them develop; secondly, what kinds of public investments—hopefully, most of them multinational public investments through the multinational institutions—still need to be made before private investment can work for these countries.

But if the question is, do we need to do more, I think the answer is yes. But then we have to look at, nation by nation, what specifically needs to be done and what they still need to do.

President Santer. I only would say that the main achievement for the Eastern countries and Central European countries would be to achieve the enlargement process. These countries, there are now 10 applicant countries, can also access—have an accession to the European Union.

As you know, we are working very hard, at this moment, precisely on this question. I think that the enlargement is a main challenge for the European Union to have to face for the 21st century. It is the first time since more than 500 years that the European Union has an historic chance to reconcile its own continent with itself in peace and freedom. And that would be the great challenge.

And therefore, we have to prepare it. We have to prepare it through the preexisting strategy which we defined with many European agreements. We have to prepare it now also after the IGC conference under the Dutch presidency. And we would put forward from the European Commission at the 15th or 16th of July under the condition that the presidency would succeed in Amsterdam—and I'm quite confident that it will succeed in Amsterdam—our opinions about the 10 applicant countries. And therefore, all elements are welcome to strengthen this intensity so that we can deal with the problems of our neighbors.

Yesterday in Paris, there was a major step on the security level. Now we have to achieve it also on the economic level for the European Union.

NOTE: The President's 146th news conference began at 11:42 a.m. in the Rolzall Room at Binnenhof Palace. The President met with Prime Minister Wim Kok of the Netherlands, President of the European Council, and Jacques Santer, President of the European Commission. Following the news conference, the three leaders witnessed the signing of a customs cooperation agreement and a chemical precursor agreement by Secretary of State Madeleine Albright, European Commission Vice President Leon Brittan, and Foreign Minister Hans van Mierlo of The Netherlands.

Remarks at a Luncheon Hosted by Queen Beatrix of The Netherlands in The Hague
May 28, 1997

Your Majesty, Prime Minister Kok, honored colleagues, on behalf of the United States, I would like to thank Her Majesty and the people of The Netherlands for this deeply appreciated commemoration. And thank you, Your Majesty, for your very fine statement.

The ties between our two nations are long and unbroken. When my country was first seeking its independence, The Netherlands was one of the first nations to which we turned. John Adams, America's first envoy to The Hague and later our second President, described the completion of a treaty of friendship with Holland as, quote, "the happiest event and the greatest action" of his life. More than 200 years later, America still takes pride in our friendship with this good land, whose compassion and generosity throughout the world is far disproportionate to its size.

I also express my gratitude to all my fellow leaders for being here today. Your presence is a very great honor to the United States and a symbol of the age of possibility which we now inhabit, thanks in no small measure to the vision and work of General Marshall and his contemporaries in the United States and in Europe.

The Marshall plan we celebrate today, as Her Majesty noted, was open to all of Europe. But for half the Continent, the dream of recovery was denied. Now, at last, all of Europe's nations are seeking their rightful places at our transatlantic table.

Here in this room are freely elected Presidents, Prime Ministers, and officials from every corner of Europe, including Russia. We are the trustees of history's rarest gift, a second chance to complete the job that Marshall and his generation began. Our great opportunity and our enormous obligation is to make the most of this precious gift and together to build an undivided, democratic, peaceful, prosperous Europe for the very first time in all human history.

The daunting challenge in Marshall's time was to repair the damage of a devastating war. Now we face the equally ambitious task of promoting peace, security, and prosperity for all the people of Europe.

As we celebrate the 50th anniversary of the Marshall plan, let us commit ourselves to build upon its success for the next 50 years and beyond. And let us now join in a toast to Her Majesty and the people of The Netherlands in gratitude for this great and good day.

NOTE: The President spoke at 1:53 p.m. in the Small Ballroom of Noordeinde Palace.

Remarks at a Ceremony Commemorating the 50th Anniversary of the Marshall Plan in The Hague
May 28, 1997

Thank you very much, Mr. Sedee, for sharing your wonderful story. I forgive you for stealing the matchbook from the White House. [*Laughter*] In fact, just before we came in, I confess that I had heard he did such a thing, so without theft, I brought him some cufflinks and some Oval Office candy for his grandchildren today. [*Laughter*]

Your Majesty, Prime Minister, fellow heads of state and leaders of government, ministers parliamentarian, Members of Congress, to the youth leaders from Europe and America, to all of you who had anything to do with or were ever touched by the Marshall plan. And I'd like to say a special word of appreciation to two distinguished Americans, former Ambassadors General Vernon Walters and Arthur Hartman, who worked on the Marshall plan as young men, who have come here to be with us today.

This is a wonderful occasion. We are grateful to the Queen, the Government, and the people of The Netherlands for hosting us and for commemorating these 50 years. The words of Mr. Sedee reach out to us across the generations, no matter where we come from or what language we speak. They warn us of what can happen when people turn against one another and inspire us with what we can achieve when we all pull together. That is a message that we should emblazon in our memories.

Just as we honor the great accomplishments of 50 years ago, as the Prime Minister said so eloquently, we must summon the spirit of the Marshall plan for the next 50 years and beyond to build a Europe that is democratic, at peace, and undivided for the first time in history, a Europe that does not repeat the darkest moments of the 20th century but instead fulfills the brightest promise of the 21st.

Here in the citadel of a prosperous, tolerant Dutch democracy, we can barely imagine how different Europe was just 50 years ago. The wonderful pictures we saw, with the music, helped us to imagine: Some 30,000 dead still lay buried beneath the sea of rubble in Warsaw; 100,000 homes had been destroyed in Holland; Germany in ruins; Britain facing a desperate shortage of coal and electric power; factories crippled all across Europe; trade paralyzed; millions fearing starvation.

Across the Atlantic, the American people were eager to return to the lives they had left behind during the war. But they heeded the call of a remarkable generation of American leaders, General Marshall, President Truman, Senator Vandenberg, who wanted to work with like-minded leaders in Europe to work for Europe's recovery as they had fought for its survival. They knew that, as never before, Europe's fate and America's future were joined.

The Marshall plan offered a cure, not a crutch. It was never a handout; it was always a hand up. It said to Europe, if you will put your divisions behind you, if you will work together to help yourselves, then America will work with you.

The British Foreign Secretary, Ernest Bevin, called the Marshall plan a lifeline to sinking men, bringing hope where there was none. From the Arctic Sea to the Mediterranean, European nations grabbed that lifeline, cooperating as never before on a common program of recovery. The task was not easy, but the hope they shared was more powerful than their differences.

The first ship set sail from Texas to France with 19,000 tons of wheat. Soon, on any given day, a convoy of hope was heading to Europe with fuel, raw materials, and equipment. By the end of the program in 1952, the Marshall plan had pumped $13 billion into Europe's parched economies. That would be the equivalent of $88 billion today. It provided the people of Europe with the tools they needed to rebuild their shattered lives. There were nets for Norwegian fishermen, wool for Austrian weavers, tractors for French and Italian farmers, machines for Dutch entrepreneurs.

For a teenage boy in Germany, Marshall aid was the generous hand that helped lift his homeland from its ruinous past. He still recalls the American trucks driving onto the schoolyard, bringing soup that warmed hearts and hands. That boy grew up to be a passionate champion of freedom and unity in Europe and a great and cherished friend of America. He became the first Chancellor of a free and unified Germany. In his good life and fine work, Helmut Kohl has come to symbolize both the substance and the spirit of the Marshall plan. Thank you.

Today we see the success of the Marshall plan and the nations it helped to rebuild. But more, we see it in the relations it helped to redefine. The Marshall plan transformed the way America related to Europe and, in so doing, transformed the way European nations related to each other. It planted the seeds of institutions that evolved to bind Western Europe together, from the OECD, the European Union, and NATO. It paved the way for reconciliation of age-old differences.

Marshall's vision, as has been noted, embraced all of Europe. But the reality of his time did not. Stalin barred Europe's Eastern half, including some of our staunchest allies during World War II, from claiming their seats at the table, shutting them out of Europe's recovery, closing the door on their freedom. But the shackled nations never lost faith, and the West never accepted the permanence of their fate. And at last, through the efforts of brave men and women determined to live free lives, the Berlin Wall and the Iron Curtain fell.

Now the dawn of new democracies is lighting the way to a new Europe in a new century, a time in which America and Europe must complete the noble journey that Marshall's generation began, and this time with no one left behind. I salute Prime Minister Kok for his leadership and the leadership his nation is giving to ensure that this time no one will be left behind. [*Applause*] Thank you.

Twenty-first century Europe will be a better Europe, first, because it will be both free and undivided; second, because it will be united not by the force of arms but by the possibilities of peace. We must remember, however, that today's possibilities are not guarantees. Though walls have come down, difficulties persist: in the ongoing struggle of newly free nations to build vibrant economies and resilient democracies; in the vulnerability of those who fear change and have not yet felt its benefits; to the appeals of extreme nationalism, hatred, and division; in the clouded thinking of those who still see the European landscape as a zero-sum game in terms of the past; and in the new dangers we face and cannot defeat alone, from the spread of weapons of mass destruction to

terrorism, to organized crime, to environmental degradation.

Our generation, like the one before us, must choose. Without the threat of cold war, without the pain of economic ruin, without the fresh memory of World War II's slaughter, it is tempting to pursue our private agendas, to simply sit back and let history unfold. We must resist that temptation. And instead, we must set out with resolve to mold the hope of this moment into a history we can be proud of.

We who follow the example of the generation we honor today must do just that. Our mission is clear: We must shape the peace, freedom, and prosperity they made possible into a common future where all our people speak the language of democracy; where they have the right to control their lives and the chance to pursue their dreams; where prosperity reaches clear across the Continent and states pursue commerce, not conquest; where security is the province of all free nations working together; where no nation in Europe is ever again excluded against its will from joining our alliance of values; and where we join together to help the rest of the world reach the objectives we hold so dear.

The United States and Europe have embraced this mission. We're advancing across a map of modern miracles. With support from America and the European Union, Europe's newly free nations are laying the cornerstones of democracy. With the help of the USIA's Voice of America, today's celebration is being heard freely by people all across this great continent.

In Prague, where listening to Western broadcasts was once a criminal offense, Radio Free Europe has made a new home and an independent press is flourishing. In Bucharest, democracy has overcome distrust, as Romanians and ethnic Hungarians for the very first time are joined in a democratic coalition government. Thank you, sir.

From Vladivostok to Kaliningrad, the people of Russia went to the polls last summer in what all of us who watched it know was a fully democratic, open, national election.

We must meet the challenge now of making sure this surge of democracy endures. The newly free nations must persevere with the difficult work of reform. America and Western Europe must continue with concrete support for their progress, bolstering judicial systems to fight crime and corruption creating checks and balances against arbitrary power, helping to install the machinery of free and fair elections so that they can be repeated over and over again, strengthening free media and civic groups to promote accountability, bringing good government closer to the people so that they can have an actual voice in decisions affecting their lives.

We have also helped new democracies transform their broken economies and move from aid to trade and investment. In Warsaw, men and women who once stood on line for food now share in the fruits of Europe's fastest growing economy, where more than 9 of 10 retail businesses rests in private hands. Since the fall of the Berlin Wall, the international financial institutions have channeled to the new democracies some $50 billion to strengthen the foundations of their market economies. And as markets have emerged, another $45 billion in private investment has flowed from places like Boston and London to help support enterprises from Budapest to Lvov.

Now, as the new democracies continue to scale the mountains of market reform, our challenge is to help them reap more fully the benefits of prosperity, working to make the business climate as stable and secure as possible, investing in their economies, sharing entrepreneurial skills, and opening the doors of institutions that enable our community to thrive.

Again let me say America salutes the European Union's commitment to expand to Central and Eastern Europe. We support this historic process and believe it should move ahead swiftly. A more prosperous Europe will be a stronger Europe and also a stronger partner for Europe's North American friends in America and Canada.

Nations that tackle tough reforms deserve to know that what they build with freedom, they can keep in security. Through NATO, the core of transatlantic security, we can do for Europe's East what we did in Europe's West: defend freedom, strengthen democracy, temper old rivalries, hasten integration, and provide a stable climate in which prosperity can grow.

We are adapting NATO to take on new missions, opening its doors to Europe's new democracies, bolstering its ties to nonmembers through a more robust Partnership For Peace, and forging a practical, lasting partnership between NATO and a democratic Russia—all these things designed to make sure that NATO remains strong, supports the coming together of Europe,

and leads in meeting our new security challenges.

Yesterday in Paris, the leaders of NATO and Russia signed the historic founding act that will make us all more secure. We will consult, coordinate, and where both agree, act jointly, as we are doing in Bosnia now.

Now, consider the extraordinary milestone this represents. For decades, the fundamental security concern in Europe was the confrontation between East and West. For the first time, a new NATO and a new Russia have agreed to work as partners to meet challenges to their common security in a new and undivided Europe, where no nation will define its greatness in terms of its ability to dominate its neighbors. Now we must meet the challenge of bolstering security across outdated divides, making the NATO partnership work with Russia, continuing NATO's historic transformation.

In less than 6 weeks, NATO will meet again in Madrid to invite the first of Europe's new democracies to add their strength to the alliance. The prospect of NATO membership already has led to greater stability, for aspiring members are deepening reform and resolving the very kinds of disputes that could lead to future conflict.

The first new members will not be the last. NATO's doors must and will remain open to all those able to share the responsibilities of membership. We will strengthen the Partnership For Peace and create a new Euro-Atlantic partnership council so that other nations can deepen their cooperation with NATO and continue to prepare for membership.

But let us be clear: There are responsibilities as well. Enlargement means extending the most solemn guarantees any nation can make, a commitment to the security of another. Security and peace are not cheap. New and current allies alike must be willing to bear the burden of our ideas and our interests.

Our collective efforts in Bosnia reflect both the urgency and the promise of our mission. Where terror and tragedy once reigned, NATO troops are standing with 14 partner nations, Americans and Russians, Germans and Poles, Norwegians and Bulgarians, all in common cause to bring peace to the heart of Europe. Now we must consolidate that hard-won peace, promote political reconciliation and economic reconstruction, support the work of the International War Crimes Tribunal here in The

Hague, and help the Bosnian peace make the promise of the Dayton accord real.

Today I affirm to the people of Europe, as General Marshall did 50 years ago: America stands with you. We have learned the lessons of history; we will not walk away.

No less today than five decades ago, our destinies are joined. For America, the commitment to our common future is not an option, it is a necessity. We are closing the door on the 20th century, a century that saw humanity at its worst and at its most noble. Here, today, let us dedicate ourselves to working together to make the new century a time when partnership between America and Europe lifts the lives of all the people of the world.

Let us summon the spirit of hope and renewal that the life story of Gustaaf Sedee represents. He has a son, Bert, who is a bank executive. Today, he is helping to fulfill the legacy his father so movingly described, for just as the Marshall plan made the investment that helped Holland's industry revive, Bert Sedee's bank is helping Dutch companies finance investments in Central and Eastern Europe. Just as the American people reached out to the people of his homeland, Bert Sedee and his colleagues

are reaching out to the people in Slovenia, Latvia, Bosnia, and beyond.

The youngest members of the Sedee family are also in our thoughts today, Gustaaf Sedee's grandchildren, Roeland and Sander, 9 months and 1½. I wonder what they will say 50 years from today. I hope that they and all the young people listening, those who are aware of what is going on and those too young to understand it, will be able to say, "We bequeath to you 50 years of peace, freedom, and prosperity." I hope that you will have raised your sons and daughters in a Europe whose horizons are wider than its frontiers. I hope you will be able to tell your grandchildren, whose faces most of us will not live to see, that this generation rose to the challenge to be shapers of the peace. I hope that we will all do this, remembering the legacy of George Marshall and envisioning a future brighter than any, any people have ever lived.

Thank you, and God bless you.

NOTE: The President spoke at 4:49 p.m. in the Hall of Knights at Binnenhof Palace. In his remarks, he referred to Gustaaf Albert Sedee, who represented The Netherlands during a visit to the White House on February 3, 1949.

Message to the Congress on Continuation of the National Emergency With Respect to the Federal Republic of Yugoslavia (Serbia and Montenegro) and the Bosnian Serbs
May 28, 1997

To the Congress of the United States:

Section 202(d) of the National Emergencies Act (50 U.S.C. 1622(d)) provides for the automatic termination of a national emergency unless, prior to the anniversary date of its declaration, the President publishes in the *Federal Register* and transmits to the Congress a notice stating that the emergency is to continue in effect beyond the anniversary date. In accordance with this provision, I have sent the enclosed notice to the *Federal Register* for publication, stating that the emergency declared with respect to the Federal Republic of Yugoslavia (Serbia and Montenegro), as expanded to address the actions and policies of the Bosnian Serb forces and the authorities in the territory that they control

within the Republic of Bosnia and Herzegovina, is to continue in effect beyond May 30, 1997.

On December 27, 1995, I issued Presidential Determination No. 96–7, directing the Secretary of the Treasury, *inter alia*, to suspend the application of sanctions imposed on the Federal Republic of Yugoslavia (Serbia and Montenegro) and to continue to block property previously blocked until provision is made to address claims or encumbrances, including the claims of the other successor states of the former Yugoslavia. This sanctions relief, in conformity with United Nations Security Council Resolution 1022 of November 22, 1995 (hereinafter the "Resolution"), was an essential factor motivating Serbia and

Montenegro's acceptance of the General Framework Agreement for Peace in Bosnia and Herzegovina initialed by the parties in Dayton on November 21, 1995, and signed in Paris on December 14, 1995 (hereinafter the "Peace Agreement"). The sanctions imposed on the Federal Republic of Yugoslavia (Serbia and Montenegro) were accordingly suspended prospectively, effective January 16, 1996. Sanctions imposed on the Bosnian Serb forces and authorities and on the territory that they control within the Republic of Bosnia and Herzegovina were subsequently suspended prospectively, effective May 10, 1996, also in conformity with the Peace Agreement and the Resolution.

Sanctions against both the Federal Republic of Yugoslavia (Serbia and Montenegro) and the Bosnian Serbs were subsequently terminated by United Nations Security Council Resolution 1074 of October 1, 1996. This termination, however, did not end the requirement of the Resolution that blocked funds and assets that are subject to claims and encumbrances remain blocked, until unblocked in accordance with applicable law. In the last year, substantial progress has been achieved to bring about a settlement of the conflict in the former Yugoslavia acceptable to the parties. Elections occurred in the Republic of Bosnia and Herzegovina, as provided for in the Peace Agreement, and the Bosnian Serb forces have continued to respect the zones of separation as provided in the Peace Agreement. The ultimate disposition of the various remaining categories of blocked assets are now being addressed, beginning with the unblocking of five Yugoslav vessels located in various United States ports effective May 19, 1997.

Until the status of all remaining blocked property is resolved, the Peace Agreement implemented, and the terms of the Resolution met, this situation continues to pose a continuing unusual and extraordinary threat to the national security, foreign policy interests, and the economy of the United States. For these reasons, I have determined that it is necessary to maintain in force these emergency authorities beyond May 30, 1997.

WILLIAM J. CLINTON

The White House,
May 28, 1997.

NOTE: The notice is listed in Appendix D at the end of this volume.

Remarks at the "Thank You, America" Celebration in Rotterdam, The Netherlands
May 28, 1997

Thank you. Mr. Mayor, Mrs. Peper; to His Royal Highness, the Prince of Orange; Prime Minister and Mrs. Kok. To all of America's Dutch friends here and my fellow Americans who are here tonight, thank you for a wonderful, wonderful welcome.

I thank Gustaaf Sedee for his words. You know, this afternoon at The Hague, he spoke and introduced me and told the story of being a young boy growing up under the Marshall plan. Tonight he spoke and spoke so well. Who knows, I may be remembered as the man who accompanied Gustaaf Sedee to Rotterdam. [*Laughter*] He did not explain to you what he told us today, which is that as a young man, he actually got to go to the United States because he won an essay contest. And each of the nations participating in the Marshall plan picked a young person who won an essay contest to go and tour America and meet the President. He met President Truman on February 4, 1949. And I have secured a copy, an actual copy of the newspaper, the New York Herald-Tribune, on that day. And I thought that I would give it to him as an expression of our gratitude for all of you and what you have meant in friendship to the United States. So here it is.

And Mr. Mayor, thank you for your wonderful reference to my campaign and my Presidency and my belief and hope in that we should never stop thinking about tomorrow. I think you would be a wonderful Ambassador to the United States. [*Laughter*]

When President Truman met with the young visitors from the Marshall plan nations years ago, he said he hoped that when they were as old as he was then, the world would know only democracy and peace. Well, today, the world knows things other than democracy and peace, but we stand closer to that dream than at any point in human history.

For the first time ever, more than half of the people on this Earth live under governments of their own choosing. And here in Europe, the Marshall plan that President Truman launched helped to rebuild a continent ravaged by war, gave strength to fragile democracies, and sparked unparalleled prosperity.

Tonight, in honoring those remarkable accomplishments begun 50 years ago, our purpose must be to summon the spirit of the Marshall generation to create a structure of opportunity and freedom and security for the next 50 years and beyond, to give the young people here in this crowd tonight, throughout Europe, and the rest of the world, as many as we can, the chance to grow up and live out their dreams.

The generation we honor tonight fought and won a war, then built the institutions and understandings that prevented war's return. Now, closer to the start of a new century than to the end of the cold war, our mission is to shape the peace they made possible, to reach for a long sought yet never realized goal: a Europe that is undivided, democratic, and at peace for the first time in all history.

America wishes to join in building a new Europe because Europe literally built America and because our futures are bound together. No nation contributed to our building more than did yours. From this great pier, more than a million Dutch men and women started their journey to America. As the mayor said, after the first Dutch vessel arrived on our shores in 1609, it was just a decade later, from the tiny port of Delft's Haven, that the Pilgrims set sail for Plymouth Rock, giving birth to the experiment that became the United States of America. The values of those early settlers became America's values: hard work and industry, individual freedom and tolerance, a willingness to take risks for boundless opportunity, a pride in country and community that knows no bounds.

Here in Rotterdam, those values faced their most terrible test 57 years ago when Nazi bombers rained fire on this city, killed 900 people, destroyed homes for 25,000 more, turned downtown Rotterdam into rubble, as we saw in the marvelous film. Even as your buildings burned, you kept your spirit going. The American people today know that the strength and courage of the Dutch Resistance helped to conquer Hitler and ensured your ultimate recovery. And I am especially proud tonight that the Allied forces had a little help from a remarkable descendant of a Dutch farmer by the name of Franklin Delano Roosevelt.

Ever since the end of World War II, Rotterdam sails have been turned to the wind. You rebuilt this city with daring modern architecture, a reflection of the daring and vision of your people. You transformed Rotterdam into the biggest and busiest port in the world. And when you did it, I might add that you took that title of biggest port in the world away from a small trading outpost you stumbled upon centuries earlier in the New World—[*laughter*]—it used to be called New Amsterdam—but we forgive you. [*Laughter*]

We are proud that the Marshall plan gave Rotterdam a new start. Through this port most of the aid flowed to the rest of Europe. Today, the generosity of the Dutch people and your courage and your commitment to build a future better than the past—in all of this, the spirit of the Marshall plan lives on. From Africa to Asia, you do not forget those who are hungry in this world, who yearn simply to put food on their table and clothes on their backs. From Bosnia to Haiti, your sons and daughters have kept the peace and helped people turn from conflict and hatred to cooperation and community. America could not hope for a closer ally or a better friend, and the world could not have a better example than this great nation, large beyond its numbers and landmass in its influence and its power of example.

Two centuries ago, our first Ambassador to your nation and our second President, John Adams, said this: "America has considered this nation as her first friend in Europe, whose history and the great character it exhibits in the various arts of peace have been studied, admired, and imitated by every State in our Union." Well, now our Union and your nation have an opportunity to practice those arts of peace as surely as past generations stood together in world war and cold war.

Together, we can complete the journey Marshall's generation began and bring all of Europe together not by the force of arms but by the possibilities of peace. Together, we have it within our power to turn the hope we share into a history we will all be proud of.

So, to all of you, the people of Rotterdam and all the Netherlands, let me say that this celebration and its simple message, "Thank you, America," is a great gift to all of us. In turn, I bring you a message from the American people. For all that you have given to my country, for all that you give to the world, for the example you set that shines so far beyond your bor-

ders, America says, thank you, and God bless you.

NOTE: The President spoke at 8:25 p.m. at Wilhelmina Pier. In his remarks, he referred to Mayor Bram Peper of Rotterdam and his wife, Nelie; Willem Alexander, the Prince of Orange; Prime Minister Wim Kok of The Netherlands and his wife, Rita; and Gustaaf Albert Sedee, who spoke prior to the President.

Remarks Greeting the British Cabinet and an Exchange With Reporters in London, United Kingdom
May 29, 1997

President Clinton. Thank you very much. Let me say that, first, I'm very appreciative of the honor of meeting with the entire Cabinet. And I have watched with enormous interest the energy and vigor with which you have all taken office and begun your work and the optimism with which you pursue it. I saw you on television last night being optimistic about peace in Ireland, which is an article of faith in my life and household, so I like that. And I agree that it is good for the United States to have a Britain that is strong in Europe and strong in its relations with the United States.

These last couple of days, not only commemorating the Marshall plan but asking the people of Europe to think about how we should organize the next 50 years to try to fulfill the unfulfilled promise of the people who envisioned the Marshall plan and signing the agreement between NATO and Russia, are part of the unfolding effort to create within Europe a continent that is democratic, undivided, and at peace for the first time ever. Europe has been periodically at peace but never all democratic and certainly never undivided.

And I see that as a way of organizing ourselves to meet the real challenges of the 21st century which will cross borders—terrorism, the dealing with racial and religious differences, and trying to minimize the extremist hatred that is gripping so much of the world and the proliferation of weapons of mass destruction and drug trafficking and the common environmental

threats that will become a bigger part of every government's agenda for the next generation.

So this is a very exciting time. And I'm glad to be here, and I thank you.

Prime Minister Blair. Thank you very much, Mr. President.

New Generation of Political Leaders

Q. Mr. President, you took office after 12 years of Republican rule in Washington. What advice do you have for these Labour Party members who have just taken office after so many years of a different party in power? You had some missteps at the beginning and probably want to share some of that advice. [*Laughter*]

President Clinton. I think they're doing very well. I'd like to have a 179-seat majority. [*Laughter*] And I'm not going to give any advice; I'm going to sit here and take it as long as they'll let me do it. [*Laughter*]

Prime Minister Blair. And I would like to make sure that we have a second term in office—[*laughter*]—so I'll take his advice, too.

Thanks very much, guys. You know there will be a press conference, of course, later where you'll be able to ask questions.

Q. Mr. Prime Minister, would you care to share with us some of your thoughts about some of the lessons you learned in getting elected from President Clinton's playbook, political playbook?

Prime Minister Blair. Well, I'm sure we'll share lots of lessons together. But as I say, you'll have an ample opportunity to ask us about them later this afternoon.

Thank you.

NOTE: The President spoke at approximately 11:30 a.m. in the Cabinet Room at 10 Downing Street, prior to a meeting with Prime Minister Tony Blair of the United Kingdom.

The President's News Conference With Prime Minister Tony Blair of the United Kingdom in London
May 29, 1997

Prime Minister Blair. Good afternoon, ladies and gentlemen. The President and I have ranged over many subjects in the hours we have had together, and we intend to continue those discussions later today.

We've discussed Bosnia and our continuing efforts to work together in addressing one of the most pressing crises on the international agenda. We've discussed, obviously, Northern Ireland and our determination to do all that we can to bring about the cease-fire that will allow all-party talks to proceed in the best possible climate and that a cease-fire is genuine and credible with all the parties there. We agreed that NATO is and will remain the cornerstone of Europe's defense. And I was grateful, too, for the President's expression of continuing support on Hong Kong. We agreed, too, that Britain does not need to choose between being strong in Europe or being close to the United States of America but that by being strong in Europe we will further strengthen our relationships with the U.S.

President Clinton will have more to say on these and other issues in a moment. But we agreed, too, and have for some time, that this is a new era which calls for a new generation politics and a new generation leadership. This is the generation that prefers reason to doctrine, that is strong in ideals but indifferent to ideology, whose instinct is to judge government not on grand designs but by practical results. This is the generation trying to take politics to a new plateau, seeking to rise above some of the old divisions of right and left. It is what, on my last visit to the United States to meet the President, I described as the radical center of politics.

The soil is the same, the values of progress, justice, of a one nation-country in which ambition for oneself and compassion for others can live easily together. But the horizons are new; the focus and agenda are also new.

We discussed how this is the generation that claims education, skills, and technology as the instruments of economic prosperity and personal fulfillment, not all battles between state and market. This is the generation that believes in international engagement, in our nations being stronger by being open to the world, not in isolationism. This is the generation that knows that it will fall to us to modernize the New Deal and the welfare state, to replace dependency by independence. This is the generation, too, searching for a new set of rules to define citizenship for the 21st century, intolerant of crime but deeply respectful and tolerant towards those of different races, colors, class, and creed, prepared to stand up against discrimination in all its guises. This is the generation, too, that celebrates the successful entrepreneur but knows that we cannot prosper as a country unless we prosper together, with no underclass of the excluded shut out from society's future. It's a generation that puts merit before privilege, which cares more about the environment than about some outdated notion of class war. New times, new challenges, the new political generation must meet them.

So yes, we discussed the pressing issues of diplomacy and statesmanship and peace in troubled parts of our world. But perhaps just as important was our discussion of this new agenda for the new world in which we find ourselves. We agreed that our priority as political leaders must indeed be education, education, education, flexible labor markets, welfare reform, partnership with business.

In Europe in particular, we need to reduce long-term and youth unemployment, both of which are unacceptably high. The U.S. has been more successful in creating jobs, but it too faces new challenges in seeking to assure opportunity for all its citizens.

The United States has the presidency of the G–8 in 1997. In 1998, Britain has the presidency both of the European Union and the G–8. We have agreed today to a common agenda and a shared determination to identify what action needs to be taken to tackle the problems we all face, to identify what reforms have worked where, what reforms have failed, and how we can learn the lessons both of success and of failure. As part of this process, Britain will host a G–8 conference of finance and social affairs ministers in the early months of our G–8 presidency next year, and the Chancellor of the Exchequer will be announcing further details today.

We have a shared language. We have a shared outlook on many of the issues that face us. We are determined, too, to share our ideas, our expertise, and our commitment to a new era of cooperation and of understanding.

Thank you.

President Clinton.

President Clinton. Thank you very much, Prime Minister. First, let me say it's an honor and a pleasure to be here today. I've looked forward to this for a long time. I have read countless articles about how Prime Minister Blair and I have everything in common, and I'm still looking for my 179-seat majority. I have been all ears in trying to get the advice about how such a thing might be achieved.

On a more serious note, let me say that one of the most important and meaningful responsibilities of any American President is to carry forward the unique partnership between the United States and the United Kingdom. Over the last 50 years, our unbreakable alliance has helped to bring our people unparalleled peace and prosperity and security. It's an alliance based on shared values and common aspirations.

In the last 4 years, I was privileged to lead the United States in pursuing that partnership. I had a good and productive relationship with Prime Minister Major, and I am very much looking forward to working with Tony Blair. I have asked him in pursuance of this to come to Washington as early as is convenient for both of us, and I expect that there will be an official visit pretty soon. And I know that the people of the United States are looking forward to having him there.

I have been impressed by the determination of the Prime Minister and his Cabinet to prepare this nation for the next century, to focus on economic growth, to make education the number one priority because, without it, you can't guarantee every person in any country the chance to compete and succeed in the world toward which we're moving. I have been impressed by his understanding that in order for the United Kingdom to fulfill its historic leadership role in Europe and the rest of the world, the needs and concerns of the people here at home have to be adequately addressed.

As you know, this corresponds with my own views. Our first task must always be to expand opportunities for our own citizens, to expect them to behave in a responsible manner, and to recognize that we have to maintain a community in which people's differences are respected but in which their shared values are more important.

We talked about how we could work together to shape a peace for the coming generation. We reviewed our efforts to complete the work that began 50 years ago with the Marshall plan: building an undivided, peaceful Europe for the first time in history, through NATO's enlargement through its new partnership with Russia, its new agreement with Ukraine; a strengthened Partnership For Peace; an expanding European Union that reaches out to Europe's newly free nations.

We agreed on the importance, as he has already said, of helping the parties in Bosnia fulfill their commitments under the Dayton accord and continuing our support for all elements of it.

We discussed Northern Ireland. As all of you know, when I visited Northern Ireland 18 months ago, I was profoundly moved by the palpable desire of people in both communities for peace. I applaud the Prime Minister's initial efforts in this regard. There is a sense of hope and reassurance that has been conveyed here. And I know that he is committed in partnership with the Irish Government to bring about a lasting resolution to the conflict.

The goal of this peace process is inclusive talks because they are the ones most likely to succeed. But I have said before, and I'd like to say again, that can only succeed if there is an unequivocal cease-fire in deed and in word. Again, I urge the IRA to lay down their guns for good and for all parties to turn their efforts to building the peace together.

The concerns we share extend far beyond our borders. Today's global challenges require global responses. Indeed, one of the reasons that we are working so hard to organize NATO in the proper way, to unify Europe in the proper way, is so that our nations will all be prepared to meet the challenges to our security in the new century which cross national lines: terrorism, international crime, weapons proliferation, and obviously, global environmental degradation. More and more, we are focusing our attention on these challenges. Again, we are going to deepen our cooperation between our two nations and in the forums in which we're members. I am very pleased with the proposal that the Prime Minister has made to pursue an economic agenda within the Group of Eight, and I intend to support that.

Let me say, finally, that we discussed Hong Kong, and I commended the United Kingdom to work to implement the word and the spirit of the 1984 agreement. All of us who care about the future of Hong Kong have a stake in making sure the agreement is fully met. We will keep faith with the people of Hong Kong by monitoring the transition to make sure that civil liberties are retained, that democratic values and free market principles are maintained. Those are the things for which the United Kingdom and the United States stand, and those are the things that the agreement guarantees.

This is a hopeful time for the people of the United Kingdom and for the people of the United States. It is a hopeful time for the world. More people live free and have the chance to live out their dreams than ever before in human history. But we face daunting new challenges, and we have to face them together. I say repeatedly to the American people, we may be at the point of our greatest relative influence in the world after the cold war, but we can exercise that influence only if we acknowledge our interdependence on like-mined people with similar dreams. I feel that very strongly here today with Prime Minister Blair, and I intend to act upon it.

Thank you very much.

Prime Minister Blair. Thank you very much, Mr. President.

Right, gentlemen, questions? Michael.

New Generation of Political Leaders

Q. Mr. President, Michael Brunson of ITN [Independent Television News]. As you probably know, during our recent election here, there was a good deal written on both sides of the Atlantic about Mr. Blair being the "Clinton clone," or the "British Clinton." I wonder, now you're here, how the American original thinks that the British version is shaping up. [*Laughter*]

President Clinton. Well, I have a couple of reactions to that. First of all, a lot of the columns that were written about that were not altogether flattering to either one of us, and I had half a mind to call Mr. Blair during the election and offer to attack him in the harshest possible terms, if he thought it might free him of an unwanted yoke. [*Laughter*] And now, I also told you today that there is one big difference, and that's the enormous parliamentary majority that the Prime Minister enjoys. So I should be here learning from New Labour instead of the other way around.

Let me just give you a serious answer. I believe that the people—free peoples in the world are interested in democratic governments that work, that have constructive economic policies, that try to reconcile the imperative of growth with the imperatives of family and neighborhood and community, that do not accept the fact that our social problems will always worsen and cannot be made better, that do not promise to do things which responsible citizens must do for themselves but which don't run away from their own responsibilities. That's what I think people want.

And I think that requires us to move beyond—I don't think that it's the end of ideology, but I think it's the end of yesterday's ideology. And I think the more people see the issues framed in terms of attacks of parties on each other and yesterday's language that seems disconnected to their own concerns, their own hopes, and their own problems, the more faith is lost in politics. The more people see the political process is relevant to their lives and their future, the more energy you have. And what I sense in Great Britain today is an enormous amount of energy.

So if you're asking me to rate the beginning, I'd say that's a great thing. It's a great thing when the people of a democracy believe in its possibilities and are willing to work for them. That is about all you can ask. No one has all the answers, but you want people to believe in the possibilities of a nation and be willing to work for them.

Yes, Ron [Ron Fournier, Associated Press].

Northern Ireland Peace Process and Iran

Q. Sir, you told us this morning that the Northern Ireland peace process is an article of faith in your life. Given that, is there anything more the U.S. can do to nudge the process along? And what's your take on Iran's new President, a moderate cleric who won in a landslide?

President Clinton. Well, let me say, first of all, we have a new British Government that has taken what I think were wise and judicious steps and made statements that I think are clear, unequivocal, and appropriate. There is about to be an election in Ireland. The United States—I have restated what the polestars of our position are today: an unequivocal cease-fire, inclusive talks. But I think before I say or do anything more, as with every peace, this is a peace that has to be made by the parties themselves, and we need to let this unfold a little. But we'll be there, active and involved, along the way.

Now, as to Iran, obviously it's a very interesting development, and for those of us who don't feel privy to all the details of daily life in that country, it's at least a reaffirmation of the democratic process there. And it's interesting, and it's hopeful. But from the point of view of the United States, what we hope for is a reconciliation with a country that does not believe that terrorism is a legitimate extension of political policies, that would not use violence to wreck a peace process in the Middle East, and would not be trying to develop weapons of mass destruction.

I have never been pleased about the estrangements between the people of the United States and the people of Iran. And they are a very great people, and I hope that the estrangements can be bridged. But those are three big hurdles that would have to be cleared, and we'll just have to hope for the best.

Prime Minister Blair. Robin.

Northern Ireland Peace Process

Q. Robin Oakley, BBC. Mr. President, you've appealed again strongly today for the IRA to call a cease-fire. How soon after the calling of an IRA cease-fire would you want and expect to see Sinn Fein in inclusive talks? How long

a verification process would you see as being correct? Would this be a matter of months or weeks or days?

President Clinton. I don't believe I should make a public comment on that at this moment. Tony Blair's government has just come into office. As I said, I think they've taken some very impressive and appropriate steps. There's about to be an Irish election. I think, at this moment, for the American President to start specifying that level of detail would be inappropriate.

Defense Cutbacks and NATO Expansion

Q. Mr. President, Gene Gibbons of Reuters. This may be a time of new politics, but there are some immutable old laws, like the military doctrine of not stretching your forces too thin. Both of you are involved in downsizing your militaries. How do you do that and at the same time credibly make a vast new defense commitment that is involved in NATO expansion?

And the second part of the question for President Clinton, there are reports that NATO enlargement will cost American taxpayers as much as $150 billion over the next 5 years. What is your estimate of the cost?

President Clinton. Well, first—and I think the Prime Minister and I both should answer your first question—so let me answer the second question very briefly. Our last estimate was—or more than an estimate—in the last defense report we got, the estimate was more in the range of $150 to $200 million a year. They are reviewing our defense commitments now.

I should point this out. The cost will be important because for most European countries, the relative costs will be greater than for the United States because we've already done some of the structural things that European countries have to do, most of them. So I do not expect that the larger figure is anywhere close to the ballpark.

Secondly, the security umbrella we have is really no longer dependent upon stationing large armies along the eastern frontier of NATO. What kept any NATO nation from being attacked, in my judgment, was the larger nuclear deterrent that was present during the cold war. Now, we are also trying to reduce that, but keep in mind—see the NATO expansion in the context of the following things: There's an agreement between NATO and Russia about what our relationship is going to be. President Yeltsin just agreed to detarget the nuclear missiles against all the NATO countries. We will have an agreement on conventional forces in Europe which will further reduce those forces. And after the Russians ratify START II, we will move on to START III which will involve an 80 percent reduction in nuclear forces from their post-cold-war high.

So, in that context, I think the expansion of NATO is quite affordable and really should be seen not only as a cooperative security guarantee but as a cooperative commitment to try to deal with the other security problems of our times, like Bosnia.

Prime Minister Blair. I agree very much with that, and I think what is important is to see NATO enlargement, and indeed, the Joint Council between NATO and Russia, as part of building the security and defense of our countries and, indeed, making sure that the commitments that we have are fully realizable.

Now, we announced just a couple days ago a strategic review of our defense, which is foreign policy led. It's not about downsizing our armed forces, but it is about making sense of the commitments that we have. But I think that NATO enlargement is a very, very important part of bringing in those emerging countries in Eastern Europe and ensuring also, through cooperation with Russia, that we're doing it in a way that preserves the security of the world. And I can't think of anything more important than that. So I don't see these as conflicting objectives. On the contrary, I see them properly implemented as entirely complementary.

Yes, Charles.

European Economy and the President's Visit

Q. Charles Wright, the Evening Standard. Mr. President—[*inaudible*]—want cooperation—[*inaudible*]—with Northern Europe there is a conflict—[*inaudible*]—on the way being pushed by the Prime Minister for more flexible labor markets and a call from Brussels for more social legislation. Is the Prime Minister right to warn against the dangers of this? And secondly, while you're in London, you said you wanted to go out and about a bit. What is it you're looking forward to see most?

President Clinton. Well, I've already seen part of what I want to see most, which is the unique and unspeakably beautiful British spring. I was so hoping it would be sunny today.

Let me say on the other question, there is not a simple answer. The great challenge for

Europe—and more for other countries even than for the United Kingdom because your unemployment rate is already lower than some—but the great challenge you face is how to create enough jobs to be competitive and to promote not only economic growth but to have a good society. A successful society requires that able-bodied adults be able to work. Successful families, successful communities, low crime rates all require that able-bodied adults be able to spend their energies a certain number of hours a day at work, quite apart from the economic considerations.

So the question is, how do you do that? How do you become more flexible? How do you have more entrepreneurs, more flexible labor markets, and still preserve the social cohesion that has made community life strong in Europe, justifiably?

In the United States, we've had enormous success—and I'm grateful for this—in creating jobs—and more in the first 4 years of my term than in any previous 4-year term in history—but we're struggling to come back the other way. We're struggling to find a way to give these working families—make sure they can all afford health care for their children, make sure they can have some time off when there is a baby born or a parent sick. You know, we're trying to deal with the arguments from the other way.

But the imperative of reconciling work and family and providing some social safety net so that the conditions of community can be met while having growth, that is the balance-striking that every advanced economy has to do.

And I think what the Prime Minister has said that I thoroughly agree with is, the one option that is unacceptable is denial. That's the only unacceptable—there is no perfect answer. I would be the last person to tell you that we've drawn the perfect balance. We're better at creating jobs than nearly anybody, but we don't have quite as much family security and support as I'd like to see in the area of child care and family leave and other things.

The one thing there is not an option to do is to deny that this is an issue anymore. The United States wants a higher growth rate in Europe. We don't feel threatened by it. We think it would help us, and we hope you can achieve it.

Prime Minister Blair. If I could just add one thing to that—I mean, I think what is absolutely essential is to realize this is part of the reason for the G–8 initiative that we want to take. We are all facing, as modern, developed countries, the same challenges. Work is changing. Industry is changing. We live in a new type of world economy. There are different pressures putting together work and family life. Now, what we're all trying to do is to make sure that we can be fully competitive as we need to be in this new economy while preserving the essential foundations of a humane and decent society. Now, that is the very goal. That's why education and welfare are important. That's why the type of different agenda that I think that a different generation of politicians is reaching towards is actually what is necessary not just here, not just in the United States, but all over the developed world. And if we can bring together some of those lessons from the U.S., from Britain, and from Europe, then we'll find better ways of going forward in Europe as well as the U.S.A.

President Clinton. John [John Donvan, ABC News]. I'll take both of you, but only one at a time.

New Generation of Political Leaders

Q. Mr. President, Prime Minister, as you've said already, a lot has been made of the notion that the two of you are similar. My question is—sometimes the press gets a story and keeps going with it; are you just a little bit sick of this story line? How far can this thing go? [*Laughter*]

President Clinton. Yes, I'm sick of it because he's 7 years younger than I am and has no gray hair. [*Laughter*] So I resent it. But there doesn't seem to be anything I can do about it.

Prime Minister Blair. Look, I think it's a perfectly healthy thing if we realize that these are common developments the world over. I mean, this isn't just something that's to do with the United States or to do with Britain. There is a different generation of political leaders. I mean, I grew up—was born 10 years after the end of the Second World War. I grew up with Eastern Europe on our doorstep. I never thought that the politics of my type of political aspiration was the politics I saw in Eastern Europe. But what I took from my own political traditions was a belief in community, in justice, in a hatred of discrimination. But I want to apply those types of values in the different world.

Now, if you take the welfare state, which we're trying to reform now here in Britain and which President Clinton has done so much to reform in the United States, we believe in the values of that, but 1997 is not 1947 or 1937. So that's why the New Deal has to be updated for today's world, the welfare state has to be updated for today's world. And in Europe, you'll find the same issues being addressed today.

Q. Mr. Prime Minister, are you the student in this relationship?

Prime Minister Blair. Well, I think we can both learn from each other and develop together. I think this is good. But I would pay tribute to the way that Bill Clinton blazed the trail in this area.

President Clinton. Let me say on that point, as all of you know—all of the American journalists here know—before I became President, I was not a Member of our Congress. I was a Governor for a dozen years. And the Founding Fathers of the United States wrote in the "Federalist Papers" that they expected the States to be the laboratories of democracy, which is an elegant 18th century way of saying that all Governors should be students of one another. They should borrow from each other shamelessly. They should learn from each other without arrogance.

And what I think is—if you get a generation of leaders—and it's not necessarily determined by age; I consider Prime Minister Kok in the Netherlands in this category, a little bit older than we are, the young Prime Minister of Portugal, a little younger than we are, a number of others who are thinking in the same way and trying to move toward the same place and have a common understanding of the kind of changes that are sweeping through the world—then we should fairly be expected to—in fact, our people ought to demand that we do the best we can to learn from each other and cherish that, celebrate that, and say that nobody has got all the answers, but if we can get our countries headed in the right direction, free people usually do the right thing if they're going in the right direction. Eventually, they figure it out.

Northern Ireland Peace Process

Q. Ken Reid, Ulster Television in Northern Ireland. Prime Minister, what role do you envisage the President playing in furthering the peace process? And Mr. President, you were obviously very disappointed when the IRA cease-fire collapsed. Do you think the other parties should now move forward without Sinn Fein if another cease-fire is not forthcoming?

Prime Minister Blair. I'll answer the first part of your question, Kenneth. The United States has played, and I've no doubt will continue to play, a helpful role. And we obviously are carrying forward the process. We want to make sure that we can get into all-party talks. We've laid down the conditions for that, and I know that the United States is fully behind that. And I think that that is always helpful.

I remember, too, the visit that President Clinton made some 18 months ago, when the huge optimism and hope that he ignited there in the province was tangible. And we want that back again. We want that sense. Peace in Northern Ireland and ensuring that we get a lasting political settlement that endures is what the vast majority of people in Northern Ireland want. This is the great burning frustration of it, that we are so keen to make sure that the voice of that majority that wants a lasting settlement, that doesn't want to do it by anything other than democratic means, is heard.

Now, I believe it's possible that we can move this process forward, but it's got to be done with care. And I'm sure, as they've played a helpful role before, the United States will play a helpful role again.

President Clinton. Obviously, I think that Sinn Fein should participate in the talks. And I think the IRA should meet what I think has to be the precondition. You can't say, "We'll talk and shoot; we'll talk when we're happy and shoot when we're not." And every political process in the world is a struggle for principled compromise, which means when it's over, no one is ever 100 percent happy.

So that is the decision that obviously all of them will have to make. But the people there do not want to be led in a destructive path anymore. I'm convinced the Catholics don't. I'm convinced the Protestants don't. And I'm convinced the young are more insistent than the old. And to trap people in the prison of those past patterns—we talk about changing economic policy—a far greater tragedy is to move into the wonders of the 21st century with the shackles of what can only be characterized as almost primitive hatred of people because they are of different religions than you are.

I promised you next; I'm sorry. Then we'll go on. Go ahead. I apologize. My memory is not what it used to be.

Q. You're older now.

President Clinton. That's right. [*Laughter*] I've got a cane. [*Laughter*]

Centrist Politics

Q. John Harris with the Washington Post. As a followup to some of the previous questions and answers, Mr. Prime Minister, your party won election by promising no new taxes and by endorsing many of the privatization policies of your Conservative predecessors. Mr. President, you've just signed off on a budget deal that has tax cuts but basically precludes any large new spending initiatives over the next several years. Both of these compromises have made people within your own parties—a lot of them have great misgivings about them. How can you convince these people that what you've described as the radical center is not really just the dead center and this new pragmatism isn't just another name for old-fashioned expediency?

Prime Minister Blair. Well, I think you can do it very easily, by sharing how it derives from conviction and principle. What we decided to do when we created New Labour was to be honest with people. There were certain things the 1980's got right, an emphasis on enterprise, more flexible labor markets. Fine; accepted; they got it right. There should be no mileage in trying to undo things that are basically right. But there were some very fundamental things that we got wrong, education, the creation of a large pool of people of underclass cut off from society's mainstream, a negative isolationist view of foreign policy—these things we change—overcentralized government. These things we change.

And what is different about it, and I think potentially exciting and radical about it, is that it does try to get past a lot of the divisions of the past. And you got out there, and you talk to people in the street about what concerns them—I often think the people are a thousand miles ahead of the politicians. They know that what matters to them is to get their schools right, their hospitals right, tackle crime in their streets. They know that there are certain things that government can't do about jobs and industry but certain things they can do. They want us to do those things.

Now, I don't think that's a dead center, I think that is a radical center. And it's—the big changes that we were able to make in the Labour Party, we made out of principle. It was electorally necessary, but it was also the right thing to do. If it hadn't been the right thing to do, it would never have taken root in the way that it did.

Now, sure, whenever you make changes, there are people that disagree, and there will be those that say we just want to go backwards. Well, the job of political leadership is to explain to people why that's not sensible, why you should move forward.

President Clinton. First of all, let me just remind you of what it was like when I took office. We had high unemployment, low growth, a country with rising crime, rising welfare, and increasing social division. We now have the lowest unemployment rate in 24 years, the biggest decline in income inequality—something the progressive party should care about—in over 30 years. We have declining crime rates. For every year I've been President, the crime rate's gone down, and our crime bill is fully funded and is implementing that. We've got the biggest decline in welfare rolls in history. And we have fought against the divisive forces of race, religion, and all the other forces that are used to divide people in a complex society like ours.

So I think that what we have done is both progressive and effective. And yes, we have a smaller Government; we have the smallest Government since the Kennedy administration. But we're spending more money on education, more money on medical research, more money on technologies. I think we're doing the right thing. That's first.

Second, on the budget agreement itself, to my fellow Democrats—before they criticize me, I would ask them to read what the conservative Republicans have said about the Republicans for signing off on the budget agreement. One conservative periodical accused the moderate Republicans of being Clintonites, which is a fate worse than death for them, you know, and then said that, "I guess we're all new Democrats now."

Look at what this budget does. You say it has no—it leaves no room for big spending; it has the biggest increase in education in a generation, a big increase in environmental protection. It has enough—$17 billion to insure half

the kids in America who don't have health insurance.

Now, beyond that, does it allow for big spending, new programs? No, it doesn't. If we want to spend any more money, big money, in the next 3½ years, what do we have to do? We either have to grow the economy or we've got to raise the money. That's what a balanced budget is for. I support that. I support that. I want the American people—if I could—we would come closer to solving our social problems if we can maintain unemployment at or under 5 percent for the next 4 years than nearly anything else I could do.

And I want us to be in a position—as the progressive party—where we can't launch a big new program unless we raise the money for it or grow the economy to fund it. That's the way we ought to do it. That is the fiscally responsible way to do it. So I am happy with that criticism, and I plead guilty, and the results are good.

Prime Minister Blair. I like that. I like that very much, indeed.

Lessons of the U.S. Economy

Q. Mr. Blair, you talked early on about lessons that you can learn from America, and you said that they've been better at creating jobs. I just wondered why you thought they had been better at creating jobs, what lessons specifically we could draw from that—their attitudes to it?

Prime Minister Blair. I think there is a very strong commitment to entrepreneurship there, which is very important. They've pursued, of course, a stable economic management policy. That is very important. And Bill said something there just a moment ago that I think is very, very important, that the progressive parties today are the parties of fiscal responsibility and prudence. You don't do anything for anybody by making a wreckage out of the economy.

Now, I think these are all things that we take to heart. And what is interesting to me is, again, if you look around not just the U.S.A. or what we're doing with New Labour here in Britain, but if you look around Europe, there are center—center-left parties there, again, as the parties of fiscal prudence and responsibility. And what you can do is make changes within the budget.

You see, the questioner a moment ago was saying, "Well, you know, you're not going for big tax increases and all the rest of it"—but people have had large tax increases. You know, state expenditure has grown to a very large extent. Why has it grown? Well, it's grown here because you've got massive welfare bills that you're paying out, often with people who would like the chance to get back into the labor market if we have the imagination and vision to try and give them the chance to do so, so that they're not any longer reliant on state benefits but are standing on their own two feet, raising their family in some type of decent set of circumstances.

So I think that these elements of job creation, of economic management, of creating the type of enterprises and industries of the future, they're interlinked. And we see those links very, very clearly, indeed.

President Clinton. If I could just say one thing. I would like to give credit where I think credit is due, which is not primarily to me in this. And I think we have been successful in creating jobs for several reasons.

One is, we maintained, earlier than a lot of other countries, a reasonably open economy, not perfectly open but reasonably open, so that we suffered a lot of painful restructuring in the 1980's due to competition. But as a result of that, both our business managers and our working people have dramatically improved their productivity—first.

Second, America is a relatively easy place to start a small business, and we get a lot of our new jobs from starting small businesses.

Third, we have been blessed by having sort of incubators of the future in computers, in telecommunications, in electronics, increasingly in biotechnology. That is important.

Fourth, we've had a good, stable monetary system. I think the Prime Minister did a good thing by—and he'll be criticized for it the first time interest rates are raised, but he did a good thing, I think, by trying to take the setting of interest rates out of politics, because it will create the feeling of stability and make Britain more attractive for investment. That's been a big factor for us.

And finally, we've had good Government policies, which were: reduce the deficit, expand trade, invest in people. So I think all those things, together, will give you a job creation policy.

Prime Minister Blair. We'll take one more each, shall we?

President Clinton. Yes.

Q. Thank you. That was shameless. Ann McFeatters with Scripps-Howard.

President Clinton. That's good.

Bosnia

Q. Mr. President, you have promised to withdraw our troops from Bosnia a year from now. And yet the British Prime Minister's Foreign Secretary says if you do that, the British will withdraw their troops, too, and that could lead to renewed fighting. Is there a dispute between Secretary of State Albright and Defense Secretary Cohen, and are you going to keep your commitment to withdraw?

President Clinton. Well, when we—first of all, when we adopted the second mission, the SFOR mission, after our first full year in Bosnia, we cut all the forces in half and stayed; we said we expected that mission to last about a year and a half. I still accept that.

Here is the problem, the basic issue. I think we would all admit that a lot of the elements of the Bosnian peace process, the Dayton process, are not going as fast as they should. We have just completed a comprehensive review of our policy. We've identified a number of things we want to do better. The Prime Minister and I talked about, for example, the police training and the placement of police there.

If you look at what our military people do today, since we are not presently today actively involved, for example, in escorting and protecting refugee returnees, a lot of that could be done by civilian police, if we were on schedule. We're not on schedule. We're not on schedule in the economic implementation. We're trying to put—very hard, all of our allies—we're trying to put together a team that will get us back up and going.

And so I would agree, to this extent, with the Prime Minister, which is that I don't think we ought to be talking about how we're going to leave. I think we ought to be talking about what we're going to do tomorrow and next week and next month. And if we work like crazy in the next 13 months, do I believe we can fulfill our mission and that they can go forward? Yes, I do. But I think we're going to have to make some very tough decisions. We can't play around with this. We can't just sort of hang around and then disappear in a year and expect the Dayton process to go forward. We have a lot of work to do in the next year. And so what I want to do is stop talking about what date we're leaving on and start talking about we're going to do on the only date that matters, which is tomorrow.

Prime Minister Blair. I agree with that very strongly, indeed.

Last question.

Advice for Prime Minister Blair

Q. President Clinton, I know you're reluctant to offer advice to our Prime Minister, but could I tempt you? You became—I want to be polite—rather unpopular during your first term after a brief honeymoon. Which mistakes do you think you made that our Prime Minister could avoid?

Prime Minister Blair. Well, he did one thing very right, which was to win again, and I hope I repeat that. [*Laughter*]

President Clinton. Well, for one thing, it was a brief honeymoon; it lasted about 35 seconds. [*Laughter*] So, again, I don't know that I have any advice to offer. I think that the errors that we made, or at least the political decisions we made that caused us problems, are fairly well-known.

Also, keep in mind, we have a different system than you do. I had to pass my first economic program with only Democrats, but the Democrats basically got credit for being divided in their support of me when the facts are that they have supported me more strongly than they supported the last three Democratic Presidents before me. But our friends on the other side were opposed in even more unified fashion.

So the things that happened to us were so unique, I hope, to the American political system—I wouldn't wish them on anyone else—that I don't really think it's very instructive for me to give advice.

Prime Minister Blair. If I could, I just say one final thing to you. I think when you heard President Clinton speak about the record that he has achieved in Government earlier, I think that is the reason why he was reelected. And the important thing is that that record stands as testimony to the leadership that he gave.

We'll have one last question then, shall we?

President Clinton. My only advice on that would be to try to keep people focused on the policies and the consequences and that we should all be willing to work on that basis, because real people out there who have to get up every day and wonder how they're going to feed and educate their children and whether they're safe in their neighborhoods and what the future is going to be like for their kids, they want to know that we're at the task. And so my only advice would be to maintain the same level of concentration in the administration that was shown by all of Labour in the campaign, that relaxing concentration is fatal in this business. It's an important thing, and it's complicated. You got to concentrate all the time.

Representative Richard A. Gephardt

Q. Mr. President—I'm sorry, Rita Braver with CBS News. Bearing in mind your comments on the budget, I was wondering if you had been listening to your own minority leader. He is against you on the budget. He is against you on MFN. He is against you on expansion of NATO on a fast track. And I wondered if you could explain maybe whether you think it's you or he who represents the hearts and minds of the Democratic Party and whether maybe you think it's time for a new minority leader, or maybe you don't really want that Democratic majority you talked about at the beginning of the news conference.

President Clinton. No, I think—for one thing, I think—you know, I disagree with him about the budget and MFN for China, and we've had some trade differences since I came here; otherwise, he's supported me on just about everything. I would point out, however, that well over 60 percent of the Democratic caucus in the House voted for the budget agreement and that 82 percent of the Democratic caucus in the Senate voted for it. We had a higher percentage of Democrats than Republicans voting for it in the Senate, a higher percentage of Republicans than Democrats voting for it in the House, and a two-to-one majority overall.

So that's something—the American people ought to feel comfortable—we had an overwhelming bipartisan agreement. Individual people will have differences on individual issues. They'll see the world in different ways. But I think I did the right thing, and I think we're going to—I think the country will be immensely benefited by it. And I think everybody that voted for it, in retrospect, will be happy and those who didn't vote for it will be pleased that what they thought was wrong with it, wasn't. That's what I think will happen.

Prime Minister Blair. Okay, thank you very much indeed, ladies and gentlemen. And thank you, in particular, to President Clinton.

President Clinton. Thank you.

NOTE: The President's 147th news conference began at 3:05 p.m. in the Winter Garden at 10 Downing Street. In his remarks, he referred to John Major, former Prime Minister of the United Kingdom; President Boris Yeltsin of Russia; Prime Minister Wim Kok of The Netherlands; and Prime Minister Antonio Guterres of Portugal. A reporter referred to President-elect Mohammad Khatami of Iran.

Message to the Congress on Most-Favored-Nation Trade Status for China
May 29, 1997

To the Congress of the United States:
I hereby transmit the document referred to in subsection 402(d)(1) of the Trade Act of 1974, as amended (the "Act"), with respect to the continuation of a waiver of application of subsections (a) and (b) of section 402 of the Act to the People's Republic of China. This document constitutes my recommendations to continue in effect this waiver for a further 12-month period and includes my determination that continuation of the waiver currently in effect for the People's Republic of China will sub- stantially promote the objectives of section 402 of the Act, and my reasons for such determination.

WILLIAM J. CLINTON

The White House,
May 29, 1997.

NOTE: This message was released by the Office of the Press Secretary on May 30. The Presidential Determination of May 29 is listed in Appendix D at the end of this volume.

Statement on the Verdict in the Megan Kanka Trial
May 30, 1997

This has been a terrible tragedy for the Kanka family and their community. Megan's family took their pain and helped guide the Nation to adopt legislation that is going to protect other children from those who would harm them. We owe the Kanka family not only our sympathy but a debt of gratitude as well.

Message to the Congress on the Generalized System of Preferences
May 30, 1997

To the Congress of the United States:
The Generalized System of Preferences (GSP) program offers duty-free treatment to specified products that are imported from designated de- veloping countries. The program is authorized by title V of the Trade Act of 1974, as amended.
Pursuant to title V, I have determined that Cambodia should be designated as a least devel- oped beneficiary developing country under the GSP program because it has taken steps to im- prove worker rights and the protection of intel- lectual property. I have also determined, as a result of the 1995 Annual Review of petitions for changes that three products should be added to the GSP list of eligible products and that the competitive need limits on 22 products should be waived. As a result of a review of 1996 imports of GSP products, I have deter- mined that de minimis limits on 79 products be waived and 11 products, whose imports no

longer exceed the program's competitive need limits, should be redesignated as GSP eligible. Finally as a result of certain provisions of the legislation enacted in August 1996 reauthorizing GSP, I am granting GSP eligibility to an additional 1,783 articles not previously included under GSP, provided that they are imported directly from the least developed beneficiary developing countries.

This notice is submitted in accordance with the requirements of title V of the Trade Act of 1974.

WILLIAM J. CLINTON

The White House,
May 30, 1997.

NOTE: The proclamation of May 30 modifying duty-free treatment under the Generalized System of Preferences is listed in Appendix D at the end of this volume.

Message to the Congress Reporting on the National Emergency With Respect to the Federal Republic of Yugoslavia (Serbia and Montenegro) and the Bosnian Serbs
May 30, 1997

To the Congress of the United States:

On May 30, 1992, by Executive Order 12808, President Bush declared a national emergency to deal with the unusual and extraordinary threat to the national security, foreign policy, and economy of the United States constituted by the actions and policies of the Governments of Serbia and Montenegro, blocking all property and interests in property of those Governments. President Bush took additional measures to prohibit trade and other transactions with the Federal Republic of Yugoslavia (Serbia and Montenegro) by Executive Orders 12810 and 12831, issued on June 5, 1992, and January 15, 1993, respectively.

On April 25, 1993, I issued Executive Order 12846, blocking the property and interests in property of all commercial, industrial, or public utility undertakings or entities organized or located in the Federal Republic of Yugoslavia (Serbia and Montenegro) (the "FRY (S&M)"), and prohibiting trade-related transactions by United States persons involving those areas of the Republic of Bosnia and Herzegovina controlled by the Bosnian Serb forces and the United Nations Protected Areas in the Republic of Croatia. On October 24, 1994, because of the actions and policies of the Bosnian Serbs, I expanded the scope of the national emergency by issuance of Executive Order 12934 to block the property of the Bosnian Serb forces and the authorities in the territory that they control

within the Republic of Bosnia and Herzegovina, as well as the property of any entity organized or located in, or controlled by any person in, or resident in, those areas.

On November 22, 1995, the United Nations Security Council passed ("Resolution 1022"), immediately and indefinitely suspending economic sanctions against the FRY (S&M). Sanctions were subsequently lifted by the United Nations Security Council pursuant to Resolution 1074 on October 1, 1996. Resolution 1022, however, continues to provide for the release of funds and assets previously blocked pursuant to sanctions against the FRY (S&M), provided that such funds and assets that are subject to claims and encumbrances, or that are the property of persons deemed insolvent, remain blocked until "released in accordance with applicable law." This provision was implemented in the United States on December 27, 1995, by Presidential Determination No. 96–7. The Determination, in conformity with Resolution 1022, directed the Secretary of the Treasury, *inter alia*, to suspend the application of sanctions imposed on the FRY (S&M) pursuant to the above-referenced Executive orders and to continue to block property previously blocked until provision is made to address claims or encumbrances, including the claims of the other successor states of the former Yugoslavia. This sanctions relief was an essential factor motivating Serbia and

683

Montenegro's acceptance of the General Framework Agreement for Peace in Bosnia and Herzegovina initialed by the parties in Dayton on November 21, 1995 (the "Peace Agreement") and signed in Paris on December 14, 1995. The sanctions imposed on the FRY (S&M) and on the United Nations Protected Areas in the Republic of Croatia were accordingly suspended prospectively, effective January 16, 1996. Sanctions imposed on the Bosnian Serb forces and authorities and on the territory that they control within the Republic of Bosnia and Herzegovina were subsequently suspended prospectively, effective May 10, 1996, in conformity with UNSCR 1022. On October 1, 1996, the United Nations passed UNSCR 1074, terminating U.N. sanctions against the FRY (S&M) and the Bosnian Serbs in light of the elections that took place in Bosnia and Herzegovina on September 14, 1996. UNSCR 1074, however, reaffirms the provisions of UNSCR 1022 with respect to the release of blocked assets, as set forth above.

The present report is submitted pursuant to 50 U.S.C. 1641(c) and 1703(c) and covers the period from November 30, 1996, through May 29, 1997. It discusses Administration actions and expenses directly related to the exercise of powers and authorities conferred by the declaration of a national emergency in Executive Order 12808 as expanded with respect to the Bosnian Serbs in Executive Order 12934, and against the FRY (S&M) contained in Executive Orders 12810, 12831, and 12846.

The declaration of the national emergency on May 30, 1992, was made pursuant to the authority vested in the President by the Constitution and laws of the United States, including the International Emergency Economic Powers Act (50 U.S.C. 1701 *et seq.*), the National Emergencies Act (50 U.S.C. 1601 *et seq.*), and section 301 of title 3 of the United States Code. The emergency declaration was reported to the Congress on May 30, 1992, pursuant to section 204(b) of the International Emergency Economic Powers Act (50 U.S.C. 1703(b)) and the expansion of that national emergency under the same authorities was reported to the Congress on October 25, 1994. The additional sanctions set forth in related Executive orders were imposed pursuant to the authority vested in the President by the Constitution and laws of the United States, including the statutes cited above, section 1114 of the Federal Aviation Act (49

U.S.C. App. 1514), and section 5 of the United Nations Participation Act (22 U.S.C. 287c).

2. The Office of Foreign Assets Control (OFAC), acting under authority delegated by the Secretary of the Treasury, implemented the sanctions imposed under the foregoing statutes in the Federal Republic of Yugoslavia (Serbia and Montenegro) and Bosnian Serb-Controlled Areas of the Republic of Bosnia and Herzegovina Sanctions Regulations, 31 C.F.R. Part 585 (the "Regulations"). To implement Presidential Determination No. 967, the Regulations were amended to authorize prospectively all transactions with respect to the FRY (S&M) otherwise prohibited (61 *FR* 1282, January 19, 1996). Property and interests in property of the FRY (S&M) previously blocked within the jurisdiction of the United States remain blocked, in conformity with the Peace Agreement and UNSCR 1022, until provision is made to address claims or encumbrances, including the claims of the other successor states of the former Yugoslavia.

On May 10, 1996, OFAC amended the Regulations to authorize prospectively all transactions with respect to the Bosnian Serbs otherwise prohibited, except with respect to property previously blocked (61 *FR* 24696, May 16, 1996). On December 4, 1996, OFAC amended Appendices A and B to 31 C.F.R. chapter V, containing the names of entities and individuals in alphabetical order and by location that are subject to the various economic sanctions programs administered by OFAC, to remove the entries for individuals and entities that were determined to be acting for or on behalf of the Government of the Federal Republic of Yugoslavia (Serbia and Montenegro). These assets were blocked on the basis of these persons' activities in support of the FRY (S&M)—activities no longer prohibited—not because the Government of the FRY (S&M) or entities located in or controlled from the FRY (S&M) had any interest in those assets (61 *FR* 64289, December 4, 1996). A copy of the amendment is attached to this report.

On April 18, 1997, the Regulations were amended by adding a new section 585.528, authorizing all transactions after 30 days with respect to the following vessels that remained blocked pursuant to the Regulations, effective at 10:00 a.m. local time in the location of the vessel on May 19, 1997: the M/V *Moslavina*, M/V *Zeta*, M/V *Lovcen*, M/V *Durmitor* and M/V *Bar* (a/k/a M/V *Inviken*) (62 *FR* 19672, April

23, 1997). During the 30-day period, United States persons were authorized to negotiate settlements of their outstanding claims with respect to the vessels with the vessels' owners or agents and were generally licensed to seek and obtain judicial warrants of maritime arrest. If claims remained unresolved 10 days prior to the vessels' unblocking (May 8, 1997), service of the warrants could be effected at that time through the United States Marshal's Office in the district where the vessel was located to ensure that United States creditors of a vessel had the opportunity to assert their claims. Appendix C to 31 CFR, chapter V, containing the names of vessels blocked pursuant to the various economic sanctions programs administered by OFAC (61 FR 32936, June 26, 1996), was also amended to remove these vessels from the list effective May 19, 1997. A copy of the amendment is attached to this report.

3. Over the past year, the Departments of State and the Treasury have worked closely with European Union member states and other U.N. member nations to implement the provisions of UNSCR 1022. In the United States, retention of blocking authority pursuant to the extension of a national emergency provides a framework for administration of an orderly claims settlement. This accords with past policy and practice with respect to the suspension of sanctions regimes.

4. During this reporting period, OFAC issued seven specific licenses regarding transactions pertaining to the FRY (S&M) or assets it owns or controls. Specific licenses have been issued (1) to authorize the unblocking of certain funds and other financial assets previously blocked; (2) for the payment of crews' wages, vessel maintenance, and emergency supplies for FRY (S&M)-controlled ships blocked in the United States; and (3) to authorize performance of certain transactions under pre-sanctions contracts.

During the past 6 months, OFAC has continued to oversee the maintenance of blocked accounts and records with respect to: (1) liquidated tangible assets and personalty of the 15 blocked United States subsidiaries of entities organized in the FRY (S&M); (2) the blocked personalty, files, and records of the two Serbian banking institutions in New York previously placed in secure storage; (3) remaining tangible property, including real estate; and (4) the 5 Yugoslav-owned vessels recently unblocked in the United States.

5. Despite the prospective authorization of transactions with the FRY (S&M), OFAC has continued to work closely with the United States Customs Service and other cooperating agencies to investigate alleged violations that occurred while sanctions were in force.

Since my last report, OFAC has collected six civil monetary penalties totaling nearly $39,000 for violations of the sanctions. These violations included prohibited imports, exports, contract dealings, and payments to the Government of the FRY (S&M), persons in the FRY (S&M), or to blocked entities owned or controlled by the FRY (S&M).

6. The expenses incurred by the Federal Government in the 6-month period from November 30, 1996, through May 29, 1997, that are directly attributable to the declaration of a national emergency with respect to the FRY (S&M) and the Bosnian Serb forces and authorities are estimated at approximately $400,000, most of which represents wage and salary costs for Federal personnel. Personnel costs were largely centered in the Department of the Treasury (particularly in OFAC and its Chief Counsel's Office, and the United States Customs Service), the Department of State, the National Security Council, and the Department of Commerce.

7. In the last year and a half, substantial progress has been achieved to bring about a settlement of the conflict in the former Yugoslavia acceptable to the parties. UNSCR 1074 terminates sanctions in view of the first free and fair elections to occur in the Republic of Bosnia and Herzegovina, as provided for in the Peace Agreement. In reaffirming Resolution 1022, however, UNSCR 1074 contemplates the continued blocking of assets potentially subject to conflicting claims and encumbrances until provision is made to address them under applicable law, including claims of the other successor states of the former Yugoslavia.

The resolution of the crisis and conflict in the former Yugoslavia that has resulted from the actions and policies of the Government of the Federal Republic of Yugoslavia (Serbia and Montenegro), and of the Bosnian Serb forces and the authorities in the territory that they control, will not be complete until such time as the Peace Agreement is implemented and the terms of UNSCR 1022 have been met. Therefore, I have continued for another year the national emergency declared on May 30,

1992, as expanded in scope on October 25, 1994, and will continue to enforce the measures adopted pursuant thereto.

I shall continue to exercise the powers at my disposal with respect to the measures against the Government of the Federal Republic of Yugoslavia (Serbia and Montenegro), and the Bosnian Serb forces, civil authorities, and enti-ties, as long as these measures are appropriate, and will continue to report periodically to the Congress on significant developments pursuant to 50 U.S.C. 1703(c).

WILLIAM J. CLINTON

The White House,
May 30, 1997.

The President's Radio Address
May 31, 1997

Good morning. I've just returned from Europe where I commemorated the 50th anniversary of the Marshall plan, which joined America's investment to Europe's commitment to rebuild and, in so doing, helped to spark 50 years of prosperity, not only for Europe but for America as well.

I also had the opportunity to discuss with leaders of Europe the present success of our economy and what we can do together to promote prosperity in the new democracies of Central and Eastern Europe in ways that will ensure their prosperity and ours for the next 50 years.

This morning I want to talk with you about the new economic policy we brought to America for the last 4½ years and how our balanced budget and tax cut plans can help in creating jobs, raising incomes, strengthening business, and moving America forward in the years to come.

Recall for a moment what America's economy looked like 4 years ago: high unemployment, few new jobs, stagnant wages, exploding budget deficits. I took office determined to replace trickle-down economics with invest-and-grow economics. There were three principal elements to our strategy: reduce the budget deficit; and invest in the education, training, and security of working men and women and our children; and open new markets for American-made goods and services through tough trade agreements. I believe all three were necessary to create the conditions for private sector prosperity and to ensure that all our people have the opportunity to reap the rewards of growth.

We made tough, often controversial decisions in 1993 and afterward to implement our new invest-and-grow economic policy. Some fine Members of Congress lost their seats because they had the courage to change course and vote for the future. But just look at the results. Today our confidence has returned and our economy leads the world.

In 1992, the deficit was $290 billion. Today, we expect it to drop to $67 billion, a 77 percent reduction. In 1992, unemployment averaged 7.5 percent. Today, it's 4.9 percent, the lowest in 24 years. In 1992 there were few new jobs. Since then, the economy has produced 12.1 million of them, including the most ever in a single Presidential term. And while the years before our plan took effect saw sluggish growth, yesterday we learned that in the first quarter of this year the economy grew at a 5.8 percent rate, the highest in a decade. Inflation is at a 30-year low; business investment, a 30-year high. Each year we've had a record number of new businesses started. Wages are rising. In the last 2 years, over half the new jobs have paid higher than average wages and inequality among working people has seen the biggest drop since the 1960's. Our economy is the healthiest in a generation.

All this didn't just happen. We've had better managed, more competitive businesses; more productive working people; the entrepreneurial spirit of small business; a Federal Reserve committed both to low inflation and to economic growth; and continued advances in technology. Americans' hard work and high energy, smart decisions in tough choices, and our invest-and-grow strategy, all these have worked together to produce this success.

Now, in the coming months, America will have to decide whether to stick with this strategy. Will we continue to engage the world economy by continuing to give normal trading status to China? Will Congress give the President the tools necessary to open new markets abroad for American products through tough new trade agreements? And above all, will we finish the job of balancing the budget while protecting our values?

Earlier this month, I reached agreement with the leaders of Congress on a bipartisan balanced budget plan that will continue our economic strategy into the next century. This is a balanced budget plan that also is in balance with our values. It will eliminate the budget deficit by 2002, honor our parents by securing the Medicare Trust Fund for a decade, preserve our environment through strong enforcement and the cleanup of 500 toxic waste sites, and protect the next generation by extending health insurance coverage to as many as 5 million uninsured children. And most important of all, it will invest in the skills of our people through the most significant increase in higher education since the GI bill half a century ago, the expansion of Head Start, and an investment in higher national academic standards for our children.

Both Houses of Congress moved forward on this budget before they left town for the Memorial Day recess. I was pleased that a strong majority of both parties supported this bipartisan plan. When Congress gets back to work, it's time to finish the job of enacting the broad outlines of the budget plan. Then in the weeks to come, Congress will fill in the details and begin writing this budget and its tax cut into law. I want a tax cut that helps families raise their children and send them to college and keeps the economy growing. That's my goal.

I look forward to continuing to work together with the Republican and Democratic Members of the tax writing committees in Congress to meet this goal as we write the details of the tax cut into law. As that process begins, I want to tell you three of the things this final tax cut plan should include.

First, with education our most important goal, our tax cut must help open the doors of college to every American. Our bipartisan budget plan includes $35 billion in tax relief, targeted to help families pay for higher education. Our HOPE scholarship is a $1,500-per-year tax cut to help pay for the first 2 years of college and

open them to all Americans. I will also recommend that students who already receive Pell grant scholarships can still receive the HOPE scholarship for education costs beyond those covered by their Pell grant. With this step, we'll make sure that our tax cut reaches all those who want to take responsibility for their own lives and go on to college. Beyond that, I favor a tax deduction for the cost of any education after high school for people of any age.

Second, as many families as possible should have a chance to receive the dividend created by economic growth. Our plan will give families a $500 child tax credit. This is the kind of tax relief we need, targeted to helping families raise their children and meeting the competing demands of work and family. As we craft this tax cut, I believe it's especially important that we make sure that the child tax credit is fair to working families, especially those with lower incomes.

Third, the tax cuts must be consistent with a balanced budget and must not be written in such a way that they reopen the deficit and bust the budget in years to come. This was absolutely key when we reached a budget agreement, and I will continue to insist on it as we write the agreement into law. Fiscal responsibility helped to produce a strong economy. Fiscal irresponsibility will surely undo it. We cannot put our prosperity at risk through time-bomb tax cuts that explode the deficit in 5 or 10 or 20 years. We must continue with discipline. We tried it the other way before, and it failed.

We are now nearly 5 years into our economic strategy of invest and grow, and it is working, well beyond our most optimistic expectations. We have now an historic chance to continue this growth and give the American people the dividends of expansion through a tax cut. We can protect our values as we expand our economy. The American people deserve a tax cut, and they need a balanced budget. We can give them both. If we make sure that this tax cut helps all working families, that it opens wide the doors of college, and that it never, never throws the budget out of balance, we can propel our country into the 21st century even stronger than it is today.

Thanks for listening.

NOTE: The address was recorded at 7:30 p.m. on May 30 in the Map Room at the White House for broadcast at 10:06 a.m. on May 31.

Commencement Address at the United States Military Academy in West Point, New York
May 31, 1997

Thank you very much. Please be seated; relax. Thank you, General Christman, for those kind introductory remarks and for your truly extraordinary service to your Nation throughout your military career. Here at West Point and before, when we had more opportunities to work together on a daily basis, I have constantly admired your dedication and your ability.

General Reimer, Secretary West, Senator Reed, Chairman Gilman, Congressman Shimkus, Congresswoman Kelly, Congressman Sessions, former Congressman Bilbray, parents and families and friends of the cadets, and especially to the class of 1997, I extend my heartfelt congratulations.

This has been a truly remarkable class. As General Christman said, you wrote an unparalleled record of academic achievement in the classroom. I congratulate you all and particularly your number one honor graduate and valedictorian, David Ake. Congratulations to all of you on your accomplishments.

Now, General Christman also outlined the extraordinary accomplishments of your athletic teams, and he mentioned that I had the privilege of seeing Army win its first 10-win season in football and reclaim the Commander in Chief's Trophy in Philadelphia. And he thanked me for that. But actually, as a lifelong football fan, I deserve no thanks. It was a terrific game, and I'm quite sure it was the first time in the field of any endeavor of conflict where the Army defeated the Navy not on land but on water. [*Laughter*]

I know that in spite of all of your achievements as a class and in teams, a few of you also upheld West Point's enduring tradition of independence. It began in 1796 when President Adams' War Department ordered the first classes in fortification. And the troops here thought they already knew all about that, so they burned the classroom to the ground, postponing the start of instruction by 5 years. [*Laughter*]

Today I am reliably informed that though your spirits are equally high, your infractions are more modest. Therefore, I hereby exercise my prerogative to grant amnesty for minor offenses to the Corps of Cadets. [*Applause*] The cheering was a little disconcerting—now, the operative word there was "minor." [*Laughter*]

Men and women of the class of '97, today you join the Long Gray Line, the Long Gray Line that stretches across two centuries of unstinting devotion to America and the freedom that is our greatest treasure. From the defense of Fort Erie in the War of 1812 to the fury of Antietam, from the trenches of Argonne to the Anzio and Okinawa, to Heartbreak Ridge, the Mekong Delta, the fiery desert of the Gulf war, the officers of West Point have served and sacrificed for our Nation.

In just the 4 years since I last spoke here, your graduates have helped to restore democracy to Haiti, to save hundreds of thousands of lives from genocide and famine in Rwanda, to end the bloodshed in Bosnia. Throughout our history, whenever duty called, the men and women of West Point have never failed us. And I speak for all Americans when I say, I know you never will.

I'd like to say a special word of appreciation to West Point and a special word of congratulations to the students in this class from other countries. We welcome you here, we are proud to have you as a part of our military service tradition, and we wish you well as you go back home. We hope you, too, can advance freedom's cause, for in the 21st century, that is something we must do together.

Two days ago, I returned from Europe on a mission to look back to one of the proudest chapters in America's history and to look forward to the history we all will seek to shape for our children and grandchildren. This week is the 50th anniversary of the Marshall plan, what Winston Churchill described as the most unsordid act in all history.

In 1947, Americans, exhausted by war and anxious to get on with their lives at home, were summoned to embrace another leadership role by a generation of remarkable leaders, General George Marshall, Senator Arthur Vandenberg, President Harry Truman, leaders who knew there could be no lasting peace and security for an America that withdrew behind its borders and withdrew from the world and its responsibilities. They provided the indispensable leadership to create the Marshall plan, NATO, the first global financial institutions. They, in effect, organized America and our allies to meet the challenges of their time, to build unparalleled prosperity, to stand firm against Soviet expansionism until the light of freedom shone all across Europe.

The second purpose of my journey was inextricably tied to the first. It was to look to the future, to the possibility of achieving what Marshall's generation could only dream of, a democratic, peaceful, and undivided Europe for the first time in all of history, and to the necessity of America and its allies once again organizing ourselves to meet the challenges of our time, to secure peace and prosperity for the next 50 years and beyond.

To build and secure a new Europe, peaceful, democratic, and undivided at last, there must be a new NATO, with new missions, new members, and new partners. We have been building that kind of NATO for the last 3 years with new partners in the Partnership For Peace and NATO's first out-of-area mission in Bosnia. In Paris last week, we took another giant stride forward when Russia entered a new partnership with NATO, choosing cooperation over confrontation, as both sides affirmed that the world is different now. European security is no longer a zero-sum contest between Russia and NATO but a cherished common goal.

In a little more than a month, I will join with other NATO leaders in Madrid to invite the first of Europe's new democracies in Central Europe to join our alliance, with the consent of the Senate, by 1999, the 50th anniversary of NATO's founding.

I firmly believe NATO enlargement is in our national interests. But because it is not without cost and risk, it is appropriate to have an open, full, national discussion before proceeding. I want to further that discussion here today in no small measure because it is especially important to those of you in this class. For after all, as the sentinels of our security in the years ahead, your work will be easier and safer if we do the right thing, and riskier and much more difficult if we do not.

Europe's fate and America's future are joined. Twice in half a century, Americans have given their lives to defend liberty and peace in World Wars that began in Europe. And we have stayed in Europe in very large numbers for a long time throughout the cold war. Taking wise steps now to strengthen our common security when we have the opportunity to do so will help to build a future without the mistakes and the divisions of the past and will enable us to organize ourselves to meet the new security challenges of the new century. In this task, NATO should be our sharpest sword and strongest shield.

Some say we no longer need NATO because there is no powerful threat to our security now. I say there is no powerful threat in part because NATO is there. And enlargement will help make it stronger. I believe we should take in new members to NATO for four reasons.

First, it will strengthen our alliance in meeting the security challenges of the 21st century, addressing conflicts that threaten the common peace of all. Consider Bosnia. Already the Czech Republic, Poland, Romania, the Baltic nations, and other Central European countries are contributing troops and bases to NATO's peacekeeping mission in Bosnia. We in the United States could not have deployed our troops to Bosnia as safely, smoothly, and swiftly as we did without the help of Hungary and our staging ground at Taszar, which I personally visited. The new democracies we invite to join NATO are ready and able to share the burdens of defending freedom in no small measure because they know the cost of losing freedom.

Second, NATO enlargement will help to secure the historic gains of democracy in Europe. NATO can do for Europe's East what it did for Europe's West at the end of World War II: provide a secure climate where freedom, democracy, and prosperity can flourish. Joining NATO once helped Italy, Germany, and Spain to consolidate their democracies. Now the opening of NATO's doors has led the Central European nations already—already—to deepen democratic reform, to strengthen civilian control of their military, to open their economies. Membership and its future prospect will give them the confidence to stay the course.

Third, enlarging NATO will encourage prospective members to resolve their differences peacefully. We see all over the world the terrible curse of people who are imprisoned by their own ethnic, regional, and nationalist hatreds, who rob themselves and their children of the lives they might have because of their primitive, destructive impulses that they cannot control.

When he signed the NATO treaty in 1949, President Truman said that if NATO had simply existed in 1914 or 1939, it would have prevented the World Wars that tore the world apart. The experience of the last 50 years supports that view. NATO helped to reconcile age-old adversaries like France and Germany, now fast friends and allies, and clearly has reduced tensions between Greece and Turkey over all these decades. Already the very prospect of NATO membership has helped to convince countries in Central Europe to settle more than half a dozen border and ethnic disputes, any one of which could have led to future conflicts. That, in turn, makes it less likely that you will ever be called to fight in another war across the Atlantic.

Fourth, enlarging NATO, along with its Partnership For Peace with many other nations and its special agreement with Russia and its soon-to-be-signed partnership with Ukraine, will erase the artificial line in Europe that Stalin drew and bring Europe together in security, not keep it apart in instability.

NATO expansion does not mean a differently divided Europe; it is part of unifying Europe. NATO's first members should not be its last. NATO's doors will remain open to all those willing and able to shoulder the responsibilities of membership, and we must continue to strengthen our partnerships with nonmembers.

Now, let me be clear to all of you: These benefits are not cost- or risk-free. Enlargement will require the United States to pay an estimated $200 million a year for the next decade. Our allies in Canada and Western Europe are prepared to do their part; so are NATO's new members; so must we.

More important, enlargement requires that we extend to new members our alliance's most solemn security pledge, to treat an attack against one as an attack against all. We have always made the pledge credible through the deployment of our troops and the deterrence of our nuclear weapons. In the years ahead, it means that you could be asked to put your lives on the line for a new NATO member, just as today you can be called upon to defend the freedom of our allies in Western Europe.

In leading NATO over the past 3 years to open its doors to Europe's new democracies, I weighed these costs very carefully. I concluded that the benefits of enlargement—strengthening NATO for the future, locking in democracy's gains in Central Europe, building stability across

the Atlantic, uniting Europe, not dividing it—these gains decisively outweigh the burdens. The bottom line to me is clear: Expanding NATO will enhance our security. It is the right thing to do. We must not fail history's challenge at this moment to build a Europe peaceful, democratic, and undivided, allied with us to face the new security threats of the new century, a Europe that will avoid repeating the darkest moments of the 20th century and fulfill the brilliant possibilities of the 21st.

This vision for a new Europe is central to our larger security strategy, which you will be called upon to implement and enforce. But our agenda must go beyond it because, with all of our power and wealth, we are living in a world in which increasingly our influence depends upon our recognizing that our future is interdependent with other nations and we must work with them all across the globe, because we see the threats we face tomorrow will cross national boundaries. They are amplified by modern technology, communication, and travel. They must be faced by like-minded nations working together, whether we're talking about terrorism, the proliferation of weapons of mass destruction, drug trafficking, or environmental degradation. Therefore, we must pursue five other objectives.

First, we must build a community of Asia-Pacific nations bound by a common commitment to stability and prosperity. We fought three wars in Asia in half a century. Asia's stability affects our peace, and Asia's explosive growth affects our prosperity. That's why we've strengthened our security ties to Japan and Korea, why we now meet every year with the Asia-Pacific leaders, why we must work with and not isolate ourselves from China.

One of the great questions that will define the future for your generation of Americans is how China will define its own greatness as a nation. We have worked with China because we believe it is important to cooperate in ways that will shape the definition of that great nation in positive, not negative, ways. We need not agree with China on all issues to maintain normal trade relations, but we do need normal trade relations to have a chance of eventually reaching agreement with China on matters of vital importance to America and the world.

Second, we are building coalitions across the world to confront these new security threats that know no borders: weapons proliferation, terrorism, drug trafficking, environmental degradation.

We have to lead in constructing global arrangements that provide us the tools to deal with these common threats: the Chemical Weapons Convention, the Non-Proliferation Treaty, the Comprehensive Test Ban Treaty, and our efforts to further reduce nuclear weapons with Russia. Now our great task is also to build these kinds of arrangements fighting terrorism, drug traffickers, and organized crime. Three weeks from now in Denver, I will use the summit of the eight leading nations to press this agenda.

The third thing we have to do is to build an open trading system. Our security is tied to the stake other nations have in the prosperity of staying free and open and working with others, not working against them. In no small measure because of the trade agreements we have negotiated, we have not only regained our position as the world's number one exporter, we have increased our influence in ways that are good for our security. To continue that progress, it is important that I have the authority to conclude smart new market-opening agreements that every President in 20 years has had.

Some of our fellow Americans do not believe that the President should have this authority anymore. They believe that somehow the global economy presents a threat to us, but I believe it's here to stay. And I think the evidence is that Americans—just as we can have the world's strongest and best military, we have the strongest and best economy in the world. The American people can out-work and out-compete anyone, given a free and fair chance.

Not only that but this is about more than money and jobs; this is about security. The world, especially our democratic neighbors to the south of us, are looking to us. If we don't build economic bridges to them, someone else will. We must make it clear that America supports free people and fair, open trade.

Fourth, we have to embrace our role as the decisive force for peace. You cannot and you should not go everywhere. But when our values and interests are at stake, our mission is crystal clear and achievable, America should stand with our allies around the world who seek to bring peace and prevent slaughter. From the Middle East to Bosnia, from Haiti to Northern Ireland, we have worked to contain conflict, to support peace, to give children a brighter future, and it has enhanced our security.

Finally, we have to have the tools to do these jobs. Those are the most powerful and best trained military in the world and a fully funded diplomacy to minimize the chances that military force will be necessary.

The long-term defense plan we have just completed will increase your readiness, capabilities, and technological edge. In a world of persistent dangers, you must and you will be able to dominate the conflicts of the future as you did the battlefields of the past.

Fifty-five years ago, in the early days of World War II, General George Marshall, the man we honored this week, spoke here at your commencement about the need to organize our Nation for the ordeal of war. He said, "We are determined that before the Sun sets on this terrible struggle, our flag will be recognized as a symbol of freedom on the one hand and of overwhelming power on the other."

Today, our flag of freedom and power flies higher than ever, but because our Nation stands at the pinnacle of its power, it also stands at the pinnacle of its responsibility. Therefore, as you carry our flag into this new era, we must organize ourselves to meet the challenges of the next 50 years. We must shape the peace for a new and better century about to dawn so that you can give your children and your grandchildren the America and the world they deserve.

God bless you, and God bless America.

NOTE: The President spoke at 10:20 a.m. in Michie Stadium. In his remarks, he referred to Lt. Gen. Daniel W. Christman, USA, Superintendent, and Adam K. Ake, valedictorian, U.S. Military Academy; and Gen. Dennis J. Reimer, USA, Chief of Staff, U.S. Army.

Statement on the Department of Justice's Report on Crime
June 1, 1997

Four years ago, my administration made a commitment to take our streets back from crime and violence. We have a comprehensive anticrime plan, and it is working. More community police, tougher punishments, and fewer guns in the hands of criminals are making a difference. Today's Justice Department release marks the largest one-year decline in murder, aggravated assault, and violent crime in the past 35 years. The continued downward trend over the past 4 years is further evidence that we are on the right track with increased community policing, tougher penalties, and greater juvenile crime prevention efforts.

Much work remains to be done, however. Juvenile crime and violence must be our top law enforcement priority for the next 4 years. My anti-gang and youth violence strategy declares war on juvenile crime and gangs, with new prosecutors and tougher penalties; an extension of the Brady bill, so violent teenage criminals will never have the right to purchase a handgun; and resources to keep schools open after hours, on weekends, and in the summer. While the House-passed juvenile crime legislation falls short of the goals outlined in my strategy, I am hopeful that the Senate will improve on this measure and pass it without delay. We must keep the crime rate coming down, and every child's prospect of a bright future going up.

NOTE: This statement was made available by the Office of the Press Secretary on May 30, but it was embargoed for release until 6 p.m. on June 1.

Letter to Congressional Leaders Reporting on the Deployment of United States Forces to Sierra Leone
May 30, 1997

Dear Mr. Speaker: *(Dear Mr. President:)*

On May 25, soldiers from the Republic of Sierra Leone Military Forces (RSLMF) mutinied against the country's democratically elected President, Ahmed Tejan Kabbah. Battles between the mutineers and the President's Nigerian security guard resulted in several rocket propelled grenade rounds hitting the U.S. Embassy. In addition, the RSLMF soldiers have engaged in looting, rape, armed robbery, and carjackings throughout the city. Sporadic gunfire and looting diminished with the arrival of additional Nigerian military forces that attempted to restore order. However, the security situation is deteriorating as tensions rise between Nigerian troops on the one hand and the mutineers and their supporters on the other hand. While there is no evidence that Americans are being directly targeted, the disorder and violence in Freetown subjects American citizens to continued risks ranging from criminal acts to random violence.

On May 29 and May 30, due to the uncertain security situation and the possible threat to American citizens and the American Embassy in Sierra Leone, approximately 200 U.S. military personnel, including an 11-member special forces detachment, were positioned in Freetown to prepare for the evacuation of certain U.S. Government employees and private U.S. citizens. Evacuation operations began on May 30, as U.S. military helicopters transported U.S. citizens and designated third-country nationals to immediate safety aboard the U.S.S. *Kearsarge* from where they will be taken to Conakry, Guinea, for further transportation. In addition to those evacuated by helicopter, 18 U.S. citizens departed Sierra Leone on May 29 via a British charter airline flight.

The Marines involved in this operation are from the Marine Expeditionary Unit currently embarked aboard U.S.S. *Kearsarge*, operating off the west coast of Africa. Special forces personnel are from the U.S. Army Third Special Forces Group, Fort Bragg, North Carolina. Although

U.S. forces are equipped for combat, the evacuation has been undertaken solely for the purpose of protecting American citizens and property. United States forces will redeploy as soon as evacuation operations are complete and enhanced security at locations in and around Freetown is no longer required.

I have taken this action pursuant to my constitutional authority to conduct the foreign relations of the United States and as Commander in Chief and Chief Executive.

I am providing this report as part of my efforts to keep the Congress fully informed, consistent with the War Powers Resolution. I appreciate the support of the Congress in this action to protect American citizens and the American Embassy in Freetown, Sierra Leone.

Sincerely,

WILLIAM J. CLINTON

NOTE: Identical letters were sent to Newt Gingrich, Speaker of the House of Representatives, and Strom Thurmond, President pro tempore of the Senate. This letter was released by the Office of the Press Secretary on June 2.

Statement on the Oklahoma City Bombing Trial
June 2, 1997

I cannot comment on the jury's verdict, but I will say that this is a very important and long overdue day for the survivors and families of those who died in Oklahoma City. And I am very, very proud of the work of Attorney General Janet Reno, the prosecutors, the FBI, and the ATF.

Two years ago, I spoke to the families of 168 people who lost their lives at the Murrah Federal building. I told them that though they had lost much, they had not lost everything—and they had not lost America. I pledged then and I pledge now that we will stand with them for as many tomorrows as it takes. Today I say to the families of the victims, no single verdict can bring an end to your anguish, but your courage has been an inspiration to all Americans. Our prayers are with you.

Interview With Sarah Staley and Bill Brand of VH1
June 3, 1997

President's Musical Interests

Q. Starting off with just present day, being President, it comes with a lot of "Pomp and Circumstance" and "Hail to the Chief." What has music meant to you personally and publicly as President?

The President. First of all, it gives a lot of meaning to being President, because the President has the Marine Band, and then whenever we have a state visit here a marching band from the Army in colonial costumes with old instruments performs. So a lot of being President is the reminder of the music here. The Air Force, the Navy, the Army, all have dance bands; they play here at the White House for events. So that's a good part of it.

The second thing that I would say is that one of the nice things about being President is nearly anybody will come perform for you. So I've gotten to be friends with people that I've loved for 20 or 30 years, James Taylor, Carly Simon, Barbra Streisand, Aretha Franklin, countless others, and then to bring a lot of other new people in and give people a chance to be heard. We've had—working with public television here, we've had a country music concert reflecting women in country music; we've done jazz music; we've done blues. It's just been fascinating. Just last week we had Yo Yo Ma, Edgar Meyer, and Mark O'Malley in here to do their wonderful Appalachian music. So all of that has been very, very important.

And then, of course, I've gotten to bring some of the most wonderful gospel and religious singers in the country in my two Inaugural services, and there are other times. So for me, one of the best things personally about being President has been the music and the way I could just sort of swallow up all my musical interests. It's been great.

Q. Let's get back to where the musical interests started. Warren Moss was here during the Inauguration, and we were talking to him. He tells a hysterical story that—was it George Grey was handling out instruments in, like, third or fourth grade. And he grabbed the trumpet, and you were left with the saxophone. Did you always want to play the saxophone?

The President. Yes, I did. Actually, I started on the clarinet when I was 9 with George Grey—who was a friend of mine all his life; we were pen pals forever—my grade school band director, and he had a daughter who was also a musician. So I played clarinet for a while, and frankly, I wasn't very good at it. And they switched me to saxophone when I was 9 years old. So I've been playing since I was 9.

Q. Mr. Spurlin said you were made for the saxophone.

The President. It suited me. It suits me emotionally, intellectually. I always liked it.

Q. There are some great videos that we have—Virginia put home videos on tape and gave them to David, and we were looking at them—of you dancing in the living room. Virginia's there, and I guess it's Roger Clinton, and little Roger is running around. What was the music that would have been playing then? I think you might have been 12, 13.

The President. Oh, when I was 12 or 13, it would have been—gosh, that was back in 1958—it would have been Elvis Presley, Bill Haley, Fats Domino, all those people.

Q. What did the music mean for you growing up? I mean, all your friendships——

The President. I loved it. I loved the whole rock and roll thing. And I was—a lot of parents in the fifties didn't like it very much. They thought there was something vaguely bad about it, you know. And my mother thought it was wonderful. She loved Elvis Presley from the first day she saw him. She thought rock and roll was great for kids. So music was always encouraged in our home, and we had—until I was 15, when I lived in a place that actually had a hardwood floor and a big room where you

could have dances. So we had kids dancing there all the time. It was great.

Q. Was it your mom who got you hooked on the musical bug? I mean, with her love for music, or was it——

The President. I think so. Neither of my parents had a particular interest, obsession with music like I did. My mother loved rock and roll and loved Elvis Presley in particular. And my father actually had played saxophone as a little boy. And I own a soprano saxophone, believe it or not, that is playable today—I've had it restored—that was made in 1915. I also have an old C-Melody saxophone that my father played. That was the only family connection, but he didn't play anymore when I started. And I just fell in love with it and just kept on doing it.

Q. Now, you mentioned, when we were talking about the Presidency, your love for gospel and spiritual music. And a lot of people—of course, I know about it, but a lot of people hadn't known about that love. You know, they just always saw you on Arsenio playing saxophone. You've mentioned—an interesting sort of reference to that was you all—that you've mentioned many times—that we all need to be repairers of the breach. What role does music play in that?

The President. Oh, I think that, for me, there is nothing that's any more emotionally healing. When I'm blue or down, I can hear some good gospel music; it immediately just lifts me up. And I've always felt that way. One of the greatest things about my being Governor of a Southern State with a lot of gospel roots is that I heard a phenomenal amount of fabulous church music from my childhood all up through my public service, both in black churches and in white churches. And that's where I got involved with the Pentecostals, who have contributed so much to my religious music education and so much to the enrichment not only of me but Hillary and Chelsea as well.

Q. What's it like during those Inaugural prayer services or anytime that you hear your friends, such as Janice or Micky or even my mom—what's it like to hear them, friends who love you, singing those songs?

The President. It's different and better. I think it's really nice when you get to know people, particularly if you've known them a long time— you just take a lot of joy in their talent, and they can touch you in a way when they're singing to you they can't when they're talking to you. It's an amazing thing. It's quite wonderful.

I also feel an immense pride. Whenever I see someone perform now that I know, who's a personal friend of mine, anywhere, especially my childhood friends or people I've known for a long time, but even people I've gotten to be friends with in the last 5 or 10 years, and I know how hard it is and I see how good they are, it really makes me proud.

Q. That's wonderful. You mentioned black artists, black music. Was that—you mentioned Virginia loved Elvis, and there was sort of the Beatles. Going into black music, was that different, Motown?

The President. When I was a child, I just—I was elated by all those Motown artists. I loved them all. And in the late eighties, I once got to play in Michigan, "Dancing in the Streets" with the Four Tops, Martha and the Vandellas, and Junior Walker. And I never will forget—I never will forget playing a saxophone riff with Junior Walker. It was a great thing. And I always loved that. I loved Ray Charles, and I loved that, and then I loved all the religious music.

One of the most memorable concerts in my entire life was a concert I attended as a young man when I was living in England. I went to the Royal Albert Hall, and I heard Mahalia Jackson sing. And all these British kids came to hear it. And I thought, you know, most of them had never even been exposed to anything like Mahalia Jackson. And when she finished singing, they stormed the stage. It was unbelievable. It was like she was a young rock star or something. So that's a big part of what music is to me, is my whole relationship with African-Americans and the roots that we share, and it always has been.

Q. It sounds like there was a real change not only in what was going on in your heart but musically when you went to Georgetown. Of course, Tom Campbell says you still came in with your little portable record player. But the discussions were longer at dinner about——

The President. Yes, and the music began to change. And the people became more serious. They got involved in the discussions about civil rights, and there were riots in the streets, and then there was the war in Vietnam. We literally had riots in Washington when Martin Luther King was killed. But there was a lot of music around all that.

I remember—you have these little songs I guess you associate with different periods in your life. When I came to Georgetown, on Sunday afternoon there was a place called the Cellar Door right down from where I lived. And you could go down there on Sunday afternoon, and for a dollar you could go in and get a Coke and listen to whoever was playing. And one group that played a lot there was a group called the Mugwumps. The lead singer of the Mugwumps was Cass Elliot, who later became Mama Cass of the Mamas and the Papas. And two other people in the Mugwumps became two of the four people in the Lovin' Spoonful. So when the Mamas and the Papas came on later in my college career, they always—every time I hear the Mamas and Papas, I think about Georgetown, I think about college, I think about "Monday, Monday" and all those old great songs.

And I think there is some of that at each stage of my life. The last week—last month I was in England, when I lived in England, was June of 1970, and that's when the Beatles broke up. So every time I hear "Let It Be"—every time I hear "Let It Be," I remember those endless lines of people who lined up to see the last movie that the Beatles made right when they announced they were breaking up.

Q. Now, the Beatles landed in America, I guess, the year you went to Georgetown.

The President. '64.

Q. Yes, yes.

The President. My senior year in high school.

Q. Do you remember that?

The President. Oh, yes.

Q. I mean, were you really into the Beatles?

The President. Oh, absolutely. I remember when they came in. I remember going over to a friend of mine's house and playing some Beatles records. I remember when they went on the Ed Sullivan Show. I remember—I was interested to see them on the Ed Sullivan Show, because you know when Elvis Presley went on the Ed Sullivan Show they could only show him from the waist up because they thought he was too lewd for the times.

Q. What's the difference between—was it a hard transition between Elvis and Beatles and Motown?

The President. Not for me, but I've always had very eclectic interests in music. And most people didn't choose, that I knew. I felt a real special relationship to Elvis Presley because he was from Mississippi; he was a poor white kid; he sang with a lot a soul. He was sort of my roots—"Heartbreak Hotel" and "Hound Dog" and "Don't Be Cruel" and "Love Me Tender," that was sort of the beginning of the awakening of America to rock and roll.

And then when the Beatles came, I just thought they were so—they were full of energy, but they were also brilliant. I mean, you go back and listen to Sergeant Pepper's album today—they were brilliant. I still think "Eleanor Rigby" is one of the most powerful songs I ever heard. They were just brilliant.

Q. You were talking about your mom, Virginia, and her love for music and how she loved rock and roll. Did that have—I mean, it must have made a huge difference not only in your life but in Roger's life now that he's gone into music.

The President. Huge. Yes. I mean, we both felt encouraged to like music and to be involved in it. And our mother had a lot to do with it. But it was something that lifted us up. We had some hard times, and we could always get out of them if we had enough good music playing.

Q. Did you ever consider going into music?

The President. I did. When I was 15 or 16, I thought about it a lot. I even thought about going to Europe to study, because in France you could study classical saxophone and actually develop a career that would be both classical and jazz and all that. And that's very rare. Wynton Marsalis is the only world-class musician in my lifetime, I think, who was preeminent in classical and preeminent in jazz music.

But I made a very—I decided not to do it for two reasons. One is, I didn't know if I'd like the lifestyle. I didn't want to get my days and nights mixed up. And back then the idea of somebody like Kenny G., who has become a good friend of mine—he's a marvelous person—the idea of someone like him actually making a living just doing concerts and records was—it seemed so remote. And I didn't want to have to just do clubs and stay up all night and sleep all day. All the saxophone players I knew did that. Even the ones that made a lot of jazz records basically had their days and nights mixed up, as far as I was concerned. And I just didn't want to do it.

And the other reason I didn't do it is I didn't think I was—I just wasn't sure I was good enough. I didn't think I would be truly great

at it. And I thought if you're going to sacrifice your life to it and give your life to it, then you should know that you could really be great at it.

Q. It's kind of cool that Roger is doing music.

The President. Yes. Saw him on television last week, singing away.

Q. What's it like?

The President. I like it. I'm very happy for him, because it's all I think he's ever really wanted to do. He really just—once he started doing it and realized he was pretty good at it, he didn't care about anything else.

And one of the things that I want for every young person in this country is I want them to be free to be able to do what they want to do to live out their dreams. He's had to work hard and make a lot of sacrifices, but he's been able to do a lot of that.

Music Education

Q. I want to talk about Mr. Spurlin——

The President. Yes, that's good.

Q. ——and music education. You were talking about change and how when you were 16 you really had to think about it hard. Mr. Spurlin said that he realized that because you came back from Boys Nation, and he could see a difference, that you were still really committed to music, with all the bands you were in.

The President. When I went to Boys Nation, it sort of crystallized for me something that I had been thinking a long time, which is that I really—I had always been interested in politics; I had always been interested in public service; I had always been consumed with the issues that dominated my childhood, which were, in rough order, basically, first, the cold war, then the civil rights revolution, then the whole—all the social upheavals and the war in Vietnam. And all these things were—you couldn't be alive in the fifties and sixties and not be concerned about great public issues. And I thought I could make a difference, and I thought I could be really good at it. I thought I could do better at that than anything else. And it's something I thought I'd never get tired of, because you're always learning something new. There's always new people coming; there's always things happening.

And the judgment I made when I was 16, I have to say now that I'm 50 I feel—I don't know why I knew it then, but I was right. And I'm glad I did it. I never stopped loving music, but I just knew I couldn't—that I wouldn't be a musician.

That's the great thing about music, though. Most—90-some percent of the people who do it don't become musicians. But I must say— I know that you talked to Virgil Spurlin, my band director, for this show, and he's a man who had a profound, positive influence on my life and on so many other people. And one of the things that's really disturbed me about education in America today is that so many schools have not been able to maintain their music programs, their arts programs, even their basic physical education programs, because these things are very important to human development, to emotional development, and to intellectual development. And they complement the academic programs.

And I must say, even after I decided, well, I'm not going to do this for a lifetime, the time I spent with my band directors and with the boys and girls that played with me, and then the men and women that have played with me since and sung with me and done all these things, they've made my life a lot richer. And I wish that—one of the things I hope we can do is find a way to give that back to the students, particularly students who come from disadvantaged backgrounds. They ought to have a chance to do music and to do art and to do— and to exercise their God-given abilities.

And whenever I think of Virgil Spurlin, for the rest of my life I'll always think about what a gift he gave to me and hundreds of other people.

Q. With all due respect, I just have another question. VH1 is launching a campaign to save the music in our public schools. Too often it's being considered a luxury, yet it does raise the math scores, the reading scores, the attendance, and team-building skills. What do you want Americans to know—what can they do to help save the music?

The President. Well, there are several things Americans can do. First of all, they can make sure that their school districts, to the maximum extent possible, preserve these music programs, because they are a lifeline to learning and to life for so many young people.

Secondly, if it's necessary, they can be willing to vote for local—increases necessary to preserve those programs while the academics are preserved.

The third thing they can do is to go around and either donate or get others to donate instruments or other things which will make it possible for these band programs and these other music programs to go on. I think it is very, very important to education. I think all young people should be exposed to music and to the arts. And as I said, I think it's even wrong to get rid of these physical education programs, to treat physical health as if it's just the providence of athletes. That's also wrong.

But the music, in particular, we know there's so much evidence that it has a positive impact on academic performance, on social skills and how you relate to other people, on self-confidence, that anything we can do in every community in this country to save these programs for the schools and for the children should be done.

Q. Thank you, Mr. President.

President's Musical Interests

[*At this point, the President looked through some record albums.*]

The President. It's got "Ruby" in it, doesn't it? "She's Funny That Way." "I'll Be Seeing You," one of my favorite songs. Glenn Yarborough was the heartthrob of the early sixties. Nancy Wilson. This is the best Judy Collins album ever made, I think, although I also like that one. "Bridge Over Troubled Water"—did you see that in "The Graduate" in 1967? Joe Cocker—I was—Joe Cocker was on Johnny Carson in 1988 when I did Johnny Carson, and I love to hear Joe Cocker sing.

Q. What were you and the First Lady thinking of when you—was it listening to Joni Mitchell, "Chelsea Morning"?

The President. I liked the song and—now we—I loved the song. And she—Joni Mitchell wrote it, and Judy Collins recorded it. And it was great because Judy Collins later became a great friend of ours, which was wonderful. And I heard it first when Judy Collins sang it, and then I later heard Joni Mitchell's recording of it.

And then after I was elected Governor in 1978, we went to London, Hillary and I did, and spent 10 days around the Christmas holidays. And all we did was walk and go to restaurants and go to plays and go to museums and galleries. That's all we did. It was a great 10-day vacation. And one day we were walking in Chelsea, and then we started singing that song, just walking down the street alone in Chelsea. And I looked at her, and I said, "You know, if we have a daughter, we ought to name her Chelsea." And that's how we decided to do it, walking in the borough of Chelsea in London in 1978 in December.

Q. A wonderful story.

The President. That's how our child got her name.

Q. Thank you for sharing it. It really was——

The President. Thanks.

NOTE: The interview was recorded at 3:50 p.m. on March 11 in the Cabinet Room at the White House, and it was released by the Office of the Press Secretary on June 3. Portions of the President's remarks were broadcast during the VH1 special "Bill Clinton: Rock & Roll President," which was televised on June 3. The interviewers referred to Warren Moss, David Leopoulos, Janice Sjostrand, Micky Manguin, and Carolyn Staley, friends of the President; and his Georgetown University roommate Tom Campbell. A tape was not available for verification of the content of this interview.

Statement on the Northern Ireland Peace Process
June 3, 1997

Today in Belfast, Senator George Mitchell reconvened the talks on the future of Northern Ireland that began almost a year ago. I call on the political leaders to seize this precious opportunity and begin the hard but worthwhile work of negotiating a just and lasting settlement. To engage in serious negotiations, to be willing to make principled compromises, requires courage and creativity. Now is the time for the representatives of the people to show the good sense and good will that I saw in such abundance when I visited Northern Ireland. The United States will continue to stand with them

as they take on, with the two Governments, the demanding task of shaping a peaceful and prosperous future in which all the people of Northern Ireland will have an equal stake.

As I have said so many times, ideally all the elected parties should be at the table when the decisions that shape the future are made. If the IRA declares and implements an unequivocal cease-fire, I am confident that Sinn Fein will be invited to add its voice to the other parties' at the table as they forge a new future for themselves and their children.

Message to the Congress Transmitting a Report on Emigration Policies of Certain Former Eastern Bloc States
June 3, 1997

To the Congress of the United States:

I hereby transmit a report concerning emigration laws and policies of Armenia, Azerbaijan, Georgia, Moldova, and Ukraine as required by subsections 402(b) and 409(b) of title IV of the Trade Act of 1974, as amended (the "Act"). I have determined that Armenia, Azerbaijan, Georgia, Moldova, and Ukraine are in full compliance with subsections 402(a) and 409(a) of the Act. As required by title IV, I will provide the Congress with periodic reports regarding the

compliance of Armenia, Azerbaijan, Georgia, Moldova, and Ukraine with these emigration standards.

WILLIAM J. CLINTON

The White House,
June 3, 1997.

NOTE: The related determination of June 3 is listed in Appendix D at the end of this volume.

Message to the Congress Transmitting Documentation on Most-Favored-Nation Trade Status for Certain Former Eastern Bloc States
June 3, 1997

To the Congress of the United States:

I hereby transmit the document referred to in subsection 402(d)(1) of the Trade Act of 1974, as amended (the "Act"), with respect to a further 12-month extension of authority to waive subsections (a) and (b) of section 402 of the Act. This document constitutes my recommendation to continue in effect this waiver authority for a further 12-month period, and includes my reasons for determining that continuation of the waiver authority and waivers currently in effect for Albania, Belarus, Kazakstan, Kyrgyzstan, Tajikistan, Turkmenistan, and Uzbekistan will substantially promote the objectives of section 402 of the Act. I have submitted a separate report with respect to the People's Republic of China.

WILLIAM J. CLINTON

The White House,
June 3, 1997.

NOTE: The related determination of June 3 is listed in Appendix D at the end of this volume.

Remarks on Signing the Individuals with Disabilities Education Act Amendments of 1997
June 4, 1997

Thank you very much. He did a great job, didn't he? Thank you, Josh, for your story. Thank you, Judy, for your work and the power of your example. And thanks to your mom. [*Laughter*]

I thank Secretary Riley. I thank all the children who are here with me on the platform who have come to symbolize what this legislation is all about and all the children who are out there in the crowds. I thank those of you who have helped me over the years to know and understand what is at stake in this issue more clearly. I thank especially the people who deserve the credit for what we're doing today, the Members of Congress, the committee chairs: Senator Jeffords and Congressman Goodling and Senator Kennedy and Senator Harkin, Congressmen Clay and Martinez and Riggs. I'd like to say a special word of thanks to all the staff people who worked on this but especially to David Hoppe, Senator Lott's chief of staff, who did such a fine job here. Thank you, David.

I would like to ask—they're all going to come up here later when we sign the bill, but there must be 30 Members of Congress here. And this bill, as you know, received virtual unanimity of support across party lines and regional lines. And in addition to the Members whose names I mentioned, I'd like to ask all the Members of Congress to stand here and be recognized for what they did. Thank you all.

I thank all the advocates who are here. I dare not start to identify you all, but I will say I am glad to see Eunice Shriver here, and thank you for what you have done to help me understand this issue better.

For 22 years now, the IDEA has been the driving force behind the simple idea we have heard restated and symbolized here today, that every American citizen is a person of dignity and worth, having a spirit and a soul, and having the right to develop his or her full capacities. Because of IDEA, disabled children all over America have a better chance to reach that capacity. And through IDEA, we recognize our common obligation to help them make the most of their God-given potential.

We are here today to reaffirm and to advance that goal. Education clearly will become even more important to our people in the days ahead; that is why I have made it my number one priority as President. That is why last month, when we announced the bipartisan agreement to balance the budget, I was most proud that we could do that and include an historic investment in education, the most significant increase in funding for education at the national level in 30 years.

America Reads, a massive volunteer effort to help make sure all of our children can read independently by the time they're 8 years old; millions of families getting a tax cut to help them pay for a college education; hundreds of thousands more deserving students getting Pell grants; tens of thousands of schools across America now will be wired to the Internet; support for raising academic standards—we know that this is the right thing to do for every American. But just as we heard from Judy, for far too long children with disabilities were closed out of those kinds of opportunities, trapped in a system without guideposts, influenced by stereotypes, dominated by assumptions that people like Josh couldn't take the courses that he just enumerated.

In 1975, Congress began to change that when the IDEA was enacted. It has meant the right to receive an education that all children deserve. It has given children who would never have had it the right to sit in the same classrooms, to learn the same skills, to dream the same dreams as their fellow Americans. And for students who sat next to them in those classrooms, it has also given them the chance to learn a little something, to get rid of the baggage of ignorance and damaging stereotypes, and to begin to understand that what we have in common is far more important than what divides us.

Since the passage of the IDEA, 90 percent fewer developmentally disabled children are living in institutions; hundreds of thousands of children with disabilities attend public schools and regular classrooms; 3 times as many disabled young people are enrolled in colleges and universities; twice as many young Americans with disabilities in their twenties are in the American workplace. We have to continue to push these trends, to do everything we can to encourage our children with disabilities not only to dream of doing great things but to live out their dreams.

Our job is not yet done. All of you know that despite this progress, young people with disabilities still drop out of high school at twice the rate their peers drop out of high school and into less certain futures. For those who stay in school, lower expectations and exclusion still are far too common. Too many parents still find themselves fighting for educational resources and services that are their children's right and their hope for a brighter future.

Today we are taking the next steps to do better. The expanded IDEA reaffirms and strengthens our national commitment to provide a world-class education for all our children. It ensures that our Nation's schools are safe and conducive to learning for children, while scrupulously protecting the rights of our disabled students.

First, this bill makes it clear once and for all that the children with disabilities have a right to be in the classroom and to be included in school activities like work experience, science clubs, and field outings. It requires States and school districts to help to get disabled children ready to come to school and to accommodate them once they are there with services ranging from preschool therapy to sign language interpreters, from mobility instructors to an extended school year.

Second, this legislation mandates that with appropriate accommodations, children with disabilities learn the same things with the same curricula and the same assessments as all other children. We know from every teacher and every principal, from every parent and every coach, that children rise to expectations when they are set high. And children with disabilities are no exception.

I have asked America to embrace high national academic standards for all our children. So far, education leaders from California to Carolina, from Michigan to Maryland have endorsed this effort. I believe very strongly that all children can make progress. Today I call upon those States to give every child the chance and the expectation of meeting those standards.

Third, we know our children's success depends upon the quality of their teachers and the involvement of their parents. This legislation will help more regular classroom teachers get the full range of teaching skills they need to teach children with disabilities. And it will require regular education teachers to be involved in the development of individual education plans to help disabled children succeed.

This legislation also gives parents a greater voice in their children's education. At long last, it will give them something other than what parents have expected from their schools for decades. It will give them what we know all parents should be entitled to: simply, regular report cards on their children's progress.

High school is a make-or-break time for all young people, but teenagers with disabilities often need more help to succeed as they make the transition from school to work. This legislation will require schools to give students that help by developing individual plans that may include independent living skills, job training, and preparation for higher education. And because acquiring these skills may take extra time, these plans must begin by the time the students with disabilities reach the age of 14.

Now, that is what the expansion of the legislation these Members of Congress have passed will achieve. In a few moments I will sign it into law. As I do, I want you to think about what it really accomplishes.

To the 5.8 million children whose futures are in the balance, we are saying: We believe in you. We believe in your potential, and we are going to do everything we can to help you develop it.

To the millions of families who are depending upon us to help them prepare their children to take their place in the world, we are saying: We are proud of you for your devotion to your children, for your belief in them, for your love for them, and we are going to do everything we can to help you succeed in preparing them.

To the teachers and the administrators who make all the difference, we are saying: We are depending upon you, and we are going to do what we can to support you.

To the American people, we are saying that we do not intend to rest until we have conquered the ignorance and prejudice against disabilities that disables us all.

And to the world, we are sending a message, the same message that the FDR Memorial I was honored to dedicate last month will send: In America, you are measured by what you are and what you can achieve. In America, the American dream is alive for all our people. In America, we recognize that what really counts is the spirit and the soul and the heart, and we honor it with this legislation.

Now I would like to ask the children and the people here with me on the platform to join me as I sign the legislation. And I would like to ask the Members of Congress who are here, every one of them, to come up, along with Tom Hehir, the Director of the Office of Special Education, as we sign into law the Individual with Disabilities Education Act of 1997.

NOTE: The President spoke at 11:12 a.m. on the South Lawn at the White House. In his remarks, he referred to student Joshua Bailey, who introduced the President; Assistant Secretary of Education Judith E. Heumann; and Eunice Shriver, founder, Special Olympics International. H.R. 5, approved June 4, was assigned Public Law No. 105–17.

Statement on Signing the Individuals with Disabilities Education Act Amendments of 1997
June 4, 1997

It is with great pleasure that I have today signed into law H.R. 5, the "Individuals with Disabilities Education Act Amendments of 1997." This Act reaffirms and strengthens our national commitment to the education of children with disabilities and their families.

Since the enactment of Public Law 94–142 over 20 years ago, the Individuals with Disabilities Education Act (IDEA) has made it possible for millions of children with disabilities to receive an education, helping them become productive adults. The bill before me today builds on that success story by:

—putting an even sharper focus on improving educational results for these children through greater access to the general curriculum and inclusion in State and district-wide assessments;

—giving parents more information, including regular reports on their children's progress, and a greater role in decisions affecting their children's education;

—reducing paperwork and increasing administrative flexibility;

—asking children with disabilities, along with schools, teachers, and parents to assume greater responsibility for the children's success; and

—promoting the use of mediation to resolve disagreements between parents and schools.

This bill also gives school officials the tools they need to ensure that the Nation's schools are safe and conducive to learning for all children, while scrupulously protecting the rights of children with disabilities. It also includes a substantial commitment from the Federal Government to support the professional development of special and regular education teachers who work with children with disabilities, research and technological innovations to improve their education, the training of parents, and the provision of technical assistance.

This bipartisan legislation is the result of a unique process involving the Congress, the Department of Education, parents, educators, the disability community, and other interested parties. I thank all who played a part in this great achievement. Successful implementation of the revised IDEA is the key to the future for children with disabilities and it will help them become successful and contributing members of their communities.

WILLIAM J. CLINTON

The White House,
June 4, 1997.

NOTE: H.R. 5, approved June 4, was assigned Public Law No. 105–17.

Statement on Supplemental Disaster Assistance Legislation
June 4, 1997

In moving ahead on this flawed legislation, the Republican leadership is once again delaying the disaster assistance needed by people and communities in the Dakotas, Minnesota, and 30 other States. With individuals, families, and businesses awaiting the assistance they need to rebuild, I urge the Republican leadership to set politics aside and pass a clean disaster assistance bill.

If the Republican majority is set on this course of adding contentious and extraneous provisions, they should send me this bill as quickly as possible. I will veto it as soon as it arrives and send it back so they can send me a clean disaster assistance bill immediately that keeps aid flowing to those in need. Americans in need should not have to endure this unnecessary delay.

Letter to the Federal Election Commission Requesting Action To End the Soft Money System in Domestic Politics
June 4, 1997

To the Members of the Federal Election Commission:

I am writing to you, pursuant to 11 CFR Part 200, to request that you take action under your existing statutory authority to ban "soft money" and end the system under which both political parties compete to raise unlimited sums from individuals, labor unions, and corporations.

The rules governing our system of financing Federal election campaigns are sorely out of date. Enacted more than two decades ago when election campaigns were much less expensive,

the rules have been overtaken by dramatic changes in the nature and cost of campaigns and the accompanying flood of money.

Today, money is raised and spent in ways that simply were not contemplated when the Congress last overhauled our campaign finance laws. We must bring the rules up to date to reflect the changes in elections and campaigning.

An important step in this process would be to change the rules governing the use and solicitation of "soft money"—funds not subject to the contribution limitations and prohibitions of the Federal Election Campaign Act of 1971, as amended (FECA). Currently Federal Election Commission (FEC) regulations (11 CFR 106.5) allow political parties to raise and spend soft money in elections involving State and Federal candidates by providing an allocation formula between Federal and non-Federal expenses incurred by party committees.

These regulations, and limited additional guidance provided through advisory opinions, are the basis upon which party committees make expenditures and raise funds with respect to Federal and State elections. The use of soft money by party committees is largely based on the direction provided in these regulations.

Whatever the merit of these regulations at the time they were adopted, it has become abundantly clear today that they are no longer adequate to the task of regulating campaigns. The role of soft money has grown dramatically in the past several elections so that by the 1996 elections the two parties raised more than $250 million, more than triple the total of 4 years before.

The current allocation system, in short, is simply outmoded. Accordingly, I propose that the FEC adopt new rules requiring that candidates for Federal office and national parties be permitted to raise and spend only "hard money"—funds subject to the restrictions, contribution limits, and reporting requirements of FECA.

The soft money ban I seek achieves similar goals as provisions of the "Bipartisan Campaign Reform Act of 1997," introduced by Senators John McCain and Russell Feingold, and Representatives Christopher Shays and Martin Meehan. Specifically, I am requesting that the FEC consider new rulemaking to accomplish the following:

1. Prohibit national political parties (and their congressional campaign committees or agents) from soliciting or receiving any funds not subject to the limitations or prohibitions of FECA. (This action would preclude, for example, contributions directly from corporate or union treasuries, or contributions from individuals in excess of the amount an individual can give to a national party's Federal account.)

2. Prohibit any Federal officeholder or candidate (and his or her agents) from soliciting or receiving any funds not subject to the limitations or prohibitions of FECA.

3. Provide that any expenditure by any national, State, or local political party during a Federal election year for any activity that influences a Federal election (including any voter registration or get-out-the-vote drive, generic advertising, or any communication that refers to a Federal candidate) must be paid for from funds subject to FECA. (This would end the allocation system, currently authorized by the FEC, under which hard and soft money are mixed for campaign activities that affect both State and Federal elections.)

These steps, available to you under your existing statutory authority, will enable our election laws to catch up with the reality of the way elections are financed today, and along with new campaign finance reform legislation, will take significant strides toward restoring public confidence in the campaign finance process.

Sincerely,

WILLIAM J. CLINTON

NOTE: This letter was released by the Office of the Press Secretary on June 5. An original was not available for verification of the content of this letter.

Statement on Requesting Federal Election Commission Action To End the Soft Money System in Domestic Politics
June 5, 1997

Today I have asked the Federal Election Commission to act, within its current legal authority, to end the soft money system. Currently, both parties compete to raise large sums from corporations, individuals, and labor unions.

There is too much money in politics, and the problem worsens with every election. This escalating arms race must stop, and I am determined that we will reform campaign finances, by every means we can.

Such an action by the FEC cannot be a substitute for comprehensive campaign finance reform legislation, which is currently before the Congress. In my State of the Union Address, I challenged Congress to act by July 4th and pass bipartisan reform. That deadline is now one month away, and there is still time for Congress to move forward on this priority. I call on Congress to pass legislation that institutes voluntary spending limits, provides free broadcast time to candidates who abide by those limits, restricts special interest contributions, addresses independent expenditures, and bans soft money.

It is clear that the current campaign finance system has been overwhelmed by an unprecedented volume of money. If we are to restore the public's faith in our institutions and the political system, we must reform the campaign finance system. This request to the FEC makes clear my determination that, one way or another, we will see reform, and we will end the soft money. I want to work in the coming days with Members of Congress to pass bipartisan and comprehensive campaign finance reform.

Statement on Supplemental Disaster Assistance Legislation
June 5, 1997

By attaching a political wish list to the much-needed disaster relief legislation, the congressional majority has chosen politics over the public interest.

The people of the Dakotas and Minnesota have been hit hard by devastating floods. They, and the people in other States around the country that have suffered disasters, urgently need funds from the enactment of a straightforward disaster relief bill. I have asked the Congress for such legislation.

Instead, the Republican majority in Congress has insisted on attaching to this vital legislation political provisions that they know are unacceptable. Among them, the bill would violate our balanced budget agreement, cutting critical investments in education and the environment instead of providing important increases in investments in these and other areas. In addition,

it would prohibit the Commerce Department from taking steps to improve the accuracy and cut the costs of the year 2000 decennial census. There are other unacceptable provisions as well. None of them have any place in this legislation.

Disaster relief legislation is neither the time nor the place for these matters. Congress needs to appropriate this disaster relief, so communities can begin long-term recovery, and funds can continue for families to rebuild homes and businesses and farmers to dig out their fields to plant crops.

I call on the Republican leaders of Congress to keep the politics off disaster relief legislation. They should now, without delay, send me straightforward legislation without provisions that are not in the interest of the American people and that they know I will not accept.

Message to the Congress Transmitting a Report on Proliferation of Weapons of Mass Destruction
June 5, 1997

To the Congress of the United States:

As required by section 204 of the International Emergency Economic Powers Act (50 U.S.C. 1703(c)) and section 401(c) of the National Emergencies Act (50 U.S.C. 1641(c)), I transmit herewith a 6-month report on the na-

tional emergency declared by Executive Order 12938 of November 14, 1994, in response to the threat posed by the proliferation of nuclear, biological, and chemical weapons ("weapons of mass destruction") and of the means of delivering such weapons.

WILLIAM J. CLINTON

The White House,

June 5, 1997.

Memorandum on Use of Project Labor Agreements for Federal Construction Projects
June 5, 1997

Memorandum for the Heads of Executive Departments and Agencies

Subject: Use of Project Labor Agreements for Federal Construction Projects

The National Performance Review and other executive branch initiatives have sought to implement rigorous performance standards, minimize costs, and eliminate wasteful and burdensome requirements. This Presidential memorandum continues those efforts, by encouraging departments and agencies in this Administration to consider project labor agreements as another tool, one with a long history in governmental contracting, to achieve economy and efficiency in Federal construction projects.

Therefore, by the authority vested in me as President by the Constitution and the laws of the United States of America and to ensure the economical and efficient administration and completion of Federal Government construction projects, it is hereby directed as follows:

Section 1. Executive departments or agencies during this Administration authorized to award a contract for the construction of a facility to be owned by a Federal department or agency may, on a project-by-project basis, use a project labor agreement on a large and significant project, (a) where a project labor agreement will advance the Government's procurement interest in cost, efficiency, and quality and in promoting labor-management stability as well as compliance with applicable legal requirements governing safety and health, equal employment opportunity, labor and employment standards, and other matters, and (b) where no laws applicable to the specific construction project preclude the use of the proposed project labor agreement.

Section 2. If an executive department or agency during this Administration determines that use of a project labor agreement will serve the goals set forth in section 1(a) of this memoran-

dum on a large and significant project, and that no law precludes the use of a project labor agreement on the project, the executive department or agency may require that every contractor or subcontractor on the project agree, for that project, to negotiate or become a party to a project labor agreement with one or more appropriate labor organizations. The executive department or agency has discretion whether to include such a requirement.

Section 3. Any project labor agreement reached pursuant to this memorandum:

(a) shall bind all contractors and subcontractors on the construction project through the inclusion of appropriate clauses in all relevant solicitation provisions and contract documents;

(b) shall allow all contractors and subcontractors wishing to compete for contracts and subcontracts on the project to do so, without discrimination against contractors, subcontractors, or employees based on union or nonunion status;

(c) shall contain guarantees against strikes, lockouts, and similar work disruptions;

(d) shall set forth effective, prompt and mutually binding procedures for resolving labor disputes arising during the project;

(e) shall provide other mechanisms for labor-management cooperation on matters of mutual interest and concern, including productivity, quality of work, safety, and health; and

(f) shall fully conform to all applicable statutes, regulations, and Executive orders.

Section 4. This memorandum does not require an executive department or agency to use a project labor agreement on any project, nor does it preclude use of a project labor agreement in circumstances not covered here, including leasehold arrangements and federally funded projects. This memorandum also does not require contractors to enter into a project labor agreement with any particular labor organization.

Section 5. The heads of executive departments or agencies covered by this memorandum, in consultation with the Federal Acquisition Regulatory Council, shall establish, within 120 days of the date of this memorandum, appropriate written procedures and criteria for the determinations set forth in section 1.

Section 6. This memorandum is not intended to create any right or benefit, substantive or procedural, enforceable by a nonfederal party against the United States, its departments, agencies or instrumentalities, its officers or employees, or any other person.

Section 7. (a) "Construction" as used in this memorandum shall have the same meaning it has in section 36.102 of the Federal Acquisition Regulation.

(b) "Executive department or agency" as used in this memorandum means any Federal entity within the meaning of 40 U.S.C. 472(a).

(c) "Labor organization" as used in this memorandum shall have the same meaning it has in 42 U.S.C. 2000e(d).

(d) "Large and significant project" as used in this memorandum shall mean a Federal construction project with a total cost to the Federal Government of more than $5 million.

Section 8. This memorandum shall be effective immediately, and shall apply to all solicitations issued after notice of establishment of the procedures and criteria required under section 5 of this memorandum.

WILLIAM J. CLINTON

NOTE: This memorandum was released by the Office of the Press Secretary on June 6.

Commencement Address at the Sidwell Friends School
June 6, 1997

Thank you. Well, Mr. Bryant, I may not hit a homerun today, but I won't be quite as off as Teddy Roosevelt was. Even good people have bad days. [*Laughter*]

Mr. Harrison, Mr. Noe, friends, family, and guests, members of the Class of 1997: Thank you for inviting me. Hillary and I especially want to thank Sidwell's faculty and staff, students and families for making our family feel so at home here, when we came under somewhat unusual circumstances.

Also, I thank the school for its superlative commitments to academic excellence, to diversity, and to service, to the welfare of all students here, to the maintenance of good character, good citizenship, and good spirits.

In particular, I have come to appreciate the school's observance of the Quaker practice of meaningful worship—an hour spent in reflective silence, broken only when someone has something truly meaningful to say in a respectful way. After the parents had a chance to participate in meaningful worship this week, I left wishing that Congress were in control of the Quakers. [*Laughter*]

I asked the senior in this class I know best what I should say today. Her reply was, "Dad, I want you to be wise, briefly." [*Laughter*] Last night she amended her advice, "Dad, the girls want you to be wise; the boys just want you to be funny." [*Laughter*] That's what I get for asking.

Members of the class of '97, you are not the only graduates here today. Even though we're staying home, your parents are graduating, too. Just as your pride and joy in this day must be tempered by the separation from Sidwell and the daily contact with the wonderful friends you have made here, our pride and joy are tempered by our coming separation from you.

So I ask you at the beginning to indulge your folks if we seem a little sad or we act a little weird. You see, today we are remembering your first day in school and all the triumphs and travails between then and now. Though we have raised you for this moment of departure and we are very proud of you, a part of us longs to hold you once more as we did when you could barely walk, to read to you just one more time "Good Night, Moon" or "Curious George" or "The Little Engine That Could."

We hope someday that you will have children of your own to bring to this happy day and know how we feel. Remember that we love you, and no matter what anybody says, you can come home again.

We celebrate your passage into the world in a hopeful time for our Nation and for people throughout the world. For the first time in history, more than half of all the world's people live free, under governments of their own choosing. The cold war has given way to the information age, with its revolutions in technology and communications and increasingly integrated economies and societies. Scientific advances and a growing global determination to preserve our environment give us hope that the challenges of the 21st century can be met in ways that will permit us to continue the advance of peace and freedom and prosperity throughout your entire lives.

Admittedly, we face serious threats to humanity's forward march, threats that go beyond the possible outbreak of disease or environmental catastrophe. They include the spread of weapons of mass destruction; terrorism; the worldwide network of crime and drug trafficking; awful ethnic, racial, tribal, and religious rivalries that unfortunately are most appealing to people your age throughout the world who feel poor and dispossessed. With vision, discipline, and patience, we can meet these challenges as well.

Here at home, our economy is strong. Crime and welfare rolls have dropped steeply. We are on the leading edge of emerging technologies. People are living longer, fuller lives. America is leading the world toward peace and freedom and progress, but you know well that we, too, have our challenges.

We still have yet to give all our children the chance you have had to develop their God-given capacities. We still have to deal with the coming retirement of your parents' very large generation and the appalling rates of poverty among young children. We have to develop the proper balance of discipline and freedom, of creativity and stability necessary to keep our economy growing, to make our society less crippled by crime and drugs, to help our families and communities to become stronger. And perhaps most important as you look around this class today, we have to make out of our rich diversity the world's first truly great multiracial, multiethnic, multi-

religious democracy. No one has ever done it before, and I hope our country can do as well as you have done with each other.

Now, all these are formidable tasks, but we are moving in the right direction. What I want to say to you is that now that you're adults, you have to do your part to keep it going. There are decisions to be made by Americans and, in a democracy, citizenship is not a spectator sport.

But what an exciting world awaits you—from cyberspace to the frontiers of artificial intelligence, from mapping our genetic structures to exploring other galaxies. With your ability and your education, your choices seem limitless. But you will have to choose. And you will have to choose not just what you will do but how you will live. No one else can make your decisions for you, and they will make all the difference—for you, for your country, and for the world. To make the right ones, you will need a lot more than knowledge and access to the Internet. You will need wisdom and resolve.

For what it's worth, here is my advice: First, be brave. Dream big and chase your dreams. You will have your failures, but you will grow from every honest effort. Over three decades ago I sat where you are. I can tell you without any doubt that in the years since, my high school classmates who chased their dreams and failed are far less disappointed than those who left their dreams on the shelf for fear of failure. So chase on. Even if you don't get what you think you want, amazing things will happen.

Second, be optimistic and be grateful. Some bad things are going to happen to you—to some of you, unfair things, perhaps even tragic things. Some of you have faced tragedy already. When these things happen, try to remember that each new day is still a gift, full of the mystery and magic of life. Try not to waste even one of those days trapped by hatred, the desire to get even, self-pity, despair, or cynicism. We all give in to them now and then, of course, but you need to work at snapping out of it and going on. Hatred and self-pity give victory to the very dark forces we deplore. Despair guarantees defeat. Cynicism is a cowardly cop-out. And no ever really gets even in life; that is God's work.

No matter how bad it gets, don't forget there's someone who's endured more pain than you have. No matter how unfair it gets, remember that most of us are far better off than we would be if we only got what we deserve. And

707

don't stop at admiring a Mandela or a Cardinal Bernardin. Strive to be more like them. Keep your spirits up. There is profound truth in the proverb, "A happy heart maketh good medicine, but a broken spirit dryeth the bones."

Third, be of service to others. Much has been given to you already, and a lot more is coming your way. You owe it to yourself to give something back, to help to build a society and a world in which more people have your chance to live out their dreams, and all people in need at least know the touch of a caring hand and the embrace of a kind heart. From your service here, many of you already know that it not only gives more joy to others, it will bring more joy to you than you can even imagine.

Fourth, be both humble and proud. Be humble because you're human, subject to error and frailty, incapable, no matter how intelligent you are, of ever knowing the whole truth. Show mercy as well as judgment to those with whom you disagree in life. Keep in mind Benjamin Franklin's adage that even our enemies are our friends, for they show us our faults.

Be proud because your life is God's unique creation, worthy of its journey, graced with a soul the equal of every other person's. Eleanor Roosevelt once said that no one can make you feel inferior without your permission. Do not give them permission.

I regret that in our time, the essential role of constructive criticism often degenerates into what Deborah Tannen has called "the culture of critique," where too many brilliant minds and prodigious energies are spent simply putting people down. Do not be put down.

Thirty-seven years ago, I was a student in Vernon Dokey's eighth grade science class. On first impression, Vernon Dokey, to put it charitably, was a very physically unattractive man. [*Laughter*] He knew it. He laughed about it. And he used it to teach us a valuable lesson in life I still remember. He told us that every morning when he woke up, he went to the bathroom and he shaved, and then he looked at himself in the mirror and he said, "Vernon, you're beautiful." [*Laughter*]

Well, Class of '97, you're beautiful. Go out and live like it. Be humble and be proud. Be of service. Be optimistic and grateful. Be brave, and dream your dreams.

God bless you.

NOTE: The President spoke at 11:07 a.m. in the gymnasium at the school. In his remarks, he referred to Ralph Bryant, chairman, board of directors, Earl Harrison, head of school, and Bernard Noe, upper school principal, Sidwell Friends School.

Statement on the National Economy
June 6, 1997

Four years ago, we put in place an economic strategy that has helped give America the strongest economy in the world. That strategy had three critical components: cutting the budget deficit; making smart investments in education, the environment, and our children; and opening new markets through tough trade agreements.

Today we received one more piece of solid evidence that this invest-and-grow strategy is working. We learned that our economy added 138,000 new jobs and that unemployment dropped to 4.8 percent, the lowest in 24 years. The American economy has now added 12.3 million new jobs since I took office, and unemployment has now been below 6 percent for

almost 3 years. America's economy is the strongest it has been in a generation.

Now we must press forward with the economic strategy that we adopted in 1993 and that has helped create the conditions for sustained growth. The balanced budget agreement I reached with leaders of Congress embodies our strategy. It is a balanced budget that is in balance with our values, and yesterday's strong endorsement of it by the House and Senate ratifies that economic strategy. This bipartisan action is a hopeful sign that both parties can work together to keep our economy growing. I look forward to working with leaders of both parties to write our balanced budget plan into law.

The progress of the balanced budget shows what America can accomplish when we reach across party lines and work together. Unfortunately, the Republican leaders of Congress have chosen the path of partisanship and confrontation in their actions on the disaster relief bill. Because congressional leaders chose to attach unacceptable political items to vital disaster relief legislation, I have no choice but to veto that measure. Once again, I call on the Congress to honor the sacrifice and aid the recovery of the families in the Dakotas, Minnesota, and across the country by passing straightforward disaster relief legislation and sending it to my desk.

The President's Radio Address
June 7, 1997

Good morning. This morning I want to talk about one of America's greatest challenges and greatest opportunities: conquering the forces of hatred and division that still exist in our society so that we can move forward into the 21st century as one America.

We are clearly the world's most diverse democracy, bound together across all of our differences by a belief in the basic dignity of every human being's life and liberty and the right of every American who lives by our laws and lives up to his or her responsibilities to share in the full promise of the greatest nation on Earth.

Especially as we move into a new century, with its global economy and its global society, our rich diversity is a powerful strength, if we respect it. We are clearly stronger as a nation when we use the full talents of all of our people, regardless of race or religious faith, national origin or sexual orientation, gender or disability. Much of America's story is really the stories of wave after wave of citizens struggling over our full history for full equality of opportunity and dignified treatment.

We stand today in sharp contrast to the racial, ethnic, tribal, and religious conflicts which continue to claim so many lives all around the world. But we have still not purged ourselves of all bigotry and intolerance. We still have our ugly words and awful violence, our burned churches and bombed buildings.

In a predominantly white suburb of Atlanta, Georgia, last month, an African-American couple was greeted with racial epithets as they moved into their new home. Just a week later, their home was sprayed with gunfire in the middle of the night. In a recent incident right here in Washington, DC, three men accosted a gay man in a park, forced him at gunpoint to go under a bridge, and beat him viciously while using antigay epithets. Last fall in Los Angeles, a Jewish student's dormitory room was bombed with a quarter stick of dynamite, and a swastika was drawn near the door.

Such hate crimes, committed solely because the victims have a different skin color or a different faith or are gays or lesbians, leave deep scars not only on the victims but on our larger community. They weaken the sense that we are one people with common values and a common future. They tear us apart when we should be moving closer together. They are acts of violence against America itself. And even a small number of Americans who harbor and act upon hatred and intolerance can do enormous damage to our efforts to bind together our increasingly diverse society into one nation realizing its full promise.

As part of our preparation for the new century, it is time for us to mount an all-out assault on hate crimes, to punish them swiftly and severely, and to do more to prevent them from happening in the first place. We must begin with a deeper understanding of the problem itself. That is why I'm convening a special White House Conference on Hate Crimes this November 10th. We'll bring to the White House victims of hate crimes and their families to understand why the impact of these acts runs so much deeper than the crimes themselves. We'll bring together law enforcement experts and leading officials from Congress and the Justice Department to take a serious look at the existing laws against hate crime and consider ways to improve enforcement and to strengthen them. We'll bring together community and religious leaders to talk about solutions that are already making a real difference in communities all across our Nation.

In preparation for the conference, Attorney General Reno has begun a thorough review of the laws concerning hate crimes and the ways in which the Federal Government can make a difference to help us to build a more vigorous plan of action. But of course, the fight against hatred and intolerance must be waged not just through our laws but in our hearts as well.

A newborn child today does not know how to hate or stereotype another human being; that behavior must be learned. And intolerance does not generally begin with criminal acts. Instead, it begins with quiet acts of indignity: the bigoted remark, the African-American who is followed around the grocery store by a suspicious clerk, the gay or lesbian who is denied a job, the Hispanic or Asian who is targeted because of unfair stereotypes. To truly move forward as one community, it is just not enough to prevent acts of violence to our bodies; we must prevent acts of violence to our spirits.

By convening the very first White House Conference on Hate Crimes this November, America can confront the dark forces of division that still exists. We can shine the bright light of justice, humanity, and harmony on them. We'll take a serious look at the laws and remedies that can make a difference in preventing hate crimes. We'll have the frank and open dialog we need to build one America across all difference and diversity. And together, we will move closer to the day when acts of hatred are no longer a stain on our community or our conscience, closer to the day when we can redeem for ourselves and show to the world the 220-year-old promise of our Founders, that we are "One Nation under God, indivisible, with liberty and justice for all."

Thanks for listening.

NOTE: The address was recorded at 11:47 a.m. on June 5 in the Oval Office at the White House for broadcast at 10:06 a.m. on June 7.

Remarks Announcing Proposed Human Cloning Prohibition Legislation
June 9, 1997

Thank you very much, Dr. Shapiro, for that fine set of remarks and for your report. I thank all the members of the President's Committee of Advisers. I'd also like to thank Secretary Shalala and Dr. Varmus for being here today, along with the President's Adviser on Science and Technology, Dr. Jack Gibbons. And I thank Congressman Brown and Congresswoman Morella for being here and for their interest in this important issue. But mostly let me say again, I am profoundly grateful to the National Bioethics Advisory Commission and to Dr. Harold Shapiro for preparing this report on a difficult topic in a short period of time, requiring an extensive inquiry. Your commitment and your courage in breaking new ground in policy is deeply appreciated.

As the Vice President has said and all of us know, we live in an era of breathtaking scientific discovery. More and more, our future in the world depends upon advances in science and technology. And more and more, the scientific community will influence the course of the future and the lives that our children will lead in the new century that is upon us.

As I said in my commencement address at Morgan State University last month, our scientific explorations must be guided by our commitment to human values, to the good of society, to our basic sense of right and wrong. Nothing makes the necessity of that moral obligation more clear than the troubling possibility that these new animal-cloning techniques could be used to create a child. That is why I acted in March to ban the use of Federal funds for cloning human beings and to urge the private sector to observe the ban voluntarily while we initiated a national dialog on the risks and the responsibilities of such a possibility, and why I asked this Commission to issue this report.

For 3 months, the Commission has rigorously explored the scientific, moral, and spiritual dimensions of human cloning. It has talked to leading scientists and religious leaders, to philosophers and families, to patient advocates and to the general public. From many opinions and beliefs, as Dr. Shapiro said, one unanimous conclusion has emerged: Attempting to clone a human being is unacceptably dangerous to the child and morally unacceptable to our society.

I believe strongly that this conclusion reflects a national consensus, and I believe personally that it is the right thing to do. Today I am sending legislation to the Congress that prohibits anyone in either public or private sectors from using these techniques to create a child. Until the day I sign the legislation into law, the ban on Federal funding I declared in March will remain in effect. And once again, I call upon the private sector to refrain voluntarily from using this technology to attempt to clone a human being.

I want to make clear that there is nothing inherently immoral or wrong with these new techniques—used for proper purposes. In fact, they hold the promise of revolutionary new medical treatments and life-saving cures to diseases like cystic fibrosis, diabetes, and cancer, to better crops and stronger livestock. This legislation, therefore, will not prohibit the use of these techniques to clone DNA in cells, and it will not ban the cloning of animals. What the legislation will do is to reaffirm our most cherished belief about the miracle of human life and the God-given individuality each person possesses. It will ensure that we do not fall prey to the temptation to replicate ourselves at the expense of those beliefs and the lives of innocent children we would produce.

Finally, the legislation will ensure that we continue the national dialog we began 3 months ago and will provide the Nation and the Congress another opportunity to take a look at this issue in 5 years. To make sure that all our voices are heard as we explore human cloning, the legislation specifically requires the National Bioethics Advisory Commission to continue its study and report back in 4½ years. At that time, we will decide how to proceed based on what has been accomplished and agreed upon and debated and discovered in the intervening period.

Banning human cloning reflects our humanity. It is the right thing to do. Creating a child through this new method calls into question our most fundamental beliefs. It has the potential to threaten the sacred family bonds at the very core of our ideals and our society. At its worst, it could lead to misguided and malevolent attempts to select certain traits, even to create certain kinds of children, to make our children objects rather than cherished individuals.

We are still a long way from understanding all the implications of the present discoveries, but it is our moral obligation to confront these issues as they arise and to act now to prevent abuse. Today I hope other countries will see what we are doing and do the same, and I pledge to work with them to enforce similar bans around the world that reflect these values.

Once again, let me say a heartfelt thank-you on behalf of our entire Nation to the National Bioethics Advisory Commission for the remarkable work you have done and the work you have agreed to continue doing in the coming years.

Thank you very much.

NOTE: The President spoke at 11:56 a.m. in the Rose Garden at the White House. In his remarks, he referred to Harold T. Shapiro, Chairman, National Bioethics Advisory Commission.

Message to the Congress Transmitting Proposed Human Cloning Prohibition Legislation
June 9, 1997

To the Congress of the United States:

I am pleased to transmit today for immediate consideration and prompt enactment the "Cloning Prohibition Act of 1997." This legislative proposal would prohibit any attempt to cre-

ate a human being using somatic cell nuclear transfer technology, the method that was used to create Dolly the sheep. This proposal will also provide for further review of the ethical and scientific issues associated with the use of somatic cell nuclear transfer in human beings.

Following the February report that a sheep had been successfully cloned using a new technique, I requested my National Bioethics Advisory Commission to examine the ethical and legal implications of applying the same cloning technology to human beings. The Commission concluded that at this time "it is morally unacceptable for anyone in the public or private sector, whether in a research or clinical setting, to attempt to create a child using somatic cell nuclear transfer cloning" and recommended that Federal legislation be enacted to prohibit such activities. I agree with the Commission's conclusion and am transmitting this legislative proposal to implement its recommendation.

Various forms of cloning technology have been used for decades resulting in important biomedical and agricultural advances. Genes, cells, tissues, and even whole plants and animals have been cloned to develop new therapies for treating such disorders as cancer, diabetes, and cystic fibrosis. Cloning technology also holds promise for producing replacement skin, cartilage, or bone tissue for burn or accident vic-

tims, and nerve tissue to treat spinal cord injury. Therefore, nothing in the "Cloning Prohibition Act of 1997" restricts activities in other areas of biomedical and agricultural research that involve: (1) the use of somatic cell nuclear transfer or other cloning technologies to clone molecules, DNA, cells, and tissues; or (2) the use of somatic cell nuclear transfer techniques to create animals.

The Commission recommended that such legislation provide for further review of the state of somatic cell nuclear transfer technology and the ethical and social issues attendant to its potential use to create human beings. My legislative proposal would implement this recommendation and assign responsibility for the review, to be completed in the fifth year after passage of the legislation, to the National Bioethics Advisory Commission.

I urge the Congress to give this legislation prompt and favorable consideration.

WILLIAM J. CLINTON

The White House,
June 9, 1997.

Statement on General Joseph W. Ralston's Withdrawal From Consideration as Chairman of the Joint Chiefs of Staff
June 9, 1997

I respect General Joe Ralston's decision to remove his name from consideration as Chairman of the Joint Chiefs of Staff.

I am pleased that General Ralston has agreed to Secretary Cohen's request to continue in his current post as Vice Chairman. For 32 years, in war and in peace, General Ralston has served our Nation with uncommon distinction. As Vice Chairman, he is a valued adviser to me, and he has played a key role in the Pentagon's review of its post-cold-war mission. The Joint

Chiefs and our country will benefit from his continued service. He is an outstanding officer.

I also welcome Secretary Cohen's action to forthrightly and thoroughly review the military's standards and procedures involving personal conduct. It is essential that our system is reasonable, consistent, and fair for those who serve our country and that it is perceived to be so by the American people.

I look forward to receiving Secretary Cohen's recommendation for the Chairmanship of the Joint Chiefs.

Message to the House of Representatives Returning Without Approval Emergency Supplemental Appropriations Legislation
June 9, 1997

To the House of Representatives:

I am returning herewith without my approval H.R. 1469, the "Supplemental Appropriations and Rescissions Act, FY 1997." The congressional majority—despite the obvious and urgent need to speed critical relief to people in the Dakotas, Minnesota, California, and 29 other States ravaged by flooding and other natural disasters—has chosen to weigh down this legislation with a series of unacceptable provisions that it knows will draw my veto. The time has come to stop playing politics with the lives of Americans in need and to send me a clean, unencumbered disaster relief bill that I can and will sign the moment it reaches my desk.

On March 19, 1997, I sent the Congress a request for emergency disaster assistance and urged the Congress to approve it promptly. Both the House and Senate Appropriations Committees acted expeditiously to approve the legislation. The core of this bill, appropriately, provides $5.8 billion of much-needed help to people in hard-hit States and, in addition, contains $1.8 billion for the Department of Defense related to our peacekeeping efforts in Bosnia and Southwest Asia. Regrettably, the Republican leadership chose to include contentious issues totally unrelated to disaster assistance, needlessly delaying essential relief.

The bill contains a provision that would create an automatic continuing resolution for all of fiscal year 1998. While the goal of ensuring that the Government does not shut down again is a worthy one, this provision is ill-advised. The issue here is not about shutting down the Government. Last month, I reached agreement with the Bipartisan Leadership of Congress on a plan to balance the budget by 2002. That agreement is the right way to finish the job of putting our fiscal house in order, consistent with our values and principles. Putting the Government's finances on automatic pilot is not.

The backbone of the Bipartisan Budget Agreement is the plan to balance the budget while providing funds for critical investments in education, the environment, and other priorities. The automatic continuing resolution would provide resources for fiscal year 1998 that are $18 billion below the level contained in the Bipartisan Budget Agreement, threatening such investments in our future. For example: college aid would be reduced by $1.7 billion, eliminating nearly 375,000 students from the Pell Grant program; the number of women, infants, and children receiving food and other services through WIC would be cut by an average of 500,000 per month; up to 56,000 fewer children would participate in Head Start; the number of border patrol and FBI agents would be reduced, as would the number of air traffic controllers; and our goal of cleaning up 900 Superfund sites by the year 2000 could not be accomplished.

The bill also contains a provision that would permanently prohibit the Department of Commerce from using statistical sampling techniques in the 2000 decennial census for the purpose of apportioning Representatives in Congress among the States. Without sampling, the cost of the decennial census will increase as its accuracy, especially with regard to minorities and groups that are traditionally undercounted, decreases substantially. The National Academy of Sciences and other experts have recommended the use of statistical sampling for the 2000 decennial census.

The Department of Justice, under the Carter and Bush Administrations and during my Administration, has issued three opinions regarding the constitutionality and legality of sampling in the decennial census. All three opinions concluded that the Constitution and relevant statutes permit the use of sampling in the decennial census. Federal courts that have addressed the issue have held that the Constitution and Federal statutes allow sampling.

The enrolled bill contains an objectionable provision that would promote the conversion of certain claimed rights-of-way into paved highways across sensitive national parks, public lands, and military installations. Under the provision, a 13-member commission would study the issue and provide recommendations to resolve outstanding Revised Statute (R.S.) 2477 claims. R.S. 2477 was enacted in 1866 to grant rights-of-way for the construction of highways over public lands not already reserved for public uses. It was repealed in 1976, subject to "valid, existing rights."

This provision in the enrolled bill is objectionable because it is cumbersome, flawed, and duplicates the extensive public hearings conducted by the Department of the Interior over the last 4 years. In addition, the proposed commission excludes the Secretary of Defense, but military installations are among the Federal properties that would be affected by the recommendations of the commission. Furthermore, there is no assurance that the proposed commission would provide a balanced representation of views or proper public participation. Under the provision, the Secretary of the Interior can disapprove the commission's recommendations, preventing their submission to the Congress under "fast-track" procedures in the House and Senate. I believe—and my Administration has stated—that a better approach would be for Interior to submit a legislative proposal to the Congress within 180 days to clarify R.S. 2477 claim issues permanently, with full congressional and public consideration.

The enrolled bill contains an objectionable provision that funds the Commission for the Advancement of Federal Law Enforcement. I agree with the Fraternal Order of Police and other national law enforcement organizations that certain activities of the Commission, such as evaluating the handling of specific investigative cases, could interfere with Federal law enforcement policy and operations. This type of oversight is most properly the role of Congress, not an unelected review board. If external views about law enforcement programs are needed, a better approach would be to fund the National Commission to Support Law Enforcement.

I also object to two other items in the bill. One reduces funding for the Ounce of Prevention Council by roughly one-third. This reduction would substantially diminish the work of the Council in coordinating crime prevention efforts at the Federal level and assisting community efforts to make their neighborhoods safer. The Council is in the process of awarding $1.8 million for grants to prevent youth substance abuse and of evaluating its existing grant programs. The Council has received over 300 applications from communities and community-based organizations from all across the country for these grants. In addition, the bill reduces funding for the Department of Defense Dual-Use Applications Program. That program helps to develop technologies used and tested by the cost-conscious commercial sector and to incorporate them into military systems. Reducing funding for this program would result in higher costs for future defense systems. The projects selected in this year's competition will save the Department of Defense an estimated $3 billion.

Finally, by including extraneous issues in this bill, the Republican leadership has also delayed necessary funding for maintaining military readiness. The Secretary of Defense has written the Congress detailing the potential disruption of military training.

I urge the Congress to remove these extraneous provisions and to send me a straightforward disaster relief bill that I can sign promptly, so that we can help hard-hit American families and businesses as they struggle to rebuild. Americans in need should not have to endure further delay.

WILLIAM J. CLINTON

The White House,
June 9, 1997.

Remarks on National Education Standards
June 10, 1997

Thank you very much. Let me say, first of all, I'm glad to be here with Pat Forgione, the Commissioner for the National Center for Educational Statistics. I thank him for the fine work that he has done. I thank the educators who are here, Linda Vieth, Lourdes Monegudo, and Sharon Simpson. I thank Secretary Riley for his excellent work. And I want to thank all of those out in the audience who have done so much to make this day come to pass, those who were introduced, the leaders of the NEA and the AFT and the other education groups who are here. All of you, thank you very much for being here.

Today is a good day for American education. Today we announce the new results from the Third International Mathematics and Science Study for fourth graders, showing that America's fourth graders are performing above the national average in math and science. In fact, in science they are doing very well, indeed. According to this report, just issued today, our fourth graders rank second in the world in the Third International Math and Science Tests, just behind Korea. We are making great strides. We've built a solid foundation in our national effort to establish standards of excellence in education.

In 1989 and 1990, when I was a Governor, I worked with the other Governors and the White House and the Department of Education to establish national education goals. I remember the night we spent staying up all night at the University of Virginia, asking ourselves whether we should have a goal in math and science and, if so, what should it be. You remember, don't you? You were there. We were up all night long, and people said to me, "There's no way in the world we can have a goal that we should be first in the world of math and science because we have a more diverse population, we have more poor children, we don't have uniformity of"—so I remember looking at the person who made the argument— it was a perfectly sane and rational argument— I said, "Well, what do you want me to say, we're going to be third in the world in math and science? That's our goal? We'll be fourth? We'll be eighth?" So we decided we would embrace the goal that we would be first.

These fourth grade examinations proved that if our educators, our parents, our schools, the rest of us in a supporting role, if we all do the right thing, that our children can achieve if we give them the chance to do it and if we have high expectations for them. So again, I want to say, I thank the educators who are here. And I think that if you look at where we were—just in 1991, there was a test similar to the TIMSS test in which our fourth graders were below average in math, above average in science, but nowhere near where they are today. So this shows you what can happen in a few short years if people are working together for the right things for our children and the future of this country.

So I just want to say again to all those who were serving with me, the Republicans and Democrats alike who were Governors back then,

I still think we did the right thing, and now we have to do what it takes to make sure we meet the goal. We have to have the conviction that every child in America can learn. And we have to know that this report proves that we don't have to settle for second class expectations or second class goals.

Now, we also have to remember that we've got a long way to go. Last November, when Secretary Riley and Commissioner Forgione released the first results from the eighth grade test, we found that we were above the international average in science but still below the international average in mathematics. That is why I have asked us to begin not just participating in the TIMSS test with a few thousand of our students but to voluntarily embrace national standards beginning with reading and mathematics and begin with examinations that would embrace every child in America with fourth grade reading and eighth grade math by 1999.

Since I issued that call, six States—education leaders or Governors—in Maryland, Michigan, North Carolina, California, West Virginia, and Massachusetts, along with the Department of Defense schools, have adopted this plan of embracing national standards and agreeing to participate in the testing program. I'm pleased to announce today that the State of Kentucky is joining the national standards movement, becoming the sixth State to agree to participate in the examinations. And I want to especially thank Governor Paul Patton, who has been a national leader in education, for joining in this endeavor.

The results today give us a roadmap to higher performance. In no other country in the world did performance in math drop from above average in fourth grade to below average in eighth grade. That didn't happen anywhere else, which means that we are doing a very good job in the early grades but we've got a lot more work to do in the later ones. We know parents have to remain involved in their children's education as they move through schools, not withdraw when their children reach adolescence. We know our curriculum will have to be more focused and more demanding. We know we'll have to hold all of our students to higher standards as they grow older and measure the schools and the students against the standards.

As the school year comes to a close, I want to thank the many thousands of parents and teachers, principals who have done the hard work necessary to achieve these positive results. They have told us over and over and over again that if we can redouble our efforts, especially now in middle school and high schools, we can meet our goals of national excellence. Bipartisan progress on education shows what we can accomplish here in Washington, too, when we reach across party lines, to balance the budget but to invest more in the education of our young people as well as our adults who need more access to education.

So let me just say, before I go on to make one or two more points, there are a lot of people who never believed the United States children would score in the top two in the world on any of these international tests. And now they know that they were wrong and they underestimated our children, underestimated our teachers, underestimated our schools, underestimated our parents. But let's not kid ourselves. We are still nowhere near where we need to be in these other areas, and all this fourth grade test does is to show us that we can be the best in the world if we simply believe it and then organize ourselves to achieve it.

This ought to be a clear challenge to every single State that has not yet come forward to agree to participate in the national standards movement and the test in 1999 that they ought to do it. We don't have to hide anymore. We don't have to be afraid of the results anymore. We're not trying to punish anybody. We're trying to lift the children of this country up, and the TIMSS test proves that they will lift themselves up if we who are adults and in charge of their future do what we ought to do to give them a chance to do it. And I hope all of you will take that message out across the country now.

Let me finally say that whether we in the National Government continue to do our part for education depends upon our good faith in implementing the budget agreement that overwhelming majorities of both parties have voted for and, specifically, what we do with the tax portion of the agreement, which overwhelming majorities agree would be used to help working families to pay for education, to buy and sell a home, to raise their children. That is fair to all Americans.

Yesterday the Republican majority on the House Ways and Means Committee released their plan to fill in the details of the tax cut

agreed to by the Congress and by me. I have reviewed this plan, and I believe that in its present form, it does not meet the tests that I would hold myself to: one, being faithful to the budget agreement; second, having a tax cut that will grow the economy; third, having a tax cut that is fair to middle class families; and fourth, having a tax cut that genuinely helps to increase the quality and volume of education in America today for people of all ages. I do not believe it meets those tests for the following reasons.

Number one, it falls $13 billion short in the amount of higher education tax cuts specifically agreed to in the balanced budget agreement. We agreed to roughly $35 billion. You might say that $34 billion is roughly $35 billion, but $22 billion is not—not even roughly $35 billion—[*laughter*]—and if that were a question in the fourth grade TIMSS test, I'm quite sure what the answer would be. [*Laughter*]

Second, it shortchanges those in the work force who want to gain new skills and those who want to go on to community colleges. Those who go to less expensive schools, like community colleges, would have the HOPE scholarship I proposed, specifically agreed to in the budget agreement, cut in half by the House plan.

Third, the plan falls short for working families in other ways. I favor a $500-per-child tax credit. We have people favoring the $500-per-child tax credit all the way from the most liberal coalitions in the Democratic caucus to the Christian Coalition. But I want to make it even more fair. I think it ought to be refundable, so it's fair to working parents with lower incomes. Instead, the Republican plan would deny the full child tax credit to millions of the hardest pressed working families simply because it is not refundable. And they would deduct the availability of the child's tax credit from the earned-income tax credit that lower income working families already earn.

Moreover, and unbelievably to me, they would reduce tax benefits to working families where both the father and the mother are working and paying for child care and getting some credit for that. They want to deduct the child tax credit from the credit people already get to pay for child care, apparently designed to make it more difficult for people who are parents to work outside the home. I think most working families will tell you, it's hard enough already; what we'd like is a little help raising our children. I do not believe we should discriminate against parents who are working and raising their children in the availability of the children's tax credit.

In short, the tax plan cuts in half the tax cuts for those who go to community college. It shortchanges 6 million families who are already in the work force and having to pay for their child care. That does not meet the standards of fairness to families and promotion of education, nor do I believe it is consistent with the budget agreement. So I hope that the House Democrats and Republicans and the Senate Democrats and Republicans will work with us to meet those tests.

Finally, let me just say one other thing. The people of the Dakotas and Minnesota earned the great compassion and concern of all Americans because of what they went through this year. We've worked hard to help them stave off the worst, to get their communities back together, to rebuild. It has been 80 days since I forwarded to Congress my request for disaster relief to allow the process of recovery to begin. Instead of giving me a disaster relief bill, the

congressional majority insisted on weighing it down with a political wish list. In the name of the people who have had to face the floods, in the name of the families who suffered and need their help now, I ask the majority to put aside the political games, to set aside the political wish list—we can negotiate on all this later— and instead just send me a straightforward disaster relief bill. Again, I believe if this were a question on an elementary school exam, 90 percent of the fourth graders in America would say, do the right thing, and have your political arguments later.

So as we celebrate today, let's do the right thing and resolve that we're not going to stop until we get those TIMSS tests and we're first in the world at the 4th grade level, at the 8th grade level, at the 12th grade level. Our fourth graders have proved that we can do it. We dare not let them and the other children of this country down.

Thank you very much.

NOTE: The President spoke at 11:24 a.m. in the Rose Garden at the White House. In his remarks, he referred to Gov. Paul E. Patton of Kentucky.

Remarks at the Juvenile Justice Conference
June 11, 1997

Thank you very much, Attorney General Reno, Ray Kelly, Father O'Donovan. Let me say to my good friend Father O'Donovan, I never know when I come to Georgetown whether being introduced as the university's most well-known alumnus will be a liability or an asset. It just depends on what month I come, I think. When Ray Kelly said he considered the Jesuits the Marine Corps of the Catholic Church, I never really thought of that. And then he went through that litany, you know, "the few, the proud" and all that, I was thinking about the ones who taught me in class. I was thinking, "the few, the proud, the brutal." [*Laughter*] But brilliantly brutal.

I love this place, and I thank Father O'Donovan for having us here at the conference. I also want to thank the Attorney General and Ray Kelly for the truly unprecedented partnership that they have established with local law

enforcement officials and others who are interested in the safety of our streets and our children throughout the United States. We have here representatives of the Fraternal Order of Police, of the Major Cities Chiefs Association, the law enforcement community, a lot of other people who just work with young people and try to help give them something to say yes to.

I'm glad to see our friend Jim Brady here. The country owes a lot of thanks to Jim and to Sarah, for with courage and persistence and good humor, they have saved a lot of lives with the Brady bill, the assault weapons ban, and others.

We are here today to talk about what we can do together to build safer neighborhoods and stronger neighborhoods as part of the preparation of America for a new century. Today I want to talk about violent youth gangs and the illegal guns they use, the biggest problem, perhaps, we still face in that ongoing struggle.

But as Ray Kelly said, this is a good time to be involved in law enforcement because the good guys are winning and the tide of crime is being rolled back. Four and a half years ago, I can honestly say, when I went around the country in 1992 seeking the Presidency and began to talk about the importance of more police and effective prevention programs along with tougher punishment—and actually I said I was confident that we could bring the crime rate way down over a sustained period of time—most people did not believe me.

You might be interested to know that every national survey I've seen says that most people still don't believe it. [*Laughter*] Even though those of you who are involved in this endeavor know that crime is now down for several years in a row and we had the largest drop in 35 years last year, most people still don't believe it. It may be because a crime story still leads the evening news. It may be the accumulation of personal experiences; nearly everybody has someone in their family who has been victimized. It may be an instinctive feeling that whether the crime rate has gone down or not, it's still too high and there are still too many of our children at risk.

But nonetheless, it has gone down. And a lot of you in this room have helped to make it so. And we tried to work with you and also to learn from you what actually works, not what sounds good in a television ad, not what sounds good in a political campaign, but what actually works: putting more police on the street, taking gangs and guns off the streets, having proven, effective prevention programs that keep our children out of trouble and prevent crimes from occurring in the first place.

That's what we tried to do with the crime bill and the Brady bill, with the assault weapons ban, with the violence against women act, and the other things that the Attorney General spoke about. It's what we've tried to do with our strongest effort ever to make our schools drug-free and gun-free, to have zero tolerance for guns in schools, to make it illegal for minors to possess handguns and for adults to transfer handguns to minors. It's what General McCaffrey is working so hard on in his position as our Nation's drug czar.

And thanks to all of you, the strategy is working. Even the juvenile crime rate showed some decline in 1995, and the juvenile crime arrest rate has begun to go down as a result of your unceasing efforts. But we know that juvenile violence is still a huge problem. We know violent youth gangs still terrorize our streets. We know innocent children are still being swept up in them and may soon be innocent no longer.

According to a report released by the Justice Department, unless we act and do more now, the number of juveniles arrested for violent crimes will more than double by the year 2010. We have got to show the same progress with young people, with juvenile crime, with violence, that we have seen in the overall crime rate with adults in the last 5 years. Keep in mind, this year when school started, we had the largest class of children starting school and the largest number of people in school in the history of America. This year is the first year that the number of schoolchildren exceeded the high watermark of the baby boom, which means that demographically we have just a few years to deal with our young people and give them a future and something to say yes to and to deal with this gang and drug and gun problem before the sheer change in population will begin to overwhelm our efforts.

So I think we know enough and a lot of you have shown us enough to be just as optimistic about this as we now can be about the general problem of crime. But we also have seen enough and we know enough to know that we have to move and move now.

In February, I sent juvenile justice legislation that I felt was very smart and very tough to Congress to declare war on gangs and guns but to do things that you say and that you have shown will work. It was largely modeled on Boston's famous Operation Cease-Fire. It guarantees new antigang prosecutors that are desperately needed to pursue and prosecute violent juveniles. It gives prosecutors the right to seek tougher penalties. It supports initiatives like Operation Night Light in Boston, where police and probation officers actually make housecalls to young probationers and their families to make sure that they live up to the rules of their probation. And when I was in Boston, not very long ago—we spent over a half a day there—the people said that their compliance rate was around 70 percent, which I'm quite confident is the highest in the country. But these things will work.

Because about 40 percent of juvenile crime occurs after school closes and before parents come home—so much for the argument that parents don't make any difference—the youth violence strategy we presented would help to launch 1,000 after-school initiatives all over the country, again, modeled on what is working today—not rocket science, just following the leader to save lives.

We know now that children should be allowed to stay in school or involved in other activities rather than left on street corners until their parents come home from work. We know now that it would be better if our children had teachers or community leaders or team leaders as role models, not gang leaders. We know that our children should be supervised by caring adults, not young people who have entered a gang culture.

The bill that I presented dealt with all this. It also is just as tough on guns as on gangs. I don't care what anybody says—guns are still at the heart of the gangs that strike at the hearts of our communities and families. Every year thousands of children and young people are killed by them, even more wounded and maimed. Listen to this: Teenage homicides by firearms tripled in the 10 years between 1984 and 1994, and the number of juveniles actually killing with guns quadrupled during the same period.

When the National Center for Health Statistics tells us that teenage boys are more likely to die from gunshot wounds than from any other cause, we know that we have more than a duty, we have a moral obligation to keep fighting against this terrible scourge of gun violence, to build on the pathbreaking work done by Jim Brady and others, and to go beyond what we have done so far.

That's why the juvenile crime bill I presented to Congress extends the Brady bill to prevent juvenile criminals from purchasing guns when they reach legal age. You shouldn't be able to commit a violent crime at 16 or 17, then buy a handgun for your 21st birthday. This bill would make that illegal, and I hope all of you will help us pass it.

The bill also requires that child safety locks be sold with guns to keep children from hurting themselves or each other. Unbelievably, a third of all privately owned handguns in our country are left both unlocked and loaded. Every one of them has the power and the potential to

make the life of one of our children lost by accident or design. Child safety locks are simple and inexpensive, but they do have the power to prevent tragedy.

I feel so strongly about them that in March I ordered Federal agencies to give them to our agents. Today, every FBI and ATF agent has such a child safety device, and by the 15th of October, every Federal agent, from the DEA to the U.S. Marshal, to the Border Patrol, to the Park Police, will have one as well. If a child safety lock is good enough for law enforcement, it ought to be good enough for the general public. These commonsense measures will help to cut off young people's access to guns that can cut short their lives.

Today we are taking comprehensive action to protect our children and our communities from juvenile crime and gun violence. In Boston, where many of these efforts are already in place, youth murders have dropped 80 percent in 5 years and not a single, solitary child has been killed with a handgun in a year and a half— in a year and a half. We can do that. Again I say, this is not rocket science; this is replication.

You know, when I was in Houston a couple years ago and I saw the juvenile crime rate going down there when it was going up everywhere else, the mayor said, "It's not very complicated. I've got 3,000 kids in a soccer league and 2,500 in a golf league, and most of them didn't know anything about either sport before we started." This is not rocket science; it is replication. We know what works. There is no excuse for not doing what works. And there is no excuse for the Congress not giving you the tools to do what works.

Now, I believe the approach embodied in the legislation I presented gives us the best chance to prevent more of this violence and to actually break its back. That's what I believe. I believe it because I have seen so many of you do it. Now, the bill that passed the House of Representatives, I think, falls far short of the goals of the bill that I presented and far short of reflecting what you have proved works. A juvenile crime bill that doesn't crack down on guns and gangs, that doesn't guarantee more prosecutors, more probation officers, and more prevention programs after school is a juvenile crime bill in name only.

I understand you can pass a bill and make it very popular if all it does is seem to penalize people. And I am not against tougher penalties; we have toughened a lot of penalties since I have been President. But to pretend that you can do that and not guarantee the police, the prosecutors, the probation officers, and the prevention programs and expect to have results is simply wrong. You work in this area, and you know it. So let's go back to the Congress and get a bill that will give you the tools to give our children their futures back and our people their neighborhoods and their streets back. We can do it together.

Let me just say something about one specific problem. The illegal guns that youth gangs use do not just come out of thin air. They are bought and sold, traded and given in trade, just like any other guns. And all too often, it is adults who are making the transfer. So today, I'm directing the Secretary of the Treasury, Bob Rubin, to require all federally licensed gun dealers to post signs in their stores and issue written warnings with each gun they sell to put adult gun purchasers on clear and unambiguous notice that selling or giving a handgun to a minor is dangerous, it is wrong, but it is also against the law, and it is a felony so serious that it can carry a penalty of up to 10 years in prison. I want every adult who buys a gun to see that sign and think about it before they give a child a gun that could wind up in gang violence.

In the last 4 years, we have proven that if we work together and learn from each other, we can begin to turn the tide and win the war, as Ray Kelly said. Now we have an opportunity that is real and genuine to build on that progress. Your presence here, your enthusiasm, and what I know about the work you have done back home give me great hope that we can give our children a safe and orderly environment where they can make the most of their lives.

We know that a lot of this will have to be done at the community level. When we did the Summit of Service that the Presidents sponsored in Philadelphia, one of the five things we said we wanted for our children was a safe environment for every child in America to grow up in. And we know that a lot of that has to be done by you. But we also know that we at the national level have our responsibility, too. And our responsibility now is to continue to implement the crime bill and put the community police officers out there, to be faithful in our enforcement of all the Federal laws that we can, and to deal with the special problems of guns and to pass a smart, balanced juvenile justice crime bill that does more than talk tough.

I pledge to work with Congress of both parties to pass such a bill. I look forward to working with all of you to get the job done, but I say again: The most powerful argument for doing it is the experience you have already had, the successes you have already achieved, the lives you have already saved.

When you know what works and you do it and you see children's lives reclaimed, it becomes unconscionable not to do more. I am determined that we will do more and that we will win this incredibly important struggle.

Thank you, and God bless you all.

NOTE: The President spoke at 12:09 p.m. in Salon H of the Conference Center at Georgetown University. In his remarks, he referred to Under Secretary of the Treasury for Enforcement Raymond W. Kelly; Father Leo O'Donovan, president, Georgetown University; Sarah Brady, chair, Handgun Control, Inc., and her husband, former White House Press Secretary James S. Brady; and Mayor Bob Lanier of Houston, TX.

Memorandum on Enforcing the Youth Handgun Safety Act
June 11, 1997

Memorandum for the Secretary of the Treasury

Subject: Enforcing the Youth Handgun Safety Act

A major problem in our Nation today is the terrifying ease with which our young people gain illegal or unattended access to guns. Firearms are now responsible for 12 percent of fatalities among all American children and teenagers. Criminal use of firearms by young people is a national tragedy. Between 1984 and 1994, the number of juvenile offenders committing homicides by firearms nearly quadrupled. Moreover,

firearms are the fourth leading cause of accidental deaths among children ages 5 to 14 and
are now the primary method by which young
people commit suicide. A recent study supported by the Department of Justice found that
slightly more than half of all privately owned
firearms were stored unlocked and approximately one-third of all handguns were stored
both loaded and unlocked. We must do all we
can to prevent both illegal and unintended access to guns by juveniles.

To address this issue, my Administration has
consistently called for toughening our laws to
help reduce youth gun violence. Specifically, we
have fought for and gained passage of: (1) the
Brady Law, to allow local law enforcement to
conduct background checks before handguns are
sold; (2) the Assault Weapons ban, to keep
deadly assault weapons off the streets; (3) the
Gun-Free Schools Act of 1994, to establish a
policy of "zero tolerance" for guns in our
schools; and (4) the Youth Handgun Safety Act,
Subtitle B of the 1994 Crime Bill, to prohibit,
in most circumstances, the transfer to or possession of a handgun by a juvenile.

More recently, we proposed comprehensive
juvenile crime legislation that, among other
things, would continue to crack down on youth
gun violence by increasing penalties for transferring a firearm to a juvenile, prohibiting violent
juveniles from owning firearms as adults, and
requiring Federal firearms licensees (FFLs) to
provide a child safety lock with every gun sold.
I hope the Congress will enact these important
measures as soon as possible.

Until the Congress acts, however, there is
more we can do to keep handguns out of the
hands of our Nation's youth. Existing law already

bans the transfer of handguns to minors and
juvenile possession of handguns, except in specified circumstances, and grants the Department
of the Treasury authority to prescribe rules and
regulations to implement this provision. I direct
you to take the authorized steps necessary to
enforce the provisions of the Youth Handgun
Safety Act—and specifically, consistent with your
statutory authority, to promptly publish in the
Federal Register proposed regulations requiring
that signs be posted on the premises of FFLs
and that written notification be issued with each
handgun sold to non-licensees warning that:

(1) Federal law prohibits, except in certain
limited circumstances, anyone under the
age of 18 from knowingly possessing a
handgun, or any adult from transferring a
handgun to such a minor;

(2) violation of the prohibition of transferring a handgun to a minor is, under certain
circumstances, punishable by up to 10 years
in prison;

(3) handguns are a leading contributor to
juvenile violence and fatalities; and

(4) safely storing and locking handguns
away from children can help ensure compliance with Federal law.

I also direct you to provide me with a written
status report within 60 days on how you will
carry out this directive.

Your implementation of this directive will help
inform gun purchasers about their responsibility
under Federal law to keep handguns from our
children. It will also ensure that gun purchasers
are warned about the frequency with which
handguns kill or injure our kids.

WILLIAM J. CLINTON

Remarks at a Democratic National Committee Dinner
June 11, 1997

Thank you very much. Let me say to all of
you how very grateful I am for your presence
and for your support. I appreciate what the Vice
President has said, and I associate myself with
his remarks. I think that's what they say in the
Congress. [*Laughter*]

I would just like to make two very brief
points. First of all, the country is in better shape

than it was 4½ years ago. It is a direct consequence, in my view, of the hard work of the
American people combined with the policies and
the changes which have been instituted here.

I want you to know that my plan is to keep
working on this until the last day I'm in office.
And as far as I'm concerned, all these good

things that have happened are not constant unless they can be sustained, so that we still have to put the meat on the bones of the balanced budget agreement. In the abstract, it is a very good agreement because it contains an investment strategy for education, for science and technology, for the environment we can be proud of and it will balance the budget with conservative estimates. But we have to put the meat on the bones.

I'm proud of the fact that we've had the biggest drop in crime in 36 years, but juvenile violence is still way too high, and we have to put the meat on the bones. We have a lot more to do there.

I'm proud of the fact that we've had the biggest drop in welfare in history by far, but we've still got to make sure when all those people run out of their welfare checks they can go to work, and we've got to put meat on the bones.

I'm proud of the fact that this budget agreement restores what I thought were unconscionable cuts in benefits to legal immigrants, but we've still got to put the meat on the bones in terms of the details of the legislation. So there's a lot to be done here.

In the world, I'm gratified by the agreements we've reached with Russia on the NATO-Russian partnership and reducing the nuclear tensions between us and the meeting that will occur in a few weeks in Madrid to expand NATO. But I'm troubled that we have not completed the Bosnian peace process; we've got a long way to go there. I'm troubled at the stagnation of the peace process in the Middle East. There's a lot of things that this administration has done that cannot be sustained unless we all keep working and moving forward.

And the second point I would like to make to you is a more abstract one, but I hope you can take some pleasure in it. I really believed in 1991 and 1992, when I went around and asked so many of you to help me run for President, that we had to modernize the approach of the Democratic Party consistent with our values, that we had to take a new approach but it had to be rooted in our values. There was nothing wrong with our values, but we had to be relevant and effective in the modern world.

We had to prove that we were capable of producing a strong defense, a credible foreign policy, a disciplined management of the economy, particularly on fiscal matters. And we had

to prove that you could cut the deficit and invest in America's future at the same time. We had to prove that we could be for high standards of personal responsibility in the criminal justice and welfare system and still believe that we should be an inclusive nation, where everybody should have a fair chance. We had to prove you could grow the economy and preserve the environment. We had to take a different position.

And when I was in Europe recently and I was doing this press conference with the new Prime Minister of Great Britain, Tony Blair, who as you know has been subject to almost savage criticism from time to time for having adopted ideas similar to mine—[*laughter*]—but the only people that like it seem to be the people over there; the voters thought it was all right—I had the feeling for the very first time that the people in the press who were asking us questions really believed that we might have changed the country and our political party and that there was some organized, principled direction to this.

And I've been working on this long before I even thought I would run for President, for a good 10 years or more now. And I think that once we believed that we had—we not only have good results but we know we're on a course that will work and we can expect it to keep working with sustained effort, that is the beginning of real hope because then you don't have to see the gains evaporate when elections change things or when term limits come up or when momentary difficulties come up in the economy or other problems.

So I would ask you to keep that in mind. I believe you have helped to contribute to a profound, almost revolutionary positive change in the direction of our country because you helped to revitalize the party that we're all proud to be a part of. And I hope you will never forget that.

And I had the feeling for the very first time that a lot of those who interpret us for the rest of the country and the world were coming to that understanding, because I was standing there with the new Prime Minister of Great Britain and we were saying the same things and we had just left the Prime Minister of The Netherlands and he said the same things and because they came along after the '92 election and had also seemed to get quite satisfactory results in their own country. So you were also part of changing the world. And for that, I am very, very grateful.

Thank you.

NOTE: The President spoke at 8:37 p.m. at the Mayflower Hotel. In his remarks, he referred to Prime Minister Wim Kok of The Netherlands.

Statement on the Mortgage Insurance Premium Reduction Initiative
June 12, 1997

Today, we are making it even easier for thousands of young families to buy their first home. I am pleased to announce that the Department of Housing and Urban Development is reducing the FHA's up-front mortgage insurance premium by 12.5 percent. This reduction, coupled with two previous reductions and savings passed on to homebuyers because of better Government efficiency, will save families buying a first home a total of $1,200. Just last year, FHA premium cuts reduced the downpayments for 550,000 families across the country.

In 1994, I called upon the Department of Housing and Urban Development to develop a strategy to boost homeownership to an all-time high—to produce 8 million new American homeowners by the year 2000. Through our National Homeownership Strategy, more than 2.5 million American families have already become homeowners. Today, more Americans are homeowners than at any time in history.

We know homeownership is strengthening families and stabilizing neighborhoods. As part of that strategy, I challenged HUD to do what it could to remove some of the barriers young families face when buying their first home. Too often, front-end closing costs, not monthly payments, stand between a hard-working family and a new home. Our goal was to cut those up-front costs by $1,000; with today's action, we have cut those costs by $1,200.

I applaud Secretary Cuomo for going the extra mile, surpassing the challenge I set in 1994 and providing the extra boost needed to make the dream of homeownership a reality for thousands more families.

Statement on the Federal Election Commission Decision To Consider Action on the Soft Money System in Domestic Politics
June 12, 1997

I applaud the Federal Election Commission's unanimous decision to begin to consider my request that they act to ban soft money in Federal elections. This is an important step in our effort to reform our elections and restore the trust of the American people in their political system.

As I said in my petition to the FEC, the rules governing our system of financing Federal election campaigns are sorely out of date. The system has been overwhelmed by a tide of money, raised in amounts and in ways that could not have been contemplated when the system was created two decades ago. I believe that the FEC has the authority and the obligation to take dramatic action, and I am pleased that five congressional sponsors of bipartisan campaign finance reform, led by Congressmen Shays and Meehan, have filed a similar petition before the Commission.

I urge the FEC to take the next step and begin the process of writing new rules that will ban soft money. I hope this action will encourage Congress to enact comprehensive, bipartisan campaign finance reform.

Statement on Enlargement of the North Atlantic Treaty Organization
June 12, 1997

After careful consideration, I have decided that the United States will support inviting three countries—Poland, Hungary, and the Czech Republic—to begin accession talks to join NATO when we meet in Madrid next month.

We have said all along that we would judge aspiring members by their ability to add strength to the alliance and their readiness to shoulder the obligations of NATO membership. Poland, Hungary, and the Czech Republic most clearly meet those criteria—and have currently made the greatest strides in military capacity and political and economic reform.

As I have repeatedly emphasized, the first new members should not and will not be the last. We will continue to work with other interested nations, such as Slovenia and Romania, to help them prepare for membership. Other nations are making good progress—and none will be excluded from consideration.

We look forward to working with our NATO Allies to reach agreement on this important issue.

Statement on Congressional Action on Emergency Supplemental Appropriations Legislation
June 12, 1997

I applaud the United States Congress for passing the disaster relief bill that the families of the Midwest and other parts of the country desperately need. I am especially pleased that the congressional majority heeded the call of common sense by ensuring that the people who need this assistance will get it and by ensuring that the controversial and extraneous provisions of the bill were dropped. Anyone who has toured the flood-ravaged areas of the Midwest, as I have, knows that these needed funds will help put America's families and communities on the road to recovery. Above all, today's vote shows that while we may not agree on everything, we can still work together and move forward on those crucial priorities that are beyond dispute. I thank the Congress for its willingness to do so, and I hope we can continue to work together in that spirit in the weeks and months to come.

Statement on Signing Emergency Supplemental Appropriations Legislation
June 12, 1997

I am pleased to sign into law tonight the disaster relief bill that Congress has just sent to me.

This bill provides the desperately needed resources for hundreds of thousands of people who have suffered terribly from the flooding and other natural disasters in the Dakotas, Minnesota, California, and 29 other States. It also includes the necessary funds for the Department of Defense in connection with our peacekeeping efforts in Bosnia and Southwest Asia. It does not include the unacceptable political provisions of the bill I vetoed that had nothing to do with the goal of providing disaster relief.

When our people are in need, we Americans come to their assistance as one nation. I applaud the Congress for heeding my call to remember that fundamental principle.

NOTE: H.R. 1871, 1997 Emergency Supplemental Appropriations Act for Recovery from Natural Disasters, and for Overseas Peacekeeping Efforts, Including Those in Bosnia, approved June 12, was assigned Public Law No. 105–18.

Remarks to the Business Roundtable
June 12, 1997

Thank you very much, ladies and gentlemen. Thank you, Don, for your introduction and for the good work that you do and that we have tried to do together. I'm delighted to be joined here today by several members of the administration. I see Secretary Daley; Secretary Herman; our NEC Chair, Gene Sperling; my Presidential Adviser for Public Liaison, Maria Echaveste; and Mack McLarty, who is known to many of you for the many hats he has worn and now, among other things, is my special envoy to Latin America.

I wanted to come today to talk to you, at what we all know is a very hopeful time, about what we have to do together to keep our economy growing and to prepare America for the 21st century, with the lowest unemployment in 24 years, the lowest inflation in 30 years, the highest corporate profit in more than two decades, the biggest drop in inequality of incomes among working people last year since the 1960's, and a stock market that has done reasonably well. [*Laughter*] We also have had the biggest drop in crime last year in 35 years and now 5 years in a row of crime going down, by far the largest drop in the welfare rolls ever since 1994 when it reached its all time peak. Our country is also leading the world again in exports and cutting edge technologies. And we can be forgiven if we now hope that we can make the 21st century, like the 20th century, another American century.

The great credit for this remarkable economic turnaround goes primarily to American businesses and workers, to small businesses and entrepreneurs, to those on the cutting edge of research and development, to the responsible policies of the Federal Reserve. But I also like to think that our new economic policy had a little something to do with it as well.

In 1993, we replaced trickle-down economics, which had quadrupled the Nation's debt, with invest-and-grow economics, starting with cutting the deficit. We cut it from $290 billion a year to what is estimated to be about $67 billion this year. That is a 77 percent reduction based on the 1993 plan. Now, with the balanced budget agreement that the administration has reached with the Congress, it will go to zero.

Second, we have invested in the skills and education of our people, beginning to put in place a system of lifelong learning for all Americans, which starts with expanding Head Start and includes raising academic standards, opening wider the doors of college, improving job training for employees, and developing with the business community, in every State, school-to-work partnerships for those who don't go on to 4-year colleges or universities.

Third, we have vigorously worked to open markets for American products. With NAFTA, GATT, and over 200 other hard-won trade agreements, our exports are at an all-time high and will be further advanced by the agreements recently reached in telecommunications and information technology. Fiscal responsibility, investing in people, free and fair trade, that has been our economic strategy.

We have also tried to modernize and improve the way the Government works with the private sector. The Federal Government now has 300,000 fewer people working for it than it did the day I became President in 1993, some 16,000 fewer pages of regulations, hundreds of fewer Government programs but, more importantly, genuine partnerships with all different kinds of industries to grow the economy and preserve the environment and to reach other genuine and legitimate aims of the American people, including moving people from welfare to work and giving our children a greater future, things to which Don alluded.

The results of your efforts and ours and our partnership have made the United States once again the envy of the world. I read the business magazines when they come out, and they're a long way from where they were in 1993, when I didn't enjoy reading them so much. Now there is a hyperbole contest. One says this is the best economy in 30 years; another says it's the best it's ever been. I don't feel the need to resolve that debate. [*Laughter*] Regardless, that's a high-class problem.

But we know that underneath that there are other challenges facing us, so I came here to say I think we can keep this going. I believe we can do better. But it will require us to make some critical choices in the coming months that will determine whether we will keep to the vision and the partnership and the forward march that we are on, or abandon it.

First, we have to finish the job of balancing the budget, and that means we have to implement this budget agreement in good faith. It will happen in two steps. In the beginning, there will be votes on what's called a reconciliation package for the multiyear spending and the multiyear tax cut between now and 2002. And then there must be votes on next year's appropriations which are faithful to the budget agreement and to the reconciliation package.

It is absolutely essential for both Republicans and Democrats, especially those who voted for the agreement—in the House, nearly two-thirds of the Democrats and nearly 90 percent of the Republicans; in the Senate, over 80 percent of the Democrats and just over 70 percent of the Republicans—it carried with overwhelming bipartisan support in both Houses, with one party having the greater percentage in one House, the other in the other House—it is essential now to implement the agreement in good faith. It is quite specific, and ambiguous on very, very few points.

If we had enough changes around the edges that some want to make, pretty soon we could make the edges ragged enough to unravel the fabric of the agreement. I do not expect that to happen. I expect it to be implemented. But you will see a lot of efforts, I think, in the next few weeks and months to get people to hold to the terms of the agreement. And since you support the agreement, I hope you will support the discipline necessary to hold to its terms.

The second test will be whether we can make good on the critical need to invest in our people and especially in education and training. This budget contains the biggest increase in educational investment since the 1960's. And arguably, in making universal access to the first 2 years of college after high school, so that it can become just as prevalent as a high school diploma is today, it is the biggest advance in opportunity for all Americans in education since the GI bill.

In addition to that, it contains the funding necessary for us to conduct a national examination of all fourth graders in reading and all eighth graders in math according to generally accepted national standards in 1999. I want to again say, of all the things the Business Roundtable has done that I am grateful for, there

is nothing that I appreciate more than your steadfast adherence to the cause of high national academic standards and the proposition that all our children can learn, should be expected to learn, and should be measured against those standards. I want to particularly thank you and thank my longtime friend and fellow Arkansan Brooks Robinson for going public on this, and thank you for mobilizing other baseball players and getting the Orioles involved. Stay with this.

Even though we just this week had evidence that our fourth graders rank well above the national average in the Third International Math and Science Test, there are States that are reluctant to participate, and it is wrong. It is wrong to pretend that this is some sort of a Government plot to take over the schools, which it isn't, or that somehow math is different in Washington State than it is in Maine and that physics is different in Miami than it is in Montana. That is not true. And we, and you especially, have an interest in our hanging tough on this.

So we can do it. Already, since I called for this in the State of the Union, we have education leaders in States reflecting about—now over 20 percent of the school students in our country willing to participate, but we ought not to stop until we have 100 percent. And I thank you for your support of that.

And let me finally say just one more word about the budget agreement. The budget agreement has a unique provision for tax relief, and I think that the amount can be afforded. And the framework of the tax relief is set out in the budget agreement. For me, the tax package that they will send to my desk should meet five tests. One, and most important, it's got to be faithful to the agreement; if you want to know what it can do, just read the agreement. Second, it should help the economy grow. Third, it should be fair to working families. Fourth, it should target our top priority of education. And finally, it should not explode the deficit in later years and make it more difficult to meet the fiscal challenges we will face as the baby boom nears retirement.

Now, the amount fixed in the agreement was $85 billion in the first year—first 5 years, and a little less than twice that in the second 5 years, which allows for natural growth. In the 10-year window that we have agreed to, this is—to give you some perspective—will provide for a lot of possibilities, but it's about one-tenth the total cost of the 1981 tax cut, much of which, as you'll remember, had to be undone in 1982 and then in subsequent years because of what happened to the deficit. We don't want to go down that road again, so there are strict limits.

Within these limits, I favor tax relief to help families raise their children and send them to college, to pay for lifetime learning, to own a home. I could support a pro-growth capital gains tax relief package, along with some help to ease the burdens of estate taxes on small businesses and family farms, as long as these tax relief measures are consistent with the budget agreement and especially consistent not only with the 5-year time window but the 10-year time window. We are trying to balance the budget over a long period of time, not just have it balanced in one year and have it bump up again the next year and leave our successors here another set of headaches.

Now, from my point of view, the tax package revealed by the Republicans in the House Ways and Means Committee does not meet all those standards. One of the biggest challenges Americans have today—and you know this, all your employees do, even upper income people—is balancing the demands of work and family, raising a child, and doing your job. I believe the package that was revealed this week by the House committee would make that job more difficult for millions of Americans for the following reasons.

First, it explicitly excludes 4 million of our hardest pressed families from receiving the child tax credit. I think that's a mistake because their incomes are so modest, they qualify for the earned-income tax credit under present tax law. Another provision actually penalizes families with working mothers by saying that parents who receive tax relief for child care under present tax law will have their children's tax credit cut. I think that is wrong. I don't think that we should single out working families who need child care for less tax relief. I cannot let that provision stand. And since a lot of you employ members of those working families, I hope you will stand with me on that in opposing it.

Nonetheless, let me say that, on balance, I think good things are happening. It is bound to be that in the beginning of this skirmish there will be a lot of particular proposals made that are inconsistent with the budget agreement.

Why? Because the budget agreement, while it was voted on by the whole Congress, was developed by just a few people. And I would dare say that not everybody who voted on it has read every word of it.

So don't get too upset or distracted or think that things are hopeless if we get into a big fight here over an issue or two, because it's part of the inevitable process of going from the terms of the budget agreement to the specifics of a reconciliation package and then to the even more specific appropriation bills that will have to pass later in the year.

The third big test, after our investment priorities and balancing the budget, is whether we will continue to lead the world in trade. I have to say that it is somewhat mysterious to me that we seem to have, if anything, even more opposition to expanding trade in 1997 than we did when we had the critical vote in 1993 and then again on GATT in 1994, when we have more evidence that our policy works.

With the 200 trade agreements that were negotiated in the first 4 years I was President went along over 12 million new jobs, the first time in history one 4-year term ever saw the American people produce over 12 million new jobs. The unemployment rate is at 4.8 percent for the fist time in 24 years, since 1973. And in the last 2 years, more than half of the new jobs created in this country have been in categories that pay wages above the average. We know that trade-related jobs pay above the average. So it's not like we don't have any evidence here.

Yet, in the face of all this evidence, it appears to me that there are some people—in both parties, I might say—who are afraid to give the President the same authority that every President since Gerald Ford has had to negotiate fast-track agreements, not just with specific countries but within the framework of the general trade regimes of which we're a part.

I do not believe we have anything to fear from more trade with Chile. I do not believe we have anything to fear from more trade with Argentina and Brazil. I believe we would be making a terrible political as well as a terrible economic mistake to walk away from the democratic and free market movement that is sweeping the world and especially our neighbors in South America, who have known so much heartache in the past from oppression and poverty and have given us a lot of heartburn in the

20th century, growing out of the governments they had and the suffering of their own people. Now we have a chance to solidify a much more positive movement, and we know it is good for us because we have the evidence. So I hope that you will help us win the fast-track vote.

I also know that there is, if anything, even more at least emotional opposition to the extension of MFN to China. You know what a lot of our fellow country men and women don't, which is that MFN is the most wrongly worded term in Government language. And that's a mouthful. [*Laughter*] We do not seek any special favors for China. We seek simply to continue the status quo, treating them as we do other normal trading partners. We believe that it will help us to maintain a stable, open, and peaceful China. We believe that our interest is having a China that is not only stable and open but one that is nonaggressive, that respects human rights, works to strengthen the rule of law, and works with us to build a more secure international order.

Now, we have great disagreements with China. The question is, can we influence China best by treating them differently from all of our other trading partners for the first time in a very long time, or can we influence them more by giving the possibility of genuine partnership?

Every President since 1980 has extended MFN to China. Ending that would end our strategic dialog, which has led to cooperation on nuclear nonproliferation issues, to stability on the Korean Peninsula, to the protection of American intellectual property rights. All of that cooperation would go by the boards. It would close one of the world's largest markets to our people and our businesses and our exports. It could put in danger some 170,000 American jobs today. It would make China more isolated and remove incentives to play by the rules of international conduct.

Revoking normal trade treatment would have grave consequences especially now, I'm afraid, as we stand on the eve of Hong Kong's reversion. In 1984, Great Britain and China made an agreement about the terms under which Hong Kong would revert and asked the United States, when President Reagan held this office, to bless the agreement. The United States did that. We expect the agreement to be honored: one China, two systems. We think it should be.

Ending MFN now would shatter any claim to influence we have on that important subject.

Half of all China's trade flows through Hong Kong. Revocation would have a more devastating effect on Hong Kong probably than China as a whole. All the political leaders in Hong Kong across the political spectrum, including the most ardent human rights and democracy advocates, have implored us to continue MFN with China and not to revoke it.

So what I say to you and what I know you agree with, but I hope you will say to Members of Congress in both parties, is that this is not about whether we agree with China on every issue; it's not about whether we have profound disagreements with them; it is about what is the interest of the American people and what is most likely to give us the largest amount of influence and cooperation with China in the years ahead.

We have to continue to speak out for human rights, and we have, and we will. We have worked with the U.N. Human Rights Commission in Geneva. Our State Department issues unvarnished annual reports. We meet with China's leaders on human rights initiatives. We talk about expanding Radio Free Asia's broadcast to China in Mandarin. And all of us have to do more on these important issues.

We have supported and will continue to support programs to advance civil society and the rule of law in China. And I ask America's business community to join with us to contribute to programs that will support the rule of law in China and in other countries where it is desperately needed. We need more educational exchanges, more training centers for lawyers and judges, more support for those who stand against corruption. You have great interest in rules that are predictable and consistent. It will help democratic society eventually to emerge and serve our values as well as our interests. But we cannot do it, I would argue, if we cut off our relations with China in trade.

The road ahead may not be entirely uniform and will be unpredictable and will be rough, but you can disagree with people and still do business with them, knowing that if you're talking to them and working with them, the incentives not to go over the edge to truly destructive behavior and a more isolated world are always there. That is what I believe is in the interests of the American people.

I would point out, too, that I have been heartened by the growing support among religious leaders in the United States for continuation of MFN status based on the ability of people in China of different religious faiths to practice their religion. So we're broadening the support. But again I ask you, please help us with this. There are a lot of people of great and genuine conviction on the other side of this issue, but I think the evidence is on our side and I hope we can prevail.

Let me say, finally, that there are a few other things that I think we have to do beyond these three issues of finishing the work of the budget, investing in our people, and expanding trade. This moment of prosperity and stability has given us an opportunity to work together to repair our social fabric, to join together to face those issues which, if we don't face them, could flare into crises and keep us from becoming the nation we ought to be in the new century.

And let me just mention a few. You were kind enough to mention the Summit of Service that President Bush, President Carter, Mrs. Reagan, and General Powell and I and others sponsored in Philadelphia. One of the things we have to do if we want to give our children a better future is to help their parents be gainfully employed. We were able to reduce the welfare rolls dramatically because of a growing economy and because of work we did with States before the passage of the welfare reform bill to help them move people from welfare to work.

Now, this welfare reform bill did two things. It required people on welfare who are ablebodied to move from welfare to work within a certain amount of time, and it gave the States, in a block grant, funds that used to be spent in a Federal entitlement so that they would have more flexibility to create incentives for people to move from welfare to work.

Forty of our States now have a windfall there because they're getting money based on how much they got when the welfare rolls were at their peak, and there has been a 20-percent-plus drop in the welfare rolls in the last 3 years. I urge you, in all the States that you're working in, to get the Governors, to get the legislators to work with the business community to spend that money in ways that, with your efforts, can move a million more people from welfare to work in the next 4 years.

We moved a million people in the last 4 when we were creating 12 million jobs. That had never been done before, the 12 million jobs; neither had the million people. Under the terms of this welfare reform law, whether we create 12 million jobs or not in the private sector, we have to move nearly another million people. We have got to have your help. But the States have the power to do things like give employers the welfare check for a year or two to use as an employment and training subsidy for people that are especially hard to place, to spend even more money on child care, to spend money on education and training.

So I implore you to help us do this. It will be a terrible thing if, having called for welfare reform and personal responsibility, the end of it is to wind up hurting poor people. That was never what was intended. The children should not suffer in this. And you are going to have to take the lead in helping to do this.

The second thing I'd like to say is, we have to—now having faced the structural budget deficit in the country, we have to deal with the generational deficit. That means we have to have long-term entitlement reform to face the realities of the baby boom generation retiring. And I will be—as soon as we get the budget out of the way, I'll be working with the bipartisan leadership in Congress on an approach to that, and I ask for your support.

It also means that we have to fulfill the mission of the Philadelphia summit, with the public and the private sectors doing their jobs. Remember what the Philadelphia summit was about: Every child ought to have a safe place to grow up, decent health care, a good education and marketable skills, a mentor, and the chance to serve.

And we live in a country where 11 percent of the people over 65 are poor, but 20 percent-plus of the people under 18 are. And we cannot do well unless we do better by our children. So this intergenerational thing is about entitlement reform, but it's also about giving our kids a better chance.

The third issue—the one I'm going to speak about in San Diego in a couple of days—and that is the challenge presented to us as we become the world's first truly multiracial democracy. We have 5 school districts in America today with kids from over 100 different racial and ethnic groups—5. We'll soon have 12.

We have—we all know this—but my Baptist minister from Arkansas came up to see me during the Inaugural, and he told me he had a cousin who had a Baptist church across the river here in Virginia that now has a Korean mission and runs English-as-a-second-language classes out of the church. There are thousands of stories like this.

And yet we know that there are still dramatically different perceptions among different racial and ethnic groups, starting with the historic tensions that have existed between African-Americans and whites in the country and layered on by the successive waves of immigrants, that pose great challenges to us.

When you look at how the world is being torn asunder in the Middle East, in Bosnia, in Northern Ireland and Africa by people who would rather kill each other over their differences than celebrate what they share, you realize that what we are trying to do here is truly astonishing.

Within the decade, more than one State in America will have no majority race—within the decade. Within three decades, the whole country will almost have no majority race. We are going to test whether what we always say about America is true, that we are basically a country founded on an idea. It's not about land. It's not about race or ethnic origin. It's about the idea that all of us are created equal. And that means, among other things, we have to deal with both the perceptions and the reality. And I don't want to get into this except to say that I hope that all of you are concerned by the consequences of the wholesale abolition of affirmative action on enrollment in higher education that we've seen in California and Texas. And I know a lot of employers at large companies have led the way in trying to preserve a sensible form of affirmative action. So I ask you to consider that, because this is not just the President and the Government. All of us are the stewards of whether we can become one America in the 21st century.

Finally, let me say on an issue that I know is a concern to some of you because I read your ad in the paper—[*laughter*]—I think that we have to prove that we can grow the economy while not only preserving but actually enhancing the environment. And I believe most of you think we can do that. And I think the message you were trying to get across in the ad is, don't

wreck the economy without knowing what you're doing. I understand that.

But let me say, I was very moved by the speech recently given by the chairman of British Petroleum on the issue of climate change. I don't know how many of you read it, but essentially what he said is, look, nobody knows exactly what the impact of climate change is, but let's not deny anymore that the climate is changing and that it can't be good and that no harm will be done if we take sensible steps to try to reduce greenhouse gas emissions and to do other things which will help us to preserve the environment.

We've had more extreme weather conditions in the United States in the last 5 years than we had in the previous 30. And we know from all the scientific studies what is happening to the temperature of the globe. What I ask you to do is to work with me in good faith to give our children a world worth living in.

A lot of you have made a good deal of money in your corporations by technologies which improve the environment. And if we have the strongest economy in the world, we will find a sensible way to grow that economy in a way that fulfills our responsibilities.

Today, with 4 percent of the world's population, we produce over 20 percent of the greenhouse gases. We're up 13 percent since 1990 when President Bush and his administration said we would try to hold constant through the year 2000.

I had an interesting conversation with Jiang Zemin in New York about a year ago, when he said, "I don't want you to have a containment policy toward China." I said, I'm not sure—I said, "I don't want to have a containment policy toward China." I said, "My biggest worry about you is that you'll get rich the same way we did. And if you do that, you might burn the air up because you've got 1.2 billion people." And we need to find an environmentally responsible way for China to grow.

So I ask you to join with us in partnership. There is no secret plan; there is no scheme here to try to put thousands of Americans out of business. I have devoted my passion and the best ideas I could come up with to try to get this country in good shape economically and socially. But I do believe it is folly for us to believe that we can go into the next century without a strategy that says we're going to be responsible and we're going to do our part and lead the world on the environmental issues—because we all know what the evidence is. We don't know what the consequences are, and we don't want to go off and do something that we're not sure makes sense. But we can do this. We can do it together. We can do it in a way that makes sense.

And I ask you not to ever ask us to back away from that but instead join hands with us and do what we've done for the last 4½ years. Let's find a way to preserve the environment, to meet our international responsibilities, to meet our responsibilities to our children, and grow the economy at the same time. I know we can do it. Look at the evidence of the last

4 years. We can do anything if we put our minds to it.

Thank you very much.

NOTE: The President spoke at 4:37 p.m. in the ballroom at the J.W. Marriott Hotel. In his remarks, he referred to Donald V. Fites, chairman, Business Roundtable; Gen. Colin L. Powell, USA (ret.), chairman, America's Promise—the Alliance for Youth; John Browne, group chief executive, British Petroleum Co., p.l.c.; and President Jiang Zemin of China. Following his remarks, the President presented a birthday cake to former President George Bush.

Remarks Prior to a Meeting With the President's Advisory Board on Race and an Exchange With Reporters
June 13, 1997

The President. I'd like to begin by thanking this distinguished group of Americans for their willingness to serve on an advisory board to me to examine the state of race relations in America over the next year, to participate in making sure that the American people have facts, not myths, upon which to base their judgments, and proceed to launching a nationwide, honest discussion that we hope will be replicated in every community in this country and that will lead to some specific recommendations for further actions on our part as we move forward.

I think this is the right time to do this, because there is not a major crisis engulfing the Nation that dominates the headlines every day. The economy is strong. Crime is down. Our position in the world is good. But if you look at where we are and where we're going, we will soon be, in the next few decades, a multiracial society in which no racial group is in a majority. And we are living in a world in which that gives us an enormous advantage in relating to other countries in the world since we have people from every country in the world here.

Already we have 5 big school districts in America with children from over 100 different racial and ethnic groups; soon we'll have 12, within the next year or so. And also, if you look at the rest of the world, all the wonders of modern technology are being threatened by

the rise of ethnic and racial and religious and tribal conflicts around the world. We'll be in a unique position to show people, not just tell people but show people, they don't have to give in to those darker impulses if we can create one America out of this incredible diversity we have.

So you all know this has been a big concern of mine for a long time, but I just believe that this is the right time for us to try to prepare for the new century and to take this time to look at it, and I have a very great group of people here, and there are hundreds, perhaps even thousands more who would like to participate in this debate, and we intend to give them the chance to do it.

State of Race Relations

Q. How bad do you think race relations are in this country today? I mean, what are the real tensions?

The President. I think they're much better than they used to be, but I think there is still discrimination. I think there is still both illegal discrimination and discrimination that may not rise to the level of illegality but certainly undermines the quality of life and our ability to live and work together. And I think there is still great disparity in real opportunity, particularly for racial minorities who are physically isolated from the rest of us in low-income areas with high crime rates and low rates of economic and educational opportunity. I also believe there are glaringly different perceptions of the fairness of how various aspects of American society operate, most clearly the criminal justice system but a lot of other areas as well. I also believe that we have not taken enough time to think about the implications of what it will mean when our racial questions are not primarily issues between African-Americans and white Americans, although still there is a lot of unfinished business there, but of the entire texture of American diversity.

So I think that there are problems. I think things are better than they used to be, but I think that we a have a lot of work to do in order to be one America.

Q. Mr. President, we have an interesting phenomenon in that a lot of Americans work in integrated work environments, but they aren't friends. I mean, they are colleagues at work, but they're not friends at home. They don't socialize together. They don't voluntarily associate with each other. Is there anything that you can do about this? Is there anything you should try to do about this?

The President. It's certainly nothing you can legislate, but I think that one of the things that I would hope that the board and I will be able to do is to show America examples where people are working together outside the workplace as friends to build their communities, and to demonstrate that in cases where that has occurred, not only are communities stronger and social problems reduced but the people involved are happier people.

I think that's one thing I hope we'll be able to talk about. It may be a little old-fashioned and Pollyanna, but I basically think that we'll all be happier as Americans if we know each other and we feel comfortable with each other and we're getting along together. I think that it will make—I think we'll have more fun. I think we'll feel better about ourselves, not just we'll feel like we're good or noble or anything, but we'll feel like we're doing what makes sense and what ought to be the better part of human nature.

President's Record on Civil Rights

Q. Mr. President, given how you've been criticized in the past on how you selected an Assistant Attorney General for Civil Rights, Lani

Guinier, and how you've been criticized by your close friend Marian Wright Edelman on welfare reform and how she essentially said it would leave poor minority children out in the dust and also how you struggled to come to a position on affirmative action that brought some rather tense moments between you and the Congressional Black Caucus and, lastly, how you were criticized on being in Texas, giving a speech on race relations on the day of the Million Man March, how much credibility do you think you honestly bring to the issue of race relations, and how much do you honestly think you can accomplish in relation to your goals?

The President. I think I ought to congratulate you. In 30 seconds, you've probably got 100 percent of the criticisms that have been leveled against me.

Q. Oh, there's a new one today. The Speaker——

Q. Besides the Speaker saying that's—[*laughter*]——

The President. First of all, I was invited a long time ago to give that speech in Texas, and I think it was a very important speech. I've had—secondly, more importantly, anybody who looks at my entire public life can see that it's been dominated by three things: economics, education, and race.

If there is any issue I ought to have credibility on, it is this one, because it is a part of who I am and what I've done, and I don't feel the need to defend myself. I think all you have to do is look at the way I constitute my administration, look at the way that we've changed the Federal bench, and look at the policies I've advocated. And I'm very proud of the process through which we went to develop the affirmative action policy with—Mr. Edley here was a part of that, and I think we did it right. After all, we not only had to come up with a position, we had to come up with a position in a way that we could defend it against those who thought we were wrong and who were determined to undo it, and we wanted to give everybody a chance to be a part of it. So I'm rather proud of that.

And on the welfare issue, time will prove whether Marian Edelman is right or I am. That's all I can tell you. All I can tell you is, even before the welfare reform bill passed, we moved more people from welfare to work than at any time in American history, and the Council of Economic Advisers says that 36 percent of them—about 30 percent of them moved because of initiatives taken by States to help people move from welfare to work. We kept the guarantee for medical care; we kept the guarantee for nutrition for poor children; we kept the guarantee that the money had to be spent on poor people; we gave the States more money to spend on welfare than they would have today under the old system. They have 20 percent more money to spend on poor people today than they would have had if we hadn't changed the law—today. And we're going to get, under the budget agreement, $3 billion more to create jobs for people who don't have them. So let's—give me a couple of years to see whether—who is right on this. She was sincere and honest in her position, and I'm sincere and honest in mine, and time will see who was right.

Expected Results

Q. Mr. President—*[inaudible]*—going to be worried that this is going to be all talk and no action. Are there going to be concrete proposals that are going to come out of this? In what areas?

The President. I expect there to be concrete proposals. I also wanted to say there will simultaneously be concrete proposals that will be debated in the context of the budget that will directly bear on this. For example, one of the things that troubles me about those in favor of getting rid of affirmative action is, I don't recall any of them coming up with any alternatives, nor do I hear any voices assuming some responsibility for the apparent resegregation of higher education in Texas and California and some places as a result of it.

So, yes, I think we are duty-bound to come up with some policy, but I also think we're duty-bound to try to mobilize the energies and the attention of the rest of America so that everybody can be a part of this.

California Proposition 209

Q. Does this mean you will specifically denounce Proposition 209 tomorrow?

The President. I've already done that, but I will make my position on that issue clear again tomorrow.

Tax Programs for the Working Poor

Q. I assume you've seen the Speaker's comment that he's looked at the advisory commission and assumes that it will come up with the—

I think he said—same old tired, liberal, big Government proposals. Would you like to disabuse him of that impression?

The President. One of the things we did in 1993, which was not an old, tired, liberal, big Government proposal—Ronald Reagan said it was the best antipoverty program in American history with the earned-income tax credit—we doubled it in 1993 to help the working poor, to reward—here is another thing I wanted to—most minorities work for a living; they are not on welfare. And there are a lot of people out there working, not making much money. So the earned-income tax credit says we're not going to tax people who work into poverty.

This new tax program that has been proposed by the Speaker's Ways and Means Committee would penalize the working poor and especially working poor mothers. So I would say that I'd be glad to have his advice, but this is a case where he needs to neaten up his own house a little bit and get those—if he's for work and empowerment and not the big Government solutions, then they ought to change that tax package and stop punishing the working poor.

Emergency Supplemental Appropriations Legislation

Q. What did you think of the Republican leaders all voting against the disaster bill? Wasn't that odd?

The President. I'm just glad it passed. Mayor Owens, the mayor of Grand Forks—I visited out there in North Dakota—called me last night after I signed it and said how glad she was the people were going to get their aid, and that's all I have to say. This never should have been political, and I don't want the politics to continue, and I don't want to talk about victories or defeat here. People are going to get help; that's all that counts. We've got to go back to working on this budget and all these other issues.

NOTE: The President spoke at 4:50 p.m. in the Oval Office at the White House. In his remarks, he referred to Christopher Edley, codirector, The Civil Rights Project, and consultant to the President's Advisory Board on Race; Marian Wright Edelman, president, Children's Defense Fund; and Mayor Patricia Owens of Grand Forks, ND. The Executive order of June 13 establishing the

President's Advisory Board on Race is listed in Appendix D at the end of this volume. A tape was not available for verification of the content of these remarks.

Statement on the Oklahoma City Bombing Trial
June 13, 1997

Since there is another trial pending, I cannot comment on the jury's decision.

But on behalf of all Americans, I thank the jurors for their deliberations and their thoroughness as they made these grave decisions. This investigation and trial have confirmed our country's faith in its justice system.

To the victims and their families, I know that your healing can be measured only one day at a time. The prayers and support of your fellow Americans will be with you every one of those days.

The President's Radio Address
June 14, 1997

Good morning. In just 17 days, after 150 years, Hong Kong returns to Chinese sovereignty. Today I want to talk to you about America's role in that and America's stake in the transition.

More than 1,100 American companies operate in Hong Kong today, making it the heart of American business in the fastest growing part of the world. Our naval ships put in dozens of port calls to Hong Kong every year. And it matters to us that the people of Hong Kong retain their distinct system with its political freedoms and its open economy, not only because we hold these principles in common with them and with a growing number of people around the world but because we are involved with them.

China has made important commitments to maintain Hong Kong's freedom and autonomy, and our Nation has a strong interest in seeing that these commitments are kept. The United States is doing its part to keep faith with the people of Hong Kong. We've negotiated agreements that will safeguard our presence and continue our cooperation. We will work with the new Hong Kong Government to maintain a productive relationship that takes into account both its changed relationship with China and its promised autonomy. We'll keep a close watch on the transition process and the preservation of freedoms that the people of Hong Kong have relied on to build a prosperous, dynamic society.

The transition process did not begin and will not end on July 1st. It will unfold over the months and years ahead. One thing we must not do is take any measures that would weaken Hong Kong just when it most needs to be strong and free.

No step would more clearly harm Hong Kong than reversing the course we have followed for years by denying normal trading status to China. That's one important reason why, a month ago, I decided to extend to China the same most-favored-nation treatment we give to every country on Earth, as every President has done since 1980. I want to just take a minute to say that even though we call it most-favored-nation treatment, that's really misnaming it. It really means normal trading status.

Why do we do this? Well, Hong Kong handles more than half of the trade between the United States and China, which makes it acutely sensitive to any disruption in our relations. The Hong Kong Government estimates that our revocation of normal trade status would cut Hong Kong's growth in half, double unemployment by eliminating up to 85,000 jobs, and reduce its trade by as much as $32 billion.

The full spectrum of Hong Kong's leaders, even those most critical of Beijing, have strongly supported normal trading status for China. As Hong Kong Governor Chris Patten, who has done so much for democracy and freedom in Hong Kong, said in a letter I received just this week, "Unconditional renewal of China's MFN status for a full year is the most valuable single gift the United States can present to Hong Kong during the handover period."

Those who oppose normal trading relations with China have legitimate concerns. I share their goals of advancing human rights and religious freedom, of promoting fair trade, and strengthening regional and global security. But reversing our course and revoking normal trade status will set back those goals, not achieve them. It will cut off our contact with the Chinese people and undermine those dedicated to openness and freedom. It will derail our cooperation on fighting the spread of dangerous weapons, drug trafficking, and terrorism. It will close one of the world's emerging markets to American exports and jeopardize more than 170,000 high-paying American jobs. And it will make China more isolationist and less likely to abide by the norms of international conduct.

I am convinced the best way to promote our interests and our values is not to shut China out but to draw China in, to help it to become a strong and stable partner in shaping security and prosperity for the future. Our strategic dialog with China has led to cooperation on nuclear nonproliferation issues, on promoting stability on the Korean Peninsula, on protecting American intellectual property rights, which is so important to our high-tech industry.

If we maintain our steady engagement with China, building areas of agreement while dealing candidly and openly with our differences on issues like human rights and religious freedom, we can help China to choose the path of integration, cooperation, and international recognition of human rights and freedoms. But if we treat China as our enemy, we may create the very outcome we're trying to guard against.

In the days ahead, the Congress will face this test as they take up the debate on China's trading status. I urge the Congress and all Americans to remember: Extending normal trading status is not a referendum on China's policies, it's a vote for America's interests. Hong Kong's leaders, present and future, understand the stakes involved. They want to maintain their freedom and their autonomy. They know they need normal trading status to do it. We need to continue to stand with the people of Hong Kong and maintain our course of pragmatic cooperation with China. That is the best guarantee of a secure, stable, and prosperous 21st century for the United States.

Thanks for listening.

NOTE: The address was recorded at 6:26 p.m. on June 13 in the Roosevelt Room at the White House for broadcast at 10:06 a.m. on June 14.

Commencement Address at the University of California San Diego in La Jolla, California
June 14, 1997

Thank you very much. Thank you. Well, ladies and gentlemen, the first thing I would like to say is that Coleen spoke so well, and she said everything I meant to say—[*laughter*]—that I could do us all a great favor by simply associating myself with her remarks and sitting down.

I would also like to thank Dr. Anagnostopoulos for reminding us of the infamous capacity of faculty members to be contrary with one another. [*Laughter*] Until he said it, I hadn't realized that probably 90 percent of the Congress once were on university faculties. [*Laughter*]

Let me say to Chancellor Dynes and President Atkinson, to the distinguished regents and faculty members, to the students and their families and friends who are here today, I'm honored to be joined by a number of people who reflect the kind of America that Coleen Sabatini called for: Senator Barbara Boxer; and Senator Dan Akaka from Hawaii; your Congressman, Bob Filner; Congresswoman Maxine Waters, the chair of the Congressional Black Caucus; Congresswoman Patsy Mink; Congressman Jim Clyburn; Congressman John Lewis, a great hero of the civil rights movement; Congresswoman Juanita

Millender-McDonald; Congressman Carlos Romero-Barceló from Puerto Rico; your Lieutenant Governor, Gray Davis; the Secretary of Transportation, Rodney Slater; of Labor, Alexis Herman; of Veterans Affairs, Jesse Brown; of Education, Dick Riley; our distinguished Ambassador to the United Nations, Bill Richardson; our distinguished Administrator of the Small Business Administration, Aida Alvarez, the first American of Puerto Rican descent ever to be in a Presidential Cabinet. I would like to ask them all to stand, along with the members of the White House staff who are here, including Thurgood Marshall, Jr., whose father has a college named for him at this great university. Would you please stand?

And I can't help but noting that there's another person here that deserves some special recognition—University of California at San Diego class of 1977—a Filipino-American woman who became the youngest captain of the Navy and my personal physician, Dr. Connie Mariano. Where is she?

I want to thank you for offering our Nation a shining example of excellence rooted in the many backgrounds that make up this great land. You have blazed new paths in science and technology, explored the new horizons of the Pacific Rim and Latin America. This is a great university for the 21st century.

Today we celebrate your achievements at a truly golden moment for America. The cold war is over and freedom has now ascended around the globe, with more than half of the people in this old world living under governments of their own choosing for the very first time. Our economy is the healthiest in a generation and the strongest in the world. Our culture, our science, our technology promise unimagined advances and exciting new careers. Our social problems, from crime to poverty, are finally bending to our efforts.

Of course, there are still challenges for you out there. Beyond our borders, we must battle terrorism, organized crime and drug trafficking, the spread of weapons of mass destruction, the prospect of new diseases and environmental disaster. Here at home, we must ensure that every child has the chance you have had to develop your God-given capacities. We cannot wait for them to get in trouble to notice them. We must continue to fight the scourge of gangs and crime and drugs. We must prepare for the retirement of the baby boom generation so that we can reduce that child poverty rate that Coleen talked about. We must harness the forces of science and technology for the public good, the entire American public.

But I believe the greatest challenge we face, among all those that Coleen talked about, is also our greatest opportunity. Of all the questions of discrimination and prejudice that still exist in our society, the most perplexing one is the oldest, and in some ways today, the newest: the problem of race. Can we fulfill the promise of America by embracing all our citizens of all races, not just at a university where people have the benefit of enlightened teachers and the time to think and grow and get to know each other within the daily life of every American community? In short, can we become one America in the 21st century? I know, and I've said before, that money cannot buy this goal, power cannot compel it, technology cannot create it. This is something that can come only from the human spirit, the spirit we saw when the choir of many races sang as a gospel choir.

Today, the State of Hawaii, which has a Senator and a Congresswoman present here, has no majority racial or ethnic group. It is a wonderful place of exuberance and friendship and patriotism. Within the next 3 years, here in California no single race or ethnic group will make up a majority of the State's population. Already, 5 of our largest school districts draw students from over 100 different racial and ethnic groups. At this campus, 12 Nobel Prize winners have taught or studied from 9 different countries. A half-century from now, when your own grandchildren are in college, there will be no majority race in America.

Now, we know what we will look like, but what will we be like? Can we be one America respecting, even celebrating, our differences, but embracing even more what we have in common? Can we define what it means to be an American, not just in terms of the hyphen showing our ethnic origins but in terms of our primary allegiance to the values America stands for and values we really live by? Our hearts long to answer yes, but our history reminds us that it will be hard. The ideals that bind us together are as old as our Nation, but so are the forces that pull us apart. Our Founders sought to form a more perfect Union. The humility and hope of that phrase is the story of America, and it is our mission today.

Consider this: We were born with a Declaration of Independence which asserted that we were all created equal and a Constitution that enshrined slavery. We fought a bloody Civil War to abolish slavery and preserve the Union, but we remained a house divided and unequal by law for another century. We advanced across the continent in the name of freedom, yet in so doing we pushed Native Americans off their land, often crushing their culture and their livelihood. Our Statue of Liberty welcomes poor, tired, huddled masses of immigrants to our borders, but each new wave has felt the sting of discrimination. In World War II, Japanese-Americans fought valiantly for freedom in Europe, taking great casualties, while at home their families were herded into internment camps. The famed Tuskegee Airmen lost none of the bombers they guarded during the war, but their African-American heritage cost them a lot of rights when they came back home in peace.

Though minorities have more opportunities than ever today, we still see evidence of bigotry, from the desecration of houses of worship, whether they be churches, synagogues, or mosques, to demeaning talk in corporate suites. There is still much work to be done by you, members of the class of 1997. But those who say we cannot transform the problem of prejudice into the promise of unity forget how far we have come, and I cannot believe they have ever seen a crowd like you.

When I look at you, it is almost impossible for me even to remember my own life. I grew up in the high drama of the cold war, in the patriotic South. Black and white southerners alike wore our Nation's uniform in defense of freedom against communism. They fought and died together, from Korea to Vietnam. But back home, I went to segregated schools, swam in segregated public pools, sat in all-white sections at the movies, and traveled through small towns in my State that still marked restrooms and water fountains "white" and "colored."

By the grace of God, I had a grandfather with just a grade school education but the heart of a true American, who taught me that it was wrong. And by the grace of God, there were brave African-Americans like Congressman John Lewis who risked their lives time and time again to make it right. And there were white Americans like Congressman Bob Filner, a freedom rider on the bus with John Lewis in the long, noble struggle for civil rights, who knew that it was a struggle to free white people, too.

To be sure, there is old, unfinished business between black and white Americans, but the classic American dilemma has now become many dilemmas of race and ethnicity. We see it in the tension between black and Hispanic customers and their Korean or Arab grocers; in a resurgent antisemitism even on some college campuses; in a hostility toward new immigrants from Asia to the Middle East to the former Communist countries to Latin America and the Caribbean, even those whose hard work and strong families have brought them success in the American way.

We see a disturbing tendency to wrongly attribute to entire groups, including the white majority, the objectionable conduct of a few members. If a black American commits a crime, condemn the act. But remember that most African-Americans are hard-working, law-abiding citizens. If a Latino gang member deals drugs, condemn the act. But remember the vast majority of Hispanics are responsible citizens who also deplore the scourge of drugs in our life. If white teenagers beat a young African-American boy almost to death just because of his race, for God's sake condemn the act. But remember the overwhelming majority of white people will find it just as hateful. If an Asian merchant discriminates against her customers of another minority group, call her on it. But remember, too, that many, many Asians have borne the burden of prejudice and do not want anyone else to feel it.

Remember too, in spite of the persistence of prejudice, we are more integrated than ever. More of us share neighborhoods and work and school and social activities, religious life, even love and marriage across racial lines than ever before. More of us enjoy each other's company and distinctive cultures than ever before. And more than ever, we understand the benefits of our racial, linguistic, and cultural diversity in a global society, where networks of commerce and communications draw us closer and bring rich rewards to those who truly understand life beyond their nation's borders. With just a twentieth of the world's population but a fifth of the world's income, we in America simply have to sell to the other 95 percent of the world's consumers just to maintain our standard of living. Because we are drawn from every culture on Earth, we are uniquely positioned to do it.

Beyond commerce, the diverse backgrounds and talents of our citizens can help America to light the globe, showing nations deeply divided by race, religion, and tribe that there is a better way.

Finally, as you have shown us today, our diversity will enrich our lives in nonmaterial ways, deepening our understanding of human nature and human differences, making our communities more exciting, more enjoyable, more meaningful. That is why I have come here today to ask the American people to join me in a great national effort to perfect the promise of America for this new time as we seek to build our more perfect Union.

Now, when there is more cause for hope than fear, when we are not driven to it by some emergency or social cataclysm, now is the time we should learn together, talk together, and act together to build one America.

Let me say that I know that for many white Americans, this conversation may seem to exclude them or threaten them. That must not be so. I believe white Americans have just as much to gain as anybody else from being a part of this endeavor, much to gain from an America where we finally take responsibility for all our children so that they, at last, can be judged as Martin Luther King hoped, not by the color of their skin but by the content of their character.

What is it that we must do? For 4½ years now, I have worked to prepare America for the 21st century with a strategy of opportunity for all, responsibility from all, and an American community of all our citizens. To succeed in each of these areas, we must deal with the realities and the perceptions affecting all racial groups in America.

First, we must continue to expand opportunity. Full participation in our strong and growing economy is the best antidote to envy, despair, and racism. We must press forward to move millions more from poverty and welfare to work, to bring the spark of enterprise to inner cities, to redouble our efforts to reach those rural communities prosperity has passed by. And most important of all, we simply must give our young people the finest education in the world.

There are no children who—because of their ethnic or racial background—who cannot meet the highest academic standards if we set them and measure our students against them, if we

give them well-trained teachers and well-equipped classrooms, and if we continue to support reasoned reforms to achieve excellence, like the charter school movement. At a time when college education means stability, a good job, a passport to the middle class, we must open the doors of college to all Americans, and we must make at least 2 years of college as universal at the dawn of the next century as a high school diploma is today.

In our efforts to extend economic and educational opportunity to all our citizens, we must consider the role of affirmative action. I know affirmative action has not been perfect in America—that's why 2 years ago we began an effort to fix the things that are wrong with it—but when used in the right way, it has worked. It has given us a whole generation of professionals in fields that used to be exclusive clubs, where people like me got the benefit of 100 percent affirmative action. There are now more women-owned businesses than ever before. There are more African-American, Latino, and Asian-American lawyers and judges, scientists and engineers, accountants and executives than ever before.

But the best example of successful affirmative action is our military. Our Armed Forces are diverse from top to bottom, perhaps the most integrated institution in our society and certainly the most integrated military in the world. And more important, no one questions that they are the best in the world. So much for the argument that excellence and diversity do not go hand in hand.

There are those who argue that scores on standardized tests should be the sole measure of qualification for admissions to colleges and universities. But many would not apply the same standard to the children of alumni or those with athletic ability. I believe a student body that reflects the excellence and the diversity of the people we will live and work with has independent educational value. Look around this crowd today. Don't you think you have learned a lot more than you would have if everybody sitting around you looked just like you? I think you have. [*Applause*]

And beyond the educational value to you, it has a public interest, because you will learn to live and work in the world you will live in better. When young people sit side by side with people of many different backgrounds, they do learn something that they can take out into the world. And they will be more effective citizens.

Many affirmative action students excel. They work hard, they achieve, they go out and serve the communities that need them for their expertise and role model. If you close the door on them, we will weaken our greatest universities, and it will be more difficult to build the society we need in the 21st century.

Let me say, I know that the people of California voted to repeal affirmative action without any ill motive. The vast majority of them simply did it with a conviction that discrimination and isolation are no longer barriers to achievement. But consider the results. Minority enrollments in law school and other graduate programs are plummeting for the first time in decades. Soon, the same will likely happen in undergraduate education. We must not resegregate higher education or leave it to the private universities to do the public's work. At the very time when we need to do a better job of living and learning together, we should not stop trying to equalize economic opportunity.

To those who oppose affirmative action, I ask you to come up with an alternative. I would embrace it if I could find a better way. And to those of us who still support it, I say we should continue to stand for it, we should reach out to those who disagree or are uncertain and talk about the practical impact of these issues, and we should never be unwilling to work with those who disagree with us to find new ways to lift people up and bring people together.

Beyond opportunity, we must demand responsibility from every American. Our strength as a society depends upon both—upon people taking responsibility for themselves and their families, teaching their children good values, working hard and obeying the law, and giving back to those around us. The new economy offers fewer guarantees, more risk, and more rewards. It calls upon all of us to take even greater responsibility for our own education than ever before.

In the current economic boom, only one racial or ethnic group in America has actually experienced a decline in income: Hispanic-Americans. One big reason is that Hispanic high school dropout rates are well above—indeed, far above—those of whites and blacks. Some of the dropouts actually reflect a strong commitment to work. We admire the legendary willingness to take the hard job at long hours for low pay. In the old economy, that was a responsible thing

to do. But in the new economy, where education is the key, responsibility means staying in school.

No responsibility is more fundamental than obeying the law. It is not racist to insist that every American do so. The fight against crime and drugs is a fight for the freedom of all our people, including those—perhaps especially those—minorities living in our poorest neighborhoods. But respect for the law must run both ways. The shocking difference in perceptions of the fairness of our criminal justice system grows out of the real experiences that too many minorities have had with law enforcement officers. Part of the answer is to have all our citizens respect the law, but the basic rule must be that the law must respect all our citizens.

And that applies, too, to the enforcement of our civil rights laws. For example, the Equal Employment Opportunity Commission has a huge backlog of cases with discrimination claims, though we have reduced it by 25 percent over the last 4 years. We can do not much better without more resources. It is imperative that Congress—especially those Members who say they're for civil rights but against affirmative action—at least give us the money necessary to enforce the law of the land, and do it soon.

Our third imperative is perhaps the most difficult of all. We must build one American community based on respect for one another and our shared values. We must begin with a candid conversation on the state of race relations today and the implications of Americans of so many different races living and working together as we approach a new century. We must be honest with each other. We have talked at each other and about each other for a long time. It's high time we all began talking with each other.

Over the coming year, I want to lead the American people in a great and unprecedented conversation about race. In community efforts from Lima, Ohio, to Billings, Montana, in remarkable experiments in cross-racial communications like the uniquely named ERACISM, I have seen what Americans can do if they let down their guards and reach out their hands.

I have asked one of America's greatest scholars, Dr. John Hope Franklin, to chair an advisory panel of seven distinguished Americans to help me in this endeavor. He will be joined by former Governors Thomas Kean of New Jersey and William Winter of Mississippi, both great champions of civil rights; by Linda Chavez-Thompson, the executive vice president of the

AFL–CIO; by Reverend Suzan Johnson Cook, a minister from the Bronx and former White House fellow; by Angela Oh, an attorney and Los Angeles community leader; and Robert Thompson, the CEO of Nissan U.S.A.—distinguished leaders, leaders in their community.

I want this panel to help educate Americans about the facts surrounding issues of race, to promote a dialog in every community of the land to confront and work through these issues, to recruit and encourage leadership at all levels to help breach racial divides, and to find, develop, and recommend how to implement concrete solutions to our problems, solutions that will involve all of us in Government, business, communities, and as individual citizens.

I will make periodic reports to the American people about our findings and what actions we all have to take to move America forward. This board will seek out and listen to Americans from all races and all walks of life. They are performing a great citizen service, but in the cause of building one America, all citizens must serve. As I said at the Presidents' Summit on Service in Philadelphia, in our new era such acts of service are basic acts of citizenship. Government must play its role, but much of the work must be done by the American people as citizen service. The very effort will strengthen us and bring us closer together. In short, I want America to capture the feel and the spirit that you have given to all of us today.

I'd like to ask the board to stand and be recognized. I want you to look at them, and I want you to feel free to talk to them over the next year or so. Dr. Franklin and members of the board. [*Applause*]

Honest dialog will not be easy at first. We'll all have to get past defensiveness and fear and political correctness and other barriers to honesty. Emotions may be rubbed raw, but we must begin.

What do I really hope we will achieve as a country? If we do nothing more than talk, it will be interesting, but it won't be enough. If we do nothing more than propose disconnected acts of policy, it will be helpful, but it won't be enough. But if 10 years from now people can look back and see that this year of honest dialog and concerted action helped to lift the heavy burden of race from our children's future, we will have given a precious gift to America.

I ask you all to remember just for a moment, as we have come through the difficult trial on the Oklahoma City bombing, remember that terrible day when we saw and wept for Americans and forgot for a moment that there were a lot of them from different races than we are. Remember the many faces and races of the Americans who did not sleep and put their lives at risk to engage in the rescue, the helping, and the healing. Remember how you have seen things like that in the natural disasters here in California. That is the face of the real America. That is the face I have seen over and over again. That is the America somehow, some way, we have to make real in daily American life.

Members of the graduating class, you will have a greater opportunity to live your dreams than any generation in our history, if we can make of our many different strands one America, a nation at peace with itself, bound together by shared values and aspirations and opportunities and real respect for our differences.

I am a Scotch-Irish Southern Baptist, and I'm proud of it. But my life has been immeasurably enriched by the power of the Torah, the beauty of the Koran, the piercing wisdom of the religions of East and South Asia—all embraced by my fellow Americans. I have felt indescribable joy and peace in black and Pentecostal churches. I have come to love the intensity and selflessness of my Hispanic fellow Americans toward *la familia*. As a southerner, I grew up on country music and country fairs, and I still like them. [*Laughter*] But I have also reveled in the festivals and the food, the music and the art and the culture of Native Americans and Americans from every region in the world.

In each land I have visited as your President, I have felt more at home because some of their people have found a home in America. For two centuries, wave upon wave of immigrants have come to our shores to build a new life, drawn by the promise of freedom and a fair chance. Whatever else they found, even bigotry and violence, most of them never gave up on America. Even African-Americans, the first of whom we brought here in chains, never gave up on America.

It is up to you to prove that their abiding faith was well-placed. Living in islands of isolation—some splendid and some sordid—is not the American way. Basing our self-esteem on the ability to look down on others is not the American way. Being satisfied if we have what we want and heedless of others who don't even have what they need and deserve is not the American way. We have torn down the barriers in our laws. Now we must break down the barriers in our lives, our minds, and our hearts.

More than 30 years ago, at the high tide of the civil rights movement, the Kerner Commission said we were becoming two Americas: one white, one black, separate and unequal. Today, we face a different choice: Will we become not two but many Americas, separate, unequal, and isolated? Or will we draw strength from all our people and our ancient faith in the quality of human dignity to become the world's first truly multiracial democracy? That is the unfinished work of our time, to lift the burden of race and redeem the promise of America.

Class of 1997, I grew up in the shadows of a divided America, but I have seen glimpses of one America. You have shown me one today. That is the America you must make. It begins with your dreams, so dream large; live your dreams; challenge your parents; and teach your children well.

God bless you, and good luck.

NOTE: The President spoke at 10:47 a.m. at Rimac Field. In his remarks, he referred to Coleen Sabatini, associated student body president; Georgios H. Anagnostopoulos, chair, academic senate; Robert C. Dynes, chancellor; and Richard C. Atkinson, president, University of California San Diego.

Remarks at a Commencement Luncheon at the University of California San Diego in La Jolla
June 14, 1997

Thank you very much for the gift. Chelsea will treasure the Dr. Seuss T-shirt, and it is an especially appropriate gift since last week I spoke at her high school graduation—believe it or not, I was much more nervous then than I was today—[*laughter*]—and I asked Chelsea and her classmates to forgive us, their parents, if we were acting a little weird that day. And I explained that we were reliving their whole lives and that, among other things, we wished just one more time we could read children's books to them. So that will always remind her of that, and I thank you.

Let me say to your student body president-to-be, and to the young woman who spoke before me at the graduation, if Coleen and Souley are emblematic of the undergraduates at the University of California San Diego, this country is in good hands, and you should be able to capture virtually every elected position in the entire State—[*laughter*]—in just a few years. It beats anything I ever saw. It was great.

Let me also thank you for making Dr. John Hope Franklin and the members of the President's Advisory Board on Race and the members of my Cabinet and the White House and the Members of Congress who are here, making us feel so welcome. We brought quite a lot of interlopers here to this event today in the hope that it would impress upon the country and the press, which will have to tell the country about it, the importance of this issue and this moment and our intentions. You have given me a great opportunity to be here today, and you've given the Nation a great gift if we can do what we set out to do here. And I will never forget that.

I'm especially glad to be here in San Diego to do this. You know, I spent a lot of time in this community over the last several years. I have come to love it and also to respect it, because I see the capacity here to make things work. One of the things I didn't get to talk about in my speech—you can't talk about everything—but in the end, we have to be judged by whether what we do makes sense or not and produces results. This community has one of the lowest crime rates of any major city in America. It deals with a whole wide range of complex problems, I think, in a very sensible way. And I see people here continually coming together across lines that divide them, and I hope that will be a model for the entire country. So for all those reasons, I'm very thankful.

And the last thing I have to say is that early this morning, when I'd had precious little sleep and my body clock was off anyway, my wife called with her last-minute criticisms of my speech—[*laughter*]—which is a routine I have come to look forward to in life. [*Laughter*] And as usual, she was right, what she had to say, and I made three changes she suggested I make in it. But the last thing she said was, she said, "Now, you remind those people that you've only been there once, and I've been there twice, and I loved it both times." [*Laughter*]

Again, Chancellor and all of you as part of the UCSD family, I thank you. I thank you on behalf of all of us who have come to visit with you today. I thank you for the ideas you have given me. Dr. Franklin, members of the board, you might be interested to know, around the table here they asked what they could do to help. And I said, well, we needed more credible research, and we needed more sources of information for the American people about basic things, delivered in understandable ways. We'll never have the kind of national conversation we want until we first agree on at least most of the facts. You know, if you have a different

view of the same set of facts than someone else, it is wonderful because you never have to give up your bias, because you can say, "The poor soul just doesn't know the facts," so you can go right on with whatever you think and whatever you believe.

We are going to need the help of the university community and groups like the National Academy of Sciences and others, and we will be back to you on that. But the most important thing is, what I saw in the eyes of the students of this great university today convinced me without any question that we are doing the right thing, first, and secondly, that we will succeed.

Thank you all. God bless you.

NOTE: The President spoke at 1:24 p.m. in the Birch Aquarium at the Scripps Institute of Oceanography. In his remarks, he referred to Souley Diallo, incoming associated student body president, University of California San Diego; and historian John Hope Franklin, Chair, President's Advisory Board on Race.

Statement on Senator Dale Bumpers' Decision Not To Seek Reelection
June 14, 1997

I have known and admired Dale Bumpers for over 25 years. He was a great Governor, and he has been a great Senator for the people of our native State and the entire Nation. We will miss his courage to stand against the tide, his vision, and his eloquence. Hillary and I wish him and Betty all the best. We will miss him. So will the Senate. So will America.

Statement on the Murder of Policemen in Northern Ireland
June 16, 1997

I am outraged by the callous murder by the IRA of two policemen in Northern Ireland. I condemn this brutal act of terrorism in the strongest possible terms. There can be no reason, no excuse for these vicious crimes. I extend my deepest sympathy to the families of the two slain officers.

There is nothing patriotic or heroic about these cowardly killings. The overwhelming majority of the people of Ireland, North and South, join me in repudiating violence and murder.

They know that a just and lasting peace is only possible through painstaking dialog and negotiation. Further violence can only play into the hands of those responsible for the vicious murders of the two policemen. The true heroes and patriots are the many people of both communities who work tirelessly and peacefully for reconciliation and understanding. I will continue to do all I can to support their efforts and the efforts of the political leaders participating in the Belfast peace talks.

Remarks at a Democratic National Committee Dinner
June 16, 1997

Thank you. Thank you very much. Mr. Mayor, my friend and neighbor, thank you for that generous introduction and for your great leadership in Memphis. I'd like to thank all of those who made this dinner possible tonight: I thank Richard and Janice and Ernie and Bob, who aren't here, and Weldon and Mel Clarke and Marianne Niles and Bill Kirk, Larry Gibson, Marianne Spragen, Jeff Thompson, everyone else who got all of you here tonight. I'm glad to see you.

You know, when you come to an event like this, even if you've been reelected President, right before you go in you're gripped with this recurring fear that you'll walk through the door and nobody will be there. [*Laughter*] So I'm very grateful to see you all here tonight. [*Laughter*]

Let me say, too, that I'm delighted to be joined tonight by two members of the White House staff, Craig Smith and Minyon Moore. And I see Carroll Willis from the DNC. There are a lot of other people from the Democratic Committee here.

I appreciate what the mayor said about my speech in San Diego, and I thought what I would try to do tonight just for a few minutes is to try to explain how that speech came to be. And we brought a few copies here tonight. If you want one on the way out, you can get it. But I thought I would like to explain how it came to be.

In 1992 when I ran for President, I had an idea that we could make this country work again if we could liberate ourselves from kind of traditional political battles and think about what we wanted the country to look like in the 21st century and then think backward and say, "Well, what would I have to do to get it that way?" Don't say in the first instance, "Well, you can't do both those things. They're inconsistent." Just ask yourself, what would you like our country to look like in the 21st century?

And I wrote a little answer down, and I have said it a thousand times since then. And every single day I think about it. I want my country to be a country where the American dream of opportunity is alive for every person, not just some. I want all citizens to be good, responsible citizens and assume the responsibilities of citi-

zenship. I want the United States to lead the world for peace and freedom 20, 30 years from now, just like we are today. And I want us to live together as one community where we respect, we even celebrate our differences, but we're bound together as Americans.

Now, those are the things I want. And I wrote it down over 5 years ago, and I've stuck with it ever since. Way back in 1991, before I made the decision to run for President, I said—nearly 6 years ago now—I said, "No point in me running unless I've got a better reason than I'd like to live in the White House." [*Laughter*] What will I say when people say, "What do you want to do? Why are you doing this?" And every single day I think about it.

So the first thing I wanted to do was to change the economic policy of the country. I said, "We can't keep on spending all this money we don't have; we're going to bankrupt the country. But we don't want to walk away from the poor or the dispossessed or the future of the country. So we have to find a way to reduce the deficit, for example, and spend more on education and spend more on preserving the environment, because they're our children and our future."

And most people didn't think you could do that. But you can, and we did. We had to do some things that weren't so popular. We got rid of hundreds of programs that I thought we could do without. And we got rid of 16,000 pages of Federal regulations. And by attrition, not firing, the Government's 300,000 people smaller than it was. But we're spending more money on education, we're spending more money on the environment, and we've cut the deficit by 77 percent. And that's a big reason, not the only reason, by any means, but a big reason the economy has done as well as it has.

On crime and social welfare, I thought to myself, there's got to be a way to protect the children and support people in moving from welfare to work but require them to do it, if they can, without hurting the kids. And that's what we've tried to do. We've had the biggest drop in welfare rolls in the history of America by far in the last 5 years.

On crime, what I wanted to do was to deal with the causes. Anybody can make a tough speech on crime and pass one more bill raising the penalties. But it was obvious to me, having been a Governor who built more prison cells than any Governor in my State's history, that there would be a limit to how far we could jail our way out of this. There are several States that are already spending more money on prisons than they are on higher education—several States.

So I said to myself, "We can't stop being tough on people who do vicious things; you have to catch them, prosecute them, and put them in jail. But we have to stop this from occurring; we have to find a way to prevent crime." And it wasn't so hard to find because already there were people who were beginning to bring the crime rate down by going back to old-fashioned community policing and reaching out to our young people and trying to find kids something to say yes to as well as something to say no to.

And so we passed a crime bill. We passed the Brady bill. We passed the assault weapons ban. I heard all the people say I was going to take all these hunters' guns away and it wouldn't do any good. Well, no hunters have lost their weapons, but 186,000 felons, fugitives, and stalkers have not been able to buy handguns. We were right about that. We're putting 100,000 police on the street. Crime has gone down every year, last year the biggest drop in 35 years.

And I say that not to be self-serving but to say, if we can get our country always to think about what do we want the country to look like when our grandchildren are our age—and we're going through a time of change, so we have to think in different ways—then I think there's a way to find good-faith solutions to these problems. And no one can seriously question that we're better off than we were 5 years ago in terms of jobs and employment, new minority businesses, biggest drop in inequality since the 1960's among working families. So I said to myself, "What do we still have to do?" because I never wanted to get a second term just to ratify the fact that I'd done a good job in the first term. You could do that with a gold watch. No one should ever want to be reelected because they've done a good job.

I remember the first time I ran for reelection—that I was successful anyway—[*laughter*]—in 1984. I went out, and things were going pretty well in my State, and this guy said, "Are you going to run for reelection as Governor?" I said, "I think so," and I said, "If I do, will you support me?" He said, "Probably." He said, "What are you going to say?" I said, "I've done a good job, and we're better off." He said, "Bill, you can't say that. That's what we hired you to do." [*Laughter*] That's pretty good, right? You think about that. He said, "You can't brag on just doing what you were hired out to do."

So I said to myself, "What are we going to do in these next 4 years? What still needs to be done?" And I'd just like to mention three or four things and end with the initiative on race, and you'll, I hope, understand why to me we're doing the right thing at the right time.

I said, "Okay, the economy is better; welfare rolls are down; crime rate is down." Another thing that was encouraging, we just saw that our fourth graders ranked way above the national average on international math and science tests, something that I was told for years would never happen because we had such a diverse student body and our kids were poor and all that. I've listened to that for years. But our teachers and others have been out there working to get these standards up, and we finally saw it manifested in international competition this year. This is something people have been working on, literally, for 10 years, since the "Nation At Risk" report was issued, now, 13 years ago. And it's finally—you're finally beginning to see people figuring out how to give poor kids the chance to prove they're just as smart as anybody, not just in town but around the world, and prove that we can make education work.

So I said, "What else do we have to do?" Okay, one, we have to keep the economy going. The best antidote to all despair and disadvantage is having a chance to make a living, because if everybody else messes up, as long as you can make a living you can at least take care of your own.

So I wanted to finish the job of balancing the budget in a way that would continue the strategy of investing in our future. And that's why I was thrilled with this budget agreement. I didn't agree with everything in it, but after all, we negotiated it with the leaders of the Republican Party in Congress and the leaders of the Democratic Party. But it will permit us to balance the budget, and it has literally—literally—over 95 percent of the investments that I recommended in my budget to the Congress.

It enables us to go on and invest in education and to invest in preserving the environment and invest in research and development and technology. It enables us to continue to try to grow the economy in the dispossessed areas—more than doubles the number of empowerment zones that have been so successful in some of our communities, including yours—more than doubles the number; has a special initiative for the District of Columbia that we have paid for there in there to try to get DC up and going again in a good way; has a brownfields initiative that all the mayors asked for to give private sector incentive to go back and invest in the inner cities in areas that had previously been unattractive because of environmental problems. It has—in this budget.

So I said, "This is a good thing"—has $3 billion to give to our communities to help put people on welfare back to work if the private sector can't pick them up. And I might add for those of you who are concerned about it, the States in this budget get the same amount of money they got in 1994, when the welfare rolls were at their all-time high, which means almost every State in America has got at least a 20 percent cushion that they can use to do things like pay prospective employers the welfare check as a wage and training supplement.

So I'd really like to see the African-American business community go out there and hit every State legislature in the country and say, "Listen, you asked for this. You got it. You've got to give these people a chance to work. Give us some of that money, and we will train them and give them a job and make sure they're not hurting their kids and they're taken care of in that way." And that ought to happen all over this country. We are spending much, much more money on welfare today than we would have spent if the old law had stayed in place because the rolls are down by more than 20 percent. But the States have it, and they will live to regret it if they don't spend the money now to make folks independent and put them into the workplace and put them into the mainstream of American life.

So all that, anyway, is in this budget. That's the first thing.

The second thing I wanted to do is to emphasize two specific things in education. One of them doesn't cost much money. And that is, I wanted to provide funds to help the Department of Education work with the appropriate experts to develop a test that would grow right out of the ones we're using now—we're just not giving them to all kids—to ask every child in the country in the fourth grade to take a reading test, in the eighth grade to take a math test by 1999, based on these international standards so we could see how our children were doing, with no adverse consequences to the kids, just a way to see whether we were really challenging our children hard enough to reach the right standards.

Now keep in mind, this last international test that showed us way above the average of math and science in the fourth grade was given to a representative sample of American students by race and income and region. Nobody's fooled with this. And what I want to do is to see every child have the chance to have the basic education necessary to succeed.

One of the things I said in my speech in San Diego—I don't know if you heard it—applies to Hispanic-Americans, who are legendary for being willing to leave school early to support their parents in low-wage jobs that they have to work long hours at. That was a responsible thing to do 10 years ago. Today, it's not a responsible thing to do. The high school completion rates of African-Americans and whites are almost identical. The high school completion rates of Hispanics are 25 percent lower—25 percent lower. And there is nothing all my social policies will do, nothing all my economic policies will do for any young person who is at least not willing to finish high school and get 2 years of further training. But a lot of people who have parents in need—their hearts are in there, they want to quit and go to work, help support their parents, but what happens is they get stuck in these jobs and their incomes go down.

So I'm trying to get people to focus on those first 12 years with a view toward, number one, everybody should finish and, number two, when you finish, your diploma ought to be worth something. And the only way to do it is to have high standards and not be afraid of them, and not punish people if they don't measure up, but just show them where the bar is and then help everybody clear it.

The second thing I want to do is open the doors of college to everyone. And that's why we proposed to give a tax credit worth about

$1,500 a year for the first 2 years of college and then a tax deduction for any cost of higher education after that. We know from the 1990 census that every young person—not every but most young people who get at least 2 years of college or more get a job with a growing income. And young people who have less than 2 years of college or who don't even have a high school diploma tend to get a job with a stagnant or a declining income. We know that's where the break was in 1990. And we know that our economy is now producing more of the high-wage jobs. In the last 2 years—that's another thing—more than half the new jobs in the last 2 years have been in higher wage categories. So that's the second thing I wanted to do.

The third thing I wanted to do that I've got some differences in our party about—and there's a lot of differences within the Republican Party; both parties are split on this—is to continue to expand the network of trading partnerships the United States has. But we negotiated 200 trade agreements to get fair and equal access to other markets in my first term, and we're now the world's number one exporter again. And one of the reasons more than half our jobs pay above average is that so many of them are tied to exports.

Now, tomorrow the First Lady and I and others are going to announce a very important initiative with regard to Africa that we've been working on for some time and that really was reinforced by her recent trip there. But I would hope that all of you who are business people would help us to continue our normal trade relations with China and to push them on things we disagree with but to keep involved with them, and to continue our reaching out to Latin America, even as we reach out to Africa. You know, we're going to have a billion people in Latin America before you know it. And they're very excited and would like to deal with us. But last year, the southern countries in Latin America, Brazil, Argentina, and the others in a group called MERCOSUR, for the first time ever did more business with Europe than the United States. Why? Because we stopped reaching out to them with our trade agreements.

So it's not like these folks aren't going to go on to create a future, and we have a great opportunity. And if we want more high-wage jobs created so that when we educate young people they'll be able to get good jobs, we have

to create the high-wage jobs. Mr. Brown's father literally gave his life for that cause. And that is the right thing to do. That is not against working people. What is good for working people is to create more high-wage jobs in America. And so I hope you will support that.

The fourth thing that we have to face is that with all of our successes, 20 percent of our kids, at least, are still living in poverty—minority children, much higher percentages. Now, in the end, no society can permit that without paying an awesome price. And that is something, by the way, that ought to factor into this affirmative action debate, when people say, "Oh, you don't need it." You cannot leave people isolated for 18 years from the mainstream of economic and social life and then tell them, "There are no barriers to your entry into colleges, universities, or starting your own business." You cannot do that.

So the reason I thought the Presidents' Summit of Service that we did, the former Presidents and General Powell did in Philadelphia was so important is it gives us a chance to mobilize millions of people around specific objectives that I'm also trying to see the Government do its part in. And let me just reiterate them real quick.

We want to see that every child has a safe place to grow up. I've got a juvenile justice bill before the Congress now that is both tough and smart, modeled on what they've been doing in Boston where our chairman, Mr. Grossman, lives, where not a single child has been killed by a gun in a year and a half. Don't tell me you can't do that. Not one.

But do we need volunteers? Yes. Why? Because look what they did in Boston. I can pass all the bills in the world, in addition to the probation officers and police officers, to have all these people walking the streets, saving these kids' lives. And you go to any city where the juvenile crime rate is going down, they have both citizens and appropriate action by the public sector.

The second thing we want is for every child to have marketable skills. I already talked about that, education.

The third thing we want is for every child to have access to health care. And I was really appreciative of that—this is one thing that General Powell and I share a common obsession with. He said, "I can't believe we let working families get by without health care. If I proposed to end the health care guarantee for people in the military when I was Chairman of the Joint Chiefs of Staff, there would have been a riot." No one in America would think about depriving military people and their children of health care. But we have 10 million kids, for example, who don't have health care. And we've got enough money in that balanced budget to cover half of them. We need to finish the job. We need to finish the job. It's not right. It's not right.

The fourth thing and the fifth thing are things that have to be done at the community level. We want every child to have a mentor, and we want every child to have a chance to serve. And I think that's important. Kids who serve feel more important; they know they matter. And 90 percent-plus of young people in a recent national poll said that they would serve in their community, even poor kids, if just somebody would ask them, if somebody would ask them and give them a chance.

So those are the things that I'm trying to get done now for our country, to keep this momentum going. But I really believe—and this brings me to the race initiative. Right now we just have one State, Hawaii, where there is no majority race. Within 3 years, California, our largest State, will be the same. Within somewhere between 30 to 50 years, depending on patterns of immigration, it will be true for the Nation as a whole. That means that we really will test whether or not we are not a nation of race or place but a nation of ideas and ideals. Politicians have been saying that in speeches for a century now—[*laughter*]—about to find out. [*Laughter*] And I don't know about you, but when we find out, I know what I want the answer to be.

Think how much time I've spent as your President and how much time I'm going to spend in the next 3½ years, dealing with hatred and mistrust in the Middle East born of ethnic and religious difference, dealing with hundreds of years of accumulated animosity in Northern Ireland born of their ethnic—originally—and religious differences, the Scotch-Irish and the Irish, the Protestants and the Catholics. How many hundreds of thousands of people died in Rwanda and how many had to be saved by us and the French and others because of the fights between the Hutus and the Tutsis? Most of us, if we walked down the street in one

of those African communities, could not tell the difference, but they knew enough to hack each other's children to death.

Or what about the Bosnians, where there is literally no biological difference between them? They are by accident of history divided because of the political forces coming together where Bosnia is now. The Orthodox became Serbs; the Catholics became Croat—or vice versa—and the people that were left in the middle were colonized by the Ottoman Empire and became Muslims. But they now are ethnically different, people who lived together as friends and neighbors for decades turned on each other like that.

So when you think everything is hunky-dory here and, oh, we might have an occasional riot when there is a controversial thing like Rodney King, but we won't really ever have a disintegrating energy in this country, you just think about how easy it was for those people to fall on each other.

Now, I know we've got a lot more to lose, you would argue, than they do. But no great nation has ever had a multiracial, multiethnic, integrated society. The Russians are doing a good job, actually, of trying to preserve their democracy with a whole lot of different ethnic groups. And they had that unfortunate difficulty in Chechnya, but there are a lot of Chechnyas over there where they don't have difficulty. But they live apart, physically apart, and normally in distinct, what we would call, States. Here we are, together.

So I said to myself, "This would be a good time to do this because we're not having a civil rights crisis, and we're not under the illusion that there's just this X little problem—even if it's a big problem—different perceptions of the fairness of law enforcement, for example—that if we fix, everything will be hunky-dory, and we'll go on. We need to imagine what it's going to be like 30 years from now." Because if you think about it, we can have a good economic policy, a good social policy, we can even begin to do the things we need to do to rescue our children, and if we can't get along together and we don't trust each other and we don't feel that people are treated in the proper way, then the rest of it could just unravel on us somewhere down the road.

Now, that's why I did this. And do I know it will be successful? Do I know that there's some mechanical way to define success? No, I don't know that, but I think it will be.

And that's how I want all of us to see this affirmative action debate. Look, if I didn't think we needed it, I'd be happy to shed it. If somebody could offer me a credible alternative and then test it for a year or so and proved that it worked, I'd be happy to shed it. What I know is that we have a vested interest as a nation, without regard to race, in having universities where people of different backgrounds get educated together, in giving people from each different ethnic group in the United States a chance to have their fair share of—not a quota but at least a share, a representative group of people in any form of human endeavor, to inspire others to come along, to have economic self-sufficiency.

You know, if you look at why—why does the United States have an unemployment rate under 5 percent and a lot of the European countries have higher unemployment rates? One reason is people like you, small-business people, independent business people, people that proved they could put together something, hire a few people, work over a lifetime, and build something. And we have a vested interest as a people in saying that there are pockets of economic self-sufficiency and entrepreneurs in every neighborhood in this country. And if we had it, we wouldn't have half the problems we've got today.

You just think about it. If every block in this country had one or two small businesses succeeding on it, there would be people on that block employed, there would be role models for those kids walking the streets to see, there would be people giving money to the school to make sure they don't have to give up their music programs. You just think about it.

So we have a vested interest, all of us, in trying to make sure we can all participate. So, to me, this affirmative action debate is somehow smaller than the larger issue. I will—I'm doing my best to honor the Supreme Court decision. I'm doing my best to have reasonable standards. I hope that there will be other things we can do as well. That's why I want the empowerment zone to double, the empowerment zones to pass. We've got a lot more economic things we need to do.

But the larger issue is, what do you want this country to look like 30 years from now? Every other question should be answered in terms of that. Once you ask the right question,

it's a whole lot easier to come to a commonsense answer.

Now, what we're going to try to do with this race initiative, just very briefly, is, first of all, stick with this vision of racial reconciliation, try to get everybody to agree on what we want the country to look like.

Second, get the facts out. Now, that's important. I think when we decide what to do with the welfare system, for example, it would be helpful if everyone in America knew that last year in Chicago there were six applicants for every minimum wage job that opened up and nine applicants in St. Louis. Don't you? I was a little concerned that over 40 percent of African-Americans and over 40 percent of whites, when asked what the percentage of the American population was black, said between 20 and 49, when the correct answer is 12. We need to know the facts.

Then the third thing we want to do is to have this kind of a dialog in every community in the country. We want to recruit and encourage local leadership.

And finally, we want to come up with some specific, concrete actions to be done at the national level and at the community level. That's what we're trying to do.

But I wanted you to understand tonight because I want you to be a part of this; I want you to feel like it's yours. And I want you to go out and find your friends and neighbors and ask them to be a part of this. And I want you to find people that don't agree with you on everything and ask them to be a part of this. Because this is a huge deal.

If we can pull this off, the United States will be by far the best positioned country in the global society of the 21st century. And if we act like we don't have to think about it until the wheel runs off, there is a chance that the wheel will run off. And even if it doesn't, we will never be what we ought to be. That is what this whole thing is about.

So I ask you, go out there and tell people— if they want to be cynical, skeptical, say, "I don't know if it will amount to anything. I don't know about that Clinton; he's got to have something to do in his second term"—whatever they're saying out there—let them say it. Tell them to participate anyway, saddle up. They don't have anything to lose by trying. I'll tell you one thing, if we all try we'll be better off than if we just let it go. So I ask you for your help.

Now, the last thing I want you to know is—that's why I want you to be proud to be here, because I think these things that our Democratic Party stands for now are the future. I think they're not just Democratic future; they're not just African-American, Hispanic-American, you name it; this is America's future. And we're going to have to make it together. And tonight, by your being here, you're making it more likely that we will do just that.

God bless you. Thank you.

Let me say one other thing before I leave. I don't know who all was here from my office before I got here, but we've got—Bob Nash, who is my Director of Personnel, is here. If you want to be Ambassador, ask him. He has the hardest job in the Government. He has to tell one person yes and 10 people no. [*Laughter*] And Maurice Daniels, the Vice President's political division person, is here.

And let me just say one other thing, too. I want you to know, because a lot of you are friends of hers, that Hillary and I were deeply saddened by what happened to Betty Shabazz, and we've been praying for her, and I know you are, too.

That's a whole other subject, but it ought to remind us that we don't have a kid to waste.

You don't want any of them to get away from you, and they do all too soon and all too easily, which is another reason we ought to think about what we came here to do tonight.

Thank you. Bless you.

NOTE: The President spoke at 8:24 p.m. in the Crystal Ballroom at the Sheraton Carlton Hotel. In his remarks, he referred to Mayor Willie W. Herenton of Memphis, TN; Richard Mays, attorney, Little Rock, AR, and Janice Griffin, vice president, Prudential, cochairs of the event; Ernest Green, managing partner, Lehman Brothers; Robert L. Johnson, chairman and chief executive officer, BET Holdings, Inc.; Weldon Latham, Jr., partner, Pittman, Potts and Trobridge; Mel Clarke, president, Metroplex; Marianne Niles, president, National Association of Investment Companies; Bill Kirk, partner, Reid and Priest; Larry Gibson, partner, Shapiro and Orlander, Baltimore, MD; Marianne Spragen, president, W.R. Lazard; Jeff Thompson, accountant, Thompson and Bazilo; Carroll Willis, director, communications services division, and Steve Grossman, national chair, Democratic National Committee; Michael Brown, son of former Secretary of Commerce Ronald H. Brown; Gen. Colin L. Powell, USA (ret.), chairman, America's Promise—the Alliance for Youth; and arson victim Betty Shabazz, widow of civil rights leader Malcolm X.

Remarks at a Democratic National Committee Dinner
June 16, 1997

Thank you very much. Steve gave such a good speech, if I had any sense I would just sit down. [*Laughter*] But I thank you for it. Let me thank Joel and David and Monte and Jeff and Ira and everyone else who is responsible for this tonight. I thank Carol Pensky and Cynthia Friedman for their leadership in our party. I thank Secretary Babbitt for coming tonight, and Ann Lewis from the White House for coming, and Craig Smith, my political director. There may be more people here. I'll hear about it tomorrow if there are. [*Laughter*] I thank Senator Lautenberg and Senator Feinstein, Dick, and Senator Lieberman and Hadassah, thank you all for being here.

I really appreciate, more than anything else I suppose, the fact that there has been established between our administration and I hope between me personally and the American Jewish community a bond of trust which is rooted in our shared values for what America ought to become here at home and for our longing for an honorable and lasting peace in the Middle East. And I thank those of you who mentioned to me, going through the line tonight, my speech in San Diego a couple of days ago. And I would like to talk a little about that and about the Middle East in what I would call a proper context.

In 1991, when I was attempting to decide whether to enter the Democratic primaries and only my mother thought I could be elected—[*laughter*]—night after night I would sit at home and say, "Why do you want to do this? You know, you could say, well, every little boy and now, I hope, every little girl can want to grow up to be President, but that's not a very good reason for other people to vote for you, the fact that you'd just as soon live in the White House as somewhere else." And I was deeply disturbed because I didn't think the country was moving to prepare for the new century.

It was an unusual time because I'd actually had a very good relationship with President Bush. I was very often the designated Democrat to deal with the White House. I had no burning, negative passions—I don't understand them very well, anyway, I think. But I really felt that my country was not preparing for the future.

And so I sat down, almost 6 years ago now, and wrote out what I wanted America to be like in the 21st century. And now I have said it over and over again probably a thousand, maybe two, three thousand times, and a lot of people are sick of hearing it. But it's important that you know that every day as President I still think about what I wrote 6 years ago.

I said that I wanted my Nation in the 21st century, first of all, to have the American dream of opportunity alive for every person here, without regard to their race, their background, their starting point in life. I wanted all of our citizens to be responsible, to take responsibility for themselves, their families, and others in their communities. I wanted America to be the world's leading force for peace and freedom and prosperity a generation from now, just as we are today. And I wanted us to become closer as one community with all of our diversity.

And I realized that if you ask the question, what do you want the country to look like 30 years from now, then you begin—and you answer that, you're much more likely to ask and answer the right questions about what are you going to do tomorrow. Because then it became clear to me that the first thing we had to do was to scrap the economic policy we were following and adopt one that made some sense, that we had to find a way to get rid of the terrible deficits we had and still invest in our future.

Most people said you couldn't cut the deficit and invest more in education and technology and research. I thought you could. We know—the record is in now. The deficit has gone down

77 percent in 4 years before this last agreement, and we have invested more. And the country is better off, and our economy has produced a record number of new jobs, biggest decline in income inequality among working families, something very important to most of you, since the 1960's.

I thought we could have a crime strategy that was more than tough talk. I mean, everybody—you can't have a free country if people are terrified of their own personal security. And I thought the Democrats had made a mistake not taking that issue on—but taking it on in a real way, not just a rhetorical way. So I worked with Senator Feinstein to ban assault weapons. And we worked to pass the Brady bill. And we heard all these talks, and a lot of our people lost seats in '94 because they had the guts to vote for the assault weapons ban and the Brady bill. And they were all told, "Oh, you're going to lose your gun." Well, as I said in '96 in New Hampshire, I said, "A lot of you voted against our people in '94 because they told you we were going to take your guns." And I said, "I want everybody who lost their guns to vote for Republicans for Congress and everybody who didn't to vote for the Democrats." [*Laughter*] And they were all laughing. But 186,000 felons, fugitives, and stalkers have lost their guns.

Last year we had the biggest drop in crime in 35 years, putting these police officers on the street, and we're moving forward with this juvenile justice strategy. Based on what's been working in Steve and Alan's hometown of Boston, there has not been a single child killed with a handgun in a year and a half.

So we're working. We had the biggest drop in welfare rolls in history. Things are moving. You may have seen last week, something that I was told by the cynics would never happen—in the International Math and Science Survey, our fourth graders scored way above the national average in math and science. They said, "Oh, no, America's kids are too poor. They're too racially diverse. You'll never get this done." But our educators have been working on this since 1984 all over America.

So then I got hired again in '96—[*laughter*]—and I said to myself, "Well, now what are we going to do?" I love to tell this story. I told this story where I was earlier tonight. When I ran for reelection as Governor one time, a guy came up to me and said, "You going to run again, Bill?" And I said, "If I do, will you vote for me?" He said, "Probably. What are you going to say?" I said, "Well, I'm going to say I did a good job." He said, "Hell, that's what I hired to you to do." He said, "That's not a reason to vote for you." [*Laughter*] You think about it. I mean, it's an interesting thing.

So I asked myself, "What are we going to do?" So I asked the right question again. Where are we going to be in 30 years? What do we still have to do? That's what this balanced budget agreement is all about. It balances the budget and has the biggest investment in education in history and opens the doors of college to all Americans and pays for examinations in math and science for every fourth and eighth grader in the country to see if we're really committed to national academic standards. It helps to bring economic opportunity and empowerment into the inner cities. It's the right thing to do. So that's the first thing I wanted to do.

The second thing I wanted to do was to continue to expand our leadership in world trade, something that's controversial in both parties. But it seems to me like we have evidence now. You know, we have a 4.8 percent unemployment, the lowest unemployment in 24 years, and we had 200 separate trade agreements in the last 4 years. And we're selling more overseas than ever before, and we're the number one exporter in the world again. And I personally do not believe we need to be afraid of making a trade agreement with Chile or Argentina or Brazil, for that matter. And I think it would be a terrible mistake for us to walk away from the chance to reach out to Latin America, to Africa, to Asia, and build closer ties and a better, brighter future.

And the fourth thing I wanted to do was to recognize that we have a problem. I don't care how well we're doing, as long as 20 percent of the kids in this country are living below the poverty line and are in physical isolation from most of the rest of us, we've got a problem. That's really what the Presidents' Summit of Service was all about in Philadelphia. It was about saying every child ought to have a safe place to grow up, ought to have a decent school, ought to have health care—all three of those things we try to deal with in our budget, by the way—ought to have a personal mentor, and ought to have a chance to serve in the community. And I thought the Summit of Service is important because it would mobilize volunteers all over America to support and reinforce and

carry out the things I'm trying to get done in this budget and in the juvenile crime bill before the Congress.

And then the last thing that I wanted to do was focus on race and ethnic and religious differences, which is why I went to San Diego. Why? Because if we have a growing economy, a good educational system, the crime rate is down, the welfare rolls are down, and we're doing better by kids, and we can't get along when there is no race in the majority in this country, the rest of it will come unraveled. And if we can't get along, we will not have the moral force we need to do what needs to be done in the Middle East, in Bosnia, in Africa, and in Northern Ireland, and who knows what's going to happen 10, 15, 20, 30 years from now.

In Hawaii—Hawaii is the only State in the country today where there is no majority race. In 3 years, there will be none in California. In somewhere between 30 and 50 years, there will be none in the United States. It depends on immigration and birth patterns, but somewhere between 30 and 50 years from now, we will test the theory that I have heard politicians talk about or read them talk about for a century, which is that this is not a nation of place or race, it's a nation of ideals. We are about to find out. And it seems to me that it would be better for us to find out at a time when we have no riots in the streets, we have no immediate emergencies, we're at the peak of our economic strength and our international influence, when we could take back—sort of step back and say, "Now, let's ask this question together one more time. What do we want to be like in 30 years?" That's what that whole business in San Diego was about.

So I hope all of you will participate in that, because this is something that has been of passionate significance to the Jewish community for a long time. I really do believe that my life is diminished every time a synagogue is defaced. And I believe when they burned that mosque in the South a couple years ago, it diminished my life. And I believe when those churches were burned, it diminished my life. And I think that you do. And so I ask you to help us participate in that.

I also have invited you all privately—I will say this publicly; I'm not ashamed to say it— you care passionately, all of you, about getting peace in the Middle East. We cannot let this process become unraveled. I cannot tell you how many nights that I have had difficulty sleeping, racking my brain trying to come up with some new thing I could do or say to try to pierce the difficulties of the moment. But you have never been shy in telling me what you thought before, so don't start now—[*laughter*]—because every one of us now has a huge stake in this.

There is some good news here in some areas, and over the next several days we'll be seeing some progress, but there are a lot of clouds on the horizon, and we have to keep working at it. But I want you to know that it's not off my radar screen. It's still right there where it was the first day I took office. And I'm going to be disappointed when I leave office if we haven't gone much further. And I still believe we can, and I want you to believe that, and I want you to help me.

But I want you also to just think, just for a moment one more time about the implications of this racial—because what I want to do is to get everybody to buy into that vision that we should be one America, that we should celebrate all the differences between us, but think that what unites us is more important; that we should get out the facts, because I've learned that we don't have the facts. I was astonished in the Gallup poll, polling African-Americans and whites just about different racial issues. They asked African-Americans and whites what percentage of our population is black. And the five choices were less than 5, between 5 and 10, between 10 and 20, between 20 and 49, or over half. Those were the five choices.

By far, the biggest plurality—there was not a majority for any answer—but by far, the most votes went to 20 to 49 percent. The most votes of whites, the most votes of blacks said between 20 and 49 percent of the American population is black. The correct answer is 12. But like 40 percent of both thought that. So if we don't even know what the facts are among us, you can imagine all the things we don't know about in more sophisticated ways, on more critical questions.

Then I want to try to get some honest dialog going in every community. And the Jewish com-

munity has been very active at this in a lot of communities, so I ask you for your help for the White House in this. Help this advisory board I have appointed to reach out to things that are working now and get something like this in every community.

And finally, we're going to try to come up with some specific, concrete solutions to go forward. But this is a huge deal. We can't hold America together and we can't maintain our position of moral leadership in the world to be for peace in a world that is coming apart around racial, ethnic, tribal, and religious differences unless we can deal with this. And we need to start now, before we have to figure out what we're going to do when things start to fray.

On balance, I'm very upbeat about our country and about the world. And there will always be difficulties. There will always be problems. It is endemic to human nature. But if we could follow the admonition of the Christian Bible to love your neighbor as yourself, or Rabbi Hillel, who said, "What is hateful to you, do not to your fellow man," which is, it seems to me, just about the same thing, then this race initiative will have been one well worth taking.

So again I say, I thank you for your support. I ask for your advice and your continued support. And more than anything else, I ask you to help your fellow Americans think about what we want this country to look like when our grandchildren are where we are.

Thank you, and God bless you.

NOTE: The President spoke at 9:54 p.m. in the John Hay Room at the Hay Adams Hotel. In his remarks, he referred to Carol Pensky, treasurer, and Alan D. Solomont, national finance chair, Democratic National Committee; David Steiner, vice chair, Monte Friedkin, national chair, D. Jeffrey Hirschberg, vice chair, Ira N. Forman, executive director, and Joel Tauber, member, National Jewish Democratic Council; Cynthia Friedman, national chair, Women's Leadership Forum; Richard Blum, husband of Senator Dianne Feinstein; and Senator Joseph I. Lieberman's wife, Hadassah.

Remarks on Signing a Memorandum on Strengthening Enforcement of Title IX of the Education Amendments of 1972
June 17, 1997

The President. Thank you very much. As you might imagine, Hillary and I have looked forward to this day with great anticipation, and we have discussed these issues together for more than 25 years now. Actually, we met before title IX; that's one thing I managed to do without the benefit of Federal law. [*Laughter*]

I thank Secretary Riley for his wonderful leadership. And thank you, Anne, for your introduction. You did so well, if you ever get tired of science I think public affairs would treat you well. Thank you, Jackie, for being a wonderful role model and a great person. Thank you, Verelett Allen and Captain Robin Forster, Dr. Nelba Chavez. And I'd like to say a special thank you to Sally Ride and tell you that tomorrow is the 14th anniversary of her famous ride.

There are so many distinguished people in the audience I hesitate to start, but I would be remiss if I did not thank former Senator Birch Bayh for his leadership in this endeavor. Thank you, sir. You're a good man.

And I'd like to thank the eighth graders from the Thomas Edison Center for Technology who are here and I hope are being inspired about the future. And I would like to ask the members of the Congressional Women's Caucus who are here to stand and be recognized. All the Members of Congress who are here, please stand. Thank you.

We are here to celebrate title IX, but even more, we're here to celebrate the God-given talent of every woman and girl who has been benefited by it. Title IX did not create their successes, but it did give them the chance to make the most of their abilities. We have heard about the difference it has made in the lives of millions of young girls and young women. We know about the confidence that it has built, the expectations it has helped to set, the achievements it has helped to inspire.

Today I also want to say that in my view title IX has had a beneficial impact on every American citizen. If we've learned anything in the last 25 years since title IX became law, it is that expanding benefits and opportunities for any American helps the rest of us. Wasted opportunity diminishes all of us.

As we prepare for the 21st century, it would be sheer folly for us not to take advantage of every ounce of energy and talent and creativity every American has to offer. As a nation, that would be our great concern. Think what we would be like if there were no Sally Rides or Jackie Joyner-Kersees or any one of the countless women whose contributions have helped to make our Nation a better place, including, I might add, the eight women which now serve in the President's Cabinet, a record number.

Every girl growing up in America today should have the chance to become an astronaut or an Olympic athlete, a Cabinet Secretary or a Supreme Court Justice, a Nobel Prize winning scientist or President of the United States. For 25 years, title IX has helped girls to realize their dreams and to achieve them—a lot of people, believe it or not, still don't know this—to achieve them not only in athletics but in academics as well.

In addition to the remarkable athletic statistics, Secretary Riley told me today that—and Jackie—in 1972, there were 300,000 girls in high school athletics. Today, there are 2.3 million. But in addition to the athletics, listen to this, in 1972, 9 percent of the medical degrees and 7 percent of the law degrees were awarded to women. In 1996, 38 percent of the medical degrees and 43 percent of the law degrees were awarded to women.

So today we celebrate how far we've come. But we must also recommit ourselves to title IX's goal of equality in education, for too many schools and education programs still drag their feet and lag behind in their responsibility to our young women and girls.

Today I'm directing every agency and executive department of our Government to strengthen their enforcement of title IX within the next 90 days, by reviewing current procedures, consulting with the Attorney General on the best way to improve them, and delivering to me a new and vigorous enforcement plan. Every school and every education program that receives Federal assistance in the entire country must understand that complying with title IX is not optional. It is the law, and the law must be enforced.

There is no question that we're better off because of title IX, but we can go even further to provide all people with the opportunity they deserve to make the most of their own lives. A lot of people don't know this, either, but currently title IX only applies to educational programs and activities that receive funding from the National Government. Ironically, it does not apply to the programs that the National Government runs itself. These include schools run by the Department of Defense, educational research conducted by the Federal Government, and educational fellowships awarded directly to students.

I believe and I surely hope that every American would agree that the National Government must hold itself to the same high standards it expects from everyone else, especially when it comes to discrimination in education. Therefore, today I have sent an executive memorandum to all the relevant Federal departments to conduct a review of their programs over the next 60 days, report the review to the Attorney General. And then after I receive her recommendation, I expect to sign an Executive order to prohibit educational discrimination on the basis of sex, race, or national origin in federally conducted education programs, thereby extending the principles of title IX to Federal programs themselves. [*Applause*] Thank you.

On the desk outside the Oval Office, there is a little sign with a quote from a woman who lives here in Washington. Here's what it says: "I rejoice in others' success, knowing there is plenty for us all." Today we are celebrating, resolving, and moving forward to make sure that all of our people, and especially every one of our girls and young women have the opportunities they deserve to make the most of their own lives. After all, there is plenty for us all. Indeed, I think you could make a compelling case that when other people succeed in a constructive manner it creates more opportunities for success for the rest of us.

Finally, let me just add one more item. There is something happening today that, like title IX, marks a significant step forward toward helping all our young people achieve their full potential. When I reached a bipartisan budget agreement with the leaders of Congress last month, one of my top goals was to extend health care coverage to millions more of our young children.

Believe it or not, 10 million children in this country still don't have health insurance, and more and more, a lot of employer-based health policies are not covering the whole family. It is no secret that this is something that Hillary and I have worked on for many years and care a great deal about.

I fought very hard to ensure that $16 billion would be set aside in the budget agreement for this purpose. But we did not prescribe in the agreement how this money would be spent. The important thing is to use it wisely and carefully so that it provides meaningful coverage to as many children as possible. I am very pleased that a bipartisan group of Senators in the United States Senate and on the Finance Committee have come up with some children's legislation that I believe offers that promise.

So today I am proud to say that I will endorse the legislation sponsored by Senators Chafee, Rockefeller, Jeffords, and Hatch. The Senate Finance Committee is voting on it today, and it will help to give a lot of our young children a healthy start in life, without which a lot of those young girls might not ever be in a position to take advantage of title IX.

This legislation will be the biggest investment in children's health care since Medicaid passed in 1965. It will be the most significant thing that we could do, I think, by committing us to providing health insurance coverage to up to 5 million uninsured children in providing health insurance today that they didn't have yesterday.

So, we've got a chance once again to prove that if we'll put politics aside and work together as we did so many years ago in the cause of civil rights, as we celebrate today with title IX, we can make America a better place.

Thank you for being here today. Thank you for the examples you set every day, and resolve tomorrow that you will give another young woman or girl a chance to make the most of her God-given abilities. Thank you very much.

[*At this point, the President signed the memorandum to the heads of executive departments and agencies.*]

The President. Thank you. Thanks for coming.

NOTE. The President spoke at 11:24 a.m. in Room 450 of the Old Executive Office Building. In his remarks, he referred to scientist Anne Jarvis Jefferson, who introduced the President; athlete

Jackie Joyner-Kersee; Verelett Allen, coordinator, YWCA/HCCE Non-Traditional Employment for Women Program; Robin Forster, fire captain, Station 10, Parkville, MD; Dr. Nelba Chavez, Administrator, Substance Abuse and Mental Health Services Administration; and former astronaut Sally K. Ride. He also referred to title IX of the Education Amendments of 1972 (Public Law 92–318).

Memorandum on Strengthening Title IX Enforcement and Addressing Discrimination on the Basis of Sex, Race, Color, and National Origin
June 17, 1997

Memorandum for the Heads of Executive Departments and Agencies

Subject: Strengthening Title IX Enforcement and Addressing Discrimination on the Basis of Sex, Race, Color, and National Origin in Federally Conducted Education Programs and Activities

As we commemorate the 25th anniversary of Title IX of the Education Amendments of 1972, we should pause to recognize the significant progress our Nation has made in increasing educational possibilities for women and girls and recommit ourselves to the goals of this important legislation. Title IX has broken down barriers and expanded opportunities—opening classroom doors, playing fields, and even the frontiers of space to women and girls across this country.

My Administration is working hard to expand further opportunities for women and girls. We have stepped up enforcement of civil rights statutes in areas such as access to advanced math and science programs. We have issued policy guidance on racial and sexual harassment and on ensuring equal opportunities in intercollegiate athletics. We have aggressively litigated cases presenting significant issues of discrimination, including cases challenging the exclusion of women from the Virginia Military Institute and the Citadel. My Administration has also sponsored an education campaign to help young girls build skills, confidence, and good health. Finally, my Administration has reaped the benefits of an ever-increasing pool of superbly qualified women, making it possible for me to appoint record numbers of women to my Cabinet, judicial posts, and to high levels of decision-making throughout the Federal Government.

Yet more needs to be done. Our Nation can reach its full potential only when all of our citizens have the opportunity to reach their full potential and contribute to our society. Today, I am announcing two important next steps in our fight to reach true equality in education.

First, I am directing executive departments and agencies to develop vigorous, new Title IX enforcement plans. We must ensure that all Federal agencies that provide financial assistance to education programs or activities take all necessary steps to ensure that programs and institutions receiving Federal money do not discriminate on the basis of sex.

I therefore direct all heads of executive departments and agencies that provide financial assistance to education programs or activities, following consultation with the Attorney General, to report to me within 90 days on measures to ensure effective enforcement of Title IX. This should include a description of department or agency priorities for enforcement, methods to make recipients of Federal financial assistance aware of their obligation not to discriminate, and grievance procedures to handle Title IX complaints. In accordance with Executive Order 12250, the Attorney General should coordinate implementation of these measures.

Second, I am asking executive departments and agencies to take appropriate action against discrimination in education programs or activities conducted by the Federal Government. Currently, Title IX generally prohibits discrimination based on sex—and Title VI of the Civil Rights Act of 1964 generally prohibits discrimination on the basis of race, color, or national origin—in education programs or activities that *receive* Federal financial assistance. However, these laws do not apply to comparable education programs or activities that are *conducted* by the

Federal Government. I believe it is essential that the Federal Government hold itself to the same principles of nondiscrimination in educational opportunities that we now apply to education programs and activities of State and local governments and private institutions receiving Federal financial assistance.

Applying these principles to appropriate Federally conducted education programs and activities will complement existing laws and regulations that prohibit other forms of discrimination in Federally conducted education programs—including discrimination against people with disabilities (prohibited by the Rehabilitation Act of 1973) and discrimination based on race, color, religion, sex, or national origin against Federal employees (prohibited by Title VII of the Civil Rights Act of 1964).

I therefore direct all heads of executive departments and agencies to report to the Attorney General within 60 days:

(1) identifying and describing education programs or activities conducted by the executive department or agency (including the approximate budget and size of the program). An education program or activity includes any civilian academic, extracurricular, research, occupational training, or other education activity conducted by the Federal Government. Examples of Federally conducted education programs would include elementary and secondary schools operated by the Department of Defense for dependent children of eligible personnel; Federally conducted educational research; and educational fellowships awarded directly by Federal agencies to students; and

(2) describing any substantive or procedural issues that might arise under these education programs or activities related to prohibiting discrimination based on sex, race, color, and national origin in the program or activity, in order to aid in determining where application of remedial efforts would be appropriate.

On the basis of these reports, I intend to issue an Executive order implementing appropriate restrictions against sex, race, color, and national origin discrimination in Federally conducted education programs. I direct the Attorney General to report to me within 60 days after receiving these reports with the results of her review and a proposal for an appropriate and effective Executive order.

WILLIAM J. CLINTON

NOTE: The memorandum referred to title IX of the Education Amendments of 1972 (Public Law 92–318).

Remarks Announcing the Africa Trade Initiative
June 17, 1997

Thank you very much, Mr. Micek, for your testimony and your work. Congressman Crane, Congressman Rangel, Congressman McDermott, thank you all for what you have said today, and even more important, for what you have done.

Mr. Ambassador, to you, thank you for your words. And to all of your colleagues, welcome and thank you for coming and for being a part of this important initiative, for testifying before the Congress and giving your ideas to help us put this together.

Thank you, Senator Lugar, for your leadership in the Senate on this issue. I thank all the Members of Congress who are here. There are so many, I think just to show you the depth of the interest, I would like to ask the Members of the House who are here to stand and be recognized so you can see them all. Thank you.

I thank Secretaries Glickman, Daley, Slater, and Herman for being here; Ambassador Richardson; Ambassador Barshefsky; our AID Administrator, Brian Atwood; the Director of the USIA, Joe Duffey; the new leader of the Ex-Im Bank, Jim Harmon, thank you for being here.

There are so many people from the business community here and distinguished American citizens—I do think I would be remiss if I did not especially thank Jack Kemp. Thank you for coming. And thank you, Jim Wolfensohn, for coming. And now he will go back to the World

Bank and write the appropriate checks, I know. [*Laughter*]

Thank you, Mayor Dinkins, for being here. Thank you, Reverend Sullivan. I thank Maxine Waters, who is chair of the Congressional Black Caucus, for the emphasis she has put on Africa. And many of the members here, most recently Congresswoman McKinney, have talked to me about Africa on a regular basis.

But I would be remiss if I did not thank four people especially who are personally responsible for making sure that I know about Africa. First, Congressman Donald Payne, thank you, sir, for all the times you have talked to me about it. Thank you, Congressman Bill Jefferson. Thank you, Andy Young, Reverend Andrew Young, thank you. Andy Young was talking to me about Africa before he ever thought I would be in a position to do anything about it. [*Laughter*] And I would like to say a special word of thanks to C. Payne Lucas and the Corporate Council on Africa for the wonderful work they have done. Thank you, sir.

This is a moment of tremendous promise for the people of Africa. For the last 4 years we have tried to put our country in a position to be more active on Africa than we have been in the past. We had the first White House Conference on Africa. We have done a number of things. I think it's fair to say that the trip that Hillary and our daughter took to Africa was one of the most meaningful experiences they have ever had. I think it changed Hillary forever. I know it changed what I now believe I know and feel about what we should be doing forever. And so, I'd like to thank her for that because I think she's done a fine job on that.

We look at Africa today as a continent full of bright hopes and persistent problems. Everyone knows about the conflicts; they make a lot of news, from Sudan to Sierra Leone. We know that we have a responsibility to continue to work for peace in Africa's troubled areas. But somehow, we have to find a way to highlight and celebrate Africa's successes, and yes, even to participate in them in ways that work to the advantage of the American people. We have to dedicate ourselves to seeing that these gains will not only be maintained but will be enhanced.

These stories don't make the headlines, but there really is a dynamic new Africa out there, and the far greater number of nations there are now making dramatic strides toward democracy and prosperity. Since 1990 the number of democracies in sub-Saharan Africa has more than quadrupled. Now more than half the region's 48 states have freely chosen their leaders. Many are embracing economic reform, opening markets, privatizing, stabilizing their currencies. Growth has more than tripled since 1990. The economies in such countries as Senegal, Ghana, Mozambique, Cote d'Ivoire are expanding at rates up to 7 percent a year. Ethiopia was not long ago gripped by famine; it grew 12 percent last year. Uganda, once a byword for tragedy, has become a magnet for investment; it grew almost 10 percent last year.

As Africa's nations join the global march toward freedom and open markets, our Nation has a deep interest in helping to ensure that these efforts pay off. An Africa that is gaining vitality while technology, trade, communications, and travel are bringing millions into the global economy is a continent of greater stability, growing markets, stronger partners. A nation that can help us work for peace, to preserve the environment, to fight disease, to grow our own economy, that's a nation, wherever it is located on the globe, that America should be a good partner to, should be involved with, should be committed to building the future with.

Today I am proud to announce our collective effort with the Congress to help fulfill the promise of a stable, prosperous, and democratic Africa. And like Congressman Rangel and Congressman Moran before me, I want to say to you, Congressman Crane, and to you, Senator Lugar, we are well aware of the numbers in the United States Congress, and we would not be here today if there weren't a number of Republicans in leadership positions who care deeply about the future of Africa. And we thank you for that.

This new initiative upon which we have agreed has five key elements.

First, at the heart of our effort will be significantly increased access to our markets for African exports. African countries will be able to export almost 50 percent more products to the United States duty free. The most committed African reformers will receive even greater access. And in the future, the United States will be prepared to negotiate free trade agreements with these countries.

Second, we will increase technical assistance to enable African countries to take the fullest advantage of these new programs.

Third, we will work to increase private investment in Africa. Through OPIC, we are creating a new $150 million equity fund to finance increased private investment, and a $500 million fund for infrastructure investment in the sub-Saharan region.

Fourth, we will work to eliminate bilateral debt for the poorest of the reforming nations, and maintain our leadership in the effort to reduce their debts to the multilateral institutions. I heard you, Mr. Ambassador, and I know that you're right.

Fifth, to maintain our momentum, the United States will hold annual economic meetings at the ministerial level with all reforming African nations.

Now, as we deepen our commerce, I believe there will be a continued need for bilateral and multilateral development assistance. We know that. I am committed to maintaining funds for the USAID programs, the international financial institutions, and IDA. But aid cannot substitute for economic reform. We know that we must have both.

Our initiative opens the door to real, positive change. Only nations carrying out serious reforms will reap the full benefits. Those who strengthen their democracies and invest in their people will see their efforts pay off in increased trade that will create new jobs, increase wages, spur growth, and improve the quality of lives of people who have suffered some of the world's worst poverty.

As these economies grow, America's prosperity and our security will benefit. The potential of a sub-Saharan market with some 700 million people is truly immense. The United States supplies just 7 percent of Africa's imports today, but already that supports 100,000 American jobs. Just imagine what this initiative can mean to the United States, as well as to Africa. Mr. Micek's company has shown what we can do for Africa and for our own people.

I also want to emphasize to all of you that this is about more than economics. A stronger, stable, prosperous Africa will be a better partner for security and peace, will join us in the fight against the new common threats of drug trafficking, international crime, terrorism, the spread of disease, environmental degradation. We need partners in Africa on every single one of these issues, and in the years ahead we will have to have more of them.

Everyone who has looked at the future, who has predicted the challenges we will face, knows that the globalization of our societies will mean that all these problems will be transnational. They will cross all borders. They will sweep across continents. They will move in the flash of an eye, and we must be ready to work together.

By transforming our trade, I'd like to say one other personal thing. We're building on the legacy of another person who is not here, the late Ron Brown, who believed so much in the promise of Africa.

It builds on our work to resolve conflicts in Liberia, Burundi, Angola; to save hundreds of thousands of lives at risk from famine in Somalia and the Horn of Africa; to save so many in Rwanda and Burundi from the adversities they have faced. We are proud of our support for democratic transition and reconciliation in South Africa and for elections throughout the continent. We are proud when President Mandela takes the lead in trying to restore peace and harmony to troubled lands. And I love to see the United States not in a leadership position but in a position of saying, we support President Mandela. And I want more of that to occur.

I do look forward to visiting Africa later this term to pay tribute to the nations that have made such historic progress. And as has already been indicated by previous speakers, I do intend in Denver in just a few days to ask our partners from the other leading industrial democracies to join us in this effort. We have to work so that all of our nations coordinate policies toward Africa so that we can all encourage reform in trade and investment and relief to heavily indebted countries and so that we can all participate not only in the responsibilities but in the benefits of a growing, prosperous, freer Africa.

I will ask our partners to join us in urging the international financial institutions, the World Bank, the IMF, the Africa Development Bank, as well as the United Nations, to create innovative new programs so that reforming African nations can succeed in integrating themselves into the global economy.

And if we all persist at this, if we keep working at this, then people will look back at this moment as a pivotal one for Africa, for America, and for the global community. The Members of Congress of both parties who have shown such leadership in this effort have recognized that a prosperous, democratic America in the 21st century needs a prosperous, democratic Africa. They are committed to cementing the ties of culture that bind us in heritage.

And I might say, this is just the latest sterling example of what happens when we put the interests of our people and the values of our country throughout the world first and foremost. When we get beyond our partisan differences and reach to the depths of the human spirit and give light to our vision, we prove that we can advance the cause of America, improve the lives of our people, and, in this case, give hope to hundreds of millions living on the African Continent.

Thank you all very much.

NOTE: The President spoke at 2:07 p.m. in Room 450 of the Old Executive Office Building. In his remarks, he referred to Ernest Micek, chief executive officer, Cargill, Inc.; Ambassador Roble Olhaye of Djibouti; Jack Kemp, 1996 Republican candidate for Vice President; James D. Wolfensohn, president, International Bank for Reconstruction and Development; David Dinkins, chairman of the board, Constituency for Africa; Rev. Leon H. Sullivan, chairman and founder, Opportunities Industrialization Centers International; Andrew Young, former U.S. Ambassador to the United Nations; C. Payne Lucas, president, Africare; and State President Nelson Mandela of South Africa.

Statement Announcing the Middle East Peace and Stability Fund
June 17, 1997

I am delighted to announce today the creation of the Middle East Peace and Stability Fund. This new U.S. fund will draw on existing allocations of economic assistance to respond to urgent new needs in that region. The fund's initial focus will be on assisting Jordan as it pursues economic modernization and reform.

King Hussein has courageously led Jordan down the path of peace, exemplifying the wisdom and tenacity necessary to negotiate and carry out peace treaties. King Hussein's concern about his people and all the peoples of the Middle East is abundantly evident in his actions to bring about peace and reconciliation.

The fund we are creating today will draw its resources from redirection of a small percentage of the economic support funds supplied to Israel and Egypt. Prime Minister Netanyahu and President Mubarak both recognize the strategic importance of supporting economic growth in the region. They share my conviction that it is extremely important for the people of the Middle East to see tangible benefits when they turn from conflict to cooperation.

We envision a fund beginning with $100 million this year, and it is our intention, in close consultation with Congress, to support the development of the fund over the next several years. In the coming days, we will work closely with the Jordanian authorities to identify the best ways to integrate these resources into existing development plans. Over time, this fund will be flexible enough to be used to support other regional priorities as needed.

We have had discussions with the Congress regarding this effort, and we will work together closely as we proceed. At a time of limited resources, we believe this fund is the most effective and practical way to respond to new needs. I will also be discussing this plan with other leaders at our summit in Denver next week, encouraging them to seek creative ways to meet the emerging needs in the Middle East.

I look forward to meeting Crown Prince Hassan on June 18 to discuss this initiative as well as other developments in the region.

Statement on Signing Emergency Supplemental Appropriations Legislation
June 17, 1997

I am pleased to have signed into law H.R. 1871, the "1997 Emergency Supplemental Appropriations Act for Recovery from Natural Disasters, and for Overseas Peacekeeping Efforts, Including Those in Bosnia."

This bill provides over $5.8 billion so that Federal agencies can help the hundreds of thousands of people who have suffered terribly from the flooding and other natural disasters that have ravaged the Dakotas, Minnesota, California, and 29 other States. The bill also provides $1.8 billion to replenish Department of Defense accounts in connection with our peacekeeping efforts in Bosnia and Southwest Asia, and to assure that the Department can maintain maximum readiness of the troops.

With regard to the funds described above, I hereby designate as emergency requirements all funds in this Act so designated by the Congress that I have not previously designated pursuant to section 251(b)(2)(D)(i) of the Balanced Budget and Emergency Deficit Control Act of 1985, as amended.

I commend the Congress for approving my request to extend Supplemental Security Income (SSI) and Medicaid benefits through the end of fiscal 1997 to all legal immigrants who would otherwise lose them. This approach ensures that the Congress has the time to restore SSI and Medicaid benefits for disabled legal immigrants, consistent with the recent Bipartisan Budget Agreement.

I am disappointed that the Congress chose to include several objectionable items that I identified in my veto message of June 9. Fund-ing included in the bill for the Commission for the Advancement of Federal Law Enforcement not only will waste valuable Federal resources but also could interfere with Federal law enforcement policy and operations. As I indicated in my veto message, this type of oversight is more properly the role of the Congress, not an unelected commission.

I am also disappointed that the Congress chose to rescind funds for the Ounce of Prevention Council and the Department of Defense Dual-Use Applications Program. The Council will be forced to reduce the level of grants for youth substance abuse prevention, for which about 300 applications are under review. The reduction in the Dual-Use Applications program will result in higher costs of future defense systems.

On balance, however, this bill is a vast improvement over the legislation that I vetoed on June 9. It includes the desperately needed resources for our Nation's hard-hit areas, but it does not include extraneous riders that had nothing to do with the goal of providing disaster relief. I am pleased that my Administration and the Congress worked together in a bipartisan fashion.

WILLIAM J. CLINTON

The White House,
June 17, 1997.

NOTE: H.R. 1871, approved June 12, was assigned Public Law No. 105–18.

Remarks at "In Performance at the White House"
June 17, 1997

The President. Thank you. Tonight we're going to have a celebration of one of the most gifted singers and performers of the last four decades, Gladys Knight.

It's a special honor to have her perform here at the White House because her music and her artistry are uniquely American. Some call it soul; some call it rhythm and blues; some may even call it rock and roll. But the music Gladys helped to popularize really has much deeper and more spiritual roots in the rich gospel and soaring harmonies of the African-American church.

Today's popular music has many different points of origin, from the dark and cynical swagger of the blues to the lilt of country music, to the stark simplicity of our folk music. As all of you know, I love them all. But the gospel strain gives the best American music its transcendent quality. That's where the soul comes from. And that's where Gladys Knight's true gift resides. That is the spark she brings to all her diverse repertoire of songs.

She had her first public performance in the church as a member of the Mount Mariah Baptist Church choir when she was all of 4 years old. She won Ted Mack's famous "Amateur Hour"—I'm old enough to remember that—[*laughter*]—at the age of 7. She continued to sing gospel, and she even performed with the legendary Gladys Knight and the Pips, with her brothers and cousins, and still continued to sing gospel on the side. It was the fusion of pop and gospel styles that made Gladys Knight and the Pips so special, that and her stunning voice. As far as I'm concerned, she could still sing the phone book, and I would like it. [*Laughter*]

As one of the earliest Motown successes, Gladys Knight and the Pips helped to lay the foundation for the close harmony groups that dominated the airways in my youth and, I'm glad to say, are topping the charts again today. She deserves a lot of the credit for bringing those sounds to a much wider audience through a long string of hit records. And she's gotten a fair amount of that credit, from gold and platinum records to Grammy Awards, to her induction last year along with the Pips into the Rock and Roll Hall of Fame.

We're delighted to have Gladys back at the White House. She's a true American original. And I'm pleased to be able to share her wonderful talent with you tonight.

Ladies and gentlemen, please welcome Gladys Knight.

[*At this point, Gladys Knight performed.*]

The President. Now, wait a minute here; this is not on the script. First, I think Bubba should run for office. You know, the shy, retiring type gets a lot of votes these days. [*Laughter*]

I want to tell you something, Gladys. When you sang that last round of Georgia songs, some of us knew the answers were Vicki Lawrence, Brook Benton, Ray Charles, and Gladys Knight. And when you started singing "Georgia on My Mind" and then you went into "Midnight Train," I leaned over and asked Hillary exactly what today was—the 17th. And I'll tell you a story: Exactly one week and 30 years ago, across the street over there at Constitution Hall, I went to hear Ray Charles sing. And you can see it made a fairly deep impression on me. [*Laughter*] I carried the ticket stub for 25 years. And I will carry the memory of this for the rest of my life. You were wonderful tonight.

Ms. Knight. Thank you so much.

The President. Ladies and gentlemen, Billboard magazine once said it is unlikely that Gladys Knight could make a bad record. And tonight she has shown us how right Billboard was. So thank you, Gladys. Thank you, Bubba. Thank you, musicians. And thank you. We're going to be cheering for you for a long, long, long time.

Thank you for joining us, and good night. God bless you all.

NOTE: The President spoke at 7:57 p.m. on the South Lawn at the White House. In his remarks, he referred to Merald (Bubba) Knight, one of the Pips; and entertainers Vicki Lawrence, Brook Benton, and Ray Charles.

Statement on the Return of Mir Aimal Kansi to the United States
June 18, 1997

I want to express my deep appreciation to the FBI, CIA, and the Departments of State, Justice, and Defense for their extraordinary work in bringing Mir Aimal Kansi to the United States. Kansi is believed to be responsible for the killing of two CIA employees and the

wounding of three others in an attack on January 25, 1993. The men and women who participated in the effort to bring Kansi here showed great courage in carrying out this mission.

The success in apprehending Kansi demonstrates that we are determined to do what is necessary to track down terrorists and bring them to justice. The United States will not relent in the pursuit of those who use violence against Americans to advance their goals—no matter how long it takes, no matter where they hide.

Today our thoughts are also with the families of the victims. Although nothing can restore their loss, we hope that the prospect of justice in this case will bring them a measure of comfort.

Remarks in Littleton, Colorado
June 19, 1997

Thank you very much. First I want to thank Robert and Erica for reminding us of what we need to do to make sure all our children have the tools they need to succeed in this new global economy, and indeed, for reminding us about what most of our endeavors are about. I think they did a good job, don't you? Let's give them another hand. [*Applause*]

Thank you, Kristy, for your very kind words and even more for the power of your example. And I want to thank my good friend Mayor Webb for being our host. He and Mrs. Webb have been good friends to Hillary and me over the years, and I'm thrilled to be in Denver. I thank my friend and former colleague Governor Romer and Mrs. Romer. Among other things, Governor Romer is recognized as the most important Governor in our country on the subject of education, which is something I want to talk to you about today, and I know you're proud of what he has done.

I thank the host committee and the honorary chairs and vice chairs of the Denver Summit. I thank Representative Diana DeGette, who is doing a good job for you in Congress and came down with me today, City Council President Cathy Reynolds. I'd like to thank the National Digital TV Center and Leo Hindry and David Beddow who showed me around through this remarkable place.

Some of you may know that I'm sort of a, to put it charitably, a movie freak. My wife used to say that I would watch anything that came on the screen if it started out and it was obviously a movie. And inside I saw 35 movies being digitalized and sent out over various channels, and I almost didn't come out. But I couldn't bear to think of you going through this.

I want to thank all the people here from the Curtis Community Project and the Mouse

Campers, thank you for being here. I'd like to say a special word of thanks to a member of my Cabinet, your former mayor, Federico Peña, who just became a father for the third time just a couple of days ago. You know how much he loves Denver, and he thinks this is important, or he wouldn't he here, although he's here with permission, I might add.

I want to thank the Director of Summit Affairs and the Executive Director of the Summit, Harold Ickes and Debbie Willhite, and their great team for what they have done. And again, Mr. Mayor and Governor, let me thank you for the incredible support that Denver and Colorado have given to the Summit of the Eight.

I don't need to tell you why we really came here. Denver is a city that America can be proud of, a city bursting with the promise of the new century that is upon us, with the most educated people in America; a city that has increased its exports to the rest of the world 60 percent faster than the rest of our country in the last 5 years; a community that, as has been said, once drew its wealth from mine shafts and factories and the land, now thriving on telecommunications, aerospace, banking, computer software, and the magnificence of its environment.

Over a century ago, Walt Whitman wrote of the Colorado pioneers, "All the past we leave behind; we enter a newer, mightier world." Today, the men and women of Denver are cutting new paths. In this very building the product of our culture is transforming from analog to digital, from yesterday's technology to tomorrow's, beamed to satellites that gird the globe, seen by billions around the world.

When the leaders of the world's leading industrial democracies arrive here for the Summit of the Eight, they will be struck not only by the breathtaking beauty of the Rockies but by the powerful optimism of a city both proud of its past and focused on the future.

With our summit partners, we'll have an opportunity to cut a new path to that future, to work to deepen and extend the benefits of the global economy and protect people more against its downsides, to reach out to bring new partners into that economy, from Africa to all other parts of the world, to spread democracy and human rights around the world, and to meet new dangers of our common security that cross all national borders now: international crime and drug trafficking, terrorism and the spread of weapons of mass destruction, the emergence of infectious diseases that can sweep the globe, and environmental decay that embraces us all.

We host our partners at a time when America's economy is the healthiest in a generation and the strongest in the world. Our economic success is a strategy that all of you have participated in. It is born of the dynamic center that has kept America moving forward for more than two centuries, a new American economic approach that required us to puncture myths and push past yesterday's stale debates, that enabled us to move earlier and more strongly than most other nations into the new global economy.

In 1993 we put in place a new economic strategy designed to help America move from the industrial to the information age, to move into a new century and a new millennium with three very simple but profound goals in mind: to make sure the American dream is alive for all of our citizens, to make sure our American community is growing more united even as it becomes more diverse, to make sure America continues to lead the world for peace and freedom and prosperity.

Our economic strategy had three elements: reduce the deficit, invest more in our people, open the world to our trade. We had to move past old ideas to embrace new thinking, to craft new approaches to achieve all three things.

First, we had to go past the old idea that if you reduced the deficit, it would be good for the economy in the long run, but it would be sheer misery in the short run and bring on a recession. Well, in the last 4 years, the deficit is down 77 percent, from $290 billion to less than $70 billion. But instead of recession, our economy produced a record number of jobs in a 4-year term, over 11 million, and now we're over 12 million and still counting.

Now we must decide to stay with that strategy, with a balanced budget that will help interest rates stay low, produce more capital for private business, and even greater confidence in the American economy. I'm pleased that our balanced budget agreement received overwhelming support from big majorities in both parties in both Houses of Congress, and I look forward to signing into law a balanced budget that is consistent with the agreement and our values before the year is over.

Second, we had to go by the old thinking that a nation couldn't bring down the deficit and make its Government smaller while still investing more in its people, its future, and its environment, and that we could not bring down the deficit and give people the tools they need to succeed at work and at home and to maintain an adequate social safety net. But by spending less and spending smart, we were able to increase the productivity of our Government.

We increased our investment in Head Start by 43 percent, spent nearly $1 billion more to provide children and their mothers with the nutrition they need so that all of our children will be able to learn when they enter school, set aside funds to help States reduce class size, began school-to-work programs in all 50 States so that we could work in partnership with business to help young high school graduates who don't go on to 4-year colleges keep learning and find good-paying jobs. We opened the doors to college wider than ever, with more scholarships, more work-study, more affordable college loans. We put more money into the National Institutes of Health to spur new medical discoveries and cures and invested more in research to keep our lead in communications and technology and environmental protection. And we did it and cut the deficit by 77 percent. It's not how much you cut but how you cut, not what you spend but where you spend it.

Hundreds of Government programs, thousands of Government regulations have been eliminated, and so help me, not a single American citizen has come up to me and said, "I just can't live without that program or that regulation you got rid of." The Government is 300,000 people smaller than it was the day I first took office. But because we had no mass layoffs and we worked with the Federal employees' union in partnership, we have seen the productivity of Government go up, and the people have been able to go on to other productive careers. I'm proud of that and proud of our Federal work force for making it possible.

We have focused not on new guarantees but on giving people new tools to help families make the most of their God-given potential. And we have shown that you can give people more opportunity for economic security and still make the economy more flexible and more adaptable.

People said that when we adopted the family leave law it would hurt the economy, but it didn't. They said that when we raised the minimum wage it would hurt the economy, but it didn't. They said when we passed the Kennedy-Kassebaum bill saying you couldn't lose your health insurance because someone in your family got sick or because you had to change jobs it would hurt the economy, but it didn't. We were able to provide greater access to health insurance for self-employed people, greater pension protection and availability, tax incentives for business to invest in high unemployment areas. It all helped the economy. If you help people succeed at home, they will be more productive at work, and the country will be stronger as a result.

But we have to finish the job and balance the budget. The new balanced budget agreement continues the strategy of cut, invest, and grow. Its centerpiece is education and investment in people. It has the single largest increase in Federal support for education since the GI bill was passed 50 years ago. Its base is a national commitment that every 8-year-old ought to be able to read independently, every 12-year-old should be computer literate, every 18-year-old should be able to get at least 2 years of higher education, and every worker should be able to keep on learning for a lifetime.

Our program includes the America Reads initiative. We're trying to mobilize a million volunteers to work with schools and parents all across America to make sure every child can read independently. And that's important in a country where we have so many children whose first language is not English. We owe it to them, and goodness knows we need every single one of them—their brains, their spirit, their energy, their self-confidence.

Our technology literacy initiative will work with schools all over the country to hook up every classroom and library to the Internet by the year 2000.

We owe it to our people to make sure that by the year 2000, 2 years of college is just as universal as a high school diploma is today. And the tax incentives in our program will do that. We will open the doors of college to all Americans for the first time in the history of this country.

We also have a proposal to put skill grants in the hands of people who are unemployed or underemployed so they can go to the nearest educational institution of their choice and get the education they need. And we recommend permanent tax deductions for employer contributions to the education of their employees. When a company goes out and invests its money to help their employees continue to be productive, and something that will benefit them whether they stay with that company or move to another one, they ought to be able to get a tax deduction for it. I hope you will support this entire educational initiative. It is good for America.

The second thing we do is recognize our special obligation to help people move from welfare to work. We now require people to do so, if they're able-bodied, within a certain amount of time. But if you're going to require them to do so, you have to protect the children, pay for child care, make sure the jobs are there when the welfare runs out. And that is in our budget, and we are committed to passing it.

The third thing we've agreed on is a tax cut designed to grow the economy, help people get an education, and give middle class families tax relief. We can do a lot of things in that tax cut, and I hope we will. When I became President, for example—we talk about the new economy—there were 3 million people making a living out of their homes. Today, there are over 12 million. Within 5 years, there will be 30 million. We ought to have an adequate home office deduction for those people. We ought to have the kind of small-business credits that will enable them to continue to expand.

I don't know what the final shape of the capital gains cuts will be, but I believe we ought to give more benefits for people who start small business, capitalize them, and then stay with them for 5 or 10 years, and create jobs and do the kind of things that you heard Kristy talking about today. That's what I think we ought to do to benefit people with that tax.

Now, all the countries in the world face the same choices we do. They're having to decide, can they reduce their deficit and still invest in their people, can they target people programs, can they maintain a social safety net? And to be fair, a lot of countries have more generous benefits for child care than we do. They cover all their children with health care, and we're going to cover half of those without insurance in this budget agreement. And I won't rest until we finish the job. They do more than that. Can they still grow their economy and reduce spending? You bet they can. Every single country can have the same impact, but you have to be willing to break through those old myths and old ideas and engage people in a committed process to get to a common goal.

The third thing we had to do that we still are fighting is to reject the false choice between protectionism, on the one hand, and unlimited free trade opening our markets with nothing in return on the other. Protectionism is simply not an option because globalization is irreversible. If we try to close up our economy, we will only hurt ourselves. We have too much to gain from opening markets, and besides, we know we can out-work and out-compete anyone, especially if we maintain our technological edge and educate all our people.

So what are we going to do? Are we going to take the lead, or wait for others to blaze the path and get the primary benefits? We have decided for the last 4 years to take the lead. But we have to decide now, are we going to do more or less to cushion the negative effects of globalization while still opening markets? Are we going to do more or less in trying to push in new areas where other countries are more protectionist than we? Or are we just going to sit around and try to close up our markets?

It seems to me difficult to imagine that this is even a serious debate now. In the last 4½ years, we have become the world's leading exporter. In the last 2 years, over half the new jobs coming into this economy have paid above average wage. And we have the lowest unemployment rate in 24 years. Who could seriously argue that our effort to open markets with 200 trade agreements, the largest number in any period in American history, is ill-advised? I say we should be doing more of it, not less of it. We ought to bear down and charge into the future and embrace the rest of the world.

Do the agreements need to be fair? Do they have to be enforced? Should we be willing to take action if people take advantage of us and don't honor their agreements? You bet. Should we continue to invest in the mobility and skills of those who might be displaced by trade? Absolutely. But should we just turn away from this? No way.

You know that we have to do these things. I also hope you know that we can grow in a way that enhances, not undermines, the global environment. We can grow in a way that strengthens, not weakens, global cooperation for the advancement of people's welfare everywhere, as well as dealing with the common security threats I mentioned a moment ago.

We have chosen to reach outward, not to be afraid of competition, to embrace the possibilities of the global economy, and to work to make sure it works for ordinary American citizens.

Let me just give you one statistic to prove we don't have an option. We are now slightly less than 5 percent [1] of the world's population, but we have slightly more than 20 percent of the world's wealth and income. There is no way to sustain that unless we sell more to the other 95 percent. This is not a matter requiring Einstein to calculate. We cannot afford not to keep reaching out to the rest of the world, and I intend to do it.

Just this morning, we reached agreement with Japan on a process to open their markets to competitive American products like telecommunications and medical equipment as they deregulate at home. Unless you think that will not come to pass, let me say that in the 20 areas where we have specific trade agreements with Japan, American exports have increased over 85 percent in the last 4 years. We can move this process forward, and we have to.

Today, Colorado has 132,000 jobs tied directly to trade—132,000. Almost without exception, they are the good jobs, the high paying jobs that we want to create more of. We must do more of this, not less.

So let me say to all of you, the success of this strategy that we have done together—and it wasn't just what the Government did. The lion's share of the credit goes to the businesses and the working people, to those people who were finding the new technologies, who were applying them, who were pushing the barriers of entrepreneurialism, to the Americans' willingness to take a risk and take a chance and to go out there and compete. We have to give

---

[1] White House correction.

credit to a Federal Reserve policy that supported both growth and low inflation. But if we had not reduced the deficit, expanded trade, and invested in our people, it would not have provided the glue to hold the whole policy together. We need to keep doing this.

America has the lowest unemployment rate in 24 years, the lowest inflation rate in 30 years, the biggest decline in inequality among working families in over 30 years. We are moving in the right direction. In the weeks and months ahead, we have to finish the job. We've got to balance the budget. We have to give—I believe strongly—we have to persuade the Congress to give the President fast-track authority. Every President has had it for the last 23 years. That's a term of art for saying I can go and negotiate a trade agreement with Chile or with Argentina or with Brazil and bring it back to Congress, and they have to vote it up or down, instead of subjecting it to 50,000 amendments which will undermine the agreement. This is very important, and we have nothing to fear from those countries. They are our partners in democracy. They are our partners in opportunity.

The second thing I believe we should do is to maintain our normal trade relations with China. We should not attenuate normal trade relations with a country just because we disagree with it. We should find ways to honestly articulate our disagreements. We should push our ideas forward, but we shouldn't imperil 170,000 American jobs today and a big chunk of America's future, not just our economic future but our ability to work with the largest country in the world in areas from arms control to making peace in Asia to dealing with problems all around the world that we share, like terrorism, by cutting off normal trading relations. We don't do it to other countries with which we disagree; we should not do it with China.

Lastly, let me say that we are uniquely placed to succeed in the global economy in the information age because our ideas and our ideals are being embraced by so many. We were the birthplace of the Internet, the biggest change in communications since the printing press. Our movies and music, our TV programming and software programs animate the lives of people all around the world—witness what goes on in the building behind me.

Much of the science and technology shaping the future is made in America. Perhaps most important, we are the most diverse large democracy in the world. There is somebody here from everywhere. Five of our school districts already have children from over 100 different racial and ethnic groups. Within 2 years, there will be 12. Within 3 years, our largest State, California, will have no majority race. We've got to learn to live together and work together, which is why I've announced this big initiative on race, and I hope you will all support it. But you have to understand, there's not just a downside here; there is a huge upside. If we're in a global economy, who will do best? The nation that has the globe living inside its borders. That's what America has, and we ought to be proud of it, lift it up, and make the most of it.

And so, my fellow Americans, that's our strategy: balancing the budget, investing in people, making the global economy work for us. That's the strategy we want everyone to embrace. We do not feel threatened by other people's success; their success is ours. And that's what we're going to work on here. Thanks for giving us a chance to do it.

Thank you, and God bless you.

NOTE: The President spoke at 2 p.m. at the National Digital Television Center. In his remarks, he referred to Robert Pinkney and Erica Gadison, students, Curtis Park Technology Center, who introduced the President; Kristy Schloos, chief executive, Schloos Environmental Consulting; Mayor Wellington Webb of Denver, CO, and his wife, Wilma; Gov. Roy Romer of Colorado and his wife, Bea; Leo J. Hindry, president, Tele-Communications, Inc.; and David Beddow, senior vice president, TCI Technology Ventures Inc.

Exchange With Reporters Prior to Discussions With Prime Minister Ryutaro Hashimoto of Japan in Denver, Colorado
June 19, 1997

Southern Baptist Boycott of Disney

Q. Mr. President, are you going to abide by the Southern Baptist vote on boycotting Disney?

President Clinton. No.

Deregulation and Trade

Q. Mr. President, the United States has been urging Japan for a number of years now to try to jump-start its domestic economy. Do you have any confidence that they're likely to be able to do so in a way that would actually improve their domestic economy——

President Clinton. Well, if the Prime Minister's deregulation initiative works, I think it could spark a lot of domestic economic activity and also increase demand in a way that would improve life for Japanese consumers and also help——

Q. Are you going to express displeasure about the trade imbalance figures that came out today?

President Clinton. Well, I wish they weren't so high. But we're going to discuss that. But keep in mind we also have made an agreement today to involve the United States in the process with Japan to evaluate its deregulation initiatives in several areas in terms of how it might affect our bilateral relations. So we're moving in the right direction, and I'm hopeful we can make some progress.

Q. Do you view it as——

Prime Minister Hashimoto. If I may say one word here. About our question, if you look at the situation in the foreign exchange market, the market has been calm, very calm. This is the answer from my side.

Q. Prime Minister Hashimoto, U.S. officials told us that you had reached an agreement with the United States under which the United States would have an advisory role on deregulating certain of Japan's industries. Do you view it as, in any sense, a violation of Japan's economic sovereignty to give the United States such a role? And why did you not insist on parity, that is to say the Japanese have got a role in U.S. deregulation?

Prime Minister Hashimoto. It's not an advisory role. We have no intention of being supervised. Deregulation is a task that we have to embark

upon for ourselves. We're friends, so we already discuss matters with the United States in that kind of process. We made a promise back in Washington, and yesterday we were able to reach an understanding to establish a framework for such a problem. So please have more confidence in the two of us.

Q. Thank you.

[At this point, one group of reporters left the room, and another group entered.]

China's Status in Future Economic Summits

Q. Mr. President, do you think that China should be a member of the summit in the future? If so, what conditions would be there?

President Clinton. Well, the short answer to that question is that these summits have always been summits of market-oriented democracies. And so it would require a whole redefinition of what this process is for a country that doesn't have democratically elected leaders to be part of it. What I do believe is that the United States and Japan should be working together to help to integrate China into the world's economic institutions and to build stable partnerships for peace and prosperity.

Q. Are you going to discuss with the other leaders or Prime Minister Hashimoto this position about China's joining?

President Clinton. The way we have this organized we will be able to discuss whatever we'd like, because we have at least one occasion, and to some extent, two, where we'll be able to sit around and bring up all of our concerns. So the Prime Minister has a lot of interesting things that he wants raised here.

Russia-Japan Territory Dispute

Q. What do you think about the territorial issue between Russia and Japan, and are you going to discuss about this issue with President Yeltsin?

President Clinton. Yes, and I have discussed it on several occasions in the past, always urging Russia to try to resolve this matter with Japan. I believe it's very much in the interest of both Russia and Japan to resolve this matter and to build a strong partnership.

The United States would feel much better about the future of the world knowing that Japan and Russia have the kind of partnership in the East that we have just tried to establish between Russia and Europe and the United States from NATO in the West. And obviously, there will have to be some plan for resolving this, but it will have to be worked out by the Prime Minister and President Yeltsin. But I have raised it before on several occasions.

Q. Would you nominate—[*inaudible*]—to the Ambassador to Japan soon, or discuss with the Prime Minister?

President Clinton. Yes, I hope to do that.

Q. Next week?

President Clinton. I don't know.

Prime Minister Hashimoto. I'm grateful to all the questioning, because you have finished most of the topics that I was going to raise with the President. [*Laughter*] But in order to pre-serve his honor, of course, I have to add some-thing. The President has been raising the issue with President Yeltsin, with the Russians on many occasions about the existence of the terri-torial issue and the urgent need for solving this issue between Japan and Russia. And of course, I sincerely hope that I can get support not only from the President of the United States but also from the other leaders participating in the summit. And I'd like to ask for cooperation from President Clinton on that account, too.

Thank you very much.

NOTE: The exchange began at 3:45 p.m. at the Hyatt Regency/Tech Center. In his remarks, the President referred to President Boris Yeltsin of Russia. Prime Minister Hashimoto spoke in Japa-nese, and his remarks were translated by an inter-preter. A tape was not available for verification of the content of this exchange.

Joint Statement on the U.S.-Japan Enhanced Initiative on Deregulation and Competition Policy
June 19, 1997

I. Basic Principles

A. In today's increasingly integrated world econ-omy, it is becoming more important to address consumers' interests in expanded choices of products and services that are readily available at lower prices, through enhanced competition and improved market access opportunities. With a view to meeting consumers' interests and to improving market access for foreign companies and foreign goods and services, the President and the Prime Minister decided in April 1997 to strengthen the dialogue between and rein-force the efforts of their governments with re-gard to deregulation and competition policy under the U.S.-Japan Framework for a New Economic Partnership ("Framework"). This En-hanced Initiative on Deregulation and Competi-tion Policy ("Enhanced Initiative") is intended to carry out that decision.

B. The objective of the Enhanced Initiative, which will address both sectoral and structural issues, is to conduct a serious exchange of views and to undertake measures, as called for in the Framework, to "address reform of relevant gov-ernment laws, regulations, and guidance which have the effect of substantially impeding market access for competitive goods and services" in order to enhance consumers' interests and to increase efficiency and promote economic activ-ity.

C. The Enhanced Initiative will be carried out through meetings of the High-level Officials Group and expert-level groups, described below, consistent with the principles of the Framework, such as achievement of tangible progress, limit-ing consultations to matters within the scope and responsibility of government, the MFN principle, and the removal of sectoral and struc-tural impediments to expanded international trade and investment flows. In addition, meetings held under this Enhanced Initiative will take place under the basic principle of two-way dialogue.

II. The High-level Officials Group and Reports to the Leaders of the Two Countries

A. A High-level Officials Group will be estab-lished to review and comment on reports by the expert-level groups. The High-level Officials Group will make utmost efforts to resolve any outstanding issues forwarded by the expert-level groups.

B. The High-level Officials Group will be chaired by the Deputy Minister, Ministry of Foreign Affairs (MOFA), and the Deputy USTR. Other principal agencies participating in the expert-level groups as described in Section III will be represented by appropriately ranked officials from the GOJ and the USG.

C. Meetings of the High-level Officials Group will be held once a year, or more frequently as agreed by both sides.

D. The progress under the Enhanced Initiative will be reported to the leaders of the two countries since the strengthening of dialogue on deregulation is based on the decision between the leaders of Japan and the United States, and the promotion of deregulation and active implementation of competition policy are issues of major importance to the GOJ.

III. Expert-level Groups

A. Overview

(1) Expert-level groups will be tasked with fulfilling the objective of the Enhanced Initiative.

(2) Initially, five expert-level groups will be included within the Enhanced Initiative: four sectoral groups—telecommunications, housing, medical devices/pharmaceuticals, and financial services—and the Deregulation and Competition Policy Working Group (the Working Group).

(3) Expert-level groups on other issues may be established or otherwise brought under the Enhanced Initiative in the future as agreed by both sides.

(4) Each experts-level group will decide the schedule and items to be taken up in its group.

(5) Officials in charge of domestic regulations within the scope of each expert-level group will participate as appropriate.

(6) Each expert-level group will report in writing to the High-level Officials Group, unless the expert-level group decides otherwise.

B. Sectoral Groups

The two governments will use existing fora to the extent possible, including the following:

(1) Deregulation in the telecommunications sector, including the implementation of the GATS commitments on basic telecommunications in each country, will be addressed in the existing experts group, co-chaired by MOFA and the Ministry of Post and Telecommunications and by USTR for the USG.

(2) Deregulation in the housing sector will be addressed in an expert-level group at the occasion of the existing wood products subcommittee, chaired by MOFA for the GOJ and USTR for the USG. The housing expert-level group will be co-chaired by MOFA and the Ministry of Construction for the GOJ and by USTR for the USG.

(3) Deregulation in the medical devices/pharmaceuticals sector will be addressed in the existing MOSS medical devices/pharmaceuticals consultations, chaired by the Ministry of Health and Welfare for the GOJ and by the Department of Commerce (DOC) for the USG.

(4) Deregulation in the financial services sector will be addressed in the existing financial services consultations, chaired by the Ministry of Finance (MOF) for the GOJ and by the Department of the Treasury for the USG.

C. Deregulation and Competition Policy Working Group

(1) The two governments will continue to address developments in the deregulation process within the Deregulation and Competition Policy Working Group (the Working Group), chaired by MOFA for the GOJ and by USTR and the Department of Justice (DOJ) for the USG.

(2) Cross-sectoral issues will be addressed within the Working Group as follows:

—Structural issues such as competition policy and distribution will be addressed in a subgroup that will be established, to be co-chaired by MOFA, MOF, Ministry of International Trade and Industry, Ministry of Transportation, and the Japan Fair Trade Commission for the GOJ and by the Department of State and DOJ for the USG.

—Issues related to transparency and other government practices will be addressed in the Working Group, which, for the purposes of this dialogue will be chaired by MOFA for the GOJ and by DOC for the USG.

(3) Other issues on deregulation which are not discussed in other expert-level groups may also be taken up within the Working Group.

Statement on Signing the Volunteer Protection Act of 1997
June 19, 1997

I have signed into law S. 543, the "Volunteer Protection Act of 1997," which will provide volunteers working for nonprofit and governmental entities certain protections from civil liability. Through citizen service, Americans recognize that we are responsible for one another and that we are members of a true community. All levels of government should encourage citizens to volunteer for service. This bill is a small part of what the Federal Government is doing to help our citizens serve as volunteers.

This legislation is a limited and targeted bill that deals with the specific concerns of individuals serving our communities without compensation. It preserves for the States, the traditional source of tort law, not only the ability to opt out of the bill's provisions in most cases, but also the right to require proper licensing and evidence of financial responsibility. It is important to note that none of the bill's limitations on liability will apply to misconduct that constitutes a crime of violence, an act of international terrorism, or a hate crime, or to misconduct that involves intoxication, drug use, a sexual offense, or the violation of any State or Federal civil rights laws. The bill does not apply to actions on behalf of any organization that engages in hate crimes. Also, S. 543 does not interfere with State law regarding the liability of volunteer organizations.

I remain concerned, however, that S. 543 contains both an absolute prohibition on joint and several liability of volunteers for noneconomic damages and elements of one-way preemption of State law. These are both modifications of tort law that make it harder for innocent injured parties to recover. I emphasize that my signing this specialized and limited bill, which is designed to promote individual citizen service, in no way mitigates the concern about these issues that I raised in my veto message on the product liability bill presented to me last year (H.R. 956, 104th Congress).

On balance, however, S. 543 will encourage volunteer citizen service without unduly affecting the rights of citizens who benefit from such service. I am pleased to have signed the bill.

WILLIAM J. CLINTON

The White House,
June 19, 1997.

NOTE: S. 543, approved June 18, was assigned Public Law No. 105–19.

Exchange With Reporters Prior to Discussions With President Boris Yeltsin of Russia in Denver
June 20, 1997

President Yeltsin. Thank you for your hospitality, for the wonderful hotel and accommodations.

Russian Support for U.N. Resolution on Iraq

Q. President Yeltsin, if we may, we understand the United States and Britain are looking for help on a resolution on Iraq with the United Nations that's being discussed. Is Russia at least willing to promise not to veto the resolution?

President Yeltsin. I'm prepared to block my answer to your question. [*Laughter*]

Russian Role in Group of Eight

Q. Mr. President, will the United States support expansion of the G–7 to a G–8 to include Russia?

President Clinton. Well, Russia is fully included. This is the first time we've ever had a meeting where the Russians were here from the beginning to the end. And we also have another happy development today: When we were in Helsinki I pledged to President Yeltsin that I would do my best to see Russia be admitted into the Paris Club within the year, and Russia and the Paris Club have just completed their negotiations, which means that now Russia will be a partner with the other members in trying to help promote the global economic growth by relieving the burden of the debt on developing countries that—[inaudible]—so what you see here is a sweeping—[inaudible]—Russia—[inaudible]—networks in the world in a way that is very positive for the rest of us.

And I must say, in the last 5 years, as Russian participation has steadily increased here, we have seen the agenda of this group broaden dramatically, and because Russia is a partner, we can talk about, for example, what we can do together to prevent the inappropriate spread of nuclear materials, and we can work together on a whole range of other options.

So I'm very positive about this and very pleased with this summit and pleased with the emergence of Russia as a leader in all these world institutions. It's a great tribute I think to President Yeltsin's leadership and to the commitment of the Russian people to democracy and reform.

Proposed Tobacco Agreement

Q. Mr. President, is there a tobacco settlement? Are you happy with it?

President Clinton. I don't believe it's been announced yet. I don't know that a settlement has been reached.

Q. But you've been briefed, sir?

President Clinton. Well, I've been generally briefed that they're approaching a settlement. But if a settlement, in fact, is announced today, then I'll make a statement about it. Until there is I don't want to make a statement.

Q. Would you intervene if there's a problem over regulation? What is your feelings——

President Clinton. Let's wait and see if they reach an agreement. If there is an agreement, I'll make a statement. I don't know that there is one.

[*At this point, one group of reporters left the room, and another group entered. When the sec-* *ond group of reporters had gathered, a question was asked and answered in Russian, and a translation was not provided.*]

Russian Role in Group of Eight

President Clinton. Let me say that until you asked that question, no one had ever suggested to me that there would ever be a time when Russia would not be a full partner in this Group of Eight.

Let me just remind you that over the last few years, as the participation of Russia in this group has grown to this moment, when for the first time we are here together from beginning to end and participating in only one press conference together and speaking with one voice—and as I'm sure you probably know, Russia has reached an agreement to join the Paris Club—it has enabled this body to go from a purely economic focus to deal with the common challenges that we have in the world we're about to enter and the one we face today.

For example, the work we're doing in nuclear cooperation would be impossible if Russia were not our partner here. And there are many other things that we're going to do together. So I think that this is a cause for celebration not only in Russia but in the other countries here.

Let me just say one final thing. I consider this day and all these things that are happening that are positive a tribute, first of all, to the support of the Russian people for democracy and reform and, second, to the unusual combination of vision and persistence that President Yeltsin has displayed over so many years. It's quite a hopeful moment for the world, I think, and I give him a lot of credit.

Thank you.

NOTE: The exchange spoke at 1:03 p.m. at the Brown Palace Hotel. President Yeltsin spoke in Russian, and his remarks were translated by an interpreter.

Remarks Prior to Discussions With President Jacques Chirac of France and an Exchange With Reporters in Denver
June 20, 1997

Proposed Tobacco Agreement

President Clinton. Let me say, first of all, I'm delighted to see President Chirac again, and I want to compliment him again on his leadership in Paris recently when we signed the NATO-Russia Founding Act. I have asked for his indulgence so that I can make a brief statement about the settlement which was announced in the tobacco case.

You all remember that it was, I think, a little less than a year ago that the Food and Drug Administration announced its proposed rule to restrain the marketing, access, and sales of tobacco to children in the United States. The jurisdiction of the FDA subsequently was upheld in court, and I believe that it was those developments which gave rise to the willingness of tobacco companies to engage in talks with the States and the other parties.

They have now reached a proposed settlement. And the first thing I'd like to do is to compliment the attorneys general and the others who were involved in the suit for their work to advance the cause of protecting the public health and protecting our children. Now what we have to do is to subject this proposed agreement to strict scrutiny.

I have asked my Domestic Policy Adviser, Bruce Reed, and Secretary Shalala to head up an administration team to review this agreement very, very carefully. And they will do that in a matter of weeks, not months. But I want them to take an adequate amount of time.

And I want to assure you that my standard will be what it always has been: We must judge this agreement based on whether it advances the public health and will reduce the number of children who are smoking cigarettes. And we will look at it from that point of view. But I do want to congratulate the parties for reaching this agreement, and I'm looking forward to looking into it.

Q. What's your first take on it, Mr. President? Does it look pretty good, or are there certain areas that you have reservations—[*inaudible*]?

President Clinton. Well, what—the money— of course, it's an enormous amount of money. And apparently, quite a bit was added just in

the last few days. I don't know much more about it than that. I would say this—what I want to look at is two things, principally, from the—[*inaudible*]—point of view: What is the scope of the FDA's jurisdiction? What is the capacity of the FDA, for example, to deal with nicotine levels in cigarettes, things of that kind? And then the second issue is, how is this money going to be paid in and spent over this period of time? What is the spending? Will it really advance the public health?

And of course, then there's some other non-financial issues: What are the nature of the warnings that they've agreed to? I've heard a little about that. But I have had no opportunity to really even see a summary of this agreement. So the number one thing for us would be the scope and nature of the FDA jurisdiction and then how will the money be spent? Will it really advance the public health?

Thank you.

Romania and NATO Expansion

Q. President Chirac, what is your position, and will you be talking to President Clinton about Romania's membership in NATO? Would you prefer Romania to be allowed into NATO right now?

President Chirac. I think it's in the interest of the world and in the interest of Romania to be part of the first set of countries admitted into expanded NATO, and I will certainly be presenting this viewpoint, which I think is fair and normal.

Middle East Peace Process

Q. Mr. President, you evidently got a bad report from President Mubarak on Mideast peacemaking. Are you bringing some urgent message to the President that the U.S. should redouble its efforts? Are you unhappy with the slow state of play?

President Chirac. This is a subject that I will be discussing with President Clinton. I am, in fact, worried about the situation in the Middle East.

[*At this point, one group of reporters left the room, and another group entered.*]

Q. Mr. President, can we ask you a question, please?

Visit of President Chirac

President Clinton. Yes. Before you do, let me say, first, I want to welcome President Chirac to the United States again and thank him for the wonderful job that he did in hosting the NATO meeting in Paris where we announced the historic partnership with Russia. I would also like to thank him for the work that we are doing together in so many parts of the world and especially on behalf of the American people to thank him for the help that France gave in the evacuation of American citizens in Brazzaville. We were very grateful for that.

The European Economy

Q. I would like to ask you, what's going to be your message to the French and to the Europeans regarding the economy? Do you have something special to say about how to have a better economy for Europe?

President Clinton. I don't think there is a uniform answer for one country you can apply to another. But I think that the trick is how do you have enough fiscal discipline and flexibility to grow jobs and have economic growth while still preserving an adequate safety net for people who deserve their support.

You know, the French have a lot of things that we Americans admire, a wonderful network of child care, for example, for working families, a provision for health insurance for all families. The question is, how can you preserve the essentials that make a society whole and give it integrity and have it be open and flexible enough to grow?

And this question will have to be answered a little differently, I think, in every country. But perhaps if we all work together in good faith, we can all make progress. The United States has a very great interest in economic growth in France and, indeed, in Europe at large. I have always supported that.

Africa

Q. Mr. President, are you planning, with President Chirac, are both of you trying to reshuffle the cards in Africa?

President Clinton. Well, I have always been impressed with President Chirac's leadership in Africa and his passionate devotion to it. And I can tell you that in every private conversation we've ever had that lasted more than 30 seconds, he's brought Africa up.

We have a proposal. We hope we can work together as we have in different ways in emergencies, in Sierra Leone, in Brazzaville, or the former Zaire. We hope we can work together to really do something for Africa.

You know, there are several countries in Africa that had growth rates of over 7 percent last year, 48 democracies now, and the rest of the world simply can't walk away from it. We need a balance of aid and trade. And we are prepared in the United States to do more. France has always been a leader, and I hope that together we can persuade other countries to join us.

NATO Expansion

Q. Do you think that it's possible to get an agreement of expansion of NATO with President Clinton before the Madrid summit? Is that possible?

President Chirac. I hope so, and I believe so.

President Clinton. Thank you.

NOTE: The President spoke at 2:50 p.m. at the Brown Palace Hotel. President Chirac spoke in French, and his remarks were translated by an interpreter.

Exchange With Reporters Prior to Discussions With Prime Minister Romano Prodi of Italy in Denver
June 20, 1997

Proposed Tobacco Agreement

Q. Mr. President, could we ask you one question again—I'm sorry—on tobacco? Apparently, Mr. Kessler is already a little bit skeptical about the agreement, particularly as it concerns regulating nicotine levels. Could the White House be in a position of rejecting this agreement? What are your concerns over nicotine levels?

President Clinton. Well, of course we could. We could be in a position of rejecting it or accepting it; I haven't seen it yet.

I received a letter—I was told that I received a letter after I left to come out here, from Dr. Kessler and Dr. Koop, both of whom, as you know, have worked with me very closely on this issue, asking for a reasonable amount of time for them to evaluate this. And I think that they should evaluate it, and of course I care very deeply about what they say. I have worked with them on a whole range of issues. And we want to see what it says.

The test should be, does it preserve clear and unambiguous jurisdiction for the FDA in important areas, and is the money spent in an appropriate way so that we advance the protection of public health and reduce children smoking? That's it. It's a simple test for me and I—but I can't comment on it because I haven't seen it. And I think that it's the same for them. You would expect them to put up a few little red flags, but we all ought to—these folks have been working hard and they've done their best, and now we should look at it and make our judgments.

Let me say to the American press, while you're here, I want to thank Prime Minister Prodi and the members of his government for the extraordinary leadership that Italy has shown in the Balkans, working with us in Bosnia, being a very effective member of the contact group, providing support for American actions there, without which we would not have been able to proceed, and then, most recently, for really an almost unprecedented effort to lead a multinational force in Albania. I will predict to you that in future years we will look back on this Italian effort and see it as a real watershed in European leadership for promoting security and minimizing disruption. I just wanted to thank him and say that to you, sir.

Prime Minister Prodi. Thank you.

Bosnia and Albania

Q. Mr. Prodi, on Bosnia, do you believe that the multinational force should stay after 1998? Do you have any concerns that fighting will still break out?

Prime Minister Prodi. I have some concerns, but we shall talk about that in our conversation. And of course, the Bosnian situation is very complex and a program to end it in a short time is not easy to solve. But we came here just to talk of this problem.

Q. Thank you.

[*At this point, one group of reporters left the room, and another group entered.*]

President Clinton. I would like to say that it's a great honor for us to have Prime Minister Prodi and the distinguished members of his government here. And I want to also say that the United States is deeply grateful for Italy's leadership in promoting peace in the Balkans, especially the work that we have done together in Bosnia. The United States could not have done its job in Bosnia without the support of Italy.

And I am especially grateful for the leadership that Italy has shown in Albania. It is an almost unprecedented effort to put together a European initiative to minimize the troubles of Albania, which are the kinds of things that we will be dealing with for a long time. And I believe that in years to come, we will look back on the Italian effort here as a dramatic historic breakthrough in the capacity of the European nations to promote peace and deal with difficulties.

NOTE: The exchange began at 4:25 p.m. at the Brown Palace Hotel. In his remarks, the President referred to David A. Kessler, former Commissioner of Food and Drugs, and C. Everett Koop, former Surgeon General.

Statement on the Proposed Tobacco Agreement
June 20, 1997

Less than one year ago, my administration announced an historic rule to protect children

from the harm caused by tobacco products. Two months ago, a court in North Carolina issued a landmark ruling confirming my decision that the Food and Drug Administration has authority to regulate tobacco products to protect our children's health. These victories for the public health drove the tobacco companies to the bargaining table and extracted concessions from them that would have been unimaginable just a short time ago.

I commend the attorneys general and other people working with them, including children's health leaders, for their hard work in negotiating this agreement in a way that seeks to advance our struggle to protect the health of children against the dangers of tobacco. They deserve our thanks for doing so.

We must now carefully consider whether approving this proposed settlement will protect the public health—and particularly our children's health—to the greatest extent possible. Until now, we have not had the opportunity to review the actual terms of the agreement, and we have

not concluded whether it is in the best interests of the public health. Over the next several weeks, we will undertake a thorough public health review. I am asking Bruce Reed, my Domestic Policy Adviser—along with Donna Shalala, Secretary of the Department of Health and Human Services—to engage in extensive consultations with the public health community and others to subject this agreement to the strictest scrutiny. They will report to me on whether this agreement represents the best means of protecting the Nation's public health interests.

In the meantime, we will fight as hard as ever to ensure that the FDA rule stands. Each day, 3,000 young people become regular smokers; 1,000 of them will have their lives cut short as a result. Protecting the health of the public and these children will be our measure of this proposed agreement.

Statement on the European Union-United States Mutual Recognition Agreements
June 20, 1997

I am pleased the United States and the European Union have initialed in Denver today landmark agreements that represent a new level of transatlantic cooperation. These accords will reduce trade barriers, increase U.S. exports, and promote more efficient regulation in sectors that account for approximately $50 billion in two-way trade between the United States and Europe, including telecommunications equipment, information technology, medical devices, and pharmaceuticals.

The Mutual Recognition Agreements will eliminate the need for duplicative testing, inspection, or certification of products destined for trade on each side of the Atlantic, while protecting the health and safety of consumers on both sides of the Atlantic. By their very nature, these accords represent and require the highest level political, economic, and regulatory

cooperation between nations. When implemented, this package will serve to increase U.S. exports by saving manufacturers up to 10 percent of the cost of delivering U.S. exports to Europe and enhance transatlantic cooperation to protect the health and safety of our peoples. This is a good agreement for the American people and is good news for manufacturers, workers, and consumers in the United States and Europe.

I want to thank the TransAtlantic Business Dialogue for its important role in supporting these negotiations. I also want to congratulate Commerce Secretary William Daley, U.S. Trade Representative Charlene Barshefsky, Under Secretary of State Stuart Eizenstat, and all the U.S. agencies that showed creativity and persistence in forging agreements that will help shape the transatlantic marketplace.

Joint Statement by France, Russia, and the United States on the Nagorno-Karabakh Conflict
June 20, 1997

On the occasion of our meeting in Denver, we, the Presidents of France, the Russian Federation and the United States of America, as leaders of the countries that co-chair the OSCE Minsk Conference on Nagorno-Karabakh, express our deep concern over the continuing Nagorno-Karabakh conflict. It has seriously undermined economic and social development and prosperity throughout the Caucasus region. It has created thousands of victims. Over a million people are still displaced from their homes.

We are encouraged by the continued observance of the cease-fire. However, the cease-fire by itself is insufficient. Without progress toward a durable settlement, the cease-fire could break down. The international community thus has repeatedly called for a settlement; we believe there should be no delay in establishing a stable and lasting peace in the region.

To that end we have committed our countries to work closely together to assist the efforts of the parties to negotiate a resolution to the conflict. The French, Russian, and U.S. Co-Chairs of the OSCE Minsk Conference have presented a new proposal for a comprehensive settlement, taking into consideration the legitimate interests and concerns of all parties. It represents an appropriate basis for achieving a mutual agreement. The primary responsibility, however, rests with the parties and their leaders. We call upon them to take a positive approach, to build upon this proposal and to negotiate an early settlement.

Letter to Congressional Leaders on the Deployment of United States Military Forces for Stabilization of the Balkan Peace Process
June 20, 1997

Dear Mr. Speaker: (*Dear Mr. President:*)

In my report to the Congress of December 20, 1996, I provided further information on the deployment of combat-equipped U.S. Armed Forces to Bosnia and other states in the region in order to participate in and support the North Atlantic Treaty Organization (NATO)-led Stabilization Force (SFOR), and on the beginning of the withdrawal of the NATO-led Implementation Force (IFOR), which completed its mission and transferred authority to the SFOR on December 20, 1996. I am providing this supplemental report, consistent with the War Powers Resolution, to help ensure that the Congress is kept fully informed on continued U.S. contributions in support of peacekeeping efforts in the former Yugoslavia.

We continue to work in concert with others in the international community to encourage the parties to fulfill their commitments under the Dayton Peace Agreement and to build on the gains achieved over the last 18 months. It remains in the United States national interest to help bring peace to Bosnia, both for humanitarian reasons and to arrest the dangers the fighting in Bosnia represented to security and stability in Europe generally. Through American leadership and in conjunction with our NATO allies and other countries, we have seen real and continued progress toward sustainable peace in Bosnia. We have also made it clear to the former warring parties that it is they who are ultimately responsible for implementing the Peace Agreement.

The United Nations Security Council authorized member states to establish the follow-on force in United Nations Security Council Resolution 1088 of December 12, 1996. The SFOR's tasks are to deter or prevent a resumption of hostilities or new threats to peace, to consolidate IFOR's achievements and to promote a climate in which the civilian-led peace process can go forward. Subject to this primary mission, SFOR will provide selective support, within its capabilities, to civilian organizations implementing the Dayton Peace Agreement. The parties to the

Peace Agreement have all confirmed to NATO their support for the SFOR mission. In particular, the leaders of Bosnia and Herzegovina have indicated that they welcome NATO's planned 18-month SFOR mission to be formally reviewed at 6 and 12 months with a view to shifting the focus from stabilization to deterrence, reducing the force's presence and completing the mission by June 1998. The first such review is to be conducted on June 26, 1997.

United States force contribution to SFOR in Bosnia currently is approximately 8,500, roughly half the size of the force deployed with IFOR at the peak of its strength. Many of the U.S. forces participating in SFOR are U.S. Army forces that were stationed in Germany. Other participating U.S. forces include special operations forces, airfield operations support forces, air forces, and reserve personnel. An amphibious force is normally in reserve in the Mediterranean Sea, and a carrier battle group remains available to provide support for air operations.

All NATO nations and 21 others, including Russia, have provided troops or other support to SFOR. Most U.S. troops are assigned to Multinational Division, North, centered around the city of Tuzla. In addition, approximately 2,800 U.S. troops are deployed to Hungary, Croatia, Italy, and other states in the region in order to provide logistical and other support to SFOR. Since the transfer of authority from IFOR to SFOR on December 20, 1996, U.S. forces sustained a total of two fatalities, neither of which was combat-related. Four American service members were also injured in accidents. As with the U.S. forces, traffic accidents, landmines, and other accidents were the primary causes of injury to SFOR personnel.

A U.S. Army contingent remains deployed in the Former Yugoslav Republic of Macedonia as part of the United Nations Preventive Deployment Force (UNPREDEP). This U.N. peacekeeping force observes and monitors conditions along the border with the Federal Republic of Yugoslavia and Albania, effectively contributing to the stability of the region. Several U.S. Army support helicopters are also deployed to provide support to U.S. forces and UNPREDEP as required. Most of the approximately 500 U.S. soldiers participating in these missions are assigned to the 2nd Battalion, 37th Armor, 1st Armored Division. A small contingent of U.S. military personnel is also serving in Croatia in direct support of the Transitional Administrator of the United Nations Transitional Administration in Eastern Slovenia.

I have directed the participation of U.S. Armed Forces in these operations pursuant to my constitutional authority to conduct U.S. foreign relations and as Commander in Chief and Chief Executive, and in accordance with various statutory authorities. I am providing this report as part of my efforts to keep the Congress fully informed about developments in Bosnia and other states in the region. I will continue to consult closely with the Congress regarding our efforts to foster peace and stability in the former Yugoslavia.

Sincerely,

WILLIAM J. CLINTON

NOTE: Identical letters were sent to Newt Gingrich, Speaker of the House of Representatives, and Strom Thurmond, President pro tempore of the Senate.

Remarks at the Opening of the First Working Session of the Summit of the Eight in Denver
June 21, 1997

I'm very pleased to welcome my fellow leaders to Denver as we open this Summit of the Eight. And I want to say a special welcome to our friend President Yeltsin, who joins us for the first time from the beginning to the end of this meeting. Russia's growing role in the shared world of market democracies reflects the progress and the potential of this age.

We meet at a moment of remarkable possibility for our nations and for the world. Powerful forces are drawing our nations closer together, delivering the promise of prosperity and security to more people than ever, changes that, like this, bring vast opportunities as we approach the new century, but we also know they bring new challenges. Our citizens must have the skills they need to succeed in a fast-changing economy. And as barriers fall, problems that start in one country can spread quickly to another, whether they are currency crises, organized crime, or outbreaks of deadly diseases.

Our challenge in this moment of peace and stability is to organize ourselves for the future, to make change work for us, not against us. We must seize the opportunities of the global economy to expand our own prosperity, bring in other nations that want to share in its benefits, and work together to meet the new threats. None of our nations can meet these challenges alone, and more than ever our summit process is an engine of common progress.

Over the next 2 days, we'll discuss the best ways to deepen and extend the benefits of the 21st century marketplace, to help our societies thrive as our populations grow older, to strengthen further the stability of the world financial system, to generate economic growth throughout the world. We'll continue our efforts to bring new partners in Africa and elsewhere into the community of market democracies. And we'll strengthen our growing cooperation to meet threats to our common security, such as our rapid response network to fight nuclear smuggling, common endeavors to combat terrorism, and initiatives to stem infectious disease, including the search for an AIDS vaccine.

It is fitting that we meet in a public library, a place where people come together to learn and share ideas without regard to their own backgrounds. If we pool our strength, we can achieve great things for all our people and the world. I look forward to addressing those challenges with my fellow leaders over the next few days, and again, I welcome them to Denver.

Thank you very much.

NOTE: The President spoke at 9:10 a.m. at the Denver Public Library. In his remarks, he referred to President Boris Yeltsin of Russia.

The President's Radio Address
June 21, 1997

Good morning. I'm speaking to you today from Denver, Colorado, where the leaders of the world's top industrial democracies are about to begin our Summit of the Eight. Over the next 2 days, the eyes of the world will be on Denver and on America, and we'll all have a lot to be proud of.

Our economy is the healthiest in a generation and the strongest in the world, with the lowest unemployment in 24 years, the lowest inflation in 30 years, the biggest decline in inequality among our working families since the 1960's, and over 12 million new jobs. Our exports are at an all time high. We cleared a new path to prosperity and security with a strategy of reducing the deficit, investing in our people, and opening the world to our trade. Now America is poised to lead in the 21st century, as we have in the 20th century, about to end.

Today I want to talk about why this summit is important to our Nation and our people and what we'll be working to achieve here. The leaders of the United States, Canada, France, Germany, Italy, the United Kingdom, Japan, the European Union, and Russia will gather shoulder to shoulder around the table. The very fact that we're gathering speaks volumes about the world today. Our homelands are thousands of miles apart, but the rise of the global economy, spurred by revolutions in technology, transportation, and communications has brought us all closer together. And the fact that this is the very first of these annual summits where a democratically elected leader of Russia joins us from beginning to end reflects just how far we've come from the days of the cold war. This moment of possibilities creates vast opportunities for all our people. Ideas, goods and services, technology, and capital fly across borders faster than ever, enriching our lives in many ways and contributing to our prosperity.

But while progress spreads quickly in our global neighborhood, problems can, too. A currency crisis in one country can send shock waves far beyond its borders, endangering jobs and stability in a completely different part of the world. Modern technology and more open borders help businesses to prosper, but they also help terrorists and drug traffickers and criminals to organize their plans and hide their tracks. Greater international travel and commerce exposes our people to new cultures and opportunities, but they also expose us to the spread of dangerous diseases from which no nation is immune. And erosion of environmental quality in one country can contribute to global problems which degrade the quality of life for all of us.

Now, we've worked hard over the last 4 years to take common action against these common threats and to make this common action a central part of our summits. Here in Denver, we'll announce further steps to protect our citizens against them. Two years ago, when we met in Halifax, Canada, we agreed to work together to help prevent financial crises from occurring and to keep them from spreading if they do. Since then, our finance ministers have agreed that we should create a global network of banking and marketing officials to monitor financial policies and police risky practices. Our cooperation will help to prevent a financial shock in a foreign country from threatening prosperity here at home.

We're also working with the developing countries to help them to adopt sound financial practices so that their markets work smoothly and they can build stable businesses and attract trade and investment. These emerging economies are the fastest growing in the world. Helping them to build their prosperity means greater opportunities for American exports and more good American jobs.

We'll also continue to advance our fight against new forces of destruction that have no regard for borders. Last year, when we met in Lyons, France, we agreed on a series of measures to combat terrorism and organized crime. Since then we've actually implemented concrete steps, from improving airline security to denying safe haven for criminals. We've also made significant progress in bolstering the safety

and security of nuclear materials, something that simply wouldn't have been possible without Russia as a partner. Together, the eight are working to tighten the management of plutonium from dismantled nuclear warheads to keep them from falling into the wrong hands. To better prevent and investigate nuclear smuggling incidents, we set up a rapid response network, stepped up law enforcement intelligence and customs cooperation, and improved our nuclear forensics capabilities so that we can identify the sources of smuggled nuclear materials. Soon, more than 20 additional countries in Europe and central Asia will be joining us in these common endeavors.

This year, we'll be taking on another global challenge: the spread of infectious disease. Many people believe this will be one of the most serious problems of the 21st century. I will press here for an agreement to develop together a global disease surveillance network to provide early warning of outbreaks so that we can respond quickly and effectively, to coordinate that response so that we get the right medicines where they're needed as fast as possible, and to strengthen our public health systems, especially those in the developing world. I will also urge my fellow leaders to join America in a vigorous search for an HIV/AIDS vaccine, as I called for at Morgan State University in Maryland last month.

Together, the meeting of the eight is part of the larger effort we're making to organize the world to deal with the global challenges in the century ahead. We know that if we pool our strength, our experience, and our ideas, we stand a far better chance of success. And for American families, that will mean greater prosperity, greater peace, and greater security for our children.

Thanks for listening.

NOTE: The address was recorded at 4:30 p.m. on June 20 at the press filing center in Denver, CO, for broadcast at 10:06 a.m. on June 21.

Exchange With Reporters Prior to Discussions With Prime Minister Tony Blair of the United Kingdom in Denver
June 21, 1997

Northern Ireland Peace Process

Q. [Inaudible]—reaction to the bombing today, especially after you offered Sinn Fein a place at the table?

Prime Minister Blair. Well, obviously, this is another appalling terrorist act, and it simply underlines the need for peace and to move this process forward, and that the longer we go on with these acts of terrorism, the less prospect there is of doing what everyone in Northern Ireland wants to happen, which is to get a lasting political settlement based on democratic and nonviolent means. And what is essential is for Sinn Fein and everyone else to realize that if they want to be part of that process, they have got to engage in purely democratic means. Now, that has been clear all the way through, it is clear now, and it is not right to make the people of Northern Ireland wait any longer for the lasting political settlement they want to achieve.

Q. Mr. President, do you have a reaction?

Q. Do you have any specific information— you say it was an act of terrorism—specific information on who caused it?

President Clinton. Let me answer your question first. First of all, you know this is something that I attach great importance to, and I have been very encouraged by the approach that Prime Minister Blair has made. We have supported consistently the efforts of the British and the Irish Governments to bring peace.

I was appalled at the murders of the two officers just a few days ago. I deplore this act today. But I, frankly, think now the ball is in Sinn Fein's court. We all have to decide now; everybody has decisions to make in life. And their decision is, are they going to be part of this peace process, or not? And so I hope the answer will be yes.

I know what the people want. Just before I came out here I had two schoolteachers from Northern Ireland, one Catholic, one Protestant, who had received awards for working for peace. That's what the people want. That's the human face of this. And I think the politicians need to get in gear and give the people the peace they want.

Prime Minister Blair. What we are doing——

Q. Can you confirm that a place was offered——

Prime Minister Blair. Michael [Michael Brunson, Independent Television News], let me just say to you that what we're doing and what we have been doing as a government is simply to try and give expression to the will of the overwhelming majority of people in Northern Ireland who want a decent, lasting, peaceful settlement to the problems there. And that chance is there, and we can do it. And I think enormous good will exists. It exists here in America, with the Irish Government, the British Government—enormous good will exists. And now it is for those people who have been holding up this process to come in and make sure that we get that lasting settlement the people want.

Thank you very much.

President Clinton. We've got to go back to work.

NOTE: The exchange began at 11:44 a.m. at the Denver Public Library. In his remarks, the President referred to teachers Gary Trew and Seamus McNeill, recipients of the President's Prize. A tape was not available for verification of the content of this exchange.

Remarks at the Presentation of the Final Communique of the Summit of the Eight in Denver
June 22, 1997

As I begin, I would like to thank the city of Denver and the people of Colorado for the wonderful work they did to make us feel welcome here. I thank the people who worked on behalf of the United States to put this together, Harold Ickes, Deb Willhite, and our whole team. And most of all, I want to thank my colleagues for their hard work and for the spirit of cooperation that prevailed here in Denver.

We've agreed on new steps to organize our nations to lay a strong foundation in the 21st century, to prepare our people and our economies for the global marketplace, to meet new transnational threats to our security, to integrate new partners into the community of free-market democracies.

Russia's role here at the summit reflects the great strides that Russia has made in its historic transformation. We look forward to Russia's continued leadership and participation, and we thank President Yeltsin for all he has done.

On behalf of my colleagues, I'd like to summarize several key points in our communique. First, as leaders of the world's major industrial democracies, we feel a special responsibility to work together, to seize the opportunities and meet the challenges of the global economy, and to ensure opportunity for all segments of our societies. We explored what we can do to create more jobs for our people, and we look forward to the conferences on employment in Japan this fall and the United Kingdom early next year. We believe we have much to learn from each other. We also discussed the challenges our nations face as our populations grow older and how we can keep our senior citizens living productive lives well into their later years.

Globalization brings with it problems none of us can conquer alone. This year we intensified our common efforts to meet new transnational threats, like environmental degradation, terrorism, drugs, crime, and infectious disease.

We are also determined to do our part to protect our environment for future generations. Among other measures, we recommitted ourselves to the principles of the Rio Summit. We intend to reach an agreement in Kyoto to reduce greenhouse gas emissions to respond to the problem of global warming. We discussed how best to protect the Earth's forests and oceans, and we are clearly committed to doing that together as well.

Last year we adopted an ambitious agenda to fight crime and terrorism. Since then we have taken concrete steps, from improving airline security to denying safe haven for criminals. This year we'll make special efforts to fight high-tech crimes such as those involving computer and telecommunications technology.

We've also made important progress in promoting nuclear safety and security, particularly in combating nuclear smuggling and in managing the growing stockpiles of plutonium from dismantled nuclear warheads.

We launched a new effort to stem the spread of infectious diseases. In the coming year, we'll be working together to improve global surveillance to provide early warning, to better coordinate our responses, and to strengthen public health systems, especially in the developing world. We've also pledged to accelerate our efforts to develop an HIV/AIDS vaccine.

As we move forward with the integration of new democracies and market economies, we're determined that no part of the world will be left behind. We agreed upon a package of political and economic measures to ensure that African nations share with us the benefits of globalization. We've also continued our efforts to strengthen and spread democracy and freedom around the world.

Finally, we discussed a number of political issues of critical importance to our nations, including Bosnia, the Middle East, and Hong Kong. Next week will represent an historic moment as Hong Kong returns to Chinese sovereignty. We reaffirmed our strong interest in Hong Kong's future and our shared conviction on the importance of China's adherence to its commitments under the 1984 agreement. We appreciate in particular the devotion that Prime Minister Blair and his government attach to this endeavor.

As we worked together to promote the progress of market democracies, we reaffirmed our intention to ensure that those states that stand outside our community, such as Iran, Iraq, and Libya, fully adhere to the fundamental norms we all agree should guide us into the next century.

We leave Denver renewed by our strength—the strength of our common efforts to prepare our people to succeed in the global economy and the global society of the 21st century. Again, let me thank my fellow leaders for their extraordinary work. I think it's been a very good summit. And again I thank the people of Denver and Colorado for their hospitality.

Thank you very much.

NOTE: The President spoke at 12:58 p.m. at the Denver Public Library. In his remarks, he referred to Harold Ickes, Director of Summit Affairs; Debbie Willhite, Executive Director of the summit; President Boris Yeltsin of Russia; and Prime Minister Tony Blair of the United Kingdom.

The President's News Conference in Denver
June 22, 1997

The President. Thank you very much. Please be seated. Let me say I have a brief opening statement, and then I will open the floor to questions. I know we also have some members of the international press here, and I'll take several questions from the American press first, and then I'll try to alternate a bit. And I think I have a general idea of where everyone is.

Let me begin by saying that over the past 4 years I have worked with our partners in these summits to focus the major industrial democracies of the world on both the opportunities and the challenges that we face as we move toward the 21st century. Together, we worked to prepare our economies to meet new transnational threats to our security, to integrate new partners into our community of free market democracies.

The summit communique I summarized just a short while ago demonstrates that here in Denver we have actually made real progress on problems that matter to our people. To prevent financial crises from one country from sending shock waves around the world, something we have seen on two different occasions in the last few years, we've strengthened our network of banking and market officials to monitor financial policies and police risky practices.

We moved forward in our fight against new security threats that confront all our people. We intend to step up our collective efforts against the growing international problem of high-tech and computer-related crime. We agreed to work more closely to stem the spread of materials of mass destruction that could be used in terror-

ist attacks. To help ensure that as we dismantle nuclear weapons, dangerous materials don't fall into the wrong hands, we'll tighten control on plutonium stockpiles and establish a rapid response network to prevent nuclear smuggling.

Together, we've begun to tackle another very dangerous threat we'll all face together in the years ahead: infectious diseases that can span the planet in the space of an airline flight. We've agreed to create a global early warning system to detect outbreaks and help us to get the right medicines where they're needed quickly.

And in all of these efforts, we believe we are stronger because we now have Russia as a partner. I'm pleased that for the first time Russia took part in our summit from the start and that this week we reached agreement on Russia's joining the Paris Club for creditor nations—evidence of Russia's emergence as a full member of the community of democracies.

The progress we've made here in Denver demonstrates again what I have said so many times in the last 5 years. In this new era, foreign policy and domestic policy are increasingly intertwined. For us to be strong at home, we must lead in the world. And for us to be able to lead in the world, we must have a strong and dynamic economy at home and a society that is addressing its problems aggressively and effectively.

To continue that path, let me say, there are some things we have to embrace on the homefront and on the international front. First, Congress must pass a balanced budget plan consistent with the agreement we made and with our values. The balanced budget must include a tax cut that is as fair as possible to middle class families and meets their real needs, providing help for education, for childrearing, for buying and selling a home. I will also insist that any tax cut be consistent with a balanced budget over the long run. We cannot afford time-bomb tax cuts that will explode in future years and undo our hard-won progress. This will be a crucial test of our will to continue the economic strategy that has produced American prosperity in the last few years: balancing the budget and investing in our people as we move into a new century.

Second, after our own Independence Day, I will travel abroad for a NATO summit where we'll take a historic step to lock in freedom and stability in Europe. In Madrid, we'll invite the first of Europe's new democracies to join our alliance, to advance our goal of building a continent that is undivided, democratic, and at peace for the first time in history.

Third, we'll move ahead with our leadership of the world economy and with the obligations and the opportunities that come with it. I urge Congress to vote next week to continue normal trade relations with China so that we can maintain our ties with one-quarter of the world's people, advance human rights and religious freedom there, continue our cooperation for stability on the Korean Peninsula and to prevent the spread of weapons of mass destruction, and keep Hong Kong's economy strong as it reverts to Chinese sovereignty.

Then I will ask Congress for the fast-track authority that every President for two decades has had, to negotiate smart new trade agreements so that we can open new markets in Latin America and Asia to American goods and services to complement the African initiative I announced just a few days ago.

In closing, let me again thank the thousands of people who put this summit together for their hard work. I thank the people of Denver for the warmth of their hospitality, the power of their optimism, and the strength of their example. And especially I want to thank Harold Ickes and Debbie Willhite and our whole team for all the work that they have done over the last several months.

And now I'll be happy to take questions. And I think we'll start with Ken [Ken Bazinet, United Press International].

Bosnia

Q. Mr. President, in the last year there have been various efforts led by the United States to try and move the Balkan States, the former Yugoslav States, into adhering to the Dayton accord. Can you tell us why you believe this summit is, in fact, going to move those leaders to do that? And also, while you have said to try and focus on what's taking place now, can you tell the American people whether or not the U.S. troops will remain in the former Yugoslavia beyond June 1998?

The President. Well, I will reiterate American policy on that. Our policy is that the SFOR mission should be completed by June of '98, and we expect it to be. But to answer your first question, which is the far more important one, I made it very clear that I think that we have all made a terrible mistake, in dealing with Bosnia, to spend all of our time focusing on June of '98 instead of focusing on tomorrow and the day after tomorrow and the day after that.

We have seen some successes in Bosnia not only in the work done by IFOR and SFOR and the absence of bloodshed but in the recent—just in the last few days we've had the Serbs agreeing to proceed with the setup of common economic institutions and to do other things which will make them eligible for economic aid. We expect there to be local elections; Madam Agnelli from Italy is doing a good job in raising the money there to conduct these local elections. And what I urge the parties to do and what our statement reflects here is our determination to spend the next year trying to implement the Dayton accords, and taking each of the seven areas—there are roughly seven areas of activity where Dayton is critical to pulling this together—and try to make headway on all fronts, and especially on the economic front.

We have pledged a lot of money, but we need to release the money as soon as it's pledged if the parties commit to do what they're supposed to do. And I'm convinced that this whole thing is always going to be a race against time and hatred and limitations, to try to get people to feel and visualize the benefits of peace and living together.

I'm not ready to give up on Dayton. I believe in it. And I feel that you will see over the next several months a number of specific examples where the people who are in the Group of Eight are trying to energize this peace process.

Terry [Terence Hunt, Associated Press].

Middle East Peace Process

Q. Mr. President, the communique says that the Middle East peace process faces crisis and that you're determined—all the leaders are determined to reinject momentum into it. The United States has tried. Egypt has recently tried. Yet, the process remains stalled on all fronts. What is it that the United States and all the partners here can do to reinvigorate this process to get things going?

The President. Well, first, let me emphasize something. You should never believe that just because you don't see high-level air transport between Washington and the Middle East that nothing is going on from our point of view. We spend—I spend quite a bit of time on this every single week. And I'm very concerned about what's happened.

But let me say, in a nutshell, here's what we have to find a way to do: We have to find a way to persuade the Palestinians that there is a basis for returning to the negotiating table and that all the final status issues are not going to be resolved out from under them. But we also have to find a way to persuade the Israelis that the Palestinians are serious about security.

In other words, the Palestinians will have to return to security cooperation with the Israelis and will have to manifest an opposition that is clear and unambiguous to terrorism, the unauthorized injury or murder to innocent civilians, and to continuing the peace process. The Israelis, for their part, have got to find specific things that can be done that show that there's a commitment to Oslo in fact, not just in words, and a commitment to getting this process going.

Now, there are several different potential scenarios that might achieve that, and we've been working very hard on trying to figure out what the most effective way to do it is. For all of us who are outsiders, including the United States, it is not always self-evident what the most effective way to exercise whatever influence you have is. And I am prepared to do anything I reasonably can to keep this peace process from going awry. I think that it's in a pivotal moment, and I think that all of the friends of Israel and the Arab States and the Palestinians need to bear down and do what we can to persuade

these people that they need to get back to the work of the peace process.

Gene [Gene Gibbons, Reuters].

China and Hong Kong

Q. Mr. President, even before next week's reversion of Hong Kong to Chinese sovereignty, there are some ominous signs that China plans to roll back some of the rights and freedoms that the people of Hong Kong now enjoy. I know that the communique here in Denver addressed that issue, but what can the United States and the other industrial democracies do if China fails to deliver on the 1984 agreement?

The President. It's interesting, we spent a lot of time talking about that this morning, and mostly we were listening to Prime Minister Blair, who obviously has the highest level of knowledge about this and the deepest experience, and a lot of personal involvement with Hong Kong, I might add.

Our sense is that, obviously, we don't exactly know what will happen, but that we have all committed to work with the British to try to continue to insist on and preserve the integrity of the '84 agreement, and we also do not want to assume the bad faith of the Chinese. I think that would be an error. China made a commitment in 1984, and they asked our country when President Reagan was in office to actually bless or endorse the commitment when China and Great Britain made the commitment to have one China but two systems. And that definition clearly included political as well as economic differences.

You know, I hate—I don't like to answer hypothetical questions, and I think anything we do will only make it worse. I think what we want to do is to encourage the Chinese to remember they have a unique, almost unprecedented place now that is reverting to their sovereignty, and that part of the fabric of what makes Hong Kong work is not just open markets and industrious people and a haven of hope for people who flee the lack of opportunity and often oppression elsewhere, but a lively and open society. And it needs to be maintained, and I hope that it will be.

Yes, Ann [Ann Compton, ABC News].

Proposed Tobacco Agreement

Q. When the tobacco deal was announced, you indicated you'd be listening for reactions from some, like Dr. David Kessler, who said this morning that he finds, in reading the fine print, that there are some hurdles, some impossible burdens. And he called parts of it a step backwards. Is there some way you can assure people that this agreement will not simply be proposed and then die? Is there something your administration can do to follow through to make sure that this represents a time of real change for the tobacco industry?

The President. Yes. I think the answer to that is yes. And let me say, obviously, I have not, myself, had a chance to review this in any detail. Bruce Lindsey has briefed me on its major provisions, and that's why I asked to have the chance to have it reviewed. I don't think any of us—at least, I hope none of us are reviewing it with the view toward either saying we're going to embrace it or kill it, and there's no other opinion.

I was impressed by some of the comments of Members of Congress in both parties that they were hoping that if they couldn't completely embrace it, that at least it could be salvaged; and by Attorney General Moore from Mississippi, who said that he thought the agreement would come apart if what he called—I think he said—radical changes or something were made in it, which would undermine its fundamental understandings.

But I think—here's bottom line for me: When two sides make an agreement—an honorable, principled agreement—they obviously both conclude that it's in their interest to make the agreement. And what we have to—those of us who are on the outside of this who represent the public interests have to do is to make sure that those things which made the tobacco interests conclude that it was in their interest to make the agreement do not compromise or undermine our obligation and our opportunity to protect the public health and especially children's health and reduce child smoking.

Now, that will particularly bear on the specific language relating to the jurisdiction of the Federal Food and Drug Administration and exactly what it means. And I just urge you all to read it carefully. We're going to be reading it carefully. And we're going to read it carefully against what the tobacco companies have already admitted about the addictive qualities of nicotine and what was known.

So you have to not only look at the legal language, but you have to look at the factual basis that's out here. We're going to work

through. But I can tell you, I'm going to do my best to see that this whole endeavor, which is massive, results in something positive for the American people. But we have to have those tests: public health, child smoking.

George [George Condon, Copley News Service].

Q. Mr. President——

The President. Just a minute, just a minute. I called on this man; then I'll call—just hold on.

NATO Expansion

Q. Mr. President, as you prepare to leave for Madrid, NATO is undergoing a rather public division over the number of nations that should be asked to join. Were you able to bridge the gap here at all with President Chirac or the Prime Minister of Italy? And secondly, do you see any lasting damage to the alliance from this split?

The President. I think my answer would be no to both questions. That is, we still have differences of opinion about whether in the first round there should be three or five nations admitted, or some favor four. But I do not expect it to do lasting damage to the alliance, if—this is a big "if"—we maintain the integrity of the process we set up; that is, if we say this is not the first entrance, there will be an open door, and if we continue to intensify the work of the Partnership For Peace, which has been wildly popular with all its members, and we have an extra outreach to those who are good prospective members.

For example, if you just take the two countries in question, Romania and Slovenia, I believe that they are excellent candidates for admission to NATO membership if they stay on the path of reform and they continue to build up their partnerships with us militarily through the Partnership For Peace, preserve democracy. Romania has resolved its problems with Hungary, has two Hungarians in the Cabinet. It's the second biggest country in Central and Eastern Europe. Slovenia is a key nation geographically, if for no other reason, between Italy and some of the other countries in Europe and Hungary and some of the difficult spots that we're likely to have trouble in.

So I think that there is not as much difference over where we think this will be 10 years from now as there is how we should proceed now. And I'm hoping we can resolve these things.

I'm confident that our position is the prudent, the disciplined, and the right one for this military alliance at this moment. But I don't think we should in any way discourage or dash the hopes of two countries that clearly are moving in the right direction and strategically located in an area where it will be very important for NATO to maintain stability in the years ahead.

Now go ahead.

North Korea

Q. Mr. President, 2 days ago the representative for the Red Cross in Pyongyang announced that there were about 5 million North Koreans in imminent danger of starvation. I was wondering if this issue was discussed at the meetings in the last 2 days and if you, as chairman of the G–7, cannot mobilize the other countries to contribute what is necessary and to create the logistical means of getting it to North Korea before a catastrophe hits.

The President. Yes, I discussed this actually personally, one on one, with a number of the leaders. And the United States has pledged more food aid to North Korea. I am very concerned about it as an humanitarian matter, and I believe you will see more action on this front. And I'm certainly committed to doing it; I'm deeply troubled.

And I also would say that in addition to that, we're hopeful that the latest statements by the North Koreans indicating that we can have a meeting to discuss how to get into the four-party talks with the Chinese and the South Koreans—that's also very hopeful. But I'm profoundly troubled by the reports that I have read about the scope of human suffering in North Korea. And whenever we've been asked, we've come up with some more food. But I'd like for us to do more, and I think you'll see these other countries willing to do more as well.

John [John Donvan, ABC News].

China

Q. Mr. President, your administration has been criticized for cutting China a break in terms of how you deal with it, using a policy of constructive engagement, that there's a double standard. You are tougher on other countries for similar transgressions, but with China, you think talk is best. The basic criticism comes down to the notion that for the sake of trade, the administration will compromise its principles. Can you respond to that, please?

The President. Yes. I don't think it's fair. For example, if you look at our policy toward Burma which, unlike China, had a democratically elected government and reversed it, and represents the most severe abuses of political and civil rights that we've dealt with recently, in terms of our actions, we've been for sanctions against Burma, but we haven't repealed MFN.

And when you look at China, we still have Tiananmen Square sanctions on China that we haven't gotten rid of. We have given up a lot of business in China, clearly—and they've made it clear that we have—by continuing to press our human rights concerns in the human rights forum. What we don't believe would be fruitful is to withdraw normal trading status from China—something we have with virtually every country in the world—in a way that would estrange us further from them, prevent us from working together on problems like North Korea, weapons proliferation, and other issues, and endanger the ability of the United States to be a partner with China in the 21st century. That's what we don't believe.

We have paid quite a price from time to time for our insistence on advancing human rights. I just don't think taking normal trading status away from them is much of a way to influence them over the long run. I think it's a mistake.

Wolf [Wolf Blitzer, CNN].

Medicare

Q. Mr. President, the Senate Finance Committee, including the Democrats, by and large, supported legislation they want you to sign that would do two very dramatic things to Medicare: raise the eligibility age from 65 to 67 and impose what's called means testing, making sure that millionaires and richer Medicare recipients pay more for the premiums than poorer Medicare recipients. Could you tell us specifically right now how you will come down on these two very sensitive, politically sensitive issues?

The President. Well, let's take them differently—separately. First of all, both of them are clearly outside the budget agreement. And if—because I felt so strongly about honoring the budget agreement, I did not try to help the advocates of the Kennedy-Hatch bill pass their child health plan, even though I strongly support it. I didn't try to help them pass it because I wanted to honor the budget agreement. So I think I can be forgiven for asking that other people honor the agreement if they voted for it. Now, if any of these Senators didn't vote for it, I can't expect them to honor it. But if they voted for it, it was very specific. And that's what concerns me about it.

Now, let's take them independently on their merits, because I wouldn't say that the administration and the leaders of both parties in Congress couldn't come back during the course of this endeavor and agree, in effect, that this should be considered as consistent with the budget agreement—not this issue, but just any particular issue. So let's take these two issues.

Number one, on the question of raising the eligibility for Medicare from 65 to 67, when that was done on a phase-in basis for Social Security back in '83, I supported that, on the grounds of increased life expectancy, changing demographic balance, and because it was part of a bipartisan process. My question here would be, apart from the fact that it's outside the agreement, is, do we know that this would not lead to increased numbers of people without any health coverage? Has there been sufficient study here? Do we really have adequate evidence that we won't have increasing numbers of people without health insurance?

On the means testing for—not for the premiums, but for the co-pays, which is what was done in the case of the cash—I have said repeatedly that, philosophically, I was not opposed to means testing Medicare. And I told Senator Lott that on the phone the other day. What my concerns are, are the following. Number one, it's outside the agreement. Number two, we have an agreement which has a lot of reform in Medicare and will realize $400 billion worth of savings and put 10 years on the Trust Fund right now. And will this imperil it because people will be opposed to it? Or would this endanger the whole Medicare deal in the House, for example, where I have reason to believe, based on our preliminary negotiations over the budget agreement, that there would be broad opposition in both parties? Thirdly, Mr. Reischauer and others have said that this particular proposal is probably not capable of being administered, that there are a lot of practical problems with it.

So again I say, I have said to leaders of both parties and to the American people, I want to take care of more of the long-term problems of the entitlement, both Social Security and Medicare. I am amenable to doing it in any bipartisan process. I have the specific problems

I mentioned on these two issues, but the number one thing is, we have got a great budget agreement. We should not alter it unless there is agreement among all the parties who made the budget agreement that it's acceptable to do because otherwise we risk undermining the prize that we have when we could achieve these other objectives as soon as the budget's done in an appropriate bipartisan forum.

Bill [Bill Plante, CBS News] and Mara [Mara Liasson, National Public Radio]. Go ahead. We'll do one, two here.

China

Q. Mr. President, there's a report out today that your administration has chosen to ignore information that China is sending missiles to Pakistan, selling them in contravention of its 1994 agreement, and also helping Pakistan to build a facility to manufacture the missiles. Is it true? If so, why did you ignore it? And will it have any effect on your MFN decision?

The President. Well, first of all, you know I can't comment on intelligence reports or alleged intelligence reports. I would remind you that when we had clear evidence that China was providing ring magnets to Pakistan in ways that we thought were plainly violative of our law and our national interest, we dealt with them about that and were satisfied. And I think it's fair to say that on all these issues we will not overlook them, we will not walk away from them, and we will make appropriate determinations and take appropriate action. The national security of the country is always going to be the most important thing.

Mara.

Proposed Tobacco Agreement

Q. [*Inaudible*]—your initial take on one of the aspects of the tobacco deal. You've said that you're concerned about the ability of the FDA to regulate tobacco as you have proposed allowing it to do in the rule. Can they do that if they have to prove that regulations would not create a black market? Some critics say that's an impossible thing to prove; the deal does require it. And isn't that just giving away the court victory that you just won?

The President. Well, you see, I don't know the answer to that. But it concerned me, because the first thing I thought was, what happens if they go to a zero nicotine ruling, and the technology is available—obviously, the technology has to be available to do it since it's otherwise a legal product—how could you prove there wouldn't be a black market? What's the definition of black market? Is a one percent penetration a black market, or does it have to be 10?

That's why I've been so reluctant to answer these questions. Not—I'll be happy to give you my opinion when I have a chance to study it, but that's why I want to take 30 days and look at this.

I've also—let me tell you, I've been involved in these agreements. It's like this long budget agreement we did. And one of the things I can tell you is, when you're dealing with something with this many complex elements, if you are dealing in complete good faith and the other side is dealing in complete good faith, it is entirely possible that there were three or four things that were put in here that will have likely consequences that neither side anticipated.

So that's why I would—I know that we're all in a hurry to sort of rush to judgment on this, and I understand that, but that's why we need to take the time to really analyze it and make sure there's not something there that would have an unintended consequence that, for all I know, neither party meant to have.

Peter [Peter Maer, NBC Mutual Radio], I'll take you next. Go ahead. We'll do both of them.

Budget Agreement

Q. Mr. President, you said that you want to avoid time-bomb tax cuts in the budget deal, that you would insist on avoiding them. Would you also insist on including the $500 child care tax credit for the 4 million working families? Is that something that you would insist upon?

And number two, regarding the budget agreement, is it made more difficult to get it done by the Republican infighting?

The President. Let me deal with the questions separately. First of all, on the tax credit, my position is that all working people should be made eligible for it—the Senate bill in that regard is better than the House bill—and that we shouldn't have some other offset, like reducing the child care credit as well as the children's tax credit in the new bill.

I understand the Republicans are arguing because they want to save money on this to pay for the capital gains and the other things that they want. They're arguing that this is, in effect,

a welfare thing because you're giving a child care credit to people who aren't paying income taxes—now, that's their argument—because of the other tax credits people are entitled to.

But let's just take the income group they are dealing with, working families with incomes between $22,000 and $25,000. Now, suppose you've got a rookie police officer in a medium-size city in the South, the average entry-level salary is about $23,000, and it's a woman or a man with two kids at home. This police officer is paying Federal taxes, a considerable Federal payroll tax. And to treat—to characterize them as welfare recipients because they would be made eligible for the same help that people making $31,000 a year would get to raise their children, I think is wrong.

So that's an area where we simply have a disagreement. I was encouraged that the Senate moved closer to us than the House. This is something I expect to work out.

On the other question, I wouldn't—do I think we're not going to make an agreement because of reported divisions within Republican ranks? No, I do not expect that to be prohibitive. I think that there was a lot of tension within their caucus, obviously, over this disaster aid bill, but in the end they did the right thing. And the leaders did the right thing. And I think that nobody likes to go through that and have your position not prevail. And so that was understandable.

But I think as time passes, they will see that their leaders did the right thing and that the country is better off and that we're moving in the right direction. So I don't expect splits to paralyze us.

Peter.

Proposed Tobacco Agreement

Q. Sir, I'd like to ask you about an aspect of this tobacco deal where you do have some expertise, the legal aspect. What's your view of this concept of protecting the tobacco industry from lawsuits, from liability? What kind of legal and what kind of constitutional precedents would that set?

The President. Well, as I understand it, it does not protect them from liability for actual damages. It protects them from liability for past punitive damages and still permits punitive damages if there is misconduct from the date of the agreement forward.

Now, in the law, the purpose of punitive damages is to deter future destructive behavior. And the concept of punitive damages is provided not because the person suing is entitled to it because of his or her injuries but because you think the injuries are not enough—compensating this person is not enough to take the profit out of whatever antisocial conduct and illegal conduct the defendant was engaging in. So you enable—you have punitive damages to take the sting out of it.

The people negotiating on behalf of the public—the attorneys general and the lawyers—as I understand it, got another $20 billion or so—Mike Moore described what it was—in a kind of advanced penalty fund—say, we're going to make you pay up front for the things you've done wrong. And that's how they—in the last few weeks, the agreement went from involving about 300 and something billion dollars to almost 370 billion.

So, that—I think—I can't answer your question except to say I'll sit down there, and I'll try to evaluate that. I will evaluate—it's an unusual and unique resolution. They got several billion dollars more out of the tobacco companies than they had been talking about getting. Can you have, in effect, an advance payment for punitive damages? Does it sort of—does that, plus all the other things that would be good from a consumer's point of view and the public's point of view, would that be enough to kind of offset the troublesome areas?

You and this man and then—[*inaudible*]—the three of you; I'll take you real quick. And then I'll take some foreign journalists back there.

Campaign Fundraising

Q. Mr. President, the hearings on campaign fundraising will begin soon. And a number of key figures—people who worked for you or old friends have either fled the country or have said they would take the fifth amendment. Is there anything you can or should do to get them to come clean?

The President. What we can do is to control what we're asked to do. We tried to be very cooperative, and all that we have asked is that the hearings be fair and bipartisan. And if they are, I think they'll serve a valid public purpose. Go ahead.

China

Q. The President, some of the critics of your decision to renew most-favored-nation trade status for China say that perhaps watching the transition of Hong Kong should have been taken into consideration before granting that status. Was that ever a consideration? And in your opinion, how realistic is a one-country, two-systems policy?

The President. Well, the answer to the first part of your question is, we have to make this decision now, and I think we should now. This thing will obviously be revisited within a year. I think if we look like we were—again, I would say to you, China is a very large country. It has great ties with the rest of the world. If we were to basically say, the United States believes we can keep you on probation all by yourself, and we're going to see what you do, we're like assuming their bad faith. I think that would be a mistake.

On the one-country, two-systems thing, I think it is realistic, but I think there will be some tensions there. And what we, of course, in the United States hope is that the tensions will steadily be resolved over time in favor of freedom and openness, free speech, personal freedom, and democracy.

But let me remind you, 25 years ago, when President Nixon went to China, or in 1979 when President Carter recognized China and worked out the understandings of how we relate to China and how we would relate to Taiwan—there is plainly a lot more personal freedom and mobility and personal well-being in China today than there was then. In other words, our frustrations with China today are not measured against the standard of 1979 or 1972; they're measured with our deep disappointment and disagreement with 1989 and Tiananmen Square and our lack of success in persuading the Chinese to, in effect, go back to the status quo before Tiananmen Square and keep moving forward. In the life of a country like China, that's not such a long time. And I'm just not prepared to give up on our engagement policy. So that's all I can say about it.

Bill.

Proposed Tobacco Agreement

Q. Mr. President, now that you have a U.S. tobacco agreement, would you favor and encourage some sort of international regulation of tobacco? And wouldn't this be a good G-7 issue?

The President. Well, it might be. But the problem is, you know, the G-7 nations are not the primary place where the market is growing. I will say this, I hope that other countries around the world that are concerned with their own public health and who have primary responsibility for the well-being of their own people will look at what we've been trying to do here and ask themselves whether they should take some similar steps if they want to avoid very high death rates, very high disease rates, and enormous social costs.

Could we have a few questions from the international press now? Would someone just stand up over here—anybody from the international press? Go ahead. We'll take a few there. Just stand up and I'll get around to you. Go ahead.

Russia-Japan Territory Dispute

Q. Mr. President, in your meetings here with the leaders of Japan and Russia, did you get the sense that the Northern Territories dispute between those two countries could be resolved? And do you see any U.S. role in that resolution process?

The President. Yes, I think—well, first of all, I think the only appropriate United States role is to try to talk to each party on behalf of the other from the point of view of being friends with both. That is, this is an area where we plainly have no personal, tangible interest of any kind. We have no territorial interest, we have no financial interest. Our only interest is seeing two friends of ours get along, and trying to stabilize one more—the future of the Asia-Pacific region by removing one more deterrent to an alliance between a free and democratic Russia and our great ally in Japan.

So I have talked to both Prime Minister Hashimoto and President Yeltsin about this on several occasions. They are beginning to talk about it among themselves. They will have to work it out. But, obviously, I'm very hopeful that it can be worked out.

Yes, sir, the gentleman standing there.

Japan-U.S. Trade

Q. Mr. President, I think you have been waiting for too long for Japan's achievement of deregulation and administrative reforms. Could you tell us your opinion, as frankly as possible, on this matter?

The President. Well, I agree with you. [*Laughter*] I agree with you.

Here's the problem we're going to run into with Japan on the trade issue. We have made real progress over the last 4 years in our trading relations with Japan. It's become a real joy to be able to meet and work with Japan where trade was an issue, but not the only issue, and where we really thought we could identify the issues and make progress on them, that there was no big structural war going on, economic war, between the United States and Japan. And I think it has obviously not been bad for Japan either. I think it's been good for both of us.

Now, the Prime Minister has reaffirmed his commitment to a domestic demand-led growth strategy for Japan and has put forward a very ambitious plan for internal reform and deregulation and opening of the Japanese economy. At the same time, he says, quite rightly, that all these advanced economies are going to face serious challenges from the aging of our populations. That's true. You've heard all the questions that were just asked of me about our medical programs. And Japan has an even older population than the United States, aging even more rapidly.

So the decisions by the Japanese Government to try to pursue a path of fiscal austerity driven in part by the desire to prepare for the retirement and the aging of the Japanese population runs the risk of going back to the old export-driven strategy of growth. And we'll just have to work through those two conflicts. We can't tell the Japanese Government or the Japanese people that they can't prepare for the aging of their population. We have to do the same.

On the other hand, I think they know that if we resort—we return to the time when we've got exploding trade deficits, then that will once again move front and center into our relations in a way that won't be good for either country, I don't think.

Yes, sir.

Russia

Q. Mr. President, Russian President Yeltsin has played an important role in the Denver Summit. What's your reading—when will Russia be totally completed into the G–7 circuit as a new member?

The President. Let me say, this year our commitment was to have Russia be a complete member of the Group of the Eight and to have the old G–7 meet only on issues that we had unique responsibility for because of our present financial standing. So I think it's fair that all of us look forward to the day when we don't even have to do that.

But, just for example, we've got this project going on to help Ukraine deal with Chernobyl, and Russia is not responsible for what we committed to do before, nor would it be fair to ask Russia to bear any responsibility for that. So we had to meet and discuss it, and we did. There was nothing secret or esoteric about it; we just had to do what we were required to do, and we did that.

But I think you will see continuing integration of Russia into full partnership. The next thing I want to see is Russia into the WTO, and we're working on that. So we'll just keep working at it, and as long as Russia keeps moving as it is under President Yeltsin, and those reformers and the people of Russia keep supporting the direction they have, I think that you'll see more and more good things ahead.

This gentleman has been here a long time, and then this gentleman, and then we'll move over here.

Q. Mr. President, what do you think? Is Russia now ready economically and politically to be a full member of the eight?

The President. I think, yes, they're ready politically and ready economically in terms of what's—like the Paris Club membership. But I think there are still some things that the old G–7 have to do that it wouldn't even be fair to ask Russia to participate in, like this Chernobyl thing that I just mentioned. So there will be a smaller and smaller role for the seven as we go forward, and a bigger and bigger role—basically, this time we had a Summit of the Eight, with a small, little afterthought for what the seven still had to do to clean up our old business. But I think that, with great prosperity, I think you'll see any last little dividing line blurring.

Yes, sir. These three gentlemen there are fine. Just take them in any order.

Q. Mr. President, I was wondering, how do you think Russia will change the balance of forces—or maybe I should say the balance of interests within the group now that Russia has joined, specifically between U.S. and Europe?

The President. Well, I hope that Russia will change in two ways that I would consider to be immensely positive. One is, I think the participation of Russia here, just like the NATO-Russia Founding Act, increases the chances that we can maintain stability in Europe in the 20th century and that we can deal with any problems that arise like we're dealing with them in Bosnia, to prevent the outbreak of widespread war in Europe.

The second thing I think is very positive is Russia, don't forget, is also a great Pacific power. So in bringing Russia into this partnership along with Japan, you will see a little more emphasis, I think, on what we can do as a group to deal with what's going on in Asia in preserving stability and freedom and opportunity there.

So in those ways, I think you'll see the texture of this change. And you could see it just in the way President Yeltsin operated here at this meeting, where I might say I thought he did an extraordinary job.

Yes, sir.

Bosnia

Q. Mr. President, can you assure us that by the time of the next summit, the main war criminals in Bosnia will finally have been arrested?

The President. I can't promise you that, but I can tell you that's what I support. And I support—generally, I think that it's going to be difficult to implement the full spirit of the Dayton accord unless you see some progress on the war criminals front, number one. And number two, as you may know, I have felt for some time, with so much ethnic and racial and religious and tribal hatred in the world, that there probably should be an international war crimes tribunal that is permanently established and goes forward, because I think that what we see in Bosnia is just one example of a whole set of very serious problems.

This young man in the back has been very patient. Let me take his question.

Summit of the Eight Accomplishments

Q. Good afternoon, Mr. President. My name is Colton Alton. I am a student taking an international course on the summit with the University of Colorado, CU On-Line. There are 450 students internationally, from each of the countries. On behalf of the 450 students, what do you feel was the most significant accomplishment with this year's summit?

The President. I think the most significant thing we did here was to commit ourselves to a growth strategy that would include not only our own countries but other countries around the world, and that would be pursued while improving, not undermining, the environment. And that's quite significant.

We've said these things specifically before, but here we said, look, we're coming up to Kyoto where we're all bound to adopt legally binding targets to reduce greenhouse gas emissions. So that means we have to grow our economies while improving our environments, number one.

And then we said, we're going to reach out to Africa, we're going to reach out to the developing countries of Asia and Latin America, that our prosperity depends upon their prosperity.

And to me, I would hope that the students who follow this on-line would look at the world in that way, would see America as a unifying, not a divisive force in the world, and would embrace the fact that our prosperity should depend upon others and upon living in harmony with our environment.

I'll take one more, this gentleman here.

North Korea

Q. The communique, just as you said, will test the importance of four-party talks. Why didn't you urge North Korea to participate in the four-party talks? And I would like to ask you, what is your prospect of the four-party meetings?

The President. Why does the communique not urge North Korea to participate? Is that the question you asked?

Q. Yes.

The President. I would say that it is an oversight and we should have, because I do every time I can. And secondly, I'm fairly optimistic now because North Korea has agreed to participate in a meeting to determine the conditions in which they would meet with the South Koreans and the Chinese and the United States to set out these four-party talks. So I'm fairly encouraged by that.

Go ahead.

China and Taiwan

Q. [*Inaudible*]—over China will definitely try very hard to sell the so-called one-country, two-system formula and hope Taiwan will be on board. And apparently the leaders in Taiwan made it clear that that formula is not acceptable for them. So I wonder what will be the U.S. policy on Taiwan after Hong Kong is turned over, and whether the U.S. will buy this one-country, two-system formula on the issue of Taiwan.

The President. Well, the most important element of United States policy will not change as it relates to Taiwan, and that is that there can be no forcible resolution of that issue, and that while we accept the idea of one China, it has always been our policy, for some years now, as you know, we also—a critical part of that policy is that the people of Taiwan and the people of China must resolve their differences in a peaceable way, agreeable to all.

So that's the only really critical element that we have to reaffirm there. I think the people of Taiwan are going to be—and the leaders of Taiwan will be watching how the Hong Kong transition goes, and I think that their attitude about what their own position should be will probably be affected by that.

Thank you very much.

NOTE: The President's 148th news conference began at 2:25 p.m. at the Colorado Convention Center. In his remarks, he referred to Susanna Agnelli, former Foreign Minister of Italy; Prime Minister Tony Blair of the United Kingdom; Attorney General Michael Moore of Mississippi; Robert D. Reischauer, former Director, Congressional Budget Office; Prime Minister Ryutaro Hashimoto of Japan; and President Boris Yeltsin of Russia.

Remarks to Summit of the Eight Volunteers in Denver
June 22, 1997

The President. Thank you.

Audience member. Teachers love you, Mr. President!

The President. Well, I love the teachers, too, so I thank you very, very much.

Let me say, first of all, my heart is full of gratitude to all of you this afternoon, to my longtime friends Governor and Mrs. Romer; to Mayor and Mrs. Webb for the astonishing work that they have done on this. I thank Lieutenant Governor Gail Schoettler and the other members of the host committee. I want to say a special word of thanks to Donna Goode and Mike Dino for the work they did. Thank you very much. And a special word of thanks to the leaders of our team here, Harold Ickes and Debbie Willhite, for the work they did.

I had this idea, when the time came for America to host the summit—you know, the easy thing to do when you host a summit like this is to go to a really big city and put everybody up in a really fancy hotel and go hear the orchestra on Saturday night or something. And I think that's a good thing to do, by the way. But what I was trying to do with this summit—I tried to figure out, where could we have this summit where people could get a flavor of the natural beauty of our country that is unique, the sort of frontier spirit of our country that is unique, but our common commitment, first of all, to shaping the future and embracing it, and secondly, to doing it together, across the lines that too often divide people in this old world? And Denver seemed to me to be the logical place to do that. And I think I made a good decision, and you helped to make it so.

The other leaders commented to me on many things. The people who got to take the train loved the train. They all loved the fort last night. They loved the buffalo meat, the horse show, and the double rainbow, which I said—and they all said they didn't know the Federal Government had control over rainbows. They were quite impressed. [*Laughter*] They loved the sort of panorama of American musical history that was put on. And I thank everybody who worked on that. That was an enormous effort and a very impressive one, and I thank you for that.

But the thing they all kept coming back to was how wonderfully friendly the people were, how genuinely glad they were to see them, and how respectful they were of the nations they represented and the work they were here to do, and what an upbeat atmosphere prevailed. I mean, the human climate and the human warmth they felt is the thing I think they'll take away from here, more than anything. And I think you can be very, very proud of that because I know that the volunteers were principally responsible for making sure that they all felt that way.

Let me just finally say, you know, these summits are interesting affairs; they rarely produce some searing headline on some great issue, but they—I have done quite a number of them now, in Japan and in Italy and in Canada and in France and now this one here, and I can tell you an enormous amount of what countries do together to make this world a better place and to beat back the problems of the world germinates from the work we do at these summits and the way we get to know each other, the way we get to understand one another's countries and cultures and political environments and the sense of common purpose we have. Again, I think it wells up more from the people than anything else.

So when you go home tonight, after you have your party and your celebration and all the things Hillary talked about and you put your head on the pillow before you go to sleep, I hope you'll take a great deal of pride in the fact that you have made a personal contribution to creating a world of tomorrow in which there is more peace, more prosperity, more freedom, and more harmony. That is what we are working for. And we made a real step forward in the last couple of days, thanks in no small measure to you.

Thank you, and God bless you.

NOTE: The President spoke at 3:53 p.m. in Currigan Hall at the Convention Center. In his remarks, he referred to Gov. Roy Romer of Colorado and his wife, Bea; Mayor Wellington E. Webb of Denver and his wife, Wilma; Lt. Gov.

Gail Schoettler of Colorado; Donna Goode, director of the host committee; and Mike Dino, executive director, City of Denver Task Force for the Summit.

Remarks to the United States Conference of Mayors in San Francisco, California
June 23, 1997

Thank you. Well, we were outside, and they played "Ruffles and Flourishes," and we had a momentary delay when we tried to decide whether Mayor Brown or I should walk in first. [*Laughter*] We finally got it right, if you saw how—[*laughter*].

I am delighted to be here. I thank Mayor Daley for his warm introduction, fulfilling one of Clinton's laws of politics: Always be introduced by someone whose brother is in the Cabinet. [*Laughter*] I'm glad to be here with Secretary Cuomo, Secretary Herman. Senator Boxer, thank you for joining us this morning. Representative Lofgren I think is here. Mayor Brown, thanks for putting on such a good show. Thanks for giving me another reason to come to San Francisco. To all the mayors here on the stage and in the audience, especially to Mayor Helmke and Mayor Corradini, who are about to assume their respective offices.

I saw my good friend Mayor Rice, and he said that today is his wife's birthday, so happy birthday. There you are. Happy birthday. [*Applause*] Thank you. I know that Mayor and Mrs. Webb are here. They hosted us at the Summit of the Eight, and if they fall asleep during the speech, I give them advance permission because they've been up for 2 or 3 days. [*Laughter*] Denver did a great job.

Thank you, Tom Cochran, for the work you've done with us. I'd also like to just make a special note of my new Director of Intergovernmental Affairs at the White House, who has been here with you, Mickey Ibarra, and Lynn Cutler, who has also been here. We're glad to have them working with you, and I know you'll enjoy working with them.

And I'd like to announce my intention to fill Secretary Cuomo's former job as Assistant Secretary of HUD for Community Planning with the mayor of Laredo, Texas, Saul Ramirez, who is right over here. Saul, stand up. [*Applause*] Thank you. Why anyone would be willing to leave Laredo to move to Washington is beyond me, but I'm glad he agreed.

I always look forward to this meeting because I do believe America's most creative and gifted and effective public officials today are to be found among the mayors. I've always thought of you as friends and allies in doing America's work, and I've always thought that a lot of my job was to help you do your jobs better.

I imagine I have been in more urban neighborhoods, meeting with more different kinds of people about more different kinds of issues than any of my predecessors. I've certainly tried to make that the case because when I ran for President, I knew that I needed to spend time in our cities, to get to know the people, the problems, and the promise of the cities, to connect our cities with our suburbs and make people understand that these problems we share are common problems and that the promise of America in this new century is a shared promise.

I also believed fervently, and I still believe, that America can never fulfill its complete promise until all our cities fulfill theirs. And I have watched you—I see out in this audience—I see Mayor White over there with his sympathetic arm injury with my leg there. Thank you very much. You'll be the company misery loves for me for a while. I have seen so many of you work so hard day-in and day-out to fulfill your own dreams, and I have seen the unique culture and richness of every city.

Mayor Abramson actually once took me to the Louisville Slugger baseball bat factory. For all you baseball fans, they have a bat Babe Ruth used in the season that he hit 60 home runs there. You can only find these kinds of things, uniquely, differently, in all of our cities in America, where the various richness and diversity of America is wound together in a wonderful fabric of strong, united values.

So, to me, when I come here I think of you the way I thought of myself when I ran as—

in the derogatory term that my opponent put on me in 1992—as the Governor of a small Southern State, because in my former life and in your present life, we did not get hired to make speeches and to posture, we got hired to mobilize people, unite people, and get things done, and denial was not an option. So I'm very glad to be here, and I want to thank you for all you have done.

What a long way we have come. It wasn't so very long ago that huge numbers of Americans had just simply given up on the prospect of our cities. But as Secretary Cuomo's compelling report, "The State of the Cities," proves, our cities are back. We've got the biggest economic resurgence in cities since World War II; the unemployment rate down by a third in our 50 largest cities; more downtowns coming back to life with sports and tourism and local business booming. Congratulation on your two new stadiums, Mayor Brown. We're taking back our streets from the worst ravages of crime. New waves of immigrants in our cities are making positive contributions with new energy and new businesses. And because of your disciplined and creative leadership, the fiscal health of our cities is stronger than it has been in decades. Our cities are literally bursting with new ideas for reform that are actually changing people's lives.

I have seen what the empowerment zone has done in Detroit. I went to Toledo to see the oldest auto plant in America up and running and bursting at the seams with new employees, selling their products to Japan in large numbers. I have been to Boston where not a single child has been killed with a handgun in a year and a half. I know what the cities are doing, and I want America to know that the mayors of this country have literally changed the shared life of America in ways that affect not only our largest cities but our smaller cities and, as I said, the relationship that is inexorably intertwined between the cities and the suburbs.

You have helped America come back, and I am grateful. But I also know, and you know, that we have much more to do. We have to have more jobs for those who must now leave the welfare rolls because they're able-bodied. We must meet the challenge of absorbing new immigrants. We must deal with the rising tide of juvenile violence and juvenile drug abuse which has in our country continued to rise even as the overall crime rate has dropped dramatically. We must deal with the continued flight

of the middle class to the suburbs. We must deal with the poor performance of too many of our schools, with the continuing health problems of too many people who live in the cities, and perhaps most important of all, with the continuing almost physical isolation of the poor in our cities, most of them young adults and little children.

During my time as President, instead of trying to either impose ready-made solutions from Washington or ignore the problems altogether, we have tried to give you and your communities the support you need and the tools you need to meet your own challenges, to use the National Government to empower local leaders, to make the grassroots progress that each and every one of you can celebrate.

We started with the economic program in 1993, which replaced trickle-down economics with invest-and-grow economics and included a number of initiatives for the cities: the empowerment zones and enterprise communities, the community development financial institutions, the earned-income tax credit, the dramatic increases in child nutrition. We continued with the urban initiatives of HUD, led by former Secretary Cuomo—former Secretary Cisneros and his able team, including Andrew Cuomo— that included an initiative on homelessness, on cleaning up our housing projects, on innovative ways to empower people who were dependent upon public housing.

We continued with the crime bill, which was largely written by big-city mayors, prosecutors, and police officers. Its strategy was hotly disputed in the Congress by people who believed in rhetoric instead of reality. But the strategy is now no longer open to doubt, as we've just seen our 5th year of declining crime, in the last year the steepest decline in violent crime of all.

We continued with the initiatives before the welfare reform law was signed, local initiatives in welfare which moved record numbers of people from welfare to work, and all the analysis showed that a great deal of them moved because of the local efforts that people were making.

The key to all this was to give individuals, families, and communities the power and the responsibility to solve their problems and make the most of their own lives. I want to press forward with this empowerment agenda. And today I would like to briefly discuss seven things that I think are important if our cities and, therefore, our country are to reach their full promise in the 21st century.

First, we've got to keep working until we extend the prosperity of this recovery to every neighborhood in America. Second, we have to do more to take back our streets from crime and especially to prevent young people from falling into a life that will destroy themselves and people around them. Third, we have to finish the job of welfare reform by creating enough jobs for all who can, and now must, work. Fourth, we have to extend the benefits of homeownership even more widely to meet our national goal of having more than two-thirds of the American people living in their own homes for the first time in history by the year 2000. Fifth, we have to raise the standards in our schools and invest more in our young people. Sixth, we have to meet public health challenges, including HIV and AIDS. And seventh, we have to create in our cities our national ideal of one America that crosses all racial, ethnic, and other lines that divide us, committed to giving every child a chance to flourish and every citizen a chance to serve.

I want to work with you to put this agenda into action. HUD must be a good partner, the Labor Department will be a good partner, the rest of our administration must be a good partner. But we are working for you, to help you and your people do what they know how to do to make the most of their lives and their prospects.

First, let's talk about extending the benefits of the economic recovery. Our national economic strategy changed dramatically in 1993. We went from trickle-down economics to what I call invest and growth: reduce the deficit but invest more in our people and technology and in the progress of people in the future and open the world to trade in American products and services.

This is clearly working. Our economy is the strongest in the world, the strongest it's been in a generation. America is now the world's number one exporter. Unemployment has been below 5 percent now for a few months for the first time in 24 years; inflation at its lowest point in 30 years; over 12 million new jobs; the largest decline in income inequality since the 1960's; a 77 percent cut in the deficit—before the balanced budget agreement—a 77 percent cut in the deficit, from $290 billion a year to less than $70 billion this year. They said we could not

cut the deficit and invest more in our people, but they were wrong. And you are reaping the benefits of that.

In this urban economic strategy that was a part, as I said, of the 1993 economic plan, the most important thing was to try to attract businesses and jobs back to our cities. We've created already 105 empowerment zones and enterprise communities, which provide a common combination of tax incentives and freedom from Government redtape for you to attract new investment. We are establishing a network of community development financial institutions to infuse our cities with capital.

It's very interesting to me—I discovered when I became President that we had been funding such efforts all over the world for years in the poorest places in the world, places with far more limited prospects than poor people in the neighborhoods of America, to grow and to build businesses and to build a future, and we had never done it in our country except on a very limited basis in Chicago and a few other cities. Now we are trying to do that all over the Nation.

We reformed the Community Reinvestment Act so that it works better to steer private capital from mainstream commercial banks into poor inner-city and rural communities. Now, since we reformed the Community Reinvestment Act there have been a number of studies which show that as much as $100 billion had been invested in these communities, which means that since the Community Reinvestment Act was passed in 1977, 70 percent of all investments it was designed to direct have been made since 1993. I am proud of that, and that also has contributed to the revitalization of many American communities.

We also recognize that a major barrier to urban economic growth is the contamination of otherwise attractive sites for development, known to you as brownfields, a word that is still a total mystery to most Americans. But you know what they are, and a lot of you have cleaned them up. We have worked hard to make those brownfields into productive assets and to clean up a record number of toxic waste sites, more in the first 3½ years of our administration than in the previous 12 years.

When I reached our historic bipartisan budget agreement with the leaders of Congress, they pledged to work with us to keep these initiatives going, to expand the empowerment zones, to expand the enterprise communities, to expand the brownfields tax incentives. Furthermore, they also agreed to funds necessary to clean up 500 more toxic waste sites, to more than double the amount of investment in the community development financial institutions, to provide for urban transportation needs for people on welfare who must travel to new jobs, and to help people on welfare get more work.

Now, all these initiatives are essential to the health of our cities. They also agreed to enough funds to cover half of the 10 million children in America who have no health insurance. That will make a dramatic difference to those of you who have severe health costs that are unmet and unfunded in your cities.

But on the tax side—that is, dealing with the brownfields and the empowerment zones and the other tax incentives for the cities—the plans put together by the House and Senate committees simply do not live up to the explicit commitment of the budget agreement, and that is wrong. I know that many in Congress do not share my enthusiasm for these programs. Many of them have never seen your reforms at work; perhaps they cannot be blamed for not voting for what they don't know about. But the truth is that that budget agreement passed by overwhelming margins of both parties in both Houses. And I would think every Member of Congress, without regard to party, would like to be known as a person who keeps his or her word. It is up to you to make sure that they have the chance to keep their words. Do not let Congress get out of the commitment they made on this issue.

The second thing we have to do is to keep up with our fight against crime and violence. You and I know that crime's been going down for years and that the strategy we put together—together—of more police on the street, tougher punishment, fewer guns in the hands of criminals, and more prevention programs to give young people a chance to say yes to a brighter future—we know this is historically effective. We know we had the largest decline in crime in 36 years last year. Murders dropped a stunning 11 percent. Cities all around the country, including our host city here, have had big declines in crime. I have been on the streets of so many of the cities here present to see you and listen to you and your police officers and community leaders talk about what you've done on crime.

But a nationally publicized poll just last week asked the American people whether crime was going up or down; 25 percent said down, and 60 percent said up. Why is that? Partly, it takes a while for public perception always to catch up with reality. Partly, it's that the local news still leads with the crime story every night. And that's a problem for a lot of you and the image you're trying to fashion for your cities. But partly it's because, with all the drops in crime, America is a place with too much violence and too much crime—still, with all the progress we have made.

We have to finish the job of putting 100,000 police on the street. I will fight to make sure we keep that commitment. We have to continue to push for real juvenile justice legislation. We put a bill before the Congress that has more prosecutors, more probation officers, more after-school and other programs for at-risk young people. It's not very long on rhetoric; it's real long on results. And it basically grew out of what I have seen working.

I mentioned the Boston program. I went to Houston, and Mayor Lanier showed me what he did, mobilizing 3,000 inner-city kids in a soccer league and, before Tiger Woods won the Masters, 2,500 inner-city kids in a golf league. Giving our children something to say yes to: that's a part of juvenile justice.

I've been to places where the probation officers and the police officers make house calls and where people walk the streets and try to keep kids out of trouble. We just need a national bill which gives you the tools to do what you know you can do to save these kids' lives. That's all I want to do. And I want you to help me pass that kind of juvenile justice bill through the Congress, so that you can save the children of your cities. And I believe we can do that.

Let me say, you can go from New York to San Diego, from Seattle and Portland, all the way to southern Florida, and if you go to city to city to city, you see that it seems to be the everyday presence of law enforcement officers on our streets, working with citizens, that has done the most to bring the crime rate down.

We have done our part by trying to help you put 100,000 more police on the street. We've come a long way from 1992, when we've seen the violent crime rate triple in the preceding 30 years, with only a 10 percent increase in police officers. And you have learned so much more about how to deploy those police officers. It's been really impressive.

I want to increase that presence even more by getting police to live in the communities they serve. Today I am pleased to announce that over the coming year we will start an Officer Next Door program through HUD. It will make it possible for police officers and their families to buy HUD-owned single-family homes in our central cities at a 50 percent discount. You have shown me how more police officers on our streets have made so many of our neighborhoods feel like home again. Just imagine what it will be like when more police make those neighborhoods their homes again.

And let me say just parenthetically—I want to give a little pat to Secretary Cuomo here—when I appointed him, I said, you know, I don't understand why HUD needs to keep all this surplus property all the time. Why do we need all this inventory? It's not doing any good just laying out there. And this is just the first of what I hope will be many initiatives. But if we can give these police officers and their families 50 percent discounts to move back into the inner cities, it will be some of the best money the Federal Government ever spent, and we want to do more of those things.

The third thing we have to do is to make sure we create jobs for the roughly one million people that have to move from welfare to work by the year 2000. Under the present welfare reform law, whatever happens to the economy, we have to move nearly a million people from welfare to work. We moved nearly a million people, about 900,000, from welfare to work in the last 4 years when we had welfare reform experiments going in 40 of the 50 States, and many of those only in part of the States. But when our economy in 4 years produced over 11 million new jobs, that had never happened before in a 4-year administration. In the next 4 years, we have to move that many people whether we produce 11 million more jobs or not. Can we do it? I believe we can.

I know a lot of you thought I made a mistake by signing the welfare reform bill. Remember, I vetoed two previous bills because I thought they were too tough on kids and too weak on work. But when we put back the guarantee of nutrition and health care to our children, when we came up with $4 billion for child care, when we agreed to leave the funding at the States equal to the amount they were getting when welfare rolls were at their all-time high, I thought it was worth the chance to change the culture of dependency.

Today, on the front page of the local newspaper, there is a study by the Federal Reserve of San Francisco saying that the rolls have dropped another 500,000 since the law came into effect, and they are now going down in virtually every State in the Union. We finally got a big drop here in California, which—because it didn't come back as quickly as the other States, it didn't have drops as soon. We can make this work. We can make this work.

In the budget agreement, we got agreement to restore the most egregious cuts in aid to immigrants, which I thought were wrong, the cuts to legal immigrants who come here, live by the rules, and work hard, through no fault of their own become disabled. We are going to restore those cuts, and I will not sign the bill unless Congress keeps its commitment in the budget agreement to do that. But that's in the agreement.

We have $600 billion through the Department of Transportation to help people on welfare travel to work, because there are a lot of cities in which right now, and maybe by the time the benefits run out, there won't be jobs but they're willing workers. There was an interesting study involving Atlanta not very long ago which said that in inner-city Atlanta, something like 80 percent of the jobs in the restaurants, fast-food restaurants, were held by low income people who lived in the cities. In the suburbs, only slightly more than 50 percent were. Obviously, if there was more transportation availability, we could do a better job of moving people that have to go to work where the jobs are, sometimes even within the cities themselves. So Secretary Slater and I are committed to that.

Most important of all, I have fought hard for—and it is in the budget agreement, and so far it's moving along nicely through the Congress—for $3 billion in welfare-to-work funds, which specifically gives our cities, working with the Department of Labor as well as with HUD and HHS and others, the resources that you need to create good jobs for people who can't get them otherwise. This is very important. Last year in Chicago there were six applicants for every entry-level job that opened up; in St. Louis there were nine. It is not true that these people don't go to work. And it is not realistic to expect that we can get all of them to work within the time deadlines unless we put this money out there where you can use it to create jobs, good jobs for people who need them. So I ask you to help me pass that in the Congress.

Finally, let me say I know a lot of you are making new partnerships with the private sector. Mayor Brown told me this morning that the private sector here in San Francisco had pledged to him that they would take 2,000 people from welfare to work on their own initiative. In this bill there is a new tax credit, very tightly drawn, that gives a 50 percent credit for up to $10,000 in wages for people who are hired from welfare to work. That also is in the budget agreement and must pass.

Let me say, finally—I want to emphasize this again, just in case there are some of you who don't know it—the States of this country are getting over 20 percent more money today for welfare than they would have gotten under the old welfare law. They are still getting the same amount of money they got when welfare rolls were at an all-time high. We have had the largest reduction in welfare rolls in the history of the United States by far. They still have that money. What are they doing with it? You have to make sure that that money is spent in a way that helps the people, most of whom live in your jurisdictions, to go to work. If they need training, get them the training.

And let me say one other thing. One of the problems we have ameliorated in this deal but not completely solved is what happens to the single men who aren't on welfare in the first place. Most Americans, when they talk about welfare reform, are thinking about all able-bodied people who are idle because of the system. The biggest social problems out there, I would argue, are with the young single men. What's going to happen to them? This money can be spent to help you put them to work.

Now, I cannot do anything directly about that, but I implore you to go back to the people who represent you in the State legislatures and see how much money your States got, and ask them to use some of that money to give these young men a chance to build their lives, too, because they need to be a part of our future.

The fourth thing we need to do is to make our cities places that anybody would be proud to call home is to make it easier for people to have homes in our cities. Homeownership is one of the most empowering things we can ever do for anyone. Since I took office, 4.7

million people across America have become homeowners for the first time. Homeownership has had big, big increases. As I said, our goal is to have more than two-thirds of the American people in their own homes by the year 2000 for the first time ever.

But you know and I know not enough homes are in our cities. In the last 4 years, we've reduced FHA mortgage premiums three times, to lower the average closing cost on a new home by $1,200. That's made a lot of difference to a lot of young people, and I'm proud of that. Today we're going to cut the premium another $200 for people if they buy homes in our central cities. This will bring the total reduction, since we took office, of closing costs to those families to $1,400.

Also, we know that there are many hard-working families who receive section 8 assistance who are ready to assume the responsibility of owning their own homes, but they can't take the first step. HUD now has a very innovative program before the Congress that would allow those families to use their rent vouchers to help to buy a home. Today I'm happy to announce that Freddie Mac is going to help us launch this homeownership empowerment voucher initiative by financing up to 2,000 of these mortgages.

Together with the Officer Next Door program, this represents almost $700 million in downpayment toward our priority of strengthening our cities family by family, by helping more people buy a home in the cities of America. And I hope you will support that as well.

The fifth thing we need to do is to make sure that our schools work and that all our children, no matter where they live, get the best education in the world. I know only a few mayors actually have any control over the school systems in your cities, but every mayor must be concerned about the quality of education in your cities. We know one of the main reasons families continue to leave cities is they simply don't think the schools are doing a good enough job.

Just this week, Hillary was visiting in a school system where junior high kids were talking to her about the problems they face. We know that these years are especially critical. But we also know our schools are capable of working.

Let me just give you one example. I hope that all of you noticed that for the very first time since we started participating in the international test on math and science, our fourth graders—only a few thousand of them, about 13,000 of them around the country, took these tests, but they are representative by race, income, and region—scored well above the international average in math and science for the first time. We can make all our schools work. You know that, and I know it, but we have to.

Our eighth graders are still below the international average, and all of you know from your own experience what happens to these kids when they're subject to difficult influences and tough circumstances, when they get into those early teenage years. That's when we're losing so many of them. And we have to make our schools work if we're going to bring them back. We just have to do it.

We're working hard to connect every classroom in America to the Internet by the year 2000. Last evening I met with some representatives of the high-tech community who were helping us to do that. We've had wonderful support from industry, and a lot of your communities are just doing this anyway. But I'm telling you, when we've got every classroom and every library and every school in America connected to the Internet, and then when we learn to teach the parents of those children how to access the Internet so they can communicate, regardless of their work schedules, with the teachers—"Was my kid in school today?"—with the principals—"What can I do to help?"—when we do that, we are going to revolutionize learning in this country. We will democratize it for the first time ever. And it won't matter whether a child is living on a Native American reservation or an inner-city neighborhood in Los Angeles or remote town in the Ozarks of north Arkansas; they will all be able to get the same learning in the same way at the same time, for the first time in history. And all of us, whether we have direct responsibility for the schools or not, have an obligation to get that done as quickly as possible.

Secretary Riley and I are working to mobilize a million volunteers, to make sure that by the year 2000 every 8-year-old, wherever he or she lives and whatever their native language is, can read independently by the third grade. That is also terribly important.

We're working to make sure that 100,000 teachers in America are certified as master teachers, so that in every school building in the country there will be at least one teacher that

you know has had the finest training available and passed the most rigorous standards that can then be imparted to other teachers in the school building. And above all, we have challenged our schools to set and meet high national standards.

Let me say, I am gratified that education officials representing over 20 percent of the children we educate in this country have agreed to participate in national exams like the international tests of reading for fourth graders and math for eighth graders by the year 1999. But a lot of people are holding back in these States. They say, "We don't want the Federal Government to take this over." The Federal Government has nothing to do with it, except we're paying for the test.

The vast majority of our States today participate in a National Assessment of Educational Progress, but they only give the test to a representative sample. They don't give it to all the kids in all the school districts in America.

Look at these last international tests. We have nothing to be afraid of. The only thing that's going to wreck our schools is if we hide our head in the sand, we don't say what the standards are, we don't measure whether our kids are meeting them, and we say, well, they just can't make it because they're poor or they come from some disadvantaged background. That is a load of bull. We need to get this out in the open and make sure all of our kids can meet these standards.

I spent a couple of hours with Mayor Daley and the people that are operating the Chicago school system not very long ago. The Chicago school system used to be known as the school system that went on strike every year whether they needed to or not. [*Laughter*] Every year in the Chicago paper—when I served as Governor and Jim Thompson was a Governor and his child was a student in the schools, there was always—you could just wait for—a certain time of the year, there would be a picture of little Samantha Thompson, who wouldn't be in school because the strike was going on. Now the Chicago schools are known for moving aggressively to stop social promotion, to raise performance, and that the city will take over the schools that are failing and straighten them up. We can do this. We can all do this.

The sixth thing we have to do is to do more to deal with issues of public health. And let me say something especially about HIV and AIDS, because it grips so many of our cities, it costs so much money, but far more important, it costs so much in human lives and trauma.

Last month I issued a call to find an AIDS vaccine within the next 10 years. We have continued to dramatically increase the amount of money we're putting into research for that purpose alone, while having dramatic increases in care, prevention, and other basic research.

Yesterday in Denver, the other leading industrial nations of the world pledged to help us meet that challenge. But until there is a vaccine, you have to help us, and we have to do more in the area of prevention. It's our strongest weapon. That's why we have to continue to identify sound public health strategies that enable local communities to address the twin epidemics of AIDS and substance abuse, and you know better than anyone how intertwined they are. We will continue to work to provide the best treatment, the best services, the finest drugs. And we will help you to meet the cost.

And let me also say, we can't stop until we find a cure to bring a permanent end to the epidemic, nor can we limit our efforts only to HIV and AIDS. We know that in the 21st century, as people move around the world more rapidly, one of the single most significant security threats of the future will be the spread of infectious diseases that are no more than the airline flight of one infected persons on another continent away from your community. We know that.

We have got to build up our public health infrastructures, and we have to make sure that we have basic health services out there for all our children, which is why I say, again, one of the most important aspects of this new budget agreement is the funds it gives us to give health insurance to half the 10 million kids who don't have it. We need to keep going until every child in every community in America has health insurance coverage and the people that are providing health care can get reimbursement so we can build a network to protect our kids to give them good health and to deal with the challenges that are bound to come to American cities in the future.

The last thing I want to ask you to do is to make our cities the model of the one America we're trying to create, which deals not only with the racial initiative that I announced in San Diego 9 days ago but also with the primary purpose of the Presidents' Summit of Service

that Mayor Rendell hosted in Philadelphia not very long ago.

Keep in mind, the purpose of the Summit of Service was quite specific. It was to save every child in America; to give every child a safe place to grow up; every child the health care he or she needs; every child a decent education so they'll be able to support themselves when they get out of school; every child a mentor who needs it—every single one a mentor, one-on-one, who needs it; and every child the chance to engage in citizen service.

Now, what's our job at the national level? An adequate education budget; a better health care effort; a crime program that will really work in the area of juvenile justice to give you the tools you need; and the work we do to help provide AmeriCorps volunteers that have done so much to help you fulfill your mission in city after city in America.

But you have to help us do that. That was not a one-time public relations stunt for me. I agreed to do that Presidents' Summit of Service because it had a very sharply defined mission and because it did not let me off the hook and it did not let Government off the hook. It said, we can't expect volunteers to replace what is the public's responsibility in education, health care, and public safety, but neither can you expect just that responsibility to change the lives of these children who are physically isolated.

I see Mayor Menino looking at me there. He may get some money from the Federal Government to hire police, but they decided that they'd have police and probation officers make house calls to kids in trouble, and they have an astonishing 70 percent compliance with probation orders in the city of Boston. I feel quite confident that that is virtually unheard of in America.

So there are things that you have to do. And there are things that even you can't do to give all these kids mentors. But you can get people to do that and then give them a chance to serve. Our national survey before that summit showed that 90 percent of the children in this country said they would—including the poorest kids—said they would be happy to engage in service themselves, but someone needed to ask them and tell them what to do. That is the job of adults.

So I want you to understand, I intend to do my job that I promised to do at the Summit of Service. You have a role to play, but we have to recognize that it doesn't matter how rich we are, it doesn't matter how successful we are, if we keep raising generation after generation of poor children that are literally physically isolated from the rest of us, this country will never fulfill the American dream. And we don't have to put up with it. And you can help us change it.

And the last thing I want to say about this dialog on race is that it is the cities that have the biggest stake in this endeavor. Today, Hawaii is the only State in America that has no majority race. But no one who has ever been there doubts it is very much an American place, patriotic, upbeat, entrepreneurial. Within 3 or 4 years, California will have no majority race. Within 30 years, there will be no majority race in the country. Today, in Mayor Archer's home county, there are people from 146 different racial and ethnic groups.

Now, people expect that in southern California. But we're talking about Michigan, in the heartland. No one—I would say no one—virtually no one has stopped to think about what America will be like in a generation. And you say, well, Bosnia at least couldn't happen here. That's probably true because we have too much stake in our shared prosperity. But don't forget how quickly people who live together as neighbors for generation after generation have turned on each other, in Africa, in Bosnia. Don't forget how totally irrational it seems to us as outsiders, especially those of us who are Irish, that our relatives in Northern Ireland continue with what we think of as madness in the face of all the evidence that the world and the 20-odd percent of us who are Americans are dying to help them rebuild a better future than they could ever imagine if they would just give up hating each other because of 600-year-old disputes rooted in their religious differences.

We have a chance here to do something that has never been done in all of human history, since people first began together in tribes before there was a written history and identified people who looked different from them and lived different from them as their potential enemies. We have a chance to rewrite the rules of human evolution, almost, by building the world's first truly great multiracial, multiethnic democracy. And it will have to be done in the cities where the people are.

So I say to you, we have an opportunity here because we're doing this not after some riots, not because we know there's a big, long legislative agenda that needs to be passed but because we know there is still prejudice and discrimination and, maybe even more important, still stereotyping which blinds us to the possibilities of our people.

Why do you really think that so many people are reluctant to belly up to the bar and participate in these national tests? Not because they're afraid that the test scores will be bad the first time, but because they're afraid they'll never get any better, because of our stereotyping, the shackles in our minds. We cannot afford it. The cities cannot afford it.

The cities of America are bursting with excitement and success. There's hardly a one you can go to that just doesn't fill you with the human potential and connections that are being made. We have to make that the rule in America. We have to make that the order of the day. We have to make that the governing public philosophy of all our citizens. And if we do, our lives will be a lot more fun and a lot more interesting. And being a mayor will be even more exciting 10 years from now and 20 years from now and 30 years from now than it is today.

So I say to you, all the other things I said, none of it will happen, and you know it won't happen, unless we learn to live together, relishing, celebrating, loving our diversity but being bound by things that are even more important.

Thank you, and God bless you.

NOTE: The President spoke at 9:50 a.m. at the Fairmont Hotel. In his remarks, he referred to J. Thomas Cochran, executive director, United States Conference of Mayors; professional golfer Tiger Woods; James R. Thompson, former Governor of Illinois, and his daughter, Samantha; and the following mayors: Willie Brown of San Francisco, CA; Richard M. Daley of Chicago, IL; Paul Helmke of Fort Wayne, IN; Deedee Corradini of Salt Lake City, UT; Norman B. Rice of Seattle, WA, and his wife, Constance; Wellington Webb of Denver, CO, and his wife, Wilma; Michael R. White of Cleveland, OH; Jerry E. Abramson of Louisville, KY; Bob Lanier of Houston, TX; Edward Rendell of Philadelphia, PA; Thomas Menino of Boston, MA; and Dennis W. Archer of Detroit, MI.

Remarks at a Luncheon for Senator Barbara Boxer in San Francisco
June 23, 1997

Thank you very much, Senator Boxer, Senator Torricelli. Delaine Eastin, thank you for being here and for supporting our educational standards and excellence movement. I thank the Saxophone Quartet and the Bacich School second grade choir. I thought they were both terrific. [*Applause*] Thank you. I guarantee you one thing, when the kids were up there singing, every one of us was saying, "I wonder if I could sing that song, if I could remember all those States in alphabetical order." [*Laughter*] Good citizenship.

When Barbara Boxer was finishing her remarks, Bob Torricelli, who is an old friend of mine—old friends talk, she should have chided us for talking—[*laughter*]—Bob Torricelli leaned over to me and said, "She is the best spirit in the entire Senate."

You know, in the spirit of campaign reform, I think you know one of the things that I favor is full disclosure. And for those of you who don't know, Barbara Boxer's first grandchild is my second nephew, so that's really why I'm here. [*Laughter*] It has nothing to do with party or conviction or anything. Therefore, I have had an unusual opportunity to get to know this woman, and what I can tell you is that everything I have ever seen of her in private is completely consistent with the face and the voice she presents to the public. And that is important. What you are seeing is exactly what you get 24 hours a day, 7 days a week, 365 weeks a year.

And while we normally but not always agree on the issues, the thing I would like for you to think about today is the spirit, the heart of the matter. I've been here a good while now in Washington, and I had a real life before I moved to Washington—[*laughter*]—and I expect to have a real life when I leave. And I have almost come to the conclusion that more important than the ideological debates or the party differences is which spirit will dominate Washington as we move into the 21st century.

I mean, here we are basically with the strongest economy in a generation, with an unemployment rate below 5 percent for the first time in 24 years; the lowest inflation in 30 years; and for us Democrats, a very important statistic,

the biggest decline in inequality among working families in over three decades; the number one exporter in the world; the lowest deficit as a percentage of our income of any major economy in the world; a crime rate that dropped—the biggest drop in 36 years last year; before the welfare law took effect, the biggest drop in welfare rolls in the history of the Republic. And yet, there are really still people in Washington who seem like they're mad about it. [*Laughter*] And they want to do whatever it takes to make sure you don't think about it. And this whole spirit, you know, are you going to be for the people who try to drive you down or the people who try to lift you up. That's really what it's about.

You know, you listen to some of these people talk in the Nation's Capital, you'd think that they spent the whole morning sucking lemons before they got up to give the speech. [*Laughter*] And you listen to Barbara Boxer talk in the middle of a rainstorm and you'd be convinced you were on the beach in some sunny resort. [*Laughter*] It's a difference in approach to life and attitude and whether you believe the purpose of politics is to elevate the human spirit and bring people together across the lines that divide them and make people believe that tomorrow can be better than today, or whether you believe the purpose of it is to carve out your little niche of power and anything that threatens it, including good news, should be crushed at the earliest possible moment with whatever means at hand.

Now, that really is the great choice here. You must not let this woman be defeated by all the people who will say, well, she's too liberal on this, that, or the other thing. If she ever made a mistake in her life, it was a mistake of the head, not the heart. And don't you ever forget it. We all make mistakes.

And that is really what is at issue. I have done everything I can as President to heal the kind of divisive, destructive, political climate that has come to dominate too much of the discourse in Washington, the automatic assumption that anybody who is different from you has got something terrible wrong with them, the feeling that anything you can do to beat somebody who is your opponent, no matter how much you have to denigrate them, is all right. I've tried to get beyond that. I've tried to treat my opponents with respect and dignity and honor. And I've tried to restore what I thought was the best tradition of this country.

But you've got a Senator that works like crazy every day, that gets things done. You heard that list. One thing she didn't mention—she'll be glad Torricelli told me this. He said she forgot to say something. She forgot to say that when she was fighting for that emergency supplemental that we got passed for all the emergencies, one of the things it had in it was money for breast cancer research in the San Francisco area to see whether environmental causes are leading the higher rates of breast cancer here than other parts of the country. She did that.

You know, I hope you'll forgive me, but I'm as high on America as those kids are. I think they're right. I think they're right. And I don't pretend to have all the answers. All I know is that this country is better off today than it was when Barbara Boxer got elected to the Senate. I know that she has made material contributions to the efforts that our administration has made to grow the economy, to give poor people a chance, to increase the availability of education, to increase the accessibility of health care, to drive the crime rate down, and to bring us together across the lines that too often divide us. That's what I know.

And that's far more important than any specific issue that you can turn into a 30-second ad one way or the other. And I know that the spirit she brings to public life is the spirit we need from all people who go to Washington to represent you without regard to their party or their philosophy. If we brought that kind of spirit into all of our endeavors, instead of thinking about how we could drive a stake into the spirit of the American people by our short-term advantage, this country would have no problems.

And also, we cannot afford to be afraid of the future. And that sort of divisive talk, you know, it makes people afraid of the future. We don't have anything to be afraid of if we just face our problems, face our challenges, realize that we've still got a lot to do, realize that we don't have a person to waste, and realize that we all deserve to be represented by people who wake up in the right spirit.

And I believe that this woman is a rare treasure for our country. Yes, we're now united by marriage. [*Laughter*] Yes, I'm personally crazy about her. That's all true. But the most important thing—I'm not running anymore, I won't be on the ballot anymore. I've been in public life for a long time. I've seen a lot of people come and go. Contrary to what you may read or feel, the overwhelming majority of people I have known of both parties and all philosophies have been scrupulously honest people who worked hard and made less money than they could've made doing nearly anything else with people of their talent and energy and ability, who wanted to make this a better country. And everybody who is trying to convince you of the contrary is wrong. And people who try to keep the American people in a bad frame of mind because they just can't bear to think that somebody is happy and successful somewhere are wrong.

And what we need to do is to be focused on our common problems and our common business. So don't let the people who trade on fear and only win when you're unhappy turn Barbara Boxer into a cardboard cutout of what she really is. Don't let that happen. And remember, it's way more important than the issues; it's about the spirit of the country. It's about the spirit of California. California did not get where it is, you didn't come back from all those disasters and a terrible recession just on my policies. I'd like to think I helped, but you didn't get there—you got there on the spirit of the people. And if everybody had sat around, being in the frame of mind that the kind of people who are going to fight her so hard want you to be in when you go vote on election day, you would not have recovered.

We cannot behave on election day in a way that is different from the way we want to behave on every other day of the year. We cannot look at the world in a different way on election day in a way different from the way we want to look at our life and expect to get the kind of elected representatives we want and the kind of collective decisions we have to make as a people. Remember that.

Remember Senator Torricelli's line. And through the ups and the downs, you stay with her and you make up your mind that you will not let the people of California be taken in by an attack on her because she is the great spirit of the Senate. And that's what America needs: the right spirit.

Thank you, and God bless you.

NOTE: The President spoke at 12:24 p.m. at the Hyatt Regency San Francisco Hotel. In his remarks, he referred to Delaine Eastin, California superintendent of public instruction.

Remarks at Mar Vista Elementary School in Los Angeles, California
June 23, 1997

The President. Thank you. I thought Mary Mendez did a good job for a parent and not a professional speaker, didn't you? Give her a hand. [*Applause*]

Hello!

Audience members. Hello!

The President. It's wonderful to be back in California and to be here in Los Angeles and to be here in this terrific neighborhood at this great school. Thank you very much for having me here. Thank you, Mayor Riordan, for your good work and your kind remarks.

I want to thank my Small Business Administrator, Aida Alvarez, who's here with me today. She's been speaking to the LULAC convention. But I brought her here to emphasize another passionate feeling of mine, and that is that we have to give every American a chance to live up to his or her God-given abilities. Aida Alvarez is the first American of Puerto Rican descent ever to be in a President's Cabinet. So I thought I would bring her today, and I'm glad she's here.

Thank you, David Lawrence and Dr. Sharon Levine, for your great citizenship. And thank you, Doris Palacio, for the wonderful work you do here at this school. I'm very, very proud of you, thank you. I want to thank the people from Children's Now, the parents, the students, and the teachers at Mar Vista.

Now, you know what we're here to talk about. Too many children all across America, too many children here in California, some children in this crowd today don't have health insurance. We are here today because Kaiser Permanente is going to make a major change in that for you in California. We want to congratulate them, but even more important, we ought to be here to resolve to do better and not to rest until every child in America has an appropriate health insurance policy and adequate health care when they need it.

The hard truth is that while America has the highest health care quality in the world, in many ways too many Americans don't have access to the best the system has to offer. You heard the good doctor outlining it. Today, over 10 million American children, over 1.6 million of them here in California, don't have health insurance. Do you know what that means? That means nearly 40 percent of the uninsured children don't get the annual checkups they need and may not find those holes in the heart or lead problems or other problems. It means one in four uninsured children don't even have a regular doctor. It means too many children who have trouble seeing a blackboard don't get the glasses they need to correct their vision; that too many nagging coughs go untreated until they worsen into more serious conditions that may require costly treatments and lengthy hospital stays later; that too many parents actually face the agonizing and impossible choice between buying medicine for a sick child or food for the rest of their family. We must do better, and we can.

Our economy is the strongest in the world. In the last 4 years we've become the number one exporter again, we've produced over 12 million jobs, we have the lowest unemployment rate in 24 years, and we are still the only advanced industrial country in the world that does not provide health insurance for every single one of its working families. It is wrong, and we have to do better.

It is true, as you have heard, that a number of children are actually covered by law under State programs like MediCal, and for some reason their parents either don't know or don't believe they can access the program. We have to do better. But it's also true that nearly one-sixth of us simply don't have health insurance. I tried hard to enact a plan that would give all American working families health insurance, and it's well known I failed. But I'm not ashamed that I tried.

So after we did, we sort of rolled up our sleeves and decided we had to try again in a different way. And we decided to try to go at this step by step. Last year we passed a law which says that families can't automatically lose their health insurance when the parent changes jobs or when somebody in the family has been sick. We've begun to make it easier for people who are self-employed to buy affordable health insurance. And we have supported efforts in States all across the country to use the Medicaid program or, in this case, the MediCal program, to try to expand coverage to working families that don't have insurance through the workplace.

We recently had a Presidents' Summit of Service in Philadelphia in which I said that the era of big Government may be over but the era of big challenges is not, and that citizens and Government had to do more to work together to give every child a fair chance at living out his or her dreams. And we said there are five things that we ought to do. One, give every child a safe place to grow up. That's one of the things that I talked to the mayors about, doing more to keep our kids out of trouble and keep our streets and our schools safe and drug free. Two, give all of our children world-class education, put computers in all the classrooms, teach all the kids to read, open the doors of college education to all young people. We can do that. I'm proud of the fact that this balanced budget agreement I reached with Congress, in addition to what it does on health care, has the biggest increase in Federal support for education in over 30 years. And we are going to pass it and bring it here to the schools of California. The fourth thing we promised to do was to do everything we can to see that every child in this country has a mentor. And we're doing our part there, trying to mobilize through AmeriCorps volunteers a million people to help make sure all of our kids can read, whatever their native tongue, read independently by the time they're in the third grade, so they can do well and go on and create a good future for themselves.

And we said that every child should have a healthy start in life, something all citizens must take responsibility for. That's what Kaiser has done. Again I say, I cannot thank Kaiser enough, not only for doing this but for challenging other people in the same line of business to do the same thing, 50,000 kids here, 50,000 there, pretty soon you're talking about a lot of families with healthy children. And we've got to do that.

But even as Kaiser does its part—you heard what they said, one of the things they're going to do—how are they going to get 50,000 kids insured every year with $20 million a year? That's $400 a child. That's less than most of you can buy health insurance for. How are they going to do that? They're going to get more kids in the existing MediCal system; they're going to work out partnerships; they're going to work out sliding fee arrangements, so that people who can afford to pay something but not the ongoing commercial rates can pay what they can afford to pay. A lot of families would gladly do that if they could just get some insurance coverage.

And what does that mean? That means that Government has to do its part, too. Telling citizens they have a responsibility will never relieve the Government of its responsibility to work with citizens who are doing the very best they can to make us one country where everybody's got a chance to raise healthy children.

So I want all of you to know that the balanced budget agreement that I reached with the leaders of Congress and that passed with overwhelming bipartisan majorities in both Houses includes the largest investment in children's health care since the Medicaid program was enacted in 1965, the largest investment in over 30 years, designed to bring to millions and millions of children health insurance coverage that they don't have, to work with companies like Kaiser Permanente, to work with States, to work with local communities to make sure that we do not leave these children and their families behind. And we have certain standards.

That budget agreement is now being written into law, and here's what we're trying to do. First of all, the coverage ought to be meaningful. It ought to cover everything from checkups to surgery so that children get the care they need. Second, we ought to make sure that coverage is affordable. People who can pay something ought to pay it, but they ought to be able to buy affordable health insurance. If people are out there working full-time and doing the best they can, they ought to be able to have the dignity of knowing that they can take care of their children. People should be able to succeed at home and succeed at work in the same way. And the third thing—and I don't expect—this won't concern a lot of you, but for people like Dr. Lawrence and me, it's a big headache—we've got to make sure that this money actually goes to uninsured children. We cannot simply see the money replacing money that already goes from Government or from private insurance or from charities to health insurance. We have to draw this bill in a way that this new money actually insures more children. And I want you to know, we're going to work hard to do all those things.

Let me just say to the young children here, you are growing up in a very hopeful time for America. Our economy is the healthiest in a generation. Crime and welfare are down. America is the world's leading force for peace and freedom and prosperity.

We have two great challenges—we have many, but there are two great challenges. First, look around this crowd today. The first is the one I talked about in San Diego just 9 days ago. We have got to prove that we can be the first truly equal, fair, harmonious, multiracial democracy in history. We have got to prove that we can do that. And the second thing we have to do is to make sure every child has a chance to live out his or her dreams. We cannot leave any of our children behind in physical isolation because they don't have decent health care, or their streets aren't safe, or their schools aren't adequate. We can't—we can't—afford that.

And this health care initiative today is very important, not only because of the children that will be covered, not only because of the challenge that others will have to meet, not only because of the energy it puts behind what we're trying to do in the Congress for millions of children but because it makes a statement about what it means to be an American on the edge of the 21st century. We're not going to leave our children behind. That's what this is about.

So again I say, thank you to the educators; thank you to the health providers; thank you, Mr. Mayor. Thanks to all of you. Remember what we're here for today. If your child needs health insurance, try to get him in this initiative. But as a citizen, don't give up until every child in America has the health care that he or she deserves.

Thank you, and God bless you.

NOTE: The President spoke at 5:08 p.m. on the playground. In his remarks, he referred to Mary Mendez, who introduced the President; Mayor Richard Riordan of Los Angeles; David Lawrence, chief executive officer and chairman, Kaiser Permanente; Sharon Levine, leader of the Kaiser Permanente pediatric unit; and school principal Doris Palacio.

Statement on the Supreme Court Decision on Federal Funds for Educational Programs
June 23, 1997

I am pleased with the Supreme Court's decision today which will raise educational standards for children across America. For the last 10 years, school districts have been barred from providing title I supplemental remedial educational programs to parochial school students in their classrooms. These special programs, which supplement the school's base curriculum, provide remedial education to students who need more than the standard school day provides.

My administration sought to overturn this unfair restriction. The Court's decision explicitly accepts the position put forth by Solicitor General Walter Dellinger, representing Secretary of Education Richard Riley, that federally funded supplemental education programs may be provided to students of both public and parochial schools without running afoul of the principle of separation of church and state. No longer will children have to leave their school buildings in order to get the assistance they need.

Because of today's ruling, all schoolchildren, whether in public or private schools, can benefit equally from the important supplemental remedial programs of title I.

Statement on the Death of Betty Shabazz
June 23, 1997

Hillary and I were saddened to learn of the passing of Betty Shabazz earlier today. She devoted a long career to education and to uplifting women and children. She was also a loving mother. Our prayers are with her family in this hour of grief.

Remarks at a Democratic Senatorial Campaign Committee Reception in Los Angeles
June 23, 1997

The President. Thank you very much. Just a minute, I have to ask Senator Boxer a question. [*Laughter*] She said, "You don't really have to say anything, it's just"——

Senator Barbara Boxer. No, I didn't, I said we want you to. [*Laughter*]

The President. She said, "I've been up here working for you for an hour, keeping the crowd"—[*laughter*]—I was back there working for her for an hour. [*Laughter*]

Ladies and gentlemen, in the interest of campaign reform and full disclosure—[*laughter*]— the real reason I'm here is that Barbara Boxer's first grandchild is my second nephew; it's just a family thing. [*Laughter*] It doesn't have anything to do with party or loyalty or agreement or anything. That's not true. I mean, it's true, but it's not the reason I'm here. [*Laughter*]

I'm so glad to see all of you here. I'm glad to see this enthusiasm for the person who is clearly the most enthusiastic member of the United States Senate. I'll tell you something, if the best Democrats in every State where there's a Senate race where we don't have a seat woke up tomorrow with a combination of Barbara Boxer's enthusiasm, self-confidence, and courage, we would win the Senate in a walk in 1998.

And I want to thank you for being here for her for a lot of reasons, but I would like to just emphasize two or three. I know Barbara gave her speech, and I know essentially what she said, even though I was in there working for her, but I want to remind you of a couple of things. When I took office in 1993, this State was not in good shape. Even more importantly, the politics of our country was dominated essentially by rhetorical and ideological name-calling,

and the whole drive of every election was basically to see how people could be divided in a way that advantaged the candidate who was trying to do the dividing. And most people just thought, well, it just doesn't matter. No one can seriously assert that now.

I said, if you'll give me a chance to serve, and you give her a chance to serve, we'll change the economic direction of this country and this State. We'll get rid of trickle-down economics. We'll replace it with an invest-and-grow strategy. We'll cut the deficit, invest in our kids and our future, invest in the environment and technology and medical research, still reduce the deficit. We'll expand our trade around the world. And we'll be stronger.

And when Barbara Boxer cast the decisive vote for my economic program in 1993—it passed by one vote, including the Vice President—as he said, "Whenever I vote, we win." [*Laughter*] I mean, the things that our friends on the other side said were just unbelievable. They said the sky would fall, the end of the world was here, nothing good would ever happen in America again. And we now know what happened. This is not a matter of dispute anymore.

Five years later, we have over 12 million new jobs, the lowest unemployment rate in 24 years, the lowest inflation in 30 years. The stock market has more than doubled. And something that's very important to us as Democrats, because you contribute to come here in large measure on behalf of those who cannot afford to be here: We've had the biggest decline in inequity among working people in over 30 years—in over 30 years. And none of that would have happened if California had sent Barbara

Boxer's opponent to the Senate in 1993, because we would have been one vote short. None of it would have happened. And I could go through example after example after example of that. So I say to you, for the following reasons, you must make sure she wins again.

Number one, she was right when you needed it, and California's back, and that's important. Number two, she always sticks up for what she believes in, and she's the same every day. She's the same in public and in private. She has integrity in the best sense: Her mind and her spirit and her words are always in the same place at the same time. And we need more of that in public life. And third, and maybe most important, as Bob Torricelli said earlier today and may have said here before I got here, she is really the greatest spirit in the Senate. And let me tell you something, after all this time I've spent in Washington, I still remember back before I moved there when I had a life. [*Laughter*] And, you know, back where people of different parties spent more time figuring out how they could work together than how they could bad-mouth each other, back where people were hired to be mayors and Governors and they were evaluated based on whether they got results, not how well they could keep people torn up and upset all the time.

And that's what I tried to bring to this country. And it's amazing. There are people in Washington—I think that it really makes them sad that America's doing so well. They wake up every day trying to think of some way to put us down, this whole country, and get us back to being angry and mad with one another. And I just keep trying to get everybody to look on the bright side and go forward. She is exhibit A. Barbara Boxer is exhibit A.

And if you think about the kind of challenges we're facing for the future, with all the things that are going well here, we still have some significant challenges. Can we really do what we need to do with the environment and still grow the economy? Yes, but we'll have to work together and be in the right frame of mind so we can have honorable, principled, and honest compromises.

Can we really find a way to stop talking about and actually do something about the real and physical isolation of the poorest of our children who have not been touched one whit by this recovery? Yes, but not if we think we can win elections by quick slogans instead of actually

doing something about it and not if we think we can do it as one party or one small group, instead of as an American commitment.

Can we really become the world's first truly great multiracial democracy where no race is a majority? That's about to happen here in a generation, about to happen here in California within 3 to 5 years. Yes, we can, but only if we have a certain largeness of spirit where we respect our honest differences of opinion, where we relish our diversity, but where we know underneath our basic humanity unites us and is more important than anything that divides us.

Now, when this election develops and the people that run against Barbara Boxer try to turn her into some kind of cardboard cookie cutout of who she really is and try to sort of perform reverse plastic surgery on her, you remember that when California was in need, she was there. You remember that every day she is up there actually getting things done. And remember most of all, she has the sort of spirit, quite apart from any vote on any issue, that is the precondition of America finishing the job of preparing this country for the 21st century and giving all our children the chance to live out their dreams and getting people to be responsible and to serve their communities and to be good citizens and bringing us together as one community.

California will send a signal to America about whether we can do what we need to do in the 21st century because you are already largely there, in ways that are all positive and ways that are somewhat negative. And you have to decide how you will approach what is left to be done. And I'm telling you, this country needs somebody in the United States Senate like Barbara Boxer, somebody who no matter how tough it gets, won't wilt; somebody who will be the same every day; and somebody who will treat her adversaries with dignity and decency and will wake up in a positive frame of mind, because that is a precondition for solving any problem that is fundamentally a human problem. And most of the problems we have left start as an affair of the heart.

So stick with her. I'm glad you're here for the kickoff. I want you to be there in the middle. And I want you to be there at the end. And I want to see you on television celebrating on election night.

Thank you, and God bless you.

NOTE: The President spoke at 8:05 p.m. at the Beverly Hilton Hotel.

Remarks at a Saxophone Club Reception in Los Angeles
June 23, 1997

The President. I thought he was going to say, "When the son of a migrant farmworker can introduce the redneck grandson of poor dirt farmers"—[*laughter*]—that's what I thought he was going to say.

Paul Rodriguez. The Secret Service cut that joke out. [*Laughter*]

The President. They take all our fun away. Thank you, Kevin. Thank you, Paul. Thank you, Campbell Brothers. Thank you, Bennett Kelley, for all your work on the Saxophone Club. I thank Lieutenant Governor Gray Davis and Congressman Brad Sherman, who were here earlier. And I thank all of you for being here.

I love the Saxophone Club. I love it. I love the idea that we've given so many people who never were in the political process before a chance to be a part of it and to help to forge your own future. I like the fact that most of the people who are in the Saxophone Club are a lot younger than I am. [*Laughter*] That's not true—I don't like that. [*Laughter*] But I do like the fact that people who have most of their days in front of them and who have a great stake in what we're doing believe enough in this to be a part of this.

You know, I was just thinking today coming out here to California how wildly different things are here than they were just 5 years ago. And I was thinking how profoundly grateful I feel to all of you for the fact that California voted for me twice, to all of you for the support you've given the policies that we have enacted, to all of you for helping to make it possible for Al Gore and Hillary and me and all of us in our administration to do things that have helped to get the unemployment rate below 5 percent for the first time in 24 years, to get the inflation rate to its lowest point in 30 years, to make America the number one exporter in the world again—and for a Democrat something that's very important—have the biggest decline in inequality among working people in over 30

years. I'm proud of that. And thank you for that.

I'm proud of the fact that we had the biggest drop in crime in 36 years, the biggest drop in the welfare rolls in history. I'm proud of the fact that we've cleaned up more toxic waste dumps in 4 years than they did in the previous 12, and we're going to clean up 500 more next time. I'm proud of that.

I'm proud of the fact that I was able, thanks to you, to get a balanced budget agreement which will have the biggest increase in health care coverage for America's children since Medicaid was enacted in 1965 and the biggest increase in investment for excellence in education in 35 years. And for the first time, if we pass this budget consistent with the agreement, we'll be able to say to every child in this country——

Audience member. What about the NEA?

The President. I'll get to that. [*Laughter*] We'll be able to say to every child in this country, when they're 10 years old, you will be able to go to college. You will be able to go to college. That's a big deal.

I'm proud of the fact that you've made it possible for us to pursue a policy that says that we can grow the economy and preserve the environment, that we can go forward together, that we don't have to do things like target the NEA or the National Endowment for the Humanities. I never could figure out why we'd want to get rid of spending $150 million a year, which is a small amount of a $1.5 trillion budget, to bring the arts and the humanities to people all across the country, in little byroads, who wouldn't have it otherwise, or to give young artists the chance to fulfill their God-given abilities. I think it's a pretty good investment.

But more than anything else, I'm proud of you. Just look around this crowd tonight. Nine days ago I had the opportunity to come to the University of California at San Diego and give a speech that was very important to me. I had been wanting to talk about it for a long time, asking the American people to join me in a national, honest conversation about race; to have in every community and every neighborhood, on every block, an honest conversation about what it is that still divides us and what unites us that's more important; to identify those laws that we ought to be enforcing that we're not, whatever changes we need to make, what new policies we need, but most important, what attitudes we have to have.

I am convinced that even more than the continuing examples of illegal discrimination, this country is being held back by things that aren't illegal but are equally damaging, that relate to stereotyping one another by race or other category. I am really concerned about it. And in California, you have both the opportunity and the obligation to lead the way in this, which is why I went to San Diego to give this speech. I mean, just look around the crowd tonight.

Today, America has one State, Hawaii, which has no majority race. In 3 to 5 years, California will join Hawaii. In 30 to 40 years, America will join Hawaii and California. And for the first time ever, we will have a chance to see whether all these things we've been saying about America for 100 years are true, that this is not about—this country is not about one race, it's not about one place, it's about a set of ideas and a set of ideals that anybody can share and be a part of and make a future on.

Well, we're about to find out. And it's high time we started thinking about it. What is the unfinished business between black Americans and white Americans? What is the unfinished business that Hispanic-Americans have growing out of their unique heritage—and they will soon be the second largest minority group when we're all minority groups in America—what about that? What does it mean to have Los Angeles County with over 150 different racial and ethnic groups? What does it mean not to be the providence of the coast anymore—Wayne County, Detroit, Michigan, has more than 140 different racial and ethnic groups in it. What does all this mean for us?

Can we become the first truly multiracial great democracy in human history? Can we shed all the historic baggage that's been with us ever since prehistory when our ancient, ancient, ancient ancestors gathered together in bands and traveled across the Earth as hunters and gathers and learned to distrust people who looked different from them because they really had reason

to be afraid of them? Why are we still living like that?

Can we get rid of those deep sort of psychological impulses that are inside? How many times did you ever have a day where you couldn't have gotten through the day if you didn't really dislike somebody? [*Laughter*] You say, "No matter how bad it is, at least I'm not as bad as that sucker." [*Laughter*] Right? How many days have you—everybody here has had a day like that, right? Everybody here has had a day like that. "I don't think much of myself today, but I sure am better than so and so." [*Laughter*] It's almost like we need this sort of thing.

And we're laughing about it. But we have been given a great gift, and those of you—particularly those of you who are younger have been given a great gift. You're going to grow up and live and raise your children and see your grandchildren grow up in an America where people have more chances to live out their dreams than ever before if we can prove that we really can live together as one America, where we not only accept, we actually celebrate what's different about us and we're secure in celebrating it because we know that what we share in common is even more important.

Now, that's really what this is all about. When we started the Saxophone Club in 1992, I had a set of simple little ideas that I wanted to bring to America. I said to myself, what do I want this country to be like when my daughter is my age in the 21st century? I want everybody to have an opportunity who is responsible enough to work for it. I want my country to be the world's strongest force for peace and freedom. And I want this country to be coming together instead of being driven apart. I am sick and tired of short-term, destructive, negative political strategies that divide people when we need to be united. That's what I wanted then, and that's what I want now.

Now, so, I say to you, I thank you for being here tonight. I want you to stay active in public affairs. I want you to, every time you hear somebody who is cynical and say it doesn't matter, say, "Compare how we are today with how we were then. This is what I supported; it was right; it made a difference; people's lives have changed." And then say, "But there's a lot more to do, and that's why I'm in it for the long haul."

Thank you, and God bless you.

NOTE: The President spoke at 10:18 p.m. at Billboard Live. In his remarks, he referred to actor Kevin Spacey; comedian Paul Rodriguez; Bennett Kelley, national cochair, Saxophone Club; and Lt. Gov. Gray Davis of California.

Message to the Congress Transmitting a Report on Federal Advisory Committees
June 23, 1997

To the Congress of the United States:

As provided by the Federal Advisory Committee Act, as amended (Public Law 92–463; 5 U.S.C., App. 2, 6(c)), I am submitting my third *Annual Report on Federal Advisory Committees,* covering fiscal year 1995.

Consistent with my commitment to create a more responsive government, the executive branch continues to implement my policy of maintaining the number of advisory committees within the ceiling of 534 required by Executive Order 12838 of February 10, 1993. As a result, my Administration held the number of discretionary advisory committees (established under general congressional authorizations) to 512, or 36 percent fewer than the 801 committees in existence at the time I took office.

During fiscal year 1995, executive departments and agencies expanded their efforts to coordinate the implementation of Federal programs with State, local, and tribal governments. To facilitate these important efforts, my Administration worked with the Congress to pass the "Unfunded Mandates Reform Act of 1995" (Public Law 104–4), which I signed into law on March 22, 1995. The Act provides for an exclusion from the Federal Advisory Committee Act (FACA) for interactions between Federal officials and their intergovernmental partners while acting in their official capacities. This action will directly support our joint efforts to strengthen accountability for program results at the local level.

Through the advisory committee planning process required by Executive Order 12838, departments and agencies have worked to minimize the number of advisory committees specifically mandated by statute. There were 407 such groups in existence at the end of fiscal year 1995, representing a 7 percent decrease over the 439 at the beginning of my Administration. However, we can do more to assure that the total costs to fund these groups, $46 million, are dedicated to support high-priority public involvement efforts.

My Administration will continue to work with the Congress to assure that all advisory committees that are required by statute are regularly reviewed through the congressional reauthorization process and that remaining groups are instrumental in achieving national interests. The results that can be realized by working together to achieve our mutual objective of a better, more accessible government will increase the public's confidence in the effectiveness of our democratic system.

WILLIAM J. CLINTON

The White House,
June 23, 1997.

NOTE: This message was released by the Office of the Press Secretary on June 24.

Statement on House of Representatives Action on Most-Favored-Nation Status for China
June 24, 1997

This past weekend, I was proud to host the leaders of the major industrial democracies at the Summit of the Eight in Denver. We discussed ways to make the 21st century safer, more secure, and more prosperous for all our people, and how we need to reach out to the world to ensure our well-being at home.

Today's vote in the House of Representatives to continue our normal trading relations with China enhances our ability to do just that—and to deepen our cooperation with the largest country in the world. I'm especially pleased to see this vote had strong bipartisan support. It sends a clear signal to our friends and foes alike that when it comes to America's security and prosperity, our Nation speaks with one voice.

Today's vote was a vote for America's interests. It makes clear that the right way to encourage further progress in China is not to cut China off but to draw China in.

China is home to nearly one-fourth the world's population and is one of the fastest growing markets in the world. Our steady engagement has expanded areas of cooperation, from stopping nuclear testing to promoting stability on the Korean Peninsula; from combating terrorism, drug trafficking, and pollution to protecting American intellectual property rights. And already, we sell $12 billion worth of exports to China every year—supporting tens of thousands of good American jobs.

Preserving normal trade relations does not mean endorsement of all of China's policies. When we disagree with China, such as on human rights and religious freedom, we will continue to speak out candidly and clearly. While we've felt all along that revoking normal trade relations would only exacerbate our differences, we are committed to work closely with Congress and others to defend and advance our interests with China as we strengthen our cooperation.

The way China evolves in the years ahead will have an enormous bearing on the shape of the 21st century. A stable, secure, open, and prosperous China that respects international norms and works with us as a partner is profoundly in America's interest. Ultimately, China will decide its own destiny. But by maintaining our steady engagement, we can play a useful role—helping China choose the path of integration that will benefit our people and the world.

Today's House vote reinforces that strategy and strengthens our ability to encourage positive change. Again, I want to thank the House of Representatives for its strong bipartisan support. I look forward to working with Members of both parties to deepen our policy consensus toward China and to advance our security and prosperity in the future.

Statement on Consumer Confidence
June 24, 1997

Today's Conference Board release, along with the University of Michigan's release earlier this month, indicate more good news on the economy.

Today's report shows that Americans are more confident about economic conditions than they have been in 28 years. With consumer confidence, unemployment, and inflation the best they've been in decades, America's economy is the strongest in the world and the best in a generation.

Unemployment is at its lowest level in 24 years, economic growth is the highest it has been in a decade, and inflation is the lowest for any administration since John F. Kennedy was President. We have already cut the deficit 77 percent since 1992, helping spark this remarkable period of strong growth and low inflation.

Now is the time to build on the bipartisan budget agreement, which will balance the budget for the first time since 1969, honor our values, and help to continue this solid economic performance.

Excerpt of Remarks During the Family Re-Union VI Conference in Nashville, Tennessee
June 25, 1997

The President. Thank you. Before we begin, let me just say briefly, of all the good ideas that Al and Tipper have ever had, this might be one of the two or three best. This is an amazing thing. It's something a President always hates to admit, but this is something I had absolutely nothing to do with. [*Laughter*] This predates our partnership even. But the fact that they recognized that the welfare and strength of the American family, upon which the whole future of the country depends, is directly affected by all these big issues we often talk about—the workplace issues, the education issues, the cultural issues—and determined to bring it down to family levels, and now this for the sixth time, I think is an astonishing and, as far as I know, unique contribution to America's public life.

And so I just want to say to you, Mr. Vice President, and to Tipper and to everybody who has worked so hard on all these conferences, you've done a great thing for our country, and I'm always glad to be here. I look forward to this every year, and I'm just grateful. And of course, because this day is about parents and education, I'm especially excited about it.

[*At this point, the discussion began.*]

The President. Unlike the rest of you, I knew what we were about to hear—[*laughter*]—because Hillary went and visited the school and she came back sort of floating. When you were talking about trying to cover that third "b", I couldn't help but think that's a perfect project for the Vice President's reinventing Government endeavor. [*Laughter*]

I don't think I can add any more to what she said, but I would like to fill in a blank that maybe needs to be filled in for some of you. When Susan was talking, I asked her if her superintendent supported what she was doing, and she said yes. It's just not true every-where that the school district supports such things or that sometimes the districts are so big they're just so overwhelmed they can't even imagine how to achieve such things.

And that is the purpose of the charter school movement that the Vice President, Secretary Riley, and I have worked so hard to support. It basically says you can create your own school within the public school system. And we have charter schools that are created in many different ways. Sometimes you just take over an existing building, and the teachers run it; sometimes a group of teachers and parents run it. But the point is, you're free to get out from under all those rules and regulations you think you have to cover yourself against.

And no one could have imagined a public school, for example, not only doing the things that were just described but actually buying out crack houses across the street or, if the parents are really poor and they want to be better role models for their kids and support them better, creating, in effect, microenterprises. And Los Angeles now has a $400 million bank that the Federal Government funded to try to help make loans to people who couldn't get loans any other way, and we'll probably be able to help to finance some of those folks.

But this is just an example of what can be done if educators and parents work together to try to create their own future in circumstances people say are hopeless. People are never in hopeless circumstances unless they have no power to do anything about it. All this charter school movement did was to give people like this remarkable woman the power to change their own lives.

So I think it's a very important component of it, and in our budget, which is part of this balanced budget amendment, we have enough funds to increase by tenfold the number of charter schools over the next 5 years. And I hope that they'll increase by a hundredfold just by local initiatives now, as these stories get out. And then of course, the real answer is for more people to be in a situation Susan is in, where the central administration just lets them do it in the first place.

Thank you. Both of you were great.

[The discussion continued.]

The President. I'm glad you took the Governor to see "Cinderella." *[Laughter]* I hope you got him home before midnight. *[Laughter]* Don Sundquist will write me about this before the week is out; I know it. *[Laughter]*

Let me ask you something. You've already done something that I think is very important, but I would like to just reemphasize it because it underlies not only what you said but, in a different way, the presentations of everyone who has spoken before you.

There is, I think, among some policymakers and—I know we've got Mr. Purcell here who might want to talk about this in a minute—and among the general public sometimes, like when a school bond issue is being voted on or something, we have an increasing divergence between the people who have money and the people who have children in the schools—or property owners. There is, I think, this underlying assumption that these kids that are in very difficult circumstances have parents that, (a) can't do better than they're doing and (b) don't want to. And both those things are just false.

But they are in different circumstances than parents used to be, and they're going to school with different kinds of people. I just think that's worth hitting home, that you and your excuse-free center—I take it once you established your excuse-free center, you got plenty of folks that want to access it. And that is something—that's a message I would like to go out across America today. It is not true that just because somebody is poor or a first-generation immigrant or has been through some rough times in their lives, has made a mistake or two, that they do not want to do a good job, number one. And it is not true that they cannot be trained to do a good job, number two. And that's the message of your work, and I think we've got to get that out.

[The discussion continued.]

The President. Just one other point I want to make here because I think it's underlying

what she's said—very important. There is a common assumption among people who are afraid of high standards that if you raise the standards, the most vulnerable children will fail more and drop out more. What she has demonstrated is that exactly the reverse is the case: If you raise the standards and you do it in the right way and you give everybody a chance to succeed, they will be more likely to stay, not more likely to quit. And I really appreciate that.

[The discussion continued.]

The President. First of all, John, thank you for establishing that fund. I'm going to be out of work in a couple years; I might apply myself. *[Laughter]*

I would like to emphasize one thing about this electronic dashboard. Now, you all haven't seen it yet, so I don't want to talk too much about it. But I want to emphasize—the fact that you're setting it up means that you believe, like all folks on this side of the stage, that all parents should be able to have access to technology and be taught to use it so they can be in communication with their children's teachers and principals. And I think that's a very important thing because a lot of school districts, in part, haven't done this because they think, "Well, maybe my parents don't speak English very well; how can they learn to use a computer?" And I think that's looking at it backwards.

So I'd like for you to just emphasize that you do not think this is just something that middle and upper middle class school districts have to use.

[The discussion continued.]

The President. I'd just like to, first of all, thank you and thank the other education reformers in Minnesota for pointing the way on the college credit initiative, which did lead to a huge increase in advanced placement, which is now being mirrored all across the country, and on public school choice and on the charter schools. And I think we were—when I was Governor of my home State, I think we were the second State to adopt a statewide school choice law. And my daughter actually took advantage of it when she was in elementary and junior high school, to the great benefit of our family and our life.

And I just want to emphasize that giving parents all these choices and all this power—the important thing, almost none of them will choose to go outside their neighborhood or assigned district, but knowing that they have the ability to do it changes the attitude of everybody in all the districts and lifts the standards everywhere. That's the key thing here.

And the charter schools, as a practical matter—we have 500 now. We had 300 when I proposed our legislation with Secretary Riley to fund 3,000 more over the next few years. What we really are trying to do is to create a critical mass which will turn every school into a school like the first two we heard about today—first three we heard about. That's what we're trying to do. And eventually we'll hit that critical mass, wherever it is, and when we do, it will be just sort of volcanic positive change in American education. And a lot of it will have started in the State of Minnesota. I'm grateful to you.

[The discussion continued.]

The President. Let me say just very briefly about Secretary Riley, first of all, as you can hear him talk, he's from South Carolina. And the Vice President and I like him because he makes us sound as if we do not have an accent when we speak. [*Laughter*]

Bill Purcell said, "Sometimes Government should lead the way; sometimes Government

should get out of the way." I agree with both those. Sometimes Government should support the way, and I believe that Dick Riley has been the best Secretary of Education our country ever had because he's been able to do all three things—all three things.

To go back to what Yvonne said at the beginning, there is no telling how many rules and regulations that Secretary Riley has gotten rid of to give the decisionmaking power back to local school districts and, to some extent, to States and ultimately to local schools. And we feel very strongly we should be doing that even as we give more support for these reform needs. And he has really done a wonderful job, and I'm very grateful to him.

NOTE: The President spoke at approximately 11:25 a.m. in Langford Auditorium at Vanderbilt University during Family Re-Union VI: Family and Learning. In his remarks, he referred to Susan Gingrich-Cameron, principal, Carson Lane Academy, Murfreesboro, TN; Gov. Don Sundquist of Tennessee; Bill Purcell, director, Child and Family Policy Center, Vanderbilt Institute for Public Policy Studies; John Doerr, partner, Kleiner, Perkins, Caufield and Byers, Menlo Park, CA; and Yvonne Chan, principal, Vaughn Next Century Learning Center, San Fernando, CA.

Remarks to the Family Re-Union VI Conference in Nashville
June 25, 1997

Thank you very much, Mr. Vice President. We built in a little time on the other end of the schedule because I knew that we'd all want to stay here longer. I'm reluctant to say anything; those 12 people were so good.

I'm reminded of the very first time I made a speech as an elected public official, more than 20 years ago now. It was at a Rotary Club in southeast Arkansas, and it was one of these officers banquets, you know, it was one of those things where we start at 6:30, and I was introduced to speak at a quarter to 10. [*Laughter*] There were 500 people there; all but 3 were introduced. They went home mad. [*Laughter*] And the only guy in the audience—in the whole crowd more nervous than me was the fellow that was supposed to introduce me. He didn't

know what to say. He was nervous, too. And so I get ready to be introduced, and the guy comes up, and his opening line is—after all the officers had been inducted, all the awards had been given, everybody had been recognized, his opening line is—in my first speech as an elected public official—is, "You know, we could have stopped here and had a very nice evening." [*Laughter*] Now, I know he didn't mean it that way. [*Laughter*] And I could have said that about myself now. We could stop right here and have had a very nice session.

What I would like to do just very briefly is to try to put this whole—what we've been talking about today in the larger context of what America is trying to do and what our responsibility is at the national level, because when

I say over and over and over again, the era of big Government is over, but the era of big challenges is not, I don't mean for people to say, as they sometimes do, that that means the Federal Government can take a powder. I don't agree with that.

What I mean is that we're going to have to do more of what we do together as partners, and we cannot succeed in a lot of these problems, which as you just heard are fundamentally human challenges that have to be dealt with child by child, family by family, street by street, school by school—that simply cannot be done successfully if the whole focus is on what is the Federal Government going to do. On the other hand, I would argue it cannot be done comprehensively and fairly to every child if there is no focus on what is the Federal Government going to do.

Now, for the last 4½ years, Vice President Gore and I and our team have worked on a simple vision for America. We've been trying to prepare our country for the 21st century with some simple goals: We want every child to have the chance to live out his or her dreams. We want every citizen to be responsible for self, for family, for community, for country. And we want a community that is coming together as one America, not being driven apart by its differences. And we think if we do all those things, we'll have—what, finally, we want is for our country to continue to be the world's leading force for peace and freedom and prosperity in the world.

And when you ask yourselves a tough question in the moment, I think it often helps to get the right answer. You say, "Well, where do I want to go?" Well, that's where we want to go. And our strategy has been to develop a National Government set of policies that would, in effect, empower citizens and families and communities and schools and workplaces to create the kind of destiny that we know we're capable of creating.

That's why I love these Family Re-Union conferences, because every one of them, fundamentally, when you get right down to it, is about empowerment. You take the two the Vice President mentioned, the television rating system and the V-chip. The Government can advocate for and even mandate, in the case of the V-chip, a law, but all it does is to empower families to be able to raise their children with a little more direction—or what we did on the family

and medical leave and what we hope to do on advancing, expanding family and medical leave, and having the right sort of flextime proposal.

Nothing is really more important to a society than raising children. But if we have a good economy, it helps people raise children. So the real—what's in the vortex there in the middle is how do you enable people to succeed at home and at work? How many times did you hear these people talking about child care, before-school care, after-school care, bringing in the parents at different times—a parent played in an orchestra concert the night before and taught orchestra the next morning. What does that mean? It means that we have to find new and creative ways to reconcile work and family and in some places to get work for families so that they can succeed as parents of students.

So that's what I like about this, because this family conference basically emphasizes what I think our central strategy ought to be, which is how are we going to give our citizens the power they need, first and foremost, to raise successful children and, secondly, to make America successful?

And let me just very briefly mention two or three things. We have tried to focus on—in addition to the economy, which was our first obsession because we knew if we couldn't get it going, a lot of these other things wouldn't occur, we tried to say, "Well, what else do families need?" One is safe streets. So we've worked hard on a grassroots crime package to empower people to keep the crime rate coming down, and last year we had the biggest drop in 36 years. And if we do it for about 3 more years, people might actually believe it's come down, as it has. And that's good. That is, it might be more than numbers and lives saved; people might actually feel safe. And that's important because if people don't feel safe, they're not fully free.

Then we focused on culture, the V-chip, the TV ratings, the work, the terrific work Secretary Riley did with Attorney General Reno to draw the lines and also amplify the possibilities for dealing with different religious convictions in our schools which are multiplying enormously. We tried to deal with cultural issues in the sensitive way that respected the differences of conviction and opinion of people on religion, on race, on other issues but still bound us together consistent with our Constitution.

The third thing we focused on, as I said, was home and work. And I mentioned that family leave, flextime, the minimum wage, a tax cut for working families with modest incomes—that's a big part of the new balanced budget plan, too. That has a children's tax cut.

The fourth thing we focused on was public health and the environment. If you think about it, the Safe Drinking Water Act, the new food safety standards, cleaning up toxic waste dumps, these things are very important. If they make children healthier, it makes us stronger. We've made a lot of strides in that in the last 4½ years, indeed, in the last 25 years. And one of the things that I was doing this morning before I came down here to be with you was to deal with the obligation of the Environmental Protection Agency to issue new regulations, as they're bound to do on a 5-year cycle, to control pollution from soot and smog. That's very important. And I approved some very strong new regulations today that will be somewhat controversial, but I think kids ought to be healthy.

Our approach on the environment, interestingly enough, has been a lot like the approach that you've heard here on the schools. We think if we have high standards for protecting the environment, but we're flexible in how those standards are implemented and we give adequate time and adequate support for technology and creativity, that we can protect the environment and grow the economy. And we know we can never be put in the position of choosing one or the other because in the end, a declining economy has always, always led to an environment that is less clean—always. So we've got to find a way to do both.

And I want to thank the Vice President for his leadership on this issue. And I know that those who have opposed the higher standards, I want to just tell you: Read the implementation schedule; work with us. We will find a way to do this in a way that grows the American economy. But we have to keep having a clean environment if we want healthy children.

Children with asthma don't do very well in school. Children with gripping allergies that they could have avoided if they hadn't had to breathe dirty air don't do as well in school. So the public health and the environment are important parts of this.

We're trying extraordinary new measures to give cities the means they need to clean up their environment so they can attract the right kind of investment. And we're determined to clean up 500 more toxic waste dumps; that will bear directly on education. And if we do it right, it will cause our economy to grow faster, not slower. So I hope all of you will support that.

And finally, let me say, in education we have focused on empowerment, on things like charter schools, public school choice, more funds for Head Start to get more kids well-prepared, better terms for college loan programs so more young people can borrow money and go to college and never worry about going broke because they couldn't pay their loans back, so they could pay them back as a percentage of their income, a huge expansion in work-study, a big expansion in Pell grants. And then, on top of what we've already done, if a balanced budget plan passes, it will be the biggest increase in funds for education in over a generation. And including funds to support the schools that are trying to set high standards, that are trying to be innovative with things like charter schools, more funds to support putting the right kind of technology with the right kind of training and software in all of our schools, more funds to support a massive volunteer effort to make sure all of our 8-year-olds have a chance to read well.

We still have some serious challenges in our schools. One of the most interesting things that we finally saw manifested in test scores this year was that the Third International Math and Science Test scores came out this year on last year's scores, and they showed that for the first time, American fourth graders scored way above the international average on math and science. And that even though this was just a few thousand of our kids who took this, it's a representative sample by race, by income, and by region, proving that our children can learn even though they are very diverse in incomes and in ethnic backgrounds and in living circumstances—way above the national average. That's the good news.

The bad news is, we were the only nation in the world to score way above the national average on the fourth grade tests and well below the international average on the eighth grade tests. It happened in no other country in the world.

Why is that? Let's be real here. The reason you stood up and clapped for Yvonne is you know that a lot of these kids are living in hellaciously difficult circumstances, right? That's why you did that. And you did it because you

want to believe that those kids can make it
if we do right by them. And she made you
believe they could, and it was thrilling to you.
But when a lot of these kids reach adolescence,
every single problem that affects every adolescent hits them multiplied by a hundred. And
we've got to find a way to keep their parents
or other concerned adults involved with them
when they reach adolescence.

The fourth grade tests should make you ecstatic. It punctures all the myths that we can't
compete globally in educational performance,
uniformly, because we have so many poor people, because we have so many immigrants, because we're so diverse. That is our meal ticket
to the future if we do it right. That punctures
the myth.

The eighth grade tests should sober us up.
These kids have a tough time out there. That's
one of the reasons that in our budget we're
determined to give half of them health insurance
for the first time and deal with some of these
health problems we're talking about. We
shouldn't stop until they all have health care.
It's unconscionable.

Let me say, in the moment, the most important thing is that you know we can do it. That's
what the fourth grade tests mean. The second
most important thing is you know that we can't
stop until every child has the kind of parental
involvement that 30 years of academic studies
have shown is pivotal in the success of children.

And so one of the things, to go back to Representative Purcell's formulation, plus my little
add-on about either leading the way, getting out
of the way, or trying to support the way—one
of the things that I think is important is that
today the Department of Education is publish-
ing a handbook to help parents everywhere understand and live up to their responsibilities and
work with the schools. And Dick gave me the
first copy here. It's called "A Compact For
Learning."

And I would like to explain something to you.
We are required under Federal law to have
a written compact for the title I schools, and
so we thought we ought to have an outline here
that would at least increase the chances that
we might be as successful in these other schools
as the ones that you've seen featured today.
But what we want to do with this is to challenge
every principal, every teacher, every parent to
have a written compact that outlines their expectations and their responsibilities for helping

every child to learn high standards, with serious,
sustained, effective parental involvement. That's
how we'll try to support the way. It is very,
very important.

I have to tell you, I feel more hopeful today—
I've been working on these educational issues
for nearly two decades now, and I have never
been more hopeful than I am today that what
I consider to be the central problem with the
system of education in America might be overcome.

The central problem is the following, as you
have just heard: Every challenge in America has
been met by somebody, somewhere. How can
that be a problem? Because if that is true, we
should be able to replicate it everywhere.

You heard the Vice President say 98 percent
of us have televisions. Well, once, just a few
of us did. We all figured out how everybody
could get a television. You heard John Doerr
say that 50 percent of the parents—more than
50 percent of the parents with children in school
now have personal computers in their homes.
Any pretty soon it will be a lot higher than
that and go way down in lower income levels.

Why is it—and I mean this as a compliment
to our first speakers, our first three speakers
who talked about their schools, and the principal
of the San Antonio school district—why is it
that we want to scream with joy when we hear
them talk, when we heard our friend from Chat-
tanooga talking about how they served the parents—and they had no excuses? Why did we
want to scream with joy when we heard that?
Because they are the exception, not the rule.

So, no offense, but I'd like it if 5 years from
now they could come back to this stage and
give all these talks and receive polite applause
and the gratitude of the Nation for getting everybody else to follow their lead so they would
no longer be the exception and not the rule.

We'll do our part. I hope you'll help us get
this handbook out and get it made alive in the
work of the school districts in the country, in
all the schools. You'll do yours. But remember,
our kids can do it. The only question is whether
we're going to do our part to make sure they
get their chance to do it. And that is, in many
ways, the central obligation of adult Americans
at this moment in our history.

And I think we owe a great debt of gratitude
to the Vice President and Mrs. Gore for every
year reminding us about what's most important
in all our lives and in our country's life.

Thank you very much.

NOTE: The President spoke at 12:40 p.m. in Langford Auditorium at Vanderbilt University. In his remarks, he referred to Yvonne Chan, principal, Vaughn New Century Learning Center, San Fernando, CA; former Tennessee State Representative Bill Purcell, director, Child and Family Policy Center, Vanderbilt Institute for Public Policy Studies; and John Doerr, partner, Kleiner, Perkins, Caufield and Byers, Menlo Park, CA.

Statement on the Death of Jacques Cousteau
June 25, 1997

Hillary and I, along with tens of millions around the world, were saddened to learn of the death of a man with rare insight and extraordinary spirit, Jacques Cousteau. While we mourn his death, it is far more appropriate that we celebrate his remarkable life and the gifts he gave to all of us.

Jacques Cousteau will be remembered for many things. He enabled mankind to truly become part of the sea and the creatures that live there, inventing scuba gear and creating the first one-person submarine. Most appropriately, he will be remembered for his service to us all on the good ship *Calypso*. Through his many documentaries, movies, and television specials, Captain Cousteau showed us both the importance of the world's oceans and the beauty that lies within. We are all far richer, and more caring, for his having shared his time on Earth with the human family.

One of his most important documentaries was titled "The World of Silence." Thanks to a life spent dedicated to serving all of God's creation, his legacy will be not silence. Rather, it will be continuing to inspire people the world over to love, appreciate, and respect the sea.

Letter to Congressional Leaders Transmitting a Report on Cyprus
June 25, 1997

Dear Mr. Speaker: (Dear Mr. Chairman:)

In accordance with Public Law 95–384 (22 U.S.C. 2373(c)), I submit to you this report on progress toward a negotiated settlement of the Cyprus question. The previous submission covered progress through January 31, 1997. The current submission covers the period February 1, 1997, through March 31, 1997.

The highlight of this reporting period was the start of U.N.-sponsored proximity talks on the island. The United States strongly supported efforts by the United Nations to engage the two Cypriot leaders productively in these talks in preparation for direct negotiations. We have stated our support for the U.N.'s undertaking on several occasions and have urged both leaders to seize the opportunity to demonstrate their commitment to the reconciliation process.

Although his appointment fell outside the current reporting period, I am very pleased that Richard Holbrooke will serve as my Special Presidential Emissary for Cyprus. He assumes his duties at a time when tensions on the island have eased due to the overflight moratorium recently agreed to by the parties, as well as their agreement to begin the U.N.-sponsored direct talks in early July. I have asked Ambassador Holbrooke to use his proven negotiating skills and superb knowledge of the region to support the U.N. efforts.

Sincerely,

WILLIAM J. CLINTON

NOTE: Identical letters were sent to Newt Gingrich, Speaker of the House of Representatives, and Jesse Helms, chairman, Senate Committee on Foreign Relations.

Message to the Senate Transmitting the Switzerland-United States Taxation Convention and Protocol With Documentation
June 25, 1997

To the Senate of the United States:

I transmit herewith for Senate advice and consent to ratification the Convention Between the United States of America and the Swiss Confederation for the Avoidance of Double Taxation with Respect to Taxes on Income, signed at Washington, October 2, 1996, together with a Protocol to the Convention. An enclosed exchange of notes with an attached Memorandum of Understanding, transmitted for the information of the Senate, provides clarification with respect to the application of the Convention in specified cases. Also transmitted is the report of the Department of State concerning the Convention.

This Convention, which is similar to tax treaties between the United States and other Orga-

nization for Economic Cooperation and Development (OECD) nations, provides maximum rates of tax to be applied to various types of income and protection from double taxation of income. The Convention also provides for exchange of information and sets forth rules to limit the benefits of the Convention so that they are available only to residents that are not engaged in treaty shopping.

I recommend that the Senate give early and favorable consideration to this Convention and give its advice and consent to ratification.

WILLIAM J. CLINTON

The White House,
June 25, 1997.

Remarks at a Dinner for Senator Carol Moseley-Braun in Chicago, Illinois
June 25, 1997

Thank you very much, Mayor and Mrs. Daley; Reverend Barrow; Representative Jones and Chairman LaPaille; Mr. Houlihan. I'm sorry Paul Simon left. I have sat in on so many of his speeches, and he sat in on so many of mine—I was sort of getting used to getting back to our old routine. I miss Paul Simon in the Senate, but I'm glad he's still here caring about Illinois. He doesn't have an ax to grind, and I think we ought to listen to his recommendations.

Let me also say that I had a good time, Mayor, when I got off the plane and I took my little helicopter to Meigs Field, soon to be Daley Park—[laughter]—and there were still people there when I got out, and they said, "Welcome home, Mr. President," and I love that. Chicago has sort of become my second home—Illinois has. And you all remember that on St. Patrick's Day in 1992 the victory we had here and up in Michigan pretty well assured the nomination, and I will always be grateful for that.

And I try to water my Chicago roots whenever I can. You know, we had the Bulls at the White House the other day, and Scottie Pippen got up and referred to me as his "homeboy"—[laughter]—after which Michael Jordan said that Hillary would always be first in the hearts of Chicagoans. That's a battle I was glad to lose. [Laughter]

The mayor was terrific leading the mayors this year. He did a great job. You should all be very proud of him. And they had a great meeting in San Francisco. I was afraid that his tenure might be tarnished by the outbreak of civil disobedience here when they started interleague play in baseball. [Laughter] And I want to congratulate you for doing whatever was necessary to avoid that. [Laughter]

Let me say—we're all among friends tonight—I want to make a fairly pointed and brief argument for why I'm here and why I hope that Senator Carol Moseley-Braun will be reelected. In 1992, when I ran for President, I had an idea that we could only change America if we changed the way we were doing politics, if we broke out of the debates which were always dividing people into yesterday's categories. It's okay to be a liberal or a conservative, but it's not okay to be irrelevant in American politics. It's not okay to be divisive for the sake of being divisive. It's not okay to be interested in rhetoric only and no reality. It's not okay to trap yourself in a pattern of conduct which never permits progress to occur.

And it was obvious to me that we had to change what we had to do and that we weren't even asking the right questions. So I started with what I thought the right question was: What would I like America to look like when my daughter is my age? How would I like America to go into this new century? What do we need to do to prepare America to go into the new century?

I still believe in what I said then: I want our country in the 21st century to be a place where every American without regard to race, gender, or background has a chance to live out his or her dreams; where our communities are full of citizens who are exercising their individual responsibilities for themselves, their families, their communities, and their country; where we are celebrating our diversity but coming together as one America in a strong united community; and where, because we did these things, we can still lead the world to greater peace and freedom and prosperity. That's what I still want for our country in this new century.

What is the principal way we have to achieve that? We have to look at every significant area of national life and ask ourselves: Does it create more opportunity for all? Does it induce more responsibility from all? Does it help us build a community of all Americans? If the era of big Government and big centralized bureaucracies is over, that doesn't let Government off the hook; far from it. In some ways, we should be more active. But it does mean we have to focus on what works, which is giving people the tools they need to empower them to seize their own opportunities and solve their own problems and build their own lives and their own community.

So we took that approach. In the economy we said we have to bring the deficit down, it's killing America. But we have to invest more in our children, in our future, in technology and science and research. We can't just stop investing in medical research because we've got a deficit. We have to cut in the right way. And

our opponents said it couldn't be done. Some of those in our own party said it couldn't be done because you couldn't cut and invest. And every single person in the other party said that if my economic plan passed in 1993 the country would go into a nosedive, we'd have a terrible recession, it would be the awfullest thing you ever saw. And so every single one of them voted against it, which means that if Carol Moseley-Braun had not been in the Senate we would not have prevailed.

Now, on that alone, she deserves your support for reelection. The State of Illinois is a lot better off today than it was on the day I was sworn in as President in 1993, and that economic program we passed by one single, solitary vote in the Senate and the House is a big reason. Vice President Gore even had to vote in that. And as he says, whenever he votes, we win. [*Laughter*]

But she was there. She stood up. She listened to all the naysayers and said, "I don't believe that's right." Well, now, before this balanced budget plan passed, we cut the deficit by 77 percent; we got a 4.8 percent unemployment rate, the lowest unemployment in 24 years; the lowest inflation in 30 years; and something that's very important to Democrats, the biggest decline in inequality among working people in over 30 years. And Carol Moseley-Braun played a major role in bringing that about, and she deserves your support because of it, and I hope you will give it to her.

We thought we could be tough and smart about crime and give the streets back to the people if we just listened to people like Mayor Daley, who had been a prosecutor, the police officers of our country, the community leaders, and fashioned a crime bill that made sense. We did it, and we supported the innovative work going on in communities all over this country. Last year we had the biggest decline in crime in 36 years—in 36 years. And not all but nearly all of the folks in the other party opposed us on that and said, "What we really need is tough talk and more jails and nothing else." We said, "What we need is more police, tougher punishment on people who are serious offenders, but more aggressive efforts to prevent young people from getting in trouble in the first place." And that strategy has worked. That strategy has worked.

Now, it's not as if this is a debatable point. You know, we've had the debate, and now we've got the evidence. And it would seem to me that the people of Illinois would want to support someone who is out there advocating policies that work and a direction that's good for the ordinary citizens of Illinois, for the business community and the working people—for the poor, the middle class, and the wealthy—because we're going together, and we're going forward together.

And I could give you example after example of that. But we have changed the way politics works in Washington. It drives some people crazy, but we've done it. There are lots of people who really, I think, in Washington who are just kind of unhappy when the country is happy. You know, they would prefer it if the world really worked like those talk shows, you know, where people scream at each other and call each other names and hurl labels around like they really meant something.

But out here in the real world, in all those little towns I visited on the bus in Illinois in '92 and '96, those people don't need talking heads screaming at each other; they need reasoned public debate by people who care deeply about their future and what their children's lives will be like, actually producing results that make a difference. And that's what we're trying to do. And that's what you ought to reward, because that's what helps the people of Illinois to build a better future.

And if you just look at this budget debate that we're having, it's a historic, marvelous thing. And I still believe, even though we're disagreeing mostly because Members of Congress, being contentious as they are—some of them don't want to adhere to the terms of the agreement at some point. But if you look at that agreement, it would balance the budget, but it would give us the biggest increase in health care investment for children since Medicaid passed in 1965. It would balance the budget, but it would give us the biggest increase in educational investment for our children since 1965 and the biggest increase in access to colleges and universities since the GI bill was passed 50 years ago. That's what's in that balanced budget. And make no mistake about it, those priorities are there because of our side and what we believe and what we brought to the table. And I think they deserve to be supported.

And I'll just give you three specific examples of things that bear the imprint of Carol Moseley-Braun: one in the past—I'll give you

four—two in the budget, and one still in the future.

Number one, she was a cosponsor of the Family and Medical Leave Act. It was the first bill I signed as President. Every month, my staff pulls for me a representative sample of mail I get from ordinary American citizens, people I've never met, people I never will meet. And among the most moving letters I have ever received are those that come from people who tell me, "My wife got sick." "My child got sick." "My father was dying." "I got to take a little time off from work without losing my job." "I got to be true and faithful to my family and true and faithful to my job, and I didn't lose it." "I'm a better employee and America is a better place because of the Family and Medical Leave Act."

Believe me, if people who thought like us had never attained the White House and kept the majority in Congress when we did, it never would have become the law of the land. The other side said, "It's going to hurt the economy." It was the first bill I signed in '93. If it's hurting the economy, it's doing a poor job of it.

I believe we're a better place when people can succeed at home and at work. This is a problem that affects Americans of all income groups. A lot of upper income people tear their hair out worrying about how they can do what they're supposed to do at work and still do right by their children. This family leave act symbolizes the values this country ought to stand for.

Two things in the budget. Number one, in 1993 we knew we would have to do something extra if we wanted our cities and people who had literally been physically isolated from the mainstream of life to have any chance whatever to participate in the free enterprise system and succeed. So we created the empowerment zone concept, which Carol Moseley-Braun supported, and Chicago is participating. We created the Community Development Financial Institutions Act to set up banks like the South Shore Bank here in Chicago all over America so that people who could otherwise never get any credit to start their own business—very often a self-employed business—in isolated inner cities and poor rural areas would have a chance to do that.

Hillary did a lot of work on these things when we were still living in Arkansas and has been all over the world promoting these kind of community financial institutions and these microenterprise businesses and loans to them in developing countries. It is amazing how much your Government has done to help people who would otherwise be desperately poor in countries all over the world to get credit to start their own businesses, and we had never done anything to help our own people do the same things. Carol Moseley-Braun was a cosponsor of that. In this balanced budget amendment we more than doubled the funds for the community development financial institutions. Everybody ought to have a chance to participate in this economic boom, and it won't be good enough for me until everybody does. And that's what she's trying to do.

Number two, the cities of this country have worked and worked and worked to bring back economic vitality, and we now see unemployment in our 50 largest cities falling by a third in the last 4 years. We've got economic growth coming back, and one of the biggest barriers to growth in the city is an environmental problem, where sites have been abandoned where economic activity used to occur, and it is not economical for someone else to come in and redevelop those sites and put people to work because of the cost of environmental cleanup. And our balanced budget—and these sites, by the way, are called brownfields. Most Americans don't know what that is. You read of brownfield—a brownfield is a place, almost always in a city, where people used to make money and they left, and it's now polluted, and people can't afford to go in and make money there again. Otherwise, the cities would very often be the most economical places to invest for new business because that's where the labor pool is—very often.

So what we have done is to come up with a strategy to give tax credits to people who invest there and also to invest a lot more money through the Environmental Protection Agency to try to help clean them up so we can have economic vitality coming back to the cities. Carol Moseley-Braun is one of the chief cosponsors of the brownfields legislation. It's a very important part of Chicago's future and important to Illinois. And you ought to be for it.

And the last thing I want to say is Carol Moseley-Braun is the first person who came to me and said, "Mr. President, I know the National Government has never done this before, but we ought to try to do something about the crumbling buildings in our country's school system." We've got too many places like a school district where I was in Florida recently, when I had my unfortunate accident, where the children were going to school in 17 trailer houses, as well as the regular school building. That's how overcrowded they were.

I was in Philadelphia the other day. The average age of a school building in Philadelphia is 65 years of age. Now, a lot of those schools are very well built, but they're in poor repair. And there are a lot of school districts that simply don't have the property tax base and simply don't have a high enough percentage of parents living in the school district as property owners to do everything they need to do to rebuild these buildings. I'm trying to put a computer in every classroom and library in the country. It will be of precious little comfort if the ceiling is leaking and the windows are cracked.

And Carol Moseley-Braun said we ought to do something about this. And she persuaded me to offer a partial solution to a huge national challenge. And in the budget agreement I could not persuade the leaders of the Congress, the majority, to go along with it. But I still believe in the end we'll get this done, especially if you reelect her, because it's the right thing to do.

But here's a case where she was out front on an issue. She said, "We have a national interest. We're fixing to have the biggest increase in investment in education from the National Government in a whole generation, and we're going to leave tens of thousands of our children in substandard physical facilities where it will be very difficult for them to learn and for the teachers to teach. And we can't solve the whole problem, but we ought to give States and localities the incentive to do more and say, 'If you will do more, we'll do more to help you. You have to carry your load, but if you will, we'll do more to help you.'"

That is leadership. That's what you hire people for. You hire people to make good decisions, to make your life better, to give you the tools to make the most of your own lives, and you hire people to look to the future and come up with leadership ideas that may not be accepted when they're first floated but that have merit, that are right, and that in the end are going to prevail if you give the people who are advocating them the chance to serve long enough to do it.

That's my simple case to you. This is a better country today because in 1992 the State of Illinois sent Carol Moseley-Braun, a Democrat, to the United States Senate instead of her opponent. If you had sent her opponent there, the economic program I advanced would have failed by one vote and this would be a different country today. You should reward people who do things that are good for this country. And it's a better country because we have someone like her up there advocating these innovating approaches in the environment, in the economy, in families, and in education. Listen, our best days are still ahead of us. Don't kid yourself; this country has got a brilliant future. But we have to face our challenges.

And I close with this point: About 10 days ago I went out to San Diego and gave a speech about race, not yesterday's racial challenges but tomorrow's. And I pointed out, among other things, that today we already have five school districts in America where the children come from over 100 different racial and ethnic groups. In a matter of a year or two, we'll have 12 school districts.

We have a large number of our biggest counties, including this one, where there are people from over 100 different racial and ethnic groups. Today, we have one State, Hawaii, where there is no majority race. In 3 years, California will join Hawaii, and they represent 13 percent of the total population of America. But within 30 years, America will have no majority race.

We must find a way to work with each other across racial lines, to sit down and talk honestly with each other, and to realize that we have a deep and profound stake in the success of each other's children. That's what I couldn't help thinking about when those kids were up here singing tonight. You didn't care what color they were, did you? And you didn't care what their backgrounds were. And they made you feel better, didn't they? You felt better when they were singing than you've felt all night long. Why? Because they represented the best of you and all of your hopes for the future.

One of the things I like about Carol Moseley-Braun is she can work with different kinds of people. She can reach across the lines that divide, and she gets up there every day and tries to get something done. And that's why I tried to become your President. That's the test that I always wanted to measure myself against. But most importantly, that's the right thing for all those children that were up here singing.

So you think about those things, and think about them today, tomorrow, and through November of 1998, and send her back to the Senate so that we can keep moving America forward.

Thank you, and God bless you all.

NOTE: The President spoke at 8 p.m. in the Ballroom at the Sheraton Hotel. In his remarks, he referred to Mayor Richard M. Daley of Chicago and his wife, Margaret; Rev. Willie Barrow of Operation PUSH; Emil D. Jones, Jr., president, Illinois State Senate; Gary LaPaille, chair, Illinois Democratic Party; and James Houlihan, Cook County assessor.

Remarks at the Funeral Service for Henry Oren Grisham in Hope, Arkansas
June 26, 1997

Reverend Hight, Duayne and Conrad and Falva and Myra and all the family, we come here to celebrate the life of one of the most truly remarkable people I have ever known, a man without wealth or power, without position or any pretense, who was, nonetheless, loved, admired, respected because he was smart and wise, profoundly good, and I might add, very funny.

There will be a lot of tears shed in the family section today, and you might say, well, how could you cry that much for a man who had God's gift of 92 years? Because he was forever young, and we wish he'd lived to be 192.

Everyone who ever knew him had a story about him, about hunting or fishing or farming, about sharing a meal or swapping a tale. One of the young men at the funeral home came up to me this morning just before we came out and said, "You know, he always kept me up. He made me laugh."

One of the members of the family said he was the salt of the Earth and the spice of life. Everyone who talks about him has clear, vivid memories of his wit and his wisdom and, I might add, his remarkable ability to be both brutally honest and always kind.

When I was a young boy, badly in need of a hand up and a little kindness and wisdom, whenever I was at his house and Ollie's, I always felt at home. But he always treated everybody that way. After I became a grown man, he only called me one time, in our whole life together, just once, to tell me that in 1979, a year before all the experts said it, that I could not be re-elected Governor because I had made people mad. And I said, "Well, what do you think I ought to do about it?" He said, "Tell them you made a mistake and undo it, for goodness sake." I said, "I can't do that." He said, "Good, after the next election, you'll have a lot more time to spend with me." [*Laughter*] And he was right.

After Ollie got sick and died, he still continued to drive around and be active. And I told Reverend Hight this morning the funny story he told me. In the last few years, he used to take two ladies who were older than he was, in their nineties, driving once a week. He said, "Nobody else would go take them out, so I would just go take them out once a week and drive them around. We have a grand time." He was about 87 at the time. And I said, "Do you like these older women?" He said, "You know, I do. It seems like they're a little more settled." [*Laughter*]

The great poet William Wordsworth said that the last, best hope of a good man's life are the little unremembered acts of kindness and love. I'll bet you every person here today who ever met that man has an act of kindness and love that you remember.

He really did the things that matter most in life very well. He was a great husband, a great father, a great grandfather, a great uncle. He was a great friend.

My most vivid memory of him, I think, will always be after Ollie got sick and they had to put her in a place where she could be cared for. And he was going through this awful period when she was failing, and he loved her so much. I stopped to see him one night in his house, and we were all alone there. We talked and shot the breeze for a long time. We laughed, and he told stories, and everything was just normal. And finally, it was real late, and I had to drive back to Little Rock, and I said, "Buddy, I've got to go." He said, "Okay." I was on my way out the door, and he grabbed me by the arm, and I turned around, and he had tears in his eyes—it was the only time I ever saw them—and I said, "This is really hard, isn't it?" And he smiled, and he said, "You know, it is. But when I married her, I signed on for the whole load, and most of it's been pretty good." I have never heard a better testament of love and devotion than that.

So I say of his great life, all of it was more than pretty good. If our country and our world had more people like Henry Oren Grisham, how much better it would be, how many more children would have a happy childhood, how much more peace and harmony there would be.

Conrad's poem said it all, and I'm pretty sure God heard it.

Thank you. God bless you.

NOTE: The President spoke at approximately 10:20 a.m. at the Brazzel/Oak Crest Chapel. Henry Oren Grisham was the President's great-uncle. In his remarks, the President referred to Rev. I.V. Hight, pastor, Unity Baptist Church; and Mr. Grisham's late wife, Ollie, his sons, Duayne and Conrad, and his daughters, Falva Grisham Lively and Myra Grisham Irvin.

Remarks to the United Nations Special Session on Environment and Development in New York City
June 26, 1997

Thank you very much. Mr. President, Mr. Secretary-General, ladies and gentlemen: Five years ago in Rio, the nations of the world joined together around a simple but revolutionary proposition, that today's progress must not come at tomorrow's expense.

In our era, the environment has moved to the top of the international agenda because how well a nation honors it will have an impact, for good or ill, not only on the people of that nation but all across the globe. Preserving the resources we share is crucial not only for the quality of our individual environments and health but also to maintain stability and peace within nations and among them. As the father of conservation in our Nation, John Muir, said, "When we try to pick anything out by itself, we find it hitched to everything else in the universe."

In the years since Rio, there has been real progress in some areas. Nations have banned the dumping of radioactive wastes in the ocean and reduced marine pollution from sources on land. We're working to protect the precious coral reefs, to conserve threatened fish, to stop the advance of deserts. At the Cairo Conference on Population and Development, we reaffirmed the crucial importance of cooperative family planning efforts to long-term sustainable development.

Here in America, we have worked to clean up a record number of our toxic dumps, and we intend to clean 500 more over the next 4 years. We passed new laws to better protect our water, created new national parks and monuments, and worked to harmonize our efforts for environmental protection, economic growth, and social improvement, aided by a distinguished Council on Sustainable Development.

Yesterday I announced the most far-reaching efforts to improve air quality in our Nation in 20 years, cutting smog levels dramatically and, for the first time ever, setting standards to lower the levels of the fine particles in the atmosphere that form soot. In America, the incidence of childhood asthma has been increasing rapidly. It is now the single biggest reason our children are hospitalized. These measures will help to change that, to improve health of people of all ages, and to prevent as many as 15,000 premature deaths a year. Still, we here have much more to do, especially in reducing America's contribution to global climate change.

The science is clear and compelling: We humans are changing the global climate. Concentrations of greenhouse gases in the atmosphere are at their highest levels in more than 200,000 years, and climbing sharply. If the trend

is not changed, scientists expect the seas to rise 2 feet or more over the next century. In America, that means 9,000 square miles of Florida, Louisiana, and other coastal areas will be flooded. In Asia, 17 percent of Bangladesh, land on which 6 million people now live, will be lost. Island chains such as the Maldives will disappear from the map, unless we reverse the predictions.

Climate changes will disrupt agriculture, cause severe droughts and floods and the spread of infectious diseases, which will be a big enough problem for us under the best of circumstances in the 21st century. There could be 50 million or more cases of malaria a year. We can expect more deaths from heat stress. Just 2 years ago, here in the United States in the city of Chicago, we saw the tragedy of more than 400 of our citizens dying during a severe heat wave.

No nation can escape this danger. None can evade its responsibility to confront it. And we must all do our part, industrial nations that emit the largest quantities of greenhouse gases today and developing nations whose greenhouse gas emissions are growing rapidly. I applaud the European Union for its strong focus on this issue and the World Bank for setting environmental standards for projects it will finance in the developing world.

Here in the United States, we must do better. With 4 percent of the world's population, we already produce more than 20 percent of its greenhouse gases. Frankly, our record since Rio is not sufficient. We have been blessed with high rates of growth and millions of new jobs over the last few years, but that has led to an increase in greenhouse gas emissions in spite of the adoption of new conservation practices. So we must do better, and we will.

The air quality action I took on yesterday is a positive first step, but more must follow. In order to reduce greenhouse gases and grow the economy, we must invest more in the technologies of the future. I am directing my Cabinet to work to develop them. Government, universities, business, and labor must work together. All these efforts must be sustained over years, indeed, over decades. As Vice President Gore said Monday, "Sustainable development requires sustained commitment." With that commitment, we can succeed.

We must create new technologies and develop new strategies like emissions trading that will both curtail pollution and support continued economic growth. We owe that in the developed world to ourselves and, equally, to those in the developing nations. Many of the technologies that will help us to meet the new air quality standards can also help us to address climate change. This is a challenge we must undertake immediately and one in which I personally plan to play a critical role.

In the United States, in order to do our part, we have to first convince the American people and the Congress that the climate change problem is real and imminent. I will convene a White House Conference on Climate Change later this year to lay the scientific facts before our people, to understand that we must act, and to lay the economic facts there so that they understand the benefits and the costs. With the best ideas and strategies and new technologies and increased productivity and energy efficiency, we can turn the challenge to our advantage.

We will work with our people, and we will bring to the Kyoto Conference a strong American commitment to realistic and binding limits that will significantly reduce our emissions of greenhouse gases.

I want to mention three other initiatives briefly that we are taking to deal with climate change and to advance sustainable development here and beyond our borders.

First, to help developing nations reduce greenhouse gas emissions, the United States will provide $1 billion in assistance over the next 5 years to support energy efficiency, develop alternative energy sources, and improve resource management to promote growth that does not have an adverse effect on the climate.

Second, we will do more to encourage private investment to meet environmental standards.

The Overseas Private Investment Corporation will now require that its projects adhere to new and strengthened environmental guidelines, just as our Export-Import Bank already does and as I hope our allies and friends soon will. Common guidelines for responsible investment clearly would lead to more sustainable growth in developing nations.

Third, we must increase our use of new technologies, even as we move to develop more new technologies. Already, we are working with our auto industry to produce cars by early in the next century that are 3 times as fuel-efficient as today's vehicles. Now we will work with businesses and communities to use the Sun's energy to reduce our reliance on fossil fuels by installing solar panels on one million more roofs around our Nation by 2010. Capturing the Sun's warmth can help us to turn down the Earth's temperature.

Distinguished leaders, in all of our cultures we have been taught from time immemorial that, as Scripture says, "One generation passes away and another comes, but the Earth abides forever." We must strengthen our stewardship of the environment to make that true and to ensure that when this generation passes, the young man who just spoke before me and all of those of his generation will inherit a rich and abundant Earth.

Thank you very much.

NOTE: The President spoke at 6:30 p.m. in the United Nations General Assembly. In his remarks, he referred to General Assembly President Razali Ismail and U.N. Secretary-General Kofi Annan.

Statement on the Supreme Court Decision on the Line Item Veto
June 26, 1997

I am very pleased with today's Supreme Court decision that turned back the challenge to the line item veto. This decision clears the way for the President to use this valuable tool for eliminating waste in the Federal budget and for enlivening the public debate over how to make the best use of public funds.

The line item veto enables Presidents to ensure that the Federal Government is spending public resources as wisely as possible. It permits the President to cancel discretionary spending, new entitlement authority, and certain types of tax provisions that benefit special interests at the expense of the public interest.

The line item veto is also a practical and principled means of serving the constitutional balance of powers. This new authority brings us closer to the Founders' view of an effective executive role in the legislative process. With it, the President will be able to prevent Congress from enacting special interest provisions under the cloak of a 500- or 1,000-page bill. Special interest provisions that do not serve the national interest will no longer escape proper scrutiny.

I was pleased to work with Congress to secure an historic agreement to balance the budget. The line item veto will help to keep the budget in balance and provide us with added discipline by ensuring that, as tight budgets increasingly squeeze our resources, we put our public funds to the best possible uses.

I intend to use it whenever appropriate, and I look forward to using it wisely.

Statement on the Supreme Court Decision on the Communications Decency Act of 1996
June 26, 1997

Today the Supreme Court ruled that portions of the Communications Decency Act addressing indecency are not constitutional. We will study its opinion closely.

The administration remains firmly committed to the provisions—both in the CDA and elsewhere in the criminal code—that prohibit the transmission of obscenity over the Internet and via other media. Similarly, we remain committed to vigorous enforcement of Federal prohibitions against transmission of child pornography over the Internet and another prohibition that makes criminal the use of the Internet by pedophiles to entice children to engage in sexual activity.

The Internet is an incredibly powerful medium for freedom of speech and freedom of expression that should be protected. It is the biggest change in human communications since the printing press and is being used to educate our children, promote electronic commerce, provide valuable health care information, and allow citizens to keep in touch with their Government. But there is material on the Internet that is clearly inappropriate for children. As a parent, I understand the concerns that parents have about their children accessing inappropriate material.

If we are to make the Internet a powerful resource for learning, we must give parents and teachers the tools they need to make the Internet safe for children.

Therefore, in the coming days, I will convene industry leaders and groups representing teachers, parents, and librarians. We can and must develop a solution for the Internet that is as powerful for the computer as the V-chip will be for the television and that protects children in ways that are consistent with America's free speech values. With the right technology and rating systems, we can help ensure that our children don't end up in the red light districts of cyberspace.

NOTE: The Communications Decency Act of 1996 is title V of Public Law 104–104.

Statement on the Supreme Court Decision on Physician-Assisted Suicide
June 26, 1997

I am very pleased with today's Supreme Court decision which accepted my administration's position that States may ban physician-assisted suicide. The decision is a victory for all Americans—it prevents us from going down a very dangerous and troubling path on this difficult and often agonizing issue.

With today's decision, the Court voices its concern that there is a significant distinction between assisting in death and allowing death to occur. Not only is this an important legal distinction, it is also a distinction of deep moral and ethical implications.

I have a great deal of sympathy and a profound respect for those who suffer from incurable illnesses and for their families. I have had a number of family members die from painful and protracted illnesses. Even so, I have always expressed my strong opposition to physician-assisted suicide. I believe that it is wrong and have always believed it to be wrong.

This issue is unavoidably heart-rendering, and we must never ignore the agony of terminally ill patients, but the Supreme Court made the right decision today. The risks and consequences of physician-assisted suicide are simply too great.

Message to the Congress Reporting on Economic Sanctions Against Libya
June 26, 1997

To the Congress of the United States:

I hereby report to the Congress on the developments since my last report of January 10, 1997, concerning the national emergency with respect to Libya that was declared in Executive Order 12543 of January 7, 1986. This report is submitted pursuant to section 401(c) of the National Emergencies Act, 50 U.S.C. 1641(c); section 204(c) of the International Emergency Economic Powers Act ("IEEPA"), 50 U.S.C. 1703(c); and section 505(c) of the International Security and Development Cooperation Act of 1985, 22 U.S.C. 2349aa–9(c).

1. As previously reported, on January 2, 1997, I renewed for another year the national emergency with respect to Libya pursuant to the IEEPA. This renewal extended the current comprehensive financial and trade embargo against Libya in effect since 1986. Under these sanctions, virtually all trade with Libya is prohibited, and all assets owned or controlled by the Libyan government in the United States or in the possession or control of U.S. persons are blocked.

2. There have been no amendments to the Libyan Sanctions Regulations, 31 C.F.R. Part 550 (the "Regulations"), administered by the Office of Foreign Assets Control (OFAC) of the Department of the Treasury, since my last report on January 10, 1997.

3. During the last 6-month period, OFAC reviewed numerous applications for licenses to authorize transactions under the Regulations. Consistent with OFAC's ongoing scrutiny of banking transactions, the largest category of license approvals (68) concerned requests by non-Libyan persons or entities to unblock transfers interdicted because of what appeared to be Government of Libya interests. Two licenses authorized the provision of legal services to the Government of Libya in connection with actions in U.S. courts in which the Government of Libya was named as defendant. Licenses were also issued authorizing diplomatic and U.S. government transactions and to permit U.S. companies to engage in transactions with respect to intellectual property protection in Libya. A total of 75 licenses were issued during the reporting period.

4. During the current 6-month period, OFAC continued to emphasize to the international banking community in the United States the importance of identifying and blocking payments made by or on behalf of Libya. The office worked closely with the banks to assure the effectiveness in interdiction software systems used to identify such payments. During the reporting period, more than 100 transactions potentially involving Libya were interdicted.

5. Since my last report, OFAC collected 13 civil monetary penalties totaling nearly $90,000 for violations of the U.S. sanctions against Libya. Ten of the violations involved the failure of banks to block funds transferred to Libyan-controlled financial institutions or commercial entities in Libya. Three U.S. corporations paid the OFAC penalties for export violations as part of the global plea agreements with the Department of Justice. Sixty-seven other cases are in active penalty processing.

6. Various enforcement actions carried over from previous reporting periods have continued

to be aggressively pursued. Numerous investigations are ongoing and new reports of violations are being scrutinized.

7. The expenses incurred by the Federal Government in the 6-month period from January 7 through July 6, 1997, that are directly attributable to the exercise of the powers and authorities conferred by the declaration of the Libyan national emergency are estimated at approximately $660,000.00. Personnel costs were largely centered in the Department of the Treasury (particularly in the Office of Foreign Assets Control, the Office of the General Counsel, and the U.S. Customs Service), the Department of State, and the Department of Commerce.

8. The policies and the actions of the Government of Libya continue to pose an unusual and extraordinary threat to the national security and foreign policy of the United States. In adopting United Nations Security Council Resolution 883 in November 1993, the Security Council determined that the continued failure of the Government of Libya to demonstrate by concrete actions its renunciation of terrorism, and in particular its continued failure to respond fully and effectively to the requests and decisions of the

Security Council in Resolutions 731 and 748, concerning the bombing of the Pan Am 103 and UTA 772 flights, constituted a threat to international peace and security. The United States will continue to coordinate its comprehensive sanctions enforcement efforts with those of other U.N. member states. We remain determined to ensure that the perpetrators of the terrorist acts against Pan Am 103 and UTA 772 are brought to justice. The families of the victims in the murderous Lockerbie bombing and other acts of Libyan terrorism deserve nothing less. I shall continue to exercise the powers at my disposal to apply economic sanctions against Libya fully and effectively, so long as those measures are appropriate, and will continue to report periodically to the Congress on significant developments as required by law.

WILLIAM J. CLINTON

The White House,
June 26, 1997.

NOTE: This message was released by the Office of the Press Secretary on June 27.

Message to the Congress Transmitting the Report of the Corporation for Public Broadcasting
June 26, 1997

To the Congress of the United States:

In accordance with the Communications Act of 1934, as amended (47 U.S.C. 396(i)), I transmit herewith the Annual Report of the Corporation for Public Broadcasting for Fiscal Year 1996 and the Inventory of the Federal Funds Distributed to Public Telecommunications Entities by

Federal Departments and Agencies: Fiscal Year 1996.

WILLIAM J. CLINTON

The White House,
June 26, 1997.

NOTE: This message was released by the Office of the Press Secretary on June 27.

Message to the Senate Transmitting the South Africa-United States Tax Convention
June 26, 1997

To the Senate of the United States:

I transmit herewith for Senate advice and consent to ratification the Convention Between the United States of America and the Republic of South Africa for the Avoidance of Double Taxation and the Prevention of Fiscal Evasion with Respect to Taxes on Income and Capital Gains, signed at Cape Town February 17, 1997. Also transmitted is the report of the Department of State concerning the Convention.

This Convention, which generally follows the U.S. model tax treaty, provides maximum rates of tax to be applied to various types of income and protection from double taxation of income. The Convention also provides for the exchange of information to prevent fiscal evasion and sets forth standard rules to limit the benefits of the Convention so that they are available only to residents that are not engaged in treaty shopping.

I recommend that the Senate give early and favorable consideration to this Convention and give its advice and consent to ratification.

WILLIAM J. CLINTON

The White House,
June 26, 1997.

NOTE: This message was released by the Office of the Press Secretary on June 27.

Remarks and a Question-and-Answer Session With the League of United Latin American Citizens
June 27, 1997

The President. Thank you very much. Thank you, President Robles. I enjoyed very much our meeting with you and your board members a few days ago, and I know since then several members of my administration have had the chance to visit with you during your convention—our United Nations Ambassador, Bill Richardson; SBA Administrator Aida Alvarez; Ida Castro, the Director of Women's Bureau at the Labor Department; and my Deputy Assistant for Legislative Affairs, Janet Murguia. Secretary Peña would have been there, too, except that he has just become a new dad for the third time, little Ryan Federico, so he now has a namesake.

I thank you for inviting me to join you in celebrating the achievements of LULAC and of Latinos across our Nation. LULAC has a proud history, and for more than 65 years now you've fought to advance the rights and the opportunities of Hispanic-Americans, and in so doing, your dedication has helped all of America.

Two weeks ago I asked all Americans to join me in thinking about and talking about how America can use our great diversity of race and ethnicity as a strength to get past our divisions and closer to what unites us so that we can become the world's greatest multiracial, multiethnic democracy in the 21st century. Hispanic-Americans must be a big part of this initiative. Latinos represent the youngest and fastest growing population in our Nation, and in many ways America's success depends upon Hispanic success. That's why we have to all work in partnership to create a plan of action to allow every child to make the most of his or her life.

Earlier this week, Aida Alvarez and I met with Belen and the LULAC executive council, as I said a moment ago. We had a very constructive talk about the work that still needs to be done to ensure that Hispanics share in the fruits of the strong economy. In the last 4 years, the Hispanic unemployment rate has gone down from 11.3 percent when I took office to about 7.4 percent in May. That's been one of the great dividends of more than 12 million new jobs created in our economy. And when we won a raise in the minimum wage, 1.6 million Hispanic workers benefited directly.

In the first 3 years of our administration, more than 220,000 new Hispanic-American-owned businesses were created. Our Small Business Administration helped even more Latino-owned businesses to get the management training and counseling they need to succeed. A new study shows that between 1987 and 1996, the number of companies owned by Hispanic women, in particular, has grown at three times the overall rate of business growth. All of this signals progress.

But our work is far from over. That's because despite a strong work ethic and a strong sense of personal responsibility, Hispanic-Americans are the only racial or ethnic group in America that has experienced a decline in income during our current economic boom. One big reason is the high Hispanic high school dropout rate. It's far above that of blacks and whites. It's holding young Hispanics back. Many times these dropouts only want to help their families by bringing in income. But long, hard hours at the low-paying jobs will never amount to the earning potential of someone who stays in school. In the new economy, education is the key and responsibility means staying in school. That's the message we must get out to young Latinos.

I know you share my concern that too many Latino youth are missing out on an education. I'm especially pleased by the interest your organization has shown for our America Reads initiative. Since our meeting on Monday, your president has spoken with Carol Rasco at our Department of Education, and we have committed to work with LULAC to ensure that LULAC volunteers are a critical part of this important effort.

Latinos know about helping others; an impressive 15 percent of the participants in our AmeriCorps program of national service are Hispanic. With your help and the participation of AmeriCorps and other volunteers, we'll be able to mobilize a million people to make sure that all of our children can read independently by the third grade. America Reads will help our children to succeed and to stay in school.

I want all young people to have the tools they need. That's why our budget agreement increases funding for bilingual education by 27 percent. It's the bridge that some students need to achieve in English. [*Applause*] Thank you. We've also worked to widen access to college, with the largest increase in Pell grants in two decades, a big increase in work-study funds, and

by proposing scholarships that would make 2 years at a community college affordable for every single family, because I believe the 13th and 14th years of school must become as universal as a high school diploma is today.

We also want every family to be able to deduct up to $10,000 a year to help pay for the cost of any higher education after high school. All that is part of the biggest increase in higher education since the GI bill 50 years ago, and it's included in our balanced budget proposal. We are working with Congress to ensure that the budget agreement does not shortchange education. And I ask you to stand with us in that. [*Applause*] Thank you.

I also want to tell you where we are in the budget negotiations on the matter of benefits for legal immigrants. As you know, when Congress enacted last year's welfare law, it included provisions affecting legal immigrants that were harsh and had nothing to do with the real goal of welfare reform, moving people from welfare to work. Since then, we've worked hard to restore SSI and Medicaid eligibility for disabled legal immigrants. I place a great deal of importance on this issue, and I'm hopeful that with the recent Senate action we will be able to restore benefits to both disabled and elderly nondisabled immigrants who were in the United States when the law was signed last August.

We all have a role to play in making a better future for coming generations. Citizens and Government must work together. We've got to give every child a fair chance to live out his or her dreams. We have to give every child a safe place to grow up. We have to give all of our children decent health care, a world-class education, and a more united, stronger America—one America.

I applaud LULAC for your commitment to improving the lives of Hispanic citizens, and I look forward to continuing our work and partnership toward the great goal of one America for the 21st century.

Thank you, and God bless you.

Ms. Robles. Thank you very much, Mr. President. And now, if you will permit us, we do have some questions from the LULAC membership. And I would like to introduce to you the national president of the LULAC youths, Alejandro Meraz, a senior at Skyline High School in Dallas, Texas, that will pose the first question.

Mr. Meraz. Good morning, Mr. President.

The President. Good morning, Alejandro.

Hispanic High School Dropout Rate

Mr. Meraz. As you are aware, the Hispanic high school dropout rate is extremely high. Allowed to continue, this problem would devastate the Hispanic community. What initiatives are you already undertaking to reduce the dropout rate in Hispanic communities? And what additional steps can be taken to alleviate this problem?

The President. First of all, let me say that I take this problem very, very seriously. I have been talking about it all across America. I raised it at the University of California in San Diego at my race speech, where 45 percent of the graduates in the class were Hispanics. I think that we all understand what we have to do here. I have charged Gene Sperling, who is the head of the National Economic Council, and Maria Echaveste, who heads my Office of Public Liaison, to make sure that our educational initiatives address the specific concerns regarding Hispanic dropouts. They, along with the Department of Education, will work with the Congressional Hispanic Caucus and other Hispanic leaders to evaluate our current programs to identify positive actions that can be taken right now to increase the percentage of Latinos graduating from high school and increase the number going on to college.

Let me just mention two or three specific things that I think can be done. Number one, if we can succeed in our goal of making sure that every 8-year-old is proficient in reading by the third grade, that will increase the ability of children whose first language is not English to do well in school, and it will increase the chances that they will stay there.

Number two, having national standards for all children will help Hispanic students. I spoke with the wonderful Latino superintendent of the San Antonio, Texas, school district the day before yesterday, and she said that San Antonio would become the first large city in Texas to participate in our national standards program, including testing fourth graders for reading and eighth graders for math in 1999. Why? Because they are learning in San Antonio that when you raise academic standards, you make school more interesting and more meaningful to people, and they are far less likely to drop out.

So I believe raising these standards and giving children a chance to get a good education in high school will, in fact, lead to a substantial reduction in the Hispanic dropout rate, especially if we've done our job on reading in the early grades.

Now, in addition to that, I think it is very, very important that we follow up on another one of the goals of the Presidents' Summit of Service. We need to make sure that all these young people who are at risk of dropping out have an adult mentor who is working with them, trying to help them and encourage them to stay in school and continue on their road in education.

So I think that that is another thing that we really need to focus on. We know from experience in community after community after community that if there is at least one caring adult which is trying to tie the young boy or the young girl to school, to school life and help them succeed, that will also make a big difference.

So those are just three things that I think we should start with. But we're going to work on it here at the White House; we're going to work with the Congressional Hispanic Caucus and the Department of Education. And we want to do everything we can to make sure that there are more young people like you as we move into the 21st century.

Ms. Robles. Thank you very much, Mr. President. And now I would like to introduce to you the district director of LULAC in Hollister, California, Ms. Micki Luna.

Ms. Luna. Greetings from the Golden State of California, Mr. President.

The President. Hello.

Affirmative Action

Ms. Luna. We applaud your recent announcement to create a commission to study race relations in our country. However, we are increasingly concerned about the effects of California's Proposition 209, which eliminated affirmative action programs in our community. What actions are you taking to lessen or to reverse the effects of Proposition 209, which have already drastically lowered Hispanic enrollment in higher education within the university system of California?

The President. Well, Micki, first of all, I've tried to continue to speak out in favor of affirmative action as I have been, as you know, for the last several years, to discourage anyone else from doing the same thing. I think that's very important.

Secondly, I have asked the Domestic Policy Council to coordinate a review by the Justice Department and the Education Department on the impact of Proposition 209 and the Hopwood decision in Texas. We need to make sure that we do everything we can to keep the doors of higher education open to all Americans, including all minorities. We are looking for specific things that we can do to ensure that higher education does not become segregated or that the progress we've made over the last 20 years is not reversed.

Secondly, I think we need to do more in secondary schools to prepare young people for college. If we can really implement the standards movement that I'm pushing for over the country and get all the schools, like the San Antonio district, to participate, what we will see is that we will do a better job of giving our young people the tools they need to get into college in the first place.

One of the things that I have noted is that so many affirmative action students have done very, very well in the universities of our country. They've also improved the quality of education there for other students by diversifying the student body. And because they do well it means that they could have done better on the entrance test, they could have done better in the beginning if we, their parents' generation, had provided them a finer elementary and secondary education. So I think that's a big part of this answer, too.

But I'm not willing to give up on affirmative action in education. I'm not about to give up on it. And we are exploring what our legal options are, as well as what policies we might implement to try to stop public higher education in America from becoming resegregated.

Ms. Robles. Thank you, Mr. President. And at this time may I introduce to you the LULAC national vice president for the Southwest from Dallas, Texas, Mr. Hector Flores.

Mr. Flores. Thank you, madam chair. Good morning, Mr. President.

The President. Good morning, Hector.

Mr. Flores. I'm glad to see you again.

The President. Thank you.

Empowerment Zones Along the Border

Mr. Flores. Mr. President, despite the general low level of unemployment throughout the country, our communities along the United States and Mexican border continue to experience high unemployment levels, ranging from as high as 12 to 15 percent. Will you work with LULAC to increase empowerment zones along the border to reduce the devastating high level of unemployment in these areas, sir?

The President. The short answer to your question is, yes, I will do what I can to increase the availability of empowerment zones, enterprise communities, incentives in all the high unemployment areas of our country.

Two weeks ago, the Vice President was in southwest Texas and hosted a townhall meeting in McAllen at the Southwest Border Conference. It was a gathering of over 200 people from the rural empowerment zones, including mayors, local elected officials, representatives from five States that are involved in these issues. And one of the things we learned is that we must have economic development along the borders to combat these double-digit unemployment rates.

We're working to find additional moneys now to fund more zones to help people help themselves. And let me say that in my budget, I call for a doubling of the number of empowerment zones and enterprise communities. We know that these things will work. [*Applause*] Thank you.

One of the continuing struggles I'm having up here in Congress to get the right kind of balanced budget is to get the Senate and the House to agree to invest funds in the empowerment zones, in the enterprise communities. Now, we've had one empowerment zone in south Texas. You know that it can work. And one of the things I'd like to ask LULAC to do is to write or call the Members of the House and the Senate who represent the border States and remind them that these empowerment zones are important and that they will work. We've got to get in the final budget coming to me—we have got to get funds for the empowerment zones and the enterprise communities, because we know we have to turn these communities that are in difficult shape, that have not participated in our economic revival. We know we've got to turn them around one by one with local leadership and private sector investment.

I will do my part. But when you leave here I want to implore you all to contact the Members of Congress, especially in the border States, and intensely argue for not only reauthorization of the empowerment zones but to expand their number. If you do, I will go in there and work with you to get these high unemployment areas fully participating in our economic recovery.

Thank you.

Mr. Flores. Thank you, Mr. President.

The President. Thank you.

Ms. Robles. Thank you, Mr. President. On behalf of all the LULAC membership, 110,000 grassroots members from across the United States and the island of Puerto Rico, I thank you. I particularly want to thank you also on behalf of the State director of the State of Arkansas, Mr. Ben Rodriguez——

The President. My longtime friend.

Ms. Robles. ——and the membership of your native State.

The President. Thank you. Tell him I said hello. Bless you.

Ms. Robles. He's here in the audience, sir. He's listening to you.

The President. Hello, Ben.

NOTE: The President spoke at 11:12 a.m. by satellite from Room 459 of the Old Executive Office Building to the meeting in California. In his remarks, he referred to Belen Robles, president, League of United Latin American Citizens.

Remarks on Signing the Drug-Free Communities Act of 1997 and an Exchange With Reporters
June 27, 1997

The President. Let me, first of all, say to you, Congressman Portman, and to Congressman Levin and Congressman Hastert and, in his absence, Congressman Rangel, and to the Senators who worked on this, this is a very important day for this legislation because it does reflect our commitment in Washington to behave in the way that people in communities behave when they do what works in fighting the drug problem, and I cannot thank you enough.

The fact that we did this in a bipartisan fashion, and we did it, to use Congressman Portman's words, based on trying to legislate nationally a system not only to empower people to do what we know works in some communities today already but to give them the incentive to do more of it, is, I think, a great thing. So I thank the Congressmen for being here. I thank the members of the Cabinet for their support. I thank Jim Copple, the president of the Community Anti-Drug Coalitions of America; Dick Bonnette, the Partnership for a Drug-Free America; and all the rest of you who are here.

Now, before I sign this bill, I have to make a couple of comments about—this has been a very interesting week of momentous decisions by the Supreme Court. Today the Supreme Court issued a ruling on the Brady bill. And since I have been so heavily identified with that

for several years now, I'd like to make a few comments.

The decision struck down the requirement that local police officers conduct background checks but left intact the Brady bill's 5-day waiting period. Since the Brady bill passed, 250,000 felons, fugitives, and mentally unstable persons have been stopped from purchasing handguns. I don't think anyone can seriously question that it has made a major contribution to increasing the safety of the American people. And I'm going to do everything I can to make sure that we continue to keep guns out of the hands of people who should not have them.

These criminal background checks make good sense; they save lives. Now 27 States, 9 more than when the Brady bill first passed, have State laws requiring them, and they will continue to do the background checks. Even in other States, criminal background checks will continue. The Brady law was drafted by our law enforcement community; they wanted it. Again, it was a community-based resolution of a difficult problem. So I know that these State and local law enforcement officials who asked us to pass the law will continue to do the background checks.

I've asked Attorney General Reno and Secretary Rubin to contact police departments across our country to make sure they know that the background checks can and should continue to be done by local police on a voluntary basis. And then the Attorney General and Secretary Rubin will immediately convene a meeting of law enforcement officers to review and develop recommendations, including appropriate legislation, to ensure that we can continue to perform these background checks. It's my understanding that the Supreme Court actually made some suggestions about how we might proceed from here.

My goal is clear: no criminal background check, no handgun anywhere in America. No State should become a safe haven for criminals who want to buy handguns.

We know that—again, I say, tremendous progress has been made. The idea that 250,000 of these sales and transfers have been stopped is a very impressive thing in just a few years, and I think it clearly contributed to the largest drop in violent crime in over 35 years last year, murders dropping a stunning 11 percent in 1996.

So we've got to keep going on this. And even though I wish we didn't have to do this extra work, I think the framework of the Court decision makes it clear that we have done the right thing, that the 5-day waiting period is legal. And let me remind you, as the Attorney General said, by November of 1998, which is not all that far away, we expect to have in place the technology and the capacity to do instantaneous background checks. Is that the date? So what we've got to do is figure out how to keep this system alive between now and November of '98. We are committed to doing it.

Let me just say another couple of words, if I might, about this legislation today and what it means to us. I think the Congressman said it's only a small part of our overall drug budget, but it clearly sends a signal that we are shifting emphasis, not to diminish what were doing on interdiction and the other work that we have to do about drugs beyond our borders, but to recognize that we will never get a hold of this problem unless we deal with the demand side here in America.

And we know that while casual drug use has plummeted over the last 15 years among adults, it has doubled among young people in just the last 5 years, and among eighth graders it has tripled. The fact that the percentage of total people trying drugs at that age level is small is cold comfort when you look at the trends and you ask yourself, how could these trends

be running in direct contradiction to the fact that drug use is going down among people between the ages of 18 and 35? That is the real threat to our future. That is the problem we face today. And the quicker we face up to it the better off we're going to be.

A study by Columbia's Center for Addiction and Substance Abuse has shown, for example, that a young person who tries marijuana is 85 times more likely to try cocaine than peers who don't try marijuana in the first place. So a middle schooler or a high schooler who mistakenly decides that it's safe to try cocaine or heroine or LSD or methamphetamine or any of the so-called designer drugs, along with marijuana, is playing a dangerous game, and we have to try somehow to do more than we have done in the past to stop this. And we know that the broadly based community antidrug coalitions have been successful at driving down casual drug use. We know that they've been more successful than anyone else and than any other approach has been.

So what we're trying to do here is to find a way to support them, to encourage them to do more, and to increase the number of such coalitions throughout our country. We know that this has got to be done person by person, family by family, community by community. That's what this legislation does. More than 4,300 communities in every State in America and our territories have organized themselves to deal with this, to help parents, to help the teachers, the coaches, the principals, all the others who are fighting for drug-free schools and communities and a drug-free future for our children.

So this is the sort of partnership we need more of. Again, let me say I am immensely gratified by the bipartisan nature of this. I also would say, if you focus on the problem, which is why juvenile drug abuse is going up while young adult drug use is going down, and the whole impact of the culture on that, I think it justifies the policy that General McCaffrey adopted that I have supported him on of having an unprecedented advertising campaign to try to get the message out to these young people. And I certainly believe it supports our juvenile crime strategy of having 1,000 afterschool programs to give our young people positive things to do, because we know that a lot of the most difficult hours are those right after school closes for criminal activity and for casual drug use.

So the Drug-Free Communities Act of 1997 is not only a good thing, but I hope it is an indication of things to come.

The last point I'd like to make, just to echo what the Vice President said about the smoking issue, is I think that this settlement was a terrific achievement. It is the result of all the work that was done before then in the public health community and the work that our administration had done. But we have to take a quick look— I mean, a careful look at it, and we will take a careful look at it. Secretary Shalala and my Domestic Policy Adviser, Bruce Reed, are heading a group that will consult with the public health community, will look at it carefully, and we will offer our judgments on it.

My preliminary take is that we do not want to paralyze the capacity of the FDA to protect the American people. That, to me, is the critical thing. And that in no way minimizes the enormous achievement of the attorneys general and the others who are involved in this in the public health community. And I have no final judgment on it. I just want to say that Secretary Shalala is going to take a serious look at it. We're going to work hard here in the White House. But if we can do more and more of these things together in a bipartisan way as we're doing today, I think this country is going to be much better off.

Thank you very much.

[*At this point, the President signed the legislation.*]

Supreme Court Decision on Handgun Legislation

Q. Mr. President, with the Supreme Court ruling today, will your administration—and can it legally—speed up the process of getting this instant background check system in place?

The President. Well, that's one of the things the Attorney General and Secretary Rubin are going to tell me in the next day or two. We're going to look at what our options are. Obviously, we've been thinking about this. I think the important thing to point out is, the Supreme Court said it was constitutional for us to have a 5-day waiting period, that we can have background checks but that five of them did not believe we could require local officials to do it. They said we could have done what we've done in the past by tying Federal funds of some kind

to the willingness to do it, sort of a contractual arrangement.

We're going to look at what our options are and see where to go from here. But in the short run, I would just implore the officials in the 23 States that don't have their own State laws requiring this to keep on doing it, because there is no longer any serious debate here; no one who needs to get any kind of weapon has been seriously inconvenienced, and a quarter of a million people who had no business with them don't have them. It's a huge public policy success for the United States. It's a part of driving the crime rate down. And we'll come up with our options as quick as we can.

Proposed Tobacco Agreement

Q. It sounds like you like the tobacco agreement.

The President. No, I don't think you should draw any conclusion one way or the other. I like the fact that they achieved it and that has— and the broad dimensions of it are quite staggering. I mean, even in Washington $368 billion is a lot of money. [*Laughter*] And I think that it's a real testament to all—to the work the attorneys general and the other parties did. But I would say that we have an obligation to look at it very carefully from the public health point of view.

Keep in mind, whenever—in any settlement in any lawsuit, both sides think they're better off settling than not, or there wouldn't be any settlement—I mean, by definition. So what we have to make—we have to be sure that the things that made the tobacco companies believe that they did the right thing to settle don't compromise the long-term interests of the public health and especially our attempts to stop children from smoking in the first place. That's all. And we're looking at it.

But I don't think—you know, even if I were to render a negative judgment on it after Secretary Shalala and Bruce Reed finish their review, I would still be immensely impressed with the work that the attorneys general and the others have done. It's quite a staggering thing. It's a long way from where we were just a couple of years ago when no one thought that any progress would ever be made on this issue.

Q. Mr. President, what are your specific concerns about the FDA provisions in this agreement?

The President. I want to wait until I get my review. I just want to make sure that they will still be able to do what is necessary to protect the public health and children's health based on the evidence that comes before them in the intervening period. Now, there is a period of years in which they cannot actually ban nicotine. But there are a lot of other options and issues which could come before them during that period, and that's what we're looking at, to make sure their jurisdiction has not been under any—[*inaudible*].

Tax Cut Legislation

Q. Sir, how do you resolve the rhetorical battle between Republicans and Democrats with the tax bill? There seems to be a stand-off going into yesterday over the income tax——

The President. Oh, I think a lot of that is—I think the best way to resolve it is, one, for everyone to say, we want a tax bill, we want a tax cut bill. We want a tax cut bill that does not explode in the out-years, does not bring the bad old days of the deficits back to us. We want one that is faithful to the agreement that was made. And I want one that, particularly within the confines of the agreement, that helps families to raise their children and that helps to fund greater education.

But you should expect a little of this skirmishing. We're going to do more, and we're going to offer our thoughts on Monday about what should be in the tax bill, and then we're going to keep working. But I'm, frankly, quite optimistic. I wouldn't—you would expect that all the parties would advance their views in the most vigorous way possible. But I think the issue is, are we likely to have a bill that meets those criteria, and I think the answer is, yes, we are quite likely to have one.

Line Item Veto

Q. You feel stronger with a line item veto, don't you?

The President. Well, I think it's the right thing to do. I was pleased that the Supreme Court didn't strike it down, although they invited the first person who gets mad enough to do so. [*Laughter*] So I guess we'll be back in court on that one. But let me—I had it when I was Governor; most Governors do. I think it should be used with great care and discipline. You have to respect the congressional process. And my experience was after having used it a few times,

that the great value of it was that it was a low—it was just another part of the framework of fiscal discipline we're trying to effect. That is, when I was a Governor, after a year or two, the most important thing about it was not when it was used, but that it existed in the first place, because it helped to keep us within a framework of fiscal responsibility. That's basically what I'm interested in.

Sending Power Back to the States

Q. Mr. President, what do you think of the Supreme Court's record on sending power back to the States, now that the term is almost over?

The President. Well, I need to have time to evaluate all the things. Basically, you know, we sent a lot of power back to the States since I've been President. Since I used to be there, I can hardly say it's a bad idea. I think the question is, what are the terms on which the power goes back, what is the framework, can the national interests still be protected? And that's how you have to evaluate all this.

But in general, it's just like this bill here. This bill basically empowers communities within the framework of an agreed-upon national objective. Why? Because this is not a problem we can solve in Washington. And every Republican and every Democrat who has ever looked at it says the same thing. So what these Members have done is to embody what seems to me to be a common-sense principle.

So I have no problem with that. I think that a lot of the operational work of life is better done where people live, at the grassroots level. The only question I would have on any of these things is, can we still pursue the national interests? If we had no capacity coming on-line in '98—let's take the Brady bill, for example—if we have no capacity coming on-line in '98 to do instantaneous background checks, then I would take the—certainly would want to take the Supreme Court up on their offer to tie the receipt of some kind of Federal money, at least, to the willingness to continue these background checks because I think that's a national interest issue.

But on balance, I think the operations, doing more operationally at the State and local level, is a good thing.

Line Item Veto

Q. Would you use the first line item veto on the tax bill?

The President. You go back and read that legislation; that was a battle over legislation—they were very artful, the Congress was, in kind of limiting the extent to which the President can use it on a tax bill. It's different. The options on spending are broader than the options on the tax bill. So I'll have to look at that.

I hope I don't have to use it at all. I hope we just make a good agreement; that's my goal. Thank you.

NOTE: The President spoke at 12:32 p.m. in the Roosevelt Room at the White House. H.R. 956, approved June 27, was assigned Public Law No. 105–20.

Exchange With Reporters Prior to Discussions With Prime Minister John Howard of Australia
June 27, 1997

Greenhouse Gas Emissions

Q. Sir, do you have any sympathy for Australia's position on greenhouse gas emissions?

President Clinton. The Prime Minister was just expressing sympathy with ours. [*Laughter*] We're going to talk about it today. I think we have to do something. I think it's a serious problem. But we've all got to—you know, what you want is everybody making a good effort. We don't want to falsely compare one person's circumstance to another. We've got from now to Kyoto to find a solution; I think we will.

Q. Sir, is differentiation the answer?

President Clinton. I want to make sure I know what I am answering when I give an answer.

Q. Different targets for different countries, sir, is that the answer?

President Clinton. I don't want to say yet; I want to have time to look through this and make a judgment.

Q. Do you think Australia and the U.S. can meet on this, then?

President Clinton. I certainly hope so. I hope we can all meet in Kyoto on it. It's what I'm working for.

Q. [*Inaudible*]—on the developing nations?

Q. Will you be discussing China today and U.S. engagement in the region?

President Clinton. Just a minute. I think the developing nations should be part of it. And I think that—we believe we can demonstrate that the developing nations can continue to grow their economies rapidly and still adopt responsible, sustainable development policies. That's

what's behind our Export-Import Bank loan policy. It's what's behind what Mr. Wolfensohn is doing at the World Bank. We can get there. What did you say about Asia?

U.S. Engagement in Asia

Q. Will you be discussing the U.S. engagement in Asia?

President Clinton. Absolutely, a lot.

Greenhouse Gas Emissions

Q. Mr. Howard, do you think you can talk the President around?

Prime Minister Howard. Well, I don't think it's a question of talking around. I think the Australian position is quite well known. We want to play a part; we don't expect a free ride. But we've argued for some kind of differentiation, because different countries are in different situations. And the concern Australia had was that the Group of Eight meeting in Denver might have preempted the outcome of the Kyoto Summit. And that clearly is not happening. And I get a lot of encouragement from the remarks that were made by the President yesterday in New York. And I think that is the basis of an understanding. I'd like to see Australia and the United States work together on it. We have a concern about domestic jobs, and I'm sure the United States does, too.

NOTE: The exchange began at approximately 1:20 p.m. in the Rose Garden at the White House. A tape was not available for verification of the content of this exchange.

Statement on the Apprehension of Indicted War Criminal Slavko Dokmanovic
June 27, 1997

I welcome the news that Slavko Dokmanovic, an indicted war criminal, has been apprehended by investigators for the International Criminal Tribunal for the Former Yugoslavia (ICTY), working with the UN Transitional Administration in Eastern Slavonia (UNTAES). Dokmanovic was one of a group of suspected war criminals who are under sealed indictment. He has been transported to The Hague. He will stand trial there for his role in the beatings and executions of Croatian soldiers and civilians taken from a hospital in Vukovar in November 1991.

I congratulate the ICTY and UNTAES on their successful apprehension. The United States continues to support fully the work of the Tribunal to bring indicted war criminals to justice. Cooperation with the Tribunal by all the parties is a cornerstone of the Dayton accords.

The President's Radio Address
June 28, 1997

Good morning. Today I'm speaking to you from the East Room of the White House, where I'm joined by hundreds of America's brightest high school students. These Presidential Scholars are here in our Nation's Capital to learn how democracy works. And we know we can make it work much, much better.

I want to talk to you this morning about steps I'm taking to open the airwaves so voters have the loudest voice in our democracy, and about responsibility of Congress to clean up the campaign finance system.

Our democracy is the oldest and most successful in the world, but we know that there is something wrong with the way we pay for elections. Our campaign finance laws were last rewritten 23 years ago. For quite a long while those laws worked well, but they have been overwhelmed by a flood of money and the changes in the way we communicate with one another and the cost of communication.

Spending in congressional campaigns has risen sixfold in the last two decades. That's more than 3 times the rate of inflation. Now both political parties are locked into an ever-escalating arms race as they compete to raise more and more money. There's simply too much money required for campaigns, it takes too much time to raise, and it raises too many questions.

In my State of the Union Address, I challenged the Congress to act to stem the rising tide of campaign money by passing comprehensive, bipartisan campaign finance reform by July 4th, the date we celebrate the birth of our democracy. Unfortunately, Congress has made little progress toward reform since that time, and it's clear that the legislation will not pass, will not even be voted on by Independence Day. That's too bad because there has been a significant number of bipartisan support for the McCain-Feingold bill, which I have also endorsed.

But now we shouldn't wait for Congress to act, and I'm not waiting. Within my power as President, I've acted to advance key elements of reform, and I'll continue to do so. First, I have petitioned the Federal Election Commission to ban so-called soft money contributions, the large contributions from corporations, labor unions, and individuals that both parties raise. Bipartisan lawmakers led by Representatives Chris Shays and Marty Meehan have asked for the same thing. I am pleased that the FEC will begin formal proceedings on our request next month.

Second, our Justice Department will fight in the courts to uphold efforts to limit campaign spending. We know how a spending spiral can have dangerous consequences, but for two decades, court cases have made it very hard to enact tough limits. Right now, strong spending limits passed for elections in Cincinnati and judicial elections across Ohio are being challenged. We believe spending limits are constitutional, and if we need to, we'll make that case to the highest court in the land.

And we're acting to address the single greatest reason for out-of-control costs, spending on television. In 1972, candidates spent $25 million for political ads; in 1996, $400 million. We're the only major democracy in the world that does it this way, and it doesn't have to be this way. We can make our most powerfully effective medium a powerful force for expanding democracy. Free TV time can help free our democracy from the grip of big money.

For years, I have supported giving candidates free time. And in fact, Vice President Gore proposed legislation to do that a decade ago, when he was in the United States Senate. Now we're working to make it happen. In March I called on the Federal Communications Commission to require broadcasters to give candidates free time as a condition of receiving a new, lucrative license for high-tech digital TV. That's the least we can ask of broadcasters, who are given access to the public airwaves, worth billions of dollars, at no cost, with only the requirement that they meet a basic public obligation. Today I'm appointing two distinguished Americans to lead a commission that will help the FCC decide precisely how free broadcast time can be given to candidates as part of the broadcasters' public interest obligations.

Les Moonves is the president of CBS Entertainment and one of America's most prominent and creative broadcasters. And Dr. Norman Ornstein, resident scholar at the American Enterprise Institute, is one of America's best known political scientists and a renowned expert on campaign finance reform. Their commission will explore the details of free time for candidates and other public interest obligations,

such as children's broadcasting, which may need to be updated.

All these steps are important, but still they're no substitute for legislation. Again I say, Congress must act to pass comprehensive bipartisan legislation. And as I said before, Senators John McCain and Russ Feingold, joined by Representatives Shays and Meehan, have strong legislation that would limit spending, end soft money, and give candidates free time or reduced-rate TV time. I'm pleased to report that Senators McCain and Feingold have announced they will bring their bill to a vote later this summer in the Senate. This will be our first chance to see who's for real on the issue of reform.

Needed change has been filibustered to death in every Congress for a decade. In my first term, it was filibustered to death each and every year. Now the same people who filibustered reform before, whose obstruction gave us the present system, have vowed to do it again. Let's let the people be heard. Let's not let them get away with it. Every Senator must realize that a vote for a filibuster is a vote to continue undue special interests influence, soft money contributions, out-of-control spending, and continued public skepticism about the way the political process works.

When it comes to fixing our campaign finance system, let's make this summer a time not of talk but of action, not of recriminations but of results. We have a rare chance to restore the trust and earn the participation of the American people. The way we pay for elections is broken; it's time to fix it. I ask for your support. And thanks for listening.

NOTE: The address was recorded at 6:09 p.m. on June 27 in the East Room at the White House for broadcast at 10:06 a.m. on June 28.

Remarks on Proposed Tax Cut Legislation and an Exchange With Reporters
June 30, 1997

The President. Ladies and gentlemen, now that the two Houses of Congress have completed action on their tax plan, I would like to make some comments and offer my plan for what I think should be done with the tax portion of the balanced budget agreement.

By way of background, let me point out again, as I have said many times, I was determined to change the economic policy of the United States Government when I became President. We abandoned trickle-down and the big deficits and instead adopted an invest-and-grow strategy: reduce the deficit, invest in the education and skills of our people, and make sure we sold more American goods and services around the world. That has contributed, along with the ingenuity, hard work, and productivity of the American people, to the healthiest economy we've had in a generation.

I want the balanced budget we ultimately pass to continue to reinforce that strategy and our values. The agreement that we signed with the Republican and Democratic leaders of Congress reflects the invest-and-grow strategy. It is in balance with our values of honoring work, strengthening families, and offering opportunity. It eliminates the deficit, it invests in education, it extends health care for more of our children while securing Medicare for our parents, and it provides for an affordable tax cut for the American people.

America's families deserve a tax cut, and they deserve one that reflects their values. It is, after all, the energy and dedication of the American people that has produced our present prosperity, that has made it possible for us to balance the budget. The American people should receive a dividend from this prosperity because they have produced the strength that has enabled us to achieve it. The dividend should be reflected in policies that help them to strengthen their families and educate their children.

Two different tax cut bills have passed the House and the Senate. The bills contain many good elements, but I do not believe they represent the best way to cut taxes, nor are they consistent with the balanced budget agreement. They are not close to the roughly $35 billion the agreement explicitly provides to help people provide for higher education costs; they do an inadequate job of opening the doors to college, therefore. They direct far too little relief to the middle class. They include time-bomb tax cuts that threaten to explode the deficit. They do not do enough to keep our economy going.

Today, as lawmakers from both Houses prepare to begin final negotiations with our administration over the details of a tax cut, I offer my plan to cut taxes. My plan reflects America's values, helping families pay for college, raise

their children, buy or sell a home, pay for health care. It honors the budget agreement. It is the right plan for America.

This reflects the approach of Democratic alternatives that were offered in Congress, but it also reflects the priorities of the Republicans as well. The $85 billion tax cut I submit has five central elements.

First, the tax cut plan will focus on education, our Nation's highest priority, with $35 billion in targeted tax cuts. To offer opportunity in the new and rapidly changing economy, we must make the 13th and 14th years of education, the first 2 years of college, as universal as a high school diploma is today. To that end, my proposal will give young people a HOPE scholarship tax credit worth up to $1,500 for the first 2 years of college. It gives further tax cuts to help pay for 4 years of college. It provides tax relief to pay for training and learning throughout a lifetime. It will allow parents to save in a tax-free IRA for their children's education, and it will use tax incentives to help communities rebuild and modernize their schools. Education is how we will meet the challenges of the 21st century, and the core of our tax cut must be to help families pay for education. The tax cuts can do for our children what the GI bill did for Americans a generation ago.

Second, my plan gives families a $500 tax credit for every child under 17. This plan, unlike the tax cut proposals put forth by the congressional majority, would give working people who earn lower salaries the child tax credit as well. A rookie police officer or a starting teacher, a firefighter or a nurse who earns $22,000 deserves a child tax credit. They are some of our hardest pressed working people. They are paying taxes now, and I will fight to give them the same tax relief that other Americans would receive.

Third, to honor our commitment to bipartisanship, the plan allows taxpayers to exclude 30 percent of their capital gains from taxation. It also gives a capital gains tax cut for buying and selling a home. The capital gains cut is targeted, more prudent, and less likely to explode the deficit in the years to come than the plan of the congressional majority.

Fourth, my plan provides estate tax relief to help parents who want to pass small businesses and family farms on to their children.

Fifth, the plan provides tax incentives to encourage businesses to hire people off welfare.

It will also provide tax cuts to businesses that clean up urban toxic waste sites known as brownfields and convert these sites to productive use. It will create 20 more empowerment zones to attract businesses into disadvantaged neighborhoods, and it includes tax incentives to revive our Nation's Capital.

The brownfields and the empowerment zones were both mentioned in the budget agreement as items that the leaders would work hard to include in the final tax bill. It is now time for all the leaders who did the agreement to work together to achieve that. Only by bringing the spark of private enterprise into our inner cities will we truly break the cycle of poverty that holds too many of our people back.

In addition, the Senate, by bipartisan agreement, departed from the budget agreement to support a 20 cents per pack tax on cigarettes. I will support this change. Unlike the Senate version, however, I believe these revenues should be used entirely in ways that focus on the needs of children and health care.

This tax cut plan that I have just outlined embodies the best ideas offered by Democrats. It reflects many of the priorities of the Republicans, such as the capital gains cut. It is balanced. It is fair to the middle class. It will foster economic growth without hurting our vulnerable citizens. And it is consistent with the budget agreement. It is the right plan for America. And I will do my best and fight hard for it in the weeks to come.

Q. What do you say to people who think you give more to the rich than the poor in this case?

The President. Well, I would just—I would ask you to compare my plan with the Republican plan. Our plan gives the vast majority of aid to the middle class, the 60 percent in the middle, and much, much more than either the plan which passed the Senate or the plan which passed the House. The people who have more money pay more taxes, and if you have a capital gains tax cut or an estate tax cut of any kind, there will be significant benefits to people in upper income groups. But our plan targets hard the middle class as well as working people who make more modest incomes.

And Secretary Rubin and Director Raines and the others on our economic team who are here will have a distributional chart, and you can compare the two. But we committed to work with the Republicans, and this is a good-faith

effort to do that, incorporating both their ideas for capital gains and some other things as well.

Q. Mr. President, could you just lay out for us what you see as the primary differences in your approach to capital gains and theirs? And also, why did you wait until now when the two Houses have finished to offer this plan? Why didn't you do it earlier?

The President. Well, because up until now I was working with both the Democrats and the Republicans in the Congress to develop their plans and to negotiate with them. But we now have two plans that, in one important respect—the amount of money allocated to help middle class families pay for higher education is clearly inconsistent with the budget agreement.

If you go back and read the budget agreement, the budget agreement says that certain things will be done, and it says other things will be worked on, that there will be best efforts. There was no ambiguity here. We said we would allocate roughly $35 billion of this to help families pay for higher education. The plans aren't close to that.

Now, can we afford to do all the things that the Republicans want to do and the things that are also mentioned in the budget agreement that are important to me and important to many Democrats? The answer is, we can if we have prudence and discipline.

The principal difference in the capital gains provisions is that I would have a 30 percent exclusion; they would have a 50 percent exclusion. It's still a very large tax cut for people who can invest money. And I think you will see that it is not necessary in terms of the stock market. It's doing quite well as it is. What I'd like to see us do is to offer more incentive for people to start new businesses and to hold on to those investments for a longer period of time to build companies.

Q. Mr. President, are you worried about the deficit rising if there——

The President. I'm worried about the deficit rising with some of the less—perhaps less publicized aspects of both plans. I think that some of the individual retirement accounts, or so-called back-loaded accounts—which means they could dramatically increase in cost to the Treasury right outside the 10-year budget window. I'm worried about the indexing of capital gains. I'm worried about the weakening of the alternative minimum tax provisions to the point where people will be making a lot of money and not paying any taxes ever. And we went through that once in the early eighties; the American people were, to say the least, opposed to it. And that could also lead to a big increase in the deficit.

Q. Mr. President, is that a list of things over which you would definitely veto a tax bill? Republicans may be wanting to know that.

The President. Well, first of all—I talked to Senator Lott and Speaker Gingrich last week, and we've had good working relationships with Mr. Archer and Senator Roth and others. I don't want to get into veto now. We knew that this, because of the unusual way in which this budget agreement was fashioned, that this would proceed, in effect, in a series of stages: the budget agreement, then the congressional committees, then we'd have final negotiations over the bill. I don't want to start talking about veto now. I want to craft an agreement consistent with the budget agreement that can be written into law and can be passed with a bipartisan majority of both sides.

We had a bipartisan majority in both Houses for the budget agreement. And I think it's important that we try to preserve that here.

Hong Kong

Q. Mr. President, are you concerned—given the letter that came from Secretary Albright to the Chinese—that the Chinese will stick to their end of the bargain on maintaining democracy in Hong Kong during this transition?

The President. Well, Secretary Albright is there, as you know, and what we have is the agreement, the 1984 agreement that the Chinese and the British asked the United States to support, and we did. And we expect that they will honor that agreement.

Q. Do you think that 4,000 troops marching in is a good sign?

The President. Well, it's a concern, I think. But we don't know yet that they intend to violate the agreement. They may be concerned about disruption, disorder. We'll just have to see what happens. But we will monitor it very closely. And everybody in the world knows what the agreement was—it's probably the most well-publicized agreement of its kind in modern history—and everybody has a pretty good feel for not only the economic but the political system of Hong Kong.

Q. Did you watch the ceremony this morning?

The President. I did not. I was not able to do it.

Q. Well, what makes you think that the Chinese——

Mike Tyson/Evander Holyfield Fight

Q. [*Inaudible*]—Federal role should be in regulating boxing, and your personal reaction to what happened in the Tyson/Holyfield fight? [*Laughter*]

The President. I saw the fight, and until what happened, it was a good fight. And I was horrified by it, and I think the American people are. And I don't know what the Federal role should be; I've not given any thought to that whatever. But as a fan, I was horrified.

Q. Why were you horrified?

Hong Kong

Q. Mr. President, back on Hong Kong, is there any reason that you have to believe that the Chinese would allow what would amount to an enclave of dissent in Hong Kong?

The President. Well, the agreement says that there will be one China and two systems. And it's hard to have a system with free elections and freedom of speech and an open press without dissent. Just look around here; I mean, people just have different views of things. [*Laughter*] I can't imagine how you could have it any other way.

Thank you very much.

NOTE: The President spoke at 9:55 a.m. on the South Lawn at the White House, prior to his departure for Boston, MA.

Remarks at the New England Presidential Luncheon in Boston, Massachusetts
June 30, 1997

Thank you. This is a pretty rowdy group today. [*Laughter*] And if you weren't rowdy before Senator Kennedy talked, you must be now. [*Laughter*]

Let me say to the mayor, to Senator Kerry, Senator Kennedy, to all the Members of the Congress that I have been with today, the State officials, Steve Grossman, Alan Solomont, Governor Mike Dukakis and Kitty, who are here, and all of you—Joan Menard—I've probably forgotten somebody behind me; I'm testing my memory, which is deteriorating rapidly here. [*Laughter*] I'm delighted to be back in Boston, and I'm glad to have the chance to say again, thank you for being the number one State in America in the support for Bill Clinton and Al Gore in 1996. I'm very grateful to you all. Thank you.

Thank you for being here for us in 1995, when everyone said that the days of our administration were numbered, the Democratic Party was on the downhill. You know all that stuff they said. You were right, and they were wrong, and I thank you for that.

But most importantly, I thank you because you have helped us to prove that it's good for America to give opportunity to everybody who's responsible enough to work for it. You've helped us to prove that it's good for America to think about the future. You've helped us to prove that it's good for America to give everybody a chance, without regard to race or gender or any other thing that divides us, if we are united by our shared values and our willingness to be good citizens. You've helped us to prove that we can lead the world and be strong at home. And I think that all of you should be very proud of that.

We are trying to prepare this country for a new century in which the young people in this audience will be able to do things with their lives that most of the rest of us could not even imagine. And I believe we are well on our way to doing it. You all know how we're doing today compared to 5 years ago. What I want us to think about is how we can be doing 5, 10, 15, 20 years from now.

I'm proud of the fact that we have the lowest unemployment rate in 24 years and the lowest inflation rate in 30 years and the biggest decline in inequality among working people since the 1960's. I'm proud of all that. The biggest drop in welfare rolls in history, the biggest drop in the crime rate in 36 years, I'm proud of that. I'm proud of the fact that we have taken dramatic strides to protect our environment with safe drinking water and new clean air standards and new food standards and record numbers of toxic waste dumps cleaned up and record land set aside in preservation forever. Only the two Roosevelt administrations have set aside as much land to preserve for our country's future.

But there is a lot to do. And you have to be a part of that. Because we're going through a transition in which we're changing so fast we can never be satisfied with where we are, we have to keep worrying about where we're going. And let me just mention one or two things, if I might.

First of all, we're debating this balanced budget plan. If we pass a balanced budget that's faithful to the agreement I made, it will have the biggest increase in health care for children since Medicaid was enacted in 1965—the biggest. Thank you, Senator Kennedy, for leading that. It will have the biggest increase in Federal support for education since 1965. It will have the biggest increase in Federal support, to help everybody in this country who is willing to work go on to college, since the GI bill was passed over 50 years ago.

It is a good budget for the American people, but it is important that we be faithful to it. If we are faithful to the agreement, it will help cities like Boston to take sites that have been polluted and are therefore useless now and clean them up and use them to provide for development and new jobs and new opportunities, to make sure this economic recovery reaches people who haven't felt it yet. If we are faithful to it, we can do all these things.

The other thing that I am determined to do, that I spoke a little about in Washington before I left today, is to get a tax bill out of this committee—out of the Congress that helps all the American people. We can pay for this tax cut.

First of all, let me say this: I would not support any tax cut that will bring back the bad old days of exploding deficits. I would not do that. This tax bill, in the first 5 years, is about one-tenth of the cost of the tax bill that was adopted in 1981, when the Reagan administration came in and asked us to adopt trickle-down economics. So we're not talking about a huge bill here. What we are talking about is a bill that is basically the dividend the American people have earned for bringing this economy back. And I believe it's important to pass a bill that will give everyone a fair chance to participate in it and that will be faithful to the budget agreement, which means among other things that we have to provide substantial resources to help middle class people to raise their children and educate them and then keep on getting an education for a lifetime. We have got to make at least 2 years of college as universal in the 21st century as a high school diploma is today.

Why did Boston come back? Why is Massachusetts coming back? Just drive around this town and look at the concentration of world-class universities. Every person in this country who gets out of high school and has at least 2 years of fine education afterward has a fair chance to get a decent job with a growing income. Everybody who doesn't is likely to get a job with declining incomes.

We must not use this tax bill to help people who don't need it too much without giving the middle class the tools they need to make higher education universal in America in the 21st century. We can do it, and we have to do it.

There are a lot of other things going on there now. We're reviewing this tobacco settlement, and again, a lot of people who have fought for the public health for years and years and years deserve a lot of credit for this. I have no final opinion on it yet, but I will say this: We cannot agree to anything which undermines the capacity of the Federal Government to protect the public health and the health of our children. If this settlement furthers it, we should be for it. If it doesn't, we should not. That ought to be the test.

In the area of crime, let me say the crime rate's going down; that's the good news. The bad news is it's still going up among people under 18 in many places, but not in Boston. And the mayor heard me in San Francisco last week saying to the mayors, I am trying to pass a crime bill for juveniles in this country that will give other cities the tools that Boston has used to take us now almost 2 full years without a child under 18 being killed by a handgun. If we can do it here, it ought to be done everywhere in America, and we can do it.

And finally, let me say we've had a remarkable amount of success moving people from welfare to work. But we have to create about another million jobs in the next 4 years. I've done everything I could to mobilize the private sector, but we can do more. Many of you have helped in this regard, and for that I am grateful. In this budget agreement there are specific provisions which will make it easier for us to work with cities and the private sector to hire people to move from welfare to work.

But I would just say on that portion of the budget, everyone who ever criticized the welfare program and everyone who ever said every able-bodied person ought to work now has a moral obligation to support laws that will make sure there are jobs there. You cannot tell people they have to go to work unless they have work. That is a big moral obligation of this balanced budget, and we dare not pass a budget that walks away from that obligation to people. We have said, "You have to work." We have to give them the jobs and the chance to build dignified, successful lives for themselves and their children.

The last point I would like to make is this: In the end, the success of the United States in the new century will depend upon a remarkable partnership between our Government, our private sector, and individual citizens. I have been very moved by the things that I have seen repeatedly here in Boston in the form of citizen service: the City Year program, the mayor's youth advisory council, all the people that I've seen volunteering in various aspects of the effort to keep juveniles out of trouble and away from violence. We need more of that.

And finally, we have got to prove that we can become the world's first truly multiracial, multiethnic democracy. A couple of weeks ago, I went out to the University of California at San Diego and asked the American people to join me for at least a year, and maybe longer, in a national conversation about where we are today on the subject of our racial differences, what we have to do to make sure that we are thinking and acting right about this and what new laws and policies we need.

I just leave you with this thought: In the United States today, there is one State only, Hawaii, that has no majority race. Within 3 to 5 years, our largest State, California, will have no majority race. Today, we have 5 school districts with over 100 different racial and ethnic groups represented among the student bodies— 5 school districts. Within 2 years, we'll have 12, maybe 15. And within 30 years, there will be no majority race in the United States. We had better start thinking about how we are going to make sure that what we always said, which is that America is a place of ideas and ideals, not a place where there is a dominant race, a dominant class, a dominant in-crowd—we better make sure that's true.

And so I leave you with this. The people of Boston and Massachusetts have embraced the vision that I have painted for the future more vigorously, more consistently, more ardently, than any other place in the United States. I ask you to stay with it. Because if you imagine what the future is going to be and how we would make it, it is clear that if we succeed in becoming the world's first truly multiracial, multiethnic, multireligious democracy, we will be better positioned in the 21st century even than we are now to lead the world toward peace and freedom and prosperity and to give our children a better future than any generation has ever known.

That's what I'm dedicated to. We've got 3½ more years to work for it, and your presence here today has dramatically increased the chances that we will succeed.

Thank you, and God bless you all.

NOTE: The President spoke at 1:18 p.m. in the Grand Ballroom at the Copley Plaza Hotel. In his remarks, he referred to Mayor Thomas Menino of Boston; Steve Grossman, national chair, and Alan D. Solomont, national finance chair, Democratic National Committee; Michael Dukakis, former Governor of Massachusetts, and his wife, Kitty; and Joan Menard, Massachusetts State Democratic chair.

Letter to Congressional Leaders on Most-Favored-Nation Status for Russia
June 30, 1997

Dear Mr. Speaker: (Dear Mr. President:)

On September 21, 1994, I determined and reported to the Congress that the Russian Federation is in full compliance with the freedom of emigration criteria of sections 402 and 409 of the Trade Act of 1974. This action allowed for the continuation of most-favored-nation (MFN) status for Russia and certain other activities without the requirement of an annual waiver.

As required by law, I am submitting an updated report to the Congress concerning the emigration laws and policies of the Russian Federation. You will find that the report indicates continued Russian compliance with U.S. and international standards in the area of emigration.

Sincerely,

WILLIAM J. CLINTON

NOTE: Identical letters were sent to Newt Gingrich, Speaker of the House of Representatives, and Albert Gore, Jr., President of the Senate.

Remarks at the St. James Theatre in New York City
June 30, 1997

I deserve that for that macarena stunt. [*Laughter*] Thank you, Whoopi. Thank you, cast. Thank you, Maestro. Thank you, orchestra.

You know, the theater is normally dark on Monday night. I think we can certify that this was most certainly not dark tonight, and we thank you from the bottom of our hearts. I thank all those who are here with our Democratic Party. And thank you all for coming tonight.

Someone told me that the last time anything like this was done on Broadway was for President Eisenhower in 1955. All I can say is, the others don't know what they missed. You have brightened all of our days. And I think you have pretty much made it a certainty that tomorrow will not be a tragedy.

Thank you. God bless you all. Thank you.

NOTE: The President spoke at 9:53 p.m. following a performance of the play "A Funny Thing Happened on the Way to the Forum." In his remarks, he referred to actress Whoopi Goldberg, who starred in the play. A tape was not available for verification of the content of these remarks.

Remarks at a Democratic National Committee Dinner in New York City
June 30, 1997

Thank you very much. Well, you heard Lauren say that Al Gore is the most influential Vice President in history—I let him have all the jokes. [*Laughter*]

I do want to thank my good friend Peter Duchin and his orchestra for being here tonight. And I want to thank Mr. Billy Porter for that wonderful song he sang, and thank you, Denise Rich, for writing the song—it was wonderful—and the group, you were all great. Thank you. You're going to hear a lot more from that young fellow, I predict. If I could sing like that, I'd be in a different line of work. [*Laughter*]

I want to thank Wynton Marsalis, who has always been there for us, repeatedly. We were having a discussion around the dinner table tonight about Wynton Marsalis, a man I admire enormously. And I said, I believe that he is the only musician in the world who is the best at what he does in both classical and jazz music. And then someone pointed out that Yo Yo Ma, with the "Appalachian Suite," had come pretty close. And he's helped us, too. So I don't care; you can take your choice. [*Laughter*] But he's a magnificent man. And thank you, Lauren Bacall, for being who you are and for being there for us for all these years. Thank you.

Thanks for being here. You know, one of my immutable laws of politics is that no one should ever have to listen to a speech after 11 o'clock at night. And I'm not running again, anyway; therefore, I will let you out by midnight. [*Laughter*] I'll be very brief.

I want you to remember the last thing the Vice President said. You have helped bring your country to this point through your support, and you are helping us to continue to take it in the direction that it is now headed, which is very different from 5 years ago.

I am so grateful to have had the chance to serve as President. I'm grateful especially to the people of New York, who gave us right at 60 percent of the vote in the last election and a huge plurality of well over 1.7 million votes, about 25 percent of our total—just under 25 percent of our total national plurality came from the generosity of the people of New York State, and I will never forget that. Judith Hope, our State Democratic chair, told me that we carried President Roosevelt's home county, which is apparently something that never happened when he was here. [*Laughter*] That's just because they didn't know me as well, and I thank them for that. [*Laughter*]

Let me say to you, when you go home tonight and you get up tomorrow and you think about why you do all this, I think the most useful question you can ask yourself is, what would you like your country to look like in 30 years? What would you like your country to look like when your children or your grandchildren are your age? That's a question I try to force myself to ask and answer every single day I do this job.

And it may sound trite now because I've said it so many times, but I don't have any better definition of that answer than I did when I started, more than 6 years ago now: I want my country to be a place where the American dream is alive for everybody who is responsible enough to work for it. I want our country to be a community that's coming together and celebrating the differences among us, not being driven apart by them. And I want us to lead the world for peace and freedom and prosperity well into the next century.

We're a lot closer to that today than we were 5 years ago because of the condition of the economy; because we are ending the structural deficit in the Government; because we have developed a serious approach to move people from welfare to work, not to punish them or their children; because we developed a serious approach to reduce the crime rate and make people safer on their streets, not just talk tough about it; because we've made a good beginning in education and the environment and done a lot of things around the world.

But we still have a lot to do. It really matters not only that we balance this budget but how we do it and whether we really empower people who need to be helped by this budget. If the budget we want passes, it will have—for people that tell you there's nothing very significant in it, you decide. It will have the biggest increase in children's health coverage since the passage of Medicaid in 1965. It will have the biggest increase in Federal support for education since 1965. It will have the biggest increase in Federal support to help all kinds of people who need it go to college since the GI bill was passed 52 years ago. I think it's a budget worth fighting for. It's a budget I'm very proud of.

We still have a lot to do in other areas. We've got a lot to do in the area of the environment. We took a tough decision last week on clean air rules, and we're going to work with our cities and our businesses to meet those clean air rules, but it matters whether the air is clean. There are too many children with asthma in this country; there are too many problems. It matters.

We're going to have to make some other tough decisions. The United States has 4 percent of the world's population; we produce 20 percent of the greenhouse gases that are warming our planet. It's led to the most disruptive weather patterns anybody can remember over the last 4 or 5 years. We owe it to our children not to take a stable universe away from them. It's not very complicated. And can we find a way to grow our economy and do that? Of course we can. We're smart. We can do that. But we have to do it.

We still have to find a way to honor the intergenerational compact that is the test of any great society. We do well by the elderly, and we don't do very well by the poor—the children in this country. Twenty percent of them are living below the poverty line, and it's hard for them to get the chances they need in life. And I am determined that before I leave office we will balance the intergenerational equities and take care of our children better, because we have to for our future.

Finally, just let me say this. I knew something—I thought I knew something about people who couldn't get along with one another because of their differences, because I grew up in the segregated South. I thought I knew something about that. And then I became President, and I saw what happened in Bosnia and Rwanda and Burundi. And I saw what happened when my kinfolks in Ireland still insist on shooting each other over 600-year-old fights that children can barely explain. And I thought after we signed that first peace agreement in the Middle East we would have an irreversible process because people would see it just did not make any sense to hold onto old hatreds. But they die hard.

And I don't care what anybody says—you know, yes, there is an entitlements issue that we have to face on Social Security, but my generation is not going to bankrupt our children and grandchildren. Fundamentally, that's an accounting problem; it'll get fixed. The biggest problem is whether we can muster the wisdom and strength of spirit to treat each other with respect and not just abide each other's differences of all kinds but to actually relish them and be glad that we have all this diversity in our country. Because if we can do that and then be united as one America by shared values, then we're way the best positioned democracy in the world for the next century. But this is a very important thing that you have to understand.

So as you leave here tonight, I want you to think about that. We've still got a lot of work to do before the new century comes in. There are 5 school districts in America with more than 100 different racial and ethnic groups among the students in them. Within 2 years, there will be 12. Before you know it, there will be 20. There's only one State in the country that has no majority race, Hawaii. Within 3 to 5 years, California won't. Within 30 years, the United

States won't. We always say we're bound together by our shared values. We're about to find out. [*Laughter*] Hold on, we're about to find out.

And every one of us who can be in this room tonight because of our financial or political position or whatever, we have a special responsibility to the people who will follow behind us. The United States has got an incredible opportunity here. And I'm going to keep trying to make peace in the Middle East and Northern Ireland and do what I can to help Africa. I'm going to do everything I can in this term to try to resolve the differences between Greece and Turkey over Cyprus. I'm going to support what's now going on, finally, where the Indians and Pakistanis are talking. I'm going to do all that. But just remember, all those people live in America.

And we have other differences as well. Sometimes I think that we couldn't live if we couldn't look down on somebody who is different from us. Sometimes I wonder if it's just sort of endemic to human nature, you know. Every one of you has done this, I know—at least I have. I'll plead guilty. Haven't you had a bad day when you just were really down on yourself and you said, "Well, no matter how bad I am, at least I'm not him or her"? I mean, it's almost like endemic, and we have to fight that because we are the most richly blessed country in the world. Here we are, going into this global society, and everybody's right here.

And if we have the discipline to give excellence in education, if we have the discipline to preserve the environment while we grow the economy, if we have the discipline to eliminate the intergenerational imbalance and give children health care just like we give it to senior citizens, if we have the discipline to do these things and to continue to fulfill our responsibilities in the world, the best days of this country are still ahead of us, and the people in this room will not live to see them. And that's good. That's good. That's our responsibility. And that's what this administration is all about, and that's what your presence here is helping to further. And for that, we are profoundly grateful.

God bless you, and thank you.

NOTE: The President spoke at 11:25 p.m. in the Ballroom at the Plaza Hotel. In his remarks, he referred to actress Lauren Bacall and musicians Peter Duchin, Billy Porter, Denise Rich, Wynton Marsalis, and Yo Yo Ma.

Appendix A—Digest of Other White House Announcements

The following list includes the President's public schedule and other items of general interest announced by the Office of the Press Secretary and not included elsewhere in this book.

January 1

In the morning, the President had a telephone conversation from Hilton Head, SC, with Chairman Yasser Arafat of the Palestinian Authority to express condolences with regard to the attack on civilians by an off-duty Israeli soldier in Hebron, West Bank.

In the afternoon, the President and Hillary and Chelsea Clinton traveled from Hilton Head, SC, to St. Thomas, U.S. Virgin Islands, for a vacation.

January 2

The President named the following winners of the 1996 National Medal of Arts and the Charles Frankel Prize in the Humanities, which he and the First Lady will present on January 9:

National Medal of Arts

Edward Albee;
Sarah Caldwell;
Harry Callahan;
Zelda Fichandler;
Eduardo (Lalo) Guerrero;
Lionel Hampton;
Bella Lewitzky;
Vera List;
Robert Redford;
Maurice Sendak;
Stephen J. Sondheim; and
the Boys Choir of Harlem.

Charles Frankel Prize in the Humanities

Rita Dove;
Doris Kearns Goodwin;
Daniel Kemmis;
Arturo Madrid; and
Bill Moyers.

January 3

The President declared a major disaster in Nevada and ordered Federal aid to supplement State and local recovery efforts in the area struck by severe storms, flooding, and mud- and landslides beginning December 20, 1996, and continuing.

January 4

The President declared major disasters in California and Idaho and ordered Federal aid to supplement State and local recovery efforts in the areas struck by severe storms, flooding, and mud- and landslides beginning December 28, 1996, and continuing.

January 5

The President and Hillary and Chelsea Clinton returned to Washington, DC, from St. Thomas, U.S. Virgin Islands.

January 6

In the morning, the President had a telephone conversation with Chancellor Helmut Kohl of Germany concerning NATO expansion and relations between Russia and the West.

The President announced his intention to nominate Alan M. Hantman to be the Architect of the Capitol.

The President announced his intention to nominate Donald Rappaport to be Chief Financial Officer of the Department of Education.

January 7

In the morning, the President met with Senator Daniel Patrick Moynihan in the Oval Office to discuss issues facing the 105th Congress.

In the afternoon, the President had a telephone conversation with Newt Gingrich to congratulate him on winning reelection to a second term as Speaker of the House of Representatives. The President also placed calls to Senate Majority Leader Trent Lott, Senate Minority Leader Thomas S. Daschle, and House Minority Leader Richard A. Gephardt.

The President announced his intention to nominate Susan E. Trees to the National Council on the Humanities.

The President declared a major disaster in the State of Washington and ordered Federal aid to supplement State and local recovery efforts in the area struck by severe ice storms November 19–December 4, 1996.

The President declared a major disaster in Minnesota and ordered Federal aid to supplement State and local recovery efforts in the area struck by severe ice storms November 14–30, 1996.

The White House announced that the President will meet with United Nations Secretary-General Kofi Annan in the Oval Office on January 23.

The White House announced that the President appointed Charles Ruff to succeed Jack Quinn as Assistant to the President and Counsel to the President. The President also appointed the following individuals to the positions listed:

Cheryl D. Mills, Deputy Assistant to the President and Deputy Counsel to the President;
Kathleen M.H. Wallman, Deputy Assistant to the President for Economic Policy and Chief of Staff

and Counselor to the National Economic Council; and

Elena Kagan, Deputy Director of the Domestic Policy Council.

January 8

In the morning, the President met with members of his economic team and Federal Reserve Board Chairman Alan Greenspan in the Oval Office to discuss economic issues.

January 9

In the morning, the President met with NATO Secretary General Javier Solana and Vice President Gore in the Vice President's West Wing office.

The President announced his intention to nominate Jeffrey Davidow to be a member of the Board of Directors of the Inter-American Foundation.

The White House announced that the President has appointed Secretary of the Interior Bruce Babbitt to lead a delegation representing the United States at the inauguration of President-elect Arnoldo Aleman of Nicaragua on January 10.

January 10

The President announced his intention to appoint Ann Lewis as Assistant to the President and Deputy Communications Director.

The President announced the nomination of Sheila F. Anthony to be a Commissioner of the Federal Trade Commission.

January 11

In the morning and afternoon, the President held a retreat with Cabinet members in the Jackson Place Conference Room at Blair House.

January 12

In the evening, the President had a telephone conversation with President Hosni Mubarak of Egypt concerning the Middle East peace process.

January 14

In the evening, the President had a conference call with Prime Minister Binyamin Netanyahu of Israel and Chairman Yasser Arafat of the Palestinian Authority concerning the Middle East peace process.

The President announced the nomination of Madeleine May Kunin to be Ambassador to Liechtenstein.

January 15

The President directed the Department of Health and Human Services to release $5 million in emergency Low Income Home Energy Assistance Program funds for North and South Dakota and the Indian tribes located in those States. The White House announced that the administration had declared North and South Dakota national disaster areas on January 10 and 11, respectively, due to extreme winter storms.

January 16

In the morning, the President had telephone conversations with King Hussein I of Jordan and President Hosni Mubarak of Egypt concerning the Middle East peace process.

The President declared a major disaster in Minnesota and ordered Federal aid to supplement State and local recovery efforts in the area struck by severe storms beginning January 3 and continuing.

January 17

In the morning, the President attended a breakfast with the U.S. Conference of Mayors in the Indian Treaty Room of the Old Executive Office Building.

In the afternoon, the President signed the Alameda Corridor loan guarantee in the Roosevelt Room. Later, the President and Hillary Clinton attended a diplomatic reception in the John Adams Room at the State Department.

In the evening, the President and Hillary Clinton hosted a dinner for outgoing Cabinet members in the Blue Room.

The President declared a major disaster in the State of Washington and ordered Federal aid to supplement State and local recovery efforts in the area struck by winter storms, land- and mudslides, and flooding beginning December 26, 1996, and continuing.

The President announced his intention to designate Jared L. Cohon as chairman and to appoint the following individuals as members of the Nuclear Waste Technical Review Board:

Daniel B. Bullen;
Florie A. Caporuscio;
Norman L. Christensen;
Debra S. Knopman;
Priscilla P. Nelson; and
Alberto A. Sagüés.

January 19

In the evening, the President and Hillary Clinton attended a pre-Inaugural festival at the USAir Arena in Landover, MD, which was taped for broadcast later that evening.

January 20

In the morning, the President and Hillary and Chelsea Clinton attended an Inaugural prayer service at the Metropolitan A.M.E. Church.

Following the Inaugural luncheon at the Capitol, the President and Hillary and Chelsea Clinton went by motorcade along the Inaugural parade route to the White House, where they viewed the parade from the reviewing stand. In the evening, they attended several Inaugural balls.

January 21

The President announced his intention to appoint Harry P. Pachon as a member of the President's Advisory Commission on Educational Excellence for Hispanic Americans.

January 22

In the morning, the President traveled to Chicago, IL, where, in the afternoon, he attended a meeting with Mayor Richard M. Daley and members of the Chicago school board in the Chicago Cultural Center. In the evening, the President returned to Washington, DC.

The President announced his intention to nominate Ellen S. Seidman to be Director of the Treasury Department's Office of Thrift Supervision.

January 23

In the morning, the President visited the office of the Presidential Inaugural Committee to congratulate the staff for its work on the Inaugural festivities.

The President declared a major disaster in Oregon and ordered Federal aid to supplement State and local recovery efforts in the area struck by severe winter storms, land- and mudslides, and flooding December 25, 1996, through January 6.

January 24

The President announced his intention to appoint Kathryn Walt Hall to the Board of Trustees of the Woodrow Wilson International Center for Scholars.

The President announced his intention to appoint Irving Greenberg and Romana Strochlitz Primus to the U.S. Holocaust Memorial Council.

January 25

In the evening, the President and Hillary Clinton attended the Alfalfa Club dinner in the ballroom of the Capital Hilton Hotel.

January 26

In the evening, the President hosted a Super Bowl party in the Family Theater at the White House. After the game, he placed a telephone call to the Super Bowl champion Green Bay Packers.

January 29

The White House announced that the President will meet at the White House with Prime Minister Binyamin Netanyahu of Israel on February 13; Chairman Yasser Arafat of the Palestinian Authority on March 3; President Hosni Mubarak of Egypt on March 10; and King Hussein I of Jordan on March 18.

January 30

In the morning, the President had a telephone conversation with President Jacques Chirac of France concerning President Chirac's upcoming visit to Moscow.

The President announced his intention to appoint Paul P. Craig to the Nuclear Waste Technical Review Board.

The President released $39 million in previously appropriated emergency funds to the Interior Department for restoration of public facilities and lands damaged by natural disasters in 1996.

January 31

The White House announced that the President invited President Jose Maria Aznar of Spain to the United States for an official working visit in the last week of April.

The White House announced that Prime Minister Antonio Guterres of Portugal has accepted the President's invitation for an official working visit at the White House on April 3.

The President directed the Department of Health and Human Services to release $210 million in emergency Low Income Home Energy Assistance Program funds for States, tribes, and territories nationwide.

February 3

In the morning, the President met with President Alberto Fujimori of Peru in the White House to discuss Mr. Fujimori's recent visit to Toronto, Canada, and the hostage crisis at the Japanese Ambassador's residence in Lima, Peru.

The White House announced that Prime Minister Jean Chretien of Canada and his wife have accepted the President's invitation for an official visit to Washington, DC, on April 8.

The White House announced that the President has accepted an invitation to visit The Netherlands on May 28 to commemorate the 50th anniversary of the Marshall plan and to participate in the U.S.-European Union Summit.

The President announced his intention to nominate Marsha Mason to the National Council on the Arts.

The President announced his intention to designate Michael J. Gaines as Chair of the U.S. Parole Commission.

The President announced his intention to appoint the following individuals to the Advisory Committee for Trade Policy and Negotiations:

Lester M. Alberthal, Jr.;
Roger J. Baccigaluppi;
John E. Bryson;
James P. (Tom) Camerlo, Jr.;
John T. Chambers;
Walter Y. Elisha;
Donald V. Fites;
Richard S. Fuld, Jr.;
Fred Krupp;
Lenore Miller;
Bernard Rapoport;
Jerome A. Siegel;
Paula Stern; and
John J. Sweeney.

February 4

The President announced his intention to nominate Theodore F. Verheggen to the Federal Mine Safety and Health Review Commission.

The White House announced that the President sent a message to Prime Minister Binyamin Netanyahu of Israel extending condolences to the Israeli people and the families of the victims of the Israeli Defense Forces helicopter tragedy.

February 5

In the morning, the President traveled to Augusta, GA. While en route aboard Air Force One, he had a telephone conversation with Prime Minister Binyamin Netanyahu of Israel to express his condolences. In the afternoon, the President returned to Washington, DC.

February 7

In the morning, the President had a telephone conversation with Chancellor Helmut Kohl of Germany concerning European security issues and the future of NATO.

The White House announced that the President will visit Mexico April 11–12 and the Caribbean and Central and South America May 6–13.

The President announced his intention to nominate Kathryn (Kitty) O'Leary Higgins to be Deputy Secretary of Labor.

The President announced the following White House staff appointments:

Thurgood Marshall, Jr., Assistant to the President and Cabinet Secretary;

Maria Echaveste, Assistant to the President and Director for Public Liaison;

Craig Smith, Assistant to the President and Director for Political Affairs;

Robert (Ben) Johnson, Deputy Assistant to the President and Deputy Director for Public Liaison;

Minyon Moore, Deputy Assistant to the President and Deputy Director for Political Affairs;

Karen Skelton, Deputy Assistant to the President and Deputy Director for Political Affairs; and

Beverly Barnes, Senior Adviser to the Chief of Staff.

February 8

In the evening, the President attended a farewell reception for Clinton/Gore '96 finance chairman Terence McAuliffe at the Hay-Adams Hotel.

February 9

In the afternoon, the President and Hillary Clinton attended a performance of "Twilight: Los Angeles, 1992. On the Road: A Search for American Character" at Ford's Theatre.

February 10

In the morning, the President traveled to Annapolis, MD. In the afternoon, he returned to Washington, DC.

February 11

In an evening ceremony in the Oval Office, the President received diplomatic credentials from Ambassadors Baktybek Abdrisaev of the Kyrgyz Republic; K.M. Shehabuddin of Bangladesh; Andrew Nicolaides of Cyprus; Bernardo Vega of the Dominican Republic; Juan Carlos Esguerra of Colombia; Andrew Sharp Peacock of Australia; Napolioni Masirewa of Fiji; Rex Stephen Horoi of the Solomon Islands; and Madame Akosita Fineanganofo of Tonga.

The President announced his intention to appoint Richard R. Parizek to the Nuclear Waste Technical Review Board.

The White House announced that the President, while on a working visit to Capitol Hill, had a telephone conversation with Senator Richard C. Shelby concerning the nomination of Anthony Lake to be Director of Central Intelligence.

February 12

The President announced that he appointed Harold Ickes as director of the 1997 summit of the world's major industrialized nations, which will take place in Denver, CO, June 20–22.

The President announced that he has given White House Director for Legislative Affairs John Hilley an expanded role as both Senior Adviser to the President and Director for Legislative Affairs.

The President announced his intention to designate Ken Kennedy as Co-Chairman of the Advisory Committee on High-Performance Computing and Communications, Information Technology, and the Next Generation Internet. He also announced his intention to appoint the following individuals as members:

Eric A. Benhamou;

Vinton Cerf;

Ching-Chih Chen;

David Cooper;

Steven D. Dorfman;

Robert Ewald;

David J. Farber;

Sherrilynne S. Fuller;

Hector Garcia-Molina;

Susan Graham;

James N. Gray;

W. Daniel Hillis;

David C. Nagel;

Raj Reddy;

Edward H. Shortliffe;

Larry Smarr;

Leslie Vadasz;

Andrew J. Viterbi; and

Steven J. Wallach.

February 14

In the afternoon, the President participated in a swearing-in ceremony in the Oval Office for Secretary of Transportation Rodney E. Slater.

The President announced his intention to nominate Stuart E. Eizenstat to be Under Secretary of State for Economic, Business, and Agricultural Affairs.

The President announced his intention to nominate Thomas Pickering to be Under Secretary of State for Political Affairs.

The President named Eric P. Goosby as Acting Director of the Office of National AIDS Policy.

The President announced his intention to appoint Gus Weill as a member of the J. William Fulbright Foreign Scholarship Board.

February 15

The President announced that he selected Robert O. Harris as Chairman and Anthony V. Sinicropi and Helen M. Witt as members of Presidential Emergency Board No. 233, established by Executive order to investigate the dispute between American Airlines and its employees represented by the Allied Pilots Association.

February 18

In the morning, the President traveled to New York City, NY. In the evening, he traveled to Boston, MA.

The White House announced that the President will visit Denmark on March 21 following his meeting in Helsinki, Finland, with President Boris Yeltsin of Russia.

February 19

In the afternoon, the President returned to Washington, DC.

February 21

The President announced his intention to designate Bill Joy as Co-Chairman of the Advisory Committee on High-Performance Computing and Communications, Information Technology, and the Next Generation Internet.

February 24

The President named Richard Socarides as Special Assistant to the President and Senior Adviser for Public Liaison.

February 25

In the morning, the President met with Second Deputy Prime Minister Prince Sultan bin Abd al-Aziz Al Saud of Saudi Arabia in the Oval Office.

The President announced his intention to nominate James B. King to serve a second 4-year term as Director of the Office of Personnel Management.

The White House announced that the President announced the formation of a Capital Budget Commission to report to the President on how best to reflect and encourage public investment while maintaining strict fiscal discipline in the Federal budget. He named Jon S. Corzine and Kathleen Brown as Cochairs. Following consultation with the Cochairs and the congressional leadership, the President will make nine other bipartisan appointments to the Commission.

The White House announced that the President will attend the New York Mets/Los Angeles Dodgers baseball game at Shea Stadium in New York City on April 15 to honor the memory of Jackie Robinson and commemorate the 50th anniversary of the integration of Major League baseball.

February 27

At noon, the President had a telephone conversation with President Boris Yeltsin of Russia concerning the upcoming Russia-U.S. Summit in Helsinki, Finland.

The President announced his intention to reappoint Brent Scowcroft as a member of the U.S. Air Force Academy Board of Visitors.

February 28

.The President declared a major disaster in South Dakota and ordered Federal aid to supplement State and local recovery efforts in the area struck by a severe winter storm November 13–26, 1996.

The President announced his intention to nominate Joel I. Klein to be Assistant Attorney General in the Antitrust Division at the Department of Justice.

The President announced his intention to appoint the following individuals to the President's Council on Sustainable Development:

Ray C. Anderson;
Scott Bernstein;
Randall Franke;
Harry J. Pearce; and
M. Susan Savage.

March 1

In the morning, the President and Hillary Clinton traveled to New York City.

March 2

In the morning, the President and Hillary Clinton returned to Washington, DC. In the evening, they attended a festival at Ford's Theatre.

The President declared a major disaster in Arkansas and ordered Federal aid to supplement State and local recovery efforts in the area struck by severe storms and tornadoes beginning March 1 and continuing.

March 3

In the afternoon, the President met with Senators Daniel Patrick Moynihan and Jesse Helms and Representatives Lee H. Hamilton and Larry Combest in the Oval Office to discuss Government security classification issues.

March 4

In the morning, the President traveled to Little Rock, AR. In the afternoon, he traveled to Arkadelphia and College Station, AR, where he toured areas of tornado damage. In the evening, he returned to Washington, DC.

The President announced his intention to appoint John R. Phillips as a member of the President's Commission on White House Fellows.

The President declared a major disaster in Kentucky and ordered Federal aid to supplement Commonwealth and local recovery efforts in the area struck by severe storms, tornadoes, and flooding beginning March 1 and continuing.

The President declared a major disaster in Ohio and ordered Federal aid to supplement State and local recovery efforts in the area struck by severe storms and flooding beginning February 28 and continuing.

March 5

In the morning, the President held a telephone interview from the Oval Office with James A. Barnes of the National Journal.

March 6

In the morning, the President traveled to Lansing, MI. In the evening, he returned to Washington, DC.

The President declared a major disaster in Indiana and ordered Federal aid to supplement State and local recovery efforts in the area struck by severe storms and flooding beginning February 28 and continuing.

March 7

The President announced his intention to appoint Dianne Welsh Bleck as a member of the U.S. Air Force Academy Board of Visitors.

The White House announced that the Russia-U.S. Summit in Helsinki, Finland, will begin with an informal dinner hosted by President Martti Ahtisaari of Finland at the Presidential Palace on March 19. The summit will continue with meetings between the President and President Boris Yeltsin of Russia on March 20. The President will depart for Copenhagen, Denmark, on the evening of March 20.

The President declared a major disaster in Tennessee and ordered Federal aid, including individual assistance, to supplement State and local recovery efforts in the areas affected by severe storms, flooding, and tornadoes that began February 28.

The President declared a major disaster in West Virginia and ordered Federal aid, including individual assistance, to supplement State and local recovery efforts in the areas affected by severe storms, heavy rains, and high winds that began February 28.

March 10

The President announced his intention to nominate Linda Tarr-Whelan, U.S. Representative to the United Nations Commission on the Status of Women, to the rank of Ambassador.

March 11

The President announced his intention to appoint Dolores Margaret Richard Spikes as a member of the U.S. Naval Academy Board of Visitors.

The President declared a major disaster in the Federated States of Micronesia and ordered Federal aid to supplement FSM recovery efforts in the area struck by Typhoon Fern, December 25–26, 1996.

March 12

The President announced his intention to appoint Aida Alvarez as a member of the Board of Governors of the American National Red Cross.

March 13

In the morning, the President traveled to Raleigh, NC. In the afternoon, he traveled to Miami, FL.

The President announced his intention to nominate Eric H. Holder, Jr., to be Deputy Attorney General at the Department of Justice.

March 14

In the morning, the President returned to Washington, DC. Later, he went to the National Naval Medical Center in Bethesda, MD, to undergo knee surgery for injuries sustained when he lost his footing on a staircase at the home of professional golfer Greg Norman in Florida the night before.

March 16

In the morning, the President returned to the White House.

The White House announced that the President and the Danish Government agreed to postpone the President's scheduled March 21 visit to Denmark, because of his recent knee surgery. The President's visit to Denmark will take place in conjunction with the Madrid NATO Summit in July.

March 17

In the afternoon, the President met with Minister of Foreign Affairs Yevgeniy Primakov of Russia in the Yellow Room to discuss issues on the agenda for the upcoming Russia-U.S. Summit in Helsinki, Finland.

The White House announced that the President extended the time for Presidential Emergency Board No. 233 to submit its report until March 19. The board was established to investigate the dispute between American Airlines and its employees represented by the Allied Pilots Association.

March 18

The President announced his intention to nominate Kenneth M. Mead to be Inspector General at the Department of Transportation.

The President declared a major disaster in Louisiana and ordered Federal aid to supplement State and local recovery efforts in the area struck by a severe ice storm January 12–17.

March 19

In the evening, the President departed for Helsinki, Finland, arriving the following afternoon.

The President announced his intention to nominate John D. Trasviña to be Special Counsel for Immigration-Related Unfair Employment Practices at the Department of Justice.

The President announced his intention to appoint Glyn T. Davies as the Executive Secretary of the National Security Council.

The White House announced that the President asked the Congress to provide nearly $2 billion in emergency funding to meet urgent needs created by recent natural disasters across the country.

March 21

In the evening, the President departed for Washington, DC, arriving early the following morning.

The President declared a major disaster in Illinois and ordered Federal aid to supplement State and local recovery efforts in the area struck by severe storms and flooding beginning March 1 and continuing.

March 24

The White House announced that the President will meet with King Hussein I of Jordan at the White House on April 1.

March 25

The White House announced that the President's scheduled visits to Mexico, Brazil, Argentina, and Venezuela have been postponed to facilitate his recovery from knee surgery. The President will visit Mexico May 6–7, and Brazil, Argentina, and Venezuela October 12–17.

The White House announced that the President will open his national service conference, the Summit for America's Future, at Independence Hall in Philadelphia, PA, on April 28, after participating in a cleanup day with AmeriCorps volunteers in Germantown, PA, on April 27.

March 28

In the afternoon, the President met in the Oval Office with John Sweeney, president, AFL–CIO; Morton Bahr, international president, Communications Workers of America; Gerald W. McEntee, president, American Federation of State, County, and Municipal Employees, AFL–CIO; and Andrew Stein, president, Service Employees International Union, AFL–CIO, to discuss welfare reform issues.

April 2

The President declared a major disaster in the State of Washington and ordered Federal aid to supplement State and local recovery efforts in the area struck by heavy rains, snow melt, flooding, and land- and mudslides March 18–28.

April 3

The President announced his intention to appoint Janet L. Yellen as Chair of the Interagency Committee on Women's Business Enterprise.

April 4

The President announced his intention to reappoint Robert A. Gaines as a member of the National Capital Planning Commission.

April 6

The President appointed James B. King to be Director of the Office of Personnel Management as a recess appointee.

April 7

The President announced the appointment of Ambassador Robert S. Gelbard as Special Representative of the President and the Secretary of State for Implementation of the Dayton Peace Accords.

The President declared a major disaster in North Dakota and ordered Federal aid to supplement State and local recovery efforts in the area struck by severe flooding, severe winter storms, heavy spring rain, rapid snowmelt, high winds, ice jams, and ground saturation due to high water tables beginning February 28 and continuing.

The President declared a major disaster in South Dakota and ordered Federal aid to supplement State and local recovery efforts in the area struck by severe flooding, severe winter storms, heavy spring rain, rapid snowmelt, high winds, and ice jams beginning February 3 and continuing.

April 8

The President declared a major disaster in Minnesota and ordered Federal aid to supplement State and local recovery efforts in the area struck by severe flooding, severe winter storms, snowmelt, high winds, rain, and ice beginning March 21 and continuing.

April 9

In the afternoon, the President met with Leah Rabin in the Oval Office to discuss the Middle East peace process.

The President announced his intention to nominate Elizabeth Moler to be Deputy Secretary of the Department of Energy.

April 10

The President announced his intention to appoint Katherine Bryan and Howard Torgrove to the Advisory Committee on the Arts of the John F. Kennedy Center for the Performing Arts.

The President announced his intention to appoint Diane Asadorian, Albert Abramson, Gerda Klein, and Leonard Wilf to the U.S. Holocaust Memorial Council.

The President announced his intention to appoint James D. Cunningham, Sr., as a member of the National Partnership Council.

The President announced his intention to reappoint Victoria Murphy as a member of the J. William Fulbright Foreign Scholarship Board.

The President announced his intention to nominate Ruth Yone Tamura to be a member of the National Museum Services Board.

The President announced his intention to nominate Andrew J. Pincus to be General Counsel for the Department of Commerce.

The President announced his intention to nominate Yerker Andersson, Gina McDonald, Bonnie O'Day, and Shirley Welsh Ryan to the National Council on Disability.

April 11

The President announced his intention to nominate Edward William Gnehm, Jr., to be Director General of the Foreign Service.

The President announced his intention to nominate Karl F. Inderfurth to be Assistant Secretary of State for South Asian Affairs.

April 13
In the evening, the President had a telephone conversation with professional golfer Tiger Woods to congratulate Mr. Woods on winning the PGA Masters golf tournament.

April 14
The President announced his intention to appoint J. Randall MacDonald as a member of the Advisory Commission on Consumer Protection and Quality in the Health Care Industry.

The President declared a major disaster in Arkansas and ordered Federal aid to supplement State and local recovery efforts in the area struck by severe storms and flooding beginning April 4 and continuing.

April 15
In the morning, the President traveled to Brooklyn, NY. In the evening, he traveled to Queens.

The President had a telephone conversation with King Fahd of Saudi Arabia to express his sympathy for the victims of the fire at Mina. Later, he returned to Washington, DC.

The President announced his intention to nominate Brian Dean Curran to be Ambassador to Mozambique.

The President announced his intention to nominate Olivia A. Golden to be Assistant Secretary for Family Support (Administration for Children and Families) at the Department of Health and Human Services.

The President announced his intention to appoint Jack Roderick as a member of the Arctic Research Commission.

The White House announced that the administration is requesting nominations for representatives to serve on the Advisory Commission on Public Interest Obligations of Digital Television Broadcasters.

April 16
In the evening, the President attended a foreign policy retreat with Members of Congress at Blair House.

The White House announced that Prime Minister Ryutaro Hashimoto of Japan accepted the President's invitation for an official working visit in Washington, DC, April 25.

April 17
The President announced his intention to appoint Emily Malino as a member of the Commission of Fine Arts.

April 18
In the morning, the President attended Vice President Al Gore's meeting with Hong Kong Democratic Party Leader Martin Lee in the Vice President's West Wing Office.

The President announced his intention to reappoint Daryl L. Jones as a member of the Board of Visitors to the U.S. Air Force Academy.

The President announced his intention to appoint the following individuals to the Board of Directors of the Presidio Trust:

Edward Blakely;
Donald G. Fisher;
Amy Meyer;
Mary G. Murphy;
William K. Reilly; and
Toby Rosenblatt.

April 22
In the morning, the President traveled to Grand Forks, ND. Following his arrival, he took a helicopter tour of areas damaged by severe flooding in North Dakota and Minnesota.

In the evening, the President returned to Washington, DC.

The President amended the April 7 and 8 major disaster declarations for the flood-ravaged upper Midwest by authorizing direct Federal funding for emergency work performed in response to the flooding in Minnesota, North Dakota, and South Dakota.

April 23
In the afternoon, the President briefly attended the Vice President's meeting with His Holiness the XIV Dalai Lama.

The President announced his intention to nominate W. Scott Gould to be Chief Financial Officer and Assistant Secretary for Administration at the Department of Commerce.

The White House announced the President's intention to send legislation to Congress to modify the Franklin D. Roosevelt Memorial, to be dedicated on May 2, in order to provide a permanent depiction of President Roosevelt's disability.

April 24
The President announced his intention to appoint James D. Cunningham, Sr., as a member of the Federal Salary Council.

April 25
The President announced his intention to nominate Michael J. Armstrong to be Associate Director of Mitigation at the Federal Emergency Management Agency.

April 26
The White House announced that the President asked U.S. Representative to the United Nations Bill Richardson to lead a special mission to Zaire.

April 27
In the morning, the President and Hillary Clinton traveled to Philadelphia, PA.

April 28

In the evening, the President and Hillary Clinton returned to Washington, DC.

April 29

The President announced his intention to nominate Robert L. Mallett to be Deputy Secretary of Commerce.

The President announced his intention to appoint Ray C. Anderson as Cochair of the President's Council on Sustainable Development.

The President announced his intention to appoint William A. Bible, Robert Wayne Loescher, and Richard Carl Leone as members of the National Gambling Impact Study Commission.

April 30

In the morning, the President met with Vice Premier and Minister of Foreign Affairs Qian Qichen of China in the Oval Office.

The White House announced that the President and Hillary Clinton announced that their daughter Chelsea will enter Stanford University in the fall as a member of the class of 2001.

May 1

In the afternoon, the President participated in a swearing-in ceremony in the Oval Office for Secretary of Labor Alexis M. Herman.

The White House announced that the President will issue a formal apology to the 14 surviving members of the original Tuskegee Experiment in a Rose Garden ceremony on May 16.

May 5

In the afternoon, the President traveled to Mexico City, Mexico, arriving in the evening.

The President announced his intention to nominate Richard Sklar to be U.S. Representative to the United Nations for U.N. Management and Reform at the State Department, with the rank of Ambassador.

May 6

In the afternoon, the President participated in a wreath-laying ceremony with President Ernesto Zedillo of Mexico at the Altar to the Nation.

In the evening, the President met with Mexican opposition leader Felipe de Jesus Calderon, president, National Action Party (PAN), at the El Presidente Intercontinental Hotel. Later, he met with Humberto Roque Villanueva, president of the ruling Institutional Revolutionary Party (PRI).

Later in the evening, the President and Hillary Clinton attended a cultural presentation at the Palacio de Belles Artes with President Zedillo and Mrs. Anilda Zedillo.

The President announced his intention to nominate Jackie M. Clegg to be First Vice President and Vice Chairman of the Export-Import Bank of the United States.

The President announced his intention to nominate James A. Harmon to be President and Chairman of the Export-Import Bank of the United States.

The President announced his intention to nominate Kathy Karpan to be Director of Surface Mining Reclamation and Enforcement at the Department of the Interior.

The President announced his intention to nominate Patrick A. Shea to be Director of the Bureau of Land Management at the Department of the Interior.

May 7

In the afternoon, the President and Hillary Clinton traveled to Tlaxcala and Teotihuacan, Mexico. In the evening, they returned to Mexico City.

Later, the President and Hillary Clinton traveled to San Jose, Costa Rica.

May 8

In the morning, the President visited the Museum of Costa Rican Art.

The White House announced that the President will give commencement addresses at Morgan State University in Baltimore, MD, on May 18; the U.S. Military Academy in West Point, NY, on May 31; and the University of California San Diego on June 14.

May 9

In the afternoon, the President and Hillary Clinton traveled to Bridgetown, Barbados.

The White House announced that in connection with his trip to The Netherlands May 28 for the U.S.-European Union Summit and the commemoration of the 50th anniversary of the Marshall plan, the President accepted an invitation to meet with newly elected Prime Minister Tony Blair of the United Kingdom in London.

May 10

In the afternoon, the President met with President Rene Preval of Haiti at the Sherbourne Center in Bridgetown, Barbados.

May 12

In the afternoon, the President returned to Washington, DC, arriving in the evening.

May 13

The President announced his intention to appoint Betty Bednarczyk as a member of the Advisory Commission on Consumer Protection and Quality in the Health Care Industry.

The White House announced that the President invited President Kiro Gligorov of the Former Yugoslav Republic of Macedonia to Washington, DC, for a working visit on June 17.

May 14

In an afternoon ceremony in the Oval Office, the President received diplomatic credentials from Ambassadors Saad Muhammad al-Kubaysi of Qatar; Pengiran Anak Dato Haji Puteh of Brunei; Osbert W. Liburd, of Saint Kitts and Nevis; Francisco Xavier Aguirre-Sacasa of Nicaragua; Riaz Hussain Khokhar of Pakistan; Aleksandr Vondra of the Czech Republic; Alfred Defago of Switzerland; Grigore-Kalev Stoicescu of Estonia; Valery Tsepkalo of Belarus; Joseph Diatta of Niger; Mark Micallef of Malta; and Le Van Bang of Vietnam.

May 15

The President announced his intention to appoint Ann Todd Free as a member of the Commission on Fine Arts.

The White House announced that the President invited NATO Secretary General Javier Solana to Washington, DC, for a meeting at the White House on May 19.

May 16

In the afternoon, the President met with President Leonid Kuchma of Ukraine in the Oval Office.

The President announced his intention to nominate George Munoz to be President of the Overseas Private Investment Corporation.

The President announced his intention to nominate Terry D. Garcia to be Assistant Secretary for Oceans and Atmosphere, National Oceanic and Atmospheric Administration, Department of Commerce.

The President announced his intention to appoint Mickey Ibarra as Assistant to the President and Director of Intergovernmental Affairs at the White House.

May 18

In the morning, the President traveled to Baltimore, MD, and he returned to Washington, DC, in the evening.

May 19

The President announced his intention to nominate Catherine Woteki to be Under Secretary for Food Safety at the Department of Agriculture.

The President announced his intention to nominate Shirley Robinson Watkins to be Under Secretary for Food, Nutrition, and Consumer Services at the Department of Agriculture.

May 20

The President announced his intention to nominate David J. Scheffer to be Ambassador at Large for War Crimes Issues at the State Department.

The President announced his intention to nominate James W. Pardew to be U.S. Representative for Military Stabilization in the Balkans with the rank of Ambassador at the State Department.

The President announced his intention to nominate Ambassador Peter Burleigh to be Deputy Representative of the U.S. to the United Nations with the rank of Ambassador Extraordinary and Plenipotentiary.

May 21

The President announced his intention to nominate John Christian Kornblum to be Ambassador to Germany.

The President announced his intention to nominate Marc Grossman to be Assistant Secretary of State for European and Canadian Affairs.

May 22

In the morning, the President traveled to Clarksburg, WV, and he returned to Washington, DC, in the evening.

The President announced his intention to nominate David R. Andrews to be Legal Adviser at the State Department.

The President announced his intention to nominate Stephen R. Sestanovich to be Ambassador at Large and Special Adviser to the Secretary of State on the New Independent States at the State Department.

May 23

The President announced his intention to nominate James Phillip Rubin to be Assistant Secretary for Public Affairs at the State Department.

The President announced the nomination of Stanley Owen Roth to be Assistant Secretary of State for East Asian and Pacific Affairs at the State Department.

The President announced the nomination of Kenneth S. Apfel to be Commissioner of the Social Security Administration.

The White House announced that the President has named Anne Luzzatto as Deputy Press Secretary for Foreign Affairs and National Security Council Senior Director for Public Affairs and that Joseph P. Lockhart will replace Mary Ellen Glynn as Deputy Press Secretary.

May 26

In the morning, the President traveled to Arlington National Cemetery in Arlington, VA, where he laid a wreath at the Tomb of the Unknowns. In the afternoon, he returned to Washington, DC.

In the evening, the President and Hillary Clinton traveled to Paris, France, arriving the following morning.

May 27

In the morning, the President met with President Jacques Chirac of France in President Chirac's office at the Elysee Palace.

In the afternoon, the President attended a luncheon hosted by President Chirac in the State Dining Room at the Elysee Palace.

In the evening, the President met with President Boris Yeltsin of Russia in the Samuel Bernard Room at the U.S. Ambassador's Residence. Later, the President and Hillary Clinton traveled to Amsterdam, The Netherlands.

The President announced the nomination of Bonnie R. Cohen to be Under Secretary for Management at the State Department.

May 28

In the afternoon, the President and Hillary Clinton took a brief walking tour of a shopping district in The Hague. In the evening, they took a walking tour of downtown Delft.

The President announced his intention to nominate Susan E. Rice to be Assistant Secretary for African Affairs at the State Department.

The President announced the appointment of Christopher J. Queram as a member of the Advisory Commission on Consumer Protection and Quality in the Health Care Industry.

The White House announced that the President will meet with Prime Minister John Howard of Australia at the White House on June 27.

May 29

In the morning, the President and Hillary Clinton traveled to London, United Kingdom. Later, the President met with Prime Minister Tony Blair in the White Room at 10 Downing Street.

In the afternoon, the President and Hillary Clinton visited the U.S. Ambassador's Residence, where the President addressed the Embassy staff. In the evening, they returned to Washington, DC.

The President announced the nomination of Paul Simon to be a member of the National Institute for Literacy Advisory Board.

May 30

The President announced his intention to nominate James Franklin Collins to be Ambassador to Russia.

The White House announced that Chelsea Clinton will graduate from the Sidwell Friends School in Washington, DC, on June 6.

May 31

In the morning, the President traveled to West Point, NY, and he returned to Washington, DC, in the afternoon.

June 2

The President announced his intention to nominate Janice R. Lachance to be Deputy Director of the Office of Personnel Management.

June 3

The President announced his intention to nominate Beth Nolan to be Assistant Attorney General in the Office of Legal Counsel at the Department of Justice.

June 4

The White House announced that the President will participate in an environmental summit in Lake Tahoe, NV, on July 26, and that he will attend a National Governors' Association meeting in Las Vegas, NV, on July 28.

June 5

The White House announced that the President will meet with Amir Hamad bin Khalifa Al Thani of Qatar at the White House on June 11.

June 6

The President announced his intention to appoint Jamie Gorelick as Chair and Maurice R. Greenberg, Margaret Greene, Erle Nye, and Floyd Emerson Wicks as members of the Advisory Committee to the President's Commission on Critical Infrastructure Protection.

June 9

The White House announced that the President forwarded to the Congress a package of fiscal year 1998 budget amendments for consistency with the bipartisan budget agreement.

June 10

In the morning, the President met with House Minority Leader Richard A. Gephardt in the Oval Office. In the afternoon, he met with Democratic members of the Senate Finance Committee in the Cabinet Room. In the evening, the President met with representatives of civil rights organizations in the Yellow Oval Room.

The President announced his intention to nominate George A. Omas to be a Commissioner on the Postal Rate Commission.

June 11

In the morning, the President met with Amir Hamad bin Khalifa Al Thani of Qatar to discuss the Qatar-U.S. bilateral relationship and its commitment to maintaining peace in the Persian Gulf region.

The President announced his intention to nominate Jane Garvey to be Administrator and George Donohue to be Deputy Administrator of the Federal Aviation Administration.

The President announced that Richard Garwin, Mortimer Elkind, and H. Rodney Withers are winners of the Enrico Fermi Award for a lifetime of achievement in the field of nuclear energy.

June 12

The President announced the nomination of Timberlake Foster to be Ambassador to Mauritania.

The President announced the nomination of Ralph Frank to be Ambassador to Nepal.

The President announced the nomination of John C. Holzman to be Ambassador to Bangladesh.

The President announced the nomination of Nancy J. Powell to be Ambassador to Uganda.

The President announced the nomination of Amelia Ellen Shippy to be Ambassador to Malawi.

The President announced his intention to nominate Bill Lann Lee to be Assistant Attorney General for the Civil Rights Division at the Department of Justice.

The President announced his intention to nominate Raymond C. Fisher to be Associate Attorney General at the Department of Justice.

The President announced his intention to appoint the following individuals as members of the President's Advisory Board on Race:

Linda Chavez-Thompson;
Suzan D. Johnson Cook;
John Hope Franklin;
Thomas H. Kean;
Angela E. Oh;
Robert Thomas; and
William F. Winter.

In addition, the President asked Christopher Edley to serve as a consultant to the Board and the President.

June 13

In the evening, the President traveled to San Diego, CA.

The White House announced that the President will meet with Crown Prince Hassan of Jordan on June 17 at the White House to discuss developments in the Middle East and Jordan-U.S. economic cooperation.

The President announced his intention to appoint Abraham H. Foxman, Jay Mazur, and Aletta Schaap to the U.S. Holocaust Memorial Council.

June 14

In the evening, the President returned to Washington, DC, arriving after midnight.

June 15

In the afternoon, the President attended the final round of the U.S. Open golf tournament at the Congressional Country Club in Bethesda, MD.

June 16

In the evening, the President attended a book release party for Texas Land Commissioner Garry Mauro at the Willard Hotel.

June 17

In the morning, the President met with President Kiro Gligorov of the Former Yugoslav Republic of Macedonia in the Oval Office to discuss a wide range of bilateral and regional issues.

June 18

In the afternoon, the President met with Crown Prince Hassan of Jordan in the Oval Office to review the Jordan-U.S. bilateral relationship and developments in the Middle East.

The President announced his intention to nominate Louis Caldera to be Managing Director and Chief Operating Officer for the Corporation for National and Community Service.

June 19

In the morning, the President met in the Oval Office with teachers Gary Trew and Seamus McNeill, the first winners of the "President's Prize" in Northern Ireland for efforts to promote cross-community understanding.

Later, the President traveled to Denver, CO. In the evening, he attended a Denver Summit host committee reception at a private residence in Cherry Hills, CO.

The President announced the designation of James J. Hoecker as Chairman of the Federal Energy Regulatory Commission.

The President announced his intention to appoint Ruby G. Moy as Staff Director of the U.S. Commission on Civil Rights.

June 20

In the morning, the President had a telephone conversation with President Fernando Cardoso of Brazil from the Presidential Suite at the Brown Palace Hotel concerning Brazil's approval of the Nuclear Non-Proliferation Treaty and the President's planned visit to Brazil.

In the evening, the President attended a reception with Summit of the Eight leaders in the courtyard of the Governor's Mansion. Later, he attended a dinner with the leaders in the Music Room of the Phipps Conference Center.

The President announced his intention to appoint Jake Steinfeld as a member of the President's Council on Physical Fitness and Sports.

June 21

In the evening, the President and Hillary Clinton had dinner with Summit of the Eight leaders at the Fort Restaurant. Later, they joined the leaders for an evening of entertainment at the Western Event Complex.

June 22

In the afternoon, the President traveled to San Francisco, CA, arriving in the evening.

June 23

In the afternoon, the President traveled to Los Angeles, CA. While en route aboard Air Force One, he had a telephone conversation with the family of Betty Shabazz to offer his condolences on her death.

In the evening, the President attended a Democratic Senatorial Campaign Committee dinner at the Beverly Hilton Hotel. Later, he returned to Washington, DC, arriving the following morning.

The President announced his intention to nominate Saul N. Ramirez, Jr., to be Assistant Secretary for Community Planning and Development at the Department of Housing and Urban Development.

The President announced his intention to nominate Jamie Rappaport Clark to be Director of the Fish and Wildlife Service at the Department of the Interior.

June 24

The President announced his intention to nominate Ambassador Martin Indyk to be Assistant Secretary for Near Eastern Affairs at the State Department.

The President announced his intention to nominate Robert Orent and Larry Schumann to be members of the President's National Security Telecommunications Advisory Committee.

The President appointed 11 men and 4 women from 10 States and the District of Columbia as the 1997–1998 White House Fellows.

June 25

In the morning, the President traveled to Nashville, TN, and in the afternoon, he traveled to Chicago, IL. In the evening, the President and Hillary Clinton traveled to Hope, AR.

The President announced his intention to nominate Rudy F. de Leon to be Under Secretary of Defense for Personnel and Readiness.

The President announced his intention to nominate M.D.B. Carlisle and Darryl R. Wold to be Commissioners on the Federal Election Commission.

June 26

In the afternoon, the President traveled to Texarkana, AR. Later, he traveled to New York City.

In the evening, the President met with U.N. Secretary-General Kofi Annan in Mr. Annan's office at the United Nations.

Later, the President met with President Kim Yongsam of South Korea in the Conference Room at the U.S. Mission.

The White House announced that President Roman Herzog of Germany will meet with the President on July 24 to discuss social and political issues of importance to both the German and American peoples.

June 27

In the evening, the President and Hillary Clinton went to Camp David, MD.

The President announced his intention to nominate David A. Lipton to be Under Secretary for International Affairs at the Department of the Treasury.

The President announced the nomination of Nancy Killefer to be Assistant Secretary for Management and Chief Financial Officer at the Department of the Treasury.

The President announced the nomination of Gary Gensler to be Assistant Secretary for Financial Markets at the Department of the Treasury.

The President announced his intention to nominate Nancy-Ann Min DeParle to be Administrator of the Health Care Financing Administration at the Department of Health and Human Services.

The President announced his intention to nominate Robert G. Stanton to be Director of the National Park Service at the Department of the Interior.

The President announced his intention to nominate Kneeland Youngblood to the Board of Directors of the U.S. Enrichment Corporation.

The White House announced that the President will travel to Poland, Romania, and Denmark immediately following the NATO Summit in Madrid, at the invitation of the Presidents of Poland and Romania and Her Majesty the Queen of Denmark.

June 28

The President announced his intention to appoint Norman J. Ornstein and Leslie Moonves as Cochairs of the Advisory Committee on Public Interest Obligations of Digital Television Broadcasters.

June 29

In the evening, the President and Hillary Clinton returned to the White House from a weekend stay at Camp David, MD.

June 30

In the morning, the President traveled to Boston, MA. In the afternoon, he traveled to New York City, returning to Washington, DC, after midnight.

The President announced the nomination of Wendy Ruth Sherman to be Counselor of the Department of State with the rank of Ambassador.

The President announced the nomination of Maura Harty to be Ambassador to Paraguay.

The President announced the nomination of Curtis Warren Kamman to be Ambassador to Colombia.

The President announced the nomination of Anne Marie Sigmund to be Ambassador to the Kyrgyz Republic.

The President announced the nomination of Daniel V. Speckhard to be Ambassador to Belarus.

Appendix B—Nominations Submitted to the Senate

The following list does not include promotions of members of the Uniformed Services, nominations to the Service Academies, or nominations of Foreign Service officers.

Submitted January 7

Madeleine Korbel Albright,
of the District of Columbia, to be Secretary of State, vice Warren Christopher, resigned.

William S. Cohen,
of Maine, to be Secretary of Defense, vice William J. Perry.

Bill Richardson,
of New Mexico, to be the Representative of the United States of America to the United Nations with the rank and status of Ambassador Extraordinary and Plenipotentiary, and the Representative of the United States of America in the Security Council of the United Nations, vice Madeleine Korbel Albright.

Aida Alvarez,
of New York, to be Administrator of the Small Business Administration, vice Philip Lader.

Andrew M. Cuomo,
of New York, to be Secretary of Housing and Urban Development, vice Henry G. Cisneros, resigned.

William M. Daley,
of Illinois, to be Secretary of Commerce, vice Michael Kantor.

Alexis M. Herman,
of Alabama, to be Secretary of Labor, vice Robert B. Reich.

Rodney E. Slater,
of Arkansas, to be Secretary of Transportation, vice Federico Peña.

Janet L. Yellen,
of California, to be a member of the Council of Economic Advisers, vice Joseph E. Stiglitz, resigned.

Charlene Barshefsky,
of the District of Columbia, to be U.S. Trade Representative, with the rank of Ambassador Extraordinary and Plenipotentiary, vice Michael Kantor.

Donna Holt Cunninghame,
of Maryland, to be Chief Financial Officer, Corporation for National and Community Service, to which position she was appointed during the last recess of the Senate (new position).

Jose-Marie Griffiths,
of Tennessee, to be a member of the National Commission on Libraries and Information Science for a term expiring July 19, 2001, vice Shirley Gray Adamovich, term expired.

Madeleine May Kunin,
of Vermont, to serve concurrently and without additional compensation as Ambassador Extraordinary and Plenipotentiary of the United States of America to the Principality of Liechtenstein.

John Warren McGarry,
of Massachusetts, to be a member of the Federal Election Commission for a term expiring April 30, 2001 (reappointment).

Donald Rappaport,
of the District of Columbia, to be Chief Financial Officer, Department of Education, vice Donald Richard Wurtz, resigned.

Karen Shepherd,
of Utah, to be U.S. Director of the European Bank for Reconstruction and Development, vice Lee F. Jackson, to which position she was appointed during the last recess of the Senate.

Arthur I. Blaustein,
of California, to be a member of the National Council on the Humanities for a term expiring January 26, 2002, vice Bruce D. Benson, term expired.

Dave Nolan Brown,
of Washington, to be a member of the National Council on Disability for a term expiring September 17, 1998, vice John A. Gannon, term expired.

Lorraine Weiss Frank,
of Arizona, to be a member of the National Council on the Humanities for a term expiring January 26, 2002, vice Mikiso Hane, term expired.

Hans M. Mark,
of Texas, to be a member of the Board of Trustees of the Barry Goldwater Scholarship and Excellence in Education Foundation for a term expiring April 17, 2002 (reappointment).

Susan Ford Wiltshire,
of Tennessee, to be a member of the National Council on the Humanities for a term expiring January 26, 2002, vice Helen Gray Crawford, term expired.

Alan M. Hantman,
of New Jersey, to be Architect of the Capitol for the term of 10 years, vice George Malcolm White.

Eric L. Clay,
of Michigan, to be U.S. Circuit Judge for the Sixth Circuit, vice Ralph B. Guy, Jr., retired.

Merrick B. Garland,
of Maryland, to be U.S. Circuit Judge for the District of Columbia Circuit, vice Abner J. Mikva, retired.

William A. Fletcher,
of California, to be U.S. Circuit Judge for the Ninth Circuit, vice William Albert Norris, retired.

Richard A. Paez,
of California, to be U.S. Circuit Judge for the Ninth Circuit, vice Cecil F. Poole, resigned.

M. Margaret McKeown,
of Washington, to be U.S. Circuit Judge for the Ninth Circuit, vice J. Jerome Farris, retired.

Arthur Gajarsa,
of Maryland, to be U.S. Circuit Judge for the Federal Circuit, vice Helen Wilson Nies, retired.

James A. Beaty, Jr.,
of North Carolina, to be U.S. Circuit Judge for the Fourth Circuit, vice James Dickson Phillips, Jr., retired.

Ann L. Aiken,
of Oregon, to be U.S. District Judge for the District of Oregon, vice James H. Redden, retired.

Lawrence Baskir,
of Maryland, to be a Judge of the U.S. Court of Federal Claims for a term of 15 years, vice Reginald W. Gibson, retired.

Joseph F. Bataillon,
of Nebraska, to be U.S. District Judge for the District of Nebraska, vice Lyle E. Strom, retired.

Colleen Kollar-Kotelly,
of the District of Columbia, to be U.S. District Judge for the District of Columbia, vice Harold H. Greene, retired.

Richard A. Lazzara,
of Florida, to be U.S. District Judge for the Middle District of Florida, vice John H. Moore II, retired.

Donald M. Middlebrooks,
of Florida, to be a U.S. District Judge for the Southern District of Florida, vice James W. Kehoe, retired.

Jeffrey T. Miller,
of California, to be U.S. District Judge for the Southern District of California, vice Gordon Thompson, Jr., retired.

Susan Oki Mollway,
of Hawaii, to be U.S. District Judge for the District of Hawaii, vice Harold M. Fong, deceased.

Margaret M. Morrow,
of California, to be U.S. District Judge for the Central District of California, vice Richard A. Gadbois, Jr., retired.

Robert W. Pratt,
of Iowa, to be U.S. District Judge for the Southern District of Iowa, vice Harold D. Vietor, retired.

Christina A. Snyder,
of California, to be U.S. District Judge for the Central District of California, vice Edward Rafeedie, retired.

Clarence J. Sundram,
of New York, to be U.S. District Judge for the Northern District of New York, vice Con G. Cholakis, retired.

Thomas W. Thrash, Jr.,
of Georgia, to be U.S. District Judge for the Northern District of Georgia, vice Robert L. Vining, Jr., retired.

Marjorie O. Rendell,
of Pennsylvania, to be U.S. Circuit Judge for the Third Circuit, vice William D. Hutchinson, deceased.

Helene N. White,
of Michigan, to be U.S. Circuit Judge for the Sixth Circuit, vice Damon J. Keith, retired.

Submitted January 9

Genta Hawkins Holmes,
of California, a career member of the Senior Foreign Service, class of Minister-Counselor, to be Ambassador Extraordinary and Plenipotentiary of the United States of America to Australia.

Anne W. Patterson,
of Virginia, a career member of the Senior Foreign Service, class of Minister-Counselor, to be Ambassador Extraordinary and Plenipotentiary of the United States of America to the Republic of El Salvador.

Arma Jane Karaer,
of Virginia, a career member of the Senior Foreign Service, class of Counselor, to be Ambassador Extraordinary and Plenipotentiary of the United States of America to Papua New Guinea, and to serve concurrently and without additional compensation as Ambassador Extraordinary and Plenipotentiary of the United States of America to Solomon Islands, and as Ambas-

sador Extraordinary and Plenipotentiary of the United States of America to the Republic of Vanuatu.

Dennis K. Hays,
of Florida, a career member of the Senior Foreign Service, class of Counselor, to be Ambassador Extraordinary and Plenipotentiary of the United States of America to the Republic of Suriname.

John Francis Maisto,
of Pennsylvania, a career member of the Senior Foreign Service, class of Minister-Counselor, to be Ambassador Extraordinary and Plenipotentiary of the United States of America to the Republic of Venezuela.

Pete Peterson,
of Florida, to be Ambassador Extraordinary and Plenipotentiary of the United States of America to the Socialist Republic of Vietnam.

Edward William Gnehm, Jr.,
of Georgia, to be a Representative of the United States of America to the 51st Session of the General Assembly of the United Nations.

Karl Frederick Inderfurth,
of North Carolina, to be an Alternate Representative of the United of America to the 51st Session of the General Assembly of the United Nations.

Victor Marrero,
of New York, to be an Alternate Representative of the United of America to the 51st Session of the General Assembly of the United Nations.

Keith R. Hall,
of Maryland, to be an Assistant Secretary of the Air Force, vice Jeffrey K. Harris, resigned.

Joseph Lane Kirkland,
of the District of Columbia, to be a member of the Board of Directors of the U.S. Institute of Peace for a term expiring January 19, 2001, vice Allen Weinstein, term expired.

Yolanda Townsend Wheat,
of Missouri, to be a member of the National Credit Union Administration Board for the term of 6 years expiring August 2, 2001, vice Robert H. Swan, term expired.

Richard W. Bogosian,
of Maryland, a career member of the Senior Foreign Service, class of Minister-Counselor, for the rank of Ambassador during his tenure of service as Special Coordinator for Rwanda/Burundi.

John Stern Wolf,
of Maryland, a career member of the Senior Foreign Service, class of Minister-Counselor, for the rank of Ambassador during his tenure of service as U.S. Coor-

dinator for Asia Pacific Economic Cooperation (APEC).

Letitia Chambers,
of Oklahoma, to be a member of the Board of Trustees of the Institute of American Indian and Alaska Native Culture and Arts Development for a term expiring May 19, 2000, vice Roy M. Huhndorf, resigned.

Barbara Blum,
of the District of Columbia, to be a member of the Board of Trustees of the Institute of American Indian and Alaska Native Culture and Arts Development for a term expiring May 19, 2002 (reappointment).

Jeanne Givens,
of Idaho, to be a member of the Board of Trustees of the Institute of American Indian and Alaska Native Culture and Arts Development for a term expiring October 18, 2002, vice Piestewa Robert Harold Ames, term expired.

Michael A. Naranjo,
of New Mexico, to be a member of the Board of Trustees of the Institute of American Indian and Alaska Native Culture and Arts Development for a term expiring May 19, 2002, vice Beatrice Rivas Sanchez, term expired.

Nathan Leventhal,
of New York, to be a member of the National Council on the Arts for a term expiring September 3, 2002, vice William Bailey, term expired.

Gerald N. Tirozzi,
of Connecticut, to be Assistant Secretary for Elementary and Secondary Education, Department of Education, vice Thomas W. Payzant, resigned.

Robert F. Drinan,
of Massachusetts, to be a member of the Board of Directors of the Civil Liberties Public Education Fund for a term of 3 years (new position).

Susan Hayase,
of California, to be a member of the Board of Directors of the Civil Liberties Public Education Fund for a term of 3 years (new position).

Elsa H. Kudo,
of Hawaii, to be a member of the Board of Directors of the Civil Liberties Public Education Fund for a term of 2 years (new position).

Yeiichi Kuwayama,
of the District of Columbia, to be a member of the Board of Directors of the Civil Liberties Public Education Fund for a term of 3 years (new position).

Dale Minami,
of California, to be a member of the Board of Directors of the Civil Liberties Public Education Fund for a term of 3 years (new position).

Peggy A. Nagae,
of Oregon, to be a member of the Board of Directors of the Civil Liberties Public Education Fund for a term of 3 years (new position).

Don T. Nakanishi,
of California, to be a member of the Board of Directors of the Civil Liberties Public Education Fund for a term of 2 years (new position).

Leo M. Goto,
of Colorado, to be a member of the Board of Directors of the Civil Liberties Public Education Fund for a term of 2 years (new position).

Mary Lucille Jordan,
of Maryland, to be a member of the Federal Mine Safety and Health Review Commission for a term of 6 years expiring August 30, 2002 (reappointment).

David J. Barram,
of California, to be Administrator of General Services, vice Roger W. Johnson, resigned.

Kevin L. Thurm,
of New York, to be Deputy Secretary of Health and Human Services, vice Walter D. Broadnax, resigned.

Rose Ochi,
of California, to be Director, Community Relations Service, for a term of 4 years, vice Grace Flores-Hughes, term expired.

Hulett Hall Askew,
of Georgia, to be a member of the Board of Directors of the Legal Services Corporation for a term expiring July 13, 1998 (reappointment).

Ernestine P. Watlington,
of Pennsylvania, to be a member of the Board of Directors of the Legal Services Corporation for a term expiring July 13, 1999 (reappointment).

A.E. Dick Howard,
of Virginia, to be a member of the Board of Trustees of the James Madison Memorial Fellowship Foundation for a term of 6 years, vice Lance Banning.

Jon Deveaux,
of New York, to be a member of the National Institute for Literacy Advisory Board for a term expiring October 12, 1998 (reappointment).

Anthony R. Sarmiento,
of Maryland, to be a member of the National Institute for Literacy Advisory Board for a term expiring September 22, 1998, vice Benita C. Somerfield, term expired.

Sarah McCracken Fox,
of New York, to be a member of the National Labor Relations Board for the term of 5 years expiring August 27, 2000, vice James M. Stephens, term expired.

Magdalena G. Jacobsen,
of Oregon, to be a member of the National Mediation Board for a term expiring July 1, 1999 (reappointment).

Patricia M. McMahon,
of New Hampshire, to be Deputy Director for Demand Reduction, Office of National Drug Control Policy, vice Fred W. Garcia.

Daniel Guttman,
of the District of Columbia, to be a member of the Occupational Safety and Health Review Commission for a term expiring April 27, 2001, vice Edwin G. Foulke, Jr., term expired.

Denis J. Hauptly,
of Minnesota, to be Chairman of the Special Panel on Appeals for a term of 6 years, vice Barbara Jean Mahone, term expired.

Sophia H. Hall,
of Illinois, to be a member of the Board of Directors of the State Justice Institute for a term expiring September 17, 1997, vice John F. Daffron, Jr., term expired.

Sophia H. Hall,
of Illinois, to be a member of the Board of Directors of the State Justice Institute for a term expiring September 17, 2002 (reappointment).

Charles A. Gueli,
of Maryland, to be a member of the Board of Directors of the National Institute of Building Sciences for a term expiring September 7, 1999, vice Walter Scott Blackburn, term expired.

Niranjan S. Shah,
of Illinois, to be a member of the Board of Directors of the National Institute of Building Sciences for a term expiring September 7, 1998, vice John H. Miller, term expired.

Lowell Lee Junkins,
of Iowa, to be a member of the Board of Directors of the Federal Agricultural Mortgage Corporation, vice Edward Charles Williamson.

Susan R. Baron,
of Maryland, to be a member of the National Corporation for Housing Partnerships for the term expiring October 27, 1997 (reappointment).

Brig. Gen. Robert Bernard Flowers, USA,
to be a member and President of the Mississippi River Commission.

M.R.C. Greenwood,
of California, to be member of the National Science Board, National Science Foundation, for a term expiring May 10, 2002, vice Perry L. Adkisson, term expired.

Vera C. Rubin,
of the District of Columbia, to be a member of the National Science Board, National Science Foundation, for a term expiring May 10, 2002, vice Bernard F. Burke, term expired.

John A. Armstrong,
of Massachusetts, to be a member of the National Science Board, National Science Foundation, for a term expiring May 10, 2002, vice Thomas B. Day, term expired.

Stanley Vincent Jaskolski,
of Ohio, to be a member of the National Science Board, National Science Foundation, for a term expiring May 10, 2002, vice James Johnson Duderstadt, term expired.

Jane Lubchenco,
of Oregon, to be a member of the National Science Board, National Science Foundation, for a term expiring May 10, 2000, vice W. Glenn Campbell, term expired.

Richard A. Tapia,
of Texas, to be a member of the National Science Board, National Science Foundation, for a term expiring May 10, 2002, vice Phillip A. Griffiths, term expired.

Mary K. Gaillard,
of California, to be a member of the National Science Board, National Science Foundation, for a term expiring May 10, 2002, vice Marye A. Fox, term expired.

Bob H. Suzuki,
of California, to be a member of the National Science Board, National Science Foundation, for a term expiring May 10, 2002, vice Jaime Oaxaca, term expired.

Eamon M. Kelly,
of Louisiana, to be a member of the National Science Board, National Science Foundation, for a term expiring May 10, 2002, vice Howard E. Simmons, term expired.

Heidi H. Schulman,
of California, to be a member of the Board of Directors of the Corporation for Public Broadcasting for a term expiring January 31, 2002, vice Martha Buchanan, resigned.

Kerri-Ann Jones,
of Maryland, to be an Associate Director of the Office of Science and Technology Policy, vice Jane M. Wales, resigned.

Jerry M. Melillo,
of Massachusetts, to be an Associate Director of the Office of Science and Technology Policy, vice Robert T. Watson, resigned.

Johnny H. Hayes,
of Tennessee, to be a member of the Board of Directors of the Tennessee Valley Authority for a term expiring May 18, 2005 (reappointment).

Triruvarur R. Lakshmanan,
of New Hampshire, to be Director of the Bureau of Transportation Statistics, Department of Transportation, for the term of 4 years (reappointment).

D. Michael Rappoport,
of Arizona, to be a member of the Board of Trustees of the Morris K. Udall Scholarship and Excellence in National Environmental Policy Foundation for a term expiring October 6, 2002 (reappointment).

Judith M. Espinosa,
of New Mexico, to be a member of the Board of Trustees of the Morris K. Udall Scholarship and Excellence in National Environmental Policy Foundation for a term of 4 years (new position).

Ronald Kent Burton,
of Virginia, to be a member of the Board of Trustees of the Morris K. Udall Scholarship and Excellence in National Environmental Policy Foundation for a term expiring October 6, 2002 (reappointment).

Madeleine Korbel Albright,
of the District of Columbia, to be a Representative of the United States of America to the 51st Session of the General Assembly of the United Nations.

Anthony Lake,
of Massachusetts, to be Director of Central Intelligence, vice John M. Deutch, resigned.

Sheila Foster Anthony,
of Arkansas, to be a Federal Trade Commissioner for the term of 7 years from September 26, 1995, vice Janet Dempsey Steiger, term expired.

Submitted January 22

Susan Bass Levin,
of New Jersey, to be a member of the Board of Trustees of the Harry S Truman Scholarship Foundation for a term expiring December 10, 1999, vice Richard C. Hackett.

Submitted January 28

Federico Peña,
of Colorado, to be Secretary of Energy, vice Hazel Rollins O'Leary, resigned.

Submitted January 30

Ann Jorgenson,
of Iowa, to be a member of the Farm Credit Administration Board, Farm Credit Administration, for a term expiring May 21, 2002, vice Gary C. Byrne, resigned.

George W. Black, Jr.,
of Georgia, to be a member of the National Transportation Safety Board for a term expiring December 31, 2001 (reappointment).

Stanley A. Riveles,
of Virginia, for the rank of Ambassador during his tenure of service as U.S. Commissioner to the Standing Consultative Commission.

Richard J. Tarplin,
of New York, to be an Assistant Secretary of Health and Human Services, vice Jerry D. Klepner, resigned.

Submitted February 4

Jeffrey A. Frankel,
of California, to be a member of the Council of Economic Advisers, vice Martin Neil Baily, resigned.

Submitted February 5

Sophia H. Hall,
of Illinois, to be a member of the Board of Directors of the State Justice Institute for a term expiring September 17, 2000 (reappointment).

Marsha Mason,
of New Mexico, to be a member of the National Council on the Arts for a term expiring September 3, 2002, vice Louise M. McClure, term expired.

Lyle Weir Swenson,
of South Dakota, to be U.S. Marshal for the District of South Dakota, vice Robert Dale Ecoffey, resigned.

Theodore Francis Verheggen,
of the District of Columbia, to be a member of the Federal Mine Safety and Health Review Commission for a term expiring August 30, 2002, vice Arlene Holen, term expired.

Withdrawn February 5

Sophia H. Hall,
of Illinois, to be a member of the Board of Directors of the State Justice Institute for a term expiring September 17, 2002 (reappointment).

Submitted February 6

Ellen Seidman,
of the District of Columbia, to be Director of the Office of Thrift Supervision for a term of 5 years, vice Timothy Ryan, resigned.

Submitted February 11

Tracey D. Conwell,
of Texas, to be a member of the National Museum Services Board for a term expiring December 6, 2001, vice Fay S. Howell, term expired.

Joaquin L.G. Salas,
of Guam, to be U.S. Marshal for the District of Guam and concurrently U.S. Marshal for the District of the Northern Mariana Islands for the term of 4 years, vice Jose R. Mariano.

Patricia A. Broderick,
of the District of Columbia, to be an Associate Judge of the Superior Court of the District of Columbia for the term of 15 years, vice Harriett Rosen Taylor, term expired.

Mary Ann Gooden Terrell,
of the District of Columbia, to be an Associate Judge of the Superior Court of the District of Columbia for the term of 15 years, vice Richard Stephen Salzman, term expired.

Submitted February 12

Alan S. Gold,
of Florida, to be U.S. District Judge for the Southern District of Florida, vice Jose A. Gonzales, Jr., retired.

Anthony W. Ishii,
of California, to be U.S. District Judge for the Eastern District of California, vice Robert E. Coyle, retired.

Lynne Lasry,
of California, to be U.S. District Judge for the Southern District of California, vice John S. Rhodes, Sr., retired.

Ivan L.R. Lemelle,
of Louisiana, to be U.S. District Judge for the Eastern District of Louisiana, vice Veronica D. Wicker, deceased.

Submitted February 25

Wyche Fowler, Jr.,
of Georgia, to be Ambassador Extraordinary and Plenipotentiary of the United States of America to the Kingdom of Saudi Arabia.

Princeton Nathan Lyman,
of Maryland, a career member of the Senior Foreign Service, class of Career Minister, to be an Assistant

Secretary of State, vice Douglas Joseph Bennet, Jr., resigned.

Submitted March 3

Joel I. Klein,
of the District of Columbia, to be an Assistant Attorney General, vice Anne Bingaman, resigned.

Robert S. LaRussa,
of Maryland, to be an Assistant Secretary of Commerce, vice Susan G. Esserman.

Submitted March 6

James B. King,
of Massachusetts, to be Director of the Office of Personnel Management for a term of 4 years (reappointment).

Submitted March 11

Robert Clarke Brown,
of Ohio, to be a member of the Board of Directors of the Metropolitan Washington Airports Authority for a term expiring November 22, 1999, vice Jack Edwards, term expired.

Submitted March 12

Letitia Chambers,
of the District of Columbia, to be a Representative of the United States of America to the 51st Session of the General Assembly of the United Nations.

James Catherwood Hormel,
of California, to be an Alternate Representative of the United States of America to the 51st Session of the General Assembly of the United Nations.

Prezell R. Robinson,
of North Carolina, to be an Alternate Representative of the United States of America to the 51st Session of the General Assembly of the United Nations.

Submitted March 19

James H. Atkins,
of Arkansas, to be a member of the Federal Retirement Thrift Investment Board for a term expiring September 25, 2000 (reappointment).

Kathryn O'Leary Higgins,
of South Dakota, to be Deputy Secretary of Labor, vice Thomas P. Glynn, resigned.

Kevin Emanuel Marchman,
of Colorado, to be an Assistant Secretary of Housing and Urban Development, vice Joseph Shuldiner.

Richard Thomas White,
of Michigan, to be a member of the Foreign Claims Settlement Commission of the United States for a term expiring September 30, 1999 (reappointment).

Submitted March 21

Stuart E. Eizenstat,
of Maryland, to be an Under Secretary of State, vice Joan E. Spero, resigned.

Kenneth M. Mead,
of Virginia, to be Inspector General, Department of Transportation, vice Mary Sterling, resigned.

Thomas R. Pickering,
of New Jersey, to be an Under Secretary of State, vice Peter Tarnoff, resigned.

Anabelle Rodriguez,
of Puerto Rico, to be U.S. District Judge for the District of Puerto Rico, vice Raymond L. Acosta, resigned.

Michael D. Schattman,
of Texas, to be U.S. District Judge for the Northern District of Texas, vice Harold Barefoot Sanders, Jr., retired.

Hilda G. Tagle,
of Texas, to be U.S. District Judge for the Southern District of Texas.

Submitted April 7

James B. King,
of Massachusetts, to be Director of the Office of Personnel Management for a term of 4 years (reappointment), to which position he was appointed during the last recess of the Senate.

Submitted April 8

James William Blagg,
of Texas, to be U.S. Attorney for the Western District of Texas for the term of 4 years, vice Ronald F. Ederer, resigned.

Calvin D. Buchanan,
of Mississippi, to be U.S. Attorney for the Northern District of Mississippi for a term of 4 years, vice Robert Q. Whitwell, resigned.

James Allan Hurd, Jr.,
of the Virgin Islands, to be U.S. Attorney for the District of the Virgin Islands for the term of 4 years, vice James W. Diehm, resigned.

Ruth Y. Tamura,
of Hawaii, to be a member of the National Museum Services Board for a term expiring December 6, 2001 (reappointment).

John D. Trasvina,
of California, to be Special Counsel for Immigration-Related Unfair Employment Practices for a term of 4 years, vice William Ho-Gonzalez, term expired.

Submitted April 14

Eric H. Holder, Jr.,
of the District of Columbia, to be Deputy Attorney General, vice Jamie S. Gorelick, resigned.

Submitted April 15

Yerker Andersson,
of Maryland, to be a member of the National Council on Disability for a term expiring September 17, 1999 (reappointment).

Linda Jane Zack Tarr-Whelan,
of Virginia, for the rank of Ambassador during her tenure of service as U.S. Representative to the Commission on the Status of Women of the Economic and Social Council of the United Nations.

Submitted April 16

Brian Dean Curran,
of Florida, a career member of the Senior Foreign Service, class of Counselor, to be Ambassador Extraordinary and Plenipotentiary of the United States of America to the Republic of Mozambique.

Olivia A. Golden,
of the District of Columbia, to be Assistant Secretary for Family Support, Department of Health and Human Services, vice Mary Jo Bane, resigned.

Gina McDonald,
of Kansas, to be a member of the National Council on Disability for a term expiring September 17, 1998, vice Larry Brown, Jr., term expired.

Bonnie O'Day,
of Minnesota, to be a member of the National Council on Disability for a term expiring September 17, 1998 (reappointment).

Submitted April 18

George John Tenet,
of Maryland, to be Director of Central Intelligence, vice John M. Deutch, resigned.

Withdrawn April 18

Anthony Lake,
of Massachusetts, to be Director of Central Intelligence, vice John M. Deutch, resigned, which was sent to the Senate on January 9, 1997.

Submitted April 22

Elizabeth Anne Moler,
of Virginia, to be Deputy Secretary of Energy, vice Charles B. Curtis, resigned.

Submitted April 25

Andrew J. Pincus,
of New York, to be General Counsel of the Department of Commerce, vice Ginger Ehn Lew.

Submitted April 28

Michael J. Armstrong,
of Colorado, to be an Associate Director of the Federal Emergency Management Agency, vice Richard Thomas Moore, resigned.

Edward William Gnehm, Jr.,
of Georgia, a career member of the Senior Foreign Service, class of Minister-Counselor, to be Director General of the Foreign Service, vice Anthony Cecil Eden Quainton.

Submitted May 6

Jackie M. Clegg,
of Utah, to be First Vice President of the Export-Import Bank of the United States for a term expiring January 20, 2001, vice Martin A. Kamarck.

James A. Harmon,
of New York, to be President of the Export-Import Bank of the United States for a term expiring January 20, 2001, vice Martin A. Kamarck, resigned.

Richard Sklar,
of California, to be Representative of the United States of America to the United Nations for U.N. Management and Reform, with the rank of Ambassador.

Submitted May 15

Henry Harold Kennedy, Jr.,
of the District of Columbia, to be U.S. District Judge for the District of Columbia, vice Joyce Hens Green, retired.

Rodney W. Sippel,
of Missouri, to be U.S. District Judge for the Eastern and Western Districts of Missouri, vice Stephen N. Limbaugh, retired.

Submitted May 19

William P. Greene, Jr.,
of West Virginia, to be an Associate Judge of the United States Court of Veterans Appeals for the term of 15 years, vice Hart T. Mankin, deceased.

Submitted May 20

A. Peter Burleigh,
of California, a career member of the Senior Foreign
Service, class of Minister-Counselor, to be the Deputy
Representative of the United States of America to
the United Nations, with the rank and status of Ambassador Extraordinary and Plenipotentiary, vice Edward William Gnehm, Jr.

James W. Pardew, Jr.,
of Virginia, for the rank of Ambassador during his
tenure of service as U.S. Special Representative for
Military Stabilization in the Balkans.

Submitted May 22

Kenneth S. Apfel,
of Maryland, to be Commissioner of Social Security
for the term expiring January 19, 2001 (new position).

Marc Grossman,
of Virginia, a career member of the Senior Foreign
Service, class of Counselor, to be an Assistant Secretary of State, vice John Christian Kornblum.

John Christian Kornblum,
of Michigan, a career member of the Senior Foreign
Service, class of Career Minister, to be Ambassador
Extraordinary and Plenipotentiary of the United States
of America to Germany, vice Charles E. Redman.

Stanley O. Roth,
of Virginia, to be an Assistant Secretary of State, vice
Winston Lord.

David J. Scheffer,
of Virginia, to be Ambassador at Large for War
Crimes Issues.

Submitted May 23

James P. Rubin,
of New York, to be an Assistant Secretary of State,
vice Thomas E. Donilon.

Harold W. Furchtgott-Roth,
of the District of Columbia, to be a member of the
Federal Communications Commission for a term of
5 years from July 1, 1995, vice Andrew Camp Barrett,
resigned.

William E. Kennard,
of California, to be a member of the Federal Communications Commission for a term of 5 years from July
1, 1996, vice James H. Quello, term expired.

Paul Simon,
of Illinois, to be a member of the National Institute
for Literacy Advisory Board for a term expiring September 22, 1998, vice Sharon Darling, term expired.

Bonnie R. Cohen,
of the District of Columbia, to be an Under Secretary
of State, vice Richard Menifee Moose.

Submitted June 2

James Franklin Collins,
of Illinois, a career member of the Senior Foreign
Service, class of Minister-Counselor, to be Ambassador
Extraordinary and Plenipotentiary of the United States
of America to the Russian Federation.

Janice R. Lachance,
of Virginia, to be Deputy Director of the Office of
Personnel Management, vice Lorraine Allyce Green,
resigned.

Submitted June 3

Beth Nolan,
of New York, to be an Assistant Attorney General,
vice Walter Dellinger.

Submitted June 5

Robert Charles Chambers,
of West Virginia, to be U.S. District Judge for the
Southern District of West Virginia, vice Elizabeth V.
Hallanan, retired.

Christopher Droney,
of Connecticut, to be U.S. District Judge for the District of Connecticut, vice Alan H. Nevas, retired.

Janet C. Hall,
of Connecticut, to be U.S. District Judge for the District of Connecticut, vice T.F. Gilroy Daly, deceased.

Katharine Sweeney Hayden,
of New Jersey, to be U.S. District Judge for the District of New Jersey, vice H. Lee Sarokin, elevated.

Submitted June 10

Patrick A. Shea,
of Utah, to be Director of the Bureau of Land Management, vice Jim Baca.

Submitted June 11

David R. Andrews,
of California, to be Legal Adviser of the Department
of State (new position).

Timberlake Foster,
of California, a career member of the Senior Foreign
Service, class of Counselor, to be Ambassador Extraordinary and Plenipotentiary of the United States of
America to the Islamic Republic of Mauritania.

Ralph Frank,
of Washington, a career member of the Senior Foreign Service, class of Minister-Counselor, to be Am-

bassador Extraordinary and Plenipotentiary of the United States of America to the Kingdom of Nepal.

Jane Garvey,
of Massachusetts, to be Administrator of the Federal Aviation Administration for the term of 5 years, vice David Russell Hinson, resigned.

John C. Holzman,
of Hawaii, a career member of the Senior Foreign Service, class of Counselor, to be Ambassador Extraordinary and Plenipotentiary of the United States of America to the People's Republic of Bangladesh.

Karl Frederick Inderfurth,
of North Carolina, to be Assistant Secretary of State for South Asian Affairs, vice Robin Lynn Raphel.

Nancy Jo Powell,
of Iowa, a career member of the Senior Foreign Service, class of Counselor, to be Ambassador Extraordinary and Plenipotentiary of the United States of America to the Republic of Uganda.

Amelia Ellen Shippy,
of Washington, a career member of the Senior Foreign Service, class of Counselor, to be Ambassador Extraordinary and Plenipotentiary of the United States of America to the Republic of Malawi.

Robert L. Mallett,
of Texas, to be Deputy Secretary of Commerce, vice David J. Barram.

George A. Omas,
of Mississippi, to be a Commissioner of the Postal Rate Commission for a term expiring October 14, 2000, vice Wayne Arthur Schley, term expired.

Submitted June 12

Susan E. Rice,
of the District of Columbia, to be an Assistant Secretary of State, vice George Edward Moose.

Submitted June 17

Shirley Robinson Watkins,
of Arkansas, to be Under Secretary of Agriculture for Food, Nutrition, and Consumer Services, vice Ellen Weinberger Haas, resigned.

Submitted June 18

Frank M. Hull,
of Georgia, to be U.S. Circuit Judge for the Eleventh Circuit, vice Phyllis A. Kravitch, resigned.

Submitted June 19

Louis Caldera,
of California, to be a Managing Director of the Corporation for National and Community Service, vice Shirley Sachi Sagawa.

Stephen R. Sestanovich,
of the District of Columbia, to be Ambassador at Large and Special Adviser to the Secretary of State on the New Independent States.

Submitted June 23

Martin S. Indyk,
of the District of Columbia, to be an Assistant Secretary of State, vice Robert H. Pelletreau, Jr., resigned.

Submitted June 25

Rudy de Leon,
of California, to be Under Secretary of Defense for Personnel and Readiness, vice Edwin Dorn, resigned.

Sonia Sotomayor,
of New York, to be U.S. Circuit Judge for the Second Circuit, vice J. Daniel Mahoney, deceased.

Submitted June 26

Gordon D. Giffin,
of Georgia, to be Ambassador Extraordinary and Plenipotentiary of the United States of America to Canada.

W. Scott Gould,
of the District of Columbia, to be an Assistant Secretary of Commerce, vice Thomas R. Bloom.

W. Scott Gould,
of the District of Columbia, to be Chief Financial Officer, Department of Commerce, vice Thomas R. Bloom.

Maura Harty,
of Florida, a career member of the Senior Foreign Service, class of Counselor, to be Ambassador Extraordinary and Plenipotentiary of the United States of America to the Republic of Paraguay.

Curtis Warren Kamman,
of the District of Columbia, a career member of the Senior Foreign Service, to be Ambassador Extraordinary and Plenipotentiary of the United States of America to the Republic of Colombia.

James F. Mack,
of Virginia, a career member of the Senior Foreign Service, class of Minister-Counselor, to be Ambassador Extraordinary and Plenipotentiary of the United States of America to the Co-operative Republic of Guyana.

Wendy Ruth Sherman,
of Maryland, to be Counselor of the Department of State, and to have the rank of Ambassador during her tenure of service.

Anne Marie Sigmund,
of the District of Columbia, a career member of the Senior Foreign Service, class of Career Minister, to be Ambassador Extraordinary and Plenipotentiary of the United States of America to the Kyrgyz Republic.

Keith C. Smith,
of California, a career member of the Senior Foreign Service, class of Minister-Counselor, to be Ambassador Extraordinary and Plenipotentiary of the United States of America to the Republic of Lithuania.

Daniel V. Speckhard,
of Wisconsin, a career member of the Senior Executive Service, to be Ambassador Extraordinary and Plenipotentiary of the United States of America to the Republic of Belarus.

Jerome B. Friedman,
of Virginia, to be U.S. District Judge for the Eastern District of Virginia, vice Robert G. Doumar, retired.

Ronnie L. White,
of Missouri, to be U.S. District Judge for the Eastern District of Missouri, vice George F. Gunn, Jr., retired.

George Donohue,
of Maryland, to be Deputy Administrator of the Federal Aviation Administration, vice Linda Hall Daschle.

Gary Gensler,
of Maryland, to be an Assistant Secretary of the Treasury, vice Darcy E. Bradbury.

Nancy Killefer,
of Florida, to be an Assistant Secretary of the Treasury, vice George Munoz.

Nancy Killefer,
of Florida, to be Chief Financial Officer, Department of the Treasury, vice George Munoz.

George Munoz,
of Illinois, to be President of the Overseas Private Investment Corporation, vice Ruth R. Harkin, resigned.

Robert G. Stanton,
of Virginia, to be Director of the National Park Service (new position).

Catherine E. Woteki,
of the District of Columbia, to be Under Secretary of Agriculture for Food Safety (new position).

Kneeland C. Youngblood,
of Texas, to be a member of the Board of Directors of the United States Enrichment Corporation for a term expiring February 24, 2002 (reappointment).

Submitted June 27

James S. Ware,
of California, to be U.S. Circuit Judge for the Ninth Circuit, vice J. Clifford Wallace, retired.

Nancy-Ann Min DeParle,
of Tennessee, to be Administrator of the Health Care Financing Administration, vice Bruce C. Vladeck.

David A. Lipton,
of Massachusetts, to be an Under Secretary of the Treasury, vice Jeffrey R. Shafer, resigned.

Appendix C—Checklist of White House Press Releases

The following list contains releases of the Office of the Press Secretary which are not included in this book.

Released January 1

Statement by the Press Secretary on the attack by an off-duty Israeli soldier in Hebron

Transcript of a press briefing by Deputy Press Secretary Mary Ellen Glynn

Released January 2

Transcript of a press briefing by Deputy Press Secretary Mary Ellen Glynn

Released January 3

Transcript of a press briefing by Deputy Press Secretary Mary Ellen Glynn

Fact sheet: President's Title III Decision

Released January 6

Transcript of a press briefing by Press Secretary Mike McCurry

Released January 7

Transcript of a press briefing by Press Secretary Mike McCurry

Statement by the Press Secretary announcing four appointments to the White House staff

Transcript of a press briefing by Dr. Joyce Lashof and Adm. Paul Busick, USN, on the report of the Presidential Advisory Committee on Gulf War Veterans' Illnesses

Fact sheet: Gulf War Veterans' Illnesses: Presidential Initiatives

Announcement of nominations for 22 Federal Judges

Released January 8

Transcript of a press briefing by Press Secretary Mike McCurry

Statement by the Press Secretary: Meeting Between President Clinton and United Nations Secretary-General Kofi Annan

Released January 9

Transcript of a press briefing by Press Secretary Mike McCurry

Transcript of a press briefing by Education Secretary Richard Riley and Education Assistant Secretary David Longanecker on the student loan default rates report

Statement by the Press Secretary: Delegation for Nicaragua Presidential Inauguration

Released January 10

Transcript of a press briefing by Press Secretary Mike McCurry

Released January 11

Transcript of a press briefing by Press Secretary Mike McCurry, Treasury Secretary Robert Rubin, Education Secretary Richard Riley, National Security Adviser Samuel R. Berger, and Environmental Protection Administrator Carol Browner on the President's working session with the Cabinet

Released January 13

Transcript of a press briefing by Press Secretary Mike McCurry

Statement by the Press Secretary on the Chemical Weapons Convention

Released January 14

Transcript of a press briefing by Press Secretary Mike McCurry

Transcript of a press briefing by National Security Adviser Samuel R. Berger on the Israeli-Palestinian agreement on Hebron

Transcript of a press briefing by Office of Management and Budget Director Franklin Raines and Treasury Secretary Robert Rubin on the President's National Capital revitalization and self-government improvement plan

Fact sheet: The President's National Capital Revitalization and Self-Government Improvement Plan

Text of the citation read on the award of the Presidential Medal of Freedom to William J. Perry

Released January 15

Transcript of a press briefing by Press Secretary Mike McCurry

Statement by the Press Secretary: Treasury Prohibits Business Dealings With and Freezes Assets of 78 Companies and Individuals Fronting for the Cali Drug Cartel

Fact sheet: Treasury Prohibits Business Dealings With and Freezes Assets of Cali Cartel Front Companies and Individuals

Transcript of a press briefing by Treasury Secretary Robert Rubin, Assistant to the President for International and Economic Policy Daniel K. Tarullo, and Deputy Treasury Secretary Lawrence H. Summers on Mexico's repayment of loans

Fact sheet: Emergency Support Program for Mexico Concludes Successfully and Ahead of Schedule

Released January 16

Transcript of a press briefing by Press Secretary Mike McCurry

Released January 17

Transcript of a press briefing by Press Secretary Mike McCurry

Statement by the Press Secretary: United States Announces Next Steps on Antipersonnel Landmines

Fact sheet: U.S. Initiatives on Antipersonnel Landmines

Text of the citation read on the award of the Presidential Medal of Freedom to Bob Dole

Released January 21

Transcript of a press briefing by Press Secretary Mike McCurry, Office of Management and Budget Director Franklin Raines, National Economic Council Director Gene Sperling, and Health and Human Services Secretary Donna Shalala on the President's budget proposal

Released January 22

Transcript of a press briefing by Press Secretary Mike McCurry

Released January 23

Transcript of a press briefing by Press Secretary Mike McCurry

Response to questions taken at Press Secretary Mike McCurry's briefing

Released January 24

Transcript of a press briefing by Press Secretary Mike McCurry

Released January 27

Transcript of a press briefing by Press Secretary Mike McCurry

Released January 28

Fact sheet: Report on Support for a Democratic Transition in Cuba

Statement by Office of Management and Budget Director Franklin Raines on the Congressional Budget Office's new budget forecast

Released January 29

Transcript of a press briefing by Press Secretary Mike McCurry and Deputy Press Secretary David Johnson

Released January 30

Transcript of a press briefing by Press Secretary Mike McCurry and Deputy Press Secretary Barry Toiv

Transcript of remarks by the First Lady and Treasury Secretary Robert Rubin at the microenterprise awards ceremony

Released January 31

Transcript of a press briefing by Vice President Al Gore and Council of Economic Advisers member Alicia Munnell on the national economy

Transcript of a press briefing by Press Secretary Mike McCurry

Statement by the Press Secretary: Official Working Visit by Spanish President Aznar

Statement by the Press Secretary: Official Working Visit by Portuguese Prime Minister Guterres

Released February 3

Transcript of a press briefing by Press Secretary Mike McCurry and Deputy Press Secretary David Johnson

Statement by the Press Secretary: Canadian Prime Minister Chretien To Make Official Visit

Statement by the Press Secretary: President Clinton To Visit The Netherlands

Transcript of remarks by the First Lady at the microcredit summit

Announcement: White House and Governors Agree To Cooperate on Technology

Released February 4

Transcript of a press briefing by Press Secretary Mike McCurry

Transcript of a press briefing by Chief of Staff Erskine Bowles and Office of Management and Budget Director Franklin Raines on the State of the Union Address

Statement by the Press Secretary: Helicopter Accident in Israel

Advance text: Embargoed Excerpts of the State of the Union Address

Announcement of nomination for U.S. Marshal for the District of South Dakota

Released February 6

Transcript of a press briefing by Press Secretary Mike McCurry

Transcript of a press briefing by Treasury Secretary Robert Rubin, Office of Management and Budget Director Franklin Raines, Council of Economic Advisers Chairman Joseph E. Stiglitz, and National Economic Council Director Gene Sperling on the fiscal year 1998 budget

Released February 7

Transcripts of press briefings by Press Secretary Mike McCurry

Transcript of a news conference by Vice President Al Gore and Prime Minister Viktor Chernomyrdin of Russia

Transcript of remarks by the First Lady at the Education Awards ceremony

Statement by the Press Secretary: Presidential Travel to Mexico, the Caribbean, and Central and South America

Statement by the Press Secretary on the settlement of the civil case concerning Director of Central Intelligence nominee Anthony Lake's stocks

Announcement of nomination for U.S. Marshal for the District of Guam

Released February 10

Transcript of a press briefing by Press Secretary Mike McCurry

Announcement of regional finalists for 1997-98 White House fellowships

Released February 11

Transcript of a press briefing by Press Secretary Mike McCurry

Statement by the Press Secretary on the President's telephone conversation with Senator Richard Shelby, chairman, Senate Select Committee on Intelligence, concerning the nomination of Anthony Lake to be Director of Central Intelligence

Announcement of nominations for the Superior Court of the District of Columbia

Released February 12

Transcript of a press briefing by Senior Policy Adviser to the Vice President Elaine Kamarck on the aviation safety report and by Press Secretary Mike McCurry

Statement by the Press Secretary: U.S. Media Licensed To Open Bureaus in Cuba

Announcement of nominations for four U.S. District Judges

Released February 13

Transcript of a press briefing by Press Secretary Mike McCurry

Transcript of remarks by Vice President Al Gore at the swearing-in ceremony for U.S. Ambassador to the United Nations Bill Richardson

Released February 14

Transcript of a press briefing by Press Secretary Mike McCurry

Transcript of remarks by the First Lady to students at Cleveland Elementary School

Statement by the Press Secretary: Release From Detention of *Golden Venture* Detainees

Released February 18

Transcript of a press briefing by Press Secretary Mike McCurry

Transcript of remarks by the First Lady at the Chicago Children's Museum

Statement by the Press Secretary: Presidential Travel to Denmark

Released February 19

Transcript of a press briefing by Press Secretary Mike McCurry

Released February 20

Transcript of a press briefing by Press Secretary Mike McCurry

Released February 21

Transcript of a press briefing by Press Secretary Mike McCurry

Released February 24

Transcript of a press briefing by Press Secretary Mike McCurry

Released February 25

Transcript of a press briefing by Press Secretary Mike McCurry and Deputy Director of Communications Ann Lewis

Transcript of a press briefing by Office of National Drug Control Policy Director Barry McCaffrey on the 1997 National Drug Control Strategy

Statement by the Press Secretary: President's Meeting With Prince Sultan of Saudi Arabia

Statement by the Press Secretary on the availability of documents concerning the 1996 Presidential election

Released February 26

Text of a letter from Acting Secretary of Labor Cynthia Metzler to Senate Labor and Human Resources Committee Chairman James Jeffords on the proposed "Family Friendly Workplace Act"

Fact sheet: U.S.-Chile Trade Relations

Fact sheet: Chile: Political-Economy and International Relations

Released February 27

Transcript of a press briefing by Press Secretary Mike McCurry

Released February 28

Transcript of a press briefing by Press Secretary Mike McCurry

Narcotics Control Fact Sheet: 1997 Presidential Certifications for Major Narcotics Producing and Transit Countries

Narcotics Control Fact Sheet: Belize

Narcotics Control Fact Sheet: Colombia

Narcotics Control Fact Sheet: Mexico

Released March 3

Transcript of a press briefing by Press Secretary Mike McCurry

Transcript of a press briefing by Vice President Al Gore on 1996 campaign financing

Response to a question taken at Press Secretary Mike McCurry's briefing

Released March 5

Transcript of a press briefing by Press Secretary Mike McCurry

Transcript of remarks by the First Lady at the Pediatric AIDS Foundation Elizabeth Glaser Scientist Awards ceremony

Released March 6

Transcript of a press briefing by Press Secretary Mike McCurry

Released March 7

Statement by the Press Secretary: U.S.-Russian Summit Dates

Statement by the Press Secretary: McLarty Trip to Guatemala

Fact sheet: Gulf War Veterans' Illnesses: Ongoing Initiatives

Released March 10

Transcripts of press briefings by Press Secretary Mike McCurry

Statement by the Press Secretary on endorsement by three former Senators of Anthony Lake to be Director of Central Intelligence

Transcript of remarks by the First Lady and Education Secretary Richard Riley in a roundtable discussion on education

Released March 11

Transcript of a press briefing by Press Secretary Mike McCurry

Transcript of a press briefing by Office of Management and Budget Director Franklin Raines, Assistant Secretary of the Treasury for Government Financial Policy Mozelle Thompson, and Special Assistant to the President for Economic Policy Ellen Seidman on the President's economic plan for the District of Columbia

Response to a question taken at Press Secretary Mike McCurry's briefing

Released March 12

Transcript of a press briefing by Press Secretary Mike McCurry

Transcript of a press briefing by Deputy Secretary of Transportation Mortimer Downey on the proposed "National Economic Crossroads Transportation Efficiency Act"

Transcript of remarks by the First Lady on International Women's Day

Released March 13

Transcript of a press briefing by Deputy Press Secretary Mary Ellen Glynn

Transcript of a press briefing by Education Secretary Richard Riley and Defense Secretary William Cohen on education initiatives

Transcript of remarks by Vice President Al Gore to the California State Legislature

Released March 14

Transcripts of press briefings by Press Secretary Mike McCurry

Transcript of a press briefing by Press Secretary Mike McCurry and National Naval Medical Center Chief of Clinical Services Cmdr. David Wade on the President's knee injury

Transcript of a press briefing by Dr. Joel Cohen of St. Mary's Medical Center in West Palm Beach, FL, on the President's knee injury

Transcript of a press briefing by physicians attending to the President's knee injury

Released March 15

Transcript of a press briefing by Press Secretary Mike McCurry

Transcript of a radio address by Vice President Al Gore

Released March 16

Transcript of a press briefing by Press Secretary Mike McCurry

Statement by the Press Secretary announcing postponement of the President's visit to Denmark and a one-day delay in the start of the summit in Helsinki, Finland

Released March 17

Transcripts of press briefings by Press Secretary Mike McCurry

Transcript of remarks by Vice President Al Gore and Prime Minister John Bruton of Ireland at the shamrock presentation

Transcript of a press briefing by Vice President Al Gore, former Vice President Walter Mondale, and former Senator Nancy Kassebaum Baker on campaign finance reform

Statement by the Press Secretary on negotiations between American Airlines and the Allied Pilots Association

Released March 18

Transcript of a press briefing by Press Secretary Mike McCurry

Transcript of a press briefing by Secretary of State Madeleine Albright and National Security Adviser Samuel Berger on the President's trip to Finland

Released March 19

Transcript of a press briefing by Secretary of State Madeleine Albright and National Security Adviser Samuel Berger on the President's trip to Finland

Statement by the Press Secretary: Emergency Board No. 233 Submits its Findings With Respect to the Dispute Between American Airlines and its Pilots

Released March 20

Transcripts of press briefings by Press Secretary Mike McCurry

Released March 21

Transcript of a press briefing by Press Secretary Mike McCurry

Transcript of a press briefing by Secretary of State Madeleine Albright, National Security Adviser Samuel Berger, and Deputy Secretary of the Treasury Lawrence H. Summers on the Helsinki summit

Fact sheet: Joint Statement on Parameters on Future Reductions in Nuclear Forces

Fact sheet: Joint Statement Concerning the Anti-Ballistic Missile Treaty

Fact sheet: Joint Statement on the Chemical Weapons Convention

Fact sheet: Joint Statement on European Security

Fact sheet: Joint Statement on U.S.-Russia Economic Initiative

Announcement of nominations for U.S. District Judges for the District of Puerto Rico, the Northern District of Texas, and the Southern District of Texas

Released March 24

Transcript of a press briefing by Press Secretary Mike McCurry

Transcript of a press briefing by National Security Council Senior Director for Defense Policy and Arms Control Robert Bell on the antiballistic missile and theater missile defenses agreement at the Helsinki summit

Statement by the Press Secretary: Meeting With King Hussein of Jordan

Released March 25

Transcript of a press briefing by Press Secretary Mike McCurry

Transcript of a press briefing by Health and Human Services Secretary Donna Shalala on proposed Medicare and Medicaid fraud prevention legislation

Statement by the Press Secretary: Ross Travel to Middle East

Statement by the Press Secretary: Postponement of Presidential Travel to Mexico, Brazil, Argentina, and Venezuela

Released March 26

Transcript of a press briefing by Press Secretary Mike McCurry

Response to questions taken at Press Secretary Mike McCurry's briefing

Released March 27

Transcript of a press briefing by Press Secretary Mike McCurry

Released March 28

Transcript of a press briefing by Press Secretary Mike McCurry

Transcript of a press briefing by Energy Secretary Federico Peña, Assistant Energy Secretary Tara O'Toole, and Acting Associate Attorney General John Dwyer on human radiation experiments

Released March 31

Transcript of a press briefing by National Economic Council Director Gene Sperling, Pension Benefit Guaranty Corporation Acting Director John Seal, Special Assistant to the President for Economic Policy Ellen Seidman, and Assistant Labor Secretary Olena Berg on protection of pension programs and by Press Secretary Mike McCurry

Released April 1

Transcript of a press briefing by Press Secretary Mike McCurry

Released April 2

Transcript of a press briefing by Press Secretary Mike McCurry

Released April 3

Transcript of a press briefing by Press Secretary Mike McCurry

Statement by the Press Secretary: President Clinton's Meeting With Portuguese Prime Minister Guterres

Released April 4

Transcript of a press briefing by Press Secretary Mike McCurry

Transcript of a press briefing by Deputy Press Secretary David Johnson, National Security Council Senior Director for Defense Policy and Arms Control Robert Bell, and Commerce Under Secretary William Reinsch on the Chemical Weapons Convention

Released April 7

Transcript of a press briefing by Press Secretary Mike McCurry

Fact sheet: Federal Election Commission Requests for Additional Funding, Fiscal Years 1997 and 1998

Announcement of appointment for Director of the Office of National AIDS Policy

Released April 9

Transcript of a press briefing by Press Secretary Mike McCurry

Released April 10

Transcript of a press briefing by Press Secretary Mike McCurry

Transcript of a press briefing by Health and Human Services Secretary Donna Shalala, Assistant to the President for Domestic Policy Bruce Reed, and Senior Policy Advisor to the Vice President Elaine Kamarck on implementation of welfare reform

Announcement on national and State-by-State statistics on the decline of welfare caseloads during the President's first term

Released April 11

Transcript of a press briefing by Press Secretary Mike McCurry

Statement by the Press Secretary on the formation of a government of unity and reconciliation in Angola

Released April 14

Transcript of a press briefing by Press Secretary Mike McCurry

Transcript of a press briefing by National Economic Council Director Gene Sperling on the apparel industry partnership

Statement by the Press Secretary on the President and Mrs. Clinton's 1996 Federal income tax return

Released April 15

Statement by the Press Secretary: United Nations Human Rights Commission Vote on China

Statement by the Press Secretary: Opening of Border Talks Between Ecuador and Peru

Released April 16

Transcript of a press briefing by Press Secretary Mike McCurry

Transcript of a press briefing by National Security Adviser Samuel Berger and NSC Senior Director for Defense and Arms Control Policy Robert Bell on the President's upcoming meeting with congressional leaders on foreign policy issues and on efforts to secure ratification of the Chemical Weapons Convention

Statement by the Press Secretary: CWC Agreed Conditions

Statement by the Press Secretary: Official Working Visit by Japanese Prime Minister Hashimoto

Released April 17

Transcript of a press briefing by Press Secretary Mike McCurry

Transcript of remarks by the First Lady at the White House Conference on Early Childhood Development and Learning

Released April 18

Transcript of a press briefing by Press Secretary Mike McCurry

Transcript of a press briefing by Senior Policy Advisor to the Vice President Elaine Kamarck on reinventing the State Department, the Arms Control and Disarmament Agency, the U.S. Information Agency, and the Agency for International Development

Fact sheet: Reinventing State, ACDA, USIA, and AID

Clarification of Press Secretary Mike McCurry's briefing

Released April 21

Transcript of a press briefing by Press Secretary Mike McCurry

Released April 22

Transcript of remarks by Vice President Al Gore on the community right-to-know law

Released April 23

Transcript of a press briefing by Press Secretary Mike McCurry

Statement by the Press Secretary on proposed legislation to modify the Franklin D. Roosevelt Memorial

Released April 24

Transcript of a press briefing by Press Secretary Mike McCurry

Released April 25

Transcript of a press briefing by Press Secretary Mike McCurry

Transcript of a press briefing by Domestic Policy Council Director Bruce Reed on the President's upcoming summit on national service

Released April 26

Statement by the Press Secretary: Ambassador Richardson Mission to Zaire

Released April 27

Transcript of remarks by Hillary Clinton, President George Bush, and Barbara Bush on presenting the President's Service Awards in Philadelphia, PA

Transcript of a press briefing by Domestic Policy Council Director Bruce Reed, Welfare to Work Foundation President Eli Segal, and Diane Fortuna on the President's volunteer service initiatives

Released April 28

Transcript of a press briefing by Press Secretary Mike McCurry and Domestic Policy Council Director Bruce Reed on the President's volunteer service initiatives

Transcript of remarks by President George Bush, President Gerald Ford, President Jimmy Carter, Gen. Colin L. Powell, USA (ret.), Mrs. Nancy Reagan, and Vice President Al Gore at the Presidents' Summit for America's Future opening ceremony in Philadelphia, PA

Transcript of remarks by President Gerald Ford and President George Bush at the Presidents' Summit for America's Future luncheon in Philadelphia, PA

Transcript of remarks by the First Lady to students, teachers, parents, and AmeriCorps volunteers in Philadelphia, PA

Released April 29

Transcript of a press briefing by Press Secretary Mike McCurry

Correction from daily briefing on the Chair of the Gambling Commission

Released April 30

Transcript of a press briefing by Press Secretary Mike McCurry

Statement by the Press Secretary: UNHCR Ogata Meeting

Released May 1

Transcript of press briefing by Press Secretary Mike McCurry

Transcript of a press briefing by National Security Adviser Samuel Berger, Treasury Secretary Robert Rubin, Special Envoy to the Americas Thomas F. (Mack) McLarty, and Office of National Drug Control Policy Director Barry McCaffrey on the President's visit to Latin America

Released May 2

Statement by the Press Secretary: Legal Cooperation With Hong Kong

Transcript of a press briefing by the President's budget team on the budget agreement

Statement by Counsel to the President Charles F.C. Ruff Concerning the Decision of the Eighth Circuit

Released May 6

Advance text of the President's remarks at the state dinner in Mexico City

Transcript of a press briefing by Press Secretary Mike McCurry, National Security Adviser Samuel Berger, Office of National Drug Control Policy Director Barry McCaffrey, Immigration and Naturalization Service Commissioner Doris Meissner, and Special Envoy to Latin America Thomas F. (Mack) McLarty on the President's visit to Mexico

Transcript of remarks by President Ernesto Zedillo of Mexico, U.S. Secretary of State Madeleine Albright, Mexico Secretary of Foreign Affairs Jose Gurria, Mexico Attorney General Jorge Madrazo, U.S. Attorney General Janet Reno, and U.S. Office of National Drug Control Policy Director Barry McCaffrey on receiving the Binational Commission report in Mexico City

Transcript of a press briefing by Deputy Press Secretary Dave Johnson on the President's visit to Mexico

Fact sheet: President Clinton's Visit to Mexico: Building a Broad and Constructive Partnership for the 21st Century

Released May 7

Transcript of a press briefing by Press Secretary Mike McCurry

Advance text of the President's address to the people of Mexico

Released May 8

Transcript of a press briefing by Press Secretary Mike McCurry, Immigration and Naturalization Service Commissioner Doris Meissner, Deputy National Security Adviser James B. Steinberg, National Economic Council Senior Director for International Economic Policy Lael Brainerd, and National Security Council Director for Inter-American Affairs Geoffrey Pyatt on the President's visit to Costa Rica

Fact sheet: The San Jose Declaration—A Deepened Partnership Between the United States and Central America

Announcement: Immigration and Migrant Trafficking

Announcement: U.S. Support for Central American Regional Integration

Announcement: Cooperative Law Enforcement in Central America

Released May 9

Transcript of a press briefing by Secretary of Energy Federico Peña and Secretary of the Interior Bruce Babbitt

Statement by the Press Secretary: Visit by the President to London

Statement by the Press Secretary: Braulio Carrillo Joint Declaration

Statement by the Press Secretary: Sustainable Development in Central America

Fact sheet: Sustainable Development in Central America

Fact sheet: U.S.-Costa Rica Statement of Intent: Electric Transportation Cooperation

Released May 10

Transcript of a press briefing by Press Secretary Mike McCurry

Transcript of a press briefing by Press Secretary Mike McCurry and Deputy National Security Adviser James B. Steinberg on the President's visit to the Caribbean

Fact sheet: Caribbean Bananas and WTO Case

Fact sheet: Partnership for a Prosperous and Secure Caribbean

Fact sheet: Regional Security and Narcotics Interdiction

Released May 13

Transcript of a press briefing by Press Secretary Mike McCurry

Statement by the Press Secretary: Visit by President Gligorov of the Former Yugoslav Republic of Macedonia

Released May 14

Transcript of a press briefing by Press Secretary Mike McCurry

Released May 15

Transcript of a press briefing by Press Secretary Mike McCurry

Statement by the Press Secretary: A National Security Strategy for a New Century

Statement by the Press Secretary: Visit of NATO Secretary General Javier Solana

Fact sheet: NATO-Russia Founding Act

Announcement of the President's 1996 Public Financial Disclosure Report

Announcement of nominations for U.S. District Judges for the District of Columbia and the Eastern and Western Districts of Missouri

Released May 16

Transcript of a press briefing by Press Secretary Mike McCurry

Transcript of a press briefing by Chief of Staff Erskine Bowles, Treasury Secretary Robert Rubin, Office of Management and Budget Director Franklin Raines, National Economic Council Director Gene Sperling, and Council of Economic Advisers Chair Janet Yellen on the budget agreement

Announcement of nomination for a U.S. Court of Veterans Appeals Judge

Statement by the Press Secretary: Anti-Personnel Landmines

Fact sheet: Banning Anti-Personnel Landmines

Fact sheet: International Nuclear Safeguards Strengthened

Released May 19

Transcript of a press briefing by Deputy Press Secretary Mary Ellen Glynn, Deputy Press Secretary Barry Toiv, and Deputy Press Secretary David Johnson

Transcript of a press briefing by National Security Adviser Samuel Berger and U.S. Trade Representative Charlene Barshefsky on the President's announcement on most-favored-nation trade status for China

Statement by the Press Secretary: Supplemental Report of Presidential Advisory Committee on Gulf War Veterans' Illnesses

Released May 20

Transcript of a press briefing by Press Secretary Mike McCurry

Statement by Counsel to the President Charles F.C. Ruff on the White House agreement with Representative Dan Burton, chairman, House Government Reform and Oversight Committee

Released May 21

Transcript of a press briefing by Press Secretary Mike McCurry

Transcript of a press briefing by National Security Adviser Samuel Berger and Deputy Secretary of State Strobe Talbott on the President's upcoming visit to Europe

Transcript of a press briefing by Ambassadors Lincoln Gordon and Vernon Walters on the history of the Marshall plan

Released May 22

Transcript of a press briefing by Press Secretary Mike McCurry

Transcript of a press briefing by Director of Communications Ann Lewis and Mike Cohen, Special Assistant to the President for Education, Domestic Policy Council on the President's proposal for a V-chip for the Internet

Released May 23

Transcript of a press briefing by Press Secretary Mike McCurry

Released May 27

Transcript of a press briefing by Press Secretary Mike McCurry

Transcript of a press briefing by National Security Adviser Samuel Berger on the President's visit to Paris, France

Transcript of remarks by President Jacques Chirac of France, President Boris Yeltsin of Russia, and NATO Secretary General Javier Solana at the signing ceremony for the NATO-Russia Founding Act in Paris, France

Fact sheet: NATO-Russia Founding Act

Released May 28

Statement by the Press Secretary: President To Meet With Australian Prime Minister

Transcript of a press briefing by Deputy National Security Adviser James B. Steinberg, Assistant to the President for International and Economic Policy Daniel K. Tarullo, and Press Secretary Mike McCurry on the European Union-U.S. summit and mutual recognition agreements

Announcement: United States and European Union Announce Steps To Address Common Problems

Released May 29

Transcript of a press briefing by Press Secretary Mike McCurry and Deputy National Security Adviser James B. Steinberg on the President's meeting with Prime Minister Tony Blair of the United Kingdom

Released May 30

Transcript of a press briefing by Press Secretary Mike McCurry

Transcript of a press briefing by Vice President Al Gore, Treasury Secretary Robert Rubin, National Economic Council Director Gene Sperling, Council of Economic Advisers Chair Janet Yellen, and Office of Management and Budget Director Franklin Raines on the national economy

Fact sheet: Charter on a Distinctive NATO-Ukraine Partnership

Released May 31

Transcript of a press briefing by National Security Adviser Samuel Berger on the President's commencement address at the U.S. Military Academy

Released June 2

Transcript of a press briefing by Press Secretary Mike McCurry

Released June 3

Transcript of a press briefing by Press Secretary Mike McCurry

Released June 4

Transcript of a press briefing by Press Secretary Mike McCurry

Released June 5

Transcript of a press briefing by Deputy Press Secretary Barry Toiv, Deputy Press Secretary Joe Lockhart, and Deputy Press Secretary Anne Luzzatto

Statement by the Press Secretary: Meeting With His Highness Sheikh Hamad bin Khalifa al Thani, Amir of the State of Qatar

Announcement of nominations for four U.S. District Judges

Released June 6

Transcript of a press briefing by Press Secretary Mike McCurry

Advance text of remarks by National Security Adviser Samuel Berger to the Council on Foreign Relations in New York City

Released June 9

Transcript of a press briefing by Press Secretary Mike McCurry

Transcript of a press briefing by Treasury Secretary Robert Rubin and National Economic Council Director Gene Sperling on negotiations on tax cut legislation

Advance text of remarks by Deputy National Security Adviser James B. Steinberg to the Carnegie Endowment for International Peace

Announcement of amendments to pending budget requests for consistency with the bipartisan budget agreement

Released June 10

Transcript of a press briefing by Press Secretary Mike McCurry

Transcript of a press briefing by Education Secretary Richard Riley, National Center for Education Statistics Commissioner Pascal Forgione, National Academy of Sciences President Bruce Alberts, National Science Foundation Acting Deputy Director Joseph Bordogna, TIMSS Project Officer Lois Peak, and TIMSS National Research Coordinator Bill Schmidt on the results of the Third International Math and Science Study (TIMSS)

List of participants in the President's meeting with civil rights leaders

Released June 11

Transcript of a press briefing by Press Secretary Mike McCurry

Statement by the Press Secretary: President's Meeting With Amir of Qatar

Statement by the Press Secretary: Northern Ireland Peace Process

Released June 12

Transcript of a press briefing by Press Secretary Mike McCurry

Transcript of a press briefing by Deputy Chief of Staff Sylvia Mathews and Office of Public Liaison Director Maria Echaveste on the President's initiative on race

List of Members of Congress attending signing of disaster relief bill

Released June 13

Transcript of a press briefing by Press Secretary Mike McCurry

Statement by the Press Secretary: Meeting With Crown Prince Hassan of Jordan

Released June 14

Transcript of a press briefing by members of the President's Advisory Board on Race

Released June 16

Transcript of a press briefing by Press Secretary Mike McCurry

Transcript of a press briefing by National Security Adviser Samuel Berger, Assistant to the President for International Economic Policy Daniel K. Tarullo, and Treasury Secretary Robert Rubin on the Denver Summit of the Eight

Released June 17

Transcript of a press briefing by Press Secretary Mike McCurry

Transcript of a press briefing by Deputy National Security Adviser James B. Steinberg, Assistant to the President for International Economic Policy Daniel K. Tarullo, Deputy U.S. Trade Representative Jeffrey Lang, and Deputy Treasury Secretary Lawrence H. Summers on the President's Africa trade initiative

Statement by the Press Secretary: Meeting With President Kito Gligorov of the Former Yugoslav Republic of Macedonia

Statement by Counsel to the President Charles F.C. Ruff on the DC Circuit Court of Appeals decision on executive privilege to protect confidential documents

Fact sheet: President Clinton's Strategy for Economic Growth and Opportunity in Africa

Released June 18

Transcript of a press briefing by Press Secretary Mike McCurry

Transcript of remarks by the First Lady to the Friends of Art and Preservation in Embassies

Statement by the Press Secretary: President's Meeting With Crown Prince of Jordan

Announcement of nomination for a U.S. Circuit Judge for the Eleventh Circuit

Released June 19

Transcript of a press briefing by Press Secretary Mike McCurry, Deputy National Security Adviser James B. Steinberg, Assistant to the President for International Economic Policy Daniel K. Tarullo, and U.S. Trade Representative Charlene Barshefsky on the President's meeting with Prime Minister Hashimoto of Japan

Transcript of a press briefing by U.S. Trade Representative Charlene Barshefsky on the Japan-U.S. initiative on deregulation and competition policy

Statement by the Press Secretary: President Receives Winners of "President's Prize"

Released June 20

Transcript of a press briefing by Press Secretary Mike McCurry, Deputy National Security Adviser James B. Steinberg, and Deputy Treasury Secretary Lawrence H. Summers on the Denver Summit of the Eight

Transcript of a press briefing by Assistant to the President for International Economic Policy Daniel K. Tarullo on the Denver Summit of the Eight

Transcript of a press briefing by Deputy National Security Adviser Samuel Berger on the President's meeting with President Chirac of France

Released June 21

Transcript of a press briefing by Press Secretary Mike McCurry

Transcript of a press briefing by Secretary of State Madeleine Albright on the summit nations Foreign Ministers report

Transcript of a press briefing by Treasury Secretary Robert Rubin on the G–7 leaders meeting

Released June 22

Transcript of a press briefing by Press Secretary Mike McCurry, Assistant to the President for International Economic Policy Daniel K. Tarullo, and National Security Adviser Samuel Berger on the Denver Summit of the Eight

Released June 23

Transcript of a press briefing by Housing and Urban Development Secretary Andrew Cuomo and Deputy Press Secretary Barry Toiv on the President's remarks to the U.S. Conference of Mayors

Released June 24

Transcript of a press briefing by National Security Adviser Samuel Berger and Deputy Press Secretary Joe Lockhart on most-favored-nation trade status for China

Announcement: President Clinton Appoints 1997–98 White House Fellows

Released June 25

Transcript of a press briefing by National Economic Council Director Gene Sperling, Environmental Protection Agency Administrator Carol Browner, and Council on Environmental Quality Chair Kathleen McGinty on implementation of the Clean Air Act

Announcement of nomination for a U.S. Court of Appeals Judge for the Second Circuit

Released June 26

Transcript of a press briefing by Press Secretary Mike McCurry, Assistant to the President for International Economic Policy Daniel K. Tarullo, and Council on Environmental Quality Chair Kathleen McGinty on the President's address to the United Nations Special Session on Environment and Development

Announcement of nominations for U.S. District Judges for the Eastern District of Virginia and the Eastern District of Missouri

Released June 27

Transcript of a press briefing by Press Secretary Mike McCurry

Transcript of a press briefing by Assistant to the President for Domestic Policy Planning Bruce Reed and Health and Human Services Secretary Donna Shalala on the review of the proposed tobacco agreement

Statement by the Press Secretary: President Clinton To Visit Poland, Romania, and Denmark

Announcement of nomination for a U.S. Court of Appeals Judge for the Ninth Circuit

Released June 30

Transcript of a press briefing by Press Secretary Mike McCurry

Transcript of a press briefing by Treasury Secretary Robert Rubin, National Economic Council Director Gene Sperling, Office of Management and Budget Director Franklin Raines, and Council of Economic Advisers Chair Janet Yellen on the President's tax cut proposal

Appendix D—Presidential Documents Published in the Federal Register

This appendix lists Presidential documents released by the Office of the Press Secretary and published in the Federal Register. The texts of the documents are printed in the Federal Register (F.R.) at the citations listed below. The documents are also printed in title 3 of the Code of Federal Regulations and in the Weekly Compilation of Presidential Documents.

PROCLAMATIONS

PROCLAMATIONS—Continued

EXECUTIVE ORDERS

OTHER PRESIDENTIAL DOCUMENTS

Subject Index

ABC News—289
Abortion. *See* Health and medical care
ACCION U.S. Network—99
Acquired immune deficiency syndrome (AIDS). *See* Health and medical care
Addiction and Substance Abuse, National Center on—323
Adoption. *See* Children and youth
Adoption Promotion Act of 1997—515
Advisory committees, Federal. *See* Government agencies and employees
Aeronautics and Space Administration, National—148
Aerospace industry—148, 155, 159, 328, 417, 857, 858
Affirmative action. *See* Armed Forces; Civil rights
AFL-CIO. *See* Labor and Congress of Industrial Organizations, American Federation of
Africa
  See also specific country
  Economic development—169
  Relations with France—773
  Relations with U.S.—773
  Trade with U.S.—756
  U.S. trade and investment, report—169
African-Americans
  See also specific subject; Civil rights
  Church burnings. *See* Law enforcement and crime
  Education—188
Agriculture
  Cloning—712
  Grains, international trade—401
Agriculture, Department of
  Food, Nutrition, and Consumer Services—862
  Food safety, role—75
  Secretary—75, 76, 208, 283, 445, 471, 474, 756
  Under Secretaries—862
AIDS. *See* Health and medical care
AIDS Policy, Office of National—397, 856
Air Force, Department of the
  See also Armed Forces, U.S.
  Air Force Academy, U.S.—857, 858, 860
Airline industry. *See* Aerospace industry
Albania
  Civil conflict—317
  Peace efforts—774
  Trade with U.S.—699
  U.S. military role—317
Alcohol, Tobacco and Firearms, Bureau of. *See* Treasury, Department of the
Alfalfa Club—855
American. *See* other part of subject
American Airlines labor dispute. *See* Labor issues
American Heritage Rivers. *See* Conservation
America's Future, Presidents' Summit for—73, 395, 502, 503, 505, 508

AmeriCorps—16, 73, 111, 122, 185, 395, 498, 507, 509, 629, 801, 859
Angola
  Economic sanctions—386
  National Union for the Total Independence of Angola (UNITA)—385
  U.S. national emergency—385
Antigua and Barbuda, Bridgetown Declaration of Principles—594
Apparel Industry Partnership—435
April Fool's Day—371
Architect of the Capitol—853
Arctic Research Commission—860
Argentina, trade with U.S.—437
Arkansas
  Governor—227, 233
  President's visits—233, 825, 857, 865
  Storms, flooding, and tornadoes—227, 233, 857, 860
Armed Forces, U.S.
  See also specific military department; Defense and national security
  Affirmative action—738
  Base closures and conversions—618
  Europe—399
  F-22 *Raptor Fighter*—417
  Military child care system—446, 448
  Security—80
  Supreme Allied Commander, Europe—96, 364
  Terrorist bombing of U.S. military complex in Dhahran, Saudi Arabia—80, 407
  Veterans. *See* Veterans
Armenia
  Emigration policies—698
  Nagorno-Karabakh region—776
Arms and munitions
  See also Defense and national security; Law enforcement and crime; Nuclear weapons
  Arms control negotiations and agreements—116, 329, 332, 335, 337, 341, 342, 379, 387, 399, 403, 425, 428, 449, 454, 470, 476, 480, 483, 495, 600, 601, 704
  Chemical and biological weapons—8, 9, 116, 209, 252, 329, 332, 342, 379, 387, 403, 425, 428, 429, 449, 454, 470, 476, 480, 483, 495, 704
  Conventional weapons—11
  Incendiary weapons—11
  Landmines—11
  Laser weapons—12
  Missile systems and technology—332, 334, 337, 341
  Nonproliferation—538, 609
Army, Department of
  See also Armed Forces, U.S.
  Aberdeen trials—457
  Secretary—471, 474

Name Index

Document Categories List

Addresses to the Nation

Inaugural Address—43
State of the Union—109

Addresses and Remarks

See also Addresses to the Nation; Appointments and Nominations; Bill Signings; Interviews With the News Media
"Adoption 2002" report—157
Advisory Commission on Consumer Protection and Quality in the Health Care Industry—352
Africa trade initiative—756
America, Central and South, radio address to citizens—586
American Council on Education—189
American Society of Newspaper Editors—423
Apparel Industry Partnership—435
April Fool's Day—371
Arkadelphia, AR, tornado damage—233
Arts and Humanities awards
  Dinner—23
  Presentation ceremony—18
Augusta State University in Augusta, GA—119
Barbados, Bridgetown, Caribbean leaders
  Reception—584
  Welcoming ceremony—587
Bethesda, MD, medical examination at the National Naval Medical Center—316
Bosnia-Herzegovina, discussions with President Izetbegovic—350
Boston, MA, roundtable discussion on juvenile crime—172
Boxer, Senator Barbara, luncheon in San Francisco, CA—803
Bridgeport, WV, Clarksburg area community—652
Business Council—215
Business Enterprise Awards, luncheon in New York City—166
Business leaders, meeting—24
Business Roundtable—725
Campaign finance reform—145
Canada, Prime Minister Chretien
  Arrival at White House—402
  Discussions—402
  State dinner—412, 414
Central Intelligence Agency, withdrawal of nomination for Director—319
Chemical Weapons Convention—387, 476, 480
Chile, President Frei
  Discussions—207
  State dinner—215
  Welcoming ceremony—206
Clarksburg, WV
  Education townhall meeting—640

Addresses and Remarks—Continued
  Clarksburg, WV—Continued
    High school students—651
  Coalition for America's Children, public service announcement—228
  Community right-to-know law—469
  Conference on Free TV and Political Reform—277
  Congressional leaders, meeting—146
  Congressional Medal of Honor, presentation ceremony—30
  Costa Rica
    Braulio Carillo National Park—582
    San Jose
      Arrival—565
      Central American Summit, dinner—581
      Central American Summit, welcoming ceremony—565
  Croatia, 1996 aircraft tragedy anniversary—383
  Defense Department
    Military leaders, meeting—96
    Secretary of Defense, swearing-in ceremony—71
  Democratic Business Council
    Dinners—90, 376, 624
    Session—196
  Democratic Congressional Campaign Committee luncheon in Brooklyn, NY—440
  Democratic Governors' Association, dinner—105
  Democratic National Committee
    Brunch—42
    Dinners
      New York City—849
      Washington, DC—285, 525, 627, 721, 743, 749
    Meeting—49
  Democratic Senatorial Campaign Committee
    Dinners
      Aventura, FL—307
      New York City—170
    Receptions
      Los Angeles, CA—808
      Washington, DC—638
  Distilled liquor, advertising—368
  District of Columbia
    Economic plan—281
    Reading tutor initiative—182
  Dorgan, Senator Byron, reception—284
  Drug policy—199
  Earth Day—469
  Easter egg roll—362
  Economic team, meeting—48
  Economy—530
  Ecumenical Prayer Breakfast—5
  Education
    National standards—714
    Roundtable discussions
      Augusta, GA—118
      Washington, DC—372

Heterick Memorial Library
Ohio Northern University

DUE	RETURNED		DUE	RETURNED
1.			13.	
2.			14.	
3.			15.	
4.			16.	
5.			17.	
6.			18.	
7.			19.	
8.			20.	
9.			21.	
10.			22.	
11.			23.	
12.			24.